Feuding, conflict and banditry in nineteenth-century Corsica

Feuding, conflict and banditry in nineteenth-century Corsica

Stephen Wilson

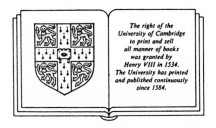

CAMBRIDGE UNIVERSITY PRESS

CAMBRIDGE

NEW YORK   NEW ROCHELLE   MELBOURNE   SYDNEY

PUBLISHED BY THE PRESS SYNDICATE OF THE UNIVERSITY OF CAMBRIDGE
The Pitt Building, Trumpington Street, Cambridge, United Kingdom

CAMBRIDGE UNIVERSITY PRESS
The Edinburgh Building, Cambridge CB2 2RU, UK
40 West 20th Street, New York NY 10011–4211, USA
477 Williamstown Road, Port Melbourne, VIC 3207, Australia
Ruiz de Alarcón 13, 28014 Madrid, Spain
Dock House, The Waterfront, Cape Town 8001, South Africa

http://www.cambridge.org

First published 1988
First paperback edition 2002

A catalogue record for this book is available from the British Library

Library of Congress Cataloguing in Publication data
Wilson, Stephen, 1941–
Feuding, conflict and banditry in nineteenth-century Corsica /
Stephen Wilson.
p.   cm.
Bibliography.
Includes index.
1. Vendetta – France – Corsica – History – 19th century.   2. Brigands
and robbers – France – Corsica – History – 19th century.   I. Title.
HV6453.F72C68   1988
944′.945–dc19   87-23288   CIP

ISBN 0 521 35033 6 hardback
ISBN 0 521 52264 1 paperback

TO THE MEMORY OF NORMAN WILSON

tua me, genitor, tua tristis imago
saepius occurrens haec limina tendere adegit

VIRGIL, *Aeneid*, Book VI

Contents

Illustrations

Figure

Maps

Tables

Acknowledgements

The conception of this book owes a great deal to the milieu which developed in the then School of European Studies in the University of East Anglia in the 1970s, and which arose from trying to teach social history by applying the insights and concepts of social anthropology to European societies of the past. My mentors and colleagues in this enterprise were Robert Rowland, Jim Casey and Morley Cooper, all of whom also directed my attention to the Mediterranean region. Teaching the history of popular culture with Neil MacMaster has also been an inspiration, as have conversations about African societies with Margo and Martin Russell.

The book's more particular debts to the researches of previous students of Corsican traditional society are obvious and are acknowledged in the text and the notes. My work builds on their foundations. Special mention should be made here of the contribution of Francis Pomponi and of Pierre Lamotte. In his capacity as director of the Archives Départementales de la Corse du Sud, M. Lamotte also provided me with general orientation and gave me invaluable advice on documentation. He and his staff at Ajaccio could not have been more helpful. My thanks are due, too, to the staffs of the Archives Départementales de la Haute-Corse at Bastia, of the Archives Nationales and the Bibliothèque Nationale in Paris, and of the British Library in London, for allowing and assisting me to use their collections. My understanding of Corsican society was enhanced by conversations with people all over the island as well as by observation of their behaviour.

Research trips to Corsica and to Paris were financed by the award of a Faculty Fellowship in European Studies from the Leverhulme Trust Fund in 1977 and by a grant from The Harry Frank Guggenheim Foundation in 1980, both of which are gratefully acknowledged. Additional financial assistance was received from the Twenty-Seven Foundation and from the University of East Anglia, which also allowed me study leave.

My somewhat complicated travel arrangements were made with his usual efficiency by Geoffrey Hooton. Tom and Malvine Evenson helped with accommodation in Paris. Christine Aldis deciphered my handwriting and assisted with the typing. My wife and daughters tolerated the anti-social consequences of my writing another big book.

Finally, I intend no endorsement of statements in the sources relating to individuals that could be construed as damaging.

] 1 [

Corsica in the nineteenth century

Corsica is the third largest Mediterranean island after Sicily and Sardinia. It measures just over 50 miles from east to west and just over 100 from north to south and is situated at about 50 miles from the present Italian and at about 100 from the present French coast. The landscape is dominated by two mountain chains, one smaller of schist in the north-east, the other much larger of granite in the south-west. The average altitude is 1,864 feet, and the highest peak, Monte Cinto, reaches 8,890 feet within 20 miles of the sea.[1]

If nature has made Corsica on this grand scale, she has by the same token made it poor. Less than a third of the territory of the island was cultivated through the nineteenth century. Of the remainder, some 20 per cent was forest and some 50 per cent maquis, natural pasture or waste.[2] The most important timber tree was the Corsican pine (*laricio*), which grows to 150–160 feet and is found at altitudes of over 3,000 feet, together with beech and fir. Maritime pine, found at lower levels, was tapped extensively for resin. Below 1,500 feet there was holm oak, used for charcoal, firewood and tannin, and cork oak. The roots of tree-heather were grubbed up for pipe wood. There were also important chestnut plantations, to which we will return. Though the forests were exploited in these ways, they were difficult of access, even after special roads had been built in the second half of the century, and they were the object of dispute between the State and local communities, attached to their grazing and use rights and opposed therefore to long-term commercial concessions.[3]

For many visitors and for homesick exiles, like Napoleon, the typical Corsican terrain was the maquis or scrub, which ranged from dense shrubbery reaching 10 or 15 feet to open heathland. The former was made up, as Maupassant described it in 1881, 'of evergreen oaks, junipers, arbutus, lentisks, broom, alaterns, tree-heathers, bays, myrtles and box, all intermingled and matted together with clematis, giant bracken, honeysuckle, rock roses, rosemary, lavender and brambles'. The more open maquis was usually produced by regeneration after fires. Many of the plants mentioned are aromatic, lending the maquis a characteristic scent. A few could be used for fuel, fodder, bedding and other purposes, but otherwise this land served only for rough pasture and for hunting small birds, which was a favourite male pursuit.[4]

The most naturally fertile part of the island was the alluvial plain running down the eastern coast, but much of the land in this and other coastal areas required draining before it could be cultivated. Plans were made in the mid-nineteenth century to drain the marshes around Calvi in the Balagna, around San-Fiorenzo in the Nebbio, and at the mouth of the Golo to the south of Bastia, but only the last had been accomplished by the time of the First World War.[5] The undrained marshes were ideal breeding places for malarial mosquitoes and all the coastal plains were for this reason avoided as places to live, though people descended from the hill and mountain villages on a temporary seasonal basis. Malaria was the main single cause of exemption from military service in Corsica, affecting up to a quarter of the young men in some districts. Effective treatment and prevention were not available until after 1900 and malaria was only eradicated in the late 1940s.[6]

The nature of the terrain meant extreme regional diversity within the island. Three main climatic zones may be distinguished: first, a mountain zone of high forests and Alpine pasture, with heavy precipitation and long winters; secondly, an intermediate zone (between 2,000 and 5,000 feet), with moderate though irregular rainfall and short winters; and thirdly, a maritime zone, with long dry summers.[7] The valleys which fast-flowing rivers or torrents cut through the mountain chains were shut off from each other by high cols blocked by snow in winter and by narrow impassable gorges. The island was thus a cluster of isolated micro-regions (*pievi*) with distinct customs and dialects.[8] From the end of the Middle Ages a broader political and cultural divide emerged between the north-east and the south-west. In the former, the *Terra qua dai Monti*, communal institutions had been established, Genoese rule later was direct, and Italian commercial and cultural contacts were evident. In the latter, the *Terra la dai Monti*, seigneurial rule had persisted, Genoese rule had been indirect, and external influences very limited. For a while during the French Revolutionary and Napoleonic period, this division had been reflected by the existence of two Corsican departments, the Golo and Liamone, an arrangement revived in 1975.[9] The *Terra qua dai Monti* contained the most densely populated and economically developed parts of the island: the Capo Corso, the Casinca and the Castagniccia. Also in the north, forming the hinterland of Calvi and Isola-Rossa, was the 'prosperous and well-cultivated' Balagna.[10]

The geographical isolation arising from natural barriers was only gradually mitigated in the course of the nineteenth century. No proper carriage roads existed in 1800, except perhaps that between Bastia and Corte, which Paoli had established as his capital. This road was not continued to Ajaccio until 1827. By the middle of the nineteenth century, these and the other three towns, Bonifacio, Calvi and Sartène, were linked by road, and the building of secondary and by-roads to villages, and of forest roads had been started; 3,500 kilometres in the former and 500 in the latter category had been built by 1870. However, road-building in Corsica was a formidably difficult task, and the majority of villages were still without roads and reliant upon mule-tracks at the end of the century.[11] Even when roads had been built, transportation remained poorly organized and very slow. The overnight journey by coach from Ajaccio to Bastia took eight hours in 1870, the journey from Sartène to Bonifacio six hours. At about the same date, however, it took Saint-Germain three hours to get from Santa-Lucia-di-Tallano to Levie, a distance of just over 5 miles, and four hours to get from Muro to Belgodère, a distance of 13 miles.[12] Railway building began in 1876, and some 185 miles had been completed by the end of the century. Again, the terrain was most unfavourable – the Ajaccio–Bastia line of just under 100 miles had 37 tunnels (one $2\frac{1}{2}$ miles long), 28 viaducts, 31 bridges and 180 cuttings – and further obstacles were provided by local obstructionism and graft.[13] Corsica has no navigable rivers, and sea transport between ports in the island hardly existed, save in the Capo Corso.[14]

The isolation of villages and *pievi* was never total. A fairly well-developed system of inter-regional barter existed. Oil merchants from the Balagna, for example, travelled all over the island, exchanging their wares for local products. Cheese merchants from Asco went to the Capo Corso and the Castagniccia. The last-named region provided much of Corsica with chestnut flour and also with wooden and leather articles. Other regions traded in a grain surplus or in live-stock.[15] Twenty or more annual fairs were held – for example, the San Pancrazio horse fair at Ajaccio and the autumn fair at Casamaccioli in the Niolo.[16]

The population of Corsica more significantly was not wholly sedentary by the start of the nineteenth century. Most villages were situated in the intermediate zone, but many of them also possessed territory in the high mountains and on the plain. As Robiquet explained in 1835, 'the cereal fields [of the mountain villages] are usually situated on the coastal plains, at a great distance from the villages. The inhabitants go down to plough and sow these lands and then return to their villages, going back again for the harvest.' Very often this involved a full-scale migration. Saint-Germain wrote that the people of Palneca 'went down in October to the plains, taking their utensils, their furniture with them, followed by their wives and children'. Of 242 villages replying to a questionnaire in 1829, 156 had a coastal satellite, where part of the population went in winter.[17] Temporary settlements were formed on the plains, their names sometimes indicating the mother village to which they were linked: Ghisoni-Ghisonaccia; Bastelica-Bastelicaccia. The pressure of rising population in the first half or two-thirds of the century tended to make these settlements more permanent. People spent longer periods of time on the coast, perhaps planting olives and vines there and building proper houses. The inhabitants of Zerubia were said around 1850 'to spend nine months of the year in the hamlets of Caldarello and Pianottole near Figari'.[18] And this process of sedentarization was reflected by the elevation of coastal settlements into fully fledged communes. So, for example, Sotta hived off administratively from Serra-Sorbollano in 1835; Afa from Bocognano in 1857; Monaccia from Aullène in 1867; and Ghisonaccia and Bastelicaccia became independent in 1861 and 1866 respectively.[19] This did not mean, however, that ties were severed with villages of origin. Much of the territory of the erstwhile satellites still belonged either collectively or in private ownership to those living in their home villages. So in 1882 nearly all the land in the newly established communes of Manso and Galeria belonged to the five mountain villages of the Niolo from which they had sprung. Most of the land at Sotta continued to be owned by a few important families from Serra-di-Scopamène. Again, there were strong matrimonial alliances between Manso and Galeria and the Niolo villages, while the people of Sotta were still registering their births and voting at Serra in the 1930s. Most important in this context, the population of the new coastal villages continued to migrate back to the mountains during the summer. Nearly all the inhabitants of Sotta, for example, left with their families at the end of June after harvest, taking their belongings in carts and on mule-back. They returned briefly in mid-September to harvest the vines, went back to Serra to harvest the chestnuts, and then returned to Sotta for the winter. The people of Conca departed from this common pattern by forming a new summer settlement at the Col di Bavella.[20] It was also customary for those citizens of Ajaccio and Bastia who could afford to do so, to move to *villeggiature* in the hills away from the heat.[21]

Towns were relatively unimportant, and only 17 per cent of the population lived in them in 1851, after a period of considerable urban growth. Bastia was the largest town with a population of around 8,000 at the end of the eighteenth century, rising to 30,000 in 1911. The administrative capital, Ajaccio, grew over the same time from around 4,000 to 19,000. Calvi, Corte and Sartène were much smaller. Only Corte and Sartène were situated inland, and only Bastia had any real significance as a commercial centre.[22] Industry was correspondingly undeveloped. Rural crafts were important in some districts, notably the Castagniccia, and there was some expansion during the nineteenth century in the preparation and processing of local agricultural products and raw materials (soap-making, milling, tanning, textiles, cork, marble). Antimony, silver and iron were mined but only for brief periods and in small quantities.[23]

Visitors, government officials and local people who had been educated abroad often regarded Corsica in the nineteenth century as 'uncivilized' or 'savage'.[24] Over the centuries the island had been governed by a series of invading powers, who had rarely extended their influence beyond the coastal towns and their hinterlands. From the late Middle Ages, the dominant sovereign power was the city-state of Genoa. A successful insurrectionary movement beginning in 1729 led to the establishment in 1755 of an independent Corsican government under the leadership of Pasquale Paoli. Genoa, however, ceded Corsica to France in 1768, and French rule was gradually established from that date, despite the turmoil of the Revolutionary and Napoleonic period.[25] It should nevertheless be stressed that at the start of the nineteenth century the effectiveness of state authority was extremely limited, particularly in the interior. French culture was also largely alien. Until the 1850s, if not later, the bulk of the population did not understand French. Interpreters were provided in the courts, and registers of births, marriages and deaths and official correspondence were still kept or carried on in Italian. A variety of local dialects existed, related to ancient Tuscan, and these remained and remain the mother-tongue of Corsicans, though by the end of the century French was established as the official and primary written language.[26] Schools were an important vehicle for the spread of French language and culture. Corsicans showed an early interest in primary schooling for boys, realizing its vocational potential. Secondary schooling and primary schooling for girls did not develop to the same extent.[27]

II

Nineteenth-century Corsica, therefore, was a predominantly rural society of a traditional kind. The economy was one in which villagers used a variety of types of land over a wide area, combining agriculture, arboriculture, horticulture and pastoralism in different proportions. At the start of the century, at Sisco in the Capo Corso, for example, only 16 per cent of the land was cultivated and at Asco 24 per cent, while at Castellare-di-Casinca the proportion was 68 per cent. Again, the proportion of the population classified as herdsmen varied from 100 per cent at Conca to less than 10 per cent at Rospigliani. Although the interests of herdsmen and cultivators were to some extent conflicting, it is important to stress that their activities were essentially complementary.[28]

We have seen that villages, situated most often between the high mountains and the plains, possessed territory or rights in territory in both these locations as well as in the vicinity of the main settlement. Land was divided into a number of categories or zones and its use was subject to a range of collective controls. Gardens or *orti* were situated in or very close to the village. These were usually privately owned and were intensively cultivated with spade or hoe to produce vegetables, fruit, and maize for poultry. This required watering, and irrigation was organized on a collective basis.[29] Fields, in which cereals were grown (wheat, barley, rye, oats and millet), were situated further from the village, and often at a considerable distance on the coast. Gardens and fields were often only roughly enclosed, with dry hedges of brambles, gorse or thorn. Some fields were continuously cultivated on a two-year rotation or with longer periods of fallow to retain fertility and moisture; others were used on a more casual basis. Here the maquis would be cut down and burned over (*diceppu*), and a crop taken for up to three years. After three to ten years, such land might be reused. Fallow land was ploughed three times annually and manured by pasturing livestock on it. Land under cultivation was sown in late autumn and harvesting was done in June or July.[30] Two types of plough were used in the island, the most common being unchanged since Roman times. Both were light and home-made and scratched rather than turned the soil. Ploughs were usually drawn by oxen, harnessed with simple throttle yokes, though other animals were used. Oxen were often hired out to cultivators by herdsmen from mountain villages.[31] Yields in these circumstances were low, ranging from under 5:1 on poor mountain soil to 20–30:1 on the plains. The average yield for wheat in the 1890s was 9:1 and for barley 12:1.[32] Grain was made into flour in archaic water-driven mills with horizontal wheels.[33]

We have referred to the ways in which the forests and maquis were exploited, but trees were also cultivated. Of these the most important was the chestnut, grown in 1846 in 300 out of 355 villages in the island. Chestnuts were most common in the Castagniccia, but became important during the nineteenth century in other areas: the south, the Cruzzini and the Vico region. In the Castagniccia, over half the cultivated land in all villages was devoted to chestnuts at the start of the century, and in some of them the proportion approached 100 per cent. Chestnuts were made into flour, which was either mixed with rye flour to make bread or used on its own in a great variety of ways. Chestnuts were a crucial complement to the island's grain crop and remained a staple element of the local diet until the time of the First World War. Young chestnut plants require watering, and harvesting is difficult and labour intensive, but otherwise the trees need little attention, leaving time for artisanal and other occupations.[34] Chestnuts were usually privately owned, but they were often planted on land in collective ownership and sometimes on private land belonging to others.[35] Olive cultivation like that of chestnuts was well-established by the start of the nineteenth century, and was particularly important in the Balagna, the Nebbio and the Bonifacio regions. We have seen that there was a significant internal trade in olive oil, but oil was also exported, though it was not of high quality. The olives were left to fall off the trees at the end of the year, and they were pressed more often than not in primitive twist or lever presses.[36] Vines were grown in many parts of the island, and some wine was produced on a commercial basis.[37] Other fruit trees were grown, especially in the Balagna and the Capo Corso. These included mulberries in the first half of the century, in association with sericulture,[38] and citrons in the second, which were exported to make candied peel.[39] Arboriculture on any scale required capital and the ability to wait many years for a crop, which meant that it was the province *par excellence* of the private landowner or notable.[40]

Livestock was kept on land around the village and also on more distant pastures. No stabling was provided and artificial meadows were almost unknown. Asses, mules and horses were used as draught or carrying animals in about equal numbers (10–12,000 in each category at the end of the nineteenth century). Oxen, we have seen, were generally used for ploughing, and 50–60,000 cattle of all kinds were kept.[41] Pigs provided an important supplement to the diet and numbers rose to about 100,000 by the end of the century. They grazed at will, especially in oak or chestnut groves and were killed with much ceremony at Christmas time. Their flesh was preserved in the form of hams, brawns and sausages.[42] Far more important than all these for the rural economy were sheep and goats. There were over 400,000 of the former and well over 200,000 of the latter by the 1890s. A few were kept in and around the villages but most were fed and managed by a system of extensive transhumance that complemented the cultivation of cereals and other crops.

Flocks were taken down to the coast in September or October, spending the winter there. In May or June, when the coastal pasture was exhausted and when the summer heats began, they were led back to the mountains, spending a short time in the vicinity of the village before proceeding to the high Alpine pastures. Flocks from particular villages followed traditional routes, trajectories ranging from 5 to 30 miles. Flocks from Bastelica, for example, spent the winter near Ajaccio and the summer on Monte Renoso. From Asco, sheep went down via Olmi-Cappella to the Speloncato district in the Balagna, while goats went via the Col of San-Colombano to the Agriates 'desert', and both returned to the high mountains surrounding the village. Flocks and herds from the Niolo travelled longer distances to the Balagna, the coastal region between Porto and Calvi, and even to the Castagniccia and the Casinca.[43] Very often, as at Bastelica, Palneca or Asco, transhumance involved the migration of whole families, but in parts at least of the Niolo only the men accompanied the flocks and herds, forming 'companies' under a leader or *capu pastore*.[44] Herdsmen and their families lived in dry-stone huts at shielings in the mountains. Accommodation on the plain was usually less substantially built of earth and straw, though, as we have seen, satellite villages developed from these settlements.[45]

The main pastoral products were wool and milk, the latter being made into cheese of various kinds. Most characteristic was *brocciu*, a soft cooked cheese, made usually from a mixture of sheeps' and goats' milk.[46] Flocks and herds were managed and owned in a variety of ways. Sometimes herdsmen owned their livestock on a family basis. Additionally, they might care for other animals for a fee, or more often for a half-share of their produce and offspring. Other herdsmen worked entirely for employers or for village communities.[47] Herdsmen almost never owned their pasture. The high mountain pasture was common land, as was some coastal grazing. Elsewhere, pasture was privately owned and was taken on lease, usually on an annual basis. Outside herdsmen also leased common grazing in lowland villages.[48] These arrangements were related to some extent to the relative importance of pastoralism in the rural economy. In the Niolo, Asco and the upper Taravo valley, for example, pastoralism was the predominant activity, but elsewhere, at Bastelica, or in the Ortolo and Rizzanese valleys in the south, it was difficult to separate agriculture from pastoralism. In the first milieu, it is possible to talk of a distinct class of herdsmen, but in the second different members of the same family would be involved in cultivation, arboriculture and livestock rearing. Villages leasing pasture to outsiders, for example in the Casinca, usually had no important flocks of their own.[49]

We have referred to collective controls over land use. Traditionally, the village lands were divided into three parts, the *presa* used for cultivation, the *circolo* used for arboriculture, and the pasture. Sometimes shares (*lenze*) in the *presa* were periodically distributed among heads of families, but more often families claimed plots within the designated area by clearing the land and roughly enclosing it. They then retained rights in such land so long as they continued to cultivate it. Times for ploughing and for harvesting cereals, chestnuts, grapes and olives were also communally regulated, as was irrigation and the guarding of fields and gardens against straying livestock. This system remained in operation in central and northern Corsica until the end of the nineteenth century, even where land had become private property.[50]

This last process was a comparatively recent development. At the end of the nineteenth century, 28 per cent of all land in Corsica was still common land. There was considerable variation within the island in this respect. In the Niolo, the Corte region, the upper valleys generally, and even parts of the Capo Corso, two-thirds or three-quarters of the land might be common. On the coast, in the Balagna and the Nebbio, the proportion was much less, and some villages in the Castagniccia and the Casinca had no common land at all.[51] A number of distinctions should be made among different categories of land in collective ownership. Some land did not belong to any particular community or *pieve* and people from over a wide area might use it for cultivation or pasture. People from some twenty villages, for example, used the plain of Taravo. Some land belonged to *pievi* and it was not unusual for two or more villages to share rights in particular territories. Zerubia and Aullène, for example, shared coastal lands in the south; Ota, Evisa and other villages shared territory around the Gulf of Porto. Most commonly, individual villages had their common lands, but it was possible for land to belong to hamlets or parts of villages, an arrangement found at Bastelica. It was also possible for rights in common land to be restricted to old or aboriginal families, as at Fozzano.[52] Here a further distinction should be made between land that belonged to the village as a corporate entity and that might be leased out *en bloc*, and land which anyone might use if he needed it. Land here was regarded in the same light as other common assets, such as water, timber and fuel supply from the forests, or facilities such as threshing floors. Access to them was open to all who belonged to the community.[53]

Land formally in private ownership was often not free from collective restraints. Much private land was held in indivision by families. Well over a third of the land in Corsica came into this category in 1962.[54] Also, as we have noted, even when land was not common, it was subject to common regulation. The most obvious manifestation of this was the custom of *vaine pâture*, whereby the flocks of the whole village (or sometimes of outsiders) were turned on to the fields after harvest. The French authorities had discouraged this practice from the end of the eighteenth century and a law of 1854 abolished it, but it survived in many villages.[55] The authorities also encouraged the partition of common lands. This had some effect on the plain, but very little in the interior.[56] Equally if not more effective in turning the tide slowly against collective and in favour of private property was the centuries-old process of usurpation of common land by local notables.[57]

Most families in Corsica owned some land, and small-scale property predominated, especially in the north. According to the Agricultural Enquiry of 1867, 93 per cent of rural properties were under 15 hectares in extent. At Castellare-di-Casinca in 1914, over 90 per cent of landowners had less than 5 hectares; while at Stazzona in the Castagniccia only 2 out of a total of 151 estates exceeded 7 hectares.[58] At the same time and related to this, estates were divided into tiny parcels. The 2,957 hectares in private ownership in the canton of San-Martino in 1867 were made up of 22,611 parcels. At Sisco, an estate of just under 4 hectares was divided in 1861 into 114 parcels.[59] Here it should be emphasized that land was regarded as family and not individual property – hence the importance of indivision; also that small landowners had access in addition to common land.[60]

Large-scale property did exist, particularly in the south. Big estates comprised 11 per cent of all Corsican land in 1867, and 38 per cent of land at Porto-Vecchio and 42 per cent of land at Levie fell into this category. By the 1880s, most of the best coastal land of Serra-di-Scopamène and Sorbollano belonged to noble families or *principali*. At Omessa in the Nebbio, estates of over 60 hectares were already common at the start of the nineteenth century, and noble and bourgeois families from Bastia owned big estates on the plain of Casinca. Some estates were very large indeed, for example the Pozzo di Borgo domain to the north of Ajaccio (1,000 hectares) and the Roccaserra estates in the Sartenais (1,500 hectares), but these were mainly rough pasture or waste.[61]

Most Corsican families worked their own land, but various modes of indirect exploitation existed, particularly but not exclusively on large estates. Cultivable land or pasture might be leased out for a year or more, and day-labourers might be hired. More common was some kind of share-cropping arrangement. Patin de La Fizelière described how this worked in La Rocca at the end of the eighteenth century: 'The landowner provides the land, the seed, the oxen and implements; and the "companion", as he is known, who is often a relative, gives only his work, ploughing and harvesting; they share the crop equally.' Elsewhere, the share-cropper (*colono*) might have to provide his own oxen, or again might be provided with a house by an important landowner in return for doing odd jobs and becoming his master's client.[62]

The traditional agro-pastoral system remained in being through the nineteenth century, though important changes did occur which heralded its ultimate collapse. First, the expansion of population stimulated a big increase in the amount of land under cereal cultivation. In the half-century between 1825 and 1875 the territory devoted to cereals in the island tripled to a maximum of just under 75,000 hectares. In many villages, the increase was even more marked. At Serra-di-Scopamène, for example, the amount of land under cultivation rose from 9 per cent at the end of the eighteenth century to 59 per cent in the 1880s, while at Sisco in the Capo Corso the amount rose from 16 to 67 per cent in 1861. As this indicates, cereal production was increased not by introducing improved methods or achieving higher yields but simply by extending existing methods to more land. Such land was usually of poor quality or difficult to use or both. Terracing of hillsides to make flat surfaces was at its apogee in the third quarter of the century.[63] Some new crops were introduced with government encouragement, notably hemp and linen, potatoes and tobacco, but none was really successful.[64]

Arboriculture also enjoyed a period of expansion and even prosperity in the nineteenth century. The area under vines doubled between 1780 and 1867. Olive-growing spread to all parts of the island and reached a maximum extension of 18,000 hectares around 1875. Chestnuts spread similarly and reached their maximum extension at about the same time.[65]

The area of land under cultivation could only expand at the expense of grazing land, and pastoralism suffered or adapted accordingly. We have seen that *vaine pâture* was officially abolished, and the practice of taking flocks and herds from the territory of one village to that of another (*libre parcours*) was also curtailed. Grazing became more strictly controlled. The number of animals per family head allowed on village pastures was limited, and flocks belonging to outsiders were often banned, unless the owners paid a fee. Legal restrictions, the influence of cultivators and population pressure combined to change patterns of transhumance in some areas. There was a tendency towards sedentarization, with herdsmen spending more time at the coast and using summer pastures closer to hand rather than returning to the mountains. Coastal settlements, we have seen, became proper villages. Traditional pastoralism had depended on the maintenance of common lands and was linked to the general extensive system of land use. From the end of the nineteenth century a more 'modern', commercial pastoralism developed, that was increasingly independent of both.[66]

By this time, however, a general crisis had developed in the Corsican economy. Between 1875 and the First World War, the area under cereal cultivation dropped from 75,000 to 15,000 hectares or below, and in some areas the fall was even more drastic. At Serra-di-Scopamène the amount of cultivated land was 1,188 hectares in 1889, but only 227 in 1914. There were 25 pairs of oxen in the village in 1830, but only one in 1914. At Sisco, only 30 per cent of the land was under cultivation by the time of the war, and terrace cultivation had been abandoned.[67] Arboriculture suffered in the same way. Vines had been badly hit by disease in the late 1860s and again by phylloxera in the 1880s. Some replanting took place in selected areas, but this was not ultimately successful in the face of North African and Italian competition.[68] Olive-growing also ran into trouble from the 1870s. Corsican oil was not saleable abroad for culinary purposes, and other vegetable oils and mineral oil were increasingly used for soap-making and lighting.[69] The area planted with chestnuts was about halved between 1850 and 1910. The internal and external markets for chestnuts and chestnut flour collapsed. Trees were felled in great numbers from about 1885 to make tannin but this destructive procedure also ceased to be viable after a while.[70] Not only did the small surpluses generated by the Corsican economy cease to be marketable, but, more grave, it came to cost less to import flour and other foodstuffs into the island than to produce them at home in the traditional laborious way.

At the same time, there was a dramatic change in the island's demography. Between 1780 and 1880, the population doubled from about 140,000 to a maximum of around 280,000. The rise was most rapid between 1825 and 1855 and varied of course from region to region.[71] Most rural areas were overpopulated in terms of their resources by the middle of the century, but densities differed widely, being related again to available resources. The average maximum population density was just over 30 inhabitants per square kilometre, but in the Castagniccia the average was over 50, in the upper Balagna 66 and in the Nebbio over 100. Some villages in these regions had even higher figures. By contrast, in the Niolo and other mainly pastoral regions, the density was lower than average. At Antisanti, for example, it was less than 20. Existing population densities affected the pattern of population decrease that came at the end of the nineteenth century. The Castagniccia reached its demographic maximum in 1851, but population growth continued strongly in the Sartenais well into the 1890s. The distribution of population in the island in fact became more even, and there was some movement of population to the towns.[72] But the most marked phenomenon was emigration. Since medieval times, men had left the island to become soldiers, priests, bureaucrats, merchants, and this traditional pattern continued.[73] Corsicans were prominent in France's nineteenth-century colonial and overseas expansion.[74] The late nineteenth- and twentieth-century exodus was different, however, both in scale and pace. Perhaps 385 people left Corsica every year between 1841 and 1880; in the decade before the First World War this figure was close to 2,000, rising to 6,000 in the 1930s. After the war, moreover, women joined men in leaving the island in large numbers. The overall fall in population took place in effect despite a continuing natural demographic surplus.[75]

III

The structure of Corsican rural society matched that of the local economy, though it was influenced, too, by external factors, notably the existence of towns and of a developing state apparatus. Where private property was important, an upper or ruling class was established. Two main patterns of stratification are evident here, according to Ravis-Giordani. First was the 'noble' type, 'characterized less by any differentiation in wealth, which need not have been very great, and more by the closed nature of the dominant class', achieved via strict endogamy. This type was found primarily in the Sartenais but also in parts of the Balagna. The Sartenais was a region where nobles or would-be nobles were thick on the ground at the end of the eighteenth century. Patin de La Fizelière counted 120 noble heads of family in the town of Sartène alone. The formal loss of feudal rights in 1789 did little to diminish the real power in the south of families like the Susini, the Ortoli, the Roccaserra and the Colonna, at least before the end of the nineteenth century when their political influence was on the wane. As we have seen, the important families in the south owned very large amounts of land. These were not always economically productive but provided the basis for maintaining a following of clients. In the Balagna, latifundia were used more frequently for agriculture and arboriculture. At Belgodere, for example, the censuses of 1851 and 1911 indicate a mass of agricultural workers employed by three noble families, and a similar situation existed at Ville-di-Paraso and at Speloncato.[76]

The second type of stratification was that of 'notables'. Here power was not hereditary or 'acquired once and for all; it had to be retained through constant efforts'. Wealth lay in land, as in the former category, but derived also from commerce, the liberal professions and state service. Social mobility was greater and there was more room for successful talent to rise. This type was found in the Vico and Corte regions, parts of the Balagna, the Capo Corso, the Nebbio, the Casinca, the Castagniccia, the Cinarca and the Cruzzini. Some of the most important of all Corsican families, those which achieved power at national level in France, fit into this category, for example, the Sebastiani, originally from La Porta in the Castagniccia, the Casabianca from the Casinca, or the Arrighi from Corte.[77]

In areas such as the Niolo, the Fiumorbo or the Venaco region, where common lands were predominant, stratification was correspondingly undeveloped. Wealth and power could not be founded there on the accumulation of private property. It was possible, however, for a stratum of 'bosses' to emerge within this egalitarian economic context. Their power was directly related to the size of their families and their ability to use physical force, but also to their skill in manipulating the political process. Control of the mayorship and thus of access to communal rights was a crucial instrument here. The power of such families was usually wholly local, though a few, like the Abbatucci from Zicavo, did achieve wider prominence.[78]

By comparison with élites in continental France, most Corsican upper-class families were poor. In 1828, only one elector paid over 500 francs in direct taxes, while only five persons in the whole island reached the property qualification to stand for election to the Chamber of Deputies in 1839. Again, during the period of limited suffrage before 1848, the number of qualified electors never reached 50.[79] There is no doubt, however, about the reality and the visibility of this top stratum of Corsican society. First, contemporaries used the special terms *jo, scio, sgio*, or *signore* to describe or address those who belonged to it. All had the original connotation of 'noble', but they were used from the early nineteenth century of both nobles, ex-nobles, wealthy non-nobles, and officials, priests and magistrates. Another sign of noble or notable status was the use of the title 'Don', found particularly in the south, the Castagniccia and the Casinca, and both were cherished and 'much coveted'. Montherot relates that a hotel keeper at Piedicroce insisted: 'Don't forget the Don, please ... I am noble.'[80] Another sign of the highest status was the possession and occupation of grand houses, most marked perhaps in the Balagna,[81] and the possession of family chapels and tombs, which we will discuss further in Chapter 13. Particularly in the first half of the nineteenth century, too, the élite enjoyed a number of privileges. As we have indicated these included the right to vote and stand for election, but licences to carry firearms, jury service and appointment as mayor were also restricted to the same narrow circle of families.[82]

Below the top stratum, a crucial difference existed between the property-owning class and those outside it. Although the term *proprietari* and its French equivalent were stretched on occasions, a real distinction was drawn in both official and popular speech and thinking between the man 'living off his property', i.e. who could live off the income derived from his property, and the man who had to complement this with other work.[83] Parallel to this and of special significance where access to communal lands was important was the distinction between old, founding or aboriginal families and newcomers who were excluded from the economic community.[84]

Below the *proprietari* in the rural social scale were various kinds of herdsmen, *pastori*, *porcai* or *caprai*, few of whom would have been entirely independent; those who worked the land: *lavatori*, *paesani* and *giornalieri*; millers; artisans; and forest workers. The important category of *lavatori* was a wide one, varying somewhat from region to region. A court case in 1852 at Antisanti involved a *lavatore* called Don Antono Mattei. More generally, they were either small land-owners who did not possess enough to 'live off', or those with no land of their own, or even herdsmen engaged temporarily in agriculture. The main thing is that they worked for others, usually on a share-cropping basis. Also unlike most day labourers and many herdsmen in the south, they had access to common lands and rights. The majority of Corsicans were to be found in this social category.[85]

At the bottom of the social scale in Corsica were Italian immigrant workers. Although they were all referred to as *lucchesi*, they came in fact from other parts of northern and central Italy besides Lucca, mainly leaving via Leghorn for Bastia. In the first half of the nineteenth century, they were nearly all seasonal migrants, arriving in October or November and leaving between April and June. They were mostly engaged in heavy manual labour: clearing land, making terraces and enclosures, general field work and sawing timber. They were also increasingly employed by the State in public works: road and later railway building. They usually worked in gangs of ten to fifteen men under a leader. Numbers rose from around 2,000 annually in 1830 to over 20,000 in the 1890s and 1900s, falling off rapidly thereafter. Most *lucchesi* remained in the eastern coastal region, but some moved further afield, especially those few who were traders or artisans. Growing numbers settled in the later nineteenth century, and some intermarriage took place. Despite this, Italians remained a despised out-group. An account of a court case in 1833 explained that *lucchese* was

> an untranslatable word that has a particular meaning in the Corsican language. A *lucchese* is less than a man, he is a species apart. One often hears it said in the interior: 'We were four men and a *lucchese*.' When they want to describe an insignificant individual, without any moral fibre, people call him *lucchese*, with an air of contempt.

Proverbs also assured dishonoured and ugly girls that they could always marry a *lucchese*. Apart from any ethnic hostility, this contempt seems to be related to the fact that Italians were without kin, associated particularly with manual work that was felt to be degrading, and engaged by employers on a purely contractual basis, which left no room for any pretence of independence.[86]

This was extremely important in Corsica, where the real hierarchy of the social structure was offset, mitigated or masked by egalitarian elements. 'Perhaps there is nowhere in the world such democratic uniformity of life as in this island, where differences of rank are scarcely perceptible', wrote Gregorovius in the 1850s, an observation made by many visitors.[87] We have seen that everyone owned some land, a vine, a garden, even in the Sartenais or the Balagna. Elsewhere most had access to common lands. Again, most people had some animals and most families owned all or part of a house. It was frequently observed, too, that Corsicans were extremely reluctant to assume roles that might imply inferiority. Réalier-Dumas noted in 1819, with special reference to the Balagna, that 'no Corsican man would consent to be a servant; and women rarely would in their place of birth'; and in recent years Corsican men, in particular, have been very unwilling to 'serve' in hotels or restaurants.[88] We have pointed, moreover, to the crucial distinction between the independent proprietor and the man who worked, albeit part-time, for someone else. Outsiders commented, too, on the easy and intimate relations between rich and poor. 'One often sees a landowner seated at table with his workers,' Mérimée wrote in 1840, 'and they call him by his Christian name and consider themselves to be members of the family.' A case in 1856 revealed that four young men from Muro were boon companions, though one was a carpenter, another from a family of petty landowners, and the other two of notable stock.[89]

However, there were strict limits to this egalitarianism, which was often more apparent than real. First, as we have stressed, some regions of Corsica were more democratic than others. In the middle of the nineteenth century, the Niolo was 'a relatively egalitarian society, where the influence of a family depended more on the number and quality of its members than on the extent of its land'. There were very few wealthy residents. Wages were almost unknown. Houses were of about equal size, and most people were listed in censuses as being of the same socio-professional status. Nevertheless, as we have seen, a ruling stratum did emerge in this milieu.[90] In other regions, such as the Balagna, where disparities in wealth were obvious, patronage, familiarity and an egalitarian ideology of honour served to cloak but ultimately to perpetuate a situation of social inequality. This is succinctly conveyed in the customary form of address, probably alluded to by Mérimée and explicitly recorded by others: 'Scio Francesco' or 'Scio Antono', that is 'Sir Francis' or 'Sir Anthony'.[91]

IV

Violent conflict, vendetta and banditry are central to the popular view of Corsica. For Maupassant, who did much to confirm the stereotype, it was 'the land of the vendetta'. 'The little that most people have heard about Corsica is largely associated with the idea of blood,' Barry agreed in 1893. 'Corsican blood vengeances have a world-wide reputation.'[92] Already established in the eighteenth century, when it was offset by the libertarian hopes associated with Paoli and the movement for independence,[93] this reputation was reinforced in the nineteenth by a combination of tourism, which produced a plethora of guide-books, accounts and journals,[94] and of literary romanticism, whose most distinguished and influential product was Mérimée's *Colomba*, published in 1840.[95]

The stereotype had a life of its own, but it was also firmly rooted in social reality. Unlike some of those who wrote fiction in a Corsican setting, Mérimée had actually visited the island and had observed its culture with some care, as had the majority of those who published factual travel books. Corsican attitudes towards what was in the main a hostile stereotype were mixed, reflecting an ambivalence towards socially sanctioned violence at least among the élite. This is emphasized in *Colomba*, the heroine remaining faithful to the traditional obligations of blood vengeance, while her brother, who has been educated outside the island, is reluctant to act in accordance with them. The vendetta was an object of reproach from the time of Paoli onwards, and some Corsican voices were eloquent in their condemnation of what was felt to be a shamefully barbaric custom. Notable here was Salvator Viale, whose mock-epic poem *Dionomachia* was first published in 1817. In others shame bred a certain reticence. 'Bandits and vendetta are the two subjects on which a Corsican is never expansive,' wrote Archer in 1924. 'They prefer the foreigner to believe that such things no longer exist,' or even, she might have added, that they never had.[96]

There is no doubt, however, of the importance in nineteenth-century Corsica of violence related to blood vengeance or of the persistent hold of the values underlying both. One of the principal and earliest aims of the French administration was to eradicate the vendetta, and a chorus of reports by police and judicial officials deplored its effects.[97] Court records and criminal statistics fully confirm such views. We shall cite the former abundantly in later chapters and will deal here only with the latter.

As in other spheres, it is difficult to arrive at reliable statistics of crime in Corsica. There were wide disparities between the number of offences and crimes committed and those reported, of crimes reported and suspects arrested, and of persons arrested and those prosecuted or again convicted. Yearly estimates of homicides in the early nineteenth century, for example, regularly exceeded actual prosecutions by a factor of 2 or 3. It is often unclear, moreover, to which category official figures refer. But we may be sure that the crime rate was consistently high throughout the nineteenth century at all levels of the court system.

The number of convictions in the lower courts in the 1820s was relatively two or three times as great in Corsica as it was in the rest of France. In the 1830s, Corsica's rate per head of population for those charged with serious crimes before the Assize Court was at least twice that for France as a whole, and Corsica figured regularly with the Seine among the departments with the highest rates, a situation which had changed little by the end of the century.[98]

Serious crimes in Corsica were mainly crimes against the person. 'The inhabitants are not at all inclined to crimes motivated by cupidity,' Governor Miot reported in 1801, and his judgment held for the rest of the century.[99] In France in the years 1826–31, the ratio of crimes against the person to crimes against property was 1:4, and the proportion of crimes against the person fell considerably during the nineteenth century.[100] In Corsica, the ratio between the two categories of serious crime was reversed through the entire century, ranging from 1:0.8 to 1:0.2.[101]

Table 1 provides figures, based on the best available evidence, of average numbers of homicides per annum and of homicides and attempted homicides per annum in Corsica, dividing the nineteenth century into five-yearly periods, and computing a rate per 100,000 of population. In some years, of course, the actual figures rose well above these averages. In 1848, 207 homicides were committed, which gives a rate of 91 per 100,000. All this gave Corsica a violent crime and homicide rate far higher than that of the rest of France. Robiquet calculated that in the years 1826–31, the incidence of crimes against the person was 9 times greater in Corsica than in the rest of France, and that there were 30 times as many cases of manslaughter (*meurtre*) and 12 times as many of murder (*assassinat*). He also noted that the proportion of homicides in which firearms, knives and daggers were used was much higher in Corsica.[102] The same disparity between Corsica and other French departments was found at the end of the century. In 1886 the rate of homicide and attempted homicide in Corsica was four times greater than it was in the Seine, the department with the second highest rate, while in 1891 the homicide rate alone in Corsica was five times greater than that in the Seine.

Corsican rates were also of course far higher than those found in Western societies today. The homicide rate in the UK has been around 0.3 to 0.4 per 100,000 since 1930, which is unusually low. In the USA, homicide rates rose to a high-point of 10 per 100,000 in 1933 and again in 1974. The rate for the city of Miami in 1948–52 was 15.[103] More helpful comparisons are probably with other traditional societies with a reputation for violence. Here, it seems that Corsican rates were generally well above those found in northern Europe in the Middle Ages or the Early Modern period,[104] though they were much closer, as might be expected, to those found in other parts of the Mediterranean world in the modern period. The homicide rate in Sardinia in the nineteenth century ranged from 22 to 80 per 100,000. The rate in the Palermo court district of Sicily in 1959 was 43, while the rate in the city of Naples in 1981, supposedly 'the highest murder rate of any city in the world', was 19.[105] Corsica was therefore at the upper end of any scale of human societies measured by the incidence of killing and interpersonal violence within them. Significantly higher homicide rates are only found regularly among certain 'primitive' peoples addicted to warfare, such as the Tauade of Papua,[106] or for very brief periods and among limited sections of 'advanced' societies.

Table 1. *Homicides and attempted homicides*[107]

	Homicides (annual average no.)	Rate per 100,000	Homicides and attempted homicides (annual average no.)	Rate per 100,000
1816–20	74	41	–	–
1821–5	65	36	139	77
1826–30	50	27	143	77
1831–5	76	39	158	81
1836–40	53	26	125	60
1841–5	62	28	122	51
1846–50	146	64	163	71
1851–5	27	12	–	–
1856–60	–	–	–	–
1861–5	33	13	–	–
1866–70	33	13	–	–
1871–5	–	–	70	28
1876–80	56	22	150	59
1881–5	73	28	130	50
1886–90	57	21	135	50
1891–5	39	14	–	–
1896–1900	–	–	66	23

A brief word is necessary about the chronology of homicides in Corsica. Our figures and analysis of a large number of administrative and other reports make it clear that homicide rates were high during the first half of the nineteenth century, continuing a trend from the previous century. There was a marked fall in the 1850s and a rise again in the last third of the century before the rate dropped definitively after the First World War.[108] How are we to explain this pattern, which exhibits no obvious unilinear progression? First, there is a correlation between periods of excessive violence and times in which the political order was relaxed, viz. the early decades of the century, the period of the Second Republic, and the early years of the Third Republic; and conversely between periods of minimal violence and times of strong government, viz. the first part of the Second Empire. Changes of régime were a particular encouragement to homicide.[109] Generally and in the long term, we are witnesses here to the process by which vendetta as a means of social control or system of customary law was replaced by the police, the courts and the law of the State. But this process was by no means smooth or simple, and the Corsican example illustrates that the introduction of state control and 'civilization' alongside a system of blood vengeance could exacerbate violence in the short term until the one definitively replaced the other.[110] The internal controlling mechanisms of the feud were undermined for a period before the policing of the State became fully effective either at the practical administrative level or at that of cultural adherence.

] 2 [

The history and incidence of feuds

It is generally recognized that feuding takes place over long spans of time. But social anthropologists cannot usually describe this essential feature of feuding directly, since they know the societies which they study only in the short term. At best, they may learn the prevailing mythological history of a feud from one or both parties to it, though even this may be missing, as feuding itself dies out and the memory of it is either forgotten or repressed.[1] As a long-term phenomenon and one that was very important in medieval and early modern Europe, feuding is therefore the proper object of historical study. Historians, however, are not usually in practice much better placed as investigators, since the indirect and fragmentary nature of their evidence precludes detailed reconstruction of the chronology of individual feuds.[2] Corsica, however, belongs to that small number of societies where feuding survived into the modern period within the purview of agents of a relatively efficient bureaucratic State. From administrative reports, judicial records and other sources, it is possible to trace the history of feuds in a number of villages from the end of the eighteenth century, thus filling a gap in our general knowledge of how feuds work as well as providing a basis for the more extended treatment of the subject in the chapters which follow. We have selected as examples those villages where the evidence is most complete or where distinctive patterns of feuding may be discerned. After presenting these chronological accounts, we shall draw some conclusions about these patterns, using a larger sample, referring also to the geographical incidence of feuding in the island.

I

ARBELLARA

Hostilities at Arbellara between the Forcioli and the Agostini on the one side, and the Giustiniani, the Camilli and the Benetti on the other, can be traced back to March 1826, when the mayor, a Giustiniani, brought a prosecution against the brothers Anton-Francesco and Don Giacomo Rutilj Forcioli 'for committing indecencies in church during the Holy Week services' and for grimacing at him when he told them to behave. In mid-May, three oxen belonging to Domenico

and Girolamo Agostini were shot dead by persons unknown. In mid-July, presumably in retaliation, two oxen and a cow, belonging to Giacomo-Alfonso and
Don Gavino Camilli, father and son, were similarly killed, while towards the end
of November three oxen belonging to Giovanni Giustiniani were killed and three
more were mortally wounded. In December, the subprefect reported that various
notables from outside, including the mayor of Sartène, had intervened to prevent
further escalation of the conflict and 'that a sincere and complete peace had
fortunately been concluded'. This peace, however, was short-lived, for early in
May 1827 an ox belonging to Francesco Rutilj, and, a week later, a horse belonging to the Rutilj Forcioli brothers, were killed. At the end of July, a shot was
fired at Don Giacomo Giustiniani 'as he was opening his window before going to
bed', though he was not hit. Again, in early October, another ox, belonging to
Angelo-Francesco Rutilj, was killed. Our next information comes in 1830. In
July, Bastiano Benetti, a relative by marriage of the Giustiniani, reported that six
of his cattle had been poisoned while they were pasturing on the plain of Baraci,
while in November the mayor called for the posting of a detachment of *voltigeurs*
to the village. He referred to 'the ill-will and strong hatred which exist between
the main families of this place' and said that the inhabitants were afraid to go out
after dark.[3]

In 1835, the feud entered a new phase. According to Versini, an offer was
made by the Giustiniani to marry their beautiful daughter Maria to the rich and
handsome Giulio Forcioli, a distant relative, known as Romano since he had
studied medicine at Rome. This offer, aimed at long-term reconciliation, was
refused. Carlo Giustiniani provided a slightly different version of events, claiming in a memoir written ten years later that a marriage had actually been arranged. 'It was never satisfactorily explained why this projected union was suddenly broken off,' he commented, 'but it is certain that this rupture prepared the
way for the sorrows which both families' were to suffer. Yet another account
attributes the initiative in the courtship to Giulio Forcioli. More certainly, some
livestock belonging to the Forcioli was killed early in July and this action was
imputed to the Giustiniani, which served as the pretext for ending the marriage
negotiations whatever their exact nature. Threats were made on both sides, and
then, on the evening of 22 July, the first killing of persons occurred. Giovan-
Battiste and Girolamo Giustiniani and their brothers-in-law, Carlo Benetti and
Don Gavino Camilli, were ambushed at a place in the country, as they returned
from Olmeto on horseback. Six shots were fired at them; Girolamo Giustiniani
was killed; Giovan-Battiste, who was mayor of Arbellara, was seriously
wounded; and Benetti, who was *adjoint* (deputy mayor), was slightly injured.
Their assailants were Antono Forcioli, the brother of Romano, and his cousin
Giulio Agostini, who went into hiding in the maquis and were later condemned
to death in their absence.

Meanwhile, following the ambush and the killing, both families fortified their
houses and their members only ventured out in armed groups. According to
Carlo Giustiniani, brother of the victims, 'the Forcioli family constructed elaborate fortifications around its domain. The doors were barricaded, the windows
blocked up leaving only loopholes, and a tower was even constructed from
which they were able to dominate their enemies and spy out their least move-

ment.' Giovan-Battiste Giustiniani reported on 6 August in the same vein to the prefect, writing that the Forcioli had 'blocked the streets of the village': 'while they boast that they have supplies to last for years and threaten us with a terrible vendetta, our relatives are forced to stay indoors and cannot get in their harvest'. At his request, a detachment of *voltigeurs* was sent to the village, but not in time to prevent a second encounter between the two families on 11 August. Rocco Forcioli, brother of Giulio and Antono, was shot in the leg at an evening gathering by Carlo Giustiniani and, in the commotion which followed, Maria Giustiniani was stabbed three times in the belly by an Agostini girl.[4]

Giovan-Battiste Giustiniani had been appointed mayor in 1833, despite misgivings on the part of the authorities and only after two other candidates had declined the post. He was at the time 'farmer of the communal lands' and cumulation of the two positions was felt to be undesirable. Despite this and the intensification of the feud at Arbellara, he was reappointed in 1835, with Carlo Benetti as *adjoint* again. Objections by the Rutilj Forcioli led to his replacement in 1837. The subprefect reported that the mayor's involvement in the feud was 'incompatible' with the exercise of his office, but the only substitute whom he could propose was another member of the Giustiniani family and 'the only municipal councillor' not ostensibly implicated in the conflict. No neutral candidate could be found for the post of *adjoint*.[5]

At the end of August 1836 or 1837, Don Gavino Camilli, an old man to whom the Forcioli had allegedly promised immunity, was shot in the back and killed while on his way to his son's wedding with a niece of the Forcioli at Olmeto. No further incidents are reported until the 1840s. In May 1841, Francesco Benetti was killed at Viggianello by Girolamo Benetti, who then became a bandit. The relationship between the two men is unclear. In November 1841, another encounter took place between the main protagonists. Giovan-Battiste Giustiniani, his son Giulio-Matteo, and Girolamo Benetti, his nephew, were searching for Antono Forcioli and Giulio Agostino who were reported to have returned from Sardinia, when they were surprised by their quarry. Giulio-Matteo and his cousin were seriously wounded. Though this incident and the return of the two Forcioli bandits 'revived' the feud, a *modus vivendi* seems soon to have prevailed, for Bertrand reports that servants and *coloni* were granted immunity and permitted to go about their normal occupations. In February 1842, Girolamo Benetti was arrested, and he was later convicted and sentenced to hard labour for life and public exhibition. Rather than undergo this last humiliation, he stabbed himself in his prison cell in Bastia in June. Meanwhile, in Arbellara, Carlo Giustiniani says that 'a kind of truce' between the main feuding families had been brought about 'by persons who had an influence over both of them', which lasted for nearly three years. In August 1842, a Forcioli was ambushed and killed between Arbellara and Fozzano, but it was reported that 'this killing has nothing to do with the feud which exists between the Forcioli and the Giustiniani, since the Forcioli who was killed is not even related to the other Forcioli'.[6]

On 31 October 1844, seven young men of the Giustiniani family (Carlo, Petro-Paolo, Matteo, Giuseppo and Giovanni Giustiniani, Carlo Benetti and Giovanni Camilli) left Arbellara for a rendezvous with their relative, Dr Peretti, the mayor of Olmeto, in order to fix the boundaries of some land which they had just acquired. At the same time, apparently by chance, a group of the Forcioli went to visit one of their properties in the same vicinity. From an elevated spot, the Giustiniani party saw and recognized the Forcioli near Pantano, the place where the 1835 encounter and killing had occurred. The Giustiniani were suspicious and decided to take pre-emptive action. The Forcioli were ambushed, and Giacomo Forcioli and his nephew Giovan-Battiste were killed. Carlo Giustiniani was slightly wounded and he was the only member of his family to be arrested immediately. Although he claimed to have been acting in self-defence, he was convicted of complicity in homicide and sentenced to eight years' imprisonment in June 1845, which was regarded as a severe sentence. This fact and 'the desire to bring about reconciliation', in Versini's words, led to the acquittal of the other Giustiniani when they were tried in April 1847. In the meantime, Antono Benetti had been shot and wounded in November 1845 on the road to Sartène by Antono Forcioli and Giulio Agostini, although he had been accompanied by four *voltigeurs*. A truce or a period of quiescence then seems to have ensued until May 1849, when Giuseppo Benetti was killed on the threshold of his house as he was washing his hands and when most people had left the village to vote in the General Election. In the early 1850s, various notables in the region undertook the task of peacemaking again. A meeting between the opposing families finally took place in March 1854. The Forcioli assured the Giustiniani that the two bandits, who had been at large for nineteen years, would cease their hostilities, and the Giustiniani, for their part, agreed not to prosecute them. A peace was then proclaimed, and solemnized by the singing of a *Te Deum* in the church at Sartène.[7]

This ended the open conflict between the two parties for some time, but, if the president of the Assize Court is to be believed, no balance had been achieved, since the Forcioli had prospered during, if not by, the feud, thanks to the support of their two bandits, while the more peaceable Giustiniani had been ruined, particularly by the successful interdict placed on their lands by the same bandits. The feud in effect remained latent and expressed itself in the early 1860s in intense political conflict. Paolo Giustiniani, who had administered the village as mayor or *adjoint* for three or more decades, died in 1861, and attempts were made to replace him with a more partisan incumbent. The prefect received a letter in May 1861 reporting that 'this unfortunate commune remains the victim of a bloody feud' and warning against the campaign to get Giovan-Battiste Giustiniani, son of the late Carlo, and 'blood enemy of the Agostini', appointed as mayor. In the event, Giovan-Battiste, who was vigorously supported by his uncle, General Councillor Galloni, was nominated and installed as mayor, which prompted the *adjoint*, who presumably belonged to the opposite camp, to resign. He was replaced by Giovanni Camilli. But this restoration of the Giustiniani to political power did not last long. Giovan-Battiste died within a year of his appointment and was replaced by a relative of neutral tendency, which brought about a comparative calm.[8]

The same period was not free of violence. In 1859, Anton-Girolamo Giustiniani exchanged shots with the officer of health, Peretti, though this was not directly related to the main feud. This was active again at the close of the century. In December 1892, Petro-Paolo Giustiniani, a schoolmaster, was killed in his house by the bandit Sorba and Simon-Giovanni Forcioli, and the latter was convicted of this crime in 1894 and condemned to 15 years hard labour. It seems, however, that by this time the distinction, discernible earlier among the Giustiniani, between those who were actively engaged in the feud and those who were neutral, had gone a stage further towards a split into two groupings, one of which sided with their erstwhile enemies; for Don Giacomo and Antono Giustiniani were said by the authorities to be protectors of Sorba.[9]

FOZZANO

The feuding at Fozzano has attracted attention, since Mérimée based his novella *Colomba* on it.[10] According to Vrydaghs Fidelis, there was conflict at Fozzano in the mid-seventeenth century involving the Tomasi among others, but feuding in modern times cannot really be traced back further than 1774, when a report referred to 'open warfare' there between the Paoli and the Bartoli, 'the two largest families': 'Many people on both sides have taken refuge in the maquis and those who have stayed in the village remain shut up in their houses.' Our next information dates from 1795, when Petro Durazzi was shot and killed by Francesco Poli (or Paoli) at Propriano, a port then dependent on Fozzano. Petro Durazzi, a member of one of the wealthiest families of the district, had recently started trading from Propriano in partnership with his brother-in-law Angelo-Fortuno, and Poli had apparently been hoping to act as their agent. When another man was appointed, Poli tried to prevent a ship laden with the Durazzi's goods from landing. This attempt, which led to general conflict between the two men's kinsmen and supporters, was frustrated, and Durazzi was killed on the evening of the same day. The judicial authorities later explained this incident in terms of 'the ancient enmities' which divided the Durazzi and the Poli families, 'enmities which had not had such serious consequences before, but which none the less inspired both sides with an implacable hatred.'[11]

By the start of the nineteenth century, if not before, these enmities among the Fozzano families, all of whom were distantly connected, had coalesced into two broad groupings. On the one side were the Durazzi and the Paoli, together with the Grimaldi, who formed the party *di sopra* or of the upper village, and on the other were the Bernardini, the Carabelli, the Tomasi and the Bartoli, who formed the party *di sotta* or of the lower village. Conflict between them must have continued through the Revolutionary period, since the authorities intervened in 1801–2 and 1805 to impose peace. In 1811, Paolo-Girolamo Paoli and Anton-Francesco Durazzi mortally wounded Lorenzo Tomasi, and, since the authorities were unable to arrest them, Paoli's father and brother and Durazzi's father and cousin were taken as hostages to the citadel in Ajaccio. Further violence was reported in 1816. In May, Bernardino Carabelli was shot and wounded in the arm by Girolamo Paoli, as he was demolishing a wall that Paoli had constructed on what Carabelli believed to be his property. In August Saverio Bernardini stabbed Bastiano Nunzi, and in September Vincenzo Bartoli was accused of hitting and threatening to kill Father Renucci, two events whose links with the main field of conflict remain unclear.[12]

In 1819, a series of attacks on animals began, similar to that which we have encountered at Arbellara. In January, Petro Paoli complained that two of his oxen had been killed with sticks and stones. In September 1820, the mayor of Fozzano, a Durazzi, reported that his mule had been shot dead. In April 1821, two oxen were killed and one seriously injured in an enclosure belonging to the Carabelli. In March 1824, an ox belonging to Antono Poli was shot dead by persons unknown, and in October a mule belonging to Antono Bartoli. Four oxen belonging to the mayor were killed in October 1826. Then, in September 1829, a bull belonging to Petro-Paolo Poli was shot dead on land belonging to Captain Carabelli, and Poli accused Antono Pasqualini, the captain's servant, of having committed the crime 'on the orders of Signora Angela-Maria Bernardini, his wife'.[13]

Conflict seems to have been building up for some years, therefore, before it erupted into new violence in the 1830s, although the Bernardini claimed that the 'enmity' between the leading Fozzano families 'appeared to be entirely extinguished, when suddenly on 6 June 1830 (the day of the patronal festival) a fight begun by the Paoli revived it'. The trouble started in the early evening as people were leaving church after vespers, and Petro-Paolo Paoli 'looked askance' at Paolo Paoli. This seems to have been because the latter had gone over to the opposing party, though Versini says that the Paoli family were always divided, which our earlier evidence would seem to confirm. The two men came to blows and their relatives quickly joined in the fighting. Shots were exchanged and daggers used. Paolo Paoli and his cousin Giovan-Battiste Bernardini were killed; Petro-Paolo Paoli, his son Giovan-Carlo and his relative by marriage, Anton-Francesco Paoli, were seriously wounded; and they, together with Michelangelo Paoli, were arrested, while seven other men, including Michel-Antono and Giovan-Paolo Durazzi on the one side, and Francesco Paoli, Francesco Bartoli and Ettore Bernardini on the other, went into hiding. Petro-Paolo Paoli died on 20 June, and the gendarmerie reported with foresight that people on both sides were so excited 'that one could only believe that this atrocity was a beginning'. In mid-August, it was reported that a house in the country, belonging to Paolo-Francesco Paoli, had been broken into and a quantity of wheat stolen from it, while in September, Giusepp'-Antono Carabelli and Anton-Michele Bernardini fired shots at Giovan-Battiste and Francesco Durazzi from behind the wall of an enclosure. Then, on 24 October 1830, Giulio Bernardini, returning from Sartène with four relatives, met Michele Durazzi with six of his relatives, apparently by chance, at a place near Arbellara. Two shots were fired; Giulio Bernardini was killed and Michele Durazzi was seriously wounded. The effect on the village was devastating. 'The houses were crenellated and barricaded, the streets deserted, and no one dared to go out.'[14] At the same time there was a political vacuum. The mayorship was vacant and the municipal council incomplete and unable to take decisions.[15]

In May 1831, Michelangelo Paoli was tried for killing Giovan-Battiste Bernardini the previous June and was acquitted. As he was celebrating this verdict afterwards in Bastia with his brother Giovan-Battiste and his nephew Paolo-Francesco, they were attacked by Saverio and Anton-Francesco Bernardini, the brother of the victim. Shots were exchanged and one of the Paoli was wounded with a dagger. The Bernardini were arrested and later prosecuted and convicted, receiving what were regarded as light sentences of two and four years' imprisonment. In December 1832, another encounter took place outside the village. Petro-Paolo Bernardini fired a shot at an armed group of the Paoli as they were passing the house of ex-Prefect Pietri in Sartène. He seems to have fired from inside the house, where his widowed aunt Magdalena Bernardini lived. Paolo-Francesco Paoli was hit in the leg and Bernardini was arrested. Robiquet and others also mention the killing of a Carabelli near Propriano in late 1831 or 1832, which was possibly a reprisal for the earlier action of the Bernardini or may have prompted this latest attack.[16]

A year later occurred the famous encounter at Tunichilla. It seems that Michele Durazzi, accompanied by his sons Giovan-Paolo, Battiste and Ignazio, his nephews Francesco-Maria and Battiste and several Italian workers, were on their way, early on the morning of 30 December 1833, to a property in the Baraci valley, when they were ambushed by a party of their enemies, including Francesco Bartoli, Francesco and Giuseppo Paoli, and Michele and Petro-Paolo Bernardini. Battiste and Ignazio Durazzi were killed outright, and their brother Giovan-Paolo was wounded. Their relatives returned the fire, and Francesco Bartoli and Michele Bernardini were killed. The Paoli and Michele Durazzi's nephews went into hiding. A year later, through the intervention of the authorities, a treaty of peace was signed by the two parties. This stipulated that those accused of crimes relating to the feud should give themselves up within two months, so that they could be tried, and the carrying of arms was forbidden in the village.[17]

However, this was by no means the end of conflict in Fozzano, either immediately or in the long term. Versini notes that although Signora Bartoli, the moving spirit of her party and the model for 'Colomba', moved to Olmeto, she did not accept the peace treaty. According to accounts related to Roger by descendants of the Paoli, she tried to hire herdsmen to kill the remaining Durazzi and she announced that she would only marry her daughter to a man who would pursue the feud. In mid-May 1835, the subprefect reported that a killing at nearby Altagène had caused 'considerable anxiety in Fozzano, where the two parties are beginning again to be wary of each other', while at the end of October, Carlino Paoli was stabbed and seriously wounded in a fight with Carlo Paoli, the son of Dono.[18]

But nothing seems to have come of this continuing animosity, and our next information dates from a decade later. In November 1846, the prefect received a letter from several members of the Bartoli and the Carabelli families, complaining of the alleged maladministration of the mayor, Paolo-Franscesco Paoli, and declaring that his supporters on the municipal council, three Durazzi and another Paoli, were unfit to hold office. The Durazzi and the Paoli had held the offices of mayor and *adjoint* through most of the period since 1815, but this does not seem to have been a prime cause of friction earlier, perhaps because more moderate members of the families were chosen. Early in 1847, Giovan-Battiste Carabelli had a meeting with the prefect, following which the mayor resigned. In his letter of resignation, Paoli claimed that his efforts to improve the village, for example by having a new road built and by leasing the communal lands, had been frustrated by the systematic opposition organized by 'the Carabelli party'.[19]

Conflict also recurred at this time between the different branches of the Paoli family. In 1846, Petro-Paolo Paoli, known as Barone, had a fight with Giuseppo-Maria Paoli of Olmeto over a boundary between their properties. Giuseppo-Maria disarmed Barone and then insulted him. Barone swore to avenge himself and was supported by his cousin, Giusepp'-Antono, who was also Giuseppo-Maria's brother-in-law. In December 1848, the two cousins killed Giuseppo-Maria on the road from Sartène to Olmeto and went into hiding. In mid-July 1849, Giusepp'-Antono's father, Paolo-Girolamo, a peaceable man aged 60, was threshing wheat with his *coloni* near Fozzano, when an unknown youth came up and shot him dead. It transpired later that his assailant had been a bandit, hired, it seems, by Giuseppo-Maria's cousin Paolo-Francesco Panzani. Barone gave himself up after four years on the run and was sentenced to 20 years' hard labour in 1853. Giusepp'-Antono was tried and convicted in 1850, but his sentence was quashed and he was acquitted at a retrial. 'He returned to the bosom of his family and lived in seclusion, afraid that his enemies would take their revenge for the terrible crime that was imputed to him.' In January 1851 his fears were realized. He went out of the house to pick up some stones that had fallen from a wall, and was shot dead by a certain Stefano Papalini. 'Since there existed no reason for enmity between the two men, it was generally believed that Papalini had [also] acted as the agent' of Giuseppo-Maria Paoli's relatives, though this was never proved.[20]

The Second Empire was a quiet period in Fozzano, and the burial of Signora Bartoli in the village in 1864 passed without serious incident. The old rivalries were still evident, however, in the form of political and electoral conflict. In 1854, a Durazzi mayor was dismissed, following disagreements over the partition and leasing of communal lands, and he was replaced by Giulio Bernardini of the opposing party, who remained in office for over a decade. He in turn was removed in 1866, after he had practised a blatant fraud during the municipal elections to give his party a majority. The declaration of the result so angered his opponents that 'armed conflict' was only prevented by a promise from the gendarmerie that Bernardini would be prosecuted.[21]

Electoral conflict also prompted the violence which recurred at Fozzano at the end of the century. Giusepp'-Antono Bartoli and Giovan-Battiste Bernardini, both municipal councillors, had fallen out over the elections of 1888. 'Bartoli, who wanted to become mayor, blamed Bernardini when his bid for the office failed,[22] and he clearly manifested his displeasure on many occasions.' Ignazio Durazzi and Michelangelo Paoli shared his resentment, and the three of them 'vowed an implacable hatred towards Bernardini'. One evening in November 1891 they shot him in a wineshop in the village, apparently following a premeditated plan, and he died next day. The public prosecutor reported that 'this odious killing revived old hatreds that had slumbered for years', and feared that it would 'be followed by terrible reprisals ... Nearly all the houses are barricaded, and people only venture out armed to the teeth.' Only the arrest of the three culprits, he suggested, could definitely prevent reprisals, but they had taken flight and were well protected. Instead, the authorities gave way to demands that relatives of the wanted men be detained, and five members of the Paoli family were arrested, treatment which they regarded as 'dishonouring'. Ignazio Durazzi and

Michelangelo Paoli did not give themselves up until 1893, when they were tried, convicted and sentenced to fifteen years' hard labour each. Giusepp'-Antono Bartoli was tried in December 1896 and received a much more lenient sentence, which led Giovan-Battiste Bernardini's brother, Francesco, to lodge an official complaint about the jury.[23]

We will pursue the general analysis of feuding in later chapters, but some comments may be made at this stage about elements in the conflict at Fozzano which have wider implications. First, although there were two clear parties, each comprised several families, and families were sometimes divided between the two, like the Paoli and probably the Durazzi earlier in the century. Moreover, both individuals and families could change sides. The Bartoli and the Bernardini, who had been allies in the 1830s, were themselves at odds in the 1890s. Secondly, despite the picture painted by some writers of the whole village being in arms, not all the members even of the leading families were combatants. Reporting a shooting incident in September 1834 between a Paoli and a Bernardini, for example, the subprefect commented that 'these individuals are not yet involved in the enmity which is desolating the village'. The administration, of course, tried to find such neutrals to fill the posts of mayor and *adjoint*. In April 1831, the subprefect proposed Antono Durazzi as mayor again, since he was 'not involved in the enmity' and was 'accessible to everyone'. In 1867, Lorenzo Paoli was prevailed upon to stay on as mayor, because he combined 'a good social position and connections' with 'a conciliatory character'.[24]

Thirdly, though feuding was centred on the village of Fozzano itself, its theatre was far wider. Conflicts between the contestants took place at Sartène and Bastia. The protagonists had allies and enemies in other villages and towns. The Durazzi were clearly on friendly terms with the Giustiniani of Arbellara, and the Bernardini with the Pietri of Sartène, relations which were often cemented by marriage ties.

SANTA-LUCIA-DI-TALLANO

A number of villages in the Tallano district experienced intensive feuding during the nineteenth century. Of these the most important was Santa-Lucia, where the Poli, together with the Giocanti and some of the Quilichini competed for supremacy with the Giacomoni and the Santalucia. Enmity between the two parties seems to have been well-established at the start of the century.

In January 1815, a house, walls and tree in Santa-Lucia belonging to the subprefect, a Giacomoni, were destroyed, while in April there was a fight between the mayor, Alessandro Quilichini, and the priest, Anton-Padova Giacomoni and his nephew, over the key to the church. In August 1816, Alessandro Quilichini claimed to have been shot at the door of his house by Giovan-Felice Giacomoni, the tax-collector, but Anton-Michele Giacomoni alleged that Quilichini had fired at him and his family. No one was hurt, but, given the 'enmity' existing between the two families, it was felt in the village that further trouble was inevitable, especially after Giovan-Felice Giacomoni was arrested. In 1819, matters came to a head over a claim by Giacomo-Francesco Giacomoni to a right of way over an enclosure belonging to the Poli. In October, Giacomoni 'ordered his herdsman to take his flock of sheep' through the enclosure in question, which provoked resistance and fighting, in which two members of the Viggiani family were wounded and Dono Orsati was killed. Following this, the leader of the Poli family was prosecuted but was only condemned to two years' imprisonment for attempted homicide, an outcome which worsened relations. The October incident also seems to have brought about a shift in alliances. Mayor Ortoli wrote later that the Viggiani and the Orsati had been on bad terms with the Giacomoni before 1819 but then joined forces with them. By 1820, moreover, according to the public prosecutor, feuding had 'extended to nearly all the families' in the village and beyond.[25]

A lengthy denunciation of the parish priest Sanseverino Giacomoni was sent that year to the prefect by the mayor. He was accused of being excessively quarrelsome, special reference being made to minor disputes with Francesco Giacomoni and Padovano Quilichini. He represented his family in extensive litigation, which meant frequent absences from the village. He had been away from October 1819 to February 1820 in connection with a suit between his brother Giacomo, who administered all the Giacomoni family property, and Giovan-Paolo Quilichini, a suit which Quilichini lost. He was also accused of going about armed, of gambling and of having relations with women, and the mayor suggested that he be moved to another parish. Sanseverino riposted by having his supporters sign a petition in his favour. The collection of signatures, which came from the Giacomoni, the Viggiani and the Orsati, was organized by Giovan-Felice Giacomoni and by Peretti, the receiver of probate, another relative. In November 1820, presumably as some form of additional retaliation, an ox belonging to the mayor was killed.[26]

In February 1821, the subprefect reported that

> the canton of Tallano is very calm at the moment, but this calm is only superficial. The partisans of ex-mayor Poli avoid the places frequented by their enemies as far as possible and go out to cultivate their fields unarmed. Similarly, the Giacomoni seem very peaceable and never mention their enemies. But the bitterness between them is still there and could develop given the slightest chance.

He added that he and others had tried to bring about a formal reconciliation but without success. Later the same month, it was reported that bandits related to the Orsati had landed in Corsica from Sardinia. The subprefect saw the leaders of various families in Santa-Lucia, including the Viggiani brothers, who had been wounded, and three close relatives of the late Dono Orsati, who had been killed in 1819, to urge them to refrain from engaging in reprisals. This warning appears to have had some effect, but the situation remained unresolved and hostilities continued through the 1820s.[27]

In November 1821, two oxen belonging to Giuseppo Quilichini were shot dead. In February 1823, there was a fight between Petro-Paolo Orsati and Giulio-Antono Giacomoni, but they 'belonged to the same party' and were quickly reconciled. In February 1824, a cow belonging to Giovan-Battiste Quilichini was killed, and a potentially more dangerous dispute occurred the following April. Giovan-Battiste Viggiani, the officer of health, attacked the parish priest when the latter stopped him singing a lesson in church, but the priest, who was a new incumbent it seems, decided to ignore the matter. In August 1826, a further quarrel caused the authorities concern. The pregnant wife of Giacomo-Filippo Ettori tried to stop a fight between her son and the son of Tomaso Quilichini, and the latter threw her to the ground, causing her to abort. The subprefect intervened, however, to reconcile the two parties. A cow belonging to Judge Alessandro Giacomoni was killed in November 1826, while a year later part of a wall belonging to Giovan-Paolo Quilichini was destroyed and the judge and the daughters of Alessandro Quilichini, cousin of Giovan-Paolo, were believed to be the culprits. In January 1827, Petro Viggiani killed a member of the Ortoli family from nearby Olmiccia, an event that was to have disastrous consequences. The introduction of charges for having chairs in the church led to hostile reaction in November 1827, in which Giovan-Battiste and Giovan-Tomaso Quilichini and Giacomo-Antono Orsati played a leading part, and their chairs were taken out of the church and burned several times in February and May 1828. In July 1828, a wall belonging to Alessandro Quilichini was demolished, and a month later there was a fight between Nunzio and Giovan-Battiste Quilichini over a right of way and gendarmes seized two pocket pistols on the person of Francesco-Maria Quilichini. Judge Alessandro Giacomoni was reported to have tried to kill Carlo-Michele Viggiani in January 1829; while in March a serious fight took place between Giovan-Battiste and Francesco-Maria Quilichini on one side, and Francesc'-Antono Quilichini and his sister on the other. Francesco-Maria was later convicted of making threats to kill and causing bodily harm and also of stealing livestock.[28]

This build-up of conflict came to a head in the early 1830s, when the Poli broke off the engagement of their eldest son to a Giacomoni girl. According to the *Gazette des Tribunaux*, a Giocanti was seriously wounded in 1830, and Faure relates that Ottavio Giacomoni, brother of the jilted girl, was killed in the same year by a Poli, who was subsequently tried but acquitted. In July 1831, Giovan-Battiste Giocanti was killed and Giovan-Battiste Quilichini was wounded; both belonged to the Poli party, and their assailants were reported to be the Ortoli brothers, Giovan-Battiste and Antono, from Olmiccia. The mayor, a Giacomoni, banned the festivals usually held at the end of July, and the subprefect proposed sending a detachment of *voltigeurs* to Santa-Lucia. This prevented further trouble until the autumn. Then, in October, Giovanni Poli was killed, and at the beginning of November, Giovan-Battiste Quilichini was again attacked and, this time, killed, by Luca-Luigi Giacomoni. The subprefect reported later that month that the village was 'in a state of desolation difficult to describe: the doors of the houses are barricaded, the windows crenellated, the streets entirely deserted'. The mayor seems temporarily to have abandoned his functions and the local gendarmerie were helpless. They failed to arrest the bandit Pietrino Giacomoni early in December in the face of resistance from his relatives, and Father Don Giovanni Santalucia, charged with instigating the killing of Giovanni Poli, left Corsica temporarily rather than stand trial. However, no further incident was reported for two years though rivalries persisted at the political level. Since 1830, if not before, the Giacomoni had been in power locally, and in December 1831 Severino Giacomoni was confirmed as mayor and Marc-Antono Giacomoni became *adjoint.* The latter became mayor in May 1832, when Severino was appointed justice of the peace, but, probably with the idea of establishing some kind of balance, the authorities appointed Giovan-Bernardino Viggiani, who belonged to the opposing party, as *adjoint* in his place. This led to friction between the two men over the demarcation between their respective functions, and the subprefect reported in 1834 that Giacomoni was reluctant to invest Viggiani with his mayoral authority when he was absent, which was the usual procedure.

Meanwhile, an armed encounter between members of the two parties took place at Fontanella in January 1834. Paolo-Natale Poli on the one side, and Giulio-Martino and Giulio-Angelo Giacomoni, the brother of Pietrino on the other, were seriously wounded, and the two Giacomoni died soon afterwards. The authorities intervened, however, and a peace was signed at Sartène in December 1834. It was agreed that Petro-Francesco Poli and another relative still on the run should not be prosecuted for their part in the Fontanella incident, and a general disarmament was effected in the village, which then enjoyed four years of calm.[29]

According to a press report,

> the Poli had welcomed the peace with enthusiasm. Since they owned a large amount of land and had nearly always been victims in the terrible conflict, they were keen to stabilize a situation which enabled them to cultivate their fields and go about safely. They therefore socialized with the Giacomoni and the Santalucia and even aided them in their enterprises.

However, the enemies of the Poli, and particularly the Giacomoni, were less satisfied. They retained political power. Giovan-Felice Giacomoni became mayor in 1835 and was reappointed in 1837, and Marc-Antono Giacomoni became *adjoint* again in the same year. But they apparently felt that, although they had fulfilled their side of the peace treaty by not prosecuting the Poli, the latter had not made a sufficient response. More specifically, the Giacomoni wished the peace to be cemented by certain advantageous marriages, which had not been stipulated in the treaty, though promises may have been made informally. Giudice Giacomoni called Sarrello, father of Giulio-Martino killed in 1834, wanted to marry his daughter Colomba to Petro-Francesco Poli, while the brothers Don Giovanni and Antono Santalucia, both close relatives of Sarrello, wanted to marry their sister to another Poli. They also planned to marry a cousin, Eufrosina, to Giacomo Quilichini. But all these proposals were rebuffed by the wealthier Poli, who also intervened at the end of 1838 to prevent Giuseppo Quilichini called Buccino, the half-brother of Giulio-Martino Giacomoni, from arranging a marriage between his son and a cousin.[30]

In February 1839, a quarrel occurred between Petro-Francesco Poli and Giacomo-Antono Giacomoni, the younger brother of Giulio-Martino, in which Antono Santalucia was also involved. Poli reproached Giacomoni with not avenging his brother's death, an insult known as the *rimbeccu* which was grave in any circumstances but much exacerbated when made by a blood enemy. At about the same time, Giovan-Battiste Quilichini, the brother of Giacomo, was allegedly discovered to have had illicit sexual relations with a Giacomoni girl. Moreover, a double wedding was planned to take place at Easter 1839 between Petro-Francesco Poli and his cousin, Giacomo Quilichini, and two girls from Levie, an Ortoli and a Roccaserra. The Giacomoni attended the preliminary festivities but soon took a terrible revenge. On the Easter Monday after the wedding, the two grooms set off unarmed to fetch one of the brides from Levie. Petro-Francesco Poli had strangely accepted an offer to borrow a horse from Father Don Giovanni Santalucia, and they went first to find this animal in an enclosure, but on the way there they were ambushed. Petro-Francesco Poli was killed by Giacomo-Antono Giacomoni, aided by his cousin Antono Santalucia, and Giacomo Quilichini was wounded. Quilichini turned back to the village but was attacked again and killed before he arrived. The Poli believed that this double murder had been planned by the Giacomoni party as a whole and, in addition to Giacomo-Antono Giacomoni and Antono Santalucia, they accused the former's father Giudice, his half-brother Giuseppo Quilichini, and his cousin Pietrino, and the latter's brother Don Giovanni, the priest. Don Giovanni, who was regarded as the leader of his party, and Giudice were arrested and put on trial early in 1840. Testimony was given that Giudice had let his beard grow after the Fontanella affair and had preserved his son's bloody shirt, both indications of an intention to seek vengeance. He was also reported to have said: 'Giulio-Martino is dead and his murderers are still alive; but I am not wearing horns. The Poli promised to go into exile, and one of them must marry my daughter, or else.' After the double killing in 1839, he appeared in public with his beard cut and wearing new clothes. He was nevertheless acquitted of complicity in the killings, though Don Giovanni Santalucia was convicted and sentenced to ten years' imprisonment. With this consolation, the Poli returned to Santa-Lucia triumphantly, expecting the rest of the Giacomoni to be arrested very soon, but their triumph was short-lived.[31]

Antono Santalucia and Giacomo-Antono Giacomoni had taken to the maquis. At the end of July 1840, they shot dead Anton-Quiliano Ortoli, of the Poli party, who had testified for the prosecution at the trial, as he was returning from Altagène. 'On learning of this, the partisans of the Poli and the Quilichini armed themselves,' and Petro-Francesco Quilichini, Ortoli's first cousin, looked for someone to kill in retaliation. The only person he could find was Battina Giacomoni, Giacomo-Antono's aunt, whom he shot and mortally wounded as she stood defenceless at the door of her house. He was arrested the following year and sentenced to five years' imprisonment for this crime. Meanwhile, in mid-August 1840, another prosecution witness in the 1840 trial, Antono Ortoli, was attacked by Antono Santalucia and Giacomo-Antono Giacomoni on the road from Propriano to Olmiccia and had his eyes gouged out. The same two bandits, joined by Giuseppo Quilichini called Buccino, and operating from the neighbouring villages of Altagène and Mela rather than from Santa-Lucia itself, then established what was described as 'a reign of terror' in the region. Giacomo-Maria Poli, Vincenzo-Girolama Ortoli, Petro Viggiani and Francesco-Maria Quilichini complained to the prefect that their lives and those of their relatives were under constant threat, that their property was being appropriated and that their land had been placed under an interdict. In November 1841, three women gathering olives for Francesco-Maria Quilichini were threatened with death by

Giacomo-Antono Giacomoni. A relative by marriage of the Poli, Dr Roccaserra, was threatened in a similar way and moved to Ajaccio, where he was shot, however, in mid-August 1842, apparently also by Giacomo-Antono. In 1842 again, a member of the Quilichini family was forced by Antono Santalucia to marry a girl of lower social standing, whom he had allegedly seduced. Well before this, the Poli had been granted special permission to carry arms, for self-defence. Later in 1842, Father Santalucia, who was regarded as directing the operations of his brother and the other bandits, was pardoned, and they left Corsica for the Italian mainland and then Sardinia. In 1843, Giuseppo Quilichini was captured and returned to Corsica for trial, but he was acquitted. He was arrested again after an encounter with *voltigeurs* and sentenced to six months' imprisonment in September 1844, which led to a renewal of the interdict against the Poli. The following year, Antono Santalucia was back in Corsica, and in September he shot Antono Quilichini, the sixth of the witnesses against his brother in the 1840 trial to be killed. In revenge, Antono Quilichini's sister, Maria-Francesca, shot and killed Marc-Antono Giacomoni, who was then mayor of Santa-Lucia. She was tried early in 1846 and convicted of justifiable homicide. By this time there was a general desire for peace and, although no formal treaty was made, the bandits Giacomoni and Santalucia once more went into exile, returning only occasionally to Corsica. Giacomo-Antono Giacomoni became a smuggler and was spotted and wounded by gendarmes near Bonifacio in July 1847; his corpse was discovered in February 1848. Antono Santalucia was reported to have gone to America, where he died, it seems, in 1856.[32]

This was not the end of feuding in Santa-Lucia, however, though later conflict took a political and electoral turn. In a letter to the prefect in September 1846, Giovan-Antono Roccaserra and Simonpetro Quilichini referred to the determination of the Giacomoni 'coterie' 'to govern the canton of Tallano at all costs'. They had accumulated an impressive array of offices. Severino Giacomoni was justice of the peace and his son, Don Giacomo, was postman, while Giovan-Felice Giacomoni and his son, Francesco-Maria, had successively held the post of tax-collector. After ten years as mayor, Giovan-Felice had been suspended from office for alleged malpractice in April 1845, and Giovan-Bernardino Viggiani of the opposing party, who was again *adjoint*, became acting mayor. He quickly resigned, 'his complete blindness' making him unfit for the position, and intense lobbying took place to find a successor who would ultimately become mayor in his own right. As we have seen, Marc-Antono Giacomoni became mayor at the end of 1845, when Giovan-Felice was formally removed from office. His death shortly afterwards at the hands of Maria-Francesca Quilichini of course set off another competition for the mayorship. The Giacomoni, who had a majority on the municipal council, hoped to have Francesco-Maria, the tax-collector, nominated, but the candidate favoured by their opponents and not previously involved in the party struggles, Francesco Cesari, was appointed at the end of 1846.[33]

The introduction of universal male suffrage in June 1848 widened the scope of political conflict and the first municipal elections held at Santa-Lucia under the new system in July led to violence. Petro-Francesco Quilichini knocked over the urn in which the ballot papers were placed, which caused 'general commotion'.

Two shots were fired at Rocco Quilichini, the schoolmaster, and another member of his family. A house was surrounded by the gendarmerie and Giacomo-Napoleone Peretti, first cousin of Severino Giacomoni, and another man were discovered there with recently used guns. Prosecutions followed, but no convictions were brought.[34] No reports of violence at Santa-Lucia in the second half of the nineteenth century have survived and conflict there seems to have subsided into routine political competition.

The feuding at Santa-Lucia made an impact, we have seen, on the whole district of the Tallano. The Giacomoni party, for example, was reported in 1846 to be making a bid to win municipal offices at Altagène, Olmiccia, Poggio, Zoza and Sant'Andrea. The leading families of Santa-Lucia, moreover, had branches and affinal connections in the surrounding villages, the Quilichini, for example, in Olmiccia and Poggio, the Poli and the Viggiani at Olmiccia, and the Giacomoni at Poggio. It is not surprising, therefore, that many of these villages also experienced lengthy periods of feuding. That at Olmiccia between the Ortoli, on the one hand, and the Quilichini and their allies on the other can be traced back to 1802 and was still active in 1850.[35] That at Poggio is known to have run from around 1820 to the middle of the century and beyond.[36]

FRASSETO

The Antona and the Franceschi had been political rivals at Frasseto since at least the first decade of the nineteenth century. The Franceschi, with their relatives and affines who included the Mariani, the Susini and the Benedetti, had the majority on the municipal council during the Restoration period and held the mayorship, and the Antona had to be content with the occasional appointment as *adjoint*. It seems that the July Revolution strengthened the political hold of the Franceschi still further, since, although Paolo-Giordano Franceschi was replaced as mayor in 1830, his position went to a relative, Petro-Francesco Franceschi, and Antono Mariani replaced Giuseppo Antona as *adjoint*.[37] Probably in response to this setback, the Antona had recourse to violence against their rivals the following year.

In August 1831, Giuseppo Antona, called Fiaccone, with the aid of relatives, abducted Maria-Francesca Franceschi, the daughter of Angelo-Francesco. The Antona were persuaded to give the girl back after 20 days and Fiaccone was apparently about to leave for Sardinia as a *quid pro quo* for having dishonoured her when he was persuaded that he would become a laughing-stock if he did so. Instead he stayed in the vicinity as a bandit, and, again with the aid of relatives, and particularly his cousin, called Griggio, 'began to commit all kinds of offences against the Franceschi'. Houses, mills and vines were burned, the walls of enclosures were destroyed, and an interdict was placed on their lands, which remained uncultivated. Maria-Francesca was abducted a second time but managed to escape. At the end of 1832, Fiaccone encountered the girl with her brother-in-law Antono Mariani, killed them both after Mariani had taunted him, and 'horribly mutilated their corpses'. They were the first of twelve members of the Franceschi family and its connections to be killed over the next 14 years.

Domenico Sanviti and Natale Franceschi were killed in 1834. In 1835, An-

gelo-Francesco Franceschi was seriously wounded, and the following year he and
his twelve-year-old son, Pasquale, were killed in a garden by their house. In 1843,
Carlo Benedetti was killed, and, in 1844, Felice Mariani, another affine of the
Franceschi. By this time, Fiaccone and Griggio had been joined by three or four
other members of the Antona family, and these bandits achieved a position of
dominance in the district, terrorizing the local population and cowing their
opponents, who retained formal political power. The Antona bandits also acted
as agents for third parties and, in particular, they championed the claims of an
Ajaccio businessman, Felice Bianchi, to lands on the coast, which the people of
Frasseto regarded as their communal property. This was probably the beginning
of the Antona's downfall.

The bandits also intervened in another matter involving Bianchi. The latter's
nephew, Domenico Canavaggio, coveted a girl who was being courted by a
Lanfranchi, a relative of the Franceschi. Fiaccone kidnapped the girl and forced
her to change prospective marriage partners. This roused the Franceschi to their
first reported act of violence. In August 1845, Giusepp'-Antono and Domenico
Franceschi killed Canavaggio, but the Antona exacted a terrible revenge. Three
cousins of Giusepp'-Antono Franceschi, including a 14-year-old boy, were killed
in January 1846. Their bodies were mutilated and parts of them hung on surrounding bushes. This treatment of the corpses of their victims was characteristic
of the Antona and was taken to signify 'their wish to destroy the entire lineage' of
their opponents. Also in 1846, Bianchi denounced the 'law-abiding' Franceschi
for an alleged fraud committed in 1841 to get Giusepp'-Antono's elder brother,
Francesco-Saverio, off military service. The young men's father, Rebulio, and
their uncle, Antono-Domenico Lanfranchi, were arrested and prosecuted for
this, but were acquitted.

Meanwhile a split had developed in the ranks of the Antona connection. The
appalling nature of the crimes committed by the bandits caused revulsion among
some of their own relatives and, in particular, among the Miliani, who had also
been the victims of their depredations. The Miliani agreed, therefore, to help the
authorities to capture or destroy Fiaccone and his gang. In August 1846, Scalone
Antona was captured in the village by gendarmes. In October, Fiaccone, Griggio
and a third bandit called Muzzole, all of whom had apparently been drugged
with opium, were surprised. All three were killed, but Muzzole shot and mortally wounded Santo Franceschi and Giacomo Mariani before he died. Shortly
afterwards, *voltigeurs* found and killed the two remaining Antona bandits, Pasquale and Bastiano. When the bodies of the Antona were laid out in the village
church, the Franceschi had them removed. Five more members of the Antona
family took to the maquis in order to carry out reprisals against the Franceschi
and their allies for the killings and for this additional insult. Troops were sent to
the village to try to prevent further bloodshed, and this aim seems to have been
achieved.

Some kind of immunity from prosecution had been offered those who had
helped to destroy the bandits, but the Antona pressed successfully for charges to
be brought. Six members of the Miliani family and their associates were therefore
put on trial in July 1847 and convicted of homicide and complicity in homicide.
Most received light sentences, but Giuseppo Miliani was given 15 years' hard

labour. This trial and its outcome should be seen in the context of efforts being made by the authorities to bring about a peace settlement in Frasseto. Using various intermediaries, negotiations continued through 1847 with Rebulio Franceschi and Dr Lanfranchi, leaders of their party, and with Scalone and Paolo Antona. The Franceschi were extremely suspicious of their enemies, with some reason, while the Antona demanded that Giusepp'-Antono and Domenico Franceschi, who were still at large, should surrender or go into exile. There was also argument about the common lands and seats on the municipal council. In September 1847, a peace treaty incorporating articles on all these topics was agreed, and it was then signed, at the insistence of the prefect, by all the adult men in the village. This suggests that the reconciliation was felt to be fragile, and the killing of Bianchi in Ajaccio early in October put it further in jeopardy. However, the leaders of both parties wrote to the prefect together to refute rumours that the peace was about to be broken. In December, Giusepp'-Antono Franceschi, who was wanted in connection with both the killing of Canavaggio in 1845 and that of Bianchi, was arrested, it seems as he was about to give himself up. His father Rebulio complained about this and told the mayor that 'it would be very advantageous to the maintenance of peace if this individual were to be acquitted'. In the event, he was tried in September 1848, convicted and sentenced to twenty years' hard labour. Domenico Franceschi remained at large. The treaty of 1847 required the acceptance and enforcement of earlier court decisions on land disputes, which seems to have met with resistance. The prefect referred in 1848 to 'the usurpers of common lands', as though they were maintaining their claims. Despite this, the peace endured, though when Dr Lanfranchi became mayor in the 1860s he was the object of sustained denunciation on the part of the Antona and their allies.[38]

This transformation from feuding to political conflict is familiar from the other examples which we have described, but in other ways the conflict at Frasseto was different. The struggle was very one-sided, and the Antona relied very heavily on their bandits, whose behaviour was extreme by local standards. Moreover, community interests were at stake in some way, and the bandits' support of an outside interest, together with their brutality, turned even their own relatives against them. Despite heavy loss of personnel, the Franceschi were not dislodged from local political power by the feud.

PILA-CANALE

The feuding at Pila-Canale between the Poli, the Giancarli and the Feliciaggi on the one side, and the Bruni, the Bozzi and the Susini on the other, dates back at least to the end of the eighteenth century, for a document of 1801 refers to 'enmities which have been going on for over twenty years'.[39] Unusually, we have two accounts of the feud provided at about the same time by the leaders of each party, and these are worth following in detail.

According to Francesco-Maria Bruni, 'the cruel massacre' of his relatives began when Vincenzo Poli shot and killed Francesco Gelignani in 1779 or 1780. Six years later, Vincenzo's brother Pasquale deliberately wounded his brother-in-law Santo Giocondi in the arm. Both men escaped arrest and fled abroad. The example of their crimes, however, led one of their cousins, Francesco Poli called Tavalone, to emulate them. Tavalone was friendly with a second Francesco-Maria Bruni, a youth of about 14 who was married to a woman with 'a considerable dowry'. While the two were walking together one day, Tavalone killed Bruni, so that he could arrange a marriage between his cousin, Alberto Giancarli, and Bruni's widow. Giancarli was already married, but he killed his first wife in order to make this new marriage possible. The Bruni family 'addressed itself to the government, not wishing to engage in private vengeance', and Tavalone was arrested, prosecuted and condemned to death, but, like his cousins before him, he was able to escape and went to Sardinia. He stayed there until the outbreak of the Revolution in France, when he returned to his native district. A little earlier, Pasquale Poli had also returned to Pila-Canale and he killed Giovanni Bozzi, young Bruni's uncle, in order to pre-empt any act of vengeance on his part; he also killed Giuseppo Bozzi of Prugna shortly afterwards. However, the Bruni, who were 'endowed with a pacific temperament', pardoned both men and made peace with them and their family around 1790.

In 1791, Domenico Biaggi and Giovan-Domenico Feliciaggi stole two oxen from Giuseppo Susini. Instead of using force in return, Susini sought help from the authorities, but this 'only encouraged an excessive pride in Feliciaggi, who later shot and mortally wounded him'. Attempts to reconcile the parties after this were wrecked by Feliciaggi, who embarked on a career of crime in company with his cousin, Simone Poli. In 1794, Feliciaggi killed Giovanni Bozzi, aged 13, although the boy was a cousin of Tavalone, and a few days later Vincenzo Casabianca of Guarguale, related by marriage to the Bozzi, was killed by Giacomo-Santo and Pasquale Poli. The Bozzi and the Casabianca pardoned the perpetrators of these crimes, however, and a treaty of peace was concluded between the parties in the same year. This brought a short period of calm, which was broken by Tavalone. Aided by his first cousins, Giuseppo the son of Giulio, and Petro the son of Giovan-Battiste Poli, he killed his wife Rosa, née Bozzi, who was five months pregnant at the time, in 1795 or 1796. Her family still refrained from taking revenge against the Poli and offered to maintain the peace on condition that Pasquale Poli and Tavalone left Corsica. This they feigned to do, assuring the Bozzi that they could go about their normal affairs without danger. Very soon after having received this assurance, Domenico-Ignazio Bozzi, Rosa's brother, was returning from Olmeto, accompanied by a cousin, when they were ambushed by Pasquale Poli, Tavalone and five of their relatives and seriously wounded. The Bozzi then realized that 'the more they pardoned their enemies, the more likely they were to be insulted and attacked by them'; indeed, the Poli deliberately taunted them for their failure to react more positively, 'provoking them with cat-calls, shots fired in the air and horn-blowing'. The Bozzi also came to see that the government was too weak to give them any real protection, so, at last, they and their relatives 'resolved to meet force with force' and declared a general state of enmity between the two families and their allies.

In May of the same year, 1797, Simone-Filippo Poli killed his uncle Giovan-Filippo, and Giacomo-Santo Poli killed his uncle Felice. These actions, according to the Bruni, were calculated to inspire their enemies with terror. 'If these wretches were so cruel and barbaric towards their own blood, what would they not be capable of towards their declared enemies?' Events in the autumn provided an answer to this question. In late September, a group of the Bozzi and their relatives were ambushed near Cauro by over a dozen members of the Poli family and their relatives, including Tavalone, Pasquale and Simone-Filippo Poli. Carlo Bozzi was mortally wounded and had his ears cut off before he died. Giovan-Felice Bruni, who had given himself up after being promised that his life would be saved, was also killed. The Poli and their allies then returned to Pila-Canale in triumph, bearing as trophies the clothes of their two victims and Bozzi's ears. In mid-October, the Poli shot dead Anna-Maria Bozzi, as she was walking along a road with a bundle of firewood on her head. A few days later, Antono Bozzi was killed. He was related to the Poli and had been given 'a written promise of immunity'. In mid-March 1798, Antono the son of Felice and Antono the son of Carlo Feliciaggi killed a twelve-year-old herdsman of the Poli. The following month, Tavalone, and three other Poli, the two Feliciaggi and Santo Fieschi killed Domenico Bozzi and Maria Poli, Tavalone's own godmother, by shooting at them from a house. Hostilities were suspended between the two parties in September 1798 at the instigation of the Paolists, who were recruiting supporters in the region. Pasquale Poli and eight other members of his party joined the Paolists, and a peace was agreed. One of the conditions of this was that the Poli should return the arms which they had taken from the Bozzi and the Bruni, but this was never implemented. Indeed, Tavalone gloried in walking about carrying weapons acquired from his enemies. Within a short while, Pasquale Poli was killed in the village and Tavalone near Ajaccio. Their relatives blamed the Bozzi and the Bruni for their deaths, but the latter denied responsibility, alleging that the two had made many other enemies 'through their acts of brigandage'.

The Poli provided the authorities with a full refutation of and alternative to this account, in which they figured as the wronged party, acting only in self-defence and under provocation. Their account also gives information about the offences committed by the Bozzi and the Bruni, which do not appear in the latter's story. First, the Poli denied that Tavalone had killed Francesco-Maria Bruni or that Alberto Giancarli had killed his wife; her relatives had testified in court to his innocence. They also denied that Pasquale Poli had killed Vincenzo Casabianca in 1794; a court had acquitted him, despite 'the pressing demands of his enemies'. Moreover, the hostilities of the Feliciaggi in 1791 had been a response to the killing of a member of their family by the Bruni in 1790. The Poli also claimed that the Bruni had killed Simone Poli and Giuseppo Paoli in 1792. In accepting the peace which was offered in that year by Giuseppo Bozzi and his relatives, therefore, it was the Poli who were being conciliatory rather than their enemies, who broke the same peace within about a month of its conclusion. Francesco-Maria Poli was shot dead by Stefano Bozzi, in the latter's house and with the collusion of Carlo and Ignazio-Domenico Bozzi and Domenico Giordani. 'This murder committed in 1793 during the peace by the satellites of the Bruni reopened recent wounds among the Poli, and a cruel vengeance would certainly have resulted, had not various citizens interposed themselves as mediators.' The Poli were thus prevailed upon against their better judgment to accept a second peace agreement, which lasted for two years.

This peace was broken, not by the Poli, but by Francesco-Maria Bruni himself, who was 'municipal officer', the Revolutionary equivalent of mayor, at the time. He attacked two members of the Fieschi family with a posse, as they were working their vines not far from the village, but both escaped injury. A few days later, Carlo and Domenico-Ignazio Bozzi and Girolamo Giordani killed Magdalena Biaggi in a garden, and Giuseppo the son of Giuseppo Bozzi killed Agostino Pianelli. And further violence followed. In 1796, the Poli and the Fieschi were fired at from a house belonging to the Colonna, and one of them was wounded. A group of Bozzi, Bruni and their allies killed Giovan-Battiste Giancarli, having persuaded him to surrender his arms 'on the pretext that he was related to them' and, a little later, the same group also killed Matteo Poli 'in the most barbarous manner, stabbing him in the face with a dagger, and drawing out his teeth after he was dead'. In the same year again, a group of a dozen Bozzi, with Giacomo-Filippo Vincenti, killed Giacomo-Santo Poli; while Angelo-Santo Bozzi killed his nephew Paolo, and Domenico-Ignazio and Carlo-Antono Bozzi, Girolamo Giordani and others killed their relative Giuseppo-Maria Casabianca and his twelve-year-old son as they were working in a field. Like their adversaries, the Poli drew attention to the enormity of killing one's own relatives. They also remarked that their own peaceful approach only made their enemies more ferocious, and they referred to being 'generally insulted' and to 'having our houses burned and devastated'.

The Poli mention a peace made in 1797. According to them, it was arranged by General Casabianca and was concluded at Ajaccio in a solemn manner, but it lasted barely two weeks. By the end of that time Carlo Bruni, who had returned from Rome under cover of the peace, and four members of the Bozzi family had killed another Giacomo-Santo Poli and his mother. Later, the same Carlo Bruni, called Falchino, Francesco-Maria Bruni, Domenico-Ignazio and Giovan-Battiste Bozzi, Girolamo Giordani, Alfonso Colonna and others killed the two daughters of Alberto Giancarli, Livia and Angelica-Maria, who was seven months pregnant. The women's breasts were cut off. In the same year, the Bozzi claimed three further victims: Petro Casanova, Magdalena Fieschi, who was shot 'while she was gathering olives', and Maria-Magdalena Paoli, aged 70, who was stabbed to death. In addition, Antono Bruni wounded the priest Domenico Bozzi with a firearm.

In 1798 or 1799, according to the Poli, mediators from the surrounding district intervened to arrange another peace, which was again concluded 'with the greatest solemnity'. This peace lasted a little over two years at the most and was again broken by the Bruni and the Bozzi, 'whose thirst for human blood was not yet satisfied'. Early in 1801, Carlo, Vincenzo-Giovanni, Giovan-Michele and Father Giovan-Girolamo Bruni, Leopoldo Susini and three members of the Bozzi family killed Francesco-Maria Poli at Campidiloro near Ajaccio. Having done this, they 'cut his throat with a dagger, committed other abominable outrages' on his corpse, and took his arms and his money. The following day, Domenico-Ignazio and Carlo-Antono Bozzi and Giovan-Michele Bruni killed Petro Poli.[40]

The two accounts not only complement but also to some extent corroborate each other as to the facts, and other documents add confirmation and additional information. In June 1801, Saverio Simoni, a day-labourer, was tried on the charge of firing shots earlier in the year at Giovan-Antono, Antono Torre, Alfonso Colonna and another man 'as they were working in the vineyard of Giovan-Santo Fieschi'. It appears that Simoni was employed by the Bruni brothers and was acting on their behalf. Speaking 'in the name of his party', Antono Feliciaggi had warned Simoni 'that he should not work either in the vines or on the land of the Bruni', which led Giovanni Bruni to declare a similar ban. In August, it was reported that Antono the son of Mario Bozzi had died from wounds. Later the same year, the authorities arrested twelve people from Pila-Canale as hostages. These were relatives of those believed to be responsible for the killings in the village but who had themselves eluded capture. From the interrogation of the hostages, we learn that Giovan-Michele Vincenti had also been implicated in the killing of Francesco-Maria Poli, and that Antono Bozzi's assailant was Simone Fieschi, who had fired at him as he was leaving the house of Petro-Andrea Pierandrei, where he had gone to discuss an exchange of property with Bonaventura Poli. We also learn that some time in the summer of 1801, Giuseppo Poli, who had been driven out of his house in the village by the Bozzi, had broken into the Monferrini house with Simone Fieschi and others. The widow Monferrini and her children, and Giuseppo Monferrini, were expelled from the house, which Poli then occupied. In December 1801, another peace treaty was concluded between the parties at Pila-Canale.[41]

Like earlier ones, this settlement seems to have lasted only a few years, for in the summer of 1805 the mayor of Pila-Canale, Tomaso Quilichini, and Colonna Bozzi, a judge at the court in Ajaccio, were both killed. It appears that these killings were in retaliation for the acquittal of three members of the Bruni family tried for homicide earlier in the year before the Court of Criminal Justice. In March 1810, Cosimo Colonna, tax-collector and a former mayor, was killed, apparently by Petro and Giovan-Gregorio Monferrini; and a further killing was reported in May. In June, two Monferrini and two Bozzi were taken as hostages to the citadel in Ajaccio, since they were 'the closest relatives' of the presumed culprits. Simone Feliciaggi and Bastiano Poli of Pila-Canale were among those in preventive detention two years later, probably in similar circumstances.[42]

In 1816, the prefect intervened to try to bring about yet another peace. This provided the occasion for further accounts of the feuding by some of its protagonists. Giacomo-Filippo Vincenti traced back his involvement in the conflict to 1802. 'By my hard work', he wrote, 'I had assured my well-being,' and he had four sons of whom he could be proud. However, 'the debauchery of a woman called Maria-Magdalena was then used by an implacable enemy to cause a series of calamities for my family'. This enemy was Matteo Bruni, Maria-Magdalena's first cousin. When she became pregnant, Bruni claimed that one of Vincenti's sons (most probably Paolo) was responsible and called on Vincenti 'to repair the damage' by agreeing to a marriage between the two. Vincenti denied that his sons had ever had anything to do with the woman and rejected the proposal out of hand. Worried by Bruni's intentions, friends intervened and suggested that compensation be paid. Vincenti then offered a sum which 'the father of Magdalena gratefully accepted'; she was found a husband, and 'calm seemed to have been restored'. But beneath a friendly exterior, Bruni was plotting revenge, and he later instigated the killing of Paolo Vincenti by Saverio Bozzi, 'a vile agent'. Bozzi was condemned to death. Bruni's complicity could not be proved, but he was nevertheless exiled by General Morand, at first temporarily and then in perpetuity. While Morand remained military governor (that is, until 1811), Bruni did not dare to return to Corsica, but one of his uncles persuaded Morand's successor, General Berthier, to lift the ban. On his return, Bruni again behaved in an apparently conciliatory manner, though 'banishment had actually redoubled his inner fury and he was only waiting for the moment to give it full reign'. This time Bruni chose as his agent Luigi Bozzi, who had already killed his own wife. In mid-May 1816, Bozzi ambushed and killed Giacomo-Filippo Vincenti's son, Anton-Lorenzo, who was a doctor by training and tax-collector for the canton.

Giacomo-Filippo's account adds that, in pursuing his vengeance against the Vincenti, Bruni 'had dissipated his fortune and contracted numerous debts', which led him to engage in highway robberies. Vincenti also claimed that Cosimo Colonna was killed by the Monferrini in 1810, because he had welcomed Bruni's banishment. Bruni had also instigated the killing of Domenico-Ignazio Bozzi and of Antono Feliciaggi, who was well-known 'for his attachment to the Vincenti family'. Another letter to the prefect, written by Giovan-Battiste Poli, Feliciaggi's nephew, provides further details here. Anton-Lorenzo Vincenti's murder had been witnessed by the son of Antono Feliciaggi, who had had later to testify in court against Luigi Bozzi, and it was for this reason that he had been killed – by Bozzi, who was still at large, together with his brother Matteo and Bruni. The Feliciaggi, the Poli and the Vincenti thus lived under constant threat and could not leave their houses or go about their normal business. Poli confirmed Vincenti's view that Luigi Bozzi was simply 'the passive but terrible instrument' of his brother and of Bruni.

The Bruni, the Bozzi and the Monferrini naturally presented a different version of these events, which also takes the story further. They denied that Luigi Bozzi had killed Anton-Lorenzo Vincenti. Moreover, in June 1816, a peace had been arranged by the authorities, which the Vincenti had almost immediately broken. In July, Giovan-Michele Vincenti and his brother Luca, Ignazio Bozzi and Antono Colonna had attempted to kill Giovan-Gregorio and Benedetto Monferrini. There is independent corroboration that such an attack took place, and both the Monferrini appear to have been seriously wounded. An attempt was made to arrest the Vincenti brothers in September at their father's house in the village. They escaped but Giacomo-Filippo was taken into custody. The Bruni and their allies also referred to many other unspecified crimes committed against them by the Vincenti and by Ignazio Bozzi, and affirmed that no definitive peace would be possible unless Giovan-Michele Vincenti were punished. They also made some interesting claims about Antono Feliciaggi. He had not been a party to the peace agreement, which was in effect when he had been killed, and he did not belong to the Vincenti party at all; indeed, the Feliciaggi and the Vincenti were enemies, since the Vincenti had killed Feliciaggi's sister, nephew and first cousin. Nevertheless, a peace treaty was finally concluded in November 1816 and was signed in the presence of the mayor, the justice of the peace and a representative of the prefect. The parties, on the one side, were Giacomo-Filippo, Giovan-Michele and Luca Vincenti, Ignazio Bozzi (son of the late Lorenzo), and Antono and Giuseppo Colonna; and, on the other, Matteo Bruni, Benedetto, Giovan-Gregorio and Petro Monferrini, and Luigi Bozzi, representing all their 'relatives and allies'.[43]

Pila-Canale then enjoyed a period of uneasy calm. Luigi Bozzi committed a further murder in 1819 and went to Sardinia. Following a fight in the village in 1824 between Giovan-Battiste Quilichini and Martinetto Bozzi, the mayor asked for a detachment of *voltigeurs* to be sent, a request which the subprefect supported, 'given the enmities which have existed and which unfortunately still exist there'. In 1829 the village was given a permanent station of gendarmes.[44]

Party rivalry also continued at the political level. In 1821, Enrico Colonna was mayor, with Antono Giancarli of the same party as *adjoint*, but in 1825, their opponent, Giovan-Felice Bruni, became mayor, and his party had a majority on the municipal council. Matteo Bruni himself became mayor in 1831 or 1832. An official complaint was lodged against him in 1835 for taking bribes. Probably for this reason he was replaced by his relative Carlo Bruni, who was reappointed in 1837. The opposing party held the office of *adjoint*.[45]

In the middle of the 1830s, there was a renewal of violence in Pila-Canale. Giulio Bozzi had quarrelled around 1830 with Domenico Leonetti, a herdsman from Ciamannacce, who appears to have been related to the Santoni of Pila-Canale, and had killed him, allegedly in self-defence. Bozzi was arrested, tried and sentenced to five years' imprisonment. Leonetti's relatives, however, found this punishment inadequate and took their own revenge. In December 1836, Domenico Santoni called Malanotte and two other men killed Filippo Bozzi, Giulio's first cousin, and in January 1837, Simone-Giovanni Fieschi, another relative. Then, in November 1837, Malanotte and his brothers Simone and Petro killed Giovanni Foata, Giulio's uncle and a man 'who had never carried weapons in his life'. Malanotte remained in the vicinity of Pila-Canale as a bandit, until he was killed by gendarmes in October 1841.[46]

From the next decade we have information about a number of incidents involving families earlier engaged in feuding. In July 1841, a group of villagers on their way to work in the fields were called on to halt by a detachment of *voltigeurs*, who were looking for a bandit. Instead two men in the party, probably Giulio Colonna and Pasquale Poli, fired at the *voltigeurs*, two of whom were mortally wounded. Colonna took to the maquis and 'inspired such terror in his own village [until he was captured in October] that many families stopped going about their affairs'. This suggests that he was involved in conflict locally as well as with the authorities, a view which is supported by evidence relating to another member of his family. Carl-Antono Colonna had married the widow Fieschi in about 1840 and had persuaded her to cede certain of her properties to him, which had particularly annoyed her son Antono. In September 1841, a quarrel occurred between Antono Fieschi and his brother Alberto, on the one hand, and Michelangelo Colonna, the brother of Carl-Antono, on the other. Following this, Antono Fieschi fired a shot from his house, which was intended for Michelangelo Colonna, but which in fact hit and killed Matteo Monferrini, who was beside him and who had tried to pacify the protagonists. Fieschi then took to the maquis.[47] In March 1843, Carl-Antono Colonna was killed by Antono Fieschi as he was on his way to a vineyard. Fieschi remained at large for another seven years, during which time he committed further crimes, including an attempt to kill Andrea Santoni by shooting at him from the Giancarli house in Pila-Canale. Fieschi was arrested in 1850 and sentenced to hard labour for life.[48]

By this time, feuding in the village had revived in earnest. The president of the Assize Court reported in July 1850 that 'the civil war at Pila-Canale seems to have reached the last degree of fury and barbarism ... No man sets foot in the street without a loaded shot-gun and without keeping his eyes on the surrounding houses, ready to shoot to kill at the slightest sign or suspicious movement.' The church no longer provided neutral ground, and 'for some years services were attended only by women, those from each party occupying different sides'. In January 1850, Angelica Giordani, aged 15, was abducted, while in the company of her aunt Rosa Casanova, by Antono Feliciaggi and Domenico Camilli. Feliciaggi later claimed that the abduction was feigned and had been arranged with the girl's consent, but she denied this and said that he had raped or tried to rape her. The girl's father, Petro-Andrea, and other relatives helped the gendarmerie to track down her abductors and, in a series of encounters, Camilli was killed and Petro-Andrea Giordani and a close relative were wounded. Feliciaggi was eventually captured and he received a ten-year prison sentence. Following the death of Domenico Camilli, his relatives 'and notably Felice Benedetti, the miller, his first cousin, declared a state of enmity against the Giordani'. Benedetti left his mill in the country and came to live in the village itself, making his intentions quite clear. 'He was friendly with the famous bandit Marco-Matteo Maestroni [who came from Pila-Canale] and told him of his plans. However, Maestroni had no quarrel with the Giordani and secretly warned them, so that they were able to avoid being ambushed.' Antono Torre, first cousin of the abducted girl, was also warned in this way, but Benedetti assured him that 'he had no evil designs towards him'. Torre therefore took no precautions and was shot dead by Benedetti in November 1850, as he was ploughing. Benedetti then remained at large as a bandit for three years, and was sentenced to hard labour for life in 1853.[49]

The other main conflict in the early 1850s related to that of the previous decade, if not earlier. Vincenzo Santoni was told by his sister one day in August 1850 that his father, Andrea, had been killed on the road to Ajaccio. Without waiting to ascertain the truth of this report, which was in fact false, Vincenzo went to fetch a gun, met Giovanni Giancarli and shot him dead. 'The Giancarli and the Santoni families were on bad terms, since Andrea Santoni had been shot at from the Giancarli house' by Antono Fieschi in 1848. We have seen that Antono Fieschi had been arrested and convicted earlier the same year. In March 1851, an encounter took place between Andrea Santoni on the one hand, and Alberto Fieschi, Antono's brother, Paolo Pierandrei and Nicola Quilichini on the other, in which Santoni was wounded in the right arm. His three assailants were arrested a few months later and received three-year prison sentences. The trial summary commented that 'a bloody enmity has for a long time divided the Quilichini and the Pierandrei families on the one hand, and the Santoni and the Maestroni on the other'. In the same session, Vincenzo Santoni was also convicted and sentenced to ten years' imprisonment.[50]

This judicial *quid pro quo* seems to have restored a measure of calm to Pila-

Canale, though conflict among the leading families still simmered at the political level. After nine years in office, mayor Arrighi was accused in 1853 of the usual petty abuse of that office by Filippo Bozzi and Francesco Filippi. He offered to resign but was persuaded by the prefect to stay on another year. He was replaced by Tomaso Quilichini, whom he had recommended as his successor, with Antono Giancarli as *adjoint*. Quilichini became involved in conflict with the parish priest, who accused him in 1856 of 'behaving scandalously during religious services'. The mayor's 'party' was reported to have responded by 'removing and hiding the church bells'. In 1860, Quilichini was the object of what the gendarmerie regarded as an unjustified complaint on the part of Giovan-Gregorio Monferrini, but he nevertheless resigned – 'for family reasons'. He was replaced by Michel-Antono Bozzi, the ex-schoolteacher. This appointment had been vigorously opposed in a letter to the prefect by Paolo Pierandrei, who asserted that Bozzi 'had been involved in all the terrible events and all the enmities which the village had suffered'. In 1864, Anton-Domenico Poli became *adjoint* to replace a Giancarli who died. Poli had not been on the list of names recommended by Mayor Bozzi. Bozzi was reappointed as mayor in 1865 without any enthusiasm on the part of the prefect and despite further opposition from Pierandrei and others, and shortly afterwards Girolamo Bruni became *adjoint*. Bruni and Bozzi failed to co-operate. Bozzi complained in 1866 that Bruni had twice refused to stand in for him when he was ill and that he had also refused to take on the responsibility for supervising building alignments and wineshops delegated to him. A number of denunciations of Mayor Bozzi also reached the prefect, emanating mainly, it seems, from members of his own family. These were Giuseppo Bozzi and Michel-Antono's son-in-law Paoletti, whom he described as the leader of the cabal opposed to him, which also included the Filippi. The mayor also alleged that Paoletti tried to kill Marc-Antono Bozzi in 1866.[51]

The history of feuding at Pila-Canale displays a number of important features, not all of which are so clear in our previous examples. The conflicts seem to have been more exclusively focused on the village itself than was the case elsewhere, though one 'enmity' did involve people from Ciamannacce some forty kilometres away in the mountains. There is some suggestion in the sources that feuding occurred between those living in the two different parts of the village, a pattern that is found at Fozzano and elsewhere. Intrafamilial conflict was also present despite the intensity of feuding between families. The main contenders were to some degree interrelated by marriage and, perhaps for this reason, some individuals were dissociated from their main family groupings. Ignazio Bozzi, for example, stood with the enemies of his family in the peace of 1816. Though intrafamilial killings undoubtedly occurred, it is nevertheless significant, too, that they were used as propaganda against those who perpetrated them. The Pila-Canale feuding also indicates that women and children could well be victims in feuds, especially when conflict escalated to an extreme level; at this level also mutilation of corpses occurred. Attacking women and children may also have been a deliberate act of provocation when one side refused to respond to normal insult and the killing of men. The impression from Francesco-Maria Bruni's account that his family relied on governmental protection and judicial redress against the violence and banditry practised by the Poli, and that they met attacks on them by pardoning those who made them, may not be entirely misleading. And such behaviour may well have been taken by their enemies to be a kind of insult, provoking them to new outrages. It is significant here that Bruni mentions ritual insults against his family, akin to those incorporated in the charivari.

The Pila-Canale feuding also shows how different parties in the feud had their own 'memory' of its history, which they could recount in some detail. But it shows, too, that a process of selection and development inevitably took place over time. Original affronts and grievances were overlaid by new ones, which might introduce different families or bring different ones to the fore, and thus change the emphasis and direction of the conflict. Some families might even eventually change sides. Such a switch occurred in the second decade of the nineteenth century, when the accusation of seducing a member of the Bruni family was made by the latter against the Vincenti. The Vincenti, who had been allies of the Bruni–Bozzi connection then joined that of the Poli, which involved drawing a veil over their earlier enmity with the Feliciaggi. The Colonna figure among the allies of the Bruni–Bozzi in the 1790s but are found among their opponents from the 1800s to the 1840s. In the 1790s and 1800s the Fieschi were allies of the Feliciaggi and others against the Bruni–Bozzi party, but in the late 1830s a Fieschi was killed because he was a relative of a Bozzi. Most striking of all, by the late 1860s the long-standing alliance of the Bruni and the Bozzi seems itself to have broken up. It is also obvious that some families simply moved in the orbit of other more important ones and were drawn into their quarrels, while others behaved much more independently. One can also detect a long-term tendency for the more important families, like the Poli, to abandon feuding as such as a mode of competition.

VENZOLASCA

So far our examples have all been taken from southern Corsica, but feuds did occur elsewhere in the modern period. Our remaining case-studies are of villages in the Casinca (Venzolasca and Penta) and the Balagna (Muro).

Conflict at Venzolasca between the Petrignani and the Ciavaldini on the one hand, and the Filippi, the Grimaldi and the Sanguinetti on the other was well-established by the middle of the nineteenth century, though little information is available about it before that date. Bourde relates it to an older and broader competition for political power in the Casinca between the *Bianchi* and the *Nevi*. The Petrignani were *Nevi* and formed the larger and more important party locally, while the *Bianchi* were led by the important Casabianca family, to whom the Filippi were allied. It is clear that blood had been shed around 1815, for Luigi and Giacomo Sanguinetti were prosecuted for homicide in 1816, while Antono Petrignani was still wanted in 1823 for a homicide committed in 1819. The murder of the poet Alessandro Petrignani also occurred at about this time. The Petrignani seem to have monopolized political power in the village after 1830, though their exercise of it did not impress the departmental authorities. In 1837, the subprefect reported that no member of the municipal council was suitable to serve as mayor. Francesco Petrignani was eventually invited to serve again, but he declined and the post went to Giovan-Carlo Petrignani, who remained mayor until 1845.[52]

By this time, violence had once more broken out between the parties. Angelo Petrignani, the vine guard of the village, had several times reported Giovan-Tomaso Sanguinetti for stealing grapes, which prompted the latter to shoot at him in November 1844. Sanguinetti was convicted the following year of attempted homicide but was sentenced to only one year's imprisonment.[53]

With the outbreak of the February Revolution in 1848, 'sentiments of friendship and confraternity appeared to replace the ancient animosities', which had divided the leading families of Venzolasca. In the last days of February, Giuseppo Petrignani and Stefano Filippi, young men 'on whom the future of their families depended, found themselves together in Bastia, effected a reconciliation', and returned to the village to inform their relatives. The next day, a celebration was held outside the Filippi house and youths fired salvos 'as signs of joy', as was usual on such occassions. Unfortunately, one of these hit and killed Giuseppo Petrignani, who was watching the proceedings from a window of his house opposite. A man called Peretti was arrested and convicted of involuntary homicide, but the Petrignani refused to believe that the killing had been an accident and Giuseppo's father 'manifested the intention of seeking revenge'. In March 1848, a quarrel developed between two youths belonging to the hostile parties, who were also rival suitors. After an exchange of insults outside the village between groups supporting each, Francesco Filippi fired his pistol at Giovan-Antono Ciosi and at the latter's cousin, Giuseppo-Maria Petrignani, but neither was hit. In mid-July, Stefano Filippi was shot and killed while on the way to one of his properties, and some relatives accompanying him were injured. The Filippi accused Giuseppo Petrignani's widow, his cousin Antono Cipriani, and Giovan-Carlo Grimaldi, 'a distant relative [by marriage] but one of the most devoted partisans of the Petrignani'. The following month, fighting broke out between the two parties during the elections to the departmental council held at the neighbouring village of Vescovato; 'two people were killed and many wounded'. By this time, the houses of the contending parties at Venzolasca were heavily fortified, and much of the rest of the population of the village had been 'dragged into the war'.[54]

A year later, the situation appeared to have eased somewhat, and those involved in the feud were taking fewer precautions. Then, one evening in August 1849, Luigi Ciavaldini was shot dead in the main street, as he was passing the Filippi house. His cousin, Giovan-Battiste Ciavaldini, who ran to his assistance, was also shot and killed. Luigi Ciavaldini had recently assumed leadership of the Petrignani party, which made him a prime target. The Filippi were also 'absolutely convinced' that he had been directly implicated in the killing of Stefano Filippi in 1848, though the authorities had taken no action against him. It is reasonably certain that those responsible for the Ciavaldini killings were Stefano's brothers, Giuseppo and Antono, and three other men including a hired agent, Angelini, on whom they managed to cast the entire blame when the affair was brought to court. In October 1849, Giovan-Battiste Sanguinetti and his cousin, Cristoforo Ciosi, who was wanted in connection with one of the killings at Vescovato in 1848, were ambushed on the path from Venzolasca to Querciolo on the plain. Their assailants were Anton-Francesco Ciavaldini, the nephew of Luigi, Francesco Petrignani, who had succeeded as leader of his party, and two other men. Sanguinetti later died from his wounds. In December 1849, Giovan-Carlo Grimaldi was convicted of killing Stefano Filippi and sentenced to 20 years' hard labour. Further arrests and prosecutions took place in the first half of 1850, but other members of the main families were acquitted, thanks to 'influence'. Anton-Francesco Ciavaldini and Antono Filippi 'remained at large'.[55]

In July 1850, two youths, Giovan-Francesco Sanguinetti, brother of Giovan-Battiste, and his cousin Giovan-Antono Ciosi surprised Anton-Francesco Ciavaldini at a place in the country and fired at him, though without hitting him. About a week later, Ciavaldini and Michele Papini, a bandit from another village, tried to kill Andrea Sanguinetti, cousin of Giovan-Francesco, in an ambush. These events 'exasperated the parties'. On the evening of the ambush, Giovan-Francesco, Andrea and Agostino Sanguinetti and Lorenzo-Luigi Ciosi all went to Oletta, 'where Antono Filippi, the leader of their party was staying', presumably in order to consult with him and receive orders. They returned to Venzolasca two days later, and on the morning following their return, the priest Mucius Ciavaldini, brother of Luigi and uncle of Anton-Francesco, was shot and killed as he was returning from saying his daily mass in the village church. Although all four men appear to have participated in the crime, only Giovan-Francesco Sanguinetti was later convicted. In October 1850, an act of vengeance was carried out that was related to one of the killings at Vescovato in 1848. Domenico Buttaci had been acquitted in March 1850 of killing Giovan-Battiste Luciani on that occasion. Luciani's son, Matteo, regarded the acquittal as 'a denial of justice', warned Buttaci 'to be on his guard', and, when the opportunity arose, ambushed his enemy and shot him in the arm. In 1850 also Francesco Petrignani, called Pedone, the field guard, was convicted of killing Domenico Padovani and sentenced to twenty years' hard labour. The killing followed a dispute at a drinking party at the house of Valerio Petrignani over who should pay for some cheese, and its connection with the main feud is not clear. According to one official report, there had been 15 murders and as many attempted murders in and around Venzolasca between February 1848 and the end of 1850. This fact alone may have occasioned the period of informal truce which followed, though violence recurred in 1853.[56]

In February of that year, Maria Albertini was abducted by Francesco-Antono Emanuelli. He was 'passionately in love with her', and, since 'their social conditions were similar, nothing could have opposed their union, had party spirit not divided their two families'. The Emanuelli, one of whose members had been an important local bandit in the early 1840s, appear to have been related by marriage to the Ciavaldini, while the Albertini were supporters of the Filippi. Following her father's advice, Maria 'had rejected all Emanuelli's proposals and let him know that she could never be his wife', which had provoked him to his desperate action. However, he had taken her to his parents' house and had 'carefully refrained from any affront to her honour', and he was therefore leniently treated by the courts. This incident may have been part of a wider conflict involving the Albertini, since we have a report from the same year of a bandit called Besignani attempting to kill a member of the Albertini family, and then succeeding in killing one of their servants. Further acts of violence are reported in the 1850s, mainly between those belonging to the same party, which probably indicates the cessation or decline of feuding proper.[57]

However, if feuding by violence disappeared in the 1850s, political conflict took its place. In 1858, Mayor Guerrini, a man with 'no known enemies' resigned and was replaced by Antono Filippi, who continued to act in the same spirit with which he had led his party in the enmities of a decade earlier. The subprefect reported that the village was run from the Filippi house, which was 'still fortified', and to which the mayor's enemies were naturally reluctant to come. The field guards were 'agents of his desire for vengeance and have been instructed to harass all those who resist him'. The village's communal assets were treated as the mayor's property. Not surprisingly, Filippi was the object of many denunciations from those of the opposing party, and he was eventually removed from office early in 1866. His place was taken by Anton-Carlo Rinaldi, a younger man who belonged to the same party but was of a more conciliatory temperament. The name of Giovan-Andrea Sanguinetti was put forward for the post of *adjoint*, but the report that 'he was a very passionate partisan' put him out of the running. Though the Filippi party had a clear majority on the municipal council in this period, Anton-Carlo Grimaldi became mayor in 1867. Much attention was devoted in the late 1860s and early 1870s to the composition of the electoral list, each side seeking to have its own supporters included and to exclude those of its opponents. The advent of the Third Republic does not seem to have immediately affected the balance of power locally, though by the early 1880s the Petrignani, who had espoused the advanced Republican cause, appear to have been in the ascendant.[58]

In other villages, we have seen that the substitution of political for violent conflict in the second half of the nineteenth century was definitive. Venzolasca departed from this pattern, experiencing a revival of violence precisely in the 1880s. This was related to the feuding earlier in the century, though we have no detailed information about the exact links between the two. The main protagonists in this later period were the Sanguinetti, who were allied to the Peretti and the Paterni, and the Paoli, who were allied to the Albertini, the Battini and the Petrignani. The Paoli do not figure at all in accounts of the earlier conflicts, while the Albertini appear to have changed sides. According to Marcaggi, the conflict between the Sanguinetti and the Paoli began with an argument between Tomaso Sanguinetti and Anton-Francesco Paoli over the boundary between their contiguous chestnut groves. An armed confrontation took place between the two men in 1880, but neither appears to have been hurt and a reconciliation was effected, marked by the marriage of Anton-Francesco's son Salvatore to a Sanguinetti girl. Quarrelling over minor matters continued, however, between the two families, and in 1888 Giuseppo Paterni fired a shot at Giovan-Tomaso Paoli, who retaliated a month later by killing Paterni's brother, also called Giovan-Tomaso. This led to the declaration of 'a state of enmity' between the two parties. At about the same time, another son of Anton-Francesco Paoli, Carlo-Riccardo, had been fined for allowing his livestock to stray, and he retained a grudge against the field guard, Ambrogio Sanguinetti. During sheep-shearing in 1889, he picked a quarrel with Ambrogio and seriously wounded him with a revolver. Carlo-Riccardo Paoli was condemned to one year's imprisonment for this, while Giovan-Tomaso Paoli received a sentence of 20 years hard labour for the Paterni murder, but these verdicts did not satisfy the Sanguinetti. In March 1890, Ambrogio Sanguinetti, his brother and two other relatives, a Paterni and an Orsatilli, surrounded the Paoli house and killed Salvatore Paoli, who was, of course, directly related to them by marriage. When he was released from prison in 1900, Carlo-Riccardo avenged his brother by killing a Sanguinetti and was killed in his turn. The Paoli then left Venzolasca, abandoning their land and taking refuge in Bastia. In December 1900, the municipal council voted for the recall of the brigade of gendarmes that had been stationed in the village during the trouble, since 'public tranquillity' had been restored.[59]

This calm was broken nine years later when Domenico Sanguinetti deserted from the army after shooting a sergeant and returned to Corsica. He began to carry out minor acts of vengeance against the Paoli family and its supporters in the Casinca. At the same time, Giovan-Tomaso Paoli, who had completed his prison sentence but was still officially banned from returning to the island, broke that ban and also arrived in the Casinca. He was joined in the maquis by his brother Nunzio, while Domenico Sanguinetti was aided by Timoteo Peretti, formerly a reputable shopkeeper. A series of acts of violence followed. In July 1910, Giovan-Tomaso Paoli killed Ambrogio Sanguinetti, and in September Domenico Sanguinetti killed Francesco Albertini. In July 1911, Paoli killed Giovanni Albertini, who had earlier been acquitted on a charge of killing Carlo-Riccardo Paoli. Later the same month, a Peretti relative of the Sanguinetti killed a certain Orlandi, described as a 'protector' of Paoli, while Giovan-Tomaso Paoli attacked or threatened Maria-Angela Giafferi, the fiancée of Petro Albertini. In October, Antono Paoli, the brother of Giovan-Tomaso, attempted to kill a certain Fava. Then, fearing reprisals, three relatives of the Paoli, Pasquale Albertini, Vincenzo Petrignani and Pasquale Bucchini, decided to emigrate to America, but they were ambushed at the railway station at Arena and Petrignani was killed. By this time, the renewed feuding at Venzolasca had claimed nearly 30 victims and had caused major disruption in the area. Houses were barricaded, people only ventured out armed, and agricultural work was for a time abandoned. The authorities made determined efforts to track down the two main bandits, Sanguinetti and Paoli, but were not successful in doing so until 1916. According to Marcaggi, both families involved in the feud were almost exterminated and only one Paoli survived, in Bastia.[60]

PENTA-DI-CASINCA

Penta-di-Casinca lies a few miles to the south of Venzolasca and was the scene of feuding between the Viterbi and the Frediani, leading families of the district. One report traces the conflict back to 1768, but detailed information is only available from 1790. In January of that year, when the general political situation was extremely unsettled, the 'notables' of the canton met in assembly at the convent of St Francis. According to the account provided by the English traveller Benson, which was at least partly inspired by the Viterbi, trouble began when a formal vote was taken to exclude the Frediani from the meeting on the grounds that they did not qualify as notables. After some vacillation, Simone Viterbi had agreed to the exclusion, which earned him reproof from a certain Serpentini, a friend of the Frediani. When Viterbi answered Serpentini back with an insult,

Serpentini stabbed and killed him. Simone Viterbi's sons, Luca-Antono and Petro then arrived, and the former killed Francesco-Andrea Frediani in retaliation. A different account of these events is provided in a memoir published in 1818 by Carlo-Felice Frediani, the son of Francesco-Andrea. No mention is made of the doubts cast on the status of the Frediani, though the Viterbi are dubbed 'base in their origins'. It is specifically denied that there was any previous hostility between the two families. Indeed, when Simone Viterbi was stabbed by a third party, unnamed, Carlo-Felice asserts that his father went to his assistance and that Simone Viterbi himself then stabbed Francesco-Andrea fatally in the heart. A third account prepared by the public prosecutor in 1818 suggests that Simone Viterbi survived his wounds and was only killed some years later by the brothers Giovan-Domenico and Angelo-Santo Antonmarchi, called Giametti, of Porri, who were acting as 'the hired agents' of the Frediani.

Meanwhile, in May 1790, a group of supporters of the Frediani from outside the canton went to Penta and occupied the house of Venturino Suzzarini. He was a partisan of the Viterbi and his house was situated opposite theirs. The intruders mounted an attack on the Viterbi house, which was repulsed by force. Suzzarini and others were wounded in the fighting, and two of the opposing party were killed. At the end of 1790 or the start of 1791, Petro Viterbi was hit in the shoulder by a musket-ball, as he was riding past the house of Donato Frediani. However, with the return of Paoli to Corsica in mid-1791 and the general mood of reconciliation, the feud subsided for a while. But the Viterbi were pro-French and Republican and opposed Paoli's alliance with the English, which the Frediani supported. When the English occupied Corsica at the end of 1793, therefore, the Viterbi went into exile in France. Once they had gone, the Frediani 'made themselves sole masters of Penta', burned down four houses belonging to their enemies and laid waste their property. The departure of the English in 1796 reversed the fortunes of the two families. The Viterbi returned in triumph. Proceedings were begun against the Frediani for their crimes and they were also placed on the list of émigrés, which meant that their property was liable to confiscation. The leading members of the family went into hiding.

At this stage, it appears, the father of Francesco-Andrea Frediani intervened with a proposal to end the feud by a marriage between one of his grandsons and the daughter of Luca-Antono Viterbi. This offer was accepted, and a member of the Viterbi family set off for Bastia to halt the court proceedings. However, his intentions were misunderstood and he was ambushed and mortally wounded. Eventually, a number of the Frediani were arrested and successfully prosecuted, and Carlo and Donato, who remained at large, were condemned in their absence to nine years in irons, a dishonouring punishment. At the same time, the courts ordered the Frediani to indemnify the Viterbi for the damage to their property. In September 1797, Carlo Frediani, who had taken refuge in the coastal marshes, 'succumbed to the bad airs', and it is reported that Luca-Antono Viterbi went to the church where his body was laid out and stabbed the corpse several times, while uttering curses against it. In 1798 or 1799, Luca-Antono Viterbi became public prosecutor, while his brother Petro became the equivalent of prefect in the northern half of the island, which was then a separate department. It was later claimed that they abused these offices not only to enrich themselves and to quash or delay legal proceedings against their family and its members but also to pursue their revenge against the Frediani, much of whose property was confiscated in this period. Luca-Antono gave up his post when Napoleon became Emperor in 1804 and returned to Penta, where a period of calm seems to have ensued.

Hostilities resumed towards the end of the next decade. Each side engaged in denunciation of the other for disloyalty to the régime. In 1812, Luca-Antono Viterbi was arrested and kept for a while in prison, while seven members of the Frediani family were put on trial but acquitted in 1813. When the Giametti returned to Corsica in 1814, the Viterbi, whose hatred for their old enemies had in no way abated, at once 'set on foot judicial proceedings against them' for murder and theft. They were eventually prosecuted on a few minor counts only and then acquitted. This outcome led the Viterbi 'to lose hope of getting even with the Giametti through the courts', while the latter were provoked by 'prosecutions which they regarded as vexatious'.

Later in 1814, the Viterbi were accused of killing Donato Frediani, in circumstances of which there are conflicting accounts. It appears that on his father's death, Donato Frediani had formally renounced his share in 'the paternal inheritance'. His three brothers therefore acquired the estate, and they sold a piece of land which they owned jointly to a widow Campana from Castellare. However, Donato then reclaimed a right to this property and made threats against its new owner. Fighting broke out there in September 1814 between two groups of armed men, each supporting a rival claimant. Frediani and his party appear to have been worsted, for he made an official complaint to the military authorities afterwards and asked for protection, alleging 'that he did not dare leave his house' because of the threats that had been made against him. Other reports suggest, however, that, far from being confined to his house at this time, he committed various acts of arson to the prejudice of his opponents. In early November 1814, he was killed on the threshold of his house. His brother, Carlo-Felice, and other relatives accused Luca-Antono Viterbi and his son Orso-Paolo, but the Viterbi claimed that 'the two families had lived for a long time, if not on good terms, at least without bitterness and without any new trouble having reanimated their old enmities'. They pointed to more recent conflict which had earned Donato Frediani many enemies. Witnesses testified later, however, to having seen Orso-Paolo, on the night that Donato was killed, in the house of Giovan-Stefano Battiglione, *adjoint* of Penta and 'the close friend and relative' of the Viterbi, which was right opposite the house of the Frediani.

Also in 1814, the Viterbi intervened in a dispute between the Ceccaldi of Vescovato, already their enemies for local political reasons, and the Arena, over the inheritance of Ursula-Felicita Arena. The powerful Ceccaldi believed that they could simply take possession of the property in question, but, according to the public prosecutor in 1818,

> the Arena found protectors in the Viterbi, who claimed a lease on it. This contest led to considerable bitterness between the families concerned ... They formed themselves into groups to take the produce of the disputed lands by force ... The Viterbi and the Ceccaldi had each as usual involved all their friends and clients in their quarrel. It was natural, therefore, for

the Giametti, enemies of the Viterbi, to take the side of the Ceccaldi, while, on the other side, the Mari ... one of whom, Brandimorte, was married to Luca-Antono's sister, figured among the most ardent partisans of the Viterbi, although they were also related to the Ceccaldi.

The threat of violence between the parties came to nothing, however, until wider political events provided an opportunity.

At the news of the embarkation of Napoleon in France in March 1815 at the start of the Hundred Days, there was a general insurrection in Corsica, only the coastal towns remaining faithful to the monarchy, which had been restored the previous year. The Bonapartists set up a camp on the plain of Bevinco just north of the Casinca. Francesco Colonna-Ceccaldi, his nephew Bastiano, and the Giametti brothers, together with their followers, were among the first to assemble there, under the leadership of General Casalta. The Viterbi, with their followers, also proceeded to the camp, though Casalta, fearing the eruption of violence between the two armed groups of enemies, tried without success to get them to turn back. A skirmish took place between the rival families and their supporters, which resulted in about ten casualties. On the Viterbi side, a nephew of Luca-Antono and another man were killed, and Marc-Antono Mari and another man were wounded. On the other side, three of the Giametti were wounded and the two Colonna-Ceccaldi were killed. The Viterbi claimed that they had been the victims of aggression, but this was denied by their enemies, who alleged, too, that the Ceccaldi had been killed after they had surrendered. General Casalta took the latter view and a decree of the revolutionary junta was issued, on his advice, which ordered the arrest of the Viterbi and their associates and the sequestration of their property, the destruction of the houses of the Viterbi and the Mari and the erection of columns of infamy on their sites. Luca-Antono and Orso-Paolo Viterbi were also sentenced to death in their absence. None of these measures appears to have been put into effect, not least because the Viterbi attached themselves to the cause of the Bourbon monarchy, which was again restored in June 1815.

Orso-Paolo Viterbi remained at large at the head of 'a gang of brigands', which included Giovan-Paolo Mari called Cappato, two members of the Casalta family and three members of the Campana family. In June 1816, they attacked the Giametti in the village of Porri, and Giovan-Agostino Giametti was killed. The Frediani alleged that they committed a series of other crimes in the district, including the burning of property and attempted murder. As a result of pressure from the Ceccaldi, charges were brought in 1818 against Luca-Antono and Orso-Paolo Viterbi and Brandimorte and Cappato Mari for their part in the events at the camp of Bevinco. Luca-Antono and the two Mari were arrested. Thanks to the efforts and influence of their ally, Judge Arena, and, it was alleged, by bribing some of the other judges and suborning witnesses, the Viterbi were acquitted at the trial, while the Mari, who had acted more or less as their agents, received only light sentences for killing the Colonna-Ceccaldi 'in response to violent provocation'. This was seen as a triumph for the Viterbi, who staged celebrations at Penta in front of the houses of the Colonna-Ceccaldi and the Frediani. In 1821, moreover, Luca-Antono and Petro Viterbi obtained possession, via a civil suit begun in 1798, of a property that formed part of the estate of Carlo Frediani, and they were also granted very extensive damages amounting to 40,000 francs from the Frediani. Marc-Antono Frediani, Carlo's heir, at once took steps to have this decision reversed, and a long legal battle, centring on the exact date of Carlo's death, began, which was still pending in the mid-1830s.

Meanwhile, proceedings were begun against Luca-Antono Viterbi and his son for the killing of Donato Frediani in 1814. Orso-Paolo escaped to Italy, but Luca-Antono was again arrested. The two families engaged in a pamphlet war, each providing its own account of the conflict between them, as we have seen. The trial, which became a *cause célèbre* in Corsica, took place in September 1821, and Viterbi was convicted and sentenced to death. Rather than suffer the shame of a public execution, Viterbi starved himself to death in December. His brother, Petro, who had made strenuous and fruitless efforts to save him, died at Penta before the trial began. Orso-Paolo is reported to have died in Naples around 1830. This appears to have been the end of the feuding at Penta, although Luca-Antono in his testament had called on his relatives to avenge his death. There are echoes of the old conflict, however, in disputes which occurred later in the century. The Frediani benefited from their Bonapartism during the Second Empire, and Francesco Frediani became mayor in 1863. A new road to the village was built at this time and most of the villagers gave the land required to the commune for nothing. Frediani and his brothers, however, obtained financial compensation. The municipal council formally appealed against this settlement in 1870 and had the amount of compensation greatly reduced. Francesco Frediani was also prosecuted for erecting a water trough which extended on to the new road. One of the main inspirers of this action against the Frediani was Petro-Paolo Battiglione, *adjoint* and then acting mayor, whose family had been actively engaged in the feuding at the start of the century as allies of the Viterbi.[61]

Four general comments may be made about the feuding at Penta. First, it involved those at the highest levels of Corsican society. The main protagonists were notables. The Viterbi were at once actively engaged in violence and the holders of high offices, albeit under a revolutionary régime. Secondly, and related to this, the conflict at Penta was part and parcel of the wider political and constitutional conflict that Corsica experienced between 1789 and 1815, each side choosing its options in the latter with its eyes very clearly on advantages to be gained in the former. Thirdly, and again connected with these previous points, the feuding itself was not confined to Penta. The Ceccaldi came from Vescovato and the Giametti from Porri, which were also theatres of conflict; while the Viterbi had supporters at both Vescovato and at Taglio. Finally, the Penta example illustrates very clearly how violence and court action could alternate as modes of feuding, a point to which we will return in Chapter 10.

MURO

Feuding was almost unknown in the Balagna later in the nineteenth century, but this had not always been the case. One of the feuds there about which we have most information, was that between the Tortora and the Maestracci of Muro. An official account of it exists, which allows one to see how the conflict gradually escalated.

The Tortora were an old family of landowners, well-established in the village. The Maestracci, by contrast, who came from the Niolo, 'had lived at Muro
for only two generations, and they made a living from trading and peddling'.
The Maestracci 'were more numerous, and more powerful within the village',
while the Tortora 'had more influence outside it through their marriage ties with
a number of respectable families' in the region. Both families had links with the
anti-Revolutionary and Royalist party in Corsica, but, while the Tortora had
emigrated, the Maestracci had not. The active hostility between the families
seems to have started during the First Empire. One of the Maestracci was
churchwarden and, when 'the Tortora pointed out a discrepancy in the parish
accounts, their friendship began to wane'. Then, a Maestracci youth engaged
himself to replace a conscript. He had second thoughts and failed to present
himself when required, was arrested but escaped. A relative, fearing official
enquiries as a result of this escape, arranged to hide what appears to have been
contraband in the Tortora house, 'but when he came to recover this merchandise,
he claimed that part of it was missing'. A little later, one of the Tortora's guard
dogs was shot dead at the door of their house during the night, which was 'a very
serious offence' in Corsica. The culprit remained undiscovered, but the Tortora
suspected the Maestracci. An incident arose next over the tethering of a goat.
One of the Tortora children attached a goat to an olive tree belonging to the
Maestracci, one of whom came up and gave the child a beating. Shortly after this,
a Tortora found a hen belonging to the Maestracci in his field and killed it. In
retaliation, the fence around his field was destroyed at night, and trees were cut
and plants uprooted. The Tortora made an official complaint, but no proof was
found against the Maestracci. 'The animosity between the two families was
growing, and the possible consequences were viewed with alarm at Muro; people
of goodwill intervened, therefore, and peace seemed to have been restored.'

However, at about this time, General Berthier, the military governor, ordered a general surrender of arms in Corsica, giving subprefects the authority to
allow certain notables to retain theirs. The subprefect of Calvi, Guibega, granted
this privilege to the Maestracci but not to the Tortora, against whom he apparently bore a grudge following an incident in 1796 or 1797, in which he had been
captured, disarmed and humiliated by a group of 40 men led by the Tortora and
their relatives, the Filippi. His decision, which was later revoked, was seen by the
Tortora as an insult, which favoured their enemies, and it led to 'a fight between
the women of the two families'. In the last months of the First Empire, in March
1814, the arrest of a number of notables in the Balagna was ordered on political
grounds. The list of those to be arrested, which had been drawn up by the
subprefect, remained secret, but the Tortora and the Filippi believed that they
were on it and remained on their guard. In due course, the head of the Filippi
family was 'surrounded in his vineyard by the gendarmerie', to whom the Maestracci had acted as guides, but he was rescued by the Tortora. On news of the
First Restoration in May, the Maestracci and the Tortora took different sides, but
no overt hostility between them occurred during the insurrection which followed. In July, however, shots were fired at the house of the Giuliani in Muro
and the Maestracci were suspected. When the official representative of the new
royal government arrived in the village there was rejoicing, in which the Maes-

tracci played a prominent part; they fired shots into the air, and a large oil jar belonging to the Tortora was broken. In mid-August, a fight took place between two of the Maestracci and a member of the Tortora family minding livestock at Zilia near Muro. At about the same time, anonymous letters were sent to certain businessmen in Bastia, creditors of the Maestracci, in an attempt 'to undermine confidence in them'. The Maestracci believed that the letters had been written by Father Giovan-Andrea Tortora and told him 'to get his penitent's robe ready', which was a threat of death. After that, the feud entered a violent phase.

At the start of September, Saverio Maestracci, his nephew Domenico, aged about twelve, and Giuseppo Napoleoni were killed at a place called L'Erbaggio near the Marsolino pass. An anonymous complaint sent to the authorities, it seems by the Maestracci, explained that they had been taking a train of mules loaded with olive oil over the mountains to Vico when they had been ambushed by seven armed men. Among these were Domenico Tortora called Toli, and a certain Marchione Acquaviva from the Niolo, who may have been a priest, although they were not absolutely clearly identified. When the news of the killings reached Muro on the afternoon of the same day, Antono Tortora and his brother Marc-Antono at once 'retired into their house and put it into a state of defence'. Three other members of the family, including Domenico, arrived later, looking exhausted. But no official accusation was made against the Tortora by the relatives of the victims, and no prosecution was immediately set on foot. At the end of September, Colonel Broussier, the military commander at Calvi, went to Muro ostensibly 'to reconcile the two families'. He summoned the heads of each and asked them 'to make peace. The Tortora agreed to this request, but the Maestracci said that they could not speak for their relatives.' The next day, however, Colonel Broussier issued warrants for the arrest of certain members of the Tortora family and ordered all the armed forces in the *arrondissement* to Muro to disarm the inhabitants. On the evening of 29 September, 300 gendarmes arrived; the village and its hamlets were surrounded; the local people were instructed to hand in their arms; and orders were issued to seize Giovanni Tortora and others. The Tortora remained barricaded inside their house and sent out a letter saying that they would only surrender their arms if and when their enemies did the same. When they were reassured on this point, they gave themselves up. While this was happening, armed partisans of the Maestracci appeared on the mountain above the village, shouting that help was at hand, and the colonel decided to leave at once with ten prisoners, including Antono Tortora and Marchione Acquaviva. Antono Tortora at first believed that he and his relatives had been tricked and that they were going to be shot by the gendarmes or handed over to their enemies, so he refused to move. He was eventually persuaded to leave when the gendarmerie clearly indicated their hostility to the Maestracci and promised that neither he nor Acquaviva would be handcuffed. About half-way to Calvi, however, at Lumio, gendarmes and prisoners were attacked in force by the supporters of the Maestracci. Antono Tortora and Acquaviva apparently took the opportunity to escape in the confusion and were fired at by the troops. Acquaviva was killed. Tortora was wounded but got away.[62]

The continuous account ends here, but we can trace the sequel from more fragmentary evidence. In February 1815, Giovan-Andrea Filippi of Muro was ambushed at a place in the country and shot in the shoulder by Giovanni Maestracci, a young man described as an oil merchant. This was in retaliation, according to the local gendarmerie, for the killing at L'Erbaggio the previous September of Saverio Maestracci and of Giuseppo Napoleoni, who was Giovanni Maestracci's nephew. A similar incident occurred in May 1816, when Giovan-Agostino Tortora was shot and seriously wounded on the road to San-Fiorenzo. He identified Giovanni and Martino Maestracci as his assailants. Two months later, an encounter between two large groups belonging to each family took place at the chapel of San Cesario just outside the neighbouring village of Cateri. Father Giovan-Andrea Tortora and another supporter of the Tortora were wounded, and they accused Giovan-Martino, Giacomo-Francesco and Petro-Francesco Maestracci. In 1819, Marc-Antono and Antono Tortora and a third man, Rocco Pasqualini, were prosecuted for the killings at L'Erbaggio. Marc-Antono and Pasqualini were acquitted, but Antono Tortora, who was tried *in absentia*, was convicted and condemned to death. He went into exile in Tuscany but returned to Corsica in 1827 to give himself up. He was retried and again convicted and sentenced to death. The conviction was quashed on procedural grounds, and, at his third trial at Aix-en-Provence in December 1827, he was finally acquitted. The Maestracci were also presumably prosecuted for the offences which they had committed, but no record of these proceedings has been found.[63]

Further reports of violence at Muro include an abduction in 1832 and a homicide in 1845, but neither of the feuding families seems to have been involved. The summary of a trial in 1848 notes that 'the village of Muro is divided into two parties, who attack each other through songs and written "satires"', but again makes no mention of the Maestracci or the Tortora. This suggests that more serious conflict had subsided by the middle of the nineteenth century, and that the old antagonists were no longer overtly at odds with each other.[64]

II

In addition to these eight feuds, there is evidence that others occurred in at least 57 places in Corsica in the nineteenth century. Enough information is available for 47 of these 65 to establish that feuds generally continued over long periods of time.[65] Five (11 per cent) lasted for over a century; 22 (47 per cent) for from fifty to a hundred years; while, of the 20 others (42 per cent), all but one lasted over ten years and most for at least a generation. Moreover, these calculations almost certainly underestimate the duration of feuds, since they are based on incomplete documentation, and many feuds were going strong before 1800.

Our information on the duration of individual feuds also allows us to compute the incidence of feuding in Corsica as a whole by decades (Fig. 1). It will be seen that feuding increased in importance from about 1810, reaching a peak in the 1830s and 1840s and then declining significantly from about 1870. This pattern fits the hypothesis, suggested by other information and analysis, that feuding in Corsica was exacerbated by the process of incorporation into a modern state. The power of blood vengeance sanctions to prevent or contain conflict

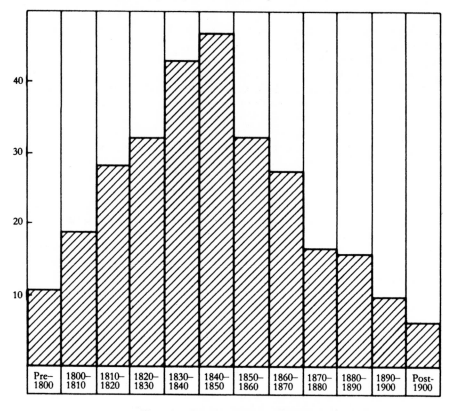

Fig. 1 Incidence of feuds, by decade

was seriously weakened for a time, and the internal balancing mechanisms of the traditional system were disrupted, all of which meant an increase, in the medium term, of feuding of a fairly unrestrained kind. We shall return to this central issue in later chapters.

Analysis of the individual feuds also permits us to draw a number of other general conclusions, some of which have been adumbrated in relation to particular villages. Feuds went through distinct phases: a phase of escalation very often, then a period of active and violent conflict, followed by reconciliation, quiescence, and then renewed violence, often after a lapse of many years. For example, low-level conflict was present at Arbellara through the early decades of the nineteenth century; the feud went into an active phase between 1835 and 1841; a truce ensued until 1844, when the feud again became active, being terminated by a peace in 1854. The feud at Pila-Canale was active in the 1790s, in 1801, in 1805, for some years up to and including 1816, in the 1830s and 1840s, and again later in the nineteenth century; and these phases of activity were punctuated, at least in the early period, by formal peace treaties, in 1792, 1797, 1798 or 1799, 1801 and 1816. However, attention should also be drawn to those villages where no such alternating pattern seems to be present, though they had a high incidence of violent conflict. This may reflect the existence of a plurality of antagonistic families rather than two clear rival groupings, which was always more common, however.

This at once raises a number of other points. Even where clear rival kindreds existed, conflict between them could be cut across and complicated by other forms of conflict. Reporting on feuding at Santa-Lucia-di-Moriani in 1809, the public prosecutor commented on 'the passionate hatreds which reign, even between close relatives'. At Olmiccia, the Ortoli, who were in a state of feud with the Quilichini, were themselves divided generally into two rival groupings and engaged in intrafamilial killing. In addition to other feuds at Levie between unrelated families, 'a terrible enmity' was said to exist in 1852 between two branches of the Peretti. At Ocana, feuding occurred within the Muselli family and between them and their affines, the Rossi, in the 1850s and 1860s.[66] Inter-village conflict could relate to feuding in a variety of ways. Sometimes general conflict with another village coexisted with feuding in one or both of them without the two apparently impinging on each other. In the 1840s, for example, when its own internal feuding was in an active phase, Venzolasca was also engaged in a dispute with Vescovato over the respective limits of their territory.[67] Sometimes, as we have seen in a number of cases, feuding between families from different villages occurred as an extension of feuding within one of them, as relatives and affines from outside became drawn into the original struggle. But, by contrast, conflict with outsiders could also stimulate solidarity within the community and thus mitigate internal conflict, at least in the short run. In 1801, for example, the Paoli of Fozzano were engaged in a feud with the Giacomoni of Santa-Maria-Figaniella. A peace was arranged between them in 1802, in which the Paoli were associated both with their relatives the Durazzi but also with their enemies the Bernardini, and this peace heralded a cessation of hostilities in Fozzano itself.[68] One also finds proper feuds between whole communities, such as that between Casalta and Silvareccio around 1830, or the war between Borgo and Lucciana earlier in the century immortalized in Viale's *Dionomachia*.[69] Feuding also took place between hamlets or parts of the same village, another important point to which we will return.

We have also seen that long feuds frequently changed their character over time, often probably without the protagonists being aware of it. Families switched sides; families divided; the mode of feuding altered from attacks on property to attacks on persons and vice versa, or from direct attacks on both to conflict in the electoral and judicial arenas. In many villages, factionalism and feuding seem to have been contemporary and virtually interchangeable patterns of behaviour, but, in general, as we have noted in our particular accounts, political and other forms of non-violent competition tended to replace feuding proper in the last third of the nineteenth century. By then, the system based on traditional sanctions was being effectively replaced and not simply dislocated by its bureaucratic rival.

A further related characteristic of Corsican feuding, which emerges from our study of individual feuds, is that generally speaking those who conducted them were members of the leading families. They involved agents, tenants, poorer relatives, clients, in their quarrels to some extent, but there was a feeling that the role of the latter in the pursuit of vengeance should be distinctly subsidiary. During a court hearing related to the feuding at Arbellara, one of the Forcioli was asked whether he knew that a share-cropper had been disfigured by shots fired probably by one of his relatives. 'We kill the masters and not the servants,' he replied. It is obvious, too, as Lear commented in connection with Fozzano, that only the wealthy could afford to engage in fighting over long periods.[70] In Sartène, the leader of the 'Sant' Anninchi' party was the mayor of the town, Vincentello Roccaserra, who was actively seconded by the subprefect, Peraldi. Following an armed encounter between the two parties in September 1830, in which two men were killed and five wounded, Roccaserra and twelve of his supporters were prosecuted. But they were easily acquitted, as the public prose-cutor complained, since they were 'connected by kinship, affinity or influence with all the important families of the island and with nearly all those of Corsican origin in the public service', including judges and magistrates.[71] In Corte at about the same time, the Mariani party, which was again involved in a violent feud, comprised the subprefect, Anton-Domenico Mariani, and his brother, the *curé*; Arrighi, the tax-collector; Giuseppo Benedetti, the mayor and nephew by marriage of the subprefect; Francesco Benedetti, the justice of the peace and the mayor's brother; District-prosecutor Poli, another nephew by marriage of the subprefect; Montera, his deputy and yet another relative by marriage of Mariani; and Casabianca, the court bailiff and an uncle of Poli's wife. 'Indeed', in the words of the public prosecutor, 'this party is made up of all the civil servants [of Corte], who are all closely related.'[72] The same pattern is repeated on a lesser scale in nearly every one of the villages which we have studied. Competition for control over local property and for local political power was usually, in effect, the essence of the feud.

A more extended analysis of property distribution has been undertaken for one village: Venzolasca, details of which are given in Appendix 1. Venzolasca was unusual, however, in a number of ways, with its large size, its lack of communal lands, its proximity to Bastia and its large amount of good agricultural land, some of which was owned by absentee landlords. Of the families active in feuding, the Petrignani and the Sanguinetti were middling proprietors, well above the general run of villagers in the amount of land and the number of houses and parts of houses which they owned but well below the biggest land-owners, the Casabianca and the Cipriani. The Ciosi and the Ciavaldini were considerably poorer, while the Filippi were wealthier, the brothers Antono and Giuseppo owning over 67 hectares.[73] The families actively engaged in feuding, moreover, belonged to the local élite proper, having only the odd member resident in Bastia or on the continent, while the wealthier families, with whom they were connected but who were not actively engaged, and notably the Casabi-anca, were mainly non-resident and belonged to the island or the French national élite.[74] There was a general trend during the nineteenth century for members of increasingly educated local élites to disengage from active feuding and to switch their efforts to the political arena, as we have noted. In Venzolasca, this process appears to have happened early as far as the very wealthiest were concerned, though some of them undoubtedly continued to participate indirectly in violent conflict. At the same time, the less wealthy élite families continued to practise violence for much longer than was normal in Corsica.

III

Map A shows the incidence of feuding in the nineteenth century by cantons. It will be seen that the heaviest concentration was in the south-west and particularly in the southern part of the *arrondissement* of Ajaccio and the northern part of that of Sartène. Feuding was also important in the north-east in the Casinca and the Castagniccia. Feuding was absent or unimportant in the Bonifacio region, the east and the north, including both the Capo Corso and the Balagna. If account is taken of the relative size of the population of these different parts of Corsica (using the *arrondissement* as the unit of measurement), this geographical pattern is only reinforced (see Table 2). The proportion of feuds to total population was eight times greater in the *arrondissement* of Sartène and four times greater in the *arrondissement* of Ajaccio than it was in the *arrondissement* of Calvi.

Table 2. *Feuds by arrondissement*

Arrondissement	Number of feuds	Ratio of feuds to population in 1852
Ajaccio	20	1:2,750
Bastia	12	1:5,720
Calvi	2	1:12,170
Corte	12	1:4,730
Sartène	19	1:1,560

In general, this confirms the view of contemporary observers and officials and of later writers, though these do not always take sufficient account of changes over time. Feuding does seem to have been most prevalent in the south-west throughout the period from 1800 to recent times,[75] though Pomponi suggests that in the early eighteenth century it was more important in the north-east.[76] There seems little doubt that feuding was never important at Bonifacio, which was a Genoese settlement, though Maupassant made it the setting for his celebrated short story.[77] The situation in the Capo Corso and the Balagna is more problematic and introduces the question of how the pattern of feuding in Corsica is to be explained.

'No example may be found among the inhabitants of the ancient province of Capo Corso of those enmities which have desolated the mountainous interior of the island,' wrote *La Gazette des Tribunaux* in 1828. As we have seen, the odd example may in fact be found, but this does not alter the general picture of an absence of feuding that was well-established by the start of the nineteenth century and which was linked in the eyes of most observers and students to the involvement of the inhabitants in maritime trade and an 'advanced', commercialized agriculture.[78] It is also significant that alternative forms of conflict were present, and notably inter-village disputes over the use of chapels.

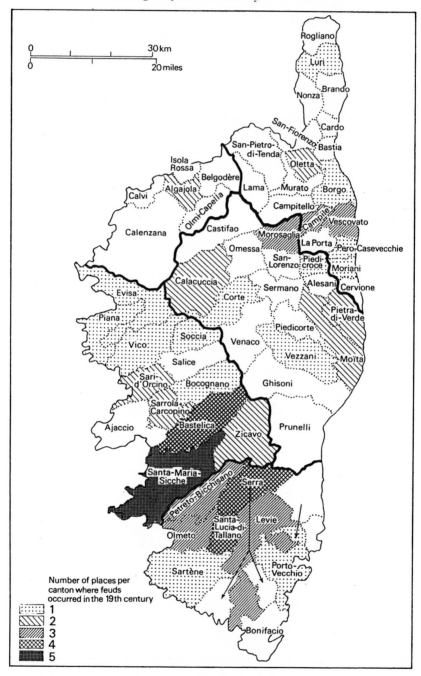

Map A Incidence of feuds, by canton

The reputation for non-violence of the Balagna was more recently acquired.[79] Serious conflict was endemic in the region through the Revolutionary and Napoleonic period[80] and, in addition to the two feuding villages included in our list, acts of violence against the person were committed in at least nine other places in the first half of the nineteenth century.[81] The lack of belligerence, which prevailed generally from the time of the July Monarchy, was attributed, as in the case of the Capo Corso, to a more advanced state of 'civilization' and a prosperity, which were in turn related to the Balagna's commercialized agriculture and arboriculture. At the same time it was pointed out that the people of the Balagna remained 'excessively quarrelsome', though this propensity found an outlet in this later period in litigation and political intrigue.[82]

The correlation between wealth and feuding may be pursued further on the cantonal and on the village level, though the results here are less conclusive. Of the ten richest cantons in terms of land, as calculated by Robiquet in 1835, five figure on Map A, and of the ten richest in terms of personal wealth, seven figure. But four and five of the ten poorest cantons, by the same criteria, also figure. Among our 65 feuding villages, similarly, examples of both wealth and poverty are found. Fozzano, for instance, was one of the richer villages in Corsica in the 1830s, measured by its tax assessment; Olmeto was described at the end of the eighteenth century as 'the richest and most populous community' in the *arrondissement* of Sartène; while Venzolasca was said in the 1840s to be 'remarkable for its wealth'. By contrast, both Ota and Loreto-di-Tallano were bywords for poverty.[83]

More significant than wealth or poverty as such were the type of economy which a place enjoyed, its size and its social structure, and any changes which occurred in these. Comprehensive information on all these topics is not available, but a number of pointers do exist. First, feuding occurred both in predominantly pastoral communities, such as Albitreccia, Ciamannacce, Cozzano or Zerubia,[84] and also in places where pastoralism was only ancillary. Indeed, a significant number of feuding villages were noted later in the nineteenth century for their relatively advanced agriculture and/or arboriculture.[85] This does not invalidate the general explanations offered for the lack or decline of feuding in the Capo Corso and the Balagna. Rather, it indicates that conflict was generated in a variety of economic contexts, and perhaps ran in more peaceful channels in the north simply because the process of agricultural development was more advanced. The example of Olmeto and the rest certainly suggests a parallel correlation between relatively advanced agriculture, and hence a high degree of private property in land, and intense and prolonged feuding, which may be more characteristic of early stages in this process. And here it is relevant that, although some feuding villages, such as Zerubia, Santa-Maria-Sicche and Olmeto had important common lands, others, such as Penta-di-Casinca, were deficient in a type of property which demanded co-operation as well as provoking conflict in ways which we shall discuss. In others, such as Fozzano or Ocana, the common lands belonged not to the whole population of the place but to a small group of aboriginal families, the main protagonists in their feuds. Moreover, villages where common lands were important saw that importance diminish in the course of the nineteenth century to the benefit again of a minority.[86] Some, like Levie or Marignana,

Table 3. *Population of feuding villages*

Population of village	Under 350	c. 500	500–1000	1000–1250	c. 1750	Over 2000
Number of villages	14	16	19	6	2	4
Number of villages as percentage of total	23	26	31	10	3	7

experienced the hiving-off of coastal satellites. Such fission may have been produced by internal tensions which were thereby reduced, but equally detachment from the plain and sedentarization may have thrown the inhabitants of the villages of the interior more in on themselves, their grudges and their quarrels.[87]

Sometimes the trend away from pastoralism or a balanced pastoral and agricultural economy towards agriculture and/or arboriculture was linked to a process of social stratification, as we have suggested, and thus of competition within an élite. But the same trend could be prompted simply by population growth, as it appears to have been at Ota. A study of land use there from the mid-nineteenth century reveals a fairly egalitarian property structure, with few big landowners and many small ones, a fair incidence of private property in land but affecting only small pieces, mainly gardens, and a continuing predominance of communal property and indivision.[88] But population growth by itself can do little to explain why feuding occurred in some villages and not others, since it was nearly universal in Corsica down to the last third of the nineteenth century. Nor does the size of places where feuds occurred appear to tell us very much. As Table 3 demonstrates, feuding took place in settlements of all sizes, from large villages like Bastelica, Levie, Olmeto or Venzolasca, down to virtual hamlets like Loreto-di-Tallano or Casalabriva. It also took place, we have noted, in the two towns of the interior, Corte and Sartène. On Map A, moreover, five of the ten most populous cantons in 1835, and four of the ten least populous, figure equally as ones with a high incidence of feuding.

If they do nothing else, therefore, our investigations into the geographical incidence of feuding in Corsica demonstrate that no easy explanations of the phenomenon exist. As Montherot noted in 1840, a peaceful village like Piedicroce might be found in the close vicinity of one torn apart by terrible enmities (probably Carcheto), with no apparent reason for the contrast.[89] Marcaggi was tempted in this impasse to look to ethnic explanations or the influence of malaria.[90] The way out or forward would seem to lie rather in two directions. First in more detailed comparative studies of villages and secondly, which is our present course, in the location of feuding and discussion of it in the wider context of conflict in Corsica. In this perspective, the problem becomes less why conflict as such occurred in one place rather than another and more why conflict, which had general causes and was very widespread, took different forms in different places and at different times.

] 3 [

Conflict and its causes:
conflicts of material interest

We turn now therefore to a consideration of conflict generally in nineteenth-century Corsica, of which feuding was only a part. Here we will distinguish conflicts of material interest, conflicts of honour, intrafamilial and inter-community conflict.

I

Writing in 1841, Léon Griffon, a former teacher at the college of Calvi, isolated the unremitting pursuit of material interest as a particular Corsican trait, linking it to the island's poverty and lack of natural resources: 'Corsicans need to practise the strictest economy ... and they have thus become sordidly materialistic to the point that they will never agree to anything unless they see an advantage in it for themselves.'[1] Other observers shared this view and pointed to the intense competitiveness which reigned at all levels of Corsican society. Again and again, trial summaries make the point that conflicts arose from 'reasons of interest' or 'differences of interest', and causing deliberate damage was probably the commonest form of offence against property all through the nineteenth century.[2] As we have seen, moreover, attacks on material resources were part and parcel of feuding. 'How many affronts were inflicted on you!', a wife told her dead husband in a lament. 'Walls pulled down, / Grange set on fire, / Trees cut down ... / Then they killed your oxen / Asleep in the straw; / Alas, it was on that day ... / [that you said] "I have had enough. / The blood of my oxen / Will be avenged".'[3] Of course, this fierce competition over material resources characterizes other similar societies in the Mediterranean region and elsewhere.[4] Nor was the pursuit of material interest incompatible with the strictest regard for 'honour'. What the Corsican material allows one to demonstrate is both how firmly rooted in conditions of scarcity were conflict and violence but also how they took on specific cultural forms.

First, conflict was extremely common over the use and ownership of land. We have already seen that disputes over land were an important ingredient in feuds.[5] Two cases from the 1860s must serve as typical examples of disputes of the same kind which did not have quite such serious consequences. At Ciamannacce, Paolo-Santo Bartoli contested the ownership of a piece of land with his aunt Dolinda. This land was 'sown with barley and, since it was necessary (in June 1862) to harvest it without delay, Dolinda and her nephew's share-croppers made an agreement to do so and to deposit the crop with a third party, Buresi, who would hand it over later to whoever had established the right to it.' While Dolinda was taking the barley to Buresi's house, she was met by Paolo-Santo, who had not been informed of the agreement and who therefore thought that she was taking it for herself. He 'addressed a few sharp words to her' and at the same time fired his pistol, causing a perforation in her cheek. In September 1864, Giacomo Bernardi, the *adjoint* of Alzi, went with his son and his first cousin Risterucci 'to sow a crop on an enclosed property called Meli' about ten kilometres from the village. Meli apparently belonged or had belonged to the Marcantoni family and Bernardi claimed that he had the permission of Giulia Marcantoni to use it. However, the three Palmesani brothers, one of whom was mayor, laid a rival and absolute claim to the property which they alleged they had obtained in an exchange with Giulia's brother, Don Giovanni. The Palmesani had therefore prepared the land for cultivation the previous July and now followed Bernardi and his relatives to Meli and ordered them off the land. Fighting broke out between the two parties, in which Bernardi was shot dead, Risterucci was stabbed and one of the Palmesani seriously wounded with an axe.[6]

Underlying such disputes over land was the extremely complex system of property which we outlined in the first chapter. Land was widely if not equally distributed, and most land belonged to families and to communities and not to individuals. 'Owners' frequently had rights in land rather than absolute property of it, and their rights were shared with others. These rights were mainly transmitted at marriage and death through dowries and inheritance, but they were also leased and might be sold. At every point conflict could emerge, and this likelihood seems in the nineteenth century to have been increased by two general trends: first the rise in population which intensified competition for already scarce resources; and secondly the gradual strengthening of individualistic and absolute notions of property as against the complex of traditional use rights. Our sources give some insight into both the traditional structure and the process of its weakening.

Disputes to some extent reflected the fact that property rights were uncertain and could be acquired by occupation over a relatively short period of time.[7] Blanqui noted in 1841 that 'very few citizens possess authentic titles to their properties and lands, and prescription is the only guarantee of most fortunes'.[8] Such a situation invited usurpation and forcible occupation, especially in times of exceptional disorder. The domain of Migliacciaro on the plain of Fiumorbo, for example, was legally owned by notables from the Casinca and Bastia but, as Robiquet explained, 'the inhabitants of the neighbouring villages had always maintained claims over it, and took it over by force during the troubles [of the Revolutionary period] ... When order was re-established, the proprietors and their *coloni* resumed their rights.'[9] More generally, Feydel referred in 1799 to 'the Corsican custom of only respecting private property out of fear of reprisals or when it is directly protected'. Here we may note that such a system clearly inhibited the development of private property in land and served to maintain a certain egalitarianism. 'What is the point of a Corsican's doubling the extent of his field', asked Malaspina in 1876, 'if his enemies prevent him from cultivating it?'[10]

A case from Isolaccio illustrates the importance of occupying and using disputed land. A field called Chiosella, 'whose ownership was uncertain, had been ploughed in 1842 by a certain Valentini and Astolfo Colombani'. The following year the land was left uncultivated, and the brothers Petro-Paolo and Suzzone Tomasi approached Valentini and obtained from him the cession of his rights to it. Negotiations also took place with Colombani via his brother Don Marco in an attempt to persuade him to sell his share, but these were not successful. While things were thus still unsettled, the Tomasi ploughed the whole of the property in question, an 'act of possession' which surprised and annoyed Astolfo Colombani. He went to Chiosella, where the Tomasi were proceeding to sow their crop with the aid of relatives, and began 'to plough the field in the opposite direction to that taken by the ox-team of the Tomasi ... this act of flagrant hostility caused havoc' and provoked general fighting with daggers and shotguns. Both Astolfo Colombani and Suzzone Tomasi were wounded, while Don Marco Colombani, who had tried to pacify them, later died of stab wounds.[11]

Conflict over land frequently arose in the context of inheritance,[12] and a special cause of dispute here was disagreement over the management or the partition of undivided property. In August 1841 shots were fired at a house in Carbini apparently in an attempt to kill Dr Paolo Fraticelli. The culprits were Francesco Cucchi and another man 'with whom the doctor was in dispute over property which they had to divide on the plain of Figari'. Father Franchi of Moca-Croce shared an undivided enclosure with Giusepp'-Antono Istria. Several attempts to divide up the property had failed through the ill-will of the latter, and an enmity existed between their families for this and other reasons. When Istria began to cultivate the land with the aid of labourers in August 1849, Father Franchi went there to protest and was wounded when shots were exchanged.[13]

Land was not uncommonly leased on a short-term basis among small proprietors, or for longer periods by wealthy landlords to *coloni*, and this, too, could generate conflict. The enmity between the Cartucci and the Rutilj of Arbellara arose from the seduction of Cornelia Cartucci by Antono Rutilj in 1840, but it was compounded by Antono's readiness to replace Cornelia's brother Angelo-Santo as a share-cropper of Signore Rutilj-Forcioli when his lease was not renewed.[14]

Land belonging to richer landowners and worked by *coloni* or labourers was also particularly vulnerable to being placed under 'interdict', and we have seen that this weapon was a feature of many prominent feuds. Interdicts were usually announced by notices placed on church doors. That posted at Canale-di-Verde in 1832, for example, read: 'The village is warned that whoever goes to cultivate the lands of the Giavacchini will be punished by death.' Interdicts seem more often than not to have been complied with, and threats against those who refused to be intimidated were carried out. In the course of the feud between the Coronati and the Susini of Sartène in the 1830s, Anton-Francesco Coronati killed a poor labourer, Giuseppo Péché. Coronati was particularly 'incensed by the fact that Péché continued to plough the Susini lands', which he had been warned not to do, and he was actually killed as he was returning from tending one of their vines.[15]

The sale of land was also potentially contentious. Carlo Poggi promised to sell a property to the notary Giuseppo Peretti of Cauro, but there was some disagreement about when the purchase price should be paid, so Poggi sought and found another buyer, Santo Riesi. The notary at first tried to get the local justice of the peace to intervene to prevent the sale and, when this failed, ambushed and killed Riesi in November 1850.[16] Sales could also conflict with the claims of kin[17] or complicate disputes within the inheritance and dowry system, as a case at Serra in the 1840s demonstrates. Petro Carlotti had sold his brother-in-law, Giacomo Carlotti, a piece of land which seems to have been part of his late wife's dowry. Although she had consented in her lifetime to the sale, Petro denied this after her death and maintained therefore that the sale had been invalid. He tried unsuccessfully to recover the land by litigation and then turned to violence, killing Giacomo's wife in 1845 and attempting to kill Giacomo himself in 1849.[18]

In most of the cases discussed so far, the land in question was in private ownership, but conflict was more likely to occur over the use of common land. This was usually cultivated on a temporary basis, those who cleared plots acquiring certain rights over them. In a case in 1827, brought against Giuseppo-Luigi Sabiani of Casamaccioli, a witness testified that Sabiani 'had cut the maquis ... I am not sure exactly when, but this sort of work, which is done so that the land may be cultivated later, usually takes place between May and August' and most often in August. Sabiani himself said that he had done the work in May 'with the intention of enclosing the plot with a hedge and sowing the land the same year'. He had returned there in mid-August 'to mark out the plot and to appropriate it definitively as was customary' only to find that it had been burned over by someone else.[19] As this shows, such a system could easily produce conflicting claims or tempt people to try to keep others away from particular plots or to use land prepared by others. We learn from a case in 1850 that 'the village of Rospigliani possesses vacant land at Ajalonga where each inhabitant has the customary right to make assartments'. Anselmo Calendini had put two parcels under cultivation and objected when a group of other men began working the parcel between them. Three of these intruders were frightened off but the fourth persisted and was shot and killed by Calendini. At Bustanico, similarly, it was 'an immemorial custom that whoever among the inhabitants brings into cultivation a piece of the common land of the village retains possession of that land so long as he continues to cultivate it'. Salabrio Taddei and his brother-in-law Michele Sarrocchi had cultivated such a plot in 1852 and taken the produce from it. In November that year, Salabrio was preparing to cultivate the same plot again when he learned that Filippo-Maria Taddei and his relatives were ploughing it. He and Sarrocchi went to try to stop them, and fighting broke out in which Salabrio and a cousin of Taddei were wounded.

Other cases show that such plots were not necessarily cultivated by groups of relatives (though this was the usual arrangement), and also that in some villages plots were not claimed but regularly distributed. 'On 1 January 1857, the villages of San-Pietro and San-Gavino proceeded, as was customary, to share out the common undivided lands by lot among the different heads of families.' A certain parcel with a hut on it was allotted to three unrelated men who began to cultivate it a week later. A fourth man, Ignazio Costa, then tried to prevent them, saying that he had marked the land with a furrow and that it was therefore his. When his appeal to the alternative mode of acquiring rights in common land failed, he attempted to demolish and set fire to the hut.[20]

As we have seen, within the whole extent of a village's common lands, a certain area, the *presa*, would be allocated for agriculture, while another, the *circolo*, would be set aside for arboriculture, and yet another for pasture. This zoning, which was periodically readjusted or altered, might be contested or ignored. In 1827, for example, the Paoli brothers and another man from Serraggio were prosecuted for cutting and damaging trees. The mayor of Serraggio, Matteo Stefani, testified that he had learned that the three men were 'preparing to cultivate a piece of land, that had [recently] been included in the part that was not to be cultivated ... but was reserved for pasture, which was upsetting other people in the village'. He therefore spoke to them about it on a Sunday after mass and, since 'the general opinion had shown itself to be against them, they desisted'. He added that 'the land in question is part of the common lands that are leased out; and that those who opposed its cultivation were the herdsmen'. This case is of especial interest since it indicates how such disputes could be, and perhaps normally were, settled without recourse to violence. It also points to another area of possible contention, since testimony was also heard from Saverio Stefani, who had taken lease of the land and who was probably a relative of the mayor.[21] The profitable lease of common lands for pasture was frequently determined by mayors in a partisan way, as we will see in detail in Chapter 11. This could arouse great hostility among those who were excluded, and doubtless explains some attacks made on the persons and the property of mayors and other officials. When ten olive trees were cut down in an enclosure belonging to the mayor of Levie in 1819, he supposed 'that this must have been done by people with whom he was in dispute over the common lands'.[22]

Finally under this heading we should mention conflict arising from the break-up or permanent division of common lands, which was encouraged by the state authorities, and the related conflict arising from the usurpation of common lands. Usurpation was 'traditional' and endemic. Patin de La Fizelière referred to the resentment occasioned in the 1770s by the usurpations of the Peretti at Figari, and the charge of usurpation was frequently laid against mayors, priests and others by their opponents in the nineteenth century. Pernet and Lenclud note that the partition of common lands was effected earliest and most easily in places like Antisanti, where 'enclosure was generalized, there was no *presa* system, and most of the inhabitants had become *coloni* or day-labourers' by the 1870s.[23] Partition, in effect, set the seal on a lengthy process of usurpation, which transformed the common lands into private property. An incident at Lano in 1841, however, shows the strength of opposition that could exist to this process and also indicates that its time-span could be shorter. A meeting was called by the mayor on the church square to discuss 'the desirability of dividing up the common lands'. A large part of these had been usurped, and the meeting was marked by intermittent violence and stone-throwing, as a result of which a man was killed.[24]

Conflict over land, private and public, often centred on limits or boundaries. For example, Giovan-Francesco Astolfi and a certain Massiani quarrelled over their relative shares of an enclosure at Pietralba in 1852. Massiani owned one-third of the property and Astolfi two-thirds, but it was not formally divided. Astolfi claimed that Massiani had cultivated more than his share, and when Massiani ignored his complaints, hit him on the head twice with a pickaxe. If lack of obvious boundaries led to dispute, so did attempts to provide them. In a case in 1821, a *colono* of Alessandro Quilichini of Olmiccia testified that when he was ploughing a field for his landlord, the Ortoli brothers came up and told him that he was on their land, and threw down small stones on the ground to indicate the line beyond which he should not go. When they found another *colono* of Quilichini ploughing in the same place a few days later, the Ortoli drove him off by throwing stones at his oxen. The Ortoli brothers were actually prosecuted for 'removing landmarks', and this was an equally common cause for dispute. A fight, in which one contestant was seriously injured, took place at Castineta in 1849, because 'Giulio-Cesareo Santini claimed that a boundary mark had been moved to his disadvantage by Costantino Ambrosi'. In a case in 1858, it was established that Francesco Giafferi of Monaccia had conducted a campaign of intimidation against Giovan-Battiste Tomasini, whose property lay alongside his: 'Sometimes he sent his flocks to devour the pasture belonging to Tomasini, sometimes he moved the boundary marks.'[25]

Our sources do not suggest that boundaries in Corsica were reinforced by making them 'sacred', as was done in Albania,[26] but they clearly had symbolic significance. Attention should be drawn here again to the common practice of destroying walls, hedges and enclosures as a specific act of vengeance or provocation, whether the property was in dispute or not. We have seen that the destruction of walls was a recurring feature of the feud between the Giacomoni and the Quilichini at Santa-Lucia-di-Tallano in the period before 1830. Walls or hedges were also destroyed in the course of feuding at Olmeta-di-Tuda, Fozzano and Moca-Croce.[27] Such actions, of course, would usually have exposed land and crops to the depredation of animals. For, as we have noted, only gardens and plots used for cereal cultivation were permanently or temporarily enclosed, and the commonest form of enclosure was a dry hedge of staves and brushwood[28] that was very easy to damage or to remove either deliberately or accidentally. A fatal quarrel in 1851, for example, between two men from Antisanti arose 'over a hedge belonging to one of them which had been damaged by oxen belonging to the other'.[29]

Related to disputes over boundaries are those over rights of way, which were also very frequent, reflecting the extreme fragmentation of property in Corsica. In 1839, for example, Natale Meria of Bastia was shot dead and his father wounded as they were taking brushwood from their property near Lucciana to the road. Their assailants were two men from Ortiporio who had objected to the Merias crossing land over which they had no right of way.[30] We have seen that it was a dispute of this kind which precipitated the feuding at Santa-Lucia-di-Tallano in 1819. Conflict under this heading seems to have been particularly common among relatives, which supports our suggestion about its connection with the fragmentation of property. For example, Simone-Paolo Cotoni, from an unspecified village, claimed a right of way across an enclosure belonging to Paolo and Giulio Quilici, his brother-in-law and cousin respectively. In October 1841, as Cotoni had just opened the entrance to the enclosure in order to cross it with a mule loaded with must from one of his vines, he was shot at by the Quilici and slightly injured. They were prosecuted and convicted of attempted homicide but received only light sentences in view of the fact that the right of way in question was contested, which implies that the situation was fairly typical.[31] Some cases of disputed rights of way involved the more immediate space around houses and we will return to these.

Dry farming predominated in Corsica, but some fields, and particularly gardens in the vicinity of villages, were irrigated. Competition could be intense over the supply of water to these, and in many villages this was communally organized and regulated in an attempt to mitigate conflict. At Vezzani in the 1860s, the gardens were 'watered from a spring some distance from the village, the water being carried in small channels constructed with great intelligence'. Here the water was used on a 'first come, first served' basis, but at Bastelica about the same time: 'Every year, the mayor with the older men makes a regulation for the distribution of water, which gives every owner of a garden in the village the right to the exclusive use of the water supply for a determined time, infraction of the regulation being punishable by the mayor using his police powers.'[32] Both Saint-Germain and Bigot noted that such communal control did not always prevent 'violent disputes and fights', particularly among women who usually did the watering. In a case in 1854, Dono Nicolai of Levie went with his mother and sister 'to water a garden. By local custom they had the exclusive right to use the water of a stream that day. But Giovan-Paolo Nicolai was already using the water and told Dono Nicolai that he did not want to give it up.' Other relatives joined in the argument, and Dono's brother was eventually shot dead. But our sources also demonstrate the existence of private property rights in water and confirm that men were directly concerned in their acquisition or defence. In a case in 1818, for example, Anton-Petro and Paolo-Maria Pietri, uncle and nephew, of Sartène, were accused of wounding Giovan-Battiste Pietri on the head and arm with a billhook. Anton-Petro explained that, on passing by an enclosure at Forcioli, he saw that the plaintiff had 'diverted from its ordinary course', by means of a ditch, a stream which had 'from time immemorial watered a garden which he possessed there'. This action would have rendered cultivation of the garden impossible, so he told his nephew to fill in the ditch, which provoked a fight with Giovan-Battiste. Nearly five years later this dispute continued, for Anton-Petro was reported to have fired a pistol at Giovan-Battiste Pietri at Forcioli in 1823. Very many similar cases could be cited from all over Corsica, and civil litigation over water rights seems also to have been common.

Further aspects of conflict related to agriculture are revealed by our sources. Many poorer cultivators relied on mutual aid or on borrowing from wealthier neighbours or patrons in order to accomplish basic tasks. In 1821, for example, Giuseppo-Maria Istria, a landowner from Moca-Croce, brought a charge against Antono Luciani for starting a fire at his threshing floor, in which a large quantity of Istria's barley was destroyed. It seems that Luciani was threshing his own barley at the floor without having asked special permission, and had lit a fire to burn some thistles, which had got out of control. Such arrangements could also lead to more direct conflict, as another case in 1821 demonstrates. Anton-Battiste Chiarelli of Olmeto testified that one morning,

> needing a kind of cart, called a *cassa*, to level some land where I was going to sow millet, I went to reclaim the one which belonged to me, from Carlo and Domenico Peretti ... who were using it for the same job on the plain of Taravo. They had taken it from a certain Chicchiolo [from a different village] ... who had borrowed it from my ploughing companion, Carlo Poli.

However, the Peretti refused to return the cart; fighting took place in which Chiarelli was worsted, and he went away 'leaving the cart to my enemies'. Two days later he was fetching his oxen from an enclosure when the Peretti came up out of the maquis, insulted and blindfolded him, pushed him in a ditch and mutilated his nose. Similar disputes could arise over the loan of animals, a point to which we will return, and over communal facilities. For example, two men from Peri quarrelled in August 1855 'over the use of the communal threshing floor called San Pancrazio', and fought with their wooden grain shovels.[33]

This last case shows, too, how agricultural tools were often used as weapons. The favourite here was the billhook or *rustaghja*, and there is a specific word in Corsican to designate a blow from this instrument,[34] but reference is also made to axes, spades and other tools. It would be natural to use these as weapons if men quarrelled while working with them, but it is significant that this mode of fighting does seem to have been distinguished from the 'nobler' and more serious use of firearms and daggers. The blow from the billhook was most characteristic of quarrels of men with women or among relatives, while unrelated men who fell out seriously while working in the country tended to return to the village to fetch their guns if they were not already armed.

II

Arboriculture produced its own forms of conflict. Most simply, disputes arose over possession of trees or plantations. In February 1836, for example, a fight took place between Petro and Anton-Petro Leca, both of Ota, 'over the owner-ship of an olive tree'. Anton-Petro was wounded and Petro was prosecuted but acquitted for lack of evidence. Anton-Petro continued 'to nourish an implacable hatred against him' and hired agents to kill him the following October. Again, at Bastelica, Giovan-Maria Valle and Angelo-Maria Pantaloni had engaged in an inconclusive civil suit over the ownership of a chestnut grove. When Valle's son went to gather chestnuts there in October 1844, Pantaloni warned him off and threatened to kill his father. The next day, the parties again confronted each other at the grove, Pantaloni was shot in the arm; and he shot and killed Valle's daughter in retaliation.[35]

Chestnuts were a staple food in many parts of Corsica, and the trees were often in multiple ownership and thus subject to complicated arrangements for their cultivation and the harvesting of their produce. Similar arrangements existed for walnuts, a valuable source of oil. In December 1819, Anton-Maria Peretti of Levie was charged with using violence against Ignazio Giacopelli, his uncle, in a quarrel the previous September, over the harvesting of walnuts from two trees which they owned 'in common'. According to Peretti, he went to gather the nuts with his brother-in-law, who was also to have had his share, while Ignazio was accompanied by another of his nephews. Peretti arrived first and climbed the larger tree. Ignazio Giacopelli arrived later and climbed the second, smaller, tree, which he soon complained was difficult to harvest, ordering Peretti to change places with him. He also observed that Peretti should not have started without him and that they should have then followed an agreed plan of collection. After further argument, the four men started fighting with sticks. In another case in 1842, we learn that Simone-Paolo Paoli, Domenico Vignoli and others had rights to the produce of a walnut tree at Pianello. One year Paoli was entitled to the whole crop while every other it was divided equally among all the interested parties.[36]

A further complication and a further ground for conflict were provided where trees and the land on which they grew belonged to different owners. This situation was found, with variations, in many parts of the island. Sometimes the land was privately owned, but more frequently it was common land. Here there was some attempt at communal regulation of tree planting and of harvesting. At Pastricciola, for example, reference was made in 1853 to the custom by which chestnuts could not be planted closer to each other than the distance that a *rustaghja* could be thrown. At Bastelica, the ground beneath chestnuts was carefully cleared in the autumn prior to the harvest and the perimeter within which each owner could gather nuts was clearly marked on the ground with sticks and leaves. But much uncertainty remained, which was compounded by the existence of communal grazing rights and by the fact that planting chestnuts was a favoured mode of usurping communal property.[37] Two cases involving the village of Bisinchi illustrate some of these points. At the end of 1846, the *adjoint* of Bastia complained to the prefect about the behaviour of the Paoloantoni, a leading family in the village. He owned land there which was planted with chestnuts and expected to have the crop, but they apparently claimed possession of the trees and took the nuts by force. Francesco Gianninelli from Pastoreccia had planted a piece of land called Debbione with chestnuts, thereby laying some kind of claim to it. The people of Bisinchi regarded the land as part of their communal property, and the mayor therefore led a group of them to Debbione in 1852 and the chestnuts were destroyed.[38] Here we see also the fundamental conflict, which we have already encountered and which we shall encounter again and again, between notions of absolute property and of use rights open to a wide circle of kin and neighbours. The action taken in the last case was also typical in another way, for the destruction of fruit trees and vines was a common mode, we have seen, of taking revenge against enemies and/or those in authority.[39]

Timber forests were another extremely common field of conflict, though here disputes were largely centred on the opposing claims of local people and of the French State.[40] In 1834, the State began a formal delimitation of its forest domain, but this was a slow and lengthy process. As the *Gazette des Tribunaux* reported in 1841, 'many landowners claim that their patrimonies have been wholly or partly taken over in this operation', and the discrepancy between the area of forest claimed by the State and that conceded by individuals and by communes was enormous.[41] It was frequently argued therefore by those accused of felling trees or pasturing animals in domanial forests that the area in question belonged to them or to the village. Giacomo-Paolo Paoli, for example, prosecuted in 1822 for allowing 37 of his sheep to graze in the forest of Zonza, claimed that it did not belong to the State and had been used by herdsmen 'from time immemorial'. Thousands of formal contestations of the claims of the State were lodged in the civil courts in the 1830s and 1840s, and while these were pending confusion reigned, since each party acted as though it had possession. 'The task of our administration', wrote the inspector of forests for the Ajaccio region to his superior in 1846, 'is painful and difficult to fulfil. Ownership of most forests is contested and is the subject of civil litigation, which renders the prosecution of forest offences in the criminal courts ineffective.'[42]

A general settlement was arrived at in this matter in 1852, which reduced the extent of domanial claims by over half, but prosecutions for forest offences remained at an extremely high level throughout the second half of the century, which indicates that local acceptance of the settlement was less than whole-hearted.[43] Unauthorized felling of forest trees, which had assumed serious proportions earlier in the century,[44] was much reduced, but illegal grazing continued unabated. A British visitor commented in 1884: 'The most troublesome part of the duties of the forest guards seems to be the task of keeping cattle, and especially sheep and goats, from straying within the forest bounds, and imposing fines on the owners or caretakers if their flocks are caught so trespassing.' Fines were severe, he noted, and in the forest of Valdoniello, for example, an average of 160 cases per annum were pursued. Viewing the same situation from the other side, Father Bartoli in 1898 deplored the general neglect of Corsica's forest resources by the State, which wasted its energy instead 'in prosecuting those unfortunate people who accidentally let their animals stray in the forests, often forcing them to give up their miserable flocks altogether ... and thus ruining the pastoral economy'. There is clearly an element of special pleading here, for other writers refer to 'official tolerance' of trespass in the exercise of traditional grazing rights. It remains true, however, that these were being progressively eroded at a time when demand for pasture was growing. It is also clear that the term 'forest' was used to describe much land that was not covered with trees or even with scrub, since neither woodland proper nor scrub provided good pasture for cattle or sheep.[45]

We will return to these problems in discussing conflict related to pastoralism, but one further aspect should be mentioned. Woolsey claimed that 'grazing trespass [was frequently] ... winked at in order to induce the local population not to set fires'; while Father Bartoli asserted that arson was often a specific act of retaliation against the State's increasingly rigorous prosecution of forest offences. Forest fires were certainly common in the later nineteenth century. Bournet calculated that, between 1878 and 1886, there were 91 serious fires in domanial forests, affecting 2,676 hectares, and 148 in communal forests, affecting 5,574 hectares, and he agreed that most fires were deliberately started.[46] It can rarely be shown, however, that forest fires had any 'social' dimension, though some cases point in this direction. When over 1,000 trees were burned in the forest of Tacca near Aullène in 1846, local people were suspected of having started the fire, and the mayor refused to co-operate with forest officials in extinguishing it. Again, a fire in the communal forest of Ota in August 1848, in which a large number of trees had been destroyed, was said to have been 'an act of revenge [by Paol'-Antono Fieschi] against the authorities', who had been trying to capture two of his cousins who were bandits.[47] We will continue our discussion of arson in the context of pastoralism, to which we now turn.

III

Like agriculture and arboriculture, pastoralism produced its own forms of conflict, and conflict also arose when the interests of each were at odds. Our sources reflect these structural tensions and indicate too that, with the extension of agricultural land and governmental interference to control the activities of herdsmen, pasture was becoming scarcer and competition for it more intense.

Disputes over access to pasture were endemic. In 1830, for example, Matteo Calzaroni, a herdsman from Ucciani, was accused of trying to kill Martino Bastianesi. Calzaroni 'had been pasturing his herd in an open pasture, when Bastianesi, who claimed to have leased the grazing, arrived, forced him to quit, and demanded a goat as an indemnity. When Calzaroni refused this, Bastianesi released his dog, which grabbed a goat by the neck and killed it.' Calzaroni had then fired a shot. Sometimes the very complexity of arrangements gave rise to conflict. In December 1811, Dono-Francesco Vargioni from Olmiccia was guarding a flock of sheep belonging to Giovan-Felice Panzani in an enclosure. Giovan-Battiste Muzziconacci was guarding his flock in another enclosure called Acovaro not far away. Vargioni had left his small brother in charge of a herd of goats at the latter place, 'part of which he had leased'. One evening, Vargioni went to Acovaro to check on the goats and found that Muzziconacci and his father had set their dog on them. He protested, saying that, 'according to the agreement made between Signore Panzani, owner of the goats ... and Muzziconacci senior, their common herds were to use the same enclosure for pasture in bad weather', and it had snowed. Vargioni then fired his pistol, he claimed in the air, in order to frighten the dog, but the Muzziconacci maintained that the shot had been aimed at one of them. In another case, Giovanni Valle from Bastelica had leased an enclosure at the coast, which was 'the undivided property of the brothers Giovan-Paolo and Antono Gambarelli and of the minor children of another brother, deceased, whose guardian was a fourth brother called Francesco', but which had always been managed by Antono. When Valle's verbally agreed lease came up for renewal, Battiste Ottavi, who wished to supplant Valle as the tenant, addressed himself to Battiste Gambarelli, the son of Francesco, who promised him the lease. However, Antono Gambarelli and his brothers agreed to continue the old arrangement with Valle. When Ottavi, nevertheless, took his flock into the enclosure in October 1863, Valle and his herdsman went to protest, and fighting with sticks, stones and billhooks ensued, in which Valle was mortally wounded.[48]

It will be noted that these cases refer to pasture that was leased, and the practice of leasing was spreading, particularly in the second half of the century. Bigot wrote in 1869 that the herdsmen of Bastelica were being forced, much against their will, to pay rent for pasture, which was increasingly difficult to obtain. This trend was confirmed a generation later by Forcioli-Conti. The 1,200 herdsmen of the village with their 15,000 animals leased the vast domanial territory of the town of Ajaccio in the winter, but even this was insufficient, and they also rented any private properties to which they could gain access.[49] Much the same situation existed for the herdsmen of the Niolo, and attention has been drawn to the tensions engendered not only among herdsmen but more between the herdsmen from the Niolo and the owners of the winter pasture in the Balagna, which they had to rent. As a proverb expressed it: 'If Christ had come from the Balagna, he too would have been a robber.'[50]

This leads us not only to 'the archetypal conflict between herders and tillers' common to the Mediterranean region[51] and which recurred throughout Corsican history,[52] but also to the complicating factors represented by the lease of common land for pasture and by common grazing rights and their erosion. Such conflict arose most often during transhumance or on the coastal plains, and more rarely on the uplands. The first type is illustrated by a dispute which developed in 1801 or 1802 between the people of Speloncato, who were harvesting their grapes, and a group of herdsmen from the Niolo, who had come to the territory of Speloncato 'to pasture their animals'. One of the herdsmen, called Flori, accused the people from Speloncato of stealing one of his sheep. They accepted the charge and promised to pay for the animal but refused to tell him the name of the culprit. The herdsmen then tried to enter a house occupied by their adversaries in the middle of the night, and in the resulting affray Flori was shot. As we have indicated, the Niolo herdsmen were very frequently engaged in such disputes throughout the century.[53] Again, in a case in 1857, we learn that 'animals belonging to the herdsmen of Palneca living at shielings on the territory of Sollacaro ... were often allowed to pasture freely and thus got into enclosures, where they caused considerable damage'. On one such occasion, clashes between herdsmen and local people occurred as the offending animals were being rounded up, the herdsmen were 'pursued by public clamour', and one of them fired a shot at his assailants. In another case, Giovan-Andrea Valentini and his father 'had leased the pasture of the estate of La Giustiniana' on the territory of Linguizetta on the eastern coastal plain, and the three Rossi brothers, probably from Linguizetta, 'had leased the ploughland of the same estate. Frequent arguments arose all the time between the two parties', which came to a head in an armed encounter in March 1893, in which the elder Valentini and two of the Rossi were killed.[54]

Much pasturing took place on common land or on land subject to common grazing rights, and villages attempted either to restrict the access of outsiders to it or to charge them for its use. In 1823, for example, the municipal council of Penta-di-Casinca introduced a tax of one franc per head on 'foreign' livestock, 'considering that during the winter many animals belonging to outsiders are brought in to take advantage of the *vaine pâture*, which causes trouble without the slightest advantage'. This scheme does not seem to have been successful, since the mayor reported in 1852 that 'foreign herdsmen were bringing flocks of sheep on to the village lands without paying anything for the grazing', and again proposed a tax on them. A case at Sorbo-Ocognano illustrates the kind of conflict which such attempts at regulation provoked. Antono Santucci from Corscia was pasturing his flock there in November 1842 when one of the village's field guards approached him and demanded a lamb, 'alleging that every herdsman from outside ... was obliged to pay this tribute'. Santucci refused, whereupon the guard began to round up his flock to take it back to the village. Santucci tried to prevent him and was eventually shot and mortally wounded. Foata noted more generally in 1856 that the exercise of *vaine pâture* caused 'bloody fights, land-owners no longer accepting that others had the right to occupy and devastate their property without special permission'.[55]

There was a tendency for officials and other observers to see this general conflict from the point of view of the cultivator. Ardouin-Dumazet wrote typically in 1898:

> The whole Evisa region is a pastoral country, and the herdsmen lead their flocks into the most inaccessible parts of the mountains. The herdsman is the real master of this district; and freedom of movement is granted to him to the great detriment of agriculture; no one would dare to undertake any land clearance, large or small, for fear of alienating the herdsmen, who are only too ready to damage fields and destroy crops. The sheep, the goat, and the half-wild pig are scourges, and no one dares to protest against their depredations, because the herdsmen, always armed with their guns and quick to use them, are feared too much.[56]

Our sources indicate that such predominance was more a local than a general phenomenon by this date, for one of the features of Corsican rural history from the mid-nineteenth century was the tipping of the balance through legislative action against the herdsman and in favour of the cultivator.

The complexities of this development have been explored by Pomponi. He stresses that population pressure combined with State policy to favour the spread of agriculture and that there was some divergence, most marked in the first half of the nineteenth century, between local efforts to control the pasturing of animals and those of the French administration. While the latter relied on the enforcement or the creation of private property rights, local authorities, as we have seen, often sought to strengthen or adapt traditional modes of land regulation. Private enclosures were already protected, and common lands and also lands in which various owners had rights were usually subject to the *presa* system. Livestock was either permanently excluded from land used for agriculture and arboriculture, or only allowed on it after crops had been harvested. In some communities, a change in emphasis occurred as to the function of enclosure, and rather than enclosing crops to exclude animals, an attempt was made to keep animals in enclosed pasture to prevent them from entering land with crops on it. This trend was encouraged in prefectoral circulars in 1823 and 1850. But the most important governmental intervention in this area was the law of 1854 abolishing *vaine pâture*. In many parts of Corsica, the law was very generally resisted or ignored. Bigot relates that there were 120 prosecutions for infraction of the law at Bastelica in the first year in which it was applied. Reactions to the 1854 law, of course, and the incidence of agro-pastoral conflict generally, depended very much on the socio-economic structure of the community in question. Purely or mainly pastoral communities, such as Bastelica or those of the Niolo, suffered from being excluded from traditional pasturing areas elsewhere or from having to pay for using them. In mixed communities, divisions between herdsmen and cultivators might be exacerbated. Such divisions were often between poor and marginal herdsmen and rich cultivators, but not always, for in some villages, especially where they had won control of the municipality, notables with large flocks might use or abuse traditional *vaine pâture* at the expense of small cultivators. Here Pomponi cites the long-drawn-out civil suit started in 1827 between the Orabona brothers of Novella and the inhabitants of neighbouring Urtaca, where the brothers owned some land. On this basis, the Orabona claimed and exercised the right to pasture a flock of some 200 sheep on the common fields of Urtaca. The local people objected that their regulations allowed grazing for only two head of livestock for every hectare of land owned in the village. The municipal council of Penta-di-Casinca reasserted a similar 'very ancient' regulation in 1823, which allowed 'every inhabitant to keep one or two goats outside the *presa* and the *circolo*', commenting that 'today they have up to six each which causes a serious threat to agriculture and provokes frequent arguments to which we must put an end'.[57]

Agro-pastoral conflict became enmeshed here with local factionalism, mayors and *adjoints* using their offices to favour one party or the other. In 1846, the mayor of Santa-Lucia-di-Moriani was reported to be in the hand of outside herdsmen 'who devastate our lands with their animals'. When the field guards of Levie found two flocks of sheep in the common pasture in May 1851 which were not being supervised, they proposed to take them off to the village pound. Their owner, Paolo Berretti claimed that he had the mayor's permission to leave his animals there. The mayor confirmed this; an altercation ensued, in which Berretti shot and wounded one of the guards; and the mayor then used his influence to have Berretti acquitted of the crime. Again, at Piana in 1852, Antono Ceccaldi became engaged in a 'discussion' with the mayor on the church square 'over the frequent damage caused by herdsmen in the fields and reproached him with not showing enough energy in the repression of these offences'. Shortly afterwards, the mayor was shot and wounded by Ceccaldi's son. On the other hand, we may cite cases in which local officials suffered or were believed to have suffered retaliation as the result of their actions against herdsmen. When two straw ricks belonging to Mayor Guerrini of Venzolasca were burned in 1854, suspicion fell first on the Albertini, herdsmen who had been prosecuted by him in the village court and who had made vague threats against him.[58]

In most of these cases, herdsmen were deliberately using land for pasture that was contested, but it was also extremely common for animals to stray accidentally on to cultivated and other land, although in practice the two categories cannot always be distinguished. Animals were particularly likely to stray during transhumance, although most of our cases involve animals grazing near villages or on the coastal plains. One day in February 1852, for example, Giovanni Santelli, a landowner from Castellare, learned that some goats being looked after by Giovan-Paolo Emmanuelli, a young herdsman from Erone, had strayed into one of his fields that was sown with a crop. He went there at once, drove the goats out and gave the boy a beating. This prompted retaliation from Emmanuelli's elder brother, Saverio, who shot and wounded Santelli. Next day, Giuseppo Santelli, head of his family, 'assembled a group of ten relatives and friends, provided them with arms, and they set out, they said, to ... arrest Saverio Emmanuelli'. He was later found dead from multiple shot wounds at a place on the coast. In 1848, the municipal council of Penta-di-Casinca decided to ban all goats from its territory, explaining that 'herds of goats were causing intolerable damage to property whenever they passed. Not only did they damage young fruit trees and crops of all kinds, but they also made gaps in hedges, knocked down walls and filled in the ditches surrounding fields.'[59] Conflict of this kind on the coastal plain was encouraged by the fact that cultivated land there was left unprotected for much of the year. The trend towards settlement on the coast meant better protection but increased competition for land.

There, and elsewhere too, we find conflict over straying animals occurring between herdsmen. A dispute took place, for example, in 1848 between Orso-Giacomo Preziosi, a herdsman from Piedicroce, and the Raffali brothers, whose field of rye was repeatedly invaded by Preziosi's goats. We learn from the fact that Preziosi killed one of the Raffali at their 'sheep fold' that they too kept livestock.[60] This is a reminder that in most Corsican communities no absolute distinction may be made between herdsmen and cultivators. The sedentary population kept livestock and herdsmen engaged in subsistence agriculture. Domenico-Andrea Graziani of Campitello, for example, who was prosecuted for his part in violence during the elections in 1884, was described as 'a cultivator and a herdsman'.[61] The division of labour within the Bastelica family described by Bigot was probably typical here. The father exercised overall control of the family enterprise, negotiated the lease of pasture, made cheese and *brocciu* and took these products for sale in Ajaccio. The eldest son was concerned almost exclusively with the cultivation of land on the plain; the second looked after the pigs; and the third was the shepherd.[62] Nevertheless, herdsmen could be outsiders even in their own communities. Giovan-Francesco Muzziconacci of Moca-Croce, accused of stealing livestock in 1806, was asked in court if he knew to whom a certain enclosure belonged, and he replied that he did not, explaining 'that as a herdsman he lived nearly all the time outside the territory of the village'.[63] And if herdsmen did not constitute 'an inferior caste' of 'savages', a stereotyped view very common among French officials and observers,[64] it remains true that they were frequently despised by the more settled inhabitants. A fight occurred in 1852 between two men from Santa-Lucia-di-Moriani, in which one was wounded with an axe and the other more seriously with a pistol shot. The trouble began when Tittino Grimaldi 'thought he heard Francesco-Saverio Antonmarchi talking about him in a disrespectful manner' to a third person. 'Don't you dare pronounce my name, you hulking herdsman!', he shouted, to which Antonmarchi replied: 'Come over here, if you want to find out what herdsmen are really like.'[65]

We discussed arson in the context of forest offences and must return to it now, since herdsmen were frequently accused of starting fires both in forests and elsewhere. For example, a fire on the plain of Taravo in September 1823 damaged hedges, haystacks, olive stocks and pasture. The information of local officials was that herdsmen from Petreto-Bicchisano had started the fire 'in order to burn off straw ... and procure for themselves the exclusive use of the marshes for their pigs'. In 1861, two herdsmen from Sisco were convicted of 'deliberately setting fire' to 25 hectares of woodland and maquis. 'It happens only too often', the trial summary stated, 'that herdsmen, wishing to provide themselves with some meagre pasture in the mountains, set fire to the maquis in this way, causing considerable damage, and they usually manage to escape being prosecuted.' That had not happened here, because local people, whose agricultural land had been threatened, had, for once, provided evidence against the incendiaries. In another case in 1862, an old herdsman from Oletta was sentenced to two years' imprisonment for setting fire to a stretch of maquis belonging to the parish church. He claimed that, having leased the land, he had the right to do this, 'in order to procure a more abundant pasture for his animals'. The president of the Assize Court confirmed that this was normal practice and considered the sentence inappropriate.[66] As this indicates, the firing of scrub to make pasture or to clear ground for cultivation was customary in Corsica. It usually took place in late summer and was subject to well-established controls.[67] When a large straw rick was burned down at Tasso in August 1841, blame was attached to Francesco Giovannoni who had 'lit a fire to clear land not far from the rick without taking the usual precautions'. Cultivators at Santa-Lucia-di-Tallano were firing scrub in the normal way in August 1820 when 'suddenly the fire spread to neighbouring enclosures and beyond. In such circumstances', the mayor reported, 'it was usual to ring the church bell in order to bring everyone to help.'[68] Such accidents were particularly common in years of drought and high winds, such as 1821 or 1828, but it is clear that very few fires were accidentally started and that those that spread by chance were also comparatively rare. Arson was a weapon in the struggle between herdsmen and cultivators as it was in that between herdsmen and forest officials. The mere exercise of traditional rights became a threat and a nuisance as the extent of cultivated, and particularly enclosed, land grew. As Chiva suggests for a later period, too, the attempts of the French administration, already evident in the 1820s and 1830s, to prevent 'slash and burn' techniques, whether used by herdsmen or cultivators, tended to deregulate the situation, encouraging clandestinity and probably increasing the number of fires which got out of control.[69] But arson was no prerogative of herdsmen and could indeed be used against them. Responsibility for a fire in June 1823 on the territory of Quenza, for example, was attributed to 'two landowners' trying to frighten off 'the herdsmen who wished to enter the district'.[70] We shall see also that arson was quite frequently used as a weapon in enmities and feuds.

IV

Conflict over animals overlaps considerably with the previous category but may nevertheless be usefully distinguished. Pastoral and agricultural interests were often at odds within as well as across communities, and disputes over abusive grazing or straying sheep and goats were as common among co-villagers as among 'strangers'. Some animals were kept in the villages permanently, and since they were usually left to fend for themselves without any stabling[71] or enclosure, they inevitably caused trouble from time to time. Here special attention may be drawn to straying by animals other than sheep or goats. At Matra in 1848 or 1849, for example, a sow belonging to Angelo-Giuseppo Battaglini got into the garden of Paolo-Maria Matra. Matra set his dog on the sow, which was bitten. Members of the two families exchanged insults over the affair and then shots. No one was hurt but the families remained in a state of 'enmity'. A case at Cozzano a few years later indicates how common such incidents must have been. Petro-Maria Renucci had apparently been trying for some time to seduce his sister-in-law Brandolina, and in May 1853 he tricked her into going to an enclosure away from the village (where he tried to rape her), by telling her that her husband's horse was damaging the property of the Cesari brothers there. A further case illustrates how animals might stray even if they had been fenced in or otherwise secured. Rocco-Francesco Roccaserra, a landowner from Cargiaca, testified in a case in 1822 that

> he kept his oxen on land next to that belonging to Paolo Alessandri and Paolo Quilichini from Poggio, the two properties being separated by a dry hedge and part of a river. Since the hedge had been carried away by the river, he had taken the precaution of hobbling his animals securely; but, despite this, they had entered the property of the two other men, who threatened to kill them if the offence were repeated.[72]

Hobbling, especially of pigs and goats, seems to have been common practice and was noted by visitors.[73]

In these cases, the straying of animals was accidental, though it might be regarded as an act of hostility. It was on occasions, however, malicious. We have seen, for example, in a case already referred to, that Francesco Giafferi of Monaccia deliberately sent his animals into the pasture of a neighbour against whom he was conducting general hostilities. And conflict over straying animals could be an element or form an episode in full-scale feuds. Enmities were provoked by damage done or allegedly done by animals or even poultry, and once an enmity existed it might be pursued by allowing livestock to devastate crops and fields.[74]

It was not uncommon for straying animals to be killed by those whose property they damaged, particularly after persistent offending. In 1821, for example, a case was brought against the brothers Antono and Don Giacomo Serra of Serra for killing a sow belonging to Valerio Vincentelli. Don Giacomo admitted the offence but said that he had committed it 'out of necessity': every night pigs ruined his garden, and he had warned that he would take action against them.[75] Paolo Alessandri and Paolo Quilichini of Poggio threatened the same retaliation against straying oxen belonging to Rocco-Francesco Roccaserra. Later one of these was found dead in an enclosure owned by Quilichini, who denied having killed it but said that since Roccaserra's animals often damaged crops, such an outcome was not surprising.

The killing or wounding of animals was also an important mode of vengeance *per se*, as Mérimée pointed out, and as our accounts of the feuds at Arbellara, Frasseto and elsewhere illustrate.[76] In July 1825, the mayor of Sorbollano reported that three mares belonging to Father Giulio Comiti and his nephew had been shot dead and a stallion wounded with a dagger or knife. A sequel was feared since such actions indicated 'the existence of a passionate hatred'. In some cases, as in Mérimée's fictional example, an animal was mutilated rather than being killed. One night in May 1823, 'a mule belonging to Dr Tomasi (of Zerubia) had its ears cut'; this was part of a ritual death threat and was in retaliation for an official complaint lodged by Tomasi against a certain Quidani. Versini mentions a similar case in which such a threat was carried out. A horse owned by Dr Risticoni of San-Gavino-d'Ampugnani had its left ear cut one night in 1822, and a few months later Risticoni himself was killed.[77]

Here we can see an honorific element being built upon a material one. Animals are no longer simply regarded as destroyers of crops or other resources, but represent their owners and their honour, though a distinction was made, it seems, between lower animals, which actually did most damage, such as pigs and goats, and higher animals, such as horses and dogs. Cattle occupied an intermediate position and were treated according to their quality and sexual status. In a case in 1830, for example, involving the killing of a bull which had damaged an enclosure, a witness reported a comment made when the carcase was discovered to the effect that 'the animal was too fine to be killed' in the circumstances.[78]

Conflict involving dogs deserves special mention. Dogs in Corsica were working animals and were used by herdsmen and for general guard duties. At Venzolasca, for example, in the last third of the nineteenth century, all dogs in the village – and there were over a hundred of them – were classified as working dogs.[79] We have seen in discussing pastoral and agro-pastoral conflict that dogs naturally became involved. They were used to drive off invasive livestock and they might be injured or killed in the process. There might be material reasons for attacks on dogs in other circumstances, too. It was reported in February 1850 that three dogs belonging to members of the Grimaldi family of Marignana had been killed on successive nights, and it was suggested that this had been done by Francesco Grimaldi and other bandits 'so that they would not be troubled in future when they passed through the village'. It was very common, moreover, for serious conflict between persons to arise from disputes over dogs. At Santa-Maria-Sicche, in 1844, members of the Emilj and the Tenneroni families, who lived opposite each other, came to blows after 'repeated fights' between their dogs, and one of the Emilj was eventually shot and killed. Again, Santo Mattei was attacked by a dog as he was crossing a square at Sari-d'Orcino one evening in 1852 and he shot it dead. He was then accosted by the dog's owner, Francesco Raffini, who shot and mortally wounded him in return. Testimony at Raffini's trial revealed that the killing of the dog had been only the latest episode in a lengthy 'enmity' between them.[80] Shooting a guard-dog, moreover, played a part in the build-up to the feud between the Tortora and the Maestracci at Muro, while the feud between the Tafani and the Rocchini of Porto-Vecchio in the 1880s began with each family killing a dog belonging to the other.[81] Even threats against dogs might prompt violent retaliation, and attacks on or insults to dogs could be taken to be attacks on or insults to their owners, who reacted accordingly. Tomaso Lanfranchi and Nicolaio Arasti were talking with others on the church square of Linguizetta in January 1846, when Arasti's dog ran up to its master. Lanfranchi made some critical remarks about 'the vivacity of the animal, adding that it was a real herdsman's dog, since it howled every night like a soul in torment'. This led Arasti to cast serious aspersions on Lanfranchi's honour, which in turn led Lanfranchi's brother to shoot Arasti dead.[82] The very close association between men and their dogs frequently came out when the former died. Vuillier refers to dogs going to howl at the graves of their masters, while Viale collected a lament from Prunelli, in which a woman threatens to cut off the tails of her late husband's two dogs, because they failed to keep death from him.[83] It does not appear from our sources, however, that the activities of dogs in Corsica were subject to the same kind of complex local regulation that was found for example in Albania,[84] and which existed, we have seen, in the sphere of arboriculture. This would confirm the view that dogs belonged very much to the personal and family realm over which the rights of the collectivity were very limited.

Another category of conflict was that engendered by disputes over the ownership of animals. Outright and obvious theft of livestock took place in Corsica and special terms associated with rustling are found,[85] but this never assumed anything like the importance which it had in modern Sardinia or some Balkan countries.[86] If Governor Miot insisted in 1801 that stealing animals had to be regarded as a serious crime, he was thinking less therefore of its incidence than of its consequences.[87] A fight at an unspecified village in 1814, for example, was 'the result of the theft of some pigs and one of the alleged robbers, a herdsman, was killed'. A case of fratricide at Corte in 1841 had been provoked when one brother took two kids belonging to another and ate them. Such cases usually involved people from different communities. A general conflict between the inhabitants of two villages in the Fiumorbo broke out in 1840, when the Marchetti brothers of Isolaccio took a cow belonging to the Dari brothers of Taglio. Again, in November 1843, several people from Zicavo, 'armed with pistols and daggers, went to the village of Loreto to reclaim a mule that Francesco Peretti had lost'; they accused Piero Susini of having stolen the animal and attacked him and his family.[88]

More common, it seems, and of more interest, are cases where ownership was less clear-cut. Where animals were left to graze unsupervised, they might stray into fields and gardens causing damage, as we have noted, but they might also get lost. In theory, they should have been clearly marked, and reference is made to thieves 'who alter the marks' on animals;[89] but in practice there was room for real confusion. A widow Mattei from Antisanti lost an ox in 1849 and announced that she would give six francs to anyone who helped her to find it. Giulio Angelini took up her offer and was given half the money, the rest to come when the animal was actually recovered. When he eventually produced the animal, the widow's son-in-law, Tristani, suspected him of having stolen it in the first place and persuaded her not to pay him the remainder of the reward. Angelini was not surprisingly aggrieved and later shot dead Tristani's cousin. Disputes could also occur where straying or stolen animals were subsequently sold. For example, in May 1835, Giacomo-Francesco Pietri of Stazzona-d'Orezza was mortally wounded at a place between Sartène and Monaccia, far away from his village. It was reported that he had been shot by the mayor of Ortiporio, Paolo Campani, 'whose mule had been stolen and then bought by Pietri's father. An argument had developed over the validity of the sale,' and Pietri had resisted Campani's attempt to take the animal back. The feud at Zerubia between the Guidicelli and the Roccaserra was rekindled in 1839 by a similar dispute over the sale of allegedly stolen animals.[90] Contested ownership could also arise where herdsmen kept animals for other people, which they frequently did in the south, with some kind of sharing arrangement over products and offspring. One of the reasons behind a serious quarrel which developed in 1802 between the Marchi from Serraggio and the important Ortoli family was a disagreement over their respective shares in a flock of sheep, which the former looked after for the latter.

Further complications might be introduced in this area by the practice of lending out draught animals, which parallels the loan of agricultural implements. This is illustrated by a case in 1805, in which Giovan-Maria Ciafferi of Aullène was accused of stealing an ox from the Sinibaldi of Sartène. According to Ciafferi, Petro Sinibaldi had come to Aullène early the previous November 'to procure two plough oxen'. Ciafferi refused to lend him his ox but offered it for sale, an offer which Sinibaldi turned down. Ciafferi then sold the ox to Vincenzo Paoli of Aullène, but before being handed over to this new owner it was apparently lent to a certain Tafani. Tafani was using it for ploughing at Monaccia near the coast when Sinibaldi came up and took it, claiming that he had orders from 'the master' (presumably Ciafferi). By then Ciafferi was obliged to deliver the ox to Paoli and went to ask Sinibaldi for it, even offering to pay compensation for the loss of its labour. When Sinibaldi refused to surrender the ox, Ciafferi took it by force. Conflict at Peri between Giulio Tavera and the Tusoli also involved the loan of draught oxen. Carlo Tusoli had lent two oxen to Tavera early in 1853, which Tavera had allowed to stray, leaving Tusoli to pay for the damage. Tusoli was thus reluctant to agree when Tavera asked to borrow the animals again and yielded only under duress. This time, Tavera lent the oxen to a third party after he had used them and refused to return them to Tusoli. When Tusoli had recourse to the gendarmerie to recover his property, Tavera fired shots at his house apparently with homicidal intentions. This kind of dispute was exacerbated where animals were in multiple ownership, which was often the case among relatives. For example, when Angelo Gervasoni of Olmeta-di-Tuda lent an ass in 1843 to his son-in-law Antono Bastiani, his own son Giovan-Battiste objected. They came to blows; other relatives joined in; and an elderly uncle of Bastiani's was shot and killed as he tried to pacify them.[91]

V

Buildings were another contested resource, and particularly houses and mills. We have seen that disputes over the possession of houses played a part in the feud at Pila-Canale in 1801. Again, at Venzolasca in 1845, the brothers Guglielmo and Giovan-Battiste Sanguinetti laid claim to a house occupied by a certain Bastiani and took possession of it while he was away. When he returned to the village, Bastiani assembled a group of relatives and tried to reoccupy the house, but the Sanguinetti resisted with firearms. Another case illustrates how intrafamilial conflict was often enmeshed with dispute over houses. In 1862, Anton-Francesco

Codaccioni of Sartène and Domenico Codaccioni of Foce-di-Bilia came before the justice of the peace to try to settle their dispute over the ownership of a small house. According to Domenico, the house 'is and always has been my exclusive property: it was built on my orders and at my expense ... Signore Anton-Francesco Codaccioni, who belonged for some years to my family, having married my daughter, lived in the house during the whole period of his marriage, but only on sufferance ... When the link which joined us was broken by the premature death without posterity of my daughter,' Anton-Francesco was asked to leave, which he did without protest, though he subsequently claimed that the house was his.[92]

Small houses were not the rule in Corsica, and, as Domenico Codaccioni's insistence on 'exclusive property' rights indicates, houses were frequently held in indivision among relatives, itself a cause of tension, or were divided among different owners, not necessarily related. According to Molinari in 1886, 'nowhere was real estate so subdivided. Apart from the very poor, everyone is the owner, if not of a whole house, then at least of a lodging. Houses are sold in bits and pieces ... One person buys a storey, another is content with half or quarter of a storey, according to his means.'[93] We will discuss this phenomenon more fully in a later chapter, confining ourselves here to the kinds of dispute which arose where houses were divided by sale or inheritance and/or were sublet to tenants. We learn, for example, from a case at Castineta in 1852 that Giovan-Tomaso Tomasi had owned 'a house in indivision with his brother-in-law Ambrosi'. During the latter's absence from the village, the house had been wholly occupied by Tomasi and his family, but Ambrosi had ceded or sold his share to a relative by marriage called Santini. Disputes then arose between the Tomasi and the Santini, culminating in a minor feud in which one member of each family was killed. Again, Petro Marsilj of Cauro was killed in 1856 by Francesco-Maria Paolini, who had apparently mistaken him for another man 'with whom he had had frequent arguments over the ownership of a cellar which belonged to a house that they had previously held in indivision'. Among cases involving tenancy, we may cite one at Bisinchi in 1854. Domenico Anziani bought two rooms in a house inhabited by Filippo Anziani, his relative, and rented them out. This displeased Filippo and his family and they wrote a letter to Domenico, ordering him to evict the tenant under threat of death. Domenico refused to comply and was later mortally wounded in a fight by Filippo's son.[94] Simple disputes between landlords and tenants were not uncommon though they might involve peculiar claims by tenants. Petro-Luigi Pietri, for example, a tenant in a house belonging to Giovan-Francesco Casabianca of Casabianca (Ampugnani) in 1797–8, apparently believed that his tenancy entitled him to remove the rafters from the house. As he was in the process of doing this, Casabianca and his relative Orso-Battiste Pietri arrived to prevent him, and in the resulting fracas he shot Orso-Battiste dead.[95]

House building was another fruitful source of conflict. Sometimes the ownership of building land was in dispute. For example, Leonardo Simoni and others from Levie and Giovanni Simoni, mayor of Figari, both claimed a piece of land at Figari and attempted to build a house on it. In March 1802, shooting lasting an hour took place between the two parties. Giovan-Domenico Giovanangeli of

Granace quarrelled violently in 1861 with his former friend Don Giovanni Leandri, the mayor of the village, 'over the site on which he wished to build a house'. Complications could arise here, too, where houses were divided or extended. At Tomino, Giovan-Girolamo Costa 'had constructed a wooden staircase to provide access to some rooms which belonged to him; this staircase rested on land which Giovanni Morazzi claimed belonged to him, which led to arguments between them.' One day in April 1814, Morazzi tried to cut down the staircase with an axe, which led to fighting in which Morazzi was seriously wounded and his wife killed.[96]

The actual building process, often a co-operative effort in which neighbours joined,[97] could also lead to trouble. Bartolomeo Colonna from Petreto-Bicchisano was helping Andrea Benedetti to build a house in 1850 and had also lent him some planks for the purpose. The two men fell out somehow over this, and Benedetti shot Colonna dead. Giulietta Gavini, an older woman, and Paolo Benedettini from Pietralba quarrelled in 1857 over the supply of stones for a house that the latter was building or extending. Benedettini began to take stones from a site nearby, but Gavini claimed to own the place and the stones and tried to prevent him. He then obtained a written authorization from the mayor, who confirmed that the site was common village property. She riposted by dropping a large stone on him, as he was continuing his work, which knocked him out.[98]

Conflict over houses and house building was exacerbated by the fact that owners of existing houses claimed rights of view or exclusive use over land around those houses, even when it did not belong to them. This is related to the custom of relatives building houses in clusters, one against the other, and the complementary resentment against intruders into such agglomerations and refusal to allow new buildings to be attached to old ones.[99] In particular, house owners laid claim to the 'square' in front of their houses. Bigot noted that this was regarded as belonging to the house next to it at Bastelica, even if it was in fact communal property,[100] and such spaces often carried the names of the families associated with them.[101] Officials later in the century inveighed against such 'encroachments', but appear to have made little headway against such a well-established tradition.[102] Our sources confirm the significance of the house 'square', as well as illustrating other aspects of the claim to space around houses. After Giacomo-Francesco Santucci of Ciamannacce had attacked the wife of Paolo Leonetti in 1844, the latter 'promised not to prosecute on condition that Santucci abstained from appearing on the square of his house', an onerous and humiliating provision that he adhered to for less than a year. Among the factors behind the hostility between the Ficoni and the Decori of Perelli-d'Alesani in the 1870s was the fact that Damiano Ficoni 'had asked the Decori to let him have a strip of land in order to round off the square in front of his house, offering to pay double its value, and that the Decori had refused to part with it at any price'. Cases may also be cited in which rights of way over such land were disputed, as at Ota in 1846. Claims could also be extended to buildings on such squares. In a case involving rival claims to a family chapel at Cauro in 1829, counsel for one branch of the Pietri family argued that since the chapel was situated on their 'square' it was 'dependent on their house'. A case at Pietra combines such claims to space with the more general kind of dispute generated by simple proximity that must have been extremely common. Giuseppo Straboni 'had a right of view via a window over the roof of the house of Simone-Paolo Castelli. It seems that water and even refuse was habitually thrown out of this window on to the roof, which led to frequent arguments between the two men.' A fight between them occurred in August 1841, in which Castelli was disarmed 'with the help of some women'. Castelli sought to avenge this affront the following October by hitting Straboni on the head with a heavy stick as he was shoeing a horse.[103]

Building houses or making extensions to them frequently interfered therefore with existing rights and claims and encountered hostility for this reason. Giovan-Giacomo Quilichini of Santa-Lucia-di-Tallano, for example, was accused in 1801 of having opposed the building of a house by Giovan-Paolo Quilichini 'capriciously and by force'. He denied this general charge but admitted opposing the construction of a stairway up to 'the door of the said house which is placed right next to his ... despite the narrowness of the common passage-way'; and he also declared, as if to demonstrate his reasonableness, that he had 'permitted' the building of the house itself and the making of doors and windows which overlooked his house, though of course the plaintiff disputed this. Walls built in the vicinity of houses were a particular bone of contention. When Mariano Galloni d'Istria of Olmeto began to dig a ditch around his house in November 1848 in order to build a retaining wall, his neighbour Leone-Giovanni Peretti protested that this would cause water to run into his house. Work was suspended while a discussion took place. This quickly turned into a fight, in which other protesting neighbours were involved, and one of these was killed. Again, a dispute over a wall played an important part in the development of a feud at Campi. It seems that in 1873 the Pietri had authorized Carlo Lanfranchi to build a wall 'to hold up the ground in front of his house', but, following conflict over other matters, they ordered him to demolish it in 1882. This he vigorously refused to do and an attempt was made to kill him shortly afterwards.[104] As these cases show, walls were not simply used to mark boundaries, but, given the hilly terrain, might be essential structural features.

Houses could also be a more direct focus of conflict. Not only were they fortified and besieged in the course of feuds, but they might also be burned and otherwise attacked. The Pozzo di Borgo sacked and threatened to burn the Bonaparte house in Ajaccio in 1793, and the Arena house at Isola Rossa was twice burned in the same period by their enemies, the Savelli.[105] Many less distinguished examples may also be cited. The house of the Albertini at Sari-d'Orcino was pillaged and set alight in 1800 and 1801, while that of Malaspina, the *adjoint* of Occhiatana was burned down in 1815.[106] Such actions were often committed by bandits.[107] In some cases, houses were deliberately set on fire with people inside them, a type of vengeance killing, or attempted vengeance killing, which will be discussed further in Chapter 10. More often, only damage or destruction of property was intended, and this motive was most obviously uppermost where more restricted targets were chosen. In 1828, for example, the wooden staircase of the presbytery at Ortale was set alight 'out of interest and the spirit of vengeance'.[108] Attacks might also be made on huts in the country that were used to store produce or as temporary accommodation.[109] Houses themselves, of course, had great symbolic as well as material value, since they represented the families which owned them,[110] and some kinds of attacks on them should be interpreted in this light. For example, the common practice of shooting at the doors of the houses was not always intended to injure or kill the occupants, but was a way of registering enmity or indicating ill-will.[111]

Apart from churches, the only other buildings of importance in rural Corsica were grain and oil mills,[112] and they were the object of all the kinds of dispute with which we are familiar. Anton-Leonardo Mancini of Occhiatana, for example, laid claim to a mill that belonged to his sister-in-law and pursued the matter in the courts without success. He then sought to obtain a share in the income generated by the mill, and, when she resisted this claim too, he did serious damage to it one night in August 1845. Mills seem nearly always to have been leased out by their owners to tenants. We learn, for example, from a case in 1860 that the mill on the Rizzanese owned by the Giustiniani of Arbellara was worked by a certain Renucci.[113] This perhaps explains the lack of hostility to millers as middlemen and notables that is found in other Mediterranean societies,[114] though tenancy produced its own difficulties, as we would expect. Petro-Domenico Vincenti of Isolaccio 'made great efforts to acquire the tenancy' of an important mill on the Fium'Alto at Acitaja, 'which was in multiple ownership and which brought in more profit' than the mill which he was presently leasing. When another miller was preferred, Vincenti shot him in the knee at the mill in August 1844. Mills in tenancy could also be placed under an 'interdict' like land, in order to harm their owners. Two 'landowners' from Olmiccia and Poggio apparently had a quarrel with Paolo-Natale Roccaserra of Santa-Lucia-di-Tallano in 1812 and, in pursuit of this, they went one night to a mill which he owned and told the miller to quit within three days or they would kill him.[115] We have referred to damage done to mills and here a favourite target was the crucial water supply. It will be remembered that the lawyer Barracini and Colonel Ghilfuccio in Mérimée's *Colomba* contested 'the ownership of a certain water course that turned a mill',[116] and here, as elsewhere, Mérimée was a faithful observer of Corsican *mores*. After the municipal council of Urtaca decided on measures in 1841 to prevent herdsmen from using a local forest for grazing, the herdsmen decided on reprisals, which included destroying part of the water channel of a mill belonging to the *adjoint*. In another case the same year, Federico Pellegrini, who leased a mill at Cervione, refused to mill some grain taken there by a Peretti girl. 'She reported this refusal to her relatives, also claiming that the miller had insulted her,' and one evening in November 'three of them went to obstruct the mill stream in order to avenge her'.[117]

VI

We come now to disputes over movable property and miscellaneous resources. As many writers on Corsica have stressed, theft, especially of movables, was rare, which reflected the archaic nature of property.[118] The general pattern of crime in the nineteenth century was heavily weighted, as we have seen, towards crimes against the person. Of 366 fugitives reported in 1833, for example, only 72, that is 20 percent, were wanted for theft or robbery, and Bournet wrote in 1888 that 'out of the multitude of offences and crimes less than a third can be explained by theft'.[119] Theft indeed was regarded as dishonourable, and the president of the Assize Court commented in 1857 on 'the general repugnance' which it inspired.[120] This may be illustrated from specific cases. Pantaleo Pasqualini of Silvareccio claimed in 1852 that some wood being used 'to repair a small bridge on the local road' belonged to him. This led to a bitter argument between Pasqualini and Domenico Terrighi, who believed that the accusation was levelled against him, and who vigorously denied it, saying: 'I am a man.' Another case in 1858 brings out the same association of theft with dishonourable status. Giovan-Cesareo Romani, accused of breaking into a shop at Petreto-Bicchisano and stealing 63 francs, was suspected because he was 'a young man with nothing to do, who spent his time in wine-shops and already had a bad reputation'.[121] In this context, it is significant that those tried for theft were often Italians.

It is characteristic, too, that theft was often practised against people from other villages or by outsiders. Bandits, we shall see, usually committed robberies away from their home regions, and our sources include a number of cases of attacks on those who travelled all over Corsica from the Balagna selling olive oil. Francesco Calixti was robbed and killed near Azzana in 1838, for example, by the son of a notary in the village, while another oil merchant, Alessandro Antonini was tricked in 1855 into spending the night in the company of a young herdsman from Palneca, who knocked him unconscious while he was asleep and stole 150 francs from him. Merchants in general were victims of theft. Goods and 25 francs in cash were stolen from the house of Signore Oroselli, merchant at Pila-Canale, one night in February 1850, it seems by Giuseppo-Marco Pieraggi, a local man. Giacomo-Natale Fumaroli of Cauro was accused of various thefts in the village in 1856 but only admitted to one of them, that of 50 francs from the house of Antono Leccia, a wholesale merchant.[122] And many other cases could be cited of thefts from shopkeepers.[123] It may seem obvious that it was those who possessed an accumulation of goods and money who should have had them stolen, but cultural as well as economic factors are involved, and there was a clear difference in attitude towards expropriating the property of traders and taking that of relatives and other neighbours. This may be related to a general distrust of money and money-makers, inherent in an agro-pastoral society. The normal rules of behaviour did not apply to traders, and since they were robbers by profession they could be repaid in kind. Montherot reported his guide's condemnation of a cousin who had become a rich merchant but had had no children: in a life of robbing and cheating, he had thus 'worked entirely for the devil', since he had only enriched himself and not his family.[124] Another example of the hatred which the *nouveau riche* could attract was seen at Ampriani in 1832, where the mayor Giovan-Battiste Lota was killed by Pasquale Negroni. Lota was a wealthy pharmacist who came originally from Penta-di-Casinca, and 'the fortune which he had acquired, the influence which he exercised in the region, excited the envy of Negroni, who could not stand seeing an outsider dictating to the inhabitants of his village'.[125] We have seen, moreover, that the mercantile Balanini were the object of hostile stereotyping as well as of actual attack. In this context, Filippi cites a more general proverb: 'Merchants and pigs are weighed when they are dead', which, while implying again that merchants are not fully men, seems also to carry an implicit threat of violence against them. Traders of all kinds must have become increasingly necessary intermediaries in the course of the nineteenth century but this appears to have done little to mitigate traditional distrust of them, for Lorenzi de Bradi drew attention as late as 1928 to Corsican distaste for the commercial as opposed to the liberal professions.[126]

A similar distaste was shown for domestic service, which was also regarded as dishonourable. Theft by servants from employers was a fairly common category of theft and probably reflects this. It is certainly the case that servants worked and robbed well away from home. Petro-Francesco Tristani from Pietraserena was convicted, for example, in 1852 of stealing money and effects from his employer, Signore Michele Pianelli of Olmeto, while Francesco-Maria Fumaroli of Eccica-Suarella was convicted in 1854 of stealing wine from his employer in Bastia. In a more interesting case in 1851, an Italian, Gaetano Poggioli, the servant of Father Giacomoni of Santa-Lucia-di-Tallano, was accused and convicted of stealing money from the priest's house, but serious doubts were expressed about the verdict. 'Poggioli maintained that he had had intimate relations with his employer's sister, a woman of a certain age, and that ... Giacomoni had accused him of theft falsely in order to ruin his reputation and thus make it impossible for his sister to go to live with him.'[127]

This brings us back to theft and disputes over movables within the community, to which we should add disputes over crops. These were well guarded as harvest approached, which is itself significant. We learn, for example, that two men from Casalabriva went out one evening at the end of August 1851 to watch over their vineyard in the country; they found a third man stealing grapes and one of them shot him dead. Crops were also vulnerable once they had been harvested, particularly since they were often stored away from villages in huts and at threshing-floors. A man from Moca-Croce was shot at in September 1842 as he was guarding his wheat at a place in the country. Despite these precautions and despite the general antipathy to theft, crops and animal products were stolen. In 1805, for example, Giovan-Andrea Castiglione of Montemaggiore was accused of stealing 66 cheeses and other goods, and pieces of the cheeses in question were discovered in the house of Francesco Renucci, whose wife was said to have been Castiglione's accomplice in this and other thefts from neighbours. But much more characteristic than theft here was quarrelling over shares in crops or products. In 1802 or 1803, for example, a charge was brought against the brothers Como and Anna-Maria Pietri of Sartène by the daughters of the late Giovan-Agostino Pietri. According to witnesses, who were working a wine-press belonging to the women, the two men came up and demanded their 'share of the wine, that is to say one-third of the produce of the press', and although this claim was not accepted they took away 27 *boccali* or about 7 gallons of wine. A more serious conflict occurred in 1834 when Domenico Giampierini of Ampriani went to collect his share of the wheat grown on land belonging to the Negroni, who came from another canton. A large group of the Negroni, all armed, also arrived and an argument developed over the exact division of the crop between them. On the intervention of the mayor and the parish priest of Ampriani, it was agreed to allow arbiters to divide the crop, but further argument then arose over how they should proceed, and shooting began in which two people were killed.[128]

More generally, since competition over material resources was usually expressed via direct personal conflict, theft was difficult to perceive or to react to, save in the same terms.[129] Relatively minor thefts could thus directly or indirectly lead to extreme acts of vengeance. Giovan-Francesco Giacoboni of Cambia, for example, discovered a man removing wheat from one of his fields in 1812, and hit him with a billhook. This prompted the man's brother to kill Giacoboni shortly afterwards in retaliation. Again, Giuseppo Giaminelli of Canale stole some honey in 1841 from a hive belonging to Giovan-Battiste Giaminelli. One of the latter's relatives, Domenico Olmiccia, discovered and reported this to Giovan-Battiste, and Giuseppo was made to pay 24 francs for the honey. As a result, he 'retained the greatest resentment against Olmiccia' and fired a shot at him later the same year. In some cases, moreover, it is clear that theft was itself being used as a mode of vengeance. A herd of pigs belonging to Petro Frassati of Bastelica damaged a field of maize belonging to Francesco Coti. Frassati refused any 'arrangement', so Coti had him summoned before the justice of the peace in October 1845. One night before the date set for this hearing, Frassati with two of his nephews and another man broke into a hut belonging to Coti, and took his rifle, some clothing and other items, at gunpoint. The theft of the rifle was a particular insult. In a more difficult case at Isolaccio (Castagniccia), Giuseppo Bardelli 'was engaged in illicit relations with the wife of Michele Papini'. In February 1848, however, the Papini couple went together 'to the [carnival] dance at Taglio, a neighbouring village', leaving their house unattended, and while they were away Bardelli went to the house and stole a sum of money, jewellery, tools and foodstuffs. 'These objects were returned, though not spontaneously' and a disagreement remained over the amount of money taken. The trial summary relates that 'it was supposed that the thefts were rather an act of vengeance against the Papini woman, who had annoyed Bardelli by going to the dance'. Papini reported the affair to the authorities, and Bardelli bacame a bandit and threatened to kill him. A further case shows how theft among relatives could fit the same pattern. Francesco-Andrea Muzi, aged 19 of Piobbeta, was courting a girl in 1858 'whose social position was inferior to his'. His mother, who was presumably a widow, made it clear to him that a marriage in such circumstances was unacceptable. This prompted him to leave home, taking 40 francs. When his mother later found Francesco-Andrea and reproached him with the theft, he pointed a pistol at her and fired it, hitting and wounding a bystander.[130]

Two other categories of offence are found under the heading of theft in the judicial records, which are really assertions of rights to communal assistance. One is begging, of which an example occurred in 1845. Petro-Santo Valle, known locally as 'the madman of Albitreccia', used to stop people on the main road near the village, armed with a shot-gun, and ask them for food and money. He was accused and convicted of highway robbery, but the jury took an indulgent view of his case and he received only a light sentence.[131] In general, begging was extremely rare in Corsica,[132] which almost certainly reflects the strength of the ties of kinship and clientage. The second closely related category is what might be called the informal community levy, of which Robiquet provides an example. At Vivario in April 1827, according to the village priest, the poor were obliged to take livestock from the richer inhabitants 'out of extreme necessity'. They took goats and other animals as food, telling the owners that poverty obliged them to do so and offering their houses and chestnut trees in exchange.[133]

This mechanism may well have been a long-term factor which served to create or to strengthen clientage as a debt relationship, but debt appears in our sources mainly in a more straightforward way as a source of conflict among equals. For example, two young men from Ortiporio quarrelled in December 1844 over a debt of three francs between them. After exchanging threats and insults, they began shooting at each other and one of them was wounded, while the other's father, who intervened, was killed. In another case, Giovan-Antono Ferruletti was owed ten francs by Marco Vincenti of Pila-Canale. Having asked for the return of the money in vain, Ferruletti went in February 1845 to the mill where Vincenti lived, and took an umbrella, which was probably a status symbol. Vincenti then made various attempts to recover the umbrella. Ferruletti refused to give it back until he got his money, which eventually provoked Vincenti to shoot him dead. Failure to pay for objects which had been sold may well have been behind such quarrels over small debts. This becomes clear in a case in 1848. Pellegrino Mattei of Casabianca had sold a violin to Giovan-Petro Mattei, who then refused to pay the price agreed. This led to a heated argument between them on a square, and later, when the instrument was being used to accompany dancing at Giovan-Quiliano Casabianca's house, one of the two came to claim it. Further argument took place, stones were thrown, and a relative of Casabianca was shot dead. Conflict could also occur over refusal to pay for services, though here the parties would probably not be social equals. In 1849, Petro Poli, a 60-year-old day labourer from Ciamannacce killed Giuseppo Peretti in a quarrel provoked by Peretti's refusal to pay six francs due for work done by Poli. Again, in May 1847, three men from Sant'Andrea-di-Cotone crossed the Tavignano on the ferry operated by Simone Andrei. They then refused to pay the fare which he demanded, and in the subsequent dispute one of them shot Andrei dead.[134]

Finally, our sources reveal a miscellaneous group of professions where rivalry led to serious conflict, suggesting that intense competition over material resources was not confined to cultivators and herdsmen. When Dr Risticoni of San-Gavino-d'Ampugnani was shot dead on the road to Pruno in 1822, one of the prime suspects was Dr Micheli, who had returned to the district a few months earlier after a spell in prison, and who was trying to rebuild his clientèle. Similarly, we learn that two doctors, 'Mannei and Vizzavona exercised the profession of medicine in the village of Bocognano' and that 'they did not for long remain on good terms'. In 1825, shots were fired at Dr Vizzavona. This was seen as attempted homicide and the initiative for it was attributed to Dr Mannei, though no prosecution was brought for lack of evidence. In 1831, Dr Mannei was killed, and his relatives suspected his rival, Dr Vizzavona, but again could produce no firm evidence to confirm their suspicions. 'The state of enmity between the two families persisted until 1833', when third parties brought about a reconciliation. However, one of Mannei's brothers and another relative were not included in this 'peace', and they killed Dr Vizzavona on the square at Afa at the end of 1833. Two cases in 1893 involved less prestigious occupations. In one, two rival hunters of thrushes from Ghisonaccia, Rocco Andreani and Saverio Constantini, fell out. Constantini then apparently stole some nets from Andreani, and to avoid retaliation ambushed and killed him. In the second, material interest was combined with honour. Francesco-Antono Benedetti and Francesco-Natale Savignoni were both barbers at Murato. Savignoni owed Benedetti a sum of money and, on top of this, they began to argue in a wineshop as to who was the better barber. They came to blows outside, and Savignoni struck Benedetti with a stone, which proved fatal.[135]

VII

We may conclude our discussion of conflicts of material interest with some interpretative comments, which link them with those involving honour. First, the conflict which we have described reflects an intense competition for scarce material resources, and this was perceived by actors and observers at the time. 'The ordinary acts of revenge carried out in the Tallano district for some time now', the subprefect commented in 1820, 'are to destroy livestock, to throw down enclosures, to cut fruit trees and to damage vines. Everyone seeks to impoverish his antagonist.'[136] But land and property were not (if they ever can be) simply an economic resource; they were a means to power and prestige. 'Everyone is excessively keen to have property,' Blanqui noted in 1841, 'much less for the profit to be obtained from it – which is very often non-existent – than from the importance which it gives.'[137] This is well conveyed by an anecdote from a village in La Rocca, reported by Lamotte. A young boy heard that a man had been killed and asked his father why. 'He had cleared some land,' was the only reply. The man had in effect wished to increase the amount of the land which he cultivated. This would have in turn increased his income and thus enhanced his political influence, something which his enemies could not tolerate.[138] The same point was made, with different emphasis, by the Corsican writer Salvator Viale in 1853: 'The wealth and dignity of a man, and his credit, can create enmities towards him among the people of his village; sometimes the acquisition or extension of a field, a new house or the improvement of an old one, even putting up shutters or hangings by windows, can be the origin of envy and ill-will.'[139]

Conflicts of material interest and conflicts of honour were thus inextricably linked in Corsica, as they were elsewhere. Sensitivity to notions of honour provided the mechanism for triggering conflict but also for controlling it. Honour denoted the ability and the will to defend and promote one's family's interests by force, if need be. For a crucial element in the cultural imperative not to let any insult or attack pass was to ensure protection by deterrence. As Brögger has written in a similar context, what is involved is the 'communication of readiness to fight' by fighting or other means. A reputation for swift and firm retaliation was the ultimate basis of power, and revenge was undertaken at all levels 'in order that other men may learn to leave us unharmed'.[140] Failure to meet challenges at the honorific level led correspondingly to material loss and disadvantage. As a proverb ran: 'Whoever has honour can be harmed by no malice; whoever has no honour cannot enjoy anything.'[141] In the case at Linguizetta to which we have referred, when Tomaso Lanfranchi made disparaging remarks about Nicolaio Arasti's dog, Arasti became angry and called Lanfranchi *rimbeccu*, a term denoting a serious fault of omission and particularly the failure to take vengeance when this was expected. The trial summary explained that calling a man *rimbeccu* implied that he was 'a social outcast, an object of scorn, whom anyone can insult with impunity because he lacks the courage to retaliate against such insults'. More particularly, Arasti meant 'to allude to the pusillanimous character of the Lanfranchi family as a whole, for one of them had been beaten up a little earlier and another had had his property devastated, and no attempt had been made to avenge this double insult.'[142] Honour arose from and mediated conflict over material interests but it then generated its own semi-autonomous conflict, to which we now turn.

] 4 [

Conflict and its causes: conflicts of honour

'Every Corsican', Benson wrote in 1825, '... has a set of fixed principles of action, and determinate notions of honour, from which he seldom swerves'.[1] The importance of individual and family honour was stressed in proverbs[2] and perhaps even more in laments for the dead. 'You were the honour of the *pieve* / And the object of respect for all your kin,' a sister sang, for example, of her schoolmaster brother from Zicavo.[3] Recommendations, legal pleadings and petitions for clemency also commonly made reference to the honourable status of the families of those on whose behalf they were made.[4] Complementary to and contrasting with the notion of honour (*onore*) was that of dishonour or shame (*bergogna*). As elsewhere in the Mediterranean world,[5] shame was both a proper quality of some persons in some situations, for example young girls in the presence of strange men, and also described a derogatory condition, which it was sometimes possible or even imperative to repair by performing an act of honour to cancel out the offence which had caused it. So, at the extreme, 'dishonour could only be washed away by blood', i.e. killing.[6] Dishonour or shame in this sense was distinguished from disgrace (*disgrazia*) or misfortune, which was often the consequence of following the requirements of honour and implied no moral or social disapprobation. Those who had met violent deaths were often referred to as 'disgraced' in this sense.[7] Male and female honour were complementary but may be distinguished for the purposes of analysis.

I

The importance of honour in quarrels among men is often explicitly referred to in our sources. In a petition for clemency on behalf of a Bastia café-owner convicted of wounding in 1835, for example, it was said that he had been 'carried away by an excess of offended honour'.[8] In 1846, Amadeo Costa went to Balogna as schoolteacher, as a protégé of the mayor, Antono Colonna. When Costa began 'to compose satirical verses against certain girls in the village', relations between them were soured and Costa apparently shot and wounded Colonna in 1847. No prosecution was brought for lack of evidence. Costa expressed the wish to move to another post but said that 'he would only leave Balogna with his honour intact', and he was still there six years later.[9] Conflict at Bastelica in 1852 between two branches of the Folacci developed from a quarrel between two children over a cap. Natale Folacci, the elder brother of one of them, told his father: 'It isn't because of the cap that I insist [on paying them back], but because they are boasting of having put me down.' He therefore challenged his opponents and was killed. In another case in 1852, Stefano Guerini of Piano confessed to having tried to kill Angelo-Francesco Raffalli following a quarrel over cards. On the day after the quarrel, he was returning from work in the country when he saw Raffalli at his window and 'the memory of the violence which he had suffered revived in his mind, and, dominated by the idea of the humiliation to which he had been subjected, he fired his gun'.[10]

As this indicates, the corollary of maintaining one's own honour intact was the attempt to damage that of one's competitors, and the humiliation of enemies was often almost ritually demonstrative. Giuseppo-Maria Paoli of Olmeto disarmed Petro-Paolo Paoli of Fozzano in a fight in 1846 and 'spat into the barrel of Paoli's shot-gun as a sign of contempt ... This was the depth of humiliation for Petro-Paolo', and he refused any kind of reconciliation and felt obliged to avenge himself. Again, when Mayor Campana of Penta dismissed his secretary Carbuccia in 1861, 'he placed a notice to this effect on the door of his house, wishing in this way to inflict a public humiliation on Carbuccia, who retaliated by denouncing the mayor to the prefect' for alleged financial irregularities.[11]

It is significant here that the judicial process itself might inflict humiliations that Corsican men could not accept. A witness in a trial at Corte in 1825 declared, after his cousin had been charged with perjury, 'that he himself would not be a man of honour if he did not in turn give false testimony'. When the Pietri, father and son, were given comparatively light sentences in 1829 for having insulted and assaulted the mayor of Sartène (they tried to throw him down a staircase), he wrote that : 'I feel much more humiliated by this judgment of the court than by the ill-treatment which I received.' A particular concern here was to avoid the humiliating punishments that were extant until well into the nineteenth century. When Francesco-Antono Battaglioni of Perelli was sentenced to death in 1797, for example, it was ordered that the judgment should be 'displayed on a gibbet to be set up for this purpose on the public square of the port' of Bastia. Convicted criminals might themselves be exhibited before serving their sentences. Girolamo Benetti of Arbellara, we have seen, stabbed himself in his cell in 1842 to avoid exhibition. 'My enemies wanted to confound me,' he declared. 'They were already looking forward to seeing me exposed to public ridicule. But they will be disappointed. They will never have that pleasure. I will rather die than submit to that infamy which I have not deserved.'[12] Luca-Antono Viterbi of Penta-di-Casinca starved himself to death in similar circumstances, and unsuccessful suicide bids to avoid exhibition are also reported in 1827 and 1843.[13]

The importance of honour and shame in conflict among males is confirmed when the nature and context of that conflict are more closely examined. First, and perhaps most obviously, male honour demanded that men be armed. 'For a long time, a gun has been and, for many men, still remains an object not of luxury but of necessity,' Mérimée wrote in 1840. 'Today, the flintlocks are disappearing, and it is common to see a peasant in rags with an excellent double-action percussion rifle.'[14] The *Gazette des Tribunaux* commented at about the same time that 'the right to carry arms is considered in Corsica to be one of the least contestable prerogatives of the citizen'.[15] The rural population was armed in other French territories of course,[16] but the tradition was particularly important in Corsica and had been strengthened by the War of Independence and the prolonged civil strife of the Revolutionary and Napoleonic eras. Successive governments associated the persistence of vendettas and banditry with this local custom and sought to license or to ban the carrying of arms, but the ban was rarely complete and never effective.[17] The district prosecutor at Bastia concluded typically in 1879: 'Carrying firearms is unfortunately an old habit in Corsica, which the courts are powerless to eradicate.'[18] The possession of firearms (which did not preclude also owning and using daggers) meant that quarrels could quickly lead to serious violence and killing. And, as we have seen, notions of honour were attached to the possession and use of firearms. A tale collected in 1882 suggests that boys were given their first gun as a sign of coming of age,[19] and male prowess in the use of guns was demonstrated in hunting as well as in direct conflict with other men.[20]

Secondly, the challenge and the insult were crucial elements in male quarrels. After a period of bad relations between their families, Paolo-Orso Paoli of Carpineto challenged Giacomo-Paolo Torre 'to measure his strength against him' on a square in the village, where they subsequently exchanged shots in 1849. In August 1861, an argument developed at a threshing-floor between Ignazio Mori and Anton-Carlo and Luigi Renucci of Sorio over a sheaf of wheat which Mori claimed had been taken from one of his fields. When the Renucci denied responsibility, Mori declared: 'You are rubbish men!', to which Luigi Renucci replied: 'By the blood of the Madonna, just wait for me, if you have the courage!' A fight then took place in which Mori was shot dead. In the course of the feud between the Pietri and the Lanfranchi of Campi, Don Giovanni Lanfranchi returned surreptitiously to the village in 1882 and was heard calling to his son by Giovan-Giuseppo Pietri, who challenged him in these terms: 'Coward, robber, empty belly that you are! Show yourself, if you have any courage. Come and shoot at me as you did in such an underhand way at my staircase.' On this occasion, the challenge was ignored.[21]

The ritual exchange of insults was a part of Corsican culture, at least in some areas. We learn, for example, from a case in 1822, that three men from Sartène engaged in hoeing vines had been 'joking together with cutting remarks'.[22] However, Chiari stresses, with reference to a later period, that Corsicans were not argumentative: 'words are taken very seriously and not bandied about ... one rarely witnesses a violent quarrel in words with each opponent hurling abuse. In fact, death often strikes before one single word has been uttered, and people who know that certain insults are likely to lead to violent issues restrain their tongues.'[23] Our sources confirm both that insults were used with some care in order to intimidate and provoke and also that they could quickly lead to violence. A witness in a trial in 1802 testified that the Majorchini had stolen certain agricultural implements from the Brandi brothers of Cervione, and that when they asked for them back, the Majorchini 'replied in an unfriendly way, making ingenious remarks', which served as a provocation to homicide. In a less serious quarrel in 1821, Martino Peretti of Levie knocked out Carl'-Antono Peretti. They had met to try to settle a dispute, but 'instead of so doing, they had taunted each other with insulting remarks'.[24]

In some cases, we have information about the kind of insult employed in such quarrels. According to a witness, a fight at Bilia in 1815 had been provoked when one party had been called 'son of the shit'.[25] In a dispute in 1824 between Anton-Pasquino Pietri and the mayor of Santa-Maria-Figaniella, the mayor is reported to have said to Pietri: 'Look at you, how badly dressed you are!', to which Pietri riposted: 'At least I don't smack of the church like you broken-down fence!'[26] We know also that more elaborate written 'satires' were composed and circulated. After such a lampoon had been written in 1811 about an alleged affair between Giovan-Gavino Casalta of Casalta and a woman in the village, he 'believed that he had been wounded in his honour ... and that it was necessary for the outrage to be paid for with the blood of the supposed culprit', which it subsequently was.[27]

Not all, perhaps not most, insults were verbal, as Chiari's remarks suggest. In his account of the feud between the Leca and the Poli of Guagno at the end of the eighteenth century, Grimaldi describes the reaction to the courtship of a Poli girl by Giovanni Leca. He sang a serenade by her window with some companions, as was customary, but rather than letting his daughter open her window and offer refreshments, which again was usual, her father ordered all the windows of the house to be closed and the lights extinguished, 'and a voice from an upper part of the house then made the *scuoccolo* resound over the entire village'. This was a long high-pitched shout and 'a very serious insult and affront'.[28] Insults could also take the form of gestures, such as spitting on the ground or into the barrel of a gun, as we have seen. The insulting gesture could become an act of violence, most obviously when one man hit another. Muzzarettu became a bandit in his maturity after he had killed a much younger man in 1931. This man had slapped him in the face in the course of an argument on the square of Grossa, and Muzzarettu had felt obliged 'to save his honour'.[29]

Male conflict was to a large extent in effect an extension of male sociability, as a consideration of some further aspects will show. Bournet noted in 1888 that many quarrels derived 'from insults exchanged after drinking',[30] and the judicial records confirm both the importance of the pastime and its deleterious effects. Sometimes incidents arose from the drinking context itself. A dispute at Tavera in 1854, for example, occurred when the company refused to pay the full bill for the wine which they had drunk during the evening, which prompted the shop's keeper to shoot one of them. In this category, one should perhaps also place cases of accidental woundings and killings under the influence of drink. Agostino Vincenti and Gennaio Pinetti of Penta, for example, had been celebrating the festival of San Pancrazio in May 1848 and both had been drinking copiously. Towards the end of the day, Pinetti took out his pistol and fired it in the air 'as a sign of rejoicing'. When Vincenti tried to make the same customary gesture, he shot Pinetti dead by mistake. But such disputes could also arise from pre-existing enmities, aggressiveness being released by drink. In August 1851, Giovan-Santo Ventura and Giovan-Bastiano Colombani of Penta-Acquatella fired shots at each other on the way back from 'the patronal festival of Ortiporio', which they had both celebrated by drinking a great deal. However, the reason for the quarrel lay in the fact that one of Ventura's nieces had been made pregnant by Colombani's brother-in-law. Again, at Ocana, a savage fight occurred in a wineshop where several men were drinking. The protagonists were Giovan-Battiste and Giuseppo Muselli, and the former first threw a flaming brand at the latter and then stabbed him several times about the head, which proved fatal. A serious enmity already existed between them, which 'originated in testimony given in court by Giovan-Battiste in a case involving another family to which Giuseppo was related by marriage'.[31]

Though alcohol consumption increased in Corsica, especially from the 1870s, heavy drinking among men was normally confined to Sundays and feast-days,[32] and drunkenness could be regarded as shameful. In a case at Oletta in 1852, Giovan-Michele Fieschi arrived at a dance with his uncle, who was drunk. Those present reproached him for this, and Giovan-Michele felt obliged to defend his uncle from ridicule, which led to his being fatally stabbed. Habitual drunkenness, moreover, brought lasting dishonour. Paolo Morelli of Bocognano was described in 1856 as a 'man addicted to drink, who had lost the respect [even] of his own relatives', who had given him a beating.[33]

An important feature of male sociability at wineshops was cardplaying. Bigot commented that 'all Corsicans were inveterate cardplayers and gamblers', and he noted that while games were in progress, 'each player had a weapon within arm's reach, a pistol or a dagger, the sight of which reminded everyone to adhere closely to the rules of the game'.[34] The most popular game was *Scopa*, which was akin to *Vingt-et-un*, and was played for money.[35] This and other games do not seem to have had the same social significance as some that were played in other parts of the Mediterranean region,[36] but the combination of drinking and playing cards for money by armed men frequently led to violence, as might be expected. Cases of homicide or attempted homicide, related to quarrels over cards, were thus extremely common throughout the nineteenth century. Mention may also be made here of violence committed in order to finance gambling or gambling debts.[37]

Festivals, when drinking and other pastimes were indulged in to excess, were most conducive to male competitiveness and quarrelling, and none more so than Carnival. A case at Lozzi in 1883 illustrates how the licence of Carnival might itself provoke conflict. It was reported that the *adjoint* Fernando Acquaviva and three younger men, all unmarried, 'went through the streets of the village (on two evenings in late February) making all kinds of threats, such as: "Come on out, you cowardly Pollachi! We want to see your blood on the square! Bring out the faggots, we want to burn the village down!"' They stopped, too, in front of the house of the schoolmistress and 'sang obscene couplets, which were most insulting to this honourable lady'. They were also said to have whistled and sounded a horn on another occasion, as she was taking her pupils for a walk. The fact that the four were prosecuted and later convicted for what was almost certainly regarded as permissible behaviour in the context of the festival was attributed to malicious and misleading gossip emanating from those who wished to have the *adjoint* removed from his post. A more violent outcome to Carnival quarrels was not infrequent. 'During the Carnival of 1835 at Castirlà', we learn,

> the young men took sides. Each side wanted to organize a more brilliant dance than the other. Taddeo Taddei was the leader of one side, while Domenico Grimaldi headed the other. Taddei was angry with Grimaldi when he managed to get hold of the only person in the village who could play the violin and, as Grimaldi was leaving the dance which he had organized, he was shot from behind at close quarters [by Taddei] and mortally wounded.[38]

Again, at Penta in 1865, various people were gathered at the start of Carnival at the house of the widow Gherardi, around the hearth of 'the big room that was used for drying [chestnuts]'. A number of youths joined the company from time to time, including Pasquale Torre, who came disguised as a woman. He gave an orange to the widow's youngest daughter and then retired to a corner of the room. Several young people of both sexes approached him and touched him on the breasts, but he did not react until Giovan-Petro Fabbi followed suit. Torre then struck Fabbi and stabbed him three times, killing him at once. He explained that Fabbi had tried to lift the veil which covered his face as well as attacking him with a knife.[39] It is understandable in such a context that a special chest was supplied at a Carnival dance at Ortale in 1864, 'in which all the weapons of those participating had to be deposited'.[40]

Conflict also occurred at other kinds of festival: New Year,[41] Easter,[42] and celebrations associated with the completion of agro-pastoral tasks.[43] But most important here were conflicts at weddings and funerals and at local saints' festivals. During a wedding at Pietralba in 1852, a certain Angelo Cristofini collapsed while a speech was being made at the new couple's house. Since the customary salvoes were being fired at the time, it was not at once obvious that he had been shot dead by Paol'-Antono Mancini, who had harboured a grudge against him for some time and had cunningly chosen this occasion to act on it. Again, fighting between the Paoli and the Pasqualini of Castineta broke out as they were returning from a funeral at Saliceto in November 1840. One man was killed and another seriously wounded.[44] Examples of violence occurring at patronal festivals have been cited and could be multiplied. We have seen, too, that the feuding at Fozzano entered a new phase in 1830 following violent and fatal exchanges during the patronal festival, while at Santa-Lucia-di-Tallano in 1831 the mayor actually banned the festival for fear of similar trouble.[45]

Most of the cases which we have mentioned here were of conflict, which occurred in a fairly random fashion at festive gatherings, or where the festival increased the vulnerability of potential victims. One of the first crimes of the bandit Romanetti from Calcatoggio was to kill his enemy Giulio-Cesare Carbuccia in January 1914, as he was walking with others to the chapel of San Bastiano near the village, 'where the feast of the saint was being celebrated'.[46] But religious occasions also gave rise to specific kinds of conflict, since they provided an arena for male competitiveness. Privat relates that quarrels occurred every year at Pastricciola over who should carry the statue of the patron saint in the festival procession, and such conflict must have been common elsewhere.[47] 'A dispute developed in March 1853 in the church of Pozzo, a hamlet of Brando, over the conveyance of the Christ in the Good Friday procession.' It was agreed that the privilege should go to the person who offered the largest gift of alms to the church, but Antono Sisco, who had been drinking, refused to accept this decision and swore that 'the Christ would only be carried by him and his friends'. After he was made to leave the church, he appeared at the window of his house and fired a shot at one of his opponents.[48]

A particular focus of male rivalry in church was the singing of the 'lessons' during mass, especially at Easter and other festivals. Some men achieved a particular reputation as singers, and they and others were anxious to display their talents.[49] The fight at Fozzano in 1811, in which Lorenzo Tomasi was stabbed, took place on Holy Thursday. It seems that the parish priest had chosen Durazzi 'to sing the lesson, but Sgio Tomasi stepped forward and sang it instead'. Afterwards Tomasi was insulted and then assaulted on the square by the church 'for singing the lesson, when it was not his place to do so'. Again, at Cauro during the patronal festival in December 1869, things were apparently running late and the priest suggested that the service of the confraternity be cut short. His advice was ignored, so he then tried 'to interrupt Santo Peraldi who was singing a lesson as he was accustomed to do'. This prompted a general commotion, in which the priest was jostled and abused. Conflict also occurred in churches on a more everyday basis. In an incident in 1879, for example, Giacomo Faggionelli of Zicavo 'maliciously pulled away a chair on which his neighbour Giuseppo Piazza was about to sit'. Piazza hit him, 'and a certain tumult ensued', which temporarily interrupted the service.[50]

The publicity of conflict in wineshops, during festivals or in church meant that questions of honour were paramount. The same consideration applies more generally when conflict arising in the countryside, whether spontaneous or contrived, is contrasted with that which occurred in villages. The latter was nearly always more serious in its implications, and retaliation in this arena was a more deliberate assertion or reassertion of male honour. The square or church square was not an important central area in most Corsican villages, but it could serve nevertheless as a kind of forum where men met and where matters of general interest were discussed. For example, several men were talking about a recent arbitration decision of the mayor on the square of the hamlet of Chioselli (Coti-Chiavari) in July 1857. This led to an argument between Pasquale Antona and Giovanni Poggi, who dissented from the general approbation expressed, and Poggi later fired shots at Antona in the maquis. The public nature of the square also meant that encounters there between those in a state of enmity were usually avoided, and when these did occur therefore they often led to further conflict. One day in October 1843, Santo Bernardi was on the square at Alzi when Angelo-Michele Sarrochi from another village entered it. 'Fifteen years earlier, Sarrochi had accidentally killed Bernardi's brother', so both men were at once on their guard. 'Sarrochi feared some act of vengeance and Bernardi resented the fact that Sarrochi had come to Alzi at all, regarding it as an insult. When Sarrochi made a suspicious movement, Bernardi fired his pistol at him, grazing his chin.' When Bernardi was later put on trial for attempted homicide, the jury accepted his claim that Sarrochi's behaviour in coming on to the square in the first place had indeed been provocative. At Castineta, Petro-Maria Paoli's brother had been killed in a fight by Filippo-Maria Pasqualini, who was convicted and sentenced to three years' imprisonment. After serving his sentence, Pasqualini returned to the village, and one day in October 1844 he and Paoli met unexpectedly on the square. Neither would give way to the other and, at three or four paces, Paoli fired a pistol and killed his opponent. Again, the jury at Paoli's trial took the view that he had acted under extreme provocation, and he received a very lenient sentence.[51]

More extensive conflict could occur on squares. General fighting took place in 1850 at Moita, for example, between the young men of the Marcelli and the Gaffajoli families 'who are enemies', while at Castellare in the same year a man was killed in a similar fight between rival factions on the church square. It is significant, however, that such public encounters were often prevented, at least temporarily. 'A lively argument developed on New Year's Day 1864 on the square of Sant'Andrea-d'Orcino between the partisans of the mayor and those of the *adjoint*, who were competing for the services of a violinist' at the celebrations. The situation was defused when a certain Graziani intervened and led the mayor and his supporters away, though Graziani was afterwards attacked and stabbed.[52] All of this underlines the seriousness of deliberately choosing to carry out vengeance in such an arena. Perhaps the most striking example of this was the 'execution' of Antono Canarelli by the Cucchi from Carbini in July 1851. Canarelli had seduced one of the Cucchi's sisters and was also suspected of having betrayed another member of the family to the gendarmes. He was kidnapped, paraded through several villages in the region with a rope around his neck, and then shot dead on the square of Poggiale in front of all the villagers who had been assembled for the purpose.[53] Several cases are reported of women choosing this mode of vengeance. Maria-Francesca Quilichini of Santa-Lucia-di-Tallano shot the mayor in 1845 as he was walking in the square. Again, at nearby Loreto, Saveria Rossi accosted Angelo Angelini in August 1846 on the public square in front of several people and tried to shoot him. Angelini had raped her earlier in the year and had reneged on a subsequent promise to marry her.[54] The absence of other opportunities may have been a factor in their choice here, but it seems likely, too, that women were attracted by the chance to right their wrongs in public.

Before we turn to a full discussion of female honour, however, some other aspects of male honour should be made clearer. Honour was not something that all men were expected to be too demonstrative about. In the words of a proverb: 'Whoever boasts of his honour loses it.'[55] There is some evidence, as we would expect, that men of gentle or easy-going disposition might have their standing lowered and lay themselves open to attack. At Muro in 1857, Giuseppo Girolami, a muleteer of peaceful character, was provoked by another man who made disparaging remarks about his fiancée's father. When Petro Giovanelli of Calcatoggio was wrongly accused in 1832 of killing a man with whom he had no grounds at all for hostility, he explained his predicament by saying: 'It is because I am a lamb [*agnello*].' This term was also used as a nickname.[56] It is also significant that mental as well as physical disability might attract humiliating treatment. In a case in 1853, we learn that Giovanni Acquaviva, a young herdsman from

Evisa, 'had for some time been the butt of ridicule in the village. He was an obvious target, being simple-minded and having a weak constitution'. Again, at Poggio-di-Tallano in 1822, Anton-Silvestro Quilichini and his wife were subjected over a long period to 'a grand charivari with whistling and banging of pots and pans'; the wooden staircase of their house was twice removed; stones were thrown and shots fired. According to the few sympathetic witnesses at the trial which ensued when the couple brought charges against some of their persecutors, the reason for this treatment lay in the personality of the victims and particularly of Anton-Silvestro. He was 'too good-natured, and that is why he is being got at; they want to make out that he is soft in the head, in order to get hold of his property' – yet another reminder this of the direct link between honour and material interest. However, physically weak or peaceful men were not always without honour. Giovanni Foata of Pila-Canale, 'who had never carried a weapon in his life', was nevertheless regarded 'as the model of honour' in 1837.

Here, it should be pointed out that aggressive concern over honour was more especially expressed by young men, and they were the main agents in feuds, something to which we will return. Certain kinds of competitive behaviour were restricted to the youths or unmarried men of a village, often acting in groups, as we have seen in connection with Carnival festivities. Young men on these and other occasions sought to show off among their peers, prospective brides, or the population generally. To provide another example, at the start of November 1848, 'three youths climbed on to the roof of the church at Oletta and rang the bells, as is customary at All Saints'.' They refused to come down when the mayor and the priest asked them to do so, and one of them was killed when force was applied against them. Much of the fighting in wineshops also involved youths, and it is clear that Corsicans themselves recognized a kind of quarrelling specific to youths. A dispute at Silvareccio in 1841 'between the Paoli and the Agostini brothers' was reported to have begun 'over remarks such as young men make'.[57] Concomitantly, older men did not as a rule participate directly in violent conflict. This did not, of course, mean that older men were without honour, but only that their honour was expressed or manifested in different ways. Honour was a quality, moreover, that took a lifetime to establish: 'One only celebrates a man at his death.'[58]

If male honour was related to temperament and to age, it was also linked more generally to status in the objective sense. Griffon noted in 1841 that Corsicans 'believed themselves to be dishonoured by engaging in field work'. The dishonour was compounded when such work was done for someone else, which would frequently be the case. 'Any landowner, however small, would consider himself dishonoured if he went to work for another person,' a police official reported in 1817.[59] This relates in turn to the high premium set upon a life of leisure by Corsican men, which is reflected in the outsider's charge of idleness made so frequently against them,[60] and to the fact that much heavy labour was carried out by women and by Italian immigrants. *Lucchesi*, we have seen, remained a despised out-group through the nineteenth century, and, as such, might be the butt of humiliating attacks on the part of Corsican men. In May 1863, for example, several Italian workers were repairing a road near Renno when a group of Corsicans passed by, escorting a bride to her wedding. One of these, a certain Francesco Benedetti from Piana, 'felt obliged, in order to honour the bride, to indulge in witticisms at the expense of the foreign workers'. They were provoked by this and one of them replied sharply, which 'wounded the pride' of Benedetti, who fired his pistol at him.[61] This case is also interesting since it indicates how shaming other men could be a form of sexual display.

Male honour commonly had a sexual reference. Most obviously, the notion of being cuckolded was directly linked in common parlance with the failure to avenge affronts. In the course of a long-running quarrel at Moca-Croce, which involved the destruction of enclosures, fruit trees and buildings, Paolo Franchi had been threatened and insulted at the door of his house in 1822 'and even called *"cornicone"* [or cuckold]'.[62] After the revenge killings in April 1839 at Santa-Lucia-di-Tallano, Giudice Giacomoni is reported to have declared: 'Giulio-Martino [his son, killed in 1834] is dead, and his murderers are still alive; but I am not wearing horns any more!'[63]

Evidence in a case in 1852, relating to the killing of a certain Belfini from Bastelica, makes the point very clear. Paolo Giordani testified that he had had a quarrel with another Giordani, his relative.

> The latter had told Paolo that he had horns, which refers in local parlance to an affront that has not yet been avenged. 'If I have two horns', Paolo replied, 'it is because of you lot,' referring thus to the killing of the relative's brother by Belfini. 'If we did have horns, we knew how to get rid of them,' was the reply which Paolo Giordani received. This expression may appear vague, but for Corsicans its meaning is clear and precise. It means that revenge has been taken and, in effect, the conversation (here reported) took place after Belfini had been killed.[64]

Men also engaged in direct sexual rivalry. The bandit Bardelli from Isolaccio was asked in 1847 by his cousin Ignazio Capponi to help him to kill the mayor's nephew, Felice Massiani. Capponi had his own reasons for seeking vengeance against the mayor and he knew that Bardelli had a grudge against Massiani, since they had both been lovers of the same woman. We shall see, too, that rivalry between suitors was an important source of conflict. A consistently dissolute life, or adultery in certain circumstances, could cause a man, and potentially his family, to lose honour. In a case in 1862, Anton-Pasquino Ortoli of Poggio was said to have lost the trust even of his relatives because of his way of life. In particular, he consorted with 'a woman of bad reputation'. When Natale Aliotti of Ciamannacce was prosecuted for adultery in 1856, it was suggested that his behaviour had lost him 'the esteem of his fellow-citizens'.[65] It was not unknown either for wives to react publicly against erring husbands with what seems to be a degree of community approval. When Pierrina Carlotti of Isolaccio came to suspect her husband Orso-Matteo 'of carrying on illicit relations with Claudia Colombani ... she manifested her jealousy in violent scenes. After one of these in 1881, she left her husband and went to live with one of her nephews in a neighbouring village.' When she learned that the Colombani woman and her mother 'were making remarks about her which impugned her honour', Pierrina returned to Isolaccio, and killed Claudia's ten-year-old son when she was unable to find any other target. She then gave herself up and received a very lenient sentence, which reflected the view that she had been largely justified in her action.[66] However, to a certain extent male sexual exploits outside marriage were expected and a matter of pride. A certain Degiovanni from Silvareccio killed his wife when he found her with another man, Vincenzo Angeli. According to a female witness at the subsequent trial in 1833, Angeli had expressed suicidal intentions, saying that he had been the cause of the death of the Degiovanni woman, to which the witness had replied: 'You want to kill yourself for that? It isn't any shame for a man to go to see another man's wife!' Again, after his conviction in 1839 on various serious charges, the bandit Antono Lucchini boasted that he had left a bastard son to avenge him. More generally, a song collected recently in the Ampugnani district proclaimed: 'Raising a bastard / Is not a shameful thing. / We are more interested here about people / Than about property and things.'[67]

A double standard operated in effect not only between the sexes but also depending on the relationship between the man and the woman concerned. Men might seek to dishonour other men's wives, sisters and daughters, but they sought even more vigorously to defend the honour of their own womenfolk. In this competition among men via women, the emphasis in Corsican culture seems to have been much more on the latter rather than the former. A higher value was set on family as against individual or peer-group interest. Indeed, the honour displayed or generated in the second arena accrued to the families of those concerned, and we shall see that those who transgressed the sexual rules of the family rarely did so in order to flout them absolutely and were much more frequently engaged in attempts to manipulate them to their own advantage.

II

The honour of men was thus intimately associated with that of the women related to them by blood or marriage. Father Galletti wrote in 1863 that the Corsican 'shows himself to be excessively jealous of the honour of his wife, his sister, his daughter, and even of other close female relatives; and he requires that they be treated with the most rigorous respect', a view that many other observers confirm.[68] Lorenzi de Bradi explained in 1936 that 'to cast any slur on a woman is to dishonour her hearth, her family; and the family must be without taint, united ... in prosperity and adversity', while a proverb put the same point more positively: 'A good woman in the house is the honour and the wealth of a family.'[69] Since female honour reflected, measured and proclaimed the 'wealth' of a family in this way, it is not surprising to find it closely involved with the practice of feuding. 'Respect for women is the basis of all other customs,' Malaspina declared in 1876; 'one could say that it has created the vendetta.'[70] From the other side of the equation, as it were, Black-Michaud has argued more generally that 'of all conflicts which occur in feuding societies, those which occur over women and shame are among the least adulterated by realistic [or what we have called 'material'] factors. They are consequently those in which hostilities are the most intense.'[71]

Female honour was expressed in a variety of ways: general comportment, adequate fulfilment of female roles, sociability; and it could be attacked or questioned in as many ways: by gossip, by physical violence, and so on; but its essential expression was sexual. This is already evident from cases that we have discussed. It is also clear that the notion of honour was explicitly present in the minds of actors, male and female. At Peri in 1853, an unmarried sister of Giuseppo Peres 'showed evident signs of being pregnant, and public opinion attributed her state to the relations which she had had ... with the parish priest. Afraid that he would share in the shame and dishonour of his sister, [Peres] ... first tried to kill the priest.' Again, excusing an attack made on his uncle and another man as they returned home late one night in 1860, Angelo-Paolo Orsini of Lento said that he had thought they were robbers 'or individuals who wished to attack his sisters' honour'. In a more complicated case in 1805, the *adjoint* of Tomino 'was led by various women of the village to believe that Angela-Maria, the nubile daughter of Signore Giuseppo-Maria Marinetti, sea captain, was pregnant, and he instructed the girl to present herself at the house of the mayor ... in order to be examined by midwives and doctors', as the law required. As soon as the girl's father, who was in Bastia, 'was informed of the suspicions being spread against his daughter', he returned at once to the village, established that the suspicions were entirely unfounded and accused the *adjoint* of maliciously seeking 'to dishonour an honest woman and thus humiliate a family, which had always lived honourably and peacefully'. The active role of women themselves in this whole sphere is highlighted by a case in 1857, in which Giovanna-Francesca Felici from Murato sued Celidonia Ristorcelli and Maria Amedei for defamation. Witnesses testified that there was a rumour in the village that the Felici woman, who was unmarried, was engaged in a correspondence with Maria Amedei's husband and that meetings had taken place between them. The rumours had been spread in particular by Celidonia Ristorcelli, Maria Amedei's mother-in-law, who claimed to have some of the letters in question. It was said that 'all these suggestions have had a serious effect on the Felici woman and have caused her to lose part of the reputation for honour which she enjoyed in the village'. Giovanna-Francesca's mother intervened at some stage to defend her daughter's honour and hit Celidonia Ristorcelli with a stick.[72]

Conflicts arising from attacks on female honour may be divided into the following categories: those involving unmarried women, where dispute might be provoked by seduction and particularly by pregnancies that were not followed by marriage, by disagreements in marriage negotiations, and by abduction; and those involving married women. Cutting across these categories was rape, which we will discuss separately.

Young girls in Corsica were ideally brought up under strict supervision. According to Father Bartoli, 'the young girl ... grows up beside her mother, learning obedience and virtue. She meets no one but her relatives socially, and she is forbidden to be demonstrative, or to show herself off. She hardly dares, timidly, to greet a young man in the street; and, even then, he must be closely related to her.' In a lament for a 16-year-old girl from Zuani, her mother boasted that she was both beautiful and attractive, and modest and unassuming: 'The young men of the district / Burned like flames / In your presence / But they were respectful ... / In church everyone, / From first to last / Looked only at you, / But you looked at no one / And hardly was mass finished / Than you said: Mother, let's go ... You were so esteemed / So full of honour.' The sons and daughters of the Bastelica family studied by Bigot went in winter to the masked ball in Ajaccio but he comments: 'It is not necessary to point out that all these young people were carefully masked and costumed, because, if such indiscretions had been known about in the village, discredit would soon have fallen on the young girls. The wearing of a mask was sufficient there to allay suspicions; but, in the village, any girl who was known to have danced would have lost her reputation', and he added that dances never accompanied festivals in the village itself except at Carnival.[73]

Not all villages were as strict as Bastelica and our evidence suggests that a significant gap could exist between ideal and real behaviour in this sphere. Whatever the size of this gap, we may suppose that the strict ideal had the function of acting as a sanction against behaviour that was thought more or less likely to occur. Here Pomponi has suggested a connection between the concern for the honour of young girls and an early age at marriage. However, while apparently more common in earlier centuries, precocious marriages were definitely not the rule in the nineteenth century, and the concern seems better explained in terms of the need to maintain girls in a state of sexual quiescence until they were married in their early or mid-twenties.[74] It is significant here that local wedding customs, notably in the south, included washing rituals which emphasized the purity of the bride.[75] Also relevant is the fall in nuptiality rates during the course of the nineteenth century,[76] which presumably made controls stricter and the tensions within the situation being controlled greater. Pointing in the same direction is the late age at first marriage of men, which meant that their sexuality had to be repressed over an even longer period of their life-span than was the case for women. We have seen that sexual expression before and outside marriage was an element in the ideology of male honour, but in practice little outlet was provided for the sexuality of unmarried men. Liaisons with 'concubines' were possible, but, as we shall see, these were generally reserved for the well-to-do and for older men.

In these circumstances and given the nature of marriage making, which we will explore further below, it is not surprising to find that the seduction of young girls was both common and a matter of serious consequence. Often a girl's father or brothers or some other authoritative person would warn off unsuitable suitors and probable seducers at an early stage. Valéry relates that the parish priest of Speloncato, 'noticing the attentions paid to a girl by a young man, offered his mediation in order to obtain her hand; but, seeing that the youth was little disposed towards matrimony, the priest pulled a pistol from his pocket and declared that he would blow the youth's brains out if he saw him near the girl again'. Following a more common pattern, Giovan-Matteo Simoni of Sorio, 'having learned that Paolo-Giuseppo Padovani claimed to be courting one of his sisters, warned him [in 1852] to cease his assiduities', and Giovan-Domenico Salvadori of Castellare warned Bastiano Tomasi in 1858 to stop frequenting the house where his half-sister, aged 15–16, lived, since his visits were compromising the girl.[77]

Once a girl had been compromised or seduced, and particularly if she were pregnant, pressure was brought on the man and his family to agree to a marriage. This was a fairly common situation and 'rules of procedure' existed. In a lullaby from Palneca, sung by a grandmother to her grandson, she boasts: 'No woman of your kindred / Will pass thirty years / Without being married, / For anyone impertinent enough / To touch his hat at her / Will not survive the fortnight / Unless he puts on her the ring.'[78] This compulsion may be seen at work in detail in court cases. Sometimes the mere rumour that a seduction had occurred was sufficient to set this procedure in motion. In 1840, for example, 'at the time of the wheat hoeing', Cornelia Cartucci of Arbellara had gone down to the plain of Taravo with several other people, including Antono Rutilj. Although they claimed that they had not even spoken to each other, some children spread the story that there had been intimacy between the two. 'From that moment Cornelia believed not only that her honour had been compromised, but also that it was Rutilj's duty to marry her.' Her brother and her uncle concurred in this view and informed Rutilj accordingly. When he protested that he had had nothing to do with her as she well knew, she agreed but added that 'the fact is that because of you, no one else will marry me'. Rutilj maintained his refusal despite further threats and was eventually killed by Cornelia's brother.[79]

In this case an attempt was also made to marry the girl to another man, and this was a possible option more generally. For example, after Domenico Benedetti of Santa-Lucia-di-Mercurio had been killed in 1824, the public prosecutor reported that he 'had had embroilments with several families as a result of his philandering [but that] ... he had been reconciled with the relatives of the seduced women. The child born of the last affair had died; and the girl had been found a husband.' Such a solution was not always regarded as satisfactory, however. In a case in the Orezza region described by Marin-Muracciole, a member of the Bonifaci family seduced a girl in 1856 and refused to marry her. He left the village and she married another man, but this was not the end of the affair; for her nephew shot the original seducer dead thirty years later when he returned to the village.[80]

Sometimes men agreed or were forced to agree to marry women from whom they separated immediately afterwards once the formal demands of honour had been met. Cristoforo Ferrandi of Giglio, for example, married his cousin Maria-Imperatrice Orsini in 1801 'to cover her honour', having consorted with her over two years. The facts of the case are not entirely clear, but it seems that he was carried off by force by her relatives and married to the girl at Alesani, in another district; and, when he was later charged with killing his wife, he said that the marriage had never been consummated and that they had not even lived together. In 1852, Anton-Pasquino Quilichini of Poggio-di-Tallano married Maria-Antonietta Quilichini, with whom he had had earlier sexual relations. 'This civil marriage was contracted to repair the honour of the girl and was not followed by an ecclesiastical marriage or by cohabitation of the spouses.' Anton-Pasquino left the village a few days after the wedding and went to Ajaccio. A third example indicates that forced mariage was very much a *pis-aller* that might do little to resolve a conflict. After Simone Lucchini of Ciamannacce 'had relations' with Maria-Angela Santucci, he 'was forced to marry her'. To achieve this outcome, her brothers had threatened his father at gun-point, and as soon as the wedding had been celebrated she returned to her relatives. Hostility between the two families remained strong and Lucchini's brother was killed in an armed encounter between them at the end of 1881. Mention may be made here of an unusual case of forced marriage, in which a woman appears to have exploited the normal procedure in order to obtain a husband. According to Bertrand, a spinster aged 35 claimed to have been seduced by an adolescent and then enlisted the support of a well-known bandit to whom she was related to make the boy and his mother agree to a marriage.[81]

This introduces the element of calculation present in such matters, which is of more general relevance. Seduction like abduction could be a ploy used to pursue or to frustrate marriage strategies, or perhaps one should say marriage tactics. Where the latter was the case, relatives of seduced girls might put difficulties in the way of their marriage, particularly trying to hold back on payment of the dowry. Luisa Sebastiani was the designated heir of Angela-Santa Sebastiani and a niece of the marshal. While staying at Borgo with her sister, she contracted a relationship with the latter's brother-in-law Domenico Morati, son of the local justice of the peace. In 1839, she left the paternal home at Porta to live with Morati. She was at once threatened with disinheritance, and though her father, Bartolomeo, later agreed to a marriage 'to end the scandal', he refused to provide a dowry. The whole affair led to a breach between the two families, and when Bartolomeo Sebastiani was killed in 1841, Morati and his brother were prime suspects.[82] In a similar case, at a less elevated social level, Antonietta Napoleoni from Muro left home to live with Giacomo-Santo Mattei. He was 'a stranger', having lived in the village for only two years, 'and he was said to have a criminal record, so that the prospect of his marrying into the Napoleoni family was viewed with repulsion ... especially by Paolo-Giovanni', Antonietta's brother. 'However, their father Giovan-Battiste was disposed reluctantly to agree to a marriage, because he believed it to be necessary to his daughter's honour.' In March 1852, an interview took place between the Napoleoni and Mattei, but 'while they were arguing in a lively manner about the constitution of the dowry', a double explosion was heard, and it was discovered that Giovan-Battiste Napoleoni had been shot dead by Mattei, who had himself been fatally wounded by Paolo-Giovanni.[83]

Similar difficulties could be used by seducers to extricate themselves at the last moment from marriages to which they had agreed. At Poggio-di-San-Gavino, for example, Tomaso Tomasini had 'carried on intimate relations' for three years with Maria-Antonietta Filippi. 'Surprised one evening in her house by the girl's father, the young man did not hesitate to let him know that his intention was to marry her. The young people were of roughly equal social condition and thus suited each other admirably, and no serious reason could be invoked against their marrying.' The two families seemed agreed on this and the banns were published. However, some difficulty then arose over provision of the girl's dowry, and Tomasini used this as an excuse to back out. Maria-Antonietta's brother then attempted to kill the reluctant groom and was subsequently treated with extreme leniency by the Assize Court.[84]

Before following this pointer to what was seen as proper behaviour where a seduction was not mended by marriage, we must consider other circumstances in which an 'arrangement' was possible. First, there were cases where a close relationship between seducer and seduced precluded marriage and where, within a family, recourse to blood vengeance was inappropriate. This does not mean that violence did not also characterize some such cases. At Bisinchi, for example, Feliciano Vecchioni was rumoured 'to be carrying on illicit relations' with Cleonice Bernardi, his wife's sister, who lived with them. One evening in March 1846 her brother came to the Vecchioni house to fetch Cleonice away, hit his other sister when she tried to stop him and then fired a shot at Vecchioni himself. Secondly, where the woman was of definitely lower status than the man, maintenance might be a substitute for marriage and legal action a more appropriate response than violence in the event of non-cooperation. At Antisanti, Michele Giacobetti, who 'belonged to a wealthy family in the village' had a long-standing and open liaison with Beatrice Alessandri, 'who had no fortune in this world save the charms with which nature had endowed her'. When she gave birth to a son, however, Giacobetti broke off his relations with the girl at once, drove her off when she attempted to see him, and refused to enter into negotiations which she attempted to open via an uncle of his. It is not absolutely clear whether she was trying to force him to marry her or to provide for the child, which seems much more likely. Finally, in January 1858, she went again to his house with the baby dressed in its best clothes. Giacobetti was exasperated and attacked them both, mortally wounding the child by hitting its head against the stone door frame of the house. That maintenance was or ought to have been the issue here is suggested by another case in 1853, in which Ignazio Leca, the mayor of Lopigna, who had been educated at the University of Pisa, was killed by Antono Rutilj, a carpenter. Rutilj 'was angry with Leca, because he had impregnated his sister, although he was married' and had then refused 'to give her any help'. Here, the significant factor was less Leca's married status than the social distance between the two families, and it seems that 'concubine' status for the girl would have been tolerated by her family had material support been forthcoming. In a further case at Venzolasca in the same year, social distance seems to have been the factor which determined a less vigorous response than might otherwise have been expected. Paolo Giafferi had frequented the house of a branch of the Petrignani family and had made 'dishonourable propositions' to Caterina Petrignani, aged 16, which she had rejected. He then found her one day weaving alone in a workroom and seduced or raped her. He told her to keep quiet about the incident, promising to marry her. She kept silent for a while, but when people in the village began to gossip, confessed to her father, who brought a charge of rape against Giafferi. The class differential was more clearly present in a case at Santa-Lucia-di-Moriani. Benedetta Nobili, aged 17, from Bastia, who 'belonged to the class of day labourers', had 'been placed by her parents with an uncle' in Santa-Lucia, in order to help him in his wineshop. Bastiano Marcangeli, an ex-gendarme and a married man, was a customer and saw the girl regularly. One day in the summer of 1861, he found her alone and had sexual relations with her and soon afterwards persuaded her to go away with him. He promised to find her a job in a shop in Bastia or to marry her to a friend of his in Algeria. After a week or so, she realized that she had been duped and returned to her mother, who then laid a charge of rape and abduction against Marcangeli.[85]

We now turn to the broader category of cases where affronts to female honour and seduction in particular were met by deliberate violence. First, abortion or infanticide might be resorted to where an unmarried girl became pregnant. We have established elsewhere that the incidence of infanticide in Corsica was greater than in France as a whole, that it was most prevalent in the south where the code of honour was most firmly adhered to, and that families were frequently involved in the crime.[86] When the corpse of a baby was discovered at Antisanti in 1812, a woman told the child's supposed grandmother, who inquired what it was: 'It is your daughter's honour and your own!'[87]

According to Marin-Muracciole, it had been the custom for the relatives of a dishonoured girl to retrieve the family's position by killing her. Feydel explained in 1799 that this was only done when the girl would not divulge the name of her seducer or lover.[88] Whatever the force of such a custom in the past, it was no longer operative in the nineteenth century. We have discovered only one case of a dishonoured girl being killed by her relatives. This was at Peri in 1851, and the circumstances were unusual. Maria Pinzuti had had sexual relations with a married friend of the family, Martino Tavera, and had given birth to triplets which had died. This caused a rift between the two families, which was healed when Tavera promised never to see the girl again. However, the two subsequently went off together and were then both killed at a place in the country by Maria's three brothers. There are also cases of seducers killing or trying to kill girls. Paolo-Matteo Cremona of Erbajolo was sentenced to death for such a crime in 1810, for example. He had had a liaison with Anna-Maria Natalini, who became pregnant. One night in December 1808, he went to her family house secretly and persuaded her to get up and go with him. He told her that 'he was going to take her to the house of one of his relatives', a traditional step in an elopement as we shall see, but instead, he took her into the country, strangled her and threw her body into the river Tavignano. It was more common, however, for families to dissociate themselves from dishonoured girls, most obviously by turning them out. For example, Fiordispina Padovani of Ota was found to be pregnant in 1845. Though she revealed the name of her seducer, 'her family was outraged and expelled her from the house'.[89]

These kinds of outcome were of course most likely where the man was already married, as the Peri case demonstrates. This category overlaps with that in which a man became involved with two women, since one of these was usually regarded or regarded herself as the fiancée. For example, at Serra-di-Scopamène in 1819, Giulio Susini was reported to have seduced Angela-Maria Susini, and 'then, contrary to his engagement, he took into his house another woman, Giulia Pietri, from Sorbollano'. Soon after, 'the relatives of the first woman, numbering about 200, went *en masse* to the seducer's house, and tried to break in the door with stones'. This crowd was dispersed and the Pietri woman was taken back to her village, but the subprefect feared 'troublesome consequences, for one of the women must remain dishonoured'. Another case illustrates what such consequences might be, though the choice of victim was not typical. Giovan-Carlo Pietrini of Pietricaggio

lived at Alando and was about to marry the daughter of a certain Defendini, with whom he lodged. Then, an objection to this marriage was raised by a widow, whom he had abandoned in his own village leaving her pregnant. The parish priest, who had initially been in favour of the marriage [with the Defendini girl], now urged them secretly to break it off.

Pietrini later attacked and seriously wounded the priest.[90]

It is probably significant that one or other of the partners in these cases was an outsider. Within villages people would have known each other's affairs too well to allow for much deception or confusion. Where cases of dual involvement did occur, the room for manoeuvre was correspondingly smaller and the consequences more serious. One option, to which we have already referred, was for the seducer and his family to treat the first of two liaisons as inferior. In 1840, Flaubert noted a case in which the daughter of a military doctor had been seduced and had had a child. The father of the child recognized it but refused to marry the girl. Indeed, he declared 'that he was soon going to marry someone else' and poured further ridicule in public on the family of 'his mistress', which prompted her brother to kill him 'to avenge the honour of her name'.[91] The pattern of seducing one girl on promise of marriage and then marrying another who represented a better match, particularly in the eyes of the man's family, was sufficiently common (and problematic), moreover, to figure in folk-tales. In 'The Ghost of the Fiancée', collected at Zoza in 1882, a girl in the first category dies of grief when her 'fiancé' goes through with a marriage to another woman, arranged by his father, but her ghost then comes into the couple's marriage bed one night and claims her 'husband'.[92]

In some cases prolonged confusion and conflict might ensue. At Figari, for example, Matteo Maisetti 'had lived for a long time' with Maddalena Cucchi, by whom he had had a son, Santo, in 1832. He then 'had intimate relations with Eugenia Susini, who became pregnant'. Her brothers, including Francesco, 'demanded the prompt reparation of the outrage done to the honour of their family' and Maisetti agreed to marry Eugenia. But this, in turn, annoyed the Cucchi, who saw the Susini being preferred to themselves and thus casting the dishonour on to them. As Maisetti was going to the mayor's house to be married, shots were fired at him and, suspecting the Susini, he refused to go through with the ceremony. It seems, however, that the shots had actually been fired by the Cucchi. Later, in 1841, an attack was made on Francesco Susini and he accused Maisetti, who was charged with the offence. Before the trial, however, Maisetti made his peace with the Susini and married Eugenia. Despite this, the Susini and the Cucchi agreed together to testify against Maisetti, and he was sentenced as a result in 1842 to eight years' hard labour. He served only part of this sentence and returned to Figari in 1847 or 1848. Out of pride, it seems, and because they regarded the match as a misalliance, the Susini refused to allow Eugenia to go to live with Maisetti, though they later claimed that he had been unwilling to have her. So either out of inclination or habit (there is some evidence that he had continued to see her), or, as a further trial report has it 'in order to appease the anger of the Cucchi', Maisetti returned to live with Maddalena. This decided the Susini to take decisive action against him, and Francesco Susini, who had become a bandit, killed Matteo Maisetti in July 1848 and his son Santo a few months later.[93]

More often, inability or refusal to marry a dishonoured girl led to a swift and a violent response, and many examples may be cited throughout the nineteenth century. At Conca in December 1892, Maria-Angela Masconi, who was unmarried, gave birth to a stillborn child and claimed that she had been made pregnant by Severino Susini, 'who had abused her by force one day in the country'. Susini denied this and 'refused to marry the girl'. She and her father then 'publicly declared their intention of killing him' and kept a close watch on his movements. Three months later, Susini had to go to Ghisonaccia on the plain to collect the body of a relative, which had been sent from Bastia for burial. In the procession back to the village, he rode in a closed vehicle for protection, but a halt was made on the way and this gave an opportunity to Maria-Angela who was lying in wait and she shot and wounded him as he got out.[94]

This last case is of interest since the girl avenged herself against her seducer, albeit with the aid and encouragement of her father. This course of action was not all that uncommon. After Fiordispina Padovani had been expelled from the family house at Ota, for example, she attempted to persuade her lover to marry her. When this failed, she shot him in July 1845 as he was sitting on a square watching a game of cards and he died a month later. It seems that women killed their lovers in such circumstances more readily later in the nineteenth century, and we will return to the topic in discussing the role played by women in feuds generally. We may, however, cite one further case here, which emphasizes the departure from the normal code of honour that such behaviour could represent. Around 1840, Andrea Giovannoni, the schoolteacher at Castineta, became the lover of Maria-Luisa Paoli. When her brothers learned of this, they told Giovannoni that he must marry the girl or leave the village and he chose the latter course. But this did not satisfy Maria-Luisa, who kept trying to see him and, when he would not agree, decided to kill him. She ambushed him and fired a pistol at him, but missed. Her brothers then felt doubly dishonoured and insisted on a marriage.[95]

More generally, it was often assumed as a matter of course that acts of violence could be attributed to this cause in the absence of other obvious reasons. After Anton-Francesco Giabicconi of Santa-Lucia-di-Moriani was killed in 1801, for example, 'the crime was at first imputed to Paolo-Domenico, the son of Patricio the miller, because Giabicconi had abused his sister'.[96] As Father Galletti noted, too, the seduction and abandonment of girls was always a common cause of 'enmities'.[97] The affair at Castineta led to a feud between the two families. The feud between the Tomasi and the Giacomi at Gavignano in the 1840s originated in the seduction of a girl in 1815, while that which decimated the Lanfranchi and the Desanti at Aullène was set off in 1847 when Petro-Paolo Desanti was killed by Lilla Lanfranchi 'whom he had seduced but refused to marry'.[98]

Much of what we have said here concerning spinsters applies also where widows were compromised. For example, 'the widow Mariana Costa, née Susini, claimed to have had such intimate relations with Andrea Malerba of Bonifacio that her honour would have suffered unless it could have been rehabilitated in the eyes of the community by marriage. Seeing that Malerba was not about to accord her this reparation voluntarily, she asked her close relatives to intervene', but he ignored both their solicitations and then their threats. Finally, in January 1852, Malerba was shot and fatally wounded by Salvatore Susini, the widow's first cousin, acting as the chosen agent of her relatives as a whole. They 'were unable to countenance Malerba's failure to marry her, since it cast dishonour on them all'. Purely formal marriages were also entered into with widows. In a case in 1838, Paolo Giacomi of Olmeto had sexual relations with a 50-year-old widow with three children. Her relatives demanded that he marry her civilly 'to repair her compromised honour', which he did, but they then refused to allow the couple to live together, a situation which we have encountered before. Here the reason was clear: 'Giacomi was poor and lazy ... and the widow had a small estate which her family' and children did not wish him to gain control of.[99] Cases may also be cited in which widows demanding marriage were killed by their lovers to get them out of the way,[100] and in which widows themselves took revenge against the men who had dishonoured them.[101]

III

Our discussion so far points to the crucial importance of marriage in relation to female and family honour, and further analysis will confirm that marriage-making in Corsica followed a 'conflict model' and can be seen as another form of competition for resources among family groups. Marriage policy had an offensive side where the weapons were seduction and abduction carried out by young males and a defensive one where brides were carefully protected and marriages negotiated by older people.

Many writers on Corsica have stressed how important marriage was as a means by which families sought to extend their power and influence or at least to maintain their standing. The wealth of prospective 'allies' was a determining factor here but attention was also paid to numbers. 'The larger a family is, the better its chances in a vendetta,' a military doctor from Calvi explained in 1822. 'So marriages with families that are rich in male children are much sought after.'[102] The moral and physical qualities of individuals might also be taken into account, though these would be difficult to separate from the honour of the group to which they belonged. Giuseppo Antonmarchi of Ampriani, who later achieved notoriety as a bandit under the name of Gallochio, attracted attention in his youth as a hard worker and as a result was apparently offered the daughter of a family much richer than his own.[103] Some autonomy in courtship was allowed to young men, as we have noted, but this was generally limited by a framework in which marriages for both sexes were arranged. 'My boy, you are of the age to marry; you are thirty, and it would perhaps not be prudent to wait any longer,' a father tells his son in a folk-tale. 'I have chosen you a rich and beautiful woman ... I want you to marry her.'[104] Abeau referred here to the agency of family councils but less formal procedures appear to have been more common.[105] A range of sanctions existed to enforce desirable and to prevent undesirable matches, of which the most important was the provision or the withholding of the dowry.[106] We will return to this and other aspects of marriage and affinal relations in the next chapter, concentrating here on the many kinds of dispute which could arise in connection with making a marriage.

Arranged marriages usually require intermediaries of some kind, at least in the early stages of negotiation.[107] Priests sometimes fulfilled this function, but more often it seems to have been carried out by mutual relatives and neighbours. This is illustrated by a case in 1842, in which a self-appointed marriage broker proved to be a wolf in sheep's clothing. Giovan-Tomaso Marinetti, a native of Biguglia, was a customs official in Bastia. He proposed to an acquaintance of his, a shoemaker called Godefroy,

> that he marry young Elisabetta Poggi from his village, to whom he claimed to be related. Godefroy went with him to Biguglia, therefore, but the parents of the girl refused the good offices of Marinetti and the husband that he offered them. Marinetti was not put off by this, however, and proposed another husband to Elisabetta, who told him to mind his own business.

Marinetti's real motives in the affair were revealed when he tried to rape the girl shortly afterwards.[108]

Marriage negotiations were frequently protracted and difficult. 'Don't call him husband until the ring is on your finger,' a proverb warned.[109] Disagreements over particular marriage proposals might divide relatives, set one family against another and engender conflict between parents and children. Giovan-Girolamo Lucchini of Giuncheto was convicted in 1821, for example, of wounding his sister-in-law after she had interfered in his plans for the marriage of his son. Again, at Cervione, in 1848, a marriage between Luigi and Angela-Caterina Canari had been agreed to by his relatives and by her father, but her brother Simone objected to the match. One day in September, as Luigi was helping Angela-Caterina and her sister to thresh haricot beans, Simone came up, picked a quarrel with him and then shot him dead a few hours later.[110]

Turning to the second category, disagreement over two projected marriages was an element in the rivalry between the two doctors from San-Gavino-d'Ampugnani, Risticoni and Micheli, in the early 1820s. Dr Risticoni had quarrelled with Ottavio Agostini, who was later accused of killing him, because the latter had opposed the marriage of one of his female relatives to a Poli, which Risticoni favoured. Another man accused of complicity in the crime was a certain Cruciani, who claimed to have been on good terms with Risticoni but on bad terms with Micheli, 'since it was he who upset a marriage which I wanted for my son with the daughter of Bastiano Petrignani of Venzolasca'.[111] Similar rivalries were present among the notables of Sari-d'Orcino at the middle of the century. We learn that 'several families had viewed with displeasure and some envy the [proposed] marriage between the son of Signore Giovanni Peretti ... and the daughter of the notary Padovani'. Some went so far as to try to prevent the marriage from being concluded by using threats and intimidation against both parties.

Direct conflict between rival suitors was also fairly common. In a case at an unspecified village in 1847, one youth shot and killed another after a quarrel over 'a serenade made to some girls', such serenades being an important feature of the beginning of courtship. Rivalry became more intense, of course, at a later stage. A schoolteacher, Giovan-Francesco Alessandri, for example, aspired to the hand of Maddalena Dari of Moncale, an heiress to whom he was giving private lessons. She had been engaged at the age of 13 to marry Nicolaio Vincentelli, but this engagement had been broken off earlier. Nevertheless, when Vincentelli was shot in August 1847, Alessandri was suspected of having instigated the crime. These were preventive measures, but revenge could also follow the conclusion of a marriage. Marin-Muracciole writes that in earlier centuries cases of disappointed suitors killing or trying to kill their successful rivals were numerous and a frequent source of vendettas, and she suggests that some women preferred not to marry, if their parents opposed their first choice, for this reason.[112] The phenomenon was still found fairly frequently in the nineteenth century, which must have been a further reason for caution in marriage negotiations. 'Having unsuccessfully sought the hand of Antonietta Gazrelli in marriage,' we learn, 'Santo Poggi [of Olmo] ... had vowed an implacable hatred against Agostino Agostini, his rival who had married the girl.' After a first attempt on Agostini's life, a peace was made between their respective families, but Poggi failed to abide by it, ambushing and trying to kill Agostini again in 1839. Similar vengeance was taken at Pietracorbara in 1847, though it did not involve killing. A barn full of forage belonging to Francesco Dominici was destroyed by fire one night and Giuseppo Giuliani was immediately accused. It was believed 'that he wanted to seek revenge for the marriage which Dominici's son had contracted with a girl whose hand he himself coveted'. Cases may also be cited in which disappointed suitors took revenge against the girls who had rejected them in favour of someone else.[113]

Although family control over marriage was strict, conflict between parents and children in this area was not uncommon, a paradox which we will attempt to explain in a broader context below. At Scolca, Felice-Antono Perfetti was in love with the daughter of Petro Mattei, and although she was favourable to the young man's advances, her father was not. One day in January 1849, Mattei found the two together, reproached Perfetti and pushed him to the ground. Whereupon, Perfetti ran to fetch a weapon and shot Mattei, who died later of his wounds.[114] The same conflict is expressed in a well-known lament. Padua-Maria reproaches the mother of the young man whom she loved for preventing their marriage, and the mother tries in vain to make amends.[115] We shall see in the next chapter that some young people similarly thwarted were driven to suicide.

Occasionally something is known of the reasons for parental opposition to particular matches or to marriage in general. When Giulio Negroni of Ampriani, who was then aged about 30, asked his mother's permission to marry a woman from Orezza in the 1820s, she refused telling him that he should wait until he had avenged the death of his brother. At Piobbeta in the mid-1850s, Francesco-Andrea Muzi, aged 19, tried to kill his mother when she opposed his courtship of a girl 'whose social condition was inferior to his'. Again, in a case in 1859, we learn that 'having been left a widow with three children, Maria-Rosa Ridolfi [of Ville-di-Paraso] could hardly make ends meet. Her eldest son Vincenzo, who could have helped her, was thinking of getting married, which led to frequent quarrels and arguments in the family.'[116] The sons of widows were clearly expected to assume their fathers' role, supporting their mothers rather than taking wives.

We have referred to the use of third parties in marriage negotiations, a practice which had the effect of avoiding any direct rebuff which could be damaging to a family's honour. Where the young people did make direct contact, other formalities fulfilled the same function. At Asco, 'when a young man wants to declare his love to a girl, he speaks to her in enigmatic formulae'. If she was agreeable, she answered in kind; if not, she talked about something else. Similarly at betrothals in the south, the girl signified her assent by sitting down when asked by the young man's father if she wanted him as her husband, while the young man indicated his agreement by standing up. In some villages, the young man serenaded the girl with a violin or a guitar, and if she opened her window, this meant that she was favourable to his suit, while if she kept it closed she was not interested.[117] The need for such ritual precautions becomes clear when we consider the possible consequences of refusing offers of marriage. We have seen that the feud at Santa-Lucia-di-Tallano revived in 1839 when various marriage proposals made by the Giacomoni and their allies were rejected by the Poli, while the feuding at Arbellara entered a new phase at about the same time for the same reason. Our sources provide many other similar examples. For instance, in a case in 1857, Angelo-Luigi Orsini of Pietricaggio testified that 'the Castelli family was angry with ours because my half-brother Bernardini had refused to marry Giuditta Castelli. Some days after this refusal, we received through the post an anonymous letter abusing both by brother and myself, which we believed to be the work of the Castelli.' Orsini protested; then insults were exchanged; and finally Orsini and his brother fired shots at a Castelli youth and at the Castelli house. Again, Vincenzo-Luigi Valentini of Isolaccio 'had solicited the hand' of Ursula Pietri, and 'on being refused, he determined to attaint her honour in order to prevent her from finding another husband'. So one day in August 1864, he raped the girl as she was watering chestnut plants, telling her: 'I am doing this to injure your father and your mother.' In another case, 'disharmony' between the Ficoni and the Decori of Perelli-d'Alesani was attributed to the fact that 'Andrea Ficoni had demanded the hand of one of the Decori girls and had had his demand repulsed.' His brother Damiano had then asked for one of her sisters but had also been refused, which prompted him to kill her brother in 1877.[118]

Father Bartoli expressly noted that

> it is not the young man in Corsica who asks first for the hand of a girl in marriage; for, if he were refused, he would be the butt of ridicule among his comrades; and no other girl of his condition would afterwards consent to marry him. She would believe herself to be humiliated if she took a man whom another had refused. It is thus the father of the girl who makes the first move, addressing himself to a close relative of the young man.[119]

Though this rule does not seem to have been universally applicable, it does seem likely that in many cases where a man and his family met with a direct rebuff they were doing something out of the ordinary and were probably trying to obtain a match that was better than they could reasonably expect. This was always a temptation, if it was not positively encouraged by a competitive system which set so high a store on a girl's honour. As we have seen in discussing seduction, girls and their families could exploit the concern for honour in order to force marriages on men, but more often the pressure was applied by and the advantage lay with the latter. The most common way of trying to force the odds here was abduction, although this was also a recognized means of overcoming the opposition of parents to marriages that were socially feasible. In other words, it overlapped with a kind of elopement.[120] But before discussing these practices in detail, something must be said about wedding ritual and what constituted a marriage in Corsica.

Until well into the modern period, customary marriage or what Count Vincenti described in 1909 as 'antique marriage by *preemptio* without any official religious ritual' remained the rule, despite the opposition of both the Church and the secular authorities. Saint-Germain wrote that, in Corsican eyes, 'it is only mutual consent which binds spouses'. This consent of both the couple and their families was expressed and concluded in a ceremony of betrothal, known as the *abraccio*. Following this, he noted with special reference to Bastelica, 'the families embrace each other, fire pistols in the air and dance on the square, while the bride starts at once to live with the groom'. Most such weddings 'took place during the winter and were only given formal religious sanction at the festival of Our Lady in mid-August', by which time nearly all 'the young women were pregnant'. In 1891, Vuillier described the *abraccio* in a little more detail.

> One evening (usually in winter), the nearest relatives of the girl go to fetch the young man and bring him to their house. The young people kiss each other and sit down side by side, while the members of the two families share a repast of cake and wine, as they arrange the conditions of the marriage contract. The young man seldom returns home that night ... It is an admitted custom, for the *abraccio* binds the betrothed to each other, and the subsequent civil contract and religious ceremony merely ratify the engagement ... It is nothing unusual for the bride at that time to have just had or to be about to have her first child.

Bigot, again, confirms that 'many local people regard the civil and the religious ceremonies as formalities of no great importance, that have to be gone through because the authorities require it'. What made a marriage, in effect, was espousal followed almost at once by copulation and cohabitation.[121]

The unpublished sources confirm these accounts. In a case in 1802, for example, Anna-Felice Stefani of Linguizetta explained how she came to remarry three months after the death of her first husband: 'since she was unable to provide the basic necessities of life for herself through her dowry or her own efforts, her parents had given her Giacomo Santucci as a husband, with whom she celebrated marriage by sleeping in his bed'. In December 1855, Maria-Antonietta Casile of Valle-di-Mezzana, a young widow, 'accepted the proposal of marriage made to her by Nicolaio Leca' and the couple 'at once began to live together as man and wife', which, according to witnesses, was 'the customary way of proceeding in the district'. Similarly, 'having demanded the hand of Grizziola Giovanangeli ... and this demand having been accepted by her parents in August 1861, Giovan-Domenico Giovanangeli of Granace lost no time in taking her into his house and living conjugally with her'; a wedding ceremony followed in December.[122] More generally, a report of the inspector of foundlings noted in 1850 that four-fifths of 'unmarried mothers' in Corsica had only one 'illegitimate' child and that by far the greater proportion of 'illegitimate' children were kept by their mothers rather than being abandoned into public care.[123] In a society in which female honour was so important this clearly reflects the widespread practice of customary marriage and the consequent frequency of pregnancies that were only prenuptial in official eyes, but it also probably testifies to some relaxation of the system of local controls under external pressure, which parallels the general weakening of the whole system of blood vengeance to which we have referred.

We turn now to abduction, which had always been extremely common in Corsica[124] and remained so through the nineteenth century. Three categories may be distinguished here: elopement or feigned abduction with the girl's consent in order to overcome parental opposition or accelerate a marriage; abduction against the consent of the girl and in order to force a marriage; and abduction against the consent of the girl without a plan to marry her.

According to Marin-Muracciole, the first category was the one most commonly found, and it was almost a complement to the system of arranged marriages. Parents who refused to allow their daughter to marry after her flight with her lover – a symbolic insult to her family which only marriage could repair – would be strongly disapproved of in the village or district. Publicity was essential to this kind of abduction in order to force a marriage. Witnesses and accomplices were needed; those of the young man arranged the transportation and often accompanied the couple; those of the girl simply saw her off and returned to the village to spread the news, but they were a guarantee of the man's good faith. When opposition to the marriage came from the girl's parents, the man often took her to his parents' house, and they then sent word to her parents to indicate that she was safe and asking when the marriage could take place. No sexual intercourse occurred, but once one of the man's relatives had kissed the girl, marriage became obligatory if her honour were not to suffer. If opposition came from the man's parents, he took the girl to other relatives of his or to the priest's house and negotiations were carried on via these intermediaries. Lorenzi de Bradi noted that elopements took place at night.[125]

Elopements proper, where there was parental opposition to overcome, are distinguishable in theory but not always in practice from normal customary marriages. An elopement or abduction might be acted out where a marriage had been agreed, and 'abduction' of the bride by the groom was reported to be usual at Ciamannacce, in the Evisa region and elsewhere as late as the 1920s.[126] Moreover, ritual abduction or mock combat between the parties of the bride and of the groom was an element of wedding ritual in many parts of the island, especially where the bride was an outsider.[127] We should also mention other recognized ways in which a young couple could overcome or bypass parental opposition. One of these was the marriage *alla greca*. Here the man declared that he was taking the woman to be his wife during Sunday mass, at the elevation, and she concurred. Despite its name, this was probably a popular derivation from and tribute to the post-Tridentine clerical ceremony.[128] It was also possible for couples to take advantage of the relaxed atmosphere of Carnival to make a public demonstration of their love and thus force a marriage on their parents.[129]

There are a number of cases of elopement or feigned abduction in our sources. Marcorio Farinacci of Sollacaro, for example, brought a suit against Paolo and Carlo Galloni for abducting his daughters Rosa and Maria-Giuseppina in 1805. The authorities opposed their prosecution, however, since the girls had told the officials who questioned them 'that they had left home of their own free will to go with the Galloni brothers, to whom they were very attached'. The girls were clearly quite young, since it was agreed that their marriages should be postponed and that they should be kept in a boarding-school in Bastia until the brothers returned from military duties in Italy.[130] In a case in 1842, a Casabianca girl from Vallecalle, under 16 years of age, 'was in love with Luigi Pruneta. Her parents, who were much better off than his, opposed the match' and had indeed accepted a proposal from another suitor. 'This prompted the girl to leave the paternal house one day to join Pruneta,' who had actually tried to dissuade her. In a more complicated case at Campile in 1848, opposition to a match came from the man's parents. A Pasqualini girl was seized by Petro-Paolo Mariotti, aged 22, and another youth, as she was returning from a vine in the country. The girl was taken into the maquis, where Mariotti had sexual intercourse with her with or without her consent. On the third day, she was returned to her parents and 'Mariotti put himself at their disposition and protested his love for her and his intention to repair the damage done to her reputation and honour by marrying her. Her parents then forgave him and allowed him to spend the night in their house, and a wedding seemed imminent.' The girl was not allowed to live in Mariotti's family house, however, and a prosecution was soon launched against him for abduction. The consequent proceedings revealed that the couple had been openly courting for some time and that his parents were unhappy about this. Mariotti claimed further in his defence 'that the abduction was a device agreed to and planned between him and the girl in order to force his parents to agree to their marriage', and she and her mother lent this story some support. Again, Paolo-Francesco Angelini of Loreto had had 'intimate relations' with Maria-Vincenza Turini for two years, but her parents still refused to allow him to marry her. He therefore told her 'that there was only one way of forcing their hand and that was for her to leave her parents' house and go away with him'. The girl agreed, and one day in December 1850 she went with him to the house of one of his relatives. 'Since the couple lacked all means of subsistence, the girl's mother, after two days, allowed them to come to take their meals in her house and even gave Angelini a waistcoat and a jacket', a reminder of the economic difficulties in the way of going against parental wishes in this way. After one further attempt at obstruction, presumably by the girl's father, a wedding took place in 1851.

A case at Alata in 1852 illustrates how abduction could be used to bring a marriage forward. Octavio Casalonga, aged 25, 'had been passionately in love for some time' with Marta Casalonga and had asked for her hand in marriage. Her parents had not rejected his proposal but had told him to wait, so he decided 'to act by abduction'. With two relatives, he waylaid the girl one day as she was returning from Ajaccio with her sister. Both girls were taken, first to a herdsman's hut and then to an inn, and they were never separated. On the same night, their father arrived at the inn to fetch them and a marriage was celebrated soon after, 'freely and with the consent of all parties'. It is also significant that abductors in the second two categories frequently claimed that the girl had been consenting in order to mitigate their offences when they were prosecuted. Such pleas would have been very implausible had elopement not been customary.[131]

The existence and importance of elopement and feigned abduction emphasizes the community dimension of marriage in Corsican villages. Competition among families was intense but it took place within a framework which set limits to that competition. This dimension is also illustrated by the fact that all members of the community participated in weddings as guests,[132] and by the custom of mounting charivaris in cases of remarriage, which we will discuss in Chapter 6.

The second category of abduction is the one which figures most prominently in the judicial records, and it is perhaps the most interesting. As Marin-Muracciole has noted, a man's social status in Corsica could be determined by that of his wife if her family were of a more elevated status than his. This gave extra licence and encouragement to abduction, and both together cut across the prevailing 'patriarchalism'.[133] However, this should be seen less as the makings of an alternative system than as a corollary of that patriarchalism. It will be noted that abducted girls were often sole heiresses, who thus fulfilled male roles in the inheritance system. Abduction may also be seen as an institution reflecting 'democratic' and community values in the face of the trend towards some social stratification, since it asserted that any match was possible, provided that the would-be groom was prepared to be bold and to take certain very real risks. An expression of male violence could triumph over the best protected female honour.

Thus in many cases the girl was clearly of higher status than her abductor, who was trying to obtain a marriage over the odds. For example, Girolama Silvani, aged 16 or 17, was abducted in 1841 by Giulio-Antono Marochelli, aided by two relatives. She belonged to one of the richest and most influential families of the canton, while he was a herdsman and an orphan. He had previously made various demands for her hand but had been refused. Again, in 1843, Angeluccia Ceccaldi, just 16 and belonging to one of the wealthiest families of Marignana, was seized by the brothers Tancredo and Domenico-Antono Massoni, ordinary 'cultivators'. They took her to a hut in the country, but her noisy protests convinced them they would never persuade her to marry either of them, so she was released the same evening.[134] It is significant here that well over half the cases of this kind of abduction in the records involved girls of 17 or under, who were probably particularly desirable and sought-after matches. This pattern is also reflected in a well-known lament collected by Viale. A girl from a rich family of Penta-di-Casinca was abducted by a poor man from Pruno-d'Ampugnani, and she married him and went to live with him there. Her parents refused to see her again and she was reduced to poverty. Her mother and sister arranged a rendezvous long afterwards, but 'her husband did not allow her / To go ... / Because she did not have a suitable dress'.[135] In a case at Peri in 1882, the usual age differential between abductor and abducted was reversed but the social distance was the same. Maddalena Rossi was an only child and thus 'destined to inherit some property', and there was some competition for her hand. One of her suitors, Paolo-Giuseppo Rossi, who was ten years her junior, sought to force the issue by abducting her with the help of two relatives, but she was rescued and married someone else.[136]

A significant proportion of abductions with a view to marriage seem to have involved principals who were closely related. This is probably to be explained by the fact that cousins would be in a privileged position to know about the prospects of heiresses and would also have special opportunities to seize them. Angelica-Maria Ottavi of Fontanaccia, for example, was twice abducted, in 1841 and 1842, by her cousin Natale Ferroloni. He claimed that her father had promised her to him in marriage, but the report of his subsequent trial concluded that 'he had only been after her fortune' and that the Ottavi had always been hostile to his intentions.[137] Again, Giuseppo-Maria Pasqualini from Saliceto

> wanted to marry Maria-Giovanna Aloisi, aged 17, his first cousin. This girl, of impeccable behaviour and agreeable appearance, owned a small amount of property, which made her richer than Pasqualini and a very advantageous match for him. Afraid, no doubt, that he might be rebuffed if he made his intentions clear in the normal manner, he conceived the criminal project of forcing his young relative to become his wife.

He tricked her into going with him on the road to Bastia one evening in December 1855, and then abducted and raped her. But there are also indications that cousin marriage was preferred precisely where girls were heiresses. Widow Giuseppelli of Peri had promised her daughter Maria, aged nearly 14, to her cousin Santo Pinzuti. But another cousin, Matteo Pinzuti, alleged a prior claim and abducted the girl in September 1841. She was taken to a house belonging to 'mutual relatives in order to force her mother to agree to give her in marriage to Matteo', but this pressure proved of no avail.[138] In another case in 1830 we are provided with a little more detail. Antono Cesari, a substantial landowner from Santa-Lucia-di-Tallano, was accused by the girl's mother, a widow, and her uncle, of having abducted the 16-year-old Anna-Maria Ortoli of Olmiccia, an only child and an heiress. According to witnesses, 'several close relatives of the girl and of Cesari [who were first cousins] had planned that they should marry', and only her mother and the uncle were against the idea. Cesari may have abducted the girl in order to overcome this opposition, but it is also possible that the charge against him was fabricated.[139]

By the nature of the evidence, most of the abductions which we have considered here did not succeed, but their comparative frequency, taken together with the strenuous efforts made to mend seductions by marriage, suggests that abduction was certainly believed to be a way of obtaining valuable brides and that it must have been actually successful to a significant extent in order to sustain this belief. Abduction was also dangerous and one of the great 'sources of private enmities'.[140] We have seen that the abduction of a Franceschi girl in 1831 lay at the origin of the feud at Frasseto between her family and the Antona. That between the Nicolai and the Antonmarchi of Tox 'dated back to 1822, when two Nicolai brothers ... abducted at gunpoint the young Ferri girl, a relative of the Antonmarchi'. Natale and Francesco Cucchi of Carbini 'forcibly abducted' the

15-year-old Rosina Nicolai in 1847, but their hopes that one of them might marry her were frustrated when 'her first cousins, the Giuseppi, tracked them down and managed to free her'. A long 'enmity' between the two families then ensued. The two Cucchi became notorious bandits, and they were eventually captured in 1853 with the help of the Giuseppi.[141]

Before we leave the topic of forced marriage, we should mention the custom known as the *attacar*. Here a man publicly laid claim to a girl by touching or kissing her or by removing her head-dress, which dishonoured her and, in theory, made a marriage imperative, unless her relatives decided instead to kill the man. It was again a means of overcoming parental resistance to a proposed marriage or of obtaining a bride of superior status.[142] The custom was still extant in the south in the early nineteenth century. In July 1824, for example, a dispute occurred at Santa-Lucia-di-Tallano between Luca-Luigi Giacomoni, a youth of about 19, and the wife of Alessandro Quilichini, an ex-mayor. She had gone out early one evening with her daughter, aged 17, to see the new drinking fountain that was being built. Giacomoni saw them and came up 'and touched the young lady's elbow'. This provoked an exchange of verbal insults, and the girl's older brother threatened Giacomoni with a dagger. A further case involved a more obvious ritual element. In October 1828 it was reported that Giacomo-Santo Peroni of Mela had tried to violate Maria-Rosalinda Peroni on the high road near the village:

> The aggressor left his prey when some passers-by arrived, but he took away the kerchief which covered the girl's head. By the custom of the country, this is not theft but a pledge of love, a declaration of a wish to marry the girl concerned, and a warning to anyone else who might dare to seek her hand until the kerchief is returned.[143]

The third category of abduction leads us beyond marriage and will only be briefly discussed here. Our sources do not always make the intentions of abductors clear, but it is fair to assume that most cases where no intention to marry the girl was raised in mitigation by the defence do indeed fall into our third category. Such cases were always rarer than those in the other two categories. Abduction of this kind was frequently perpetrated by bandits,[144] and, like seduction, it could of course lead to a man's being forced into marriage, as a case at Prato in 1859 illustrates. Ermonino Nasica, aged 25, abducted Maria-Francesca Acquaviva in July of that year and a wedding quickly followed, but this was not the desired outcome on either side. The girl did not leave her father's house and, though Nasica joined her there for about a month, he then left or was expelled. According to the Acquaviva, he wished 'to end at any price a marriage which he had only consented to in order to avoid prosecution', and he later attempted to kill his wife. Also to be placed in this category are abductions of married women and abductions to prevent marriage, both comparatively rare.[145]

We turn now to other kinds of conflict relating to marriage making. If refusal of a marriage offer could impugn the honour of the demanding party, breaking off an engagement was even more serious, especially if the dowry had been constituted and the trousseau assembled. In a letter written in 1764, Paoli had described it 'as the grossest insult that can be imagined',[146] and this remained true in the following century. Faure wrote that a broken engagement was one of the four circumstances in which a vendetta might be declared. Were a family not to respond in this way, it 'would become the butt of ridicule throughout the entire district; no woman would want its men; no man would want its women; men would spit in the face of its members and children would make signs with their fingers at them in public places'.[147] Such considerations prompted some well-known feuds. The elopement of Luigia Rosola with Gallochio in 1820 followed rumours that her parents were about to break off their engagement in favour of a better match. His father wished to declare a vendetta straightaway, but in the event this was done only after the girl had returned to her family. The feud between the Giovannoni and the Paoli at Castineta originated in a broken promise to marry a Paoli girl in the early 1840s. At Carbini, according to Faure, Rosina Nicolai's father had at first engaged her to marry Natale Cucchi against her will and had then broken off this engagement, which led to her abduction and the further conflict which we have mentioned. Many other violent conflicts may also be attributed to the same cause. At Campile in 1840, for example, a certain Cagnetto, who had given up the priesthood in order to marry, killed his would-be bride's mother, a rival suitor's father and a third person, when he learned that the mother was about to go back on an engagement made with him publicly. At Arbellara, again, intimate relations had existed for some time between a certain Mariani and the sister of Luciano Cartucci. When the girl became pregnant, Mariani agreed to marry her, espousals took place and the amount of the dowry was settled, but Mariani then refused to go ahead with a wedding. This annoyed Cartucci, who mortally wounded Mariani in an encounter in 1840. Cartucci was later prosecuted but received only a light sentence for 'excusable homicide'. This last case in which the rupture was initiated by the fiancé is perhaps essentially no different from other cases, which we have discussed under the heading of seduction. It is not clear from the sources how far an important distinction was made here depending on which side initiated the rupture, though obviously in one case a man's honour was directly affected and in the other a woman's. Borel-Léandri refers to a ritual in which fiancé and fiancée together ended their engagement by breaking a piece of stick, but this could only have occurred in the rare circumstances where both agreed to the rupture.[148]

IV

Conflict involving the honour of married women seems to have been much less common than that involving the unmarried. The behaviour of wives like that of young girls was strictly controlled. Married women were not meant to meet men other than their husbands and close relatives and certainly not to be alone in their company.[149] Affronts to wives met generally with the same kind of response as those to unmarried daughters or sisters. At Levie in 1852, for example, the wife of Francesco Canarelli told him that Giacomo-Alfonso Peretti had made propositions to her, which provoked a fight between the two men in which Canarelli was shot in the hand. It is significant that Canarelli himself was not prosecuted, although he instigated the quarrel. Some cases do suggest, however, that the honour of wives was less vulnerable and might even be a matter for joking. At San-Gavino, Anton-Michele Beretti had just got married in 1859 and Francesco Pietri congratulated him on his young wife. Beretti thereupon suggested that they exchange wives, and Pietri agreed, thinking that he was being funny. But the same evening, while Pietri was out, Beretti went to his house and tried to get into bed with his wife. She raised the alarm, and he fled taking two handkerchiefs and an apron as trophies. Next day he called to apologize for what he claimed was a prank, but the Pietri were not amused and brought a charge of attempted rape against Beretti.[150]

Outright or presumed adultery by a wife was usually a killing matter. The man from Silvareccio who killed his wife in 1832 when he found her in the house with another man was sentenced only to a fine of ten francs, an indication that his action was believed to be justified. Giudici Giudicelli, a miller from Porta, was convicted in 1852 of killing his wife in similar circumstances and was sentenced to five years' imprisonment, still a fairly lenient sentence. He claimed to have found her *in flagrante delicto*, but there was a previous history of disputes and separations of which the court took account. Erring wives were usually less severely treated and revenge was reserved for their lovers. At Ocana in 1863, for example, Anton-Napoleone Muselli 'conceived serious doubts about the fidelity of his wife' and he suspected a distant cousin, Giusepp'-Antono Muselli, with whom he was already on bad terms, and whose house she frequently visited to collect provisions stored there. Returning home unexpectedly one evening, he found the door of his own house locked and his wife hesitated to open it. He realized that there was a man in the house, who escaped without being seen. Anton-Napoleone at once evicted his wife and six months later he killed Giusepp'-Antono. He also received a comparatively light sentence.[151]

Sometimes husbands reacted less strongly, which led Saint-Germain to assert that adultery by a married woman in Corsica did not dishonour her husband.[152] As a categorical statement this is obviously misleading, but it does point to the fact that adultery reflected as much if not more on the wife's blood relatives as on her husband, and that relations between a married woman and a man of higher status than the husband might perforce be tolerated. Here, however, the wife's relatives might be less tolerant than the cuckolded husband and might even direct their anger at him. Angelina Battistelli of Bastelica was married to Angiolello Pittinelli, 'but she often left his house to go to live in that of Sgio Folacci', a local notable. Her husband appears to have raised no objection to this arrangement but Angelina's brother Salvatore told Pittinelli 'that he would make him pay for not living with his sister' and made other threats in the 1840s to kill him. If lack of adequate response on the part of husbands could bring about the intervention of the wife's relatives in this way, the two parties could also act in concert, and this would surely have been more usual. At Ciamannacce, for example, Ciccarella Susini was 'carrying on adulterous relations with Natale Aliotti'. This 'scandal' seems to have been ended when proceedings were brought against Aliotti in the lower courts, but he was nevertheless killed some time later in 1856. According to the account of their subsequent trial, his wife's adultery had aroused 'the desire for revenge in the soul of her outraged husband', and her brother, Cesareo Santucci, had also 'felt the greatest resentment at

Aliotti's affront to the name and honour of his family'. The killing had been planned by these two, in complicity with Ciccarella herself, who had turned against the lover who had abandoned her.[153]

Relations on either side – usually brothers – might also intervene where husbands were unable to do so. Maria-Caterina Agostini of San-Giuliano had been married to a certain Poggi against her inclination. When he left Corsica to do his military service, she returned to live with her family. She then became involved with Angelo-Maria Cesarini, a close friend of the Agostini, and became pregnant. This angered her brother Giovan-Battiste, who made threats against both of them but agreed not to harm them if they left the village and if Cesarini brought up the child. Cesarini was later ambushed and killed, however, in 1840, and it seems that Giovan-Battiste was responsible. The obligation of a brother to avenge a sister's honour overrode promises made to a friend. In a case at Lecci, Maria-Antonietta Marchi lived with Bastiano Guidicelli and became pregnant, while her husband Paolo was serving a five-year prison sentence for homicide. Paolo's brother Paolo-Matteo reported this to the gendarmerie in 1894 'in case, he said, there should be incidents in the family in the future', and when the child was born he announced that he had decided 'to avenge the honour of his brother'. Soon afterwards, Guidicelli was ambushed and wounded in the arm; Paolo-Matteo Marchi, though not recognized as his assailant, went into hiding; and the latter's wife boasted in the village that 'he had kept his word'.[154]

V

The distinction between rape and abduction made in our sources was to some extent a false one by local standards, and we have already mentioned some cases of rape under former headings. However, our discussion of female honour should include this topic for a number of reasons. It is important in the sources, a fact which conforms with the local view that men would attempt to have sexual relations with any woman if they were not prevented by strict controls and sanctions. The circumstances of rape, moreover, suggest a connection between the great importance attached to the notion of female honour as a sanction here, and the economic or social requirement that women work in situations which made them vulnerable, something that will be discussed further in Chapter 8.

There was a category of rape that may be seen as a kind of abduction, though it only became so after the event when an offer of marriage was made by the offender threatened with reprisals and/or prosecution. In some cases, the charge might then be reduced to one of sexual assault. For example, Anton-Martino Spinosa was accused of the attempted rape of Giacinta Sabrini, aged 19, as she was gathering chestnuts near Ota in October 1848. She fought him off, although he had a knife. The jury was told that 'the accused had made marriage proposals to the father of the victim', which apparently persuaded it to convict on the lesser charge. Again, in 1864, two young men from Saliceto, Ignazio and Francesco Pasqualini, made a concerted attack on two girls, both under 15, as they were gathering firewood 'in the maquis at some distance from the village'. One was actually raped by Francesco, while Ignazio only attempted unsuccessfully to rape the other, Maria-Ursula. The relatives of the first girl proposed that Francesco marry her but he refused, and though he was acquitted of rape he was sentenced to three years for sexual assault with violence. By contrast, Ignazio 'had hurried to ask for the hand of Maria-Ursula in order to repair the outrage which she had suffered, and a civil wedding had been celebrated the day before his case came up for trial'. In these circumstances, he was acquitted of any charge.[155]

Though there was a large degree of variation here, this type of rape case may be broadly contrasted with that in which marriage was certainly not intended and where it rarely intervened. This is clearly so where the woman or the man was already married. One evening in August 1857, for example, Maria Buttavi of Venzolasca ran out of her house 'in a state of complete nudity' and went to find her husband who was busy carrying grain to a neighbouring house. She told him and the neighbours that she had been in bed with her child, waiting for her husband, when Lorenzo Ciosi had entered her room with another man and had tried to rape her. Ciosi was prosecuted and sentenced to four years in prison. Giovan-Battiste Rustini of Ota was prosecuted in 1864 on three similar charges. Two of his victims were 'honest' married women in their forties, the mothers of several children, and all came from Ota.[156]

Much more characteristic of this category was the situation where the parties came from different communities and where the men were outsiders: bandits, herdsmen or foreigners. In July 1850, for example, Cajus and Annibal Pietri of Guagno and the bandit Don Giovan-Battiste Lanfranchi arrived one night at the hut in which a family of herdsmen, the Mallaroni, lived near Serra. They demanded food and then forced two of the women to go with them by threatening a child. One of the women was raped. Again, in November 1852, Maria Paoli of Salice was travelling towards Bastelica with her young brother and another relative. Towards nightfall they stopped at a house on the territory of Sarrola and asked if they could rest there. After a while three men, whom they took to be bandits, arrived. After drinking, two of them began to touch and fondle Maria and she decided to leave, despite the fact that it was still dark. The two men followed her, however, and one of them raped her along the way, while the other kept her relatives at bay with his rifle. Among cases of rape involving foreign men we may cite the examples of an Italian day-labourer convicted of attacking a 45-year-old married woman at Luri in 1842, or of Lorenzo Mazzochi, a miller of Tuscan origin, convicted in 1853 of raping a girl who brought barley to his mill. Relevant also here is a case in 1865, in which a 30-year-old Piedmontese was convicted of trying to rape the young daughter of the English manager of the Bastia gas works. News of the crime, according to the trial summary, caused 'terror in the local population ... and everyone was agreed that suspicion could not possibly have fallen on a native Corsican'. The rape of children was a sub-category here, and a number of cases may be cited where the victims were well short of puberty. Felice-Antono Massoni, aged 29, of Cervione, for example, forced his way into a flour mill near Valle in 1855, while the miller and his wife were away, and raped their eight-year-old daughter, who had been left there with her young brother. The crime made 'a very great impression in the district', and Massoni's severe sentence of twenty years' hard labour was intended to reassure people and especially parents who had to leave children in similar circumstances.[157]

As this emphasizes, a certain type of rape occurred beyond the margins of normal society, and here victims like offenders were frequently of unusual status, being often orphans or illegitimate. Maria-Felicita Calassi, aged 21, of Poggio-d'Oletta, an orphan, testified that Ignazio-Stefano Poggi, aged 30, had entered her room one night in 1862 and had had sexual intercourse with her without her consent. The trial summary suggested that she may have been more 'sympathetic' towards Poggi than she later suggested but that she put a hostile construction on the facts 'to avenge herself on Poggi for having subsequently abandoned her', or because she became convinced that he would never agree 'to marry a woman who had no resources at all and who was obliged to supply her needs by doing day-work'. There is the implication here that an accusation of rape (or seduction) could be the female equivalent of abduction, the means by which a poor girl might obtain a better match or a match *tout court*. This ploy was explicitly present in a case in 1859, in which a 31-year-old spinster from Venzolasca accused a man of raping her, a claim that a medical examination failed to substantiate.[158] The Poggio case also points to the 'class' and family elements in the system centred on female honour. Girls or women without close relatives were more likely targets, because offences against them were less likely to meet with reprisals, but they also had less honour in the first place. Such women, too, were poorer and would be engaged in menial work, which exposed them more to sexual attack. A category familiar in other European societies, too, was that of the male employer sexually exploiting his female employee or servant.[159] For example, Pierangelo Giabiconi, a married man of Santa-Lucia-di-Moriani, hired Teresa Chiaramonti in 1854 to gather chestnuts for him. She was a poor orphan who 'had no property at all, and she was obliged to earn her living by hiring herself out to different people, usually to do field work'. Giabiconi made a sexual assault on her after she had rejected his advances.

This aspect is present in a rare case of collective rape at Petreto-Bicchisano in 1893, which also illustrates the cumulative element in the process of dishonouring. The victim was Maria-Francesca Carcopino, aged 19, who had had sexual relations successively with two Italian workers, both of whom had abandoned her, one while she was pregnant. She had a reputation for 'irregular morals' therefore when she arrived in Petreto to work as a servant in an inn and, on the day after her arrival, four local youths dragged her from the inn kitchen and raped her in a nearby field. The fact that they were all acquitted suggests a degree of approval of their behaviour in the local community.[160] It has been suggested in another context that such practices were perhaps inherent in traditional European societies which regulated legitimate sexual behaviour very strictly and maintained a late age at marriage, and thus had to allow an outlet to unmarried youths who were often organized into gangs. Collective rape here, moreover, was an avenue to prostitution for the victims.[161] This pattern fits nineteenth-century rural Corsica to only a limited extent, but it does remind us again of the existence there of latent male sexuality and of its cultural translation into notions of male honour which set high value on violence and aggression both generally and in the sexual sphere. Very few Corsican women ever became prostitutes – Bournet notes that in 1886 only 3 out of the 32 registered women in Ajaccio and Bastia were natives – but it was said later that for dishonoured village girls the urban brothel was about the only recourse.[162]

The class differential related to notions of honour is also reflected in the existence of concubinage, to which we have referred. Robiquet wrote in 1835 that 'concubinage is quite common in the interior of the island. Married men live publicly with women who take the place of their legitimate wives', and he noted that the prefect had issued a circular to mayors in 1818 asking them to take steps to end this 'scandal'.[163] This at once points to an ambiguity in the sources. It is sometimes difficult to tell whether the distinction made generally or in particular cases between wives and concubines follows local attitudes or simply reflects the outlook of the French authorities or other outsiders. Evidence in a case from Isolaccio in 1849, for example, suggests that a woman referred to as a 'concubine' was in fact a common-law wife. Francesca Marchetti worked with Giovan-Giacomo Bianchini in his garden near the village; she tried to warn him of an attack about to be made on him by a certain Raffali; and, most significantly, her family were active in the prosecution of Raffali after Bianchini had been killed by him.[164] Similarly, the target of the 1818 prefectoral circular like that of the Catholic missionaries of the late 1830s, who were also anxious 'to regularize liaisons',[165] was surely the practice of customary marriage and not concubinage in the biblical sense.

On the other hand, there is no doubt that some so-called concubines – and the word was used locally – were mistresses or even akin to prostitutes. For example, Lucia Ucciani, who was kept by Anton-Pasquino Ortoli of Poggio-di-Tallano, came from Ajaccio and was reported in 1862 to be 'a woman of bad reputation who lived in an isolated house'. She was fourteen years older than Ortoli and there is some suggestion that she also procured the services of her 17-year-old daughter for Ortoli and others. In a famous lament for two cousins collected by Viale, a singer asserts that women belonging to the family of their enemies were once the 'concubines' of the deceased and entertained them in the evenings. That this was not simply a convenient insult – which would itself be significant – is indicated by an unusual case of attempted abduction at Moca-Croce in 1829. Anton-Matteo Istria and two other men, who proved to be the girl's brother and her first cousin, went armed to the house of Luchinessa Cesari 'in order to force her to leave and go to the house of Anton-Matteo to live there as his concubine, since he was married to another woman but separated from her'. This apparent attempt by a brother and a cousin to give a woman to another man as his mistress was repeated a little later.[166]

There are, of course, strong analogies with marriage in this last case, but concubinage in the local sense implied social distance between a man of superior and a woman of inferior status and could not, in normal circumstances, be a step towards marriage. It could, however, be regarded as an acceptable complement to or substitute for marriage. Chapman related in 1908 that the landlady of an inn in the Niolo was warmly embraced by a youth who was travelling with him. 'I innocently inquired if she were a relative. "No", he replied, "not exactly a relative, but she had a child by my father". Obviously this constituted a tie which was regarded with equanimity by his family.' A lament for a wealthy man from Levie referred without embarrassment to his mistresses, at least one of whom attended the funeral. As we have seen, Antono Canarelli lived with a cousin of the Cucchi of Carbini for many years and they had four children together, and he only ran into trouble with her relatives when he seduced another female relative of theirs. In another case, we learn that Anna-Maria Saturni from Levie 'lived for fourteen or fifteen years in concubinage with Giovan-Agostino Nicolai', with whom she had four children. Although Nicolai was legally married to another woman, Anna-Maria was known after his death as the widow Nicolai.[167] It was not unknown, moreover, for a wife and a concubine to live under the same roof. Robiquet refers to this practice early in the century in the Fiumorbo, and Marcaggi and others mention specific later examples. In one instance, at Piana, Marcaggi explains that the wife consented to such an arrangement because she herself was barren, but it is clear that this was not a necessary condition.[168]

Concubines, like second wives in polygamous societies, could also, however, be the objects of extreme hostility. Legitimate wives could take action against their rivals, like Clelia Peloni who killed her husband's concubine at Levie in 1850. Or legitimate offspring might take action against women whose role cast a slur on their mothers and who threatened their interests. According to Robiquet, the bandit Giovan-Andrea Gambini's first crime was to kill his father's concubine. At Porto-Vecchio, Petro Orsini had lived for some years with a concubine, Angela-Maria Filippi, although he had a wife and legitimate children. One of these, a boy aged 16 or 17, having been reprimanded by Filippi for having taken wine and flour from the cellar, heated a pointed stake at the fire and drove it into her chest as she lay ill in bed. Here we may also cite a case at Vignale in the early 1830s, in which the legitimate relatives directed their hostility against the man. Paolo-Francesco Bonnetti had separated from his wife with whom he had had no children. His brother Michele therefore expected to inherit his property, to make sure of which he had persuaded Paolo-Francesco to make a will in his favour in 1833. Paolo-Francesco, however, had had a liaison with another woman by whom he had two illegitimate daughters. When he began to show some affection for these, even planning to have them live with him, Michele and his son became alarmed, and, when Paolo-Francesco was found dead soon afterwards, they were accused and convicted of the crime.[169]

This is very similar to conflicts arising from remarriage and leads us back to the real ambiguity in the status of the concubine. Confusion was probably most marked where social distance was small, but given the egalitarian thrust of notions of honour which was present alongside their class aspect, there was always a danger, from the point of view of a man and his family, that a bold woman (or her kin) might seek to convert concubinage into marriage. This appears to have happened at Prato in the late 1840s, where, according to the local justice of the peace, Biaggino Nasica at first seemed to be 'indifferent to the fact that his daughter had gone to live in concubinage with the mayor'. Once a child had been born, however, and playing probably on a general hostility to the mayor in the village, Nasica later persuaded him to agree to a marriage.[170] The birth of a child had the same significance in other cases, where men reacted in a negative way, entirely repudiating their erstwhile mistresses in order to prevent any matrimonial claims made by them. This was the case with Michele Giacobetti of Antisanti, as we have seen. Infanticide or abortion was another possible tactic here. Angelo-Maria Coscioli, the son of the mayor of Sant' Andrea-di-Tallano, had had 'illicit relations' for some time with an older woman, Clorinda Comiti, who became pregnant in 1856. Then 'a rumour developed in the district that the young man wished to conceal the fruits of his turpitude at any price and that he had made his mistress agree to destroy the child which she was carrying by means of an abortion brought about by taking potions and by being bled'. In all these cases, the social distance between the parties was considerable.

The general ambiguity was indicated in other ways. Relatives might avenge the deaths of concubines as if they had been wives. For example, Paolo-Francesco Fieschi, officer of health and assistant justice of the peace at Petreto-Bicchisano instigated proceedings against Francesco Istria in 1845 for having killed his father's concubine. Similarly, when Giovanni Grimaldi of Ota killed Anton-Giovanni Ambrosini in 1850, vengeance was taken against his brother by Serafino Battini, 'who had entertained illicit relations for many years with the victim's daughter'. Battini was acting here like a dutiful son-in-law. We may also cite cases in which men did eventually marry women who had been their concubines. Antono Corteggiani, a master mason from Corte, for example, had a long-term relationship with two women, his wife who had no children, and a woman married to another man, who did bear Corteggiani a daughter and whom he subsequently married after their two spouses had died.[171]

Our discussion of both customary marriage and concubinage indicates that different levels of marriage were practised locally. Alongside customary marriage, both civil and religious marriage had been introduced from outside, the latter having gained most ground, at least in rural areas. In the case at Linguizetta in 1802, Anna-Felice Stefani testified that 'she had never gone through a civil marriage [with her second husband], this not being the custom in the district'. In 1844, the parish priest of Moncale was fined 'for having celebrated a religious marriage before the civil ceremony had taken place'. It is clear that an example was made of him by the authorities in an attempt to make some inroad against the ingrained local custom of ignoring the civil ceremony altogether. Elsewhere, however, there is evidence that civil marriage was used as a kind of 'second-class' affair, often where a match was required for reasons of honour. A lieutenant aged 52 from the garrison at Sartène 'had expressed his interest in a girl aged about 20, who was attached to the household of Signore Abbati, a merchant in the town, and had even proposed to marry her in front of a priest'. Her parents indicated, however, 'that a marriage could only take place at the town hall ... and he was asked to stop visiting the Abbati house'. It is not clear here whether the lieutenant turned down an inferior offer or whether the parents were signalling that the girl was already espoused. Saint-Germain refers to a case where the existence of two types of official marriage was ingeniously exploited to find a way out of what we have seen to be a virtual impasse. A young man had seduced and made pregnant two girls. He married one civilly and the other in church, and, while the first was recognized officially as his wife, he lived with the other.[172] All of this suggests that a spectrum of types of marriage, some imposed from outside, was adapted to fit the combined requirements of stratification and honour.

Some writers have implied that the honourable reputation of Corsican women was something of a myth,[173] and reference to promiscuity is even made in folk-tales and in some factual reporting. The women of Coggia, for example, were said to have abandoned the strict rules which applied in the village when they went down to the coast to work the land.[174] We have, of course, produced abundant evidence, too, of sexual behaviour that broke the rules. The important point in the present context is that the rules were strict on the assumption that behaviour would otherwise be unrestrained and that they provided largely external sanctions. Comiti noted in 1933 that the virtue of Corsican women 'appears to be founded not on an internal discipline but on an external constraint', and this is typical of a more general reliance on external sanctions and group control which is manifested in the system of blood vengeance and in other ways, for example the charivari. According to Father Galletti in 1863, dishonoured girls might be set backwards astride an ass, paraded around the village to the accompaniment of horn-blowing, whistles and banging on pots and pans, and then driven out of the community, and actual cases of such treatment may be cited, for instance at Sartène in 1829.[175] The emphasis laid on female honour in effect was a not always successful means of controlling and protecting women in an environment where they were required to work outside the home and the village, as we have suggested, and where instinct and notions of male honour made them vulnerable. The general notion of honour may be seen perhaps as a currency in an economy of scarcity, which was used to measure the standing of families at one remove from the exercise of sheer force. Both men and women were resources in this economy, but honour was related to them in contrasting ways, focusing for men on violence and for women on marriage. Families were in competition throughout and the view of each vis-à-vis female honour in particular was thus duplex, though common adherence to general values may be supposed to have had some effect. Men upheld the chastity of their own women but this was a reason for it to be attacked by other men.[176] At every stage conflict could break out, and conflict does not simply provide an insight into how the social system worked, though it does that; it was inherent in it at the 'moral' as well as the material level.

] 5 [

Conflict and its causes:
intrafamilial conflict

Although it takes different forms in different societies and is present at varying levels of intensity, intrafamilial conflict is a universal human phenomenon.[1] It is natural both to love and to hate one's closest associates. The social significance of such conflict in simpler societies is increased by the fact that 'family relationships carry an economic load', in Davis' words,[2] and are not mainly or exclusively affective. Feuding societies are no exception. Indeed, there, as elsewhere, intra-familial conflict should be seen as an inescapable complement to kin solidarity. Gluckman quotes a Lozi proverb, which aptly makes this point: 'He who kills me, who will it be but my kinsman; he who succours me, who will it be but my kinsman?'[3]

Emphasis on kin solidarity in the feud has to some extent obscured this. Studies of other societies with systems of blood vengeance have noted that killing within the family or kindred is anomalous. It cannot be avenged in the normal way; it causes an 'impasse' or 'confusion' in relationships; and, therefore, it may either be quickly forgotten, as though it had never happened, or it may be regarded as a religious wrong, a sin, requiring or automatically inviting special retribution and attended for this reason by extraordinary purifying ritual.[4] Killing relatives, or indeed fighting with them, was regarded as extremely reprehensible in Corsica. The mayor of Santa-Lucia-di-Tallano, who was called to stop a fight between two women in 1812, testified that, 'knowing how they were related, I let them know how wrong it was for them to be fighting and treating each other in such an indecent manner'.[5] When Giuseppo Franceschini of Bastel-ica was killed by the bandit Gasparini in 1824, a local man commented: 'What is most surprising is that the unfortunate victim was a first cousin of this monster's wife.'[6] Again, a peace treaty signed at Serra in 1835 referred to 'the perfect harmony which should reign among kith and kin'.[7]

But, at the same time, killings or attempted killings among close relatives were not at all uncommon.[8] Moreover, vengeance killing and feuding also took place among relatives.[9] At Pila-Canale in 1797, Giusepp'-Antono Colonna and Petro Poli killed Antono Bozzi, 'their close friend and relative',[10] which was not the only example of such behaviour in the feuding there. In 1836, at Frasseto, the Antona killed Angelo-Francesco Franceschini and his son Pasquale. Angelo-Francesco had pleaded with them for the life of Pasquale, 'reminding them that he was their first cousin and that the same blood flowed in their veins', but his plea was without effect.[11] The feud at Marignana in the 1840s originated in a killing between cousins and was intensified by further intrafamilial killings carried out by the bandit Massoni in 1848. Faure refers to another feud among relatives around 1850 at Vignalella, in which the protagonists lamented their victims. Again, one of the last feuds in Corsica, at Balogna around the turn of the century, occurred between the Poli and the Leca, who were related within the second and third degrees Roman style.[12]

This suggests that the distinction between killing relatives and non-relatives was less sharply drawn in Corsica than in some feuding societies and that Corsicans were perhaps less sensitive to illogicalities in the blood vengeance system than say Albanians or Somali, all of which probably reflects the fact that feuding took place within villages which were largely endogamous units. This does not mean that feuding was not mainly conducted against those who were not close relatives, nor that kin solidarity was not essential to feuding, a point which we will discuss in Chapter 7. There is some indication, moreover, from the examples which we have cited and from the comments of observers that feuds among close relatives were peculiarly bitter and bloody,[13] which suggests that they did run counter to the system and that the normal controls and pacifying machinery could not easily be brought to bear on them. Given the generally high incidence of intrafamilial conflict, which was directly related to the structure of the family and the economy, it can also be argued that one of the functions of feuding in Corsica and of the kin solidarity which it required and occasioned was precisely to contain and to limit that conflict.[14] These issues will become clearer if we examine intrafamilial conflict and its context more closely, looking first at specific relationships – between fathers and sons, mothers and sons, brothers, cousins and so on – some of which were much more fraught with contention than others.

I

The force of paternal authority in Corsica was very great.[15] Adult sons, whether married or unmarried, frequently continued to live in their father's house,[16] and our sources indicate again and again that fathers and sons worked together in a family unit and defended their interests in common. Moreover, the obligation on sons to avenge fathers was particularly strong, and a proverb warned: 'Don't touch a father who has a son.'[17] This means that conflict between fathers and sons was rare and highly disapproved of. A case at Oletta in 1843 illustrates some of these points. Fighting began there when Giovan-Battiste Gervasoni tried to recover an ass which his father had lent to his son-in-law Antono Bastiani. Felice Venturini, a man of 46, and an uncle by marriage of Gervasoni, took his side in the quarrel. As stones were being thrown and blows exchanged, Luigi Venturini, 'the father of Felice, a respected and worthy old man', intervened 'to prevent further trouble. He ruled that his son and grandson were in the wrong and to end the conflict seized the ass's halter in one hand and his nephew Bastiani's collar in the other and led them both away.' However, a shot was then fired which killed the old man. The culprit was his son Felice, who had been aiming at Bastiani. When Felice appeared next day 'on the square where his father's corpse was displayed, surrounded by weeping relatives, all the women pushed him away ... as a parricide'. He approached the body, however, and addressed it, saying: 'O father, the shot was not meant for you!' We may also cite a case in 1853 in which a man from Bocognano 'had at an early age earned the nickname Tombababu [or Hits-His-Father], because it was known that he had hit and even stabbed his father with a dagger'.

Where such conflict did occur, it was usually related to matters of material interest and the use of family resources. For example, Dono Quilici of Olmiccia and his son Paolo-Francesco quarrelled in 1859 over the use of some manure, which the father wished to sell or exchange but which the son wished to put on the family garden. Dono, who actually lived apart from his wife and children, attacked his son with a stick, and a fight ensued in which Paolo-Francesco's maternal grandfather intervened on his side and in which Dono Quilici was injured. Here both the previous estrangement and the involvement of the mother's father are clearly significant. In a similar case in 1862, 'material interests had for some time divided' Giovanni Orsini of Calenzana and his father. Their dispute had come before the justice of the peace, who, seeing 'the ill temper of the father and the lack of respect of the son, had advised them to live apart'. One day in November, the father found 'two goats belonging to his son in a field sown with wheat'. As he was chasing them off, his son arrived, knocked his father to the ground and kicked him in the face. The four-year prison sentence, which Giovanni received for this otherwise comparatively minor offence, indicates again how much importance was attached to paternal authority.[18] This could only be legitimately questioned, let alone attacked, in extraordinary circumstances, and particularly where the family patrimony was threatened. Such seems to have been the case in 1823 at Sartène, where a disturbance occurred when Dr Antono Pietri tried to prevent his father, clearly a habitual gambler who had already lost large sums of money, from continuing to play cards.[19] We may also detect here signs of the tensions inherent in a situation in which sons remained dependent on their fathers until the latter died,[20] and which have been remarked on in other societies.[21] This important latent conflict is also reflected in proverbs warning fathers against yielding to the demands of impatient heirs: 'The father who gives up his property will be thrown out of doors'; or: 'To your heirs, say: "Hold on", and give them nothing.'[22]

Ties between mothers and sons were also close but they were primarily affectionate. In a well-known lament, the bandit Tramoni addresses his 'dear mother', for example.[23] Before Petro-Maria Giovanelli from an unspecified village set off to be executed in Bastia in 1833, he wrote to his mother.[24] A certain Graziani of Sant'Andrea-d'Orcino, who was stabbed to death in 1864, was on his way to Sari to fetch 'some leeches for his sick mother'. Sons also defended the honour of their mothers and avenged or sought to avenge fairly minor affronts against them. At Ciamannacce, Antono Lucchini's widowed mother was hit in a fight over the use of the communal oven in 1821 by Luciano Gabrielli. As soon as he heard of this, Lucchini returned to the village and shot Gabrielli dead. It is fair to add here that Gabrielli had killed Lucchini's father some thirty years earlier.

But filial obligations to father and mother did not always run together, and we may cite a significant number of cases in which sons protected or defended their mothers against their fathers. Giulio-Antono Angelini of Corte was accustomed to beat his wife, who was nearly blind, if his food was not at once available when he came in. Their son protested about this behaviour to his father and threatened to call in the police, which prompted a fight between father and son in 1861, in which the son was mortally wounded.[25] Pierrina Carlotti of Isolaccio had been convicted of killing the child of her husband's mistress, and her son, a Republican Guard in Paris, took her part against his father. He explained in a petition for clemency on her behalf in 1883 that she had been 'insulted, mistreated and beaten by my father, who then abandoned her to attach himself to a shameless woman'.[26] Mothers also demonstrated their attachment to their sons, most obviously in those laments for the dead in which the words 'mother's darling' or 'mother's dear' are endlessly repeated.[27] But maternal affection also took more material forms. Paola-Caterina Nicolai of Tox, for example, was shot and mortally wounded in 1831, as she was acting as a scout for her bandit son.

Although most stress is rightly laid on the affective nature of the tie between them, mothers could also exercise authority over sons. We have already encountered the conflict to which this could lead in the area of marriage but disagreement might also arise in other ways. In 1863, for example, Giovan-Camillo Pietrapiana of Peri was accused of having kicked his mother and knocked her down, when she came to fetch him at a wineshop where he was playing cards. This suggests resentment by a young man at being treated like a child in front of other men. Cases of conflict were most common where mothers were widows and where sons had assumed or were trying to assume control of the family economy or where they neglected their responsibility to support mother and siblings, categories that are not always distinguishable. At Pruno in 1852, 'family interests had led to arguments between the widow Mariani and her son Giacomo-Antono, a shoemaker. He was already married and did not live with his mother, and he only handed over to her and her other children, his co-heirs, a very small amount from their common income.' When she tried to stop him removing a quantity of hay from her house, he hit her with a stick. In a similar case at Oletta in the same year, Petro-Antono Romanacce, aged 19, was the eldest of 'three children in the care of a widowed mother. Instead of helping his family, he dissipated its resources by taking provisions from the house and even by selling livestock.' His mother reprimanded him and, when she caught him taking a cheese from a cellar, a fight developed between them in which she was injured. In the first two cases where convictions were brought, severe penalties demonstrated how far such behaviour departed from the ideal.[28]

Relations between mothers and daughters were also expected to be close, and laments again reflect affection on both sides.[29] Daughters were supposed to be dutiful and obedient too, an ideal expressed in topographical legends which attributed the origin of particular rock formations to the petrification of selfish or disobedient girls through the agency of maternal curses.[30] Mothers played a leading role in arranging the marriages of their daughters and lent them aid and protection after they had left home. Just occasionally such tutelage could lead to conflict. The mother of Elisabetta Mariani of Muro, for example, frequently criticized her daughter for her profligate life-style. Elisabetta was unmarried but had had three children and had been convicted in 1860 of exposing one of them. In a fight between mother and daughter in 1864, which caused a 'scandal' in the village, the older woman was injured and a successful prosecution followed. Another extreme case points to a further area of possible conflict: the requirement to provide for aged parents. 'The widow Graziani [of San-Martino-di-Lota] had been abandoned by the children of her first marriage but had lived for some years with a daughter of her second, Maria-Francesca.' Both women were of 'irritable temperament' and there were thus frequent quarrels between them. These were provoked particularly by 'the fact that the daughter refused to give her mother enough to eat and demanded work of her that [in her seventies] she was too old to perform.' One winter day in 1854, Maria-Francesca told her mother to go out to gather bedding for the animals and, when she refused, hit her with a stick breaking her arm. The mother received no medical attention, and unable to bear the pain, threw herself from a cliff. Her death 'caused considerable indignation' in the village.[31]

Parental authority was strict and open conflict between parents and children was therefore rare. It is significant here that the tensions latent in the relationship were sometimes passively resolved via suicide. Laura Alfonsi, aged 18, of Sartène, poisoned herself with arsenic in 1819 after her mother had 'reprimanded' and beaten her;[32] Maddalena Galloni of Olmeto seems to have killed herself in 1825 'to put an end to the pestering of her family'; while Antono Nicolaj, an 18-year-old herdsman from Foce, shot himself in 1826, because 'his parents reproached him with the marriage which he proposed to make'.[33] This was probably the commonest reason for such suicides, which were most prevalent among young people. By contrast, conflict was more frequently found among family members whose relationship was not so obviously hierarchical.

Solidarity among brothers was an important positive value in Corsica and was a crucial element in feuding. Brothers worked together and, by extension, they defended family interests in common. Armed conflict between sets of brothers was therefore characteristic. In 1822, the Nicolai brothers of Tox carried out an abduction together; 'in 1828, they killed the two Valeri brothers and in 1830 the two Ferri brothers'. Again, a general conflict between the inhabitants of Taglio and of Isolaccio in 1840 developed from a quarrel between the Dari brothers from the one and the Marchetti brothers from the other village.[34] We shall see too that bandits frequently operated in fraternal pairs. Another indicator of solidarity among brothers, though one which also points to a hierarchical component, is provided by the fact that the proper influence of an elder brother was often invoked as an extenuating circumstance when a man committed a crime. In 1842, for example, the bandit Anton-Francesco Antonini kidnapped and raped a girl with the aid of two accomplices, one of whom was his brother Giovanni. The jury convicted both accomplices but treated Giovanni more leniently, since the bandit had 'a great influence over the mind of his brother'.[35]

As has been noted for other societies,[36] the socio-economic requirement that brothers co-operate and show strong solidarity did not preclude the existence and expression of distance, rivalry and even bitter enmity between them, leading in some cases to fratricide.[37] This hostility could be psychological in origin. In a case in 1846, for example, we learn that Antono Bujoli of Ocana bore a grudge against his brother Tomaso, because their father favoured him;[38] while an 'irreconcilable enmity' between Andrea and Damiano Ficoni of Perelli in the 1870s was explained by the fact that Damiano had had adulterous relations with his brother's wife.[39] But conflict among brothers arose much more frequently and usually simultaneously from material factors, centring on their respective shares in, or contributions to, the family property and economy. As a proverb put it: 'We are brothers at prayer but not where interest is concerned.'[40] In 1800, for example, Durazzo Durazzi of Fozzano, then living in Ajaccio, laid a charge against his brother Ignazio, an ex-priest. Two years earlier, Durazzo claimed, he had sent two men to work his vines at Fozzano, but they had been ordered off by Ignazio and had then been shot at.[41] Two cases of fratricide in 1849 illustrate other forms of conflict involving material interest. Giovan-Battiste and Nunzio-Maria Franceschetti, herdsmen of Asco, quarrelled over their share of the milk produced by their flocks, and in a fight between them Nunzio-Maria was killed. Giovan-Paolo Ordioni of Corte lent his brother Giovan-Pasquino a sheep, which he refused to return. A quarrel ensued, and Giovan-Pasquino threw a stone which killed his brother.

Brothers often owned land or other property in common of course and they might live together, all of which provided further ground for conflict. In a case of 1863, we learn that Francesco and Saverio Susini of Porto Vecchio 'were not on very good terms with each other'. When Saverio, a blacksmith, aged 53 and unmarried, asked Francesco for two chairs, which were part of the furniture which they owned in common, the latter angrily refused. Shortly afterwards, Saverio went to a vineyard some way from the village where his brother was working with his in-laws, and seriously wounded one of them with a rifle shot. Leonardo and Domenico Calzaroni, both of whom were married, lived together in the same house at Ucciani. A quarrel arose in the household in November 1852, when Domenico reproached Leonardo's wife for lighting too big a fire in the common living room, and some days later Leonardo shot and killed his brother. Trouble could also occur when one brother seemed not to be contributing enough to the family economy. Pasquino and Francesco Ordioni of Corte, for example, 'lived under the same roof with their young sister Francesca; but each brother had his separate property and they had often talked about splitting up altogether'. Francesco was the elder brother, but he was unsociable, slow and perhaps slow-witted, while Pasquino, who had served in the army in North Africa, was energetic and outgoing and sought to dominate his siblings. One evening in April 1841, the three Ordioni were at a neighbour's house, when Pasquino was asked whether he had pruned his vines yet, and he replied: 'Why should I bother, since the others will get all the fruit?' This prompted a serious quarrel between the two brothers and Francesco was killed.[42]

Perhaps the most common kind of conflict among brothers, however, arose when estates were divided or inherited. A case at Levie in 1832 involved the two Maestrati brothers. Como, the elder, a forest guard, was intelligent but callous, while Pietrino was simple. 'When their father's estate was divided, a house at Levie was allotted to Pietrino, but Como was living in it with his wife and children' and obstinately refused to vacate it. Pietrino spent some time living rough in the maquis and was then allowed by Como to sleep in an outhouse. One day in July 1832, however, Pietrino took his revenge. He waited until the house was unoccupied, then barricaded himself inside, and shot Como dead when he tried to get in.[43] At Aullène, 'very bad relations' had existed for some time between Francesc'-Antono and Tomaso Desanti as a result of disagreements over the division of their father's estate and the execution of the will of an uncle. Their relatives intervened, but at a meeting arranged to accept their arbitration Francesc'-Antono fired a shot at Tomaso which seriously wounded him. Particular trouble was caused where the inheritance was divided in a manifestly unequal way. Anton-Petro Antonmarchi of Pietra, for example, had been left one quarter of his father's estate, in addition to the share which went equally to all heirs. His brother Domenico-Luigi disputed this legacy and refused to hand over the property concerned, which led to acrimony between them. Things came to a head at the grape harvest in September 1834, when Domenico-Luigi mortally wounded his brother in a fight.[44] The special dislike of younger for elder brothers must often have stemmed from the fact that traditional inheritance customs continued to disadvantage them despite the formal introduction of the Napoleonic Code.[45] Related to this, they would often be unable to marry and would be expected to work under their elder brothers. So we learn that Anton-Francesco Susini, aged 24 of Loreto, was stabbed by his younger brother Marco-Maria in 1841, 'following a slight disagreement over family affairs'; while Giovan-Maria Casabianca, aged 40 of Ficaja, was killed in 1842 by his younger brother Paolo, again after a quarrel 'over a matter of interest'.[46] It is also significant that the unfavourable situation of younger sons or brothers seems to have been a common theme in Corsican folk tales.[47]

As we have indicated, family patrimonies were kept together by restricting or postponing marriage, and the marriage of a brother might therefore precipitate a division that was inconvenient to his siblings. Fear of such an outcome was a determining factor in a case at Santa-Reparata in 1857. The two Liccia brothers lived together. Some of their family patrimony had been divided but the rest was still held in common. Giovan-Crisostomo 'had foolishly sold his separate share of the inheritance', and depended entirely for his living on his brother Francesco-Saverio's share and on what they owned together. 'But the latter wished to divide the rest of the estate and get married ... which would have exposed Giovan-Crisostomo to poverty, scorn and dishonour.' To save himself from this fate, he pretended that Francesco-Saverio was mad and chained him to his bed, treatment which soon caused his death. In another case at Lento in 1860, Marc'-Aurelio Orsini and his married brother 'had never proceeded to the division of the estates of their parents and had continued to live together in one household. Then, Marc'-Aurelio, though nearly 60, decided to get married himself, but this proposed change of condition was not taken to kindly by his brother. Marc'-Aurelio was mistreated in various ways. He was refused his share in the common family patrimony' and was eventually evicted from the family house.[48] Division of property was always potentially contentious and agreed procedures existed in order to obviate or minimize quarrels, but these were not always successful and they were not always followed. Marcaggi describes the example of the Mancini, herdsmen from Bastelica who owned extensive pasture on the coast north of

Ajaccio. After holding this land 'in community' for a long time, the brothers Marc'-Aurelio and Antono decided to divide it between them, when 'their families became too large'. However, the division was not carried out in the traditional manner by casting lots, but had been determined by the bandit Romanetti, who awarded the lion's share to Marc'-Aurelio, the father of his mistress Maddalena. This unequal division caused bitter hostility between the brothers, though while the bandit was alive Antono did not dare to complain. However, after Romanetti's death in 1926, Antono went to law and obtained a much larger share of the Mancini land, which naturally displeased his brother. Threats of violence were exchanged between them and, when Antono Mancini and two of his sons were robbed and killed in 1928, Marc'-Aurelio and Maddalena were the prime suspects.[49]

Conflict between brothers could also be occasioned by anticipation of inheritances. The brothers Paolo-Francesco and Michele Bonnetti of Vignale were both married, but Paolo-Francesco had no legitimate children and was separated from his wife. Michele, who must have been somewhat younger than his brother, was anxious to make sure that Paolo-Francesco's property went to him and his children. With this end in view, he sent his two daughters to keep house for Paolo-Francesco, who was persuaded to make a will in 1833 leaving his entire estate to Michele and to Michele's son, Carlo-Francesco. Once this was achieved, however, Michele withdrew his daughters and entirely neglected his brother. Paolo-Francesco turned therefore to his own illegitimate daughters for help and asked them to keep house for him. News of this rapprochement 'alarmed' Michele, who at first sought to keep away these potential rivals by renewing his friendly behaviour towards Paolo-Francesco. Then presumably because this did not seem to be working, Michele and his son killed Paolo-Francesco, making out that he had met with an accident.[50]

The very close ties between brothers and sisters in Corsica were commented on by many observers.[51] Sisters lamented brothers in the most passionate terms,[52] and spouses expressed affection for each other by using the words 'brother' or 'sister'.[53] The bond was also manifested in more material ways. Sisters worked alongside their brothers – a case was even reported in 1842 of a sister and a brother committing a burglary together[54] – and they aided them when they were in difficulties. Francesco-Giovanni Luporsi of Pietricaggio, wanted by the authorities for offences committed in May 1848, went into hiding at Castellare, 'where he had a married sister'. He was captured there eleven months later but not before his sister and one of her sons had tried to organize the villagers to save him. Again, Marta Bastianesi of Ucciani petitioned the President of the Republic in 1878 for the release of her brother Francesco, who had been sentenced to hard labour for life in 1849. On their side, brothers protected their sisters. Saverio Timotei of Felce, for example, had threatened to kill his wife, Maria-Antonietta, if she did not produce a son, and when a second girl was born to her in February 1861 he began to stab her. Hearing her cries, her brother, 'who was resting in a room nearby', rushed to her aid.[55] As we have seen in the last chapter, brothers were those most obliged to defend the honour of their sisters and frequently acted under this obligation. Here, as we have emphasized, they were defending the honour and indirectly the interest of the family and of themselves, but more than a hint of sexual jealousy or love seems also to have been present.[56] From this or other motives, brothers might be at odds with their own relatives in this sphere, as a case in 1834 demonstrates. Girolamo Cotoni of Campi had lost both his parents at the age of four and was brought up by his elder sister Caterina. He was a diligent boy and decided to provide his other sister Saveria with a dowry so that she could get married. With this end in view, he restored a small vineyard, and a suitable partner was found and an engagement fixed. Then a certain Mariani, a cousin of the Cotoni, returned to the village, having completed his military service. He persuaded Girolamo to postpone Saveria's wedding, and then abducted the girl himself. As a result, Girolamo, who was still only 13 and at school, was called 'cuckold' by his school-mates and felt that 'his sister's dishonour reflected on him and the whole family'. The other relatives did not apparently share this view, given the fact that Mariani was a cousin. Girolamo decided, nevertheless, to act and shot Mariani dead.[57]

It seems likely that the relatively small effective claim on the family patrimony of daughters as compared with sons, and the fact that their claims were to a large extent indirectly channelled via dowries, minimized conflict between sisters and brothers and encouraged the close affective ties which we have described.[58] Conflict between brothers and sisters over property did occur, however, though it was far less common than that between brothers. At Moca-Croce, in 1841, for example, Maria-Saveria Gianni née Cesari was threatened with a pistol and hit with an axe handle by her brother Carlo-Andrea in a quarrel 'over a piece of land whose ownership they disputed'.[59] Like brothers, brothers and sisters often held land 'in indivision' and though brothers normally managed this with their sisters' tacit consent, disputes could arise, particularly when brothers were younger than sisters or when one party wished to withdraw.[60] In a more straightforward inheritance dispute, Don Giuseppo Renucci of Feliceto had died intestate in 1832, leaving his large estate to be divided between his brother Rocco and his married sister Barbara-Maria. Rocco Renucci was dissatisfied with this prospect, claiming that his brother had intended to leave the whole estate to him. After consulting various priests who appear to have advised him that the patriarchal end justified the means, he fabricated a will in his own favour. His sister successfully contested the validity of this will and Rocco was convicted of fraud.[61] Often in such cases the conflict was essentially between brothers and their sisters' husbands or potential husbands and their relatives. Brothers' control over the honour of sisters was part of a chain that led via control over marriage to control over property and the alliances which both together could secure. Conflict was inherent at every stage in this chain not least after marriages had been concluded, and we will discuss conflict among affines in a later section of this chapter.

To continue with relationships among kin, ties between cousins and especially first cousins were close and were expected to be supportive. Once again, laments expressed the affection of female for male cousins,[62] while male cousins were obliged to avenge each other. First cousins often lived in the same house together. Cousins of both sexes also worked and went about together. Vergine-Maria Anziani of Poggio, for example, was shot by her estranged husband in October 1833 as she was gathering chestnuts with her sister and a male cousin. In another case, a certain Manenti of Pianello 'had obtained a piece of communal land ... and, in order to cultivate it, had formed an association with his first cousin Rossi'. Maria Cosini of Tox went down to work on the plain of Aleria in May 1857 and returned with her female cousin Parfini. Cousins also lent each other aid and assistance in a variety of circumstances. For example, when Matteo Tavera of Sartène was kidnapped by bandits in 1847, along with his wife, his sister and a cousin, another cousin collected and handed over the ransom money. Again, when the widow Anna-Maria Bolelli of Tavera was seduced with promises of marriage and robbed by Marco-Santo Finelli, it was her cousin Caterina Romani who persuaded her to go to the gendarmerie. Cousins co-operated, too, in illegal enterprises. Giulio-Antono Marochelli of Ucciani abducted the heiress Girolama Silvani in 1841 with the aid of his uncle and a female cousin. The bandit Francesco-Maria Castelli lodged with his first cousin Antono at Carcheto in 1912, and this cousin also acted as his accomplice. Cousins, moreover, frequently formed more permanent associations as bandits, as did Francesco and Natale Cucchi of Carbini in the late 1840s and early 1850s.[63]

The closeness – but also the ambiguity – of the cousin relationship was reflected in the extent to which cousin marriage occurred in Corsica.[64] We have seen in discussing abduction that this was often regarded as desirable, since it could be the means of keeping property within the family and preventing uneconomic division of 'the ancestral patrimony'.[65] In a case to which we have referred, 'the paternal relatives [of the heiress Anna-Maria Ortoli of Olmiccia] had always wanted to marry her to her cousin Antono Cesari. According to them, this would keep the family property together and prevent litigation'.[66] Another Ortoli girl from Olmiccia, Nunzia-Maria, was the co-heiress in the 1850s to her father's considerable fortune together with her late married sister's child. Her relatives planned to marry her to her cousin Vincenzo-Maria Ortoli, but Lisandro Peretti, her brother-in-law and father of the niece, with whom both girls lived, objected to this plan. In order to frustrate an event which would have deprived him of control over the estate, he poisoned Nunzia-Maria with arsenic.[67]

Such illustrations sufficiently indicate that cousin marriage was as likely to provoke conflict as to promote harmony among relatives. Saravelli-Retali cites the proverb: 'If you get married, beware ... friends, ritual kin and cousins.'[68] Familiarity among cousins also led to conflict in other circumstances. The cousin relationship allowed an intimacy between men and women who were not married that could be abused. At Pianello, for example, Francesco Serrachioli, who was married to another woman, had sexual relations with his cousin Maria-Ursula Picchini, aged 17, who became pregnant and who killed her baby after it was born in 1856. Petro-Maria Paoli, a shoemaker aged 50, lived in the same apartment at Castineta as his sister-in-law Maria-Felicita Paoli. Relations between them were good, until she noticed that he 'was becoming too intimate with his cousin Anna-Maria'. She gossiped about this in the village, and Petro-Maria shot and killed her in 1849. Living together in the more general sense could produce all kinds of frictions. For example, Germano Alessandri of Focicchia, who was married with two children, lived in the same house as his cousin Giuseppo-Maria Franchi. In November 1854, Alessandri moved the staircase leading up to the entrance to the house, which inconvenienced Franchi, who took the case to the justice of the peace. He ordered Alessandri to provide a new staircase for his cousin and to pay the costs of the case. This led to a serious enmity between the two men, and in May 1855 Alessandri attacked Franchi with a knife.[69]

Where they were not members of the same family enterprise, cousins in particular would be expected to render each other the kinds of service that we have encountered among non-relatives in the community, and these could give rise to the same conflicts. For example, Carlo-Maria Ortoli of Olmiccia 'borrowed a ploughshare from his first cousin Vincenzo-Maria and then refused to return it on the pretext that the latter owed him something to pay for damage caused by his oxen'. When Vincenzo-Maria called at Carlo-Maria's house in February 1844 to collect the ploughshare, a fight began and shots were fired. Another case illustrates more perfectly how the expected trust between cousins could itself set them at odds when it appeared to be abused. While Paolo-Alfonso Tomasini of Zerubia was away one night in November 1855, he left the key of his house with his cousin Marco Bartoli. The house was broken into and the sum of 3800 francs stolen, and Tomasini accused Bartoli, who was prosecuted but acquitted for lack of evidence against him. A further possible dimension to the hostility in this case was the fact that Bartoli was the *colono* of the much wealthier Tomasini.[70]

Disputes over land use were also common among cousins. In 1827, for example, part of a wall belonging to Giovan-Paolo Quilichini of Santa-Lucia-di-Tallano was destroyed in a 'boundary dispute' which he had with his first cousin Lisandro. In another case at Farinole we learn that 'in order to reach one of his properties, Giusepp'-Antono Poggi had to cross a piece of land belonging to the Battisti brothers, his first cousins. The Battisti did not contest the right of way, but they did want Poggi to use a path that would make the right less onerous for them.' With this end in view, they prevented Poggi's sisters from taking the usual way across the land one day in May 1842. The next day Poggi accompanied his sisters on the same route, armed with a rifle, and they were met by the Battisti and their father, who were also armed. Stones were thrown, and one of the Battisti was wounded by a shot fired by Poggi.[71]

Such disputes among cousins must often have been in effect inheritance disputes and this aspect is frequently more conspicuous. The bandit Domenico Mozziconacci of Loreto, for example, claimed a share in an inheritance which came legally to his cousins Giovan-Battiste and Marcuccio. In lieu of this share, he asked for 500 francs and threatened to kill his cousins unless they handed over the money, which prompted them to kill him in 1850. Again, the first cousins Giulio and Francesco Luporsi of Perelli were the sole effective survivors of a family that had been destroyed by killings and prosecutions. 'They disputed the ownership of a few chestnuts which formed their common patrimony,' each wanting to harvest the crop to the exclusion of the other. This disagreement led to a serious fight between them in October 1852, in which Francesco shot and killed Giulio and also an old aunt who intervened to try to pacify them. More was at stake in another case at Mazzola. Francesc'-Antono Franceschi and his sisters 'owned a house which they had inherited from their father' and which had been in the possession of their immediate family for at least thirty years. However, Carlo-Giuseppo Orsini and Ignazio Danesi, 'their first cousins, together with other relatives to the same degree, claimed that they also had rights in this house which (according to them) derived from the estate of the late Benedetto Franceschi, their common grandfather, and they decided [in August 1852] to take possession of it without going through any legal formality.' They found the Franceschi sisters alone there and told them that they had come to divide up and occupy the house. Francesc'-Antono then returned and was killed after an argument by Orsini.[72]

In all this, it should be stressed again that although conflict and even feuding could occur between cousins, such behaviour was generally regarded with disfavour and in its more extreme forms with horror. In 1848, the bandit Massoni killed Giovan-Battiste Grimaldi his cousin, who had given evidence against him in a trial five years earlier. After the killing, another relative remonstrated with Massoni, asking: 'Why do you shoot at your own blood?' A lament, collected in 1926, for a man from Loreto-di-Casinca, killed by a cousin over a 'question of interest', referred similarly to 'the heinous offence' of shedding cousinly blood. It is significant here that the killing in 1928 of Perfettini, a particularly bloodthirsty and mercenary bandit, by a cousin was justified by the claim that he 'had impugned the honour of the family'.[73] In other words, a family dealt with its own 'black sheep', and it might be the duty of a cousin to kill another for the sake of that family honour and solidarity, which would normally have prevented and proscribed any such thing.

The relationship between uncles and nephews was again normally a close one. Blanqui commented in 1841 on the 'affection' shown by uncles for their nephews, which he said was reciprocated by a 'filial' cult.[74] Nephews (and nieces) quite frequently lived with their uncles,[75] and whether co-residents or not uncles and nephews worked and socialized together. In 1798, for example, a priest from Lucciana and his nephew were attacked when they went into the country together 'to see to the last stages of the harvesting'. Francesco Coti of Bastelica was robbed one night in October 1845 as he was sleeping in a cabin at Campidiloro with his nephews Servi and Padovani, who were presumably helping him with seasonal work on the plain. Again, Giovan-Michele Fieschi went to a dance at Oletta in February 1852 with his uncle Simone and was fatally stabbed in the course of defending him from ridicule. Uncles aided nephews in a variety of situations. Anton-Domenico Lanfranchi of Frasseto procured a false death certificate for his nephew Francesco-Saverio Franceschi in 1841, so that he would not be conscripted. In 1896, Paolo and Petro Giovanni were reported to be 'the most faithful protectors' of their nephew, a bandit operating in the Ortolo valley. Such services were also rendered by nephews to uncles. Giovan-Francesco Zuccarelli of Corte was sentenced to ten years' imprisonment in 1822 for providing the bandit Gambini with provisions and ammunition. In a petition for clemency, he pointed out that, since Gambini was his uncle, he had naturally aided him in his misfortune and 'shared with him his daily bread'. Another and more permanent variety of assistance is referred to in a report of 1866, where Father Muzziconacci was said effectively to administer the village of Loreto-di-Tallano 'through the agency of his nephew, Anton-Quiliano Roccaserra, whom he had had nominated as mayor'. Uncles and nephews also supported each other in quarrels and disputes – with violence, if necessary, as we have seen. At Bastelica in February 1859, Antono Marietti had an argument in a wineshop with another man, which was soon settled. But Marietti's paternal uncle had heard that his nephew was being attacked and intervened in a threatening manner. Fighting broke out and a bystander who tried to separate the combatants was mortally wounded. The obligation on nephews to avenge the killing of uncles was particularly strong, and the close ties between uncles and nephews and their mutual obligations are also demonstrated in feuding situations where one was substituted as a victim for the other. For example, Ignazio Capponi of Isolaccio was the enemy of the mayor Cipriani, and in 1847 Capponi killed Felice Massiani. In the words of the summary of his trial, this 'was a way of striking at Cipriani, to kill Massiani, his nephew and his designated heir'.[76]

Nevertheless, conflict between uncles and nephews did occur and seems indeed to have been more common than that among cousins. Sometimes our sources simply mention quarrels ending in violence or other expressions of hostility. Giovan-Grando Renucci of Cozzano was accused in 1808 of 'a plan to poison his uncle'. Paolo-Matteo Cerrotti of Petreto-Bicchisano was shot at and wounded in 1850 by his nephews Giacinto and Giovan-Carlo Pianelli, with whom he was in a state of enmity. Such examples could be multiplied, and it will be noted that in most such cases the nephew was the aggressor. Very often material interests underlay conflicts of this kind, as other examples make clear. In 1822, the brothers Ugo and Don Giacomo Peretti of Levie had a dispute with their uncle Don Luigi over the ownership of a bed; he attacked them; they defended themselves with sticks and he was slightly injured. At Calenzana, the brothers Giovan-Maria and Domenico Villanova had engaged in litigation in the early 1860s with their maternal uncle Giovan-Francesco Donati over a piece of land, as a result of which the property was formally divided between them. But quarrelling continued. The three came to blows in July 1865, and Donati was stabbed in the belly and died soon afterwards, having been bound up by an unskilled man.[77]

As this last case suggests, such disputes were often related to the inheritance of family property. In 1842, for example, Paolo-Natale Ortoli of Olmiccia, reputedly 'the richest man in the *canton*', killed his nephew Francesco-Maria. Civil litigation between the two over an inheritance was pending, and they had quarrelled over the effective possession of some nut trees. Similarly, Don Antono Mattei of Antisanti and his uncle Faustino had been engaged in litigation over the division of an inheritance for two years, when Don Antono shot and killed Faustino in 1851, as he was watering a garden. The feud at Balogna in the 1900s between the Poli brothers and their uncle Leca and his sons arose from a dispute over the estate of the former's grandfather (and Leca's father-in-law).[78]

The interpretation of such incidents is not easy, since our sources rarely indicate the exact degree of relationship involved and it is not always possible to distinguish between paternal and maternal uncles from names alone. It is evident that maternal uncles could have close and working relationships with their nephews, but such ties would have been less common than those in the paternal line and would have lacked their normative backing. The role of paternal uncles vis-à-vis nephews would depend on their own married status and on whether they were elder or younger brothers. A celibate paternal uncle might be a companion figure to his nephews, or he might be the effective head of the family with full 'paternal' authority over them.[79] Here, our evidence suggests, however, that they never wielded that authority in quite the unquestioned way that prevented avowed conflict between fathers and sons. These issues will become clearer when we discuss inheritance customs, relations with affines, and family structure.

Before concluding this section, however, we should make a brief mention of conflict between aunts and nephews, though this was not common. Our few examples suggest that there was little specific about quarrels with aunts. If they were widowed, which seems usually to have been the case, they simply stood in for uncles and were treated accordingly, though probably with less respect given their sex.[80]

II

Much of the intrafamilial conflict, which we have already evoked, reflected tensions inherent in the mechanisms by which the family patrimony was preserved and transmitted from one generation to the next.[81] Corsican inheritance customs (which include the transfer of roles and resources at marriage as well as at death) are of a complexity that it is not easy to describe. This is partly because there were real regional variations and differences in practice according to 'class' but also because the system was largely carried on by custom and oral agreement, which means that the historian has little evidence of it. Where written documents conforming to official legal norms do exist – and they become more common in the course of the nineteenth century – they can be misleading, masking traditional custom in the language of the Napoleonic Code or adapting the one to the other to a degree that by themselves they do not allow us to measure. The indications from more recent studies are that it was strongly felt at all levels but especially below that of the notables, that the patrimony, the family house *par excellence*, the land, the livestock, all other resources including rights to common land, water and so on, belonged to the family as a whole. The aim of both marriage strategies and inheritance customs was to keep this patrimony intact or to expand it, and to ensure that the optimum number of family members was kept together to work it, not too many and not too few. In a sense, therefore, as Lenclud notes, there was no inheritance, no transfer of property from one person to another, but rather a continuous cycle endlessly matching family to resources.[82] A system of so-called partible inheritance had been in operation since the sixteenth century at least, but, as Spinosi has stressed, this strictly egalitarian system, in which there was no favouring of the eldest or any other son, was once again 'aimed at keeping property within the family and at avoiding splitting it up as far as possible'. 'The theoretical principle of division – "every brother has his share" as a proverb put it – allowed in practice for indivision', and proverbs or sayings warned also against 'divisions which ruined patrimonies'.[83] Only sons inherited. Daughters were excluded, receiving dowries instead, which comprised livestock or movables and less often land or houses, on the same principle that the patrimony should not be diminished. More obviously, the sale of family property was generally proscribed.[84] Again, where wills were made and where the eldest son was favoured in them with the 'disposable portion', as the Code allowed,[85] it was with the same intention of preserving the patrimony. Bigot relates that it was usual at Bastelica in the 1860s for both parents to make formal bequests of this kind, motivated by 'love of the patrilineal name and the desire to perpetuate it, together with the influence of the family'. At the same time, 'simulated sales might be made [before a father died] in order to consolidate the family property in the hands of the eldest son and prevent the alienation or excessive divisions that a legal partition would involve'.[86]

However, although the family had the characteristics of a permanent corporation, whose continuity might by ensured by a variety of means, its membership and its leadership did change, and property and power were effectively transferred on the death of the paterfamilias. Bigot noted that it was rare for old people to surrender control of property before they died, and proverbs emphasized the dangers of anticipation here.[87] Though patrimonies continued to be held by siblings and others in indivision, the eldest brother, or sometimes an uncle, assumed charge of the family holdings and economy. Occasionally, this role might be taken by the siblings' widowed mother. Malaspina declared in 1876 that when an older man died, 'his wife inherited his rights and became the head of the family community', and we have seen that Signora Bartoli exercised this function at Fozzano. Although favouring the eldest son could be a disguised way of retaining the patrimony for the whole family, there are indications that real primogeniture was spreading in the modern period, encouraged by the Code and perhaps following local aristocratic models. Lorenzi de Bradi wrote in 1928 that there were 'families in which the girls never marry so that their brother can inherit all the property. If there are several brothers, it is only one who may perpetuate the line.'[88]

The precautions taken to keep the patrimony together suggest that partition, moreover, was a constant threat and not one that was always kept at bay. Blanqui wrote in 1841 that it was 'rare for an heir to buy out his co-heirs; thus the smallest parcel of land is split up into as many portions as there are inheritors and, since each of these wishes to have the best, hatreds are bred with the division'. Even the paternal house, symbol of the family and its unity, might be divided 'by floors among the children or, where the number of children exceeds the number of floors, by rooms' or parts of rooms. Lenclud notes that in the Niolo, an area where traditional ways persisted, a tendency to divide up houses was evident by the time of the First World War.[89] Where estates were preserved in indivision by siblings after a father's death this might be a temporary phase, and a partition would occur in due course when one or more of them wished to marry or to provide for their own children. Again, the introduction of French inheritance law almost certainly strengthened the tendencies towards division, at least in the short run before massive emigration removed the competition for resources and allowed indivision to flourish again through inertia.

Many of the intrafamilial conflicts which we have discussed arose from the tensions inherent in traditional inheritance customs strictly applied, but conflict arose also from the fact that traditional customs existed alongside new legal forms. The latter could be adapted to the former as we have seen, but their coexistence also generated a degree of uncertainty about what the rules were.[90]

Further discussion of examples from our sources will amplify and elucidate these points.

First, as we have seen, preserving the family patrimony intact often involved strains, and brothers, in particular, were liable to fall out over running the family economy, once their father's authority was removed. In a case in 1820, the brother and two cousins of Anton-Marco Sinibaldi of Sartène were accused of wounding him. It was said that the men had quarrelled over property which they held in common and that Anton-Marco had not been 'in agreement with his brother since the death of their father'. Very often the division of the patrimony was the sign of a serious breach in relations. When young Filippo Agostini of Croce decided in 1850 to stop living with his sister because of her shameful behaviour, 'he demanded from her his share in the family estate'. Immediate division was more likely where heirs were not so closely related, but whatever the circumstances it easily aroused hostility and conflict as Blanqui indicates, especially since force and *de facto* possession were used to flout or pre-empt legal provisions. For example, Anton-Battiste Micheli of Noceta had claims 'on the estate of an uncle who had died a few days previously, leaving his property to another nephew Orso-Paolo Arrighi'. The latter feared that Micheli would take possession of some of the livestock involved, so he went to watch over it at a place in the country in March 1852. A day or so later, Micheli and his son went to this place and shots were exchanged between the two parties. In a case in 1853 at Porto-Vecchio, we learn that one claimant took possession of a disputed vineyard 'by placing a heifer in it', which was perhaps a ritual mode of appropriation. Another kind of conflict over the division of estates arose when sisters pressed their claims to an equal share, against traditional custom but in line with the new law. This tendency was already evident before the promulgation of the Code of 1804. Felicina, the widow of the late Rocco Filippi of Quenza testified in a case in 1802 'that she had had discussions with her brother Giuseppo Mancini [of Ajaccio] about their paternal and maternal inheritance and other matters, as a result of which she had had a writ served on him to have the estate divided and to allow her to enter into possession of her dotal property'.[91] In a more obvious case where a woman was involved as an heir rather than as a bride, we have seen that Rocco Renucci of Feliceto fabricated a will to try to prevent his sister from obtaining her share in their brother's estate. Again, some heirs might wish to divide the patrimony while others did not, and some might even wish to revert to indivision after they had taken out their shares. Giovan-Crisostomo Liccia of Santa-Reparata tried to obtain the best of both worlds in this way.

Conflict could also be engendered by the exercise of testator's rights, especially where a will ran counter to custom or interfered with the interests of close relatives in favour of spouses, illegitimate children or others. Giovan-Antono Serra, a shoemaker from Cargiaca, was accused in 1830 of wounding a horse belonging to Antono Santarelli from a neighbouring village. He denied the charge but admitted 'that relations are bad between Santarelli and myself, because he made my sister-in-law, the wife of his son, make a will in the latter's favour. I won't conceal from you that this displeased me a great deal, particularly since I was sure that she had been subjected to great pressure.' Santarelli's version was that Serra lived 'in concubinage with the sister of my son's wife'; the latter had fallen dangerously ill and made a will in favour of 'her husband with whom she had had no children'; hearing this, Serra went to see her to try to persuade her to change her will in favour of her sister (her nearest blood relative) and, when she refused, he left in anger and threatened to kill Santarelli. Just before he died, Don Giacomo Roccaserra of Levie made a will leaving his considerable fortune to Maria-Trojana, his childless wife. 'His many relatives were most indignant,' and she was subjected to threats culminating in an attempt to wound or kill her in 1842. In a more unusual case, Maria Lanfranchi of Muro made a will in 1854 in favour of Vincenzo-Domenico Marinetti, to whom she was related by marriage. Her motive is not clear, for although she had no children, she had collaterals and her husband was alive. Four years later she indicated that she wished to change her will in favour of her husband, and this prompted Marinetti to poison her and her unmarried sister with arsenic.[92] We have seen that Paolo-Francesco Bonnetti of Vignale was killed in 1835 by his brother and a nephew in order to stop him making a will in favour of his two illegitimate daughters. These cases suggest, too, that wills were being increasingly used and that written agreements were tending to replace oral ones. This view is confirmed by a feature of the dispute between the Luporsi cousins of Perelli, to which we have referred. In order to clinch his claim to exclusive ownership of chestnuts which formed 'their common patrimony', one of them alleged that he had a written agreement to that effect made by their respective fathers. It is unlikely that any such document existed, since it was never produced, but its invocation reflects the new prestige of the document, will or pseudo-will.

As one would expect, inheritance disputes were particularly likely to occur where the heirs were minors. For example, Cosimo Pietri of Sartène was prosecuted in 1802 for trying 'to usurp the property' of his cousins, the daughters of the late Agostino Pietri, who were still children. When Paolo-Giacomo-Santo Pietri, also of Sartène, damaged a mill belonging to the orphan sons of Agostino Susini in the same year, he did so, it seems, in order to persuade their guardian, Guglielmo Filippi, to reach some accommodation with him over his claim to a share in the property. Another case at Guarguale involved a will and the use of force to oppose its provisions. A relative of the Casanova brothers died in 1858, leaving his estate to the grandsons of Justice of the peace Ornano. 'Deprived of an inheritance which they had hoped to add to their patrimony, the Casanova did everything in their power to prevent the heirs from claiming their legacy.' Ornano, who acted as his grandsons' guardian, was intimidated and threatened with death on several occasions. The will was formally contested, but without success. Finally the Casanova had recourse to the bandit Quastana, whose protectors they were reputed to be. He ordered the clerk of the local court to instruct Ornano 'to hand over to the Casanova brothers most of the property which the court had awarded to his grandchildren', something which he obstinately refused to do.[93]

Inheritance disputes also frequently involved affines, and the encouragement given by the Code to the claims of daughters may well have increased this kind of conflict. Giovan-Martino Casella of Erbajolo, for example, 'had married the sister of Giovanni Micaelli. Arguments arose between them over the estate of Micaelli's father. A verbal arbitration followed, the estate was divided, and boundary marks were placed in position.' Then Casella claimed a piece of land that had been allotted to Micaelli to compensate for a debt against the estate which the latter had paid. When Micaelli refused to discuss this claim, Casella repudiated the entire partition agreement and began 'to exercise rights of ownership over the entire estate of his late father-in-law'. One day in October 1828, Casella was harvesting chestnuts at a grove that had earlier been allotted to Micaelli, when the latter's wife and son arrived and tried to stop him. Attempts at conciliation by third parties were frustrated when Micaelli himself arrived, armed with a gun. Fighting broke out between the two parties, and both Micaelli and his wife were fatally stabbed by Casella.[94] Again, Angelo-Battiste Riucelli of Alando had married the sister of Anton-Francesco Marcantoni. The two men lived on friendly terms until the death of the latter's father, when they fell out over the division of the estate. 'Anton-Francesco was not satisfied with the share allotted to him; he demanded a new partition; and, in order to obtain this, he subjected his brother-in-law to incessant vexations,' which culminated in his shooting him in 1835. Many other cases of this kind could be cited.

The claims of a son-in-law were traditional, where the wife had no brothers and was thus an heiress, a situation which we have encountered in discussing marriage and abduction. Here the daughter (and effectively her husband) was regarded as if she were a son for inheritance purposes. A case in 1865 illustrates the expectations involved in this custom and the difficulties to which it could give rise. Giuseppo Armani, a landowner from Vero, married the only daughter of the Mariani couple. A child was born of the marriage, but mother and child died. Armani, 'however, continued to live in the household of the Mariani and to administer their property, even after he had remarried', though this is less surprising when one learns that his second wife was his first mother-in-law's niece. Armani fully expected 'to become the heir of the Mariani couple', but a rupture occurred between them for some reason and he left their house with 'a strong and deep resentment against them'. This found expression in acts of violence against his former mother-in-law, and in hostility directed against Giulio Leca of Lopigna, a relative of the Mariani, who now stood to inherit their estate. Armani and Leca had several heated arguments, and in 1865, after another quarrel, Armani shot his rival with a pistol and mortally wounded him. Things could be even more complicated where there were two sons-in-law expecting to inherit. Don Giacomo Peretti, municipal tax-receiver at Ajaccio and Paolo Galloni 'had each married one of the Bianchi sisters, and they all lived together in the town house of the widow Bianchi. Peretti, who had married some years before Galloni, was thus more senior in the house than his brother-in-law, and exercised some kind of authority there,' while Galloni had very little influence even over his wife, who was dominated by her mother. This situation led to many altercations in the household, and Galloni announced at the end of 1851 that he was leaving and taking his wife to live at Olmeto, his native village. He therefore asked that the estate of his late father-in-law, which was still undivided, should be split up, a course which both Peretti and the widow Bianchi opposed. Peretti fired a shot at Galloni as he was about to leave for Olmeto, presumably in order to intimidate or prevent him.[95]

III

This brings us to the general topic of conflict with affines. As kinship terminology indicates, in-laws were regarded as members of the family, and once again one must stress that co-operation and solidarity among affines were expected and enjoined.[96] As Malaspina noted in 1876, a bride with extensive kin was more sought after than one who was simply rich, because through her access was gained to both labour and protection.[97] Uxorilocal residence was not uncommon, even where brides were not heiresses,[98] and affines worked with and for each other, as we have seen. Affines also lent each other aid in a variety of other ways. After killing a man at another village in 1808, for example, Angelo-Paolo Ottaviani took refuge 'in the house of Giovanna-Maria Lorenzi', his mother-in-law, at Campile. When Paolo-Emilio Carlotti of Pietroso wished to procure an abortion for a widow whom he had seduced, he contacted a pharmacist in Corte who was the brother-in-law of a friend. There is evidence, too, that affines supported and felt obliged to support each other at critical times in the life-cycle. In petitioning in 1860 for clemency for her brother-in-law Pancrazio Quastana, who had been sentenced to 20 years' hard labour in 1849 for complicity in a murder, the widow Angela-Maria Quastana declared that, having just lost her only son, 'the support of my brother-in-law has become a necessity for me now that I am old and for my children who are all very young'.[99] There was doubtless an element of special pleading here, but its terms of reference are significant. It is also relevant that petitions for clemency frequently came from affines.[100]

The solidarity of affines was also demonstrated in situations where they became involved in each other's quarrels and disputes. Giovan-Battiste and Giuseppo Muselli of Ocana, for example, had been on extremely bad terms following 'testimony given in court by Giovan-Battiste against the Chiodi family, to which Giuseppo was related by marriage'. Here it is likely that the Muselli were actually kinsmen, but affinal ties, albeit strong, would not usually outweigh kinship ones, though in-laws could easily be drawn, as we have seen, into disputes between kin. Affinal support in quarrels was most frequently given, it seems, by brothers-in-law to each other and by sons-in-law to fathers-in-law, which is what one would expect. In another incident at Ocana, in 1843, fighting broke out in a wineshop between Santo Costa and Antono Girardini. Hearing about this, Blasius Muraccioli, Costa's brother-in-law, at once ran up, intervened and was wounded in the head by Girardini. Paolo-Francesco Casta of Santa-Reparata sold 'a property of little value' to a certain Castellani, who agreed verbally to pay for it in instalments, the last due at Christmas 1865. However, in October Casta cited Castellani without warning before the justice of the peace at Isola-Rossa for not paying his debt, and Castellani was given a month to pay and also ordered to pay the costs of the action. His brother-in-law Francesc'-Antono Mariotti accosted Casta as he left the court and told him that, as a result of his action he never would be paid. Later the same day, Casta left for home in the company of his brother-in-law Leoni. They were followed by Mariotti, who caught up with them and provoked a fight in which he was mortally wounded. In 1858 Giuseppo Girolami of Muro was convicted of wounding Giovanni Napoleoni. He had been exasperated by disparaging remarks made by Napoleoni about the father of his fiancée.[101] We shall see in a later chapter that the obligation to take vengeance extended to affines and that they were frequently involved both actively and passively in feuds.

We must now turn to situations where conflict between affines did nevertheless occur. This could sometimes develop into full-scale feuding, as at Olmeta-di-Tuda in the first two decades of the nineteenth century or at Cozzano in the 1860s.[102] The odd case of conflict between distant affines is reported but contention was much more likely between those closely related by marriage. Since marriages were made in a competitive way and involved the combination or exchange of both honour and material resources or rights, the affinal relationship was charged with tensions and potential discord.[103]

The most direct form of affinal conflict was that between husbands and wives. Here again solidarity was of course prescribed and frequently practised,[104] but despite this, disputes, often of a violent nature, were common. Cases of husbands killing wives, to take the most extreme example, came fairly often before the courts. Paolo Polverini of Fozzano was convicted in 1807 of having shot his wife dead in the forest of Piopi, 'where she was looking after her goats'. The motive for the killing seems to have been his interest in another woman. Again, in 1809, Vincenzo Poletti from Loreto-di-Casinca, who was at that time a bandit, stopped his wife 'as she was returning to the village carrying a faggot of wood and stabbed her to death', perhaps because she refused to assist him.[105] The reasons for conflict are often much clearer and may be arranged under a number of headings.

First, trouble might arise in relation to the couple's place of residence. According to Spinosi, 'when a woman marries, she generally leaves her family to go to live in the district and in the house of her husband'. As Lenclud indicates for the Niolo, this was not an absolutely binding rule.[106] We learn, for example, in a case in 1850 that Giulio Graziani of Campile was living in the house of Giovan-Tomaso Moroselli, 'whose daughter he was going to marry'. In 1879, Anton-Quiliano Roccaserra, mayor of Loreto-di-Tallano, explained that he was 'not a native of the village'. However, 'having married an heiress from Loreto', it was in his interest to settle there. This was probably the main though not the exclusive reason for uxorilocal marriage, an arrangement that always put the husband in a more or less anomalous position. In a situation which parallels that at Loreto, Giovan-Battiste Lota from Penta-di-Casinca had married a Negroni girl and had gone to live in her village, Ampriani, where he later became mayor. But the success of this intruder was much resented and Lota was killed by one of his wife's relatives in 1833. Disagreements among in-laws here often led to the termination or attempted termination of co-residence, which in turn could lead to further conflict. In 1842, Paolo-Natale Nicoli of San-Gavino was shot dead by his son-in-law Rocco. The latter's motive, according to the gendarmerie, was that he had been expelled from his father-in-law's house the day before after an argument.[107] At Cozzano, Francesco Peretti had gone to live 'as one of the family' in the house of his daughter's husband's relatives. This arrangement proved unsatisfactory and he was asked to leave in 1865, which prompted the feud between the two families to which we have referred. A more common pattern was for the husband to take or try to take his wife away from her family's house. When Luigi

Borghetti of Velone married Vergine-Maria Anziani of Poggio, he went to live in the house of Caterina Anziani, her mother, who was almost certainly a widow. This led to constant quarrelling. Borghetti took his wife away to Velone, but she returned to her mother. Eventually in 1834, Borghetti killed his mother-in-law, whom he blamed for this outcome, and also shot and wounded his wife. At Porto, Giudice Giudicelli married a Paoli girl in 1850 and 'it appears that one of the conditions of the marriage was that the new couple should not live separately from the Paoli family'. Having agreed to this condition, Giudicelli found it irksome. He tried to persuade his wife to leave her family and set up house with him but she refused, and he later killed her, claiming to have found her committing adultery. Such cases suggest that uxorilocal marriage could deprive a man of the control over his wife that male honour demanded.

Trouble could also occur where wives followed the more usual practice of going to live with their husband's families. Guglielmo Ciosi of Venzolasca, for example, married Rosa-Maria Paoli in 1863. She 'was of a flighty temperament and dubious morality and she soon left the conjugal residence to return to her brother's house [in another village], on the pretext that she found it impossible to live any longer with her husband's family'. Again, Elisabetta Rutili of Calenzana left her husband, Giovanni Marini, in 1894 after four years of marriage, alleging severe ill-treatment. In each case, after trying in vain to get her to return, the husband eventually killed his wife.[108] Wives might also be sent back to their families of origin for a variety of reasons including difficult personality traits, such as extreme inquisitiveness, and doubts cast on their honour.[109] In 1836, Anton-Claudio Peretti, of Levie, married Maria-Angelina Peretti, but shortly after the wedding she was obliged 'to return to her father's house', where she gave birth to a daughter. There was a dispute over her dowry, but the decisive reason for the separation seems to have been Anton-Claudio's uncertainty about the paternity of the child, which seems to have been prenuptially conceived. This case also brings out another kind of conflict which was likely to arise if a wife left or was forced to leave the husband's home, or if a husband abandoned a wife. The Peretti couple lived apart without incident until 1846, when Maria-Angelina brought a suit against her husband in order to make him provide for her and the child. He then offered to take them into his house, an offer which Maria-Angelina accepted believing that he wished for a sincere reconciliation. She was immediately disabused, for on the first evening under his roof he told her that 'life in common' was impossible for them and threatened to cause her 'serious trouble if she did not again leave', a threat which he repeated on successive evenings. His intention was clearly to place the initiative in leaving 'the conjugal home' clearly on her, so that he would be relieved of any responsibility for the maintenance of wife or child. A case in 1864 reveals a pathetic but rare attempt to avoid the pressures which living with either spouse's family involved. Eugenia Orsini of Campile, aged 19, 'had left her father's house to go to live with Antono Lorenzi on the strength of a promise of marriage. He, for his part, left his mother and brothers with whom he had lived until then. The two lovers rented a small room in the village and supported themselves by their own labour without having recourse to their relatives.' They planned to marry when Lorenzi's mother lifted her objections to their match. In the event, however, he was prevailed upon by his mother to break off the relationship, and Eugenia, who was pregnant, reacted by shooting and mortally wounding him.[110]

Our examples indicate that where the question of residence was the main bone of contention between spouses, it was almost never the only one. We have seen that a husband's honour could be bound up in it, and this can be further demonstrated. In the Peretti case at Levie, Anton-Claudio eventually killed his wife and her child, and he was prompted to do so by two of his relatives who 'reproached him in a lively manner for allowing himself to be dishonoured' by her. The behaviour of the husband in the Calenzana case is even more telling. A short while after his wife had left him, Giovanni Marini met her on the road to Calvi with her old father. He drove the father off, forced her to have sexual intercourse and then mutilated her sexual parts. In a further case, Petro-Giuseppo Reginensi, a charcoal burner from Pietricaggio, had moved with his wife to Bastia around 1860. Here she worked and brought up the children, while he spent his time drinking. When she tried to get him to reform, he threatened her with violence, and he finally stabbed her to death in bed in 1865. When he was arrested, he said that he had killed her 'because he could no longer put up with her incessant affronts to his honour as a husband'. He implied that she was guilty of sexual misconduct but he was also reacting to her daring to censure him. His trial revealed that on one occasion, before they went to Bastia, he had led her through the streets of the village with a rope round her neck as a sign of her dependence. Finally, we may refer again to the case of Saverio Timotei of Felce, who killed his wife because she failed to produce a male heir. Here a husband's concern for his virility coincided with his family's concern to perpetuate itself.[111]

Disputes related to place of residence point to the fact that after marriage a woman remained to some degree a member of her family of origin, as crisis situations demonstrated. At Cauro, for example, in 1827, Santo Casanova received two stab wounds from his son-in-law Domenico Luisi when he intervened 'to prevent Luisi from beating his wife'. Again, a case was brought in 1820 by a woman's husband against Marco Mozziconacci of Loreto-di-Tallano for using violence against his 35-year-old niece, whom he had brought up as his daughter. The niece testified, for the defence, that Mozziconacci had administered 'correction' to her and her aunt after they had squabbled, and said that 'far from complaining about this treatment', she regarded it as right and proper on the part of a man who was virtually her father.[112] The economic underpinning to such ties is well conveyed in a remark attributed by Marcaggi to a Massoni woman from Marignana. In the course of the feuding between her family and the Durilli around 1850, she insulted some members of the latter family, and when one of their partisans tried to stop her, she told him: 'As for making me keep my mouth shut, that's not your business, as I well know. Do you provide me with food to eat? It's only my father who has the right to tell me how to behave.' From the other side, as proverbs stressed, a wife was always a stranger in her husband's family, often less important than his siblings and regarded as an 'intruder'.[113] Control over a woman passed in theory at marriage from her father to her husband and this was signified to some extent by the simultaneous transfer of the dowry, or resources to support her. But the ambiguity of her situation vis-à-vis her two families is reflected precisely in disputes over the dowry.

Traditionally in Corsica a dowry was required in a marriage, and only the dotal form of matrimonial régime was recognized.[114] According to Spinosi, dowries included both movable and immovable property, and in a case at Campile in 1840 we learn of local surveyors measuring up land as a prelude to marriage.[115] We have seen, however, that below the level of notables there was a reluctance to include land or houses in the dowry, and reference is made in the sources to trees, jewelry, household equipment and furniture, linen (which the girl herself made with her female relatives), and money.[116] In an arrangement at Olmeto in 1859, a brother agreed to pay 400 francs, out of which the groom was to buy a mule, but in exchange the bride ceded her rights over land which she held in indivision with her brother. This seems to be a traditional practice of raising a cash dowry from the family estate, adapted to a legal situation in which all siblings, male and female, had equal rights.[117] The number of a woman's relatives and her qualities and skills also entered into the calculation of the dowry.[118] The husband administered the dowry, but the immovable part of it did not become his property and he could not alienate it. On the death of the wife, her heirs, that is, her children, if any, her father or her brothers, inherited the dotal property unless a contract stipulated otherwise, but this rule did not again apply to movable property which remained with the husband and his family. As we have emphasized, the provision of a dowry for a girl was an alternative to allowing her a share in the family estate by inheritance, and it was generally felt also that dowries should not be excessive, putting that patrimony in difficulties. A legend attached to a mountain called La Sposata near Vico relates that a greedy bride, who sent a messenger back to her poor mother to fetch the dough scraper to add to her trousseau, was turned to stone.[119] Dowries were also given in the event of second marriages, though at a lower level. In a case at Tavera in 1859, for example, we learn of a widow aged 20, raising 300 francs via an uncle.[120]

As in other societies, dowries could give rise to all kinds of dispute. The amount of the dowry would have been arrived at by hard bargaining but, where most agreements were verbal and payment in instalments common, there was plenty of room for disagreement and subterfuge once the bargain had been struck. At Zicavo in 1810, for example, Anton-Pasquino Abbatucci, a member of a leading family, married his daughter to Giovan-Francesco Piazza and demanded from him 'a notarized receipt for the whole dowry', which Piazza supplied in good faith, though he had only in fact received part of it. When Piazza later asked for the rest, he met with a flat refusal. Again, Anton-Francesco Leca of Pastricciola married the daughter of Giovan-Santo Ottaviani, a gunsmith, in 1830. 'They all lived together in the latter's house on apparently good terms,' but after a quarrel in 1835 the couple went to live elsewhere. Leca claimed that his father-in-law had made him a verbal promise of a dowry of 1500 Genoese *lire* but had only paid one third of this sum. He threatened to kill Ottaviani unless the remainder was paid, and Ottaviani agreed to take the matter to arbitration. However, the justice of the peace and the parish priest who were consulted decided in Ottaviani's favour. Leca refused to accept their decision and killed his father-in-law in 1839. To underline the link between the dowry and a wife's maintenance it was common for a husband to return a wife to her family of origin if the dowry were not paid or paid in full, as a case at Lozzi in 1811 illustrates. Andrea Giansilj was accused of killing his wife two years earlier and was asked 'if a little while before her death, he had reason to be dissatisfied with her and to expel her from his house?' to which he replied 'that ... his father-in-law had not paid him all the dowry that he had promised and so he sent his wife back to her father following the custom of the district in such circumstances'. This was after six years of marriage. The father-in-law's response was to pay over the bulk of the sum owing and Giansilj 'had then taken back his wife'. However, four or five Genoese *lire* remained unpaid and, when the father-in-law signified his intention of not ever paying them on the grounds that the marriage contract drawn up by the parish priest was invalid, Giansilj 'again sent his wife back to her father's house'. After about a month, the father-in-law 'had a new dotal instrument drawn up, which was properly registered. Although he received no money, Giansilj felt that his claim was now secure and agreed to take back his wife, and they lived together in harmony.' The accusation subsequently made against Giansilj reflects continuing distrust between him and his wife's relatives, but it is reasonably certain that she died of an epileptic fit.[121] The case illustrates perfectly how wife and dowry were treated as equivalents, the physical presence of the one being used to negotiate payment of the other. The same linkage was explicit in the Cozzano case, to which we have referred. When Francesco Peretti was expelled from his daughter's husband's family house, his brother told the in-laws: 'If you are going to send away the father, then send away the daughter, too, and don't forget to give back her dowry!'

As this indicates, disputes over dowries were very likely to occur when a wife separated from her husband, or when she died. In a case at Castineta, Francesco Tomasi left his wife while her father Giulio-Cesare Santini was in prison. When Santini returned home, he demanded from Tomasi a half share in the property worth 1500 francs which Tomasi had acquired with the dowry money that Santini had given him. When Tomasi refused this, Santini made threats against him and eventually fired a shot at him in 1861. Many inheritance disputes involved dotal property. In the case against Cristoforo Ferrandi of Giglio in 1801, a witness declared that the public suspicion was either that Ferrandi had indeed killed his wife as charged, or that she had been killed by her brother, 'because, people say, by this killing he has regained possession of the property which he conceded with his sister as a dowry'. A conflict arose in 1806 between Dr Bernardino Peretti of Sari-d'Orcino and his brother-in-law Martino Cinarchese 'over the return of a vineyard that had formed part of the dowry of Peretti's sister and Martino's deceased wife'. Again, at Olmeto, Carlo Fiamma had married the sister of Giusepp'-Antono Istria, but no dowry had been assigned to him. When Istria's father died intestate, therefore, the Fiamma couple demanded her share in the estate. The Istria created difficulties, forcing the Fiamma to take the case to court in Sartène. There the Istria produced written evidence that Fiamma had received a dowry of 5000 francs and argued that his wife therefore had no further claim on her father's estate, but their argument fell through when it was shown that this evidence had been fabricated.[122]

Dowry and inheritance disputes frequently involved brothers-in-law, and quarrels between them were perhaps the most common form taken by affinal conflict, mainly because they were often the effective heads of their families and family interests were defended primarily by young adult males. Violence between brothers-in-law was often reported without any indication of motive beyond 'family interest',[123] which is itself significant. Where motives are indicated, they fall into familiar categories. First, there are quarrels of material interest. In July 1827, for example, a dispute took place between Silvestro Muraccioli of Muracciole and his brother-in-law Giulio-Francesco as they were threshing wheat together. Giulio-Francesco claimed a measure of wheat to which Silvestro did not think he was entitled, so Silvestro hit Giulio-Francesco on the head with a shovel and he died three weeks later. In another case tried in 1830, Martino Ristozi of Poggio-di-Venaco was convicted of killing his brother-in-law Paolo. Paolo had gone to see Martino to ask him to provide his share of the food with which they supplied their common father and father-in-law. Martino claimed to have already given two measures of wheat, which Paolo said was untrue. A fight then developed in which Paolo was mortally wounded.[124] We have cited examples of inheritance disputes between brothers-in-law in the previous section, and many others could be added to the list.

A sexual element could also be a factor in such conflict, given the fact that the affinal relationship could place men and women who were not married in situations of close proximity, often under the same roof. Anton-Giacomo Bernardi of Bisinchi, for example, was on bad terms with his brother-in-law Feliciano Vecchioni 'who was said to be carrying on illicit relations with Bernardi's [unmarried sister] Cleonice', although he was married to another sister, Paolina-Maria. Bernardi went to the Vecchioni house one evening in March 1846, found Cleonice there and fired a shot at Vecchioni. In a more complicated case, Pasquale Torre, an Ajaccio tailor, paid a visit to his native Cuttoli in July 1865 and spent the night at the house of his mother-in-law Saveria Paoletti. He was put in a room next to that occupied by Livia, the new wife of his wife's brother Paolo Paoletti, who was away at the coast. During the night, Torre went into Livia's room and tried to have sexual relations with her, telling her that he had conceived a violent passion for her and only desisting when she threatened to call for help. The next day, Paolo Paoletti returned to find his wife in distress and, after some hesitation, she told him why. 'When mealtime came, Paolo refused to sit at the common table, pretending to be ill. In fact, he felt the strongest repugnance to the idea of eating with Pasquale Torre. When everyone insisted, he did sit down, but left after swallowing only a few spoonfuls.' Paolo explained the reasons for his behaviour to his mother and told her that he could not tolerate under his roof a man 'who had tried to dishonour him'. Torre spent one more night in the house and then Saveria told him to leave, warning him that Paolo would shoot him if he returned. Torre, who had tried to make light of the affair, spent that day in a neighbouring village but came back to the Paoletti house in Cuttoli in the evening, when Paolo shot and wounded him. Torre claimed later that Paolo Paoletti had to some extent used the affair as a pretext, being put out by the preference which his mother showed for her daughter and Torre himself.[125]

Relating to the view that a wife was an intruder in her husband's family, it is significant that quarrels between brothers-in-law were frequently blamed on the women to whom they were married. In 1831, for example, Petro Codaccioni, a herdsman from Bilia, was shot dead by his brother-in-law Anton-Paolo Grimaldi in the course of a dispute which 'was caused by Grimaldi's wife who sowed dissension between them'.[126] At Palneca, Anton-Lorenzo Santoni had been on bad terms for some time with his brother-in-law Anton-Giuseppo. 'The latter was particularly hostile towards Anton-Lorenzo's wife, whom he accused of having caused the rupture between them and of having made malicious remarks about him,' and he shot her dead in 1851.

Conflict between sons-in-law and fathers-in-law seems to have been less common, inhibited perhaps by the same patriarchal principle that limited open conflict between fathers and sons. A case in 1842 at Pietricaggio involved hostility between a son-in-law and his father-in-law, but this was directed probably not by chance against a more favoured brother-in-law. Lanfranco Lanfranchi 'had had several disputes over questions of interest with his father-in-law Simone Pietrini, and with Giacomo-Santo Grazj, who, having married another daughter of Pietrini, lived in the latter's house'. One day in January 1840, when the cantonal tax-collector was at Lanfranchi's house, Grazj came to pay his taxes and those of Pietrini. As Grazj was leaving, Lanfranchi accosted him on the external stairway, reproached him with setting foot in his house, and fired a pistol at him, wounding him in the neck.[127] Cases are reported, however, of violence against fathers-in-law. We have referred to the rivalry at Pila-Canale in the 1860s between the mayor Michele-Antono Bozzi and his son-in-law Paoletti. Bozzi claimed that Paoletti had not only made false accusations against him but had also tried to kill him.[128]

We turn now to conflict involving female affines. The crucial structural conflict in virilocal marriage would be that between mothers-in-law and daughters-in-law. Lenclud relates a telling example from a village in the Niolo, where a man married aged 45, having helped his widowed mother to bring up a large number of siblings. At the wedding, the mother-in-law told her daughter-in-law: 'You have stolen my bread-winner!' and then refused to speak to her again for 15 years.[129] It is significant that this relationship, so potentially full of conflict but so inescapable and so essential to the smooth working of the Corsican system of family reproduction, should in practice have given rise to so little actual conflict, as though some avoidance mechanism were in operation. We have seen that open conflict between sons-in-law and mothers-in-law in cases of uxorilocal marriage seems to have been much more common, and it is reported in other circumstances. The bandit Capracinta, for example, was reported to have come three times into the Prunelli region in 1820 in order to try 'to kill his mother-in-law, because she had denounced him to the troops'.[130]

Violent conflict between sisters-in-law was not unknown but it seems to have been rare. We may cite an example from Rapaggio in 1882. In August that year, Anna-Vittoria Filippi née Pieri 'was receiving visits of condolence in her house following the death of a neighbour. When a certain Anna-Caterina Santini, with whom she had long been on very bad terms, arrived, Anna-Vittoria at once manifested her extreme displeasure not only with the unwanted visitor but also with her sister-in-law Cecilia-Maria Mori', who, she believed, had invited her. 'The other women present tried to calm Anna-Vittoria' but without success, and she 'threw herself on her sister-in-law, seized her by the throat and squeezed so hard that Cecilia-Maria lost consciousness and died a few days later'. As we have indicated already, conflict involving sisters-in-law and brothers-in-law was more common. Such conflict was generally inspired by the same motives as that between brothers-in-law, from which of course it must frequently have been indistinguishable, unless the sister-in-law were a widow. We should emphasize that, although conflict relating to particular role relationships among affines may be isolated and may be significant, much conflict took place in a broader context between families or between couples. For example, in a case in 1850 we learn that 'Domenico-Francesco Alessandri, his wife Maria-Nativita, his wife's brother Michele Corrazzini and his wife Francesca, all lived in common in the same house at Piedicorte', together with Alessandri's mother. The two young couples were always quarrelling and in the course of one particular dispute over a store room which the Corrazzini claimed the exclusive right to use, Francesca Corrazzini fatally stabbed her brother-in-law.[131]

We conclude this section with a discussion of conflict stemming from remarriage. Corsicans recognized the importance, even the necessity for those occupying certain roles, of having a spouse. In the words of a proverb: 'A man who does not take a wife is the half of a pair of scissors.'[132] Single women were vulnerable. When Giulio-Cesare Santini of Castineta was condemned to a long prison sentence, he arranged for his daughter to marry Francesco Tomasi, a younger man of lower standing, in order to give her and their property a protector in his absence. In these circumstances, there were compelling socioeconomic reasons for both widows and widowers to remarry. We have seen how difficult it might prove for widows to provide for themselves and their children. In a case in 1859, it was reported that the widow Ridolfi of Valle 'had difficulty in bringing up her family' of three children, and as in other examples this led to conflict between her and her eldest son. Again, at Chiatra, the widow Lucciani was 'obliged to do day work in order to feed her family', which involved going down to the plain and 'leaving two very young children at her house in the care of neighbours'.[133] Here, it is relevant that inns and hotels were frequently kept by widows and that this was an occupation that was generally felt in Corsica to be demeaning.[134] We may also cite examples of widows being seduced, insulted or attacked. In 1819, the widow Tomasini from Zerubia claimed that she had been knocked down and kicked at a place in the country by Nunzio Guidicelli, a bastard. Guidicelli complained that she had not greeted him properly.[135] Widowers would be less vulnerable but would miss the complementary work of a wife in house, garden and field. It is not surprising, therefore, to find that remarriage in Corsica was statistically important. Pomponi provides a figure of 11 per cent for the period 1814–30.[136]

Nevertheless, the remarriage of widows (and to a lesser extent of widowers) was generally disapproved of. Mérimée noted that 'mourning for a husband lasts a lifetime' and that it was 'excessively rare for a widow to remarry', and other sources concur. A proverb proclaimed that 'the widow who remarries loses esteem', while Arrighi's 'widow of Arbellara' explained her vow never to remarry as a way of honouring 'her husband's remains'.[137] Related to this, there is some evidence that where a remarriage did take place the husband's brother was the preferred choice.[138] In social terms this was a replica of the first marriage, and in spiritual terms it caused least offence to the dead. Another indication of the disapproval of second marriages was the charivari, which accompanied weddings of widows or widowers. This was known onomatopoeically as the *bagagliacciu* or *franghillacciu*, and involved serenading the couples with horns and the banging of pots and pans.[139] Benson asserted in 1825 that what was being objected to was the probability that such a union of an older couple would be infertile, thus frustrating 'one of the chief ends for which ... [marriage] was destined'.[140] Specific cases which we have found would not suggest that such a view is wrong, though they all involve marriages of widowers where other considerations might be important. Our cases also show how the charivari itself might lead to violence. Felice-Giovanni Risteracci of Alando, for example, who had been a widower for some time, contracted a second marriage in 1861. 'Following a custom traditional in most Corsican villages, a group of youths gathered together to give him a charivari ... Risteracci could have avoided this disagreeable event by paying them a small sum of money, but he refused,' and the trouble began. One of Risteracci's nephews, however, tried to stop the proceedings and, exasperated by his failure to do so, fired a pistol loaded with nails at the participants in the charivari, one of whom was hit in the eye and blinded. Similarly at Mela in February 1895, a wedding had been arranged between a certain Verduschi, an Italian who had lived in the village for some time, and a local woman, Rosa Santelli. 'Verduschi was a widower, and several people gathered together' on the eve of the wedding opposite the house occupied by the groom, in order to mount a charivari. In the course of this, a pistol shot was fired by the bride's grandfather, which severely wounded one of Verduschi's party. It seems that he was taking advantage of the circumstances to settle an old score.[141]

We may point to examples of solidarity among step-relations. In a case in 1858, Giovan-Domenico Salvadori of Castellare took on himself to warn Bastiano Tomasi that he was in danger of compromising the former's step-sister Maria-Camilla Petrucci with his assiduities. When neither took any notice of this warning, Salvadori beat Maria-Camilla and had a fight with Tomasi. However, the weight of evidence in our sources suggests that conflict was perhaps more common. Remarriage could lead to a break with relations formed via a previous marriage, even between parents and children. In a case in 1841, we learn that after Petro Favaletti's mother remarried, he was brought up by his late father's sister at Valle. Again, in a case at San-Martino in 1855, 'the widow Graziani had been abandoned by the children of her first marriage' when she contracted a second. This reflects the view that children belonged primarily to the family of their father. However, conflict seems in practice to have been more common where, following this principle or not, stepchildren lived in the same house with a stepparent or where a second marriage by a man threatened the inheritance prospects of his existing offspring. At Fozzano, Paolo, the son of Captain Bernardino Carabelli and said to be 'of very mild character', struck and wounded his father's second wife in 1820. Another case reveals the lengths to which a man might go in order to conceal a second marriage from his children. As we shall see, the neighbouring villages of Tomino and Rogliano in the Capo Corso were bitter rivals engaged in endemic hostility over their respective limits and other matters. When the father of the mayor of Tomino, Giovanetti, himself an ex-mayor and a great champion of the rights of his village, 'wished to get married again at an advanced age to a young woman', the only way he could devise of circumventing the opposition of his children was to arrange to have the wedding in Rogliano. He spent several months in the summer therefore over consecutive years in the 'enemy' village, and by this means he acquired the technical residence qualifications laid down in the Civil Code and could be married by the mayor of Rogliano. It seems, too, that the relationship between the sons of widows who remarried and their stepfathers was peculiarly difficult. At Zigliara, Laura Foata, a widow with three children, married Carlo-Antono Poli, a hawker. It seems that Poli had only agreed to a match with a woman much older than himself in order to get hold of her considerable fortune, the Foata being one of the leading families in the canton. Whatever the truth of this, 'from the time of the marriage, the widow's eldest son Anton-Felice conceived an implacable hatred for and made wild threats against his stepfather'. Finally, in May 1843, Anton-Felice ambushed and mortally wounded Poli as he was returning from Ajaccio. Significantly, the jury took a favourable view of this crime, regarding it as 'excusable homicide'. In another case, Giuseppo Marcantoni, aged 18 of Rebbia, 'had left the house of his [widowed] mother', when she started living 'as the common-law wife of a certain Ristericci, but he went to the house from time to time to be given or to take provisions that he needed'. On one of these visits in August 1852, when he had gone 'to ask for a little wheat', an argument developed between Marcantoni and his mother, in which Ristericci intervened, threatening his stepson with a stick and an axe. Marcantoni left the house, challenged Ristericci to show himself and then fired a pistol at him.[142]

We have established that intrafamilial conflict was very important in Corsican society throughout the nineteenth century. To a large extent such conflict was structural, reflecting tensions inherent in the family economy and being directly related to the performance of roles within it. Here our hypothesis stands that feuding acted to contain intrafamilial conflict in a situation where co-operation within the family was an economic and political necessity. But intrafamilial conflict, like feuding, was also a symptom of change and of dysfunctioning. The performance of strict roles in the family, and particularly the operation of a 'patrimonial' system of inheritance, was undermined by the introduction of the new law of the State. At the same time, by the end of our period, the traditional economy was in decline and losing its determining grip on social structure and cultural behaviour.

] 6 [

Conflict and its causes: inter-community conflict

We turn now to the third type of conflict, which coexisted in Corsica with intrafamilial conflict and with conflict between families. In order to understand conflict between communities, it is necessary first to know what constituted a community and how strongly the sense of community was expressed. Some writers have stressed the lack of association in Corsica at the village and higher levels in the face of family loyalty, individualism and patronage, while others have emphasized the force of local solidarity.[1] The truth is that both centripetal and centrifugal forces, tendencies towards unity and towards separation or segmentation, complemented each other in a variety of ways. Conflict between communities, moreover, was only one way in which community was demonstrated and reinforced.

I

More generally, community found expression in the physical lay-out of villages, and in political, economic, social and ritual terms.[2]

First and perhaps most obviously, Corsican villages were isolated by the nature of the island's mountainous terrain. They were situated in high valleys, on the slopes of foothills and on spurs. Sometimes they were clustered together, as in the Tallano; and they had been grouped together for ecclesiastical and administrative purposes in parishes or *pievi* in the pre-Revolutionary period,[3] but, although such ties might be important, villages within sight of each other could be hours apart on foot and unconnected by roads, while rivalries and fission within *pievi* were constant. We shall see that reciprocal and sharing arrangements between villages were also very common, but this did not seriously weaken a basic self-sufficiency. Village identity, moreover, was proclaimed and reinforced by the perched and agglomerated pattern of settlement.

Outside the Balagna, Corsican villages are rarely of the fully centralized type formed around a single square, such as is found, for example, in parts of Provence,[4] and we shall see that their internal divisions into hamlets, quarters and clusters of houses are very significant in understanding how feuds were carried on. But squares of various kinds did exist, very often by the church. As the name of one of the squares at Venzolasca – the 'common square'[5] – indicates, these acted as arenas for general sociability. The square of Dominicacci, a hamlet of Bastelica, served as a meeting place for people from this and other hamlets, especially in summer, and it was furnished with stone benches on which they could sit under the trees. Itinerant tinkers mended pots and pans on the square of Peri's hamlet of Poggio, while amusements, such as throwing at cocks, took place there on festive occasions, and people slept there in the hot weather during the day or even the night. At Cauro in the 1880s the men chatted, smoked and played cards on the 'large square', while the women regularly crossed it as they went to fetch water at the fountain. Lorenzi de Bradi presents a more general picture of the village square as 'a sort of agora', where men sat, played cards, told stories, sang songs and discussed local and national politics.[6] The judicial records, moreover, provide many instances of male sociability centred on the square,[7] and we saw in Chapter 4 that conflict occurred on the square both accidentally because men happened to meet there and more deliberately because it was a public place.

Villages also had communal buildings and other facilities. These included bread ovens, water fountains, olive presses, threshing floors and later laundries,[8] but the most important communal building was the church. Churches had originally served *pievi* comprising several villages, but progressively from the later eighteenth century possession of its own church or vicarial chapel became the mark of a community's independent status. There were many demands, especially in the 1820s and 1830s, for permission to build such churches or chapels or to upgrade existing ones.[9] There was also concern about the status of a village church within the *pieve* once hiving-off or some other rearrangement had occurred. In 1873, the mayor of Penta-di-Casinca expressed a longstanding grievance. Before 1802, the church at Penta had been the main church of one of the two *pievi* into which Casinca was divided. When these two were amalgamated into one, however, the church at Venzolasca became the seat of the *pievan* or *curé* and that at Penta thus lost its old status.[10] In physical terms, the importance of the church as an expression of village pride is reflected in the building of belfries, which seems to have taken place all over the island, particularly in the second half of the nineteenth century.[11] Internally, too, churches served important community functions. Attendance at church services was normal, and non-attendance could therefore signify deliberate withdrawal from the community. Grimaldi recounts that a Lecà youth from Guagno carried out the *attacar* against a Poli girl by cutting a lock of her hair when her father opposed their courtship. The father, who was prior of a confraternity, then announced that 'no member of the Poli family would appear in church or have anything to do with the confraternity' until the girl's hair had grown again.[12] It was common, of course, for families in a state of enmity to avoid meeting together in church. In addition to common religious functions, churches also served important secular ones. Churches were still being used in the nineteenth century as the venues for electoral meetings, meetings to select conscripts and so on, despite attempts by the bishop to end the practice,[13] and church squares were places of general assembly. Here it should be emphasized that Corsican churches were not usually located in the centre of villages and that different quarters or hamlets often had their own chapels, all of which qualifies the significance of the church as a symbol and arena of village solidarity.

Politically, the sense of community was indicated by the use of the term *paese* to describe it, which parallels the Andalusian *pueblo*.[14] The *paese* was run in the nineteenth century by the municipal council and municipal officials. The council was the heir to older communal assemblies,[15] and this filiation is reflected in the fact that the process of consultation and decision-making in the community went or was supposed to go beyond the council to include notables and others. At Moita in 1841, for example, an attempt to resolve a dispute with the parish priest was made by 'a meeting of the municipal council and the twelve men paying most in taxes', while at Bastelica the mayor was reprimanded by the prefect for taking a decision to renovate a chapel after consulting with only 'twelve of your supporters and four other notables', and not a larger number of local people.[16] Blanqui noted at the same time that the isolationism of Corsican villages was such 'that they all want to have a justice of the peace as well as a mayor and are willing to bear the cost of this ... Each village also wishes to have its own tax collector, schoolteacher, forest guard and so on.'[17] We shall see in Chapter 11 that municipal councils and posts were frequently used as instruments in factional struggles within communities but this should not obscure their primary communal function. It is also relevant to note again that not all residents in Corsican villages might be full members of the community with political and economic rights. At Fozzano, for example, only members of the original seven families were full 'citizens'. The rest were 'foreigners', who were 'excluded from sharing in the land as well as from the community in general', which meant no intermarriage and no burial in the old burying place.[18] In addition to such exclusion from access to common land, there was also in some villages an extreme reluctance to sell or even to let property to outsiders. Elsewhere, in the Castagniccia, the Nebbio and especially the Casinca, this communal attitude towards village land and property had long ago been eroded by the progress of stratification and of private property. At Venzolasca in the third quarter of the nineteenth century, one-third of those assessed for direct taxes were non-residents, while at Castellare, where there were no common lands, about half the land was owned by outsiders. It is significant, however, that nearly all these 'foreigners' came from neighbouring villages, and that residents and non-residents were carefully distinguished and separately assessed and taxed.[19]

This takes us on to the village as an economic community. Perhaps the most important function of the municipal council was to regulate the use or the lease of communal lands, woods and pastures, together with irrigation. This regulation required the appointment of communal agents. Most common were field guards, whom we have already encountered. Penta-di-Casinca had three in the mid-nineteenth century and also a person whose job it was to milk animals being kept in the village pound.[20] We learn from a case in 1845 that Venzolasca had a 'vine warden', while Prunelli had a communal herdsman in the 1830s. These people were sometimes paid a money wage, as at Penta, or they might be supported with direct contributions from other members of the community. At Prunelli, the leader of the Raffaelli faction, having been defeated in the municipal elections in 1834, 'withdrew in pique from the community'. He and his followers 'stopped giving the customary bread every Sunday to the field guard and the priest, and they took their goats away from the communal herdsman'.[21] Among communal resources in mountain villages, we should also mention the collection and marketing of snow, to provide ice in the towns in summer.[22]

On the social level, which can hardly be distinguished from the economic, the community found expression in a variety of further ways. First, there was a strong tradition of mutual aid and exchange of services.[23] We have seen that this was a feature of agricultural work. Friends and neighbours, as well as relatives, helped each other with clearing the maquis, lent equipment and labour on a reciprocal basis, and harvested crops together. The last was probably the most important and involved both cereals and tree products. At Venzolasca, for example, an attempt was made to rape Maria Buttavi in August 1857, while her husband was helping a neighbour to carry grain to his house. Also at Venzolasca, Matteo Luciani encountered his father's killer in October 1850, as he was going 'to help one of his neighbours to bring in his chestnuts'.[24] Mutual aid was also characteristic of pastoralism. Sometimes, herdsmen who were not necessarily related grouped together into 'companies', particularly for transhumance and for the hiring and use of winter pasture. Where this more formal organization was absent, co-operation in shearing, rounding up flocks and herds on the mountains, the use of shielings and transporting cheeses was usual. More generally, killing pigs and preserving their meat was a collective enterprise.[25] Again, community or neighbourly aid was provided on special occasions, such as the building or alteration of a house or in the event of some disaster such as a fire,[26] and it might also be given on a more regular basis in cases of need. Robiquet noted in 1835 that land belonging to widows and orphans was cultivated by relatives and friends on Sundays and festivals after mass, and in the Niolo the men of the village assembled every Sunday morning to do jobs for widows and families in hardship: fetching or cutting wood, gathering and cleaning chestnuts and so on, a practice known as the *chiamata*.[27] We should also mention the more formal practice of the municipal *corvée*. In 1839, for example, the council at Penta-di-Casinca resolved that every male between the ages of 18 and 60 should be liable to three days' labour or 'prestation' in order to repair the roads in the village. Heads of households were additionally required to provide carts and draught animals for this work. Again, in a case in 1852, we learn of a similarly drafted work-force from Silvareccio being occupied 'in repairing a small bridge on the local road'.[28]

Mutual aid was only one aspect of a sociability where competition was balanced or complemented by reciprocity. Ravis-Giordani writes that female sociability in Corsica was 'made up of exchanges of services and information. A person who lives apart, *ritirata*, is thus viewed askance, even regarded with suspicion, for she puts herself beyond the common rule of taking and giving, of mutual aid, and of the control exercised by the other women over her actions.'[29] These remarks are of more general application and relate to the importance of gift exchange and the tradition of hospitality, both frequently commented on by visitors to the island. Corsicans would be offended by attempts to pay them for their services, but they would accept gifts in exchange for gifts.[30] However, more calculation entered into such matters than many visitors perceived. Griffon connected the tradition of hospitality with the general scarcity of resources and stressed its strictly reciprocal basis. As if developing this point, Montherot related that many Corsicans had told him that they would have liked to have seen an end to the old hospitality, since it created such onerous obligations: 'Having granted hospitality, people use this as justification for claiming important services from the guest at a later date. Hospitality is only free for strangers; but among Corsicans it is paid for, not in money, but in services. For example, one would ask a lawyer for a free consultation, a mayor to discharge a conscript, a magistrate to acquit a guilty person.'[31] The strength of the obligations of hospitality is indicated by the fact that in theory they overrode those of the feud, a point to which we will return in Chapter 8. In such a context, refusal of hospitality or assistance could be a very serious matter.[32]

As Ravis-Giordani's remarks indicate, neighbourly or community assistance implied surveillance, and this was particularly important in a society which set such a high store on honour and reputation. An area where community control via women's gossip is very obvious is that of breaches of the sexual rules by women, to which we have already referred. An official reported in 1850 that 'it was virtually impossible in Corsica for a girl's unreported pregnancy to escape the notice of neighbours and thus of all those living in the same locality'.[33] In cases of suspected infanticide, again and again an unmarried woman's pregnancy and then her failure to give birth regularly and to show her baby were remarked on first by neighbours informally. In 1859, for example, Lucia Vitali of Santo-Pietro, who had already given birth to one illegitimate child, became pregnant again, but she dissimulated her state and even denied it. Her neighbours, however, had no doubts about it, 'and, seeing that she was making no preparations for the baby, suspected that she must be thinking of getting rid of it'. She then shut herself up inside her house one day in April 1860 and 'refused to accept the visit of several women who went to offer their assistance', believing either that she was ill or that she was about to give birth.[34] Neighbourly surveillance (or type-casting) might also lead to the detection or supposed detection of other misdemeanours. After the theft of money from a shop at Petreto-Bicchisano in 1858, for example, 'public opinion at once identified the culprits. People were saying openly in the village that if the thief came from Bicchisano it could only be Giovan-Cesare Romani, while if he came from Petreto, it must be Giacomo-Filippo Vellutini', and both men were later prosecuted.[35]

Other forms of community control existed. First, nicknames were very generally used. These were a necessary complement to an official naming system which employed a very limited number of Christian names and surnames, but their significance extends beyond such a rationale. Nicknames were names given and used within the community, and they often referred to behaviour or qualities, which implied a communal judgment on or assessment of a person. They would also be used to designate outside origins.[36] The community was also involved in the settlement of disputes. Not only was an obligation laid on people to act as arbiters, mediators and peacemakers in each other's conflicts, but the community itself might act formally or semi-formally. Village tribunals had existed in the past, and some peace treaties from the early nineteenth century were sponsored and guaranteed by the community.[37] We will return to these questions in Chapter 9. A further manifestation of community control was the charivari, to which we have referred in the context of male and female honour and of remarriage. It could also be used in other circumstances, for example to demonstrate hostility towards secular officials or the parish priest. The charivari brings us to the ritual expressions of community.

Of these the most obvious and important was the patronal festival. Church services were held in honour of the local patron saint or virgin, and the saint's statue was processed along a route that took in the significant points of the village territory. Games were played and other forms of merrymaking took place, which included the eating of special food. The function of festivals in making or reinforcing the sense of community is indicated in two further ways. First, villagers who had left home would make special efforts to return for the festival. Beaulieu-Delbet noted that at Santa-Maria-Sicche around 1890 the festival of Santa Reparata was very much an occasion for such 'exiles', and this trend has become very general in recent times.[38] Secondly, where villages were divided into hamlets, these very often had their own festivals, but on these occasions the people from one hamlet played host to those from others, a practice which stressed their common ties.[39] Two other community rituals had similar functions. On the Day of the Dead, in addition to the usual rites associated with the dead themselves to which we will return in Chapter 13, ritual begging by children took place, and meat and other food was sometimes distributed by bigger landowners to their clients.[40] At a time when common solidarity with the ancestors was being emphasized, solidarity across living age groups and classes was also expressed. Carnival stressed community in different ways, notably by suspending normal relations and controls. Lorenzi de Bradi noted that it was a time of licence, when people donned disguises and abandoned restraints and respect for age, rank and sex. All doors were opened, and men could approach girls whom they would not normally speak to. Such expressions of the fundamental equality of all members of the community were important, but there was an order in Carnival behind its apparent licence which also demonstrated the force of the community and its values. The leading role in Carnival was taken by the village youths, constituted in more or less formal groups. They were sometimes led by 'kings' and they disguised themselves in specific and recognized ways, as women, animals or characters such as 'Turks' or 'Moors'. So disguised, they might perform well-articulated rituals and dances, as at Bastelica. Very often they singled out specific individuals or families for attention or attack, capturing people for ransom or performing outside chosen houses until refreshment was provided.[41] This would seem to be a way of sanctioning unpopular or anti-social behaviour much like the charivari, and relates to the composition and circulation of satires taking place, we have seen, at the same time. More generally, though festivals could be occasions for tensions to erupt into violence, in Corsica as elsewhere they must have served ordinarily to channel conflict in a ritual and cathartic way.[42] Moreover, conflict was often explicitly seen to be antagonistic to communal involvement in festivals. Lorenzi de Bradi noted that in his own village of Belvedere 'only families engaged in a vendetta bolted their doors' during Carnival. Since the festival was an expression of community, those in a state of open hostility with each other were excluded from it. In other cases, however, the festive time could be a period of truce, in which enmities were temporarily set aside or even brought permanently to an end. Discussing the feud between the Grimaldi and the Vincenti at Monte-d'Olmo, Gregorovius wrote that the patronal festival temporarily 'put a check on all hostile actions between them'.[43]

In addition to general festivals, rites of passage in Corsica were important community occasions. This is less true of baptisms than of weddings and funerals, though they too involved processions through the village, banquets with music and the exchange of gifts well beyond immediate kin. Godparents, moreover, according to Malaspina, were never chosen from within the family, and ritual kinship was thus used to create ties at the village level and beyond.[44]

We have already seen that, although marriages were made by families, the community had an important say too, and might even sanction matches of which parents disapproved. In the nineteenth century, moreover, the customary marriage was usually solemnized by a wedding ceremony, in which state, church and community each had a part to play. Of these, as Casanova notes, the participation of the community was the most important, ensuring publicity and public approval and ultimately conferring legitimacy.[45] The communal nature of weddings also reflected the basic fact that village endogamy was the rule in Corsica for all but the wealthiest, though even they might not go far afield. According to Finelli, the important Tavera family of Tavera intermarried with families from villages in the same valley and from Ajaccio, the nearest place on the coast, while Lamotte notes the preference of the seven aboriginal families of Fozzano for intermarriage among themselves.[46] The predominance of village endogamy was noted by a succession of residents and visitors. The parish priest of Rusio wrote typically in 1850 that the population of the village was 'united by ties of kinship and marriage, hardly any marriages being contracted outside'.[47] Preference for village endogamy is reflected in folk-tales and expressed in proverbs, such as 'Marry a neighbour!'; or 'Wives and oxen should come from your own place.'[48] Higher ecclesiastical sources paint the same picture. The Church's strict rules against consanguinous marriage met with persistent resistance in Corsica, and technical incest, that is, union within the prohibited degrees, was the most common offence noted in visitations in the eighteenth century. It was recognized that Corsicans were too poor to obtain the necessary dispensations from Rome, and in 1819 the bishop of Ajaccio was authorized, on a year to year basis, to grant such dispensations for marriages within the third and fourth degrees of kinship. In the two decades ending in 1945, Corsica was still the French department with the highest proportion of consanguinous marriages measured by requests for ecclesiastical dispensations.[49] We may point again to the paucity of surnames as a further sign of strict endogamy.[50]

Finally, local demographic studies provide incontrovertible confirmation of the other evidence. At Calenzana in the Balagna between 1800 and 1850, both spouses came from the village in the case of over 90 per cent of marriages. At Albertacce between 1850 and 1900, 86 per cent of marriages united partners from within the village, and rates of 80 per cent or more applied in other villages of the Niolo at this time and more recently. At Poggio-di-Venaco just south of Corte purely endogamous marriages again accounted for 80 per cent of all marriages in the period just before the First World War.[51] It is significant here that at Cargèse the trend towards village endogamy eventually overcame hostility between Greek settlers and local inhabitants, between whom intermarriage had become normal by the second half of the nineteenth century if not earlier.[52] Where strict village endogamy was less important, spouses were rarely chosen outside the district.[53] Where exogamous patterns appear to be strong outside the ranks of the élite, moreover, they can be shown to have an endogamous basis. Matrimonial alliances were common, for example, after 1875 between the inhabitants of Manso in the Fango valley and of the Nioline villages of Corscia and Lozzi and between those of the coastal village of Galeria and of Albertacce, but both Manso and Galeria were coastal 'colonies' of the three Nioline villages in question.[54]

The fact that exogamy was unusual and perhaps something of a threat was expressed in wedding rituals. Symbolic combats between horsemen from the two villages concerned took place at Bastelica, in the Sartène region, the Capo Corso and elsewhere. Obstacles were placed in the way of bridal processions from 'strange villages', both at the exit from the bride's and at the entry to the groom's village. These might be purely symbolic ribbons or effective wooden barriers. 'Foreign' brides were also required to 'pay' for their entry with gifts and might have stones thrown at them. Charivaris might be mounted, too, against exogamous couples.[55] Community involvement was general, however, in all weddings. At Santa-Maria-Sicche around 1890, 'all the women of the district came to the bride's house and assisted with her clothes', while the groom was accompanied by the men. In the Balagna, all the village expected to attend the ceremonies and enjoy the festivities. The provision of gifts on the occasion of marriages was another expression of community, a kind of mutual aid. 'In the West and notably in the Ajaccio region,' Casanova writes,

> the guests (that is all the village) pour wheat, dried vegetables, chestnuts into the bride's apron. The products, which had to overflow on to the ground and spread over as large an area as possible, were brought in sufficient quantities to provide for the upkeep of the young couple for a whole year. These ceremonies expressed the solidarity of the village.[56]

The custom would also seem to have a magical significance, seeking to ensure the bride's fertility by filling the apron over her abdomen to overflowing with the fruits of the earth.[57]

Funerals were also community occasions. There was an obligation, sometimes on all adults, sometimes on one representative from every family, to attend the administration of the last sacraments, the wake, and the church funeral. Burial in common ground was by no means the rule, however. We shall return to these questions in Chapter 13.

A leading role in funeral ritual was played by confraternities, and these represented and articulated community solidarity on other occasions, notably the patronal festival and at Easter. It was reported in an eighteenth-century source that there was 'at least one confraternity in each parish. Nearly all the inhabitants belong to it. Usually it possesses a private oratory, which is decorated and furnished with more care than the church itself'. Confraternities continued to be very widespread through the nineteenth century, though not every village had one, and the possession of separate chapels seems to have been mainly confined to wealthier villages in the Balagna, the Nebbio, the Capo Corso and the Castagniccia; in the south, a chapel inside the parish church was the rule. An enquiry in 1810 confirms that one confraternity per village was normal and that a good proportion of the adult male population belonged, since numbers of members ranged from 60 to well over 400. Sororities for women also existed.[58] Confraternities had often been established or encouraged by the clergy specifically to restrain conflict within communities,[59] but they could themselves provoke conflict. Fighting broke out, for example, in 1809 at a municipal council meeting at Sorbo in the Casinca when the financial administration of a confraternity chapel was discussed, and three men were killed.[60] At Monte-d'Olmo, the truce, to which we have referred, was in fact broken when the rival families began to quarrel over who should wear the robe and cowl of the confraternity and who should lead the procession.[61] More germane to the concerns of this chapter, confraternities sometimes conducted disputes on behalf of their communities either with their own priests or with confraternities from other villages.[62]

Community also found expression in resistance to external authority. This ranged from maintaining a 'wall of silence' in the face of official investigations into alleged offences[63] to the use of force against the military and the police. In 1819, for example, the gendarmerie went to Rusio to arrest three men, wanted on serious charges, including homicide. One of these was the son-in-law of the mayor, who was suspected of harbouring him and his companions. The mayor's house and that of the parish priest were surrounded and shots were fired from the latter, one of which killed a gendarme. Two of the wanted men then escaped. The mayor was asked to provide a guide to fetch reinforcements, but he refused. The gendarmerie, who were still besieging the third man in the priest's house, were finally attacked by a large body of local men and forced to retire from the village.[64] Harbouring deserters or men resisting conscription seems to have been particularly widespread at this time, and a number of similar incidents were reported. Tacit encouragement by local officials seems to have been characteristic of these 'acts of rebellion'. At Corscia, where the gendarmerie were attacked in 1820 while trying to arrest a deserter from the Corsican legion, the local officer of health was reported to have poured hot water on to them from a window, and 'neither the mayor nor the *adjoint* appeared to enforce respect for the law or to attempt to dissipate the unlawful assembly'.[65] Similar acts of violent resistance occurred later in the century. Three were reported in the Balagna in 1832[66] and three came before the Assize Court in 1849.[67] However, they were not confined to, though they may have been encouraged by, periods of political instability, and further examples occurred during the Second Empire.[68] In the Rusio example, the parish priest acted as the representative or leader of the community against outsiders but it was also possible for the community to take action against priests as outsiders, as we shall see in Chapter 8. Acts of rebellion against the central authorities could also overlap with inter-village conflict,[69] to which we now turn.

II

The situation of Corsican villages vis-à-vis each other parallels that among families. They were in competition for scarce resources and they distrusted each
other, but a degree of co-operation was often essential to their functioning.
Conflict between villages stemmed from these factors, and a spectrum of antagonism is found ranging from general hostility and rivalry to actual feuding.

On an everyday level, hostility between villages was expressed through the
use of mocking or abusive sobriquets, of which Arrighi has collected over 200.
So, for their neighbours, 'Zoza, Conca and Lecci [were] the last villages God
made', 'the people from Renno [had] no sense', those from Ghisonaccia were
'loonies', while Calcatoggio was the place 'where you get a bad dinner and a
worse bed'.[70] Similar hostile stereotyping occurred in folk-tales, for example in
three stories about the stupidity of the people of Bastelica collected by Ortoli in
Altagène, Olmiccia and Porto-Vecchio.[71] Like nicknaming, of course, such characterization of other villages implied a measure of contact with and concern
about them. More generally, proverbs expressed an extreme caution about any
such contact with outsiders, who were presumed to be *ipso facto* unfriendly. 'With
the people beyond the river, neither take nor give,' warned one; 'Don't go out of
your own territory with an empty bag,' warned another.[72] In a case in 1812, a
man from Pastoreccia-di-Rostino was asked about his relationship with the Capo-
rosi brothers from Frasso and he replied 'that he could not trust them since they
came from a different village'.[73] We have seen that intermarriage between villages
was rare, and this meant that immigration to them was also very limited, particularly since outsiders might not have full rights in the community. Very occasionally non-natives might achieve positions of power but even then they were not
fully accepted. Giovan-Battiste Lota of Penta-di-Casinca, who became mayor of
Ampriani, was killed by Pasquale Negroni, 'who could not stand to see an
outsider laying down the law' in his village.[74] It is probably significant in this
context that rape was usually an inter-community offence.[75]

In many parts of Europe, inter-village rivalries were institutionalized in the
form of sporting contests, regular fights between youth groups and competition
at common festivals or pilgrimages.[76] Only the last seems to have been of any
importance in Corsica, and we shall return to it. Collective litigation between
villages occurred but does not seem to have been common.[77] Long-standing
rivalries between particular villages sometimes achieved legendary status. That
between Borgo and Lucciana near Bastia was the subject of Viale's *Dionomachia*,[78]
while that between Renno and Chigliani in the canton of Vico was more literally
explained by a legend which was also a 'noodle tale' directed by the people of
Renno against their neighbours. There was an eclipse of the sun, and the people
from Chigliani thought that their rivals from Renno had taken it. The herdsmen
from Renno then appropriated some meadowland that had belonged to Chigliani, and said that they would return the sun if the meadow were ceded to them in
writing. The people from Chigliani agreed, later realizing that they had been
duped. They tried to get their own back by sending frogs to croak at night in
Renno, hoping that the people there would imagine that this was vengeance on
the part of the spirits and thus return the meadow which they had wrongfully

acquired. But the canny inhabitants of Renno knew that the frogs were harmless and in retaliation diverted a local stream to make a noisy waterfall near Chigliani.[79] Before considering the material interests at stake in such rivalries to which the legend refers, we should mention the well-known competition between Ajaccio and Bastia, which was in many ways simply an inter-village rivalry writ large. Bastia never accepted Ajaccio's position as chief administrative centre, which it held from 1811 until 1975. Much argument took place over the location of the Assize Court in the years before and after its transfer to Bastia in 1816, and this controversy resumed in 1848. Bastia was also successful in obtaining nomination in 1838 as head of the Corsican 'academy' or educational division, with a college, later given the status of *lycée*. Bastia, too, was the seat of the military headquarters. A report in 1823, when this was still in doubt, shows the public prosecutor countering the claims of Ajaccio and singing the praises of Bastia as if he had been a native. Bastia was 'the capital city of the island. Bastia is superior in both wealth and enlightenment. Bastia is the centre of urbanity and good manners ...'[80]

Like conflict between families, conflict between villages may be divided into two broad categories: that which concerned material and that which concerned non-material interests. Most inter-village conflict stemmed from disputes over land, as the Renno/Chigliani example illustrates. 'The boundaries between villages have remained till now very uncertain,' Réalier-Dumas declared in 1819. 'This uncertainty is a real calamity, since it gives rise to daily contestations, in which, all too often, people get killed.'[81] Sometimes such disputes were comparatively simple ones over the limits between contiguous settlements, like that between Venzolasca and Vescovato, which was settled by official agreement in 1845.[82] More often, however, two or more villages shared rights in territory situated far away from the main settlements. Conflict over the use of these was traditional and continued into the nineteenth century. In 1727, for example, the inhabitants of Olmi-Cappella, men, women and children, took part in a punitive expedition against the people of the neighbouring villages of Forcili and Pioggiola and killed 230 head of livestock belonging to them. This prompted the governor to intervene to partition the *prese*, in which they all had rights. In 1817, however, Olmi-Cappella was still engaged in similar disputes 'over common lands' with other villages.[83] Patin de La Fizelière referred at the end of the eighteenth century to disputes over coastal land in the south-east between the communities of Aullène and Zerubia on the one hand, and the town of Bonifacio on the other, and between the inhabitants of Sartène and those of the *pievi* of Scopamène and Zicavo over the valuable pasture on the mountain of Coscione. These disputes again persisted into the next century, though the lines of battle were not always drawn in the same places. Several examples are reported, for instance, of conflict in the early nineteenth century involving the inhabitants of Aullène. In June 1818, ten armed men stole a quantity of cheese, *brocciu* and bread, and ten sheep from two herdsmen from Aullène. 'Out of fear', neither they nor the mayor would say who the robbers were, but 'there is every reason to believe that they come from Zicavo, whose inhabitants are accustomed to perpetrating such excesses at this time of year'. The following March the people of Aullène and Zerubia damaged and burned each other's property on the coast in the territory of Figari, and they were said to be preparing for a full-scale war with each other over their conflicting claims to land in the area. Again, in September 1827, the inhabitants of Olivese went *en masse* to certain mountain pastures 'situated between the two villages and carried off about 350 animals belonging to the herdsmen of Aullène, who were pasturing them there, as they claimed, by right. This action led to altercations between the small number of herdsmen and the crowd of aggressors. The herdsmen were beaten with sticks, and three of them were tied up and taken back to Olivese.' Echoes of these collective disputes clearly lingered on, since in a case in 1850, in which Marco-Matteo Roccaserra of Aullène was shot at and mortally wounded, he at once accused the Guidicelli, 'his enemies from Zerubia'.[84] A similar, if not more complicated, situation existed vis-à-vis the coastal lands in the north-east. At the start of the nineteenth century, the territory of Galeria was used for winter pasture and agriculture by eight villages of the interior, while lands at Girolata, Sia and Filosarma were shared and disputed by five herding communities from the Niolo, by the villages of Calenzana and Moncale in the Balagna and by those of Ota and Evisa.[85]

Inter-community conflict centred on the use of common lands was exacerbated in the early nineteenth century as the State intervened to impose or encourage partition or stricter demarcation.[86] In a letter to the prefect in 1825, for example, the district prosecutor of Bastia referred to an increasing number of 'collective acts of violence between the inhabitants of different villages or of hamlets belonging to the same village, occasioned by disputes over rights to common lands'. The prefect had set up a special committee 'to bring all such claims to an end by settling these disputes once and for all'. But in the interim people had been encouraged 'to occupy the contested territories by force and to usurp them for their exclusive use'. For instance, the people of Olmo had gone '*en masse*' in mid-August to a piece of land called Valle and had cut down the maquis and the trees growing there, as if to prepare it for cultivation, 'although the land was in fact property that was common to the villages of Olmo and Prunelli-di-Casacconi'. The people of Prunelli had been prevented by the gendarmerie from mounting an expedition to recover the land and had had to remain content with making an official complaint. Such pre-emptive actions were so common at this time that the prefect issued a special notice relating to them.[87]

Other elements, which we have already encountered, entered into these conflicts. First, there was hostility between villages that had once formed part of a single community. Lamotte refers here to conflict in the early eighteenth century between Bisinchi and Vignale.[88] The subprefect of Calvi explained in 1821 that the animosity of the inhabitants of the Niolo against those of Galeria, whose settlement they had many times ravaged, was an animosity directed 'not against outsiders, as one might think, but against their own compatriots whom they wished to prevent from settling there'.[89] Again, we learn in 1854 that 'their undivided lands were the cause of continual conflict' between Levie and its former hamlet Figari on the plain.[90]

Secondly, these conflicts were often also conflicts between pastoral and agricultural interests. Bisinchi was a pastoral and Vignale an agricultural community. The herdsmen from the Niolo wished to prevent the creation of agricultural villages on their traditional pasturing territories. Opposition and conflict also existed between dual transhumant communities and sedentary villages through which they regularly took their flocks, for example between Ciamannacce, Cozzano and Palneca on the one hand, and Olmeto, Arbellara and Fozzano on the other, or between Asco on the one hand, and Castifao and Moltifao on the other.[91] Similar trouble occurred where herdsmen from one village pastured their flocks legitimately or illegitimately on the lands of another. In May 1841, for example, the municipal council of Urtaca took steps to try to stop 'the devastations which [outside] herdsmen were causing in the communal forest'. These, from an unspecified village or villages, retaliated by taking action against Urtaca's municipal officers. A mule belonging to the mayor was killed and the watercourse running to a mill belonging to the *adjoint* was diverted. A number of conflicts are reported in the 1840s and 1850s between herdsmen from the Niolo and elsewhere and the inhabitants of villages in the Casinca. Antono Santucci, a herdsman from Corscia, was killed, for example, in 1843 by the field-guard of Sorbo-Ocognano when he refused to hand over the lamb which was allegedly 'the customary tribute due from any herdsman from outside who took his flock on to the territory of the village'. Damage done by straying goats belonging to herdsmen from Silvareccio and from Erone caused serious affrays at Castellare in 1841 and 1852, in each of which a man was killed. In another case in 1857, we learn that 'animals belonging to herdsmen from Palneca [who occupied shielings on the territory of Sollacaro] were often allowed to pasture at will, and thus got into enclosures where they caused considerable damage'. Following one such incident in March 1857, the herdsmen were 'pursued by local hue and cry'.[92] Sometimes, as we saw in Chapter 3, outside herdsmen were aided and seconded by groups within the villages whose lands they damaged or devastated. The municipal council of Santa-Lucia-di-Moriani had voted unanimously in 1845 to abolish common pasturing on all lands after harvest, but the mayor had failed to forward the decision to the prefecture for ratification 'because his friends, relatives and protectors from the neighbouring village of San-Giovanni would have suffered had such a measure been implemented'.[93] We should also mention here the efforts of sedentary communities sharing lands with herding, transhumant ones to take advantage of the trend towards partition to try to charge the latter a rent for using their traditional pastures. When the inhabitants of Evisa tried this tactic in 1826 in connection with lands at Girolata and Sia, the herdsmen of the Niolo resisted by force and addressed a successful protest to the prefect via their mayors. But herdsmen from Figari who used the pasture near the lagoon of Ventilegne on the territory of Bonifacio were less fortunate. They were attacked in November 1834 by four to five hundred people from the town, who burned their huts, destroyed their folds and carried off their animals. As a result they agreed to pay rent.[94]

Collective violence between villages arising from disputes over land and livestock became rare after the 1830s, though a few notable exceptions may be cited. Violent disputes between individuals or families from different villages, by contrast, occurred throughout the century. In a case in 1842, for example, Felice Nasica of Prato was convicted of homicide. 'The inhabitants of Prato and of Popolasca had, for a long time, disputed ownership of a piece of common land called *Li Monti grassi*', and Nasica and his brother were trying to prevent some men from Popolasca from ploughing there, which led to fighting between them.[95] Similar disputes were probably even more common in a pastoral setting. A fight took place in July 1826 'on the mountain called Acione' between the Calzaroni of Ucciani and the brothers Fiamnolino of Bastelica, provoked, it seems, by the latter who claimed, 'that the land on which the Calzaroni were pasturing their animals' was not part of the territory of Ucciani.[96] The report of a case in 1864 related that 'for many years the possession of the north slope of the mountain which divides the cantons of Orezza and San-Lorenzo has been the cause of conflict, often bloody, between the villages of those cantons'.[97] Stealing livestock was also an issue here, and we have referred to conflicts prompted by such theft or supposed theft between people from Zicavo and Loreto-di-Tallano in 1843 and from Taglio and Isolaccio in 1840. The latter dispute eventually involved about 150 combatants.[98] It also drew in people from Porri, and some disputes did transcend village level, even taking on an inter-regional dimension. This is true of the conflicts in which the herdsmen of the Niolo were engaged, and it appears in an incident which took place in 1834 on the plain of Marana. People from the Balagna and from the Capo Corso were harvesting their crops there and began to exchange epithets: 'nuts' for the former, and 'thickheads' and 'onion-eaters' for the latter. Stones were thrown and a man was mortally wounded.[99]

Under the heading of conflicts of material interest between communities one may also include those relating to marriage. Intermarriage between villages was unusual, as we have seen, and the subject of ritual sanctions. It might also be physically prevented by collective action. In 1816, a large number of people from Omessa and Castirlà, including 40 armed men, went to Soveria 'to prevent the marriage of the daughter of a widow' from one of the first two places, and similar action was reported more recently in the Balagna.[100] Action to prevent exogamy might also provoke conflict. A certain Nicolai, for example, wished to marry a girl from Valpajola, which was not his own village. His plans were thwarted and, as a result, he 'conceived a grudge against the whole village'. One day in May 1849 he went there with a group of other men, all armed, in order to give vent to his hostility. Shots were exchanged between the intruders and local men, and Nicolai himself was killed.[101] Where unwanted marriages did occur between villages, an inter-community dimension could compound the hostility between affines. After a girl from a wealthy family of Penta-di-Casinca married a much poorer man from Pruno-d'Ampugnani, we have seen that her parents broke off all relations with her. When she died, however, her sister went to Pruno for the wake and sang a lament in which she poured scorn on the poverty of her in-laws and on their native place: 'Is this the village / That claims to be like a town? / There are only herdsmen's huts here / Where no proper hospitality can be offered.'[102]

Conflicts of 'honour' between communities centred largely on religious resources and reflect the importance of ritual expressions of community. We have seen that a village's independence often focused on its having its own priest and parish church, and rivalries were especially intense here between old and new settlements.[103] A tale collected in 1882 about the church at Poggio-di-Tallano is instructive here. Poggio was the only village in the *pieve* without its own church and it was therefore decided to build one. Stones were assembled at the chosen site, but they kept being moved during the night. Before realizing that this was a supernatural intervention, the inhabitants of Poggio supposed that people from the neighbouring villages were to blame; they were thought to be 'envious ... they don't want us to build our own church'.[104]

The furnishing and embellishment of churches was another focus of pride and rivalry. Tommaseo referred to a 'minor war' between Castellare and Penta-di-Casinca over a church bell, and a similar dispute occurred in 1837 when the bell from the church at Alzi was stolen by the people of Favalello.[105] This bell almost certainly came from the former monastic church of Bozio, the acquisition of whose equipment led to fierce competition among a number of villages in the early 1820s. In September 1822, a bell, a stoup and other effects were removed from the church. The inhabitants of Alando, who claimed to own the church, followed the robbers to Bustanico, where they surrounded the village and were ultimately dispersed by the military. On New Year's Day 1823, various objects 'consecrated to divine service' were again taken from the old convent church. Two days later, 'a crowd of people from Sermano, led by their *adjoint*, marched to Bozio with axes [and other tools], intending to remove everything which had not yet been pillaged. The village of Alando raised the alarm, and people from there hurried to the convent to prevent further depredations'; the intervention of the local authorities and notables forced the people of Sermano to retire, and the church was left alone. But not for long, for at the end of March Bozio was again raided by people from Arbitro, Piedicorte, Mazzola and Rebbia, led by their mayors and *adjoints*, and all the remaining furnishings were removed from the church. Similar disputes over the contents of disaffected monastic churches are reported at about the same time in other parts of the north-east.[106]

Village festivals were often attended by people from other villages. We learn from cases in 1852, for example, that people from Penta-Acquatella and from Silvareccio went to the festival at Ortiporio at the end of August. This practice could lead to inter-community conflict. In September 1841, fighting broke out during the patronal festival at Ciamannacce between local people and those from Palneca, three of whom were wounded.[107] There were also regional festivals or pilgrimages, which were again a forum for co-operation and for conflict between villages. Renucci refers to the annual pilgrimage made by the villages of the canton of Tavagna to the cross above the old convent of St Francis between Pero-Casevecchie and Talasani 'in order to call down the blessing of heaven on their crops'.[108] A similar gathering took place annually in May a little further to the north on the plain of Casinca. This was the festival of San Pancrazio centred on his chapel there, which attracted people from villages in the Casinca itself, in the Castagniccia and further afield. Conflict among them was not uncommon, as we have already seen. In 1822, what was described as a 'riot' occurred as 'people were getting ready to go home' after the festival. 'A dispute arose between a man from Carpineto and another from Erbajolo as to who should use a drinking-glass first'. One of the men drew his pistol. Others quickly joined in and general fighting broke out. In all, 40 shots were fired, three people were killed and nine wounded.[109]

Another form of competition was characteristic of the Capo Corso. According to a report in 1828, 'most quarrels there have to do with religion; the possession of a particular chapel is disputed with more ardour than if the ownership of a great communal domain were at stake', and the inhabitants would rarely agree to share chapels with people from other villages.[110] The best documented dispute of this kind related to the chapel of Santa Maria della Chiapella. This small isolated chapel had been a bone of contention in the later Middle Ages between the local secular clergy and its titular monastic patrons on the Italian mainland. From the fifteenth century it had been a dependency of the parish church of Tomino, one of the oldest centres of Christianity in Corsica. By the start of the nineteenth century, however, Tomino had declined in importance vis-à-vis the neighbouring village of Rogliano on whose territory the chapel actually stood. Both villages laid claim to it and both participated in the special ceremonies which took place there annually in Holy Week. Processions went from each village to the chapel, and arguments and contestations between them were usual. 'Everyone wants to distinguish himself, if need be by fighting, on an occasion which is the subject of conversation throughout the rest of the year.' The young men from each village egged each other on, excited by wine and by the presence of girls. Usually, people contented themselves with threats and shouts, 'and sometimes the inhabitants of the one village would drown with yells the sacred songs and psalms being sung by the other'. On Good Friday 1826, however, a more serious confrontation occurred. The people from Rogliano processed first to the chapel and took possession of it. 'They had decided not to share with their neighbours from Tomino in offering prayers to the Virgin and in receiving the graces which were thus obtained; and they prepared for a struggle if necessary to keep their rivals out.' In an attempt to prevent trouble, the mayor of Tomino banned the procession from his village and the local clergy refused to lead it. At the same time, the mayor of Rogliano had a detachment of gendarmes placed on the road to the chapel to bar the route to anyone from Tomino. But these precautions had no effect, and a procession of 300–400 people from Tomino went to the chapel as usual. They were met outside by the Rogliano people, who had just finished their prayers, and fighting between them began. The men threw stones, which the women collected for them, and batons and the standards and crucifixes used in the processions were also employed as weapons. The fighting carried on for a long time and was only ended when a gun was fired on one side. Seven people were injured, one seriously. Both sides claimed victory and returned with a standard of the enemy, which was placed as a trophy in the village church. Similar, if less violent, confrontations recurred through the 1830s and after, and related boundary disputes between the two villages were still unsettled in 1855. Arrighi relates that the people of Rogliano were still known at Tomino until very recently as '*tagliacristi*' (the ones who cut us off from Christ), 'because it is said, of their claims to the chapel' of Santa Maria.[111]

Rivalry between villages divided by mountains was sometimes expressed in symbolic form. Persons with special supernatural powers from the villages concerned, known as *mazzeri*, were believed to go out in spirit form to the mountains to engage in annual fights, which in some way determined the well-being of the villages concerned. Such battles took place, for example, between Guagno and Venaco at the Col di Manganello, between Guagno and Pastricciola at the

Col di Missicella, between Bastelica and Frasseto at the Col d'Arusula, and between Soccia and the villages of the Niolo. Battles are also said to have occurred between Cozzano and Ciamannacce, which were neighbouring villages in the upper Taravo valley.[112]

Having discussed the main types of inter-community conflict, we must briefly consider how they related to other forms of conflict and to feuding in particular. Conflict between members of different communities occurred at individual and family as well as at the collective level, though the distinction is not always easy to draw in practice. Some acts of aggression seem to have been directed at strangers simply because they were strangers. This seems to have been the case with Giuseppo Canavaggio from Pila-Canale, for example, arrested in 1841 for stabbing a man from Tavera in a brawl in Ajaccio.[113] We may also cite cases in which men from different villages attacked each other while stopping at inns.[114] It was also a fairly common initial reaction to attribute responsibility for offences to outsiders. When Anton-Francesco Giabicconi of Moriani was killed in 1803, witnesses said that local people blamed 'men from Bastia' or from the Fiumorbo.[115] Similarly, following the killing of the Pietrini brothers of Olmi-Cappella, opinion was divided in the village as to who the culprits were: 'some said that it was people from Palasca and others people from Santo-Pietro-di-Tenda'.[116] In practice, such accusations were often a way of protecting local culprits and may be a better guide to general currents of hostility between communities than to actual acts of aggression. One should also stress that aggression between people from different villages was unlikely to be random and would usually take place in a context of established enmity. Thus Giacomo-Natale Pianelli of Olmeto was fatally stabbed in December 1851 by Anton-Marco Mondolini of Cozzano in the course of a fight between them over a piece of land,[117] but this personal quarrel took place against the wider background of hostility between their villages.

Such killing between villages and consequent feuding between families from different communities was rare, but it did take place. We saw in Chapter 2 that the feud between the Viterbi and the Frediani of Penta-di-Casinca around 1800 also involved families from Porri, Taglio and Vescovato. In the 1820s and early 1830s, the Antonmarchi, the Ferri and other families of Tox were engaged in an 'implacable and terrible feud' with the Nicolai of Campi, following the abduction of a Ferri girl in 1822. Five of the former and probably an equivalent number of the latter were killed. A more restricted feud occurred in the 1840s between the Raffalli of Nocario and the Campana of Campana,[118] while Chanal referred later to a long-standing enmity between the Giuncheto of Vignamajo and the Figari of Salice.[119] We may note again that the villages concerned here were all contiguous or close neighbours and that general rivalry or hostility between them was likely to have existed. In such circumstances, there would be a tendency for other members of the community to be drawn into quarrels with outsiders. At the end of 1802, for example, 'youths from the village of Piobbeta provoked and attacked another youth from Carpineto', who was slightly injured with small-shot. 'Since the two villages were next door to each other', the authorities feared that the trouble might escalate and intervened to effect a reconciliation.[120] More generally, when Dr Matteo was killed at a neighbouring village where he had gone to treat a patient, his relatives held all the inhabitants responsible and refused to greet them or to accept refreshments from them when they went to fetch his body.[121] Such preventive or avoiding action was not always successful. An attempt by Visconte Casile of Valle to ambush and kill Dr Petruschi of Sari-d'Orcino in 1842 led to a general feud between their two villages and beyond. 'This terrible crime annoyed the relatives and friends of Petruschi to such an extent that the inhabitants of the whole canton found themselves in a state of enmity. Missionaries visited the area in an attempt to pacify the parties, but this proved ineffective.'[122]

A number of such feuds between whole villages are recorded, but in most cases it seems doubtful whether the use of the term is really justified. Renucci and others refer to a 'feud' between Serra and Serrale in the Moriani district in the later Genoese period, but both places were hamlets of a larger if scattered community.[123] Even the classic example of the feud between Borgo and Lucciana described by Viale is dubious. The conflict occurred in 1812 at Easter, when a dead donkey was found blocking the route between the two villages, thus preventing the usual exchange of visits between their confraternities. Responsibility for the insulting obstruction was attributed by each to the ill-will of the other and the carcase was carried backwards and forwards between the villages in an atmosphere of mounting irritation, which culminated in bloodshed.[124] Viale himself saw this episode as a variety of vendetta, but it would seem to have more in common with the kind of inter-community conflict over religious resources that characterized the Capo Corso. Of course, both this and other forms of conflict between communities could and usually did have the long time-scale that is an essential element in feuding. To mention only one further example here, the contiguous villages of Silvareccio and Casalta in the Casinca were reported in 1830 to be 'divided by bloody enmities'. A man from Casalta was killed in 1829 in general fighting between the youths of the two places on the occasion of drawing lots for conscription, and he was not avenged until 1850.[125] We may also cite reliable references to peace treaties signed between communities, for example, between Porri and Silvareccio and between Olmeto and Ciamannacce in 1834, and between Valle and Sari-d'Orcino in 1843.[126]

The term 'feud' may more certainly be used to describe the conflict between Corsican communities and those of Greek colonists, which were endemic from the time of the latter's arrival in the late seventeenth century. The Greeks, who enjoyed official protection, were several times driven from their settlements in the Vico region, and hostilities were still evident in the early nineteenth century.[127] The subprefect of Vico was called in by the mayor of Cargèse, the main Greek settlement, in 1807 'to prevent an attack that was being launched by people from Piana'. Trouble had arisen when a Greek from Ajaccio, who owned land in Cargèse, had objected to having his horse impounded by a man from Piana. Attempts were made to capture or to shoot this Greek and another, both of whom escaped by swimming out to sea.[128] Again, the enmity between the Frimicacci and the Casalta of Renno, which led to an armed encounter between the two families in 1832, was said to derive from the fact that the former were descendants of Greek settlers.[129] A serious incident, which took place at Corte during the run-up to the General Election of 1881, cannot be linked in a general way with this earlier conflict in the Vico region, though it is probably significant that at least one of the Corte men involved was born there. A local boy got into a scrap with another from 'a group of itinerant tinkers of Greek origin' who were camped just outside the town. A rumour spread that the Greeks had killed someone, and a posse set out to exact revenge. The camp, which had been abandoned, was sacked, and its occupants, who had fled in the hope of finding protection from the gendarmerie, were pursued and attacked. At least four of them were killed, and a dozen or so injured with stones, daggers and gunshot. Two Greeks who happened to be in Corte at the same time were also attacked, one with fatal results.[130]

A number of points may be made in conclusion to this and the three previous chapters. First, the importance of inter-community conflict in Corsica emphasizes the importance of community itself. Conflict stemming from competition for scarce resources, moreover, was the complement to co-operation at both the community and the family level. Communities like families, needed, in the traditional context, to share land, facilities and services,[131] and the traditional economy had an important exchange element with particular areas or groups specializing in the production of commodities which were then distributed to other parts of the island. But inter-community conflict was not predominant. Even where it began to assume elements of the feud, interaction was nearly always articulated along kinship lines. Inter-village feuds were between families from rival villages rather than between whole communities. It is significant here that in the Casalta/Silvareccio example cited above vengeance was ultimately taken by the victim's brother. The relatively low-key nature of inter-community conflict in Corsica may also be related to the more prominent position of conflict between families from the same community. If conflict between communities was a means of strengthening village solidarity, then moderation of that conflict would remove a restraint on conflict within the community.[132] It is not therefore surprising to find that in the Capo Corso, where inter-community conflict on the religious level was intense, internal violence and feuding were markedly absent. Of equal importance is the linkage of inter- and intrafamilial conflict. Where the latter was so serious and so widespread, the former must be seen as a means of controlling it, by exemplifying and proclaiming the overriding need for family solidarity. Inter-familial conflict, in effect, was the central element of a three-tier structure and cannot be fully understood in isolation from this fact. Its most extreme manifestation, of course, was feuding, to which we now return.

] 7 [

Obligation and organization in the feud

According to Busquet and others, feuding in Corsica was subject to fairly formal conventional regulation or 'law'. This provides a guide to the conduct of feuds, though one should always distinguish between this law and actual practice.

I

First, there is the question of who was involved in a feud or the exaction of blood vengeance. Were there sharply defined feuding groups made up of specific agnatic kin, or were feuds carried on between looser *ad hoc* groupings, including affines and neighbours but not necessarily all close relatives? In order to answer this question, we must try to establish some of the main features of the structure of the family and the kindred in Corsica, though this is not easy to do with great certainty in the present state of research. Studying the feud, indeed, is one way of finding out more about kinship ties.

We have established that the family was the basic economic unit in rural Corsica, owning, having access to, and/or working the land and raising livestock collectively. The aim of the inheritance system was to maintain the family patrimony intact, and houses, land, flocks and other resources were ideally joint family property held in indivision.[1] The nature and context of the family economy, moreover: pastoralism with transhumance, polyculture involving extensive land-use, self-sufficiency, required the deployment of large family units. Bigot provides a classic description of such a unit, as it existed at Bastelica at the end of the nineteenth century. Here the working family was of the stem type, adult sons and daughters living and working with their parents, and one son later marrying and thus forming a couple to replace the latter. More recently, Lenclud and Pernet have referred to 'the association between fathers and married sons, between brothers and brothers-in-law, and between uncles and nephews' that characterized the pastoral economy down to the time of the Second World War.[2] Our own discussion of intra-familial conflict has illustrated and emphasized the economic load borne by these close kinship and affinal ties.

Whatever the make-up of the working family and the household (a point to which we will return), wider kinship ties were always socially operative. The importance of having a large number of kinsmen was stressed in proverbs, for example: 'I want to have kin, even in the devil's house.' Proverbs explained, too, why kinsmen were needed: 'Kinsmen are teeth,' or 'Kin are a defence,'[3] a view echoed by observers from one end of the nineteenth century to the other. Moore noted in 1794 that 'a man is esteemed and his alliance courted in proportion as his family is numerous. In this proportion only do they conceive themselves safe from insult and oppression.'[4] Again, as we saw in Chapter 4, numbers of prospective affines could often be a factor in marriage strategy. Réalier-Dumas commented in 1819 that, since a large circle of kin was 'the primary form of wealth. So, when the marriage of a girl is being mooted, enquiries are made first about the number and quality of her relatives; discussion of the dowry only comes afterwards.' Saint-Germain suggested later than these two operations might be combined, with dowries actually being calculated in terms of numbers of potential affines.[5] There was a negative corollary to the high valuation of kinsmen and affines, and 'reproaching anyone with not having relatives was an extreme insult'.[6]

As we shall see in more detail, such considerations loomed large in conflict between families. Referring to the rivalry at Vignale in the 1830s between the Vignale on the one hand, and the Canacci and the Valeri on the other, a judicial report noted that the latter were 'closely united ... They had a large kindred, and they firmly believed that they would always remain in a position of supremacy in the district.'[7] Again, when the bandit Massoni came out of prison in 1848, the powerful Durilli family of Marignana assured him of their support in these terms: 'We are 5 brothers and 68 male kin including first and second cousins; you can count on us.'[8] By contrast, reporting an accusation of parricide made anonymously against the mayor of Moca-Croce in 1830, the subprefect of Sartène explained that 'this official has very few relatives'.[9] The partial renewal of the municipal council of Prunelli at the end of 1834 excited intense competition between the sitting mayor, Mariotti, and Raffaelli, leader of the rival faction. Confident of his success, the latter boasted to the former: 'Remember that you are alone and without kin, that you have only one first cousin, while I have such a host of relatives that you cannot really hope to compete with me.'[10]

If there was general agreement about the importance of kinship ties, some uncertainty exists among observers about the span at which they remained significant. Bouchez, for example, claimed in 1843 that ties were respected 'beyond the tenth degree of kinship', by which he probably meant beyond the range of fourth cousins. For Barry in 1893, 'the "family" in the Corsican sense extends to third and fourth cousins', while for Blanqui in 1841 and Vanutberghe in 1904 the outer limits were third and second cousins respectively.[11] Similarly, there was some difference of opinion about the importance attached by Corsicans to lineage. Feydel asserted in 1799 that

> the only science with which they are concerned is that of genealogies. For it is upon this that the security of persons and of property in their island reposes and has done from time immemorial. Everyone knows how many male relatives he has to the fourth degree and beyond and which families in the district are more or less closely related to his.

Bourde referred in 1887 to 'the family archives preserved with care' by notables of San-Fiorenzo. And, more recently, Marin-Muracciole has written that 'knowledge of and taste for genealogy reaches a degree of perfection [in Corsica] that is very difficult [for outsiders] to imagine'.[12] We may also cite specific references to 'lineage'[13] and point to other evidence of regard for it, both looking backwards and forwards. A pregnant widow from the Ampugnani was urged in a lament for her dead husband: 'Be strong and brave. / The little one that you are carrying / May he be preserved / So that the name of his father / May be quickly reborn!'[14] However, such considerations would apply primarily to landowning notables, who would be atypical also in not having to rely on oral genealogical memory.[15] In general, the emphasis was placed on horizontal rather than vertical ties, on the family as 'those of the same blood' here present rather than on the family tree. Here it is significant that in certain circumstances sons could take the name of their mothers.[16] Kin contours were also flexible and subject to choice or accident.[17] Though the evidence should be treated with caution, one may note that it was fairly common for witnesses in court to express uncertainty on the subject. A wage-earning herdsman from Acciola, for example, testified in a trial in 1817 that he 'did not know whether he was related by kin or marriage to any of the parties', while another witness in a case in 1802 stated that he was related to one of the accused 'without recalling to what degree'.[18] Another pointer to the span of significant kinship ties is provided by the government's practice of taking relatives hostage where it was unable to arrest wanted men themselves. The dozen hostages taken at Pila-Canale in 1801–2 included no kin beyond the third degree and only two beyond the second. One hostage, however, included his wife's kin to the second and third degree among his own 'close relatives'.[19]

In addition to affines, 'family ties' might include other categories. In many Mediterranean societies or societies deriving from them, the network of kin and the protection which it provides are extended through the medium of godparenthood or ritual kinship,[20] and Corsica should be included among these. The institution was not confined to godparents of baptism, whose duties ended at the confirmation of the godchild. At Tavera and Evisa, for example, godparenthood links were forged at the midsummer festival of St John.[21] In the Niolo and elsewhere special gifts were given to a priest celebrating his first mass by his godmother, who also presided over the subsequent festivities.[22] Links were also formed between those of the same age, usually at First Communion, and these ties could be very close. In the elaborate instructions which he made for his funeral, Luca-Antono Viterbi made special reference to Father Suzzarini, 'my dear *cumpare*'; while the bandit Andrea Spada committed his first crime in 1922 in order to free his '*cumpà*' after he had been arrested at Sari-d'Orcino.[23] Godparents of baptism were usually chosen outside the family proper and among people of influence.[24] Ritual kinship *per se* was of limited importance in Corsica, given the strength of real kinship ties, and was more important as a variety of patronage.[25]

Rossi wrote in 1900 that the family 'rested in the first place on a common (biological) origin, on blood', but that it comprised also all those brought together by the obligations of friendship, hospitality or community of interest. The tenants, workers, herdsmen, all those involved in the running of a family's holding or who were obligated to it in some other way, became the dependents, the clients of that family. It was this extension of families via patron–client ties that formed the larger units known as 'clans'. 'Each family [at Bastelica]', according to Bigot, 'was part of a group, a sort of clan, deriving from an ancient common origin and known by a common generic name.' Busquet agreed that several clans were centuries old and suggested that some might have been modelled on the Genoese *alberghi*. But, with this influence in mind, he believed that most Corsican 'clans' were in fact pseudo-clans or organizations 'cast artificially into the form of the kindred. Various families which had no blood ties decided to give up their individual names and to take collectively either the name of one of them or an entirely new name.' The small number of Corsican surnames, to which we have alluded, would support this speculation. Whatever their origin, clans were clearly functional in modern times. The leader of one at San-Fiorenzo told Bourde in 1886: 'Everyone must belong to a clan in order to be able to draw on its influence at the critical moments of life.' More recently and more generally, Choury has written: 'The clan is a grouping of families, placed under the authority of a leader whose office is hereditary. One gives oneself to the clan. One remains faithful to its leader whatever his behaviour. In return ... one calls on the support of the clan in order to improve one's material situation, to obtain a pension, a job or an official position.'[26] Clans, which existed at village, district and island level, were the main vehicles of influence and patronage. To some extent, the clan system was an alternative to that of kinship. The same mayor of Moca-Croce, whose lack of kin made him vulnerable, was able to compensate to some degree by building up 'a numerous clientèle'. But, much more significantly, the clan was a means of extending kinship ties, of building smaller family units into larger ones for effective political action beyond the village level. Using the idiom of kinship beyond the strict confines of blood (or of marriage) was crucial to this process, but paradoxically the clan system created order in a potentially chaotic kinship system by selecting and underlining certain ties and blocking out or ignoring others in communities where everyone might be more or less related.

But this only applied at the outer edges of the kinship system, and the chaos was more potential than actual.

> It would be false [Lenclud and Ravis-Giordani[27] have warned] to imagine that the 'Corsican cousin' is a simple model and that, in a village, these links of cousinage are perceived and used in an undifferentiated fashion, on the supposition that in a village everyone is inter-related. The kinship code in Corsica is (on the contrary) fairly precise and diversified ... and close and distant kin are carefully distinguished.

They go on to describe in some detail the various 'nebulae' of kin as perceived in communities in the Niolo. At the most general level was the sense of relationship known as *a ceppu*. This was attached to a belief in 'a common but very distant ancestry', that is, belonging to a 'clan', but usually derived more directly from residence in the same locality. 'At Calasima, for example, all the inhabitants, who share two patronymics ... recognize that they are "all related".' This same sentiment found expression much more generally in the island in proverbs which identified neighbours with kin.[28] At the next level of differentiation, people belonged to a particular *sterpa* or lineage. This term referred 'to relationship based on the social recognition of biological links'. These were usually 'not clearly describable and depended on [vague] genealogical memory', but they were held to be indubitable links of kinship. Within the *sterpa* were sub-groupings of distant relatives known as *parentelli*, which were clearly distinguished from *parenti stretti* or closer relatives, themselves distinguished by specific kinship terms. Any individual was thus surrounded by concentric circles of kin, which included paternal and maternal relatives on equal terms. The *parentelli* relationship reached in the Niolo to the seventh degree, but both here and elsewhere the most significant thresholds lay between the immediate family as a working unit and the wider kindred, and between relatives to the third or fourth degree and those beyond. An ex-mayor of Levie even referred specifically in 1847 to a sub-grouping of the Peretti 'to the degree of brother-in-law, uncle and nephew'.[29] Intermarriage was banned, by the Church within the fourth degree, though Corsican custom did not always accept this restriction. More telling, a number of sources mention 'families' or kindreds of 70–100 persons, which must have comprised all relatives to the third or fourth degree.[30] This suggests a degree of cohesion, which was not always present. The zone between the third and fourth degrees was one of ambiguity, as our discussion of the obligations of relatives in the feud will confirm. More generally, Lenclud has recently stressed the flexibility of family ties and their linkage with the socio-economic process rather than any ideal scheme of things.[31] Consideration of the functions of kinship ties and the ways in which they were manifested shows how the two were inextricably mixed.

Kin at all levels were expected to aid each other, especially when they were in difficulties. Thus Giulia Montecattini of Olmeto solicited the help of a distant kinsman in Bastia, Dr Franzini, when she wished to cash in a bond in 1861.[32] It seems, as this example shows, that kinsmen who had achieved positions of wealth and influence were in practice the most obligated here. Lorenzi de Bradi noted that 'when a Corsican gets on, he never forgets his kin. He helps his brothers and sisters. He obtains positions for them and enriches them if he can ... and his concern extends, too, to more distant relatives.'[33] It was on the basis of this assumption that the mother-in-law of Francesco Bastianesi of Ucciani, sentenced to hard labour for life in 1849, petitioned Prince Napoleon on his behalf; she was a Martinetti, she wrote, and a relative of the prince.[34] Kinship here overlapped and reinforced the system of patronage and influence.

Kinship in depth also found expression in ritual terms. Perpetual chantries were still extant in Corsica in the early nineteenth century, although they had become a ground for conflict between the clergy and the families concerned and sometimes between rival descendants. Family chapels and altars preserved the memory of ancestors and served as ongoing symbols of family status. Pietrini Campi of Campi, for example, wrote in 1869 to both the prefect and the Minister of Cults to protest at the plans of the mayor to demolish 'the sacred edifice of St Cervone, built in 1206 by one of my ancestors, to whose posterity the chapel has always been dedicated, there being there a closed tomb bearing the inscription "di Campi" above it'.[35] An alternative to burial in family chapels or vaults in churches was burial in family tombs on family land, a custom which had the same function of marking lineage and thus providing a focus for wider kinship ties.[36] An unorthodox reversal of the link between kin across the grave, represented by masses and prayers for the dead, crops up in a pamphlet published in Bastia in 1858. Purporting to be 'a true letter from Jesus Christ', this promised among other 'favours' to those who fulfilled its instructions that they would be able to return to the world after their deaths and fetch the souls of relatives to the fourth degree to eternal glory.[37]

We have seen that funerals and weddings were community affairs, but they were also important opportunities for the expression of kin solidarity. 'At weddings and in trouble, one knows one's own people,' a proverb put it.[38] The patronal festival was also a ritual of kinship. Benson noted in 1825 that all members of a family celebrated together on that day: 'this union ... is considered a sacred obligation. A refusal to attend ... is considered a denial of their family; and produces much injury to a man's reputation.' The obligation very much included relatives from other villages, who would not otherwise be regularly seen. He adds that 'at these festive meetings, the Corsicans arrange the marriage of their daughters and other family matters'.[39] An important vehicle in such arrangements and discussions would be the family council, to which we have referred earlier and which could also have a role to play in the conduct of feuds.[40]

We come now to the relationship between family and household. These were frequently regarded as identical. A youth from Foce, prosecuted for stealing a pig in 1814, was asked 'how many people composed the family to which he belonged', and he replied that he lived with five other persons: his widowed mother, his brother and three sisters.[41] These were people at the lowest end of the social scale, poor in relatives as in everything else, but the same assumption is found among the better-off. This is most obvious in the way in which the physical house itself represented the family to which it belonged and who inhabited it. According to Privat, 'the house was the raison d'être' of the members of a family. 'If it was destroyed, it would be rebuilt as far as possible with the same materials.'[42] Houses bore the names of families, often inscribed in the granite of their doorways,[43] and the standing of a family was frequently measured by the quality of its dwelling.[44] Houses remained in the same family generation after generation, and, as we have seen, they formed 'the patrimony par excellence',[45] which it was almost unthinkable to sell. 'Perhaps the most damaging thing', to quote Privat again, 'that one could say of a man was that he had sold his father's house.'[46] It is significant that houses in the Niolo, according to Lenclud, retained their original family name, even if they came to be occupied or owned by someone else.

The traditional Corsican house, examples of which were still being built in the nineteenth century, was a large building of several storeys, sometimes four or more. Many were clearly built in stages, horizontally and vertically. One of the oldest houses in Azzana, for instance, was originally one room but came to have two storeys with five rooms, and such examples could be multiplied. Houses were primarily dwelling-places but also served to accommodate stores of produce, agricultural equipment and some livestock, there being no separate farm buildings in villages. Additionally, houses large and small were built on or next to each other in clusters, and contiguous houses might have internal intercommunication. All these features suggest that houses or clusters of houses were occupied by large groups of people and that extensions were made as these groups expanded and needed more room. There is no doubt either that these groups were groups of kin and that houses were built 'for children, grandchildren, nephews and cousins'. To these one should add affines, for, as Ravis-Giordani points out, the term used to designate relatives by marriage in Corsica, *appiciccaticci* derives from the term *appicciu,* meaning a building attached to another building.[47]

However, if Corsican houses were occupied by large family groupings three generations deep, the relationship between house and family was neither simple nor static. Lenclud has established that in the Niolo the extended family as an economic or working unit was not necessarily co-resident. Moreover, the relationship between family membership and dwelling-place changed not only through the life-cycle but also from one season to another. Among transhumant pastoralists, individuals might belong to different family groupings in the village itself, on the winter coastal pasture, and during the summer milking period in the high mountains.[48] Again, if houses expanded to accommodate growing families, they could also be split up through the process of inheritance. Fontana commented in 1905 that 'the family house is divided by floors among the children or even (where the number of children exceeds the number of floors) by rooms; and it is rare for any system of equivalents to be accepted.'[49] The result of such division may be seen in the cadastral survey of 1882 at Venzolasca. Francesc'-Antono Petrignani owned two second floors and one first floor and a whole house at Chiasso Longo; Andrea Sanguinetti's property included two first floors, one third floor and two whole houses at Chiasso Longo and one-third of a second and third floor at Santa-Luccia; and so on. Such fragmented property might well be rented out to poorer families or even sold. At Ghisoni in 1880, the widow Caterina Pancrazi sold a bedroom and half another room on the second floor of a house, while another widow and her son sold half a bedroom, half another room that was not partitioned (presumably a share in a living-room), and three-eighths of a cellar to an Italian labourer.[50]

More commonly, however, houses remained in theory undivided, with entrance doors, stairways and other parts actually in common, and married brothers or other sub-groups occupying separate storeys.[51] Such arrangements could be regarded as collections of separate households under one roof,[52] or as single households of polynuclear type, depending upon one's point of view. Confusion has been caused in the minds of demographic historians here by the fact that some census material exclusively adopts the former option. Dupâquier and Jadin thus reach the absurd conclusion that 'the "patriarchal" type of family' scarcely existed at the end of the eighteenth century, let alone later.[53] Two local quantitative studies are more nuanced and may be mentioned as points of reference. At Penta-di-Casinca in 1769, the 510 inhabitants were divided in the census into 106 *fuochi* or 'hearths' and 15 *mezzi-fuochi.* 'A *fuoco* ... comprised everyone living with the father and mother, even married children and ascendants. A *mezzo-fuoco* was a unit lacking one or both parents.' Well over half the total population belonged to hearths of more than five persons, and fifteen of these hearths included seven or more persons. At Calasima in the Niolo in 1926, half the population lived in households of more than six members and 15 per cent in households of over ten members. About a third of these domestic groups comprised other relatives in addition to the conjugal pair and its offspring.[54] In each case the importance of the extended family is almost certainly underestimated, given the artificial nature of the categories being used. 'Hearths' could really be sub-units of 'households', with each married woman, for example, having a share in a common fireplace. Conjugal units could live and work but not eat together on a regular basis, while relatives living in separate houses could be commensal. As Lenclud concludes, 'there was no sharp distinction between shared and separate occupation of houses, but different degrees of cohabitation, dynamic relations as opposed to a perceptible discontinuity'.[55]

The judicial records confirm the importance of the extended family/household and illustrate its variants. It was normal, first, for adult offspring to live with their parents and to contribute to the family economy. We learn, for example, that Matteo Ferrandi, aged 26, of Penta-Acquatella, lived in 1812 in his father's house with another brother and a sister.[56] Later in the century, the mayor of Salice was accused of misappropriating funds awarded to his village after it had been struck by a hurricane. Not only did he award generous sums to himself, despite having sustained no loss, 'but he also indemnified his grown children who live together with him'.[57] That such co-residence was the norm is indicated by a case at Calenzana in 1862. Since Giovanni Orsini, aged 27, and his father were always quarrelling, they were exceptionally 'advised [by the justice of the peace] to live apart from each other'. Moreover, even when children had left home in such circumstances, they still retained claims upon the family economy. Giuseppo Marcantoni, aged 18, of Rebbia, had left his widowed mother's house, but he continued 'to present himself there from time to time in order to be given or to take the provisions that he required'.[58]

It was also usual for married offspring to continue living in their parents' houses. According to Bigot, 'when the eldest son and the other sons marry, and if family interests do not keep them away from the paternal house, they continue to live there with their wives and their children until the death of their father. Only then do they split up.'[59] Our sources indicate that there was generally rather more flexibility in household composition and formation than this suggests. There is some evidence, for example, that sometimes only one son married, at least during his father's lifetime, and that this was not necessarily the eldest. Simone-Francesco Savelli, aged 28 of Aregno, was married with three children and lived in 1834 'with his mother and father, whose property he worked'. No mention is made of siblings.[60] We learn from a case in 1801 that the three adult sons of Petro-Giovanni Piazzoli of Terrivola (Alesani) lived in their father's house, and of these it seems that only the second, aged 28, was married.[61] The married sibling in such a multiple household could even be a woman. Don Giacomo Susini of Loreto-di-Tallano, whose house was set on fire by his enemies in 1847, lived there with his son Antono, who appears to have been single, his daughter Colomba, her common-law husband Santo, their two-year-old daughter, and a nephew.[62]

Such arrangements were usual, we have seen, where a woman had no brothers and was thus an heiress. Giuseppo Armani of Vero married a Mariani girl, who was a cousin of some kind and, it appears, an only child. She died soon afterwards, probably in childbed, followed to the grave three months later by her baby. Armani 'nevertheless continued to live with her parents and to administer their property, even after he had remarried'. This corresponded to the practice whereby brides remained in the households which they had entered by marriage after the death of their partners. When Brigida Peretti of Levie was expelled from the house of her father-in-law in 1849 after being widowed, her nearest male relative, an uncle, protested vigorously and was shot dead for his pains. Of course, neither he nor Armani would have been disinterested. Armani hoped to become heir to the Mariani property, while the alternative to a widow's remaining with her late husband's family was for her kin to resume responsibility for her maintenance. It also seems that spouses' widowed parents were not uncommonly attached to the larger households to which the former belonged. At Cozzano in 1865, for example, 'Francesco Peretti, whose daughter had married Simone Renucci, inhabited the same house as the couple and lived with them as one family', and the household also comprised Renucci's mother, who seems indeed to have been the head of it. In a more complicated situation at Piedicorte around 1850, Domenico-Francesco Alessandri and his wife, his wife's brother and his wife 'occupied the same house and lived in common together with Alessandri's mother'.[63]

Bigot's observation that younger married brothers at Bastelica hived off from the household on the death of the father is confirmed for other villages. Lenclud and Ravis-Giordani concluded that at Calasima in 1926 'there do not seem to be any domestic groups made up of married brothers living together', while Marcaggi notes that the Castelli brothers at Carcheto lived one in the upper and the other in the lower village.[64] Contrary examples may be found, however, and the *frérêche* may well have been more common in Corsica than this suggests. At Olmeto, in 1829, for instance, the Pianelli brothers lived in one household with their wives, servants and other relatives and such an arrangement does not seem to have been regarded as odd.[65] Examples may also be found without difficulty of married brothers and sister cohabiting, and of married sisters doing the same. At Muro in 1858, the three Morati sisters lived in the same house. All of them were married, and mention is made of an adult unmarried daughter of one of them, while another had six children. Each sister seems to have had separate quarters within the house, but all members of the household went in and out of these freely. The situation of unmarried adult siblings cohabiting seems to have been more common. Francesc'-Antono Franceschi of Mazzola, for example, lived in 1853 with his two sisters in a house inherited from their father. At Santa-Reparata in the 1840s, the Liccia brothers, having lived together with an uncle, continued to do so for five years after his death. At Corte in 1841, Pasquino and Francesco Ordioni 'lived under the same roof with their young sister Francesca', but, in this case, 'each of the two brothers managed his small property separately'.[66] Frequent, too, was the practice of unmarried siblings remaining in the household of a married brother and working with or for him, as they had done for their father. There was an expression in Corsican to describe this practice: *fa uzio* (to be the uncle)[67] which indicates how common it must have been, and we cited examples in Chapter 5.[68] Cohabitation of unmarried with married siblings did not, however, always betoken dependent status. In 1859, the brother-in-law of the miller Renucci was living at the mill on the Rizzanese, almost certainly as a kind of paying guest and because he was in poor health. We learn, moreover, in 1862, that the parish priest of Olmiccia lived with his sister and her husband, and such an arrangement cannot have been rare among the clergy. Situations such as these might very well in time leave a brother-in-law and a sister-in-law living together, as at Castineta in 1851, where a shoemaker, aged 50, and his sister-in-law 'occupied the same apartment and lived for a long time in perfect harmony'.[69]

Further evidence of the co-residence of married siblings is provided by reports of cousins living together. Cowen noted in 1848 that 'Corsicans ... consider their cousins as brothers, in the full sense of the word: they live in the same house from infancy to manhood.'[70] The judicial records point in the same direction. Though engaged in bitter conflict over an inheritance, the Luporsi cousins of Perelli yet lived in the same house. Evidence in another case, already referred to, revealed that Giovanni Ferracci of Porto-Vecchio lived in the same household with his brother and his first cousin. When he married, his wife Maria-Giuditta joined the household. While Ferracci was away doing his military service, Michele Pietri, another of his cousins, also married, came to live temporarily in the house, being lodged in the same bedroom as Maria-Giuditta. Cohabitation of cousins arose, too, where children were orphaned. We have seen that Petro Faveletti of Valle lost his father as a child and that when his mother remarried he was brought up in the Faveletti house by his father's sister, who hoped that he would eventually marry her daughter, his cousin.[71] Where cousins did not actually live in the same household, they might occupy contiguous or interrelated ones. At Terrivola, the houses of cousins Giuseppo-Giovanni and Paolo-Matteo Piazzoli were next door to each other, and a witness testified 'that there was an internal passage between them'. In another case, in 1865, we learn that the Antoni and Casanova cousins occupied the same house in a hamlet of Velone-Orneto, their quarters being separated only by a thin partition wall.[72]

By the same token, households included aunts and uncles, nephews and nieces. Letizia Rossi of Poggio-di-Nazza was abducted in 1845, as she was sleeping in bed with her aunt Casabianca. At Ciamannacce in 1850, Giovan-Battiste Orsini lived in the same house as his widowed aunt Serafina and her daughter Maria-Domenica. Mention is also made of a baby, presumably Maria-Domenica's, and of a younger brother or cousin of Giovan-Battiste. Again, at Isolaccio, we learn from a case in 1893, Domenico Carlotti 'lived nearly all the time' in the house of his aunt and her husband. In some cases, cohabitation of second-degree kin seems to have been unrelated to the large family house and its cycle of occupation. At Castineta, in 1843, Ignazio Pasqualini lived in 'a ramshackle house on the edge of the village' with his aunt and her daughter, who had a baby (not Pasqualini's). They lived in common to some extent, the nephew usually spending his evenings with his aunt and probably eating with her, but he also had his own 'distinct and separate' quarters. We have seen that nieces might live with uncles as housekeepers or servants.[73]

Households or houses might also contain more distant kin. In the case against Andrea Giansilj of Lozzi in 1811, Domenico Giansilj testified that he was the third cousin of both Andrea and Andrea's wife; also that he had 'a part of the house of the father of the said woman, in which he lived, the main room of the house being undivided between them'.[74] In addition, domestic groupings could include other categories of person: illegitimate children, servants, or lodgers. From a rape case in 1865, we learn that Bianca Geronini, an illegitimate child aged about twelve, lived with her uncle, first at Grossa and then at a house on the territory of Giuncheto, where the uncle's unmarried brother-in-law, who committed the offence, also lived.[75] As Bigot emphasized, servants as such did not exist in Corsica, and we have seen that those involved in court cases were extremely reluctant to admit to this status. However, kin might fill servant roles, and concomitantly non-kin employed, say to look after a flock, were put 'on the same footing as the children of the household'.[76] Non-Corsican hired labour, and in some cases workers from other villages, did not benefit from this paternalism. Lodgers or tenants seem to have been common, filling space left vacant perhaps when families contracted. In the case involving Cristoforo Ferrandi of Giglio in 1801, we learn that his estranged wife lived in a house with her mother, the mother's sister-in-law, and an unrelated woman among others. In another case, Anna-Felice Stefani of Linguizetta was asked to explain how she came to marry Giacomo Santucci only three months after the death of her first husband. She replied that she 'had rented a room belonging to Santucci's uncle' and that Santucci lived in the same house.[77] Again, in 1815, we learn that Giovan-Girolamo Costa of Tomino let the rooms on the upper floor of his house to the Bettolacce family, and that Maria Giorgi lived in the house of Giovanni Morazzi, to whom she was apparently unrelated.[78] Here there is clearly a distinction to be made between lodgers or tenants living in distinct quarters and outsiders living with the family, between lodgers or tenants who were relatives and those who were not, and between families and individuals. Families lodged if they were poor or strangers or both. For example, the Degiovanni, a couple with two young children, occupied 'a room on the first floor of the Martini house' at Silvareccio. He was a *voltigeur* and almost certainly from another village.[79] Single lodgers, of both sexes, appear to have been more common, and many of these were probably kin of some kind.

Judicial records also shed further light on the use of space inside houses, confirming the surviving architectural evidence and contemporary descriptions.[80] Most houses had only one hearth, which was the focus of sociability in the main living-room. Anna-Felice Stefani testified that 'she very often spent the evenings in the room where there was a hearth (*fuocone*), as was the custom in the village, and where the other people living in the house also gathered'. Alternatively or additionally, there might be 'sub-hearths' for sub-units of the household. We have seen that a quarrel between the Calzaroni brothers of Ucciani originated when one of them told off the other's wife 'for lighting too big a fire on a portable hearth which was in the common [living] room but had been placed too near the door of a bedroom'.[81] It is clear, too, that this common sociability included not only relatives with separate sleeping accommodation in the same house but also those from outside.[82] Sometimes visiting relatives might stay the night. When Bartolomeo Comiti of Sorbollano was accused of various nocturnal offences in 1813, he claimed that during the time in question he had 'never passed a night away from my house or those of my brothers-in-law'.[83] A high level of interaction of this kind between houses or households was encouraged by the fact that houses were built in clusters with common space around them. Arrighi has referred here to 'familial *quartiers*', and there is other evidence to support this.[84] Families could even occupy whole hamlets, as the Cucchi 'tribe' did at Orone just south of Carbini.[85]

We are now in a better position to appreciate the nature, the importance and the all-pervasiveness of kinship ties in Corsican society. With some provisos, the situation was similar to that described by Banfield in 'Montegrano'. Individuals existed as kinsmen rather than as 'egos', and

> the world being what it is, all who stand outside the ... circle of the family are at least potential competitors and therefore also potential enemies. Towards those who are not of the family, the reasonable attitude is suspicion. The parent [i.e. kinsman] knows that other families will envy and fear the success of his family and that they are likely to seek to do it injury. He must therefore fear them and be ready to do them injury in order that they may have less power to injure him and his.[86]

Abeau made the same point with reference to Corsica when he declared in 1888 that 'every family aspires to grow in wealth and importance ... This is what is called *fare la sua casa*',[87] and we have seen how success on the part of one family could lead to envy and hostilities on the part of others. In such circumstances, community was an important and necessary countervailing factor, but community loyalties were inevitably weak.

Examination of friendship in Corsican society is relevant here. The term *amicizia* referred mainly to relations between families rather than between individuals, and it was a largely negative notion, denoting the absence of hostility or *nimicizia* (enmity).[88] This is reflected in the replies made by Matteo Ferrandi of Penta-Acquatella, interrogated in 1812 in connection with the killing of a certain Fusaja. Asked if the victim had been 'the friend or the enemy of his family or of himself', Ferrandi said 'that he showed friendship, since they always spoke to each other when they met, and Fusaja's eldest son was his in-law to the third degree, having married one of his [Ferrandi's] cousins'.[89] Friendship, as this indicates, was also most likely within the circles of kindred and affinity. Innocente Cuttoli, for example, was reported in 1813 to have been 'the distant kinsman and close friend' of the man who had killed the mayor of Peri.[90] Where our sources refer to 'friends and relatives' lending each other aid and assistance, which they not infrequently do, 'friends' should almost certainly be usually read in the medieval sense of kinsmen,[91] though sometimes those designated were political associates or clients. It was probably in this latter sense that a reputed singer of laments proclaimed at a wake at San-Damiano: 'I have been the friend of the Ristori family / Over many years.'[92] Friendship between unrelated persons of a disinterested kind did occur, particularly between pairs of young men. Sometimes the relationship was particularly close. The involvement of Francesco Raffini in an ambush at Sari-d'Orcino in 1850 as the accomplice of Alessandro Padovani was 'explained by the intimate relations' existing between them. Again, in a case at Peri in 1852, we learn that Grazio Manzaggi 'was the intimate and inseparable friend of Petro-Luigi (Pinzuti), and even helped him to abduct a girl', and we shall see in Chapter 12 that such close dyadic ties were quite common among bandits. Here it is again significant, however, that such ties were often expressed via behaviour appropriate usually only among close relatives. Petro Pietri of Algajola was convicted in 1842 of accidentally killing Antono Guitona. According to the trial summary, Pietri 'lived on the terms of closest friendship with Guitona. They ate at the same table and slept together.'[93] Moreover, the ties of friendship, however close, did not overrule family obligations, as we can see in cases where brothers avenged the honour of sisters against those who had abused friendship by seducing them. A certain Mattei of Corte, for example, shot and killed his friend Perelli in 1840 after Perelli refused to marry Mattei's sister whom he had impregnated. Again, after some hesitation, Giovan-Battiste Agostino of San-Giuliano killed his friend Angelo-Maria Cesarini, who had seduced and was cohabiting with Agostini's married sister.[94]

II

Having discussed family and kinship ties in general, we now return to the specific question of the feuding obligations associated with them. There are societies, for example the Bedouin of Cyrenaica or the Northern Somali, in which the vengeance group is precisely defined.[95] There are others, such as that of the Merovingian Franks or the Turkish village described by Stirling, where one may speak of 'a small *ad hoc* vengeance-group' and where 'it is not precisely laid down who is and who is not involved'.[96] This distinction reflects fundamental differences in social structure and in the function of the vengeance group. A clearly demarcated group can only exist where there is a clearly demarcated kindred, based usually on patrilineal descent, and in such circumstances the group has other roles, notably the provision and reception of bridewealth, which often parallels the provision and reception of 'wergild' or its equivalent. As was pointed out by Bloch in the medieval European context, a bilateral kinship system itself inhibits the constitution of effective and distinct kindreds and hence of vengeance groups, and this inhibiting factor is redoubled by endogamy and/or the dispersal of kin in settlements where they are co-resident with non-kin.[97]

Modern Corsica has features in common with both these kinds of society but falls mainly into the second category. Some writers refer to tightly organized vengeance groups here,[98] but there is significantly considerable disagreement about their theoretical boundaries, which parallels the more general uncertainty about the span of kinship which we have discussed. According to Tommaseo in 1841, 'the vendetta ... extends through the furthest branches of kindred and affinity', a view echoed rather more tentatively by Gregorovius and Bourde. Others were more specific. Réalier-Dumas wrote in 1819 that the obligation to pursue vengeance extended to relatives to the fourth or even the fifth degree, and Faure in 1858 referred to involvement of kin to the sixth degree. In his comprehensive study of 1919, Busquet concluded that for the past four centuries it had been the rule for relatives to the third degree only to be actively involved in the pursuit of blood vengeance, though he acknowledged that some early nineteenth-century texts referred here to the fourth degree. He also suggested that feuds may have involved whole clans in the more distant past. He reached similar conclusions as to the range of kin properly regarded as targets for vengeance.

Here the boundary was again the third degree, and more distant relatives and clients were usually regarded as immune. He added that 'the rules today in this sphere seem to be becoming rather hazy'.[99]

This haziness may have been accentuated in the course of the nineteenth century as the nature of feuding itself changed, but it had always been present, reflecting genuine ambiguities as well as providing scope for duplicity and special pleading. Miot noted that the degrees of kinship within which vengeance had to be exercised were 'regulated by ancient custom', but that the application of such regulation to particular instances could well be problematic. He cited an example at Peri, where a man found a relative of one of his enemies in a field and announced that he was going to kill him. A discussion about the degree of kinship between the two ensued, and the first man then decided not to risk killing someone who might not be within the scope of the feud.[100] In a case in 1846, relating to the feud at Bastelica, the defence counsel of Giovan-Battiste Scapola 'attempted to demonstrate that he had no interest whatever in avenging the death of Domenico Scapola his half-brother, who had left children able to do this and with whom, moreover, he had always been on bad terms'. More than this, the two half-brothers were actually on opposing sides in the feud between their respective mothers' families.[101] Similarly, at Marignana around 1850, Caterina Grimaldi joined in the lamenting for Antono Durilli, who had been killed by the bandit Massoni. She was married to a Durilli, cousin to Antono, but she was also a first cousin of Massoni's wife. When she wailed: 'My cousin! My cousin! Poor unfortunate man!', one of Antono's brothers thought that she was referring to Massoni and thereupon shot her dead.[102]

The difficulty of knowing who was a legitimate target in a feud was to some extent overcome by requiring that protagonists make a clear declaration on the subject. Robiquet stated in 1835 that at the outset of a feud a family 'would let it be known to what degree of kinship the hostilities would extend'.[103] But even where this practice was followed, there was plenty of room for misunderstanding. The Giacomoni who were involved in a feud with the Paoli of Fozzano in 1801–2 stated unhelpfully that their enemies were 'Antono Paoli called Fagiani, his son Giuseppo, with all the other relatives of the same family'.[104] After his brother had been killed at Palneca in 1852 by Cesare Bartoli, Francesco Bartoli swore to take revenge 'on the relatives of the killer, who were informed of his intentions and kept on their guard. However, Bernardino Andrei, a first cousin of Cesare Bartoli, did not believe that he was implicated in the enmity' and therefore went about his affairs normally. He was ambushed and seriously wounded by Francesco Bartoli within two months. Sometimes misunderstandings were deliberately created. In the course of the feud between the Giacomi and the Tomasi of Gavignano, a Giacomi was killed in 1838. 'The relatives of the victim resolved to take reprisals and in order better to achieve this they declared emphatically that they wished only to punish the killer himself and not members of his family. Tricked by this deceitful declaration, the latter took no precautions' and two of them were ambushed shortly afterwards.[105]

As far as active obligation in feuding was concerned, however, such considerations were not often relevant. 'The duty of avenging a murder (or other injury) ... fell on the nearest able-bodied male relative of the victim,' in Carrington's words, and on this all writers are agreed.[106] As one would expect, the obligation radiated out from close to more distant relatives through the nebulae of kinship and affinity. This is most aptly reflected in the lament for Dr Matteo of 1745: 'The blood of Matteo / Will soon be avenged. / Here are his brothers, / His cousins, his brother-in-law, / And if they are not enough, / There will be the entire kindred.'[107] Our sources provide confirmation and many illustrations of the operation of these rules.

Perhaps the most common and binding obligation within the system was for sons to avenge fathers.[108] We may cite many examples of sons avenging the killing of their fathers, for instance at Venzolasca in 1850, at Pila-Canale in 1851, at Castineta and at Penta-di-Casinca in 1852,[109] but perhaps more telling are cases where the original injury was less serious. Ignazio Giacomoni of Loreto-di-Tallano killed a cousin in 1847, because he had testified in court against his father. Finale Pasqualini of Silvareccio stabbed and fatally injured Domenico Terrighi in 1852, following a quarrel between the latter and Finale's father over the ownership of some beams. Again, it is significant that sons might be killed in order to prevent their avenging their fathers. This was apparently the motive which led the Susini of Figari to kill Santo, the teen-age son of Matteo Maisetti in 1848. Sons who avenged fathers were also treated benevolently by the courts. Salvatore Gaffori of Pastricciola killed a man in 1848, but was acquitted of murder on the grounds that he was justified in attacking a man 'who had wounded his father'. Vengeance might also be taken against fathers for offences committed by their sons, though this seems to have been far less common. At Venzolasca, Natale Antonelli hit another youth, Giuseppo-Maria Petrignani, on the head with a stick after midnight mass at Christmas 1854. Petrignani encountered Antonelli's father, who knew nothing about the incident, soon afterwards, and, 'doubtless to take revenge for having been insulted by his son', stabbed him three times with a knife, causing him near-mortal injuries.[110]

Brothers were expected to avenge dead brothers, and our sources confirm that they frequently did so.[111] Brothers also avenged affronts short of killing. At Linguizetta, we have seen that Nicolaio Arasti called Tomaso Lanfranchi '*rimbeccu*' on the square by the church in January 1846. Tomaso's brother heard the insulting word from the window of his house, called out to Arasti and shot him dead. Brothers, too, might serve as targets for vengeance, particularly when the prime culprits proved inaccessible. In 1850, Serafino Battini of Ota killed the brother of Giovanni Grimaldi, who had killed the father of his 'concubine', because Grimaldi himself had been quick to put himself under the protection of the authorities. In 1848, a brother of Antono Serra of Sartène had been killed by Domenico Mozziconacci. In March 1850, therefore, Serra and another relative ambushed and killed Antono Mozziconacci. He 'had not been involved in the original crime committed by Domenico', the trial summary explained, 'but since the latter had managed to escape his enemies', the Serra had selected his brother as the victim of their revenge instead.[112]

The pursuit of vengeance by relatives beyond the first degree seems most frequently to have involved cousins, as one would expect, acting either alone or with closer kin. 'You may rest tranquil,' a mother told her dead son in a lament. 'You will be revenged; / Your cousins are all here.'[113] After Domenico Camilli had been killed at Pila-Canale in 1850, his relatives, 'and notably Felice Benedetti, his first cousin, declared a state of enmity against the Giordani' and particularly against Antono Torre, first cousin of a girl whom Camilli had abducted.[114] The main obligation obviously rested on cousins only when closer kin did not exist. When a cousin of the bandit Rosso of Bastelica was killed around 1820, his widow, according to Faure, asked Rosso to avenge him since he had no sons, brothers, brothers-in-law or father-in-law living, and this Rosso agreed to do.[115] We may again cite many examples of cousins fulfilling such an obligation.[116] It is also significant that cousins might react to injuries more strongly than those directly affected. When Giuseppo-Maria Paoli of Olmeto grossly insulted Petro-Paolo Paoli of Fozzano in 1848 by spitting down his rifle, we learn that 'the offence against Petro-Paolo was most deeply felt by Giusepp'-Antono, his first cousin, who refused to speak to Giuseppo-Maria, although he was his brother-in-law', and the two cousins plotted revenge together.[117] Again, at Lumio in 1879, Giovan-Antono Padovani intervened 'to incite his cousin Benedetto Morelli to avenge a wound which the latter had received on the head'.[118] In Ambrosi's fictionalized account of a feud at Rostino, cousins from another village come to offer their help when Mora's son is killed and are most unhappy when this is declined.[119] Such evidence suggests that more distant kin, if not directly involved in blood vengeance, had the important role of ensuring that closer relatives of victims met their obligations. Cousins, of course, like other relatives, might neglect their duties in this sphere, though this was unusual. Felice-Agostino Grimaldi, accused of killing Anton-Francesco Giabicconi of Santa-Lucia-di-Moriani in 1801, claimed that he had been on good terms with his alleged victim, 'despite the fact that Giabicconi had killed Don Angelo Ruffini, his first cousin'.[120] Cousins were also very frequently selected as targets by those pursuing vengeance. When Domenico Scagni of Loreto was shot in 1861, for example, a certain Agostini was at first suspected, 'because he had had a dispute a few days previously with one of Scagni's cousins'.[121] It should be pointed out, however, that cousins did not always believe that they were likely targets and that they were sometimes selected *faute de mieux*. At Campi, Don Giovanni Lanfranchi had wounded Giovan-Giuseppo Pietri in the head in 1881 in the course of a dispute over some land. After further provocations from Don Giovanni, Giovan-Giuseppo and his brother accosted Carlo Lanfranchi, a cousin of Don Giovanni, on the village square and tried to kill him. It was later reported that 'Carlo could not have expected that the vengeance of the Pietri brothers should have been exercised against himself', although Giovan-Giuseppo 'had vowed an implacable hatred for Don Giovanni Lanfranchi, which extended to all members of his family'.[122] Again, at Albitreccia, Pancrazio and Santo Quastana believed that they were unaffected by the feud between their cousin, the famous bandit, and Ignazio Borelli, and a report made after they had been killed around 1840 stated: 'The inhabitants of the village were unanimous in thinking that it was frustrated anger at not being able to reach the bandit himself which led Borelli to murder two of his cousins who had remained outside the vendetta.'[123]

A less common but significant category was that of nephews avenging uncles. Petro-Francesco Tomasi of Gavignano, for example, was given the same name as an uncle who had been killed in 1816 in a longstanding feud with the Grimaldi, and he therefore felt obliged to avenge him, which he did by killing Anton-Francesco Grimaldi in 1837. But no such special incentive was necessary. In 1848, Bastiano Guidicelli was killed by Susino Maestrati at Zonza, and later on the same day Susino's brother Napoleone was killed in another part of the village territory by Giacomo Muzi, nephew of Giudicelli, 'who thus avenged his death'. The obligation of nephews is underlined by reproaches cast at them when they neglected it. We learn in a case at Ciamannacce in 1850 that Serafina Orsini upbraided her nephew Giovan-Battiste for such a failure. 'Go and gather the bones of your uncle from Sambuchello,' she told him, referring to the place where the uncle had been killed. This was such a serious accusation that Giovan-Battiste then attempted to kill his aunt. Nephews were also potential victims of transverse vengeance. We have seen that Domenico Canavaggio was killed in 1845 by a group of men from Frasseto. They had no quarrel with Canavaggio himself, but they were in conflict with his uncle.[124] Uncles, too, were involved in avenging nephews, presumably where they were of the right age.[125]

We have seen that in-laws were included within the circle of close relatives upon whom the duty of vengeance primarily fell, and this can be further illustrated. For example, when Giovanni Gentili of Calcatoggio was ambushed and killed in 1846, it was believed that Santo Romanetti and Pasquale Ceccaldi were responsible, thus avenging the killing of Stefano Romanetti, their brother and brother-in-law respectively.[126] Sons-in-law could also be actively involved. Anton-Maria Luccioni of Bisinchi, for instance, took part in an attack on Anton-Battiste Canacci as a reprisal for the killing of his father-in-law Vignale.[127] At Fozzano, Colomba Bartoli tried to ensure that her daughter would marry a man who would continue the feud against the Durazzi.[128] Cases may be cited, too, of vengeance being carried out by fathers-in-law and more distant affines.[129] All these categories, moreover, provided targets in feuds. At Frasseto, the Antona killed Carlo Benedetti in 1843, simply because he was married to a Franceschi woman. At Cozzano, in 1840, Giovan-Battiste Pantalucci was shot dead by Anton-Marco Renucci, following a quarrel between the latter and Michele Renucci. Pantalucci was 'a peaceful man, who had taken no part in the dispute and whose only fault was to be ... Michele's father-in-law'. There is some evidence, however, that affines were or might regard themselves as immune. The father of Luigi Angeli of Penta had been killed in a fight by Anton-Andrea Fabi. After serving a short prison sentence, Fabi returned to the village, but, 'fearing reprisals from the relatives of his victim and wishing as far as possible to avoid any encounter with them, he ceded the upper floor of the house, which he had shared with the Angeli, to his brother-in-law Matteo Suzzerini'. The Angeli took no action against Suzzerini, but shot and grievously wounded Fabi when he visited him in 1852. Unscrupulous abuse of affinal immunity or non-involvement occurred at Bocognano, where Dr Mannei had been killed in 1831, it was suspected by his rival Dr Vizzavona. Mannei's brother returned to the village from doing his military service late in 1833 after a peace had been agreed between the two families. However, 'he was able to come to an understanding with Francesco-Luigi Ciamborani, his first cousin by marriage, who had not been called on to join in the reconciliation' and was not therefore bound by it, and the two men killed Dr Vizzavona before the year was out.[130]

From our discussion so far, it will have become clear that certain factors determined whether feuding should remain within the circle of close relatives or extend beyond it. One, as we have seen, was whether close kin existed or not. 'If relatives were lacking,' Rossi pointed out, 'friends might arm themselves.'[131] Female relatives and neighbours might also pursue revenge in such circumstances. More generally, the vengeance obligation followed the concentric circles of kinship, being strongest at the centre and weakest at the periphery, as one might expect. This confirms Black-Michaud's suggestion that people felt most obliged to avenge those on whom they most depended.[132] These were not necessarily kin, and there is some evidence that propinquity itself was of some significance in determining obligations. In his account of a feud in the Niolo at the end of the eighteenth century, Grimaldi puts these words into the mouth of a girl who is urging her fiancé to avenge the death of her brother, a priest:

> When I have become your wife, how shall I be able to bear the insulting reproaches of the women of your village, who will never stop telling me with scorn: 'You have no relatives; you are alone on the earth; you have no one to support and protect you; for you have found no one to avenge for you even the death of a priest; or, if you have relatives, they must be far away, on the other side of the mountains.'

Conversely, Marin-Muracciole emphasizes that the avenger was usually the closest male relative living under the same roof as the victim.[133] From this, it is one step to neighbours being involved in vengeance. In the Civil and Criminal Statutes of the Genoese period, neighbours were assumed to bear the same responsibilities in a vendetta as relatives.[134] Réalier-Dumas commented in 1819 that the solidarity of kinsmen could be extended to all those from the same village or the same district. When a Captain Morelli was killed in 1817 in Bonifacio, he reported, 'the people of the Fiumorbo, who claimed to be Morelli's compatriots, swore to avenge his death against the best man in Bonifacio'.[135] As we have seen, feuds between or across communities were not unknown, and they must have involved the co-operation of neighbours. Ortoli refers, too, to offensive and defensive alliances being made in feuds between unrelated families.[136] All of this meant that neighbours, or indeed anyone providing neighbourly help to those engaged in feuding and thus expressing a solidarity with them, might be regarded as a legitimate target by their enemies. It was alleged, for example, that Dr Luigi Tulti of Penta-di-Casinca was killed by the Viterbi many years after the event 'for having bandaged the wounds of Venturino Suzzarini', whom Luca-Antono Viterbi had attempted to kill in 1796.[137]

However, the vicinity factor should not be exaggerated. If close kin were the ones primarily engaged in carrying out vengeance, more distant kin were usually present and ready to see that they did so, for material and honorific reasons. A further element here was the tendency of feuds to escalate, which necessarily brought in a wider and wider circle of kin and affines. The enmity between Giuseppo Antonmarchi, known as Gallocchio, and the Negroni, for example, began when he abducted a girl from Ampriani around 1820. This displeased Cesare Negroni, a cousin of the girl and probably a rival suitor. Hostilities were at first confined to the two main proponents and their brothers, but by the 1830s they had spread through first cousins, uncles and nephews, and affines to more distant kinsmen.[138] An important means of escalation, reflecting belief in the collective responsibility of kin, was the practice of 'transverse vengeance', or striking at relatives, close or distant, of those who had committed hostile acts rather than directly at the culprits themselves. We have cited many examples of this practice, but it should be stressed that it was not the rule, at least in the initial stages of feuds. Busquet claims that it was on the decline in the nineteenth century, and in trial cases it attracted special comment and was often explained, we have seen, as a substitute for the direct retaliation that would have been preferred. Even in the bigger feuds it did not usually act as a short-cut to the involvement of wider kin and these were brought in gradually. When large groups of kinsmen were operating as armed groups, transverse killing was more accidental than essential.[139] A related factor here was the seriousness of the initial injury calling for vengeance. Busquet noted that the mobilization of the family could be limited or extended depending on the nature of the offence and that the degree of mobilization could be stipulated in any formal declaration. However, once feuding had begun, rules as to who was or should be involved might be set aside 'in the intensity of passion unleashed', which is perhaps the explanation for the more exaggerated ideas about the boundary of the vengeance group that we have cited.[140] Fear of such an eventuality was expressed by Angelo-Paolo Octaviani of Carogne, who was accused of having killed Giovan-Petro Antonsanti in 1808. Angelo-Paolo maintained that he was not among the Octaviani who had committed the crime and explained the incriminating circumstances of his not having attended Antonsanti's wake and having then taken to the maquis by saying that 'since he was related to the culprits, the Antonsanti, blinded by anger, might have attacked him without reflecting and without bothering to find out whether he had actually participated in the killing of their kinsman or not'.[141]

All of this demonstrates that a distinction was made between vengeance killing between close circles of kin and that which went beyond. A further case makes this very plain. In 1814, the sister and niece of Marcello Graziani were killed by Guido-Antono Orticoni of Monticello. Together with Gorgonio Orticoni, Graziani assembled a group of 40 men and went to Monticello to exact revenge, and the houses of Guido-Antono and his associates were burned and pillaged. Both men were subsequently condemned to death for this crime, but clemency was recommended for Graziani. Because of his close kinship with the original victims, the public prosecutor advised, Graziani had been 'justified' in local terms in taking the action he did, while Gorgonio Orticoni, who was only distantly related to the two women, 'did not have the pretext of blood relations or even the defence of honour to exculpate him'.[142]

III

The involvement of relatives in feuding called for a degree of organization, to which we now turn. Writing in 1801, Miot commented on the 'solidarity contracted among the members of one family or one party in order to avenge a common injury', and stated that 'the person who executes the crime which vengeance demands is usually only an instrument chosen as such by his group'.[143] Here some writers refer to a decision taken by a family council, a procedure followed when there was no obvious male relative to act as avenger. The family council might also draw up a list of reserves, in case the first choice were himself killed, or where hostilities were or were likely to be prolonged. The council might also take the initial decision whether to avenge or not and issue a declaration of a state of enmity where appropriate.[144] Direct evidence of this formal exercise of solidarity is necessarily sparse, though the judicial records do sometimes refer to collective decision-making by relatives.

A general peace had been concluded at Sari-d'Orcino in 1841, after fighting in which Anton-Francesco Padovani had been mortally wounded, 'but the relatives of Padovani' found that they could not accept this outcome 'and resolved to avenge him'.[145] Following the death of a member of the Serra family of Sartène in 1848, we learn that 'the family decided to avenge him'; while 'all or some of [his many relatives at Olmeto and Altagène] ... determined to avenge' the killing of Giuseppo Paoli of Fozzano in the same year.[146]

A feature of feuds that seems nearly always to have been present, whether any formal organization was involved or not, was their direction by older and their actual prosecution by younger men. The predominance of men under 35 among offenders put on trial for crimes of violence is very striking, and this impression is confirmed by closer analysis of those prosecuted for homicide or attempted homicide, as indicated in Table 4. We have seen in Chapter 2 that feuds were directed by older men, and further evidence can be adduced to show that such direction was normal and largely unquestioned. It was suggested in 1797 that a certain Guglielmi from the canton of Ornano should be removed from his position as a criminal judge and reference was made here to 'the vendettas which he does not carry out himself but which he controls with the greatest circumspection'.[147] One of the hostages taken by the government at Pila-Canale in 1801 was asked what he had done to try 'to get the feuds in the village stopped and to bring about a reconciliation between the families concerned', and he had replied 'that he was a young man and that these matters were the business of those older than himself'.[148] According to a report in 1822, the relatives of the bandit Teodoro Poli (though not his father) promoted his activities.[149] Again, when Antono Saliceti was killed in 1841, his relatives accused the two sons of Paolo-Maria Giacomi, who was prosecuted with them. It was argued at his trial that he was 'the head of the Giacomi family and their leader in the feud between them and the Saliceti and must therefore have instigated the crime'.[150] Other cases of vengeance killings attributable to the influence of uncles and fathers-in-law may also be cited.[151]

This pattern reflects the 'patriarchal' family structure and the respect for age and experience found in a traditional society. Malaspina noted very generally here that Corsicans 'obeyed the oldest members of their families', and this norm is expressed in proverbs.[152] Some students of other feuding societies have suggested that young men may sometimes be reluctant to act in the quarrels of their elders, or conversely that older men may be more prone to seek conciliation in conflict situations and avoid the violent action which is attractive to the young.[153] Examples of both can be found in Corsica, and the latter parallels the distinction

Table 4. *Age of those prosecuted for homicide or attempted homicide*

Year	Mean age	Median age
1830 (1st and 2nd sessions)	31	26
1853 (1st and 2nd sessions)	29	26
1865 (all sessions)	31	28

between older men's preference for negotiated marriages and the penchant of young men for abduction, which we discussed in Chapter 4. Once again, however, the behaviour of young and old should be seen as ultimately complementary, even when they appear to diverge.

Such organization within the family was part of a wider system of regulation, for in Corsica, as in most other feuding societies, blood vengeance was subject to 'law', if indeed it did not itself constitute a system of law.[154] 'Vengeance as exercised in Corsica has its rules, from which it is not permitted to depart,' Pompei declared in 1821. Father Bartoli referred in 1898 to the 'fixed and definite rules' of the vendetta, while Surier wrote in 1934 that vengeance killing 'was surrounded by an established procedure tacitly agreed to. This expeditious and partial mode of justice has its code, its rules, which no one would dream of breaking.' Busquet's classic study proclaims the same view in its title and supports it with ample evidence. Only Robiquet sounded a discordant note, commenting in 1835 that feuding 'appears to be subject to no rules, or rather if rules exist, their observation has become exceptional'.[155]

First, there were rules or conventions about the circumstances in which vengeance might properly be taken. According to Faure, there were four situations which justified or required vengeance: when a woman had been dishonoured, when an engagement had been broken, when a close relative had been killed, and when false testimony in court led to the conviction of a member of one's family. Most of the examples which we have cited fall under these headings. Feuding had to be generally approved of by the community, at least in its initial stages. 'If public opinion did not sanction a vendetta,' Saint-Germain noted, 'it became virtually impossible to carry out, since those involved would be deprived of aid and protection.'[156]

Once a family had decided to pursue vengeance, the initial step was to declare a state of hostilities against the enemy, and we have seen that such 'declarations of war' might stipulate exactly who was to be involved. The declaration was usually made after the funeral of the victim, and an oath might be sworn.[157] A number of set formulae were used, for example: 'Be on your guard and watch your step!', 'Take care or the priest will be singing for you!', or 'Take care! If you show yourself to the sun, my lead shot will strike you!' The term 'to be on one's guard' was generally used to mean that one was engaged in a feud.[158] In addition to verbal declarations, Busquet mentions the sounding of horns, and a number of reports from the Sartenais in the early nineteenth century refer to the placing of wooden crosses at the doors of houses accompanied by powder and shot, and sometimes by messages.[159] Many specific examples may be cited to support these general observations. We saw that Francesco-Maria Bruni and his relatives 'declared a general state of enmity between themselves and the Poli' at Pila-Canale in 1797.[160] Réalier-Dumas related in 1819 that, when he was at the house of a certain Battesti at Ventiseri, an armed man entered and announced formally that from that day his family was 'in a state of enmity' with that of Battesti. He gave him eight days 'in which to warn his relatives', after which period each side would have to be 'on its guard' against the other.[161] Again, after Domenico Bottaci of Venzolasca had been acquitted on the charge of killing Giovan-Battiste Luciani, the latter's son 'warned Bottaci to keep out of his way', which was taken to be a declaration of his intention to remedy the situation by taking vengeance himself.[162] It does not seem, however, that formal declarations were absolutely necessary, and they may have become less frequent in the course of the nineteenth century.[163] Nevertheless, hostile intentions were nearly always made clear and killing without warning was regarded as reprehensible. Feuding was concerned with questions of honour and status, which encouraged both demonstrativeness and sticking to the rules. It is relevant here that the accomplishment of vengeance was also publicly announced either verbally or by signs.

A warning of hostilities had only to be given once, however. After that, in the words of the fifteenth-century chronicler Cyrnaeus, if the parties to a feud 'could not accomplish their aims openly, they used ambushes, ruse and all manner of artifice'.[164] Ambushes were a common feature of the feuds which we have described, and many further examples might be cited.[165] It is possible that ambushes became more prevalent as formal declarations declined and that these two related trends were aspects of a general deregulation of feuding, points to which we will return.

Persons engaged in a feud were expected to follow certain forms of behaviour, which not only publicized their state of enmity but also indicated in a ritual way that this state was special, liminal and dangerous. Contemporaries and later authors mention the shutting up of houses, the wearing of sombre clothes by persons of both sexes and semi-fasting, all of which were extensions of normal mourning procedures and which were maintained until vengeance had been accomplished or peace concluded.[166] Two practices attracted particular notice here. First, men involved in a feud let their hair and beards grow. Versini cites an example from a trial in 1843, in which the witnesses, close relatives of a man who had been killed, wore long beards. Asked to explain why, they said that they 'had sworn an oath not to cut our beards or our hair until the death of our brother has been avenged'. Montherot referred in 1840 to a man from Bocognano having 'cut off his beard of vengeance' on concluding a peace with his enemies.[167] The second custom was the preservation of the bloody shirt or some other relic of a victim. This was kept, Mérimée explained, 'as a reminder of the need for vengeance. It was shown to relatives to excite them to punish the victim's killers' and especially to the children of unavenged men.[168] The grandmother of the two Forcioli killed at Arbellara in 1844 declared in her lament for them: 'I will put a nail in the wall / On which to hang the bloody clothes / Of our two dead, / And people will show them to the children that remain to me; / I will address *rimbeccu* to them / Until we have been avenged!' Again, a sister lamenting a brother wished that she had a son: then 'I would cut up my bloody apron / And make him a waistcoat of it; / So that he would never forget / The blood [of his uncle].'[169] Sometimes, pieces of paper were dipped in the blood of victims for the same purpose, and Bourde cites a case from the Sartenais in the 1880s in which a woman put her children's fingers in their father's wounds, daubed his blood on their faces and swore them to vengeance.[170]

Funeral ceremonies also served to perpetuate the memories of relatives to be avenged. Luca-Antono Viterbi of Penta left elaborate instructions in 1821 for his burial. The provisions included oaths not to forget and implicitly to avenge him:

> My sons-in-law will dig the first sod and will be the first to cast a shovelful of earth to fill in my grave. Each of my relatives and friends, as they pass each other the shovel next, will throw earth on my coffin, saying at the same time in a loud voice: 'I swear never to forget the manner in which my friend and relative Luca-Antono Viterbi died.' The children will be the first to take this oath.

Nor were female relatives left out, for the instructions continued: 'When my corpse has left the house, my wife will gather together all her daughters; they will kneel down and will swear eternal hatred to my persecutors.'[171] Anniversary rituals and funeral monuments performed the same function in a more enduring way, and we will discuss them in more detail in Chapter 13.

The interval between injury or declaration of hostilities and taking vengeance could be short or long as the circumstances dictated. A delay of a year or so was common. For example, in January 1843, Giovan-Bernardino Peraldi of Olmeto shot Giuseppo Paganacci on the road to Ajaccio. At first there seemed no motive for the crime, until it was learned that Paganacci had hit Peraldi twelve months previously, an assault that Peraldi had had no opportunity to avenge earlier. Again, at Ciamannacce, Giacomo-Francesco Santucci used violence against the wife of Paolo Leonetti in October 1844, but Leonetti committed no act of retaliation until September 1845. Longer delays might be caused by the imprisonment of enemies or waiting for the outcome of court action. Here the return of the offender to the village often prompted the act of revenge, as we have seen.[172] Long delays might also be occasioned by the lack of adult kinsmen and waiting for sons, nephews or even grandsons to reach maturity. Miot relates that a vengeance killing took place at Bocognano in 1801, when he was visiting the village. A man had been killed eight years earlier, leaving two sons. These had just reached the age of 16 or 17 and 'were thus in a position to avenge their father'.[173] However, external factors and obstacles are not the entire explanation for delay in taking vengeance. In a case at Campile, Giovan-Camillo Mariotti had been killed in mid-1838. Felice Mariotti and Giulio-Francesco Mattei were responsible and were later arrested. Giovan-Camillo's son Anton-Giacomo awaited the outcome of their trials before taking any action. Felice Mariotti was convicted and condemned to 20 years' hard labour, but Mattei, who had been charged as his accomplice, was acquitted at the end of 1840. Anton-Giacomo 'believed that the death of his father had only been half-revenged and resolved to complete the work of the courts'. But he nursed his plan for nearly two years more and did not kill Mattei until November 1842.[174] We may cite other cases, moreover, where revenge was not taken for 12, 15 or 20 years, and where no obvious reason for the delay is provided.[175]

This relates to the long-term nature of feuding, to which we drew attention in Chapter 2. Officials and observers emphasized this phenomenon, referring to 'perpetual enmities', 'hereditary hatreds', feuds that had existed for generations or from 'time immemorial'.[176] A Corsican might forgive but he would 'never forget an injury', Bigot wrote in 1869, and, where he did not forgive, he was quite prepared to wait, knowing in the words of a proverb that 'time would bring a time [for revenge]'. More generally, according to a lawyer cited by Réalier-Dumas, 'a Corsican realizes that he will need your help in ten years' time and acts accordingly ... patience is their favourite word'.[177] Specific examples may be found, moreover, of conflict being remembered and perhaps reactivated after two or more generations. In a case in 1801, Michele-Orso Peraldi of Rospigliani was accused, among other offences, of having shot at Santo Marchetti. He denied having had any dispute with Marchetti personally but admitted that they were not 'friends': 'On the contrary, his father and his grandfather were always opposed to the father and grandfather of Marchetti because of ancient enmities, and his grandfather, who is still alive, was wounded in the thumb and still has the scar.'[178] At Bastelica, Giovan-Francesco Pasqualini, in dispute with another man in 1862, reacted violently when the latter mentioned the name Farinati, since 'hearing this name reminded him of the killing of his grandfather many years ago by a Farinati'.[179] Again, in a lament collected by Ortoli, a wife told her dead husband: 'Between you [and your enemies] there was never peace / Since the time of your great-grandfather!'[180]

Students of feuding in other societies have argued that past conflict can only be selectively remembered, and that this occurs with reference to the present situation, old hostilities being forgotten if they have been overtaken by new alliances, or recalled, even embroidered, if conflict along the same lines is still alive.[181] The chances of selectivity or lapse of memory might predictably be small in a village-based society such as Corsica, in which family competition was perennially intense and where it would be a primary consideration to know the state of relations between one family and another, a consideration kept active also by the requirements of marriage strategy and by the various mnemonic devices that we have described. Corsicans set the highest store, too, on fidelity and not forgetting, as we have seen. However, both this insistence and the very importance of mnemonics suggest a fear of not remembering, and selectivity was clearly operative in Corsica, though to a lesser extent perhaps than elsewhere. We saw in Chapter 2 that families did change sides in feuds over long periods of time, and further evidence may be cited which suggests that local memories could be shorter and vaguer than they were ideally supposed to be. In a case in 1802, arising from the feuding between the Paoli of Fozzano and the Giacomoni of Santa-Maria-Figaniella, Sampiero Giacomoni was asked 'to tell the court why he and his relatives were enemies of the Paoli family', and he replied 'that he did not know'. Again, in a case in 1801, Dezio Valentini of Moca claimed that serious charges against him had been fabricated by Marco-Maria Franchi, also from Moca, who was a gendarme at Olmeto. Asked to explain the apparently unmotivated hostility of his fellow-villager, Valentini declared that 'his ancestors and those of the gendarme had been enemies, or so he had heard'.[182] There is no doubt also that time could abate the passion for vengeance. Montherot was told by an inhabitant of Corte:

> We remember ancient wrongs, but we don't punish them. We would avenge recent offences, but as far as old ones are concerned, we just bear a grudge. If a man seduces my daughter, I will kill him; but, if my grand-mother was abducted, and I happen to meet the grandson of her seducer, it is enough for me not to raise my hat.[183]

More generally, Bastelica was the theatre of very violent conflict early in the nineteenth century but had achieved a reputation by the start of the twentieth as a place where feuding was unknown.[184] Also relevant here is the way in which feuds went through periods of quiescence, often being revived in an accidental fashion or under the influence of external events. The lawyer and journalist Patorni claimed that many crimes committed in the years of political upheaval from 1813 to 1815 had been forgiven and forgotten, until the government launched a series of prosecutions in 1819, which stimulated new acts of vengeance.[185] More particularly, the feud between the Vignale and the Canacci of Bisinchi appeared to be over in 1842, when a chance attack on a Canacci by a dog belonging to the Vignale occurred to revive it;[186] and many other examples could be adduced. We will return to the general question of how feuds were ended in Chapter 9, concluding this chapter with further consideration of the nature of the feuding obligation.

We have seen how this related to kinship structure, but how binding was the obligation on the relatives concerned? Most writers on the subject are in no doubt that in general terms the obligation to avenge killings and other serious offences was absolute and sacred in Corsica, as it was in many other feuding societies, particularly in the Mediterranean region.[187] Busquet concluded that feuding 'was not an option but a requirement ... For the offended group, the vendetta is imperative; it is not a right but a duty.'[188] However, it was conceded that exceptions to this rule existed, which were not simply a breach of it, and this degree of optionality surely reflects the flexibility of general kinship ties and obligations.

> A man who had been provoked by a personal affront, or by the killing of one of his relatives [wrote Colonna de Cesari-Rocca in 1908] was not absolutely and inevitably required to exact vengeance. It was not very honourable to take this course, but examples are found. To refuse the enmity, it was not necessary to contact one's opponents directly or indirectly; it was sufficient not to carry a gun or any other weapon.

Busquet agreed that a person had the right not to declare or not to take part in a vendetta. This would be indicated by a statement to that effect, or by not carrying arms, by tending the hair and beard normally, and so on. Marin-Muracciole writes more positively that 'the Corsican could always choose between vengeance and pardon', though she adds that it was always thought better 'to grant pardon after vengeance had been exacted'.[189]

Proverbs allowed some scope for Christian forgiveness but also marked its limits, for example: 'Pardon the first and the second injury, but, at the third, strike back!'; or 'To pardon is the act of a Christian; to forget is that of an imbecile.'[190] As Colonna de Cesari-Rocca suggests, cases of pardoning offences did occur in the nineteenth century. Francesco-Matteo Bruni claimed, we have seen, to have pardoned the Poli more than once before eventually declaring a vendetta against them. According to Father Abeau, when the son of Marianna Pozzo di Borgo, a widow from Appietto, was killed by Andrea Romanetti, she at first sought revenge but then forgave him. Similarly, in the Moriani district, Dezio Dezii killed Luigione Venturini's father. He went into exile, and when he returned Luigione relinquished the opportunity to kill him and pardoned him instead.[191] Again, political rivalries led to the death of Domenico-Francesco Agostini of Prunelli in 1835 at the hands of hired assassins. At the trial of two of these, Agostini's old father declared that he pardoned them, since 'they would never have dreamed of killing my son, had they not been put under pressure to do so'. Since both were sentenced to life imprisonment, this pardon was some-what academic.[192] There is evidence, too, that some people were out of sympathy with the whole notion of vengeance killing. These included some but not all members of the clergy, as we shall see in the next chapter, and men who had been educated abroad like Mérimée's Orso della Rebbia, but also ordinary Corsicans. Giovan-Girolamo Sampieri, a hired herdsman, for example, gave evidence in a trial in 1817. He had seen shooting between two parties near Bilia and then the pursuit of a wounded man through the maquis 'in order to finish him off'. 'I turned back weeping,' he said, 'because I had seen men harming each other with guns.'[193] There is little evidence, however, that the decision of individuals whether or not to fulfil feuding obligations was a dilemma of general cultural significance, as it appears to have been in the world of the Icelandic sagas.[194] The dilemma is central, of course, in *Colomba*, but this only reflects attitudes found among a small acculturated élite.

More generally, involvement in a feud was regarded as a 'misfortune'. The man who kills for vengeance, wrote Bourde, is 'a man in trouble', and as such he is pitied as well as admired and supported.[195] Moreover, as we shall see in more detail below, efforts were normally made to settle disputes amicably, and vendettas themselves were punctuated by periods of reconciliation. Feuds were some-times only declared after attempts at mediation had failed, and there is evidence that those who were too keen to seek vengeance might be the objects of disapproval. At the trial in 1830 of Francesco Susini of Moca, accused of destroying vines, fruit trees and enclosures as an act of vengeance, a witness testified that he was 'a hothead who didn't know how to conduct his affairs properly'.[196]

Neutrality on the part of non-principals was more common. At Fozzano, for example, Paolo-Girolamo Paoli and Petro Bernardini were said in 1834 'not to be involved in the feuding which is desolating the village', although they were almost certainly related to the main protagonists within the degree of obligation.[197] At Venzolasca in 1911, 'the local people, who from the start have declared themselves to be neutral, have nothing to fear', the gendarmerie reported; 'the only people involved in the conflict are those who get themselves involved or who have been mixed up in some way in the quarrels of the two feuding families'.[198] Neutrality, moreover, was a characteristic which the government sought out and was usually able to find in appointing local officials in feuding villages.[199] We have seen that feuding among relatives was possible, but in general being related to both parties in a feud, presumably not an uncommon predicament, would keep people out of it. Among the hostages taken at Pila-Canale in 1801, Giacomo-Filippo Vincenti claimed 'to have always belonged to both parties and therefore to have taken no part in their enmities'; while Antono Fieschi declared that he was 'neutral in the conflict since he was related to both parties'.[200] Again, a recommendation for the nomination of an *adjoint* at Carbini in the 1860s argued in favour of a son of the late judge Nicolai. Though he belonged to a family involved in the feuding in the village, the fact that he was also 'related by marriage to all the families', meant that he could not be a partisan.[201] Neutrality in a feud could be a difficult position to sustain. In the feud between the Mattei and the Giampietri at Gavignano in the 1830s, a certain Fausti was said 'to have maintained a sort of neutrality' for some time, although his father was a staunch supporter of the Giampietri. Eventually, however, Fausti himself was drawn into the conflict, helping to ambush and kill Bartolomeo Mattei in August 1833. Room for a non-partisan stance also diminished as a feud intensified and spread through the community. At Arbellara by the 1840s, for example, 'nearly all the other families in the village had ranged themselves' behind one or the other of the main protagonists.[202]

We should emphasize that non-involvement of kin and especially failure to seek revenge or to declare a vendetta by close relatives were normally highly disapproved of. 'A man who does not carry out vengeance is reputed to be dishonourable,' Cyrnaeus declared, in words often cited by nineteenth-century writers,[203] and others spelled out what this meant in practice. 'A man who has not avenged his father or another murdered relative, or a girl who has been seduced, can no longer appear in public,' Father Bartoli noted. 'People will not speak to him ... He loses all standing, all prestige.'[204] The suicide of Giuseppo Lorenzi at Belvedere in 1834 was attributed to the strain following the killing of his brother and his failure to avenge it.[205] Such a failure and the consequent shame reflected of course on a man's family, who would bring pressure on him to perform his duty. After his cousins Gregorio and Fiordispina Grimaldi had been killed at Marignana in the 1840s, Petro-Giovanni Massoni took no steps to avenge them and 'obstinately refused to show any solidarity with his relatives'. The victims' father, who had no other children, appealed to his nephew to intervene, seconded by other relatives, mainly women, who told him that the family was the object of shame and ridicule.[206] More generally, Réalier-Dumas noted that a family council might appoint another relative to act to redeem the family honour, where sons or other close kin had failed or refused to do their part.[207]

Failure to carry out vengeance incurred a special reproach or sanction. This was the *rimbeccu*, a deliberate reminder of the unfulfilled revenge. It could take the form of a song, a remark, a gesture or a look, and could be delivered by relatives, neighbours or strangers, men or women. It was a direct accusation of cowardice and dereliction and was itself a common cause of feuding or the revival of feuding, which led to its being proscribed in legislation from the sixteenth century. Busquet noted that modern juries nearly always acquitted offenders who had been prompted to crimes by the *rimbeccu*.[208] We have seen that the feud at Santa-Lucia-di-Tallano revived in 1839, when Petro Poli reproached Giacomo-Antono Giacomoni with not having avenged his brother, killed five years earlier, and a killing at Linguizetta in 1846 was prompted by actual use of the epithet.[209] The existence of the *rimbeccu* as a custom suggests that there was a need for people to be reminded of their duty to pursue vengeance, or rather perhaps that in a society where a morality of honour and shame and not of conscience prevailed, a public sanction of this kind was required. As blood vengeance itself was an external sanction against 'antisocial' behaviour in a society of competing family groups, so its secondary sanction, the *rimbeccu*, was of the same kind, though we shall see that vengeance was also backed up by supernatural sanctions.

Failure to take vengeance or willingness to pardon affronts would usually be taken as signs of weakness, 'leaving a family the prey to every outrage in the future'.[210] Honour again was the means of defending material interest. However, within this context, it was not expected that people would seek revenge against those who were too powerful. Pompei wrote that there was 'usually a certain equality between the two parties who are at war. It is rare indeed for a vendetta to occur where there is a great disproportion of strength between the two families, unless the weaker one seeks outside support ... in order to reestablish the balance.' As a result, he added, families rarely engaged in conflict whose outcome seemed hopeless.[211] A case at Cargiaca in 1821 seems to illustrate this consideration. Don Giacomo Valerj, his wife and their son, made Carlo Luccioni and Battiste Valerj give them a barrel. 'The latter acquiesced', the subprefect reported, 'in order to avoid a dispute which would doubtless have had dire results for them; they preferred to suffer the insult rather than answer it by force.'[212] This indicates conversely that the powerful in numbers or other resources could, to some extent, ignore honour in the pursuit of interest. There were limits to the exercise of power, however, and even the domination by terror of notorious bandits was in time checked or countered. Blood vengeance, moreover, clearly had an egalitarian potentiality here, leaving room for boldness, initiative and courage against the weight of numbers or influence.

Also relevant here is the practice of employing agents to fulfil feuding obligations. This was not uncommon and was a feature of many important feuds. At Olmeta-di-Tuda, Domenico Campocasso was killed in 1817 by Girolamo Monti, 'one of the hired agents of the Casale'. At Venzolasca, the Filippi hired an Italian Angelini, to kill or help them to kill two members of the Ciavaldini family.[213] Where non-relatives were involved in vengeance killings, the authorities and local opinion nearly always assumed that they must have been hired for the job. When Giusepp'-Antono Paoli was killed outside his house at Fozzano in 1851 by Stefano Papalini, for example, 'everyone concluded that Papalini must have acted as the agent of Paoli's enemies since there was no cause otherwise for enmity between the two men'.[214] Very often notables used agents, paying them for their services, avoiding doing their own dirty work and also avoiding or trying to avoid the consequences. The Filippi attempted to cast all the blame for the Ciavaldini killings on to their hired killer, and in a number of other cases hired agents were convicted while their employers went free. The use of agents in this context was discreditable to both parties. Saverio Bozzi of Pila-Canale was referred to by his opponents as 'the vile agent' of the Bruni.[215] A special pejorative term, *taddunaghiu*, existed to describe a person who killed or betrayed for money.[216] It is significant also that hired agents were not infrequently Italians.

There were circumstances, however, in which agents might be used without dishonour, notably by those unable to fulfil vengeance themselves, such as women, especially widows, older men and priests. We have seen that Signora Bartoli tried to hire herdsmen to continue the feud at Fozzano after the peace of 1834. When Nicolaio Vincentelli was shot dead near Feliceto in 1847, Giovanni Colonna of Evisa was suspected of the crime and was believed to have acted as the agent of Giovan-Francesco Alessandri and his uncle Leca, a priest. Again, at Piobbeta, Father Vincenti was killed in 1851 in the course of a feud between his family and the Muzi. 'It seems that Father Muzi wrote to some bandits in order to get them to kill Father Vincenti,' and, this having failed, that he and his brother then 'used their cousin Luporsi to dispose of their enemy'. As this example indicates, the agents chosen were often relatives, usually distant ones, probably from a mixture of convenience and the wish to mitigate the stigma of using an agent at all. The Brignole of Olmeta-di-Tuda hired a certain Lucciani from Bisinchi to kill Orso-Santo Casale in 1830 and he proved later to have been their distant kinsman. Anton-Petro Leca of Ota, an older man and the dominant figure in his family, was worsted in a property dispute in February 1836 with Petro Leca, against whom he 'nourished an implacable hatred'. When Petro Leca was shot and killed some months later, his family accused Luca-Antono Leca and Serafino Bastino. 'No personal interest, no kind of enmity could have led them independently to attack Petro Leca, whom they hardly knew,' but they were related to Anton-Petro Leca and were presumed to have acted as his agents. Suitable relatives might also be enlisted as accomplices rather than principals. Giovanni Borghetti of Poggio-Mezzana 'addressed himself to a certain Ricciardi, his relative, who, though still very young, displayed a bold and violent character and a perverse disposition', and together they carried out a vengeance killing in 1829.[217]

Those chosen as agents were often bandits. 'It is well-known', wrote Mérimée, 'that the protection of bandits is much sought after in Corsica, and that they intervene frequently in family quarrels to oblige their friends.'[218] This was an obvious extension of the bandit's primary role as the agent in his own family's feuding, and there was sometimes a kinship link where bandits intervened in the conflict of others. Recourse might also be had to bandits where one party was much weaker than the other. In the feud between the Valerj and the Ferrali of Sant'Andrea, we learn that the latter were obviously less powerful and had therefore 'placed themselves under the protection of a number of redoubtable bandits'. A shortage of able-bodied males may also be presumed in other cases. Antono Giacobbi, from Luno, for example, deserted from the army around 1840 when he heard that his father had been condemned to ten years' hard labour for homicide, 'probably with the intention of seeking revenge, since he attached himself to two well-known bandits'.[219] More often, however, the arrangement appears to have been more mercenary. Giovan-Battiste Ornano, for example, wrote in 1840 to the prefect of 'the oppression exercised against me and my family by hired agents, bandits paid by those who hate me'.[220] Similarly, when the relatives of Giuseppo Paoli of Fozzano, killed in 1848, were looking for an agent to avenge his death, a number of bandits were approached on their behalf by a third party and one of these eventually agreed to act for them.[221] Increasing use of agents in feuds might be a sign of decadence, but there is no real evidence for the existence of such a trend. Indeed, more cases in which agents were employed appear in the judicial records before 1850 than after. One must conclude that, for the notables in particular, a degree of inconsistency with the requirements of the feud's code of honour was always possible.

] 8 [

Immunity and disruption

Certain categories of person were in theory immune from involvement in feuding.[1] They were not required to seek vengeance and they were not proper targets for it. These were guests and those protected by the laws of hospitality, children, old men, women, and members of the clergy. To these five sometimes overlapping categories may be added self-declared neutrals[2] and those to whom special assurances had been given.[3] Attacks on immune persons broke the rules of the vendetta and might incur their own penalty. According to Malaspina, 'if a vendetta involved an old man or a child, the killer was dishonoured, and his own relatives abandoned him'.[4] We shall see, however, that immunities were quite often flouted in the nineteenth century, which is perhaps a further sign of the decadence of the whole blood-vengeance system. Immunities were one factor which mitigated the disruptive effect of feuds, together with others that we will discuss at the end of the chapter.

I

We have already discussed the Corsican tradition of hospitality in general terms. As in many other societies of the Mediterranean region and beyond,[5] the stranger or guest in Corsica was 'sacred' and 'inviolable',[6] and this quality extended to enemies who asked for hospitality.[7] At Marignana, for example, a short while before he eventually killed him, Massoni sought out his cousin Stefano at the house of a certain Castellani, for whom he worked. Stefano was at first hidden. When he was produced, Castellani declared: 'He eats his bread at my house and it must be a refuge for him,' and Massoni agreed to respect this convention.[8] Chanal relates two further instances of hospitality given to enemies. In the first, his guide, a Vinciguerra from Guagno, had killed a Leca. He fled and sought refuge in a house which proved to be that of the father of his victim. He was allowed to spend the night and witnessed the lament and swearing of vengeance over the corpse. In the second, Orso Figari of Salice gave the bandit Giuncheto from Vignamajo shelter for the night, although their two families had been enemies for years. Tommaseo even cites a case in the eighteenth century in which a man killed his own nephew in order to defend an enemy who had taken refuge in his house.[9] However, it was possible for the rules of hospitality to be neglected or very differently interpreted. When Maria Paoli from Salice was molested at a house on the territory of Sarrola, her host did little or nothing, it seems, to protect her.[10] Though it could be dramatic, this category of immunity was in general relatively unimportant.

The immunity accorded to children and to old men was more significant. In some other feuding societies, children might be fully involved and examples can be found of vengeance being exacted on babies. Young children were more rarely regarded as wholly responsible for homicide, a not wholly logical position according to any strictly compensatory view of blood vengeance.[11] In Corsica, most writers agree that children were in theory excluded from feuds as actors or victims.[12] A witness in a case in 1857, in which two men were accused of shooting at the son of a certain Castelli from Pietricaggio, testified that 'people thought that it was impossible that the two accused should have tried to kill a child of sixteen'.[13] Cases may be cited, too, in which children were deliberately spared. Orso-Martino Tristani of Antisanti was convicted in 1852 of having killed Orso-Francesco Marchi. Tristani was given an extremely bad character and was sentenced to 20 years' hard labour, an unusually severe penalty. Nevertheless, in his encounter with Marchi, he had left alone the latter's younger brother and a cousin aged 13.[14] One may also point to examples which indicate that killing children was indeed extraordinary and aroused extreme aversion. When Giovan-Battiste Tramoni killed a boy of seven at Mela in 1901, he was abandoned by his own relatives and forced to go into exile in Sardinia.[15]

Despite all this, the killing of children does figure surprisingly frequently in the judicial records. It was sometimes accidental or incidental to attacks on adults. In 1851, for example, Giulio-Matteo Guiderdoni of Moca-Croce shot at Giusepp'-Antono Istria, who had seduced his sister, as he was on the 'square' of his house with his six-year-old son and killed the boy.[16] One evening in August 1855, Santo Santini of Arro and his two sons, who were in a state of enmity with the family of Antono Colonna, came across Colonna sleeping in a field with his wife and two children. The Santini fired at the Colonna, killing one of the children who was five and wounding the other who was seven.[17] Where children were not actually harmed in similar circumstances, this seems often to have been by pure chance. Luciano Gabrielli shot and killed a member of the rival Lucchini family at Ciamannacce in 1809 as he was at a window holding a child, while at Antisanti in 1851 Don Antono Mattei allegedly shot and killed his uncle Faustino as the latter was watering his garden with his five-year-old daughter.[18] Children were also selected in some circumstances as second-best targets. Pierrina Carlotti of Isolaccio shot the ten-year-old son of a woman with whom she suspected her husband was having an affair, but only after having failed to reach his mother or grandmother.[19] As often, however, the killing of children was deliberate and unqualified. According to accounts of the feud at Pila-Canale, the Bozzi killed the twelve-year-old son of Giuseppo-Maria Casabianca in 1796, the Poli killed Giovanni Bozzi aged twelve in 1797, and the Feliciaggi killed Pancrazio Ficuelle, also aged twelve, in 1798. Children aged twelve and fourteen were killed in the feud at Frasseto in the 1830s and 1840s. A boy of twelve or thirteen was killed at Muro in 1814 and a baby of two at Loreto-di-Tallano in 1847.[20] Valéry reported, moreover, that children were kept indoors during the feuding at Fozzano in the 1830s, as though they were possible targets.[21] There are indications that the killing of children characterized feuds of peculiar bitterness or 'bad feuds' aimed at the total extinction of rival families.[22] 'On adults and children, it does not matter. / Even on the women. / Rip out all their guts!', an aunt enjoined her nephew in a lament.[23] Durham's suggestion that the killing of children in feuds reflects the importance attached to making a blood-offering to the slain is also relevant to Corsica, and we shall return to it in Chapter 13. But we may also note that children were often killed in the heat of the moment. After Anton-Domenico Moroselli was killed at Tavera in 1840, his relatives sought immediate revenge. One of them met Paolo-Giovanni Casanova, aged 14, the brother of one of the suspected culprits, coming towards the village, shot at him and then stabbed him to death. At Bocognano, again, in 1852 or 1853, Giuseppo Tavera killed Francesco Morelli, whereupon one of the latter's sons went to Tavera's house and killed his son, who was only a boy.[24]

Three further points are of interest in this context. First, when did children cease to be children? Reference in court cases to 'children' of 16 is almost certainly special pleading, for youths of 17 and 18 were readily called 'landowners' and treated as adult men. In general, boys seem to have been regarded as of age in this respect when they reached 16. The two brothers who avenged their father's death, while Miot was at Bocognano in 1801, had just reached the ages of 16 and 17.[25] At Figari, the Susini killed Santo Maisetti in 1849 in order to prevent him from avenging his father. The boy was 16. Again, at Venzolasca in 1857, following a fight, Giacomo Merrighi issued a formal warning to be on his guard to Tomaso Alfonsi aged 15 or 16.[26]

A second question is whether children might act as avengers. Reference is made to boys of ten acting in this capacity in the mid-eighteenth century.[27] No modern examples of such precocity have been found, but there are some of boys in their early teens. In an encounter between the Nicoloni of Pero-Casevecchie and the bandit Robetti in 1830, one of the latter's companions was killed by Giovan-Gregorio Nicoloni, aged twelve.[28] Girolamo Cotoni of Campi was only 13 when he avenged the dishonouring of his sister by a cousin, but he was an orphan and had no brothers. Again, at Levie in the course of a feud between two branches of the Peretti family, the father and elder brother of Don Giacomo-Telemaco Peretti had been killed in 1847 when he was only eleven. From that time the boy went about armed and talked of vengeance and in 1851 he shot and killed a member of the opposing family. At his trial, it was claimed that as a child he was not fully responsible for his actions, and he was acquitted. A similar verdict was reached in other cases of this kind, which the president of the Assize Court saw as a mistaken application of 'continental' notions.[29] The circumstances in all our examples were unusual and involved no element of calculation. There are indications, however, that at a lower level of conflict minors might act as principals precisely on account of their privileged status. In a case in 1822, a boy of twelve from Cargiaca was told to kill a straying horse, since reprisals and punishment would be less serious than if his father had acted himself.[30]

Thirdly, a certain amount of conflict was generated by children, which indicates not only a strong affection for them but also a sense that they, too, were representative members of their families. At Santa-Maria-Sicche, Pasquino Massimi stabbed another man in the chest in 1857 in a quarrel which began when some children started to pull the tails and manes of the horses of a carter from Ajaccio. At Poggio-di-Nazza in 1893 two eight-year-olds began to fight over a knife. The mother of one intervened and then an adult male cousin of the other, who shot her dead. Many similar incidents could be cited. Children were also unwitting or witting purveyors of information which prompted revenge killings. They might spread gossip like their elders. We have seen that children spread the story that there had been intimacy between Antono Rutilj and Cornelia Cartucci of Arbellara in 1840, which eventually led her brother to kill him. Children might also be used by adults here to disarm or deceive their enemies. In the course of the feud between the Mattei and the Giampietri at Gavignano, a man was told by a child where he could find his brother's killer, but this proved to be a trap which led him into an ambush.[31]

Old men were also non-combatants in feuds in theory.[32] At what age men reached this status is unclear, though we have noted that in practice those actively involved in feuding were usually under 35. Before he died after being shot by another youth in 1832, a certain Tomasini of Venzolasca asked his father to avenge him, but the latter replied that he was 'too old' and that they would have to rely on God and the courts.[33] At the start of the feud at Marignana, Gregorio Grimaldi's father felt too old to avenge his son himself and called on his nephew Massoni to act, as we have seen. Later in the feud, Saverio Grimaldi, another old man, made insulting remarks about the Durilli. As a reprisal, two of them surprised him at one of his properties in the country but rather than killing they simply beat and humiliated him.[34] Here again exceptions to the rule may be found, though they seem to have been less frequent and certainly less commented upon than attacks on children. At Corbiti, a hamlet of San-Lorenzo, hostilities broke out between the Moracchini and the Agostini during the municipal elections of 1832, and Luigi Moracchini was killed. The following day, Seppo Agostini, a man in his seventies, decided to leave San-Lorenzo and go to Moriani, 'where he had a large number of kinsmen'. On the way there, he was shot and killed by Luigi Moracchini's son and two other men. Here the victim was clearly chosen and felt himself to be in danger. More often, however, old men were killed either incidentally or believing that they were immune. At Campi, a blind old man was shot and killed by the Pietri brothers because he happened to be in the company of Carlo Lanfranchi, their enemy and intended victim. Paolo-Girolamo Paoli of Fozzano, a man in his sixties, was shot dead in 1849 as he was threshing wheat. Although his son had killed an enemy, he was clearly not expecting to be a target for revenge. Bourde relates that the old father of the Rocchini was killed by the Tafani at Porto-Vecchio in the 1880s, under the same impression that he was immune and having taken no precautions. The Porto-Vecchio feud, moreover, was a 'bad feud', in which women and children were also killed.[35] Here it should be recalled that old men were sometimes killed in intrafamilial conflict, and that they frequently directed feuds in which they did not participate. In general, old age conveyed authority and required respect *per se*, as we saw in discussing family structure, but, depending on familial role, health and temperament, old men could also be regarded as ineffective,[36] and their immunity derived from both qualities.

II

The immunity of women raises a range of other questions, which must be discussed in conjunction with it. The status of women was generally inferior to that of men, but their virtue was a crucial expression of family standing and honour. And, although their virtue was fiercely guarded by their menfolk, as we have seen in Chapter 4, they were engaged in work which took them outside the house and the village and which thus made them vulnerable. The ideally passive role of women generally meant that they were theoretically non-combatants in conflict and feuding, but their actual roles ensured that they did on occasion play an active part in both. They also figured as victims.

Most observers of Corsica in the nineteenth century, short-stay visitors as well as officials, commented on the low standing of Corsican women, married and unmarried. 'The Corsican wife is little more than the slave and drudge of her haughty master,' protested Benson in 1825. Ballard referred in 1852 to 'the state of abjection' in which women were 'plunged'. Vuillier asserted in 1891 that 'the Corsican woman occupies a position of real inferiority. Her life may be summed up in three words: work, submission, and sacrifice.'[37] It has been suggested that such judgments are stereotyped, reflecting the assumptions of those making them rather than the objective situation, and there is undoubtedly some truth in this. However, as we have indicated, the best-informed observers concurred in the general view. Bigot, who was justice of the peace at Bastelica for many years, concluded that 'in the sphere of relations between spouses, the husband has an incontestable preponderance, and absolute power. For the wife, he is the boss, *il padrone*.'[38] There is also direct evidence of emic attitudes. 'You know, ladies,' a widow sang in a lament, 'The man gives the orders! / The husband wears the trousers. / We have the spindle; / If he speaks, / We must obey without complaint.' The inferior and passive status of women was expressed in proverbs, while, according to Réalier-Dumas, the birth of a son was the occasion for rejoicing but that of a daughter by contrast 'was almost considered a misfortune'.[39] The same priority was explicit in wedding ritual. Brides were offered the wish: 'Good luck and male children,' or 'Many boys and one girl,' and Rossi noted the custom of placing a small boy on the lap of the bride in order to induce the future conception of a son.[40] That such practices were performed in earnest may be gauged from the case of Saverio Timotei, who threatened to kill his wife if she did not produce a son for him, and who carried out his threat when she gave birth to a girl.

It is obvious, however, that a woman's status varied according to her age, class and circumstances, and attention has been recently drawn to these and other factors, which add nuances to this general picture.[41] Proverbs, for example, refer to female power and male fear of it as well as to female weakness: 'Woman makes man and then eats him'; or: 'A man who does not feel strong does not take a wife.'[42] Malaspina noted in 1876 that 'in Corsica, women have always led lives of work and devotion; but nowhere have they been so much respected and nowhere have they had such authority within the family ... the mother of a family is the veritable guardian and mistress of the hearth [*la padrona di casa*] ... If her husband should die, she inherits all his rights and becomes the head of the community.' The high status of older women with children was generally remarked upon, and Ravis-Giordani has indicated that unmarried women could in some circumstances assume dominant male roles.[43] Rather than subordination, there was in effect a sharp division of roles, with women being concerned primarily with the house and men with things outside it. In some villages in the Balagna, Deane has noted, houses were significantly named after the wife rather than the husband. The custom of women serving men at the table and not sitting down to eat with them should be related to this division and not to any semi-servile status. The wife is 'not the servant of her husband', Comiti declared with reference to the south in 1933, 'but his associate and her influence is often very great'.[44] The same division was expressed in ritual terms. Women did not as a rule attend public baptisms, or church weddings and funerals, save as principals, but they played a central role in the domestic side of these rites of passage, and notably in the funeral wake, as we shall see in Chapter 13.

Some allowance must be made, too, for regional variations. Juta drew a contrast in 1926 between the freedom of women in some villages, and especially 'shepherd women', and their constriction in towns.[45] Again, women in the Niolo were said to be independent, even domineering, which is explained by the fact that their menfolk were absent for much of the year, leaving the women to run households themselves.[46] However subordinate they might be within the family, it was also noted that women would rarely serve elsewhere. It was impossible to get a woman to work as a domestic servant at Bastelica, the work being regarded as 'slavery', and we have seen that this was the case more generally.[47] Women, often widows, ran hotels,[48] and domestic and farm servants existed in towns and in the Balagna, but the low status of the latter only underlines our general point.[49] Some observers, moreover, detected changes in the attitude of some women from the middle of the nineteenth century. Bigot related that the women of Bastelica had 'rebelled against the old custom of their remaining on their knees on the ground all through religious services', and had obtained chairs on which to kneel or sit. Gregorovius met a girl near Bastia in 1852 who told him that she was 'near running away to Ajaccio' in order to avoid a marriage arranged by her mother; and similar examples of incipient indocility on the part of young women could be cited from later years.[50]

A crucial element, determining the status of women and deriving from it in a mutually reinforcing way, was the kind of work which they did or were expected to do. There seems little doubt that in traditional Corsican society women worked very hard and continuously in contrast to men, though the view that the latter were 'idle' is another piece of stereotyping that requires revision.[51] Women also did work that was regarded as menial and specific to their sex. This may be amply illustrated from contemporary accounts. Benson wrote, for example, that near Vivario in 1823 'we met several parties of natives, the men riding, while their wives paced along on foot with burthens on their shoulders; indeed, wherever we saw olives gathering, or any other manual labour, on our journey, the women only were employed'. A young woman told Molinari in 1884 that she would prefer a husband from the mainland, 'because they don't work their women like oxen', a reference to a well-known proverb advising men to do exactly that.[52] Bigot provides a more detailed picture. At Bastelica, women did all the domestic work as well as a wide range of other tasks. 'The woman alone is concerned with work inside the house, with washing and laundry, with sewing and mending, with cooking, with making cloth; but she also cultivates the fields; she bakes the bread; she prepares cereals and chestnuts for milling; she spins wool and linen; she goes to collect firewood every morning from the forest and returns barefoot with the faggots on her head. On a journey, she walks on foot, with a sack of chestnuts or grain, or a packet, on her head, while her husband rides alongside her.' More particularly, he observed that the mother of the family which he studied spent two-thirds of her time on domestic tasks, which included fetching firewood. The rest of her time was devoted to haymaking in season, cleaning the ground under the chestnuts and collecting and drying the crop, and watering the garden. Her elder daughter aided her in many of these tasks, but also had the special job in winter of taking milk for sale in Ajaccio some 40 kilometres away. She also planted the potatoes, harvested the acorns from the family's oak trees, and occasionally helped to look after the flocks. The second daughter also helped her mother in and out of the house, and her special task was harvesting the olives. She sometimes replaced her sister in taking milk to town. This description of women's work is confirmed by a range of other evidence, which suggests that it is typical. To it must be added, however, caring for the children and for the domestic animals as opposed to the transhumant flocks or large herds of pigs, which were mainly looked after by the men. These domestic animals might include poultry, a milch cow or goat and a house-pig.[53] As Bigot's example shows, the sexual division of labour was fairly firm but not absolute, and the distinction between men's work and women's work was not made in the same way in all parts of Corsica. In a case in 1812, for instance, we learn that a 50-year-old miller from Olmiccia helped his wife to gather firewood,[54] and women were fairly commonly engaged, particularly in the south, in auxiliary pastoral tasks, such as milking and cheese-making.[55]

Despite women's essential association with the house, many of their tasks took them outside it and even outside the village. This is true of tasks that might be regarded as purely domestic, such as fetching water and fuel but also doing the laundry in the river or wash-place and baking bread, which was often done in a communal oven. Such work was usually performed in company and was indeed an important vehicle for female sociability,[56] but women might also work away from the house in small groups, in pairs or alone. We have seen, too, that they had non-domestic jobs to do. Of these, visitors were most struck by their work on the land,[57] something which was by no means universal in the Mediterranean region.[58] Many specific examples of this may be cited from the judicial records. In a case in 1811, we find that the wife of Andrea Giansilj 'had a piece of land which she cultivated' at some distance from the village of Lozzi and which 'she visited frequently in order to make sure that no animal strayed on to it'. In November 1832 Anton-Giovanni Roccaserra was attacked, 'as he went with his wife and mother-in-law to an enclosure which he owned', presumably to prepare it for cultivation. Again, Diana Rossi of Valle-di-Mezzana was abducted in May 1860, as she was returning from the fields, a not uncommon occurrence.[59] We have seen, too, in Chapter 3, that women became engaged in conflict with each other as they were doing field work. The involvement of women in agriculture was most characteristic of regions where pastoralism was predominant. Here the men travelled from their villages with their flocks leaving the women behind to carry out sedentary tasks.[60] In our examples above, at Lozzi in the Niolo the woman was wholly responsible for the field which she cultivated, while at Serra in the south men and women were engaged together. Archer noted, moreover, in 1924 that at Bonifacio 'the women do not work on the land except at harvest time, and when the olives are gathered in'.[61]

The more general contribution of women to harvesting included gathering hay and cereals as well as nuts and fruit. Cipressa Canaraggia of Campile was raped in April 1857 while she was on her way to collect hay. In a case in 1821, we learn that the victim of a shooting incident at Sant'Andrea-di-Tallano had left the village at 7 a.m. with his female cousin and his sister 'to harvest some barley' at an enclosure in the country. Saint-Germain even saw women threshing near Guitera in the 1860s.[62] Harvesting tree crops was a more exclusively female preserve all over the island. They gathered grapes and other fruit, acorns, but above all chestnuts and olives.[63] Luigi Borghetti of Velone shot his wife in 1833 as she was gathering chestnuts, while Anna-Maria Ortoli of Olmiccia was allegedly abducted in 1830 when she went with some female cousins to gather olives for a cousin. Women were also engaged in the important task of watering young olive and chestnut plants as well as in irrigation more generally, and in pressing olives.[64] In the Balagna especially, where olives were grown commercially, women were employed by big landowners as hired labourers, and this introduces an important proviso to our description of female field work in Corsica, for it was essentially an occupation of poor women. Teresa Chiaramonti was an orphan 'with no means at all, who hired herself out to different people, usually to do field work'. Similarly, the beautiful Beatrice Alessandri, aged nineteen, of Antisanti, was induced by poverty to become the mistress of a young man of superior station in the village but she continued to do field work even after she discovered that she was pregnant. Again, a widow Lucciani from Chiatra was 'obliged to do day work to feed her children' and left them in the care of neighbours while she went down to the plain.[65] Carlotti noted here in 1936 that Corsican women 'detested field work' and only did it when and if they had to.[66] It is also significant that in this respect they shared the lot of the despised *lucchesi*.

Marketing went beyond dairy products and was to some degree an extension of harvesting. In 1815, Anna-Maria Muzzi, a widow from Bilia, took a horse laden with corn for sale in Sartène; while Finelli relates that the women of Tavera sold chestnut flour in the market at Ajaccio on a regular basis. They were taken there by the men but stayed a week or so on their own.[67] It was also an extension of the traditional role of women as carriers or 'beasts of burden', which was remarked upon by a succession of visitors. They carried water, firewood, coal, and just about anything which needed to be transported, usually on their heads.[68] A further variation was reported by Bigot. 'When a house catches fire,' he wrote, 'it is the women who are specially charged with putting it out; they arrive barefoot, with a metal or wooden bucket on their heads; and they come and go, taking the water from the village fountain to the site of the fire.'[69]

Ravis-Giordani concludes that 'the labour of women, in the house and in the fields, [was] a harsh necessity which could hardly be accommodated with their close confinement'.[70] Indeed, the need for women to work could give them considerable independence. The nature of women's work also made them vulnerable, exposing them to situations of conflict and to attacks on their reputation and virtue, which is one reason, we have suggested, for the great emphasis placed at the ideological level on their sexual honour. This is most clearly seen in cases of rape, assault or abduction. Angelica-Maria Ottavi, aged 16 or 17, of Bastelica, was abducted in 1841, 'as she was returning from making faggots of wood' at a place in the country in company with several other girls of her age. Teresa Chiaramonti was raped by her employer in 1855, as she was gathering chestnuts for him at Santa-Lucia-di-Moriani. Maria-Angela Giafferi was threatened by an armed man early one morning in November 1911, while she was fetching water from a fountain just outside Venzolasca.[71] It was also more generally assumed that there was a connection between women working outside the family circle and their loss of honour. The women of the Balagna were supposed to be morally lax.[72] And, to take a particular example, at the trial of Angelina Francescani, aged 23 of Poggio-di-Tallano, accused of killing her lover, the mayor testified that she had a doubtful reputation, since 'she exercised the profession of a dressmaker and received a lot of people in her house, on top of which she had the misfortune to be pretty'.[73]

All of this provides a necessary introduction to the position of women vis-à-vis feuding. In some feuding societies, women might be involved in blood vengeance, though where compensation was paid they were assessed at a lower rate than men.[74] In others, including Corsica, they were not in theory implicated either as actors or victims.[75] Feydel wrote in 1799 that before the Revolution 'it was unheard of for Corsicans to involve their women in wars between kindreds. A man would feel dishonoured if he killed a woman to whom he was unrelated by blood or marriage' (an interesting indicator of attitudes towards intrafamilial killing). He claimed that this proscription had lost much of its force by the time he was writing, but his opinion is not supported by later writers, nearly all of whom affirm that it continued to be operative. Official reports on two killings of women 'inspired by vengeance' in 1821 declared that this 'kind of atrocity has always been rejected in Corsican custom', and that such acts were 'almost unknown'. In Mérimée's *Colomba* it is made clear that only cowards attack women, and Marcaggi confirms that this was the general view later in the century. He relates that, when a man from Chidazzo shot the wife of his enemy, the neighbours expressed their horror, asking: 'Are you not ashamed to fire at a woman?' Busquet judged that the rule excluding women was still effective in the modern period, though it was perhaps more often broken than in the past.[76] We must now examine this conclusion in the light of more detailed evidence.

First, it is clear that women were actually granted immunity in certain feuding situations and that advantage was taken of this. Feydel wrote that 'women took messages for their husbands, fathers, brothers or sons, walked in front of them, reconnoitred dangerous places and enemy positions, carried letters, and were generally able to move about without danger'. During the long feud at Arbellara in the 1830s and 1840s, the men remained shut up in their houses for much of the time, but the women 'were able to go about freely', and acted as scouts when men had to leave the village. During the same feud, Giulio Agostini and Antono Rutilj-Forcioli had the opportunity in 1849 to kill a woman who had witnessed their murdering her husband, but they merely insulted her. According to a military report, 'only the women had ventured out' for a six-month period at Olmeto in 1847; while for many years only the women attended church at Pila-Canale, the men being afraid to expose themselves to attack.[77] Cases are reported, too, of men trying to avoid reprisals by disguising themselves as women[78] and of men sheltering behind their womenfolk. At Bastelica, Pasquale Gasparini felt in special danger after being acquitted of killing Domenico Scapola in 1832, so he went about armed and accompanied by his daughter.[79] And there are further indications that women were generally considered to be immune. Very occasionally, as at Olmeta-di-Tuda in 1815 and Carcheto in 1912, women were attacked as they took provisions to men under siege, but usually they could do this with impunity, and such exceptions caused a sense of outrage.[80] Again, female immunity was assumed in encounters with the authorities. The house of the Giacomoni at Santa-Maria-Figaniella was surrounded by troops in 1802. The men inside eventually agreed to come out, but they 'sent one of their women to open the door'. At Rusio in 1819, the mayor provoked an attack on the gendarmerie, who had come to arrest some bandits, 'by sending his daughter to warn the latter's relatives'; and women played a leading part in similar incidents at Levie in 1813 and at Quenza in 1826.[81]

The detailed evidence also confirms Feydel's view that, despite this theoretical immunity, or perhaps because it had weakened, women could be the victims of vengeance killing, though the extent to which this was so should not be exaggerated. Reported killings and attempted killings of women were around 15 per cent of those of men in the decade 1821–31, a proportion that does not appear to have changed greatly over the course of the century.[82] Attacks on women were an especial feature of the feud at Marignana in the middle of the century. Having killed Gregorio Grimaldi, Anton-Francesco Antonini killed his sister Fiordilucia to stop her vituperation of him. He attacked her as she was washing clothes in the river. In 1848, the bandit Massoni attacked Bianchina Massoni and tried to kill her, which aroused great controversy, more it seems because she was a relative than because she was a woman. Later in 1848, Domenico Durilj shot at Alda La Bella Alessandri 'in the presence of her mother', and in April 1849 he tried to kill Anna-Maria Massoni and her relative, the widow Barbara Grimaldi. In February the same year, his cousin Francesco Fieschi had tried to shoot another widow, and in June 1850 Caterina Durilj was shot and killed by Giovan-Domenico Durilj on the church square.[83] Such a high incidence of attacks on women was unusual, but many other isolated cases could be cited from the early and mid-nineteenth century and they continued to be fairly common in subsequent years. It is significant also that women felt vulnerable in feuding situations and took precautions. For example, after Father Susini of Moca had been killed in 1839 by the bandit Luciani, his niece did not leave her house for two years.[84] The assumption that women could or would be killed in feuds took other forms. Giacomo-Antono Giacomoni of Santa-Lucia-di-Tallano, having just killed Nunzio Arrij of Olmiccia in 1841, threatened a group of women who were picking olives for another of his enemies, and 'it was only after many prayers' that he agreed not to kill them also. Again, when Mariana Desanti of Aullène was killed by lightning in 1849, her brother thought that she had been killed by their enemies, the Lanfranchi, and retaliated by shooting at Bernardino Lanfranchi.[85]

The killing of women in feuds was of different kinds. Some killings, like those of children or old men, were accidental. At Frasso in 1865, for example, Chiara-Maria Maroselli and Teresa Furiani were seriously wounded with a shotgun by Giovan-Antono Mariani. Mariani, an old man, had been drinking and hit them by mistake when he was trying to shoot a man against whom he had a grudge. It is perhaps a further indication of the general disapproval of killing women that their deaths were sometimes presented as accidents when they clearly were not. Angela-Maria Casanova was shot and killed by Mariano Galloni d'Istria in an encounter with the Peretti at Olmeto in 1848. She was said to have been a bystander who was hit by chance, but her body had eight bullet wounds.[86] In other cases, women were second-best targets, chosen only because the avengers were unable to attack their male enemies directly. Parigi Petrignani was killed by Francesco Casabianca at Venzolasca in 1798. Petrignani's relatives killed Casabianca's two daughters the same day in revenge, since he had gone into hiding. The next day they achieved their real aim by killing him.[87] In yet other cases the killing of women was quite deliberate and not a substitute for killing men. A certain Luporsi was killed in the conflict in 1834 between the Giampierini of Ampriani and people from Alesani, and his supporters then killed Francesca Giampierini in simple retaliation.[88] Though individuals were always attacked primarily as members of their family or party, some women were selected as targets because their individual behaviour had been provocative. Paola-Caterina Nicolai was killed in 1831, in the course of the feud at Tox, to avenge a killing committed by her brothers, the bandits Nicolai, but she had acted as their scout. In a case in 1900, referred to by Chapman, the widow Galloni was shot and killed near Propriano. The culprit was the brother of a man who had been convicted of an earlier killing, mainly on her evidence.[89]

Here there was little apparent difference between killing women and killing men, but other evidence suggests that important distinctions were made. It was possible to regard killing a woman as 'inferior' to killing a man and thus unworthy of the more honourable modes of despatch. In the Venzolasca case, one of Casabianca's daughters was bludgeoned to death with the butt of a shot-gun. At the other end of the scale, killing a woman broke a taboo and might be seen as the most extreme form of killing. Their enemies described the Poli of Pila-Canale in 1797 as 'wanting to dip their hands in the blood of a woman', in order to indicate their complete depravity. The same sadistic tendency would seem to be present in a case at Piazzole in 1842, in which two sisters, aged 49 and 55 respectively, were stabbed to death by a young man of 24. This was apparently a revenge killing and the women had multiple stab wounds, 17 and 25 each.[90] To return to Pila-Canale, one of the Giancarli women killed in 1796 was pregnant and she had her breasts mutilated. This may have sexual and religious meaning, but it was also indicative of a 'bad feud', in which women were involved as victims not only in themselves but also as future child-bearers. In such feuds the aim was to eliminate one's enemies completely. At Prunelli-di-Casacconi in 1820, two men and then two women of the Filippi were killed, and the gendarmerie commented that 'the savage violence' being exercised against the family 'seems to have in view their complete extinction'. Again, according to witnesses at a trial in 1890, Tullia Talvatori from an unspecified village declared of the enemies of her family: 'They must all be exterminated, men, women and children.'[91]

In order to place all this further in context, a number of other factors need to be taken into account. First, women were killed in circumstances other than feud, notably, as we have seen, in intrafamilial conflict.[92] Secondly, there seems to have been a high incidence of general violence involving women, which is not adequately reflected in the crime statistics.[93] We have seen that specifically sexual violence against women was not uncommon, and rapes, abductions or attempted abductions were often accompanied by additional brutalities. Maria-Geltrude Gaffori of Pastricciola, for example, was stabbed and seriously wounded in 1841 in what appears to have been an attempted abduction.[94] Violence against women, short of killing, was also a feature of intrafamilial conflict. The wife of Silvestro Quilichini of Poggio-di-Tallano was hit on the hand and the head with a billhook in 1816 by her cousin Giulio, as she was washing clothes. Paolo-Santo Bartoli of Ciamannacce, who was in dispute with his aunt Maria-Dolinda over a piece of land, perforated her cheek with buck-shot in 1862.[95] Women, moreover, seem to have been drawn into conflict with outsiders fairly easily. A fight developed at Tomino in 1815 between a certain Costa and others. 'Lucia, the wife of Giovanni Morazzi, ran to the scene and at once became a target for attack like everyone else. Having knocked her down, Costa hit her with stones, a stick and the butt of a shot-gun, and one of these blows broke her arm.'[96] Women were sometimes injured or even killed as they tried to prevent men from fighting. Colomba Susini, for example, from Loreto-di-Tallano was wounded in 1843 when she threw herself between Santo Susini and Simone Gaudeani of Zicavo; while Angela-Dea Suzzarini, probably from the same village, was killed in 1850 'as she was running to place herself between relatives who were quarrelling'.[97] But this does not mean that women were always the victims of violence or that they lacked aggression. Some women carried arms. In a search of the Tortora house at Muro, arms were found 'hidden in a woman's skirts', while we learn in a case in 1856 that Maria-Aurelia Lucchini, aged 25 of Aullène had a previous conviction for carrying arms.[98] They also used both guns and pistols and other weapons. Rosalinda Poli of Olmiccia fired a pistol at her brother-in-law in 1841 after an argument between them over 'family matters', while Francesca Corrazzini stabbed her brother-in-law to death in similar circumstances at Piedicorte in 1849 or 1850.[99] Aggression on the part of women was also found in conflict outside the family. In a dispute at Sant'Andrea-di-Tallano in 1823 between mayor Comiti and ex-mayor Panzani, for example, the wife and daughters of the mayor seriously injured a supporter of Panzani by hitting him over the head with sticks. Christophari relates that his grandmother, who kept a wineshop with her husband when she was a young woman, once knocked a man unconscious with the butt of a pistol when he refused to pay.[100] Some of the violence which accompanied sexual offences stemmed from the strong resistance with which women met attacks on them.[101] Most telling perhaps here is the fact that violent quarrels and fights were so common between women. One of the first cases to be tried by jury in Corsica in 1792 involved a woman from Calvi who had fatally wounded another woman in a brawl. In a case in 1812, three women from Sant'Andrea-di-Tallano became engaged in a dispute over firewood, which they were collecting, and this developed into a fight in which one of them used an axe. In 1844, Maria-Vidonia Battesti, a widow from Santa-Lucia-di-Moriani, quarrelled violently for reasons unknown with another woman and stabbed her to death.[102] Robiquet suggested more generally that the strict dependence in which men kept women in Corsica was a deliberate means of reducing conflict among them.[103]

This relates to the third point about the connection between conflict involving men only and that involving women too or women exclusively. Some sources indicate that men were reluctant to become involved in what were dismissed as 'women's squabbles'.[104] But one of the reasons for this reluctance was that the latter could lead all too easily to something more serious. A dispute at Levie between two women over the ownership of a cock led to a fight between them in 1834. The fiancé of one and the husband and brother-in-law of the other intervened to try 'to separate the women, who were pulling each other's hair and hitting one another', but instead they were drawn into the conflict and one of the men was shot and mortally wounded. The consequent enmity was not settled until twenty years later. The feud between the Crebasali and the Lisandri at Chidazzo in the 1870s originated similarly in an exchange of insults between the wives of the main contenders.[105] All of this suggests that violence involving women was not only less rare than some writers have intimated,[106] but also that it could be less specific than has been indicated above. The authorities and educated Corsicans condemned the killing of women throughout the century and they claimed to be reflecting a more general view. The Poli characterized the killing of the Giancarli women at Pila-Canale in 1796 as 'the blackest of murders ... an unheard-of act of barbarism'; while Marcaggi wrote that the killing of Giannina Malanini in 1886 was 'an odious crime ... [that] aroused a feeling of horror throughout the island'.[107] There is evidence, however, that ordinary Corsicans were not always horrified by such incidents. Official reports, for example, on the 'barbaric' killing of the Filippi women at Prunelli in 1820 make it clear that 'most of the inhabitants of the village' approved and protected the killers. When Angelica Campana from an unspecified village was shot as she crossed the threshold of a house in 1833, there was reported to have been 'a great to-do in the village', but less because she was a woman than because she had no known enemies and had been killed in an ambush without warning.[108] This nonchalance and lack of differentiation should not be exaggerated, but they are important, together with the general level of female violence, if we are to understand the role of women as avengers and as inciters of vengeance.

First, women did act as avengers. Such action was out of the ordinary, but it was not too uncommon and it was not disapproved of in the proper circumstances. It was most often expected where there were no male relatives to avenge an offence.[109] Thus Maria-Felice of Calacuccia declared in a well-known lament for her brother: 'Of so large a family / You leave only a sister, / Without first cousins, / Poor, orphaned and unarmed, / But to accomplish your vengeance / Rest assured that she alone suffices.'[110] In another lament, the sister of the bandit Canino concluded: 'I want to quit my skirt; / I want to arm myself with a dagger and a blunderbuss; / I want to put on a cartridge belt and a pistol. / Dear heart, your sister wants to carry out your vengeance.'[111] In an actual example, Maria-Francesca Quilichini tried to avenge the death of her brother by shooting the mayor of Santa-Lucia-di-Tallano, a distant relative of his killer, in 1845. It seems that she had no male relatives, and her action was described as 'astonishing' at her trial but was much admired.[112] Cases may also be cited of vengeance being carried out by daughters[113] and particularly by widows. The widow Murati of Cambia fired two shots in 1883 at Innocenzo Bariani of Corticosi, as he was leaving a blacksmith's shop. She explained that she had mistaken him 'from his voice for the man who had killed her husband', who had, it was established, been murdered 'not long before by a member of the Bariani family'. She received a light sentence, and a petition for clemency stressed that she had three young nieces to support but makes no mention of male kin.[114] However, widows seem also to have acted themselves when they did have male kin. This was sometimes because the latter were reluctant to act but not always. Vuillier recounted seeing a widow at Zicavo, whose husband had recently been killed and who 'carried a dagger all the time and used to say to her brothers: "It is not for you to help in accomplishing my revenge. I am quite capable of doing it myself!" '[115]

Probably more common were cases in which women carried out vengeance killings with male relatives, both as accomplices and as full partners in crime, and we have encountered examples of each. There are also cases, much rarer, where women actually led and organized feuds. The best-known was at Fozzano in the 1830s, where one party was effectively headed by Colomba Bartoli, née Carabelli. Contrary to the impression conveyed in Mérimée's story, she was then a woman in her late fifties. In Roger's words, she was the 'ardent inspirer of her party ... There is no evidence that she personally took part in any act of violence, but she excited the desire for vengeance in those around her and encouraged her sons to exterminate their enemies.' Although she was a widow, it is not clear why she assumed this position of command, since she had both sons and three brothers living.[116] A similar role was played by Mariana Pozzo di Borgo at Appietto in the 1790s, and by Perla Arrighi at Urbalacone and Rosa Mariani at Lopigna, both around 1850.[117] In the main, women were all here fulfilling male roles. 'I want to wear trousers,' Maria-Felice proclaimed, while Mariana Pozzo di Borgo actually dressed as a man. But women might also pursue and achieve vengeance in a specific or less 'masculine' way. Maria-Francesca Quilichini, for example, attacked her victim, as she was pretending to fetch water normally from the fountain in the village square. There is some evidence, too, of women selecting other women as targets in feuds, for example at Arbellara in 1836, and of poisoning as a favoured female mode of vengeance.[118]

This brings us to the commonest category by far of women acting as avengers, that in which they took reprisals themselves against men who had seduced and abandoned them. At least four such cases came before the Assize Court in 1865, when they aroused much comment. Fairly typical of these was the case of Rosa-Maria Nicolai of Scata, who 'had surrendered her honour' to Cristoforo Marchetti in 1858, when she was 18 and he was 16. He had promised to marry her when he was 'old enough and in the position to do so, which decided the Nicolai family to receive him under their roof. But the wealthier Marchetti did not want to agree to such a marriage, since the Nicolai had nothing to give [as a dowry].' Rosa-Maria nevertheless continued to live with Marchetti and gave birth to two children, neither of whom survived long. In 1864, a rumour circulated in the village that Marchetti was going to get married 'to a young lady of his own condition who lived in a village in a neighbouring canton', and he did not hide from Rosa-Maria that such indeed were his plans. She, for her part, did not conceal 'her plans of vengeance'. But, whether from real affection for him or through guile, she continued to see him and have sexual relations with him. The two had arranged a rendezvous in December 1864 in 'a chestnut drying loft', where she had prepared a kind of bed. While he was unguarded after intercourse, she took an axe that she had hidden and hit him three blows on the head with the blunt end of it, breaking his skull and killing him almost instantly. She then gave herself up to the gendarmerie. She was tried, convicted and sentenced to ten years' hard labour. Only the mode of killing and the severe sentence are unusual here. The public prosecutor prepared a special report on this and the other cases tried in 1865, which is of some interest.[119] He commented that when women became dishonoured in such circumstances, 'vengeance offers them a kind of moral rehabilitation, for, by the customs of this country, when they have removed the author of their infamy by homicide, they are considered virtually to have removed the infamy itself.' This explained the usual leniency of Corsican juries towards this type of crime, which the evidence of earlier cases certainly confirms. Fiordispina Padovani of Ota, for example, was convicted of excusable homicide with extenuating circumstances and sentenced to only 30 months' imprisonment. She also became the heroine in a popular lament.[120] The report also claimed that the crime was increasing, supposedly because men were no longer prepared to avenge affronts to the honour of their female relatives and risk either the severest reprisals from the victim's kin or very stiff sentences from the courts. 'When the wronged woman carried out her own vengeance, however, the same consequences did not follow; so that the woman, by a secret agreement and connivance of her family, is often chosen to play the role of avenger, which used to be reserved for men.' This analysis would seem to require some qualification. Full statistics are not available but it is doubtful whether the increase in such crimes was as significant as the public prosecutor imagined. Many examples may be cited from earlier in the century and at least eight were tried in the decade 1845–55. The importance of women punishing their own seducers was well-established in traditional Corsican culture, as he himself demonstrates, and was reflected in folk-tales.[121] Not too much credence should be given either to the idea that men sheltered behind women in such circumstances. We have seen how important it was for men to defend the honour of their women, and it is not hard to find cases, albeit from a slightly earlier period, in which women acted only because they had no male kin or where their initiative was in fact disapproved of by their male relatives.[122] Ortoli even relates that Fiordispina Padovani was killed by her brothers. Though too much should not be made of it, there was room here for some divergence between male and female attitudes and behaviour.

This brings us to the most important role of women in feuding, which was as inciters to vengeance. As many writers have stressed, women departed here from any subordinate status to assume a primary and directing function. In Corsica, as elsewhere,[123] the vendetta was 'presided over' and perpetuated by the women. 'It is the woman', wrote Bigot, 'who religiously maintains the traditions of the family, who tells her growing children of the hatreds and the friendships of their ancestors,' who kept the clothing of those killed by enemies, and reminded children by this and other means of injuries that required vengeance. Women, moreover, sang laments (*voceri*) over the corpses of victims, promising and calling for vengeance. Father Bartoli concluded in 1898 that 'women are the instigators of all acts of vengeance'. For the sake of honour, 'they sacrifice all that is dearest to them: husbands, sons, relatives; they stop at nothing, face every danger, accept every privation'.[124] We will discuss laments in Chapter 13, illustrating other kinds of incitement here.

Boswell recounted that an old man came to see Pasquale Paoli at Sollacaro in 1765 and

> told him that there had been an unlucky tumult in the village where he lived, and that two of his sons were killed. That looking upon this as a heavy misfortune, but without malice on the part of those who deprived him of his sons, he was willing to have allowed it to pass without enquiry. But his wife, anxious for revenge, had made an application to have them apprehended and punished. That he gave his Excellency this trouble to entreat that the greatest care might be taken, lest in the heat of enmity among his neighbours anybody should be punished as guilty of the blood of his sons who was really innocent of it.[125]

It would be hazardous to generalize from this instance alone, but there is corroborative evidence that women were more reluctant to pardon than men and that they were less actively involved in conciliation. And there is no doubt about the encouragement which they gave to enmities and feuding. At Peri in 1812, after the mayor had been killed, 'it was one of his daughters ... who was the most excited by resentment' and who, with her husband, planned a killing in revenge via an agent. We have seen that the mother of Giulio Negroni of Ampriani refused to give her consent to his marriage until he had avenged his brother's death. At Marignana after the killing of Gregorio Grimaldi in 1848, his mother expressed the desire 'to drink the blood of my son's killer', while her daughter prayed to the Virgin Mary and pestered the killer with insults until he murdered her too. In the course of the feud at Aullène between the Desanti and the Lanfranchi, Marco-Matteo Roccaserra, who was married to a Lanfranchi, was killed in 1850. This prompted the mother of the Desanti to declare publicly: 'The widow Roccaserra claimed that the bullets of my children couldn't hit anything; now she knows better.'[126]

Father Bartoli stressed women's attachment to honour as their prime motivation, seeing this as a personal thing or as the expression of female sensibility. Our examples confirm that women instigated acts of vengeance in order to uphold family honour but show rather how this overlapped with their role as gossips. Both were means, one more extreme than the other, of securing adherence to norms and thus maintaining social control in the community. Hence the importance of the publicity given to the intention to seek and then to the achievement of revenge, which a further example very aptly illustrates. At Lecci in 1894, Paolo-Matteo Marchi 'avenged the honour' of his absent brother by killing his wife's lover, whereupon Marchi's own wife boasted in the village: 'He made a promise and he kept his word.'[127] We have seen that accusations were often made by women, and they also employed their networks to pursue enmities. At Marignana, Gregorio Grimaldi's mother kept herself informed of the movements of his killer mainly via a network of old women and children and then passed this information on to the authorities. Turner has linked the phenomenon of women inciting men to kill each other in Icelandic sagas with the fact that women lived in and were wholly concerned with their own communities, while 'men, through their participation in juridical and legislative action on a wider scale than the local' had both the means and the incentive to reconcile rather than exacerbate enmities. This insight is relevant to Corsica. Deane subtly relates the role of women in feuding to their generally subordinate role: 'The lives of the women ... are more confined than those of the men ... so the women, having less to think about, are more sensitive to local feuds and pressures, more inclined to create and foster them.'[128] Some women were involved, however, in supra-local political activity in Corsica,[129] and we shall see in Chapter 11 that feuding and politics were by no means distinct occupations.

To conclude, there was a significant gap between the immunity in theory of women in feuds and their actual involvement, though their normal role remained that of inciters to violence not participants in it. Women could be victims and they could act in the most savage manner. Two men were killed in an encounter between the Colombani and the Vittori of the Fiumorbo in 1832 and a third man, a Colombani, was wounded. 'The Vittori women, whom grief had driven wild, threw themselves upon Colombani, who was still breathing, and finished him off with stones, to avenge the death of their relatives, they said.'[130] Despite the generally high incidence of female violence, a distinction may be drawn by and large between male and female behaviour in the context of blood vengeance. Save in certain specific circumstances, notably seduction and abandonment, female violence, especially of the kind which we have just described, was something engaged in only in the heat of the moment and a rare overflow into direct action of the emotions usually reserved for prompting men to act. The killing of women, moreover, while not all that uncommon, did not have the same meaning as the killing of men. As in Montenegro, it seems, only male blood could really satisfy the need for vengeance, and in this sense all killing of women was incidental.[131] The blood vengeance system in effect reflected the same firm differentiation of male and female roles that was generally evident in Corsican culture, but it does emphasize once more that they were complementary rather than in any simple relation of hierarchy.[132]

III

The final category of those enjoying immunity in feuding is that of the clergy. This again raises general questions which we must first attempt to answer.

Contemporaries expressed divergent views as to the position and influence of priests in Corsica, views which to some extent expressed their own sympathies. So, an anticlerical official referred in 1797 to the clergy's ability to 'manipulate the people in its favour' and to the persistence of 'the blind submission of past centuries'; and the leading role of the clergy in the War of Independence is well known.[133] Bigot declared, by contrast, that the clergy had very little influence in Corsica, where men, in particular, attended church infrequently; and popular anticlericalism was a feature of both proverbs and folk-tales.[134] Other sources confirm this suggestion of a decline of influence and their explanations are illuminating. Griffon in 1841 related a certain loss of status to his observation that 'men of distinguished families rarely enter the clerical profession today'. This in turn was related, in part at least, to the substitution of French for Italian cultural and political dominance, since the clergy had traditionally been educated in Italy. Robiquet noted in 1835 that, though the urban clergy was on the whole well-educated and of a reasonable standard, 'there are still, in the villages, a large number of priests without positions, poorly trained and at a loose end, which means that the clergy generally is not as respected by the people as it should be'.[135] The point about the large number of priests in Corsican villages is important. The disruption of the Revolutionary period did little to check 'the proliferation of ecclesiastics' already noted in the eighteenth century. By the late 1820s, Corsica had twice as many priests per head of population as the average for French departments, and numbers did not significantly decline thereafter until the 1890s or 1900s. Many of these priests had had little proper training and held no incumbencies.[136] As Bishop Casanelli d'Istria put it in 1833: 'Corsica has no lack of priests, but it does lack a clergy.' Though it did not automatically lead to advancement, the clerical career was and remained attractive as a potential avenue to wealth and influence, especially for younger sons for whom it represented an alternative to emigration. '"Having a priest at the altar" was a golden opportunity for a family,' Martelli notes of Ghisoni; 'to be the nephew of a *curé* was as good as being an only son'.[137] As this and the general abundance of postulants to clerical office show, any decline in the prestige and influence of the clergy should not be exaggerated. A report on the case at Feliceto in 1833, in which a man consulted a priest before forging a will in his own favour, stated that in the Balagna 'the clergy meddle in nearly all affairs'. Robiquet related that when he was in charge of building a new road between Ajaccio and Bastia, the parish priest of Vivario approached him with the request that he employ 'his people'. In 1851, the Italian servant of Father Giacomoni of Santa-Lucia-di-Tallano was convicted of stealing from his employer. The servant claimed that he had been falsely accused, but the testimony of the priest, without any corroboration, convinced both the jury and the president of the court. Such cases are reminders, too, of the wealth of some members of the clergy. The huge sum of 5000 francs was said to have been stolen from the parish priest of Olmiccia in 1862.[138]

A distinction ought to be made here between the influence of the priest as priest and as notable. Corsicans adhered, on the whole, to the Church for the rites of passage and were attached, as we have seen, to certain manifestations of popular Catholicism: pilgrimages, patronal festivals, confraternities. Bigot stressed the importance at Bastelica and elsewhere of the great festivals, in which men did take part, and he noted the practice of the priest blessing the houses of the village biennially on Holy Saturday. Similarly, at Tavera until 1914, it was socially obligatory to attend mass on Sundays and at the great festivals. Abeau, himself a priest, lays stress on the association of the clergy with family-orientated ritual: 'It is still usual ... for each family to reserve a part of the bread baked for its own use for the parish priest. In return, the priest celebrates a mass for the deceased every week, distributes holy candles at Candlemas and blesses olive branches on Palm Sunday.'[139] Before the Revolution this payment had been made in grain, and it later became a bone of contention. Allowing for regional variations and personal idiosyncrasies, therefore, 'the priestly function was held in very high esteem in Corsican villages',[140] and this is reflected in posthumous laments. These also indicate that that function went beyond the narrowly 'religious'. Father Santucci of Pietricaggio-d'Alesani, for example, was celebrated as a 'medical practitioner', while Father Defranchi of Soccia was remembered for promoting an irrigation scheme.[141] All of this gave a priest considerable potential influence in the community, though, as Father Casta emphasizes, if he went beyond the confines of his function, he would be quickly checked.

Churches, we have seen, had important communal functions, and were not regarded as the exclusive domain of the clergy. The office of churchwarden was of great significance here and was hotly competed for by village factions. The use of churches was governed by elaborate conventions, all of which could give rise to conflicts between priest and parishioners. Those reported in the nineteenth century centred on the collection of the priest's bread, mentioned above, funeral perquisites, the conduct of services, and the activities of confraternities, though the four categories were not always in practice distinct.

The traditional provision of bread for the priest on Sundays seems to have met with little independent opposition at village level and continued indeed in some areas into the twentieth century. Circulars from the government in 1824, 1838 and 1843, however, ruled that the practice of collecting bread was illegal if it was regarded as an obligatory payment to the priest in return for his services. Collections could only continue on the understanding that they were voluntary and did not constitute a replacement for fees. In some cases, collections were maintained under the guise of collections for the poor or for the Souls in Purgatory, but elsewhere the new jurisprudence fuelled local conflict. Some mayors, for example at Moita, Moca-Croce and La Porta, banned all collections, doubtless as a move in ongoing hostilities with the parish priest. At Penta-di-Casinca, the collection was at the centre of a prolonged and serious dispute between the municipal council and the parish priest, Father Peretti. When he was appointed, Peretti agreed 'to cede his funeral fees and have bread every Sunday from each family [in turn] instead'. He appears not to have kept to this agreement and to have demanded half the candles at funerals from the prior of the confraternity, which led to scenes in the church. At the end of 1856, 'seeing that the collection of bread for the priest had divided the village into two parties, the conformists and the non-conformists, and that at the funerals of the latter altercations, often violent, always take place between the relatives of the deceased and the priest over his perquisites', the municipal council resolved that in future the priest should have the fees to which he was legally entitled but that, in return, the collection of bread should stop.[142]

This introduces the second related category of conflict, that between parish priests and churchwardens and between priests and confraternities over their relative share in the candles used at funerals. A decree of 1813 laid down ground rules here but these were often at odds with local usage. At Moita, for example, an agreement was reported in 1841 by which the parish 'gave up its claim to half the candles left over at funerals in return for the right to make three or four collections annually at harvest times, [while] ... by an old convention the priest had surrendered his claim to the other half in return for being supplied with bread daily', a variation on what we have seen was a common arrangement. Whatever the rule or convention in force, however, there was always room for dispute. Conflicts between priest and churchwardens were reported, for example, at Zicavo in 1824, at Lavatoggio in 1830 and at La Porta in 1835; while at Bisinchi in 1849 a quarrel arose 'between the incumbent Father Angeli and some members of the confraternity over his claim to half the wax which the confraternity customarily provided when one of its members died, a claim that none of Father Angeli's predecessors had made'.[143]

The third category may be illustrated by the conflict between priest and parishioners at San-Martino-di-Lota in the Capo Corso. In September 1841, the priest, Father Guasco, was subjected to a very hostile charivari and a store room full of hay and straw underneath the presbytery was set alight. These actions, which were intended to force him to leave the parish, were the culmination of years of friction. A report by the local justice of the peace explained that relations between priest and people at San-Martino had been amicable before the appointment of Father Guasco in 1836, but 'as soon as he was placed at the head of the parish, he did all that was in his power to antagonize the local population by his contrariness and his constant attacks on the local customs to which they were attached'. Finally, in April 1841, he decided to exclude male parishioners from the two side pews in the chancel, 'which had always been occupied by them during mass and other divine services', and used force against those who resisted. His parishioners then formally asked the bishop for another priest, and Father Guasco began prosecutions against a number of them.[144] Formal complaints against parish priests were not uncommon and alleged a similar over-zealousness but also negligence and peculation. These accusations were somewhat incongruously combined in a complaint made in 1861, for example, by municipal councillors and notables of Granace against Father Giacomoni. He was said to have 'kept parishioners away from the confessional by the severe penances which he imposed', to have failed to conduct religious services regularly, 'to have kept for himself sums collected as alms and for the upkeep of the church and the presbytery', and, a political slant, to have refused to sing a *Te Deum* at Assumption in honour of the Emperor. Absence or non-residence were also common grounds of complaint, as at Monaccia in 1866.[145]

Some conflicts involving confraternities have already been mentioned, but a number of others may be cited. The church at Porretto was historically a dependency of the Order of St John Lateran and not therefore under the normal diocesan aegis. It had been granted in return for a nominal rent to several local confraternities of St John, who regarded it as 'their' church. When a new parish priest arrived in 1828 from Aix-en-Provence, he refused to recognize this situation and claimed the right to use the church as if it belonged to the parish. When he went there to establish his right, he was allegedly insulted by the chaplain and three members of one of the confraternities. Official complaints were made in the early 1860s against the parish priest of Sorbollano, Father Comiti. It was alleged that, although he took the emoluments, he never performed the corresponding services in the chapel of a confraternity at Serra. Again, the mayor of Sant' Andrea-di-Tallano reported a 'popular demonstration', occasioned by the parish priest's interference in the election of the prior of the confraternity. According to its statutes, the prior was elected annually on the first Sunday in October by all the members. In 1865, the priest at first called a meeting at short notice and tried to proceed to an election when the serving prior and others were absent. Having been forced to postpone the election for a week, he then refused to let it take place in the church as was customary, and it was held outside instead amid the reported commotion.[146]

As notables, Corsican priests had nothing of the social power, say, of some of the Breton clergy or of the Brazilian *padre-coronel*,[147] but they could and did exercise political influence, in the context of family and clan rivalries. This was evident in the Paoli period and continued to be remarked upon through the nineteenth century. Réalier-Dumas declared in 1819 that many priests 'keep up the divisions within their parishes, placing themselves at the head of the parties'. The prefect asserted similarly in 1872 that 'priests are very often still the leaders of parties' and as such they 'are involved in every political intrigue and throw themselves into every struggle'. In this, he added, they had been encouraged during his long episcopate by the late Mgr Casanelli d'Istria. Bigot also mentioned the role played by priests in party rivalries, which explained why it was so important for a family to have a priest among its members. This point has recently been enlarged upon by Pomponi, who concludes that

> having a priest among one's relatives was a trump card in the game of
> constituting the network of a clientèle. Through his function and his
> knowledge, the priest intervened at every moment in the life of the village
> and in the intimacy of family life. He played the role of adviser and
> arbiter, and, depending on the place which he occupied in the ecclesiasti-
> cal hierarchy, he was able to render very useful services ... The priest was
> rarely [however] the public leader of a clan; he was content with a more
> covert role; he reinforced or maintained alliances, acting in particular as
> the marriage strategist of the family; he participated in building up the
> dowries of the girls and he left his property to his nephews.[148]

This general picture may be confirmed and illustrated in detail. First, the appointment to clerical, as to all other, posts in Corsica was the object of patron-age and lobbying, often intense. The stage was set for this right at the start of the century with the reappointment of 'reliable' concordatory clergy in 1801. Casta demonstrates the contrasting outcomes for individuals and families by reference to two members of the Peretti della Rocca family. Antono was offered the cure of Serra-di-Scopamène but turned it down as unworthy of a man of his quality and died in indigence at Levie in 1815. His relative Giacomo-Antono, however, was given the cure of his native Levie, with which he was well satisfied. Special lobbying naturally concentrated on the more lucrative livings, such as Levie or Calenzana or Oletta.[149] Here different factions would put up rival candidates, and the appointment of outsiders or of men who did not belong to the predominant 'party' in the village could lead to trouble. At Belgodère, for example, 'the new priest, Father Luciani, was greeted by a noisy charivari when he arrived in the village in October 1847'. The mayor and the gendarmerie managed to restore calm and Father Luciani was formally installed next day by the parish council, but he was then locked out of the church. A hostile crowd forced the authorities to withdraw. The following day, a mock funeral procession went to the presbytery with a coffin in which it was intended to carry Father Luciani out of the village. He left soon after this and the bishop placed the parish under an interdict. This ban proved ineffective, however, for once Father Luciani had gone the church was opened and services and other ecclesiastical functions were performed by another priest, who lived in the village. Similar incidents were reported in at least six places in the last third of the century. At Cuttoli-Corticchiato in 1891–2, the opposition came from the partisans of the old priest, who had apparently been removed from his post, and, having at first appointed another local man, the bishop then appointed an outsider in the hope of restoring calm, but in vain, for both appointees were forced to leave the village. Here and at Bustanico in 1872, hostile demonstrations or refusals to hand over the keys to church or presbytery were abetted by the mayor, in the latter case on the grounds that the new priest had no intention of residing in the parish.[150]

Once appointed and accepted, priests could act, we have seen, as representatives of the community and defenders of its interests vis-à-vis outsiders. At Rusio in 1819, the parish priest played a leading part in local resistance to the gendarmerie.[151] More positively, a memorial statue at Occhiatana records Father Costa Savelli's successful defence of the village's title to its common lands in the mid-nineteenth century. As often, however, priests were eminent participants in local factionalism. After the attacks on him at San-Martino-di-Lota in 1841, Father Guasco went to the hamlet of Canale, where he had relatives, and 'called on all the people living there to give him their support against the rest of the community ... thus stirring up old village rivalries'. Avapessa in the Balagna was reported in 1850 to be divided into two factions, one of which was bitterly opposed to the parish priest. Conflicts occurred over the activities of the confraternity, the renting of seats in church and repairs to the presbytery.[152] Factionalism even impinged on the religious function of priests. A fatal quarrel between two men at Carogne in 1808 developed 'over the mass, the one claiming that the mass in the chapel should be celebrated by a priest of his party and the other insisting that it should be celebrated by another priest chosen by him'. Again, the bandit Giovan-Battiste Torre, facing execution in 1934, at first refused the priest sent to him, asking for 'one of his own party'.[153]

The commonest form of village factionalism involving priests was that which brought them into direct conflict with mayors. The mayor of Tolla, for example, was accused of having 'committed acts of violence' against Father Martinaggi, the parish priest, in December 1811, and he claimed in return that Father Martinaggi had stirred up a tumult of parishioners against him on Christmas night. At Serra-di-Fiumorbo, the parish priest, Father Bruni, had protested publicly against those who were systematically trespassing on land and forest belonging to the parish. These included both the mayor and the local justice of the peace, who organized a campaign to have Father Bruni removed from his post. But he enjoyed the support of many of his parishioners in his determination to defend the interests of the church, and, as a result of his efforts, the mayor was successfully prosecuted in 1856 for 'interference with church services'.[154] Cargèse was the scene of a much longer-standing conflict between those of the Greek and Latin rites and their respective priests, who had to share a single church until the mid-1860s, but there was also contention there between the clergy and the mayor. The Easter mass in 1860 was marred by angry exchanges between the mayor and the Latin priest, after the latter had criticized the mayor's singing.[155] At Luri, the quarrel between the parish priest and the mayor and their respective factions had more serious consequences. The mayor and his supporters refused to attend church, so for three months no church weddings or funerals took place.[156] Such cases illustrate some of the main areas of conflict between priests and mayors, and they also show that priests could sometimes be the overt leaders of family-based factions. Another prominent example of this type was Father Mozziconacci, who was parish priest at Loreto-di-Tallano from 1851 to 1866. He came from the village and, during his incumbency, according to the subprefect, 'he had worked ceaselessly to extend his properties and to achieve domination over his parishioners by keeping them divided'. He treated the church lands as if they were his own and he managed to have one of his nephews appointed as mayor.[157]

We should also note the open involvement of the clergy in political and electoral rivalries, particularly following the introduction of universal male suffrage in 1848. Serious trouble was reported at Piedicroce on the occasion of the election of a cantonal representative to the departmental council in 1848. The two candidates were the justice of the peace of the canton, Battesti, and a brother of the mayor of Piedicroce, called Paoli, and voting took place at the presbytery. According to the mayor, Father Nicolaio Battesti, a nephew of the justice of the peace, arrived there first and gave the signal for the building to be invaded by 50 armed supporters of his uncle. The gendarmerie and *voltigeurs* eventually persuaded them to leave, but they returned when a dispute arose about scrutinizing the voting, and shooting broke out. It appears that a former priest of the parish, who was an uncle of the mayor, played a role corresponding to that of Father Battesti on the Paoli side. Again, at Barbaggio in 1860, the electors were 'divided into two factions of about equal strength, one of which was led by the mayor and the other by Father Biaggini', who had been the parish priest for 30 years. After a series of abortive municipal elections in 1860 and 1861, both men were convicted of electoral fraud and Father Biaggini was removed from his post.[158] There is also evidence that the clergy played a more general, and sometimes orchestrated, role in elections. Two pamphlets making this allegation in 1858, with particular reference to the cantons of Soccia, Piana and Vico and to the Niolo, clearly struck home to judge by the angry response and idle threats of court action against their author.[159] Bishops Casanelli d'Istria (1833–69) and Gaffory (1872–7) were generally opposed, however, to advocating any denominational stance in elections. The same is not true of Bishop Foata (1877–99), whose episcopate coincided with a period of struggle between Church and State. Not only did he encourage the clergy to play an active electoral role on behalf of 'reactionary parties', but he was also accused of harassing and even dismissing clergy of known Republican sympathies. Such had been the fate, according to the subprefect of Corte, of Father Saliceti, who was removed as parish priest of Gavignano in 1887. This had ostensibly been prompted by allegations relating to his private life and the performance of his religious duties but, 'although there are still two years to go until the departmental elections, it is the prospect of these which is the real explanation for his disgrace. It was desirable to remove him [from a position of potential influence] in a canton which his brother Canon Saliceti represents.'[160]

All of this serves as a necessary background against which the role of the clergy in feuding proper may be understood, but first two other factors must be considered. The clergy in Corsica traditionally fulfilled the role of *paceri* or peacemakers, as they did in many other feuding societies, European and non-European.[161] In 1826, for example, the prefect paid tribute in his report to the departmental council to those members of the clergy who 'had extinguished the fatal hatreds that divided families and villages in many parts of the island', and similar commendations were made in other years. The 1858 pamphlets criticizing the political role of the clergy stressed that the proper function of a priest was to act as a conciliator and not a partisan. The litanies of the Virgin by Bishop Foata published in 1867, when he was a parish priest at Corte, expressed this pacificatory concern very strongly: 'Through you, Mary, / May the cruel / And horrible vendettas cease. / May you quieten our hearts / And take the anger and fury from them ... / You, who are always good, / Give us peace, / And bind us together in fraternal love!' Father Bartoli, again, at the end of the century emphasized the part played by the clergy in ending feuds both by preaching peace and harmony in a general way and more practically by acting as mediators between warring groups.[162]

Many particular instances may be adduced, moreover, of priests fulfilling or being asked to fulfil this role. At Lama, in 1811, when a violent protest began after a bogus auction of the lease of the communal pasture, the parish priest intervened to persuade the protesters to send a petition to the prefect instead of taking the law into their own hands. In her attempts to persuade her lover to marry her, Fiordispina Padovani of Ota 'solicited the intervention of certain influential people in the village and notably that of the parish priest'. Again, the priest of Cozzano tried to stop two men from fighting near Ciamannacce in 1852.[163] Parish priests also negotiated or attempted to negotiate peace settlements in feuds, for example at Ampriani in 1834, at Zerubia in 1848 and at Aullène in 1850,[164] and peace treaties were frequently solemnized in the parish church. At Aullène, however, the treaty was negotiated by the parish priest of Arbellara, and it is significant that peacemaking was a role associated more with outsiders than with the local clergy, themselves enmeshed so often in local strife.[165] The bishop of Ajaccio was personally involved in the settlement of many feuds in the first half of the nineteenth century, notably at Fozzano, Marignana, Moca-Croce, Olmeto and Sari-d'Orcino.[166] At Sari, the bishop's efforts were seconded by those of non-parochial missionaries, while the Marignana peace treaty was signed in the convent of Vico belonging to the Oblates of Mary the Immaculate. The role of religious orders as peacemakers, which had been important in earlier centuries,[167] enjoyed a brief revival in the second quarter of the nineteenth century. Our sources refer to peacemaking by 'missionaries' at Ucciana in 1827 and at Cuttoli in 1831, but the most remarkable achievement came with the arrival of the Oblates of Mary in the late 1830s. In 1837 and 1838, these missionary priests, led by Father Albini, brought about peace settlements at Ota, Guagno, Calcatoggio, Canale and Linguizetta.[168]

The ability of the parish clergy to act as conciliators was further limited by the absence of any strong Christian sentiment opposed to the practice of vengeance, a point to which we will return in Chapter 13. As we have seen, too, aggressiveness of a competitive kind and even violence were not by any means excluded from the 'sacred' territory of church or chapel. Violence occurring in churches, convents or other consecrated places had apparently been so common in earlier centuries that it was given a special heading in the ancient statutes, though it did earn a double penalty.[169] In 1827, the churchwardens of Santa-Lucia-di-Tallano decided that a charge would be levied in future on all chairs brought into the church and that those not paid for would be removed. This 'greatly displeased' three men in the village in particular, who refused to pay and who, for a while, successfully prevented the removal of their chairs by mounting a guard at the church door with their relatives and friends. More seriously, the mayor of Bonifacio was insulted and then hit and two gendarmes were seriously wounded in the church in 1833 during the funeral of the parish priest, while in the same year four people received stab wounds in a brawl which developed in the church at Canale, again during a funeral. According to a letter sent to the prefect, 'a bloody conflict took place in December 1849 in the chapel of the confraternity of St Charles at Avapessa, when an attempt was made to exclude a brother on the grounds that he was not a regular churchgoer'.[170] This was an episode in the general conflict in the village, to which we have referred. The non-privileged status of sacred places in this respect brings us at last to the question of the immunity of the clergy themselves.

There is much evidence that, at the popular as well as at the official level, members of the clergy were assumed to have immunity in feuds. Just before Father Ciavaldini was shot dead at Venzolasca in 1850, one of his killers had been heard to say 'We'll even get the priests,' advertising the extraordinary nature of what he was about to do. Again, when Father Vincenti was shot dead in 1851, no one at first seems to have understood why, although his family was in a state of enmity with the Muzi of Piobbeta.[171] Among Arrighi's pejorative village epithets is one directed against Carcheto, 'where they even murder priests!'[172] The neutrality of members of the clergy was also assumed where the obligation to pursue revenge was concerned. After the brother of the parish priest of Cardo had been killed around 1890 by an enemy who remained at large, 'the priest kept quiet; his sacred character did not permit him to take revenge'.[173] However, our examples demonstrate, too, that clerical immunity was readily ignored, and that priests could be the victims of acts of vengeance either as a result of their individual behaviour or through their family connections.

These were sometimes of a limited nature. Stones were thrown at Father Gabrielli of Bocognano in 1821 by relatives of the notary Serpaggi, for example.

At Aregno in 1829, olive trees belonging to Father Marcelli were destroyed, while the previous year the wooden staircase of the presbytery at Ortale was burned down. More serious arson attacks are also reported, and the presbytery at Piedigriggio was sacked and looted in 1822 by bandits acting on behalf of a man from whom the parish priest was trying to recover a loan.[174] Like women or children, too, priests might be accidentally or incidentally attacked in quarrels which did not directly concern them. Giovan-Bastiano Tomasi of Castineta, for example, fired a pistol at his enemy Giovan-Cesare Santini in 1858, as he was chatting with Father Geronimi, the parish priest. Such incidents also occurred when the priest was carrying out his sacerdotal functions. A man was shot at Ocana in 1861 and a neighbour ran to fetch the priest to administer the last rites. The priest was fired at as he approached the house and had to abandon his mission.[175] Both kinds of attack suggest that priests were held in no special awe, and this point is reinforced by the frequency of more serious threats and actions against them, usually in the context of blood vengeance.

Priests were sometimes clearly designated as intended victims in a feud. In a well-known lament, the sister of a man killed by his enemies declared that she wished in revenge 'to see the guts / Of the rector of the canton in a basket'. At Zicavo in 1820, two lead bullets, a charge of gunpowder and an anonymous threatening note were left at the presbytery. 'It is known', a police report explained, 'that the parish priest is in a state of enmity with the Losinchi family over a chapel in the church, which this family claims to have founded and to own.' A similar death threat was made against Father Renucci of Fozzano in 1816.[176] Such threats were by no means idle and cases in which priests were killed are not hard to find, particularly in the first half of the nineteenth century. In 1838, Father Giacomo-Andrea Susini was killed at Moca-Croce as he was saying mass in the village church. He had played some part in a quarrel involving the Luciani family and had particularly antagonized one of its members, a young bandit called Cioccio. When Cioccio threatened to kill him, Father Susini declared prophetically that he would only succeed in doing so if he killed him at the altar. Eleven years later, an attempt was made to kill another priest in the same village in the course of a feud between the Franchi and the Istria. Similarly at Bisinchi, Father Vignale became drawn into the feud between his family and the Canacci, who regarded him, rightly or wrongly, as the head of his family. He had been chaplain to Napoleon on St Helena and a beneficiary in his will, and he returned to Corsica a wealthy man. He was threatened, took precautions, but was shot dead in 1836 as he was emptying his chamber pot from a window of his house.[177]

We may cite other cases in which priests were able to avoid such a fate only by taking even more care or by good luck. Father Giovan-Battiste Mozziconacci was parish priest of Cargiaca but lived at his native Loreto-di-Tallano. After he had given evidence in court against the Arrii and the Giacomoni in connection with an incident in their longstanding feud with the Susini, his life was threatened. An attempt was made to ambush him and he then abandoned his parish altogether and remained shut up in his house at Loreto. Another priest stood in for him at Cargiaca, thus allowing him to 'escape the vengeance of the Arrii', but this priest was in turn intimidated. A letter to the prefect in

1850 from Father Susini of Renno told a similar story. His nephew had been killed by a certain Giovanni Casalta in an inheritance dispute. Casalta now threatened to kill the priest also and had placed his land under an 'interdict'. Father Susini asked for protection from the authorities, since his conciliatory moves had been consistently repudiated. Also relevant here is a case at Peri in 1854 in which a priest was the prime target of an avenger, escaping only because he was 'nominated to a parish' in another part of the island. It should be noted that the killing of priests was to some extent incorporated into the blood vengeance system as an action more serious than a 'normal' killing and requiring a special response. According to the gendarmerie, Father Vignale's relatives determined 'to exterminate the Canacci family' in revenge, while the trial summary relating to the shooting of Father Ciavaldini at Venzolasca stated more generally that there were barriers which prevented the killing of a priest but that 'once such a deed had been accomplished, it called for a terrible expiation'.[178]

We turn now to the active role of the clergy in conflict and feuding.[179] First, it was not uncommon for priests to carry arms. Father Giacomoni of Santa-Lucia-di-Tallano always did so, according to a report from the mayor in 1820. The new priest at Poggio-di-Nazza apparently showed his parishioners his arms at their first meeting in 1818: his shot-gun, 'Here is the Father'; his pistol, 'Here is the Son'; and his dagger, 'Here is the Holy Ghost.' Apocryphal or not, this story clearly caught a social type and was repeated years later.[180] Less flamboyant or aggressive characters might also arm themselves for protection, like Father Franchi of Moca-Croce, who was authorized to do so by the bishop in the late 1840s after his life had been threatened. Our sources also show that priests might engage in violence, using such weapons if the occasion arose. Among those detained in custody in 1812 was a young priest from Frasso, who had been involved in a brawl in the village. In disturbances at Suarella in 1825, 'during the time of the mass on the square by the church', Father Agostino Antonelli had a hand-to-hand fight with a member of the Polacci family. At about the same time at Poggio-di-Tallano, the parish priest, Father Giuliani, was reported to have fired a pistol and had a fight with a woman.[181] Some cases may even be cited in which priests killed their enemies. At the start of the nineteenth century, for example, Bernardino Peretti, a doctor and a priest, became involved in a property dispute with his affines. Having been ambushed by one of them, he shot and killed the latter's brother in revenge and went on to kill two other people. The notorious bandit Borghello, a member of Teodoro's gang, was killed by a priest.[182]

Much more common were those situations in which priests played a less exposed but often more important role in family conflict. As the mayor of Santa-Lucia-di-Tallano wrote in 1820, referring to an example to which we will return, had Father Giacomoni the best qualities in the world (which he had not), he would yet have been drawn into the bloody feuding of his relatives; 'he cannot separate his interests or detach his lot from theirs'.[183] At Muro, Father Tortora was suspected of having written anonymous letters to Bastia in order to undermine the credit of the Maestracci, and he was later killed in retaliation; while at Penta-di-Casinca, Father Suzzarini was described as an active partisan of the

Viterbi. A similar role was played in the feuding at Sartène in the 1830s by Father Paolo-Maria Pietri.[184]

In a few cases, which include some of the most prominent feuds of the century, priests were the driving force behind conflict. A peace treaty was signed in 1812 under the auspices of Count Berthier between the Lucchini of Ciamannacce and the parish priest of Sollacaro, 'chief' of his family. In the 1830s, Father Lucchini of Ciamannacce was reputed to be the instigator of the many crimes of his nephew Antono and the main promoter of the feud between the Lucchini and the Gabrielli.[185] The 'parties' at Santa-Lucia-di-Tallano in the first half of the century had a succession of clerical leaders. Sanseverino Giacomoni, described as a 'boss' during the Revolutionary period, was appointed parish priest in 1810. He appears to have been wholly unsuited for pastoral work, but he was well-connected and the effective head of his powerful family. This explains his litigiousness and his endemic quarrels with other notables. He was also fully engaged in his family's feud with the Quilichini. The shots fired at Mayor Alessandro Quilichini in August 1816, for example, which provoked a more general encounter, came from the house of the parish priest. One of Sanseverino's brothers, Anton-Padova, was also a priest, and had been involved the previous year in a dispute with Quilichini over the key to the church, which had ended in the priest's nephew firing a blank at the mayor and striking him with a dagger. Some years later, Father Santa-Lucia 'was actively involved in the enmities' of his family. He was prosecuted for instigating a killing in 1831 and became a bandit. He was also believed to have masterminded the murder in 1839 of Petro Poli and Giacomo Quilichini. In 1840, he was arrested, convicted on this latter charge and sentenced to ten years' imprisonment. His family claimed, possibly with some justice, that the prosecution witnesses had committed perjury against him, but there seems little doubt that he was their chief and the main organizer of their feuding activities.[186] We may also cite the example of Father Cerati, who was appointed to the parish of Lopigna in 1849 and who arrived there to be installed, 'accompanied by twenty armed men', explaining that he was engaged in a feud in his native Scanafaghiaccia and would have to exercise his functions through a substitute. Similar situations obtained at Campile in the 1830s and at San-Gavino around 1850.[187] In at least two of the examples which we have already cited, clerical leaders of parties in feuds were reported to have selected other priests as targets. Father Susini of Moca-Croce was at odds, we have seen, with the Luciani family, one of whose senior members was the parish priest of Sartène, and it was believed that either he or else the parish priest at Moca had encouraged his sacrilegious murder. Again, the killing of Father Vincenti in 1851 was more certainly instigated by Father Muzi of Piobbeta.

We may conclude generally that, although immunities were significant in Corsica and help to explain why feuds were not more disruptive, they were by no means always respected in practice. Expected roles of women and of priests, in particular, were not always binding on individuals, and there was a tendency as feuds escalated for people to act simply as members of a group and for enemies to attack each other indiscriminately. The behaviour of priests was also guided by the fact that they were family leaders, notables and politicians as well as pastors.

IV

Social anthropologists, who have usually studied feuding in non-European societies, have often stressed that it was too disruptive an activity to be carried on
within communities. Evans-Pritchard concluded, with reference to the Nuer,
that 'corporate life is incompatible with a state of feud'. Peters has written more
generally that feud

> is excluded from the corporate group because the activities its members
> perform, and the social relationships which develop out of them, make it
> imperative that serious breaches of the peace, whether homicide, physical
> injury, adultery, sexual misdemeanours, gross insult or false accusations,
> are dealt with at once, to prevent the spread of hostility ... In circum-
> stances where co-residents need to co-operate in their exploitation of
> natural resources ... and where their activities necessitate the movement
> of people to and from their gardens, plots and fields, without let or
> hindrance, homicide may well occur, but feud will be absent.[188]

In 1960, Stirling indicated that such conclusions did not apply to Turkish village
society, where feuds were carried on almost exclusively within communities and
where they did not cause total disruption, and the scope of his remarks can
probably be extended to the northern Mediterranean region generally.[189] What
we know of Corsica certainly lends them support and permits some attempt to
show how the disintegration foreseen by Evans-Pritchard and others was in
practice avoided. It should also be said that the observation that total feud is
impossible tends to be tautological. In the long term feuds may always be settled,
but in the shorter term (which may be decades) they take place and life is
(temporarily or to some extent) disrupted. One may argue that these are not real
feuds or that what stems from them is not real disruption, but this is to deal in
abstractions for their own sake. We wish simply to understand how feuding
could have been so prevalent in Corsican society without causing more disturbance than it did.

We have shown that feuding between villages took place and that there was a
high incidence of intrafamilial conflict, but feuding mainly occurred within villages and between distinct family groupings. There is no doubt either that such
feuding upset normal life for the combatants and their relatives, but also for
those not directly involved. Gregorovius commented in the mid-nineteenth century that 'family feuds are far more striking and terrible in Corsica [than they had
been in Italian cities in the past], because they are carried on in such small places,
in villages often possessing scarcely a thousand inhabitants, who are moreover
indissolubly bound to one another by the bonds of blood and the rights of
hospitality'.[190]

Here various levels of disruption may be distinguished. First, a killing or a
serious quarrel might lead people to take refuge inside their houses for a time.
After the quarrel between Father Anton-Padova Giacomoni and the mayor at
Santa-Lucia-di-Tallano in 1815, 'the news spread through the village and every-
one retired or sought to retire into his house'. After the killing of Antono
Gabrielli at Ciamannacce in 1828, the mayor reported that 'nearly everyone in

this place is shut up in his house'. Such confinement was obviously most necessary for those directly involved in conflicts. At Pila-Canale, the Feliciaggi and the Poli were allegedly unable to leave their houses for long periods in 1815 and 1816. Father Albini, who visited Ota in 1838 just after a vengeance killing had been committed, reported that 'public tranquillity was so compromised that the close relatives on either side all kept indoors for fear of being killed'. A lament sung by the grandmother of the two Forcioli of Arbellara, killed in 1844, commented of their enemies: 'They have kept us shut up, / So that we cannot go out.'[191] Confinement of this kind could last for months or, in the case of serious feuds, for years. Following the threats against his life in 1848, Father Giovan-Battiste Mozziconacci did not leave his house at Loreto-di-Tallano for four months. Giusepp'-Antono Paoli of Fozzano was killed in 1851, when he ventured out of his house for the first time in two years, and there are other reports of seclusion for periods of two to fifteen years.[192]

Immurement was to some extent an alternative to active feuding. Bertrand describes a case known to him in which the only remaining relative of two youths killed in a feud was their uncle aged nearly 80. He was unable to pursue vengeance because of his age, but 'he believed that a Corsican who had been offended could not live honourably without vengeance, so he decided to cut himself off from the world'. He shut himself up in his house, whose façade was painted black, emerging only ten years later when his enemy had been killed by someone else. Others have noted more generally that the houses of victims and of those in mourning were closed up and we have seen that a victim's relatives and anyone with a vengeance to pursue withdrew from normal social life.[193] The disturbance caused by all this could be considerable. In 1847, according to a military report, there were no men to be seen at Olmeto; while at Pila-Canale a few years later we have seen that only the women attended church any more and among them each 'party' kept to its own side. According to Bertrand again, 'in certain villages whole generations lived without taking any part in social life'; some individuals in the Sartenais were allegedly taken to the church to be baptized and were not seen in public again until they were old men.[194]

Confinement was often only one step from siege. Corsican houses seem to have been built with this eventuality in mind, and most observers commented on their fortified aspect. 'Corsican houses are like citadels,' wrote Agostini in 1819, while Ardouin-Dumazet noted at the end of the century that they were places 'where one can either defend oneself or be reinforced by one's supporters'.[195] As this reminds us, Corsican village houses were often large, tall buildings of several storeys, with the entrance on the first floor.[196] More important families in some villages, such as Fozzano, Arbellara or Santa-Maria-Sicche, had towers attached to their houses. These were usually old, but some were built or rebuilt in the nineteenth century, and they could be of special importance during hostilities.[197] Houses, moreover, were specifically equipped for sieges. Not only were entrances high up, but they were often machicolated. The system of domestic fortification included 'heavy shutters over the lower part of the windows, pierced by openings just large enough to allow rifle barrels to be placed through them'. Sometimes such loopholes were constructed with stone or brick and they were still a feature of houses being built at Fozzano in the late 1860s. In addition, as descriptions of Arbellara in the 1840s illustrate, the land around houses might be 'surrounded by ramparts, and crenellated parapets were added to the roofs. In several places, too, the dwellings were fitted with internal latrines, an oven and a well, so that ... all the needs of the household could be met without going out.' At Arbellara again, 'the Giustiniani house in the lower village on the slope of a small hill had a solid protective wall around it and crenellated windows; while the Forcioli house, on a more elevated site, [also] had an external wall surrounding it' and three internal courtyards, the family's living quarters being within the last and protected by loopholes. Nearby a square tower had been constructed, which dominated the approach to the village and served as both look-out and fortress. A trench had been dug between it and the Forcioli house and there were plans to make this into a covered passage.[198]

In a situation of feud or potential feud, in effect, families barricaded themselves inside their houses or compounds, where they might be besieged by their enemies,[199] or two rival families might conduct hostilities against each other from their fortified dwellings, as at Fozzano or Arbellara. Fozzano, according to the public prosecutor in 1832, 'offered an afflicting spectacle. One would have said that the whole village was in a state of siege; the houses are fortified and barricaded, the streets deserted, and no one dares go out. Everyone is on the look-out and seeks to avoid encountering an enemy.' 'The war-like aspect of the village was frightful, miserable,' wrote Valéry a little later. 'The peasants were all armed; the houses were crenellated ... with their windows blocked up with red bricks. About a quarter of the population was in a state of enmity, and the families of all those involved had to keep indoors.'[200] With variations, this description would fit most of the villages which experienced serious feuds in the period.[201]

On the face of it, the consequent disruption must have been considerable, and our sources confirm this impression. Communications internal and external might be severed or curtailed. At Arbellara, the construction of fortifications 'had blocked streets and paths and prevented normal circulation' in the village. In a case in 1801, Giovan-Giacomo Quilichini of Santa-Lucia-di-Tallano plausibly claimed that he had been unable to have recourse to legal means to prevent the building of a house next to his, 'because the state of enmity had prevented him from going to Sartène'.[202] Bourde and others related that those involved in vendettas travelled if at all in large armed groups,[203] which were always liable to ambush and attack, as we have seen. Social relations beyond the confines of the vengeance group might also be suspended. Church-going ceased. The preamble to the peace treaty at Fozzano in 1834 declared that 'whole years had gone by without a single marriage being registered'. At Porto-Vecchio in 1885 even those not involved in the feud went into isolation. 'No one dared to meet together any longer or to talk with people, since any remark was liable to be inaccurately reported, and might draw one into the conflict.' The political life of communities might also be paralysed, as at Fozzano in 1830–1.[204]

But potentially most damaging was the dislocation of economic life. Togab, who was an excise official in Corsica for five years, wrote in 1905 of 'the death of trade'. The blacksmith and other artisans and traders from Venzolasca complained in 1911 that 'they could not carry on their work and all their business had had to be abandoned'.[205] Given the nature of the Corsican economy, however, the main victim was agriculture. Report after report refers to cultivation being neglected and fields abandoned. This was sometimes because those engaged in feuds were 'giving all their strength and wit to the conduct of hostilities', but more often because they were prevented by threats and confinement. According to local officials in 1828, the Lucchini of Ciamannacce had been forced by their enemies 'to shut themselves up in their houses, exposing their land to every risk'.[206] Mayor Giustiniani of Arbellara related in 1835 that his relatives 'were forced to remain in their houses, which prevents them from getting in the harvest and is prejudicial to agriculture'. A decade later in the same village 'all those who had to work in the fields' were escorted there daily by *voltigeurs*. It was also common for parties in feuds to place the lands of their enemies under 'interdicts', as we saw in Chapter 3. The Franceschi declared, for example, that during their feud with the Antona at Frasseto they were unable to use their land for 16 years, 'because of the threats of death made against anyone who dared to work it'. Interdicts are known to have been declared in fifteen feuding villages.[207] Such bans might also include the provision of fire and water to those under siege and looking after flocks and other animals. At Ucciani in 1843, Martino Bastianesi's herdsman was told 'to abandon the care of his flock'; while Bourde noted that the livestock belonging to both parties at Porto-Vecchio in the 1880s had gone wild. This is one of the few indications incidentally that pastoral activities could be affected in the same way as agriculture, and in general they were far less vulnerable.

There is no doubt that some individuals, some families, perhaps some communities were reduced to ruin by the effects of feuding. The justice of the peace at Sari-d'Orcino was unable to carry on his functions in the 1820s and he had to resign from his post. In a letter presumably smuggled out to the prefect, three members of the Quilichini 'party' at Santa-Lucia-di-Tallano wrote that 'they and their relatives were reduced to the last extremity'. At Marignana, 'the interference with the freedom to work was translated into the direst poverty and distress ... Public life seemed to be suspended, the fields were neglected, and everyone had to make do with eating *polenta*.' A military officer, who was born there, wrote in 1809 of the 'misfortunes, miseries and calamities as well as depopulation' caused by feuding at Olmeto. The head of one family involved in feuding at Piazzole in 1852 concluded that the inconveniences were intolerable. He left his cover and appeared on the village square, 'shouting that since he could no longer go about his normal business, he might as well be dead'.[208] That such sentiments may have been more common than at first appears is suggested by the fact that the disorganization of social and economic life was often explicitly referred to as the reason for negotiating peace treaties to end feuds. 'The enmity having lasted for a long time, the war having been bloody and the damage done extensive, the parties concerned felt the need of a general peace,' the Fozzano treaty of 1834 stated; while one signed at Piana in 1848 declared: 'Everyone can go about his normal affairs again without fear.'[209]

Despite all this, it is clear that even villages like Fozzano and Arbellara were not entirely disrupted by years of feuding. Despite the claim relating to Olmeto, feuding does not seem to have stemmed the rise in population experienced by Corsican villages in the nineteenth century. Of 20 feuding villages, chosen fairly randomly, only 5 showed any decline in population in the first half of the century and only at Santa-Lucia-di-Moriani was this important or sustained. At both Arbellara and Fozzano the population rose during the troubles there, at Fozzano quite markedly.[210] We have seen in Chapter 2, moreover, that feuding villages that were prosperous to start with on the whole remained so. How are we to explain this? First and most obviously, though often long-term, feuding was also intermittent, and periods of very intensive conflict were not normally longer than a year or so and were frequently shorter. The duration and intensity of conflict is connected in turn with its proliferation within the community. Whereas at Arbellara by the 1840s 'nearly all the families' of the village were reported to be involved, at Canale in 1837, according to Father Albini, only a third of the population was affected.[211] Related to this again there was an important distinction between kinds of feuds. 'Bad feuds', in which enemies swore to exterminate each other and where immunities were flouted, were clearly the most disruptive but they were not the most common form.[212] Miot wrote, for example, that the double killing at Bocognano in 1801 'caused no sensation there ... The local people seemed pleased rather than saddened. They told me that it was fortunately the last vengeance outstanding at Bocognano and that now that it had been accomplished they need fear no further disturbances. The relatives on both sides recognized that the action had been just and within the rules, and no one interfered.'[213]

Where the immunity granted to women and other categories was respected, this allowed basic tasks to be carried out. A military report in 1827 suggested that women only did agricultural work when feuding stopped men from doing it. Malaspina, who in general took what one might call a 'maximalist' view of the feud, conceded that vendettas prevented men from working in the fields but not on the whole women.[214] And we have seen in particular instances that women might 'go about freely', while men were confined indoors. Related to this, there might be specific periods of truce to allow agricultural and other tasks to be completed. Reporting on a quarrel between two youths from Linguizetta and Carpineto in 1802, the military commissary said that there was some danger of a general conflict developing but that he had managed 'to pacify the parties concerned'. This had been facilitated by the fact that 'people were extremely anxious to get on with the harvest'.[215]

Our sources provide a basis for enquiry into the seasonal incidence of feuding, but no very obvious pattern emerges overall. In some places, such as Fozzano, Olmiccia or Olmeto, acts of hostility occurred throughout the year. April, June and September were the months when hostilities seem in general to have been rarest, which may be linked to the arrangement of the agricultural year. August, the month following the cereal harvest, was a time when feuding was often most active. February and December were the commonest times for peace settlements. It seems that concern to avoid conflict during critical periods of the agricultural year was to a degree offset by the fact that people were most likely to meet, interact and quarrel at precisely the same times, a point well illustrated in Chapter 3. Seasonal patterns seem more marked for herding communities. Hostilities were rare or non-existent at Aullène, Bastelica, Carbini and Ciamannacce in the winter months, when the men were away at the coast, and June was also a quiet month, being the time when the flocks were taken up into the high mountain pastures. By contrast, at Aullène there was a concentration of violence in the month of August, and at Carbini in August and September, when the men would have been in the villages.

Other aspects of the Corsican economy are relevant here, too. On the one hand, the economy, together with the political system, was not entirely local, being linked to that of France. Short periods of disruption could thus be lived through without disaster ensuing.[216] On the other hand, the nature of the village economy was still such that families could go through the long periods of autarky that feuding entailed. Co-operation at the community level was essential in the long, but not necessarily in the short term. As we have seen, provisions could be accumulated and were stored. Houses were very often purpose-built for sieges. Moreover, the balance between pastoralism, agriculture and arboriculture gave the family economy considerable flexibility. It is significant here that nineteenth-century administrators frequently linked Corsican dislike for sedentary agriculture with the risk of feuding.[217] Most important, the mixed rural economy was not continuously labour intensive and the withdrawal of male labour for a time may have had comparatively little impact. Especially where pastoralism or arboriculture predominated, there would always be long periods of inactivity, particularly for men.

We have seen in another context that Corsican men had a reputation for idleness. 'It is well-known', Charles Maurras wrote, following a visit in 1898, 'that the natives of Corsica have a pronounced taste for doing nothing in particular'; while an English visitor to Ghisonaccia in the 1920s exclaimed that 'the unlimited leisure of the villagers is a thing to admire and marvel at ... the sight of men at work of any sort is exceptional'. These are late examples of a common theme and, to some extent, reflect the fact that the traditional economy was declining as well as the preconceptions of those accustomed to a different approach to work. But many earlier examples could be cited, and male idleness was admitted, even bragged about, by the 'natives'. 'No Corsican works, m'sieur,' the mayor of a village in the Balagna told another English visitor with some pride, 'at least not *in* the island.'[218] Feuding in such an environment was often quite literally a pastime, a sport, a way of 'keeping the blood from stagnating', in the words of Sir Walter Scott.[219] According to a report in 1826, 'in the parts of Corsica where chestnuts are abundant, the inhabitants only depart from their normal idleness at the time of the harvest. The rest of the year they do no work at all. They smoke, they play cards, they hunt, and they occupy themselves with their enmities.' Abeau observed more generally in 1888 'that the vendetta would be far less of a scourge, if Corsicans could satisfy their devouring need for activity in another way'.[220] The 'sporting' element in feuding, which we have encountered in the importance attached to the rules and conventions and to honour, would also have acted to contain its impact.

All of these factors would depend of course on the extent to which a village was dependent on agriculture and on how much time local people needed to spend to keep their fields cultivated and harvested. The parish priest of Vivario, for example, told Robiquet that agricultural work only occupied the local population for five and a half months in all, from mid-June to mid-August and from mid-October until the end of January. More detailed information is available on this point for the Casinca, which suffered an outbreak of feuding and banditry in the years just before the First World War. According to the gendarmerie at Vescovato, 'the agricultural population of the canton remained tranquil [during this time] and carried on with its work', but reports from Venzolasca, the centre of the troubles, were less sanguine. Both agriculture and commerce had been affected in the neighbouring villages of Loreto and Sorbo-Ocognano, and the disruption at Venzolasca itself had been very serious, though this might not have been obvious to the superficial observer unacquainted with the local work routine.

> At Venzolasca and Sorbo-Ocognano, the most agricultural villages in the district, the cultivators rise in normal times around two or three in the morning, during the seasons for sowing, haymaking, harvesting and ploughing. They then go down to the plain [a distance of 4 kilometres on average], planning to arrive there an hour or an hour and a half before dawn if they are going to use oxen, or at dawn if they are working without oxen. In the evenings they remain at work until nightfall and return home three-quarters of an hour or an hour after this. During all the present month [November], which is the sowing season, they have left home at 6 a.m., and they have returned in the evenings before dark ... This means that, taking account of the time needed to look after their animals, they are losing between a third and a half of their working day. When they get home, they stay indoors and do not emerge again until it is light again.[221]

In other words, in one of the least pastoral areas in Corsica, the economy was upset but not ruined by a prolonged period of feuding. Another factor to take account of here would be the distance between a village and its fields. The villages of the Casinca overlooked the plain and it was feasible to go down there to work on a daily basis, but this was not the rule and elsewhere an expedition lasting days or weeks would be required, which might be a more risky undertaking.

This brings us to the general question of the relationship between habitat and feuding. We have seen that feuds often took the form of minor civil wars within villages with sieges and counter-sieges, and we noted in Chapter 4 that killing within built-up areas had a significant demonstrative quality.[222] But, by the same token, attempts were made to minimize the impact of acts of violence by taking quarrels away from public places.[223] The same mitigating effect was achieved on a much wider scale and at a profounder cultural level by the topography of Corsican villages, to which we have already alluded.

Corsican rural settlement followed an agglomerated 'urban' pattern, such as is found in other parts of the northern Mediterranean and which may be explained by a historical need for defence against coastal raiders as well as the hot and unhealthy nature of the plains.[224] Account should also be taken of the nature of the terrain and the requirements of the agro-pastoral system and of the fact that whatever its origins, this pattern persisted. Isolated houses were rare and aroused special comment.[225] A sharp distinction was made between the 'urban' inhabited village zone, that of gardens and fields, and that of the 'wild' beyond, and Lenclud notes that, despite the demographic expansion of the nineteenth century, nearly all villages remained within their old limits, building upwards but not outwards.[226] However, as we have seen, these villages were rarely of the centralized type with a single square. Saint-Germain wrote of Zicavo in 1869 that 'there were no squares or streets even, but passageways or rather stairways to go from one house to another' and he added that such a layout was typical. Where streets and squares did exist, they were often only semi-public areas, being regarded as appendages of the houses alongside them.[227] There were important exceptions to this rule, some of which we have come across as arenas of conflict, for example Calenzana, Speloncato and Castellare. In general, compact villages are more often found in the north of the island, and particularly in the Balagna, the Nebbio and the Casinca.[228] It will be noted that these were also regions in which agriculture and arboriculture were most advanced, and, in the first two, feuding and banditry had become rare by the mid-nineteenth century. *A priori* then compact settlement seems, together with other factors, to have inhibited feuding within villages.[229]

But the general pattern in the south, as well as in the Niolo and the Castagniccia, that is where feuding was most common, was of settlements made up of groupings of *quartiers*, hamlets or clusters of houses with no very obvious centre or centres,[230] and we have seen that the church rarely provided such a focus. In some cases, the proliferation was extreme. Corscia and Ghisoni comprised 9 hamlets; Sisco in the Capo Corso 16 or 17. Morosaglia is a collection of 20 or so scattered clusters of houses on small hillocks and ridges; while Campile is an example of what can only be called a *bocage* settlement. It is characteristic that observers disagree about the number of hamlets in some villages or cease to count them: 5, 6, even 12 are given for Bastelica. Numbers of hamlets could also change over time. Rezza in the Cruzzini had 7 in 1851 and 11 in 1931, Azzana 5 in 1851 and 16 in 1881. A further complication was the existence of hamlets away from the main site. Until 1914 Tavera comprised 6 hamlets in the village proper, 4 of which were old and 2 more recent, and the dependency of Mezzavia in the valley near Ajaccio. Levie is a large village with 5 or more hamlets at its main site, but in the past it also had a number of more distant satellites, for example Carbini, and it possessed a large coastal settlement at Figari, which only became independent around 1800.[231]

In other cases, a limited number of hamlets may be discerned: three at Valle-d'Alesani, Ventiseri and Campo, for example. In yet other cases there are only two hamlets, in close proximity and often one above the other on the side of a hill, as at Argiusta-Moriccio, Moca-Croce, Calcatoggio or Zerubia. Sometimes such pairs were called 'upper' and 'lower': *soprana* and *sottana*, or *di sopra* and *di sotta* as at Fozzano. Sometimes they were otherwise distinguished. At Sari-d'Orcino they were called Acqua in sù and Acqua in giù; at Letia, San-Rocco was the upper hamlet and San-Martino the lower.[232] As our first two examples illustrate, this type of coupled settlement, common elsewhere in the Mediterranean region and beyond,[233] is often indicated in the name of the village, though this is sometimes misleading. Pila-Canale, for example, and Petreto-Bicchisano comprise more than two hamlets. A further type of pairing, to which we have referred earlier, is really a variation on the pattern of Tavera and Levie, and that is the coupling of a settlement in the mountains with one or more on the plain.

We have seen that there was a tendency during the nineteenth century for such satellites to hive off. The dual or coupled settlement probably has a significance that outweighs its apparent numerical importance, for, as we shall see, factionalism of a two-party kind was almost universal in Corsican villages and must reflect a more fundamental dual social organization. There is also evidence that where larger numbers of hamlets existed they were grouped in pairs, as they were at Bastelica.[234]

A more systematic analysis of the correlation between patterns of settlement and feuding is pertinent here. Of 50 villages which experienced feuding or serious conflict during the nineteenth century, 21 (42 per cent) are of the multiple-site or dispersed type; 6 (12 per cent) are of the clear two-site type, all but one with an upper and a lower part; and 23 (46 per cent) are of the single-site type. But, of those in the last category, 6 were divided into *quartiers*, and a further 5 had dependent hamlets in addition to the main site, though at some distance from it, leaving only 12 (24 per cent of the whole group) as villages of a clear single-site type. Of the 50, moreover, only 16 have anything approaching a square and for only 5 of these is the space of any size. Only 14 have churches within the built-up area of the village. Of the 35 villages among these 50 which experienced prolonged feuding, 10 (29 per cent) were of the multiple or dispersed type of settlement; 6 (17 per cent) of the dual type; and 19 (54 per cent) of the single-site type. But, of these 19, 6 were divided into *quartiers* and 5 had hamlets at a distance, leaving only 8 (23 per cent) of the purely single-site type. This suggests that in most cases feuding was actually carried on either within or perhaps between disparate parts of villages. This may be confirmed by a closer examination of the nature of hamlets or *quartiers*.

These had a strong sense of identity and often considerable autonomy. Down to the end of the eighteenth century, each of the hamlets of Bastelica even had its own communal lands, and such arrangements were found elsewhere.[235] Other communal amenities of hamlets, which survived into the nineteenth century, include ovens[236] and, above all, chapels. Nearly all the hamlets contained in our 50 feuding villages had their own chapels, and many had the ambition to have their own curate also to take services there. A request was made, for example, in the 1820s by the inhabitants of Varriccio(?), a hamlet of Levie, with this end in view, but the subprefect strongly opposed the idea. Varriccio had only 130 inhabitants, he explained, and was only two miles from both Levie and Carbini, each of which had a parish priest. More important, were this request to be granted, 'the other hamlets, which are in fact further away from the centre than Varriccio, would all put forward similar demands'. Each of the four hamlets or *quartiers* of Calacuccia, which had a total population of only 800 in 1933, had its own chapel, and additionally the nave of the parish church was divided into two parts, each occupied by inhabitants from the upper and the lower parts of the village nucleus.[237] Hamlets were also political entities, sometimes having specific representation on municipal councils or even their own *adjoints*, as at San-Martino, a hamlet of Serra-di-Scopamène. It is clear that such arrangements were a way of maintaining a balance of power in villages that were in effect federations of hamlets. A group of local people wrote to the prefect in 1860 from Bastelica to try to ensure the maintenance of the system by which each of the village's three *quartiers*, made up we have seen of pairs of hamlets, was represented on the municipal council. The three *quartiers* had existed 'from time immemorial', it was asserted. They were distinct places, 'separated by large areas of uninhabited land made up of meadows, gardens and so on'; they had roughly the same population; and they had always been used as the units for allotting and dividing up the communal lands. The threefold division, moreover, was an essential means 'of preventing any single party in the village from gaining exclusive control of it'.[238] Alternation of municipal offices between or among hamlets might be used to achieve the same result. We learn, for example, from a case in 1811 that at Lozzi, which comprised three hamlets, the mayor was chosen from one and the *adjoint* from another. Pianottoli-Caldarello, a coastal hamlet attached to Zerubia, made a bid in 1846 to escape the latter's tutelage but had to settle for a similar arrangement.[239] The autonomy (and rivalry) of hamlets also found expression in the organization of wakes and festivals.[240] We may conclude that hamlets were relatively self-sufficient and might be little affected by feuding in other parts of their villages, and also that conflict between them was latent and might easily erupt into violence.

A further factor lends weight to this view, for, as we saw in discussing family structure, clusters of houses, hamlets or *quartiers* were often relatively exclusive units of sociability comprising kin and clients.[241] Specific examples may be cited. At Scanafaghiaccia, a hamlet of 13 houses in the Cruzzini, all 72 inhabitants in 1851 had the same surname as two brothers recorded there in a pastoral visit of 1733. At Scale, similarly, all 53 inhabitants were called Marcangeli, while the Cucchi family was described in 1853 as 'a kind of tribe inhabiting the place called Orone', which was a hamlet of Carbini. It is fair to assume that the combination of a single surname and the subdivision of villages into hamlets and clusters in the Castagniccia, the Niolo and elsewhere has the same significance.[242]

It can be demonstrated, moreover, that conflict did take place between hamlets and parts of villages. Finelli relates that hostilities between the inhabitants of Poggio and Canavaggio, hamlets of Tavera, led the latter to emigrate *en masse* to a site in the Castagniccia. We learn from a case in 1850 that 'the existing rivalry [between Pero and Casevecchie, which together formed a single village] was exacerbated in 1848 when the mayorship, which had belonged exclusively to the former, passed to the latter'. Conflict came to a head over the leasing of the chestnut woods, which was traditionally done by the mayor after the harvest. There was a rumour that the usual division of the income from the lease, two-thirds to Pero and one-third to Casevecchie, was not going to be followed, and the people of Pero then contested the mayor's right to lease the pasture at all. In subsequent shooting in December, the mayor killed one of his critics and a second man was killed in retaliation. In 1865, Antono Padovani from Eccica-Suarella was tried for attempted homicide. The conflict arose when children from Suarella began to throw stones at two men who came from a different hamlet. This fact was stressed by Padovani, who reacted violently when one of the men threw a stone back, narrowly missing him. 'If you are unlucky enough to hit me,' he had shouted, 'you won't be going back to Bodicasci to sleep tonight!'[243] Again, in trouble which occurred during the municipal elections at San-Lorenzo in 1884, shots were fired when electors from an outlying hamlet arrived to take part in the voting.[244] The fact that conflict took place here when inhabitants of hamlets came into the village nucleus confirms our hypothesis that this configuration must generally have limited occasions for violent interaction and mitigated its effects. Antagonism between upper and lower parts of villages was also common, if not endemic. A woman was killed and a man injured, for example, in fighting at Zicavo in 1883. This arose from the celebrations following the election of a member of the council of the *arrondissement*. He and his supporters came from the upper part of the village and their activities had annoyed their political opponents from the lower.[245] Ettori cites a lament evoking the same antagonism at Corscia.[246] In this context, we should also mention the hostilities between *quartiers* of towns, for example at Ajaccio in the late eighteenth and at Sartène in the early nineteenth century.[247]

It can also be demonstrated that such conflicts overlapped to a considerable degree with family feuding. According to Morandière, a feud at Calacuccia, which lasted for over a century and claimed 36 victims, took place between the Negroni of Leca and the Bonamanacce of Castellace, each a hamlet of the village. After Father Guasco of San-Martino-di-Lota quarrelled with his parishioners in 1841, he went to the hamlet of Canale, where he had relatives, and asked them for help 'against the other eight hamlets which composed the parish'. According to a report in 1850, 'the feud at Pila-Canale was primarily between the people of Pila and those of Canale'.[248] Feuds also took place between upper and lower parts of villages. At Fozzano, the Paoli and the Durazzi formed the party '*di sopra*', and the Carabelli, the Bernardini and the Bartoli that '*di sotta*'. At Castineta around 1840, the conflict lay between the Paoli of Castineta *soprana* and the Giovannoni of Castineta *sottana*; while a feud at Casalabriva in the 1870s involved two branches of the Ogliastroni family, residing one in the upper and the other in the lower part of the village. Where such hamlets or *quartiers* were well separated, conflict between them would be sporadic and peripheral. Although it later caused general disruption, the feud at Marignana, for example, was at first largely confined to the outlying hamlets of Chidazzo and Revenda and did not at that stage cause much concern beyond them.[249]

Conflict could also occur within hamlets that were not co-extensive with single groups, but this also had the effect of containing it. Coibiti, a hamlet of San-Lorenzo, was the residence of two rival families, the Moracchini and the Agostini. They competed for political power in the village as a whole, but when this led to violence in 1832 the confrontation, in which two people were killed and one seriously injured, took place at Coibiti. Other such cases include one of enmity between two branches of the Gaffori at Guigliazza, a hamlet of Pastricciola. They organized separate festivities in March 1848 for Carnival, which eventually led to shooting between them.[250] In all this, it is important to know where feuding families lived in the hamlet or village concerned. Unfortunately, information is not always easily available, though it is clear that feuding families often lived in close proximity. The houses of the Lucchini and the Gabrielli at Ciamannacce were close by each other, since the feud between the families began, around 1809, when a Lucchini was killed at his window by a shot fired from the Gabrielli house. Similar exchanges are reported between the houses of the Quilichini and the Giacomoni at Santa-Lucia-di-Tallano in 1816, of the Trojani and the Suzzarini at Loreto in the 1840s, and of the Arrighi and the Istria at Urbalacone in 1850. We know also that the houses of the Emilj and the Tenneroni at Santa-Maria-Sicche were contiguous, while at Venzolasca the houses of the Ciavaldini, the Filippi, the Petrignani and the Sanguinetti were all very close together.[251] At Arbellara and at Fozzano, again, the houses of the main feuding families were only about fifty yards apart.

The disruptive impact of feuding was also reduced by various forms of avoidance behaviour. We learn from a report in 1821 that 'the partisans of ex-mayor Poli [of Santa-Lucia-di-Tallano] keep away as far as possible from the places frequented by their enemies'. Anton-Andrea Fabi of Penta returned to his village in 1852, having served a three-year prison sentence for killing a man called Angeli in a brawl. 'Fearing reprisals from the victim's relatives and wishing as far as possible to avoid meeting them, he ceded to his brother-in-law the upper floor where he had lived before, since the Angeli family occupied the ground floor of the same house.'[252] It was also common for those affected by 'enmities' to leave their villages either temporarily or permanently. Dr Rocca-serra of Santa-Lucia 'went to live in Ajaccio [in a vain attempt] to escape the vengeance' of Antono Santalucia. Giovan-Agostino Nicolai left Levie after killing a man in a quarrel over irrigation in 1848. He became a bandit, residing at Carbini, where he had a house. Alessandro Peretti 'was implicated in serious enmities', also at Levie, so he went in 1848 to live at Olmiccia, where he married. Exodus from Frasseto in the 1840s and Venzolasca in 1911 occurred on a wider scale.[253] It was even more common for people to take to the maquis for short periods, a custom related to banditry, which we will discuss in Chapter 12. It is also relevant to note that exile, a formal penalty in the old legal codes, persisted into the nineteenth century in the form of exclusion orders. Those who had served prison sentences might additionally be banned for a further period from returning to the island or to their native villages. Transhumance must also have had the effect of separating enemies physically, though some feuds travelled with herdsmen and their flocks.

Finally, we should recall the element of honour, which was so important in Corsican feuding. This meant that certain rules were observed which limited the extent of conflict. The ostensible aim of vengeance, moreover, was not to destroy one's enemy but to restore one's own honour, and we have seen that this might be damaged by behaviour that was too ruthless. The Corsican data would here seem to support Black-Michaud's general view that 'the translation of conflicts over materially limited goods into conflicts in which the prize at stake is said to be honour ... prevents [conflict] ... from resulting in wide-scale destruction'.[254]

Notions of honour, the nature of the economy, the lay-out of villages and other specific devices all acted to mitigate the potentially disruptive effects of feuding in Corsica. A further factor, the machinery for conciliation and peace-making, was of equal if not greater importance and deserves a chapter to itself.

] 9 [

Conciliation and peacemaking

Wallace-Hadrill has referred to 'the natural pulls inherent in a feud-society towards settlement and composition'. In some feuding societies this pull was stronger than in others, and in some it gave rise to formal arbitration machinery that is not so obviously present elsewhere.[1] Corsica clearly belongs to this latter category, and some well-informed observers have even claimed that 'conciliation in disputes rarely occurred', and that most vendettas were not peacefully settled.[2] But this is to exaggerate the intransigence of Corsicans. Procedures to prevent and to mediate in conflicts were well-established, and these were applied to feuds.

I

Despite the prevalence of conflict and the positive valuation of violence, peace was also esteemed and appreciated in Corsican culture. It was celebrated as a good in a number of proverbs, for example: 'With work and peace one lives in plenty.'[3] In connection with a dispute over the remuneration of the parish priest in the mid-1850s, the municipal council of Penta-di-Casinca stressed not untypically in its deliberations that its aim was always to ensure 'the public peace', 'peace in the village', 'public tranquillity'.[4] Peace, moreover, had positive religious sanction in a Catholic society. Certain shrines were dedicated to peacebringing saints. The chapel of San Petro in the mountains south of Zicavo was apparently built around 1500 to commemorate the ending of a feud and is still the object of pilgrimage.[5] The Madonna of Loreto-di-Casinca was called Our Lady of Peace and reconciliations were attributed to her influence as they were to that of Our Lady of Mercy in Ajaccio. Peace treaties, as we shall see, make specific reference to religious imperatives, and the clergy played an important role as peacemakers. Lamotte dwells, too, on the role of confraternities in composing conflict.[6] Corsica does not, however, seem to have had the communal rituals for the periodic settlement of disputes and reconciliation of enemies found in other parts of Europe,[7] though funerals could sometimes fulfil this function.

But there is no doubt that the endemic conflict of the island was accompanied, complemented and contained by a complex informal machinery of avoidance, arrangement and conciliation, such as is found in other parts of the Mediterranean region.[8] The first is inherently the most difficult to document, but Lenclud and Pernet point to the preference for indivision here in circumstances where its economic *raison d'être* is hard to see, and Barry noted in 1893 that the socializing of Corsican notables was much inhibited by their wish to avoid situations where offence might be taken.[9] The machinery of arrangement and conciliation ranged from the interposition of third parties in minor quarrels to the negotiation of formal treaties of peace between feuding groups. It also included use of the courts, although increased resort to this mode of settlement, which the French State encouraged, ultimately weakened and undermined the traditional procedures. We will discuss and illustrate some of the general features of such procedures before coming to the settlement of feuds.

First, differences were not necessarily, or in the first instance, settled violently, and recognized means existed for the repair of small offences and disputes. In a case in 1861, for example, we learn that Giovan-Domenico Fumaroli invited his brother-in-law 'to drink with him in a tavern at Cauro ... in order to be reconciled and to forget the coolness between them occasioned by the municipal elections'. As in other societies, eating or drinking together was probably a common way of expressing reconciliation.[10] More often, such arrangements involved negotiations via third parties. The justice of the peace of the canton of Scopamène was asked in 1812 by the relatives of Maria Quilici 'to talk with Stefano Stefani and his relatives about compensation for an ox, which the latter had killed three years previously'.[11] After getting a widow from Pietroso pregnant in 1844, Paol'-Emilio Carlotti gave her an abortifacient. When her family was informed of this, 'they got in touch with his relatives in an attempt to settle the affair in a friendly way'. Again, the Giacomoni brothers from Loreto-di-Tallano had a difference of interest with another man in 1846 and proposed an arrangement with him, inviting him to discuss the matter at a shieling belonging to 'a mutual relative'. Very often the aim of such interventions was specifically to prevent violence. At Arbellara in 1840, the brothers Benedetti believed that their relative Francesco Benetti from Viggianello had cheated them of part of a property which they owned jointly. When a court in Sartène confirmed Benetti in his possession of the land concerned in 1841, the Benedetti were exasperated and 'mutual friends and relatives of both parties became alarmed and intervened, wishing to prevent the trouble which seemed imminent'. The Desanti brothers of Aullène were similarly in dispute in 1851 over the estate of a deceased uncle. 'In order to try to avoid a clash between the two [one of whom was a bandit], their relatives took it upon themselves to settle things amicably' and drew up an agreement which they then communicated to the two parties.[12] The same machinery might be brought into operation at the highest levels of Corsican society, even among the administrative élite. An incident during the municipal elections at Ajaccio at the end of 1864 led to a challenge to a duel between the prefect and a member of a leading family of the city, Napoléon-Levie Ramolino. It is not clear whether an encounter actually took place, but the parties were reconciled a month later through the good offices of Ramolino's relative, Princess Marie-Anne Bonaparte, the bishop of Ajaccio and other dignitaries.[13]

At village level again, the conciliation process often continued even after violence had been committed. In a case in 1811 against Anton-Francesco Durazzi and Paolo-Geronimo Paoli of Fozzano, accused of wounding Lorenzo Tomasi, a witness told the court that Michel'-Angelo Durazzi and another man from Altagène 'had been charged by the fathers of the accused ... to go to the plaintiff Tomasi to make proposals for an arrangement' and that he himself had been asked 'by Tomasi to go to Signore Giuseppo Orsini in Sartène to get him to draw up a compromise formula'. Michel'-Angelo Durazzi, himself, testified that, when he heard about the wounding incident, his 'wish to maintain peace among the families of the village, and his position as a relative common to both parties, decided him to go, without any solicitation, to see both the plaintiff and the fathers of the accused at their houses, in order to find out exactly what had happened and at the same time to try to bring about an arrangement'.[14]

It is significant here that recourse to the courts or to violence often came after negotiations for an amicable or a peaceful settlement had been tried and had failed. The account of a dispute over a private chapel at Cauro in the 1820s noted that for several years 'it had been kept out of the courts, as is usual in Corsica with contentions of this kind'.[15] Two tenants of Tito Roccaserra of Sartène were in dispute in 1855 over a cave used for storage. One of them removed from it straw belonging to the other, which led to reprisals but only 'after all the modes of conciliation had been exhausted'.[16] While most characteristic of minor disputes, the same pattern is found in more serious cases, and notably those involving female honour and marriage. The bandit Gallochio reputedly tried to get third parties to mediate after his engagement was broken off and only declared a vendetta on his fiancée's family when these attempts came to nothing. Again, Giulio-Cesare Santini of Castineta tried to kill his son-in-law in 1861, following the failure of mediators to end a long dispute between them over a dowry.[17]

As many of the examples cited indicate, conciliation in disputes was usually effected by relatives, but employers, patrons, local notables, officials or simply 'the wisest people' in the village or district could also be involved.[18] In a case in 1830, the two Paolini brothers of Zigliara were accused of stealing honey from Vincenzo Croce of Moca-Croce. Having been arrested by the gendarmerie, they asked to see their 'boss', a certain Susini, who, according to Croce, 'took me on one side, and told me that the matter must be arranged, promising to pay me both for the honey and for the damage done to my hives, if the Paolini were released'. In another case in 1814, in which a man from Granace was accused of wounding his sister-in-law, a witness was specifically asked by the magistrate 'whether mediators had intervened to conciliate the parties' following their quarrel and replied that two priests had acted in this capacity.[19] We have seen that the mayor and the parish priest of Ampriani tried to act as mediators in the dispute in 1834 between the Giampierini and people from Alesani.[20]

Sometimes the function of mediator or arbiter existed on a more regular basis. In most villages, according to Chiva, there were older men who 'dealt with all questions relating to the division of property, the fixing of boundaries, the appraisal of legacies and dowries, the evaluation and measurement of pastures, the calculation of damages, and so on'. They went under a variety of names from one region to another: *stimadòri* (estimators), *arbitri* (arbitrators), or *uòmi di bè* (good men or men of repute).[21] Such men were the natural choice as mediators in more serious conflict. Robiquet cited Cyrnaeus: 'If any dispute arises among them, Corsicans choose as an arbiter a man of probity, and they accept his judgment,' and he noted that this custom was still being followed,[22] which our evidence confirms. At Casabianca, we have seen that Petro-Luigi and Orso-Battiste Pietri fell out because the former had removed the rafters from a house which he rented from the latter's uncle. According to a witness, Petro-Luigi's father 'tried to dissipate Orso-Battiste's anger by informing him that he had just been talking with his uncle and that they had agreed to settle the whole affair by taking it to arbiters to decide'. At Casalabriva in 1852, Antono Guiderdoni and Giacomo Romangoni had agreed to settle a boundary dispute by appointing 'mutually acceptable arbiters', though they then refused to accept their decision. At Pietricaggio in 1857, the Castelli and the half-brothers Angelo-Luigi Orsini and Carlo-Filippo Bernardini were at odds over a number of matters. Eventually, the Castelli proposed 'that they settle their differences in a friendly manner', and the parties were reconciled through the offices of two apparently unrelated arbitrators. In another case in 1857 we learn of 'a decision made by the mayor [of Coti-Chiavari] in his capacity as arbiter chosen by the justice of the peace', and Bazal refers to the important role as arbiter and mediator in disputes played well beyond his own village by Giovanni Lucchini, who became mayor of Monaccia in 1899.[23]

In the early part of the nineteenth century, it was not unusual for higher-ranking officials to assume the same function. We saw in the last chapter that the military commissary 'pacified' a dispute between people from Linguizetta and from Carpineto in 1802. The subprefect of Sartène intervened fairly regularly in disputes in the first quarter of the century. In 1821, for example, following a fight between two men at Levie, he told the mayor 'to call the parties before him in order to try every means of conciliation and to encourage them to seek vengeance, if they had to, via the courts'. Again, in 1823, he stepped in directly to reconcile Petro-Paolo Orsali and Giulio-Antono Giacomoni after a brawl at Santa-Lucia-di-Tallano.[24] We shall see that prefects, military commanders and others were actively involved in pacifying feuds in the same period.

It was also common, up to the middle of the century at least, for the courts and the judicial authorities to take account of unofficial reconciliations and settlements. After Giovan-Agostino Anziani of Bisinchi made threats to kill a relative in 1854, for example, the latter reported this to the authorities, but the public prosecutor did not take immediate action 'to allow time for a reconciliation', which, in the event did not take place. Moreover, subsequent 'arrangements' might effect the outcome of prosecutions, with or without the connivance of the court. Antono Fieschi of Pila-Canale, for example, was accused of killing a gendarme in 1848, while resisting arrest. Andrea Santoni, an enemy of the Fieschi, who had been with the gendarmes, was a key prosecution witness. But, when Fieschi was brought to trial two years later, he was acquitted when Santoni, 'who had been reconciled with the Fieschi', changed his evidence.[25] Further examples will be cited in our discussion of the general relationship between feuding and the use of the courts in the next chapter. We should also mention here the role played formally by justices of the peace in settling village disputes.[26]

At the village level again, attention should be drawn to the way in which fighting was so often stopped by the intervention of third parties. A quarrel between two women at the public fountain at Cozzano in 1840 provoked their menfolk to join in, armed with pistols, 'but those present prevented any trouble and everyone returned peacefully to the village'. When two men from different villages began to fight at Mazzola in 1822, during the pilgrimage to the chapel of San Pancrazio, 'onlookers intervened to try to re-establish the peace', though in this case their efforts were unsuccessful.[27] Very often, those who intervened in this way were relatives or 'mutual friends'[28] but the sources refer equally to 'men of peace' or 'men of repute',[29] whom we have already encountered, and it is clear that there was a general obligation on those present when a quarrel, and still more a fight, broke out to try to restore calm and limit the social damage.[30]

Three further points may be made in this connection. First, intervention to stop actual fighting seems to have become less common after the 1860s, an indicator perhaps of an increasing acceptance of the gendarmerie as peacekeeper rather than the local community itself. Secondly, the phenomenon was always as common in feuding as in non-feuding villages. Of 18 instances traced in the judicial records between 1840 and 1860, at least 10 occurred in feuding villages, which supports the view that the non-violent settlement of disputes was not simply an alternative but a complement to feuding. Thirdly, the strength of the social obligation to conciliate may paradoxically be measured by the danger to which would-be mediators in quarrels exposed themselves. Giacomo Agostini of Santa-Lucia-di-Tallano was shot and mortally wounded in 1845, when he intervened to stop a fight over cards between two other men; Battiste Martinanghi was fatally stabbed in 1859 when he tried to separate combatants in a fight at Bastelica; and many other examples could be cited in which pacifiers suffered a similar fate.[31]

II

We should not lose sight of the fact, central to our whole discussion, that certain offences, and notably killing, were not susceptible to arrangement. They demanded revenge in the form of bloodshed and it would have been dishonouring to react to them, at least initially, in any other way. This at once raises the question of blood money or material compensation for the loss of life. Attitudes towards the acceptance of blood money or composition have varied in feuding societies. Sometimes a fairly well-established scale of payments was in operation, the systems of 'wergild' and 'wampum' being probably the best-known examples.[32] Perhaps more often composition was regarded as a second-best, frequently acceptable only after there had been some show of violence, or even a dishonourable outcome forced on weaker parties.[33] Corsica represents an extreme pole of this spectrum. In Busquet's words, 'blood was not for sale' and the idea of material compensation was profoundly alien.[34] A few exceptions to this rule may be cited but only in the end to confirm it.

We learn from a case in 1830 that Anton-Pasquino Quilichini of Poggio-di-Tallano had agreed to pay 2000 francs in compensation to Giuseppo Bernardini, whose wife he had killed five years earlier. Only part of the money was paid and hostility between the two families continued, leading to further killings. Moreover, the trial evidence makes it clear that the Bernardini's original acceptance of blood money was both highly unusual and regarded as shameful. None of the other cases involved such a serious offence. In 1848, Carlo and Giovan-Tomaso Tomasini, from an unspecified village, quarrelled with Francesco Santoni, whom they accused of injuring their dog. Giovan-Tomaso was shot in the thigh and 'Santoni's relatives consented to pay an indemnity of 50 francs to him, peace being concluded on this condition'. Again, in 1865, two women from Frasso were seriously injured in a general brawl by the elderly Giovan-Antono Mariani, to whom they were related. His four sons, who were all in the army, 'compensated the women financially', which led a jury to acquit him. All of this suggests that the payment of compensation was only possible either where a woman and not a man had been killed, though even here such a course was very rare, or in the case of fairly minor injuries, particularly among relatives and particularly again to women. A few other examples indicate that indemnities for injuries or offences might also be paid where there was a significant difference in status between the parties. At Zilia in 1848, Andrea Placidi, a shoemaker, accused Vincenzo Andreani of getting his sister pregnant. Andreani 'belonged to an important family' and the aim of the accusation appears to have been 'to obtain an indemnity'. Vincenzo indeed promised Placidi 1500 francs, it seems, but his brothers repudiated the promise, and Placidi then threatened to kill them. Again, at Pila-Canale in 1802, an offer of compensation was made following a seduction, which was in effect the provision of a dowry so that the woman could marry a man of her own station.[35]

Money might also be paid in other circumstances related to feuding. Courts sometimes awarded damages to the relatives and dependents of victims. So, for example, the widow of Giovanni Valle of Bastelica, who had five young children, was awarded 2500 francs in damages after her husband had been killed in a fight in 1863. Injured parties might also sue for damages themselves. Following the acquittal in 1850 of Giuseppo Filippi and others accused of killing her husband, the widow of Giovan-Battiste Ciavaldini of Venzolasca claimed damages of 25,000 francs against them, but her suit was unsuccessful. It is probably no coincidence that our examples here again involve women. Rewards were occasionally offered, too, by relatives for help or information that might lead to the discovery or arrest of wanted enemies. After Francesco-Matteo Giampietri of Gavignano killed the brother of Bartolomeo Mattei in 1832, the latter offered a reward of 100 crowns (*écus*) to anyone who could indicate the former's whereabouts. The practice of offering and paying rewards for information of this kind was widely used by the authorities in their fight against banditry, as we shall see in Chapter 12. The relative inefficacy of this policy, however, reflects the fact that it ran counter to Corsican mores. The appalling crimes of the Antona during the feuding at Frasseto led some of their relatives to help the gendarmerie to get rid of them, and they were apparently given rewards for so doing. Some of them, however, were later prosecuted, and the advocate-general reproached them with killing bandits for money.[36] Also relevant in this context is the firm opposition to attempts by French governments, from the time of Paoli onwards, to buy 'party' loyalty in Corsica.[37] We should note finally that money payments could be included among the provisions of peace treaties. A condition of the treaty negotiated at Marignana in 1848 was that Petro-Giovanni Massoni be provided with 1800 francs in 'expenses', if he went into exile as agreed. It seems that the money was raised among both parties, and that it was actually handed over to Massoni, since Marcaggi relates that the bandit returned the money later to indicate that he did not intend to abide by the terms of the treaty.[38]

However, despite this antipathy to financial or material composition, 'the fundamental idea behind the vendetta was one of compensation', an eye for an eye, a life for a life.[39] Blood vengeance and peaceful negotiation may be seen as two registers of interaction, the switch being made from one to the other only when a 'balance' had been achieved. Once serious hostilities had been engaged, there was considerable resistance to using the machinery for mediation and conciliation, and initial peace proposals might be rejected.[40] In time, however, feuding parties usually agreed to treat. Miot wrote in 1801 that

> when two parties are tired after a long period of feuding, or rather when the number of dead is equal on either side, a condition to which each of them attaches the greatest importance in order to be able to enter into negotiations without dishonour, they discuss a peace via the channel of some neutral persons. The conditions are thoroughly debated and a settlement is usually arrived at which takes account of the damage done on either side.[41]

The accuracy of this general account is confirmed by particular examples in our sources. The sense of being 'quits' might sometimes be fairly quickly achieved. Bastiano Giudicelli of Zonza, for example, was killed by Susino Maestrati in January 1848. The same afternoon Bastiano's nephew killed Maestrati's brother. Each family had one victim and one man liable to prosecution for homicide. 'They realized that they needed to reach an agreement,' and a peace treaty followed almost at once. The families then colluded in attesting 'that the two victims had killed each other'. This was an unsuccessful attempt to deceive the authorities and protect their own, but it was also the concisest summation of the notion that balance had indeed been arrived at.[42] This was more often a difficult stage to reach. As we have seen, hostilities usually involved a whole series of incidents and the calculation of equivalents was not easy. Conventions about how injuries compared with deaths, blows from one weapon with those from another, deaths of women with those of men, and so on, were only very rough, and notions of honour, which the escalation of violence brought to the fore, militated against such calculations.[43]

To sue for peace or to grant it prematurely was regarded as humiliating and suggested weakness or bad faith. After Father Giovan-Giacomo Lucchini of Ciamannacce and his brother were shot at in 1828, he announced his pardon of the offenders 'provided that the village should henceforward enjoy a sincere peace; but this pardon was not accepted'. Instead the culprits took to the maquis, threatened witnesses of the original attack, and forced the Lucchini to stay inside their houses. The 1848 peace at Marignana was only agreed to after relatives on both sides had been assured that they would not be subject to the *rimbeccu* or otherwise dishonoured. Another peace settlement in the same village two years later, moreover, was sabotaged when it was intimated to some of the signatories that they had acted in a weak or cowardly manner in accepting it.[44] In both these instances, too, there are strong indications that the peace had not been sincerely entered into by all parties in the first place, and other examples may be cited. In their accounts of their feud at Pila-Canale in the 1790s, both the Poli and the Bruni claimed to have fully pardoned their enemies and agreed to peace despite outstanding grievances, but the transient nature of the succession of peace treaties between them suggests that these were seen rather as a means of gaining temporary advantage and of trying to cast their enemies in a bad light with the French authorities. In a case in 1812, after Giovan-Felice Ferrandi of Penta-Acquatella was accused of killing Giuseppo Fusaja by the latter's relatives, his brother Matteo sued for peace on his behalf. This was apparently granted on condition that Giovan-Felice left Corsica, which he did. But Matteo Ferrandi clearly regarded this as an excessive penalty for what seems to have been an accidental killing. He was overheard to say that 'if his brother was going to have to stay in exile, it might as well be for a good reason', and, when a brother of Giuseppo Fusaja was killed shortly afterwards, Matteo was believed to be implicated. In a similar but more definite case, Petro-Felice and Domenico Andreani had killed a certain Casabianca from Lugo-di-Nazza in 1834. 'This death was not followed by an immediate vengeance, and an apparent reconciliation took place between the two families.' However, Casabianca's brother Gregorio had not really pardoned the offence, and he killed Petro-Felice's brother Michele in 1836.[45]

Offers of pardon might be more generally acceptable but only after a period of time in which an offender had, as it were, 'purged' his offence either in the maquis, in exile or in prison. In the course of a feud at Arro between the Santini and the Colonna, Santo Santini and his son had shot dead the young son of Antono Colonna in 1855, and they were later prosecuted and sentenced to hard labour for life. In 1876, however, Antono Colonna supported a petition for clemency on behalf of Santo Santini, 'according him a complete pardon and agreeing to his return to his native village'. Similarly, the descendants of his former victims and enemies made a formal declaration of amity towards Francesco Bastianesi of Ucciani in the 1870s — thirty years after his conviction — and asked for clemency on his behalf.[46]

One further instance illustrates another dimension of the process of peace settlement. Quite apart from any question of balancing offences, one side or another in a feud might have a greater interest in negotiating than another, for example if it lacked active male members or if it had more to lose through disruption. At Santa-Lucia-di-Tallano in 1834, it was the wealthier and more vulnerable Poli who wanted a peace treaty. The Giacomoni and the Santalucia were far less eager to settle and they acceded to the overtures of their old enemies with some reluctance.[47]

All of this helps to explain why peace negotiations nearly always involved third parties, who intervened independently or made it appear that they did. Natale Gasparini declared at Cauro in 1824 that 'a peace had several times been mooted by men of repute' between himself and his enemies, the Pasqualini and the Orazj, but they had always rejected such offers. At one stage during the feud between the Quastana and the Borelli at Albitreccia in 1835, each party barricaded itself in its house for several months. Then, 'alarmed by this situation, a number of honourable friends of the two families, including the bishop of Ajaccio ... undertook to restore peace between them'.[48] When Marignana became 'paralysed' by the feud between the Grimaldi and the Massoni in 1848, notables from the village and the surrounding area decided that things had become intolerable and intervened to negotiate a settlement.

We have already discussed the role of conciliators and arbiters, and much of what was said in that general context applies also to peacemakers proper. The role of peacemaker in feuding societies can be more or less formal and more or less permanent.[49] Corsica had peacemakers of both kinds until well into the nineteenth century. Seigneurs and then clan leaders acted as peacemakers from the medieval period onwards, and peacemaking magistrates were appointed in the seventeenth and eighteenth centuries. In the modern period there was a strong tendency for the publicly recognized peacemaker to be eclipsed or replaced by the courts, though for a time his role was to some extent assumed by French officials from the highest to the lowest level.[50]

Miot recalled that, during his period of government in Corsica which ended in October 1802, he had 'often been obliged to summon the heads of families divided by hereditary hatreds and to act as arbiter between them, bringing them through negotiations to a kind of treaty of peace'. The prefect made a similar boast in his report to the departmental council in 1827. Again, as late as 1865, the president of the Assize Court referred to 'energetic and intelligent intervention at the official level to prevent and bring to an end conflicts between families and parties'.[51]

Many specific examples of such intervention may be cited. Four peace treaties were signed in the canton of Ornano in 1800 under the auspices of the prefect. The settlement at Olmeto in 1809 between the Peretti and the Istria was achieved via the mediation of General Morand, then military governor of the island; while the treaty of 1812 at Ciamannacce was signed in the presence of Count Berthier, his successor. Again, a number of peace treaties were negotiated in 1816 and 1818 on the initiative of Count Willot, chief of the armed forces, and at least one of these was concluded in his presence. The prefect was involved in attempts to conciliate the feuding at Fozzano, and the treaties of Fozzano, Sartène and Serra of 1834–5 were sponsored by the military commander, Lieutenant-General Baron Lallemand, the first two being signed in his presence.[52] There was a trend, however, already evident at this time and more obvious from the 1840s, for the role of the military and the higher civilian authorities to diminish and for official peacemaking to be devolved to local officials and especially justices of the peace. Though the prefect was kept informed of attempts to arrange a peace at Santa-Lucia-di-Tallano in 1821, negotiations were left in the hands of the subprefect. When conflict at Arbellara was becoming serious in 1826, an ex-tax-collector and the mayor of Sartène intervened to bring about a peace, and the subprefect was merely kept informed.[53] The peace at Ciamannacce in 1830 was negotiated by the justice of the peace, aided by members of the clergy. Talks to settle feuding at Pietricaggio in 1848 took place in the house of the justice of the peace, with the local commanders of the gendarmerie and the *voltigeurs* present. Finally, in what may have been the last case of its kind in Corsica, the wife of the secretary-general of the prefecture was used as an intermediary in an abortive attempt in 1903 to settle a feud at Balogna.[54] Even in the early nineteenth century, moreover, official involvement in peacemaking was often reported in an apologetic manner and attention was drawn to the danger of thereby letting crimes go unpunished and thus undermining the judicial process. As the courts became more effective, the practice was therefore discouraged.

Unofficial peacemaking was always more important. Under this heading we may include that engaged in by the clergy, to which we drew attention in the last chapter and examples of which we have cited above. Where the bishop of Ajaccio was concerned, intervention had an official, a religious and an unofficial dimension. At Albitreccia, for example, the bishop was acting, at least in part, as the patron of Ignazio Borelli, who had attended the diocesan seminary. Local patrons and politicians acted more generally as 'private peacemakers'. We learn, for example, that a departmental councillor was instrumental in negotiating the peace at Casalabriva in 1835. A deputy and an ex-deputy were involved at San-Gavino in 1878–9.[55] Mutual relations also played an important role in peacemaking, but no special responsibility appears to have been assumed either by godparents or by affines and maternal kin, arrangements found elsewhere.[56] Peacemaking kin would in general be fairly remotely related to the protagonists and they often had additional qualifications of wealth, status or office. In the conflict in 1802, for example, between different branches of the Simoni family at Figari, Giovan-Battiste Nicolai, a doctor distantly related to both parties, was invited 'to try to make an arrangement', and at a later stage another relative, who was a priest at Levie, became involved in the negotiations.[57]

Very often, however, patrons or kin, however distant, would not be regarded as sufficiently disinterested, and Busquet stresses that those who acted most commonly and effectively as private peacemakers, and who were known as *paceri* or *parolanti*, were unconnected to those in conflict. They were persons of standing and honour in their communities, with large kindreds in order to enable them to assert their authority and effectively guarantee the reconciliations which they negotiated. Their actions thus had the neutrality which characterized the intervention of complete outsiders but they were backed up by power at the local level. They might intervene with or without invitation, but they would not do so without the agreement of their own kin, given the potentially serious consequences involved in guaranteeing peace treaties and punishing breaches of their clauses. Such peacemakers also acted in the less serious circumstances which we discussed in the previous section. Since *paceri* had as a rule to be unrelated to either party in a conflict, different conflicts called for different peacemakers, which explains the relative lack of success of full-time peacemakers at all but the highest level. Some individuals did, however, achieve reputations as *paceri*, based, it seems, on their special skill and personal authority. In a funeral oration for Paolo-Francesco Peraldi of Ajaccio, who died in 1827, it was said that 'people had recourse to him from all parts of the island, to clear up doubts, to arrange trials, to decide thorny questions', and to bring about reconciliations. We have suggested that peacemaking of all kinds was eventually eclipsed by the activities of formal judicial authorities, and Quantin wrote in 1914 that 'the old peacemakers' had disappeared.[58] But the transition from one mode of settlement to the other was not a simple and clear-cut process of substitution. There was a long period of overlap here, as there was between feuding and the use of the courts generally. Nor was one type of peacemaker more or less 'advanced' than another. Outsiders, religious, official or otherwise, would have to be used, for example, when local conflict became so serious that all families of consequence were involved in it.

III

If the negotiations conducted by the peacemakers were successful, peace was formally concluded via a legal instrument or treaty, drawn up before a notary, a procedure common in many parts of Europe in earlier centuries.[59] The treaty was signed by representatives of the families concerned and by witnesses and guarantors who were local notables and often public officials. The signing usually took place in solemn fashion, and reconciliation between the parties was expressed by public embracing and often by attendance at a common religious service. At Ciamannacce in 1830, we learn that this was followed by a banquet, at which the erstwhile enemies ate and drank together.[60]

Miot claimed in 1801 that several thousand such peace treaties existed. Far fewer are extant for the subsequent period, at least in the public records, though it is clear that the practice of making them continued into the twentieth century. Reference has been traced to 66 treaties for the period from 1790 to around 1935, but the actual texts of only 19 have been found. One can be sure that these represent only a fraction of the treaties actually made – and more could probably be discovered in notarial records – but there is no reason to believe that the sample is unrepresentative. Of the 66, the bulk date from the years before 1835, and only 7 are from after 1860. This would seem to be a fair reflection of the true chronological importance of the treaty and of the decline of the practice and its retreat into semi-clandestinity after the middle of the nineteenth century, when official approval was removed. Further details are supplied in Appendix 3.

Two examples may be presented as a prelude to a more general analysis. A treaty was concluded in May 1801 between the Follacci and the Rossi of Ocana and Eccica-Suarella to end what was called 'a capital enmity' between them. It was signed on one side by Giovan-Santo Follacci and two of his sons, Girolamo and Carlo, and on the other by the brothers Antono, Giovan-Battiste and Romano Rossi and by Giovan-Battiste's son Innocenzo. The Follacci also signed on behalf of a third son, Lorenzo, and a relative to the third degree, Santo Muselli, and both sides engaged their relatives in a general way. In an opening religious clause, both parties 'recognized their obligations as Christians towards Jesus Christ ... who had recommended peace and love for one's enemies in his gospels', and both swore to the peace on the Bible. The material clauses referred to 'a true, sincere and perpetual peace', agreed that both sides should renounce prosecutions for any past offences and should petition the authorities to follow suit, and laid down that Girolamo and Lorenzo Follacci should leave Corsica, not returning 'until permission was given to them to do so by the Rossi brothers'. The peace was guaranteed by three men from Cuttoli-Corticchiato, a neighbouring village, 'under the pledge of both their persons and their present and future possessions', and it was made under 'the auspices, protection and advice' of the prefect and of General Casalta, the military commander of the island, and was witnessed in the prefecture.[61]

Another treaty was signed in the church at Sartène in December 1834 between the two factions at Fozzano. The signatories were, on the one side, Michele and Giovan-Battiste Durazzi (also representing their sons), and Battiste-Michelangelo and Paolo Paoli, and, on the other, six male members of the Carabelli family, Antono Bernardini, Giuseppo Paoli and Agostino and Giovan-Battiste Bartoli. The instrument referred to the role of Lieutenant-General Baron Lallemand in bringing about the peace. Both sides promised 'to cease waging war and to live from now on as good kinsmen, friends and compatriots'. Legal proceedings were to go ahead, and those against whom warrants for arrest had been issued were to surrender within two months and be tried. 'No action was to be taken either to aggravate their situation or to shelter them from the proper legal process'. No exile was imposed explicitly on any particular person, but, 'should Petro-Paolo Bernardini or Francesco Paoli be acquitted by the courts', the authorities were to take what steps they considered necessary against them. More generally, the inhabitants of Fozzano 'and all others implicated in the enmity' agreed to forswear the carrying of arms, and the lieutenant-general was given authority to take what other measures he saw fit to ensure peace in the village. The treaty was made under the auspices of the lieutenant-general, the subprefect and other military and civil officials; it was also guaranteed by various notables from outside Fozzano. In addition, the peace was said 'to repose upon the honour, the good faith and the word of all the inhabitants' of the village, and a final clause invited 'friends, protectors and supporters' of the parties 'to lend their aid and assistance in order to ensure the execution' of the treaty, 'and, in case of an infraction of it, to break off all relations with the offenders and their partisans and to abandon them all to ignominy'.[62]

These examples are fairly typical in most respects. A religious invocation was usually present in treaties and was generally more important than in the Fozzano case. This element was particularly stressed, as one would expect, in treaties signed under the auspices of the clergy. A treaty was agreed, for example at Sari-d'Orcino in 1842, following mediation by the Oblates of Mary and the bishop of Ajaccio. It opened with religious clauses invoking the Trinity, the Blessed Virgin Mary, Saint Martin (patron of Sari) and other saints, and, in later paragraphs, placed emphasis on the notion that peace was essential to salvation. Peace, moreover, had been 'brought by Christ into the world' and was 'the finest gift of heaven'. Christ had preached that it was our duty 'to pardon injuries and to love our enemies' and, 'to lend more force to these divine precepts, He had sanctioned them by His example, pardoning from the Cross those who had placed Him there'.[63]

Treaties were also placed under a religious aegis by having them signed in churches, and this was usually done with more ceremony than the 1834 Fozzano example indicates. The Sartène treaty of 1834 between the 'Santa Anna' and the 'Borgo' factions was signed in the parish church; then, after a speech from the lieutenant-general, and 'in order to render the contract even more solemn and sacred, a *Te Deum* of thanks was sung'. Similarly the treaty at Serra in 1835 was signed in the presbytery, 'following which everyone went to the parish church, where a *Te Deum* of thanks was sung after mass had been said'. At San-Gavino in 1883, specific mention was made of the exchange of a kiss of peace between the parties. In some cases, the signing took place at or on the altar, as at Sari-d'Orcino in 1842 and Carbini in 1904. The Marignana peace of 1851 was signed at the altar of the convent of Vico, which was presumably regarded as a particularly holy place. Though signing or the swearing of oaths in church was not universal – the Pila-Canale treaty of 1816, for example, was signed outside the church – it is clear that an appeal to supernatural sanctions as well as the public expression of reconciliation were most important.[64] One may note, too, the absence in Corsica of the shaming rituals found in some other feuding societies.[65]

Other considerations mentioned in the preambles to treaties were regard for public order and especially the local disruption caused by long periods of feuding, as we noted in Chapter 8.[66]

The number of those signing peace treaties could vary considerably. It was usual, it seems, for a small number of leaders of families to sign, representing and engaging their kin and clientèle. The Sartène peace of 1834 refers to 'party leaders acting each one for his people', and at Pila-Canale in 1816 eleven principals signed for themselves and on behalf of 'their relatives and allies'. In some cases, however, larger numbers of principals signed or gave their assent to treaties. The San-Gavino treaty of 1879 was signed by 29 Nicolai, 22 Peretti, 24 Pietri and 7 Agostini. An earlier undated treaty at Pila-Canale listed the names of 38 participants, who did not sign the peace only because they were illiterate, while a peace at Ocana in 1801 included relatives 'to the third degree on both sides'. At the insistence of the prefect, the peace of 1847 at Frasseto was signed 'by all the inhabitants', and other documents refer to 'a general peace', for example at Bastelica in 1846, which presumably involved all or most families of the village. These cases probably reflect the individualistic assumptions of the French bureaucrats sponsoring the treaties and their desire to make them effective rather than any departure from patriarchal notions on the part of the contracting parties. Whatever the means, direct or indirect, there is no doubt that treaties were binding on whole families or kindreds. Signatories were nearly always men, and only one exception to this rule has been found – at Serra in 1835, where the widow of 'Giulio V.' signed, together with five men of her 'party'. We have seen that Colomba Bartoli was not a party to the Fozzano treaty of 1834.[67] Though the sanction of the whole community might be invoked in support of a treaty, as we have noted, numbers of witnesses and guarantors were usually small, since they were notables and/or officials. But again, in the case of the former, kin would have been consulted and might be indirectly engaged.

The material provisions of treaties were limited and were outlined as a rule in under ten articles or clauses. The first of these generally laid down that the two sides should cease all acts of hostility and should pardon each other for past offences. The first article of the Sartène treaty of 1834, for example, called on both parties 'to forgive and forget everything connected with the dreadful events of the past', and stipulated that 'the external signs of war and enmity should disappear immediately'. Very similar clauses are found in other treaties. According to the Piana treaty of 1848, 'fraternal peace is granted to every person, whatever his degree of kinship, who is or who could be involved in the enmity ... between the Moreschi and the Versini'; and the Sari-d'Orcino treaty of 1842 was even more fulsome. In its first article, 'the undersigned swear and have sworn spontaneously to forget for ever their mutual injuries, and to grant each other an absolute and irrevocable pardon for all the wrongs known and unknown with which they might have reproached each other, promising from this time on to love each other and to treat each other like brothers, obliging and helping each other whenever they can'.[68] More specifically, a few treaties stipulated that the parties concerned and sometimes all the inhabitants of the village should no longer carry arms in future. Clauses to this effect appear in the Fozzano and Sartène treaties of 1834 and in the Serra treaty of 1835. Only very rarely was any reference made to material reparations or the settlement of conflict over resources. The Frasseto treaty of 1847 laid down that two earlier court judgments on the distribution of private and common land in the village should be accepted and enforced, which in effect asked the parties to surrender the land which they had usurped over a period of decades.

The pardons pronounced in treaties gave immunity to those who had committed offences, as far as their enemies were concerned. Having carried out a vengeance killing in 1840, for example, Santo Minichetti of Tavera had taken to the maquis in order to escape reprisals from his victim's relatives. Once a treaty had been signed between the two sides, the latter called off their hunt for Minichetti, though he remained in hiding to avoid being arrested by the authorities. In another unusual case at Cuttoli, a peace treaty between the Crudeli and the Torre was signed around 1830, but Pasquale Crudeli, whose killing of Simone Torre had occasioned the enmity, did not accept it. He was therefore excluded from the general promise of immunity made to the Crudeli, but it was agreed that he should not be attacked by more than three of Torre's relatives at once.[69]

Some treaties went further to promise that no prosecutions would follow for those who had committed offences against the law. Miot noted in 1801 that 'prosecution in the courts was forbidden' in many treaties, and that the authorities had often to accept this condition, because no accusations or testimony would then be forthcoming. Later examples confirm this. In the conflict at Casalta between the Parsj and the Cappellini on the one side, and the Casalta and their allies on the other, the former only brought proceedings against the latter when they broke a treaty of peace, and court action was suspended in 1812 for a time after a further treaty had been negotiated. The treaty between the Scaglia and the Bucchini, and the Vincentelli and others of Zicavo in 1816 explicitly stipulated that 'all prosecutions in the courts should cease'. The treaty between the Tenneroni and the Emilj at Santa-Maria-Sicche in the mid-1840s was intended 'to prevent the prosecution that had been opened against Natale Tenneroni'; while, according to the terms of the treaty of 1854 at Arbellara, the Giustiniani undertook not to prosecute the Forcioli bandits.[70]

However, as Miot's remarks indicate, the authorities were never happy about such provisions and rarely, if at all, did they grant such immunity formally themselves. In 1801, an official specifically denied that the four treaties just negotiated in the canton of Orcino gave any guarantee against prosecution to the parties concerned, and many treaties, like that at Sari-d'Orcino in 1842, preclude prosecution by the parties but not by the authorities. Most treaties, indeed, refer to some kind of court action as inevitable but seek to mitigate its consequences. So, at Ciamannacce in 1812, both parties agreed to abstain from all acts of violence, insults or threats 'during the whole time of [a forthcoming] ... trial'. At Pila-Canale in 1816, the parties agreed to appear in court should that be neces- sary. An article in the Fozzano treaty of 1834 stated that 'justice will be allowed to take its course'; those for whom arrest warrants had been issued were to give themselves up, as we have seen, and nothing was to be done by either side to affect the outcome of the trials. Almost identical clauses appear in the Sartène treaty of 1834 and the Serra treaty of 1835. In a later treaty at Pila-Canale, in 1872, the Quilichini agreed that if a certain member of the Poli family were arrested, they would 'only testify to the simple truth' in the case and would not try to aggravate his position. The San-Gavino treaty of 1879 allowed the parties more leeway to use the legal process, each to its own advantage, 'but only by employ- ing honest and fair means', and each agreed to respect the ultimate decisions of the courts.[71]

At the same time, some treaties referred, more or less explicitly, to deals or interference in the judicial process. There was an assumption in the Sartène and Serra treaties that those to be put on trial would be acquitted and mention was made of measures that would have to be taken by the authorities in that event. The treaty at Olmeta-di-Tuda in 1818 followed the condemnation to death of Bernardo Campocasso and in it 'the Casale brothers ... wholly satisfied with this vengeance of the law, which they owed to the spirit of their father', called for a commutation of the sentence. Giusepp'-Antono Franceschi was arrested in 1847 just after the signing of the peace at Frasseto and apparently as he was about to give himself up. His father then told the mayor that 'it would be very advantage- ous to the maintenance of the peace if this individual were to be acquitted' at his trial. More openly, a clause in the Piana treaty of 1848 stated that if one or both of the bandits concerned should be caught by the authorities, 'their relatives and guarantors obliged themselves to give them all the aid and assistance in their power in order to obtain either an acquittal or a lenient sentence'. In the event, such arrangements were often successful. After many years of feuding at Bastel- ica, 'animosities lost their intensity', and a treaty of peace was concluded (in the mid-1840s) between the Scapola and the Gasparini. The bandit Giovan-Battiste Scapola then gave himself up for trial on a charge relating to a vengeance killing committed in 1836 and was acquitted. In a similar case at Aullène, Pompeo Chiaroni remained in hiding for eight years after a revenge killing and only gave himself up in 1851 when 'a peace treaty had been concluded between his family and that of his victims'. He was again tried and acquitted, an outcome which only the authorities appear to have regretted. By contrast, when Carlo Giacomoni of Petreto-Bicchisano was sentenced to ten years' hard labour in 1912 in similar circumstances, this was felt to be excessive not least by his erstwhile enemies, who had testified in court on his behalf.[72]

Clauses about legal proceedings were often related to ones about banish- ment,[73] and the exile of those who had committed homicide was frequently the most important specific provision agreed to in treaties. In a case brought in 1801 against the Luciani brothers of Giovicacce for killing Petro-Paolo Biaggi of Guitera, reference was made to a treaty of peace agreed between the parties. One of the stipulations of this was that the Luciani, together with a cousin, should leave Corsica 'in order to give satisfaction to the relatives of the dead man', not returning until invited to do so by his brothers. Treaties at Ocana and Zicavo in the same year contained similar provisions, and it was reported in the latter case that passports had been requested, 'so that the Leandri may go into exile'. Count Willot indicated to the Minister of War in 1817 that a treaty negotiated under his auspices at Peri was 'all the more secure in that the guilty party has agreed to expatriate himself'.[74] An article of the Piana treaty of 1848 laid down that two men, one from each party, should leave Corsica by the end of September and their relatives undertook 'to make them do so'. Again, by the terms of the treaty of Pila-Canale in 1872, the bandit Poli was to go into exile and his relatives promised to give him up to the authorities if he returned.

The report on the Zicavo case, referred to above, put forward the view that, although such 'arrangements were quite common, they should not directly involve public officials', but it is obvious that the authorities did often favour exile as an alternative to prosecution and that they helped actively to arrange it in a number of cases. The Serra treaty of 1835 clearly stated that should Vincenzo C. be acquitted, the lieutenant-general would then be asked 'to take the appropriate measures required for the preservation of the peace, even sending him into exile if necessary'. Again, by the terms of a treaty made at Novella in 1844 via the offices of the bishop of Ajaccio, Giusepp'-Antono Orabona and his relatives 'agreed that, if he were acquitted [in a forthcoming trial], he would leave Corsica for as long as the bishop thought fit'. These cases involved banishment from the island, but in at least one further example, a treaty at Grossa in the 1930s, only banishment from the village was required, and this may have been a more common feature of settlements than the extant texts of treaties suggest.[75]

Both Busquet and Marin-Muracciole have stressed the importance of matrimonial clauses in Corsican peace treaties before the nineteenth century.[76] This derived from the principle that there could be 'no real friendship without a tie of blood', and the giving of a bride in such circumstances does not seem to have been regarded as a form of compensation as it was in some other feuding societies.[77] Families without parties of marriageable age affianced children, and peacemakers were often known as *maritanti* or marryers. Modern peace treaties do not contain matrimonial clauses, but this does not necessarily mean that marriages were not still being used in reconciliations. Miot assumed in 1801 that a marriage would frequently be part of a peace settlement. Benson relates that a marriage was planned between the Viterbi and the Frediani of Penta-di-Casinca around 1790; while Achille Campocasso of Olmeta-di-Tuda explained in 1817 that his aunt had been married to a member of the rival Casale family, in the hope 'that their inveterate hatred might be extinguished by a marriage'. Again, the subprefect of Sartène commented in 1821 à propos the feud between the Poli and the Giacomoni of Santa-Lucia-di-Tallano: 'Marriages have always been a great resource in pacifying Corsicans in a state of enmity, but unfortunately we have none to propose in this affair.' The 1834 peace at Santa-Lucia made no reference to any marriage, but we have seen that the Giacomoni and the Santalucia believed that it should have done. Later in the century, a reconciliation between the Filippi and the Sanguinetti of Venzolasca was sealed by a marriage between them, according to Marcaggi.[78]

It has been argued that in some societies marriage and feuding are much more positively connected, a situation summed up in the adage: 'We marry our enemies.' Marriage and feud 'are two different forms of communicative behaviour which achieve very similar results', Black-Michaud argues. 'The ambiguities inherent in marital alliances often cause feuds, just as feuds are also frequently the "cause" of marriages contracted to "conclude" hostilities.'[79] We have seen that there was an aggressive, even a violent, aspect of marriage-making in Corsica; mock combats formed a part of marriage ritual and these were very significantly brought to an end by *paceri*.[80] These connections perceived by theorists, however, were at the most implicit or vestigial in reality, something belonging perhaps to an earlier period when agnatic ties and clan structure had been much stronger. We may note also the absence in Corsican peace treaties of 'the creation of fictitious kin bonds' as a means of 'quieting ... old animosities'.[81]

We turn now to the question of how binding and effective peace settlements were. Miot asserted in 1801 that treaties had in the past been sacrosanct. Robiquet wrote in 1835 that they were 'religiously observed' still, and similar observations were made later in the century. That these views were over-sanguine is indicated by the fact that the draft penal code of 1755, like the earlier Genoese statutes, included special provisions against those who broke peace agreements,[82] and that modern treaties contained explicit sanctions of the same kind.

An identical article in the Sartène treaty of 1834 and in the Serra treaty of 1835 'invited all persons in the district, who loved peace and honour, to lend their aid and assistance to ensure the loyal execution of the treaty, particularly by considering those who might break it as perjurors and by abandoning them to universal execration'. More generally, all treaties were signed by guarantors. These usually included those who had negotiated the peace, and their reputation was bound up with adherence to it. Quantin noted in 1914 that *paceri* in the past had 'had the right to punish oath-breakers by destroying their property and burning their houses'.[83] There is no evidence that this happened in the modern period, but most treaties did include financial penalty clauses. A treaty signed in the canton of Orcino in 1799 required any party breaking the peace to pay 3000 francs, and most of the treaties sponsored by Count Willot in 1816 had similar clauses. In the Zicavo treaty, the parties agreed to pay 2000 francs to the government should the peace be broken, and they also agreed to forfeit their property into the hands of the party which did keep the peace. The treaty between the Leonzi and the Lovinchi, signed at Santa-Maria-Sicche, stipulated a penalty fine of 3000 francs, to be paid by the guarantors. In the Pila-Canale treaty, the penalty fine rose to 4000 francs, but only 1000 francs were to be paid if the offending party were arrested. Of this, 400 francs were to go to the poor of the parish and the rest to the other party. The Peri treaty was reinforced by 'a sum of 6000 francs offered as a guarantee by the two guarantors on each side'.[84] It will be seen that a variety of arrangements existed, some involving the financial responsibility of the parties themselves, some that of their guarantors; penalty fines and forfeits, moreover, might go to the injured party or to the State. Treaties were also secured, as we have seen, by supernatural sanctions and by the fact that they were often negotiated and sponsored by important officials and notables.

Treaties were nevertheless very frequently broken soon after being signed. The 1792 peace at Pila-Canale was allegedly broken within a month and the 1816 treaty did not hold much longer. A peace made at Sari-d'Orcino early in 1799 was soon broken. The prefect forced the parties to agree to a new treaty a year later, but this too lasted barely a month. The peace made at Olmeto in February 1809 was broken in March. The treaty made at Ciamannacce in July 1812 was violated the following year. A peace at Canale in 1817 again survived less than a year.[85] The list could be extended. Treaties seem to have been broken in four main circumstances. First, they were vulnerable when not all parties to the feud were included in the treaty. At Cuttoli, Pasquale Crudeli killed a certain Valentini in 1831, despite the fact that his family had agreed to a peace, and he explained that not only was he not a party to the peace but he had not even been consulted about it. Secondly, a treaty's terms, explicit or implicit, might not be kept. We have seen that the 1834 peace at Santa-Lucia-di-Tallano was broken in 1839 because one side rejected the marriage arrangements wanted or expected by the other. Thirdly, a peace or peace negotiations could be entered into with duplicity, as a ploy in a feuding situation. A treaty made at Olmo between the Poggi and the Agostini was broken in 1839 by Santo Poggi, who had never been sincere in accepting it and in pardoning a rival suitor; and we have earlier cited other examples. Fourthly, a peace might be broken as the result of a misunderstanding or an accident. The Buteri and the Moretti of Lumio 'were celebrating the peace, which they had just agreed to, in a wineshop', when quarrelling broke out between the drinkers and the keeper of the shop. Those outside, however, thought that the two families had resumed their enmity, and a shot was fired into the shop, killing a youth.[86]

We should not leave the impression that treaties were ephemeral. Our evidence suggests rather that treaties were more often adhered to than not, though it might take more than one treaty to ensure a definitive pacification, as at Pila-Canale. As we have emphasized, too, feuds were inherently long-term affairs and comprised alternating phases of hostility and peace, the latter often uneasy. It was reported, for example, in the mid-1850s that 'a solemn peace treaty, sworn in the presence and under the auspices of a general of the Restoration [at Gavignano] ... has been maintained ever since without apparent infraction, but there always exists a secret antagonism, which is ready to show itself at the first opportunity'.[87] From one perspective, this suggests that peace settlements were only interludes in a situation of endemic conflict, but they may equally be seen as means of mitigating conflict and keeping it normally below the level of violence; and many settlements were genuine and lasting. To add to our conclusions in the previous chapter, the process of mediation and pacification was an essential complement to that of conflict and feuding, preventing it from becoming socially disruptive. The efficacy of traditional modes of settlement was weakened, however, in the modern period as that of the courts strengthened. It can be no coincidence here that peace treaties become so rare after about 1850. However, the relationship between settlement, feuding and the courts was far from simple, as the next chapter shows.

] 10 [

Feuding and the courts

Conflict was endemic in Corsican society, and there were many ways of attacking one's enemies and achieving vengeance, short of actual violence or killing. Both behaviour in or vis-à-vis the courts and political action could thus be modes of feuding in the broad sense. Before discussing these in detail, a broader account of these other forms is appropriate.

In some areas and more generally among the educated élite later in the nineteenth century, non-violent means of taking revenge predominated. Montherot commented in 1840 that 'vengeance killings have become very rare in Corte, but enmities continue. A local man told me: "We would like to harm one another, but in practice we no longer do so."' The *Gazette des Tribunaux* noted in 1833 that, in the Balagna, there were 'no murders as a rule, no bloody brawls, but many actions at law; acts of ruse and chicanery abound, and petty wars are fought not to destroy one's neighbour but simply to ruin him and enrich oneself at his expense. The inhabitants of this region use their pens instead of their daggers and conduct their vendettas with pieces of paper.' Elsewhere, and particularly in the south, non-violent and violent or violent and less violent means might be used together. While acknowledging, for example, that 'the spirit of vendetta' inspired many homicides in the Sartène region, Patin de La Fizelière observed at the end of the eighteenth century that 'it usually degenerates into trickery of all kinds', which included using the judicial machinery and making denunciations. Again, in the words of their ex-mayor in 1879, the inhabitants of Loreto-di-Tallano 'tore each other apart via court actions, perjuries, homicides, etc. etc.'[1]

There is no doubt that the destruction of property of different kinds could be a mode of feuding. The subprefect of Ajaccio reported in 1827 that 'the vendetta at Tavera has been carried on until now only against property, but it appears that it will be extended to persons'.[2] We encountered this pattern in other feuds described in Chapter 2. Attacks on property could also be part of and not simply the preliminary to all-out war between enemies. As Giovan-Battiste Luccioni of Tox asked Marsilio Nicolai in court in 1834: 'Have you and your brothers not ravaged our fields, cut down our olive trees, destroyed our livestock, besieged our houses and ruined our families? Have you not killed my brother, my brother-in-law, two of my nephews and my son?'[3]

Arson was a particularly common form of this destruction of property.[4] A school inspector in 1821 referred to fires as a 'type of vendetta' and, in reporting forest fires, officials usually attributed them either to the traditional 'slash and burn' practices which we discussed in Chapter 3 or to ill-will and enmities. For example, a fire in July 1828, a month of exceptional drought, spread from the forest of Tolla to those of Pancheraccia and Casevecchie and threatened the property of Filipp'-Antono Poggioli. Francesco Stefani, a herdsman from Serraggio, was held responsible for starting the fire 'either to procure winter pasture thereby or to avenge himself on Poggioli'. Climatic conditions alone were rarely regarded as a sufficient explanation for such disasters.[5]

In addition to firing forest and scrub, enemies might burn fields and crops and even houses, and many examples could be cited in all these categories. In 1830, Domenico Casanova, a herdsman from Lugo-di-Nazza, was prosecuted for having burnt 'a cabin in the fields on the territory of Tallano', belonging to Giovan-Paolo Puggeri, and was said to have 'acted from a spirit of vengeance'.[6] In 1848, Giuseppo Giuliani of Pietracorbara was accused of a similar act, perpetrated to take revenge against a man whose 'son married the young lady whose hand he himself coveted'. More information is preserved about a case at Pieve. In December 1859, a pile of firewood belonging to Antonietta Sebastiani was burned and

> she at once imputed the crime to Maria Cesari. Hostility already existed between the two families, the Cesari having furnished information to the authorities which led to the arrest of the Sebastiani's son ... Indignation at this behaviour had been general in the village and a charivari had been mounted against the Cesari couple. This had exasperated Maria Cesari, whose character was notoriously vindictive.

However, no official complaint was lodged after this first fire and no proceedings were taken. Then, in July 1860, a second fire occurred at Pieve. This time a small house, used to store forage and belonging to Stefano Casabianca, was destroyed with its contents. The Casabianca were political opponents of a former mayor of the village, Galeazzini, 'in whose house Maria Cesari had been brought up and had worked as a servant'. She was illegitimate and possibly the natural daughter of Galeazzini. 'Naturally', the trial summary explained, 'this woman must have shared the animosity felt by the Galeazzini party against that of the Casabianca. The slightest pretext led to violent arguments between them, the exchange of insults and even, on the part of the Cesari, the uttering of threats.' A few days before the fire, a game being played by the Cesari children led to an altercation, in which Cesari referred explicitly to arson; and, a little later, 'while the forage, which was afterwards burnt, was being placed in the house [which was next door to that of the Cesari], a small amount of hay fell near the door of the latter, and Cesari remarked that it would all be going up in smoke before long.'[7]

Among other attacks on buildings, we may cite the burning of a mill belonging to Anton-Francesco Paoli of Fozzano in 1800, an act attributed by witnesses to the ill-will of the Giacomoni.[8] Again, in the course of the feud at

Carcheto, Francesco-Maria Castelli and others were 'unable to kill Stefano Castelli and his brother so they burned down his house instead' in 1911.[9] Attacks on family houses were important symbolically as well as materially of course, and the burning of houses could be a form of homicide. In a dispute between herdsmen from the Niolo and people from Speloncato in 1799, threats were made to burn down a house with ten people inside.[10] At Loreto-di-Tallano, the house of Don Giacomo Susini was set on fire in 1847 by his enemies; his baby grand-daughter was burned to death and other relatives were shot as they tried to escape; and a similar incident occurred during feuding at Peri in the 1860s.[11] Citing an official report of 1961 which claimed that 60 per cent of fires in Corsica were the result of arson and a further 30 per cent of presumed arson, Wagner has concluded that 'incendiarism is the cringing descendant of the vendetta'.[12] It is probably true that arson has become more important as a mode of vengeance, to some extent replacing killing, but our evidence indicates that it was already significant in the nineteenth century.

The vindictive meaning of many attacks on property in Corsica is indicated in two further ways. In the ancient Statutes of the Genoese period as well as in the penal code of the Paoli era, devastation of trees, land and houses figures as a special penalty for crimes committed out of vengeance. Moreover, cases are reported of people destroying their own property in order to try to cast the blame on to others. At Oletta, it was said in 1846, for example, that 'some people went so far as to destroy walls and commit other acts of destruction on their own property, in order to impute such acts to their enemies'.[13]

Another very common mode of vengeance was denunciation. Delation to the authorities was not infrequent in the early years of resistance to French rule and was attributed to 'enmities'. Patin de La Fizelière wrote around 1780 that people in the Sartène region 'employed every means possible to make the courts and officials serve their desire for vengeance through denunciations of the most lurid kind'. Beaumont, who was subprefect at Calvi, noted in 1822 that 'informing and denunciation with the aim of harming one's enemies legally' were on the increase and characterized the practice as 'the vendetta accommodated to modern manners'. Such views were echoed by observers writing at the end of the nineteenth century and the beginning of this.[14] A number of examples may be cited from the judicial records, spanning much the same period of time. In 1806, for instance, Anton-Maria Santucci of Loreto-di-Casinca wrote to the Minister of Justice, denouncing a certain Casabianca as the killer of a young priest.[15] We learn from a case in 1856 that Maria-Clorinda Comiti and Caterina Giavri of Sant' Andrea-di-Tallano were enemies. As a result of a charge brought by the former, the latter had been convicted of 'making verbal insults', and, in retaliation, Giavri reported her opponent's illegitimate pregnancy to the *adjoint*, which in turn led to the prosecution of Comiti and her lover (the son of the mayor) for procuring an abortion.[16] Again, a petition for clemency on behalf of a man from Pietricaggio in 1879 claimed that proceedings had been taken against him (for carrying a prohibited weapon), 'following a denunciation signed by an enemy'.[17] As this and other cases indicate, denunciation was not necessarily wholly secret, though informers did often maintain or attempt to maintain their anonymity. Information about infanticides, for example, was very often furnished to the authorities anonymously.[18] Denunciation was often a weapon used by the weaker party in a feud, as at Carcheto in 1911–12.[19]

A particular variety of denunciation was the reporting of 'inferior functionaries ... to their superiors' for real or imaginary misdemeanours. Rocco Quilichini of Olmiccia, for example, was convicted in 1843 of complicity in the 'libellous denunciation' of Anton-Goffredo Ortoli, the local tax-collector.[20] Prosecution in such cases was rare, but this reflects the difficulty of investigating them impartially and not their infrequency. Reporting on accusations which he had been asked to look into, the subprefect of Corte wrote in 1851 that 'the facts alleged against the mayors [of Frasso and Piedipartino] are either false or extremely exaggerated and ... the denunciations only stem from private animosities which are unfortunately only too common in our villages'. Attacks of this kind on mayors were endemic and we will return to them in the next chapter. Some indication may, nevertheless, be given here of how they were used in situations of conflict or feud. Serafino Quilichini and two other men from Cozzano complained to the prefect in 1843 about the conduct of the mayor. He learned of this, went to see Quilichini and asked 'whether he had not made a denunciation against him', threatening Quilichini with 'revenge' unless he withdrew it. The mayor also put pressure on the other two by promising to get prosecutions against them for forest offences dropped. A few years later the mayor himself denounced the local road inspector to the prefect. His charges were reported to be without foundation by the village gendarme, who at the same time expressed the fear that he, too, might be the object of a denunciation by the mayor, should his views become known.[21] It is significant here that malicious denunciations of mayors are found in villages which experienced serious feuding, for example Olmeto, Ota, Penta-di-Casinca and Venzolasca.[22] We have seen, too, how common was the denunciation of priests. A case in 1851 shows how this might lead to violence, especially where anonymity was not employed or protected. Giovanni Mattei of San-Gavino was believed 'to have brought about the transfer of the parish priest, Pietri, through his incessant denunciations', and this prompted the priest's nephew and another relative to kill him.[23]

Other modes of vengeance included aiding the authorities against one's enemies,[24] mounting charivaris and composing satires.[25] In conclusion, we may note that, though escalation may be detected in any particular conflict, all modes of vengeance could be used at any stage in a feud. There is little or no evidence, moreover, of the phenomenon of secret enmity found in other societies, which may be either deflected in fictions[26] or channelled into 'magical vengeance' or witchcraft.[27] There was a religious or supernatural dimension to the pursuit of vengeance in Corsica, as we shall see in Chapter 13, but, however motivated, vengeance had to be taken openly, even demonstratively, in order to achieve its effect, which was to advance the interests or redeem the honour of a family.

II

Blood vengeance is rightly seen as a system of sanctions and social control that is logically distinct and in general terms historically anterior to a formal court system. Each operated on different principles and the one came to replace the other, as the bureaucratic power of the State developed.[28] However, in practice, systems of blood vengeance and court systems could and did coexist and interconnect over long periods of time.[29] A number of writers have drawn attention to the way in which the courts and police procedure might be used as a means of attacking and harassing one's enemies, and this may be seen, to a degree, as an extension of the more traditional situation, in which disputes might be articulated via oratorical competitions, compurgation, or displays of the strength of kindred and/or clientèle in front of general assemblies.[30] We have already seen that in Corsica the courts had by the nineteenth century become part of the arena in which feuding took place and for a significant period of time the two systems ran together. While French officials sought to implant a system of impartial justice based on the collection and assessment of evidence and the application of general rules, Corsicans succeeded in adapting the formal framework of that system to the requirements of family and clan rivalries. For some time an uneasy compromise was reached, the judicial authorities being guided like other officials by a concern to make peace and using the courts therefore to try to reconcile parties rather than to administer the French law strictly.[31] Eventually, however, the growing importance and effectiveness of the courts led to the eclipse of their rival as an autonomous system. But this happened in two stages. First, the traditional restraints upon conflict and feuding tended to be undermined or removed, and as a result violence, feuding and banditry increased. Only later did the courts secure that monopoly of settling disputes, which they enjoyed in other French departments.[32]

It was commonplace throughout the nineteenth century to attribute the existence and then the persistence of feuding in Corsica to the absence and then the corruption of official justice.[33] According to this view, the origin of the vendetta lay in centuries of Genoese misrule. 'Vengeance was a necessity in Corsica under the abominable Genoese government,' wrote Mérimée, 'for the poor could not obtain justice for the wrongs done against them.' 'One could understand why the vendetta still exists,' echoed Father Bartoli half a century later, 'if justice were still venal as it was in the time of the Genoese.'[34] As Busquet pointed out, this orthodoxy was historically inaccurate, since feuding occurred well before the Genoese took over the administration of the island,[35] but it does express a structural truth, of which many officials and a few independent observers were more aware than Father Bartoli. As we have suggested, in a general sense the feud was an alternative system of justice to that provided by the courts,[36] and its persistence was related to the continuing venality and/or ineffectiveness of the latter. 'In studying the customs of Corsica,' General Berthier concluded in 1812, 'it has been easy to see that the spirit of the vendetta which characterizes them arises from the fact that injuries remain unpunished' by the law; and he commented on two cases in 1813 where the courts had either acquitted the accused or handed down light sentences: 'These examples ... are too frequent; they embolden the guilty who, because they have connections with a family which has some influence, believe that they can act with impunity. Private acts of vengeance proliferate because people who suffer some injury have no trust in the magistrates and take the law into their own hands.' Count Willot wrote in 1816 similarly that the large number of crimes of violence committed in Corsica was directly related to 'the delays in the administration of justice, which encouraged people to revive their old custom of doing justice for themselves, as they put it'.[37]

The judicial system functioned particularly badly during the Revolutionary period and the first two decades of the nineteenth century. An official report justifying the peacemaking efforts of the prefect in 1800–1 explained that over the last two decades summonses and arrests had not been properly executed, 'witnesses refused to tell the truth, jurors refused to find offenders guilty through the spirit of kinship and party but also out of fear of reprisals, and the courts and judges were therefore reduced to being helpless spectators of killings and vendettas, that had become everyday events'. Ordinary citizens made the same diagnosis as those in authority. Complaining of the failure of Petro-Maria Colombani of Talasani to comply with a sentence of banishment imposed on him by the courts, Carlo Mari declared at the end of 1797: 'Crimes are so common in Corsica because of the slowness of the courts and the lack of exemplary punishments.' A petition for clemency made in 1820 on behalf of two men sentenced to death for crimes committed six years earlier – the delay is itself significant – made the point that 'at that time all justice had been flaunted and parties in conflict had [therefore] committed the most terrible acts of violence against each other'.[38] Despite marked improvements in the functioning of the courts, similar comments, linking the survival of feuding and the high incidence of violence to their inefficiency or venality, continued to be made into the early years of this century.[39]

Here it is significant that a basic distrust of the courts, common in other traditional Mediterranean societies,[40] outlasted increasing involvement with them. The prefect remarked in 1823 on Corsicans' 'disdainful aversion to judicial formalities', a trait noted by others and expressed in many proverbs: 'The laws are made for nincompoops'; 'In the courts, one party is stripped naked, and the other is lucky to escape with the shirt on his back'; or 'Even a bad arrangement is better than a good judgment from the courts.'[41] Yet by the mid-nineteenth century, if not before, Corsica was endowed, even over-endowed, with the full panoply of French courts and judicial officials. Robiquet noted in 1835 that the number of judges in Corsica per head of the population was twice the average for the other French departments, while the number of justices of the peace was three times as great, and these proportions had not changed very much by 1900.[42] Most of these officials were natives, and the penchant of Corsicans for careers as magistrates and lawyers was universally remarked upon thoughgout the century.[43] Again, full use was made of the courts, both criminal and civil. By 1900 again, for example, a rough average of 17,500 offenders were being prosecuted each year in the lower courts in Corsica, six times more than in the other French departments. According to a recent study, Corsica came top of the list of French departments for litigiousness in the nineteenth century at the level of justices of the peace, and the rate here was twice as high in all the Corsican *arrondissements* as it was in any *arrondissement* in continental France.[44]

It was very strongly felt, however, that involvement in court procedure could in many circumstances be dishonouring. Mottet, who was public prosecutor from 1833 to 1836, reported that Corsicans 'had recourse to the courts when they had no other choice; they are almost ashamed of doing so, and it is a confession of weakness'. He mentions here the case of a woman who came to see him after her husband had been killed. He had praised her for preferring justice to vengeance. 'You are mistaken,' she had replied. 'I would have preferred vengeance, but my son is a coward who dishonours the family. I could not persuade him to kill our enemy.' Again, in a novel published much later, a young man wrongly accused of homicide who proposes to stand trial is told by his uncle: 'You must be mad ... The court is a tunnel that you may get through without being defiled if you are well protected but from which it is more than likely that you will emerge with your name fouled and blackened.'[45]

As this indicates, Corsicans had an equally strong conviction that the courts were partial and corrupt. As another proverb put it: 'If you have money and friends, you can twist the nose of justice.' In a similar vein, Colomba Bartoli told Valéry in the 1830s that 'justice was for sale in Bastia like everything else'. 'Justice is obtained', Lorenzi de Bradi agreed a century later, 'by the person who is able to mobilize the most effective support; it depends on influence and "politicking".'[46] As a chorus of commentators, official and unofficial, pointed out over the same period, the 'impartial' French system of justice was enmeshed with local networks of kinship and patronage, which diverted or sought to divert it to serve family and party interest and/or revenge.

This is most clearly demonstrated in the assumption made by most French judicial officials that their Corsican counterparts could not be expected to be impartial. First President Mézard announced, for example, in 1816 that he would himself preside over all criminal cases involving vendettas, patronage and family matters (which meant in practice nearly all criminal cases), 'in order to try to prevent the intrigues, the solicitations, the manoeuvres and the threats which are always in evidence'. In 1836, Mottet asked:

> How can Corsican judges retain their impartiality when they have so many relatives in the island and when they are conscious of the enormous importance which a powerful suitor attaches to the success of his efforts? When people from their own district are involved, disinterestedness becomes impossible without falling out with their closest friends and often with members of their own family.

As Robiquet pointed out at about the same time, even where Corsican judges or magistrates did resist such pressure they were still believed to be partial and the effect was much the same. This overall situation appears to have changed very little over the next fifty or a hundred years. Bigot noted in 1869 that the average Corsican 'loved justice but did not believe that judges were honest. He will therefore make presents to a judge when a trial is pending or during it; he will try to get round the judge by having recourse to his friends or to those who may have some influence over his career.' Such practices appear to have been the rule at the end of the nineteenth century and by then another dimension of 'influence' had become prominent. During the Second Empire and the Third Republic, judges and justices of the peace were often appointed 'for electoral and political reasons', as a public prosecutor complained bitterly in 1871. 'The sense of justice is often lacking in those charged with administering it,' Surier wrote in 1934.

'The protection of an influential political figure and of the clientèle to which one belongs is the best of all advocates. If the ear of a judge who is a partisan of the same politician is gained, then the cause of the faithful elector is gained too.'[47]

These considerations had led the French authorities to maintain an exceptional judicial régime in Corsica in the first three decades of the nineteenth century. An Extraordinary Criminal Court (Tribunal Criminel Extraordinaire) was instituted in 1801 to try all serious cases. It was composed at first of five civilian judges, all of whom were Corsican, and three military officers who were not, but within a year all Corsicans were excluded from the tribunal. A regular civilian judicature was restored in 1810, but without a jury. From 1814 to 1831, the Court of Criminal Justice comprised six rather than the eight judges normal in an Assize Court. This reduction, which was made the grounds for several unsuccessful appeals against its decisions, was almost certainly motivated by a desire to minimize the effects of local influence on the court. Réalier-Dumas, himself a judge in Bastia from 1816 to 1819 and later public prosecutor, opposed the whole idea of having Corsican judges and argued that at the very least there should be a majority of continentals on the bench in the criminal court. As late as 1852, after all the exceptional features of the court system in Corsica had been removed, an official report on banditry recommended that the proportion of continental judges, which was only 12 out of 46, should be greatly increased.[48]

Very few dissenting voices were raised on this subject, though Corsican pressure lay behind the return of the island to French judicial normality in 1831 and Corsican magistrates did take exception to some of the more blatant criticisms levelled against them as a body. In an article published on the front page of the *Journal de la Corse* in July 1857, a primary school inspector, Cerati, asserted that judicial venality was the rule and took two main forms: 'first, that of zealous patronage, by which connections with judges and with officials at all levels were abused in order to recommend a protégé, visits being paid, pressing letters sent, and so on; and secondly that of giving gifts of various kinds: wild boar, wild sheep, ducks, etc.' If a protégé got off completely or lightly from a charge against him, his patron took the credit, whether it was due or not, and thus built up his prestige and his power for further such transactions. The first president of the Bastia court reacted strongly against what he called a 'calumny', denying that Corsican judges ever received visits or presents in the way described, and both the author and the printer of the article were successfully prosecuted. We have seen, however, that such accusations continued to be made and even Corsican judges admitted, in confidentiality, that they were well-founded. Judge Montera wrote, for example, in 1860 that 'the spirit of patronage is so deeply rooted in the customs of the country that it manifests itself in nearly all cases [before the Assize Court]; and there is no defendant, however, obscure, who does not find a protector of some kind'.[49]

The importance of 'influence' and the venality of justice generally is evident when one examines particular cases. The sternest critics conceded that financial corruption was infrequent[50] and it is rarely signalled in the sources. One would not *a priori* expect it to be of course, since those engaged in it would be careful to cover their tracks. Moreover, given the hold of patronage and kinship ties, bribery as such would have been either unnecessary or ineffective. Like blood money, it would offend the ethos of honour. In certain situations, where these factors were absent or weak, corruption might find a place, however. In 1820, President Pasqualini, who already had a reputation for dishonesty, was formally accused of taking bribes, and an extra-judicial enquiry under the chairmanship of a continental judge was set up. This revealed that Pasqualini had indeed accepted bribes ranging from 600 to 1500 francs. In one case, the money was to be paid back if the defendant was in fact indicted, terms which were apparently agreed in writing by Pasqualini's son, who was *adjoint* in Bastia; in another, the bribe was disguised as the discharge of a debt. The enquiry also uncovered payments made to another judge, Boccheciampe, via his wife and his son-in-law. Larger bribes were said to have been paid in the Morati case in 1842, but this cannot be substantiated.[51]

Much more usual was the exercise of 'influence' on those involved in the judicial procedure, though this may have involved giving money and gifts on a scale which the sources do not indicate. There is evidence particularly from the early part of our period of the French authorities attempting to take preventive measures here. In a report in 1798, for example, the commissary for the department of Golo called for the removal from office of the director of the grand jury, Pietri: he 'was the first cousin of the Franceschi brothers, whose indictment for homicide was under consideration, and he had not followed the proper procedures against them'. He also suggested that the case against the killers of the ex-priest Marietti in the canton of Marana be given to an examining magistrate from Bastia, given 'the kinship ties of citizen Bastelica, justice of the peace of this canton'. In 1807, General Morand asked for the dismissal of the president of the Appeal Court at Ajaccio, Chiappe. Not only 'did he openly protect murderers and other criminals, he even dared to ask me not to prosecute a certain Marchilesi, who had been indicted for homicide' and had then engineered the man's release from prison in Sartène.[52]

One can show, too, how such influence could have a decisive effect on the outcome of prosecutions. The public prosecutor reported that the acquittal of Bernardino Peretti on a homicide charge in 1804 'has astonished the public, who have ascribed it to all the manoeuvres, intrigues and cabals set in motion quite openly on his behalf'. General Morand added that the president of the court in this case had 'demonstrated a partiality quite unworthy of the important functions entrusted to him', and he made the same criticism of the examining magistrate Della Costa, who had initially ruled that there was no case to answer against Peretti and had ordered his release from custody, a decision which Morand had at once countermanded.[53] In a case in 1806, conflict developed between the heirs of Bastiano Viale of Bastia. His sons-in-law, Rijo and Santello, claimed that Viale's son had stolen a considerable sum of money from his father's house shortly after the latter's death, thus depriving the other heirs of their rightful share in the inheritance. The public prosecutor grumbled about the extreme delays in the proceedings against Viale *fils* and reported that 'he could not expect to see the case fairly concluded, because of Viale's great influence'. Rijo also complained of this influence, although he was a close friend of the public prosecutor and sought to put pressure on him and on other judges in his own favour. The case eventually went for trial in Marseille, where Rijo 'failed to find the same complaisance towards himself that he had enjoyed in Corsica'. The director of the Marseille grand jury commented, moreover, that 'all the Corsican judges involved in the case were suspect'. A similar situation was evoked by Anton-Maria Santucci of Loreto-di-Casinca. The killer of a young priest, whom he denounced, was said to be 'the nephew of the wife of a Casabianca, who is a cousin of the son-in-law of the Casabianca, who is a judge of the criminal court', and, of course, Santucci added, 'the author of this premeditated murder will be let off because he is a relative of a judge'. The local Casabianca, he explained again, 'had a regiment of daughters married to all sorts of people in useful positions', which reinforced the likelihood of an 'arrangement'. A final example is provided by the Morati case to which we have referred. The Morati brothers were accused of instigating the murder of Bartolomeo Sebastiani, member of a Corsican family of national importance. Their trial in mid-1842 attracted such interest that it had to be held in the church of San-Carlo, the usual courtroom being too small, and enormous influence was brought to bear to secure an acquittal. The accused were cousins of the subprefect of Bastia, who sat in court in a prominent position. A non-Corsican, Jourdan, presided over the court, but there were strong indications that he had been 'worked on' by the Morati's 'friends', for he opened the trial by 'proclaiming their innocence in a quite unprecedented way', which earned him a severe reprimand from the Minister of Justice.[54]

What we may call judicial patronage continued to operate in the second half of the nineteenth century, though it is generally referred to in vaguer terms in the sources. In 1852, Don Giacomo Peretti, municipal tax-collector in Ajaccio, was acquitted of trying to kill his brother-in-law. There was no doubt of his guilt, but 'the highest influences' had operated on his behalf. Again, in 1856, Maria-Celinda Filippi of Foce was acquitted on a charge of infanticide. The evidence was not absolutely clear, but she had 'protectors who were able to recommend her heartily to those whose task it was to judge her'.[55] Many similar cases could be cited, though in this period influence over witnesses and jurors had become more important than influence over judges.

Where judicial leniency could be attributed to partiality or influence, severity was believed to stem not from impartiality but from hostility, and attacks on judges and magistrates by those whom they had convicted or their relatives were not uncommon in the period before 1830. The old Genoese Statutes had reserved their severest penalties for violence against magistrates. Count Willot reported in 1816 that judges who tried to carry out their duties strictly and conscientiously 'were exposed to the vengeance' of those against whom they acted. One of the arguments put forward at this time for moving and then keeping the criminal court at Bastia was that the judges would be less open to threat and attack there than at Ajaccio. Moreover, specific cases of both occurred at all levels of the judicature. Judge Arena was ambushed around 1820 in the forest of Vizzavona by the bandit Poli, who had just escaped from prison, having been sentenced to hard labour for life. Arena had been one of the judges of the court which handed down this sentence and Poli threatened to kill him in retaliation. Arena managed to convince the bandit that he had not personally supported the judgment and he was spared. In a few cases, such threats were carried out. In 1820, Colonna, the examining magistrate investigating the killing of Nunzio Gasparini at Bastelica, made the mistake of staying at the house of former War commissary Pasqualini, who was believed to be hostile towards the Gasparini and friendly towards their enemies the Casanova. On his way back to Ajaccio under escort, having completed his enquiry, Colonna was shot at and mortally wounded. The case was taken over by Judge Franceschini who was recommended for the Cross of the Legion of Honour 'on account of the risks to which he had been exposed' in so doing. The same dangers were faced by justices of the peace, though we shall see that they incurred hostility as much if not more for their political as for their judicial activities. Deputy justice of the peace Fieschi of Petreto-Bicchisano was shot dead, for example, in 1848 by Francesco Istria, after he had opened an investigation into the killing of Istria's father's mistress three years earlier, with Istria as the prime suspect. Prosecutors were perhaps even more vulnerable than judges and magistrates. Notices threatening Public Prosecutor Boucher appeared on walls in Ajaccio in November 1820, for example. At the same time, it was reported that the district prosecutor at Bastia was 'obliged to take special precautions against being ambushed by the Agostini'. Again, threats were made against the district prosecutor of Sartène, Susini, after a certain Ortoli from Olmiccia had been indicted for attempted homicide rather than for wounding, a much less serious offence. For a long time, Susini was unable to leave his house save under armed escort, and he was finally killed by Ortoli's brothers.[56]

Before turning to a full discussion of influence over witnesses and jurors, we should note a number of other features of the court system in Corsica that tended to reduce its effectiveness. First, the changes in the form of the main criminal court were matched by changes in its locale. In the pre-Revolutionary period the court sat at Bastia and then from 1792 to 1796 at Corte. Between 1796 and 1801 there were two courts at Bastia and at Ajaccio. In 1801, these were amalgamated into a single court again, which sat at Ajaccio until 1816. From then on, the definitive move was made back to Bastia, as we have seen. The criminal court there was held in an old convent building, quarters that were shared with the civil court and the court of first instance and which also served as a barracks. Important cases, like that of the Morati, had to be heard elsewhere, and the premises were generally inconvenient and lacking in dignity. A purpose-built courthouse, the present Palais de Justice, was only built in the late 1850s.[57] Secondly, for French judicial officials, as for French officials in general, a posting to Corsica was more often regarded as an exile to be endured than as a challenge to be faced. There was consequently a rapid turnover and few non-Corsicans acquired any profound knowledge of the island or its customs or became fully acquainted with the local élites. Characteristic here is the unstable tenancy of the post at the apex of the island's system of criminal justice, that of public prosecutor. In the century after 1819 there were 42 holders of the post, which means an average occupancy of just over two years. Some public prosecutors, notably Boucher (1819–23), Cabet (1830–1) and Mottet (1833–6), displayed a combination of toughness and tactlessness that made it impossible for them to work with the local magistrature.[58] Thirdly, court procedure was conducted in French, which meant that many ordinary Corsicans could not understand what was going on, though they were allowed to testify in their own language. But then non-Corsican judges could not understand them. First President Mézard was at this disadvantage in 1816, and President Stefanini complained in 1843 that Judge Maniez, who had presided over the previous session of the Assize Court, 'could hardly understand the language of the country and was thus obliged to interrogate the defendants and to examine witnesses through the offices of an interpreter'.[59]

<h2 style="text-align:center">III</h2>

Partisan testimony and the intimidation of witnesses and later jurors were characteristic of the operation of official justice in Corsica and became the most important means by which conflict was carried on via the courts.

First, people were often extremely reluctant to act as witnesses at all and could maintain a wall of silence. The public prosecutor commented in 1825 on 'the extreme difficulty of obtaining from the mouths of the best-informed witnesses precise declarations on the most obvious circumstances of a case'. As one advocate-general put it later in the century, the patron saint of Corsicans in judicial matters was 'Santa Nèga': 'I know nothing' or 'I deny it.'[60] The president of the Assize Court reported on a case in 1843: 'This time, as always, great efforts had to be made to obtain the whole truth from witnesses.' A case in 1835, in which Domenico-Luigi Antonmarchi and his brother-in-law Romani of Pietra were accused of mortally wounding Antonmarchi's brother, reveals what might lie behind such reserve. A key witness, Anna-Maria Massei, admitted in court that she had withheld information from the examining magistrate. She explained that

> before going to give evidence at Corte, I went to see the mayor, a relative of Romani. He asked me what I was going to say [to the magistrate]. I told him: 'All the facts,' and when I related the remarks of Romani [about the killing], he gave a start and shouted: 'So you want to have two men condemned to death?', adding: 'But you are not obliged to disclose all these circumstances to the judges. One doesn't have to tell all one knows, where the life of a man is at stake.'

When she seemed unconvinced by this argument, the mayor then brought in the parish priest to back up what he had been telling her. Such considerations did not apply solely to capital offences, however, and, beyond the fact that local solidarity is not just taken for granted here, all that is unusual about the case is the woman's resistance to the pressure put on her. Having testified during the preliminary stages of a case, moreover, witnesses not infrequently failed to attend the public hearings, or, as we shall see in detail, they might alter or withdraw incriminating evidence in open court that they had been prepared to give in private.[61]

When witnesses did attend court and did testify, their testimony was often unreliable. False testimony was commonplace and was motivated in Corsica, as it was elsewhere,[62] by family and party loyalty, by fear of reprisals if the truth were told, or by the wish to damage one's enemies. 'Bearing false witness is, alas, all too frequent in this department,' wrote an official attached to the Extraordinary

Criminal Court in 1801, a complaint echoed by those in similar positions over the next century or more. 'In most cases', Advocate-general Sorbier declared in 1833, 'those testifying before the Assize Court commit perjury with unbelievable impudence.' Bigot confirmed later in the century that the same could be said for the lower courts: 'telling lies in court was not really regarded as lying by the people of Bastelica'.[63] It is significant, as we have seen, that some members of the clergy shared and encouraged this attitude, which prompted Bishop Casanelli d'Istria to reserve absolution in cases of false testimony to himself.[64] The deeply ingrained nature of the practice is further indicated by reference to it in proverbs, popular sayings and laments. 'May God preserve you from fire, flood and false witnesses', ran one salutation; while to say that someone was prepared 'to go to Bastia' meant that he or she was ready to give hostile testimony in court there.[65] Perjury by witnesses was frequently adduced, too, as grounds for clemency. Five mayors of his canton claimed in 1852 that Francesco Bastianesi of Ucciani had been 'the innocent victim of false testimonies made through hatred and malice'; while Martino Cristini, ex-mayor of Castiglione, declared on his own behalf in 1885 that he had been convicted of electoral fraud 'through false statements sworn by my political enemies'.[66]

Witnesses did not behave as individuals telling or seeking the truth but as members of a family or a clientèle with interests to further or defend. The public prosecutor commented on a case in 1820 that they 'lied for the defence or for the prosecution with no other motive than their hatred or their affection for the defendant and in fulfilment of their reciprocal duties as patrons and clients'. In another case in 1841, a boy of around thirteen was asked by the president of the Assize Court why his evidence contradicted that of other witnesses and he replied: 'They are lying, which is natural enough; what would you do, sir, if someone had killed your cousin?'[67]

It was usual for opposing sides in a case to produce witnesses with contradictory versions of the same events. In a case in 1844, for example, Felice Venturini of Olmeto was accused of having accidentally killed his father in a brawl. Sixty witnesses were heard and they provided flatly conflicting evidence. In particular, three witnesses swore that they had seen Venturini fire a pistol killing his father, while three others testified that the fatal shot had been fired by Venturini's cousin. Again, in a case related to the feuding at Venzolasca, two women testified that they had seen Paolo-Francesco Angelini fire the shot that had killed Giovan-Battiste Ciavaldini in 1849, while another witness was equally sure that he had seen the homicide committed by Antono Luciani. As a result of the conflicts of evidence in this case, it came before the Assize Court three times and five witnesses were arrested for perjury.[68] Related to this, it was also common for witnesses to change their evidence. The new clerk to the court of first instance at Bastia addressed a significant query to the Ministry of Justice in 1799. 'Was it admissible', he asked, 'for witnesses in court about to testify, and who were afraid of contradicting themselves, to have read to them their original declarations made to the examining magistrate or to the director of the grand jury?'[69] Many particular instances of this practice may be cited. Antono Santoni of Palneca, for example, was accused in 1850 of trying to kill Guidonia Santoni, and she changed her evidence four times in the course of the investigation. She claimed at first that Antono, who had had sexual relations with her but then refused to marry her, had tried to drown her in a river. Then, under pressure from his relatives, who promised that he would marry her, she told the parish priest and the mayor that she had fallen into the river and that Antono had tried to save her. Later, she told the examining magistrate that she had not even seen Antono near the river. Later still, after she had been arrested herself under suspicion of perjury, she returned to her original story, on the basis of which Antono was convicted. In 1853, Simone Renucci of Ciamannacce was shot dead while returning from Zicavo with Santo Francisci. Giovan-Battiste Mondolini informed the examining magistrate that Francisci had told him the following day that he and Renucci had quarrelled over a water course, but Mondolini denied this when the case came to court. Similarly, in the case against the Palmesani brothers of Alzi in 1865, the public prosecutor reported that 'the witnesses have not been as affirmative [at the trial] as they were during the preliminary enquiry'.[70] As we have seen in the previous chapter, such behaviour was sometimes explained by the fact that a reconciliation had intervened. For example, in a case brought before the Tribunal Correctionnel of Corte in 1829, a surprise acquittal on a charge of wounding drew this comment from the district prosecutor: 'The pacification of the parties after the charge was brought explains why the witnesses said nothing at the trial about facts which they had earlier sworn to be certain.'[71] It is also significant in this context that, although prosecutions for perjury were occasionally brought, they were rarely successful.[72].

Within this general framework, there is no doubt that evidence was often given by witnesses with deliberately hostile intention. The president of the Assize Court in 1844 noted that there were many witnesses who testified 'in order to satisfy a desire for vengeance, which they had been unable or unwilling to achieve by force or violence, and who cleverly fabricated evidence against defendants whom they wanted to injure or destroy, hoping thus to make the court the involuntary accomplice of their passionate hatreds'. And we may cite specific examples. In the course of the feud between the Serra and the Susini at Loreto-di-Tallano, the house of Don Giacomo Susini was set alight, as we have seen, while it was occupied by several of his close relatives. One of those charged with this act of homicidal arson was Giovan-Antono Susini, and Antono Susini testified at his trial in 1848 that he had actually seen him taking wood to the house in question in order to get the fire going. This testimony helped to get Giovan-Antono convicted and sentenced to 20 years' hard labour. However, four years after the trial, Antono Susini fell seriously ill and declared publicly, after having confessed to a priest, that 'he had been advised to testify falsely against Giovan-Antono Susini, who was in fact innocent', and following this declaration the latter was pardoned. It follows from all this, as we have seen, that giving false testimony that led to a wrongful conviction often provoked retaliation and could be grounds for the formal declaration of a vendetta.[73]

Pressure on witnesses was thus very general and ranged from the recognized obligations to kin, clients, community and party to intimidation and coercion. A case in 1833 is a good illustration both of the expected partisanship of witnesses and also of the fear of reprisals which might guide the giving of testimony. At the trial of Pasquale Negroni of Ampriani, who was accused of killing the mayor, Giovan-Battiste Lota, the latter's father-in-law was asked about the moral standing of the accused and he replied: 'I cannot say: I am his enemy; others will tell you.' Another witness, Maddalena Leonetti testified that her husband had confessed on his death-bed to having overheard Negroni and another man plotting to kill Lota. She was asked why her husband had not revealed this when he was interrogated by the examining magistrate. 'My master wanted to live,' was her answer. In a case in 1844, a young herdsman, Mozziconacci, who was protected by the Tramoni bandits, was accused of poisoning members of the family of Girolamo Roccaserra at Sartène by putting arsenic in their domestic water supply. A certain Aldroandi, inspector of weights and measures at Bonifacio, testified that he had been at the Roccaserra house on the day in question and had not seen the accused there. But his evidence was discounted by the public prosecutor, who commented in court that 'the witness, a most honourable man, was obliged by his position to travel about all the time in the environs of Sartène where the Tramoni bandits are at large. The jury will therefore understand that he has not told the court all he knows.'[74]

It was usual in cases involving serious conflict for the positive ties of loyalty affecting defence witnesses to be complemented by threats against those in a position to testify for the prosecution. After protracted investigations, Paolo Follacci of Ajaccio and two associates were put on trial for premeditated homicide in 1822, but the behaviour of the witnesses ensured their acquittal. Many of them had criminal records themselves; those who seemed most honest were 'blood enemies of Follacci'; while 'the others were more or less intimidated by him and his followers, or else were seduced, corrupted, or swayed by the demands of clientship'. Many other examples may be cited, in which intimidation of witnesses is implied or actually described. During the trial of Bernardino Peretti of Sari-d'Orcino in 1804, his relatives 'went off into the mountains from where they continually threatened the witnesses in order to stop them from talking; at the same time, in Ajaccio, the agents, friends and protectors of the Peretti briefed those who did come to give evidence, confirmed the threats against those who remained hostile, and engaged in other outrageous man-oeuvres on behalf of their protégés'. Giovan-Dario Bazziconi from Feliceto was convicted in 1851 of killing Domenico-Francesco Renucci. The verdict was something of a surprise, since Bazziconi was protected by the bandit Massoni and his gang, 'then terrorizing the Balagna ... The intimidation to which witnesses had been subjected may be gauged from their attempts to retract their statements and from their hesitation in answering questions. All of them had been threatened.'

Expert witnesses were included in these manoeuvres. In a case in 1833 against Don Antono Leca from Occhiatana, who was accused of wounding Maria Orsolani, the doctor who examined the victim made two contradictory reports, one in writing and another later in court. When he was asked to explain the discrepancy, he said:

A certain person in our canton, whom one had reason to fear because of his character and his influence [probably Justice of the peace Malaspina, the account adds], got in touch with me and, without form or ceremony, invited me in a threatening manner to change my report. And, since I wanted to be able to go about my business freely ... But let me tell you that it doesn't really bother me that these discrepancies make me appear an ignoramus to my medical colleagues. I would rather live as an ignoramus than die as a good doctor!

Suborners of witnesses were even less commonly prosecuted or convicted than perjurers, and the light penalties which they received on conviction once again reflect how normal intimidation was and how little disapproved of among Corsicans. An advocate from Ajaccio, Coti, for example, was condemned to 40 days' imprisonment in the early 1860s for subornation, which seems not to have damaged his professional or political career.[75]

Nor were threats against witnesses idle, as some of our examples have already indicated. In a case in 1858, we learn that the enmity between Giovan-Battiste and Giuseppo Muselli of Ocana 'stemmed from testimony given in court by Giovan-Battiste against the Chiodi family, to which Giuseppo was related by marriage'. The ill-feeling between them culminated in a fight, in which Giuseppo was fatally stabbed in the eye. This outcome may have been accidental, although the choice of target suggests a connection with more deliberate acts of reprisal. The bishop of Ajaccio referred in 1848 to 'unfortunate individuals who have had their eyes gouged out by their enemies as revenge for having testified against them in the courts', and cases in which tongues or ears were mutilated are also recorded.[76] Hostile witnesses were also killed. After Father Santa-Lucia was convicted in 1840 of complicity in a double killing, his brother 'swore to exterminate the prosecution witnesses whose testimony had secured his conviction', and we have seen that he managed to kill six of them within five years. In a still more extreme case, a notary from Novale was convicted of homicide on false testimony and subsequently died in prison. His brother became a bandit and over a period of years killed all 14 prosecution witnesses. Many other less spectacular examples could be cited.[77]

IV

Before discussing the direct relationship between feuding and judicial procedures further, something must be said about the role of the jury. For much of the early part of the nineteenth century, as we have seen, there was no trial by jury in Corsica,[78] and it was only reintroduced in 1831 as a result of a long and lively campaign by Corsicans influential in Paris.[79] Moreover, controversy about the viability of the jury system in Corsica continued into the 1840s and 1850s, and the 1852 Commission on banditry proposed that the jury be once again suspended in cases of homicide, though the government did not adopt this idea.[80]

The main argument against having trial by jury was that jurors were reluctant, for one reason or another, to convict and that there was therefore an unacceptably high rate of acquittals as well as a tendency to give light sentences for serious offences. No conception of impartial justice existed and jurors, like witnesses, either followed party or family interest or else succumbed to tacit or open intimidation. 'The clearest proofs, the most blatant evidence of a crime', Miot wrote in 1801, 'have never decided a jury made up of men of the same family or the same party as the accused to pronounce against him, because, according to the dominant opinion in Corsica, whoever denies his party or his blood, as the expression goes, is thereby dishonoured'. 'During the assizes', Advocate-general Sorbier lamented in 1833, 'people from all classes of society converge on Bastia to sound out the dispositions of the jurors, besieging their places of residence, seeking to enter their consciences by force and wring from them culpable promises of support.' 'Those jurors who were believed to be the weakest or the most accessible were the ones who were most actively solicited and most boldly threatened,' Public Prosecutor Mottet continued in 1836. 'Hence, so many scandalous acquittals and so many convictions with extenuating circumstances, a kind of transaction that is sometimes even more scandalous than an acquittal.' Many similar observations could be cited by judicial officials and others through the nineteenth and into the twentieth century. Bourde related in 1887 that it was common for an accused person to choose a lawyer to defend him from the opposing 'party'. His own relatives would then work on the jurors of his party and the lawyer on those of the other. In 1896, the public prosecutor inveighed against the lobbying of jurors in the same terms as Sorbier or Mottet:

It is painful to have to report that in nearly all cases of the slightest importance the jurors are openly laid siege to from the start of the session; they are pursued by solicitations, importuned, made promises, even threatened. The most outrageous deals, the most shameful agreements are hatched in the corridors of the Assize Court, and the soundest and best-substantiated charges, where the culpability of the defendant is evident, meet with an invincible prejudice that leads to an acquittal.[81]

The 'unreliability' of juries can to some extent be measured by the acquittal rate in criminal cases (see Table 5). The average rate for the 40-year period was 32 per cent, but this and the five-year averages conceal much higher rates in some years: 60 per cent in 1831, 53 per cent in 1849, 51 per cent in 1856 and 50 per cent in 1850. The 1831 figure as well as the five-year average for 1831–5 clearly reflect the impact of the introduction of the jury, but the rate then dropped considerably. It should be pointed out, too, that the acquittal rate in Corsica was not very different from that found elsewhere in France at the same time[82] or in other comparable societies, for example early modern England.[83] In the first case, however, there was a significant contrast in the proportion of crimes resulting in arrests and prosecutions, and in the proportion of serious crimes.

A number of cases will illustrate the ways in which juries were influenced, confirming this general picture. Nine men from Campitello were acquitted in 1849 on charges arising from an electoral conflict, in which a bystander had been killed.

The jury had been worked on all the more assiduously in that the outcome of the trial had become a local political issue [between the factions led respectively by the mayor and the justice of the peace]. Both parties were present in court; and friends on either side were assigned to

Table 5. *Acquittal rates*[84]

Years	Acquittals as percentage of those tried
1826–30	34 (40 according to Robiquet)
1831–5	46
1836–40	24
1841–5	21 (or 24)
1846–50	42
1851–5	30
1856–60	33
1861–5	19

lobby in the exclusive interest of one or the other; the result of all this was the acquittal of all the defendants.

In the case against Ignazio Borelli of Albitreccia, in the same year, the jury brought in a tied verdict. The six jurors from Bastia found Borelli guilty of homicide, but the six jurors from the country ensured his acquittal; they took the view, it seems, that he had acted legitimately in killing his enemies, but they were also afraid of reprisals. The president of the Assize Court drew attention to a flagrant contrast between two cases in 1851. In the case of Felice Agostini of Piana, accused of premeditated homicide, the jury had been subjected to pressure both before and during the trial, as a result of which the defendant was found guilty of simple homicide only under 'violent provocation' and received a short prison sentence. A certain Bozzi from Zigliara was found guilty, however, of a similar crime by the same jury and was condemned to death. After being sentenced, he told them: 'You have condemned me, members of the jury, because I am only a poor devil. If I had had powerful protectors, you would have let me off, even if I had been a hundred times guilty.' Again, at the end of the century, three men from Fozzano were tried for a homicide which they had committed together. In 1893, Ignazio Durazzi and Michelangelo Paoli were convicted and sentenced to 15 years' hard labour each, but in 1896 Giusepp'-Antono Bartoli received a much more lenient sentence. A police enquiry was instigated, following objections by the family of their victim. This confirmed that 'repeated solicitations had been made to the jurors by Bartoli's relatives with a view to securing his acquittal', but also revealed that the family of his victim had acted in the same way 'in order to try to obtain his condemnation'.[85]

A further indication of the pressure placed on jurors is the attention drawn to those occasions on which such pressure was resisted. Commenting, for example, on the last session of the Assize Court in 1832, when the jury system was still very new, the *Gazette des Tribunaux* declared that 'during the whole period [of the session, which lasted a month], the zeal of the jury never slackened' and it showed itself to be 'impartial, firm and above all intrigue'. Giovan-Dario Bazziconi had been convicted in 1851, despite intimidation of both witnesses and jurors. The latter had been 'stopped on their way to Bastia by bandits protecting him' and 'requested' to act in his favour.[86]

As some of these examples show, intimidation of or patronage over jurors meant that they were generally indulgent towards defendants. In 1870 Bertrand wrote:

> The reports of both public prosecutors and the presidents of the assize courts draw attention in each session to acquittals and mitigations, which weaken the law's power to intimidate. Not only is the benefit of extenuating circumstances almost never refused, but the banal excuse of 'violent provocation' is usually admitted, all of which reduce the punishment for murder to the level appropriate for minor offences.[87]

This view is amply confirmed by detailed study of the judicial records. President Miravail commented, for example, of the second session of 1851: 'The jury admitted extenuating circumstances in all the cases but one, in which it did not acquit or recognize the existence of provocation.' In a case in 1849, Francesco Graziani of Monticello had shot and killed a man, who had, he believed, been party to the abduction of his sister. The circumstances of the killing were not entirely clear, but the jury readily accepted the defence's pleas of provocation and of legitimate defence, 'Graziani having presented himself in court under the cover of an active and powerful patronage'.[88] Many more individual cases of this kind could be cited, but a statistical account is more telling. In the first two sessions of 1853 and all four sessions of 1865 – and the period of the Second Empire was the one in which the jury system probably operated most strictly during the nineteenth century – the mean sentence for homicide was ten years' imprisonment and the median sentence five years, while the mean sentence for attempted homicide was four years and the median $2\frac{1}{2}$ years.[89] It was also common for juries to forward petitions for clemency after defendants had been convicted and sentenced.[90]

There is a significant contrast, too, between types of case, where juries did show leniency and those where they did not. In the former category, as we have emphasized, were cases where family or 'party' pressure was brought to bear but also where jurors' views of what constituted criminal behaviour differed from that assumed by French law, though in practice the two often overlapped. A case in 1851, for example, involved charges against several men who began fighting and shooting at each other during the municipal elections at Olmiccia. No one was seriously injured, and the jury 'saw nothing criminal in these acts of violence and acquitted all the accused'. In a case against a man from Suarella in 1861, the jury accepted that he had committed perjury in a lower court but asked for the minimum penalty, given 'the close kinship links between him and the person on whose behalf he was testifying'. By contrast, other offences might be very severely punished, especially where the culprit benefited from no protection. So, whereas those responsible for vengeance killings at Venzolasca in the middle of the century were leniently treated by the courts, Luigi Ciarini, an Italian day-labourer, received a seven-year prison sentence in 1857 for burning two straw ricks belonging to the mayor.[91]

The indulgence of jurors but also their enmeshment in local networks and values can be seen, too, in their reluctance to be party to capital convictions. Death sentences were commonly passed and carried out in Corsica in the three decades before 1830. Over the following century, however, according to Bazal, only 38 death sentences were passed, of which 22 were carried out, the last being that of Andrea Spada in 1935.[92] There is no doubt that the change in pattern is to be attributed to the introduction of the jury. Witnesses in a case in 1852, for example, testified that Anton-Giuseppo Santoni of Palneca had killed his sister-in-law with premeditation, but the jury refused to accept this, for no other reason than to avoid bringing in a verdict that would mean a capital sentence. The trial summary of another case in 1854 was quite specific. The jury accepted that Giovan-Agostino Nicolai of Levie, convicted of various serious crimes including two homicides, had acted in extenuating circumstances, a decision motivated by 'a repugnance for the death penalty that has become almost systematic'.[93] Earlier, in 1819, the public prosecutor had complained that the Corsican clergy were telling witnesses 'that one should never contribute to a capital condemnation', and jurors almost certainly received the same advice later.[94] As in other feuding societies, this reluctance on the part of jurors must mainly have stemmed from the belief that if they did contribute towards a judicial homicide they would be legitimate targets of blood vengeance.[95]

Similar considerations may explain the unwillingness of men to serve as jurors, though this had other motives, too, and was offset by the prestige which jury service could convey. The *Gazette des Tribunaux* noted in 1834 that 'all the jurors were present' for the second session of the Assize Court that year. This diligence, which was almost unprecedented, deserved 'to be remarked upon'. The president of the court reported in 1849 that only half or two-thirds of the jurors who were summoned actually attended, and that of these the ones coming from any distance only expected to stay for a day or so. Permission to leave was readily granted by the court via the medium of 'influence', and by the end of the session therefore the jury was almost entirely composed of citizens of Bastia. Again, of the 30 jurors summoned for the fourth session of 1856, only 22 were properly qualified and actually turned up, and the president commented: 'People are in general less than enthusiastic in this department about fulfilling the juror's function.' He added that a fair number of those excused on grounds of ill-health and unfitness to travel made use of false certificates. Real impediments were compounded by the effects of patronage and influence.

These perennial features intervened once more where the drawing-up of jury lists, prior dispensations and the right to object to individual jurors were concerned, though efforts to reduce their effects had some success. President Gaffory observed in 1852 that the lists of jurors for the first session 'had not been drawn up with the care and attention to the rules that such an important operation demands'. The list included men who had already served for three years and men over 70, both categories excused from further service, as well as men without the required educational qualifications. 'All these irregularities had often interfered with the course of justice.' Gaffory noted five years later that there had been some improvement in the composition of the jury, which he and his colleague Fabrizzy attributed to 'the happy influence of the 1853 law'. This allowed the judicial authorities more effective control of the drawing up of the lists at the local level. The 1857 list nevertheless included one man who had been dead for over a year, another who had left for America three years previously, and, among those who did present themselves, three who had previously attended court in the dock. By 1864, Gaffory could report a further 'marked improvement in the establishment of the jury lists', which meant that jurors were beginning to show 'the zeal, the care and the impartiality' that their task required.[96] As we have suggested, this was an over-sanguine view as far as the behaviour, if not the constitution, of Corsican juries was concerned.

After some reduction during the July Monarchy, dispensations from jury service seem to have multiplied again, even during the stricter régime of the Second Empire. According to the *Gazette des Tribunaux* at the start of 1835, men were much more anxious to fulfil their duties as jurors in Corsica than had previously been the case and demands for dispensation had accordingly become rarer; it had even come to be a question of honour to serve on a jury. In the last session of 1865, however, the public prosecutor reported that, as a result of dispensations, he had had to call on the services of 25 additional jurors, whose names had not been on the original list. Numbers of jurors were further depleted, he added, by the exercise of the right to object to up to 12 jurors out of a possible 30 per case. This right belonged to both sides and was nearly always used, by the prosecution in an attempt to secure jurors who were independent and intelligent, and by the defence to eliminate those with 'moral sense, strength of character, or general ability', in the words of President Montera in 1857.[97]

We have not undertaken any systematic analysis of jurors along social and occupational lines, but something may be gathered again from the reports of the presidents of the Assize Court. In the 1830s and 1840s and even the 1850s, jurors were not necessarily members of Corsica's small educated élite. 'Never was a jury so poorly composed,' President Giordani complained at the end of the second session of 1844. Very few notables had served; the rest 'lacked both intelligence and firmness'; and some did not understand French. Again, President Poli noted that the jury for the third session of 1850 'had been generally weak and unintelligent', with the result that over half the defendants had been acquitted. Reports of this kind predominated until the 1860s, when juries took on a definitively notable complexion. The lists for 1864, for example, comprised landowners, professional men, retired army officers, mayors and local council-lors. President Gaffory suggested that this was 'some guarantee that justice would be done', though he added cautiously that the best of Corsican juries tended to be 'indulgent'.[98]

v

Influence with judges, perjury, pressure placed on jurors could all be weapons in ongoing feuds conducted via the courts, and Busquet referred in this context to the 'judicial vendetta'.[99] Here a distinction may be drawn between cases in which the courts were simply used and influenced in the course of feuds, an extension of the general situation which we have described, and those in which a special aggressiveness was displayed. The first category mainly comprises cases where it was necessary to get an accused killer acquitted. As Mattei put it in 1912:

in Corsica, those who appear before the Assize Court are those who wish to appear there. And those who wish to appear there are, of course, those who are almost sure of being let off ... During the time that they are at large, they have plenty of opportunity to recruit obliging witnesses, and thus to prepare a strong defence based on alibis or pleas of mitigation.

Arrangements might also have been made with judges and/or jurors.[100] Such attempts to manage the courts, often successful, were made in the course of some of Corsica's most important feuds. The police reported in 1818, for example, that two agents of the Viterbi of Penta-di-Casinca had been acquitted thanks to the support of Deputy-prosecutor Arena. When Luca-Antono Viterbi was himself prosecuted in 1821, Arena, who had been moved to Aix-en-Provence, returned to Bastia, 'where he will doubtless spend most of his time soliciting on behalf of Viterbi'. Judge Pasqualini was also said to be taking 'a warm interest' in Viterbi and his family.[101] A number of cases arising from the feuding at Venzolasca came before the courts in 1850 and 1851. In the second session of 1850, Francesco Petrignani, Federico Federici and Francesco Antonetti were prosecuted for killing Giovan-Battiste Sanguinetti in an ambush in January 1849. Despite evidence of the guilt of all three defendants and of premeditation, only Antonetti was convicted and he was allowed the excuse of 'provocation' and received a lenient sentence. The trial summary commented that 'intrigue in this case has reached new levels'; each side in the feud 'had relatives in the highest circles at Bastia', which meant among the judges of the court; false testimony was blatant, and two witnesses had been arrested for perjury. In another case in the same session, involving a killing by the opposing party, again 'everything had been done to obtain an acquittal'. Here the arrest of three reluctant or unreliable witnesses had led to a postponement of the hearing, but acquittals were secured in the following session. Those responsible for killing Luigi Ciavaldini in August 1849 were not tried until 1851, the case having been twice postponed to allow for the prosecution of would-be witnesses for perjury. Antono Filippi and Giovan-Battiste Ciosi were prosecuted, together with Paolo-Francesco Angelini, an Italian ex-gendarme in the pay of the Filippi. In the words of the trial summary, 'the Filippi family wielded great influence through its connections and its relatives', and it used that influence effectively. First, the weight of the accusation fell on Angelini rather than on the members of the Filippi family for whom he had acted but who were merely cited as his accomplices. Then, as we have seen, witnesses were put under pressure, and also court officials. The clerk to the examining magistrate in the case was 'devoted to the Filippi' and had obstructed the summoning of a crucial eye-witness. In the event, both Filippi and Ciosi were acquitted, a verdict that was seen as 'inevitable' in the circumstances, while Angelini was convicted and sentenced to 20 years' hard labour 'in compensation'. Even he benefited to a degree, however, from his patrons' influence, since the charge of premeditation, which might have cost him his life, was rejected by the jury.[102]

Moving to the second category, where vengeance was more actively pursued through the courts, we find that it was not uncommon in the early nineteenth century for feuding parties to make a show of force during the trial of one of their members. Serious conflict occurred, for example, in the early 1830s at Corte between the Gaffory and the Mariani parties. Various armed encounters took place, including one in May 1833, in which two members of the Gaffory party were killed. The following month a trial was held in connection with this incident and another in which the victim had been on the other side. The alleged culprit here was defended by the leader of his party, 'the advocate Gaffory himself [who] went down from Corte to Bastia, like a clan chieftain with an escort of armed mountaineers'.[103] The courts were more commonly used in this context, however, in an attempt to secure the conviction and punishment of enemies. The president of the court commented in 1849 on the extreme passion shown at the trial of Ignazio Borelli of Albitreccia: 'Hatred and the desire for revenge were written on the faces of the witnesses, and all their depositions were marked by these emotions.'[104] Again, Saverio Castelli of Carcheto attributed the very severe sentence passed on his son in 1910 or 1911 to the machinations of their enemies. Very often judicial action and violence would be alternated as means of pursuing vengeance. In a case at Cuttoli-Corticchiato, Giuseppo Torre killed Pasquale Borelli in May 1851 and took to the maquis. Three months later, Borelli's brother, Giulio-Matteo, surprised Torre's son and one of his cousins in the country and fired at them without hitting them. They only reported this attack more than a year later, however, after Giuseppo Torre had himself been arrested and sentenced to hard labour for life. Giulio-Matteo was then tried and sentenced to three years' imprisonment for attempted homicide, and this can be seen as a revenge for the severity with which Torre had been treated.[105] As we saw in Chapter 4, moreover, prosecutions could ensure not only the punishment but also the dishonouring of enemies.

Mérimée noted in 1840 that most killings were preceded by some kind of procedure in the courts.[106] The opening of legal proceedings, which might include denunciation, could be seen on either or both sides as the opening of hostilities, and many cases may be cited in which legal action, court proceedings or judicial decisions prompted or exacerbated conflict and feuding. We have seen that the feuding at Penta-di-Casinca entered a new phase in 1814, following unsuccessful judicial proceedings initiated by one side against the other.[107] A feud at Poggio-Mezzana began in the late 1820s when Giovanni Borghetti was accused of stealing a cock belonging to an Italian woman. He was convicted and sentenced to three months' imprisonment, all of which he blamed on his enemies the Taddei. He swore vengeance and killed one of them in 1829, with the aid of a relative, who was a bandit. Borghetti was arrested, convicted and executed for this crime, and this in turn prompted further killings over the next four years, Borghetti's own father and the father of his victim being among the targets. At Olmeto in 1865, animals belonging to several people strayed on to the land of Filippo Balisoni, causing slight damage. He took legal action selectively against the Pacchiarelli brothers but not the others. They found this provocative and asked a cousin of theirs, who had a similar complaint against Balisoni, to bring an action against him in retaliation. While this was pending, Balisoni was shot in the face and one of the Pacchiarelli was fatally stabbed. Other examples may be cited of civil suits leading to or exacerbating feuds. The penultimate phase of the conflict at Olmeta-di-Tuda between the Campocasso and the Casale took the form of litigation over property, and Pio Casale was a judge and his father an advocate in Bastia. Again, the long-standing feud between the Muglioni and the Chiapperoni of Valle-di-Rostino was reported in 1851 to have originated in a 'civil litigation'.[108]

Judicial intervention in local conflicts could have a more general disruptive effect, even when it was intended to be conciliatory. Busquet noted that rulings by justices of the peace often caused vendettas, and the armed conflict between the Alfonsi and the Susini of Albertacce in 1883 certainly followed 'a discussion of material interests before the justice of the peace at Calacuccia'.[109] We learn from a case in 1864 that the Orsini and the Raffaelli of Ortiporio had been on very bad terms for a long time and that their enmity had been fuelled and then fanned to violence by a number of condemnations at the correctional level. Again, the proposed marriage of Giovanni Peretti of Sari-d'Orcino to the daughter of notary Padovani had aroused intense hostility locally, presumably from families of disappointed rival suitors, and threats were made against both parties to the match. These in turn led to the prosecution of those responsible and their condemnation to short prison sentences, but 'the condemnations, far from calming things down' as intended, only made them worse, as did the solemnization of the marriage. The families concerned entered 'into a state of flagrant hostility', and an attempt was made to kill Peretti at the end of 1850. It was argued, too, that over-zealous prosecutions brought by the authorities, particularly long after the event, could revive enmities that had died down. Patorni claimed that this happened around 1820, 'when summonses were issued all over the place. People thought that they had been denounced by former enemies; and violent hatreds were thus reanimated.'[110]

A much more common pattern was for violence to ensue when judicial action failed to produce the results required by one party in a conflict. Proceedings might be dropped before they came to court. An enmity had existed, for example, between the Peretti and the Susini of Olmeto since at least 1847. A son of Don Giovanni Peretti had been killed allegedly at the instigation of Giuseppo Susini, but the case against him did not come to court for lack of evidence. 'This decision merely exacerbated the hatred which Don Giovanni nourished for the Susini,' and he took revenge in 1849 by shooting Giuseppo Susini's son Giovan-Domenico. After Giovan-Battiste Arrighi of Urbalacone had been killed in 1848, his relatives accused Carlo-Francesco Istria, but proceedings against him were not pursued. When Istria was released from custody, Arrighi's widow, who 'regarded this as the denial of all justice, uttered various threats against him, saying [among other things] ... that she would dye the clothes of Istria's wife as black as her own'; and Istria was later ambushed by the bandit Santo Quastana, who was Arrighi's cousin.[111]

Once a case came to court, it was generally assumed that failure to convict an accused killer would lead to reprisals. After the acquittal of Napoleone Paoli in 1842, the trial summary commented: 'it is to be feared that the Agostini family will meet this impunity by taking vengeance itself'. After the acquittal of Anton-Felice Quilichi of Speloncato on a charge of attempted homicide in 1849, the president of the court expressed the fear that the relatives of his victim might 'seek through violence the reparation which they had been unable to obtain in the courts'. Again, in the course of the feud at Moca-Croce between the Franchi and the Istria, Giusepp'-Antono Istria had wounded Father Franchi with a shotgun. When he was later acquitted, despite clear evidence of his guilt, the verdict was described as 'deplorable and likely to be followed by bloody reprisals'.[112]

Actual reprisals following acquittals were very common. As we saw in Chapter 2, Michelangelo Paoli of Fozzano was acquitted in May 1831 of having killed Giovan-Battiste Bernardini. The day after the verdict was announced, Paoli was attacked in Bastia by Giovan-Battiste's brother and two other relatives. When they were eventually tried themselves for attempted homicide, the jury took account of the 'provocation' which the earlier verdict had represented for the close relatives of the victim, and lenient sentences were applied. Paola-Caterina Nicolai was killed in 1831 in the course of the feud at Tox. Two members of the Antonmarchi family were accused and put on trial the same year. When they were acquitted, one of them was immediately killed by the Nicolai. Again, Giovan-Battiste Luciani of Venzolasca had been killed in fighting during the 1848 elections by Domenico Bottaci and others. When Bottaci was tried for his part in this crime and acquitted in 1850, this seemed to Luciani's son Matteo 'a denial of all justice and inspired in him the idea of taking revenge directly himself'. He therefore 'warned Bottaci to be on his guard' and later ambushed him. Matteo Luciani was then in turn tried for attempted homicide and, though convicted, he received the very light sentence of three years' imprisonment on the grounds that he had been justifiably provoked.[113]

We have seen that reprisals might be taken against witnesses, or even judges, held to be responsible for convictions. Reprisals following acquittals might also be directed against persons other than the principals. Petro-Paolo Vittini was killed at Poggio-Mezzana in 1847, and Domenico Dominici was convicted of this crime and sentenced to hard labour for life. However, the verdict was quashed on appeal, and 'the Vittini family attributed this regrettable outcome to the agency of the commander of the Voltigeurs Corses, Battisti, who was Dominici's relative' and patron, and an attempt was made on Battisti's life in 1850 by a cousin of Vittini.[114]

Where convictions were brought, the reactions of wronged parties would depend on what they regarded as the appropriateness of the sentence. In 1843, for example, Fiordispina Canacci of Bisinchi had been accidentally killed in a brawl. Anton-Maria Luccioni was convicted for his part in this affair and sentenced to two years' imprisonment for 'excusable homicide'. But 'this reparation did not seem sufficient to the Canacci family', and after Luccioni had returned to the district, having served his sentence, he was shot and very seriously wounded by Fiordispina's brothers.[115] In a feud at Lecci, a member of the Cirendini family was killed and two of his relatives wounded in 1895. Three Furioli brothers were prosecuted and condemned to periods of eight to twenty years' hard labour, but, in Marcaggi's words, 'the Cirendini cannot have regarded the judicial satisfaction as adequate to compensate them for the killing of one of their number, for three years later they ambushed Francesco Furioli and his 16-year-old son', who was fatally wounded in the encounter.[116] It is characteristic of this transactional attitude that little distinction was drawn at village level between accidental and deliberate killings, though the courts drew the distinction very clearly. Antono

Belfini of Zicavo, for example, was sentenced to only eight months' imprisonment around 1830 for the accidental killing of Silvestro Giordani of Bastelica. The latter's family saw this as a totally inadequate punishment and arranged to have Belfini killed by bandits when he came out of prison. Courts and combatants in feuds also differed in the view which they took of accomplices. Whereas judges – and juries – treated them leniently as a rule, on the grounds that their responsibility was limited, relatives of victims saw them as more fully accountable. Giovan-Camillo Mariotti, for example, had been killed at Campile in 1838 by Felice Mariotti, who was sentenced to 20 years' hard labour for the crime; but Felice's alleged accomplice Giulio-Francesco Mattei, was tried separately later and acquitted. The victim's 15-year-old son did not accept this unequal verdict; 'he believed that his father's death had only been half-avenged and he resolved to complete the work left unfinished by the courts'. In 1842, therefore, two years after the acquittal he shot and killed Mattei as he was gathering chestnuts.[117]

These cases indicate that punishment by the courts could be fitted into the traditional systems of blood vengeance and the same notions of balance applied. In a case which we have already encountered, Matteo Maisetti of Figari and his son had been killed in 1848 and 1849 to avenge the dishonouring of a woman. Three of the culprits were prosecuted and convicted in 1854, receiving long or life sentences to hard labour, but the fourth went into exile in Sardinia. When he gave himself up in 1860, he was acquitted, a verdict explained or justified by the trial summary in these terms: the two victims had no close kin and 'their distant relatives seemed to be satisfied with the three previous convictions and not to be insisting on the condemnation of the last defendant'. Offenders and their relatives took such responses into consideration in their more general negotiations with the judicial authorities prior to surrender, proportioning the length of their stay in the maquis accordingly, as Barry explained in 1893. More rarely, the courts might be immediately preferred as a safer option or a refuge. Giovanni Grimaldi of Ota, for example, killed Anton-Giovanni Ambrosini in 1850 and, 'fearing the vengeance of Serafino Battini [who lived with his victim's daughter] more than the action of the courts, he quickly gave himself up as a prisoner'.[118]

This brings us again to the pacificatory role of the courts. In this perspective, the trial was a period of truce in the hostilities between the two parties. The peace treaty of 1812 at Ciamannacce laid down that no violence would be committed during the coming trial and that no pressure would be placed on witnesses or principals; both parties agreed 'to submit absolutely to the decision of the court'.[119] The aim was to reconcile the parties by judicious and balanced verdicts, and the actual court proceedings here were usually preceded by careful negotiations, as we have seen.

Explaining official sponsorship of a number of peace treaties in 1817 which had involved the deportation of two men from Corsica, Count Willot wrote that this was 'preferable to bringing them before the courts, where witnesses would not dare to testify against them and they would simply be acquitted'. Concomitantly, however, peace treaties and arrangements were taken account of in judicial proceedings, especially by juries. In a case in 1814, Battiste Bojoli of Ocana was killed by Innocenzo Rossi in retaliation, it seems, for Bojoli's having wounded the mayor who was Rossi's relative. At the trial, however, two first cousins of the victim testified that Rossi had killed Bojoli in self-defence, and the case against him was dismissed. This decision, the public prosecutor commented, was 'very suspect, since it was clear that the accused had come to some arrangement with the relatives of his victim in order to defeat the ends of justice'.[120] Visconte Casile of Valle shot and seriously wounded Dr Petreschi of Sari-d'Orcino in 1842, which led to an enmity between their families. This was ended by the intervention of the bishop of Ajaccio, and a peace treaty was concluded. When Casile was subsequently prosecuted for the original attempted homicide, the jury rejected his plea of 'violent provocation', but 'considered that it had to admit extenuating circumstances in his favour, following the convention so deeply rooted in Corsican custom of respecting peace treaties in order to prevent worse misfortunes'. In a more blatant case in 1845, Natale Tenneroni of Santa-Maria-Sicche was charged with trying to kill Giovan-Battiste Emilj in the course of a feud between their families, which had subsequently been concluded with a peace treaty. 'In accordance with the terms of this treaty, the Emilj and other witnesses testified in court that Giovan-Battiste had been wounded by his own pistol exploding in his hands' as he was shooting his own dog. The jury was by no means taken in by this unlikely story but, nevertheless, took account of the rapprochement, finding Tenneroni guilty of simple wounding, which carried a sentence of only four months' imprisonment. Many other examples could be cited, and the same principle applied to less formal reconciliations between relatives.[121]

Some further cases are slightly more complicated and raise other issues. Two branches of the Anziani family of Bisinchi had quarrelled over the ownership and tenure of rooms in a house and threats of death had been exchanged between them. However, prosecutions for this offence were suspended 'to allow time for a reconciliation', a decision which proved to be ill-judged since, in the interval, one of the protagonists was killed. In some cases, reconciliations were feigned in order to achieve a favourable verdict in the courts. Agostino and Domenico Anziani of San-Martino, for example, were charged in the lower courts in 1841 with interrupting religious services and insulting the parish priest, behaviour which had caused the latter to leave the parish. 'In order to obtain an acquittal, they pretended to make their peace with him,' a successful manoeuvre. But soon afterwards they made threats against him to dissuade him from returning to San-Martino and they started a fire in a stable under the presbytery when he did come back. It was also possible for arrangements stemming from peace treaties to be ignored or broken. The widow Pianelli of Olmeto had been shot and killed in January 1853 as she was returning from a shieling in the mountains. Her relatives accused Carlo Balisoni, a youth, who had been a friend of the family, and alleged a sexual motive. At the trial in June, it was learned that 'the Pianelli had made their peace with the Balisoni', but this did not affect their attitude towards the prosecution, which they continued to pursue. Again, the peace treaty at Piana in 1849 between the Moreschi and the Versini was drawn up and signed after there had been one killing on each side. It bound each party to eschew prosecution and to work for the acquittal of either murderer if he were caught. However, the Versini did not keep to these terms following the arrest of Lorenzo Moreschi, but instead revealed to the authorities 'all they knew that could aid his prosecution'. The Moreschi riposted by divulging the terms of the treaty, which had remained secret, in order to damage the position of Matteo Versini, who had also been arrested. The treaty was, in effect, in the words of the trial summary, 'a treaty of insurance against the action of the courts'. In the event, both men were convicted and sentenced to the same sentence of hard labour for life, and the equality of this double condemnation satisfied both families.[122]

The courts could try to play a more actively conciliatory role, and sentences might be arrived at with this intention clearly in mind. A judicial official complained indeed in connection with a case in 1801: 'the parties concerned are closely related, the plaintiff being the sister-in-law of one of the defendants, which should have led the judges to pronounce a less rigorous verdict in order to reconcile these families'. The public prosecutor commented more generally at the end of 1825 that 'moderate sentences for acts of violence have been found by experience to suffice to re-establish calm in the villages and peace among families'. Again, a petition for clemency for Giovan-Achille Santucci of Ciamannacce, sentenced to five years' imprisonment and ten years' 'surveillance' for homicide, was opposed by the public prosecutor in 1882. The sentence, he argued, had been handed down by the court 'with the express aim of preventing further trouble and the continuation of the blood enmity between the two families', and any diminution of the penalty would undermine this aim.[123]

The notion of balance inherent in settlements at the local level also guided the authorities in their attitudes towards granting pardons generally. A petition for clemency on behalf of Simone-Petro Agostini of San-Lorenzo in 1833 was supported by its sponsors on the grounds that it 'would contribute powerfully to restore concord in a canton riven by terrible dissensions', but the public prosecutor disagreed. Political rivalry in the hamlet of Corbiti had led to two killings, and a double prosecution had been felt necessary in order to keep the peace. Any difference in penalties between the two sides, brought about by acts of clemency, might revive the enmity. A less serious case at Olmeto arose after a demonstration in 1863 when Bartoli, the opposition candidate in the legislative elections, visited the village. Five of his opponents and five of his supporters were prosecuted on minor charges and all were sentenced to a few days in prison and small fines. Appeals were launched separately, and the sentences against four of the Bartoli supporters were remitted, while that of the fifth was reduced to a simple fine. In considering the appeals from the other side, therefore, the public prosecutor insisted that a rough balance be kept, although the opponents of Bartoli had clearly started the trouble. All their prison sentences were then remitted and the fine of one of them was reduced.[124]

We have seen how exile was used by the civil and military authorities in the early nineteenth century as an element in their attempts to conciliate feuds, and periods of exile were often laid down in peace treaties. In this scheme of things, prison tended to be assimilated to exile at the official and the local levels. This identification was reinforced by the fact that long prison sentences were nearly always served on the 'continent', partly because prison conditions in Corsica were so bad.[125] Periods spent in prison were treated like periods spent in exile or as bandits in the maquis and were referred to in the same terms as a 'temporary disgrace' or an expiation. A petition for clemency in 1842 on behalf of two men from Bocognano, sentenced to five years' imprisonment in 1839 for wounding with intent, stated that 'they believed that they were sufficiently purified of their offence by the punishment which they had already suffered'.[126] In this perspective, prison sentences did not need to be long, and they were adjusted to take account of time spent in voluntary exile or in the maquis. After he had killed Giovan-Bernardino Codaccioni in 1834, Giacomo Chiaroni of Casalabriva fled to Sardinia. After remaining there for nine years, he returned to Corsica to face trial in 1843 and was sentenced to three years' imprisonment for excusable homicide. The sentence assumed that Chiaroni had acted under provocation or had even killed his victim accidentally, but it also took account of his years of self-imposed exile. Paolo Tafanelli of Moca-Croce was convicted of homicide in 1853, for a crime committed in 1834, and sentenced to only two years' imprisonment. This was felt to be a sufficient sentence 'against a man who had already suffered 19 years' exile'. In 1860, Francesco di Quiliano Susini of Figari was even acquitted on a homicide charge, where all the evidence was against him, because he had already spent twelve years abroad and his victim's relatives appeared to be satisfied with this.[127]

This last condition would always have been a crucial element in such calculations. For exile or prison was both 'a measure of prudence' as far as the offender was concerned, removing him from the reach of possible reprisals, and a penalty exacted for the offence, depriving a family of one of its members for a lapse of time that had to match the gravity of that offence; it also provided a cooling-off period in which a reconciliation might be effected or hostilities be mitigated. In the Bocognano petition for clemency, the victim associated himself with the plea on behalf of his erstwhile enemies after they had served only part of their sentence. In a more extreme case, Antono Colonna of Arro made a formal declaration in 1876, 'according à complete pardon to Santo Santini, an accomplice in the killing of his infant son, agreeing to his return to the village, and soliciting his speedy release'. Santini's life sentence passed in 1857 had been reduced to 20 years in 1875 and it appears that, following this guarantee, he was allowed to return to Arro, an old man of 75, when his new sentence expired. But enemies could be far less conciliatory, insisting that sentences be adhered to, particularly, it is likely, where these were not considered severe enough in the first place. We have seen that it was common for prison sentences to be accompanied by further periods of 'surveillance', which prevented or sought to prevent offenders from returning to their villages or even to Corsica. Paolo-Damiano Ficoni of Perelli-d'Alesani was sentenced to eight years' imprisonment and five years' surveillance in 1878, following his conviction for homicide. A plea to remit the second part of his sentence was rejected in 1884 on the grounds that it would not have been acceptable to the relatives of his victim. They were 'utterly opposed to the idea that Ficoni should come to live in Corsica when he leaves prison, and they let it be known that his presence in the island could lead to bloody reprisals'.[128]

Patronage and political conflict

I

Various aspects of patronage and clientship have been discussed by historians, social anthropologists and political scientists.[1] For the modern Mediterranean world, most emphasis has been placed on the role of patrons as mediators between poor, backward and isolated regions and the central state apparatus. Local patrons with their exclusive outside contacts controlled access to the benefits which the State had to offer in the form of official positions, grants, public works, etc., and they channelled these benefits towards their followers, offering the State and its representatives loyalty, local information and votes in return. The form of the patronage phenomenon was altered with increasing state intervention, the introduction of universal suffrage and the creation of political parties, but these only introduced complexities into the system and added further layers to it; they did not fundamentally change it.[2] Patronage took different forms, depending on the structure and culture of the society in which it was found. Patronage always acted as a counterweight to class consciousness and class conflict, but it could assume an outwardly egalitarian mode where land ownership was widely diffused and economic relationships indirect, or it could act as a buffer system segregating an élite from a labouring class via a stratum of bailiffs, middling petty bourgeois and domestic servants.[3] Patrons, moreover, could be aristocrats or notables of obviously higher standing than their clients (though not in the modern period of different legal status), a situation quite compatible with informal personal ties; or they could be brokers more on a social level with their clients, being superior only in special political skill or know-how.[4]

Some writers have argued that a patronage system acts to prevent violent conflict not only on a class but on a general level,[5] but in Corsica, where much of the analysis outlined above applies, this was certainly not the case. Many observers, indeed, specifically linked patronage and feuding. 'The system of vendetta', wrote Robiquet in 1835, 'makes each family into an independent "power", which its leaders seek to extend and strengthen; the most distant relatives are sought out and protected. Families then group together into "parties", and the powerful men of each party protect all their adherents.' More vaguely, Father

Galletti in 1863 related the persistence of feuding and banditry into the second half of the nineteenth century to 'this accursèd patronage which certain families exercise in the island'. In the more penetrating diagnosis of Bourde, competition between 'clans' and their leaders operated equally via influence and bloodshed, politics and violence.[6] Although they were, to an extent and at a fundamental level, complementary modes of conflict within the same overall system, we may distinguish between them, and a more detailed description of the Corsican patronage system is a prerequisite to understanding political conflict there.

'Here, the coterie, the cabal and patronage are everything,' reported the commander of the gendarmerie in 1821; while Father Abeau declared two generations later that 'patronage and clientship are practised in Corsica as they were in the days of ancient Rome'.[7] Kinship ties were supplemented or reinforced everywhere by ties of dependency between landowners and tenants or labourers, between richer and poorer neighbours, and between notables and officials and the rest of the population. Although most people had access to land, as we have seen the best agricultural land was owned by notables, who leased it to share-croppers or farmers. These might be selected because they already were clients, and they certainly became so by the nature of the tenancy. A patron, whom Bourde interviewed at San-Fiorenzo in 1886, explained that his family's scattered properties were let out 'on fairly generous terms, whose conditions we do not always strictly enforce'. The fifty or so households of share-croppers thus 'depend on us for their living and are entirely devoted to us'. *Lucchesi* labourers were also clients working year after year for the same families. Ties between neighbours were expressed by the provision of hospitality around the hearth in the evenings or of doles on ritual occasions. Gregorovius writes here of the survival of a kind of vassalage, of 'retinues of dependents and friends bound to important families and rendering them service, known as "*patrocinatori*" or "*geniali*"'. Thus, in a letter to one of his supporters, Luca-Antono Viterbi referred to 'my people from Taglio'.[8]

Whatever their basis or historical origin, such ties were often not overtly hierarchical and left room for the expression of some independence on the part of clients. Griffon noted in 1841 that the better-off landowners of the Balagna were extremely powerful but that they needed great skill in order to 'rule', because the local population was 'so proud'. On the material plane, Montherot was told by a priest near Belgodere that the owners of the rich olive groves of the same district 'were obliged by local custom to allow one-third of the crop to the peasants who harvested it and transported it to the presses'. Indeed, the 'egalitarianism' of Corsican society was often remarked upon by visitors, as we have seen. 'Nowhere else do the different social classes mingle so frequently and so intimately,' Mérimée noted. Abeau wrote later in the century that a poor client 'recognized and respected social rank', but relations between clients and patrons were 'of a free and easy-going kind that we would find difficult to imagine'.[9] Only occasionally was it suggested that such familiarity was a sham. A Corsican official in the highways department in 1871, for example, described the system as a 'petty feudalism without a trace of glory or grandeur, guided by no moral principle, which throws to its clients a few minor places, the odd favour, the odd gift, a smile – always ironic – like bones to dogs'.[10]

Patronage and clientship in Corsica had a number of overlapping functions. First, the system provided mutual protection for both parties. According to Public Prosecutor Mottet in 1836, patronage was a response to the failure of the government to provide protection, which led

> everyone to seek some other power to look after them. The powerful men from each canton group around them the rest of the population and make a kind of local guard of them. At the patron's call, all the clients take up arms; they accompany him on his travels; they protect him against his enemies, share in his hostilities, and often act as the instruments of his vengeance. In return for this dependence, for this blind devotion, the patron acts as the zealous defender of his clients in all circumstances.

Bourde made the same analysis half a century later:

> Having no legal protection to rely on, a man felt lost if he remained isolated; so everyone strengthened the ties which linked him to his relatives, looked for alliances, gave himself to an influential family that already had a clientèle. The greater the number of its clients and the more powerful therefore that a clan was, the better protected the individual member would be in the struggle for life.[11]

The extension of kinship ties into a wider circle of protection was most obviously effected via godparenthood. Malaspina noted in 1876 that

> Corsicans never choose godparents from within the family; they prefer to address themselves to a powerful man or, even better, to the young heir of some powerful family, who will protect both them and their child ... For their part, influential men themselves seek out this honour, for a godchild or *cumpare* can turn out to be very useful to them.

'From the day of its birth', Abeau agreed, 'a powerful protector is sought for a child, and the choice of godparents is dominated by this thought. A simple labourer often has an important person as his godfather, a millionaire, a judge, a deputy, a senator.'[12] As this indicates more generally, by the later nineteenth century patronage was related less to the lack of central authority than to the indirect nature of state presence. According to Bigot, the Corsican 'turned, in pursuit of his interest, to someone who would, he believed, be useful to him in obtaining jobs for his children, in giving him "influence", in helping him at law, and here he looked to a person with pull in official circles, judicial or administrative, either in the department or further afield'. And, although such a patron might initially be sought out of interest, Bigot stressed that, once the relationship was formed, the client – and his children – offered unconditional and lifelong loyalty.[13]

The range of reciprocal services involved was enormous. Most simply, as we have seen, patrons acted as generous landlords in return for allegiance. As Colomba told the prefect to explain why she was letting a water mill at a very low rent: 'My father was dead, and in my position I had to keep the family's clients happy.' Patrons also provided loans, gifts and favours. A notable from Venaco told Bourde that 'when the tax-collector threatened one of his clients with seizure because his payments were in arrears or because fines had not been paid, he made the client an advance of the sum in question. The client pays back the money if he is able.' While Bourde was in the village, a client in such straits arrived, having brought a hectolitre of wine over 50 kilometres in order to borrow 30 francs, and he was put up overnight. Baptismal and wedding presents were very often afforded, whether patrons were godparents or not. Clients were visited and looked after when they were ill, and 'the influence of a family or clan was greatly enhanced by having a doctor among its members', who could dispense free medical care in return for support. Bennet relates in this context that when Dr Manfredi, a leading surgeon in Bastia, visited his family house in Orezza, crowds of people gathered to see him and to ask for advice and help. Legal services were similarly furnished. 'Once or twice a month', Bourde's Venaco patron 'went to Corte to arrange affairs for his clients with his lawyer.' We have discussed patronage and the courts quite fully in the last chapter and need add little here. Judicial patronage was always part of a much wider network, and its successful deployment reinforced patrons' power both individually and generally. As a police report commented on an acquittal of a defendant from Sartène: 'The local patrons had to retain their name and their credit in the eyes of their following.' Nearly all petitions for clemency for convicted offenders were supported by letters from mayors, deputies and other officials or notables, and such support was expected. Giovan-Felice Graziani, for example, convicted for his part in a brawl during the municipal elections at Campitello in 1883, had boasted that he would be pardoned, saying that 'his friends Messrs Laguerre and Laisant, the deputies, are ready and waiting to protect him and obtain for him what he wants'.[14]

The courts also provide illustrations of the two-way nature of patronage and clientship. Clients expected patrons to procure pardons, mild sentences or acquittals, but clients were also expected to give false testimony, act as pliant jurors or even appear in the dock. In a case in 1834, Carlo-Michele Rossi of Bastelica was convicted of wounding a woman in an affray and was sentenced to five years' imprisonment. After an appeal had failed, the Rossi wrote to the public prosecutor claiming that the shot in question had been fired by a certain Giulj. He was 'a simple peasant, completely devoted to the Rossi family', who had apparently agreed not to deny the accusation on the understanding that he would receive a very light sentence. Rossi was released, and Giulj was tried, convicted and sent to prison for two months for 'involuntary wounding'. The following year these two contradictory verdicts were both quashed and both men were sent for retrial at Aix-en-Provence.[15] A similar pattern is sometimes found in connection with military service. Clients expected patrons to obtain exemptions for them, but they might also have to stand in (before the last third of the nineteenth century) as replacements. We learn, for example, from a case in 1844 that a young herdsman, who was a client of the Roccaserra family of Sartène, had agreed to serve instead of a member of the family for 1200 francs, well below the normal rate for buying military substitutes.[16]

Patrons were the intermediaries through whom state obligations and benefits were channelled. The number of these grew, of course, as the century progressed, and the latter category included exemptions from paying school fees, certificates of indigence, and hunting permits.[17] But the favourite field for the exercise of patronage here was undoubtedly that of public office. Already at the end of the eighteenth century, Patin de La Fizelière commented on the proliferation of local officials in the Sartène region. 'The love of public office is pushed to the furthest extremes,' Glatigny noted in 1870. Most 'Corsican peasants would sacrifice everything for a position even as a field guard'. Again, according to Vanutberghe in 1904, Corsican society was 'divided into two branches: one "noble", comprising those holding a place of some kind; and the other vulgar, made up of those who do not. The first enjoys the greatest prestige. Titles, gold braid, an ordinary caretaker's hat, all are universally coveted'. Inside and outside the island, Corsicans flocked into the civil service, the army, the customs and excise, the police, the church and, as we have seen, the judicature, so that by the later nineteenth century theirs was the French department with the highest proportion of persons engaged in these and the liberal professions. The local press published information on every appointment, transfer or promotion in the whole of France involving Corsicans. There was hardly a family without one member in government service of some type and such news was avidly followed. The importance attached to education from the early nineteenth century is related to this general phenomenon, since, in Versini's words, 'even when jobs were obtained by "influence", their occupants increasingly came to require the right diplomas'.[18]

Observers also pointed to the reasons for this penchant for places. Réalier-Dumas wrote in 1819 that Corsicans were 'very keen to have official positions, because they are poor and because they acquire in them the means to help their friends and humiliate their enemies at the same time'. 'Our country is poor,' a local man told Maurras in 1898:

> We have no industry; our agriculture is short of markets. We are thus obliged to live under the reign of patronage, but we want to reap the benefits of this situation as well as suffering its disadvantages. Our big families ... hold all the top positions, but with their help, the rest of us can hope for some of the less elevated ones, and these are not to be sneezed at.

A Franciscan informed Molinari more succinctly on a boat from Isola-Rossa to the Capo-Corso: 'Good people, the Corsicans. They pull strings to get places. They need places to have enough to eat. But good people!'[19]

As this makes clear, positions were normally acquired through patronage. Until election was introduced under the Third Republic, the appointment of mayors and *adjoints* was the occasion for intense lobbying from all quarters: the candidates themselves, their local adherents, their opponents and, most decisively, their patrons. For example, the prefect received a recommendation in 1840 on behalf of Agostino Stefanini for the post of mayor of Sari-d'Orcino from Count Colonna Cinarca, and in 1847 on behalf of Dr Antono Stefanini for that of *adjoint* from Cuneo d'Ornano, a local notable. Both candidates were successful. In 1846, Baron de Cesari wrote to the prefect with a long list of recommendations for these posts at Casalabriva ('my native place'), at Serra, at Zerubia and at Petreto-Bicchisano. In the same year, Francesco-Maria Ceccaldi, a notary from Ota, wrote to recommend himself as mayor, putting forward reasons that patrons also usually emphasized: 'my family has always enjoyed an influence which no one could think of denying ... and that influence would be wholly at the disposition of the government'. The administration tried sometimes to bypass these networks of influence, but this was virtually impossible and anyway self-defeating if the island was to be governed at all. Appointments, moreover, as we shall see in detail, were bitterly contested. A particularly fierce competition took place at Penta-di-Casinca in 1866, in which the sitting mayor Frediani was opposed by a candidate supported by Limperani, father of the consul-general at Genoa and by Deputy Gavini, a relative of the Limperani.[20]

Other posts were obtained through the same machinery. Italiani became justice of the peace in his own canton of Orcino in 1884 – something not usually encouraged – through the patronage of Senator Peraldi. The correspondence relating to the filling of ecclesiastical posts had become so time-consuming by the mid-1830s that Bishop Casanelli d'Istria, who was opposed to patronage on principle, announced publicly that he would no longer acknowledge letters of recommendation. What is more, it was made known that 'any cleric who solicited a post directly or indirectly would *ipso facto* be excluded from consideration for it, whatever his qualifications'. This had some immediate effect, but solicitations by third parties and wire pulling of the most blatant kind was in full swing by the end of the century. This may be illustrated by the intense lobbying for the rich living of Oletta in 1887. The subprefect referred to four main candidates, one of whom was related to the bishop, and a letter from a fifth, Father Maraninchi, parish priest of Nonza, soliciting on his own account, has been preserved. He stressed his loyalty and usefulness to the Republican régime. His elder brother was mayor of Moncale and also deputy justice of the peace in the canton. 'My family has always voted and got others to vote for the government. At the last general election, M. Arène and the other deputies [on the Republican list] obtained 62 votes at Moncale.' Maraninchi wanted to be nearer to his family 'above all, in order to be able to give them my support during elections'.[21]

For reasons that we have mentioned, access to educational resources, clerical and secular, fell within the same ambit. There was great pressure during the Restoration period on the small number of scholarships offered to Corsicans in the seminary of Aix-en-Provence, and Casta notes that candidates were selected via patronage, which favoured 'nephews of *curés* and younger sons of good families'. Presumably the same principles operated more or less strongly once Ajaccio had its own seminary, which it did effectively from 1835. As far as other institutions are concerned, we may cite again the article attacking judicial and other forms of patronage published by Cerati, a primary school inspector, in 1857. He said that he received thousands of letters and visits every year trying to engage his influence in connection with the public examinations for entry into state colleges and *lycées* and the teachers' training college in Ajaccio.[22]

A case in 1839 involving one of the leading families of the island provides a good insight into how patronage worked (or failed to work) more generally. Girolamo Casalonga, called Poveruomo, was the bailiff and land agent at Alata for Felice Pozzo di Borgo, departmental paymaster and nephew of the Russian ambassador. In 1823, Casalonga publicly insulted a female member of his patron's family, and,

at the insistence of his brother the colonel, Felice Pozzo di Borgo removed Casalonga from his position, but without ostentation and without
breaking other ties with him, for fear of incurring his hostility. Poveruomo continued to accompany his old employer on his travels and to
advise him on the running of his rural business. He had the reputation of
being an able man and influential in Alata.

It is not therefore surprising to learn that, after the July Revolution, he acted for
a short while as mayor there, though apparently without any direct recommendation from the Pozzo di Borgo. Casalonga 'believed, however, that his standing in
Alata and the services which he had rendered the paymaster gave him special
rights to the latter's benevolence, and he asked for this to be exercised in favour
of his only son Antono', who had joined the army in 1831. Pozzo di Borgo
helped Antono to get various advantageous postings as well as promotion to
corporal, but the young man believed that he was not being helped enough and
began to murmur against his patron. In 1834, Antono was invalided out of the
army and returned to the village. He had hoped to obtain a comfortable position,
such as that of clerk to the local justice of the peace, and was annoyed when
Pozzo di Borgo offered instead to get him work on the main road from Ajaccio
to Bastia, which was being rebuilt, or a job as a *voltigeur* at Pruno which was
reputed to be unhealthy. Relations between patron and ambitious clients became
strained and then broken. Finally, when another man in the village obtained a
post in the *voltigeurs* in a congenial place, the Casalonga decided to take action
against Pozzo di Borgo. Poveruomo declared publicly at the end of 1836 that a
man who kept promising without ever providing anything deserved to be killed.
The paymaster was also blamed early in 1837 when the usual largesse in the
district of Ambassador Pozzo di Borgo (in the form of gifts, payment for college
places in France, dowries, funds for local byways, food parcels, etc.) temporarily
dried up. At the last moment, Dr Pozzo di Borgo, a relative of the paymaster,
intervened to effect a rapprochement, and Antono Casalonga was promised a
commission in the army of Don Carlos in Spain. But this fell through, and later in
1837, the paymaster was ambushed and killed.[23]

   This is a reminder that patronage did not always run smoothly. But, to return
to the usual pattern, once installed in their positions clients continued to enjoy
protection. Mayors and other local officials who had acted illegally, for example,
were often retained in office through influence. A letter to the prefect in 1846
from Zerubia complained that the subprefect was doing nothing to investigate
accusations of malpractice laid against the mayor; indeed, the former was 'actively sheltering the mayor whose *cumpare* he is, and he boasts openly that he is
his protector'. Again, Mayor Arrighi of Noceta answered complaints made
against him in 1850 by invoking protection from a similar quarter. He agreed
that he had not officially reported the death of the *adjoint* as he should have done,
but this news had been communicated to the former subprefect, 'who knows our
family well'.[24]

   The partisanship of those in official positions was adduced in arguments for a
totally non-Corsican civil service advanced in the early decades of French rule.
'There is too much being related in posts,' Antono-Maria Santuccj of Loreto-di-

Casinca declared in a letter to the Minister of Justice in 1805. 'The father, the son, the cousins, they are all in it together. No Corsican should have an official post in Corsica.' 'To be able to count on a Corsican official in Corsica,' agreed a French police report in 1817, 'he would have to have no relatives, no friends, no party.' More specifically, in a letter in 1803, defending himself against 'calumnies' spread by the Mariani, the manager of the military hospital at Corte informed the public prosecutor that they were 'very closely related to the Arrighi family; and it has always been the practice of that family to abuse the powers entrusted to it by the government in order to oppress all those who declare that they will not be its slaves and who will not follow its whims'.[25] Later in the century, as we have noted, there was more emphasis on procuring benefits from the State, of which Bourde provides a striking example. The board established in 1886 to assess compensation for the expropriations of land, which would be required for the proposed east coast railway line, was made up of supporters of the powerful Casabianca family, one of whose members was also the railway company's lawyer. Friends, relatives and clients of the Casabianca were therefore awarded very large indemnities while their enemies or those who did not belong to their following were offered much smaller sums for the same amounts of land. The board set up the following year, however, to assess compensation for the Bastia–Corte line was controlled by opponents of the Casabianca, who turned the tables on them. 'If we had not given our friends payments as great as those which Mr de Casabianca gave to his,' Bourde was told, 'people would have concluded that we had failed in our duty to them and we would have been regarded as bad patrons.'[26] More generally, Francesco Susini of Olmeto wrote in 1847 that 'so long as family patronage exists in Corsica, intrigue will always triumph and lesser functionaries will be in the tow of party leaders',[27] which brings us to the broader issue of the connection between patronage and politics and thence to political rivalry and conflict.

II

To some extent, patronage networks were a mafia-like alternative to the bureaucratic organization of the State. 'The oldest and most important Corsican families continue to live in the villages,' wrote Robiquet in 1835,

> but they have many representatives in the towns, either in the administration or the judicature. It is around these families and a few others that have arisen more recently that the 'parties' form themselves. The leaders of these parties or factions usually seek to circumvent the official channels of government, to keep the authorities in a dependent position so far as the affairs of their canton are concerned and thus to rule the roost in their little world.

Yet, the extent of state 'patronage' was considerable even at this time, providing local patrons with additional resources with which to reward their clients, and reinforcing their role as intermediaries.[28] The terms 'clan' and 'clanism' have been used to describe these networks in which ties of kinship and alliance, of friendship and of mutual economic and political obligation overlapped, and clanism has been seen by some as a purely modern phenomenon.[29] Volney, for example, in 1793 attributed the symbiosis of local clanism and state patronage to the hiatus in effective government during the Revolutionary period, and Santoni has distinguished more recently between later political clanism and the situation in the early nineteenth century even, when the clan was still based on the community and the family and was free of involvement in the apparatus of the State. Though Pomponi has demonstrated that political clanism was a phenomenon found in Corsica well before the nineteenth century, this distinction has some validity and the modern period saw a significant process of adaptation of the local clan system to new predominating political and administrative structures.[30] Critics of French 'rule' in Corsica, indeed, have seen clanism as an essential condition of dependency. Complementing large-scale emigration as the main linkage between the island and metropolitan France, it provided a form of political and administrative incorporation which actually prevented any wider or more profound social and economic integration.[31]

The successful working of the system in its developed form required friends and agents at all levels of the French administrative and political system, starting at the top. In the wake of the Bonapartes and the Pozzo di Borgo, members of various Corsican families achieved high office in church and state especially in the early and mid-nineteenth century. Louis Sebastiani was bishop of Ajaccio from 1802 to 1831. One of his nephews, Tiburce, became a general and a peer of France and commander of the important military division of Paris, while another, Horace, followed a successful military career during the First Empire by becoming Minister for Foreign Affairs and a marshal of France during the July Monarchy.[32] Xavier de Casabianca was Minister of Agriculture and then of Finance during the Second Republic and became Minister of State in 1852. Jacques Abbatucci, a former judge at Bastia, was Minister of Justice from 1852 to 1857, and his son, Jean-Charles, served as his private secretary before becoming a Councillor of State. Another family to benefit in a similar way under the régime of Napoleon's nephew was that of the Pietri from Fozzano. The brothers Joachim and Joseph-Marie served as prefects in metropolitan France before each becoming Prefect of Police in Paris, the first in the 1850s and the second in the 1860s.[33]

At the next level and occupying a crucial linking position were deputies and senators. These sometimes came from the same families as those at the top, and they might even be the same people. Xavier de Casabianca and Jean-Charles Abbatucci were deputies in the late 1840s and again during the early Third Republic. Jacques Abbatucci was a senator, and another of his sons, Séverin, was a deputy throughout the Second Empire. Saint-Germain describes a journey undertaken in the late 1860s with Séverin Abbatucci and a group of local notables in the Zicavo region, the district from which his family came. Everywhere they went, 'herdsmen and others rushed to greet their representative; often he was obliged to descend from his horse in order to shake hands with old men too infirm to come to him or to go to visit invalids on their sick-beds'. This brings out the importance of the face-to-face relationship with the patron. A later report emphasizes the pressure on the politician to 'deliver the goods' that we saw was so necessary in the earlier Pozzo di Borgo example. Abbatucci and his fellow deputy Gavini, both officially sponsored by the administration, were said to have refused to support a government proposal to maintain the ban on carrying arms in Corsica in 1867, mainly because the prefect had failed to satisfy 'all their demands for places for their protégés'.[34] A number of writers have commented on the unrivalled influence in the following generation of Emmanuel Arène, deputy for various Corsican constituencies from 1880 to 1904 and then a senator. He was a friend of Gambetta and a leading figure in the 'Union des Gauches' in Paris, and even the prefect was said to be 'under his orders'. He was known in Corsica as 'Manna', because of his ability to obtain favours for his constituents.[35]

Further down the chain came departmental councillors. Maurras reported in 1898 that 'no festival or market attracted such a crowd from all parts of the island' as a full session of the General Council of the department:

> Not only are there sixty cantons to be represented, but every councillor arrives in Ajaccio with a train of friends, servants and, above all, clients and petitioners. Thus the patricians of Ancient Rome used to come to their assemblies. Every councillor presents his clientèle to the prefect and to the parliamentary representatives of his political colour. He puts forward face-to-face the recommendations that he has communicated in writing, usually more than once. For his part, the client, if he is wise, does all he can to boost the standing of his patron.

The streets and cafés around the prefecture were crowded and clients waited attentively. 'If they saw their councillor in the company of a deputy or a senator, they would be overjoyed, supposing that their business was "sown up".' 'A shake with a famous hand, or conversely, failure to touch or raise a hat, either could mean life or death, a career opened or closed.'[36]

At the village level, the agents of formal political patronage were mayors, *adjoints* and justices of the peace. We will discuss their local activities in detail in the next section, being content here to establish their role in the system as a whole. In return for local power, they mustered votes for elected representatives at all levels. Bourde's San-Fiorenzo patron does not appear to have held local office directly, though he called himself his clan's 'political manager' and explained that whereas 'in the past our clients would have followed us into battle, now they follow us instead to the voting urn'. Concomitantly mayors and other officials had political patrons, whose fortunes determined their own. At the end of 1846, Mayor Petro Renucci of Cozzano reported that news of the defeat of the governmental candidate in the general elections by Judge Abbatucci had convinced the villagers that he was going to be replaced as mayor by Giovan-Andrea Renucci, the pharmacist, whose supporters were staging noisy celebrations. Again, the subprefect of Bastia confirmed in 1865 that complaints of partisan maladministration laid against Mayor Filippi of Venzolasca were justified. However, it would be difficult to remove him, since 'he is related to and placed under the patronage of certain influential figures that you know, who will tell you, if you touch him, that the administration is trying to harm them'. The system allowed some room for manoeuvre for the skilled local politician. Mayor Manetta of Palneca, a renowned 'fixer' of elections in the early years of the Third

Republic, was careful to maintain some balance between the old Bonapartist and the new Republican 'parties'. 'If I eliminate Arène's enemies altogether,' he is reported to have said, 'the prefect won't need me any more, and then farewell to our influence!' But showing too much independence could be risky. When Formoso Giacobbi, mayor of Venaco and deputy justice of the peace, refused to support P.-P. Casabianca, who was standing in the local constituency in the general elections of 1881, Casabianca prevailed upon Gambetta to have him removed from his post as a magistrate.[37]

Different clans and their leaders predominated at different periods through their monopoly of governmental patronage. So, no jobs, favours, pardons, and so on were granted under the Restoration without the recommendation of the Pozzo di Borgo, under the July Monarchy without that of the Sebastiani, and under the Second Empire without that of Abbatucci or Gavini. The power of the last survived for a while under the Third Republic but was eventually eclipsed by that of the Casabianca and then of Arène. Though clan loyalty was important, Corsicans could not afford to be in real opposition to the government for any length of time, since this would have cut them off from official favour.[38] This meant that national political upheavals in France were felt even at village level in large-scale reshuffles of posts,[39] but also that politics were largely non-ideological. The characterization of a mayor of Levie by an opponent in 1846 must have been very generally applicable: 'he has never persisted in any political allegiance but has changed his party according to the times, always playing the wily fox'. Even towards the end of the nineteenth century, observers noted the absence of both political programmes and public meetings in Corsica. Political labels were used but they reflected the changing constitutional and governmental situation in France more than anything else and, where ideological opinions existed, they remained subservient to family or clan allegiances. So, in the 1870s and into the 1880s, for example, to be Republican was to be 'Casabianquiste'.[40]

In a sense, as Bourde suggests, politics was too serious a business in Corsica to be guided by theoretical considerations. Corsican men were trained in other circumstances of life – and especially perhaps as pastoralists[41] – in basic political skills. Like many others, Lorenzi de Bradi referred in 1928 to 'the Corsican genius for intrigue – resolute, ingenious, tortuous intrigue. No good Corsican can live without it. Success in life depends on it. Merit counts for nothing; intrigue counts for everything. It has become a science, a doctrine. One must know how to intrigue not only to obtain favours but more importantly in order to obtain one's rights.' The wholehearted participation of Corsicans in politics was noted by a succession of writers from Patin de La Fizelière onwards. Metz-Noblat commented in 1885 that 'abstention from elections and political apathy were virtually unknown'; while Count Vincenti declared in 1909 that 'all Corsican proprietors without exception are engaged in politics, which is, for them, an absolute necessity. Were they to refuse to involve themselves in every labyrinthine intrigue, they would be treated as fall-guys and pariahs by everyone else.' Proverbs reflected but also censured the national obsession.[42] Lack of ideology did not, however, mean lack of rivalry or conflict. To some extent, politics were an alternative to violence, but political struggles were passionate and generated their own violence.[43] We must turn now to a full discussion of the political rivalry, or factionalism, which accompanied the patronage system in Corsica.

III

Factionalism is a phenomenon with which historians of the Roman Republic and the Italian city states – to go no further – are familiar,[44] and its presence at village level has been signalled in many parts of Europe and beyond.[45] Social anthropologists have examined it in more detail and have begun a comparative explanatory analysis that is of help in understanding the Corsican situation in the nineteenth century. In his study of rural Brazil, Gross relates factionalism to the existence of a patronage system channelling resources from the central government to the localities. This situation generates competition, and 'modernization' thus provides a stimulant to factional conflict. Gross also links factionalism with the process of the expansion and fission of villages. Not only do factions hive off to form new villages where circumstances allow it, but factional divisions within established villages may be based on distinctions between 'original' inhabitants and later settlers. In a more general discussion, Siegel and Beals have isolated types and levels of factionalism and have sought to identify the circumstances in which 'pervasive factionalism' is found, in terms of strains within a community and of threats to or interference with it from outside. Others have noted the absence of any marked factionalism in some societies and have explained this by reference to deliberate mechanisms for promoting community, or to a mode of social structure that inhibits the formation of permanent or semi-permanent groupings.[46]

It is fair to characterize Corsica as a society of 'pervasive factionalism', and we have seen that the politicized patronage system involved the existence of rival 'clans', though one was usually predominant at island level. The Pozzo di Borgo were ousted by the Sebastiani in 1830. The third quarter of the century was marked by a struggle between the Abbatucci and the Casabianca. During the Second World War, the Pietri clan supported Vichy and the Landry the Gaullistes and the Resistance. As Lorenzi de Bradi asserted in 1928, 'there had only ever been two parties in Corsica and there always would be two parties'.[47] Nearly all sources agree, moreover, that the same is true at village level. 'At Prato, the population is divided into two parties,' the local justice of the peace reported in 1848, 'as it is in almost all the villages of the island.' 'The village of Speloncato is divided into two factions, like all Corsican villages without exception,' a trial summary stated more categorically the following year. More recently, Chiva found only one example of a village without two competing factions in a sample of over forty.[48] Nor is there any doubt about the linkage between factions at the different levels. Of the two 'parties' at Speloncato, 'one is led by Sr Arrighi, a rich landowner and brother of a judge of the Court of Appeal, while at the head of the other is Sr Malaspina, also a rich landowner and the son-in-law of Sr Pietri of Isola-Rossa, a member of the departmental council'. At Venzolasca during the Second Empire, the dominant Filippi faction belonged to the 'Casabianca party'. At Porri, according to a report in 1879, the inhabitants were divided into two parties, the Blacks and the Whites, or Republicans and Bonapartists, and shouts of 'Long live the Whites!' and 'Long live the Blacks!' were exchanged during the municipal election campaign of that year.[49]

Though adapted to and exacerbated by modern circumstances, factionalism, like patronage, was an old-established feature of Corsican society.[50] It was very evident in the struggles for independence and in the subsequent conflicts of the Revolutionary and Napoleonic period.[51] There would also seem to be a historical connection in Corsica between 'old' and 'new' inhabitants,[52] and between factions and residential groupings, whether within villages or between main village and coastal satellites. At San-Lorenzo in the 1830s both factions were centred on the hamlet of Coibiti but one of them predominated at Tribbio. In a report of a clash between the two rival factions at Zicavo in 1883, it was said that one of them 'came from the upper village', and we have pointed to the significance of such divisions as far as feuding proper is concerned. According to the parish priest in 1846, 'the inhabitants [of Zerubia] were divided into two parties, one of the mountain and the other of the coast',[53] and these divisions with their inherently fissiparous tendencies are also familiar. Factions might also be related to different interest groups in villages, particularly herdsmen and agriculturalists, though they might also be identified with the rival 'companies' into which transhumant pastoralists were organized.[54] A class element might also be present. A political opponent described the rival faction at Sari-d'Orcino in 1860, for example, as 'a party ... composed of insubordinate people from the dregs of society'.[55]

As one would expect, village factions were primarily family-based. At San-Lorenzo the two rival parties, though to some extent geographical, were formed around two families, the Moracchini and the Agostini. The former 'had for a long time exercised in the village a patronage which no one had dared to contest, but the latter had emerged from its modest status through hard work and successful agricultural enterprise and had acquired a fortune equal or superior to that of the Moracchini. This allowed the Agostini to contest the supremacy which the Moracchini had formerly enjoyed without hindrance', and particularly its control of the municipal council. Ravis-Giordani has shown that the rival factions at Calacuccia from the mid-nineteenth century belonged to two main family clusters, but both belonged to the same regional party or clan. This leads him to stress the importance of ties of friendship and reciprocal services in the formation of parties and of qualities of education and political skill in leaders, all of which complemented links of kinship and alliance. The leadership factor may be confirmed for other places. According to the prefect in 1816, Ignazio Marini, mayor of Calenzana, 'a simple peasant without fortune, had risen by strength of character to be leader of a party'. Similarly, the 'large clientèle' of Mayor Susini of Moca-Croce was attributed in 1830 to his personal influence, and the popular faction at Sari-d'Orcino in 1860 was said to have been created by its leader, Stefano Petreschi.[56]

We come now to the relationship between politically oriented factionalism and feuding. The two may be seen as distinct, even contrasting, forms of social behaviour. We have seen that there were important regional variations in the incidence of violent conflict, and there was clearly a long-term trend towards the replacement of feuding by other forms of competition. Coppolani wrote, for example, in 1949 that there had been no vendettas at Cargèse for at least a century, but that 'the spirit of the vendetta survived in the bitterness of political struggles'. There is overwhelming evidence, however, that political rivalry and feuding went together in the short term and that, as Coppolani implies, they were different modes of conducting the same struggle within a village. We saw in Chapter 2 that periods of political conflict often alternated with periods of violence in feuding villages. It is arguable, too, that increasing politicization exacerbated feuding in the short term. The public prosecutor wrote in 1805 that 'municipal officers harass their constituents every day in the most revolting way, and this feeds the factional spirit which still reigns in the villages of the interior breeding vendettas'. Surier noted in 1934 that 'cynical political considerations were often at the root of feuds', and the point has been amplified recently by Ettori and Pomponi. Ettori suggests that even before the Revolution the decline of community structures allowed 'bitter struggles for preponderance' to develop between rival families using both violence and political means. Pomponi notes that 'the pursuit of vengeance frequently underlaid political and electoral struggles and also dictated the way in which power was exercised'. Here he cites a report by the parish priest in 1870 on the situation at Avapessa: 'the mayor of this unfortunate village has for many years acted out of pure vengeance, and anyone else would only want to be mayor in order to avenge himself in the same way against those who happen to belong to the opposing party ... Thus discord is propagated, enmities are perpetuated and disputes are multiplied.'[57] It was in a usually vain attempt to prevent such a state of affairs that governments in the early nineteenth century tried to appoint mayors in feuding villages who did not belong to either warring party. Cases may even be cited in which mayors were outsiders, for example at Loreto-di-Tallano in the 1850s and 1860s, though whether this was on local or official initiative remains unclear.[58] Once clientèles became established or reinforced for political reasons, moreover, they could easily become involved in quarrels between families that had no original political motive. At Sant'Andrea in the late 1840s, for example, it was reported that 'the Valerj and the Ferrali were in a state of open enmity', which it was feared would escalate, since 'each had a numerous following'. Obligation in feuds, moreover, might extend to clients. Morandière referred in 1933 to a case in the Niolo in which a family expected a client to kill one of their enemies.[59]

Many examples may be cited in detail, in which factionalism, violence and feuding went together. According to the summary of a trial in 1861, 'a long-standing rivalry between the Corsi and the Renucci families divided the inhabitants of Pero-Casevecchie into two enemy camps'. A secret society, hostile to the government of the Second Empire, had recently been discovered in the canton, led by the advocate Patriccia de Corsi, an extreme Republican in 1848. The most prominent members of this society, all belonging to the Corsi party, had been prosecuted in the courts, and this had been seen as a hostile action inspired by the Renucci, particularly since the local justice of the peace was a Renucci. Elections for the departmental council in 1861 were seen by the Corsi as an opportunity to even the score against their enemies, and they stirred the population into a 'paroxysm'. There were two candidates for the local seat: Justice of the peace

Renucci, and a nephew of Patriccia de Corsi, for whom his uncle campaigned 'with all the ardour that the passionate desire for vengeance provides'. During the campaign, a group of Renucci supporters ambushed Patriccia de Corsi as he was going to another village with three companions. One of these was killed, and Corsi was hit by a stone and knocked to the ground but managed to escape. As this indicates, political occasions easily turned into violent ones. During a meeting of the municipal council of Sorbo-Ocognano one evening in February 1809, an argument developed over the disposition of income belonging to a chapel. Giovan-Antonio Casabianca and his nephew 'harangued the councillors and called them "robbers, cheats and assassins", which started a brawl; the lights were extinguished; blows with sticks were exchanged, and then daggers were used'. Three men were killed and another wounded, all it seems by the Casabianca. Again, at the time of the February Revolution of 1848, Pietricaggio was divided into two parties, led by Gianmassimo Luporsi and Timante Colombani. Colombani was mayor before the Revolution, but Luporsi was then nominated to replace him. Colombani protested, however, and was reinstalled. 'All of this got everyone extremely excited.' Colombani's supporters staged 'demonstrations of joy', during which they insulted their adversaries. On the following day, the partisans of Luporsi assembled in armed groups; the mayor tried unsuccessfully to disperse them; and shooting eventually broke out between the two parties on the church square, five people being wounded.[60]

In some cases, political conflict led via violence of this kind to vengeance killing and feuding proper. We have seen that rivalry between the Agostini and the Moracchini lay behind factionalism at San-Lorenzo in the early 1830s. In 1832, each party won five seats in the municipal elections. Competition then switched to the nomination of the mayor, and when a partisan of the Agostini was appointed, this was seen as a triumph for their party. The usual demonstrative celebrations were held in honour of the new mayor. During them shooting between the two parties began, in the course of which a Moracchini was killed and an Agostini woman seriously injured. The following day, an elderly member of the family was ambushed and killed as he was fleeing the village, in a deliberate act of vengeance. The serious feuding at Bisinchi, which lasted ten years and involved the 'virtual extermination' of the Vignale family, was provoked when a Vignale was appointed mayor in 1835, thus challenging the erstwhile supremacy in the village of the Canacci. To make matters worse, the new mayor threatened to open an official investigation into the municipal accounts on the supposition that his predecessors had been guilty of peculation. After peace had eventually been restored seven municipal councillors wrote to the subprefect in 1845, warning that 'the old animosities would soon be revived' were not great care taken in appointing a mayor from those among their number 'who have friendly relations with all the inhabitants'.[61] We have seen that the administration shared this general concern.

IV

These examples show that conflict within villages focused more often than not on control of the office of mayor. Like other French mayors, those in Corsica had administrative, police and judicial functions, and, where villages had communal assets, they effectively controlled these. As in other Mediterranean societies in the modern period,[62] they were able to use these powers to build up or to consolidate positions as local 'bosses', to some extent replacing the leadership of the *sgio* or important landowner. Save for a brief period during the Second Republic, mayors were nominated by the Ministry of the Interior or directly by the prefect, in a context of intense lobbying by patrons and local people that we have described. Only in 1882 was the practice of election definitively established. The same procedures applied to the selection of deputy mayors or *adjoints*.[63]

A few cases may be cited in which mayors stood or tried to stand above the mêlée of factional conflict. In a letter of resignation in 1852, Mayor Sandamiani of Peri declared that 'he had done all that he could to eradicate the partisanship there' but without success. We have seen that mayors occasionally acted as mediators in conflicts and that the administration tried to appoint 'neutrals' in feuding villages. Individuals, moreover, whether in this category or not, sometimes protested their reluctance to serve as mayor. A.-G. Quilichini of Poggio-di-Tallano told the prefect in 1846 that he had accepted the office of mayor more than ten years earlier out of a sense of public duty and 'against the interests of my family'.[64] But these were exceptions. According to Bourde, the main aim of Corsican 'parties' was to gain possession of 'the mayor's seal of office, for it is this which procures most for them in terms of immediate gains'.[65] In general, therefore, the position of mayor was much sought after and much contested, and men relished the opportunity to exercise the power and influence which it conveyed.

Again and again contemporaries referred to the 'tyranny' or 'despotism' of mayors.[66] When Pompeo Franceschi, the leader of his party, was nominated as mayor of Piazzole in 1852, 'he announced that, if previous mayors had ridden the local people with silver spurs, he would do so with ones of iron'. It was said of the mayor of Vivario in 1850 that 'he considered the mayorship as his property, his fief, his thing'. Indicative of such an attitude is an incident reported at Cozzano in 1855. The mayor, Giovan-Felice Renucci, met an opponent Antono Pantalacci, who walked with a stick, on the square. Renucci told Pantalacci that a new by-law made it illegal to walk with a stick in the village, grabbed his stick and threw it away. Pantalacci was later prosecuted for failing to show proper respect to the mayor – he had addressed him in the second person singular – and fined three francs. Among many complaints made against the mayor of Zerubia in 1846, more seriously, was the claim that 'he had not held a meeting of the municipal council for six years and had signed councillors' names himself on budgets' and other documents.[67] The 'tyranny' of mayors could be exacerbated by long tenure of office. Mayor Casalta of Muro, for example, remained in office throughout the July Monarchy. According to his brother, Mayor Maraninchi of Moncale occupied his position for thirty years; while Paolo Olivieri was mayor of Tavera from 1884 to 1929.[68]

Since the exercise of power by individuals and through them by parties was the main function of the office, a high level of incompetence by bureaucratic standards was displayed by mayors, though the accusations of enemies in this area should be treated with caution. With reference to filling the vacant post of mayor at Santa-Lucia-di-Moriani in 1840, the subprefect reported: 'We are faced with a municipal council filled entirely with men of no principles, of doubtful morality and of total incompetence,' and his remarks applied much more generally. Of 91 mayors replaced by Prefect Vignolle in 1818–19, for example, 71 were removed for misbehaviour or incapacity.[69] Many mayors and *adjoints*, particularly in the first half of the nineteenth century, were illiterate or unable to read or write French.[70] This meant, of course, that they were unable to keep the registers of births, marriages and deaths. According to Réalier-Dumas, these were 'kept unmethodically and inaccurately in most villages', while in some they did not exist or 'had disappeared'. It was said in 1850 that Mayor Arrighi of Noceta did not bother to keep a proper register of marriages, and his distaste for paperwork meant that, when his deputy died, he failed to report the fact and kept the post vacant. Sexual immorality seems to have been fairly common among mayors and deputy mayors, a reflection perhaps of their powerful status, and they had sometimes committed various crimes or offences before being appointed. In 1867, for example, the prefect turned down the candidature of Carlo Paoli for the post of *adjoint* at Fozzano because he had a number of convictions, but he was appointed nevertheless the following year.[71] As we shall see, there was more scope for illegal activity following appointment, and convictions of sitting mayors and *adjoints* were not uncommon. Deputy mayor Simoni of Figari was replaced in 1839 after he had been 'condemned to five years' imprisonment by the Assize Court'. Mayor Quilichini of Poggio-di-Tallano was convicted in 1845 of complicity in aiding two prisoners to escape and was later dismissed from office for this and other misdemeanours; while Mayor Giovansilj of Peri was suspended in 1858 following his conviction for keeping an illegal gambling house.[72]

Some degrees of incompetence would seem to contradict the idea of mayoral power. When the *adjoint* of Santa-Lucia-di-Tallano resigned in 1845, it was explained that 'his state of complete blindness made it impossible for him to manage his own affairs let alone carry out administrative functions'. Quite often in fact what one might call 'stooge mayors' were appointed, men who did not arouse the administration's suspicions as party leaders but through whom effective power was exercised by local bosses. The councillors of Aullène wrote to the prefect in 1846, urging him not to make Giovan-Battiste Simoncelli mayor. Not only was he 'a very poor man, irreligious, vindictive, immoral and ignorant, but he would also be a mere front-man for his cousin, ex-Mayor Susini'. The prefect was told similarly the same year that were Giovan-Paolo Susini to be made mayor of Serra-di-Scopamène, 'the village would in fact be run by his brother the priest'. More generally, the cousin of Mayor Tomasi of Zerubia testified in answer to an enquiry that he was 'a very weak man, who was entirely in the hands of an entourage of fanatics'.[73]

As a rule, however, mayoral power was exercised directly by local leaders to their own benefit or that of their families. Versini cites a song composed about the wife of a herdsman who became mayor of Pied'-Orezza: 'Rosa will be happy now / And all her brood. / They will have something better to wear now / Than rags on top of more rags ...' Public Prosecutor Mottet reported in 1836 to the same effect though in different language, that 'too many mayors turned what were intended to be wholly voluntary functions into very lucrative ones', and Spalinowski asserted in 1909 that mayors of small villages could make small fortunes on the side during their terms of office.[74] It was for this reason that the administration always enquired into the income of candidates and favoured wealthy men for the job, who might be less prone to financial malpractice. Such men were not easy to find in the poor villages of Corsica, however, and our sources illustrate in detail the many ways in which mayoral control of the local budget, communal resources, state benefits and so on, could be exploited for personal profit.

Mayor Mattei of Penta-Acquatella was threatened with dismissal in 1822, after he had left his own contribution off the village's annual tax assessment. In 1836, the mayor of Moca-Croce was reported to have pocketed the 300 francs voted by the municipal council as wages for the field guards; while the mayor of Balogna was alleged to have appropriated to his own use funds provided for school equipment. The military authorities were informed in 1844 that the mayor of Gavignano was charging soldiers on leave five sous per day for the certificates of good conduct which they required.[75] Among the misdemeanours for which Mayor Quilichini of Poggio-di-Tallano was dismissed in 1845 was forging a signature in order 'to appropriate a sum of 150 francs earmarked for the repair of the presbytery'.[76] In 1860, a forest guard from Calacuccia was awarded the sum of 100 francs by the government, because his son had been born on the same day as the Prince Imperial. The order for the money was sent to the mayor, who, instead of passing it on to its proper recipient, forged the latter's signature and obtained the money for himself from the tax office in Corte. Giacomo-Andrea Mariani was prosecuted in 1861 for various offences committed while he was mayor of Moro-saglia. These included charging 40 francs for marrying a couple without the right papers, receiving substantial bribes in cash and kind in connection with his judicial functions, and putting pressure on the local court bailiff to hand over all or part of his fees. Here it is very likely that the bailiff owed his position to the patronage of the mayor.[77] And the list could be continued.[78]

Until well into the Third Republic, it was rare for there to be any special municipal office building and mayors conducted their business in their own houses. This enabled them to draw an indemnity from the State, which was increased if the house was also used as the village school. In addition to pro-curing further financial benefit, this practice also reinforced the idea that the mayor's office belonged to him personally and established a setting in which all kinds of influence could be exerted on villagers. It was even possible to exclude opponents from meetings, elections and general access to municipal services.[79]

The house, of course, represented the family, and holding the position of mayor was a means of furthering family interests as well as of personal aggran-disement. A letter to the prefect from Ciamannacce declared in 1846 that 'the whole population had been oppressed for a long time by a single family, whose leader was the mayor'. It was frequently asserted that mayors packed municipal councils and other bodies with their relatives. According to his opponents in 1847, the mayor of Balogna 'had placed all municipal power in the hands of his family'; both his brother and his father-in-law had been made councillors and members of the parish committee (the *fabrique*); his brother-in-law was also a councillor, while the *adjoint* was his 'creature' and all the other councillors but three his relatives. Again, at Noceta in 1850 the municipal council was described as 'a family council', comprising the kinsmen and in-laws of the mayor, 'who signed everything which he presented to them'.[80] Municipal posts were also distributed to relatives, another means of obtaining resources for the family and of extending its power. We have seen that a bitter struggle divided supporters of the Greek and Latin rites at Cargèse. The latter were led by the Papadacci brothers, one of whom was mayor from 1808 and the other Latin priest from 1829. The municipal council was made up of their relatives, and they were also able to prevent Greek being taught in the local school, since the schoolteacher was their relative by marriage.[81] Field guards were appointed by the mayor and were usually his clients or relatives. At Moca-Croce in 1836, for example, both the field guards were related to the mayor. At Figari, according to a complaint made in 1854, the new mayor, Vincenzo Simoni, 'a capricious and terrible man', had appointed his young brother-in-law as field guard and was using him 'as his instrument'. Field guards were sometimes cypher appointments, wages in cash or kind being taken by the mayor, as we have seen.[82] More often, the post was of considerable importance (in the context which we have described in Chapter 3), and we will return to the partisan ways in which it could be exercised. Where mayors were unable to appoint or get their relatives appointed to local posts, they could make the position of their occupants extremely uncomfortable with a view to replacing or outflanking them. The candidature of Agostino Pulvarelli as mayor of Petreto-Bicchisano in 1847 was opposed by the state schoolteacher, on the grounds that he had a nephew who ran a private school, and would therefore keep the public school short of funds.[83]

This brings us to the more general ways in which mayoral power was used to advance factional interests and to disadvantage opponents. Pomponi and Ravis-Giordani have pointed out that many mayors used their control of common lands to win the political allegiance that large landowners derived from their tenants.[84] Mayors might themselves usurp common lands and their products, notably timber,[85] but more significant here was their toleration of usurpation by their followers. Among many complaints made against the mayor of Zerubia in 1846, for example, was one that he 'tolerated and encouraged the usurpation of common land'. The local gendarmerie commander told the prefect in the same year that 'usurpation of the common lands (at Olmeto) had been flagrant and continuous' for many years and that a strong and independent mayor was required to stop the practice. More generally, according to Bourde in 1887, parts of the common lands in most villages had been converted to permanent private use 'and, so long as one was on good terms with the mayor, nothing was said', and of course no rent was paid.[86]

The mayor also effectively controlled the leasing of remaining communal lands and assets, and arrangements were made which benefited him and his supporters rather than the village as a whole. Opponents of Mayor Giampietri of Gavignano, for example, complained in 1854 that he leased the chestnut woods after harvest to outside swineherds, thus depriving local people of their grazing rights. Mayors frequently received presents from such lessees or kept back part of the rent or obtained some other 'kick-back'. At Serra-di-Scopamène in the 1830s, Mayor Pandolfi was accused of taking money paid by herdsmen for the lease of common lands, though the subprefect found that at least in 1836 130 francs had been taken rather by the *adjoint* and other councillors, the mayor's accusers. More clearly, at Luri, where, according to Pomponi, 'the mayor had an important bakery business, he obliged those taking the concession to cut wood in the village to sell him what he needed at a specially low price'. Such formal leases of pasture or felling concessions, moreover, were frequently granted to friends of the mayor or to relatives on the most advantageous terms.[87] A case at Lama in 1811 indicates how this might be done while preserving a simulacrum of proper procedure. It was announced that the lease of 'grazing on the sides of the lanes of the village' would be settled at a candle auction to be held at the mayor's house on a certain day starting at 9 a.m. A would-be lessee arrived there on the day, however, at 8 a.m. to find a candle burning, which signified that the auction had begun, but no one else was there save the mayor, his son and the mayor's secretary. He protested, but meanwhile the candle went out and the grazing was allotted to the mayor's son as the highest (and only) bidder.[88]

Communal grazing rights, as we have seen, included that of *vaine pâture*, or rights of common on all the fields of a village after harvest. Mayor Folacci of Bastelica was 'reproached [in the 1860s] with numerous abuses, notably in the regulation of *vaine pâture* and in the allotment of the tax on livestock' making use of it. Similarly, the 'tyrannical' Mayor Filippi of Venzolasca ignored the law abolishing *vaine pâture* and leased the grazing to outsiders in return for money, a proportion of which he kept, spending the rest as he saw fit on various communal projects. One can see here how this practice might be the means of attracting a following both outside and within the community. Mayor Frediani of Penti-di-Casinca was accused in 1867 of having 'handed over the village to five or six families of herdsmen, who live off the devastation caused by their animals'. These outsiders had been given electoral rights in Penta and had received their privileges in return for giving the mayor their votes. Where local people did continue to enjoy traditional grazing rights, moreover, these could be managed to the advantage of the mayor's partisans. Bourde noted that at Casamaccioli in 1886, 34 supporters and 37 opponents of the mayor had livestock grazing on the common lands. The former had the larger flocks but paid less than a tenth the amount which the latter were charged. This practice was apparently widespread and points again to the importance of having field guards and assessors of one's own party, since they did the counting.[89] The convenience of this resource meant that mayors often resisted the partition of common lands. Mayor Durazzi of Fozzano was dismissed in 1854, for example, when he refused to implement a division and tried to retain at least part of the common lands for leasing out. And, where partition was carried out, it provided further opportunities for favouritism. The candidature of Ignazio Leca as mayor of Ota was opposed in 1860 on the grounds that 'in the division of the common lands at Sia ... he used his influence as a municipal councillor to allot a share to his mother', who had in fact left the village twenty years earlier.[90]

A related but also more general grievance was that mayors allowed their own livestock and that of supporters to stray without being checked. A complaint against Mayor Antonini of Marignana in 1848 referred to 'his devotion to goats', which were permitted to devour chestnut saplings. A large landowner at Olmeta-di-Tuda claimed in 1869 that his property was being devastated by animals belonging to the mayor, and the mayor of Venzolasca was accused of 'tolerating' similar acts of trespass and damage by others in the late 1870s.[91] As local police officials with the field guards under their control, mayors could operate legal sanctions in this sphere selectively to their own advantage and that of their followers. Mayor Giampietri of Gavignano was said to have allowed owners of straying goats to pay him 50 centimes per head rather than face prosecution. A number of landowners from Bisinchi complained to the prefect in 1874 that a local herdsman called Marchetti took goats 'to pasture every day on their property and on that of other inhabitants' and that the field guards did nothing to stop him; while two other herdsmen who did the same thing were prosecuted and forced to abandon their occupation. 'Because he was looking after the goats of the mayor's partisans,' it was explained, 'and had voted for him and his candidates, Marchetti could let his goats do every kind of damage with impunity.' The other herdsmen, by contrast, were 'looking after the goats of the mayor's opponents' and were treated accordingly. Bourde made it clear in 1887 that this was a well-nigh universal pattern.[92]

We have here only one example of selective use of the police and judicial process as an instrument of mayoral power. Bourde again pointed out that official police reports (*procès-verbaux*) relating to offences committed by 'friends' might be mislaid. Offenders who were 'friends' were nearly always given official warnings, whereas enemies and opponents were summonsed straightaway. Mayors could also exercise influence, as we have seen, in the higher echelons of the judicial system. Following a killing at Pietra in 1834, the mayor, who was a relative of one of the suspects, called in a crucial witness and told her that she should not give testimony that might put a man's life in danger. Mayor Quilichini of Poggio-di-Tallano was reported in 1845 to have offered 'a person in custody immunity in return for his vote'. More legitimately, mayors supported (or failed to support) petitions for clemency. For example, letters on behalf of Francesco Bastianesi, condemned to hard labour for life in 1849, were written by five mayors of the canton of Bocognano in 1852, while the mayor of his own village of Ucciani organized a petition with 74 signatures in his favour in 1877.[93]

Further opportunities for favouritism stemmed from the mayor's administrative functions, and first from his role as local registrar. As Pomponi has noted, falsification of the registers of births, marriages and deaths in order to raise income for the mayor and do favours for relatives and clients was common. We learn from a case in 1863 that the mayor of Gavignano had refused to provide a villager with false documents in order to allow him to serve as a military replacement despite being married, but that the man had been able to obtain them elsewhere. This suggests that mayors did normally provide such services, at least for their 'friends', and that forged documents were not hard to procure, and other examples support this view. Among the reasons given for dismissing Mayor Campana of Penta-di-Casinca in 1862 was the fact that he had issued Signore Frediani with a falsified copy of his birth certificate. Frediani wished to marry a girl in the village, but her family hesitated to accept him because he was too old and there were doubts about his family's claim to nobility. The mayor thereupon issued a certificate, which reduced Frediani's age by ten years and gave both his parents the *particule*. Again, Francesco Antonmarchi, *adjoint* of Venzolasca, was dismissed in the same year for falsifying birth certificates in order to permit three local youths to engage in the army while under the age of 17.[94] Falsification of the register in this area, however, was more often aimed at getting young men off military service. Several instances may be cited in which mayors were dismissed during the Consulate and First Empire for declaring young men to be dead so that they could avoid being conscripted, and the practice survived this period. According to Bourde, certificates were regularly issued later in the nineteenth century declaring men to be the eldest sons of widows when they were not, while the births of sons were often only registered once the age of military service had passed.[95]

Also much abused was the 'certificate of indigence', which was freely granted to relatives and supporters in order to let them off paying fines and taxes and later to enable them to qualify for school and other grants. The mayor of Balogna, for example, it was claimed in 1836, had provided a certain Felicita Carlotti with 'a false certificate to relieve her from paying a fine and costs ordered against her by the court of first instance in Ajaccio'. The mayors of Zerubia and of Ota were accused of providing certificates in similar circumstances, the first to a well-to-do supporter in 1846 and the second to his brother-in-law in 1853. The issue of other papers could be manipulated in the same kind of way. In an extreme example, the mayor of Cozzano was reported in 1843 to have provided a relative who was wanted for homicide with papers that enabled him to live in Sardinia, as well as conniving at his periodic visits to the village. Again, governmental grants and indemnities could be channelled by these and other means towards friends and relatives. A 'workshop' set up at Moca-Croce in 1836 with governmental backing was staffed by four relatives of the mayor, while he himself acted as supervisor. At Salice in 1868, Mayor Paoli was reported 'to have shown a revolting partiality in sharing out the relief accorded to the inhabitants' after a hurricane had destroyed a number of chestnut trees in the village. Those who had suffered most received only a few francs each, while relatives and followers of the mayor, some of whom owned no trees at all, obtained large amounts. In the same spirit, a friend of the mayor of Bastelicaccia was awarded generous compensation in 1887 for cattle lost in an epizootic outbreak, when in fact he had never owned any livestock, and the mayor of another, unnamed village, according to Spalinowski, placed his own wife on the list of unmarried mothers in order to claim for her. Indemnities were also available where land was requisitioned for road-building, and the same favouritism prevailed in their allocation. Other opportunities also arose here. The route taken by a road at Balogna was allegedly altered in a very inconvenient way in the 1840s to avoid a piece of land belonging to the mayor's father-in-law, a manoeuvre made possible by the fact that the road surveyor was also his relative. Again, at Penta-di-Casinca in the late 1860s, Mayor Frediani successfully held up the completion of a road because it would encroach on his property and had a drinking trough built at communal expense in a place which suited himself. The Balogna case is also a reminder that jobs as road surveyors, gendarmes, schoolteachers, postmen and so on, which became increasingly available from the mid-nineteenth century, were only obtainable as a rule, inside and outside the village, on the recommendation of the mayor.[96]

More general and pervasive was the role of the mayor in fixing local tax

assessments. Taxes on movable property were calculated by municipal committees, usually dominated by the mayor, and friends were favoured and enemies
disadvantaged in the usual way. In 1885, nearly 1500 appeals were lodged against
such assessments, of which nearly 1000 were upheld, and similar statistics obtain
for other years. Many of those unfairly assessed, moreover, did not appeal, either
through fear or because they were content to wait until their party won power,
when they could turn the tables on their opponents. At Casamaccioli, for example, in 1887, 56 partisans of the mayor and 41 opponents figured in the tax
registers. Although each party was assessed at an equivalent rate for the tax on
immovable property, which was independently assessed, and had a roughly equal
share of the total property of the village, the opponents of the mayor were
assessed for five times as much tax on movable property as his friends. Another
form of local 'taxation' was the *prestation* or liability to provide labour and
animals for road and bridge building and other public works. Here again favouritism could operate in the selection of men for particular tasks and in determining
liability. A denunciation of Mayor Tomasini of Zerubia in 1847 claimed that, in
revising the register of draught animals for the *prestations*, he left off as dead two
horses belonging to his cousin and another relative.[97]

To an extent, mayors had to appear as patrons and benefactors of the entire
community, and failure in this respect might undermine their authority. We learn
from a case in 1839, for example, that Girolamo Casalonga had resigned as mayor
of Alata 'because he had been unable to make the claims of his village prevail in a
dispute with the people of Bocognano'. It is also significant that mayors engaged,
particularly from the mid-nineteenth century, in improvements and schemes such
as the building of bell-towers, with which all the inhabitants could identify.[98]
More obviously, however, mayoral partisanship, as some of the above examples
have already shown, took the form of hostility to enemies as well as favouritism
to friends and could go as far as excluding or trying to exclude them from the
community altogether. As a song from the Ampugnani district put it: 'We have
won the mayorship / And the other party / Is in mourning!'[99]

Vexation of opponents falls into the categories with which we are already
familiar. A complaint from Balogna in 1847 illustrates some of the difficulties for
the opposition in having the mayor's functions centred in his personal residence:

> Our mayor only calls meetings of the municipal council now at ten
> o'clock in the evenings. We never know which room they will be held in,
> since he never tells us. He has all his own way in the meetings anyway,
> because most of the councillors are his relatives. When Councillor Dani-
> elli [an opponent] went to the room normally used for municipal affairs in
> order to pay his taxes, the mayor told him off for coming into his house
> [without being asked].

Mayors again abused their powers in connection with communal usages and
minor infractions relating to them. 'Moved by hatred and animosity towards
some local inhabitants,' according to further charges made against Mayor Tomasini of Zerubia, 'he has had a large number of poor people condemned in the
police court for gathering acorns in the woods belonging to the village.' Mayor
Filippi of Venzolasca had played a leading part in the 'terrible enmities' in his

village; in 1865, 'his house was still crenellated and he was widely feared. The field guards were the agents of his acts of vengeance and had been told ruthlessly to pursue all those who resisted him.' After Serafino Quilichini and others had complained to the authorities about the conduct of the mayor of Cozzano in the early 1840s, Quilichini was openly threatened by the mayor who said 'that he would take his revenge', while his associates were charged with fictitious forest offences.[100]

More blatant use of police powers in private quarrels seems to have been quite frequent. Mayor Frimicacci of Renno, for example, had the house of his enemies, the Casalta, surrounded by gendarmes in 1832, and two of them were subsequently prosecuted for acts of violence committed while resisting arrest. In the 1840s, the mayor of Balogna was in dispute with the Leca family over a right of way which they claimed over his land. When the Leca obtained a court judgment in their favour, the mayor accused three members of the family of cutting down some of his vines and had them arrested. They denied the charge and claimed that the mayor had paid witnesses to testify against them. They were convicted in the correctional court in Ajaccio but appealed. Whereupon the mayor offered to get his witnesses to withdraw, if the Leca family gave up their claim to the right of way, which they did.[101]

Registration and other administrative functions were also carried out or not carried out in a hostile manner. When his enemy Pasquale Negroni wanted to get married in 1831, Mayor Lota of Ampriani refused to issue a copy of his birth certificate, on the grounds – adding insult to injury – that the document in question stated that Negroni was a girl. Again, Mayor Tomasini of Zerubia refused to register a death and two births in the family of Tomaso Tomasini, 'his enemy'. We also hear of mayors having troops billeted on opponents. In a case in 1833, Petro Giovanelli claimed that Mayor Romanetti of Calcatoggio, 'his enemy ... had never missed an occasion to persecute and humiliate him. When his [Giovanelli's] father had been alive and there was a detachment of troops in the canton, officers had been billeted with the family, but, following his father's death, Romanetti only ever sent ordinary soldiers to the house.'[102] An opportunity to make a much more serious attack on the honour of opponents was provided by the mayor's legal obligation to enquire into cases of pregnancy among unmarried women as a precaution against infanticide. We have seen, for example, that the *adjoint* of Tomino ordered an examination in 1805 of a daughter of Giuseppo-Maria Marinetti, an action which her father took to be a deliberate attempt to dishonour the family by a man whom 'he knew to be his enemy'. Often a combination of means of official harassment was chosen. According to Giulio Renucci of Cozzano in 1846, the mayor had listed him for five oxen rather than the two which he actually owned on the register for *prestations*, and had taken no account of Renucci's age in assessing the number of days' work due from him; the mayor had also put difficulties in the way of the marriage of one of Renucci's daughters, claiming that the banns had not been properly published and demanding a special licence; finally, the mayor had underestimated the value of Renucci's property 'in order to prevent him from being an elector'.[103]

In the main, we have so far been discussing the non-violent use or abuse of mayoral power, but mayors also engaged in violence and were not infrequently

involved in feuding proper. Examples may be cited of mayors who had been
bandits or who were the protectors or protégés of bandits,[104] and, of course, of
mayors who went about habitually armed. In an extreme case, Mayor Marini of
Calenzana was arrested in 1816, following numerous complaints about his 'acts
of violence and arbitrary exactions'; he was reported to patrol the district at the
head of a large posse of armed men, and was known as the 'Viceroy'.[105] Mayors
not infrequently used the force available to them as officials or leaders of 'parties'.
Mayor Renucci of Ciamannacce was engaged in a property suit in the late 1850s;
when assessors were sent by the court to the disputed land he kept them off by
force, an act for which he was later prosecuted.[106] Nor is it difficult to find
examples of killings or attempted killings in which mayors and deputy mayors
were implicated as principals or accessories. At Piazzole in 1852, Mayor Franceschi shot and wounded the leader of the opposing party in the village. Mayor
Folacci of Bastelica was accused of complicity in homicide in 1852;[107] while the
adjoint of Canale-di-Verde shot at and then stabbed an opponent in 1884.[108]

Many of these acts of violence occurred in the context of overt and formal
political competition. As we have stressed, the mayorship with its extensive
powers was the object of fierce contest between factions that it is often difficult to
distinguish from feuding. The bitter rivalry between the two medical officers at
Bocognano in the 1820s was described as 'a vendetta', and 'the functions of
mayor, which one of them, Vizzavona, carried out with honour for eight years,
together with his large clientèle, made him the object of an implacable envy on
the part of his colleague'. 'At Prato', according to the justice of the peace in 1848,
'there was a constant war of influence, and each party aspired to retain or to get
hold of the mayorship.' In these circumstances, it is not surprising to learn of
armed confrontations between mayors and ex-mayors and their supporters, for
example at Sant'Andrea-d'Orcino in 1823 and at Sari-d'Orcino in 1841. In the
latter fray, the mayor and the ex-mayor were both badly hurt, and a man was
killed by the *adjoint*, who subsequently took to the maquis.[109]

Traditional celebrations took place when mayors or *adjoints* were appointed,[110] and these, like other festivities, could generate violence. At Corte, a
new mayor and *adjoint* were appointed in February 1832, although they were the
only members of their 'party' to be elected to the municipal council. The usual
celebrations in their honour were therefore countered by a charivari mounted by
their opponents. This hostile demonstration lasted several days; placards insulting the mayor were posted; the door of his house was broken in with axes, and
shots were fired. Similar demonstrations recurred on at least three occasions over
the next eighteen months and resulted in three serious casualties. 'A tumultuous
scene' of a similar kind was reported at Carpineto in 1841; while the incident at
Canale-di-Verde in 1884, referred to above, took place during festivities outside
the new *adjoint*'s house, where a maypole had been erected.[111]

Even where mayors assumed a position of dominance in their villages, they
did not usually escape criticism, and our account has been based on the numerous
complaints against and denunciations of mayors in the administrative and judicial
archives. According to Bourde, the actions of mayors stimulated such protests
from between one-third and one-half the villages of Corsica every year. Many
examples may be cited where complaints were motivated by hostility and malice

or proved to be unfounded or both. The mayor of Zerubia, the object of several denunciations in the late 1840s, as we have seen, claimed that these emanated from a family whose members he had prosecuted for usurping common lands, and the subprefect of Sartène agreed that they were 'the work of ill-will'. The subprefect of Corte reported in 1851 that the facts alleged against the mayors of Frasso and Piedipartino, which he had been asked to investigate, were 'either false or extremely exaggerated' and 'the result of the private animosities which are unfortunately so common in our villages'.[112]

Hostility might also be directed against mayors and *adjoints* in other ways. As we saw in Chapters 2 and 3, attacks on property and livestock were fairly common.[113] The mayor might also be affronted in his person. In 1826, two of the Rutilj Forcioli brothers and another man pulled faces at the mayor of Arbellara in church. The mayor of Piana was insulted on the church square in 1852 and later wounded, following a disagreement about damage caused by herdsmen, and a similar incident occurred at Coti-Chiavari in 1857.[114]

More serious threats or attempts were made against mayors. Marco-Maria Susini was arrested at the end of 1841 for threatening to kill the mayor of Loreto. Mayor Susino of Mela was shot and seriously wounded in 1827, following a quarrel. In 1847, the schoolteacher of Balogna, Amedeo Costa, fired a shot at the mayor, probably with the intention of killing him. Costa had been a protégé of the mayor, but had turned against him 'and made common cause with his political opponents, who exploited this animosity and probably provoked the crime'.[115] Nor were such attempts always unsuccessful. The mayor of Peri was killed by his enemies on the road to Ajaccio in March 1812. Again, Marc'-Antono Giacomoni was shot and killed shortly after being appointed mayor of Santa-Lucia-di-Tallano in 1846; while Giuseppo Leca, mayor of Lopigna, was killed by an enemy in 1852.[116]

In a number of these cases, killing the mayor or the *adjoint*, during or after his term of office, was a direct response to the way in which he had acted as an official. Mayor Costa of Bastelica was shot in front of his house and mortally wounded in 1816, apparently by two men hired by Domenico Porri, 'for whom the mayor had refused to sign a certificate of good conduct and political soundness, which was necessary for him to obtain his military half-pay'. After Domenico-Francesco Renucci of Feliceto had been ambushed and killed in 1850, 'people then recalled that he had carried out his functions as *adjoint* with rare but imprudent zeal. In particular, he had been tough on the herdsmen, and one of them had shown his resentment', and was later convicted of the crime. In other cases, though the overlap is considerable, mayors were clearly involved in on-going pre-existing enmities. At Loreto-di-Tallano in the 1840s, Mayor Serra was engaged in a 'feud' between his family and the Susini. Mayor Leca of Lopigna had an enemy in Petro-Ignazio Padovani. The two men had been friends when they studied together at the University of Pisa, but had fallen out 'after Leca had married the daughter of a man with whom Padovani was on the worst of terms'. Leca had also incurred the hostility of the widow Mariani, Padovani's mistress, by ordering her to fill in an obstructive ditch outside her home. The two combined with another man with a score to settle with Leca in order to kill him. Mayoral involvement in feuds and enmities proper is also indicated where attacks were made on their relatives. After Mayor Cipriani of Isolaccio had made Ignazio Capponi 'take down a construction which he had begun to build on the public highway', Capponi 'declared himself to be Cipriani's enemy' and later shot and killed his nephew in retaliation.[117]

Another variety of conflict related to both feuding and factionalism is that which set mayors against deputy-mayors. Ravis-Giordani notes that in recent times mayors and *adjoints* have nearly always come from the same party. It is unlikely that this generalization holds good for the period before these officers were locally elected, though examples may of course be found.[118] The administration frequently chose mayors and *adjoints* quite deliberately from opposing parties in villages where feuding was prevalent in an attempt to prevent the monopolization of power locally, and our sources reveal many cases of serious conflict or enmity between the two, both in feuding villages and elsewhere. The mayor and his deputy were at odds at Santa-Lucia-di-Tallano in the mid-1830s, the mayor refusing to invest the *adjoint* with his powers when he was absent. *Adjoint* Petreschi of Sari-d'Orcino was among those who denounced Mayor Stefanini to the authorities in 1858 for a series of alleged malpractices, and we have seen that he played a violent part in a fight between the same mayor and one of his predecessors in 1841. Again, at Pila-Canale in the 1860s, the mayor and the *adjoint* belonged to rival families. The *adjoint* refused to stand in for the mayor when the latter was absent and would not carry out the responsibilities delegated to him by the mayor, because he thought them beneath his dignity.[119] Serious conflict was also evident in villages not noted for feuding. The mayor of Lama and his deputy quarrelled in 1810–11 over the leasing of pasture belonging to the village and other matters. The mayor prosecuted the *adjoint* and others for obstructing him in the exercise of his duties and claimed that they had tried to kill him. At Alzi in the 1860s, 'a great animosity' existed between Mayor Palmesani and *Adjoint* Bernardini and their families. Palmesani 'believed that Bernardini aspired to the position of mayor', and relations were worsened by a dispute over the ownership of an enclosure. A fight occurred there in 1864, in which the mayor's brother shot the *adjoint* dead, while the mayor himself stabbed the *adjoint's* cousin.[120]

Other leaders and officials might also serve as rival foci of power in the community. We have seen in Chapter 8 that parish priests were not infrequently in conflict with mayors, very often over the administration of property belonging to the *fabrique*. In some cases, for example at Loreto-di-Tallano during the Second Empire, priests were effectively leaders of factions and acted as such either against mayors or else ran villages themselves through 'stooges'.[121] Another independent source of power was the district justice of the peace, and we will discuss his role more fully in the next section. Suffice it to mention that although justices of the peace and mayors were often allies and some mayors were justices of the peace, examples of conflict between them are not hard to discover. Justice of the peace Costa of Bastelica, for example, officially reported the mayor in 1846 'for failure to show him the proper respect in the exercise of his office', and the mayor was summoned to appear before the correctional tribunal in Ajaccio. Again, at Penta-di-Casinca, former Justice of the peace Limperani appears to have played a leading role in the campaign of denunciation against Mayor Frediani in the late 1860s.[122]

Conflict involving mayors was also frequently mixed up with broader kinds of conflict in the community. We have seen, for example, that mayors might support the interests of herdsmen against those of agriculturalists. The location of the mayor's house could cause further difficulties when it highlighted geographical divisions within villages, as it did, for example, at Pero-Casevecchie in the late 1840s. Similar rivalries could exist between mountain settlements and their coastal satellites. A letter to the prefect in 1846 from several inhabitants of Ota pointed out that Giovan-Francesco Leca, the present *adjoint*, would be a most unsuitable person to be mayor since he was 'a cultivator on the plain of Sia ... and was almost always away from the village'. A faction of the community of Zerubia at the same time 'wanted both the mayor and the *adjoint* to be established at Caldarello and Pianottoli on the coast' rather than in the 'mother' village, claiming that the bulk of the inhabitants actually spent most of their time there. Opponents of Mayor Scipio of Figari complained that he spent most of the year at Levie, which had ceased to have any formal connection with its former colony. As Bourde noted in 1887 in connection with a similar complaint from the inhabitants of Conca, it was extremely inconvenient for those remaining on the plain if the mayor spent all or much of his time in the mountains, and they were often effectively deprived of his services.[123] The practice of appointing *adjoints* in coastal settlements obviated this difficulty to some extent but was not widespread.

On occasions, mayors resided in totally unrelated villages. The mayor of Carcheto was said in 1912 to reside at Stazzona, a neighbouring village, but separated by a steep river valley. A complaint about the mayor of Noceta in 1850 alleged that 'he resides at Arca, a hamlet of Muracciole [several kilometres away], where he married and where his family lives, and he therefore only makes rare appearances at Noceta, so that one might say that he is a ghost-mayor. If anyone needs the mayor's signature on a document, he has to go to Arca.'[124]

V

We have discussed the judicial role of justices of the peace in the previous chapter, but justices were also important political figures at the cantonal level and were often the effective leaders of their party or clan. Indeed, these roles reinforced each other. In the judicial sphere, friends were treated leniently and enemies with severity. If the former were prosecuted and convicted of offences, which was unlikely, then their fines would remain uncollected, while enemies were made to pay or had their goods seized or were sent to prison. A police report concluded in 1817 that justices were 'useless or worse in the area of rural policing because of their ties of kinship, clientship and neighbourhood and above all because of the enmities which these foster'. Later in the century, partisan exercise of their judicial role, in the face of official disapproval, was maintained through the device of appointing deputies (*suppléants*), whose actions could always be disavowed. Probably the most important political role of justices arose from the fact that it was they who decided disputes about the composition of the electoral register, but they also had a more general 'electoral and political mandate' vis-à-vis their clan and their connections in the political hierarchy.[125] A few examples will illustrate the role played by the justice of the peace as local patron or boss, though this is less well documentated than is the case for mayors. Nor should the formal and informal role of justices as mediators in local conflict be overlooked.

Irregularities in the municipal elections at Corte in 1827 led to the provisional replacement of Justice of the peace Benedetti, described as 'the leader and the most inept and least conciliatory member of his party'. The doctor, who altered his report on a woman seriously wounded at Occhiatana in 1833, said that he had been persuaded to do so by 'a very formidable person in our canton because of his personality and his influence', referring, it was believed, to Justice of the peace Malaspina. From a case in 1849, we learn that the two rival factions at Campitello in 1849 were led by Mayor Lorenzi and by Justice of the peace Bugnoli respectively.[126]

Until they were declared ineligible as departmental councillors in 1871 and as delegates to the electoral colleges in senatorial elections in 1875, justices of the peace were actively engaged in formal politics,[127] and it was common in Corsica for justices to stand and to be elected to the departmental council.[128] After 1875, their political and electoral activities continued, albeit in less direct form. In a report in 1876, for example, criticizing the electioneering on behalf of Deputy Gavini by various members of the judicature, the public prosecutor singled out Vincenti, justice of the peace at Valle-d'Alesani, and called for his dismissal. Justice of the peace Italiani had been appointed in his native canton in 1884, we have seen, through senatorial patronage. The judicial authorities had opposed his appointment, as they usually did in such cases, on the grounds that 'with his political connections, his impartiality would be suspect'. And this certainly proved to be the case. He was accused of interfering in the municipal elections at Sari where he had been mayor, and in 1892 he managed to get his son elected as departmental councillor for the canton. A dispute over the election of a departmental councillor in the canton of San-Lorenzo in 1883 shows how the powers of a justice of the peace vis-à-vis the composition of the electoral register might be abused or give rise to objection. The mayor of Corticoli, who presided over the voting, admitted two electors who had been removed from the register by the justice of the peace and refused to admit four whose names he had placed on it. In his defence, the mayor claimed later that the justice had only made these changes to the register a few hours before polling started and that they were motivated by 'pure contrariness'.[129]

Given their political role, it is not surprising that justices of the peace often fell short of the expected bureaucratic standards. As magistrates, they might be markedly partisan, or, as the police report of 1817 notes, they might 'find a thousand reasons for not making decisions, so as to avoid making enemies'. Like mayors, justices and their clerks might be poor keepers of records, out of incompetence or for partisan reasons. A case in 1861 revealed, for example, that the register of the decisions of the justice of the peace of Vico had not been regularly kept, though the clerk explained the lacunae by saying that his daughter had accidentally burned one of the log books. More generally, Réalier-Dumas wrote in 1819 that 'most justices of the peace are quite unsuited to their functions. Some are unable to write. Several have convictions for theft and forgery, and others for homicide. I have even been told of one justice who holds court with his arms beside him.'[130]

This brings us to the involvement of justices in conflict and violence. First, justices were objects of the same kinds of attack as mayors. When Justice Estella of Luri was wrongly accused of electoral malpractice in 1840, according to Patorni he held on to his post through 'influence'; but his pride was fatally wounded and he died the following year. Justice Stretti of Moita was subjected in the 1890s to 'lively attacks and groundless denunciations' by Mayor Morandini. Their disagreement stemmed from an attempt by the justice to investigate alleged irregularities in the composition of the electoral register, and physical threats were made against him. Justices might also be insulted. Luca Pianelli of Olmeto was prosecuted in 1812 for having 'verbally insulted' the justice of the peace of Vallinco, Giustiniani, and testimony at the trial reveals something of the circumstances. In a general public discussion, Pianelli had complained of the justice's combination of partiality against himself and 'inaction'. The justice explained the latter by the fact that his clerk had resigned, but Pianelli riposted that this had happened because the clerk had been 'expected to deal not only with official business but also with Giustiniani's domestic affairs'. In another case, various members of the Danieri family of Olmo had been trying to get the justice of the peace of Campile 'to appoint a family council', in order to settle the affairs of one of them who had gone to live abroad. They suspected the justice of prevarication; so they went one day in 1879 to Campile and 'hurled invective at him in his court'. It seems likely that such attacks often reflected pre-existing enmities, as did the partiality or supposed partiality referred to here. Certainly, in the Vico case which we have mentioned, the justice's clerk claimed that the local police officer and the departmental registrar, who had made the accusation against him, 'were his enemies and had acted through hatred and the spirit of vengeance'. In a rather different case, two satires against the new justice of the peace were posted on the church door at Carbini in 1825, while a guy representing him was placed nearby. Here, the objection was to 'the appointment of a justice from outside the canton'.[131]

More serious attacks are also reported, extending to attempted homicide and homicide itself. At Olmeto in 1848, Justice of the peace Peretti intervened as a would-be mediator in the dispute over a ditch between his nephew Don Giovanni Peretti and Mariano Galloni d'Istria. His decision in his nephew's favour and his observation that the ditch also impinged on land which he owned himself infuriated Galloni d'Istria, who abused the justice verbally, 'threatened to pull off his moustache' and fired several shots, one of which wounded him. Later in the century, an attempt was made to kill the justices of the peace of Piana in 1880 and of Zicavo in 1882. This last example was clearly an episode in a feud, since a 'peace' was later made between the two families concerned. A case at Sari-d'Orcino in 1860 was more akin to that at Carbini in 1825. Justice Agostini was ambushed by a youth, Matteo Raffini, who later claimed that he had only wished to frighten him. Raffini was nevertheless charged with attempted homicide, and the trial summary explained that Agostini's 'firm and impartial administration of justice had aroused the animosity of several influential families in the district, including that of the accused'. These people, some of whom had been brought before the courts at his behest, 'tried to make his job as difficult and his general situation as uncomfortable as possible, hoping to force him to leave a district where he was an outsider by birth and had no "interests"'. Earlier, it was reported, Agostini 'had been booed and jeered at as he crossed the village square, and many people habitually "cut" him when they met him'.[132] These cases, where hostility was directed against disinterested outsiders, point again to the value to the district of having 'political' justices of the peace meshed in to the prevailing clan and patronage system.

A few instances may be cited in which justices were killed by their enemies. Two justices of the peace of Orezza were killed within the space of five years, Justice Piazzole in 1813, who became the subject of a well-known lament, and Justice Battesti in 1818. The justice of Sagro was killed in 1823 by three people from Sisco. In 1848, the deputy justice of the peace of Petreto-Bicchisano, Fieschi, was killed by Francesco Istria. Three years earlier, Fieschi had started proceedings against Istria for killing his father's mistress, a crime which he had hoped to pass off as an accident.[133] Justices of the peace also occasionally committed homicidal acts, though our examples are again confined to the early nineteenth century. A property dispute between Justice Vittini of Tavignano and the Renosi brothers led to 'a serious enmity' between them and their families. Two armed encounters took place between the parties in 1815, in which the justice played an active part. In the same year, Justice Lucciani of Vallinco was suspended following a charge that he had tried to kill a man from Piedicorte.[134]

VI

We come now to local elections, which in the Corsican setting were like pitched battles in the ongoing factional 'wars' that we have described. 'Municipal elections in the villages are the cause of more bloodshed, excite more passion and provoke more enmities than family quarrels ever did,' Facy asserted in 1933 with only a degree of exaggeration. Elections were not only contests for power in the village or the canton; they were also the crucial point where local politics was geared in to the wider system. Bourde and others explained how the patronage network focused on elections and their management. Important families 'disposed of an "influence"', which allowed them to control the votes of a significant number of electors'. Patrons offered their various services to clients in return for votes, and, if these votes were delivered, especially in general elections, then they obtained a share of the 'manna' of state benefits for themselves and their followings.[135] A modern system of representation in effect was adapted to a society where ties of kinship and patronage were paramount. Moreover, elections at the different levels, municipal, cantonal, general, were all interlocking, and successful management at one level depended on previous success at another. Most important for our purposes, mayors played an important role in mustering votes in cantonal and general elections, and this gave municipal elections a supra-local significance, especially during the Third Republic.

Not surprisingly in these circumstances, what the authorities regarded as 'electoral fraud' was 'traditional' or 'endemic'.[136] Some commentators have seen this as particularly characteristic of the Third Republic again; but already during the July Monarchy 400 electoral cases were coming before the Appeal Court every year; and the public prosecutor referred to 'a peak in the number of frauds and in their audacity' in the elections of 1865. He also made two further related remarks, which are of interest. The offences in question, committed mainly by mayors or *adjoints*, did not usually involve corruption or the subornation of electors; they were rather 'dishonest manoeuvres or mechanical frauds perpetrated during the election itself in order to affect or alter its outcome'; and they were committed in a relatively open way. Such offences, moreover, 'had always been treated in Corsica with a certain indulgence, partly in order to try to restore calm to villages once the electoral crisis was over'.[137] Santoni notes here that electoral fraud was not regarded as reprehensible in Corsica, and penalties for electoral offences were not severe. Sentences of two to four months' imprisonment seem to have been normal in the later nineteenth century, but these were often reduced to fines on appeal, and, where fines were originally imposed, these again might be scaled down. In an extreme case, Mayor Cesari of San-Fiorenzo was fined 150 francs for threatening and suborning electors in the 1881 general elections, but the fine was successively reduced to 50 and then to 10 francs.[138]

We will now examine the various 'manoeuvres' or 'frauds' employed in the electoral battle, starting with the composition of the electoral register. The aim here was to increase the number of voters belonging to one's own party and to reduce the number belonging to that of one's opponents. During the Restoration and the July Monarchy, of course, the right to vote was based on property qualifications, and the intense but restricted conflict over the composition of registers tended to focus on these. Public Prosecutor Mottet referred in 1836 to 'frauds of all kinds: simulated sales and leases, bogus divisions of property and cessions of usufruct'. In a typical case in 1830, Colonel Sebastiani-Capellini appealed against his removal from the register. According to the *Gazette des Tribunaux*, following their defeat in the elections of 1827 and 1828 the 'ministerial' party, headed by Pozzo di Borgo, determined to achieve victory in 1830 by means of a thorough purge of the electoral registers. All opponents of the government, 'who had managed to survive the regular annual revisions of the lists', were removed in one fell swoop, including the colonel. Five mayors from his canton, said to be 'his personal enemies', testified that 'he did not in fact own the bulk of the property in the canton, with which he laid claim to his voting rights'. A further complication in Corsica at this time was that, given the high level of income required to qualify for the vote (and more so to stand for election), such a poor department had very few inhabitants in either category. In 1824, there were only 32 *éligibles* in the whole island. The constitutional charter laid down that where numbers fell below a certain minimum for this reason, they should be supplemented by choosing additional names from among the less wealthy. But, as an objector in a pamphlet issued in 1828 complained, this meant that the prefect and others could select supporters of the administration and their clients.[139]

The introduction of universal suffrage in 1848 completely altered the context in which rigging the electoral register occurred, enormously extending the range of the operation and transferring it decisively to the local level. Men were often listed on more than one register, which was to some extent a *bona fide* reflection of the fact that 'many Corsicans did have two villages', one on the plain and one on the mountain, and that fission into two distinct administrative units was usually fairly recent. But the ambiguity inherent in this situation was fully exploited, together with other ploys. Registers might be packed with 'friends' who no longer lived at all in the villages concerned. They might be brought in to vote, from outside the island if need be, or others might vote in their names. The official criterion of paying taxes in the village was generally ignored. Sometimes men who had never lived in a village were placed on its electoral register, and the list could always be inflated by leaving on those who were dead. Conversely, the names of 'enemies' were removed from the register on the slightest pretext, for example, if they had not been spelled 'correctly', or if men spent any time during the year away from the village.[140]

The register was annually reviewed by a committee comprising the mayor, a municipal councillor and a representative of the prefect. Anyone could propose changes in the list, and such proposals were made in significant numbers every year. At Venzolasca, for example, in 1867, Petro-Paolo Nicolai and Agostino Sanguinetti called for the removal of six names from the register on the grounds that they were 'all the sons of foreigners and thus not qualified'; they also asked for the exclusion of Stefano Petrignani, whose domicile was in Bastia, and wanted six names added to the list. Giovan-Mattei Nicolai asked for 15 names to be added, including that of Stefano Petrignani who was said to be a resident of the village. Carlo-Giuseppo Grimaldi and Giovanni Albertini called for the removal from the register of 17 'individuals who were not French subjects and had never been naturalized' and also of four leading members of the Casabianca family, two Ciosi and Luigi Sanguinetti, on the grounds that none of them lived in the village. Other requests were also received by the mayor. It seems clear here that political rivals were trying to place their own clients on the register and to keep off those of their rivals, and also that the voting rights of leading figures on both sides were being directly challenged. The solution of the municipal committee (which included members of the Grimaldi and Sanguinetti families) was one of compromise, slanted very much towards the status quo. A few clients were removed or added to the list, but on the whole the fact that an elector had voted before ensured his right to do so again, even if his nationality were in doubt. And none of the notables of the village had their rights infringed. It was pointed out that Stefano Petrignani had at least been born in Venzolasca; the four Casabianca spent part of the year there; while, as customs officers, the two Ciosi came under the military category and could therefore spend long periods of time away from the village without losing their voting rights. A similar pattern is evident in other years, and for one village at least this reveals a normal situation of fierce but regulated competition. Appeals against the municipal committee were settled in the first instance, we have seen, by the justice of the peace, and conflict between the justice and the mayor did occur. More often, however, the two acted in concert, and justices rejected appeals against what was in effect the mayor's committee.[141]

Often, too, things lacked the respectable veneer we find at Venzolasca, and manipulation of the register by the mayor could be quite blatant. Forty-two electors or would-be electors from Salice complained that no electoral register had been made public in 1848 and that no consultation had taken place over its composition. The municipal elections in the same year were held in the mayor's house, and 'on polling day, realizing that he did not have enough votes to be re-elected to the council, the mayor placed two *lucchesi* on the register'. At Piedicroce in 1865, the mayor altered the register in favour of his own party during the municipal elections and refused to allow some of his opponents to vote. At Barbaggio before the 1884 elections, which were decided by 37 votes to 33, the mayor failed to call the committee to establish the register, refused to accept notifications of suggested changes, and omitted to publish any list. Attempts by his opponents to get him to produce a register in the proper manner were thwarted by the justice of the peace and even by the prefecture and only succeeded after the case had been taken to the Cour de Cassation.[142]

Exclusions or attempts at exclusion from the electoral register could themselves lead to violence. Angelo Marchetti of San-Nicolai-di-Moriani was hoping in the late 1830s to oust Agosto Poli, district prosecutor at Ajaccio, as departmental councillor, and with this aim in view 'took steps to have his name removed from the local register'. Marchetti and his supporters formally lodged their objection at Cervione in a demonstrative, 'bragging' way that added to the annoyance of the Poli and their friends. Later the same evening the two parties encountered each other, and fighting broke out, in which Marchetti was wounded. A man from San-Lorenzo, who believed that he had been excluded from the electoral register at the behest of the Moracchini, ambushed a member of the family during the 1884 elections and killed him. Again, a herdsman, Cristiani, from Morsiglia was taken off the register after he had quarrelled with his old patrons, the Paoli, and gone over to the camp of their rivals, the Pietri. The local justice, a Paoli supporter, gave Cristiani no redress, and he shot and killed one of the Paoli just before the elections in the same year.[143]

Even if electors were inscribed on the register, attempts might be made to prevent them from voting. The prefect believed that Mayor Quilichini had excluded a number of inscribed electors in the municipal elections of 1846 at Poggio-di-Tallano. Four electors were barred at Salice in 1865. At Alando in the elections of the same year, the mayor refused to allow the *adjoint* to vote, claiming not to recognize him. And other examples could be cited.[144]

Electors who did vote were subject to all kinds of pressures. First, votes were solicited by those with influence. Dr Zuccarelli, whose family was involved in local politics in the inter-war period, recalled that:

> I quite often wrote to patients to ask them if they would vote for my brother or for a friend. I always received a reply and I was allotted either all or part of the family's votes. In Corsica, a family always holds a meeting in order to decide how to vote and is always flattered if a well-known person solicits its votes.

According to Ravis-Giordani, it was customary for the party leader to pay a call on all his followers before the elections, 'even on those who were most faithful and most certain. If he failed to go to solicit their votes for himself or for the candidate whom he supported and would introduce to them on this occasion, they might well say to themselves: "He never came to tell me for whom I should vote."' Others refer to the practice of electors going to the houses of 'the notables' on the eve of elections for refreshments and 'to receive instructions from their clan leaders'. These visits were 'indispensable', and they were the occasions also, on which *quid pro quo* promises about dispensations, pensions, jobs and so on were made to voters.[145]

Sometimes pressure was rather more heavy-handed. Mayor Cesari of San-Fiorenzo was convicted of threatening electors in the general elections of 1882. A postman, Ghiglioni, testified that he had promised Cesari that he would vote for his party, but that Cesari did not trust him and had come round to his house with a printed voting slip 'with a word written on it by hand, and had warned him that he would recognize the slip when it came out of the voting urn'. Ghiglioni also claimed that Cesari had given him another marked voting slip 'for his son who was a schoolmaster at Valpajola, telling him that he [Cesari] was in a position to bring about the prosperity or the ruin of the Ghiglioni family'. In another case at Campitello in 1905, the mayor was accused of warning herdsmen via the field guards that they should vote for his brother as departmental councillor or else face 'persecution and ruin'.[146]

Complaints were also made in this sphere against members of the clergy and the judicature, though their real role was probably less important than that of mayors. Father Nicolaio Battesti, who was the nephew of one of the candidates, Justice of the peace Battesti, was reported to be actively involved, for example, in electioneering at Piedicroce, where the polling took place in the presbytery. Two pamphlets, to which we have referred, claimed that the clergy were widely involved 'in electoral intrigues' and drew specific attention to the departmental council elections in the cantons of Vico and Piana in 1852 and in the canton of Soccia in 1852 and 1858, in which relatives of the bishop were standing. More definitely, the mayor of Nonza informed the prefect in 1891 that the parish priest 'is the leader of the forces of reaction [in the village] and is out campaigning in the municipal elections, as he always does'. The public prosecutor complained in 1876 that various judges of the Appeal Court, as well as lesser magistrates, had used their influence on behalf of the Bonapartist Gavini in the general elections, and we have cited examples of similar behaviour on the part of justices of the peace. Not only did Justice Italiani of Sari-d'Orcino hold electoral meetings in his own house, but he was said to have postponed all cases pending during the departmental elections of 1892, 'seeking thereby to win over some voters by promises and to frighten others with threats'.[147]

In extreme cases force might be used to prevent electors from voting. 'In order to obtain the majority [in the municipal elections of 1884 at Poggio-di-Tallano], the opponents of Mayor Quilichini conceived the idea of kidnapping his son, Dono, who was simple-minded, to stop him from voting.' The plan was carried out, and, not surprisingly, 'provoked the mayor and his supporters to the highest degree'. Again, four days before polling in the municipal elections at Ozzano in 1892, Giovanni Pinelli, 'who until then had voted for Giovan-Antono Marcangeli, was enticed into the house of the outgoing mayor, Battesti, and it became impossible for his political friends to communicate with him'.[148] We will see in the next chapter, too, that the services of bandits might be called on by party leaders in elections. The general point should be made, however, that in most cases such pressure was unnecessary. Ritual soliciting of votes might be required for honour's sake, but most electors voted out of solidarity with family, clan and party.

Given this premise, further opportunities for manipulation existed before the election was actually held. First, the announcement of the election might be made at short notice or without full publicity. At Venzolasca in 1872, for example, the official notice calling the municipal elections was only posted in the village three days before polling day, which 'prevented the opposition party from having enough time to compose its list'. Inadequate advance notice of elections also interfered with another procedure which had become common by the early twentieth century, if not before, for general and then local elections, and this was paying for electors to return from continental France to vote and arranging their transportation. Then, the election might be held in a place which favoured one party, or the venue might be changed without prior warning. Mayor Frediani of Penta-di-Casinca, for example, held the cantonal elections of 1867 in the girls' school, which communicated directly with a house belonging to his uncle. The mayor stationed himself with a number of partisans in this adjacent building on the day of the election, hoping to oversee if not to overawe the voting. A particular advantage accrued to a mayor's party if the elections were held in his house. When they objected to the inclusion of two foreigners on the electoral list, the opponents of the mayor of Salice were ejected in 1848 from the mayor's house, where the municipal election proceeded without them. In 1884, 'contrary to instructions from the prefect telling him to hold the municipal elections in the boys' school, the mayor of Pianello announced that polling would take place in his house'. This prompted the opposing party to block all access to it, which prevented most electors from voting. Again, at an unnamed village in 1893, the acting mayor opened the polling in his own house rather than in the boys' school, the expected venue, and later declared that a proper election had taken place, although only a cabal of his own supporters had attended.[149]

We come now to the polling itself. It should be made clear at the outset that, whatever the requirements of French law, voting in Corsica was not secret. In accordance with French practice, voting slips with their names on them were distributed by candidates before polling day or handed out at the door on the day. During the Third Republic, these slips were all meant to look alike to avoid identification of them during voting, which consisted of placing them in a locked ballot box or urn. In practice, they could often be distinguished, and the 'urn' was not necessarily secure, as we shall see. When voting booths were introduced in this century, they were 'disdained'. As a recent commentator explained, 'if anyone passes through the yellow calico curtains into the booth itself, he is instantly suspect to his own side'. It seems that voting in secret was regarded as unmanly or dishonourable. Male participation in politics had to be open to view.[150]

Polling was organized and supervised by a committee or 'bureau', composed in theory of two members of each party and presided over by the mayor or his delegate. Mayors seem very often to have delegated what was a crucial role for their continuation in office, in order to avoid subsequent prosecution for malpractice. In the 1936 general elections, for example, the bureau for the *arrondissement* of Ajaccio was presided over by the *adjoint*, ostensibly on the grounds that the mayor was absent. But the mayor was present during the polling, and it is clear that the *adjoint's* presidency was something of a fiction. To win elections, according to Bourde, it was essential to control the bureau, in order to prevent the other side from committing fraud while allowing one's own party to do so. If one controlled the bureau, one could allow votes from absent or deceased electors and stop opponents from voting on various pretexts, as we have seen. A further range of ploys was also available, as some examples will show.[151]

First, the president or members of the bureau might put additional voting slips of their own party into the urn before or during the count. In the 1865 municipal elections at Bastelica, the *adjoint*, who was acting as president, was seen to introduce some extra slips into the piles assembled for the final count, and these were readily identifiable since they had not been perforated, as the slips presented by electors regularly were. Again, for the elections of 1884, Mayor Cristini of Castiglione formed a bureau entirely of his own partisans. His supporters, 31 in all, voted 'by giving their slips to the mayor, who did not check them against the register as he was supposed to do, but instead quickly deposited them in the soup tureen, which served as the urn'. At the count, 90 slips were found in the tureen, although only 74 electors had voted.[152] Conversely, slips of opponents might be marked and thus invalidated. During the elections of 1865 at Prunelli-di-Fiumorbo, the mayor (who was also deputy justice of the peace) 'marked 16 voting slips with the aim of annulling them and thus assuring the triumph of his party'. Then, instead of sending the supposedly spoiled slips to the prefecture, as required by the law in such circumstances, he substituted 16 valid slips from his own list.[153]

An alternative manoeuvre was the deliberate miscount. In the cantonal elections at Fiaja in 1855, one of the candidates, Dr Casabianca, son of the justice of the peace of Campile, tried to prevent this by getting those who had voted for him to affirm orally that they had done so, during the count. Though at least twice as many made such an affirmation, when the result was declared Casabianca was credited with only 17 votes. Again, in the municipal elections of 1866 at Fozzano, the mayor, Giulio Bernardini, appointed as scrutineer a Carabelli, 'who was devoted to him'. At the count, the mayor 'dictated to him names belonging to his own party, which were not on the voting slips in front of him, and omitted to read the names of those belonging to his opponents'. During this manoeuvre, the mayor kept the slips close to his chest and allowed no one to come near but the scrutineer. The mayor's party thus obtained a handsome majority, though his opponents then prompted a judicial investigation. A mayor of Nocario around 1900 was said to have put his skill at card tricks to good use in such manoeuvres.[154]

Where a count had been fraudulent, there was a temptation, not always followed, to destroy the evidence. Partial municipal elections were held at Balogna in 1837, in which the mayor was opposed by notary Colonna. The bureau was composed of 'friends of the mayor' plus the notary. After the count, a proposal was adopted that the voting slips be burned before the result was announced. When this had been done, the mayor declared that his party had won all five vacant seats on the council by a majority of 16 to 14. Whereupon 16 electors swore that they had voted for the Colonna party and offered to vote again, which provoked 'general tumult'. Again, at Pietricaggio in 1865, having realized that the party opposed to the mayor and himself had the majority of votes, the *adjoint* burned all the voting slips before the count could take place. It was common by this century for each party to collect and guard its own voting slips, presumably in an effort to eliminate or reduce frauds of this kind. Mention should also be made of the possibility of making false accusations against opponents under this head. The public prosecutor commented in connection with a case at Figari in 1865:

> Experience has shown that sometimes in Corsica, when men of one party see that an election is escaping them, they will then vote for the other. But afterwards they will swear before a notary, a police officer or a justice of the peace that they voted for their friends. The aim of this tactic is to compromise the members of the bureau; such declarations are in contradiction with the official result and suggest, of course, that frauds have been committed during the count.[155]

A further possibility at the disposal of the president of the bureau was to write and forward an official report announcing the results of the election, which bore no resemblance to what had actually happened. In the 1893 case, to which we have referred, the *adjoint* ostensibly adjourned the elections when objections were made to holding them in his house. But the prefecture nevertheless received a report next day signed by members of what appeared to be a regularly constituted bureau and announcing that they and four of their political friends had been duly elected. Again, in the Ajaccio election of 1936, in which the contestants were Chiappe and Landry, the latter seems to have obtained most votes, but in his report to the prefect the *adjoint* altered the figures to make Chiappe the victor in his district. What is more, instead of drawing up two identical copies of this report agreed by both parties, he produced one giving the real figures, which he showed to Landry's supporters and another giving Chiappe the lead, which he sent to the prefect.

So far we have discussed fraudulent ways of winning or trying to win elections. It was also possible to retain power by not holding elections. At Palneca in the 1880s, the mayor, who was a notorious 'fixer' of elections at all levels, postponed the municipal elections three times, because he was in the minority on the electoral register. Sometimes a combination of manipulation and delaying tactics could be used, as at Campitello, where there were six attempts to elect a new council in the early 1880s. In January 1881, members of the bureau were caught putting extra voting slips in the urn, and the elections were annulled. In March, when new elections were held under the same president, more votes were found in the urn than there were electors. In May 1882, the mayor's party voted in the early morning and polling was then closed, excluding the opposition. In October that year, the mayor, who was going to preside over the elections, resigned on the morning of polling day. In March 1883, the councillor, who was to have presided, claimed to be ill. In April 1883, the mayor's party, having falsified the register, admitted outsiders to the poll, and the opposition tried to exclude them by force. In each of these cases again, the elections were annulled or postponed, and the old mayor's party remained in power. According to Surier, one mayor this century kept his position for 25 years without having a majority on the council by the systematic use of such tactics.[156]

Although elections were managed in these ways with considerable finesse, violence was always potentially or actually present, as many informed observers noted. Felix Bertrand, who had been advocate-general at Bastia, wrote in 1870 that 'the introduction and then the extension of electoral institutions had occasioned many crimes, profound divisions and bloody confrontations. This outcome was quite predictable in a country where the conquest of positions is an overriding concern and where the least antagonism awakens the most violent passions.'[157] Bourde and others noted a more exact correlation between years of municipal elections, in particular, and peaks in the statistics of crimes against the person. Such considerations prompted calls for the suspension of these elections either on a long-term basis or temporarily, as happened in 1884.[158]

Electoral violence took a variety of forms. Some was of a ritual or limited kind, though this could provoke more serious trouble. Demonstrations or skirmishes between the parties, called *zarghe*, were a feature of the pre-electoral period, and 'special satirical songs were composed and then shouted in chorus in each camp'.[159] In the period just before the municipal elections at Calvi in 1896, a group of about 40 electors, belonging to the party opposed to the mayor, created a disturbance by drinking together and then going up and down the streets singing. When a police officer tried to disperse them he was attacked. At nearby Calenzana, two groups of electors clashed during 'certain electoral demonstrations'. Insults were exchanged and stones thrown, one of which hit and fatally wounded the *adjoint*. Again, Archer described Vescovato during election time in the early 1920s: 'Bands of the rival parties paraded the streets day and night ... shrieking insults at one another and firing salvoes into the air. The excitement reached a climax one night, when a man was set upon by the opposite party.'[160] Similarly, victory in elections was ritually celebrated, as we have seen, and this, too, might end in violence. After Dr Murazzani had been elected to the council of the *arrondissement* in 1883, the usual celebrations at Zicavo 'were prolonged over several days, which annoyed his political opponents'. The festival of Assumption intervened and provided the occasion for counter-demonstrations Taunts, threats and then shots were exchanged, and a woman was killed and a man injured.[161]

Other forms of violence lacked this ritual aspect, although they were very common. First, we may mention the use or attempted use of force during the election itself. Trouble was expected during the municipal elections of 1848 at Campitello, where the mayor's party was thought to be in the minority and fraudulent manoeuvres on his part were anticipated. Gendarmes were sent into the village as a precaution, but the mayor sent them back, and he was rumoured to have summoned a force of friends and relatives from another village. Voting was arranged in the house of a partisan of the mayor, which was surrounded on polling day by a large number of the mayor's suspicious opponents, all armed. He ordered them to surrender their weapons and disperse, but they refused.

General fighting then broke out, in which a bystander was killed. At partial elections at Olmiccia in 1850, there were the usual arguments over the register and the composition of the bureau, but all went fairly well until the count, when two extra voting slips were discovered. When the president of the bureau tried to annul them, protests were made; the room was invaded by a crowd of men; the urn was overturned and voting slips torn up. Fighting then spread to the square outside, and shots were fired. At Antisanti in 1878, 'the electors were all armed with pistols under their jackets, as is the custom in Corsica, and they began to shoot each other at a certain stage in the proceedings'. Four or five men were killed. Many similar incidents could be cited, particularly from the last third of the century.[162]

Very often, as we have noted, violence was a response to excessive or flagrant fraud. When the mayor at Campitello proposed to allow 15 Italian workers to vote in April 1883, the exasperated leader of the opposing faction, Departmental Councillor Graziani, announced that he and his supporters 'would do everything possible to prevent the intruders from voting, even if they had to use guns'. 'Thirty of them surrounded the polling station' and challenged voters as they arrived. When one of the Italians refused to stop, he was shot dead. Graziani explained later that 'the underdogs wanted finally to defeat fraud by violence'.[163] The obviously fraudulent miscount at Fozzano in 1866 provoked a furious reaction from the mayor's opponents, and violence was only prevented by the intervention of the gendarmerie and the promise of an official enquiry.

This raises again the general question of the relationship between political and electoral conflict on the one hand, and violence and feuding on the other. A number of writers have associated electoral malpractice with the introduction of universal male suffrage in 1848 and with the extension of the power of mayors under the Third Republic.[164] But these only widened participation in behaviour that had assumed its characteristic forms much earlier.[165] Throughout the nineteenth century and after the phenomenon is found, too, at all levels of the electoral system. Fraud or force or a combination of the two was reported, for example, in the course of elections to the departmental council at Piana in 1833, at Bonifacio, Petreto-Bicchisano and Serra in 1836, and at Albertacce, Calacuccia, Campitello, Piedicroce and Vescovato in 1848.[166] It is probably true also that electoral violence declined during the modern period in the long term, as violence declined in general, but it is hard to see that violence and voting or violence and fraud were ever regarded as clear alternatives at the village level. Miot wrote that elections around 1800 'were always the pretext and the occasion for troubles, often accompanied by bloodshed. Once elections were over, the winning party then used its power to take revenge on the losers', which engendered further conflict. Commenting on a number of cases tried in 1865, the president of the Assize Court, Fabrizzi, concurred: 'crimes increase, together with the party divisions and hatreds which go with them, and all are fuelled by the prospect of the coming electoral struggles; elections ... have become the touchstone by which the influence of the principal families is measured, not only in the villages of the interior, but also in the towns'. And, as far as the villages were concerned, similar comments were still being made in the 1930s.[167]

Consideration of particular examples confirms that elections could be both sources of and episodes in vendettas. The feud between the Nicolai and the Pietri at San-Gavino-di-Carbini was triggered off in 1878, according to Bourde, by a quarrel over a contested voting slip. At Fozzano, Giusepp'-Antono Bartoli, Ignazio Durazzi and Michelangelo Paoli 'conceived an intense dislike of Giovan-Battiste Bernardini, following the municipal elections of 1888', which led them to kill him three years later. The two competing parties in the municipal elections at Santa-Lucia-di-Tallano in 1848 were led by the Giacomoni and the Quilichini, who were in a state of feud with each other. When a Quilichini knocked over the urn in the polling station, shooting began both there and outside. Again, 'a long-standing enmity existed at Piobbeta between the Muzi and the Vincenti. On the occasion of the municipal elections of 1851, this animosity became an active hatred and terrible threats were made.' Soon after the elections, Father Vincenti, parish priest at Tallone, was killed by a distant relative of the Muzi, acting on their behalf.[168]

A further factor linking electoral conflict and feuding was honour. As well as being a counter in a game of political calculation, the right to vote was a matter of honour, a sign of masculinity, and to deprive a man of his vote therefore was an affront of a serious kind. This may be gauged from a case involving Departmental Councillor Peretti of Levie. He was sentenced to four months' imprisonment and had his electoral rights suspended in 1856, following an incident in which he had fired a shot at the director of the penitentiary of Chiavari. He protested vigorously against his suspension and in fact continued to vote in elections, being prosecuted for this in 1861. The same combination of interest and honour is evident in an example cited by Dr Zuccarelli. He relates that he performed an operation with a colleague on a man in a village in the Bastia region in the inter-war period. As soon as the operation was over, the patient spoke to the other doctor 'and told him in a decisive manner: "Doctor, you must keep an eye on the electoral register..." Then his wife appeared in the doorway of the room, where the operation had taken place and added: "Doctor, make sure that he lives until May, so that he can cast his vote against the mayor; after that he can die."' Success or failure in elections also had an honorific aspect, as President Fabrizzi indicates. A popular mayor, A., according to Ravis-Giordani, was a candidate in the cantonal elections around 1900, and he went to the polling at the main village in the canton with 200 armed partisans. His rival was the mayor of this village, who in fact won the election but refused to announce the result. A. told his followers that he himself had been elected, in order to avoid trouble, and they returned to his village to celebrate. When they arrived home, A. admitted that he had not been elected. His followers responded by telling him: 'If you had told us that when we were there, we would have burned down the mayor's house and taken to the maquis. But since you didn't want it that way, we will never vote for you again.'[169] This brings us conveniently to the subject of banditry.

] 12 [

Banditry

General accounts of banditry have alluded to its connection with 'vengeance and family honour', but this has rarely occupied a central place in their description and analysis.[1] The Corsican example suggests, by contrast, that although banditry had other aspects, its essential significance cannot be appreciated unless it is situated in a society where blood vengeance was operative and the defence of family interest and honour by violence a common imperative. The Corsican example also lends weight to the view elaborated by a number of writers in criticism of Hobsbawm,[2] that, where banditry had a political dimension, it was less as a protest against the rich and the powerful in pursuit of liberty and justice and more as a component of intensified competition among local élites in the circumstances of incorporation into a modern state. In Corsica, too, when banditry did become distanced from the system of blood vengeance and honour, this may be seen as a sign of serious social crisis.[3]

I

This is not the place to deal with the history of banditry in modern Corsica in detail, but some rough chronological outline is required. The struggle against the Genoese in the mid-eighteenth century had, to some extent, fostered banditry, and it continued to be an important phenomenon during the Paoli administration (1755–69), as evidenced by the draconian decrees issued against it. Banditry was again prominent in the resistance to the imposition of French rule after 1768, and during the French Revolutionary and Napoleonic periods, when external intervention exacerbated 'internal dissensions' and conscription filled the maquis with draft-evaders and deserters.[4] However, banditry declined steadily in importance from the 1820s and many writers in the mid-nineteenth century announced its demise. This proved premature, for banditry (like violent crime generally) regularly proliferated in periods of political instability or governmental weakness (around 1850, the 1870s, the First World War), and it became a problem of longer-term significance from the 1880s to the 1920s, associated here with the undermining of the traditional economy and way of life by the onset of massive emigration.[5] This chronology can be given no exact statistical basis, though some figures are available from a variety of sources (Table 6).

Table 6. *Numbers of bandits*[6]

Date	Numbers of bandits or fugitives from justice
1770	200 bandits
*c.*1800	Over 1000 bandits
1822–3	366 sentenced fugitives (of which 70 had left Corsica)
1825	342 fugitives
1826	400 bandits
1830	320 fugitives (of which 250 had been convicted)
1845–50	500–600 fugitives
1851	250 bandits
1880	190–240 bandits
1887	Up to 600 bandits
1893	Over 200 'outlaws'
1896	50 'dangerous bandits'
1899–1900	125–200 bandits
1933	100 bandits

Account should also be taken of the connection, uppermost in the minds of the authorities, between the fortunes of banditry and governmental action against it. The French employed a variety of measures in their fight against banditry in Corsica, often after setting up special committees of enquiry.[7] These ranged from general 'development' to specific tactical measures, and the latter particularly tell us a great deal not only about official attitudes but also about the nature of banditry itself.

The most obvious was the deployment of military or semi-military force. The military presence was very marked in the first three or four decades of the nineteenth century, and throughout the period a proportionately larger number of military and police was stationed in Corsica than in any other French department.[8] Residential stations of gendarmerie were built in or near many of the larger villages, especially in 'violent' areas. Increasing the numbers of such forces yet further was commonly advised, but the authorities generally recognized that this could rarely be effective by itself,[9] and emphasis was placed instead on specialist units and on concerted campaigns against bandits in particular areas. A special force of 'scouts' had been set up in 1801 to track down bandits, but did not survive the Napoleonic period. In 1822, the Voltigeurs Corses were constituted on a similar basis. This force included a high proportion of native Corsican volunteers, who knew the terrain, the language and local customs. Additionally, many of them were motivated by having old scores to pay off against bandits. According to Marcaggi, the *voltigeurs* reached a strength of 1000 men before they were disbanded in 1850. The reasons for their eclipse seem to have been their excessive zeal in killing bandits rather than capturing them alive and difficulties in co-ordination between them and the mainly 'continental' gendarmerie. The prefect suggested reviving them in 1874, but by this time the gendarmerie had adopted a number of their features, including, for a while, local recruitment,[10] and later governments preferred localized and then more general military-style campaigns. These had sinister precedents in the notorious 'flying columns' of Sionville in the Castagniccia in 1774 and of Morand in the Fiumorbo in 1808,[11] which inhibited their use for a time. However, Mottet advocated their revival in 1836, and a special mobile column of *voltigeurs* and gendarmes was employed to track down and destroy Massoni and his associates in 1849–51. In 1882, two infantry companies were sent to deal with bandits in the Sartène region, and further campaigns of a similar nature took place in the same region and in the Fiumorbo in the late 1880s and the mid-1890s. Finally, an expedition of 640 troops, armed with rifles and six machine-guns, was despatched to Corsica in 1931 to end its last significant wave of banditry.[12]

The success of such campaigns depended on cutting bandits off from their lines of supply and support, and this could best be done by arresting or detaining their relatives and friends. This policy had been applied in brutal fashion in the earliest period of French rule, and it remained an important feature of governmental action against banditry off and on throughout the modern period.[13] Sometimes people were simply detained; in other cases, charges of harbouring bandits were made, particularly after this became a specific offence in 1854. A large number of Massoni's relatives in Marignana were arrested and imprisoned in 1850 for harbouring, which forced Massoni to leave his home district. Again, those suspected of associating with him in the Balagna in 1851 were arrested, which made him move to the Niolo.[14]

A third and complementary policy was to provide money to induce local people to supply information about bandits or otherwise to co-operate in their capture or destruction; and large secret funds were made available to the authorities in Corsica for this purpose by successive governments.[15] From the other end of the operation, we have evidence of rewards being offered and paid and of some important successes for the authorities as a result. It appears that those responsible for tracking down and killing the Antona bandits in 1846 received financial inducement from the gendarmerie, and a reward of 10,000 francs was offered in 1851 for the capture or killing of the Massoni brothers and Arrighi a few months before they were 'betrayed' and killed.[16]

We have more information about this general policy from the 1870s. In 1874, the military and the police were said to require 10,000 francs to pay for local help and information against bandits, and funds were allotted from Paris and by the departmental council (though probably not to cover the full amount). Prominent bandits had prices placed on them, usually on the understanding that they be taken alive. In 1875, when a certain Casimiri claimed the reward of 4000 francs that had been offered for the capture of the bandit Fiaschetto, he was given only 1000 francs, because the bandit had been killed. The central government seems to have been less happy about this policy than its local representatives, cutting off funds once 'the problem' subsided and only renewing them after repeated requests. However, payments of 3000–5000 francs per month were being made through most of 1880, and annual sums of 20,000 to 40,000 francs were made available in the mid-1890s.[17]

Fourthly, there were judicial measures. Bandits were fugitives from justice, but though physically beyond the influence of the courts, they could be tried in their absence. Mottet complained in 1836 that this was too rarely done on the specious grounds that, once convicted, bandits would become desperate and yet more violent. Moreover, large numbers of bandits were allowed to go into exile in Sardinia and elsewhere and were never extradited. Indeed, as we have seen, banishment was still regarded by the authorities in the early nineteenth century as an acceptable alternative to prosecution.[18] In the second half of the century, however, 'executive' measures against bandits were generally abandoned. Fugitives were regularly prosecuted and given severe, even capital, sentences, and it appears that extradition became more common. The limited effectiveness of the courts in the prosecution of those who were arrested has been discussed in Chapter 8, but there was progress here from the government's point of view. The police could refer in 1900 to the 'energetic measures' being taken by the judicial authorities against bandits and those who harboured them.[19]

A fifth measure is the only one that can be called preventive: banning or controlling the carrying of weapons. Much of the population had been armed during the Wars of Independence and the French authorities had never, despite strenuous efforts, managed to disarm it. Reviving a system which had existed under the Genoese, the French introduced licensing in 1806 to control the possession and carrying of guns. Licences cost 10 francs, and 3000–4000 per annum were being issued to 'notables' in 1809–10. After that, applications dried up and the scheme was dropped. During the Restoration period prefects attempted to ban the carrying of arms altogether, but they were unable to overcome local opposition. The authorities continued to believe, however, that such a measure was necessary if banditry were to be eradicated, and some pressure was placed on officials in the first half of the century to show a good example in this area. A circular to mayors in 1847, for example, called on them to use their influence to prevent primary school teachers from going about armed, as they usually did. Only in 1853 was the authoritarian Second Empire able to impose a formal ban on carrying arms, which, the Republican prefect conceded in 1872, had given Corsica nearly 15 years of 'peace and prosperity'. He called then for the reintroduction of the 1853 ban but local politicians were unanimously opposed to what they regarded as a derogatory 'exceptional' measure and the proposal was successfully blocked. By-laws banned the carrying of arms in particular villages, but these were very difficult to implement. Further official proposals to reintroduce a general ban were made later in the century, but they foundered again on local opposition, which claimed that guns were necessary for hunting and for protection *against* bandits.[20] Carrying guns was still customary in many parts of the island until a generation ago.

Changes in policy through the modern period indicate serious differences of opinion over the suitability and the efficacy of these various kinds of measure. For example, the prefect wrote in 1874 that the policy of offering rewards was useless against the really dangerous bandits, since no one would take the money.[21] The very entrenchment of bandits in Corsican society militated against the success of most governmental anti-banditry policies. Moreover, nearly all of these were unpopular locally, for this and other reasons, and with liberal opinion on the 'Continent'. A typical article in *La Presse* in 1879 argued that the real remedy lay in good local administration and the development of the economy;

other measures were palliatives at best and derived from misconceptions about the nature of banditry.[22]

The basic misconception here – and one of much wider currency – was to see 'banditry' simply as a variety of criminality. Braudel has written that banditry is 'an ill-defined word if ever there was one'.[23] The trouble is rather that is has precise but multiple meanings. Following current French usage from at least the early eighteenth century,[24] the authorities in Corsica used the term to categorize certain kinds of violent or potentially violent behaviour in a pejorative way. Such behaviour was by no means necessarily regarded or perceived at the popular level in the same light. As Moss has explained with reference to Sardinia, banditry as a term 'is part of the metalanguage of crime rather than a crime itself'. At the élite and official level again, banditry may have stricter legal meanings equivalent to banishment, outlawry or the state of being a fugitive from justice.[25] A number of writers stressed that an element of banishment or outlawry still attached to banditry in nineteenth-century Corsica,[26] but the last of the three is more obviously relevant. Banditry here was a status that formed part of the two overlapping systems of sanctions that we have described: the system of the police and the courts, and the system of blood vengeance. A military report of 1826 defined a bandit 'as a man who responds to a summons by taking to the maquis'.[27] Tommaseo provided the other side of the picture in 1841, writing that 'a bandit is a man who has killed an enemy and who takes to the maquis, abandoning wife and family, village and normal life, to avoid public justice *and* private revenge'.[28] In practice the first category here nearly always included the second, and the essential material element in the bandit's condition was that he was 'in the maquis'[29] though he remained a member of the local 'moral community'.[30] Additionally, different types of banditry have been identified by scholars,[31] and were recognized within local cultures. At the popular level in Corsica, a distinction was drawn between the 'bandit of honour' and the 'mercenary bandit' or *parcittore*. Giovan-Simone Ettori, active in the Petreto-Bicchisano area in the early decades of this century, refused an offer to join the mercenary Bartoli gang and warned them off his territory with the words: 'We are not the same kind of bandit.'[32]

II

We will begin our discussion of the reality behind such distinctions by considering in what circumstances men became bandits and how they then managed to live.

Some Corsican bandits fit into Hobsbawm's category of the man who offends against the law of the State but not that of the community,[33] in the obvious sense of coming into direct conflict with the authorities. Montherot's guide told him in the late 1830s that he and a cousin had been wrongly accused of a crime in their youth; they had been arrested, but had escaped from prison and had then spent three years in the maquis. There is some evidence that such confrontation with the 'police' enjoyed special local approval. A lament sung for Gallocchio, who was killed in 1845, distinguished between his 'dishonourable' and his 'honourable' actions. Killing gendarmes and *voltigeurs* came into the latter category.[34]

Resistance to conscription and desertion seem to have been common avenues into banditry here. Teodoro Poli became a bandit in 1820 after killing a local gendarme who had had him arrested as a draft-evader. Domenico Sanguinetti deserted from the army at Toulon in 1909, returned to Corsica 'in search of a refuge' and became actively engaged in feuding in and around Venzolasca. An important motivation in such cases generally, to which we have referred in Chapter 8, was the feeling that justice was not likely to be had from the State and its courts.[35]

In other cases, a man became a bandit following an action in defence of his personal or family honour. For example, Giovan-Domenico Giovanangeli of Granace quarrelled in 1861 with Don Giovanni Leandri, the mayor, following the latter's attentions to his wife. Having tried to kill Leandri, Giovanangeli took to the maquis from where he later successfully achieved his revenge. Muzzarettu took to the maquis in 1931, we have seen, after killing a younger man, who had slapped him in the face.[36]

The distinction between these two ways into banditry was frequently blurred in practice. Conflict with the authorities was often related to the wider mesh of conflict in communities. Although Teodoro Poli's main initial quarrel was with the gendarmes, he had been denounced to them by a fellow-villager, with whose family his brother subsequently waged a feud. Antono Bonelli (Bellacoscia) became a bandit after killing the mayor of Bocognano, against whom he had a grudge because the latter had not enabled him to avoid doing military service. The mayor had also turned down Antono's proposal to marry his sister. Of course committing a vengeance crime was also to commit a crime against the State. After Natale Tenneroni of Santa-Maria-Sicche was accused locally of having shot and wounded Giovan-Francesco Emilj in 1845, he took to the maquis 'in order to avoid being arrested by the police'.[37]

A third and far less common category is made up of those who were attracted by the bandit's life of apparent liberty, power and fame. According to Gregorovius, Giacomino, called Bracciamozzo, was 'intoxicated by the renown of the brave bandit Massoni, [and] got it into his head that he would play a similar part, and gain the admiration of all Corsica. So he killed a man ... and became a bandit.' Francesco Raffini, a youth of 16, helped an established bandit, Alessandro Padovani, to ambush Giovanni Peretti of Sari-d'Orcino in 1850. 'There was no specific reason for hostility between Peretti and Raffini, and the latter's participation in the crime can only be explained by his close association with Padovani and the desire which he had expressed ... of becoming a bandit.'[38] Marcaggi has suggested that some of those in this category were mentally ill and had a pathological attraction towards violence.[39] This may be so, but more significant is the fact that Corsican society provided such men with a legitimate role.

In their own perceptions, most bandits, including those in the last category, seem to have seen their predicament in passive rather than active terms. They and others expressed this via two related notions: 'disgrace' and 'destiny' or 'fate', the first notion being primarily social and the second personal and cosmic. In his lament, Colombani called himself 'the poor disgraced one' (*poveru disgraziatu*) and similar expressions were used by other bandits.[40] Natale Gasparini declared in a public letter in 1824 that 'my fate wills it that I should be a criminal and do wrong'. A century later Andrea Spada told his brother: 'We did not become bandits from choice; destiny pushed us into it.'[41]

Hobsbawm's observation that bandits were usually young is confirmed by the Corsican example, though it is less certain that they were also 'single and unattached'.[42] No complete statistics are available of course, but a fairly random sample of 50 bandits, mainly from the period 1850–1930, indicates that well over half were under 30 when they became bandits or when they were captured or killed. Since ages at capture or death predominate in the older age-groups in the sample, it is clear that the normal age for becoming a bandit must have been 25 or younger. The sample also suggests that banditry was virtually absent among mature adult men, though some old men were or became bandits.[43]

Female bandits are said to occur in some societies.[44] The phenomenon is reported for Corsica,[45] but must have been extremely rare. We have seen, however, that women might more commonly themselves avenge affronts to their honour, and this might sometimes be assimilated to banditry. Ortoli suggested that Maria Fiordispina Padovani, who shot her lover on the square at Ota, actually took to the maquis and was later seized and killed by her brothers to prevent her from further 'disgracing herself', though the lament sung after her death suggests rather that her bandit status was only a symbolic and posthumous one.[46] In other cases, where women clearly did take to the maquis, it was as the companions of male bandits. The wife of a bandit from Pietrapola joined him in the maquis for a period in the 1890s. According to Bourde, when all the adult males of the Chiaverini family of Mela had been killed in their feud with the Mattei, an 18-year-old girl took on the obligation to avenge them. She became the mistress of the bandit Giovanni Pietri, joining him in the maquis, and achieving her vengeance with his help in 1885.[47]

It has often been pointed out that Corsican bandits might well belong to the upper educated class of landowners, notables and officials. Teodoro Poli's family 'was one of the richest and most honourable in the region'. Gallocchio's rival Peverone was an accomplished poet. Both Antono Forcioli and Giulio Agostini, who became bandits in the course of the feud at Arbellara in the 1840s, were young men of high social position and good education. Francesco Bastianesi of Ucciani 'belonged to an honourable family and one of some substance' and had been a medical officer before becoming a bandit in the early 1840s. Giovan-Tomaso Lanfranchi of Aullène was an important landowner, while his relative Giovan Battiste Lanfranchi bore the honorific title of Don.[48]

This list of upper-class bandits could be extended considerably, but most Corsican bandits of the modern period were of less elevated social status. Faure noted that most members of Teodoro Poli's gang in the 1820s were poor men who did not belong to influential families,[49] and scattered evidence from official sources suggests that this pattern was general. Reports from the later nineteenth century mention bandits who were cultivators, *lavatori*, artisans, muleteers and day-labourers.[50] A higher proportion were herdsmen, a point to which we will return. Upper-class bandits could still be found in this later period,[51] but it seems that the highest stratum of the élite had generally ceased to be directly involved in banditry as it had ceased to be involved in feuding. The leading bandits of the inter-war period all belonged to the middle stratum of Corsican society or below.

Romanetti came from a family of small landowners but was poorly educated. Giuseppo Bartoli's family was important in the village of Palneca – we have encountered his grandfather as mayor – but he had no education beyond primary school. He engaged in the colonial infantry at the age of 18 and did not rise beyond the ranks. Andrea Spada's father was a Sardinian woodcutter and charcoal-burner. He also failed to progress beyond primary school and the height of his ambition, before he became a bandit, was to obtain a post as a customs officer.[52]

Well before this, moreover, there is evidence of banditry being used as a weapon in local power struggles by poorer and less important families against their richer and more influential rivals. Gallocchio had trained for the priesthood and later adopted an upper-class life-style, but he belonged to a family that was distinctly inferior in status to those of his enemies.[53] The Multedo brothers, who belonged to Teodoro Poli's gang, were poor herdsmen from Calcatoggio engaged in a feud with the Pozzo di Borgo and the family of the justice of the peace for the canton of Sari-d'Orcino.[54] We have seen, too, that the force and violence employed by the Antona bandits at Frasseto more than compensated for their family's lack of wealth and status compared with the Franceschi. The same pattern is found in the feud between the Massoni and the Durilli at Marignana, though here the terroristic style of banditry practised by the Massoni was counterproductive and their wealthier opponents ultimately prevailed.[55]

In contradistinction to their 'class', no data on the family status of bandits is available to indicate, for example, whether they were predominantly younger sons. It is clear, however, that banditry ran in families to some extent. Paolo-Andrea Buresi of Ventiseri, convicted of homicide in 1862, was said to 'belong to a family of delinquents which has already produced two notorious bandits'.[56] There are many examples of sons succeeding fathers as bandits, and rather fewer of nephews following in the footsteps of uncles.[57]

This brings us to the more general associations between bandits and their kin. As we have seen, men frequently became bandits in the course of prosecuting feuds and they acted here as members of families or kindreds. Whether this was the case or not, once in the maquis a man's main source of support came from his kin. Giacomo Bonelli (Bellacoscia), who was at large for 40 years, was 'harboured and protected by an infinite number of relatives'. When Giuseppo Bartoli became a bandit in 1927, Marcaggi relates that 'the whole Bartoli kindred rushed to give him help and protection'. Muzzarettu declared that when he became a bandit, 'my relatives and friends in the canton took on the task of hiding and feeding me'.[58] Here it is significant that very few bandits were foreigners, since foreigners would not usually have had extensive kin in the island.[59] The policy of arresting and detaining the relatives of bandits was a direct response, of course, to this reliance upon kin. A former mayor of Marignana reported in 1850 that the imprisonment of the kin of the Massoni bandits had forced the latter 'to leave their native district [as we have seen] and [even] to become suspicious of their closest relatives whom they have caused to suffer such hardship'.[60]

Relatives helped bandits in a variety of ways. First, they served as scouts, messengers and look-outs. For example, the two brothers of Domenico Santoni, called Malanotte, of Palneca, acted as his scouts, and the gendarmerie expected to capture him easily after they had been arrested in 1841. Female relatives played an important part here. The Nicolai brothers of Campi, called Bartoli, were skilfully supported by their male relatives but also by their sister, who not only provided them with food and shelter but acted too as a scout. When A. Besignani of Venzolasca demanded 100 francs from the local excise collector in 1853, he sent the demand via his 17-year-old sister.[61]

Relatives also joined bandits in the maquis, and kinship was an important element in the formation of bandit gangs or associations in Corsica, as it was elsewhere.[62] Rovère notes that of 33 partisans of Pace Maria in the 1770s, 11 were definitely related to him while 29 came from the same village. Teodoro Poli's gang was a supra-kinship organization at its height but reverted to reliance on kin in its final difficult years. Moreover, Poli was joined in the maquis in 1823 by his uncle and then by his brother Borghello. Ignazio Giacomoni and Giovan-Antono Arrii from Loreto-di-Tallano operated as bandits together in the 1840s, although they were not related. But Ignazio's brother Paolino acted as their messenger and scout, and sometimes as their accomplice, while a wider range of relatives was involved in the more important crimes committed by the two bandits, including another brother of Giacomoni and the father and two brothers of Arrii. Again, Francesco-Maria Castelli, who was active in the Carcheto district in 1911–12, was aided by two cousins as well as by two other bandits, Pietrantoni and Albertini, who appear to have been unrelated to him; but Pietrantoni was aided in turn by his father and his son.[63]

Certain kinship relationships seem to have been particularly significant in banditry, a reflection to some extent of their general importance in Corsican society. Of these the most obvious was the fraternal tie. At least 16 sets of bandit brothers may be identified in the century between the 1820s and the 1920s, and most common was the association between a pair of brothers, the simplest form of 'fellowship' in a kin-oriented society.[64] The tie between uncle and nephew seems also to have been important. Petro Giovanni, for example, enjoyed the active support of three uncles, and Francesco Caviglioli was joined in the maquis in 1930–1 by two nephews. The solidarity of affines with bandits seems to have been less marked than that of kin, as one might expect, but examples may be cited. Gallocchio's most faithful scout and messenger was said to be Bastiano Micheli of Noceta, the brother-in-law of his first cousin, who was for this reason killed by the bandit's principal enemy in 1834.[65]

In some cases, bandits were clearly agents of their families and acted on instructions from elder relatives. A common pattern in the organization of feuds, this was of wider significance and could have mercenary implications. It was alleged that 'the relatives of Teodoro Poli ... were the instigators of his robberies' and especially his uncle Lario, who was reported to have declared: 'My dog is on the loose, so anyone who gets on the wrong side of us should look out!' Giovan-Antono Arrii appears to have acted under directions from his father. When he demanded money from Guelfo Panzani in 1847, for example, Panzani's brother went to negotiate matters with the bandit's father who was in prison in Sartène, and it was the latter who agreed to the sum of 100 francs which Panzani eventually paid.[66] Gregorovius noted generally in 1855 that bandits 'enrich their relatives and friends with the money they extort'. Such contributions might also be in kind and of a comparatively humble nature, but they were much appreciated. Gaffori, for example, a one-time companion of Teodoro Poli, obtained clothes and sheets for his mother and sister. In a lament for Teodoro himself, his wife declared that, thanks to him, she 'had not lacked meat or bread / Or slippers and fine stockings / Ear-rings and necklaces / Handkerchiefs ... of cotton / Muslin or Indian stuff'; while two female relatives of Cecco Mattei lamented after his death in 1885: 'No more hams, / No more sacks of flour.'[67]

Conversely, the aid of related bandits might be invoked in quarrels by distant kin. When the dispute between the Paoli and the Vignoli of Pianello became critical in 1841, for example, Simone-Paolo Paoli contacted his relative, the bandit Giacomolo Griggi, which seems to have prompted the Vignoli to take pre-emptive action against him.[68] We have seen that the authorities countered or exploited the bandit's reliance on his kin by placing them in detention. Attempts were also made to persuade relatives, who were often alone in a position to do so, to betray or to kill bandits, and these sometimes succeeded in overcoming the fundamental principle of kinship solidarity. We have seen that the Massoni became 'suspicious of their closest relatives' after the latter had been imprisoned. Teodoro Poli's uncle, Uccelloni, accepted money to kill him and other related members of the gang. He shot one of these, but in circumstances that led to his being discovered. Teodoro and his brother then summoned and assembled their remaining kin and killed Uccelloni in front of them as a deterrent to further betrayal. Again, Giuseppo Bartoli was eventually betrayed by two cousins and probably killed by them in 1931.[69]

Though aided primarily by their relatives, bandits also enjoyed more general support. 'In Corsica', the prefect reported in 1874, 'the killer who has taken to the maquis does not inspire the same revulsion as in France; people regard him as a person more to be pitied than blamed and they help him in every way ... in the villages everyone acts as a look-out, warning the bandit of any move made against him.'[70] Here it is significant that songs about bandits (which were very popular) often stressed the 'hardships' of bandit life. 'When I saw you take up / The bandit's gourd and heavy cloak / His pistol and shot-gun', a mother sang of her son, 'I felt my heart go cold / ... And I nearly died of grief.'[71] Again, Mottet noted in 1836 that the authorities were unable to enforce the confiscation of the property of bandits condemned by the courts in their absence, because no one was willing to acquire or even to use such property.[72] Family enemies would not be included in this 'universal sympathy' of course, and sympathy could be used up by persistent hostile actions, recognition of which fact could act as a powerful check on mercenary bandits. Nevertheless, a kind of support could be won 'through inspiring fear as well as [genuine] sympathy'. Marcaggi wrote that 'the terror which Massoni evoked occasioned demonstrations of sympathy in his favour wherever he went', and when he and his gang moved down into the Balagna in 1850–1 they were presented with gifts and fêted in the villages. Again, the bandits extorting money and goods from the local people in the Fiumorbo in the mid-1890s, were reported to be 'nevertheless very hospitably treated there'.[73]

A further indication of local solidarity with bandits is the way in which they were able not only to remain in contact with their relatives but even, in some cases, to continue to perform their roles in the family and the community.

Malaspina noted in 1876 that most bandits were married and visited their wives and children regularly. Aurenche observed in 1926, with tongue slightly in cheek, that had bandits remained continuously in the maquis they would all have contracted malaria and rheumatism and probably died of cold and boredom, adding that they 'never failed to attend family reunions, baptisms, weddings and funerals, nor, of course, to participate in elections'. And specific examples can be found to illustrate such general claims. Pasquale-Antono Benedetti of Ota 're-mained in the vicinity of his village and returned there to spend the night from time to time'. Giovan-Agostino Nicolai lived in the village of Carbini, where he had built a house, allegedly using money which he had earned for killing a man from Fozzano. In the inter-war period, Giuseppo Bartoli did not live in the maquis but in the houses of 'friends' at Palneca and Ciamannacce.[74]

A parallel indicator of solidarity with bandits is the fact that they were able to remain at large for long periods of time. Of sentenced fugitives at large in 1822–3, 41 or 11 per cent had been at large for over 20 years (including seven for more than 25 years and one for 32 years); while 82 or 22 per cent had been at large for between 10 and 19 years. Thus one-third of these bandits had spent over 10 years in the maquis or in exile.[75] For the period 1828–1930, our sources provide twenty-five examples of bandits who remained at large for 10 years or more. Of these, two were in the maquis for 30 years and two for over 40 years. All of this confirms the general view that 10 to 15 years in the maquis was usual.[76] It is also significant that a fair proportion of bandits eventually gave themselves up and were not captured by the authorities.

This local solidarity and dependence meant that bandits could normally oper-ate only within fairly limited areas. Most probably stuck to the neighbourhood of their own villages, and their range very rarely extended over more than one or two cantons. Camillo Ornano, for example, operated in the cantons of Zicavo and Santa-Maria-Sicche from 1815 to 1829, and Domenico Santoni in the same two cantons around 1840. In the inter-war period, the leading bandits each had their own clearly demarcated 'fiefs', Bartoli in the canton of Zicavo, Romanetti and then Andrea Spada in the Cinarca, and so on. In warning Bartoli off his territory, Ettori declared: 'You stay in your place and I will stay in mine.'[77] It has been remarked that the relationship between bandit and local population changed very much when he moved or was forced to move away from his native terri-tory.[78] Away from home, the bandit could no longer rely on kinship or commu-nity ties. He had to fend for himself, which meant forming gangs and carrying out extortion, robbery and various kinds of intimidation, points to which we will return. Nevertheless, there were supra-local elements of solidarity with bandits, expressed in the creation and propagation of legends about them, in the conferr-ing of nicknames on them and in actual networks of protection. The security of Natale Gasparini was not affected, it seems, when he moved from his native Bastelica to La Rocca in 1824, and Serafino, from Ota, enjoyed powerful protec-tion and support first in the Asco valley and then in the Balagna, which is not entirely to be explained by the fear which both bandits undoubtedly inspired.[79]

Many bandits operated singly or in pairs, as we have seen, but gangs were also common. These never reached the size apparently found in some other societies,[80] except possibly in the period of the struggle for independence in the mid-eighteenth century. Rovère mentions large gangs of up to 30 men each in the Niolo, the Guagno region and elsewhere in the 1770s, but no gangs in the nineteenth or twentieth centuries were so large.[81] Teodoro Poli's gang in the 1820s numbered at least a dozen.[82] The Durilli and the Massoni gangs in the Evisa region in the late 1840s comprised seven to ten men each, though Massoni's rose to around a dozen when he moved into the Balagna in 1850–1. Much more common was the small gang of less than six men, a pattern that Hobsbawm has observed more generally. Antono Lucchini of Ciamannacce was associated in the 1820s with his cousin Giuseppo and with Giuseppo Bonacorsi called Tambino. The Nicolai brothers of Campi were associated around 1830 with Ricciardi. Giovan-Agostino Nicolai of Levie joined forces around 1850 with four other bandits, the Cucchi and the Tramoni. Among the gangs operating in the later nineteenth century, those of Colombani and of Achilli each comprised four to five men.[83]

In these larger groupings men formed associations with unrelated persons, but it is not clear how this was done. Cases of unrelated pairs are also found; for example, Antono Fieschi of Pila-Canale, a youth of 18, joined the famous bandit Quastana in 1841. Vuillier suggested that something akin to blood-brotherhood was involved, writing that 'the bandits, who generally work in pairs, cement their partnership by a common crime, which forms an indissoluble bond between them'. However, these and other ties were not always stable and shifts in associations among bandits seem to have been quite frequent. The Colombani and the Achilli gangs, for example, had at one time formed a single unit. Teodoro Poli's gang broke up in the face of police action against it. In the inter-war period, having acted as a scout for Andrea Spada for two years, Francesco Caviglioli then fell out with him and organized his own gang with his nephews and others.[84]

The larger gangs were autocratically run. Teodoro Poli was formally elected leader of his, according to Faure, but his authority was complete. Romanetti was 'a respected leader who imposed his will on his followers and was obeyed by them'. Gregorovius suggested that Corsicans did not take happily to the wielding of too much authority here as in any other sphere, and the position of the bandit leader in Corsica vis-à-vis his followers must have been analagous to that of the patron vis-à-vis his clients. 'The bandit has an entourage,' Francesco Bornea explained in a letter to a local newspaper in 1930, and he had to keep that entourage happy by supplying it with benefits.[85]

It is difficult to substantiate Malaspina's claim that Corsican banditry *per se* represented a 'formidable organization', though we shall see that it could be an important adjunct to the political power of notables and important families. Mafia-type organizations seem to have been largely absent from Corsica, at least before 1914, though Faure suggests that Teodoro Poli and others belonged to the Carbonari and that the gang's organization was underpinned by that of the secret society.[86]

III

The bandit of honour became so following an action in defence of his personal or family reputation, and he maintained an 'honourable' mode of life. 'Here a bandit is ordinarily the most honest man in the district,' wrote Flaubert in 1840, a view echoed by later writers.[87] More particularly, as many observers again noted, and as the local press, with its eye on tourism, insisted later in the period, 'true' Corsican bandits never attacked people indiscriminately and they respected the property of those with whom they had no particular quarrel.[88] A lament sung by a widow declared proudly: 'He was a bandit of honour ... / And harmed no one (except his enemies).' Petro-Ignazio Padovani avenged the seduction of his sister in the mid-1840s by killing both the seducer and the latter's father. According to Marcaggi, 'he enjoyed general public esteem' after this and was regarded as a 'model bandit'; 'he only accepted food, munitions and clothing if he could pay for them', and he gave his services as a medical man freely. He was also a man of religious convictions, a point to which we will return. Even greater self-restraint was attributed to Giovan-Battiste Scapola of Bastelica, who became a bandit after committing a vengeance killing in 1836. He stayed in the maquis for about ten years 'without ever troubling or threatening those who accused him of the crime or the enemies of his family'.[89] At least two examples of bandit codes of practice are referred to in our sources: the Convention of Aitone agreed to by members of Teodoro Poli's gang in the Restoration period, and the code supposedly written down by Feliciolo Micaelli in 1927 after twenty years in the maquis, and which proscribed attacks on the honour of women, kidnapping, drunkenness and robbing from rich or poor.[90] Exclusive reliance on kin or community was also characteristic of the bandit of honour. As a corollary to this, the bandit of honour usually avoided association with other bandits. The bandit Capa from the Niolo was a 'loner', begging for his food and drink and deliberately eschewing luxuries like alcohol and tobacco that might have tempted him from the path of honour; while Ettori told Bazal that he could have joined a gang in the early 1900s, but had preferred to remain on his own, since he did not want to engage in robbery and extortion.[91]

The bandit of honour seems at first sight to have much in common with the 'noble' or 'social bandit', but further investigation reveals that the former was motivated primarily by adherence to the traditional values of blood vengeance and had little concern with social justice in any wider sense. Moreover, the notion of 'social banditry' as a 'primitive' form of protest and rebellion, popularized by Hobsbawm,[92] seems to be of limited applicability to nineteenth-century Corsica.

Some actions of bandits were directed against the agents of the State – but largely in self-defence. 'The bandits wage a terrible war against the police and the armed forces,' wrote Mottet in 1836, but in the context of a specific campaign against them.[93] The occasional bandit does seem to have had a particular animus against the police, like Teodoro Poli who declared that the gendarmes were his only enemies and who carried out an attack on a police barracks,[94] but in general very few police or gendarmes seem to have been killed by bandits. We have seen that conscription was resented and that draft-evasion provided recruits for banditry, but there is no evidence that this was regarded as a form of deliberate protest. The same is true of bandit attacks on the fisc. Tax officials were harassed and robbed, for example in the mid-1890s in the Fiumorbo where payment of all taxes was suspended for over a year. But the bandits concerned attacked tax-officials because they had supplies of ready cash, and the local population continued to pay taxes in effect, but to the bandits rather than to the State.[95]

Wider movements of political opposition in Corsica in the eighteenth century had included a bandit element, as we have seen. However, there is little or no evidence of any real protest element of this kind in banditry there between the time of the French occupation in the 1770s and that of the Italians during the Second World War. Teodoro was apparently involved in Carbonarism and was seen by some of his contemporaries, according to Faure, as a Corsican nationalist and by others as a Bonapartist opponent of the Bourbons, but this is an isolated and uncertain example.[96] Some bandits engaged in 'revolutionary' causes outside Corsica. Gallocchio, for example, fought in the Greek War of Independence, while Antono Santalucia was reported to be serving in Garibaldi's army in 1851. However, the main attraction here seems to have been mercenary service as such and not the particular cause which was involved, and bandits seem to have enrolled as readily in 'reactionary' armies. Antono Lucchini, for example, left Corsica in 1831 and later joined the papal army. All of this fits in with our discussion of the non-ideological nature of Corsican politics, though it may be significant that one of the places where Communism gained support after the Second World War was the Fiumorbo, a traditional bandit area.[97]

Rich and influential persons were of course attacked and sometimes killed by bandits. We have seen that Judge Colonna was killed by bandits on his return from a visit to Bastelica in 1820; the manager of a silver mine at Argentella was killed in 1887; and the station-master of Ghisonaccia was held up in 1895.[98] But these and similar episodes can hardly be regarded as political acts and must be seen rather in a context of feuding or of extortion from the rich because only the rich could pay.

Similarly, the common practice of placing the property of wealthy families under an interdict had little or no element of 'class conflict' in it. We have seen that it was a powerful weapon in the conduct of feuds and one that bandits were peculiarly well-placed to use, either in that context or on their account. Furthermore, interdicts harmed the employees, tenants and clients of notables as much as the notables themselves. Giovan-Tomaso Lanfranchi of Aullène, for example, placed the property of Tomaso Lanfranchi under a general interdict in 1850 in order to force him to pay a large ransom. Towards this end, he threatened to kill 'the *coloni*, the herdsmen and the house-tenants of Tomaso Lanfranchi unless they abandoned the land which they cultivated for him, the flocks which they looked after for him and the houses in which they lived'.[99]

Examples are cited of bandits who confirmed to the 'noble' or 'social' type. Malaspina described Teodoro as 'the Robin Hood of Corsica'.[100] But such characterizations derive almost entirely from popular songs and bandit laments, that is from legends about bandits rather than from direct experience of them. Moreover, bandits of a mercenary kind liked to be thought of as 'Robin Hood' figures. Romanetti is reported to have killed one of his scouts who had tried to extort money in his name, in order to demonstrate that he, Romanetti, was not a mercenary bandit. Francesco Bornea, who operated a protection racket with Giuseppo Bartoli in the Zicavo region, claimed in a letter to the local press that they only ever 'demanded money from those who had plenty of it'.[101] We will discuss such contradictions further below.

There is one sphere, however, in which bandits do appear to have defended popular rights. An official reported, for example, from Aullène in 1846 that an attempt was being made 'to paralyse the activity of the forest administration, by means of threats issued by bandits'. In 1882, a certain Begliomini acquired a concession in the communal forests of Levie and Carbini, which conflicted with the rights claimed by local people. When Italian woodmen arrived to fell the trees, they were threatened and frightened off by bandits. This manoeuvre was repeated in subsequent years and forced Begliomini to abandon his concession in 1886. In 1895, Armand Royé of Lyon wrote to the Minister of the Interior to complain that he was unable to operate his family's plantations of cork oak in the Fiumorbo, as a result of the activities of the Colombani gang. Both the share-croppers and the estate guards had been warned to stop working for or co-operating with the owners. 'Our forests are being robbed by accomplices of the bandits, who act as look-outs for them; the cork is cut by them at night, and we are unable to do anything about it, since our guards are shot at if they try to intervene.' If cork was loaded on to carts for the landlord, the carts were ambushed and forcibly unloaded. Similar action was taken at the same time against other private owners of forests in the region, while the functioning of the state forest administration in the canton of Ghisoni was seriously disrupted; forest guards were intimidated and forest offences went unchecked.[102] Here, bandits were aiding local resistance to the policing of forests designated as belonging to the State, to the concession of felling and other rights to outsiders rather than to local people, and to the exclusion of livestock and people from forests in public and private ownership.

But bandit interests or those of their relatives were often the primary concern rather than the rights of the community or social justice *per se* – the Colombani gang was said to be acting on behalf of friends and relatives – and in some cases mercenary and other interests are very clear. In 1874, the bandit Casanova demanded 1000 francs from a certain Pozzo, a banker and businessman and the Italian consul in Ajaccio. When he refused to pay, Casanova placed his extensive concessions in the forests of Aitone and Valdoniello under an interdict. At first, the workers concerned, Corsican and Italian, ignored the bandit's threats, but when these were renewed, work ceased. In fact, the workers benefited from the bandit's actions, since they had been paid in advance for work which they did not do, but this does not seem to have been Casanova's intention. Such actions might also be ploys by those with forest concessions. When the bandit Achilli, for example, 'placed a ban' on tree-felling in the forests of Laparo and Malanotte via a note to the foreman, the gendarmerie did not take the affair seriously, believing that there was collusion among all the parties concerned in order to try to get the terms of the concession improved. Forests, moreover, were often places of refuge for bandits, and they naturally resented invasion of them. Andrea Spada, for example, was annoyed when the concession to exploit the communal forest of Calcatoggio was granted to Giuseppo Faggianelli of Ajaccio. His brother explained later that Spada 'intended these woods, situated near his hide-out, to be reserved for himself. So when Faggianelli ... sent Italian workers to cut firewood

and make charcoal, Spada had their hut burned down and warned them never to
set foot in the forest again.' Faggianelli responded by hiring another bandit to
support his claims against Spada.[103]

At least one important case exists where bandits intervened in a conflict
involving rival claims to agricultural land, but the circumstances were peculiar.
The fertile lands of Migliacciaro on the coastal plain below the Fiumorbo had been
the object of dispute between the local inhabitants and absentee landlords since the
eighteenth century, if not before. During the Revolutionary period and the 'war'
of the Fiumorbo (1800–9), the lands had been occupied and used by the local
people, and, in the course of suppressing the 'war', General Morand had negotiated a compromise settlement or partition in 1808 by which the legal owners, the
Frediani of Penta-di-Casinca and the Morelli of Bastia, made certain concessions in
return for local recognition of their rights. But this settlement was by no means
definitive, for in 1818 the Genoese noble family, which sold the lands to the
Frediani and the Morelli in about 1755, began court proceedings to obtain the
residue of the purchase money, which had not been paid on the grounds that the
purchasers did not have free access to Migliacciaro. At the same time, the Frediani
and the Morelli sued for possession against the villages of the Fiumorbo. The case
seems to have gone against the villages, and by 1820 the two notable families were
in possession and had let the land to share-croppers via 'farmers' or local agents.
But the authority of the government was still very weak in the district, which had
attracted a large number of fugitives from justice who were 'protected by local
officials, whose relatives and clients they were'. In 1821, these bandits 'came down
to the plain at harvest time to take the share in the harvest which each *colono* owed
his landlords or their farmers. The *coloni* were threatened with death if they refused
to obey.' A letter from one such bandit explained that:

> our circumstances oblige us to provide for our own subsistence. We
> know that you have to pay a rent in wheat for the part of the estate of
> Messrs Morelli and Frediani which you cultivate; we invite you to give
> this instead to the person whom we will send to you ... We warn you that,
> if the slightest obstacle is put forward to the accomplishment of this
> measure, in particular by the police forces, you and your family will suffer
> in your persons and property.

Most of the 'farmers' had already paid their rent to the landlords' 'farmer-
general' in Corte and stood to suffer if they did not in turn receive their rent in
kind from the *coloni*. One of these tried to get the gendarmerie to intervene and
had to go into hiding.

> On some threshing floors [where the harvest was divided], the bandits
> found the *coloni* armed and ready to resist, and they did not dare to take
> anything. Moreover, nowhere did the bandits demand more than that
> share of the crop which was due to the landlords or to the farmers. The
> share of the *coloni* themselves was respected, and, if they could prove that
> they had already paid it, nothing more was demanded.

The bandits also singled out the farmer-general for special treatment. All his
grain stores were raided and emptied, and an attempt was made to make him

'hand over to the bandits all the documents relating to loans which he had made to the inhabitants of the Fiumorbo', but he claimed that the Frediani and the Morelli had these in Bastia.[104]

There are echoes here of an agrarian movement but they are faint, and the bandits had in effect replaced the landlords and farmers whom they only temporarily ousted. The estate was acquired not long afterwards by a French company, which seems to have successfully introduced modern methods of cultivation. There is some evidence that *coloni* and herdsmen from the Fiumorbo ceased payments to their landlords and employers in a similar way in the 1890s, but it seems again that these, like tax payments, were simply transferred to the bandits themselves. Bazal provides an example of a bandit defending a community – but against another bandit. When their district was being terrorized in 1930 by a certain Toma, the villagers of Petreto-Bicchisano sent a delegation to the local bandit Ettori asking him to rid them of the intruder, which he did; but this may be seen as a case of a bandit defending his fief as much as the act of a 'Robin Hood'.[105]

Several authors have noted the close links between banditry and pastoralism, notably in modern Sardinia. There the connection is not found before the nineteenth century, Day argues, and reflects 'the progressive degradation of the position of the herdsman following the establishment of a capitalist property system'.[106] Was there any such link in Corsica, which followed a similar evolution in the modern period?

We have mentioned that a high proportion of bandits were herdsmen, and the identification was a commonplace of official reporting and of local guide-books, and predates the nineteenth century, as Rovère establishes.[107] It is not surprising that bandits and herdsmen frequently associated with each other, since both lived and operated in the same maquis, forests and mountains. Herdsmen were the obvious contacts, supporters and protectors of bandits, while shielings were obvious places of refuge. Antono Ciavaldini of Venzolasca, for example, was surprised by his enemies in 1850 as he was eating with a herdsman at Chiosone on the territory of Vescovato. Around 1825, the bandit Bartoli of Ciamannacce was reported to be staying at the shieling of Carbonaccio on the territory of Pila-Canale. The shieling at La Punta in the Cinarca served as the headquarters of Romanetti and then of Andrea Spada in the inter-war period, and after La Punta had come under attack from the authorities, Romanetti moved to another shieling at Lava on the coast near Ajaccio.[108]

In return for such aid and assistance, bandits used their power to protect or further the interests of herdsmen and of pastoralism. The owners of La Punta were substantial herdsmen, the Leca, who benefited from having two well-known bandits as virtual members of the family – two daughters in succession were mistresses of Romanetti; one of them bore him a child and the other transferred her affections to Spada after Romanetti died. Thanks to the fear or sympathy which the two bandits evoked, the Leca were able to obtain pasture at low rents, to avoid any judicial or other consequences when their flocks strayed and caused damage to crops, and to obtain and keep a valuable contract to supply the Roquefort cheese company with processed sheep's milk.[109] Other examples may be cited from the nineteenth century. The Massoni gang supported the herdsmen of Feliceto in their struggle with the sedentary interest there. The same gang responded in 1851 to a request for help from four herdsmen from the Niolo, who had been excluded from their usual pasture at Montemaggiore, and made the mayor agree to restore 'free pasture' (*libre pacage*) on the communal lands for all comers. Bourde reported that bandits supported the claims of herdsmen against the owners of vineyards in the Sartène region in the 1880s. Colombani and his associates in the Fiumorbo in the 1890s operated in association with local herdsmen. The herdsmen supplied the bandits with food and ammunition and, in return, were allowed to pasture their flocks on land placed under interdict by the bandits.[110]

This close relationship meant that bandits were not uncommonly betrayed by herdsmen. The two Massoni and Arrighi were eventually tracked down and killed after their hide-out had been revealed by a local herdsman whose ram the bandits had killed for food. The public prosecutor reported in 1874 that most of the money being paid out by the authorities to obtain information for use against bandits was being paid to herdsmen. More particularly, the prefect suggested in 1893 that Giacomo Bonelli could be captured if money was forthcoming to pay local herdsmen to betray him. Apart from personal and family enmities, all this reflected the fact, as Natali notes, that bandits were often parasites upon herdsmen.[111] There is no clear evidence that banditry generally had any particular connection with the difficulties of pastoralism in the modern period, and the Sardinian phenomenon of *abigeato* or livestock rustling is not found to any significant degree in modern Corsica, though it occurred in earlier centuries.[112]

The role of the bandit as a justiciar has been identified as another feature of social banditry,[113] and here there is considerable overlap with the emic notion of the bandit of honour. There is no doubt that some Corsican bandits regarded themselves as righters of wrongs and were so regarded by others. Renucci related a story told about Gallocchio in his lifetime. A poor *lucchese* on his way home via Bastia was robbed of his season's earnings by a man pretending to be the famous bandit. The real bandit happened to meet the distressed victim, pursued, caught and punished the robber, and restored the money to its rightful and grateful owner. Muzzarettu referred to himself as a 'justiciar', and told Bazal that bandits in Corsica were regarded 'as medieval knights, who dealt out sentences of death, in their own good time and for good reasons; they were righters of wrongs who laughed at the gendarmes sent to catch them'. According to Aurenche, bandits were sometimes referred to in common parlance as 'the just men'.[114]

There is evidence, too, that some bandits actually performed this role, though it is scant. First, bandits acted as arbiters and mediators in disputes. Faure related that bandits used their influence to restore harmony between spouses, to prevent or to end litigation, and to reconcile enemies. He referred, too, to 'courts' held in the maquis by Teodoro Poli and by bandits in the Ortolo valley around 1850, though in the first case the main function of the 'court' seems to have been to try offences among and against bandits themselves. An official report in 1894 stated that bandits 'did not hesitate to set themselves up as arbiters in local quarrels and in private disputes'; and both Romanetti and Ettori seem to have performed this function in the 1920s. However, examples may also be found of bandits refusing to accept local arbitration procedures. A. Arrighi mentions a bandit who killed an arbitrator from Urbalacone, who had decided against him in a dispute over a water course.[115]

Secondly, and related to this, bandits acted to make sure that others adhered to local codes of conduct. Serafino, for example, intervened around 1850 in a village in the Balagna to make two sons look after their aged mother. We have an actual example, too, of a bandit intervening to reconcile spouses and to assert the authority of a husband. Giovanna Guerini of Rospigliani, the wife of Ristoruccio Ristorucci, had left her husband and returned to her father's house. A meeting was arranged in 1840 between husband and wife and their respective relatives, in order to attempt a reconciliation. However, quarrelling broke out between the two sets of affines, and Giovanna refused to go with her husband. Thereupon, the bandit Giacomolo Griggi appeared on the scene, apparently having been forewarned by Ristoruccio. He told the Guerini to disperse, saying: 'The husband is master of the wife,' and shot dead a youth who failed to obey him.[116]

The most frequently reported type of intervention in this area concerns affronts to female honour. Benson relates that Gallocchio took a herdsman, who had raped a girl while pretending to be Gallocchio himself, before the mayor of the village concerned and made the man marry her. The bandit warned that punishment would follow if the wife were ill-treated, and, when the man and several of his relatives were later killed, it was assumed that the bandit's instructions had been ignored and that he had therefore carried out his threat. In the mid-1830s, Maria-Lilla Antonmarchi, a widow from Santa-Lucia-di-Moriani, became pregnant, and Diogene Bonavita, the father-in-law of one of her sons, Petro-Paolo, was said to be responsible. Petro-Paolo asked Bonavita to repair the situation by marrying Maria-Lilla, and backed up his request with a letter from the bandit Franchi Rinaldo, a friend of the Antonmarchi family. Rinaldo stated that Bonavita's behaviour 'displeased him and was an affront to the woman's relatives'. When Bonavita ignored these threats, he was killed by the bandit. In another case, the 18-year-old daughter of a widow from L'Acquale, a relative of Massoni, was impregnated by the son of a rich landowner and herdsman from Albertacce, Fra Jura. Following a request for help from the widow, the bandit paid a visit on Fra Jura and his son, told them that, since the girl had no other male relative, he was acting on her behalf, and made them agree to a marriage despite the great disparity in wealth and status between the families. When Fra Jura made no preparations for a wedding, he was reminded of his promise and then killed by Massoni in 1851.[117] It will be noted that in these examples bandits were defending their own reputations and/or their family interests as well as upholding the honour of defenceless women. In a further case, reported by Saint-Germain, not always a reliable source, Serafino helped a girl to kill one of his own relatives who had seduced her,[118] but such disinterestedness must have been rare.

Bandits themselves, for one thing, were notorious offenders against female honour. Abductions and rapes by bandits were fairly common,[119] and bandits frequently had mistresses, concubines and passing liaisons. 'Women are crazy about us bandits,' Mérimée's Brandolaccia boasts to Della Robbia. 'I have three mistresses in three different cantons.' We have seen that the two Leca sisters served as Romanetti's mistresses, and when he moved from La Punta to Lava, he seduced the daughter of the house there. Andrea Spada also had and cultivated a reputation as a womanizer.[120] All this reflects the power of bandits, but also it seems a special attraction. A woman testified, for example, in a case in 1836 that she was the mistress of the bandit Felice Nicolai and proud of it, thus flouting the proper female norms.[121] On the other hand, the behaviour of bandits here conformed to one 'ideal' of male honour, the predatory conquest of women. In this context, it may be significant that some bandits were originally rejected suitors, like Gallocchio or Matteo Arrighi,[122] and had a point to prove in this area. Whatever its motivation, this aspect of bandits' behaviour could make them vulnerable. Bandits were not infrequently betrayed or captured with the help of women, and their sexual exploits provoked hostility from men that could be disastrous. An ex-mayor of Isolaccio in the Fiumorbo, Captain Laurelli, told Flaubert that he had himself killed a bandit who had been notorious in this respect, ordering local men to send him their womenfolk at stated times 'like an Asiatic despot'. News of his death led to universal rejoicing, 'and peasants from the whole district between Bastia and Isolaccio came to see Laurelli to thank him'. Romanetti was ambushed and killed in 1926 thanks largely to the efforts of a man from Bocognano whose wife he had seduced.[123]

Corsican bandits were reported to be 'religious', a phenomenon found elsewhere,[124] and one that might be taken as another sign of 'honourable' status. 'All bandits, without exception', wrote Marcaggi, 'had a deeply-rooted superstitious belief in scapulars, rosaries, crucifixes, holy medals, prayers sewn into their jackets or waistcoats, all in order to preserve them from being killed.' Ortoli refers to daily prayers to the Virgin Mary, the wearing of scapulars and relics, placing guns under the protection of a saint or the Virgin, and the transmission of verbal charms from one bandit to another.[125] Bandit laments, moreover, frequently invoke God and the saints and express religious sentiments.[126] And there is abundant testimony of the religious sentiment and practice of particular bandits. Teodoro Poli recited prayers morning and night. Gallocchio, an ex-seminarian, had a similar reputation for piety and was supposed to have killed an inn-keeper who served him meat on a Friday. Among later bandits, Giacomo Bonelli had a large collection of amulets, holy images and prayers; Francesco Bocognano 'filled his pockets with crucifixes and statuettes of St Francis and never went to sleep without first saying his rosary'; while Andrea Spada also 'said his rosary every evening ... and wore scapulars and religious medals'. Spada was wearing an enormous crucifix round his neck when he was arrested in 1932.[127] It is also reported that both Andrea Spada and Francesco Bornea performed the role of the Grand Penitent in the Good Friday procession at Sartène.[128] Bandits also displayed the normal concern not to die without the performance of the proper religious acts. Several cases are reported of bandits arranging to make their final confessions when they felt that the end was near. Massoni asked for the prayers for the dying to be said after he had been mortally wounded, while his companion Arrighi, in the same straits, requested that some of the money on his person be used to pay for 20 masses for his soul.[129]

Most of these practices were intended to procure protection, if not invulnerability, as Marcaggi suggests. Petro-Ignazio Padovani is said to have declared in the late 1840s of bandits in general: 'So long as we are in God's hands, we can

walk about boldly and no bullet will harm us. But once God withdraws his holy
protection from us, our eyes cloud over, our arms shake and our last hour has
come.'[130] This kind of faith was clearly 'useful' to bandits, as was their general
reputation for possessing supernatural power. The latter was not so important in
Corsica as it was elsewhere perhaps, but it did exist. Mérimée's Brandolaccio had
the evil eye; while Muzzarettu told Bazal: 'I know all the names of the stars. One
of my dogs is called Saturn. I can predict the weather!' Faure relates that bandits
were often regarded as 'sacred beings', which meant that any hostile action
against them was supernaturally as well as materially dangerous. 'The very word
bandit throws people into a panic,' Marcaggi elaborated.

> The bandit, the man of the maquis strikes the popular imagination with a
> superstitious dread. He is a being who has placed himself on the margin
> of society, who no longer accepts any law, who is constrained by no
> responsibilities, who has sacrificed his life in advance, who will perish
> sooner or later by violent means, and whose only guide is his own
> whim.[131]

However, this exaggerates both the marginality of the bandit and the awe in
which he was held, which depended more on his acts of terror than on his status
as such, as we shall see. Bandit religiosity was a closer reflection of popular
religiosity than Marcaggi allows, albeit heightened by the bandit's precarious
mode of existence. It had its uses, and it did not denote any adherence to a
superior moral code or any attachment to a goal of social justice. It is significant
here that there seems to have been no link in Corsica between banditry and
millenarianism, such as is found in other parts of the world.[132]

The notion of banditry as a sacred status takes us on to banditry in popular
myth or legend. The propensity to make bandits into legendary heroes seems to
be almost universal, both in societies which have real bandits and in those which
do not,[133] and Corsica was no exception. According to a guide-book in 1881, 'the
word bandit was synonymous with hero for most of the population': while a
military observer wrote similarly in 1904 that 'admiration for bandits is very old
and very much alive ... their often unbelievable exploits, their courage, their skill
and their energy are legendary'.[134] This heroic view of banditry was expressed
and preserved in an extensive oral literature. Muzzarettu recalled that he had
'been brought up on stories of bandits', and such stories, told at *veillées* and on
other occasions are referred to in many other sources.[135] There also existed a
special genre of song or *lamento* composed by or about bandits and sung all over
Corsica.[136] The texts of a number of these have been preserved, and they stress
the bandit's original innocence and the hardship to which his fate condemned
him as well as his boldness and bravery.[137]

The significance of bandit legends had been disputed, some like Hobsbawm
taking them to reflect a real libertarian element in banditry itself, others regarding the reality of and the legends about banditry as distinct or related only in so
far as complimentary legends served to disguise or legitimize the exercise of
brute force.[138] Here attention has been drawn to wide discrepancies between the
real lives of bandits and their images in popular literature and later accounts, and
Corsica provides some remarkable examples of such divergence. Versini claims

with reason that Teodoro Poli was a mercenary bandit in his lifetime and notes that there was public celebration when he was killed by *voltigeurs* in 1827. But from that time, if not before, a myth of a 'Robin Hood'-type hero was created via a series of popular songs and anecdotes, which are reflected in literary accounts such as those by Flaubert and by Gregorovius. Faure could write in 1858 that Teodoro's reputation in Corsica was only equalled or excelled by those of Sampiero, Paoli and Napoleon, and his 'renown' was still the object of notice in 1928.[139] Much the same pattern is found with Gallocchio. He became a bandit for reasons of honour, it is true, and he was engaged in a feud; but he behaved with particular brutality and was said to have killed 45 people during his time as a bandit. In the words of a lament sung at his funeral, his 'nickname / Broadcast such terror ... / Hearing the name of Gallocchio / Was enough to terrify people.' For this reason, according to Tommaseo, he could only be overcome by stealth and was killed in his sleep by a scout with the support of local people, who rejoiced when the deed was accomplished. After Gallocchio's death, however, songs began to circulate which celebrated 'his misfortunes, his courage, his probity and his piety'. It is significant that later accounts disagree about his status. Colonna de Cesari-Rocca stresses that Gallocchio was motivated by questions of honour, while Versini categorizes him as a mercenary bandit.[140] The Santalucia and Giacomoni bandits of the Tallano,[141] and Massoni and his associates[142] were extolled after their deaths in a similar way. The making of legends about bandits was mainly a posthumous phenomenon, though Massoni was glorified in popular songs in both the Niolo and the Balagna in his lifetime, and several bandits of the inter-war period were granted legendary status before they died.[143]

The Corsican evidence suggests that bandit legend was an idealization of bandit reality. 'People forgot their exactions and their interference with everyday life,' Privat wrote in 1936, 'and wanted to remember only their defiance of established things and the acts of kindness which they carried out.' Nor did people fail to perceive the distinction, as this perhaps implies. To some extent the legend asserted what bandits ought to be, the ideal of the 'bandit of honour' as against what bandits were actually like. In a society where banditry was a reality, moreover, bandit legends also served as a natural vehicle for the declaration and discussion of social values. As Dalmas has written of *lamenti* from San-Gavino-d'Ampugnani, they 'evoke the spectacular activities of personalities who are both feared and admired'.[144] Like other folkloric heroes, the bandit of legend was both an atypical fictional creation and the embodiment of central and universally shared values.

IV

Contemporaries in the later nineteenth and early twentieth centuries lamented the decline of the bandit of honour. The subprefect of Corte, for example, looked back nostalgically in 1896 to an earlier period when bandits had lived frugally, respected the property of others and acted chivalrously. 'Today the situation is quite different ... The bandit has become an ordinary malefactor, a brigand who holds up mail coaches, robs travellers and lives from theft and rapine'. Again, according to a bandit in the 1920s, 'true banditry was in the doldrums ... Some of the so-called bandits of today are just interested in money! They extort ransoms, they commit the worst robberies ... They are famous, it is true, and the newspapers write all about them, but I am ashamed of these bastard bandits.' Albitreccia referred more generally to banditry after the First World War in Corsica as a 'neo-banditry', distinct from the traditional kind linked to the system of blood vengeance and honour. The bandit of honour was still occasionally found in the twentieth century, but he was significantly often an old man, following behaviour patterns of the past. Though some of them liked to be thought of in the old way, the bandits of the inter-war years were essentially *parcittori*, and *parcittori* on a new scale. In this period also, the links between Corsican banditry and the continental French underworld were established.[145]

This fundamental change was reflected in the way in which bandits ended their careers. We have seen that it was common in the early and mid-nineteenth century for bandits to give themselves up, after arrangements had been made with their enemies and with the authorities. This procedure was still sometimes followed in the 1880s and 1890s and even in the 1930s, but in the post-1870 period generally bandits were much more often reported to have been arrested (presumably involuntarily) or to have been killed by the police. Figures are available relating to 88 bandits captured or killed in eighteen of the years between 1873 and 1900. Of these, 12 (13.6 per cent) gave themselves up, 47 (53.4 per cent) were arrested, and 29 (33 per cent) were killed by the police.[146]

The perception of a change in the nature of banditry undoubtedly reflected something real and was related to radical transformations in Corsican society, but an element of illusion enters into it. Banditry had always been ambiguous and its honourable and mercenary aspects had co-existed. As Hobsbawm observes, 'one sort of bandit can easily turn into another'.[147] Driven from his own territory, separated from his network of support, the bandit of honour would be forced to attack travellers, to prey on local people, in order to survive. Even if he did stay in his own region, he might be 'caught up in a web of crimes ... in defending himself against his enemies or escaping the pursuit of the authorities'.[148] For example, Giovan-Agostino Nicolai of Levie became a bandit in the late 1840s after refusing to do his military service. His first 'crime' was committed in August 1848 in support of his family's interest and honour. He came to the help of his brother who was involved in a dispute over a water-course, and shot one of those with counter-claims to the irrigation supply. Following this, however, he joined up with other bandits in the region and committed further 'non-honorific' crimes. It appears that he killed Giuseppo Paoli of Fozzano in December 1848, for which he was paid 4000 francs by the latter's enemies, and in 1849 he tried to extort money from two notables in Sartène by threatening to kill them.[149] Here one can see the local bandit closely involved with his kin and its quarrels evolving into the bandit operating on a wider front with other bandits and being employed by members of the élite.

Very often, however, there is no obvious evolution as far as any individual bandit is concerned. The bandit is both a bandit of honour and mercenary, depending in part on circumstances and on who is looking at him. We have seen that Teodoro Poli gained a posthumous reputation as a 'Robin Hood' figure, and incidents in his actual career can be found which fit this picture. However, many of those living in the districts where he was active had a different view of him. In February 1823, for example, Father Pinelli, the parish priest of Soccia, wrote to the prefect to protest at the way in which Teodoro and others were 'tormenting honest folk' in the canton. He himself had been unable to leave his house for a month because the bandits had been lying in wait in the vicinity. Other victims of Teodoro and his gang included the justice of the peace of the canton of Cruzzini and his brothers, the parish priest of Salice, and the priest at Pastricciola, from all of whom money had been extorted, as well as the relatives of three women who had become Teodoro's 'concubines'.[150]

We have observed that it was very much in the interest of bandits to cultivate an honorific image. The bandit's reputation for honour could be a means of sustaining support from a local population which he was in fact exploiting.[151] The complementarity is neatly reflected in the phenomenon of pairs of bandit brothers, like Teodoro and Borghello, or Antono and Giacomo Bonelli, one of whom had the reputation of being 'good and honourable', while the other was regarded as 'bad and mercenary'.[152]

We turn now to a fuller discussion of the mercenary side of banditry, which, despite these links, can be distinguished as a type. By contrast with the bandit of honour, the mercenary bandit or *parcittore* paid only lip-service to traditional codes of behaviour. Rather than relying exclusively on kin and community support, *parcittori* also formed their own gangs and networks and acted as agents for the notables. They were notorious womanizers and drunkards. They used their power to enrich themselves at the expense of the community through extortion and robbery, and some of them exercised deliberate reigns of terror. Though some may nevertheless have achieved legendary status, most, according to Marcaggi, were the 'objects of public execration'.[153] As we have seen, some observers believed that the mercenary bandit was a modern phenomenon, but mercenary banditry existed in all periods, though especially, as Rovère notes – and this would include the modern period – in times of economic and social upheaval when traditional ties were weakened or broken.[154]

As we have seen in the case of Teodoro Poli and his associates in the 1820s, Corsican bandits frequently extorted money. Teodoro levied sums ranging from 20 to 300 francs or more from members of the clergy and others in his area. 'In the province of Vico / All paid tribute, / Priests ... and herdsmen, / Deans, *curés* and misers, / Rich people, justices of the peace, / Substitute judges and secretaries.'[155] According to the Franceschi, the Antona bandits of Frasseto 'were accustomed to make forced levies on the inhabitants of the canton and beyond, where they exercised complete authority by force'. In February 1847, Guelfo Panzini was ordered 'by means of a notice fixed to the church of Loreto-di-Tallano', to pay the bandit Giovan-Antonio Arrii 2000 francs. 'Friends intervened and the demand of the bandit fell to 200 francs'. When Panzini continued to resist payment, he received several letters from the bandit threatening to kill him and to 'dishonour his sister', and he eventually handed over 100 francs. The following year, Arrii made similar demands on Dono Mozziconacci, mayor of Loreto, who was asked to hand over 'the income deriving from the lease of the communal lands', and, when this demand was ignored, to pay 300 francs. Both demands were accompanied by threats of death. When the affair was eventually brought to court, Arrii was ordered to pay 200 francs damages to Dono Mozziconacci, 'who was of course not so foolish as to require that this sum be actually paid to him, though he gave Arrii a receipt for it'.[156]

Many similar examples of extortion or attempted extortion could be cited from the later nineteenth century. By then and particularly in the inter-war period, the development of tourism had provided a new target in the form of hotels and thermal establishments. Three bandits tried to extort 3000 francs at gun-point at the Hôtel de Bellevue in Ajaccio in 1886. Giuseppo Bartoli demanded 20,000 francs from the manager of the Grand Hôtel Continental there in 1931; while Francesco Cavigliolo and his gang, having occupied the Hôtel Miramar at Tiuccia, attacked the baths at Guagno in the same year in an attempt to force the payment of a ransom.[157]

As these and the Loreto example indicate, such extortion was accompanied by serious threats. Bourde noted in 1887 that most landowners paid up levies to bandits when asked and then kept quiet about it for fear of reprisals. When the parish priest of Murzo refused to hand over the 20 francs demanded of him by Teodoro Poli and the Multedo brothers in 1822, the bandits removed all his furniture, bedding and other belongings and burned them in front of the presbytery, which induced him to change his mind. In some cases, victims were kept virtually besieged in their houses, like Father Pinelli of Soccia. According to his patron Count Colonna Cinarca, Agostino Stefanini of Sari 'had been forced to stay in his house for more than three months following a demand for 250 francs made by the bandit of the same name'. Sometimes people were forced to leave home. Ex-Prefect of Police Pietri moved his residence from Sartène to Ajaccio after money had been extorted from him in 1886, and in 1895 the rich mayor of Ventiseri left the village to avoid paying a 'ransom'.[158]

Kidnapping accompanied by a ransom demand was not uncommon. Borghello and Cipriani demanded 100 francs from Mayor Colonna of Balogna in 1827. When he refused to pay, the bandits kidnapped his son and his cousin and only released them when a promise to hand over 600 francs was forthcoming. Agostino Stefanini 'kidnapped the mayor of Sari-d'Orcino' in 1841 and kept him for over forty days, always on the move, until his relatives had paid a ransom of 4000 francs. In 1847, Matteo Tavera, a rich merchant from Sartène, was kidnapped by the bandits Giovan-Antonio Arrii and Ignazio Giacomoni. A ransom of 9000 francs or more was demanded from his relatives, and after negotiations lasting a week 6000 francs were handed over. In the 1880s, Giacomo Bonelli and Stefano Suzzeri kidnapped the mayor of Nocario and obtained a large ransom from his brother, a priest, only one of several kidnappings in which the Bellacoscia were involved.[159]

Four members of the Ferracci family from a village near Bonifacio were convicted in 1835 of having kidnapped an English traveller and extorted money from him, but such attacks on foreigners were said both then and later to be extremely rare. Spada's 'autobiography' states that there was a strict rule among inter-war bandits against molesting tourists.[160] This was in accordance with the traditional obligation to provide hospitality to strangers, but was also motivated by the well-placed fear that action against tourists, who were becoming one of the island's main sources of income by this time, would prompt serious governmental intervention, which of course it eventually did.

However, although foreign visitors were not usually victims of banditry, outsiders working in areas where bandits were active often were. In 1895, for example, Colombani and Bartoli called at the house of a non-Corsican contractor at Prunelli-di-Fiumorbo, and ordered him to pay them 200 francs and leave the district. He stalled on the first demand, but left for Corte the next day. We also learn of 'ransoms' being paid by pipe manufacturers operating in eastern Corsica in the 1890s, and tax-officials were common targets more generally. The bandit Brusco demanded money from Pozzo di Borgo, paymaster of Corsica, when he was taking the waters at Guagno in the 1820s. When he left the paymaster was given an armed escort, which did not prevent his party from being ambushed.[161]

As one would expect, these cases of extortion relate mainly to the wealthy, whether local people or outsiders. However, wealth as such seems to have been a less important criterion in the selection of victims than vulnerability, which would explain why members of the clergy and later schoolteachers were favourite targets. And by no means all the victims of bandits under this heading belonged to the élite. The bandits of the Fiumorbo in the 1890s took money and goods 'from the herdsmen, peasants and small landowners' of the region, and the tax-collector of Prunelli gave as the main reason for his failure to collect taxes in his area in 1896 'the profound poverty of the unfortunate inhabitants' following three years of extortion and pillage by bandits.[162]

In many cases, Corsican bandits received regular rather than *ad hoc* payments, whether from notables or the population at large. Gregorovius wrote that: 'The bandits levy contributions; they tax individuals nay whole villages and parishes, according to an assessment, and rigorously call in their tribute.'[163] The word *parcittore*, most commonly used to describe the mercenary bandit, means literally a collector of tribute, tax or revenue. Teodoro Poli's extortions from priests were part of a systematic levy imposed on the clergy and others, and force was applied only against those who refused to pay. At the end of the century, it was reported that the parish priest of Isolaccio in the Fiumorbo was similarly required to pay part of his salary on a regular basis to the gang of bandits led by Giovanni, while according to Bourde, Giacomo Bonelli 'taxed' all entrepreneurs engaged in public works in his area, including those involved in building the railway between Ajaccio and Bastia. More generally, it was reported in 1895 that Giovanni was levying a kind of general tax on the inhabitants of the region in which he operated, and the inhabitants of the cantons of Prunelli, Ghisoni, Porto-Vecchio and Moita were paying a similar regular tribute to 'two gangs of bandits led by Achilli and by Bartoli'.[164] It is not quite clear what form this tax or tribute took, though such levies do seem to have replaced legitimate rents and state taxes for periods of a year or more in the Fiumorbo both in the early nineteenth century and in the 1890s. There is no evidence of the formal bandit taxes on marriages and land sales referred to by Brögger for southern Italy,[165] but a lament collected by Ortoli mentions bandits 'raising taxes / At the crossing of bridges, / On the roads, at the shielings', which suggests a kind of toll.[166]

More details are available on the protection money raised by bandits in the inter-war period. According to Andrea Spada, 'we acted almost in the capacity of an insurance company. In return for an agreed sum of money, we gave our protection to the various shopkeepers, hotel-keepers and businessmen. So great was the power of Romanetti's band that once a shopkeeper had paid his toll to Romanetti and come under our protection, the lesser bands never dared to molest him.' He added that the big bandits like Romanetti never tried to get rid of the small bandits because they served the crucial function of frightening people into paying for this protection. However, the big bandits also placed their own pressure on their protégés, as Spada's subsequent career, once he had served his apprenticeship under Romanetti, illustrates. During his last seven years in the maquis, Spada lived mainly on protection money obtained from those running the postal and carrier services between Ajaccio and Lopigna. In 1926 the concession for these services was awarded for one year to Delmo Franchi. Spada held up his vans and effectively suspended the service for three months, until Franchi agreed to pay the bandit half the postal subsidy of about 1000 francs per month. The concession came up for renewal in 1930 and was awarded to Francesco Sorbo, mayor of Lopigna, who refused to continue payments to Spada. In May 1930, Spada and his brother held up the post van and killed the driver and two gendarmes who were supposed to be ensuring his safety, and in December Sorba abandoned the concession to a certain Malandri, who was in effect a stooge operating for Spada himself. In September 1931, Malandri backed out of this arrangement, and the concession passed to another stooge, who paid Spada the whole of the subsidy. Giuseppo Bartoli and his associates operated a more extensive protection racket in the Palneca region but also further afield in the cantons of Zicavo, Santa-Maria-Sicche and Sartène and in Ajaccio. This involved industrialists, tradesmen and businessmen as well as the concessionaries of postal and carrier services and felling rights.[167]

We have seen that theft was uncommon in Corsica and that thieves were held in contempt. The bandit of honour eschewed stealing. Of the sentenced fugitives at large in 1822–3, 68 per cent had been convicted of homicide and only 24 per cent of robbery.[168] The mercenary bandit, however, regularly carried out robberies, as a few fairly random examples will indicate. Pietrorso and Angelo Massini were reported to have committed various serious robberies in the canton of Nonza in 1827–8. The bandit Feliciolo called Bartolo of Tox was killed in 1839 in the house of a merchant from Antisanti, which he was trying to burgle. Petro Bartoli, called Piriggino, from Isolaccio was sentenced to hard labour for life after being convicted in 1846 of several robberies with violence. Later in the century, the bandits of the Fiumorbo were notorious for their hold-ups. Here and elsewhere in this later period, robbery from post-offices and postal officials was particularly frequent. The post-office of Prunelli-di-Fiumorbo was robbed so often that it was eventually closed. Bandits also tried to derail a train in 1899 on the line between Ajaccio and Bastia in order to rob the mail which it carried.[169]

Extortion, robbery, the raising of protection money do not exhaust the means of intimidation available to Corsican bandits. We have seen that they placed interdicts on the lands and livestock of their enemies or those who resisted them. Victims might also be confined to their houses and thus prevented from going about their affairs.[170] Alternatively, they might be forced to leave their

native districts or even to quit the island.[171] Again, bandits engaged in the
intimidation of jurors and witnesses, either on behalf of others or on their own
account, and women were abducted and marriages forced on unwilling families.
In 1861, Paolo Mondolini of Olmeto obtained the support of the bandit Antono
Paoletti for his attempt to marry Nunzia Andreani. Her relatives 'were intimidated into breaking off her engagement to Francesco Andreani', and, when they
'persisted in refusing the demands of Paolo Mondolini' and engaged the girl to a
third man, Paoletti and Mondolini ambushed the engaged couple, stabbing and
seriously wounding her fiancé and abducting the girl.[172]

   In this general context, official, press and other reports referred to bandits
creating or inspiring 'terror'.[173] This was in part a cliché reflecting the difference
between official and popular notions of banditry, but there is no doubt that in
Corsica,[174] as elsewhere, terror was a part of the image of some bandits and acted
as a basis of their power. We have seen that Gallocchio's reputation depended on
the fear which he inspired, and, in a serenade collected in the early nineteenth
century, a young man tries to impress his would-be fiancée with the boast: 'I
want to become a fierce dog / A hundred times more cruel than Galeazzino
[another well-known bandit].' Serafini and Massoni in the mid-nineteenth century and Castelli in the early years of this also fell within this category. All three
broke the conventions that applied to vengeance killings, selecting as victims
relatives, old men, women and those under age. All displayed a sadistic pleasure
in killing (to which we will return), and all committed killings with the deliberate
intention of causing horror.[175] Although bandit violence generally fitted into a
traditional context rather than representing sheer criminality or a 'nihilistic release' as Hobsbawm suggests,[176] a distinction does seem to have been made
between such 'terrorism' and what one might call 'normal' violence, and this may
have been reflected in divergent responses to each.

   Bandits like Massoni, who wished to create terror, were often successful in
doing so, and there is much evidence, as we have seen, that populations were
cowed into protecting those who preyed on them or into maintaining a wall of
silence around their activities. A newspaper reported in 1828 that Francesco-
Giovanni Guidicilli of Serra-di-Fiumorbo had 'escaped arrest for seven years,
thanks to the terror which he inspired in the local people'. The gendarmerie
reported in the same terms about Giacomo Bonelli in 1893, adding 'that no one has
ever dared to resist him in any way or to give the slightest piece of information that
would allow us to take action against him'. The same state of affairs existed more
generally in the Fiumorbo in the mid-1890s and in the Casinca in 1910–11.[177]

   Overt passivity might conceal covert resistance. As we have noted, bandits
did incur local hostility and this was the usual reason for their downfall. 'People
feared him,' Marcaggi wrote of Matteo Poli of Balogna, 'but he had no sincere
support; everyone secretly wanted him to be destroyed.' Here we may refer first
to cases where local people appealed to the authorities for protection against
bandits. The mayor and municipal council of Loreto-di-Tallano wrote to the
prefect in 1882, complaining that 'law, order and tranquillity in the village were
under threat from local bandits' and asking for a detachment of gendarmes to be
posted there. A letter from San-Gavino-di-Fiumorbo in 1895 begged the prefect
not to withdraw the gendarmes, lest the village be attacked by bandits and its

inhabitants either killed or forced to leave. More generally, the public prosecutor reported at the end of 1895 that 'in the face of the unprecedented audacity of the bandits, opinion in all quarters is demanding that exceptional measures be taken. The local press, which usually tends to draw a veil over banditry and its excesses, is now calling on the authorities to intervene.' However, such appeals usually remained private and discreet, and advisedly so. An anonymous letter in 1911 called on the public prosecutor to protect 'the honest and peaceful section' of the population of the Casinca, and especially of Venzolasca, against the threats, intimidation and depredations of local bandits. According to the district prosecutor, this letter in fact came from Mayor Moracchini of Venzolasca, whose life, he said, would be in danger if his anonymity were not protected.[178]

We also have a number of reports of local people welcoming the killing of bandits by the authorities. When the bandit Stefanini, called Torto, was killed by gendarmes in 1816 near Vico, for example, the latter reported: 'Although he was a native of Vico, the death of this individual has caused no trouble in the area; on the contrary, everyone is pleased to be rid of a man who only robbed and threatened them.' We have seen that there was rejoicing in the same region when Teodoro was killed in 1827, and a local newspaper reported that the 'destruction' of Borghello in 1829 'had been greeted with joy in our department, and especially in the cantons of Vico, Salice and Soccia, where the bandit was most troublesome'. According to the lament for Gallocchio, the people of Altiani 'were happy' at the news of his death 'and prepared festivities', and a later press report also refers to more demonstrative jubilation following the killing of Giacomolo Griggi by *voltigeurs* in 1842:

> Such was the horror which this bandit inspired in the whole population that, once the news of his death was broadcast, there were celebrations and public demonstrations of joy in every village where he had made his presence felt; and several municipal councils met to demand a reward for the members of the armed forces who had shown such bravery and tenacity [in tracking him down].

An example from 1844 introduces another expression of hostility against a bandit who was an outsider though from the region. After Giorgi, called Scarlino, from Venzolasca was killed at Biguglia in June 1844, 'the horror which he inspired in the local people meant that he was refused proper burial there. His body was simply placed in a shallow ditch and covered with earth and quickly attracted birds of prey.'[179]

Going a step further, local people also aided the authorities in their campaigns against bandits. This practice was fairly common in the 1770s and Robiquet referred in 1835 to the many occasions on which bandits were captured and convicted with local assistance, despite the terror which they evoked. According to a report filed by the local police in 1825, Teodoro and his associates 'had attracted the hostility of various inhabitants of Orto, Poggiolo, Guagno and Salice as a result of their crimes and vexations, and use may be made of the hatred of these persons in order to effect the arrest of the bandits'. The persons mentioned were those from whom money had been extorted or whose womenfolk had been dishonoured. Among the former, a retired officer 'had specifically offered his services in the fight against the bandit'. Flaubert relates that Borghello was actually killed by a priest from whom he had extorted or tried to extort money.[180]

In some cases it was less a question of local people co-operating with the authorities than of both joining forces to achieve the same objective, and a few cases seem akin to the phenomenon found in Icelandic sagas of action against the *ojafnadarmadr* or the disruptive overbearing personality who may be killed for the sake of the community.[181] Barry wrote in 1893 that 'the usual end' of the mercenary bandit was 'that of being trapped and shot by the inhabitants' – without any reference to the authorities; while Bourde noted that bandits reported to have been killed by the police had often in fact been killed by their enemies. Petro Giovanni, whose exactions in the Sartène region over a period of 15 years had been notorious, was finally killed in 1899 by local people. He was invited to a banquet, held ostensibly in his honour, and given too much to eat and drink. He was then shot and his body was placed in a prominent place in the maquis for the authorities to find. In the inter-war period, Romanetti incurred general dislike within his own 'fief' as a result of his excessive demands and his womanizing, and he was eventually ambushed and killed in 1926, as we have noted, by a man whom he had offended. The activities of Giuseppo Bartoli also stirred up hostility, and Bartoli was killed in 1931 in similar circumstances.[182] Comprehensive information about the place of capture or destruction of bandits is not available, but in a small sample of 18, spanning the period from 1816 to 1899, two-thirds were arrested or killed on their home territory and only one-third away from home. Bandits might tend to head for home when the police were closing in on them, and not all those who met their end on home territory were necessarily the victims of local hostility, but the figures are nevertheless of interest.

Co-operation against bandits between the authorities and local people often involved the exploitation of pre-existing enmities, a point to which we will return. It also involved persuading bandits' associates to betray them. As we have seen, the provision of money for this purpose was an important element in governmental policy through the nineteenth century, and bandits themselves were always afraid of being betrayed. *Lamenti* dwell on the possibility of betrayal, while funeral laments for bandits frequently allege that they had met their end through treachery.[183] Moreover, bandits reacted very strongly against those whom they believed to be traitors. Teodoro killed scouts whom he suspected of disloyalty and cut off the ears of three Italian woodcutters who gave information about him to the authorities. Massoni killed a herdsman in 1849 because he thought that he had done the same.[184] Of course, there was great moral resistance in Corsica to the idea of betraying a bandit, especially for money, and sums that were offered might find no takers.[185] But in many instances, as we have already indicated, such resistance was overcome, and a number of notable bandits, including both Gallocchio and Teodoro, were captured or killed by means of treachery. In 1893, after Giacomo Bonelli had been at large for 40 years, the gendarmerie reported that one of his scouts, 'whose fidelity had been until now unshakeable, has been deeply hurt in his affections by the bandit', and was ready to betray him in return for the 4000 francs offered by the authorities. A later report referred to 'several herdsmen' in this context and added that, in addition to the money, 'they wished to be taken immediately to the Continent or to Algeria in order to escape reprisals from Bellacoscia's relatives'. The following year the bandit was captured.[186]

V

Having discussed different types of bandit, we turn now to the 'political role' of bandits in the broadest sense. Banditry did on occasion and in some areas become a predominant force.[187] According to Marcaggi, Serafino Battini of Ota and his companion Dominiquello Padovani, 'reigned as despots over the gentle and hardworking population of the Balagna' in the years 1850–1.

> [Serafino's] secret power was immense; he put pressure on the public services, intervened in court cases, settled disputes between landowners and peasants. A word from him scrawled on a scrap of paper was enough to break down any resistance, to weaken the toughest resolve. His wishes, his slightest desires, his caprices even, were catered for with servility. At the courts of Calvi and Bastia, he recommended prisoners to the benevolence of the judges, who showed themselves indulgent towards his clients and were afraid to incur his hostility.

Serafino, moreover, was often seen in the cafés of Isola-Rossa, where his mistress kept a grocery shop patronized by officials and notables, all anxious to curry favour with the bandit. In the 1870s, the prefect reported that Fiaschetto and Germani 'ruled' in a similar way over the Castagniccia, while Casanova did so in the Evisa region. In the mid-1890s, bandits were described as the 'masters' of many villages in the Sartène region, while the Fiumorbo and surrounding districts were 'completely at the mercy' of gangs led by Colombani, Achilli and Bartoli. As we have seen, the collection of taxes and other public services were suspended in the Fiumorbo in 1895–6. Again, it was reported from the same district in 1907:

> Never, even at the time when the Colombani and Achilli gangs were at the height of their influence, have bandits exercised such a reign of terror here: requisitions, armed robberies, rapes, are the least of their misdeeds; the security and the life of travellers are seriously at risk; the local police look on, helpless and afraid ... and, in an unbelievable reversal of roles, it is not the police who set out to stop the bandits, but the bandits who harass the police.

The payment of taxes was once more 'almost entirely suspended' both in the Fiumorbo and also in the cantons of Vezzani and Santa-Maria-Sicche.[188] A similar situation existed in some areas in the inter-war period, notably in the Cinarca and the Palneca region, as we have indicated.

Though it sometimes represented a temporary loss of control over bandit clients, such independent 'rule' by bandits was probably more often apparent than real and was rarely achieved if at all without the connivance and encouragement of local notables. Students of banditry elsewhere have remarked that it was frequently sponsored by local élites, and some have argued further that, far from acting as a force of 'popular protest', bandits were 'highly integrated with established power-holders' being used as instruments in their internal power struggles and also serving to defend the collective interests of the élites against movements from below on the part of peasants or against state intervention from outsiders.[189] The Corsican evidence in this area is patchy but seems to point in the same direction.

There is no doubt, first, that bandits very often enjoyed the support of important persons at all levels, despite the existence of official policies designed to extirpate banditry. Some distinction should be drawn here at the governmental level between turning a blind eye or not pursuing local bandits who did no particular harm and might even be useful to the authorities, accepting the temporary and local predominance of bandits *faute de mieux*, and working with bandits in order to maintain the political order. The categories are not in practice always separable and much depended on the attitude of local people towards the bandits in question. There was divergence, too, between the attitude of 'continental' officials like the prefect and the public prosecutor and that of local officials, and policies also changed over time. Faure noted that in the early nineteenth century popular sympathy for bandits was generally complemented by élite and governmental tolerance; whereas the fact that local officials habitually 'tolerated' bandits in their areas was a matter for complaint on the part of the prefect in 1872 and of adverse comment by Bourde again in 1887. In the early nineteenth century, moreover, the authorities were prepared to 'treat' with bandits as they were prepared to sponsor peace settlements between feuding parties. The military, for example, negotiated with Pasquale Gambini and Gallocchio in 1823 and allowed them safe passage out of Corsica on condition that they remained in exile.[190] As we have seen, too, it was common in this period for Corsican bandits to be allowed to take refuge in nearby Sardinia. They even formed a special colony at Longo-Sardo, where they were provided with land. They remained under surveillance but were not subject to extradition. During the Second Empire, this toleration of self-imposed exile in Sardinia ceased.[191] More generally, official toleration later in the century became less formal, less direct, less obvious, taking the form, for example, of tacit agreements whereby bandits gave themselves up in return for lenient sentences. Some examples will illustrate this and other points.

We have already encountered the Bonelli or Bellacoscia brothers of Bocognano, who were probably the best-known bandits in Corsica in the second half of the nineteenth century. Antono Bonelli took to the maquis in 1848 after a quarrel with the mayor of Bocognano, who refused to provide various false certificates and who also demanded payment from the Bonelli for the use of communal lands at Pentica. The mayor was soon afterwards killed by Antono and his brother Martino. In 1849, Antono kidnapped the father of a girl whom he wanted to marry but who refused to agree to the union. When she later married another man, he was killed – by Antono and his brother Giuseppo, who also took to the maquis in 1850. Immediately following their initial crimes, attempts were made to capture the Bonelli, but soon 'a sort of *modus vivendi* was established between the authorities and the wanted men'. Saint-Germain noted in 1869 that they were 'very odd bandits; they cultivate their land quite openly; they sow their crops, pasture their flocks, and even play cards with the gendarmes whose job it is to arrest them'. They travelled about freely, acquired large amounts of land and other assets, and were visited in their fortified headquarters at Pentica by continental celebrities, and even in 1871 by the prefect himself. In a report in 1874 another prefect explained some of the reasons for this official tolerance: 'they work the forest and communal lands, maintain excellent relations with the notables of Ajaccio, are protected by departmental councillors, pay visits to them in town using their carriages for the purpose, and act as excellent electoral agents for them'. This policy lasted until the late 1880s when a special campaign was mounted against the Bellacoscia. Pentica was besieged and, after five or six attempts, captured, and relatives of the bandits were detained. In 1892, Antono gave himself up, was tried and acquitted, while Giuseppo was captured, as we have seen, in 1894.[192]

The toleration of Serafino and the Massoni in the Balagna around 1850 reflected the well-established position of the first in the local power structure and the fact that the terror caused by the latter prevented the authorities from intervening. Both factors seem to have lain behind the passive behaviour of the authorities, at local and island level, vis-à-vis banditry in the 1920s. When Romanetti, for example, invited all the mayors of the canton of Sari-d'Orcino to the wedding of his illegitimate daughter, none of them dared to decline. The local press at this time regularly published bandits' demands and threats. Moreover, the protection rackets run by Romanetti, Spada, Bartoli and others depended on a fair degree of official compliance, notably in the granting of government contracts and concessions.[193]

This brings us back to the links between banditry and local notables. The prefect wrote in 1872 that

> people appreciated the friendship of a bandit; he would be entertained at table, provided with clothing, food and powder in the maquis, for he was a means of exercising influence locally and of obtaining standing. So, he would be helped if he were brought before the courts, and, if he were convicted, a pardon would be solicited for him. All of this indicated that one had powerful connections and 'social credit'.

Earlier in the century, he added, 'bandits had actually been in the pay of influential families, who rewarded them in cash or with open protection'. Fifteen years later, Bourde indicated that this picture did not belong to the past: '"He had a bandit at his service" is a very revealing Corsican expression. Since the law is powerless and justice scorned, the bandit replaces them. You feed and protect a bandit, and the bandit puts his gun at your disposal. It is an exchange of services.' Thus bandits were used by notables to collect debts, to put off creditors, to enforce claims to property or pasture, to keep herdsmen and their flocks off land, and so on. 'The bandit, in a word, is a kind of grand social regulator.' Among others, Bourde related a particular instance from the Sartène region. Some local landowners had rented out land on long leases to a Parisian company to establish large-scale commercial vineyards. This development interfered with traditional grazing rights in the area, and bandits intervened on behalf of the herdsmen affected to place the vineyards under an interdict. The gendarmerie attempted to protect the company and its employees from the effects of this ban, but normal working was not resumed until the company, presumably in collusion with its landlords, itself hired bandits to protect its interests against the herdsmen and their agents. A submission to a local committee of enquiry into banditry in 1896 declared that 'the continued existence of banditry results from the fact that all bandits find the help and protection which they need ... from the village bosses and their masters; the encouragement, aid and protection which they receive put them beyond the reach of the law'.[194]

Banditry, in effect, as a perceptive president of the Assize Court remarked in 1850, was or could be an aspect of patronage, and the banditry of the 1920s in particular has been compared more recently with a 'mafia', leading bandits having 'friends' in all the right places.[195] And many specific examples can be adduced in support of such views. First, there is no doubt that bandits often had influential protectors or patrons. The mayor of Bastelica reported in 1824 that, since moving from his home territory to La Rocca, Natale Gasparini had become the protégé of the Follacci family of Propriano, of ex-Subprefect Bartoli of Sartène and of Captain Casabianca of Arbellara. Marcaggi related that 'the herdsmen and big landowners' of Evisa openly sought the friendship of Massoni in the late 1840s, and that, when the bandit moved to the Niolo, 'the rich landowners of Calacuccia, Albertacce and Lozzi competed for the honour of inviting him to their tables and courted him in order to obtain his friendship'.[196]

It was very common for mayors to protect local bandits, or to be accused of doing so. Mayor Francesco Quilichini of Poggio-di-Tallano was said to be a notorious protector of bandits in the 1840s. The mayors of Casalabriva and of Bilia were arrested in 1896 for harbouring bandits. Despite the evident disruption in the district caused by the Sanguinetti and Paoli bandits, the mayor and other notables of Vescovato made various declarations in 1911 to the effect that they had neither seen nor been bothered by the bandits. There is also some evidence of links between bandits and members of the magistrature. According to a report in 1887, for example, the mistress of Massué, an examining magistrate in Ajaccio, was the daughter-in-law of one of the Bellacoscia. Achilli, deputy justice of the peace of Prunelli-di-Fiumorbo, was a relative of the Colombani bandits, and when he was removed from his post in January 1895, he joined them in the maquis.[197]

Specific examples may also be cited of notables drawing on the services of bandits in return for their protection. First, material interests might be directly defended by bandits, as we have seen in the case of the vineyards of the Sartenais. Some bandit interventions in forests and on behalf of large-scale pastoralists fall into the same category. Secondly, as we saw in Chapter 7, bandits might act as agents in feuds which notables were unable or unwilling to conduct themselves. The public prosecutor commented in 1823 on the news that a number of bandits had gone to the Balagna: 'Everywhere that the slightest hostility exists, it is to be feared that their passage may lead to bloodshed, for unfortunately there is no place in Corsica where the services of a hired killer are not from time to time welcome.' The general protection afforded to the bandits of the Fiumorbo in the 1890s, despite their extortions, was attributed in large part by officials 'to their usefulness to certain inhabitants whose vendettas they abet when they do not actually implement them'.[198] In most cases, we are dealing with bandits acting as hired agents or as clients, but this is not always possible to distinguish absolutely from bandit involvement in feuds through kinship loyalty. As in other contexts, the networks of kinship and clientage overlapped. Bandits were involved on both sides, for example, in the feuding between the Arrighi and the Istria of Urbala-cone. In 1848, Giovan-Battiste Arrighi was killed, it seems by the bandit Maestroni of Pila-Canale, who was acting on behalf of the Istria, to whom he was not related; but in July 1850, Carlo Istria was ambushed and wounded by Santo Quastana, the *doyen* of Corsican bandits, who was a first cousin of Giovan-Battiste Arrighi. In other circumstances, distant kinship ties might 'cover' interventions of a purely or mainly mercenary kind, which we have seen were deprecated. It was reported in the 1840s, for example, that while some members of the Antona family were appalled by the crimes committed by the bandits to whom they were related, others profited from their activities and 'used them as agents in order to carry out their acts of vengeance'.[199]

Thirdly, bandits played a role, and a generally conservative role, in Corsican politics.[200] In his report of 1872, the prefect noted that bandits were protected by 'the leading figures of all the political parties', but especially by the Bonapartists. Bandits intervened in elections at all levels, either on their own account, or more commonly on behalf of these protectors. 'Since universal suffrage now plays so large a part in our political institutions,' in the words of the same report, 'bandits have become electoral agents,'[201] and we have seen that the Bellacoscia were prime examples of this in the early years of the Third Republic. However, this development can be traced further back, at least on the municipal level. Accord-ing to the gendarmerie in the 1840s, Dr Stefanini and his brother-in-law Pado-vani had been elected to the municipal council of Sari-d'Orcino 'solely through the influence of the bandit Stefanini, their relative'. Moreover, when municipal councils were temporarily granted the right to elect mayors in 1848, Stefanini was chosen as a result of pressure placed on the other councillors by the same bandit. Bandit interference in municipal politics remained important later. For example, when Guerrini, leader of a bandit gang, learned that his candidates had been defeated in the municipal elections at Antisanti in 1878, he at once reacted by shooting the president of the polling committee and four other men, includ-ing the secretary to the mayor. According to Bourde, the council of Lozzi was selected by two local bandits over a period of seven years around 1880, and the bandit Manani had his list elected at Bustanico in 1884. Romanetti was involved as a young man in disorders related to the municipal elections at Calcatoggio in 1906, and in 1920 his influence was said to have been decisive in the elections in four or five villages in the Cinarca. We have seen that the Bartoli controlled the municipality of Palneca in the first two decades of the Third Republic, and Giuseppo Bartoli resumed this control in the 1920s.[202]

Many examples may be cited of bandit intervention in departmental and general elections in this later period. Bandit Benedetti intervened in the senatorial elections of 1885, making it known to the municipal council of Lugo-di-Nazza that he favoured a particular delegate to the electoral college. The departmental elections of 1895 were contested in the canton of Vezzani by Dr Carlotti from

Bastia, who owned some property there, and by Senator Fazinola. It appears that both candidates had bandits working for them, since it was reported that Dr Carlotti had been warned by bandits via his sister not to meddle in the affairs of Vezzani, while the senator was robbed and held to ransom by another group of bandits shortly afterwards. Many of the leading bandits of the inter-war years were similarly involved. The perfumer François Coty, a candidate in the 1923 senatorial elections, had a meeting in the maquis with Romanetti, at which he allegedly paid for the bandit's neutrality if not his support. Candidates in the 1924 legislative elections also bought Romanetti's support. Bartoli is reported to have received 100,000 francs from the millionaire Paul Lederlin, who was a candidate in the senatorial elections of 1930, and in return to have 'delivered' the votes of the five delegates to the electoral college from his 'fief'. Again, Spada is said to have aided the election of Jules Leca to the Senate in 1931.[203]

We have seen that some bandits became mayors and municipal councillors, and that bandits were the virtual rulers of some areas of the island on an unofficial basis for quite long periods of time. But on the whole they acted as auxiliaries to local power groups, and independent political activity on the part of bandits was rare and not something which the notables encouraged. Francesco-Maria Castelli exercised what Marcaggi called 'a real dictatorship over the entire Orezza region' between 1911 and the mid-1920s and 'politicians solicited his intervention in municipal and cantonal elections there', but when he put himself forward as a candidate in the 1924 general elections and obtained a respectable number of votes, a careful operation was mounted to get rid of him.[204]

VI

We earlier emphasized the links between banditry and feuding in Corsica, and we have referred to the role played by bandits as agents in the feuds of others. In concluding this chapter, we must examine this aspect of banditry in more detail.[205]

According to Faure, the bandit was primarily 'a man who, having avenged his family's honour with blood, took to the wandering life of the maquis and defended himself against his enemies'; while Marcaggi declared that 'the vendetta engenders the bandit', who took to the maquis not only in order to escape reprisals, but also to defend his own kin. This view was endorsed by many other observers, and it can be very fully substantiated with specific examples, as our discussion of bandits of honour has already indicated.[206]

First, many bandits, including the most notorious, became so following actions in defence of family honour or interest. As we have seen, Gallocchio became involved, it seems reluctantly, in a feud with the Rosola and the Negroni families after the former broke off his engagement to their daughter in favour of a member of the latter. He killed the girl's father and then the rival suitor, and embarked on the bandit career. Gallocchio's sometime companion Sarocchi became a bandit following a quarrel with his father-in-law, Frederici, over the pasturing of some oxen in an enclosure. Sarocchi fired shots at Frederici and killed his sister-in-law. After he joined a gang of bandits, Sarocchi continued his feud, for Robiquet reports that he and other bandits pillaged Frederici's house in the summer of 1822 and then commandeered his grain harvest. Men might also become bandits specifically to enable them to carry out vengeance killings. Santo Romanetti of Calcatoggio, for example, took to the maquis in 1846 following the killing of his brother, and he was able to take his revenge on those responsible a few years later. In a similar case, a man from a wealthy and educated family in the Santa-Maria-Sicche district became a bandit in the 1890s in order to avenge the death of his father, which he managed to do after ten years in the maquis.[207]

As some of these examples show and as we have seen at greater length in Chapter 2, feuds were frequently conducted by bandits and banditry was a consequence and an exacerbating feature of many important feuds. This salient point deserves further illustration. Bandits were involved on both sides in the feuding at Bastelica in the 1820s and 1830s. Natale Gasparini became a bandit in 1820 after he was accused of killing Judge Colonna, and he was joined in the maquis by his brother Pasquale after another killing. On the other side, Giovan-Battiste Scapola became a bandit in 1830 and remained at large until 1846. In the same period, the Ribetti bandits of Casevecchie were involved in an all-out feud with the Nicoloni. The bandit Don Luigi Ricciardi of Pero-Casevecchie, said to be 'the most formidable bandit' in Corsica when he was killed in 1832, was similarly engaged in a feud with the Taddei and most of his crimes were directed against them.[208] Francesco Bastianesi of Ucciani became involved in a bitter feud with the Calzaroni in the early 1840s, and most of the crimes of which he was convicted in 1849 were committed in pursuance of it.[209] The strict connection between feuding and banditry is also found later. Bandits had been prominent in the feuding at Venzolasca in the middle of the century and they were to be so again in that which so seriously upset the whole Casinca in 1910–12. Again, Francesco-Maria Castelli of Carcheto became a bandit for the first time in 1906 after killing a cousin. He gave himself up and received a short prison sentence, after which he returned to Corsica in 1911, determined to take revenge on all those who had testified against him at his trial and also to take reprisals for an alleged slight against his father 20 years earlier.[210]

In some cases feuds conducted via bandits became petty wars between rival bandits. When Gallocchio's young brother was killed by the Negroni in 1833, he returned to Corsica from exile and killed one of the Negroni in return. Giulio Negroni, called Peverone, then became a bandit too, and he and Gallocchio engaged in what was called a 'war' lasting several years. After Gallocchio had been killed by the police, Peverone ceased his hostilities and gave himself up. Tambino Bonacorsi and Michele Sampiero were fighting each other in a similar fashion in the Palneca region in the late 1820s. One of Tambino's victims had been a member of the Poli family of Olmeto, and in 1838, Francesco Poli called Fiadone killed Tambino's son, Giovan-Battiste, in revenge, and then remained at large as a bandit until 1845. The bandits Achilli and Colombani had co-operated for a while in the Fiumorbo in the 1890s, as we have seen. Then each formed his own separate gang and they became rivals. Seven or eight men were killed in a shoot-out between them at Pietrapola in May 1895.[211]

Such rivalries between bandits sometimes reflected a difference in style, the old distinction between bandits of honour and bandits of prey. It was reported, for example, in 1842 that the bandit Stefanini had returned to Corsica from Sardinia with Santo Quastana. Unknown to Quastana, Stefanini forced the mayor of Sari to pay a ransom of 4000 francs, as we have seen. When he learned of this 'unworthy' conduct on the part of his associate, Quastana left Stefanini, aided the armed forces in their hunt for him, and ensured that the money was repaid. But rivalry between bandits could be simply a rivalry of interest. We have seen that Serafino was already established in the Balagna when Massoni descended on the region with his gang in 1850–1, and Serafino resented this intrusion, since Massoni's influence inevitably reduced his own. 'The rich landowners who were paying him protection money, whom he kept under his thumb, began to lift their heads again, now that they had the option of protection from Massoni. Even Serafino's influence over local officials began to escape him. Massoni became the only man to worry about, the only man to fear. He was getting the courts to take account of what he wanted; he was getting his nominees appointed' to all kinds of positions in the local administration. In these circumstances, Serafino began to co-operate with the authorities to destroy his rival. He kept a close watch on Massoni and his gang, through his scouts, and passed on information about their whereabouts to the gendarmerie. After the killing of Fra Jura, which was generally disapproved of, he redoubled his efforts. Two ambushes of Massoni were planned in collaboration with the authorities and via the agency of Serafino's brother who was a gendarme. At the same time, Serafino acted against his rival on his own account and in collaboration with Massoni's other enemies. He tried on one occasion to get some herdsmen to poison him, and in 1851 he joined forces with the two Durilli bandits from Marignana who were still pursuing their feud with Massoni.[212] Rivalry between bandits in the inter-war period often stemmed from the same competition for control over the resources of 'fiefs'.

Not surprisingly in all these circumstances, bandits often met their end at the hands of their enemies, that is, those in a state of formal enmity from them. The bandit Giovanni Cristinacce of Sant'Andrea-d'Orcino, for example, was shot and killed in 1822 by Angelo Vincenti. Their families 'had become enemies' after a goat belonging to one had strayed on to land belonging to the other. Domenico Mozziconacci of Loreto-di-Tallano threatened to kill two of his cousins, we have seen, when they refused his demand for 500 francs as his share in an inheritance, and he made similar threats against three herdsmen when they claimed back a cave or cabin that the bandit was using. These five men eventually joined together to kill Mozziconacci in 1850. Where bandits could not themselves be reached, enemies might strike at their auxiliaries. In a case in 1836, Paolo-Girolamo Balisoni of Olmeto was convicted of killing a scout of the bandit Sorba. Sorba had killed Balisoni's cousin, and Balisoni had sworn revenge but had been unable to achieve it directly.[213]

As the Serafino example reminds us, the authorities were frequently able to make use of a bandit's enemies in order to capture or to kill him. The exploitation of revenge was one of the main causes of the extinction of banditry, according to Malaspina in 1876, and he noted that the success of the *voltigeurs* derived from the fact that 'each one of them had reasons to pursue revenge against some bandit or other'. Bartolo Martinetti of Olmeto was 'the enemy of the bandits Francesco

Gabrielli and Petro Poli [of Ciamannacce] and sought to have them arrested and brought to justice'. He gave information about them to the gendarmerie and was killed in 1830 by the bandits as he was guiding gendarmes to their hide-out. Giacomo Ottavi of Casevecchie helped the gendarmerie in their attempts to capture Natale Ferloni of Bastelica, a bandit who had abducted his daughter, threatened him with death, and placed an interdict on his land. Again, both Antono Fieschi of Pila-Canale and Giovan-Andrea Giansili of Lozzi were captured and brought to trial in 1850 thanks to the assistance given to the gendarmerie by their enemies. Where such local co-operation was lacking, as in the Fiumorbo in the mid-1890s, attempts to capture or to kill bandits were likely to fail. There, the enemies of the bandits were so afraid of them that they maintained the same wall of silence as their friends, and those few who did contact the authorities did not know where the hide-outs of the bandits were.[214]

It can also be confirmed that enemies of bandits did join the local police in order to oppose them. When the Nicolai brothers of Campi became bandits in the late 1820s, their enemies, the Morelli and the Antonmarchi of Tox, 'enrolled deliberately in the *voltigeurs* in order to be better able to track them down', and when they were disappointed in this aim, they left the force. Of course, some officials were wary of the policy of using revenge to destroy bandits, since it very often created new enmities and exacerbated the situation. But we have seen that it continued to be used off and on throughout the nineteenth century.[215]

Though the odd contrary example may perhaps be found,[216] there is little doubt, finally, that Corsican bandits were involved with blood vengeance in one way or another, and that their behaviour and their very existence are inexplicable unless they are seen in this context. Men nearly always became bandits as a result of some dispute or action involving honour. Once they were in the maquis, they were available to pursue revenge or might have to do so in self-defence. Any wider social roles which they may have performed derived from this basis.

The close connection between banditry and blood vengeance is reflected in two other ways. First, there was a parallel decline in both as alternative ways of settling disputes and punishing offenders were provided or imposed. Secondly, there is a fair correlation between the geographical incidence of feuding and of banditry. Maps B and C provide a picture of the incidence of banditry by canton for the two periods 1815–1850 and 1870–1931, based on a variety of sources. As the prefect commented in 1880, bandits could be found 'scattered about almost everywhere in the island',[217] and the maps refer only to banditry as a more important and persistent phenomenon. In addition, more detailed information is available from the 1820s, and we will begin with an analysis of this.

It will be seen from Table 7 that the largest number of fugitives was in the *arrondissement* of Corte, which was followed by that of Ajaccio, but, if account is taken of the relative population density of the different *arrondissements*, then the highest incidence of fugitives is found in that of Sartène, followed by that of Corte. Similar figures on 342 fugitives at large in 1825 provide much the same pattern,[218] which conforms with what we know about the incidence of feuding in this period. There was of course uneven incidence within *arrondissements*, according to the 1822–3 list, but this too fits in with our picture of feuding. In the *arrondissement* of Corte, for example, about one-third of fugitives came from the

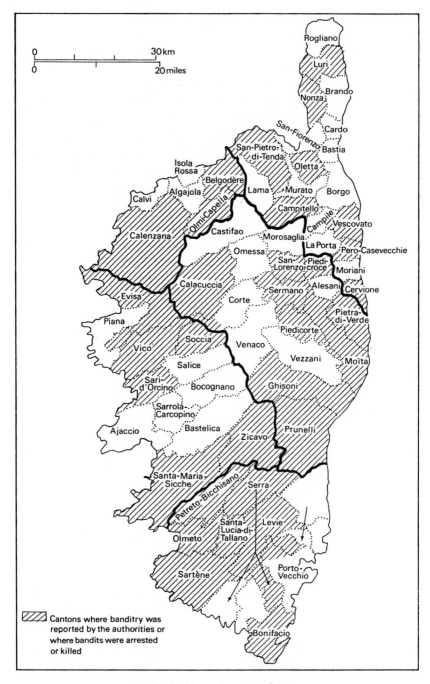

Map B Banditry 1815–1850, by canton

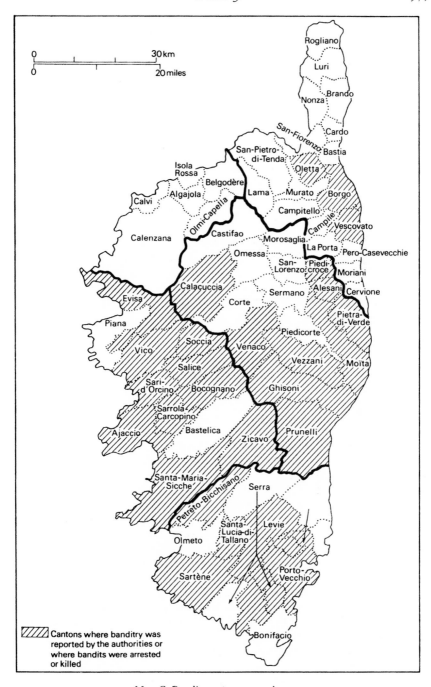

Map C Banditry 1870–1931, by canton

Table 7. *Sentenced fugitives by arrondissement, 1822–3* [219]

Arrondissement	Number of fugitives	Percentage of total	Incidence in proportion to population of arrondissement
Ajaccio	74	21	1:561
Bastia	67	19	1:826
Calvi	23	7	1:879
Corte	115	33	1:370
Sartène	67	19	1:320

Castagniccia. In that of Bastia, over one-third came from the Casinca, while less than one-fifth came from the Capo Corso. Moreover, 36 villages provided more than one fugitive in the 1822–3 list. These included nine of the feuding villages identified in Chapter 2, and four of these provided seven or more fugitives: Levie (7), Serra (9), Olmeto (13) and Santa-Maria-Sicche (13).[220]

The same correlation is found if the maps of the incidence of banditry by canton are considered, though there are also some differences in the patterns. Some areas remained important centres of banditry through the nineteenth century and into the inter-war period, for example the Fiumorbo, the upper Taravo valley (Zicavo, Palneca, Guitera), the Evisa and Vico regions, the Casinca, the Sartenais generally. These were mainly isolated areas, with difficult terrain and poor communications where the penetration of state authority was slow, factors which also explain the survival of feuding in these and similar places. The Niolo and the Asco valley are also mentioned as bandit areas through the nineteenth century,[221] though Blanchard argues that areas such as the Sartenais and the Castagniccia were always more important than the high mountains where the climate inhibited the outdoor life.[222] Some bandits, however, probably moved from the mountain to the plain and back with the seasons like or with herdsmen. But there were also changes in the geography of banditry in Corsica during the nineteenth century.[223] Most obviously, the *arrondissements* of Calvi (the Balagna) and of Bastia (including the Capo Corso), already the least affected by banditry in the 1820s, became areas where bandits virtually disappeared. The subprefects explained this change in 1896 in terms of the factors previously mentioned (easier terrain, better roads) but referred also to the development of agriculture and of education, all of which, of course, contributed, too, to the disappearance of feuding.[224] However, the progress of 'civilization' was not always inimical to either, at least in the shorter term. As we have seen that feuding was exacerbated during the earlier stages of state penetration, so the important bandits of the inter-war period thrived on the diversion of resources created directly or indirectly by the French government, and a number of them operated in an urbanized environment, particularly in and around Ajaccio itself.[225]

] 13 [

Death and the dead

No discussion of conflict in Corsica and of the operation of the system of blood vengeance there would be complete without a consideration of the wider notions about death and the dead, which formed the context for homicide. How was death by violence accommodated in funeral ritual and burial practice, and how did it relate to beliefs about the ultimate cause of death and about links with the ancestors? Our data here is often sparse and difficult to interpret, though there is no doubt that death was of central importance and 'one of the axes of Corsican religious culture'.[1]

I

We may begin on relatively firm ground with a description of funeral ritual, based on the many accounts which exist from the nineteenth and twentieth centuries,[2] and dealing in the first instance with the ritual followed where deaths were not caused by violence.

When a person was dying, relatives, friends and neighbours were in attendance, and the last rites were administered by a priest. In most parishes there was a priest 'whose special function was to administer such aid to the moribund',[3] and much importance was attached to this service. In many villages, when the priest set out with the last sacraments, a bell was rung, 'and everyone, men and women, accompanied him to the house of the dying person'.[4] News of the death itself was similarly quickly broadcast, by word of mouth, by tolling bells or by blowing horns. Those not already at the house then hastened towards it, either singly or in groups. While the bell tolled, Vuillier wrote of a death in Zicavo around 1890, 'a procession of women clad in black ... moved silently towards the house of mourning'.[5] Ortoli says that widows, in particular, were obliged to attend in their own and neighbouring villages, going to the latter as a group. Female prominence at this stage (as later) is generally reported, as is the attendance of men and women from villages roundabout.[6] Women traditionally wore the *faldetta* on such occasions, a long skirt in black or dark blue wool or cotton, the tail of which could be pulled over the head like a nun's veil, and which was the usual dress of widows.[7]

Meanwhile, as soon as the person had died, a relative or friend lit a candle and placed it successively in each hand of the deceased and then snuffed it out. The hearth fire in the house was also extinguished and was not rekindled for three or more days.[8] Mirrors were covered; and doors and sometimes windows were opened, in order, it was said, to enable the soul or spirit of the deceased to get away easily. But the blinds were drawn and the house darkened, lit only by torches and an uneven number of oil-lamps or candles around the corpse.[9] This was washed and laid out on a couch, a table or a special trestle called a *tola*[10] in the main or public room of the house, known sometimes as 'the room of strangers'.[11] In summer or where the house was small, the corpse might be laid out on the 'square' in front of the house, being brought inside at nightfall. Some sources refer to priests being laid out on stone slabs, probably in churchyards. For the laying out, the eyes of the corpse would be closed, its jaw tied with a handkerchief or ribbon, a rosary and/or a special herb[12] placed in its hands and sometimes a crucifix on its breast, and it was sprinkled with holy water. There are early reports of the corpse being dressed in a white shift, but from later in the nineteenth century confraternity robes or a person's best clothes were the rule. 'We have put on your shoes / And your finest dress, / Your hat and your good gloves, / The embroidered ones,' a woman was told in a lament collected at Zonza in 1926.[13] Young women and girls wore their wedding dresses, and the corpses of unmarried girls were covered with flowers, ribbons and garlands. Priests were laid out in sacerdotal dress, with a chalice in their hands.

Those women present at the moment of death and other female mourners on first hearing the news performed gestures of extreme grief, which were repeated at other stages of the funeral rites. These were loosening and/or tearing the hair, lacerating the cheeks until the blood ran, and uttering loud shrieks and strident guttural cries. On arriving at the house of the deceased, the female mourners repeated these gestures. Inside the house, men and women were segregated, with women on one side and men on the other side of the room, or men sometimes stayed outside the house altogether or remained by the door, leaving women to take the central role in the proceedings. On arriving at the wake, each mourner would go to greet the corpse, men shaking it by the hand, women hugging and kissing it, all saying a few words of greeting, farewell or reproach for dying. In some cantons, gifts of wine, chestnuts or tobacco were offered to the deceased to underline this point: 'Did you go short of wine, bread, etc.? I have brought you some.'[14] Next, the rosary would be said, and the priest would arrive to say further prayers. By this time, large numbers of people would be present. Two cases are reported in 1841 and 1842 at Cozzano and Ciamannacce respectively of the floors of houses collapsing during wakes under the weight of 'over two hundred people'.[15]

The women would now be grouped around the corpse in a circle, and one of them would then break away and approach it. She held a handkerchief or apron in her hands and her face was initially obscured by her *faldetta* or her veil, though it became uncovered very soon. She cried and bent over the body, and then began to sing a lament or dirge, known variously as a *vocero, buceru, buceratu* or *ballata*. The *vocero* usually comprised strophes of six octosyllabic lines, though these were sometimes interspersed with quatrains and eight-line verses, and it was chanted to a simple melody in a uniform, impersonal, vibrating voice that some observers have compared with that of a medium.[16] At Altiani, *voceri* were sung by pairs of women, but elsewhere they sang alone and successively, each woman signalling to another to continue when she was exhausted. Some reports refer to singers going into trances or falling unconscious. The singing went on for hours, and the rest of the women provided a chorus, interjecting cries and phrases. Vuillier notes that at Zicavo the women also 'put their mouths to the ear of the deceased', while the *voceri* were being sung, 'and talked to it in low voices'. More generally, the women swayed rhythmically to the chanting, and in some places performed a dance around the corpse, known as the *caracolu*.[17] The term *ballata* or *baddata* used generally in the south and sporadically elsewhere instead of *vocero* means both 'funeral dirge' and 'dance', and this usage suggests that assimilation of the two was once more widespread.[18] When a person died away from home and it was not possible to return the corpse, a wake might be held nevertheless, at which *voceri* were 'addressed either to an empty bed or to a picture [or effigy] of the deceased'.[19]

The singers of dirges or *voceratrici* were usually close relatives: sisters, mothers, wives, female cousins; or neighbours; but specialists also performed, and some women, like Mérimée's Colomba, achieved a reputation over whole districts for their improvisatory talent. However, such specialists would nearly always know the deceased, and there was no positive value attached to having a stranger among the lamenting women, such as one finds in Greece.[20] There is some evidence of a greater reliance on specialists from the later nineteenth century, at least among notable families, whose women were losing the capacity to sing themselves. Traditionally, all women learned a repertoire of dirges from an early age, adapting them to particular circumstances. Southwell Colucci provides an example of a *vocero*, collected in 1923, in which a 17-year-old girl mentions the fact that she is improvising a real lament for the first time. A large number of *voceri* were collected and published from the 1840s onwards.[21]

At a certain stage of the wake, sometimes after the priest had said further prayers over the corpse, the bulk of the company would depart, leaving only close relatives and friends to watch over the body through the night. Elsewhere, people would come and go, or all but those closest to the deceased would leave when the Angelus rang. Refreshments were served to those keeping vigil at or around midnight. These were brought in from the houses of relatives and neighbours and consisted of bread or pancakes, vegetable pasties (*bastelli*), soup, cheese or ham. Some drinking of wine or spirits occurred, but most observers stress the sobriety of the proceedings and there are no hints of the burlesque diversions associated with Irish, Scottish, Rumanian and other wakes.[22]

In the morning, the bells tolled again at first light, and the corpse was taken up by men and placed on a bier or in an open coffin. Though they are occasionally referred to in the eighteenth century, coffins only came into general use in the second half of the nineteenth century and were not used in some villages for children and young people as late as the mid-1920s.[23] The bier or coffin was then carried to the church, usually by members of a confraternity dressed in their robes. At the taking up of the body and as it left the house, the women renewed their cries and extreme gestures of grief, 'raising an immense clamour'.[24] It is also reported that they scratched or knocked on the coffin as if to try to reawaken the corpse. The body was usually carried to the church in a formal procession, and the composition of and route taken by this procession were of great significance. Relatives and friends would take it in turn to bear the coffin, and men and women were again segregated, the men preceding and the women following the corpse. In some cases, women did not participate at all in the funeral procession or the church service.

This service was attended by representatives of every family in the community and sometimes by nearly the whole population, though some people did not stay for all of it. It was very long, lasting for up to five hours. All the priests in the parish said low mass together or successively; the office for the dead was then sung; and high mass was performed. During the service, the closest relatives remained standing at the head of the coffin, and female relatives and others frequently repeated their lamentations. Large numbers of candles were burned.

Next, the body was taken from the church, and the coffin lid was finally nailed down. This again provoked cries and extreme gestures of grief from the women. Sometimes, Vuillier reports, they 'threw themselves on the body, which they covered with kisses and vehemently embraced', and they had to be forcibly removed before the coffin could be closed. The procession to the place of burial was again formal with the men following the coffin first and then the women. The clergy did not in more recent times usually accompany the body on this final stage. Burial might take place in a church, a churchyard, a communal grave, a common cemetery or on family land, and we will return to these various options. Save in exceptional circumstances, burial took place within 24 hours of death.

After the burial, the mourners returned to the house of the deceased for the funeral feast, called the *conforto* or *magnaria*, though occasionally this might be postponed if the date were inconvenient. In addition, special cakes or pasties called *coccioli* or *bastelli* were made and distributed on the day of burial to the whole village and beyond. We have seen that they were also eaten at the wake. In some places, small quantities of food were left on the grave on the evening of burial, which were in practice consumed by the grave-diggers. The funeral feast was an elaborate affair, attended by large numbers of people from the village and outside. Lamotte has noted the special importance attached to the presence of the clergy, who in the past received the skin and a specific proportion of the animals killed for it.[25] The scale of the feast reflected the standing of the family and the honour being paid to the deceased. According to Versini, it was sometimes called 'the share of the dead'; while Bartoli wrote that 'the main aim of these feasts is to expiate the sins of the deceased; they are a kind of sacrifice, a religious act'.[26] Tommaseo relates that one man had two oxen killed and over 100 loaves baked for a funeral feast, and other observers noted that a succession of such feasts could ruin a family. The food served at the *conforto* was fixed by tradition: meat broth with noodles, one or two meat stews with olives and carrots or with haricot beans, cheese, coffee and brandy. No roast meat and no fruit were served. At the end of the meal, a priest said the *De profundis*, thus expressing thanks to the deceased for being invited. Guests from outside the village sometimes stayed on for several days after the feast.

Further ritual marked specific intervals after a death, the seventh day, the thirtieth day, and, more commonly, the anniversary. Luca-Antono Viterbi asked in his testament that his relatives should 'celebrate the anniversary of my death every year, gathering together with all the children in the paternal house and going from there together to the cemetery'. 'In some villages', according to Father Casanova, 'bread, cheese, water and a coin are placed on the tomb a year after the death.'[27] Sometimes such ritual offerings were made to the community, bread, wine and meat being given to all the families in the village in a kind of repetition of the funeral feast. Religious services, usually masses for the souls of the deceased, were also held at anniversaries and other intervals. At Bastelica, an elaborate simulacrum of the funeral service was held one year after a death. Everywhere, as we shall see in a later section, all the dead were commemorated annually on All Souls' Day.

Where a death had occurred by violence, the funeral ritual inevitably differed in some important respects. First, there was no death-bed scene, and a clear distinction was drawn in Corsica between the 'good death' experienced in the midst of one's kin and the 'bad death' or *mala morte* suffered away from home. If a person were killed, moreover, he or she might not receive the last rites. The announcement of the death came as more of a shock, and the reactions to it were more extreme. Some reporters suggest that the more exaggerated gestures, such as tearing the hair and lacerating the face, were reserved for cases of homicide, at least in the modern period. Different terms were used for the lamentations, *scirrata* referring to lamenting for those who had died naturally and *gridata* to lamenting for the victims of violence.[28] In the case of the latter, too, the corpse was not washed or dressed for the wake. A man 'is left in his bloody and dirty clothes ... His hair and his beard are not arranged, nor his face composed.'[29] During the wake also the women soaked handkerchiefs in the blood of the victim, and their dirges became specific incitements to vengeance. The men involved themselves by drumming their rifle butts on the floor during the singing of the *voceri*. Reports also refer to men trembling, 'tearing their beards, scratching their faces and uttering cries of grief',[30] all of which contrasts strongly with their behaviour at ordinary wakes. Vuillier noted, too, that the *caracolu* was only performed at Zicavo when the deceased had been killed. Those responsible for the killing and their relatives did not, of course, attend the wake or any other part of the funeral ritual, which again contrasts with the normal stress on community in the rites.

The body of a person who had met a violent death was buried without much ceremony. In the early nineteenth century there was no public funeral service, and Ortoli wrote in 1887 that 'a man who has been killed is assumed to have died in a state of mortal sin and cannot be buried with the usual rites. The bell is not tolled, and the priest does not say prayers over the corpse.'[31] Orthodox clerical concerns appear to have coincided here with a popular belief that the victim was or could not be properly consigned to the other world until after vengence had been accomplished.

Corsican funeral ritual, with its extreme gestures of grief, its dirges, its wake, belongs to a pattern of behaviour, found much more widely in the Mediterranean world,[32] in other parts of Europe[33] and beyond.[34] As Lawson and De Martino have stressed, the ritual was very ancient in the Mediterranean world.[35] Both world religions which became established in the region expressed opposition to the ancient practices, but neither was able to extirpate them. Our description shows that some kind of accommodation had been arrived at in modern Corsica between the old ritual and that of Christianity. From the sixteenth century onwards, however, the ecclesiastical authorities had issued severe and repeated condemnations of the extreme gestures of grief and of the singing of *voceri*; they also banned funeral feasts and the distribution of food and drink at intervals after a death, all of which were seen as 'pagan'.[36] But this repeated censure was largely ineffective, save in one important respect: the traditional rituals were generally excluded from churches and restricted to private houses.[37] There are indications that this process had not yet been completed by the start of the nineteenth century. A pedlar testified, for example, in 1801 that, on hearing the news of the killing of a man at Zicavo, he 'turned back to the village, went to the place where the dead man was, and accompanied the corpse to the church as was customary'.[38] In general, however, corpses were only laid out in churches in the modern period in exceptional circumstances, often when a person had died away from home or there was some other reason for delaying the funeral.[39]

We have seen that members of the clergy attended the death-bed and part of the wake and that their attendance at the *conforto* was regarded as crucial. Lamotte suggests that the previously condemned funeral feast had been Christianized by this stress on clerical participation and by the practice of giving food on this occasion to the clergy instead of to the dead. Like the last rites, the funeral service in church was an important part of the whole ritual of death. *Voceri* for members of the clergy, moreover, were not uncommon, and deaths were popularly and obliquely referred to in terms of clerical participation in funerals via such phrases as 'the priest will be singing'.[40] However, the clergy also maintained their distance from the traditional ritual. They did not accompany the corpse to its place of burial, which was often in unconsecrated ground. Lamentations in church during the funeral service were reproved. And, in general, a fairly clear division may be seen between the traditional, 'secular' aspects of the funeral and those involved with formal Christianity.

Here we may see two factors at work. First is a syncretism that was characteristic of popular religion in the island generally. Like most peoples of Catholic Europe, Corsicans were attached to the cult of saints often associated with wayside shrines and chapels,[41] to village festivals,[42] to pilgrimages[43] and to confraternities.[44] Underlying many of these cults and practices was a concern to procure and preserve the well-being and fertility of the community and its inhabitants, and, to this end, the religious power of the Church or the clergy was inserted into a framework that was pre- or non-Christian. F.O. Renucci, for example, relates that the confraternities from the villages of Tavagna used to go annually to the cross above the convent of San Francesco in order

> to call down the blessings of heaven on the productions of the soil ... The priest blesses a quantity of small metallic stones, which are found all over the mountain, and the pilgrims carefully gather them up in order to take them back with them to their houses or to distribute in their fields, believing them to possess a miraculous power.[45]

Death customs, as we shall see, were to some extent the converse of this kind of ritual, seeking to propitiate or to ward off the potentially harmful influence of the spirits of the departed.

Secondly, a divergence remained between clerical and popular attitudes, which is especially conspicuous where vengeance is concerned. The clash between the demands of honour which require revenge and the religious ideal of forgiving one's enemies is inevitable in feuding societies that have formally adopted Christianity,[46] and was frequently pointed to in connection with modern Corsica. 'Corsicans are religious,' Robiquet noted, 'yet they remain attached to a custom which is diametrically opposed to Christian morality.' 'I don't believe that it is a sin / To wipe out ... / Those who have deprived me / Of my treasure,' a widow declared in a *vocero* for her murdered husband.[47]

We have noted the role of the clergy as peacemakers, and the Church consistently opposed the vendetta and its ideology. In Arrighi's novel *La Veuve d'Arbellara* (1856), for example, the parish priest asks the widow of a murdered man to forgive the killer, while she insists on vengeance. Malaspina describes a wake after a *mala morte*, where the laments drowned the priest's attempts to utter words of reconciliation as the body was lifted.[48] More significantly, the message of Christian forgiveness sometimes entered the universe of the *vocero* itself. In the well-known lament for Dr Matteo, one singer calls for vengeance in the usual way, but she is countered by another, an old woman, who says 'O my sisters, calm yourselves, / And stop all this noise. / Matteo does not wish to be avenged, / For he is in heaven with the Lord. / Look well at this coffin, / Look, dear sisters. / Jesus Christ is above it, / He who teaches forgiveness. / Do not excite your menfolk, / The sea is agitated enough.'[49]

However, Christian influence in this context more commonly took the form not of preaching forgiveness but of trusting in divine or saintly vengeance. In the *vocero* already cited, the widow who calls for human revenge is told by another woman: 'Calm your grief, / Don't make your troubles worse. / Let the Lord act / To avenge your wrongs ... / The vengeance of the Lord / Will be sure and prompt.' A later lament included the lines: 'I hope that the Madonna / Will take care of my revenge.'[50]

More often still, Christian values were amalgamated in *voceri* with those of blood vengeance.[51] *Voceri* sung for members of the clergy called for vengeance on their behalf.[52] *Voceri* inciting secular vengeance also referred to the saints, the Virgin Mary, Jesus and God.[53] A literary *vocero* of this type, very popular all over Corsica according to Viale, opens with the words: 'Jesus, Joseph, Mary, / Most Holy Sacrament,' and was said to have been composed by a monk. Another from the Rostino district in the 1920s promises: 'We swear, my treasure / That you will be avenged. / The killer will be plagued / Always by bad luck, / And will be rejected and abandoned / By the Virgin Mary.' In the same vein, Mérimée cites the *vocero* sung by Beatrice of Piedicroce for Justice of the peace Piazzole of Orezza in 1813: 'Who killed him? Was it a Turk, or a Lutheran?', as though an 'enemy' must also be an infidel or a heretic and beyond the religious pale.[54] More extreme but quite numerous are *voceri* in which God or the saints are invoked in order to aid in the pursuit of human vengeance. A sister sang for a murdered brother, for example: 'I am going to pray to the Lord / And I am going to pray to all the saints / For the Ricci to be exterminated.' 'O holy Virgin, grant me this favour,' declared another sister, 'That I may rip out the guts [of my brother's killer].'[55] *Voceri* also challenged or threatened God: 'If I am not going to see vengeance, / I will no longer believe in God'; or 'If I do not see him avenged, / I wish to undo my baptism.'[56] This is similar to a mechanism noted by Pareto in Sardinia, whereby the cursing of an enemy by a woman acted to incite her brother to commit a vengeance killing.[57] In the realm of action, Malaspina noted that Corsicans carrying out acts of vengeance often made the sign of the cross as they aimed their weapons at their enemies, in order to make sure that they hit them.[58] More generally, though references to the dead being 'in Paradise' are fairly common in *voceri*, such references nearly always apply to those who had died non-violently, and reference is also made, sometimes in the same *voceri*, to an after-life status of a less orthodox and comfortable kind. For example, after making the conventional reference, the mother of Chilina of Carcheto declared that 'there where she must go / Is a sad place. / The sun never appears there / And no fire is lit.'[59] This Homeric note seems to reflect a profound uncertainty about the fate of the dead at the heart of popular Catholicism, and we shall return to some of its implications in discussing relations between the living and the dead in a later section.

Our description of funeral ritual, secular and religious, indicates its import-ance as an expression of community. News of the individual's death was of general interest, spreading quickly and bringing people from the village and beyond to the house of mourning, and at every subsequent stage members of the community were involved. We have earlier noted the importance of the confra-ternity as an expression of community, and its role in funeral ritual underlines this point. Most villages still had confraternities in the 1930s if not later, and their most important role was to officiate at funerals.[60] This is frequently referred to in *voceri*, and it is significant that the dead themselves were believed to congregate in confraternities.[61] Community was also very directly expressed in the commensal-ity of the funeral feast. At the time of the loss of one of its members, as Jean Guiart has written more generally, 'the collectivity reaffirms its permanence'.[62]

Here it is significant that funerals could become 'a time for reconciliation' between those in a state of hostility, and that 'enemies' participated together in the public and the private parts of the funeral ritual where death was from natural causes. Ettori has argued further that *voceri* could express tensions within families and communities in a cathartic way that tended to dissipate them and to obviate real conflict.[63]

In this context, failure to attend a funeral or to invite someone who ought to have been invited was a serious insult. Moreover, those in a state of active enmity, and, most obviously, as we have seen, those guilty or believed to be guilty of killing a person would not participate in his or her funeral. After the killing of a certain Bernamonti of Matra in 1832, his brother-in-law 'did not attend the funeral ... which is regarded in Corsica, in such circumstances, as a sign of deep hatred or a grave presumption of guilt'. In another case, the mother of the supposed killer of a woman from Olmeto did not go to the latter's wake, which was again taken to be evidence of the son's guilt.[64]

As in many other societies, not only in the Mediterranean region,[65] women in

Corsica were more directly involved in religious observance than men,[66] and
their central role in funeral ritual, stressed by all observers, may be seen as an
extension of this. At the same time, the active role played by women and the
passive role played by men in funeral ritual is clearly another example of the
sharp differentiation of gender roles in Corsican society, though it reverses the
usual pattern. Where everyday life is concerned, men are dominant and women
outwardly submissive, but where death is concerned women dominate and men
are passive, indifferent or undemonstrative.[67] In cases of violent death, men have
to be incited to pursue revenge by the women through the medium of the *vocero*.[68]
However, not all men are excluded from funeral ritual or restricted to a subsidiary role in it, and women do not predominate at all its stages. Women lead and
officiate at the domestic, 'secular' ritual concentrated on the *vocero*,[69] but their role
is subordinate or they may even be absent, once the corpse leaves the house. The
priest, of course, leads the ritual in church, and he is explicitly viewed by the
women as a rival. A *voceratrice* addressed a priest who tried to silence her at the
time of the taking-up of the corpse: 'And you, your reverence, / You keep saying:
Be quiet! Be quiet! / But it is we who lose all we have at a death / While you draw
benefits from it.'[70] On a profounder level, as we have seen more generally, the
women are celebrants at non-Christian rites, which naturally puts them at odds
with the official representative of the Catholic Church. In some cases they were
even excluded altogether from participating in either the funeral procession or
the church service, presumably in order to prevent their lamenting from disrupt-
ing these more seemly liturgical occasions. It is also significant that beyond their
own domestic sphere the women begin to be treated as something of a nuisance
by men, who pull them away from the corpse or coffin and otherwise try to
restrain what are seen as their excesses.

Here we may mention the assimilation of funerals with weddings, which is
also found in other Mediterranean societies.[71] We have seen that young girls were
dressed on their biers in wedding clothes and decked with flowers and garlands,
and *voceri* made the significance of this quite clear. 'I had made you a garland', a
mother told her dead daughter, 'So fine and so honourable, / For when you got
married: / I was going to put it on your head. / You can wear it today, / O your
mother's pride and treasure.' Another singer addressed another unmarried girl:
'Come on! get up, O Chilina, / For the mare is saddled; / Let us ride to Carcheto /
Where you will be married; / The banns have been published / And the cavalcade
is ready.' Again, in an example collected at Agnerone in 1925, a mother says to
her daughter: 'You will not be going as a bride, / You will not be going to France
[after all], / For you have been abducted by a civil servant [i.e. death] / Whose
ship I see / Ready in the harbour.' Other examples indicate that more was
involved than a convenient metaphor; marriage and death actually had much in
common. In a *vocero* collected at Castello-di-Rostino in 1928, a dead girl is said to
have been 'married without house furniture' or dowry. Another composed at
Venzolasca for the daughter of a neighbour, the second to die in succession,
commented on 'the unfortunate fact / That in this house / No brides go out, / But
[instead] the girls go out / In closed boxes.'[72] No laments were sung in Corsica
when a bride left her family of origin to enter the house of strangers, but the
parallel between this event and her death was obviously felt, and may once have

found ritual expression. The *caracolu* was similar to another circular dance performed around the couple at betrothals, and both are related to the more general spiral dance, the *granitula*, performed by the community on Good Friday and on other occasions and which Father Casta sees as a symbolic representation of the opposition between the principles of life or fertility and death.[73] These complex connections, in which death and marriage were both analagous and opposed, are illustrated in a further *vocero*, collected by Southwell Colucci and analysed by Ettori. Here a young man's parents had refused to allow him to marry the girl whom he had chosen, Padua Maria, and had kept him shut up in their house for three months in an attempt to end the relationship. This confinement was believed to have caused his death from consumption, and at the wake his would-be fiancée and the boy's mother, Faustina, confront each other. Padua Maria asserts to Faustina: 'Rather than give him to me, / You left him to death,' to which Faustina replies: 'It is true; it is not a lie; / I confess my sin: / Rather than give him to you, / I preferred to see him buried.' Padua Maria then addresses the corpse ironically: 'Don't you hear your mother? / ... Get up. / All is forgiven. / Now I am your legitimate wife ... / We are going to exchange rings, / For your father and your brother / Now give their consent.'[74]

Observers of Corsican funeral ritual disagree about the extent to which it expressed 'real' emotion in a spontaneous way. Referring to a funeral procession, which he saw at Bocognano in 1801, Miot wrote that the men held up the most grief-stricken women, 'but with an insensibility which gave the impression that it was all a game or an empty ceremony'. Bigot noted in 1863 that the wailing and shouting of the women was 'required by custom'. Lorenzi de Bradi related of *voceratrici* in the inter-war period: 'There is no tear of emotion; their faces stay dry', and referred to them as 'tragic actresses'.[75] Moreover, as Galletti points out, assembling the 'chorus of lamenters or *schiera*' required a degree of deliberate organization, especially when women came from other villages. Against this, we have evidence from many writers of unbridled emotional behaviour. Forcioli-Conti describes the actions of the women around the corpse in these terms: 'They weep, lament, shout, address each other; they get up and sit down; they stride about; they return to the corpse, they collapse on it, wetting it with their tears, subjecting it to kisses, knocks and hugs.' Vuillier reported that the *caracolu* was performed as if those present had been seized by a kind of vertigo. Here it is significant, too, that the *vocero* was not performed at any set stage during the wake, and that *voceratrici* are reported to have gone into trance-like states or to have fainted during their performances. Again, some authors have stressed the element of improvisation and spontaneity in the singing of *voceri*, while others have emphasized instead the element of role-playing by the singer and her reliance on conventional phraseology.

The truth is that the ritual was both spontaneous and conventional. The set forms provided an expected, indeed a compulsory, framework, through which personal grief and anger could be channelled. Moreover, as De Martino has demonstrated in a more general context,[76] the ritual contained and controlled the emotions which it expressed in a specific way, passing through two alternate phases, the *planctus* or phase of paroxysm and extreme gestures, and the *lamentatio* proper, that is, in the Corsican context, the *vocero*. Forcioli-Conti noted that it was the job of the *voceratrice* to bring about calm and acceptance (where no revenge was required), and she sometimes failed to do this, in which case 'shouting and disorder would recommence, chairs would be thrown about and broken', and the women would crowd about the corpse again, and later renew their singing.[77]

As far as the *vocero* itself is concerned, like all oral poetry or prose[78] it contained both improvised and traditional elements. The singer built up the particular *vocero* according to a set pattern which she had learned, and using a number of stock phrases, lines or even verses. For example, the *vocero* 'Eu filava la mio rocca', which figures, with minor variations, in most collections and two verses of which serve as the epigraph to Mérimée's *Colomba*, is an edited version of one sung in the late eighteenth or early nineteenth century by Maria Filici or Felice of Calacuccia for her brother. According to Bertrand, the *vocero* sung by their grandmother for two members of the Forcioli family killed at Arbellara in 1844 began with four lines from this earlier *vocero* and also included another line in common, but was otherwise quite different, and was of course related to quite different circumstances in another part of the island.[79] Other examples of this kind may be cited.[80] But local details had always to be improvised, and a singer of talent could be creative within the set framework. No one who has read the extant collections could fail to recognize poetry of a high order in *voceri* at their best.[81]

Nineteenth-century observers noted changes in the funeral ritual, for example in the dress worn by the deceased or in the lesser or greater reliance upon specialist *voceratrici*. In general, the ritual became simpler, and the more extreme gestures were modified or abandoned, especially in the towns and among the notables. However, the main corpus of ritual seems to have survived in the villages, like much of Corsican traditional culture, until about the time of the First World War.[82] Much the same may be said of the singing of *voceri* in particular. Forcioli-Conti claimed in 1897 that they were 'still sung in town and country, big houses and small', but he admitted that 'the new generation does not know them', a view confirmed by other writers.[83] After the lapse of the actual performance of *voceri* at wakes, they seem to have survived a little longer as 'folk songs' sung on other occasions.[84]

II

As we have noted, Corsican burial customs in the nineteenth century were far from uniform. More research is required before a definitive picture can be arrived at, but sufficient information is available to make a start in that direction. It seems that notables were buried by preference in the pre-nineteenth-century period in churches, a custom that lingered on, to be replaced by burial on private land in family mortuary chapels. This custom in turn may be traced back into the eighteenth century, if not earlier. The rest of the population was buried in common graves or vaults in churches and churchyards, which were replaced during the course of the nineteenth century by communal cemeteries.

According to Patin de La Fizelière, at the end of the eighteenth century 'all the dead' of the *pieve* were customarily buried in the church of the convent of Tallano, while those of Sartène were similarly buried in the convent church there.[85] Other monastic churches fulfilled the same function in other parts of

Corsica.[86] Patin de La Fizelière also mentions the tombs of 'many noble and non-noble families' at Sartène, suggesting a distinction between these and common burial in the same church. The religious orders disappeared during the Revolutionary period, and the official opposition to burial in churches, already evident earlier and successfully resisted by them, strengthened. A royal decree of 1776 had restricted burial in churches and chapels to the clergy and to lay patrons and had laid down that such burial had to be in properly paved vaults. During and after the Revolution, all burial in churches became illegal. In a circular of 1818, the prefect 'reiterated that burials should never be made in churches, chapels or hospitals. He had learned, however, that this custom was continued in many localities, vitiating the air of the buildings concerned and compromising the health of citizens.' In order to prevent covert attempts to get round the law, all burials at night were barred.[87] And there is other evidence that burial in churches continued until well into the nineteenth century, despite the law. At Ghisoni, people were buried in the convent church of San Francesco until at least 1811 and in the old parish church of Santa Maria until at least 1813. Tommaseo cites a *vocero* from 1818, in which a woman declares: 'On this holy day / We want to see / Your belovèd body interred / At Santa Reparata, / So that we may often go / To continue our prayers [for you] there. / Over your sepulchre / I want to stand to hear mass.' The *adjoint* of Foce reported in 1828 that the body of Angela-Maria Nicolai, 'which had been buried in the place which served as a cemetery, had subsequently been disinterred, and had been found in a burial place in the church'. Marcaggi asserted that the practice of burial in churches was not finally discontinued until around 1840, though even this may be an optimistic view.[88]

This process of reluctant adherence to French law coincided sometimes with the building of new churches with no tradition as burial places. At Bastelica, for example, a new church replaced the old convent church which was demolished. At Zicavo, another new church was built, and the convent church was simply abandoned.[89] Nevertheless, the popularity of the old sites remained, and the churchyards of some old convent churches have continued in use as burial places to the present day. It is significant also that the word *cunbentu* came to have the meaning of 'burial place'.[90] Mention should be made here too of family chantry chapels, which had also been abolished in theory during the French Revolution, but which survived to become the object of much litigation during the Restoration period, as we have seen.[91] With their endowed chaplains, they were aimed primarily at providing masses for the souls of their founders, but they also served as family burial places, the precursors perhaps of later mortuary chapels. The mayor of Bastelica was reported to the authorities in 1864 for showing 'partiality in the matter of burials'. He had allowed the widow Berfini to be buried alongside her husband in a private chapel, which was situated just inside the confines of the village and which was no longer an authorized burial place.[92] In medieval Genoa, another feuding society, the need to avoid the dangerous environment of ordinary churches but also 'to keep inviolate the family's graves' was put forward as a reason for having private chapels,[93] and the argument might equally apply to modern Corsica.

Where non-notables were concerned, burial in church might well have been in a common vault. Borel-Léandri writes that 'until the middle of the eighteenth century, burial took place in the crypts of churches and convents, or in communal graves under stone slabs', and she cites a *vocero* from Mariana: 'This morning in our church / A hole was dug under the stone floor.'[94] According to other writers, collective burial in the common grave or *arca* within the church survived in certain villages down to the end of the nineteenth century or even to the 1930s.[95] The subprefect of Sartène reported a burial at Loreto-di-Tallano in 1866, which had taken place without the permission of the municipal authorities but with the connivance of the priest, who had charge of the key to 'the cemetery which consists of a crypt or vault'. Vuillier noted in 1891 that it had been 'the practice in many parts of Corsica [until quite recently] to throw the bodies into the charnel-pit'. Such pits existed, we know, in the old churches at Zicavo, Ghisoni and Bocognano and were in use until about 1870. Archer noted that 'very often the *arca* was in the aisle of the village church, and [was] separated into four parts, for men, women, children, and strangers'. In a similar arrangement in the church of Santa Reparata near Calenzana, there were three divisions, for clergy, lay adults, and children.[96]

Sometimes the charnel-pit was situated outside the church, though usually close to it. Bigot wrote that there was 'no cemetery at Cauro or Ocana, but only, for those who own no land, a common grave into which the corpse is thrown covered in a shroud'. Saint-Germain noted at the same time that Cauro had 'neither cemetery nor [private] mausoleums ... the dead are dropped pell-mell into a kind of well, which is then closed over with a large stone slab'. Archer referred to the dead having been 'thrown into a common tomb or *arca*' at Venaco, a custom still extant in the 1840s. There the *arca* seems to have been a large stone construction, the bodies being thrown in through two holes in the roof, which was reached by a stairway. Elsewhere, Father Casanova mentions 'cylindrical' *arca* closed by large stone discs, which did not prevent the odour of putrefaction from escaping.[97]

In a few villages, natural apertures served as collective burial places. Archer again reported that 'formerly' the inhabitants of Campodonico near Orezza, 'having no cemetery, threw their dead into a deep gulley'. Carrington writes that, until well into the nineteenth century, the people of Giuncheto in the Sartène region used to place corpses in caves or holes in the rocks, which they closed up with stone slabs. The bandit Muzzarettu, who died in 1952 aged 85, said that the dead were still being thrown into a natural chasm at Grossa in his time.[98]

The communal burial ground or cemetery as opposed to the communal vault or charnel-pit is also a very old institution in Corsica, though the two cannot always be clearly distinguished. The public cemetery of Ajaccio was probably the first to be established in Corsica – a petition to this effect dates from 1770 – but in the middle of the nineteenth century it contained a number of common graves 'in the form of long trenches, gradually filled up'.[99] The traditional communal burial ground was usually situated by or near a church, often monastic as we have seen.[100]

The use of the churchyard (though it was not enclosed)[101] seems to have been a stage between burial inside churches and in public cemeteries proper, as it was in contemporary Portugal.[102] There was pressure on villages to establish their own independent public cemeteries from the end of the eighteenth century, and they gradually but reluctantly complied. In the circular of 1818, already cited, the prefect prescribed burial in public cemeteries especially established for the purpose away from dwelling-places, and he called on communes to abandon burial places which did not fulfil these conditions. This policy apparently had some effect, since the number of legally established cemeteries in Corsica rose from 9 in 1818 to 91 in 1819, but this meant that the vast majority of communes were without them, and their geographical distribution was very uneven. There were 49 cemeteries in 1819 in the *arrondissement* of Ajaccio, but only 6 in that of Sartène and none at all in that of Bastia.[103] It is significant here that there was a change of terminology during the nineteenth century, but one that could and can lead to confusion. A number of *voceri* published later in the period refer to burial in *lu campu santu*,[104] a term which held its own against the novel *cimiteriu* and which could apply to either churchyard or public cemetery.[105] Concomitantly, French officials used the word *cimetière*, where it is not always clear that a public cemetery is involved. A woman from Foce, accused of infanticide in 1856, for example, testified that she had placed the remains of her stillborn baby 'in one of the vaults in the cemetery of the commune'.[106] Most public municipal cemeteries still in use today seem to date from the later nineteenth century, and this impression can be confirmed in some instances. A decision to construct a municipal cemetery at Ghisoni was taken in 1853, but this was only acted upon in 1868 after long arguments about the site. At Tavera, the municipal cemetery was laid out around 1890 on the initiative of the mayor, and the site chosen was 'the hill where the dead were buried', that is, it seems, a place already in use as a burial ground. However, Vanutberghe noted in 1904 that 'cemeteries are still recent and uncommon'; and there were still villages without cemeteries in 1930.[107]

Few visitors to Corsica in the last hundred years or so have failed to comment on the ubiquity of private burial grounds, mortuary chapels and tombs. 'Corsicans dislike being buried in public churchyards,' wrote Edward Lear, for example, in 1870, 'and prefer interment in their own land. The whole island is dotted over with little mausoleums as a result.' 'At Zicavo', Vuillier reported in 1891, 'burial crosses are to be met with everywhere, under the chestnut trees, and on the borders of fields, even by the side of the highway.' Again, in 1930, Colonel Rankin 'noted the custom of burying the dead in the paternal acres'. A handsome monument 'in the middle of a barley field is quite a common sight'.[108] How are we to explain such a custom? An obvious answer would seem to be the lack or inadequacy of public cemeteries. 'When there is no cemetery,' wrote Bigot, 'many families bury their dead on land which belongs to them.' 'No wonder that the well-to-do Corsican prefers his private mortuary chapel,' remarked Murray after visiting the public cemetery at Ajaccio in the 1860s.[109] However, there is evidence that where cemeteries were few and far between, corpses might be taken considerable distances for burial in them. In the past, Archer relates,

> when certain villages possessed no cemeteries or churches, and were obliged to bury their dead in distant communes, the corpse, dressed in its best clothes, was seated on a horse, propped up by a forked stick fastened to the back of the saddle, and led down the mountain paths to its burial place ... This custom was still in use as recently as 1887 in the Fiumorbo district.

Chiari more prosaically describes coffins from hamlets without churches or cemeteries being 'carried on men's shoulders along mule-paths over distances of up to ten or twelve miles'.[110]

Moreover, even where public cemeteries did exist, burial in private land is also found. More plausible as a general explanation here would be the historical argument that the French Revolution upset traditional customs by banning burial in churches. With this outlet blocked, Corsicans, rather like pre-nineteenth-century French Protestants,[111] adopted burial on private land, which had existed earlier as a minority custom, as a general or preferred practice, only later accepting the public cemetery and even then with important qualifications. At Ghisoni, for example, the construction of mortuary chapels and the use of private burial plots became common in the period after the ban on burial in churches and before the municipal cemetery was established in 1868.[112]

A number of other factors are relevant here. First, as we have noted, burial in private ground was primarily a custom of the well-to-do and, crucially, of those who owned land in which to bury. The *arca*, as Bigot said, was 'for those who own no land', and the same was true of the public cemetery. When the mayor of Zonza, a herdsman, attempted to have his relatives buried in the nave of the parish church in the late 1840s in violation of the law, this evoked the following comment from a local notable: 'As if the public cemetery were not good enough to receive the remains of persons who have spent their lives in a sheep-run!'[113] The cemetery at Ajaccio was reported in 1893 to be 'used by few but the poor and the Protestants'.[114] Once more was involved than a simple enclosure, wealth again became significant. Spalinowski reported in 1904: 'There are tombs everywhere on the larger properties ... but only the rich can afford to construct these little mortuary chapels; the poor join each other in the cemetery.' Janine Renucci refers to an interesting example from the 1860s of what appears to be an adaptation of the *arca* in the face of the new vogue for private tombs. The mayor of Brando had 'a communal tomb with racks' built for the inhabitants of the hamlet of Pozzo, 'because they were too poor to pay for private tombs or even for coffins'. The private burial ground and the private tomb were 'ways of marking social distance', of claiming social 'superiority',[115] which could also be manifested, especially from the later nineteenth century, within the cemetery itself. A tale collected at Zoza in 1882 relates of a young girl: 'They dug her grave in the cemetery, and since she possessed nothing, she did not even have a wooden cross.' The land for the cemetery at Tavera, to which we have referred, was presented to the commune by its owners, the Luterani, 'who reserved a place for their dead, and who later built their chapel in the upper section of the cemetery'.[116] This pattern of notables and the general population of a village sharing a cemetery, but with the former having chapels and separate plots within it, is fairly common in Corsica today.

The private burial ground was also an assertion of family as against community. Abeau wrote in 1888 that the cult of the family was expressed through the family tomb: 'no one, who has a patch of ground and can afford a few sous, would dream of entrusting the remains of his relatives to the common cemetery'. Maurras in 1898 celebrated the Corsicans' attachment to burial in private enclosures 'in the midst of the dead of their blood'; while Bigot in 1869 noted how returning emigrants used their wealth to build 'a patrimonial tomb where each relative, past, present or to come, will have his or her place'. Tombs, moreover, were usually inscribed with the family name in a prominent place. A *vocero* for a member of the Filippi family of Venzolasca, collected in 1931, referred to their tomb as a 'grand property' displaying their name.[117] The house-like aspect of most tombs made the same point. As the domestic house represented the family in secular terms, so the house-tomb did in relation to the dead. Burial 'in the paternal acres' also formed a sacred link between land and family. 'This sacred ground', wrote Abeau of the family's private burial enclosure, 'will remain part of the family patrimony for ever, and will be the best guarantee that it will never pass into the hands of strangers'. This point has been taken up more recently by Caisson. Tombs, he argues, were signs of ownership, and the placing of tombs in fields was 'a means of appropriating land that was contested, or of preventing its sale by descendants. The tomb fixes the lineage to the soil.'[118] The existence of other symbolic links between the soil and the dead would lend support to this view.[119]

The same considerations explain the importance attached to being buried in the right place – in one's own village and in the family land or tomb. Although the odd person might affect indifference towards his place of burial and although cases are recorded of people being buried away from home for no good or obvious reason, these were clearly exceptions.[120] According to one source, Luca-Antono Viterbi himself stated that he did not care whether he were buried in Bastia or his native Penta, but 'his relatives', the police reported in 1821, were most anxious to obtain his body 'in order to bury it in style in Penta'. Some 600 people set out for Bastia with the aim of escorting the body home, which prompted the authorities to dispose of it post-haste in quick-lime.[121] The mayor of Eccica-Suarella reported in 1824 that 'the inhabitants of his commune having learned that a certain Michele Bastelica had been killed ... on the territory of Tolla, hastened out of a feeling of piety to fetch the body and bring it back to their village'. A *vocero* for Stefano Ceccaldi of Evisa, collected in 1928, states that he died at Ocognano in the Casinca, 'a foreign place', but was brought home for burial. Other *voceri* reflect the same practice but also the related anxieties aroused by the death and possibly the burial of family members away from home. In a *vocero* dating from before 1918 for a girl from Asco who died of malaria in Bastia, her mother says: 'I ask, but no one replies, / Whether you have stayed in Bastia / And do not wish to rest in Asco / Beside the church of Santa Maria, / Where so many souls / Make a great company?'. Some *voceri* actually suggest that those who are not brought back to the local burial place will not be reunited with their relatives and ancestors in the after-life. As Bigot reported, too, emigrants usually returned to the island in old age, being 'especially concerned to be buried near the paternal house'.[122] This introduces what may be a further explanatory factor. Corsican society had always experienced a high incidence of emigration and this became much more marked in the later nineteenth century. As Bloch has argued for the Merina of Madagascar, dispersal of population of this kind may reinforce attachment to burial in the ancestral place or tomb as the only remaining link with the past and with stability.[123]

The identification of family and tomb also meant that families might be attacked via assaults on their tombs. In 1841, for example, 'a tomb belonging to

Giovan-Battiste Benedetti ... of Aullène, and situated on one of his properties near the village, was entirely demolished'. Benedetti suspected Giovan-Battiste Bacciocchi of the same village, 'with whom he is in a state of enmity', and Bacciocchi was arrested and charged a few days later.[124]

If the tomb or private burial ground was quite literally the memorial of the landowning family, what about evidence that suggests that the aim of burial in fields and elsewhere was to forget the dead? Vuillier writes that

> at Ghisoni, the better-off people bury their dead on their property, leaving a corner of land uncultivated for this purpose. The graves are marked by a wooden cross, but ever afterwards the place of sepulture is shunned by the survivors, who even take the greatest care to avoid mentioning the name of the deceased, as if they vowed the dead to eternal oblivion.

He notes that Ghisoni's customs were unusual, but there is other evidence to suggest that commemoration, at least via the place of burial, was avoided elsewhere in Corsica. Lorenzi de Bradi related that people buried in fields or vineyards had a cross at their heads, to which a paper was attached with their names written in ink, and a stone at their feet. 'Tomorrow men will forget this mound. Nature will cover it with brambles and flowers.'[125] And even tombs were no guarantee of continued commemoration of individual or family. Spalinowski noted as early as 1904 that most of the tombs which he saw were in ruins. His comment that it was believed that anyone who restored a tomb would die suggests that there was more involved in this than the simple failure of human memory over more than three or four generations. Perhaps we can see commemorative burial in private land as the mark *par excellence* of landowning notables, a reflection of private property, of agricultural interests and of family, while communal burial or oblivion-orientated burial in private land reflected rather the traditional communal socio-economic practices of herdsmen. The division predated the French Revolution but was exacerbated during the nineteenth century, the spread of 'notable' burial customs keeping pace with the expansion of private property, enclosure and the local exploitation of state power, though the older customs lingered on and exercised an inhibiting effect to some extent, as Spalinowski's observations indicate. Here the impression that family tombs developed first and were most prominent and elaborate in the 'advanced' Capo Corso and the Balagna would be significant. Corsican burial customs, in effect, reflected and underpinned secular social arrangements, and the cemetery, in the widest sense, was a map of society.[126]

But, more germane to the particular focus of this book, nineteenth-century Corsicans, and notables in particular, were averse to being buried in the vicinity of their enemies. It is not always clear how this difficulty was overcome in earlier periods, when burial inside churches was the rule.[127] Sometimes rival families occupied distinct parts of the church, rather as local people and strangers, and the sexes, were kept apart in the charnel-pits. At Ghisoni, for example, the leading families each had their own chapels within the convent church where they were buried.[128] Perhaps the church was sometimes regarded as sufficiently sacred territory to force a final reconciliation in death, though we know that rival families in life would frequently refuse to attend church services together. Whatever the answer to this question, which must depend on further research, there is no doubt that burial on private land, so characteristic of the nineteenth century, was an obvious way of avoiding the promiscuity of the common burial ground, whether of the traditional or the modern type, and as such would have appealed to social groups prone to feuding. Burial on private land, moreover, could be a strong expression of family entity and pride and could also reinforce and express family enmities and feuds. The most striking example of this is provided by the village of Olmeta-di-Tuda. The road into the village from the south is dominated by the huge octagonal mausoleum of the Campocasso family, while that of their enemies, the Casale, overlooks the road to the north.

The placing of tombs and burial places generally in the landscape is of great significance and reminds us that even family tombs belonged to communities. It is noticeable today that tombs are very often located on the edge of villages, sometimes in commanding positions overlooking valleys or the sea. To some extent this reflects the scarcity of suitable terrain within or near the village, but it seems also to have a more positive significance. As Caisson has written: 'The dead keep watch on the boundaries; they ... guard the territory of their communities';[129] which brings us to attitudes towards the dead and the after-life.

III

Confirming Frazer's generalization on the subject, some observers of Corsican society have stressed that the attitude of the living towards the dead was 'dominated by fear rather than by affection' and guided by the conviction that the dead were 'touchy' and 'irritable' by nature, if not envious and vindictive.[130] This view has been most strongly stated by Carrington, who writes that: 'Terror of the dead is expressed in innumerable Corsican customs,' and who sees all of the rituals which we have described as aimed primarily at placation or at disguising that terror 'as respect and love'.[131] It has been pointed out further that the dead are a 'source of terror' in Corsican folk-tales. The living are often afraid to go near burial grounds; ghosts, whose return is common, are nearly always hostile; and there is a solidarity among the spirits of the dead which is exercised against the living.[132] It would seem that this takes too exclusively negative a view of a situation that was more complicated. One would not wish, for example, to deny that the corpse was regarded as dangerous in the period between death and burial and that elements in the funeral ritual may be seen as a placation of it, but the corpse was also itself in danger and the ritual was aimed, too, at protecting it and ensuring its safe passage.[133] Frazer argues plausibly, moreover, that where fear of the dead, including the ghosts of one's 'own kinsfolk', was strong, then people would be 'at great pains to drive them away, to keep them at a distance, and to bar the house against their unwelcome intrusions'. This would imply the avoidance of burying the dead close at hand and also of symbolic commensality with them,[134] both customs that were important in Corsica. Going further, some writers have referred to a positive or 'religious cult of the dead' in Corsica.[135] Many have repeated Tommaseo's comment that Corsican folk-poetry is essentially a poetry of death, while Römer has noted that the music for ordinary festival masses is modelled on that of masses for the dead.[136] Some aspects of the burial and commemoration of the dead would also support the view that 'the dead are not considered ... as those who have gone but rather as relatives who are in a special condition and that one must associate with the various activities of daily life'.[137] They were still active in promoting and defending family interests and relations with them were an important expression of family solidarity.[138]

Many of these contradictions are more apparent than real and will be resolved by more detailed consideration of the evidence. Students of other similar societies have stressed that fear of and affection for the dead go together and that friendly and inimical relations between the living and the dead may be complementary.[139] Attention should also be paid to the process by which the dead are desocialized or purified, ultimately ceasing to be close relatives and joining the anonymous dead or the ancestors. In some societies this process is much more rapid than in others, and the dead at different stages in the process possess different degrees of danger for the living. Among the Kaingáng of Brazil, for example, the spirits of the dead were especially dangerous immediately after death and to their spouses whom they would wish to take with them into the after-life. Widows and widowers therefore received special ritual protection. But once the period immediately following the death was over, affectionate laments were sung expressing regret for deceased persons and even the desire to see them again.[140] The danger represented by the dead also depends closely on their mode of dying and on the funerals which they have been given or failed to be given. This factor is of particular significance in Corsica, where it was the spirits of those who had died by violence and who were not at rest that, above all, aroused fear, and where the dead were generally honoured and revered.

We will begin our more detailed discussion with some salient aspects of the latter tendency. First, Corsicans had a strong sense of 'the ancestors'. *Voceri* referred fairly often to forbears whom the deceased would be meeting and to whom messages might be sent through his or her agency. These were sometimes parents or grandparents, uncles, aunts or cousins. In an example from Venzolasca from about the time of the First World War, an aunt tells her nephew: 'When you arrive, / O nephew in those places / And you meet / All your cousins, / If someone recognizes you, / Say: I am Agostino Landolfini.'[141] But more distant co-laterals are also mentioned.[142] The usual term here was *antichi* or *antinati*, but sometimes *arci* is found, which must surely have been connected in people's minds with the *arca*, though it was etymologically distinct.[143] Another link with the ancestors was provided by the practice of having masses said for the dead, which was combined with belief in visits from ghosts to provide a two-way channel of communication. In a tale collected at Zoza in 1881, a man is visited by the ghosts of his father, his aunt and a cousin, who inform him that, thanks to the masses that have been said for them, they are now in Paradise: while a *vocero*, collected at Castello-di-Rostino in 1928, refers to a message from a dead mother to her surviving children: 'When I am no longer with you, / From the sempiternal life, / From the other world, / I will order some masses to be said.'[144] Links with forbears were also reflected in naming customs. Corsicans were frequently known as N, son of the late M, and so on. Tommaseo drew attention, too, to the practice of giving or using dual Christian names, which seems to have been almost universal in Corsica (and which of course is found elsewhere). He suggested that this was a means of obtaining for the person so named the double protection of the ancestors whose names they had. It is not clear on what basis the names were chosen, but a systematic anthroponymous linkage across generations and between affines seems likely.[145] Finally, there is evidence from earlier centuries of general assemblies of communities being held in churchyards or cemeteries and of legal documents being written and sworn to on 'arringo stones', which seem to have been the tombs of the ancestors or founders of the village concerned. Such practices survived in some cases until the mid-nineteenth century.[146]

Underlying much Corsican funeral ritual and reflected in some burial customs is the idea that the dead were still in some sense present. Indicative of this intimacy with death and the dead is the relative absence of specialized vocabulary for use in the funeral context. The same words are used for 'table' and 'bier', for 'ditch' and 'grave', for 'sheet' and 'shroud', and so on, and the sense only changes with the context.[147] Also significant is the familiarity with the corpse at the wake, which we have described, the men shaking it by the hand as they might a living friend or relative, the women kissing and caressing it, and the *voceratrici* even laying their ears to its mouth as if to catch its requests or demands, or asking it to concern itself 'with their grievances'.[148] One of the obvious functions of the funeral ritual, too, was to express the intense grief felt at the loss of the deceased, which explains the extreme gestures of anguish, the attempts to awaken the corpse, the refusal to let it leave the house or enter the grave.[149] This sense of bereavement was also verbalized in the remarks addressed to the corpse and in *voceri*, in a characteristically familiar idiom. In Mérimée's description of the wake in *Colomba*, 'from time to time, someone broke the silence to address a few words to the corpse. "Why have you left your good wife?", asked one old woman. "Didn't she look after you well? Why didn't you wait another month, and your daughter-in-law would have given you a son?"'[150] Again and again in *voceri*, the deceased is reproached with dying. 'Don't you know that I am your wife,' a woman asked a man from Vescovato, 'And that you are my husband?... / Does my company no longer please you?... / If you don't want to stay in the village, / I will send you [to our daughter's] in Bastia.' Another widow censured her husband similarly for abandoning her and the children: 'Why break the bonds / Of so faithful a union, / And leave your children / And their mother to destitution?' A parishioner blamed Father Santucci of Pietricaggio-d'Alesani for abandoning his parish and asked him who would act as doctor there in the future. Sometimes the corpse was addressed as though it were still alive and only feigning to be dead. A young widow from the Tallano told her husband, into whose house she had not yet moved: 'I arrived at your door / And you treated me badly! / You did not even come out / To help me off my horse.' 'We all came / From far away this morning,' another *vocero* chided. 'Get up and / Shake hands with us; / For the friends and relatives / Are upset [at your failure to do so]. / If you do not do this, / We will go away discontented. / All the friends and relatives / Have come. / Say something to them / To make them happy.' Less frequently, a singer indicated that she could not or did not wish to live on without the deceased.[151]

To be interpreted in a similar way is the notion that the deceased attended the post-burial feast in his honour. In a lament, collected at San-Gavino-d'Ampug-nani, a cousin tells the dead man: 'When you leave the church, / You know what you have to do: / Come back with me to the house / Where the meal will be ready.' Alternatively, or at the same time, as we have seen, a viaticum might be left at the grave. Bartoli noted that 'in some villages, according to a very ancient custom, bread, water, and a little money are left for a dead person; they are his provisions for the journey'; but leaving food on graves may also be seen as a way of continuing to include the deceased in the family and the community.[152]

More generally, the funeral ritual, including the feast, was intended to boost the prestige of the family performing it by demonstrating the honour in which the deceased had been and was still held. Here the number of clergy officiating, the lavishness of the hospitality, the number of candles burned, and so on, were all carefully assessed within the community. A *vocero* by a mother for an unmarried daughter, for example, boasted that her father had spent the equivalent of her dowry on candles.[153] It followed that failure to observe the required ritual was extremely rare and risked most serious consequences. We have seen that when the bandit Scarlino from Venzolasca was killed at Biguglia in 1844, he was given perfunctory burial in 'a shallow ditch', but his mother 'gathered her friends and relatives and went to fetch his remains, so that they could be given the proper funeral honours'.[154]

Burial customs also reflected a continuing association between the living and the dead, especially, as we have emphasized, where burial was on family land and/or among the living in prominent and frequented places. Like lavish funeral ritual, moreover, the erection of costly and elaborate tombs or funeral monuments was a further means of pleasing and honouring the dead as well as of promoting the family; indeed, the two went specifically together.[155] And even where tombs were built 'in wild places', they were frequently visited. In a *vocero*, cited by Ortoli, a widow promises to visit the tomb of her husband every day to weep over his bones. Such promises may not have been fulfilled to the letter, but the fact that they were made is significant.[156]

We have seen, too, that anniversary masses were performed and that graveside rituals were carried out at intervals after a death. Women also recollected their own dead when singing *voceri* at the funerals of others.[157] But the most important commemoration of the dead occurred collectively in Corsica on the Day of the Dead. On this day, usually 2 November, graves and tombs were tidied up, decorated and visited, sometimes in solemn procession.[158] In some places, two other ritual elements were present. First, during the night of 1–2 November, the church bells were pealed by the youth of the town or village concerned. In some areas, for example the Nebbio, 'large bonfires were [also] lit in front of churches', and everyone gathered around them and a collection was made.[159]

This takes us to the second characteristic ritual associated with the Day of the Dead, the distribution of food, that is, another variety of commensality with the dead. Lamotte relates that at Bocognano, where food and drink were placed on graves after burial, 'tables with food on them were also set out on the Day of the Dead, and the dead were believed to eat from them during the night'. More commonly, however, this gift of food to the dead was disguised. Borel-Léandri notes that in some regions, the *bastelli* served at wakes and post-burial feasts were also made and consumed on the Day of the Dead 'in honour of the dead and for the rest of their souls'.[160] Very often this or other food was distributed in the community. At Tavera, for example, 'for the Feast of the Dead on the eve of All Saints', it was customary in all the hamlets to prepare ovenfuls of "*zuccatti*", or pumpkin turnovers, which were offered to neighbours, friends, and especially the poor'. In the south, according to Lorenzi de Bradi, 'the big landowners, the Jo of the village, send to every hearth joints of meat and "*chacci*", a kind of round turnover full of *brocciu* and raisins'. Chiari remembered that on All Souls' Night, a pail full of boiled chestnuts would be left outside the entrance to the house, 'so that any beggar or hungry person can help himself and allay his hunger'. There seems little doubt that the poor or the beggars in this context represented the dead. Rossi wrote in 1900 that the custom of the wealthy giving bread and wine to the poor on the eve of the Day of the Dead was the vestige of an older custom of leaving food and drink for the dead themselves; while Lorenzi de Bradi recorded a dole custom that was quite explicit. At dawn on the Day of the Dead, he relates,

> a troop of children, barefoot and very lightly dressed, and shivering as a result, goes about the village knocking on doors and asking for: 'Charity for our poor dead! Give, give, for the repose of your dead!' The children, some of whom were from the village and others from neighbouring shielings, were brought into each house, warmed, and told: 'You are welcome ... The souls of our dead welcome you into this house, which was theirs and which they still visit.'

The children were then given nuts, dried figs and small coins 'in memory of the dead', whom they stood for. At Asco, special cakes were offered generally, with the words: 'For our dead.'[161]

Some sources refer to longer rituals or ritual periods involving the dead. Arrighi, for example, mentions a week of the dead at Arbellara. In some parts of southern Corsica, too, the Day, or rather the Night, of the Dead was 31 July–1 August, the Feast of the Maccabees. At Palneca, Tavera and elsewhere, bonfires were lit in front of the houses; at Tavera, a procession took place round the house with a church candle, and the sign of the cross was made at all the doors and windows. 'On the same day, sharp instruments are set out to preserve one from the dead.' These included axes, sickles and billhooks and were placed on window sills, thresholds and behind doors. At Cargiaca and elsewhere, these implements were put out on 2 November and salt was also placed on thresholds. Here the family rather than the community ambience of the ritual is evident, and it is clear that precautions are being taken against the dead. The contrast with the commensality of All Souls', as we have previously described it, is highlighted by a common cautionary tale. In this a man who forgets to put water out on the Day of the Dead receives a terrible visitation and is nearly carried off by the dead, who require the water 'to drink and to purify themselves from their sins'.[162] But even such manifest fear of the dead was not unqualified, for, in some cases at least, rituals implying association with the dead and rituals implying dissociation are found together.

In addition to commemorating the dead at intervals, Corsicans observed strict mourning customs. 'I want to dress in black / And put the *faldetta* on my head,' a sister declared in a *vocero* for her two brothers, and she promised never to show any joy again. The wearing of black or dark colours was required for five years or more for close relatives and for two years or more for distant ones, and much of the population dressed in sombre tones as a result. As the reference to the *faldetta*, the widow's dress in the modern period, indicates, mourning by widows was particularly strict. 'I must wear / Black colours; / So long as my life lasts, / I will be covered in them from head to toe,' a widow from the Tallano district declared in 1838, and we have seen that widows rarely remarried unless they were very young.[163]

Other mourning customs involved the hair. Women sometimes let their hair down as a sign of mourning. 'I intend to wear my hair loose / And flowing on my shoulders,' declared another widow. The alternative option was to cut the hair off, a common practice in the Niolo, according to Fée. We have seen that tearing the hair was a traditional gesture of grief, and this was sometimes replaced by cutting the hair.[164] Here the hair might be used (probably figuratively) to staunch the wounds of those killed by violence. A grandmother in her *vocero* for two members of the Forcioli family, killed in the Arbellara feud, declared: 'Bring me scissors / And come quickly with them; / I want to cut a lock of my hair / To close the wounds of my boys.' In another *vocero* from the Piana district, a girl told her father: 'I want to cut my hair / To fill up your wounds.' Tommaseo refers to a pre-nineteenth-century custom of women throwing their hair on to the bier on which the corpse was carried away from the house.[165] The parallel mourning custom for men was to let their beards grow. Corsican men normally wore beards, and the mark of mourning was not to cut them. So a *vocero* by a sister for a murdered brother complained: 'His distant relatives / Will trim their beards.' Bigot also refers to men not cutting the hair on their heads. Not cutting the beard was of course both a sign of general mourning and of a vengeance unfulfilled.[166]

Rituals occurring on the Day of the Dead and mourning customs were only part of a more general day-to-day intercourse between living and dead. According to Gregorovius, it was believed that 'the dead love society ... They are seen in churchyards and visit the living at night'. Father Bartoli expanded on this belief in 1898, providing further explanation of the custom of leaving water out for the dead, which he said was done every night.

> People are persuaded that the dead come to the house at night. They think that they hear them talking, walking about, breathing; under cover of darkness, they visit their relatives and their old house; and they leave in the morning at cockcrow. And they would curse their relatives, if they found nothing to quench their thirst: dearth would ensue as a punishment. Sometimes, too, ghosts nip people and suck their blood, leaving large black marks.

Sometimes the dead called the living by name in the night, and if that person answered, he or she would fall ill or even die. Rossi agreed more generally that 'Corsicans believe that the dead continue to take part in the various activities of the family'; while others noted that the dead were thought to wander about at night, often in groups, returning to the places where they had lived.[167] In this connection, it is probably significant that a number of *voceri* take pains to emphasize the orthodox Christian view that the dead have gone 'to the place / From which no one returns'. One may suggest that the dead may have become objects of fear in this context in the face of clerically inspired disapproval of the old notion of familiarity with them, though this notion was sometimes able to adapt itself to modern conditions surprisingly well. According to a recent account from a village in the Balagna: 'The living-room is also a room of the dead. There, marching across the walls in rows ... are framed photographs of the deceased,' parents, grandparents, uncles and aunts of the present occupants. 'All the people in the photographs are old, and all of them are dead,' and the author surmises that old people must have their ancestral photographs taken just before they were about to die.[168]

We turn now to the opposite pole of attitudes towards the dead, where fear or obligation is uppermost, and this was mainly so where deaths had occurred by violence. We have noted significant variations in the funeral ritual performed for 'natural' and for violent deaths. In the modern period, there seems not to have been any distinction in the way in which the corpse was buried in each case. However, a well-established practice suggests that in the past such a distinction probably was made. Mérimée noted that

> in several cantons of Corsica, especially in the mountains, an extremely old custom obliges passers-by to throw a stone or a branch of a tree on to the spot where a man has perished by violence. Over the years and so long as his tragic end remains in men's memories, this singular offering accumulates from day to day. People call this the 'heap' or *mucchio* of such and such a person.

The practice persisted through the nineteenth century, notably in the Niolo and the Castagniccia. Sometimes a tree might be planted at the place instead; sometimes crosses were put there, a practice later observed in the case of those killed during the Second World War.[169] The custom of erecting cairns or making crosses at sites of violent death is found widely in the Mediterranean world and elsewhere,[170] and there seems little doubt that it is a symbolic representation of burial at the site, which did actually occur in some societies in the past. There are references to such burial, for example, in the Icelandic Sagas, and Dante relates that Manfred, who was killed excommunicate at the battle of Benevento in 1266, was buried on the battlefield and that every soldier threw a stone on to his corpse.[171] In modern Corsica itself we have encountered the case of the bandit Scarlino, who was initially buried 'at the spot where his body had been found'.

Two related considerations seem to have underlain this custom. First, as Mérimée suggests, the heap of stones (or its equivalent) had a mnemonic function. In a *vocero* from the Ghisoni region, the sister of a murdered man says: 'In the district of Nazza / I want to plant a thorn-tree / So that none of our kindred / Will pass by the place,' the implication being either that the spot will be deliberately avoided or, more likely, that when kinsmen do pass it, they will be reminded of the death and of their obligation to avenge it.[172] We have seen that actual burial might very occasionally take place at the site of death and this could significantly serve to perpetuate a feud. At Arbellara, according to the president of the Assize Court in 1850, 'the memory of the conflict which began the feud is preserved by the tomb for two of the Forcioli, which was built on the very spot where they were killed.' Another case also indicates the close connection that existed between the place of a killing and the taking of revenge. After Gregorio Casabianca's brother was killed in a brawl at Lugo-di-Nazza in 1834 by a member of the Andreani family, 'an apparent reconciliation took place between the two families'. However, Casabianca frequently 'visited the place where his brother's blood had been spilled', and soon afterwards killed an Andreani in revenge. Victims might also be buried at the site of death by their killers. For example, Bartolo Renucci of Ciamannacce was killed on the territory of San-Paolo in 1828 in the course of a feud. His throat was cut and he was buried under a large stone.[173] However, this type of action had rather different implications, to which we will return.

As the *vocero* cited above suggests, the indications are that more was involved in the general custom than a simple reminder. In Corsica, as in other societies where similar practices existed, it seems that the special commemoration of the site of a violent death was related to beliefs about the whereabouts and the intentions of the victim's spirit.[174] In a tale to which we referred in Chapter 6, the people of Poggio-di-Tallano assembled stones at a chosen place to build a church. These are moved, however, by a supernatural being, who reveals himself to be St John and who explains that a murderer is buried on the site, which is therefore unsuitable. Here the would-be church builders involuntarily mimic the creation of a *mucchio*, which perhaps itself provides the indication of the previous burial, and the site remains contaminated, or haunted, though we are told that the burial occurred a hundred years earlier. It is also relevant, as Carrington and Lamotte note, that stones were also thrown in Corsica when people passed by rivers and fountains at night in order 'to keep away evil spirits'.[175]

More directly, we have many indications that the spirits of the slain were believed to be deprived of rest and to inhabit the vicinity of their graves and to revisit their erstwhile homes.[176] As such, of course, they were dangerous to the community, to their own kin and to their enemies. As Van Gennep observed, those who had met their deaths by violence, together with those who had not received the proper burial rites, had left the world of the living but were unable to enter the world of the dead. This meant that they were often extremely hostile towards the living, 'sometimes having an intense desire for vengeance' against them.[177] In some societies the anomaly found expression in the further belief that homicide polluted the whole community, and public rituals of protection, purification and placation were performed.[178] At one extreme, these sought to obliterate the slain entirely, removing them from both the worlds of the living and of the dead.[179] Where such notions were very strong, as among the Cheyenne, homicide could come to be regarded as a public 'crime' to be dealt with by the community rather than as a matter to be settled by the kin taking vengeance. Or some compromise between the two systems might be arranged, the community intervening under some religious aegis, for example, to force or persuade the kindreds concerned to make peace.[180] The idea that homicide was a communal offence in both senses of the word was also reflected in the belief that it incurred supernatural sanctions. The slayer was 'pursued by the Furies, or by the ghost of the slain, or some other supernatural being'.[181] In Corsica, where the sense of community was relatively weak and where blood vengeance was correspondingly important, these supernatural sanctions operated less on the general level represented by communal pollution and pursuit by Furies and more as reinforcements of the blood vengeance system itself, though of course all such beliefs have a communal dimension. We are here particularly concerned with the pursuit of vengeance, directly or indirectly, by 'the ghost of the slain'.

Gough has shown that among the Nayars 'the spirits of those who died prematurely and violently' occupy a special place among the lineage ghosts. Only they are 'still interested in this life', and, though all ghosts may punish, they are most prone to do so and are thus most in need of cult and propitiation. This belief, she argues, 'probably formed a sanction against intra-lineage murder', but this inhibiting effect may have extended further. Feuding between lineages occurred among the Nayars, and it was also believed that the ghosts of non-lineage members were dangerous if they had been killed on the land of the lineage group. In ancient and modern Greece, societies both geographically and culturally closer to Corsica, feuding and the belief in avenging ghosts seem to have been more closely associated. In Greek belief, according to Lawson, the ghost of a murdered person 'plagues his murderer' and seeks his own revenge against him; but 'the idea of vendetta is ... perfectly harmonious' with this. 'The acknowledged power of the dead man has never ... served as an excuse for his kinsmen to sit idle; rather it has been an incentive to them to assist more strenuously in the task of vengeance, lest they themselves also should fall under the dead man's displeasure.' Among the Maniotes in particular, it was believed that 'a man who has been murdered cannot rest in his grave until he has been avenged, but issues forth as a *vrykolakas* [or vampire] athirst for his enemy's blood ... To secure his bodily dissolution and repose, it is incumbent upon the next of kin to slay the murderer or, at the least, some near kinsman of the murderer.' Until this is done, the next of kin lies under the victim's curse, and, if he dies in this state, becomes a *vrykolakas* too. 'Thus, the belief in powerful and vindictive *revenants* forms the very mainspring of the vendetta.'[182] The same syndrome is found in a large number of other feuding societies.[183]

These comparisons help us to make sense of the less consistent picture that we have of Corsican beliefs in this area. First, those who died by violence had died 'a bad death'. Most obviously, they had not received the full and proper funeral and burial rites, and as such they were in 'disgrace' and might be destined 'to wander the earth', to occupy that 'limbo' between the living and the dead to which we have referred.[184] In an attempt to avoid or mitigate this fate, victims of violence or others might try to ensure that at least some of the last rites were performed. In a *vocero* collected in 1928 for a man killed at Perelli-d'Alesani, his mother emphasized that he had asked for 'confession' before he died. When Battiste Rossi of Tolla was shot and mortally wounded by his nephew in 1861, a neighbour, 'seeing that his eyes still had some life in them, ran at once to fetch the priest, wishing to procure for him the last succour of religion'. However, we have seen that the funeral ritual for victims of violence had specific features, which distinguish them and which relate to their need to be avenged. In the *vocero* for Dr Matteo, the victim's cousin urges vengeance against the killer, so that Matteo may be at rest.[185]

Most graphically, this idea was expressed in *voceri* and elsewhere via the notion that the blood of the victim itself called for vengeance. So, in the same *vocero*, the singer declares: 'The blood of Matteo / Cannot remain without vengeance.' In another *vocero*, a mother reassures her son: 'You can rest tranquil; / You will be revenged / ... Your precious blood / Will not shout out for ever [*grida*].' In another, the singer says: 'The blood of your brother / Cries to me from the earth.'[186] Leaving the corpses of victims bloody and unwashed assumes a special positive significance in this context and cannot be seen as a sign of negligence as some commentators suggest. As in medieval Florence where the same custom was followed, the aim was for 'the blood to irresistibly attract the vengeance of the relatives'.[187] The blood is seen as the instrument of vengeance. 'From his blood, / His rose-coloured blood / Your sad spouse / Will draw vengeance!', sang one wife to her husband; while another declared: 'But your gentle blood / ... your innocent blood / Will soon make vengeance / Against the cruel people / Who wrongly killed you.' Less directly and evoking notions of pollution, the sister of Massoni proclaimed: 'If I could collect your blood / And put it in my bosom, / I would sow it all over the Niolo / Like a poison.'[188] In this context also, the laceration of the cheeks of the female mourners may be seen as an imitation of the wounding of the victim and another call for revenge.

In a complex symbolism, the blood, the most obvious sign of the violence of the death, here stands for the spirit of the victim which must be appeased by offering it vengeance. Again and again, vengeance is referred to as a satisfaction offered to the dead, as an appeasement, as an expiation. The peace treaty of 1818 between the Casale and the Campocasso of Olmeta-di-Tuda referred to 'the vengeance which they [the Casale brothers] owe to the spirit of their father'. In the course of the feud at Albitreccia, after Ignazio Borelli had killed two members of the Quastana family only remotely connected with previous conflict,

> people were convinced that, in his fury at being unable to slake his thirst for vengeance [on those more immediately involved] ... he had sacrificed these two innocent victims to the spirits of his dead brothers. 'He needed his bread!', a witness said, in figurative language. 'Blood demands blood; the blood of his brothers demanded two victims; and he took them where he found them.'

More generally, Falcucci wrote in 1915 that the blood of an offender must be shed in revenge 'to placate the spirit of the person killed'.[189] All of this further elucidates Corsican distaste for the payment of money instead of blood in the settlement of homicide. It also explains a man's particular anxiety, in a feuding society, to have sons who would survive him. Corsicans prayed, Forcioli-Conti noted, that they might leave someone behind to avenge them, for, if they did not, their souls might never be at rest.[190]

However, where a person was not avenged, his or her spirit might act on its own initiative, either to haunt or to kill the murderer. In a *vocero* already cited, a woman tells her husband: 'You may trouble / Your enemies / Till the day of my joy,' that is, until the death is avenged in reality. In a court case in 1832 a certain Bernamonti from Matra saw a white figure in the maquis and 'was terrified, thinking that it was the ghost of the late Pieri, his old enemy, come to get him'. Again, in a case in 1853, it was reported that the supposed murderer of a woman from Olmeto had been unable to sleep on the night of her wake and had been 'agitated by dreams'; while in a story by Viale, the ghost of a man without kin to avenge him actually carries out vengeance himself. The notion of revenge taken by the dead was not restricted to the domains of belief or fiction but was also reflected in practice. Versini suggests that the wearing of amulets by bandits was aimed in part at obtaining protection from such vengeance, and a case in 1832 lends support to this view. Petro Giovanelli was reported by the brother of a man whom he had killed to have been afraid to go into the maquis on his own, because 'he was afraid of the dead'. Moreover, a particular protective ritual was sometimes used in this context. An oil merchant from the Balagna was robbed and killed near Ajaccio in 1838 and a small coin was found, which had been placed deliberately on the victim's shoulder by his killers. 'In several places in Corsica', a press report explained, 'it is believed ... that one will be unable to walk or to get away after committing a murder unless one leaves something behind, as if to appease the evil spirits.'[191] More generally, here, one may draw attention, too, to the commonly expressed view in Corsica that a murderer had fallen into 'misfortune' and was perhaps more to be pitied even than his victim, a view that otherwise becomes very difficult to understand.[192]

The spirits of the slain could also trouble their own relatives. Luca-Antono Viterbi addressed verses to the ghost of his brother Petro, who appeared to him in the prison at Bastia in 1821. In Grimaldi's story, 'The Fiancée of the Niolo', the girl is torn between her obligation as sole surviving relative to avenge her murdered brother and her wish to get married. When the latter option appeared to be about to prevail, 'it seemed to her that the bloody corpse of her brother rose up before her to censure her weakness'. There is evidence, too, of more extreme sanctions applied by ghosts against defaulting kin. According to Comiti, if a victim is not appeased by blood, 'the soul of the dead man becomes hostile and pursues its living relatives [and] the only escape from its vindictiveness is to carry out vengeance for it'. In the words of Carrington, 'the living must kill if they hope to keep alive', and, adding another dimension, she relates the opinion of a middle-aged landowner: 'Of course one would be afraid of meeting the murdered man in the next world if one had failed in one's duty to him here on earth.' Hogg suggests that these beliefs survived the decline of feuding and may even have been exacerbated by it. He was told at Fozzano that there was 'a specific type of dead man who becomes a *revenant*: he is the lost soul of someone killed in the course of an inter-family feud. His advent is ... greatly feared, for ... people believe that death will soon come, without other explanation, to some member of a family whose threshold is crossed by one of these unwelcome guests.' Such ghosts were most likely, of course, to cross the thresholds of the houses of their surviving kinsfolk and, by the time at which Hogg was writing in the 1970s, these were unlikely to have avenged a killing in any direct way.[193]

Belief in these supernatural sanctions clearly reinforced the imperative to take revenge and served to underpin the whole system of blood vengeance.[194] At the same time, it objectified the links between the living and the dead. Vuillier wrote in 1891 of a widow with a revenge to fulfil: 'Her husband was not dead to her, so long as she had his death to avenge.' Concomitantly, while a family had a death to avenge, its members were themselves socially dead.

> If someone is killed in Corsica [wrote Bartoli] his death is a blot on his family; and his relatives are dishonoured; they cannot go outside without feeling shame ... it will seem to them that everyone is looking at them and reproaching them with the murder which they have not avenged ... In effect, a person who has not avenged a close relative who has been killed or a girl who has been seduced can no longer appear in public; no one will speak to him; he must keep quiet ... he is himself dead.

Here it is significant that an accidental death, which also deprived the victim of the proper rites, had the same effect of dishonouring or disgracing a family, though to a lesser degree. It is important, too, to note that the link between religious sanction and social situation or action was noted by contemporaries. Sorbier stated in the mid-nineteenth century that 'the vendetta is a kind of religion ... The Corsican takes revenge ... because the affront which he has suffered separates him from his peers, and renders him impure, like a social excommunicate.'[195]

We turn now to a more detailed consideration of further aspects of vengeance killing, which some observers regarded as inexplicably horrific, but which make sense in the framework of our discussion of religious sanctions and of relations between the living and the dead.

Some killers took precautions to ensure that their victims died in a state of grace (in the orthodox religious sense), presumably in order to mitigate any supernatural retaliation from them. The spirit of a person who accomplished at least some of the last rites would be less dangerous than one who had omitted them all. Thus after Massoni and his associates had shot and apparently mortally wounded Antono Durilli in 1848 or 1849, Massoni told the others not to finish him off immediately, saying: 'People will find him; he will be able to make his last confession and remit his soul to God.' Again, Massoni told another victim to make his act of contrition before he was shot.[196] However, in other cases, a contrary motivation is evident, though based on the same general assumptions. According to G. de Champgrand, writing in the mid-eighteenth century, some Corsicans wanted to kill their enemies precisely while they were in a state of mortal sin, so that they would suffer eternally after death.[197]

The same concerns seem to have underlain another practice. Those engaged in feuding sometimes mutilated or otherwise mistreated the corpses of their victims. The body of a man from Cargiaca was found in 1809 'cut in half and with the viscera divided into four parts'.[198] During the feud at Frasseto, the bodies of several members of the Franceschi family suffered in the same kind of way. In 1832, the Antona bandits 'horribly mutilated' the bodies of Maria-Francesco Franceschi and Antono Mariani. In 1846, Giovan-Natale Franceschi's head was cut off and his viscera ripped out, while the body of his 14-year-old son and another relative were similarly treated. A press report refers to 'the heart and lungs of these three unfortunate victims ... being hung on the branches of shrubs in the maquis', and suggests also that their sexual organs had been cut off. The bodies of victims might also be burned. The Durilli burned the body of Francesc'-Antono Grimaldi in 1848. Bodies were found at Cuttoli-Corticchiato in 1893, which had been burned after the brains and entrails had been removed from them.[199] Clearly matter-of-fact considerations of avoiding detection may have sometimes entered into the thinking of those who carried out such actions, but their gestures were usually in fact demonstrative and other explanations must be sought. Cremation was totally alien to Corsican funeral customs, as we have seen, and may have been believed to relegate the spirit of the victim to an uneasy after-life, if it did not annihilate it altogether. Mutilation was much more central to the practice of the blood feud and requires further elucidation.

Singers of *voceri* frequently called for the bodies of those responsible for killings to be mutilated in particular ways. This was a main theme in one of the most popular and most published *voceri*, 'O Matteo di la surella'. 'Why do you wait, Cecc' Anto?', the sister of one victim asks the brother of the other. 'Rip out the guts / Of Riccioto and of Mascarone, / And throw them to the crows! / O let a flock of crows / Eat their flesh and strip their bones! / ... O Mattè / I wish I could see in a basket / The bowels of the priest [a relative of the killers]! / I wish I could tear them with my teeth / And squeeze and feel them with my hands!'[200] In another, a mother, whose son has been killed, declares: 'Seize the murderer. / I hunger for his heart! / Bring me his entrails; / I want to throw them to the crows! / Tear out his eyes; / They have looked at my child.'[201]

Such mutilation has been practised in most societies where homicide has had some kind of positive value, from Ancient Greece and America to medieval and modern Europe, where, of course, it was a prominent feature of the established penal system before the mid-nineteenth century.[202] More particularly, it occurs in other modern feuding societies.[203] A number of suggestions have been made as to the significance of mutilation for these societies, some of which are helpful also in the Corsican context. First, mutilation of the corpse may be seen as an extreme retaliatory action. The call by *voceratrici* to disembowel or otherwise mutilate the corpses of the murderers of their relatives was triggered off by the sight of the victims' wounds and followed the pattern of balanced response. In 'O Matteo di la surella,' his sister notes, after calling for the mutilations: 'They have shot lead / Into Matteo's brain / And into Pasquale's lungs, / Worse than if they were sparrows.' In another *vocero* of a sister for a brother, she calls for the hearts and guts of his killers to be 'ripped out' and, at the same time, she dwells on the brother's wounds: 'I can see your chest with the hole in it, / Your discoloured lips, / Your mouth full of dust; / I see your wounds, O my brother! / And I will not live long enough / To destroy you all, you wretches! / ... [and to] see you disembowelled.'[204] Needless to say, in addition to reflecting actual practice, such wishes were often purely expressive.

Secondly, it is probably right to see mutilation, when carried out, as a further means of dishonouring one's victim. In Shakespeare's *Romeo and Juliet*, it will be recalled, Paris supposes that Romeo has entered the Capulet tomb 'to do some villainous shame / To the dead bodies' of Tybalt and of Juliet.[205] Here a trophy might be taken for subsequent display.[206] It may also be the case, as Lawson suggests it was for contemporary Greece, that mutilation was a means by which 'the murderer sought to deprive his victim of the power to exact vengeance for his wrongs', the mode there being to cut off the hands and feet and place them under the armpits or tie them round the chest.[207] It should be noted, however, that elsewhere mutilation might increase the danger represented by the victim's ghost.[208]

Two particular forms of mutilation are prominent in the Corsican sources. First, as we have seen in discussing false testimony in Chapter 10, betrayal or alleged perjury might be punished by mutilation of the responsible organs. The Antona of Frasseto were accused of 'burning off the ears of their victims and filling their mouths with grass'. Giovan-Paolo Chiari was killed in the Fiumorbo in 1885 by the Colombani gang. His eyes were gouged out and his tongue and nose were cut, to indicate that he had been killed for trying to betray the bandits.[209] A serenade published in the mid-nineteenth century shows that this practice might be extended, in fantasy at least, to other contexts. The man threatens that if the girl leaves him he will become violent and commit murders: 'I want the tongues of mediators [who might try to prevent this] / Cut in bits and fed to the dogs.'[210]

Secondly, ears were cut off as a humiliation and to serve as trophies. As we have seen, Carlo Bozzi of Pila-Canale had his ears cut off before he was killed by his enemies in 1797, and these were kept by the latter and shown to Bozzi's mother on several occasions. Bozzi's body and that of another victim were also stripped as a further humiliation. According to Marcaggi, F.-A. Grimaldi of Marignana was killed in the late 1840s by Domenico-Maria Durilli, at the request of the widow of a certain Negri, whom Grimaldi had killed. Durilli cut off one of Grimaldi's ears and presented it to the widow after the deed was done. Ears were also cut off people who were not killed, usually those of low status for whom killing was not perhaps deemed appropriate, or who represented an important family in the way that its dogs or livestock might have done. Caisson notes here that cutting or marking the ears was a common way of indicating the ownership of animals.[211] In the feud between the Multedo of Calcatoggio and a leading family from Sari-d'Orcino, one of the latter's servants had his ear cut off and this was then nailed to the church door. Teodoro Poli, we have seen, cut off the ears of three Italians whom he suspected of betraying him. Concomitantly, mutilating a notable like this might be a particular way of dishonouring him. The Multedo again captured Justice of the peace Domenico Casanova, beat him and cut off his left ear before letting him go. A further demonstration of the association of this form of mutilation with honour is provided (in a ludic and fictional context) by a tale collected at Santa-Lucia-di-Tallano in 1882, in which two men wager that the first to get angry will have his ears cut off by the other.[212]

We return now to the broader problem of the links between the dead body, vengeance and the spirit of the victim, of which mutilation forms only a part. It is sometimes reported that corpses were stabbed after death, for example, at Mezzana in 1797 or at Santa-Maria-Figaniella in 1801.[213] Such actions may be seen simply as the gestures of those overcome by uncontrollable feelings of hatred, but other meanings are possible. They could be intended to disarm the spirit of the victim along the lines suggested by Lawson for Greece. But, without excluding these explanations, stabbing the corpse is, in the first instance, more plausibly related to the need to shed blood, which, we have already shown, was the central ritual element of the vendetta in Corsica. Apart from stabbing corpses some time after death, it was very commonly reported that victims of vengeance killings were both shot and stabbed. For example, Nunzio-Maria and Giacomo-Paolo Acquatella of Bisinchi were killed in 1801 by the Vecchioni. They were shot and then 'had their throats cut with a dagger'. The mayor of Ciamannacce reported the discovery in 1824 of the body of Francesco Renucci, who 'had been killed with a firearm and had also had his throat cut'.[214]

Thirst for blood is a common metaphor in *voceri* and other sources. 'I am thirsty for blood ... / I am hungry for carnage!', sang the sister of Matteo. It was also fairly common for enemies and bandits to be described as 'bloodthirsty', and this was not a mere hackneyed expression. Before an actual revenge killing at Silvareccio in 1812, Giovan-Gavino Casalta was reported to have declared that 'he would drink the blood of his enemies before the day was out'.[215]

Actual physical contact with the blood of victims was also usual. Cloths were dipped in it and kept as memorials. Mérimée cites a *vocero*: 'Where is his dear daughter? / Let her buy a handkerchief / And dip it in his blood, / And let her wear it round her neck / When she is tempted to laugh.' This relates of course to the customs of keeping the bloody clothes of victims and of daubing the face and hands of would-be avengers with their blood. Faure and others report that mourning women 'kissed' or 'sucked the wounds of victims of violence'.[216] This was presumably in order to obtain liquid blood for the purposes just mentioned, but the practice also applies to the victim the treatment that women wished to perform on the killer.

The idiom of blood, real and figurative, brought together a number of related notions that were central to the feud.[217] Extending its biological meaning, the term 'blood', *sangue*, stood for the family, the kindred.[218] So Angelo-Francesco Franceschi pleaded with the Antona bandits in 1836 not to kill him or his son, reminding them 'that he was their cousin and that the same blood flowed in their veins'. Massoni's sister, while evoking the power of the bandit's own spilled blood in her *vocero*, addresses a relative of Saverio, 'who is of our blood'.[219] Killing a person thus released the element in him or her that represented not only individual life but also, in the words of Djilas, the 'life that had flowed together from generations of forbears [and which] ... coursed in all members of the clan'.[220] The shedding of blood was also highly visible, as we have noted, and proclaimed the disgrace and dishonour of the victim's kindred in the most obvious manner. 'O Matteo,' sang his sister, 'With your precious blood / They have washed the square, / They have bathed the enclosure.' 'The blood of Giovan-Petro / Is spattered over the plain,' sang his mother, in another *vocero*.[221] The shedding of the blood of one kindred thus doubly required that the blood of the killer or killers be shed in return. In Corsica, as in other feuding societies, a feud was an 'enmity of blood'[222] and the notion of the 'debt of blood' was strong. Filippi cites the proverb: 'Blood demands blood,' and 'having a debt of blood to pay' was a common phrase used to indicate that a family had a killing or another serious offence to avenge. Here we encounter again the notion of balance or reciprocity. Before ambushing and killing a gendarme in 1830, the bandit Ricciardi was heard to say: 'He has upset my blood; I must upset his in return!' And fine calculations could be made within this framework. Réalier-Dumas refers to a case in 1817 in which a Captain Morelli was killed at Bonifacio. 'The people of the Fiumorbo, who claimed to be his compatriots, swore to avenge his death upon someone from the best circles in the town: "A noble blood is required", they said, "to avenge the blood of Morelli properly."'[223]

But the concept of reciprocity went much deeper than this and has other aspects, which take us back to the sphere of the dead. First, in a patrilineal context, identifying the kindred with the blood meant that killing a woman in revenge was both inappropriate and ineffective, since her blood was 'without virtue'.[224] Secondly, there are suggestions that in Corsica, as in Albania,[225] it was felt necessary to literally replace the blood which the kindred had lost through a murder of one of its members, by making offerings of blood in a variety of ways, of which vengeance killing was only one. Here the clawing of the face at the funeral may be seen as a kind of blood-offering. Such a notion would also seem to be connected with the theme of symbolic cannibalism which occurs in *voceri* and other sources. The bodies of those freshly killed, relatives but more often enemies, were referred to as meat. In a *vocero* for a man from Loreto-di-Casinca, killed by his cousin, his mother addresses another surviving son: 'Mercantio, dear to your mother, / Write to your brothers / That we have fresh meat / Without going to the butcher's.' Old Signora Bartoli told a member of the Durazzo family, her enemies, after the ambush at Tunichilla: 'Run quickly ... there is fresh meat for you over there.' And the same expression is recorded in other sources.[226] Moreover, what is here implicit could become explicit. In a dispute between the Ottaviani and the Antonsanti of Carragno in 1808, one of the Antonsanti arrived on the scene saying: 'Do you want to eat us?', to which a voice replied: 'We eat bread and not men.' Again, Corsicans not infrequently referred to their enemies as 'cannibals'. Most obviously, the theme appears in *voceri* and laments. 'We will make tripe and sausages / Of our enemies,' boasted a grandmother. I want to see his heart / In pieces,' declared a widow of her husband's killer. 'A morsel in the morning, / A morsel at night, / I will consume ... / I hunger for his entrails.' Don Giacomo Chiaverini, a bandit who had the deaths of two brothers to avenge, expressed this wish for his enemy: 'I hope that his blood / Will redden the ground. / I want to dip in it / All the clothes I am wearing. / I want to kill him / With fury, if I can, / And then disembowel him / And take his heart. / I want to eat it / To avenge my honour.'[227]

Here, as with the notion of the relatives' thirst for blood, it is possible to see both the principles of reciprocity and of countering pollution at work. 'Dishonour in Corsica', wrote Lorenzi de Bradi, 'is washed away by blood'.[228] And the survivors' need for flesh or blood corresponds to or stands in for the need of the victim. As in the Balkans or in modern Greece, where the victim might become a vampire,[229] in Corsica the spirit of the slain needed blood, and, in shedding the blood of his killer, the avenger was satisfying this need. Here it will be recalled that it was imperative to put out water for the dead on All Souls' Night or other occasions, so that they could slake their thirst. More directly, *voceri* refer to blood being 'drunk' by the earth,[230] in which the dead were generally laid. We are familiar from Homer with the notion that the lifeless and helpless dead may be temporarily reanimated by providing them with blood, that of sacrificial animals or that of those who brought about their deaths. Tiresias, himself reanimated in this way, tells Odysseus: 'Any ghost to whom you give access to the blood will hold rational speech with you, while those whom you reject will leave you and retire.'[231] In Corsica, of course, animal sacrifice was never employed as a substitute for homicide[232] but, with this proviso, the Homeric model demonstrates how shedding blood in vengeance within such a system would not only placate the dead but also restore friendly and familiar relations with them.

All of this emphasizes the religious dimension of the feud, recalling Durkheim's comment that in Corsica 'offences against the family were regarded as sacrilege'.[233] The dead themselves required that they be avenged with the blood of their killers or offenders. Without diminishing the significance of this sanction on the religious or supernatural plane, we may point to the way in which it converged with the family's defence of its material interests. In a case in 1856, Carlo-Giuseppo Carlotti of Poggio-di-Venaco 'had been heard making the most terrible threats [against a man with whom he had a dispute about a chestnut grove] and to have announced that the chestnuts must be watered with blood'.[234] Here the linkage between landownership and burial place, which we discussed in the previous section, has become transposed to one between ownership and shedding blood. In each case, death sets the seal on property.

IV

We come now to a final and complicating feature of Corsican beliefs concerning death. As has been the case elsewhere, death was not regarded in traditional Corsican society as a 'natural' or accidental phenomenon.[235]

First, deaths were announced by signs or omens.[236] 'When you were ill,' a daughter sang in a *vocero* to her father, 'The killer bird [owl] cried out / And your soul flew away / At his sad cry.' In another *vocero*, a wife compares herself to a bird of ill-omen announcing a death; and Ortoli refers to a bird (*malucella*) crying on three consecutive nights on the roof of a sick person's house.[237] In addition to an owl screeching, such omens included a dog barking in the night, a drum or drums heard beating at night (sometimes at midnight), a strange light shining in or on a house or in the church, the appearance of a person's 'double' or *spirdo*, a vision of a death-bed scene or a wake, and a vision of the dead in a group either going to a place of burial to recite a rosary for the person about to join them or visiting a particular house. In the last instance, the dead were dressed in the robes of members of a confraternity, and were known variously as the *cumpagnia*, the *squadra d'Arrozza* or *d'Erode*, or the *mumma* or *mubba*.[238] Corsicans also had more general presentiments of death. In a case in 1853, for example, reference was made to a man having had such a presentiment and having therefore turned back from a rendezvous, thus avoiding an ambush.[239]

Secondly, it was believed in many places that all deaths in a community were predicted and 'caused' by a person or persons who had this specific role to fulfil. They were known as *culpadori*, *culpamorti*, *acciatori* or, most commonly, *mazzeri*, that is 'strikers' or killers.[240] They were distinct from diviners or healers (*signadori*) and from witches (*streghi*). Actual people in the village, men or women, young or old, knew themselves to be and were generally recognized as *mazzeri*. *Mazzeri* went hunting at night, in dreams or as 'doubles', since their bodies did not usually leave their beds. They hunted either alone or in groups, and their hunting grounds were the wildest parts of the maquis and especially near rivers or springs. They found and killed the first animal which they saw. This was often a wild boar, but it might be another wild, or even a domestic, animal, or a bird. As they slung their quarry on to their backs, the *mazzeri* recognized by its face or its voice that it was the 'double' or *spirdo* of someone in the village, for the 'doubles' of non-*mazzeri* also travelled about at night. The person so recognized would die shortly after the hunt and always within the year. Illness might be caused by simply wounding the animal. Male *mazzeri* usually killed their victims with guns, and women with sticks or knives, or 'even with their own teeth like hunting dogs'. Some sources refer to *mazzeri* actually turning themselves into dogs or other animals. Vuillier writes of *mazzeri* killing people 'by drinking up their souls', if they encountered them 'at noonday in a solitary place'. Whatever the means, *mazzeri* only killed members of their own community. In some parts of Corsica, it was believed further that on one night in the year, usually the night of 31 July–1 August, the *mazzeri* from different villages met to fight each other, using normal weapons or in one case stems of asphodel. Those killed in this dream-conflict would themselves die during the coming year. This belief seems to reflect suspicion or antagonism between contiguous villages from different cultural areas. Some *mazzeri* were 'odd' and were regarded with hostility, but most seem to have led normal lives, at least during the day, working, marrying, having children, and so on, though they were treated 'with a certain respect'.

There are analogies here with beliefs about causing deaths by sorcery found in other societies. The Azande believe that witches destroy their victims in dream-happenings, in which the witches assume the shape of animals. The victims have the dreams, but it is thought that the 'souls' of the witches do roam about while they are asleep. Among the Garia, 'the sorcerer temporarily, but at will, becomes invisible or transforms himself into an animal and "shoots" missiles into the body of his victim'. A single 'shooting' produces illness and several death. Among the Nayars, certain persons are believed to be able to use the power of patron spirits 'in order to take the form of a bull, dog, jackal or other animal. In this form he touches his foe in the night, causing him to fall ill with terror, to become insane, or even to die.'[241] But unlike such sorcerers or witches, *mazzeri* have no evil intentions towards their victims. Most accounts stress that the role of the *mazzeri* was involuntary and implied no hostility. Chiari noted that they would sometimes have to kill close relatives, though they sought to avoid this, by warning them and by endeavouring 'to live on the best of terms with them when they are conscious, so as not to breed a subconscious ill-will which could be fatal'. It is also reported that some *mazzeri* sought to be cured or exorcized by undergoing special rituals of penance in the church, sometimes on Good Friday. *Mazzeri* were simply the agents of a mysterious power and were thus not held responsible for deaths in the village, although they brought them about. This contrasts not only with sorcery, but also with the system of blood vengeance, which makes a whole circle of kin responsible for a death brought about by one of its members.

There is some uncertainty about how people became *mazzeri*. Some accounts say that the role was hereditary or that one could be initiated into it, which would seem to contradict the idea that the *mazzeri*'s activity was involuntary. More commonly, *mazzeri* are said to be persons who had not been properly baptized, or whose godparents were *mazzeri*. They were thus outside or in opposition to the Christian community, although they might formally attend church and take the sacraments.

Mazzeri beliefs were found in many parts of Corsica, and particularly in some villages and districts, where there was a high incidence of feuding. These include the Sartenais (especially La Rocca), the Fiumorbo, and the Niolo. The beliefs were generally absent in the Capo Corso and the Balagna, where feuding was also rare or non-existent. It is therefore legitimate to ask what connection, if any, existed between the two.

Carrington asserts that the beliefs relating to the *mazzeri* and those relating to the spirits of the dead 'cannot be co-ordinated' and 'derive from different layers of culture'. Both are agents of death, but while the *mazzeri*, as we have seen, kill without animosity or volition, the dead 'are spiteful and cunning'. However, links between the beliefs associated with *mazzeri* and beliefs about the dead and funeral ritual are not hard to find. When a person dies, for example, as Ettori noted, mirrors are covered over, lest seeing the image or the 'double' of the deceased provoke another death in the entourage. *Mazzeri* are not baptized or not properly baptized, and we have seen that *voceratrici* sang of undoing their baptism in order to achieve vengeance. *Mazzeri* hunt in the wild places and by water, where the spirits of the dead are also found. Bartoli reported that the latter could take the form of animals, for example, that of hares, and that they 'travelled in the company of witches, looking for a victim. If they met someone, they would strike him or her', which meant that that person would die. Casanova explicitly states here that *mazzeri* joined the spirits of the dead in their nocturnal activities. The battles between *mazzeri* from different villages take place on the old Day or Night of the Dead, and in the Cruzzini the fires lit in front of houses on this occasion were said to be intended 'to burn the *mazzeri*'. The *squadra d'Arrozza* announced a death or deaths like the *mazzeri*, and they sought victims among those whom they encountered, often at night and in the wild.[242]

There seems indeed to be some correspondence, if not identity, between the three kinds of 'killer', the *mazzeri*, the spirits of the dead, and those with a vengeance to fulfil or a ghost in the family to placate. The *mazzeri* belief brought the same predictability and ineluctability to normal deaths that the system of blood vengeance brought to deaths by violence. The vengeance killing thus provided a model for all deaths, or vengeance killing and 'natural' death were brought within the same conceptual system. In rural Greece, as Du Boulay explains, dying is similarly conceptualized as being killed and having one's blood spilled by Charós or the Angel of Death.[243] In Corsica, death was often personified in *voceri*, held responsible for those whom it had 'killed' and even threatened with revenge.[244] In contrast to situations where death may be attributed to sorcery, with the sorcery feud as the most extreme example,[245] the element of uncertainty as to the agent of death is removed. But since that agent is not held responsible, the need for retaliation is also excluded. Vengeance killing is thus to some extent contained and reserved to the secular everyday world, with one important exception: the requirement to placate the spirit of a person killed by violence by taking another life by violence in return. This requirement was expressed, we have seen, in the idiom of blood, and may be seen as an assertion of the link with the ancestors, thus boosting and strengthening, indeed expressing, the cohesion of the kindred across the generations.

Mazzeri beliefs may be seen here as another expression of community, whereas feuding represents the pursuit of family interests and values. The *mazzeri* serve the whole community, representing the view that 'death comes to all', 'death is not partial, / But straightforward and sincere with everyone!'[246] Moreover, like the *benandanti* of the Friuli studied by Ginzburg with whom they have much in common,[247] they serve only the community to which they belong, and they represent that community in annual symbolic conflict with other communities, where communal well-being is at stake. As Carrington has stressed, too, *mazzeri* acting as *mazzeri* are indifferent to family ties and loyalties, which are otherwise so pervasive in Corsican society. They share this characteristic with the *squadri d'Arrozza*, whose behaviour is autonomous and unaffected by any ties with the living.

Mazzeri beliefs also have the function of regulating deaths. The *mazzero* seems to be analogous to the 'watcher of the churchyard' found in many parts of Britain or to the Breton *ankou*. The 'watcher of the churchyard' was a role taken on by any person buried there 'until such time as he was relieved of his task by the interment of another corpse'. The watcher did not go to his rest but stayed in the parish in order 'to summon all those ... who were about to die'. This was done by the watcher travelling 'by night through the countryside in a cart, the sound of which was a sure omen of death', and stopping outside the house of the person summoned. The role of the *ankou* was very similar. The *ankou* was the last person to die in a parish during the year. He also travelled about at night in a cart, whose sound was an omen of death. But the *ankou* touched his victims or sometimes struck them with a scythe made of human bones, and some accounts make it clear that the *ankou* did not simply announce deaths that had been preordained; he actually caused them. Moreover, the *ankou* was sometimes regarded as an independent supernatural being rather than the ghost of a particular deceased person.[248] Attention may be drawn, too, to a custom reported by Chiari for Corsica:

> On All Souls' Night, the tradition is that before going to bed the youngest girl of the house has to stand on the threshold of the house and call out the names of all the members of her family and those of her near relatives; and she has to be extremely careful not to forget anybody, for any person left uncalled is supposed to die within the year.

If there are no girls in the house, a boy may perform the role, and if there are no children, an adult.[249] Here we can see the same regulating mechanism represented by *mazzeri* beliefs on the community level operating within the family, with the latest recruit acting to predict the next to die, almost as if the one replaced the other.

Such customs and beliefs introduced conceptual order into an area that was inherently unpredictable. Sorcery could have the same function but generated its own feuding and consequent disruption, offset usually by the rapid payment of compensation. *Mazzeri* beliefs, which admit the supernatural causing of deaths but exclude the disruptive consequences of this, may thus be seen as a necessary complement to actual feuding which allowed no payment of compensation. Envy, ill-will and conflict in Corsican society were thus channelled into only one of two alternatives. Actual feuding caused real local disruption, as we have seen, but by providing a model for all deaths, it also contributed in an important way to the creation of general religious order.

] 14 [

Conclusion

In this chapter, we will try to draw together and re-emphasize some of the main conclusions of our study.

First, feuding in Corsica was part of a wider complex of conflict, which occurred with some frequency between communities and within families as well as between families. Conflict within families reflected tensions inherent in the performance of roles. Marriage-making also had a strong competitive element akin to feuding. These different forms of conflict were complementary. Kinship solidarity, which was threatened by intrafamilial conflict, was reinforced by feuding, while community solidarity, threatened by feuding, was reinforced by conflict with other villages. This confirms but refines the view that feuding generally could have a socially integrative function at one 'segmental' level, while being disruptive at another, and lends support to the thesis that feuding may be seen as a means by which conflict is contained.[1]

The basis of conflict was always competition over access to or control over scarce material resources, but this was translated into an honorific idiom which took on a large degree of autonomy. This is relevant to scholarly debate over the definition of feud, which we have so far avoided. As Boehm notes for Montenegro, the idea of feud as a series of retaliatory actions of specific form, length or intensity is usually one imposed on an area of native behaviour from outside (like banditry). Montenegrins perceive and think of being 'in blood', and their notion is not related to the duration or the level of violence of the conflict concerned. Being 'in blood', and the same is true of the Corsican state of 'enmity', refers to both low-level or short-term disputes and to homicidal conflicts lasting many years. It can also refer to a relationship where conflict is only potential. The external form which the resentment or conflict happens to take is less important than the ethos which informs and inspires it, and which is couched in terms of honour.[2] In Corsica, one can say too that the distinction drawn by Peters and Black-Michaud between finite and 'endless' feud is one of circumstance and not of principle.[3] This is not to say that Corsicans did not perceive and experience the very different effects and consequences of more or less serious enmities, and we have seen that feuds were 'declared'.

Germane here is the uneven incidence of feud and conflict across societies. Why do people in some societies normally settle or try to settle their differences by using

415

force, while in others violence is either absent or deliberately avoided?[4] We cannot
hope to encompass here a problem which involves well-nigh every human grouping,
but a number of relevant points may be made. The Corsican example shows that
demographically buoyant communities making extensive use of resources over a
wide area can tolerate levels of violence that would be difficult to live with in more
restricted habitats. It also suggests that conflict may be intensified where land and
other resources are reduced or access to them limited, or where population increases
in proportion to resources. The cultural stress on honour, moreover, militated
against the peaceful settlement of disputes, which were inherent in the system of land
use. However, against this, even in Corsica where so much stress was laid on honour
and where material compensation for injuries was not acceptable, there were well-
established procedures for preventing and resolving conflicts, and there also existed
a variety of modes of conflict, not all of which were violent.

Again, feuding is not unregulated conflict. Rather, in intensely competitive
societies, it is precisely a regulator of conflict, a system of primitive law and
restitutive justice, providing sanctions against anti-social behaviour in the absence of a strong central authority. It operates to a degree here as a deterrent to
violence, although it must probably be brought into action from time to time in
order to maintain this function. Its success also requires the promotion of vindictiveness and the bearing of grudges as a cultural trait, though one may agree with
Rivers that it is essentially feuding which explains the high value set on revenge
rather than vice versa.[5] The Corsican example illustrates, too, that there may be
a considerable gap between the customary 'law' of the feud and actual practice,
for instance in the area of respecting immunities. Like any increase in the incidence of violent feuding, this may be a pathological phenomenon, a sign of
decadence and of the collapse of the traditional system of sanctions, associated
usually with 'modernization' and state incorporation. But this is not the only
possible reason for the gap between theory and practice. Feuds in the traditional
context could have a tendency to escalate and to degenerate into more extreme
forms (the 'bad feud'). Nor should the truism that feuding cannot in general be
allowed to become too disruptive obscure the fact that particular feuds could
produce local situations of very serious social and economic dislocation.[6]

The general argument that fear of escalation and disruption moves actors in
conflicts towards compromise[7] fits the Corsican situation with all its paradoxical
force, given the reluctance there to contemplate material compensation for homicide. Peacemaking was institutionalized and peace treaties were being made well
into the modern period. This supports the view that feuding takes place essentially within 'jural communities'.[8] Despite distaste for blood payment, even when
cast in honorific form, a clear sense of needing to achieve a balance, even of
vengeance as an exchange, was present.[9]

The same flexibility appears when the relationship of feuding and action in
the courts is considered. These may be regarded as radically and exclusively
alternative modes of dispute settlement and the 'punishment' of offenders. But in
nineteenth-century Corsica, as elsewhere, the two modes co-existed and inter-
meshed over a long period of time. Some students like to see feuding as a way of
minimizing or settling conflict between two parties, where no third party exists
to mediate or to impose peace.[10] We have seen that third parties were needed in

Corsica, as elsewhere, to settle feuds, and the role of third party could be assumed by the representatives of central authority. It is true as a very general proposition that feuding is in the end incompatible with 'modernization' and the development of the State, or even 'that the higher the level of political complexity in a society, the less frequently feuding is found'.[11] But the process by which one form of justice is replaced by another is itself complex and goes through a number of stages that are not irreversible. The two systems may exist side by side without interaction. Then, rulers or governments, unable or unwilling to ban feuding, may intervene to encourage settlements within the feuding context and to generally regulate the system.[12] Once external interference of this kind reaches a certain level, it may exacerbate rather than limit feuding, since it undermines the traditional controls on the old system of sanctions before supplying an effective replacement. One can see this process in operation in modern Corsica.[13]

Like most modern European examples of feuding, that in Corsica was mainly a rural phenomenon, associated with a traditional 'backward' society. But Corsica also demonstrates that this association is to some extent accidental. Feuding was also found in the towns[14] and among the élite, and it was a special feature, together with banditry, of the crisis period from around 1880 to around 1930, when the traditional economy collapsed. We saw in Chapter 2 that feuds usually involved the leading families of the villages and towns where they took place, and at the start of the nineteenth century these comprised the highest stratum of all. Here we may point to the well-known enmity between the Pozzo di Borgo and the Bonapartes of Ajaccio.[15] This accords with evidence that feuding elsewhere in the Mediterranean region at the same time was a mode of power-struggle indulged in by the 'gentry'.[16] The connection of feuding with an élite milieu in Corsica may help to explain its emphasis on honour, since, where such conflict was of wider provenance, it seems that its honorific aspects (for example, the refusal to accept blood money or the absolute obligation to pursue revenge) were most pronounced among, if not restricted to, the élite.[17] Over the course of the nineteenth century, the highest stratum ceased to be directly involved in feuding and its members competed instead via patronage and the manipulation of the political and administrative system.[18] The two modes were not, however, mutually exclusive, and the introduction of formal political democracy could also exacerbate violent conflict.

Does this mean that feuding (with patronage) operated to smother group or class conflict, as Tarrow, for example, claims it did in southern Italy?[19] Certainly, in nineteenth-century Corsica there was little 'social homicide' or killing across the boundaries of social stratification.[20] There was sometimes an element of 'class struggle', however, in the competition within the élite, with new rising families seeking to oust older established ones via a combination of feud and political contest. Pomponi suggests further, from a Marxist perspective, that feuding can be the means by which a wider class struggle is expressed in a society dominated by patronage and clientship. In the conflict which broke out in Sartène following the July Revolution in 1830, the 'party' of the Roccaserra, the Durazzi and ex-Prefect Pietri represented the aristocracy, while that of the Ortoli, the Susini and another branch of the Pietri represented the bourgeoisie. The aristocrats rallied their mainly rural clients, while the bourgeois had the support of many of the artisans and rural workers living in the town. Similarly, in the villages, one party in a feud might represent herdsmen and another the sedentary peasants or large landowners.[21] Such class interests, however, were rarely, if at all, predominant, and they were not reflected at the ideological level.

A connection has been made by others between feuding and egalitarian elements in both ideology and social structure. Here feuding may be seen as a way of creating leadership in a non-stratified society, such as medieval Iceland.[22] Here, superiority relies directly on the exercise of force, and the model clearly applies to some Corsican situations. Feuding may also be seen as a means of asserting or maintaining egalitarianism in the face of the development of private property and state incorporation. Black-Michaud has written, with Corsica in mind, that feuding can 'provide a means of equalizing opportunity and sur-mounting the barriers created by economic differentiation even when those barriers are theoretically sanctioned and reinforced by an inefficient ... government [employing] ... a system of indirect rule, in which authority is wielded locally by those who are economically more favoured than others'.[23] This parallels interpretations of the ethos of honour, which see it as the preserver of a community of theoretical equals. By its criteria, status is accorded not on the basis of wealth but of male combativeness and female virtue.[24]

Our discussion of banditry reveals something of the same pattern. Banditry is an institution complementary to feuding and would not exist without it. It is a means by which men can obtain status and power through the use of force. However, in practice, banditry served the interests of the élite or factions within it, and this aspect of banditry became more pronounced later in the nineteenth century and early in this. If there was a tendency for banditry to assume some autonomy as a social or political force, it was certainly not as an instrument or expression of popular aspirations or protest.

Finally, the Corsican example directs attention to the religious sanctions which underlay feuding. Corsica was a society in which vengeance was a duty, a sacred obligation.[25] Under its auspices, violence and killing were given positive cultural meaning, and feuding there expressed and reflected the highest values: male courage, female honour, family loyalty and obligations to the dead, and the last of these was by no means the least.[26] In some societies, supernatural sanctions are the resort of the non-violent; in others they are a clear alternative to vio-lence;[27] but in Corsica they reinforced and legitimized violence. However, Corsica (like many other feuding societies) should be contrasted here with other kinds of society, in which violence, and homicide in particular, are given positive value. These would include those like the late Mexican civilizations, in which ritual killing was a central feature of 'state' religion,[28] and warrior groups, say in medieval Europe or in New Guinea, where killing was a sport-cum-initiation rite among men.[29] The high incidence of homicide in Corsica should be distin-guished, too, from that found in societies, not exclusively modern, where killing was an outcome of anomie or cultural breakdown.[30] To reiterate, homicide in Corsica was regulated via feuding. Indeed, *mazzeri* beliefs sought to regulate all deaths. And, while killing in certain circumstances was a duty, death and dealing death were never lightly regarded. The homicide was always in a state of misfor-tune and suffered accordingly, while his or her victim received not only funeral honours but help beyond the grave.

Appendices

Appendix 1. Analysis of tax register for Venzolasca, 1882 (ADHC E.18/18).

A

Family	Resident members on register, both sexes	Assessment in francs				
		Nil	0–10	10–50	50–100	Over 100
Albertini	34	9	10	11	2	2
Casabianca (and de C.)	4	–	–	–	–	4
Ciavaldini	8	2	2	4	–	–
Ciosi	10	4	3	1	1	1
Cipriani	2	–	–	–	1	1
Filippi	8	3	3	1	–	1
Grimaldi	7	1	1	1	1	3
Paoli	6	2	1	2	–	1
Petrignani	24	6	6	7	2	3
Sanguinetti	8	3	–	2	1	2

B

Tax assessment (francs)	No. in category	% of total	% of residents	Details
Over 2,000	2	0.3	0	Both Casabianca, res. Bastia.
1,000–2,000	7	1.2	0.7	Four non-res. Includes two Casabianca; widow of Giuseppo Petrignani, res. Bastia; and Ant. and Gius. Filippi.
500–1,000	6	1	0.5	Four non-res.; two Casabianca.
400–500	5	0.8	0.2	Four non-res. Includes one Casabianca; Col. Giovan-Felice Filippi, non-res.; Stefano Petrignani, advocate, res. Bastia; and Andrea Sanguinetti.
300–400	4	0.7	0.7	One non-res.; two Casabianca.
200–300	15	2.5	2.2	Six non-res. Includes two Albertini; and Giovan-Carlo Petrignani.
100–200	35	5.8	4.2	18 non-res. Includes one Casabianca; Giovan-Carlo Ciosi; Doria Grimaldi, née Filippi; Giovan-Andrea Paoli; Giovan-Matteo

B Tax assessment (francs)	No. in category	% of total	% of residents	Details
				Petrignani; C.-Luigi di Giacomo-Marco Petrignani; and Guglielmo Sanguinetti.
50–100	52	8.6	7.6	21 non-res.
10–50	191	31.6	29.5	71 non-res.
0–10	162	24.6	62	62 non-res.
Nil	125	20.6	29.5	5 non-res.

The total number of taxpayers on the register is 604, of which 198(33%) were non-resident. Among non-residents, 82% came from other villages, mainly in the Casinca; 13% lived in Bastia; and 5% outside Corsica.

Appendix 2. Corsican nicknames from judicial and other sources.

Name	Meaning	Place
Agnello	Lamb	Carpineto
Angeletto	Little angel	Nocario/Occhiatana
Animalonga, L'	Big beast	Cozzano
Antonietto	Little Tony	Lozzi
Aquila, L'	Eagle	Quenza
Augellone	Bird of ill-omen	Guagno
Bacucco	Little Bacchus (winebibber)	Pastoreccia?
Bagarisso?	?	Carbini
Baggliacone	Flashy?	Pancheraccia
Bajone	?	San-Andrea-di-Cervione
Barba-in-orecchie	Hair in the ears	?
Barbetta	Little beard	Guagno
Baritonnu	Baritone	South
Barone (2)	Baron, big shot (cheat?)	Fozzano; Lumio
Bastone	Stick	Pastoreccia
Battolo	Clapper of mill	Croce
Bavigliolo (2)	Slobberer?	Alata; Bastelicaccia
Bellacoscia (father and sons)	Fine (fruitful) thighs	Pentica
Bellamore	Black?	Bilia
Bianco/one (2)	Whitey/ish	Ciamannacce; Morosaglia
Biondino	Fine fellow	Porta
Borghello	?	Guagno
Borticase, La? (fem.)	?	Fozzano
Bracciamozzo	Crippled arm	?
Bracone	Great gossip	Casinca
Brandone	Like a sword	Taglio or Penta-di-Casinca
Bravino	Brave, good chap	Arbellara
Brico	Coffee-pot	South
Brusco (3)	Brusque	Guagno; Vico; ?
Bucchino (2)	Smoker (of cigarettes)	Santa-Lucia-di-Tallano; Poggio-di-Tallano

Name	Meaning	Place
Buccino (2)	Little pig, gossip?	Santa-Lucia-di-Tallano; Zicavo
Buciardone	Thrower of balls, bowls or bullets?	Olmiccia
Bujatello	Little liar	Evisa
Burrasca	Gust of wind	Figari
Cagione (2)	?	Bocognano; Zicavo/Cozzano
Calandro (2)	Lark, ninny	San-Gavino; Levie
Canielo or Cannello	Grafting tube (illiterate?)	Fozzano
Canino	Puppy	Isolaccio
Cannone	The cannon	Figari
Cantaretto	Skinny	Moca-Croce
Capobianco (2)	White head	Aullène; Cozzano
Cappato	Wearing cap	Taglio or Penta-di-Casinca
Capricinta	Goat with black stripe	Prunelli
Carlacchioli (brs)	Little Charles	Alata
Carlino	ditto	Fozzano
Carlotti	ditto	Serra-di-Fiumorbo
Carluccio	ditto	Corscia
Carne rosso	Red meat	Azzana
Caruccio?	?	Olmeto
Casamoze	Broken-down house	Cozzano
Cascioli?	Thighs	Pila-Canale
Cascioni	Coffers or coffins	Santa-Maria-Figaniella
Cataleta	Stretcher (in the way?)	Stazzona
Catone	Cato, of strict principles	Asco
Ceccecco	Little magpie or prattler, Frankie	Gavignano
Cecc(h)o (4)	ditto	Venzolasca; Pancheracia; Casinca; Rusio
Cecco Griggio	Grey Cecco	Croce
Ceccone (2)	Little magpie, Frankie	Orto; Lozzi
Ceccuccio	ditto	Olmeto
Cec(h)ino	Darling, nice fellow (ironic), or little blind man	Foce
Ceco	Blind	Aullène
Cesuccio	?	Pila-Canale
Chatiré?	Butterfly?	Olmeto
Chiaccharone	Braggart	Ortiporio
Chi(u)chino	Little donkey	Fozzano
Chiappato	?	Calcatoggio
Chiappina	Little thighs	Cozzano
Chicchio	Hairy?	Levie
Chiodono	Nailer?	Corte
Chirino or Chizione	?	Venzolasca
Ciacciarello	Light-weight, all talk	Sollacaro
Ciammannelli	Weak-willed	Muro
Ciancano	Talking rubbish	Brustico
Cianotte?	?	Monte (Casaconi)
Ciccarella (fem.)	Vivacious?	Ciamannacce
Cicchetto	ditto?	San-Andrea-di-Cervione
Ciccolo	Hairy	Valle-di-Rostino
Cioccio	Owl	Moca-Croce

Name	Meaning	Place
Cipriano	Made up like a woman	Ocana
Cirolo?	Waxy?	Zicavo
Cocco	Hair (in bun?)	Ocana
Conzaja?	?	Venzolasca
Corsicco	?	Moca-Croce
Corticone	From Corte	Fozzano/Santa-Maria-Figaniella
Costivecchio	Old hillside?	Zicavo
Cozzè	Corner?	Levie
Creatura	Animal	Novale
Croce	Wooden-leg?	Moca-Croce
Crudele	Cruel	Santa-Maria-Sicche
Cuiulo	?	ditto
Donzella	Young girl	Santa-Maria-Figaniella
Dragone	Dragoon	Campi
Fagiano/i	Pheasant	Fozzano
Falchino	Little falcon	Pila-Canale
Falconetto	ditto	Isolaccio
Falcuccio	ditto	Venzolasca
Falone	Blazer (fire)	Marignana
Faniano	?	Santa-Maria-Sicche
Farfarello	Little coltsfoot or butterfly	Olmeto
Faziano	Helping hand?	Sollacaro
Feliciolo/i (2)	Happy	Tox; Monte (Casaconi)
Felicone (2)	Dark-coloured dog	Piana; Antisanti
Ferrato	Iron-like, brave	Petreto-Bicchisano
Fiaccone	Fagged out?	Frasseto
Fiadone	Type of cake	Olmeto
Fiaducce	Loyal	Carcheto
Fiaschetto	Worn out?	?
Filippolo	Little Phil	Bustanico
Finmazzo	Little stick or cane	Sartène
Fiordispina/o	Thorn flower	Olmeto
Fissonello	Steadfast or Stick-in the mud?	San-Gavino (San Pietro)
Forchetta	Fork	Omessa
Formicolusa	Swarming with (parasites) or bubbling over?	Arbellara
Francichello	Frankie	Vescovato
Frasso	Place name	Levie
Fratato	Little friar	Frasseto
Frate (2)	Friar	Tavera; Serra
Frontiglione	Large brow?	Ota
Fumicone (2)	Smoky, reeking	Venzolasca; Porri
Gallochio	Little cock (with voice like)	Ampriani
Ghiacarone	Bad dog	?
Giacomello	Little James	Ocana
Giambatti	Legs (an itinerant singer)	Occhiatana
Gianballo/i	?	Moca-Croce
Giannetti	Sticks or pikes	Porri
Giovannone	Little John	Zicavo?
Griggio	Grey (haired)	Frasseto
Grillo	Grasshopper	Ocana
Grossitano, Il	The little big one	Grossa
Juda(s)	Judas	Olmeto

Name	Meaning	Place
Lazaretto	Pauper	Foce-di-Bilia
Lollo (2)	Bogeyman	Sartène; Albertacce
Loro/i	Dirty?	Ocana
Lucione	Little Luke	Venzolasca
Luiginiccio	Little Louis	Piedipartino
Macchiaiolo	Man of the maquis, i.e. bandit	Ozzano
Mafrino	?	Corte
Malafide	Bad faith	Olmeto
Malafina	Thin?	Levie
Malanotte (3)	Unfortunate	Pila-Canale; Palneca; Ciamannacce
Mandrano	Shepherd?	Cauro
Mangiapane	Bread eater	Grossa
Mannarino (2)	Domestic pig	Levie; Salice/Guagno
Marangoni	Diver	Cozzano
Marcuccio	Little Mark	Zerubia
Martinetto	Little Martin	Monaccia/Aullène
Mascarone	Dog or ox with dark face	?
Mastellone	Little tub	Cozzano
Matteccio	Little Matthew or loony	Piedipartino
Mazzole	Hammer	Frasseto
Migiskia	Smoked meat (long scar like)	Santa-Lucia-di-Tallano
Minanno	Grandpa	Bastelica
Minghitello	Little penis	Peri
Miniuccio	Kitten?	Arbellara
Minninello	?	Bastelica
Mischione	Mongrel or spotted	Venzolasca
Moco	Kind of vetch	Olmiccia
Moscaneva	Snowflake?	Porto-Vecchio
Mucchiolo	Like cistus	Near Corte
Muletto	Young mule	Cozzano
Muracchiolo	Fire-crest	Cozzano
Musascabrusa	Dangerous muse?	Orone-di-Carbini
Musello	?	Olmeto
Mustacciolo	Moustached	Bilia
Mutecchi	Dumb?	Ucciani
Muzzarello	Mutilated?	Bocognano
Muzzarettu	ditto	Grossa
Muzzichjata or Muziliaqui	With piece cut out of hair	Santa-Maria-Sicche
Muzzola?	?	Frasseto
Narbosa	Nervous	Petreto-Bicchisano
Nasino	Big nose	Sartène
Nasone	ditto	San-Martino-di-Lota
Nazzacchiolo	Bird catcher	Muro
Nino	Baby	Santa-Maria-Sicche
Niollo	From the Niolo or head-in-the-clouds	Olmeto
Orsone	Little Orso, little bear	Bilia
Pacchiolo	Glutton	Santa-Maria-Sicche
Palazzone	Big house	Venzolasca

Name	Meaning	Place
Pallone	Lump of flour	Poggio-di-Tallano
Pampalone	?	Loreto-di-Tallano
Pantalucci	Buffoon?	Bastelica
Panzano	Paunchy	Fozzano
Paoluccio	Little Paul	Vero
Paravicini	?	Levie
Pastorello	Little herdsman	Venzolasca
Pecchino	Little bee?	Ampriani
Pedone	Walker	Venzolasca
Pellegrino	Pilgrim (an orphan)	Peri
Pendino	Ear-ring	Piedicorte
Pentacosta	Pentacost	Pila-Canale
Peppo	?	Corte
Pernoco	?	Alesani
Persichetto	Little peach tree (pejorative)	Campile
Petrone	Strong man, Little Peter	Grossa
Peverino	Little pear	Oletta
Peverone (2)	Pimento	Ampriani; Serra-di-Fiumorbo
Picchiato	Pock-marked	Zicavo
Piedigialla, La (fem.)	Yellow feet	Olmiccia
Pierone	Little Peter	Albertacce
Pietrino	ditto	Levie
Piriggino	?	Isolaccio
Polverello	Dusty	Frasseto
Pontello	Little bridge	Bilia
Poppre?	?	Lozzi
Portovecchio	Place name	Renuso
Poveruomo	Pauper	Alata
Prugnolo	Plum tree	Serra
Quirino	?	Piedipartino
Racchione	Skulker or wearing amulet	Albertacce
Rambotto	Made of copper	Cargese
Rialto	Levee	Casinca?
Riccioto (2)	Burned over or beaten	Fiumorbo?
Ricisulto	?	Sari-d'Orcino
Risticoni	?	Fozzano
Rognoni il Venacesmo?	Kidneys or scabby from Venaco	Pozzi
Romano	Roman, i.e. had studied in Rome	Arbellara
Rosalicato	Itchy?	Vero
Rosso/i (5)	Red or red-haired (pejorative)	Pila-Canale; Bastelica; Ajaccio; Petreto-Bicchisano; Corte
Ruffino	Ruffian, reckless	Santa-Lucia-di-Tallano
Rusgo	Holly oak	Serra-di-Fiumorbo
Sampiero	Name of Corsican hero	Olmeto
Sarrello	?	Santa-Lucia-di-Tallano
Scalone	Stair?	Frasseto
Scambaronu	Old or ill-fitting shoe	?
Scarlino	?	Venzolasca

Name	Meaning	Place
Scazzolo	?	Appriciani
Segnatu-di-Diu	Marked by God, i.e. simple-minded	Levie
Seppa	Hedge?	Venzolasca
Stacchetta	White speck in the eye	Bocognano
Strimpoli	Out of tune?	Evisa
Tagliuccio	Cutting, good with knife or dagger	Orone-di-Carbini
Tamb(ell)one (2)	Blockhead?	San-Andrea; Fozzano
Tambino	?	Olmeto
Tangone	?	Carbuccia
Tappo or Toppo (2)	Cork, very small person	Altagène; Olmeto
Tattone (6)	Sly fellow	Loreto; Antisanti; Erbajola; Olmeta-di-Tuda; Asco; Perelli
Tavolone	?	Pila-Canale
Testa	Head	Peri
Titto	Mischievous	Matra
Tombababu	Hits his father	Bocognano
Toroso	Sturdy?	Corte
Torto or Storto (3)	Twisted	North; Vico; Prunelli
Tosti	Cheeky	?
Tramini	?	Lugo-di-Venaco
Tribulino (2)	Sufferer, always in trouble	Castineta; Porri
Trompetto	Trumpet	Olmeto
Tuscano	Tuscan	Porta (Ampugnani)
Tuzzino	Little morsel	Lugo-di-Nazza
Varrino	?	Petreto-Bicchisano
Vescovato	Place name	Niolo
Vicchiolo	Old fellow	Ocana
Zuanello	Wearing garters?	Calcatoggio
?	Loony	Albitreccia
?	Wild man	Olmo

Only three on the list are women's names, which reflects the bias of the judicial records.

Analysis of the 209 names whose meaning is established reveals that 40% refer to psychological or social attributes, 26% to physical attributes, 17% to names of animals, birds or plants, and 4% to place of origin. A further 8% are diminutive Christian names and the rest are miscellaneous. The categories have been treated as if they are distinct, though in practice they are overlapping. A few names were shared by brothers, and fewer were inherited.

Appendix 3. Peace treaties.

Date	Place	Parties concerned	Text extant	Source
1790/2	Pila-Canale	Bozzi/Aigui and Poli		AN BB[18]236
1794	Pila-Canale	Bozzi/Bruni and Poli		AN BB[18]236
1797	Pila-Canale	Bozzi/Bruni and Poli		⎰AN BB[18]236
1798	Pila-Canale	Bozzi/Bruni and Poli		⎱and ADCS 1.M.224
c.1800	Sari-d'Orcino	Cacciguerra/Stefani and Marchi		AN BB[18]236

Date	Place	Parties concerned	Text extant	Source
c.1800	Bastelica	General		*Gaz. Trib.*, 16/4/1846
1800	Canton of Orcino (4)			AN BB[18]236
1800	Levie/Figari	Peretti, Simoni and Susini		ADCS 1.M.224
1800/1	Ocana/Suarella	Follacci and Rossi	*	AN BB[18]236
1801	Saliceto/Casalta	Casanova and Benedetti		ADCS 7.U.1/9
1801	Gioviccace/Guitera	Luciani and Biaggi		ADCS 7.U.1/4
1801	Pila-Canale	Bozzi and Poli	*	ADCS 1.M.224 and Busquet (1919)
1802	Olmiccia			ADCS 1.M.224
1809	Olmeto	Istria and Peretti		AN BB[18]241
1812	Ciamannacce	Lucchini/Gabrielli and Susini	*	Busquet (1919)
1813	Casalta/Silvareccio	Casalta and Parsj		AN BB[18]241
1816	Zicavo	Scaglia/Bucchini and Vincentelli/Leandri	*	AN BB[18]1014
1816	Santa-Maria-Sicche	Giovanacci/Leonzi/Ornano and Aiqui/Lovichi	*	AN BB[18]1014; and ADCS 1.M.224
1816	Casinca	Casanova and Casalta	*	AN BB[18]1014; and ADCS 1.M.224
1816	Cardo/Grosseto	Pichetti and Clementi/Pitroli	*	AN BB[18]1014; and ADCS 1.M.224
1816	Pila-Canale	Bozzi/Bruni and Vincenti	*	ADCS 1.M.224
1816	Pila-Canale	Vincenti and Bruni/Monferrini	*	AN BB[18]1014; and ADCS 1.M.224
1816	Peri	Peres and Sandamiani	*	AN BB[18]1014; and ADCS 1.M.224
1817	Canale	Vincenti and Manfredi		Franceschini (1923)
1818	Olmeta-di-Tuda	Casale and Campocasso	*	AN BB[18]242
c.1820	Calcatoggio/Sari-d'Orcino	Multedo and Pozzo di Borgo		Faure (1858)
1821	Prunelli-di-Casaconi			ADCS 4.M.74
c.1825	Gavignano	Mattei and Giampietri		ADCS 2.M.127; and AN BB[20]121
1827	Ucciani	General		ADCS 4.M.91
1830	Ciamannacce	Lucchini/Gabrielli and Susini		ADCS 1.M.224
c.1830	Cuttoli-Corticchiato	Crudeli and Torre		*Gaz. Trib.*, 22/9/1833
1833	Tivolaggio	Capponi		Marcaggi (1932)
1834	Porri/Silvareccio	General		Marcaggi (1932)
1834	Olmeto/Ciamannacce			Marcaggi (1932)
1834	Gavignano	Mattei and Giampietri		*Gaz. Trib.* 2/10/1834; and Valéry (1837)
1834	Fozzano	Carabelli/Bartoli and Durazzi	*	Busquet (1919); Marcaggi (1932); and Roger (1945)
1834	Sartène	Durazzi/Roccaserra and Ortoli/Susini/Pietri	*	Busquet (1919); Marcaggi (1932); and Versini (1972)

Date	Place	Parties concerned	Text extant	Source
1835	Casalabriva	Barboni and Istria		ADCS 4.M.100
1835	Serra		*	Busquet (1919)
1842	Sari-d'Orcino	Petreschi and Stefani/ Casile	*	ADCS 2.M.149; AN BB[20]125; and Busquet (1919)
1842	Levie	Roccaserra		AN BB[20]130
1843	Olmo	Poggi and Agostini		AN BB[20]121
1845	Cervione			Fée (1850)
c.1845	Bastelica	Scapola and Gasparini		AN BB[20]134
c.1845	Novella	Massiani and Orabona		AN BB[20]130
c.1845	Santa-Maria-Sicche	Tenneroni and Emilj		AN BB[20]130
1847	Frasseto	Franceschi and Antona		ADCS 1.M.224
1848	Zonza	Giudicelli and Maestrati		AN BB[20]142
1848	Lumio	Buteri and Moretti		AN BB[20]142
1848	Marignana	Massoni and Grimaldi		Marcaggi (1898b)
1849	Piana	Moreschi and Versini	*	AN BB[20]146
c.1850	Aullène	Lanfranchi and Lucchini		AN BB[20]152
c.1850	Levie	Peretti		AN BB[20]158
1851	Tavera	Maroselli and Casanova		AN BB[20]152
1851	Marignana	Massoni and Durilli		Marcaggi (1898b)
1854	Arbellara	Forcioli and Giustiniani		Versini (1972)
1872	Pila-Canale	Poli and Quilichini		AN F[7]12849
1878/9	San-Gavino-di-Carbini	Nicolai and Pietri	*	AN F[7]12849; Bourde (1887); and Busquet (1919)
1883	San-Gavino-di-Carbini	Nicolai and Pietri	*	Busquet (1919)
1904	Carbini	Nicolai and Giuseppi	*	Busquet (1919)
1912	Petreto-Bicchisano	Giacomoni		Bazal (1973)
1923	Lopigna	Emmanuelli and Rutili		Bazal (1973)
c.1935	Grossa	Alfonsi and Giannini		Bazal (1973)

Abbreviations used in notes and bibliography

AA	*American Anthropologist*
ACNSS	*Actes du Congrès National des Sociétés Savantes*, Section d'Histoire Moderne et Contemporaine
ADCS	Archives Départementales de la Corse du Sud
ADHC	Archives Départementales de la Haute-Corse
AG	*Annales de Géographie*
AN	Archives Nationales
Ann	*Annales*
AQ	*Anthropological Quarterly*
BJS	*British Journal of Sociology*
BN	Bibliothèque Nationale
BS	*Balkan Studies*
BSSHNC	*Bulletin de la Société des Sciences Historiques et Naturelles de la Corse*
CH	*Corse Historique*
CSSH	*Comparative Studies in Society and History*
EC	*Etudes Corses*
EF	*Ethnologie Française*
ER	*Etudes Rurales*
ESS	*Encyclopedia of the Social Sciences*
Gaz. Trib.	*La Gazette des Tribunaux*
JAR	*Journal of Anthropological Research*
JCR	*Journal of Conflict Resolution*
JRAI	*Journal of the Royal Anthropological Institute of Great Britain and Ireland*
MS	*Mediaeval Studies*
P and P	*Past and Present*
RGA	*Revue de Géographie Alpine*
SJA	*Southwestern Journal of Anthropology*
TIBG	*Transactions of the Institute of British Geographers*
TM	*Temps Modernes*

Notes

1 Corsica in the nineteenth century

1 Bennet (1876), pp. 15–16; Baedeker (1895), p. 260; Ratzel (1899); Woolsey (1917), p. 113; Villat *et al.* (1951), pp. 13–14; and Renucci (1974), pp. 15 and 24.

2 Hauser (1909), p. 541; Albitreccia (1942a), p. 57; Ardouin-Dumazet (1898), pp. 99–100; and Vanutberghe (1904), p. 342.

3 Campbell (1868), pp. 121–2; Ardouin-Dumazet (1898), pp. 152–60; Bartoli (1898), pp. 98–101; Woolsey (1917), esp. pp. vii, 8, 115–22 and 153–5; Albitreccia (1942a), pp. 32–3 and 95–7; and Pomponi (1975), pp. 26–30.

4 Maupassant (1962), I, pp. 44–5; also Campbell (1868), p. 8; Bennet (1876), p. 23; Barry (1893), pp. 186–201; and Albitreccia (1942a), pp. 29–32.

5 Hernoux (1852); Deliberations, Municipal Council, Penta-di-Casinca, 26 October 1856; 6 March 1859; and 24 May 1866. ADHC E.28/8; Ardouin-Dumazet (1898), pp. 22 and 221–5; Blanchard (1926), pp. 57–60; Albitreccia (1942a), pp. 99–103; J. Pomponi (1962), p. 81; Luciani (1969), pp. 52–3; and Renucci (1974), pp. 44–5.

6 Fée (1850), p. 219; Pierangeli (1907); Léger and Arlo (1914); Lorenzi de Bradi (1928), pp. 279–82; Albitreccia (1942a), pp. 99–103; Renucci (1974), pp. 41–4 and Fig. 6; and Pomponi (1979a), pp. 256–8.

7 Woolsey (1917), p. 113; Villat et al. (1951), pp. 20–1; Renucci (1974), pp. 29–31 and 40; and Lücke (1982), p. 88.

8 Ardouin-Dumazet (1898), p. 179; Morandière (1933), pp. 41–2; Villat et al. (1951), pp. 16, 23–49 and 50–2; Spinosi (1956), p. 159; Luciani (1969), p. 38; P. Arrighi (ed.) (1971), p. 7; Renucci (1974), p. 28; and Lenclud (1979), p. 9.

9 Rémy (1930), pp. 8–10 and 21; P. Arrighi (ed.) (1971), pp. 190–1; Renucci (1974), pp. 28–9; and Pomponi (1979b), pp. 324 and 414.

10 Campbell (1868), pp. 65 and 69–70; Black (1892), pp. 12–13; Girolami-Cortona (1893), p. 249; Ardouin-Dumazet (1898), pp. 8–21 and 228–31; Blanchard (1926), p. 46; Luciani (1969), p. 32; and Bernardini (1970), I, pp. 40–4.

11 Bartoli (1898), p. 85; Maurice (ed.) (1904), p. 122; Hauser (1909), pp. 555–63; Albitreccia (1942a), pp. 114–31 and Figs. 8 and 9; Coppolani (1949), p. 96; Reparaz (1961), p. 37; J. Pomponi (1962), pp. 80–1; Rossi (1962), pp. 52–3; Vidalenc (1966), pp. 74–5; Luciani (1969), pp. 38–44; Renucci (1974), pp. 25–7; and Pomponi (1977), p. 103.

12 Campbell (1868), pp. 45–8 and 150–3; and Saint-Germain (1869), pp. 381, 388 and 411–12.

13 Ardouin-Dumazet (1898), p. 10; Albitreccia (1942a), pp. 134–45; Luciani (1969), pp. 44–6; and Finelli (n.d.), p. 51.

14 Blanchard (1915), pp. 25–33; Villat et al. (1951), p. 19; Luciani (1969), pp. 46–51 and 63; and Vidalenc (1966), pp. 75–6.

15 E.g. Simi (1966), p. 179; Viale et al. (1966), pp. 72 and 75; Finelli (n.d.), p. 34; Pernet and Lenclud (1977), p. 84; and Lenclud (1979), p. 11.

16 *Journal du Département de la Corse*, 21 January 1830; Deliberations, Municipal Council, Penta-di-Casinca, 26 May 1864. ADHC E.29/8; Campbell (1868), pp. 138–43; Black (1892), p. 7; Albitreccia (1942a), pp. 239–40; Renucci (1974), p. 244; *Le Provençal Corse*, 8 September 1977; and *Corse-Matin*, 24 May 1979; and 5 and 12 August 1981.

17 Robiquet (1835), pp. 392 and 465–7; Saint-Germain (1869), pp. 154, 224 and 383; Ortoli (1883), p. ii; Bigot (1890), pp. 497–8; Maurice (ed.) (1904), p. 154; Southwell Colucci (1933), p. 148; J. Pomponi (1962), pp. 6–7; Patin de La Fizelière (1963), pp. 60–2; F. Pomponi (1974b), pp. 14–17; Renucci (1974), pp. 224–6; Finelli (n.d.), p. 26; and Pernet and Lenclud (1977), p. 78.

18 Letter, V. Roccaserra to Prefect, 1846(?). ADCS 2.M.88; Robiquet (1835), p. 392; Comiti (1933), pp. 163–72; Albitreccia (1942a), pp. 165–7; Luciani (1969), pp. 32–3; Pomponi (1974b), pp. 28–31; Pernet and Lenclud (1977), pp. 81–2; Geoffray (1982), pp. 61 and 64; and Lücke (1982), p. 104.

19 Albitreccia (1942a), pp. 166–7, 187–8 and 191; J. Pomponi (1962), pp. 82–6; Luciani (1969), p. 33; Renucci (1974), pp. 59–60; and F. Pomponi (1975), pp. 32–40 and 51 (map). The commune was the smallest French administrative unit, having a major and a municipal council.

20 Faure (1858), pp. 151–5; Blanchard (1926), pp. 129–30; Comiti (1933), pp. 147–55 and 208; Reparaz (1961), pp. 66–71; J. Pomponi (1962), pp. 86 and 91–2; Finelli (n.d.), p. 49; and Geoffray (1982), pp. 67–8.

21 E.g. Campbell (1868), pp. 36, 46 and 107.

22 Albitreccia (1942a), pp. 172–87; Reparaz (1961), p. 31; Kolodny (1962), pp. 153 and 155; Vidalenc (1966), p. 75; and Bernardini (1970).

23 Ardouin-Dumazet (1898), pp. 30–1, 237, 268, 286 and 291; Girolami-Cortona (1893), pp. 25–6, 110 and 259; Hauser (1909), pp. 564–7; Albitreccia (1942a), pp. 103–13; Perry (1967), pp. 212–13; Luciani (1969), pp. 65–7; and Pomponi (1977), p. 83.

24 E.g. Rossi (1962), p. 50; Patin de La Fizelière (1963), p. 72; and Vidalenc (1966), p. 67.

25 P. Arrighi (ed.) (1971), chs. IX–XI; and Pomponi (1979), pts II and III.

26 E.g. Tommaseo (1841), p. 56; Cases v. P.-M. Paoli; and D. Leca, Assize Court, 4th session 1843. AN BB20121; Faure (1858), p. 214; Barry (1893), p. 56; Beaulieu-Delbet (1897), p. 40; Bartoli (1898), p. 287; Franceschini (1919), p. 36, citing Letter, Commissaire spécial, 1818; Ross (1948), p. 31; P. Arrighi in Villat et al. (1951), pp. 99–134; Martelli (1960), p. 252; Delarue (1970), p. 169; Emmanuelli (1971b), pp. 403–6; Renucci (1974), p. 158; and Thiers (1977), esp. pp. 15, 33–5 and 39.

27 Robiquet (1835), pp. 572–9; Campbell (1868), p. 20; Girolami-Cortona (1893), pp. 317–19; Bartoli (1898), pp. 287–8; Rossi (1962), pp. 50–2; and Thiers (1977), pp. 15 and 19–20.

28 Saint-Germain (1869), pp. 135–6; Reparaz (1961), pp. 34, 41 and 51–4; Casanova (1965), I, pp. 12–13; Simi (1966), pp. 75–86; Viale et al. (1966), p. 79; Defranceschi (1974), pp. 545 and 548; Casanova (1978), p. 64; and Lenclud and Pernet (1978), p. 60.

29 E.g. Saint-Germain (1869), p. 332; Coppolani (1949), pp. 83–4; Ravis-Giordani (1974), pp. 43–4; and Lenclud and Pernet (1978), p. 56.

30 Montherot (1840), p. 16; Bigot (1890), pp. 503–4; Comiti (1933), pp. 255–7; Coppolani (1949), pp. 82 and 89–90; J. Pomponi (1962), pp. 87–91; Patin de La Fizelière (1963), pp. 62–3 and 82; Casanova (1965), I, pp. 14–15; Bevilacqua (1967), pp. 48–50; Luciani (1969), pp. 60–1; Finelli (n.d.), pp. 33–4; Ravis-Giordani (1974), pp. 43–4; and Lenclud and Pernet (1978), pp. 56.

31 Saint-Germain (1869), p. 330; Bourde (1887), p. 17; Bigot (1890), p. 467; Hauser (1909), p. 545; Luciani (1969), pp. 61–2; Ravis-Giordani (1974); and Franzini (1975).

32 Campbell (1868), p. 65; Girolami-Cortona (1893), pp. 100–1; Coppolani (1949), p. 82; and Pomponi (1978b), pp. 279–80.

33 Casanova (1971).

34 Ardouin-Dumazet (1898), pp. 200–2; Blanchard (1926), p. 34; Albitreccia (1942a), Fig. 27; Reparaz (1961), pp. 48–51; Perry (1967), pp. 211–12; Méria (1970), pp. 47–55; Renucci (1974), pp. 195–7; Finelli (n.d.), pp. 37–8; Pomponi (1975), pp. 18–19 and 24–5; Borel-Léandri (1978), pp. 199–201; Pomponi (1978b), pp. 281–2; and Perry (1984).

35 Lamotte (1956b); Chiva (1958), p. 143; Chiva (1963), p. 105; Casanova (1965), I, pp. 11–12; and Favreau-Cancellieri (1975), pp. 15–16.

36 Campbell (1868), p. 34; Girolami-Cortona (1893), p. 103; Quantin (1914), pp. 65ff.; Albitreccia (1942a), pp. 69–71 and Fig. 28; Coppolani (1949), pp. 84–5; Patin de La Fizelière (1963), p. 63; Casanova (1968a); and (1968b); Renucci (1974), pp. 197–8; and Pomponi (1978b), pp. 283–4.

37 E.g. Comiti (1933), pp. 260–6; Albitreccia (1942a), pp. 71–5 and Fig. 26; Coppolani (1949), pp. 84–5; Renucci (1974), pp. 198–9; and Pomponi (1978b), pp. 282–3.

38 E.g. Girolami-Cortona (1893), p. 106; Albitreccia (1942a), pp. 77–81; and Luciani (1969), p. 57.

39 Campbell (1868), pp. 55–6; Ardouin-Dumazet (1898), pp. 97–8 and 121–5; Albitreccia (1942a), p. 86; and Coppolani (1949), p. 85.

40 Casanova (1968a), pp. 256–7; and Renucci (1974), pp. 57–9.

41 E.g. Girolami-Cortona (1893), pp. 105–6; Patin de La Fizelière (1963), p. 63; Simi (1966), p. 184; Pernet and Lenclud (1977), p. 51; and Pomponi (1978b), pp. 284–5 and Figs. 82–98.

42 Bigot (1890), p. 500; Comiti (1933), pp. 281–3; Finelli (n.d.), pp. 36–9; Deane (1965), pp. 15 and 28–47; and Renucci (1974), pp. 203 and 212.

43 Bigot (1890), p. 497; Forcioli-Conti (1897), p. 60; Blanchard (1915), pp. 48–57; Comiti (1933), pp. 140–7; Albitreccia (1942a), pp. 256–62 and Fig. 23; Coppolani (1949), p. 87; Patin de La Fizelière (1963), p. 64; Viale et al. (1966), pp. 73–4; Finelli (n.d.), p. 49; Renucci (1974), pp. 32–3; and Pernet and Lenclud (1977), pp. 76ff.

44 Robiquet (1835), pp. 400–1; Case v. S. Bartoli, Assize Court, 3rd session 1857. AN BB²⁰194 (Palneca); Campbell (1868), p. 127; Saint-Germain (1869), p. 154; Blanchard (1915), pp. 59–62; Morandière (1933), p. 73; Villat et al. (1951), p. 34; Carrington (1971a), p. 310; Renucci (1974), pp. 220–4 and 228; and Pernet and Lenclud (1977), pp. 128–9.

45 J. Pomponi (1962), pp. 62–3; Renucci (1974), p. 171; Pernet and Lenclud (1977), pp. 130–1; Borel-Léandri (1978), pp. 189–97 and photos; and author's fieldwork.

46 Galletti (1863), pp. 48–9; Campbell (1868), pp. 27–8; Saint-Germain (1869), pp. 140–1; Bigot (1890), pp. 498–502; Archer (1924), pp. 139–40; Lorenzi de Bradi (1928), pp. 191–2; Morandière (1933), p. 73; Natali (1934), pp. 142–7; Coppolani (1949), pp. 88–9; and Lenclud and Pernet (1978), pp. 84–5.

47 Robiquet (1835), pp. 400–1 and 427; Case v. G.-T. Lanfranchi, Assize Court, 1st session 1852. AN BB²⁰158 (Aullène); Saint-Germain (1869), p. 124; Léger and Arlo (1914), p. 51; Comiti (1933), pp. 143–7; Natali (1934), pp. 55–62; Chiva (1963), pp. 108–10; Patin de La Fizelière (1963), p. 64; and Rovère (1978), p. 84.

48 E.g. Comiti (1933), p. 142; Natali (1934), p. 54; J. Pomponi (1962), p. 75; Deane (1965), pp. 10–11; and Renucci (1974), p. 251.

49 Robiquet (1835), pp. 399–400; Bigot (1890), esp. pp. 464–7; Girolami-Cortona (1893), p. 277; Piobb (n.d.), pp. 65–70; Natali (1934), p. 49; Reparaz (1961), pp. 61–4; J. Pomponi (1962), p. 62; F. Pomponi (1975), pp. 20–4; Pernet and Lenclud (1977), pp. 80–1, 123–7 and 138–9; and Lenclud and Pernet (1978), pp. 59–60.

50 Bigot (1890), pp. 462 and 503–4; Lamotte (1956b); and (1956c); Chiva (1963), pp. 106–7; Pomponi (1974b), pp. 17–21; and Lenclud and Pernet (1978), p. 56.

51 Albitreccia (1942b), Map 3; Lamotte (1956b), p. 57; Reparaz (1961), pp. 33, 41, 49, 55

and 62–3; J. Pomponi (1962), pp. 60 and 99–100; Bevilacqua (1967), p. 51; and Lenclud and Pernet (1978), p. 62.

52 E.g. Albitreccia (1942a), pp. 167–71; Lamotte (1957b), pp. 73–5; J. Pomponi (1962), pp. 76 and 101–2; Patin de La Fizelière (1963), pp. 59–60, 62 and 72; Bevilacqua (1967), p. 50; and F. Pomponi (1974b), pp. 8–17.

53 Cases v. M. Franceschi, Assize Court, 4th session 1853. AN BB^{20}164 (Loreto); and v. D. Santini et al., 4th session 1855. AN BB^{20}177; J. Pomponi (1962), p. 100; F. Pomponi (1974b), p. 8; Pernet and Lenclud (1977), pp. 63–4 and 95–6; Lenclud (1979), p. 12; and Lenclud (1985), p. 36.

54 E.g. Maestrati (1964), pp. 54 and 56; Bevilacqua (1967), pp. 53 and 55; Ravis-Giordani (1976a), p. 172; Pernet and Lenclud (1977), pp. 97–8; and Lenclud and Pernet (1978), pp. 70.

55 Bigot (1890), pp. 501–2; Lamotte (1957b), p. 70; J. Pomponi (1962), p. 74; Chiva (1963), p. 112; Luciani (1969), p. 25; Renucci (1974), pp. 253–4; Favreau-Cancellieri (1975), p. 52; F. Pomponi (1976b); Pernet and Lenclud (1977), pp. 77–8; and F. Pomponi (1977), p. 85.

56 Albitreccia (1942a), pp. 65–7; Lamotte (1957b), p. 68; J. Pomponi (1962), pp. 76ff; Rossi (1962), p. 55; Chiva (1963), pp. 103–4; and F. Pomponi (1975), pp. 32 and 40–3.

57 Robiquet (1835), pp. 514–15; Bourde (1887), p. 107; Lamotte (1956b), p. 56; Chiva (1963), pp. 103–4; Patin de La Fizelière (1963), pp. 61, 73 and 81; Pomponi (1974b), p. 34; Pomponi (1975), pp. 17–18; and Pernet and Lenclud (1977), pp. 96ff.

58 E.g. Robiquet (1835), p. 392; Lorenzi de Bradi (1928), p. 168; Albitreccia (1942a), pp. 223–4; Reparaz (1961), pp. 43, 49–51 and 63; J. Pomponi (1962), pp. 105–6; Bevilacqua (1967), pp. 51 and 57; and Renucci (1974), p. 179.

59 Bigot (1890), p. 440; Albitreccia (1942a), p. 224; Coppolani (1949), pp. 89–90; Reparaz (1961), pp. 36–7, 43 and 54; J. Pomponi (1962), pp. 120–1; Bevilacqua (1967), p. 61; Luciani (1969), p. 61; and Renucci (1974), p. 179.

60 Bigot (1890), p. 462; and Lenclud (1985), pp. 36–7.

61 Cadastre 1851–1914, Venzolasca. ADHC 3.P.852; Bourde (1887), pp. 11–17; Comiti (1933), pp. 154–5; Reparaz (1961), pp. 42, 54–6 and 69–72; J. Pomponi (1962), pp. 68–73, 91, 105–6 and 114; Luciani (1969), p. 61; and Renucci (1974), p. 180.

62 Bigot (1890), p. 442; Albitreccia (1942a), pp. 227–8; Coppolani (1949), pp. 93–4; Chiva (1963), pp. 107–8; Patin de La Fizelière (1963), p. 63; and Pomponi (1978b), pp. 280–1.

63 Reparaz (1961), pp. 34 and 41; J. Pomponi (1962), pp. 86–9, 90–1 and 151–3; Pernet and Lenclud (1977), pp. 69–74; and Pomponi (1978b), pp. 275–80 and Annexe 4.

64 Case v. A. Lucchini, Assize Court, 2nd session 1839. *Gaz. Trib.*, 20 July 1839 (Ciamannacce); Girolami-Cortona (1893), pp. 100–2; Albitreccia (1942a), pp. 75–86; Bizouard (1964); and Renucci (1974), pp. 191–5.

65 Albitreccia (1942a), pp. 69–75; Coppolani (1949), pp. 84–5; Renucci (1974), pp. 198–9; Pomponi (1978b), pp. 281–4 and Figs. 76 and 79–81; and Perry (1984), pp. 80–1.

66 Deliberations, Municipal Council, Venzolasca, 31 August 1853. ADHC E.18/26; and Penta-di-Casinca, 16 February 1861. ADHC E.29/8; Blanchard (1915), pp. 53–6; Casanova (1965), I, pp. 14–15; Luciani (1969), pp. 53–4; Bernardini (1970), I, p. 43; Ettori (1971), pp. 278–82; Pomponi (1975), pp. 30–2; Pomponi (1976b), pp. 28–9; and Pernet and Lenclud (1977), esp. pp. 70–9, 81–2, 86, 93 and 151.

67 Carlotti (1936), pp. 4–5; Albitreccia (1942a), pp. 265–6; Coppolani (1949), p. 82; Reparaz (1961), pp. 35, 37–40 and 55–6; J. Pomponi (1962), pp. 93–4; Bevilacqua (1967), pp. 448–9; Pernet and Lenclud (1977), p. 18; F. Pomponi (1977), pp. 76–7; and F. Pomponi (1978b), p. 281.

68 Girolami-Cortona (1893), p. 272; Comiti (1933), pp. 260–6; Coppolani (1949), pp. 84–5; Renucci (1974), pp. 198–9; Pomponi (1977), pp. 81–2; and Pomponi (1978b), pp. 282–3.
69 Pomponi (1977), pp. 80–1; and Pomponi (1978b), p. 284.
70 Woolsey (1917), p. 122; Renucci (1974), pp. 196–7; Pomponi (1977), pp. 77–9.
71 Robiquet (1835), p. 455 and Tables XXX–XXXIV; Ardouin-Dumazet (1898), p. 323; Callon (1931), pp. 281–4; Lefèbvre (1954); (1955); and (1957); Luciani (1969), pp. 30–1; Le Mée (1971), p. 26; Emmanuelli (1971b), p. 415; Renucci (1974), pp. 106 and 108–9; Pomponi (1975), p. 17; Pernet and Lenclud (1977), p. 82; Pomponi (1978b), pp. 271–3 and Annexe I. As Lefèbvre has demonstrated, Corsican census figures are unreliable and must be carefully interpreted. In the recent period particularly, official figures have been inflated for political and electoral reasons, while earlier it was genuinely difficult to count a population that was not sedentary or friendly towards bureaucracy.
72 Anfossi (1918), pp. 84–9 and 94–7; Morandière (1933), p. 72; Albitreccia (1942a), pp. 159–65 and 172–7; Lefèbvre (1955), p. 90; Perry (1967), pp. 214–18; Le Mée (1971), p. 40; Méria (1970), pp. 40–1; Renucci (1974), pp. 114–18 and Fig. 14; and Pernet and Lenclud (1977), p. 82.
73 Albitreccia (1942a), pp. 206–10; P. Arrighi (ed.) (1971), pp. 215–16. 236–7, 270 and 276–8; Braudel (1972), I, pp. 158–60; Casta (1974), pp. 26, 60, 62, 79 and 165; and Renucci (1974), p. 69.
74 Olivesi (1969).
75 Renucci (1974), esp. pp. 133–54; and Pomponi (1977), pp. 84–91.
76 Saint-Germain (1869), p. 378; Girolami-Cortona (1893), pp. 117 and 283–4; Susini (1906), pp. 242–3; Comiti (1933), pp. 154–5 and 208; Patin de La Fizelière (1963), pp. 68–71 and 78–9; Renucci (1974), pp. 135, 171, 180, 246 and 257–8; Ravis-Giordani (1976a), p. 171; Casanova (1978), pp. 66–7; and Ravis-Giordani (1978c), pp. 33–4 and 37.
77 In addition to previous note, see List of tax payers, Penta-di-Casinca, 1866. ADCS 2.M.140; Southwell Colucci (1933), pp. 146–7; Robinet et al. (1899); and Versini (1979), pp. 39–41 and 46.
78 Casanova (1965), I, pp. 20–6; Lenclud (1979), pp. 12–13; and Ravis-Giordani (1979a), pp. 63–9.
79 Robiquet (1835), p. 388 note; Maestrati (1964), pp. 50, 53–4, and 57–9; and Versini (1979), p. 39.
80 Robiquet (1835), pp. 387–8; Montherot (1840), pp. 73–4; Barry (1893), p. 124; Girolami-Cortona (1893), p. 117; Lorenzi de Bradi (1928), pp. 157 and 167; Finelli (n.d.), p. 91 note; and Renucci (1974), pp. 257–9. Of 21 instances in which the title 'Don' was used in judicial records between 1807 and 1864, 14 cases came from the south (with 6 from the village of Levie and 3 from Olmeto), 5 from the Castagniccia and the Casinca, and 2 from the Balagna.
81 Lenclud and Ravis-Giordani (1973), p. 210; and Raulin and Ravis-Giordani (1978).
82 AN F⁷3247 (1807); Lists of jurors, e.g. AN BB²⁰260 (1864); and Pomponi (1976c), p. 166.
83 E.g. Cases v. P.-L. Pietri, Extraordinary Criminal Court, 29 Fructidor An IX. ADCS 7.U.1/17 (Casabianca); and v. P.-A. Veccioni, 6 Floréal An X. ADCS 7.U.1/21 (Bisinchi); Piobb (n.d.), p. 47; and Lamotte (1956e), pp. 40–3.
84 Chiva (1963), p. 111.
85 Case v. Don A. Mattei, Assize Court, 2nd session 1852. AN BB²⁰158; Girolami-Cortona (1893), p. 117; Deliberations, Municipal Council, Venzolasca, 26 August 1900. ADHC E.18/3; Albitreccia (1942a), p. 227; Pomponi (1976c), p. 166; and Pernet and Lenclud (1977), pp. 87–8.

86 Case v. P. Coti, Assize Court, 4th session 1833. *Gaz. Trib.*, 30 December 1833, cit. Sorbier (1863), pp. 66–9; Robiquet (1835), pp. 511–13; Mérimée (1840a), pp. 494–5; Montherot (1840), pp. 84–6; Gregorovius (1855), p. 111; Mattei (1867), pp. 23 and 26; Campbell (1868), p. 15; Bennet (1876), pp. 73–4; Girolami-Cortona (1893), p. 106; Vuillier (1896), p. 214; Ardouin-Dumazet (1898), pp. 99–101, 142–3 and 320; Vanutberghe (1904), p. 342; Piobb (n.d.), pp. 86–90; Bazin (1913), p. 181; Anfossi (1918), pp. 89–90; Albitreccia (1942a), pp. 199–200 and 228–9; Deane (1965), p. 119; Vidalenc (1966), p. 72; Finelli (n.d.), p. 31; Bernardini (1970), I, pp. 37–8; Emmanuelli (1971b), pp. 415–16; Ceccaldi (1974), p. 213; Renucci (1974), pp. 79–81 and 154–63; Pomponi (1977), pp. 86–7; Pomponi (1978a), p. 17; Ravis-Giordani (1978a), p. 151; and Versini (1979), pp. 107–8.

87 Gregorovius (1855), p. 269.

88 Réalier-Dumas (1819), p. 24; Hogg (1973), pp. 62–5; and Renucci (1974), p. 79. Réalier-Dumas was a judge at Bastia and later public prosecutor.

89 Mérimée (1840b), p. 668 note; and Case v. G. Antoniotti et al., Assize Court, 2nd session 1856. AN BB20185.

90 Lenclud and Ravis-Giordani (1973), p. 214; and Ravis Giordani (1979a).

91 E.g. Griffon (1841), pp. 24–5; and Barry (1893), p. 124. We shall return to the very large topics of patronage and honour in subsequent chapters.

92 Maupassant (1928), p. 185; and Barry (1893), pp. 28 and 49; also Fée, (1850), pp. 64 and 216; Busquet (1919), p. 493; and Lorenzi de Bradi (1928), p. 18.

93 See Brady and Pottle (eds.) (1955); McLaren (1966), esp. p. 21; Thrasher (1970), esp. Ch. 6; Arrighi (ed.) (1971), esp. p. 356; and Pomponi (1979b), pp. 272–4.

94 E.g. Gregorovius (1855), p. 101; Joanne (1881), p. 470; and Baedeker (1902), p. 498.

95 Roger (1945); Roger (1947); Carrington (1971a), esp. p. 89; and Jeoffroy-Faggianelli (1979).

96 Emmanuelli (1969); Valéry (1837), p. 204; Viale (1842), esp. Canto VIII, Stanzas VI–VIII; Letter, Ottomani to Prefect, 25 June 1896. ADCS 1.M.230: 'Our island is the scene of continual human butchery and horrific carnage ...'; and Archer (1924), p. 209.

97 E.g. Letter, Councillor, Cour Royale, Ajaccio, to Minister of Justice, 1815. AN BB18241: 'The vendetta is at the root of all the crimes which desolate this country'; also Report, Commander, Gendarmerie, 8 November 1820, cit. Franceschini (1919), p. 60; Letter, Procureur-général to Minister of Justice, 3 June 1833. AN BB181333, and President of Assize Court, Address to jurors, April 1834. *Gaz. Trib.*, 3 July 1834, No. 2769.

98 Robiquet (1835), pp. 412–13 and Tables XLIX and LI; Rapports au Roi sur l'administration générale de la justice criminelle, 1828, 1831, 1835, 1836 and 1839. *Gaz. Trib.*, 5 November 1829, No. 1323; 24 January 1833, No. 2322; 6–7 November 1837, No. 3794; 26 December 1838, No. 4147; and 5 June 1841, No. 4913; and *Annuaire Statistique de la France* (1879); (1884); (1889); and (1892–4).

99 Letter, Administrateur-général des Départments du Golo et du Liamone to Minister of Justice, 20 Brumaire An X. AN BB18236. Miot governed Corsica with special powers from December 1796 to March 1797 and from January 1801 to October 1802.

100 Robiquet (1835), Table XLIII; and Zehr (1976), esp. pp. 120–33.

101 These figures are compiled from the following sources: List of crimes, 1816. AN BB181095; Arrests, 1819–21. Franceschini (1919), Appendix; Report on crimes committed in 1822, Prefect, 24 March 1823. AN BB181095; Crimes tried, 1826–31. Robiquet (1835), Table XLII; Crimes tried, 1830–48. Bernardini (1970) II, p. 18; Crimes tried, Assize Court, 1852–65. AN BB20; and Crimes and 'délits' of recidivists before tribunaux correctionnels, 1862. AN BB301212.

102 Robiquet (1835), pp. 409–10 and Table XLVIII. The important legal distinction

between *meurtre*, where there was no premeditation, and *assassinat*, where there was, is difficult to apply in the Corsican situation. We have generally used the term homicide, therefore, rather than their English equivalents.

103 See Gibson and Klein (1961), p. 4, Table I; Graham and Gurr (eds.) (1969), p. 375; and Given (1977), pp. 38–9.

104 Rates for selected counties of thirteenth-century England range from 9 through 12, 17, 22 and 23 to 47 per 100,000. Indicted homicide rates in the Elizabethan Home Counties reached a maximum of 16. Given (1977), p. 36, Table 2; and Cockburn (1977), pp. 55–6.

105 Ferracuti et al. (1970), Appendix B, Table I and p. 49, Table II; Pirastu (1973), pp. 106–7 and 112; Dolci (1963), p. 313; and Steinberg (1982), p. 3.

106 See Hallpike (1973), p. 462, suggesting a figure of over 550 per 100,000 over a fifty-year period for the Tauade; or Nash (1967), p. 456; and Given (1977), pp. 38–9, recording rates of 250 for some Mexican villages.

107 These figures are compiled from the following sources: Franceschini (1919), Appendix; Report, Prefect, 24 March 1823. AN BB[18]1095; Vidalenc (1966), p. 79, citing military report; Robiquet (1835), Table LV; Versini (1979), pp. 77 and 166 (Rapport Mottet); Bernardini (1970), II, p. 18; 'Tableau indiquant le nombre d'assassinats ou tentatives d'assassinats, de meurtres ou tentatives de meurtre, commis du 1 janvier 1821 au 31 décembre 1851, Département de la Corse'. ADCS 4.M.88; 'Crimes contre les personnes, statistique annuelle 1843–52'. ADCS 4.M.90; Report, President, Assize Court, 13 July 1850. AN BB[20]149; Reports, Prefect, 23 December 1872; 30 October 1874; 15 March 1882; and Sûreté Générale, 1887. AN F[7]12849: *Annuaire Statistique de la France* (1879); (1884); (1889); and (1892–4); Bourde (1887), pp. 133–4; and Reports, Prefect and Gendarmerie, 1894–9. AN F[7]12850.

108 Thrasher (1970), pp. 63–4 and 225; Renucci (1974), p. 71; Reports, Commissaire du gouvernement, Golo, to Minister of Justice, 20 Brumaire An VII. AN BB[18]237; Substitut, Commissaire du gouvernement, Germinal An IX. AN BB[18]236; Miot (1858), II, pp. 4–5; Reports, General Brulard to Minister of Justice, 9 February 1815. AN BB[18]950; and Minister of Justice to Emperor, 3 May 1815. AN BB[18]242; Patorni (1842), pp. 69–70; Report, Prefect to Conseil-général, 1826. AN BB[18]1146; *Journal du Département de la Corse*, 29 January 1829; Sorbier (1833), pp. 6–7; Blanqui (1841), p. 500; Sorbier (1845), p. 60; Report, President, Assize Court, 14 September 1857. AN BB[20]194; Galletti (1863), p. 563; Reports, President, Assize Court, 24 May 1864; and Procureur-général, 5 July 1864. AN BB[20]260; and President, Assize Court, 29 December 1865. AB BB[20]273; Mattei (1912), pp. 1–2 and 6; Busquet (1919), p. 411; and Marcaggi (1932), pp. 27 and 43.

109 *Gaz. Trib.*, 1 May 1827, No. 508; and 18 January 1834, No. 2629; Marcaggi (1932), pp. 11 and 13; Report, Prefect to Minister of Justice, 21 April 1852. AN BB[18]1473; Grandchamps (1859), p. 71; and Albitreccia (1942a), p. 211.

110 See Pareto (1935), IV, p. 1518; and Hobsbawm (1972), pp. 65–6.

2 The history and incidence of feuds

1 For a discussion of some of these problems see Black-Michaud (1975), esp. pp. 33–5; also Campbell (1964), pp. 96–7 and 193–9; and Stirling (1965), pp. 247–54, for two N. Mediterranean examples.

2 See, for example, the admirable studies by Petit-Dutaillis (1908), Brunner (1943), Davies (1969) and Wormald (1980).

3 See Reports, Subprefect, Sartène, 28 March, 23 May, 22 July, 25 November and 19 December 1826; 8 and 12 May, 31 July and 13 October 1827; and 30 July and 22

November 1830. ADCS 4.M.99 and 4.M.100. It is possible that the poisoning of Benetti's cattle, from drinking river water, was accidental but this seems unlikely in view of what followed, and the important thing is how he and his relatives interpreted the event. Though first names are usually given in French in the documents, we will use the Corsican or Italian equivalents throughout. The *voltigeurs* were a special locally recruited force formed in 1822, primarily to combat banditry.

4 See Versini (1972), pp. 95–9; Report, Subprefect, Sartène, 24 July 1835. ADCS 4.M.100; Printed memoir by Sr Carlo Giustiniani in support of his appeal before the Cour de Cassation (no date – 1845?). AN BB^{24}219–55; *Gaz. Trib.*, 22 April 1847; and Bertrand (1870), pp. 13–20. Bertrand was appointed first *avocat-général* at Bastia in 1858. Giustiniani's reference to the construction of a tower by the Forcioli in 1835 is probably misleading, since their tower was already a very old building at this time; what he probably means is that they repaired and put it to use again; see photograph in Vrydaghs Fidelis (1962), p. 57.

5 Letters, Subprefect to Prefect, 17 January 1832; and 28 October and 24 December 1836. ADCS 2.M.79 and 2.M.65.

6 Cases v. A.-S. and L. Cartucci, Assize Court, 1st session 1843. AN BB^{20}121; Reports, Gendarmerie, 26 February, 23 and 27 August 1842. ADCS 4.M.126; *Gaz. Trib.*, 12 December 1841, and 4 June 1842.

7 Cases v. C. Giustiniani, Assize Court, 2nd session 1845. AN BB^{20}130; and v. A. Rutilj Forciolo and G. Agostini, 2nd session 1851. AN BB^{20}152; Petition for clemency for Carlo Giustiniani. AN BB^{24}251–85; *Gaz. Trib.*, 27 April 1847, No. 6177; and Versini (1972), pp. 99–107.

8 Letter, President of Assize Court, 13 July 1850. AN BB^{20}149; ADCS 2.M.87 (Arbellara); ADCS 2.M.115 (Arbellara).

9 Cases v. Peretti and Giustiniani, 1st session 1860. AN BB^{20}221; and Report, Procureur-général, 21 August 1896; and other documents. AN BB^{18}2041.

10 Mérimée spent seven weeks in Corsica in 1839 as Inspector of Historical Monuments and visited Fozzano and Sartène. *Colomba* was published in July 1840. Roger (1945), pp. 153–72.

11 Vrydaghs Fidelis (1962), p. 217; Rovère (1978), pp. 73 and 95; and Case, Extraordinary Criminal Court, 6 Fructidor An IX. ADCS 7.U.1/17; Renucci (1974), pp. 49 and 55. Earlier sources refer to the Durazzi and later to the Durazzo; for the sake of consistency we employ the former throughout.

12 Versini (1972), pp. 85ff; Letter, General Morand to Ministry of General Police, 13 June 1810. AN BB^{18}214; and Reports, Gendarmerie, 14 May, 26 August and 23 September 1816. ADCS 4.M.102.

13 Reports, Subprefect, Sartène, 27 January 1819; 30 September 1820; 14 April 1821; 9 March and 5 October 1824; 17 October 1827; and 22 September 1829. ADCS 4.M.98–99.

14 Reports, Subprefect, Sartène, 8 and 22 June, 16 August, 8 September, and 26 October 1830; Dossier: 'Fozzano: Affaire Colomba'; and Reports, Gendarmerie, 10 June and 26 October 1830. ADCS 4.M.99–100; Petition for clemency for A.-F. and S. Bernardini, 1832. AN BB^{24}116–35; Robiquet (1835), p. 429; Valéry (1837), pp. 202–3; and Versini (1972), pp. 85–8.

15 Reports, Subprefect, to Prefect, 5 February, and 12 April 1831. ADCS 2.M.82.

16 *Gaz. Trib.*, 30–31 May 1831, No. 1808; 13 October 1831, No. 1924; and 28 March 1832, cit. Sorbier (1863), pp. 15–18; Report, Procureur-général, 26 May 1832. Petition for clemency for A.-F. and S. Bernardini; Reports, Voltigeurs, Gendarmerie and Subprefect, Sartène, 11 December 1832; and Report, Gendarmerie, 1 January 1833. ADCS 4.M.100 (Dossier: 'Fozzano: Affaire Colomba'); Robiquet (1835), p. 428; and Roger (1945), pp. 181–2.

17 Reports, Gendarmerie, 30 December 1833; and 1 January 1834. ADCS 4.M.100; Versini (1972), pp. 88–90; Marcaggi (1932), pp. 86–9, citing reports by the gendarmerie and the mayor, Anton-Francesco Durazzi; and Busquet (1919), pp. 624–7, citing the text of the treaty (13 December 1834), which is also provided by Roger (1945), Appendix III, pp. 281–5.

18 Roger (1945), pp. 276–80; Reports, Subprefect, 19 May, and 30 October 1835. ADCS 4.M.100.

19 ADCS 2.M.57 and 2.M.65; Letters, 26 November 1846; 24 January, and April 1847. ADCS 2.M.82.

20 Cases v. P.-P. Paoli, Assize Court, 3rd session 1852. AN BB[20]158; v. P.-P. Paoli, 17 February 1853. AN BB[20]164; v. G.-A. Nicolai, 1st session 1854. AN BB[20]170; and v. S. Papalini, 1st session 1856. AN BB[20]185.

21 Saint-Germain (1869), p. 386; Roger (1945), Appendix III; ADCS 2.M.126; Petition for clemency for G. Bernardini, 16 June 1866; and Report, Procureur-général, 12 July 1866. AN BB[24]717.

22 By this time, mayors were no longer appointed, but elected by municipal councils.

23 Reports, Procureur-général to Ministry of Justice, 14 and 30 November 1891; 2 February 1892; 9 February, and 27 March 1893; Charges, J.-P. Paoli, 12 December 1891; and F. Paoli, 18 January 1893; Telegrams and letters, F. Bernardini to Ministry of Justice and Procureur-général, 18 October, and 23 December 1896; and 5 January 1897; and other official reports and telegrams, December 1896. AN BB[18]1870; and Case v. G.-A. Bartoli et al., Assize Court, 20–1 December 1893. AN BB[20]286.

24 Report, Subprefect, 15 September 1834. ADCS 4.M.100; Letters, Subprefect to Prefect, 20 April 1831. ADCS 2.M.82; and 22 March 1867. ADCS 2.M.126.

25 Report, Subprefect, Sartène, 4 February 1815. ADCS 4.M.98; Reports, Gendarmerie, 3 August, and 19 September 1816. ADCS 4.M.102; Versini (1972), pp. 109–12; Letter, Mayor Ortoli to Prefect, 9 February 1821; and Acte d'accusation, 16 September 1820. ADCS 1.V.44.

26 Notice sur Mr Giacomoni; Letters, Mayor to Prefect, 9 February, and 5 March 1821; Letter, Mayor to Minister of the Interior, 1820. ADCS 1.V.44; and Report, Subprefect, 14 November 1820. ADCS 4.M.98.

27 Letters, Subprefect to Prefect, 1, 18 and 24 February, and 3 March 1821; and Letter, Prefect to Subprefect, 24 February 1821. ADCS 1.M.224.

28 Reports, Subprefect, 7 and 30 November 1821; 23 February 1823; 6 February, and 20 April 1824; 29 August 1826; 13 November 1827; 12 February, 17 May, 26 July, 8 and 9 August 1828; 3 January, and 24 March 1829; and 30 May 1830. ADCS 4.M.98–99; Case, Tribunal correctionnel, Sartène, 1829. AN BB[30]1211: and List of 'contumaces', 1830. AN BB[20]49.

29 *Gaz. Trib.*, 18 April 1840, No. 4559, cit. Sorbier (1863), pp. 166–77; Faure (1885), II, pp. 291ff; Versini (1972), pp. 112–13; Reports, Subprefect, 25 July, 11 November and 22 December 1831; and 19 and 21 January 1834. ADCS 4.M.100; ADCS 2.M.65; and Letter, Subprefect, to Prefect, 27 August 1834. ADCS 2.M.87.

30 ADCS 2.M.65; and Sorbier (1863), pp. 167–71.

31 Versini (1972), pp. 113–21, following the account of the trial in *Gaz. Trib.* The killing of Quilichini provided the occasion for the well-known lament or *vocero*, 'O caro di la surella', sung by his young bride; see Mérimée (1840b), pp. 739–45; and Ortoli (1887), pp. 300–11.

32 Letters, Giovan-Francesco Poli to Subprefect, 16 October 1840; Giacomo-Maria Poli et al. to Prefect, 10 March 1842; Prefect to Procureur-général, 21 March 1842; Petro Viggiani to Prefect, 18 October 1843; Vincenzo-Girolamo Ortoli to Prefect, 6 November 1843; and Procureur-général to Prefect, 13 August 1845. ADCS 1.M.229; Reports, Gendarmerie, 23 November 1841; and 4 January 1842. ADCS 4.M.125; and

15 August 1842. ADCS 4.M.126; Cases v. P.-F. Quilichini, Assize Court, 4 March and 16 May 1842. AN BB²⁰116; v. M.-F. Quilichini, 1st session 1846. AN BB²⁰134; and v. A. Santalucia, 2nd session 1851, Cases tried *in absentia*. AN BB²⁰152; Versini (1972), pp. 122–42; and Marin-Muracciole (1964), pp. 211–12. Lemps (1844), p. 68, refers to a pacification brought about by the bishop of Ajaccio, presumably in the early 1840s, but this is not mentioned elsewhere.

33 Letter, G.-A. Roccaserra and S. Quilichini to Prefect, 9 September 1846; and other documents. ADCS 2.M.87.

34 Letters, Avocat-général to Minister of Justice, 9 August, and 18 September 1848. AN BB¹⁸1466; and Case, Assize Court, 1st session 1849. AN BB²⁰146.

35 E.g. Letter, Mayor to Prefect, 28 Prairial An X; and other letters. ADCS 1.M.224; and Cases v. F.-M. Ortoli et al., Assize Court, 1st and 2nd sessions 1851. AN BB²⁰152.

36 E.g. List of 'contumaces', 1823. AN BB¹⁸1095; and ADCS 2.M.144.

37 List of licences to carry arms, 1807. AN F⁷3247; ADCS 2.M.53; *Journal du Département de la Corse*, 13 November 1830.

38 ADCS 2.M.69; and 2.M.82; Cases v. A.-D. Lanfranchi, Assize Court, 4th session 1846. AN BB²⁰134; v. G. Miliani et al., 2nd session 1847. *Gaz. Trib.*, 18 July 1847, No. 6252; v. G.-A. Franceschi, 3rd session 1848. AN BB²⁰142; and v. D. Franceschi, 3rd session 1852, Cases tried *in absentia*. AN BB²⁰158; Letters, Franceschi and Mariani to Prefect, 9 January; Mayor Stefani to Prefect, 18 August; Gendarmerie to Prefect, 20 September; Prefect to Mayor, 20 September; Franceschi, Antona and others to Prefect, 18 October; Mayor Stefani to Prefect, 20 December 1847; and Prefect to Mayor, 5 January 1848; and other documents. ADCS 1.M.224; Report, Gendarmerie, 6 December 1847. ADCS 1.M.229; Versini (1972), pp. 143–64; ADCS 2.M.127; and 'Réclamations et plaintes par personnel ecclésiastique contre certains maires ... 1837–1871'. ADCS 2.V.19.

39 Letter, 11 Fructidor An IX. ADCS 7.U.1/3.

40 Letters, Francesco-Maria Bruni to Miot, and the Poli to Miot, no date (but enclosed with documents dated Fructidor An IX). AN BB¹⁸236.

41 Case v. S. Simoni, Extraordinary Criminal Court, 8 Messidor An IX. ADCS 7.U.1/16; Letter, 11 Fructidor An IX. ADCS 7.U.1/3; Interrogation of hostages, Vendémiaire An X. ADCS 7.U.1/3; Réquisition, Substitut commissaire du gouvernement près le Tribunal Criminel Extraordinaire, 8 Vendémiaire An X; and Correspondence, 8 Brumaire An X. ADCS 7.U.1/4; ADCS 1.M.224; and Busquet (1919) pp. 615–17.

42 Letter, General Morand to Minister of Justice, 5 Floréal An XIII; and other documents. AN BB¹⁸240; List of licences to carry arms, 1807. AN F⁷3247; Letters, General Morand to Minister of General Police, 30 May, and 13 June 1810. AN BB¹⁸241; and List of those in detention. AN F⁷3282.

43 Letters, Giacomo-Filippo Vincenti to Prefect; Giovan-Battiste Poli to same; Dr Casabianca to same; and Matteo Bruni, Benedetto Monferrini and Matteo Bozzi to same; anonymous letter to Colonel Peraldi. No dates (1816). ADCS 1.M.224; Reports, Gendarmerie, 21 May, 31 July, and 18 September 1816. ADCS 4.M.102; and Acte de paix, Pila-Canale, 15 November 1816, drawn up by notary Leopoldo Susini. ADCS 1.M.224; and AN BB¹⁸1014.

44 List of 'contumaces', 1823. AN BB¹⁸1095; Reports, Subprefect, Ajaccio, 29 April 1824; and 14 January 1828. ADCS 4.M.91; and *Journal du Département de la Corse*, 2 July 1829.

45 ADCS 2.M.53; ADCS 2.M.69; and Pomponi (1976c), p. 160.

46 Letter, Giulio and Bonaventura Bozzi and Martino Foata to Prefect, no date (1837?). ADCS 1.M.229; and *Gaz. Trib.*, 23 October 1841, No. 4535.

47 Case v. S. Majoli and P. Poli, Assize Court, 1st session 1842. AN BB²⁰116; Reports, Gendarmerie, 8 September, and 21 October 1841. ADCS 4.M.125; and Case v. A. Fieschi, 2nd session 1850. AN BB²⁰149.

48 Case v. A. Fieschi, 2nd session 1850. AN BB^{20}149. Testimony in the case also referred to the Sanviti house.

49 Letter, President La Cour, 13 July; Case v. A. Feliciaggi, 2nd session 1850. AN BB^{20}149; and Case v. F. Benedetti, 11 June 1853. AN BB^{20}164.

50 Cases v. V. Santoni, and v. A. Fieschi et al., 4th session 1851. AN BB^{20}152.

51 Various letters and documents, 1853–68. ADCS 2.M.144; Marin-Muracciole (1964), p. 190, which provides no names; and Telegram, Prefect, 2 April 1880. AN F^{7}12849.

52 Bourde (1887), pp. 53–4; Robinet et al. (1899); List of cases, 1816(?). AN BB^{18}1014; Tommaseo (1841), p. 93; Viale (1842), pp. 155 and 175; Cavallucci (1930), pp. 58–9; List of 'contumaces', 1823. AN BB^{18}1095; *Journal du Département de la Corse*, 27 November 1830; and ADCS 2.M.88.

53 Cases v. G.-T. Sanguinetti; and v. G. Sanguinetti, Assize Court, 2nd session 1845. AN BB^{20}130.

54 Case v. G.-C. Grimaldi, 4th session 1849. AN BB^{20}146; Petitions for clemency, for G.-C. Grimaldi, 1850 and 1866; and Various reports. AN BB^{24}374–80; Cases v. F. Filippi, 1st session 1853. AN BB^{20}164; and v. C. Ciosi and A. Buttaci, 2nd session 1850; and Letter, President of Assize Court, 13 July 1850. AN BB^{20}149.

55 Cases v. M.-G. Rocchi et al.; and v. G. Filippi et al., 3rd session 1850. AN BB^{20}149; v. P.-F. Angelini et al., March-April 1851. AN BB^{20}152; v. C. Ciosi et al.; and v. F. Antonetti et al., 2nd session 1850. AN BB^{20}149; and v. G.-C. Grimaldi, 4th session 1849. AN BB^{20}146.

56 Cases v. G. F. Sanguinetti et al.; v. M. Papini; and v. M. Luciani, 1st session 1851. AN BB^{20}152; and v. F. Petrignani, 3rd session 1850. AN BB^{20}149.

57 Case v. F.-A. Emanuelli, May 1853. AN BB^{20}164; *Gaz. Trib.*, 5 January 1845, No. 5522; Cases v. L.-M. Besignani, 1st session 1854. AN BB^{20}170; v. P. Giafferi, 4th session 1853; AN BB^{20}164; v. G.-M. Petrignani, 2nd session 1855. AN BB^{20}177; and v. L. Ciosi, 1st session 1858. AN BB^{20}204.

58 Case v. L. Ciarini, 2nd session 1857. AN BB^{20}194; Letters, Subprefect to Prefect, 2 May, 14 and 28 December 1865; and other documents. ADCS 2.M.158; Venzolasca, Correspondence 1850–1889. ADHC E/18/26; and L. Lorenzi, 'Il y a cent ans', *Corse-Matin*, 10 August 1981. E. Petrignani stood as a Left-wing Radical at Bastia in the 1881 General Elections against the Bonapartist D. Gavini.

59 Marcaggi (1932), pp. 52–5; Report, Procureur-général to Minister of Justice, 16 October 1912. ADCS 1.M.231, 'Banditisme 1911–1917'; and ADHC E/18/3.

60 Press cuttings, 1911–12; Report, Procureur-général to Minister of Justice, 16 October 1912; and other documents. ADCS 1.M.231; Mattei (1912); Marcaggi (1932), pp. 52–5; and Régis and Martin (n.d.), pp. 8–9.

61 *Gaz. Trib.*, 18 January 1834; Benson (1825), pp. 62–70 and 165–82; Report, Procureur-général to Minister of Justice, 1818; Printed Memoirs by Carlo-Felice Frediani, no date (1818); by Captain Frediani, 1820 and 1821; and by Viterbi, no date and 1820; Reports, Maître des requêtes to Minister of Justice, 10 April 1821; and Procureur-général to same, 29 March 1820; 19 December 1821; and 27 February, and 6 March 1822; and miscellaneous documents. AN BB^{18}243; F. Renucci (1833–4), II, p. 142; Franceschini (1919), pp. 36–41; List of those in detention, July 1812. AN F^{7}3282; Report, Commissaire spécial, 14 January 1818, cit. E. Franceschini (1923), pp. 18–19; List of 'contumaces', 1823. AN BB^{18}1095; ADHC E.29/8; List of criminal procedures, 1816. AN BB^{18}1014; and ADCS 2.M.140.

62 Report, Bruslart to Minister of Justice, 4 January 1815. AN BB^{18}242; and Tommaseo (1841), pp. 105–7. Bruslart was military commander in Corsica from July 1814 until March 1815.

63 Reports, Gendarmerie, 11 February 1815; 25 May, and 7 July 1816. ADCS 4.M.102; and *Gaz. Trib.*, 1 May, No. 508; 12 May, No. 519; and 15 December 1827, No. 733.

64 Robiquet (1835), pp. 591–2; ADCS 1.M.222; Report, Subprefect, Calvi, 23 June 1832; Cases v. A. Calisti, Assize Court, 4th session 1845. AN BB[20]130; v. G. Antoniotti et al., 2nd session; and v. G.-B. Maestracci, 4th session 1856. AN BB[20]185; and v. D. Tortora, 28 November 1893. AN BB[20]286.

65 The full list of 65 is as follows: Albitreccia, Antisanti, Arbellara, Aullène, Balogna, Bastelica, Bisinchi, Borgo-Lucciana, Calacuccia, Calasima, Campile, Canale, Carbini, Carcheto, Casalabriva, Casalta/Silvareccio, Castineta, Cauro, Ciamannacce, Corte, Cozzano, Cuttoli-Corticchiato, Eccica-Suarella, Feliceto, Fozzano, Frasseto, Gavignano, Guagno, Levie/Figari, Linguizetta, Loreto-di-Casinca, Loreto-di-Tallano, Marignana, Moca-Croce, Moita, Muro, Ocana, Oletta, Olmeta-di-Tuda, Olmeto, Olmiccia, Ortiporio, Ota, Penta-di-Casinca, Peri, Petreto-Bicchisano, Pila-Canale, Pino, Poggio-di-Tallano, Porto-Vecchio, San-Andrea-di-Orcino, San-Gavino-d'Ampugnani, San-Gavino-di-Carbini, Santa-Lucia-di-Moriani, Santa-Lucia-di-Tallano, Santa-Maria-Sicche, Sari-d'Orcino, Sartène, Serra, Sorbollano, Tavera, Tox, Urbalacone, Venzolasca and Zerubia.

66 Report, Procureur-général, 20 January 1809. AN BB[18]239; Miscellaneous letters, An X.ADCS 1.M.224; Report, Gendarmerie, 3 February 1842. ADCS 4.M.126; Cases v. C.-M. Ortoli, Assize Court, 2nd session 1844. AN BB[20]125; v. Don G.-T. Peretti, 2nd session 1852. AN BB[20]158; v. P.-A. Rossi, 4th session 1861. AN BB[20]229; v. A.-N. Muselli, 4th session 1863. AN BB[20]249; v. J.-P. Renucci, 4th session 1865. AN BB[20]273; and v. Don G. Cesari, 2nd session 1893. AN BB[20]286.

67 'Procès-verbal de délimitation de la commune de Venzolasca avec plan, 1845.' ADHC E.18.25. Dossier 1.

68 Case v. G.-F. Giacomoni et al., Extraordinary Criminal Court, Sartène, Floréal An X. ADCS 3.U.5/129; and Denunciations. ADCS 7.U.1/9.

69 See Case v. G.-F. and P. Moracchini, Court of Criminal Justice, 1830. AN BB[20]49; Viale (1842); and Cavallucci (1930), Ch. III. The latter case is actually less clear-cut than this suggests; see Ch. 6, p. 175.

70 Versini (1972), p. 104; and Lear (1870), p. 44 note.

71 *Gaz. Trib.*, 30 July 1835, No. 3103; and 4 May 1836, No 3315; Robiquet (1835), pp. 429–30; AN BB[18]1205; Versini (1972), pp. 49–83; and Sacquin-Moulin (1982), p. 653.

72 Report, Procureur-général to Minister of Justice, 16 February 1833; and other documents. AN BB[18]1333.

73 In addition to the tax register used in Appendix 1, cadastral surveys of land and buildings, dating from 1851 and 1882, have been consulted. ADHC 3.P.852 and 3.P.854.

74 See Robinet et al. (1899); and J. Balteau et al. (1933), VII, which has nine entries for members of the Casabianca family.

75 See, e.g., Miot (1858), I, p. 151; Murray (1868), p. 26; Metz-Noblat (1885), p. 54; Vuillier (1896), p. 238; Comiti (1933), p. 240; and Morel (1951), p. 167.

76 Pomponi (1974a), p. 17.

77 See, e.g., Lear (1870), p. 65; Metz-Noblat (1885), p. 385; Bazin (1913), pp. 225–6; and Archer (1924), p. 83.

78 *Gaz. Trib.*, 8 October 1828, No. 988; see also Vidalenc (1966), p. 71; Valéry (1837), pp. 29–30; Martini (1921); Martini (1922), p. 156; and Bernardini (1970), I, pp. 40–4. Wine, fruit and silk were produced and exported.

79 See Marcaggi (1932), p. 48, who asserts that no vendettas occurred there.

80 See, e.g., Letters, Commissaire du directoire exécutif, Golo, to Minister of Justice, 8 Vendémiaire An VII. AN BB[18]237; President, Tribunal de première instance, Calvi, to same, 4 October 1813. AN BB[18]242; and Miot (1858), I, pp. 144–5; and II, p. 4.

81 At Aregno, Belgodere, Calenzana, Moncale, Montemaggiore, Monticello, Occhiatana,

Olmi-Cappella and Speloncato; see also Gaste (1965), p. 54, who assumes that feuding was still important in the region in 1822.

82 Report, Bruslart to Minister of Justice, 8 February 1815. AN BB[18]242; Gaste (1965), pp. 50–1 (1822); *Gaz. Trib.*, 18 July 1833, No. 2472; and 20 June 1838, No. 3986; Valéry (1837), p. 65; Report, Inspector Carlotti, 3 June 1843. ADCS 3.X.37c; Ortoli (1883), pp. 146–7; and Girolami-Cortona (1893), p. 249.

83 Robiquet (1835), pp. 457 and 458, and Table XXX; Patin de La Fizelière (1963), p. 59; Valéry (1837), p. 200; *Gaz. Trib.*, 5 January 1845, No 5522; Girolami-Cortona (1893), p. 193; and Saravelli-Retali (1976), p. 188.

84 See Vuillier (1896), pp. 215–18; and Morandière (1933).

85 E.g. for Olmeto: Galletti (1863), p. 156; Campbell (1868), pp. 76–7; Saint-Germain (1869), p. 387; Joanne (1881), pp. 546–7; and Lorenzo de Bradi (1928), p. 86; for Santa-Lucia-di-Tallano: Lear (1870), pp. 100–1; Bennet (1876), p. 129; Black (1892), p. 45; and Girolami-Cortona (1893), pp. 287–8; for Levie: Lear (1870), pp. 99–100; for Santa-Maria-Sicche: Joanne (1881), p. 550; for Sari-d'Orcino: Saint-Germain (1869), p. 158; Girolami-Cortona (1893), p. 189; and Bazal (1973), p. 122; and for Oletta: Mancini (1883), p. 114.

86 Lamotte (1956b), p. 55; ADHC E.29.7 (Penta-di-Casinca); Patin de La Fizelière (1963), pp. 61, 73 and 81 (Levie); Pomponi (1974b), esp. pp. 9–12 and 21–3; and Pomponi (1975), esp. pp. 24, 25, 29, 35 and 43–6.

87 Comiti (1933), pp. 163–72; Pomponi (1974b), p. 17; and Pomponi (1975), p. 38.

88 Bevilacqua (1967).

89 Montherot (1840), p. 74; see also Bonaviri (1980), p. 100, on the same phenomenon in Sicily.

90 Marcaggi (1932), pp. 42–3, 48–9, 51–2 and 187.

3 Conflict and its causes: conflicts of material interest

1 Griffon (1841), p. 21; also Deane (1965), p. 38.

2 E.g. Cases v. G.-A. Anziani, Assize Court, 4th session 1854, Extraordinary sitting. AN BB[20]170; and v. S. Papalini, 1st session 1856. AN BB[20]185; and Bournet (1888), pp. 9 and 17–18.

3 Ortoli (1887), pp. 238–9.

4 See e.g. Bialor (1968); P. Schneider (1969); Cohen (1972); Lisón-Tolosana (1973), pp. 825–9; and Du Boulay (1979), p. 17; and, for medieval Iceland, Turner (1971), p. 335; and Byock (1982).

5 See also the general comments of Réalier-Dumas (1819), p. 18; Blanqui (1841), pp. 511 and 532–3; and a speech made by the Procureur-général in 1847. Dufresne (1847), p. 2.

6 Cases v. P.-S. Bartoli, Assize Court, 3rd session 1863. AN BB[20]249; and v. F., G.-F. and L. Palmesani, 1st session 1865. AN BB[20]273.

7 The *Statuts Civils* of 1571 recognized property acquired by *de facto* possession for as little as ten years. Fontana (1905), pp. 83–6.

8 Blanqui (1841), p. 511.

9 Robiquet (1835), pp. 419–20. We shall return to this example in Chapter 12.

10 Feydel (1799), p. 85; and Malaspina (1876), p. 372.

11 Case v. S. Tomasi, Assize Court, 4th session 1843. AN BB[20]121.

12 We will discuss inheritance disputes in detail in Chapter 5.

13 Report, Gendarmerie, Ajaccio, 7 August 1841. ADCS 4.M.125; and Case v. G.-A. Istria, Assize Court, 2nd session 1850. AN BB[20]149.

14 Case v. A.-S. Cartucci, 1st session 1843. AN BB²⁰121.
15 Bertrand (1870), pp. 178–9; and Case v. A.-F. Coronati, Assize Court. *Gaz. Trib.*, 4 May 1836, cit. Sorbier (1863), p. 81.
16 Case v. G. Peretti, 3rd session 1851. AN BB²⁰152.
17 The *Statuts* of 1571 had sanctioned the institution of *avvocazione*, by which paternal relatives to the third degree of the vendor of land or buildings had the first option of buying, a right which had a time limit. If no relatives wished to acquire the property the option passed to the owners of contiguous land. Fontana (1905), pp. 78–80.
18 Case v. P. Carlotti, Assize Court, 3rd session 1853. AN BB²⁰164.
19 Case v. G.-L. Sabiani, Appeal Court, 10 December 1827. ADCS 2.U.1/60. As we shall see, firing scrub for cultivation or pasture was a common procedure.
20 Cases v. A. Calendini, Assize Court, 2nd session 1850. AN BB²⁰149; v. M. Sarrocchi and F.-M. Taddei, 2nd session 1853. AN BB²⁰164; and v. I. Costa, 3rd session 1857. AN BB²⁰194.
21 Case v. G. Ratoni et al., Appeal Court, 26 September 1827. ADCS 2.U.1/60.
22 Report, Subprefect, Sartène, 20 November 1819. ADCS 4.M.98.
23 Patin de La Fizelière (1963), pp. 73 and 80; and Pernet and Lenclud (1977), pp. 92–4. The common lands at Antisanti were partitioned in 1811.
24 Report, 7 October 1842. Petition for clemency for Angelo-Giuseppo Ruggeri. AN BB²⁴195–218.
25 Cases v. G.-F. Astolfi, Assize Court, 1st session 1853. AN BB²⁰164; v. Don Giacomo Ortoli and brothers, Tribunal correctionnel, Sartène, 21 January 1821. 3.U.5/170; v. G.-B. and P.-F. Ambrosi, Assize Court, 3rd session 1850. AN BB²⁰149; and v. F. Giafferi, 2nd session 1858. AN BB²⁰204.
26 Hasluck (1954), Ch. IX.
27 Report, Subprefect, Sartène, 25 August 1823. ADCS 4.M.99.
28 See e.g. Raulin and Ravis-Giordani (1978), p. 61 and illustration.
29 Case v. O.-M. Tristani, Assize Court, 2nd session 1852. AN BB²⁰158.
30 'Chronique', *Gaz. Trib.*, 18 May 1839, No. 4270.
31 Case v. P. and G. Quilici, Assize Court, 4th session 1842. AN BB²⁰116.
32 Saint-Germain (1869), p. 332; Bigot (1890), pp. 440–1; Deliberations, Municipal Council, Penta-di-Casinca, 11 August 1861, etc. ADHC E.29/8; and Venzolasca, 10 June 1900. ADHC E.18/3; Bevilacqua (1967), pp. 49–50; and author's fieldwork; see also generally Comiti (1933), pp. 267–8; Patin de La Fizelière (1963), p. 63; Renucci (1974), pp. 38–9; and Favreau-Cancellieri (1975), p. 48.
33 Cases v. G.-A. Nicolai, Assize Court, 1st session 1854. AN BB²⁰170; and v. A.-P. and P.-M. Pietri, Tribunal correctionnel, Sartène, 11 August 1818. ADCS 3.U.5/167; Report, Subprefect, Sartène, 29 March 1823. 4.M.99; Cases v. V. Vellutini, Tribunal correctionnel, Sartène, 22 September; v. A. Luciani, 27 October 1821; v. C. and D. Peretti, 16 May 1821. ADCS 3.U.5/170; and v. G.-S. and D. Santini, Assize Court, 4th session 1855. AN BB²⁰177.
34 Ceccaldi (1974), p. 341; on the billhook itself, see Finelli (n.d.) p. 34; Cristofini et al. (1978), p. 96; and Abelleira (1981), p. 113, Fig. 14.
35 Cases v. L.-A. Leca, Assize Court, 2nd session 1842. AN BB²⁰116; and v. G.-M. Valle and A.-M. Pantaloni, 2nd session 1845. AN BB²⁰130.
36 Cases v. A.-M. Peretti, Tribunal correctionnel, Sartène, 11 December 1819. ADCS 3.U.5/168; and v. D. Vignoli, Assize Court, 3rd session 1842. AN BB²⁰116.
37 Lamotte (1956g); and Bigot (1890), pp. 440 and 505–8.
38 Letter, F. Lambruschini to Prefect, 29 December 1846. ADCS 2.M.79; and Case v. 13 persons from Bisinchi, Assize Court, 4th session 1852. AN BB²⁰158.
39 E.g. Reports, Subprefect, Sartène, 26 June 1820 (Olmeto); and 13 September 1828 (Mela). ADCS 4.M.98 and 99.

40 See e.g. ADCS 2.U.1/60, 'Délits forestiers 1827'; and 3.U.5/224–7, 'Jugements forestiers 1855–95'; and Albitreccia (1942a), pp. 95–7.

41 *Gaz. Trib.*, 3 September 1841, No. 4992, re Case, Tribunal correctionnel, Corte, 16 July. The State claimed 129,000 ha. in 1841, of which only 21,554 ha. were uncontested.

42 Case v. G.-P. Paoli, Tribunal correctionnel, Sartène, 9 November 1822. ADCS 3.U.5/171; *Gaz. Trib.*, 3 September 1841; and Letter, Sub-inspector of forests, Ajaccio, to Keeper of forests, 3 August 1846. ADCS 2.M.79.

43 See Ballard (1852), esp. pp. 11–15; Bournet (1888), pp. 11–13.

44 7,000 trees were said to have been felled illegally in the northern half of Corsica in the winter of 1797. Letter, Commissaire du Directoire exécutif, Department of Golo to Ministry of Justice, 5e jour complémentaire An VI. AN BB[18]237.

45 Tuckett (1884), p. 457; Bartoli (1898), pp. 100–1; Woolsey (1917), pp. 154–7; Viale et al. (1966), pp. 80–8; and Pernet and Lenclud (1977), p. 93. On the last point, see e.g. the testimony of a Sicilian shepherd cited by Dolci (1963), p. 173: 'Woods are bad for sheep-grazing. The sheep catch their wool in the briars and come out stripped of their coats. Shepherds don't like woods as thorns and scrub tear the fleece ... and the grass underneath trees is no good.'

46 Woolsey (1917), p. 154; Bartoli (1898), pp. 100–1; and Bournet (1888).

47 Letters, Sub-inspector of forests, Ajaccio, 3 August; and Forest Administrator to Prefect, 6 August 1846. ADCS 2.M.79; and Case v. P.-A. Fieschi, Assize Court, 1st session 1849. AN BB[20]146.

48 Cases v. M. Calzaroni, Court of Criminal Justice, 1st session 1830. AN BB[20]49; v. D.-F. Vargioni, Ajaccio, 17 April 1812. ADCS 2.U.1/42; and v. B. Ottavi, Assize Court, 1st session 1864. AN BB[20]260.

49 Bigot (1890), pp. 501–2; and Forcioli-Conti (1897), p. 77; see also Foata (1856), where the *curé* of Bocognano and future bishop of Ajaccio prophesied this development.

50 Lenclud and Ravis-Giordani (1973), pp. 200–5.

51 Davis (1977), p. 21; see also J. Schneider (1969), pp. 115–16; and J. Schneider (1971).

52 See, for example, Feydel (1799), pp. 52–3; Defranceschi (1974); and Pomponi (1979b), pp. 147–51, 157, 160, 166, 200, 234–6 and *passim*.

53 Case v. J.-M. Saladini, Extraordinary Criminal Court, 3 Messidor An X. ADCS 7.U.1/22; see also e.g. Letter, Commissaire du Directoire exécutif, Department of Golo to Ministry of Justice, 8 Vendémiaire An VII. AN BB[18]237; and Case v. M. Nicolai et al., Assize Court, 22 April 1834. *Gaz. Trib.*, 3 July 1834, No. 2769.

54 Cases v. S. Bartoli, Assize Court, 3rd session 1857. AN BB[20]194; and v. G.-A. Valentini, 25 May 1893. AN BB[20]286.

55 Deliberations, Municipal Council, Penta-di-Casinca, Year VIII – 1853. ADHC E.29.7; Case v. A.-M. Antonmarchi, Assize Court, 4th session 1843. AN BB[20]121; and Foata (1856), p. 4.

56 Ardouin-Dumazet (1898), p. 152; see also Rapport Mottet, 1836, cit. Versini (1979), pp. 188–9; Ballard (1852), pp. 5 and 10–11; and Piobb (n.d.), pp. 67–8 and 70.

57 Pomponi (1976b); Ballard (1852), p. 11; Bigot (1890), pp. 501–2; and Deliberations, Municipal Council, Penta-di-Casinca, 8 March 1823. ADHC E.29/7; also Albitreccia (1942a), pp. 64–5; and Luciani (1969), pp. 53–4.

58 Letter, A. Vincentelli to Prefect, 3 December 1846. ADCS 2.M.87; and Cases v. P. Berretti, Assize Court, 2nd session; and v. N. Ceccaldi, 4th session 1852, Extraordinary sitting. AN BB[20]158; v. G.-D. Bazziconi, Assize Court, 1st session 1851, AN BB[20]152; and v. L. Ciarini, 2nd session 1857. AN BB[20]194.

59 Bertrand (1870), pp. 144–5; Case v. G. Santelli et al., Assize Court, 3rd session 1852. AN BB[20]158; and Deliberations, Municipal Council, Penta-di-Casinca. ADHC E.29/7.

60 Case v. O.-G. Preziosi, Assize Court, 4th session 1849. AN BB[20]146.

61 Petition for clemency for D.-A. Graziani. AN BB[24]886.

62 Bigot (1890), pp. 465–6; see also Comiti (1933), p. 142.

63 Case v. G.-F. Muzziconacci, Extraordinary Criminal Court, Sartène, 11 April 1806. ADCS 3.U.5/131.

64 Piobb (n.d.), p. 69; and Feydel (1799), pp. 35–6; see also Blanqui (1841), p. 509; Forester (1858), p. 60; Blanchard (1915), p. 57; and Blanchard (1926), p. 115.

65 Case v. F.-S. Antonmarchi and T. Grimaldi, Assize Court, 1st session 1853. AN BB[20]164.

66 Report, Subprefect, Sartène, 11 September 1823. ADCS 4.M.99; and Cases v. R. Paoli and C. Tomasini, Assize Court, 4th session 1861. AN BB[20]229; and v. S.-M. Vaccarezza, 1st session 1862. AN BB[20]239.

67 See e.g. Blanqui (1841), pp. 508–9 and 513–14; Faure (1858), pp. 264–7; Bigot (1890), p. 42; Simi (1966), p. 42; and Chiva (1963), p. 112.

68 Reports, Gendarmerie, 14 August 1841. ADCS 4.M.125; and Mayor, Santa-Lucia-di-Tallano, 1 November 1820. ADCS 1.V.44.

69 Report, Gendarmerie, 8 September 1821, cit. Franceschini (1919), p. 83; and *Journal du Département de la Corse*, 19 July and 9 August 1828. It is significant here that Francesco Stefani, a herdsman from Serraggio, was sentenced to death in 1830 for starting a forest fire in July 1828. This extremely severe sentence was clearly intended to have deterrent value. See Case v. F. Stefani, Court of Criminal Justice, 2nd session 1830. AN BB[20]49.

70 Report, Subprefect, Sartène, 22 June 1823. ADCS 4.M.99.

71 See Mérimée (1840a); Bigot (1890), p. 438; Méjean (1932), pp. 659, 664, 668 and 670; Raulin and Ravis-Giordani (1978), pp. 37 and 40; and Ravis-Giordani (1978a), p. 136.

72 Cases v. P.-M. and G.-B. Matra, Assize Court, 4th session 1849. AN BB[20]146; v. P.-M. Renucci, 2nd session 1854. AN BB[20]170; and v. P. Alessandri and P. Quilichini, Tribunal correctionnel, Sartène, 13 February 1822. ADCS 3.U.5/171.

73 See e.g. Lear (1870), p. 133, with illustration; Vuillier (1896), p. 175, with illustration; D'Este (1905), p. 69; Rankin (1930), p. 17; and author's fieldwork (Speloncato, 1981). Lear and Vuillier refer to special collars attached to pigs at Ota and Zicavo.

74 Report, Procureur-général to Ministry of Justice, 14 January 1815. AN BB[18]242 (Ocana); Valéry (1837), pp. 210–22; and Case v. D. Nicolai, Assize Court, 1st session 1853. AN BB[20]164 (Levie); Case v. D. Mondolini, Court of Criminal Justice, 1830. AN BB[20]49 (Cozzano); Pomponi (1976c), p. 160 (Pila-Canale); Case v. B. Buresi, Assize Court, 1st session 1842. AN BB[20]116 (Ciamannacce); Case v. D. Mozziconacci, 2nd session 1853, Extraordinary sitting. AN BB[20]164 (Loreto-di-Tallano); Cases v. B. Giordani, 1st session 1860. AN BB[20]221; and v. A.-M. Tavera and G.-A. Pinzuti, 1st and 4th sessions 1863. AN BB[20]249 (Peri); Case v. A.-V. Pacchiarelli, 4th session 1865. AN BB[20]273; and Carrington (1971a), pp. 83–4; and Bazal (1973), pp. 183–9 (Moca-Croce).

75 Case v. A. and Don G. Serra, Tribunal correctionnel, Sartène, 8 September 1821. ADCS 3.U.5/170.

76 Mérimée (1840a) p. 525; see also Marin-Muracciole (1964), p. 11; and Carrington (1971a), p. 84. It also figured in the feuds at Aullène, Levie, Moca-Croce and Santa-Maria-Sicche; see Reports, Gendarmerie, Ajaccio, 15 September and 8 October 1841. ADCS 4.M.125; and 5 July 1842. ADCS 4.M.126; and Reports, Subprefect, Sartène, 18 November 1826 etc. ADCS 4.M.99.

77 Reports, Subprefect, Sartène, 14 April 1821, 9 April and 16 July 1825, and 26 May 1823. ADCS 4.M.98 and 99; and Versini (1972), pp. 21–47.

78 Case v. G. Ortoli and G.-A. Poli, Tribunal correctionnel, Sartène, 22 January 1830. ADCS 3.U.5/156.

79 'Rôles des taxes municipales sur les chiens, 1872–1909', Venzolasca. ADHC E.18/22. The tax on working or guard-dogs (introduced in 1855) was 1 franc and that on other dogs 5 francs, which must have discouraged registration under the second category, but it is unlikely that the degree of fraud was such as to alter the overall pattern significantly. See also for the Sartenais in an earlier period, Patin de La Fizelière (1963), p. 63.

80 Letter, Massoni to Prefect, 5 February 1850. ADCS 1.M.229; and Cases v. N. Tenneroni, Assize Court, 2nd session 1845. AN BB[20]130; and v. F. Raffini, 1st session 1853. AN BB[20]164.

81 See the somewhat discrepant accounts of Bourde (1887), pp. 161–80; Cesari-Rocca (1908), p. 22; and Marcaggi (1932), pp. 41–2.

82 Cases v. A.-M. Lucioni, Assize Court, 1st session; and v. P.-F. Giannetti, 2nd session 1843. AN BB[20]121; and v. G.-F. Lanfranchi, 1 June 1846. *Gaz. Trib.*, 21 June 1846, No. 5914.

83 Vuillier (1896), p. 174; and Viale (1855), p. 21.

84 Hasluck (1954), Ch. VII, 'The law of the dog'; see also Luomala (1960) on Polynesia; and Bieler (1963), p. 175, citing a mid-seventh century Irish canon.

85 E.g. Lamotte (1964), p. 60; Bournet (1888), p. 9; judgment of Special Military Commission, 3 May 1808. AN BB[18]241; and Ortoli (1887), pp. 188–9.

86 Moss (1979), pp. 490–2; and Hasluck (1954), p. 203.

87 Letter, Administrateur-général Miot to Ministry of Justice, 10 Fructidor An IX. AN BB[18]236.

88 Report, Procureur-général, 17 December 1814. AN BB[18]242; Letter, Mayor, Corte, to Prefect, 18 April 1841. ADCS 4.M.125; Cases, Assize Court. *Gaz. Trib.*, 23 September 1840, No. 4695; and v. S. Gaudeani, 4th session 1844. AN BB[20]125.

89 See Gregorovius (1855), p. 329; Caisson (1978b), p. 162; and Ortoli (1887), pp. 164–5.

90 Case v. G. Angelini, Assize Court, 3rd session 1849. AN BB[20]146; Report, Subprefect, Sartène, 29 May 1835. ADCS 4.M.100; Case v. G. Guidicelli, Assize Court, 3rd session 1842. AN BB[20]116.

91 Cases v. G. Marchi et al., Extraordinary Criminal Court, 20 Nivôse An XI. ADCS 3.U.5/130; and v. G.-M. Ciafferi, Brumaire An XIV. ADCS 3.U.5/131; v. Giulio Tavera, Assize Court, 4th session 1853, Extraordinary sitting. AN BB[20]164; and v. F. Venturini et al., 2nd session 1844. AN BB[20]125.

92 Cases v. G. Sanguinetti, 2nd session 1845. AN BB[20]130; and 21 September 1862, 'Conciliations 1861–80'. ADCS 4.U.3/60.

93 Molinari (1886), p. 237; see also Pernet and Lenclud (1977), p. 116 note 12.

94 Cases v. G.-C. Santini and v. M. Tomasi, Assize Court, 4th session 1852. AN BB[20]158; v. F.-M. Paolini, 3rd session 1856. AN BB[20]185; and v. G.-A. Anziani, 4th session 1854, Extraordinary sitting. AN BB[20]170.

95 Case v. P.-L. Pietri, Extraordinary Criminal Court, 29 Fructidor An IX. ADCS 7.U.1/17. It is not clear whether this was a right of tenants in Corsica in some circumstances, as it was, for example, among the Swat Pathans; see Barth (1965), p. 74; and also Barley (1961), pp. 70, 84, 89 and 154.

96 Cases v. G. Simoni et al., Extraordinary Criminal Court, Sartène, Thermidor An X. ADCS 3.U.5/129; and v. G.-D. Giovanangeli, Assize Court, 3rd session 1862. AN BB[20]239; and Indictment of G.-G. Costa et al., 23 November 1815. AN BB[18]241.

97 Robiquet (1835), p. 445; and Raulin and Ravis-Giordani (1978), p. 62.

98 Cases v. A. Benedetti, Assize Court, 3rd session 1850. AN BB[20]149; and v. G. Gavini, Appeal Court, May 1857 (Procédures correctionnels). ADCS 2.U.1/61.

99 Raulin and Ravis-Giordani (1978), p. 67; see also Mattei (1867), pp. 59–60.

100 Bigot (1890), p. 471; and see Caisson et al. (1978a), p. 134 (photo).

101 E.g. 'the square of Domenico Muselli' at Ocana (Letter, P. Muselli to Prefect, 2 November 1840. ADCS 2.M.84), the 'square called Antoni' at Pila-Canale (Report, Gendarmerie, Ajaccio, 8 September 1841. ADCS 4.M.125), or 'the square called Santoni' at Palneca (Report, same, 30 June 1842. ADCS 4.M.126).

102 E.g. Letter, Mayor, Venzolasca to Subprefect, 26 March 1875. ADHC E.18/26; and author's fieldwork (Carbini, Cozzano, Santa-Lucia-di-Tallano, Santa-Maria-Sicche and Serra).

103 Case v. P. Leonetti, Assize Court, 2nd session 1853, Extraordinary sitting. AN BB^{20}164; Report on case before Assize Court, August 1878, Petition for clemency for D. Ficoni, 1883. AN BB^{24}875; Cases v. G. and A.-M. Subrini, Assize Court, 3rd session 1846. AN BB^{20}134; Appeal Court, 6 May 1829, *Gaz. Trib.*, 25–26 May, No. 1184; and S.P. Castelli, Assize Court, 3rd session 1842. AN BB^{20}116.

104 Cases v. Don F. Quilichini, Tribunal correctionnel, Sartène, 30 June 1824. ADCS 3.U.5/174; and v. M. Galloni d'Istria, Assize Court, 2nd session 1851, Cases tried *in absentia*. AN BB^{20}152; and 4th session 1852. AN BB^{20}158; and Reports, February 1883, Petition for clemency for G.-G. Pietri. AN BB^{24}887.

105 Maestrati (1962), p. 13; and Thrasher (1970), pp. 233–4 and 269.

106 Letters, 28 Nivôse An IX. AN BB^{18}236; and Report, Gendarmerie, 8 November 1820, cit. Franceschini (1919), p. 60.

107 E.g. *Journal du Département de la Corse*, 2 July 1829; *Gaz. Trib.*, 23 December 1832, No. 2297; and Letter, Castelli to Procureur-général, 27 May 1912. ADCS 1.M.231.

108 Case v. S. Reginendi. Court of Criminal Justice, 2nd session 1830. AN BB^{20}49.

109 E.g. Cases v. C.-P. Paoli, 4th session 1844. AN BB^{20}125; and v. B. Buresi and G.-B. Zerubia, 2nd session 1852. AN BB^{20}158.

110 See Pernet and Lenclud (1977), p. 116, note 12; and Raulin and Ravis-Giordani (1978), esp. pp. 71–3.

111 E.g. cases reported by the subprefect of Sartène at Arbellara, 31 July 1817; at Olmiccia, 13 November 1827; and at Poggio, 23 August 1828. ADCS 4.M.98 and 99.

112 See Robiquet (1835), pp. 536–7; Bigot (1890), pp. 504–5; Casanova (1971); Borel-Léandri (1978), pp. 222ff; and Raulin and Ravis-Giordani (1978), pp. 58–9, 106–13 and 146–9.

113 Cases v. A.-L. Mancini, Assize Court, 1st session 1846. AN BB^{20}134; and v. G.-B. Peretti, 1st session 1860. AN BB^{20}221.

114 See Davis (1977), p. 59.

115 Cases v. P.-D. Vincenti, 3rd session 1845. AN BB^{20}130; and v. N.-M. Ortoli and F. Quilichini, Tribunal correctionnel, Sartène, December 1812. ADCS 3.U.5/166.

116 Mérimée (1840a), pp. 468 and 507.

117 Cases v. Don J. Bonavita et al., Assize Court, 4th session; and v. F. Pellegrini, 1st session 1842. AN BB^{18}116.

118 E.g. Benson (1825), p. 60; Chiari (1960), p. 110; and Arrighi (ed.) (1971), p. 410. On the latter point, see Hallowell (1943), pp. 132–3.

119 List of 'contumaces', 23 July 1833. AN BB^{18}1095; and Bournet (1888), p. 17. See also Chapter 1, p. 15.

120 Assize Court, Report on 2nd session 1857. AN BB^{20}194.

121 Cases v. F. Pasqualini, 4th session 1852, Extraordinary sitting. AN BB^{20}158; and v. G.-C. Romani and G.-F. Vellutini, 3rd session 1858. AN BB^{20}213.

122 Cases v. D. Battisti, 1–2 June 1838. *Gaz. Trib.*, 20 June 1838, No. 3986; v. G.-B. Santoni, 4th session 1855. AN BB^{20}177; v. G.-M. Pieraggi, 2nd session 1850. AN BB^{20}149; and v. G.-N. Fumaroli, 2nd session 1856. AN BB^{20}185.

123 E.g. Cases v. G.-B. Maestracci et al., 2nd session 1856. AN BB^{20}185 (Muro); and v. C.-A. Peretti, 3rd session 1859. AN BB^{20}213 (Levie).

124 Montherot (1840), pp. 67–8.

125 Case v. P. Negroni, Assize Court, 3rd session 1833. *Gaz. Trib.*, 30 October 1833, No. 2562.

126 Filippi (1906), p. 34; and Lorenzi de Bradi (1928), pp. 139–40.

127 Cases v. P.-F. Tristani, Assize Court, 4th session 1852. AN BB²⁰158; v. F.-M. Fumaroli, 1st session 1854. AN BB²⁰170; and v. G. Poggioli, 2nd session 1851. AN BB²⁰152.

128 Case v. I. Barboni, Assize Court, 2nd session 1851. AN BB²⁰152; Report, Gendarmerie, Ajaccio, 14 September 1842. ADCS 4.M.128; Report on case v. G.-A. Castiglione, Tribunal correctionnel, Calvi, 15 Messidor An XIII. AN BB¹⁸240; and Cases v. C. and A.-M. Pietri, Tribunal correctionnel, Sartène, An IX. ADCS 3.U.5/132; and v. D. Giampierini, Assize Court, 4th session 1834. *Gaz. Trib.*, 25 January 1835, No. 2942.

129 A point made in another context by Cohen (1972).

130 Cases v. P.-M. Vincenti, Assize Court, 1st session 1833. *Gaz. Trib.*, 19 April 1833, cit. Sorbier (1863), pp. 30–4; v. G. Giaminelli, 1st session 1842. AN BB²⁰116; v. J. Lucrezj, 4th session 1846. AN BB²⁰134; v. P. Frassati, 1st session; and v. G. Bardelli, 2nd session 1849, Extraordinary sitting. AN BB²⁰146; and v. F.-A. Muzi, 4th session 1858. AN BB²⁰204.

131 Case v. P.-S. Valle, 4th session 1845. AN BB²⁰130.

132 E.g. Benson (1825), p. 38.

133 Robiquet (1835), pp. 392–3. The same plea of poverty was made by two men convicted of stealing part of a monstrance from the church of Ortiporio in 1829. *Gaz. Trib.*, 20 August 1829, No. 1257.

134 Cases v. D. Gionnotti and C. Massoni; and v. M. Vincenti, Assize Court, 2nd session 1845. AN BB²⁰130; v. O.-B. Pietri, 2nd session 1848. AN BB²⁰142; v. P. Poli, 4th session 1851. AN BB²⁰152; and v. P.-M. Ortoli et al., 2nd session 1848. AN BB²⁰142.

135 Versini (1972), pp. 21–44; and Cases v. F.-F. Ciamborani, Assize Court, 1st session 1853. AN BB²⁰164; and v. S. Constantini; and v. F.-N. Savignoni, 2nd session 1893. AN BB²⁰286.

136 Report, Subprefect, 14 November 1820. ADCS 4.M.98.

137 Blanqui (1841), p. 511, see also Piobb (n.d.), p. 47; and Pomponi (1978a), p. 17.

138 Lamotte (1956e), p. 42.

139 Cit. Pomponi (1978a), p. 13; see also Réalier-Dumas (1819), p. 25.

140 Brögger (1968), pp. 232–3; and Burckhardt (1944), p. 276, citing an unnamed source; see also Dolci (1963), pp. 81 and 241; and P. Schneider (1969) (Sicily); Barth (1965), pp. 82–6 (Swat Pathans); Du Boulay (1979), pp. 110–11 (modern Greece); Breteau and Zagnoli (1979), p. 294 (Calabria and Algeria); Byock (1982), pp. 72–3 (medieval Iceland); and Black-Michaud (1975), pp. 177–9, 181, 184 and 190ff.

141 Saravelli-Retali (1976), p. 135.

142 For further discussion of the *rimbeccu*, see Ch. 7, pp. 203–4.

4 Conflict and its causes: conflicts of honour

1 Benson (1825), p. 51.

2 E.g. Mattei (1867), pp. 57–8, 91 and 118–20; and Saravelli-Retali (1976), p. 56.

3 Cit. Viale (1855), p. 38.

4 E.g. Report, Procureur-général, 10 September 1863, Petition for clemency for P. Balisoni. AN BB²⁴687–709; and Letter from A.-Q. Roccaserra to Ministry of Justice, 3 January 1879. AN BB²⁴852.

5 See Pitt-Rivers (1971), esp. Ch. VIII.

6 Lorenzi de Bradi (1928), pp. 167–8.

7 E.g. Southwell Colucci (1933), pp. 93 and 209–10.
8 Petition for clemency for L. Barberini, 1835. AN BB²⁴155–69.
9 Case v. A. Costa, Assize Court, 2nd session 1853. AN BB²⁰164. For examples of such verses, see Dalmas (1978), pp. 21–2.
10 Cases v. D. Folacci, 1st session; and v. S. Guerini, 2nd session 1852. AN BB²⁰158.
11 Case v. P.-P. Paoli, Assize Court, 1st session 1853. AN BB²⁰164; Note, Prefecture, 1861(?); and Report, Procureur-général to Prefect, 11 April 1862. ADCS 2.M.140.
12 Report, Procureur-général to Ministry of Justice, 2 January 1826. AN BB¹⁸1132; Letter, Mayor, Sartène, 1 December 1829. ADCS 4.M.99; Printed Judgment, Criminal Court, Bastia, 1 Vendémiaire An VI. AN BB¹⁸237; *Gaz. Trib.*, 4 June 1842, No. 4729; and Versini (1972), p. 105 note.
13 *Gaz. Trib.*, 14 August 1827, No. 612; and 30 November 1843, No. 5186.
14 Mérimée (1840b), p. 710; see also Robiquet (1835), p. 387. It is not always clear whether the weapons in question were muskets or rifles.
15 *Gaz. Trib.*, 8 November 1837, No. 3795.
16 See e.g. Goubert (1968), p. 144.
17 See Chapter 12, p. 338.
18 Petition for clemency for G. Dionisi (sentenced to one month's imprisonment for carrying arms), November 1879. AN BB²⁴868.
19 Ortoli (1883), p. 278.
20 It is significant here that the lower courts in Corsica firmly rejected a ruling of the *Cour Royale* in 1841, which included hunting guns in the ban on carrying firearms, restricting the ban effectively to 'weapons of war'. *Gaz. Trib.*, 24 October 1841, No. 4536. On the unrestrained nature of hunting in Corsica, see Comiti (1933), pp. 290–2.
21 Cases v. P.-O. Paoli, Assize Court, 4th session 1849. AN BB²⁰146; and v. L. Renucci, 4th session 1861. AN BB²⁰229; and Report, 13 February 1883, Petition for clemency for G.-G. Pietri, AN BB²⁴887.
22 Case, Tribunal correctionnel, Sartène, 1822. ADCS 3.U.5/171; see also Gil (1978), pp. 198–9, citing a well-known folk-tale.
23 Chiari (1960), p. 109.
24 Case v. A. and A.-B. Brandi, Extraordinary Criminal Court, 22 Vendémiaire An XI. ADCS 7.U.1/24; Report, Subprefect, Sartène, 28 July 1821. ADCS 4.M.99; and Bazal (1973), p. 141.
25 'O figliuolo di cacasoquiule.' Case v. G. Codaccioni, Tribunal correctionnel, Sartène, 24 July 1817. ADCS 3.U.5/167.
26 'O spaghia chiusa' – literally 'ruined enclosure'. Case v. A.-P. Pietri, Tribunal correctionnel, Sartène, 6 October 1824. ADCS 3.U.5/174.
27 Letter, Sebastiano Cappelini to Count Berthier, no date. AN BB¹⁸242.
28 Bouchez (1843), p. 52.
29 Cases v. C.-M. Balisoni and G.-A. Galloni, Assize Court, 3rd session 1857. AN BB²⁰194; and v. M. Galloni d'Istria, 2nd session 1851. AN BB²⁰152; and Bazal (1973), pp. 50–1.
30 Bournet (1888), p. 17.
31 Cases, Assize Court, 4th session 1849. AN BB²⁰146; v. G.-B. Martinetti, 4th session 1854. AN BB²⁰170; v. A. Vincenti, 4th session 1848. AN BB²⁰142; v. G.-S. Ventura and G.-B. Colombani, 1st session 1852. AN BB²⁰158; and v. G.-B. Muselli, 2nd session 1858. AN BB²⁰204.
32 Bournet (1888), pp. 26–9 (providing figures for spirits); and Bigot (1890), pp. 474–5.
33 Cases v. P.-D. Vacarezza, Assize Court, 4th session 1852, Extraordinary sitting. AN BB²⁰158; v. B. Morelli, 1st session 1856. AN BB²⁰185.
34 Bigot (1890), p. 475; see also Robiquet (1835), p. 445; Miot (1858), II, pp. 35–6 (Bocognano); Beaulieu-Delbet (1897), p. 48 (Cauro); Lorenzi de Bradi (1928),

pp. 143–4 and 155–6; Arrighi (1970), p. 247; Saravelli-Retali (1976), p. 135; and Finelli (n.d.), p. 53 (Tavera).

35 Saint-Germain (1869), p. 293 (Campile); and Versini (1979), pp. 121–2, who provides a description of the game. Dominoes was also played.

36 See Davis (1964), criticizing the account provided by Vailland (1957); also Falassi (1980), pp. 213–23.

37 E.g. Case v. B. Peres, Assize Court, 1st session 1857. AN BB^{20}194.

38 Petitions for clemency for F. Acquaviva et al., 1884. AN BB^{24}882; and for T. Taddei, 1836. AN BB^{24}155–69.

39 Case v. P. Torre, Assize Court, 2nd session 1865. AN BB^{20}273. Bigot (1890), p. 516, notes the same practice of young men dressing up as women or as Turks or Moors with black faces, and engaging in ritual begging, mock captures, etc.

40 Report, Procureur impérial to Prefect, 20 February 1864. ADCS 2.M.138.

41 E.g. Case v. G.-A. Mariani, Assize Court, 2nd session 1865. AN BB^{20}273 (Frasso).

42 E.g. Bertrand (1870), pp. 164–8, referring to fighting during the Passion play at Orezza in 1808.

43 E.g. Marcaggi (1932), p. 53, referring to a violent conflict at Venzolasca during the sheep-shearing festival in 1880.

44 Cases v. P.-A. Mancini, Assize Court, 4th session 1852. AN BB^{20}158; v. A. Giovannoni and G.-B. Pasqualini, 2nd session 1841. *Gaz. Trib.*, 5th June 1841, No. 4913.

45 Report, Gendarmerie, Ajaccio, 13 September 1841. ADCS 4.M.125; and Case v. A.-M. and P.-F. Vecchioni, Assize Court, 2nd session 1854. AN BB^{20}170; see also Marcaggi (1932), pp. 145–7 and 238ff.

46 Marcaggi (1932), pp. 159–60.

47 Privat (1936), p. 48; and see, for comparison, Hertz (1983), pp. 65–7.

48 Case v. A. Sisco, Assize Court, 3rd session 1853. AN BB^{20}164.

49 Casanova (1931), I, p. xxii; Southwell Colucci (1933), pp. 148–9, citing a *vocero* collected at Evisa; and Casta (1974), p. 171.

50 Case v. A.-F. Durazzi and P.-G. Paoli, Tribunal correctionnel, Sartène, July 1811. ADCS 3.U.5/165; Report, Subprefect, Sartène, 20 April 1824. ADCS 4.M.99; Letter, Mayor to Prefect, 16 December 1869. ADCS 2.V.20; and Report, Procureur de la République, 20 April 1885, Petition for clemency for G.-A. Piazza. AN BB^{24}888.

51 Cases v. G. Poggi, Assize Court, 3rd session 1857. AN BB^{20}194; v. S. Bernardi, 2nd session 1844. AN BB^{20}125; and v. P.-M. Paoli, 2nd session 1845. AN BB^{20}130.

52 Cases v. D. and G. Gaffajoli and C.-G. Marcelli, 1st session; and v. Don P. Carlotti, 3rd session 1851. AN BB^{20}152; and v. F. Giovannoni, 3rd session 1864. AN BB^{20}260; also v. A. Fieschi, 2nd session 1850. AN BB^{20}149.

53 Case v. N. and F. Cucchi, 4th session 1853. AN BB^{20}164; and Bertrand (1870), pp. 120–7.

54 Cases v. M.-F. Quilichini, 1st session; and v. A. Angelini and S. Rossi, 4th session 1846. AN BB^{20}134. The general question of women exercising vengeance is discussed in Chapter 8, pp. 219–21.

55 Filippi (1906), p. 11.

56 Cases v. G. Girolami, 2nd session 1858. AN BB^{20}204; and v. P. Giovanelli, 4th session 1832. *Gaz. Trib.*, 3 January 1833, No. 2305; also *Gaz. Trib.*, 30 November 1843. No. 5186.

57 Cases v. G. Acquaviva, Assize Court, 2nd session 1853, Extraordinary sitting. AN BB^{20}164; v. G. Quilichini et al., Tribunal correctionnel, Sartène, 31 July 1822. ADCS 3.U.5/171; Letter, G. Bozzi et al. to Prefect, no date (1837). ADCS 1.M.229; Cases, v. D. Romanacce, Assize Court, 2nd session 1849, Extraordinary sitting. AN BB^{20}146; and v. N. Paoli, 1st session 1842. AN BB^{20}116.

58 Filippi (1906), p. 12.

59 Griffon (1841), p. 15; Report, Commissaire spécial, 29 September 1817, cit. Franceschini (1922), p. 288; and Fée (1850), p. 217.

60 See e.g. Montherot (1840), pp. 17 and 61–2; and Beaulieu-Delbet (1897), p. 14.

61 Case v. F. Benedetti, Assize Court, 4th session 1863. AN BB^{20}249.

62 Case v. P.-A. Franchi et al., Tribunal correctionnel, Sartène, 29 January 1825. ADCS 3.U.5/175. Literally *cornicone* means 'wearing horns'.

63 Versini (1972), p. 120; and Southwell-Colucci (1933), pp. 207–8.

64 Case v. G.-B. Martinetti and P. Giordani, Assize Court, 1st session 1851, Extraordinary sitting. AN BB^{20}152.

65 Cases v. I. Capponi, 3rd session 1848. AN BB^{20}142; v. C.-M. Balisoni and G.-A. Galloni, 3rd session 1857. AN BB^{20}194; v. A.-P. Ortoli, 3rd session 1862. AN BB^{20}239; and v. G.-C. Santucci et al., 1st session 1857. AN BB^{20}194.

66 Report, Procureur-général, 19 September 1861, Petition for clemency for P. Carlotti. AN BB^{24}876.

67 Cases. v. Degiovanni, 1st session 1833. *Gaz. Trib.*, 5 April 1833, cit. Sorbier (1863), pp. 26–30; and v. A. Lucchini, 2nd session 1839. *Gaz. Trib.*, 20 July 1839, No. 4236; and Dalmas (1978), p. 18.

68 Galletti (1863), pp. 230–1; and also Brady and Pottle (eds.) (1955), p. 159 (1765); Flaubert (1973) [1840], pp. 325–6; Bennet (1876), pp. 36–7; Busquet (1919), p. 112; Marin-Muracciole (1964), esp. pp. 196–201; and McLaren (1966), pp. 47–8.

69 Lorenzi de Bradi (1936), p. 12; and Mattei (1867), p. 34; see also Ravis-Giordani (1978b), p. 196; and Martin-Gistucci (1976), p. 179.

70 Malaspina (1876), p. 372; see also Mérimée (1840a), pp. 495–6; and Saint-Germain (1869), p. 250.

71 Black-Michaud (1975), pp. 227–8; see also, more generally, Cozzi (1910), pp. 673–6; Yalman (1963); and Papanek (1973), esp. pp. 317–19.

72 Cases v. G. Peres, Assize Court, 2nd session 1854. AN BB^{20}170; and v. A.-P. Orsini, 1st session 1861. AN BB^{20}229; Letter, Procureur-général, Golo, to Ministry of Justice, 18 Thermidor An XIII. AN BB^{18}238; and Cases v. G.-F. Felici, C. Ristorcelli and M. Amedei; and v. T. Felici, Appeal Court, May–June 1857. ADCS 2.U.1/61.

73 Bartoli (1898), p. 259; Viale (1855), pp. 27–8; Saravelli-Retali (1976), p. 49; Chapman (1908), p. 138; and Bigot (1890), pp. 475 and 516.

74 He provides examples of teen-age brides from the seventeenth and eighteenth centuries, but his statistics for Verdese give a figure of 23 for the early nineteenth century and 25 for the decade 1890–1900; men at Verdese married on average at 28 *c.* 1805, at 26 *c.* 1860 and at 29 *c.* 1900. Pomponi (1976a), pp. 329–31 and 336. See also Le Mée (1971), pp. 32–3; and Lenclud (1985), pp. 39 and 41, who provide similar figures.

75 Vuillier (1896), p. 239; and Casta (1978), p. 178.

76 Callon (1931), pp. 281–4; Orsini (1981), pp. 43–4 (Valpajola); and Geoffray (1982), pp. 58, 61, 64 and 67 (Manso and Galeria).

77 Valéry (1837), p. 76; and Cases v. G.-M. Simoni, Assize Court, 1st session 1853, 2nd sitting. AN BB^{20}164; and v. B. Tomasi, 3rd session 1858. AN BB^{20}204.

78 E.g. Feydel (1799), pp. 68–9; Vuillier (1896), p. 220; Bartoli (1898), pp. 256–9 and 374; and Marin-Muracciole (1964), pp. 196ff.

79 Case v. A.-T. Cartucci, Assize Court, 1st session 1843. AN BB^{20}121.

80 Report, Procureur-général to Ministry of Justice, 2 January 1826. AN BB^{18}1137; and Marin-Muracciole (1964), p. 199.

81 Cases v. C. Ferrandi, Extraordinary Criminal Court, 25 Floréal An IX. ADCS 7.U.1/14; and v. P.-J. Piazzoli and sons, 17 Messidor An IX. ADCS 7.U.1/16; v. A.-P. Quilichini, Assize Court, 2nd session 1854. AN BB^{20}170; Letter, Subprefect to Prefect, 20 August 1852. ADCS 2.M.144. Report, Procureur-général, 11 April 1882, Petition for clemency for G.-A. Santucci. AN BB^{24}881; and Bertrand (1870), pp. 190–3.

82 They were tried in 1842 and acquitted. Case v. D. and C.-F. Morati, Assize Court, 2nd session 1842. AN BB²⁰116; and Versini (1979), pp. 90–7.

83 Case v. P.-G. Napoleoni, 1st session 1853. AN BB²⁰164.

84 Cases v. O.-P. Filippi, 3rd session 1861. AN BB²⁰229; and v. M. Grimaldi, 3rd session 1865. AN BB²⁰273.

85 Cases v. A.-G. Bernardi, 4th session 1846. AN BB²⁰134; v. M. Giacobetti, 2nd session 1858. AN BB²⁰204; v. R. Mariani and A. Rutilj, 2nd session 1853; v. P. Giafferi, 4th session 1853. AN BB²⁰164; and v. B. Marcangeli, 1st session 1862. AN BB²⁰239.

86 Wilson (1988).

87 Case v. M.-F. Franchini, Cour Impériale, Ajaccio, January 1813. ADCS 2.U.1/43.

88 Marin-Muracciole (1964), p. 198; and Feydel (1799), pp. 68–9.

89 Case v. P. Pinzuti, Assize Court, 2nd session 1853, Extraordinary sitting. AN BB²⁰164; Extract from Register of cases. Court of Criminal Justice, 26 March 1810. AN BB¹⁸239; and Case v. F. Padovani, 4th session 1845. AN BB²⁰130.

90 Report, Subprefect, Sartène, 26 March 1819. ADCS 4.M.98; and Case v. G.-C. Pietrini, Court of Criminal Justice, 1st session 1830. AN BB²⁰49.

91 Flaubert (1973) [1840], pp. 325–6.

92 Ortoli (1883), pp. 329–33.

93 Cases v. M. Poli, Assize Court, 3rd session 1853. AN BB²⁰164; v. M. Maisetti, 1st session 1842. AN BB²⁰116; v. F. Susini and D.-N. Marcilesi, 3rd session 1854. AN BB²⁰170; and v. F. di Q. Susini, 2nd session 1860. AN BB²⁰221.

94 Case v. M.-A. and S.-F. Masconi, Assize Court, 4th session 1893. AN BB²⁰286.

95 Case v. A. Giovannoni, 2nd session 1841. *Gaz. Trib.*, 5th June 1841, No. 4913.

96 Case v. A. Ruffini and F.-A. Grimaldi, Extraordinary Criminal Court, 27 Floréal An XII(?). ADCS 7.U.1/22.

97 Galletti (1863), p. 55.

98 Cases v. P.-F. Tomasi, Assize Court, 2nd session 1840. *Gaz. Trib.*, 11 June 1840, No. 4604, cit. Sorbier (1863), pp. 177–81; and v. N. Chiaroni, 1st session 1851. AN BB²⁰152.

99 Cases v. S. Susini, 1st session 1853. AN BB²⁰164; and v. N. Olivesi, 1st session 1861. AN BB²⁰229; and Special report, *Gaz. Trib.*, 3 October 1838, No. 4076.

100 E.g. Case v. S. Colonna, 4th session 1864. AN BB²⁰260.

101 E.g. Case v. A.-M. Saturni and F. Nicolai, 1st session 1855. AN BB²⁰177.

102 Gaste (1965), p. 54; also Lenclud (1979), p. 44; and Lenclud (1985), p. 39.

103 Saint-Germain (1869), pp. 229–30.

104 See note 92.

105 Abeau (1888), pp. 11 and 16; see also Beaumont (1822), p. 36; Benson (1825), p. 40; Gregorovius (1855), pp. 107–8; Spinosi (1956); Marin-Muracciole (1964), esp. pp. 73–4 and 92–100; Deane (1965), pp. 69ff; and Pomponi (1976a), pp. 333–5.

106 Marin-Muracciole (1964), pp. 87ff; and Antonetti (1979), I.

107 See Westermarck (1922), I, pp. 426–7; Arensberg and Kimball (1940), p. 110; and Mair (1971), p. 91.

108 Case v. G.-T. Marinetti, Assize Court, 1st session 1842. AN BB²⁰116.

109 Filippi (1906), p. 21; see also Flaubert (1973) [1840], p. 333.

110 Cases v. G.-G. Lucchini, Tribunal correctionnel, Sartène, 1821. ADCS 3.U.5/170; and v. S. Canari, Assize Court, 4th session 1849. AN BB²⁰146.

111 Versini (1972), pp. 26 and 33, citing Case, Court of Criminal Justice, 1824.

112 Cases v. F. Raffini, Assize Court, 2nd session 1851. AN BB²⁰152; v. M.-A. Leoni, 3rd session 1848. AN BB²⁰142; v. G.-S. Soavi and F. Luigi, 1st session 1842. AN BB²⁰116; and v. G. Colonna et al., 2nd session 1848. AN BB²⁰142; and Marin-Muracciole (1964), p. 93.

113 Cases v. S. Poggi, Assize Court, 1st session 1843. AN BB²⁰121; and v. G. Giuliani,

2nd session 1848. AN BB^{20}142; and see, for example, Case v. B. Zuccarelli, 2nd session 1845. AN BB^{20}130.

114 Case v. F.-A. Perfetti, Assize Court, 4th session 1849. AN BB^{20}146.

115 See Southwell Colucci (1933), pp. 137–9; and Ettori (1979), pp. 187–9.

116 Cases v. G. Negroni, Assize Court, 4th session 1839. *Gaz. Trib.*, 5 January 1839, No. 4156; v. F.-A. Muzi, 4th session 1858. AN BB^{20}204; and Tommaseo (1841), p. 18

117 Saint-Germain (1869), pp. 407–8; Cesari-Rocca (1909), pp. 109–10; Bartoli (1898), p. 261; Finelli (n.d.), p. 54; and Christophari (1981), p. 149.

118 Cases v. A.-L. Orsini and C.-F. Bernardini, Court of Appeal, Bastia, May–June 1857. ADCS 2.U.1/61; v. V.-L. Valentini, Assize Court, 1st session 1865. AN BB^{20}273; and Report, Procureur-général, 14 April 1883, Petition for clemency for D. Ficoni. AN BB^{24}875; see also Marcaggi (1932), pp. 24–6, note; and Chiari (1960), p. 138.

119 Bartoli (1898), p. 260.

120 For parallels in other societies, see Martinez-Alier (1972); and Ferguson (1981), p. 215.

121 Piobb (n.d.), p. 22; Saint-Germain (1869), pp. 238 and 127–30; Vuillier (1896), p. 240; and Bigot (1890), p. 445; see also Robiquet (1835), pp. 590–1; Faure (1858), pp. 50–1; Bonaparte (1891), p. 87; Cesari-Rocca (1909), pp. 109–11; Spinosi (1956), pp. 48–9; Marin-Muracciole (1964), pp. 94 and 96; Bernardini (1970), II, p. 12; Delarue (1970), pp. 122–3, 185, 191, 198–9 and 265; Carrington (1971a), p. 305; Casta (1974), pp. 109–10 and 195–7; and Pomponi (1976a), p. 346.

122 Cases v. G. Santucci and A.-F. Stefani, Extraordinary Criminal Court, 27 Pluviôse An X. ADCS 7.U.1/19; v. M.-A. Casile et al., Assize Court, 4th session 1856. AN BB^{20}185; and v. G.-D. Giovanangeli, 3rd session 1862. AN BB^{20}239.

123 Report, Inspector Carlotti, 1849–50. ADCS 3.X.37c, 'Enfants trouvés'.

124 It was specifically catered for in Paoli's legislation; see Emmanuelli (1969), p. 92.

125 Marin-Muracciole (1964), pp. 191–4; and Lorenzi de Bradi (1928).

126 Marcaggi (1932), pp. 191–2 and 268; and Juta (1926), p. 110.

127 Robiquet (1835), pp. 451–2; Galletti (1863), pp. 62–3; Malaspina (1876), p. 373; Andrei (1893), pp. 255–7; Bartoli (1898), pp. 263–4; and Rossi (1900), pp. 154–5.

128 Bigot (1890), pp. 512–13; and Vinciguerra (1967).

129 Casanova (1973), pp. 93–4.

130 Report, Procureur-général to Ministry of Justice, 9 September 1806. AN BB^{18}238.

131 Cases v. L. Pruneta, Assize Court, 4th session 1842. AN BB^{20}116; v. P.-P. Mariotti and G. Graziani, 3rd session 1849. AN BB^{20}146; v. P.-F. Angelini, 4th session 1851. AN BB^{20}152; v. O. Casalonga, 1st session 1853, Second sitting. AN BB^{20}164; and v. A. Feliciaggi, 2nd session 1850. AN BB^{20}149.

132 Galletti (1863), pp. 54ff; Bartoli (1898), pp. 262–5; and Deane (1965), p. 189.

133 Marin-Muracciole (1964), pp. 34–5; and Ravis-Giordani (1978b), p. 199.

134 Cases v. G.-A. Marochelli, Assize Court, 4th session 1841. *Gaz. Trib.*, 18 December 1841, No. 4584; v. G.-D. Marchetti, 1st session 1842. AN BB^{20}116; and v. T. and D.-A. Massoni, 1st session 1844. AN BB^{20}125.

135 Viale (1855), pp. 43–8.

136 Report, Procureur de la République, Ajaccio, 16 July 1883, Petition for clemency for P.-G. Rossi et al. AN BB^{24}876.

137 Reports, Gendarmerie, 12 August 1841; and 8 and 26 November 1842. ADCS 4.M.125–126; and Case v. N. Ferroloni, Assize Court, 1st session 1849. AN BB^{20}146.

138 Case v. G.-M. Pasqualini, 2nd session 1856. AN BB^{20}185; Report, Gendarmerie, Peri, 14 September 1841. ADCS 4.M.125; and Cases v. M. Pinzuti; and v. P. Borelli, Assize Court, 1st and 4th sessions 1842. AN BB^{20}116.

139 Case v. A. Cesari, Tribunal correctionnel, Sartène, 31 March 1830. ADCS 3.U.5/156.

140 Report, Administrateur-général Miot to Ministry of Justice, 10 Fructidor An IX. AN BB^{18}236.

141 Cases v. Antonmarchi and Morelli, Assize Court, 4th session 1831. *Gaz. Trib.*, 1 January 1832; and v. F. and N. Cucchi, 4th session 1853. AN BB²⁰164; Report, Procureur-général, 22 September 1871, Petition for clemency for N. Cucchi. AN BB²⁴843; and Faure (1885), II, pp. 337–57.

142 See Bouchez (1843), p. 53; Busquet (1919), p. 112–18; and Marin-Muracciole (1964), pp. 172–5.

143 Reports, Subprefect, Sartène, 19 July 1824; and 4 October 1828. ADCS 4.M.99.

144 Marcaggi (1932), pp. 158–9; and Marin-Muracciole (1964), p. 189.

145 Case v. E. Nasica, Assize Court, 1st session 1861. AN BB²⁰229; Printed judgment, Special Military Commission, Ajaccio, 26 November 1807. AN BB¹⁸241; and Case v. G.-A. Mercuri and O.-M. Angelofranchi, Assize Court, 4th session 1861. AN BB²⁰228.

146 Letter, Pasquale Paoli to Casabianca, 29 June 1764, cit. Arrighi (1971), pp. 364–5.

147 Faure (1885), I, p. 44; and Faure (1858), p. 54; also Cesari-Rocca (1908), pp. 110–11.

148 Saint-Germain (1869), pp. 231–3; Faure (1885), II, pp. 11–49; Case v. O. Giovannoni, Assize Court, 2nd session 1843. AN BB²⁰121; Chronique départementale, Corte, 3 June 1840. *Gaz. Trib.*, 10 June 1840, No. 4603; Case v. L. Cartucci, Assize Court, 1st session 1843. AN BB²⁰121; and Borel-Léandri (1978), p. 250.

149 Deane (1965), pp. 107, 149 and 182–4.

150 Cases v. G.-A. Peretti, Assize Court, 2nd session 1852. AN BB²⁰158; and v. A.-M. Beretti, 3rd session 1860. AN BB²⁰221.

151 Cases v. Degiovanni, 1st session 1833. *Gaz. Trib.*, 5 April 1833, cit. Sorbier (1863), pp. 26–30; v. G. Giudicelli, 1st session 1852. AN BB²⁰158; and v. A.-N. Muselli, 4th session 1863. AN BB²⁰249; and Zuccarelli (n.d.), p. 76.

152 Saint-Germain (1869), p. 238.

153 Cases v. A. Antonietti, Assize Court, 4th session 1845. AN BB²⁰130; and v. G.-C. Santucci et al., 1st session 1857. AN BB²⁰194.

154 Cases v. G.-B. Agostini, 1st session 1841. *Gaz. Trib.*, 10 April 1841, No. 4865; and v. P.-M. Marchi, 2nd session 1895. AN BB²⁰286.

155 Cases v. A.-M. Spinosa, 1849. AN BB²⁰146; and v. I. and F. Pasqualini, 1st session 1865. AN BB²⁰273.

156 Cases v. L. Ciosi, 1st session 1858. AN BB²⁰204; and v. G.-B. Rustini, 4th session 1864. AN BB²⁰260.

157 Cases v. C. and A. Pietri, 2nd session 1852. AN BB²⁰158; v. A.-F. Pettinelli and G. Giordani, 2nd session 1853. AN BB²⁰164; v. ..., 3rd session 1842. AN BB²⁰116; v. L. Mazzochi, 2nd session 1853, Extraordinary sitting. AN BB²⁰164; v. G.-B. Chiaretta, 4th session 1865. AN BB²⁰273; and v. F.-A. Massoni, 2nd session 1856. AN BB²⁰185.

158 Cases v. I.-S. Poggi, 4th session 1863. AN BB²⁰249; and v. D. Fanucchi, 3rd session 1859. AN BB²⁰213.

159 See, for example, Depauw (1972), pp. 1167–9.

160 Case v. P. Giabiconi, 2nd session 1855. AN BB²⁰177; and v. A.-N. Fieschi et al., 4th session 1893. AN BB²⁰286.

161 See Rossiaud (1976), pp. 292–301, referring to fifteenth-century Rhône valley towns.

162 Bournet (1888), p. 19; and Christophari (1981), p. 62.

163 Robiquet (1835), pp. 590–1; see also Bourde (1887), pp. 211–12; Marin-Muracciole (1964), pp. 384–93; and Ravis-Giordani (1978b), p. 199.

164 Case v. Raffali, Assize Court, 2nd session 1849, Extraordinary sitting. AN BB²⁰146.

165 Delarue (1970), pp. 185, 191, 198–9 and 265.

166 Case v. A.-P. Ortoli et al., 3rd session 1862. AN BB²⁰239; Viale (1855), p. 96; and Report, Subprefect, Sartène, 13 June 1829. ADCS 4.M.99.

167 Chapman (1908), pp. 191–2; Ettori (1979), p. 178; Cases v. F. Cucchi, Assize Court, 4th session 1853. AN BB²⁰164; and v. A.-M. Saturni, 1st session 1855. AN BB²⁰177; and Bazal (1973), p. 188.

168 Robiquet (1835), pp. 590–1; Marcaggi (1932), p. 279 note; Bazal (1973), p. 198; and Marcaggi (1898a), p. 15.
169 Case v. C. Peloni, Assize Court, 2nd session 1852. AN BB²⁰158; Report, Subprefect, Sartène, 15 February 1824. ADCS 4.M.99; and Case v. M. and C.-F. Bonnetti, Assize Court, July 1835. *Gaz. Trib.*, 2 August 1835, No. 3106.
170 Letter, Juge de paix Gabrielli to Prefect, 15 February 1848. ADCS 2.M.88.
171 Cases v. M.-C. Comiti and A.-M. Coscioli, Assize Court, 2nd session 1856. AN BB²⁰185; v. F. Istria; and v. S. Battini, 2nd session 1851. AN BB²⁰152; and v. A. Corteggiani et al., 1st session 1854. AN BB²⁰170.
172 Dossier, 12 October 1844. AN BB¹⁸1426; Report, Subprefect, Sartène, 15 September 1827. ADCS 4.M.99; Special report, Sartène, *Gaz. Trib.*, 3 October 1838, No. 4076; and Saint-Germain (1869), pp. 220–1. We should add that in the towns of Ajaccio and Bastia civil marriage seems to have become normal early on in the nineteenth century, while the religious ceremony was commonly ignored. A number of cases may be cited in which men resisted pressure from women and priests to go through the religious ceremony, sometimes when the woman was about to die; see, for example, Petition for clemency for Luigi Barberini. AN BB²⁴155–69; and Case v. Maria Garbini, Assize Court, 4th session 1863. AN BB²⁰249.
173 E.g. Beaumont (1822), pp. 40–1; and Surier (1934), p. 52.
174 E.g. Ortoli (1883), pp. 39–43, 242–6 and 258–66; and Delarue (1970), p. 173.
175 Comiti (1933), pp. 242–3; Galletti (1863), pp. 55–6; and Report, Subprefect, Sartène, 27 September 1829. ADCS 4.M.99.
176 Deane (1965), p. 188 suggests that maintaining the chastity of daughters was a 'masculine dream' and that women themselves were much more realistic and interested primarily in obtaining husbands.

5 Conflict and its causes: intrafamilial conflict

1 E.g. Philpotts (1913), p. 30; Siegel and Beals (1960b), p. 396; Bialor (1968), p. 112; Gellner (1969), pp. 116 and 118; Boram (1973); Du Boulay (1979), p. 153; Wormald (1980), p. 69; and Duby (1985), pp. 93–4.
2 Davis (1977), p. 49; see also pp. 188–9; and Sabean (1976), p. 111.
3 Gluckman (1973), p. 154; see also Philpotts (1913), p. 70; and Kent (1977), pp. 188ff.
4 See e.g. Lawson (1910), p. 457, citing Plato's *Laws*; Gray et al., (1909), pp. 721 and 731; Westermarck (1934), p. 367; Colson (1953), p. 203; Hasluck (1954), Ch. XXI; Schapera (1955); Lewis (1967), p. 257; Peters (1967), pp. 263–4, 272–3 and 275; Winter (1970), pp. 152–3; Black-Michaud (1975), pp. 228–34; and Ferguson (1981), p. 227. We return to this question in Chapter 8.
5 Case v. I. Fagianelli, Tribunal correctionnel, Sartène, 1812. ADCS 3.U.5/166.
6 Letter, Pasqualini to Prefect, 1 December 1824. ADCS 1.M.228.
7 Busquet (1919), p. 634; see also proverbs cited by Mattei (1867), pp. 29 and 62.
8 Molinari (1886), p. 260. We will provide many examples in what follows.
9 As it did in medieval Iceland; see for example, *The Saga of Gisli*. According to Brown (1983), pp. 165–6, 15% of feuds in Scotland around 1600 occurred within the kindred.
10 Letter, F.-M. Bruni to Miot, An IX(?). AN BB¹⁸236.
11 Case v. G. Miliani et al., Assize Court, 2nd session 1847. *Gaz Trib.*, 18 July 1847, No. 6252.
12 Marcaggi (1898b); Faure (1858), pp. 49–58; and Marcaggi (1932), pp. 133–43.
13 See Busquet (1919), p. 103; and Pomponi (1976c), p. 156.
14 A point hinted at by Malaspina (1876), p. 372; see also Barth (1965), pp. 108–14.

15 See, for example, Valéry (1837), pp. 177–8; and Comiti (1933), p. 237.
16 At Calasima in the Niolo in 1926, 77% of households lived under the authority of a man of over 45, and 20% under a man of over 70. Lenclud and Ravis-Giordani (1973), p. 220.
17 Filippi (1906), p. 32.
18 Cases v. F. Venturini et al., Assize Court, 2nd session 1844. AN BB²⁰125; v. G. Riuscuto, 3rd session 1853. AN BB²⁰164; v. P.-F. Quilici and P.-A. Capponi, 3rd session 1859. AN BB²⁰213; and v. S. Orsini, 1st session 1863. AN BB²⁰249.
19 Report, Gendarmerie, 22 December 1823. ADCS 4.M.99.
20 This situation did not always pertain, however. In the Niolo, sons obtained their own flocks when they married. Lenclud and Ravis-Giordani (1973), p. 218.
21 See, for Mediterranean societies, Skinner (1961); and J. Schneider (1971), pp. 10–11; and, for others, Bateson (1958), pp. 40–2 (Iatmul); and Brody (1973), p. 110 (Ireland).
22 Filippi (1906), p. 19. We will return to the general topic of inheritance in the next section of this chapter.
23 Southwell Colucci (1933), p. 125.
24 *Gaz. Trib.*, 18 April 1833, No. 2395.
25 Cases v. F. Giavannoni, Assize Court, 3rd session 1864. AN BB²⁰260; v. A. Lucchini, 2nd session 1839. *Gaz. Trib.*, 20 July 1839, No. 4326; and v. G.-A. Angelini, 2nd session 1862. AN BB²⁰239.
26 Petition for clemency for P. Carlotti, 20 June 1883. AN BB²⁴876.
27 E.g. Southwell Colucci (1933), pp. 207 and 209–10.
28 Cases v. Morelli and Antonmarchi, Assize Court, 4th session 1831. *Gaz. Trib.*, 1 January 1832, No. 1992; v. G.-C. Pietrapiana, 2nd session 1863. AN BB²⁰249; v. G.-A. Mariani; and v. P.-A. Romanacce, 1st session 1853, 2nd sitting. AN BB²⁰164.
29 E.g. Southwell Colucci (1933), pp. 140–2 and 191–2.
30 E.g. Chanal (n.d.), pp. 123–8.
31 Cases v. E. Mariani, Assize Court, 2nd session 1864. AN BB²⁰260; and v. M.-F. Casanova, 2nd session 1855. AN BB²⁰177.
32 Report, Subprefect, 3 July 1819. ADCS 4.M.98; and Case v. M.-V. Pietri (the apothecary's wife who had sold the girl the poison), Tribunal correctionnel, Sartène, 1 September 1819. ADCS 3.U.5/168. The reason for the reprimands is not divulged, but autopsy showed that the girl was *not* pregnant. Arsenic was used as a remedy for malaria.
33 Reports, Subprefect, Sartène, 18 October 1825; and 25 April 1826. ADCS 4.M.99.
34 Cases v. Morelli and Antonmarchi, Assize Court, 4th session 1831. *Gaz. Trib.*, 1 January 1832, No. 1992; and v. Cesari and Ciavaldini, 3rd session 1840. *Gaz. Trib.*, 23 September 1840, No. 4695.
35 Case v. G. Antonini and P.-G. Massoni, 4th session 1842. AN BB²⁰116.
36 E.g. Pocock (1957), p. 298 (Gujerat); Bateson (1958), p. 213; Nash (1967), p. 412 (Mexico); Gellner (1969), pp. 46–7 (Atlas region); and Girard (1977), pp. 61–4, referring to myths of the 'enemy brother'.
37 See Pomponi (1976a), p. 342; and Pomponi (1978a), p. 13.
38 Case v. A. Bujoli, Assize Court, 3rd session 1846. AN BB²⁰134.
39 Report on Case v. D. Ficoni, 3rd session 1878. Petitions for clemency, 1883–5. AN BB²⁴875.
40 Saravelli-Retali (1976), p. 39.
41 Case v. I. Durazzi, Indictment, 23 Pluviôse An VIII. ADCS 3.U.5/132.
42 Cases v. G.-B. Franceschetti; and v. G.-P. Ordioni, Assize Court, 4th session 1849. AN BB²⁰116; v. S. Susini, 1st session 1863. AN BB²⁰249; v. L. Calzaroni, 3rd session 1853. AN BB²⁰164; and v. P. Ordioni, 3rd session 1841, *Gaz. Trib.*, 19 October 1841, No. 4506.

43 Reports, Subprefect, Sartène, 4 and 27 July 1832. ADCS 4.M.100; and Case v. P. Maestrati, Assize Court, 4th session 1832. *Gaz. Trib.*, 27 January 1833, No. 2326.

44 Cases v. F.-A. Desanti, 4th session 1852, Extraordinary sitting. AN BB^{20}158; and v. D.-L. Antonmarchi, 4th session 1832. *Gaz. Trib.*, 26 February 1836, cit. Sorbier (1863), pp. 72–6.

45 This stipulated that all children should receive an equal share of the family patrimony but, additionally, allowed a man to bequeath between a third and a quarter of his estate (depending on the number of his children) to a particular one of them. This additional share was known as the 'disposable portion'. For further discussion, see the following section.

46 Reports, Gendarmerie, Ajaccio, 3 July 1841. ADCS 4.M.125; and Bastia, 19 November 1842. ADCS 4.M.126.

47 Ortoli (1883), pp. 171ff.

48 Cases v. G.-C. Liccia, Assize Court, 1st session 1857. AN BB^{20}194; and v. A.-P. Orsini, 1st session 1861. AN BB^{20}229.

49 Marcaggi (1932), pp. 180–5; see also Bazal (1973), pp. 220–4. Marc'-Aurelio was acquitted but Maddalena was convicted and sentenced to life imprisonment. She was later exonerated.

50 Case v. M. and C.-F. Bonnetti, Assize Court, July 1835. *Gaz. Trib.*, 2 August 1835, No. 3106.

51 E.g. Tommaseo (1841), pp. 39–40; Privat (1936), p. 17; and Marin-Muracciole (1964), p. 9.

52 E.g. Tommaseo (1841), pp. 35–9, 107–9 and 116–19; Viale (1855), pp. 88–9, 90–7, 100–2 and 102–5; and Southwell Colucci (1933), pp. 180, 187 and 225–6; see also Ravis-Giordani (1978b), p. 197.

53 Mérimée (1840b), pp. 739–40; Tommaseo (1841), pp. 122, 124 and 125; Fée (1850), p. 208; Gregorovius (1855), pp. 135–6; Ortoli (1887), pp. 248–55 and 300–11; Saint-Victor (1925) [1887], p. 351; and Carrington (1971a), p. 91.

54 Reports, Gendarmerie, Bastia, 14 and 27 April 1842. ADCS 4.M.126; see also Cases v. A. Lucchini, Assize Court, 2nd session 1839, *Gaz. Trib.*, 20 July 1839, No. 4326; and v. F.-M. Paolini, 3rd session 1856, AN BB^{20}185, for examples of men being killed while returning from working in the country with their sisters.

55 Case v. M.-G. Bernardini et al., Assize Court, 3rd session 1849. AN BB^{20}146; Petitions for clemency for F. Bastianesi, 1874–85. AN BB^{24}798; and Case v. S. Timotei, 1st session 1862. AN BB^{20}239.

56 A suggestion made by Ravis-Giordani (1978b), p. 203 note 7; see also Rivière (1967), pp. 576 and 578–9.

57 Case v. G. Cotoni, Assize Court, 4th session 1834. *Gaz. Trib.*, 18 January 1835, No. 2936.

58 See Djilas (1958), pp. 311–12, for the similar but more extreme situation in Montenegro.

59 Report, Gendarmerie, Ajaccio, 23 September 1841. ADCS 4.M.125.

60 E.g. Case v. F. and G.-S. Agostini, Assize Court, 1st session 1853, 2nd sitting. AN BB^{20}164. For an example of property held in indivision and effectively controlled by the brother, see Case v. P. Pianelli (of Olmeto), 1st session 1864. AN BB^{20}260.

61 Case, Cour Royale, Bastia. *Gaz. Trib.*, 18 July 1833, No. 2472. His conviction was quashed on appeal, however, and brother and sister were then persuaded to divide the estate amicably.

62 E.g. Tommaseo (1841), pp. 98–101; Viale (1855), pp. 48–51, 84–8 and 106–10; and Ortoli (1887), pp. 276–89.

63 Cases v. P. Giacomoni et al., Assize Court, 2nd session 1848. *Gaz. Trib.*, 12 and 22 July 1848, Nos. 6559 and 6568; v. L. Borghetti, 2nd session 1854. *Gaz. Trib.*, 3 July

1834, No. 2769; v. F.-A. Giudicelli, 4th session 1856. AN BB²⁰185; v. M. Cosini, 3rd session 1857. AN BB²⁰194; v. P.-T. Maroselli et al., 1st session 1859. AN BB²⁰213; and v. G.-A. Marochelli and G. Pompeani, 4th session 1841. *Gaz. Trib.*, 18 December 1841, No. 4584; Letter, S. Castelli to Procureur-général, 27 May 1912. ADCS 1.M.231; and Case v. F. and N. Cucchi, Assize Court, 4th session 1853. AN BB²⁰164.

64 See, for example, Lamotte (1956e), p. 39, who notes that Fozzano spouses were often first, second and third cousins at once.

65 Marin-Muracciole (1964), p. 260. See Davis (1977), pp. 211–17, on preferential cousin marriage in other parts of the Mediterranean region.

66 Case v. A. Cesari, Tribunal correctionnel, Sartène, 31 March 1830. ADCS 3.U.5/156. This case was complicated by the fact that there was no register of Anna-Maria's father's marriage.

67 Case v. A. Peretti, Assize Court, 1st session 1854. AN BB²⁰170.

68 Saravelli-Retali (1976), p. 41.

69 Cases v. M.-U. Picchini, Assize Court, 3rd session 1856. AN BB²⁰185; v. P.-M. Paoli, 4th session 1851. AN BB²⁰152; and v. G. Alessandri, 4th session 1855. AN BB²⁰177.

70 Cases v. C.-M. Ortoli, 2nd session 1844. AN BB²⁰125; and v. M.-M. Bartoli, 2nd session 1856. AN BB²⁰185.

71 Reports, Subprefect, Sartène, 13 November 1827; and 9 June 1835. ADCS 4.M.99 and 100; Case v. G.-A. Poggi, Assize Court, 4th session 1842. AN BB²⁰116; and Marcaggi (1932), pp. 145–7.

72 Cases v. G.-B. Mozziconacci et al., 2nd session 1851. Extraordinary sitting. AN BB²⁰152; v. F. Luporsi; and v. C.-G. Orsini and I. Danesi, 2nd session 1853. AN BB²⁰164.

73 Marcaggi (1898b), pp. 95–102; Southwell Colucci (1933), pp. 205–10; and Marcaggi (1932), p. 185.

74 Blanqui (1841), p. 490.

75 E.g. Case v. G.-C. Liccia, Assize Court, 1st session 1857. AN BB²⁰194.

76 Report, Commissaire du Directoire exécutif, Golo, to Ministry of Justice, 30 Messidor An VI. AN BB¹⁸237; Cases v. G. Lucrezj, Assize Court, 4th session 1846. AN BB²⁰134; v. P.-D. Vacarezza, 4th session 1852, Extraordinary sitting. AN BB²⁰158; and v. A.-D. Lanfranchi, 4th session 1846. AN BB²⁰134; Report, Gendarmerie, 24 May 1896. ADCS 1.M.230; Petition for clemency for G.-F. Zuccarelli, no date. AN BB²⁴18–33; Report, Subprefect, Sartène, to Prefect, 4 May 1866. ADCS 1.V.44; Cases v. M. Valle, Assize Court, 4th session 1849. AN BB²⁰146; v. A. Marietti, 4th session 1859. AN BB²⁰213; and v. I. Capponi, 3rd session 1848. AN BB²⁰142.

77 Printed judgment, Special Military Court, 3 May 1808. AN BB¹⁸241; Case v. G.-C. Pianelli, Assize Court, 1st session 1851. AN BB²⁰152; Report, Procureur-général, 30 May 1893. AN BB²⁰286; Letter re case, Extraordinary Criminal Court, 15 Brumaire An X. ADCS 7.U.1/4; Cases v. U. and Don G. Peretti, Tribunal correctionnel, Sartène, 30 November 1822. ADCS 3.U.5/171; and v. G.-M. and D. Villanova, Assize Court, 4th session 1865. AN BB²⁰273.

78 Report, Gendarmerie, Ajaccio, 3 February 1842. ADCS 4.M.126; Cases v. P.-N. Ortoli, Assize Court, 1st session 1843. AN BB²⁰121; and v. Don A. Mattei, 2nd session 1852. AN BB²⁰158; and Juta (1926), p. 49.

79 Lenclud (1979), p. 30; and Lenclud (1985), p. 42.

80 Cases v. P. Favaletti et al., Assize Court, 3rd session 1841. *Gaz. Trib.*, 4 September 1841, No. 4993; v. G.-B. Orsini, 3rd session 1850. AN BB²⁰149; v. G. Casabianca, 3rd session 1854. AN BB²⁰170; and v. P.-S. Bartoli, 3rd session 1863. AN BB²⁰249.

81 For parallels, see Bialor (1968), p. 112; and J. Schneider (1971), p. 16.

82 Lenclud (1985), esp. pp. 35–8; also Casanova (1965), II, pp. 3–5; Casanova (1968a), pp. 64–5; Renucci (1974), p. 179; and Lenclud (1979), pp. 39ff.

83 Spinosi (1956), p. 184; Lenclud (1985), pp. 38 and 41–2; Mattei (1867), pp. 56–8; and Saravelli-Retali (1976), p. 95.

84 Bigot (1890), pp. 460–1 and 478; and Lenclud (1985), pp. 37 and 40.

85 See note 45.

86 Bigot (1890), pp. 449, 478 and 452–3; and Fontana (1905), p. 93.

87 E.g. Filippi (1906), p. 19.

88 Malaspina (1876), p. 371; and Lorenzi de Bradi (1928), p. 167.

89 Blanqui (1841), pp. 497–8; Fontana (1905), p. 75; and Lenclud (1979), pp. 16–17.

90 For a parallel situation, see Brandão (1983), p. 83.

91 Cases v. F.-M. Sinibaldi et al., Tribunal correctionnel, Sartène, 6 May 1820. ADCS 3.U.5/169; v. P. and G.-B. Agostini; and A.-B. Micheli, Assize Court, 1st session; and v. G. and G.-C. Terrazzoni, 2nd session 1853, Extraordinary sittings. AN BB²⁰164; and v. G. Rossi, Extraordinary Criminal Court, 4 Messidor An X. ADCS 7.U.1/22.

92 Cases v. G.-A. Serra, Tribunal Correctionnel, Sartène, 6 May 1830. ADCS 3.U.5/156; v. G.-A. Roccaserra, Assize Court, 3rd session 1846. AN BB²⁰134; and v. V.-D. Marinetti, 2nd session 1859. AN BB²⁰213.

93 Cases v. C. Pietri, Extraordinary Criminal Court, Pluviôse An X. ADCS 7.U.1/4; and v. P.-G.-S. Pietri, Court of First Instance, Sartène, Ventôse An XI. ADCS 3.U.5/130; and Reports, Procureur-général, 20 May and 14 July 1863. AN BB²⁴674–86.

94 Case v. G.-M. Casella, Court of Criminal Justice, 1st session 1830. AN BB²⁰49.

95 Cases v. A.-F. Marcantoni, Assize Court, 4th session 1835, *Gaz. Trib.*, 2 January 1836, cit. Sorbier (1863), pp. 69–72; v. G. Armani, 2nd session 1865. AN BB²⁰273; and v. Don G. Peretti, 2nd session 1852. AN BB²⁰158.

96 Lenclud (1979), p. 42; and Blanqui (1841), p. 450.

97 Malaspina (1876), p. 372.

98 Lenclud (1979), p. 22.

99 Cases v. G.-M. Susini et al., Tribunal correctionnel, Sartène, 16 October 1813. ADCS 3.U.5/166; v. A.-P. Ottaviani, Court of Criminal Justice, Department of Golo, 1809; and Ajaccio, 1813. ADCS 2.U.1/43; v. P.-E. Carlotti et al., Assize Court, 3rd session 1845. AN BB²⁰130; Letter to Prefect, 15 August 1860. ADCS 2.M.140; and Petition for clemency for P. Quastana, 14 September 1860. AN BB²⁴605–21.

100 E.g. Petitions for clemency for Angelo Defendini, ex-mayor of Alando, convicted of electoral fraud, from his wife and his brother-in-law, 1865. AN BB²⁴718; and for Anton-Andrea Polidori of Morosaglia, convicted of electoral offences and carrying an illegal weapon, from his father-in-law, 1885. AN BB²⁴888.

101 Cases v. G.-B. Muselli, Assize Court, 2nd session 1858. AN BB²⁰204; v. D.-A. Antonmarchi, 4th session 1835. *Gaz. Trib.*, 26 February 1836, cit. Sorbier (1863), pp. 72–6; v. B. Muraccioli, 2nd session 1844. AN BB²⁰125; v. P.-F. Casta, 4th session 1865. AN BB²⁰273; and v. G. Girolami, 2nd session 1858. AN BB²⁰204.

102 For Cozzano, see e.g. Case v. G.-P. Renucci, Assize Court, 4th session 1865. AN BB²⁰273.

103 See generally, e.g. Pocock (1975), p. 71; and, for Corsica, the evidence of laments: ·Ettori (1979), pp. 179–86.

104 See again the evidence of laments: Viale (1855), pp. 23–6.

105 Printed Judgments of Special Military Commission, Ajaccio, 26 November 1807. AN BB¹⁸241; and of Court of Criminal Justice, Bastia, August 1810. AN BB¹⁸239.

106 Spinosi (1956), p. 177; and Lenclud (1979), pp. 22, 31 and 40; see also Mérimée (1840b), pp. 739–45; Viale (1855), pp. 77–81; and Ortoli (1887), pp. 300–11, all citing laments.

107 Case v. R. Casabianca, Assize Court, 3rd session 1850. AN BB²⁰149; Letter, A.-Q. Roccaserra to Minister of Justice, 3 January 1879, Petition for clemency. AN BB²⁴852; Case v. P. Negroni, Assize Court, 3rd session 1833. *Gaz. Trib.*, 30 October 1833, No. 2562; and Report, Gendarmerie, 19 February 1842. ADCS 4.M.126.

108 Cases v. L. Borghetti, Assize Court, 2nd session 1834. *Gaz. Trib.*, 3 July 1834, No. 2769; v. G. Giudicelli, 1st session 1852. AN BB²⁰158; v. G. Ciosi, 3rd session 1865. AN BB²⁰273; and v. G. Marini, 2nd session 1895. AN BB²⁰286.

109 See Ortoli (1883), pp. 39–43 and 267–73.

110 Cases v. A.-C. and C. Peretti, 2nd session 1853, Extraordinary sitting. AN BB²⁰164; and v. E. Orsini, 4th session 1864. AN BB²⁰260.

111 Cases v. P.-G. Reginensi, 4th session 1865. AN BB²⁰273; and v. S. Timotei, 1st session 1862. AN BB²⁰239.

112 Report, Subprefect, Ajaccio, 14 January 1828. ADCS 4.M.91; and Case v. M. Mozziconacci, Tribunal correctionnel, Sartène, 27 December 1820. ADCS 3.U.5/169.

113 Marcaggi (1898b), p. 204; Ravis-Giordani (1978b), p. 197; and Davis (1977), pp. 190–3.

114 See Mattei (1867), citing proverbs; Fontana (1905), pp. 86–91 and 94; and Spinosi (1956), pp. 75, 93–5, 104, 126–46 and 181.

115 Chronique départementale, Corte, 3 June; *Gaz. Trib.*, 10 June 1840, No. 4603; also Lenclud (1985), p. 40.

116 See, for example, laments cited by Tommaseo (1841), pp. 230–1; Viale (1855), pp. 30ff; Ortoli (1887), pp. 44–57; and Ettori (1979), pp. 181–2; and Borel-Léandri (1978), pp. 228–9, on the trousseau.

117 Case v. P. Pianelli, Assize Court, 1st session 1864. AN BB²⁰260.

118 Saint-Germain (1869), p. 252; and Malaspina (1876), p. 272.

119 Chanal (n.d.), pp. 113–21.

120 Case v. P.-G. Maroselli, Assize Court, 1st session 1859. AN BB²⁰213.

121 Note, General Morand, 1810. AN BB¹⁸241; Cases v. A.-F. Leca, 2nd session 1840. *Gaz. Trib.*, 15 August 1840, No. 4659, cit. Sorbier (1863), pp. 204–5; and v. A. Giansilj, Court of Criminal Justice, Ajaccio, 1811. ADCS 2.U.1/42.

122 Case v. G.-C. Santini, Assize Court, 1st session 1862. AN BB²⁰239; Petition for clemency for Dr B. Peretti, 20 January 1807. AN BB²⁴8–17; and Case v. G.-A. Istria, Assize Court, 4th session 1849. AN BB²⁰146.

123 E.g. in a case at Olmiccia in 1827. Case v. A.-G. Ortoli, Court of Criminal Justice, 2nd session 1830, Cases tried *in absentia*. AN BB²⁰49.

124 Cases v. S. Muraccioli; and v. M. Ristozi, Court of Criminal Justice, 1st session 1830. AN BB²⁰49.

125 Cases v. A.-G. Bernardi, Assize Court, 4th session 1846. AN BB²⁰134; and v. P. Paoletti, 4th session 1865. AN BB²⁰273.

126 Report, Subprefect, Sartène, 26 June 1831. ADCS 4.M.100.

127 Cases v. A.-G. Santoni, Assize Court, 4th session 1852. Extraordinary sitting. AN BB²⁰158; and v. L. Lanfranchi, 1st session 1842. AN BB²⁰116.

128 Letter, M.-A. Bozzi to Prefect, 18 March 1868; and other documents. ADCS 2.M.144; and Robiquet (1835), pp. 431–2.

129 Lenclud (1985), p. 40.

130 Report, Military officer, Prunelli, 12 August 1820. ADCS 1.M.228.

131 Petition for clemency for A.-V. Pieri, 1884. AN BB²⁴877; Report, Gendarmerie, Ajaccio, 12 October 1841. ADCS 4.M.125; Cases v. S. Colonna, Assize Court, 1st session 1865. AN BB²⁰273; and v. F. Corrazzini, 3rd session 1850. AN BB²⁰149.

132 Filippi (1906), p. 20; see also Martin-Gistucci (1976), p. 181.

133 Cases v. V. Ridolfi; and v. S.-F. Campana, Assize Court, 3rd session 1859. AN BB²⁰213.

134 E.g. Montherot (1840), p. 31; and Lear (1870), pp. 63, 66, 105 and 107–8.

135 Case v. N. Guidicelli, Tribunal correctionnel, Sartène, 15 July 1820. ADCS 3.U.5/169.

136 Pomponi (1976a), pp. 326–8; and Lenclud (1979), p. 42.

137 Mérimée (1840b), p. 743; Filippi (1906), p. 19; and Arrighi (1856b), pp. 4–5 and

passim; see also Viale (1855), pp. 77–81, citing lament; Ortoli (1887), pp. 133–5; Radclyffe Dugmore (n.d.), p. 52; Lorenzi de Bradi (1928), p. 298; and Marin-Muracciole (1964), p. 139.

138 See Southwell Colucci (1933), pp. 137–9; and Christophari (1981), pp. 24–5.
139 Martelli (1960), p. 296; Finelli (n.d.), p. 55; Borel-Léandri (1978), p. 251; and Christophari (1981), pp. 10–12.
140 Benson (1825), p. 41.
141 Cases v. G. Guelfecci, Assize Court, 3rd session 1861. AN BB^{20}229; and v. A.-P. Mattei, 2nd session 1895. AN BB^{20}286.
142 Cases v. B. Tomasi, 3rd session 1858. AN BB^{20}204; v. P. Favaletti et al., 3rd session 1841. *Gaz. Trib.*, 4 September 1841, No. 4993; and v. M.-F. Casanova, 2nd session 1855. AN BB^{20}177; Report, Subprefect, Sartène, 21 November 1820. ADCS 4.M.98; Deliberations of municipal councils of Rogliano and Tomino, January and February 1836. ADHC E.6/25; Report, Procureur-général to Minister of Justice, 28 December 1814. AN BB^{18}242; Cases v. C.-F. Foata, Assize Court, 2nd session 1845. AN BB^{20}130; and v. G. Marcantoni, 1st session 1853. AN BB^{20}164.

6 Conflict and its causes: inter-community conflict

1 For the former view, see Piobb (n.d.), p. 55; Busquet (1919), p. 543; and Carlotti (1936), pp. 30–1; and for the latter, Finelli (n.d.), pp. 41 and 59.
2 For the components of community in other parts of Europe, see e.g. Tax Freeman (1968); Blum (1971a); and (1971b); and Raulin (1972).
3 Casta (1974), pp. 33–4; and Pomponi (1979b), pp. 205–6.
4 See e.g. Roublin (1970), pp. 538–9.
5 Report, Gendarmerie, Bastia, 4 July 1842. ADCS 4.M.126.
6 Forcioli-Conti (1897), pp. 46–7; Finelli (n.d.), pp. 34 and 53–4; Beaulieu-Delbet (1897), p. 48; Lorenzi de Bradi (1928), pp. 143–4; and Christophari (1981), pp. 22 and 59.
7 E.g. Case v. N. Graziani et al., Court of Criminal Justice, Ajaccio, 1812. ADCS 2.U.1/43.
8 In addition to author's fieldwork, see, for bread ovens, Archer (1942), p. 142 (Piana); Martelli (1960), p. 289 (Ghisoni); Deane (1965), p. 115 (Balagna); Dalmas (1978), p. 7 (Ampugnani); Raulin and Ravis-Giordani (1978), pp. 35 and 249 photo (Bastelica); and Finelli (n.d.), pp. 35 and opp. 38 photo (Tavera); for olive presses, Deane (1965), p. 134; and for threshing floors, Case v. G.-S. Santini, Assize Court, 4th session 1855. AN BB^{20}177 (Peri). These facilities sometimes belonged to a hamlet rather than a whole village.
9 See Patin de La Fizelière (1963), referring to Foce, Granace, Giuncheto, Bilia and Belvedere, all in the Sartenais; and ADCS 2.V.17, 'Chapelles An XIII – 1873'.
10 Mayor, Report to Municipal Council, Penta-di-Casinca, 23 November 1873. ADHC E.29/8.
11 See Finelli (n.d.), p. 25; and author's fieldwork.
12 Bouchez (1843), p. 53.
13 Casta (1974), p. 171; and Martelli (1960), p. 259.
14 See Pitt-Rivers (1971), Chs. I and II.
15 Lamotte (1956a), pp. 35–9.
16 Letter, Subprefect to Prefect, 28 May 1841. ADCS 2.V.25; and Letter, Prefect to Mayor, 19 July 1841. ADCS 2.V.19.
17 Blanqui (1841), p. 496.
18 Lamotte (1956e), p. 39; see also Vrydaghs Fidelis (1962); and Pomponi (1974b); and Lenclud (1979), p. 41, more generally.

19 See ADCS 2.M.79 (Bisinchi); ADCS 2.M.137 (Olmeta-di-Tuda); ADHC E.18/18, 'Matrice générale des contributions foncière, personelle et mobilière et des portes et fenêtres', 1866–85; ADHC E.18/3 and E.18/27, 'Conseil Municipal', 1890–1944; and ADHC 3.P.852, 'Cadastre, Régistre des propriétaires, 1851–1914' (Venzolasca); and Reparaz (1961), pp. 41–2 (Castellare).

20 ADHC E.29/7–8.

21 Cases v. G.-T. Sanguinetti, Assize Court, 2nd session 1845. AN BB²⁰130; and v. Agostini, 3rd session 1835, *Gaz. Trib.*, 28 October 1835, cit. Sorbier (1863), pp. 55–60; see also, for communal herdsmen, Pernet and Lenclud (1977), pp. 89–90; and Dalmas (1978), p. 9.

22 Planhol (1968).

23 See, for Corsica generally, Pomponi (1976a), p. 332; Pernet and Lenclud (1977), p. 87; and Lenclud (1979), p. 25; and for parallels elsewhere, Freitas Marcondes (1940); and Brody (1973), pp. 26–7 and 134–43.

24 Cases v. L. Ciosi, Assize Court, 1st session 1858. AN BB²⁰204; and v. M. Luciani, 1st session 1851, Extraordinary sitting. AN BB²⁰152; see also Cristofini et al. (1978), pp. 99–100; and Finelli (n.d.), pp. 37–8.

25 Pernet and Lenclud (1977), pp. 89–90; Lenclud (1979), pp. 24–5 and 29–31; and Deane (1965), pp. 42 and 158.

26 Robiquet (1835), p. 443; Bigot (1890), p. 478; Borel-Léandri (1978), p. 11; Lenclud (1979), p. 18; and Christophari (1981), pp. 56–7; and, for a parallel, Barley (1961), p. 265.

27 Lenclud and Ravis-Giordani (1973), p. 205; see also Finelli (n.d.), pp. 41 and 49.

28 Municipal Council, Penta-di-Casinca, May 1839. ADHC E.29/7; and Case v. F. Pasqualini, Assize Court, 4th session 1852. AN BB²⁰158.

29 Ravis-Giordani (1978a), p. 7.

30 Montherot (1840), p. 42; Gregorovius (1855), pp. 402–3; Lear (1870), p. 133; Bennet (1876), pp. 131–2; and Chapman (1908), pp. 361–3. A man at Ostriconi, to whom Chapman offered a cigar, insisted on giving him a huge pumpkin in return.

31 Griffon (1841), p. 21; and Montherot (1840), pp. 12–13. See also, for hospitality in Corsica, Maurice (ed.) (1904), pp. 43, 46, 119 and 151; Versini (1979), pp. 30–3; and Christophari (1981), p. 18; and, generally, Barth (1965), p. 77.

32 E.g. Case v. P.-D. Mondolini, Assize Court, 1st session 1855. AN BB²⁰177, where a man from Arbellara shot another from Olmiccia, when he was refused hospitality.

33 Report, Inspector Carlotti, 1850. ADCS 3.X.37c.

34 Case v. L. Vitali, 3rd session 1860. AN BB²⁰221; see also Wilson (1988).

35 Case v. G.-C. Romani and G.-F. Vellutini, 3rd session 1859. AN BB²⁰213.

36 See Pitt-Rivers (1971), pp. 161–8. A list of Corsican nicknames is provided in Appendix 2.

37 See Lamotte (1964), p. 60; and Martini (1964a), on tribunals; and Roger (1945), pp. 281–5.

38 Beaulieu-Delbet (1897), pp. 123–6; and Lorenzi de Bradi (1928), pp. 155–6; and, more generally, Borel-Léandri (1978), pp. 272–3; and author's fieldwork.

39 E.g. at Campile; see Case v. A.-M. Vecchioni et al., Assize Court, 2nd session 1854. AN BB²⁰170.

40 E.g. Lorenzi de Bradi (1928), p. 157.

41 Lorenzi de Bradi (1928), pp. 161–2; also Robiquet (1835), pp. 445–6; Bigot (1890), p. 516; Franceschini (1923), pp. 30 and 34; Casanova (1973); and Finelli (n.d.), pp. 54–5.

42 See Malcolmson (1973), pp. 82–3; Girard (1977), p. 125; and Roubin (1977), p. 176.

43 In the event, as we shall see, the parties quarrelled over the festival ritual itself and broke the truce; see Gregorovius (1855), pp. 419–23.

44 Malaspina (1876), p. 374; and Beaulieu-Delbet (1897), pp. 29–30.

45 Casanova (1965), II, pp. 14–18.

46 Finelli (n.d.), p. 15; and Lamotte (1956e), p. 39.

47 Cit. Pomponi (1976c), p. 156; see also Blanqui (1841), p. 496; Quantin (1914), p. 248; Casanova (1965), II, p. 2; Deane (1965), p. 187; Carrington (1971d), p. 305; Pomponi (1978a), p. 23; and Ravis-Giordani (1978b), p. 197.

48 Archer (1924), pp. 151–2; Tommaseo (1841), p. 367; Arrighi (1970), p. 228; Borel-Léandri (1978), p. 250; also Mattei (1867), p. 24.

49 Casta (1974), pp. 109–10, 123 and 170; Casanova (1931–2), II, p. 82; Marin-Muracciole (1964), pp. 260–1; Pomponi (1976a), pp. 341–4; Letter, 25 November 1819 and other documents. ADCS 2.V.25, 'Dispensations de mariage 1819–25'; and Lenclud and Ravis-Giordani (1973), p. 232 note 20.

50 Patin de La Fizelière (1963), pp. 60, 61 and 68; see also Beaumont (1822), pp. 36–7; and Chapter 8, pp. 244–5.

51 Leca (1978), p. 122; Lenclud and Ravis Giordani (1973), p. 209; Lenclud and Pernet (1978), p. 58; Lenclud (1979), pp. 40–1; and Pernet and Lenclud (1977), p. 89.

52 Coppolani (1949), pp. 78 and 80–1.

53 Pomponi (1976a), pp. 343–4.

54 Geoffray (1982), pp. 67–8.

55 Benson (1825), p. 41; Flaubert (1973) [1840], pp. 327–8; Gregorovius (1855), pp. 182–4; Viale (1855), p. 37 (*vocero*): Vuillier (1896), pp. 239–41; Andrei (1893), pp. 275–7; Rossi (1900), Ch. IX; Juta (1926), p. 110; Casanova (1965), II, pp. 11–13; and Versini (1979), p. 139, citing Bigot.

56 Beaulieu-Delbet (1897), pp. 101–3; Deane (1965), pp. 77 and 185; Casanova (1965), II, p. 14.

57 The well-recorded and ancient custom of throwing rice or other grains at or over the bride had the same significance; see Galletti (1863), p. 65; Richardson (1894), p. 519; Lorenzi de Bradi (1928), pp. 154–5; Spinosi (1956), p. 172; and Maestroni (1978), p. 71.

58 Casanova (1931–2), III, p. 376; ADCS 2.V.27, 'Confréries An XIII – 1881'; Robiquet (1835), pp. 404 and 592; Griffon (1841), pp. 42–3; Saint-Germain (1869), p. 292; Bigot (1890), pp. 515–16; Casta (1976), p. 295; and author's fieldwork.

59 Lamotte (1956a), p. 37; Lamotte (1961); and Casta (1974), pp. 83–5, 112–13, 165 and 199–200.

60 Printed Judgment, Court of Criminal Justice, Bastia, August 1810. AN BB18239.

61 F. Renucci (1838), pp. 15–19; and Gregorovius (1855), pp. 419–23.

62 E.g. Case, Appeal Court. *Gaz. Trib.*, 31 August 1828, No. 956.

63 E.g. Report, Inspector Carlotti, 12 November 1847. ADCS 3.X.37c, on frauds related to the nursing of abandoned children.

64 Report, Procureur-général to Ministry of Justice, 17 February 1819. AN BB181049.

65 Reports, Procureur-général to Ministry of Justice, 15 November 1820. AN BB181069; and 21 February 1821. AN BB181072; see also Report, Gendarmerie, 9 December 1820, cit. Franceschini (1919), p. 61 (Altagène).

66 Report, Subprefect, Calvi, 23 June 1832. ADCS 1.M.222.

67 Cases v. Abbé Lanfranchi et al., Assize Court, 1st session (Aullène); v. M.-G. Bernardini et al., 3rd session (Pietricaggio); and v. Mannoni et al., 3rd session 1849 (Felce). AN BB20146.

68 E.g. at Vescovato (1859) and at Olmeto (1864). ADCS 1.M.222.

69 E.g. Fighting in 1798 between the inhabitants of Speloncato and a neighbouring unspecified village. Letter, Commissaire du Directoire exécutif, Golo, 8 Vendémiaire An VII. AN BB18237.

70 Arrighi (1976), Ch. III; also Filippi (1906), pp. 34–5; and Dalmas (1978), p. 11; and, for English parallels, Porter (1969), p. 376.

71 Ortoli (1883), pp. 242–54. Briggs (1971), Part A, Vol. 2, pp. 3, 5, 349–60 and *passim*, presenting English parallels, uses the generic term 'noodle tale'.
72 Saravelli-Retali (1976), p. 124; and Filippi (1906), p. 16.
73 Case v. P.-M. Casali et al., Court of Criminal Justice, Ajaccio, 1812. ADCS 2.U.1/43; see also Deane (1965), p. 130.
74 Case v. P. Negroni, Assize Court, 3rd session 1833. *Gaz Trib.*, 30 October 1833, No. 2562; also Privat (1936), p. 48.
75 See e.g. Cases v. C. and A. Pietri, 2nd session 1852. AN BB²⁰158; and v. A. Flori, 3rd session 1854. AN BB²⁰170.
76 E.g. Boissevain (1965), pp. 27, 33–4 and 67–9 (Malta); Porter (1969), pp. 102, 142–5, 231 and 240 (Cambridgeshire); Morel (1972), pp. 70 and 75 (Picardy); G. and A. Duby (1973), pp. 26 and 40 (fifteenth-century Lorraine); Malcolmson (1973), pp. 83–4 (England); Riegelhaupt (1973), esp. pp. 844–5 (Portugal); Cuisenier (1978), p. 29 (Brittany); and AN BB²⁴868 (various parts of France in 1879).
77 E.g. Case v. G.-B. Ramacciotti, Assize Court, 4th session 1865. AN BB²⁰273 (Canale); or the litigation in the 1860s between Silvareccio and Penta-di-Casinca over a spring. ADHC E.29/8.
78 See p. 175.
79 Chanal (n.d.), pp. 133–40. Rivalry was also expressed in laments; see Ettori (1979), pp. 179–82 and 193–4.
80 Pomponi (1979b), pp. 324 and 414; Rémy (1930), pp. 25–57 and 71–4; Lacroix (1981), p. 26; and Report, Procureur-général to Minister of Justice, 13 April 1823. AN BB¹⁸1096.
81 Réalier-Dumas (1819), p. 32.
82 Tommaseo (1841), p. 128; and ADHC E.18/25. Dossier 1, 'Procès-verbal de délimitation de la commune de Venzolasca avec plan, 1845'.
83 Pomponi (1974a), pp. 19–20; and Report, Commissaire spécial, 6 October 1817, cit. Franceschini (1922), p. 293; and, more generally, Pomponi (1974b); and Pomponi (1975).
84 Patin de La Fizelière (1963), pp. 73 and 80; Robiquet (1835), pp. 465–7; Pomponi (1974), pp. 14–15; Arrighi (1976), p. 88; Reports, Subprefect, Sartène, and Gendarmerie, 17–18 June 1818; and Subprefect, 30 March 1819; and 8 September 1827. ADCS 4.M.98 and 99; and Case v. T. Desanti, Assize Court, 1st session 1852. AN BB²⁰158.
85 E.g. Defranceschi (1978), p. 85; and Leca (1978), pp. 106–7.
86 Pomponi (1974b), esp. pp. 24–31; also Defranceschi (1974), pp. 552–6, for the earlier eighteenth-century phase of this development.
87 Letter, Procureur du Roi, Bastia, to Prefect, 22 August 1825; and Notice, 26 August 1825. ADCS 1.M.222.
88 Lamotte (1961), pp. 47–8; see also, more generally, Defranceschi (1978), pp. 93–4.
89 Cit. Geoffray (1982), p. 68.
90 Letter, Municipal councillors, Levie, to Prefect, 3 December 1854. ADCS 2.M.126.
91 E.g. Defranceschi (1974), p. 551; and Viale (1966), p. 73.
92 Cases v. Don G. Bonavita et al., Assize Court, 4th session 1842. AN BB²⁰116; v. A.-M. Antonmarchi, 4th session 1843. AN BB²⁰121; v. F. Zecchini et al., 3rd session 1842. AN BB²⁰116; v. G. Santelli et al., 3rd session 1852. AN BB²⁰158; and v. S. Bartoli, 3rd session 1857. AN BB²⁰194.
93 Letter, Antono Vincentelli to Prefect, 3 December 1846. ADCS 2.M.87.
94 Letters, Subprefect, Calvi, to Prefect, 6 and 7 March 1826; and Letters, Mayors, Niolo, to Prefect, 20 March 1826; and other documents. ADCS 1.M.222; and Versini (1979), pp. 79 and 165–6, citing Rapport Mottet.
95 Cases v. Gavini et al., Assize Court, 4th session 1852. AN BB²⁰158; and v. F. Nasica, 4th session 1842. AN BB²⁰116.

96 Report, Subprefect, Ajaccio, 6 July 1826. ADCS 4.M.91.

97 Case v. P.-P. Raffali, Assize Court, 1st and 2nd sessions 1864. AN BB²⁰260.

98 Cases v. S. Gaudeani, 4th session 1844. AN BB²⁰125; and v. G.-V. Dari, 3rd (?) session 1840. *Gaz. Trib.*, 23 September 1840, No. 4695. Conflict early in the nineteenth century between Fozzano and Santa-Maria-Figaniella involved cattle-rustling by the latter. 'Dénunciations'. ADCS 7.U.1/9; and Case, 9 Floréal An X, Extraordinary Criminal Court, Sartène. ADCS 3.U.5/129.

99 Case, Assize Court, 1st(?) session 1835. *Gaz. Trib.*, 8 March 1835, No. 2979. '*Ghioccari capocorsini ... cipullai*' and '*ziparai*'; see also Arrighi (1976), pp. 43 and 71.

100 Report, Gendarmerie, Bastia, 10 May 1816. ADCS 4.M.102; and Deane (1965), p. 187.

101 Case v. M. Mattei, Assize Court, 2nd session 1849, Extraordinary sitting. AN BB²⁰146.

102 Viale (1855), pp. 43–8; and Ettori (1979), pp. 179–82.

103 See e.g. Patin de La Fizelière (1963), p. 66.

104 Ortoli (1883), p. 304; and Borel-Léandri (1978), p. 262. The culprit was St John, who was indicating the ill-omened nature of the site.

105 Tommaseo (1841), pp. 143–5; and Versini (1979), p. 79.

106 Letter, Prefect to Ministry of Interior, 22 September 1822. AN BB¹⁸1066; Reports, Procureur-général to Ministry of Justice, 29 January, 14 and 16 April; and to Ministry of the Interior, 13 May 1823. AN BB¹⁸1093.

107 Cases v. G.-S. Ventura, Assize Court, 1st session; and v. O.-G. Chipponi, 2nd session 1852. AN BB²⁰158; and Report, Gendarmerie, Ajaccio, 13 September 1841. ADCS 4.M.125.

108 Robiquet (1835), p. 405.

109 Case v. A. Vincenti, Assize Court, 4th session 1848. AN BB²⁰142; and Report, Police, 27 May 1822. ADCS 4.M.75.

110 *Gaz. Trib.*, 8 October 1828, No. 988, referring in particular to conflict between Centuri and Morsiglia. For an important parallel, see Hertz (1983).

111 'Dossier sur l'église de Santa Maria della Chiapella 1790–1825', Collection Franceschi. ADHC 1.J.2/1; Martini (1922); Report, Procureur-général to Ministry of Justice, 1 April 1826. AN BB¹⁸1137; Case, Tribunal correctionnel, Bastia, 1826. *Gaz. Trib.*, 7 January 1827, No. 396; ADHC E.6/25. Tomino 1835–55; and Arrighi (1976), p. 75. The present building probably dates from the sixteenth century and is ironically neglected and in disrepair.

112 Carrington and Lamotte (1957), p. 85; and (1958), pp. 66–7; Chiari (1960), pp. 134–5; Caisson (1978b), p. 160; Ravis-Giordani (1978a), p. 146; Finelli (n.d.), p. 48; and Giacomo-Marcellesi (1979), p. 114. *Mazzeri* are discussed in Chapter 13.

113 Report, Gendarmerie, Ajaccio, 13 December 1841. ADCS 4.M.125.

114 E.g. Cases v. D. Mariotti; and v. P.-F. Guerrini, Assize Court, 3rd session 1852. AN BB²⁰158; and v. B. Peres, 1st session 1857. AN BB²⁰194.

115 Case v. F. Grimaldi et al., Extraordinary Criminal Court, 22 Floréal An XII. ADCS 7.U.1/22.

116 Transcript, Case v. G.-A. Castiglione, Tribunal correctionnel, Calvi, 15 Messidor An XIII. AN BB¹⁸240.

117 Case v. A.-M. Mondolini, Assize Court, 2nd session 1852. AN BB²⁰158.

118 Cases v. Morelli and Antonmarchi, Assize Court, 4th session 1831. *Gaz. Trib.*, 1 January 1832; v. Nicolai, 1st session 1834. *Gaz. Trib.*, 3 July 1834, No. 2769; and v. P.-P. Campana, 4th session 1842. AN BB²⁰116.

119 Chanal (n.d.), p. 87; see also Rossi (1900), pp. 185–8.

120 Letter, Commissaire des guerres Antoni to Commissaire du gouvernment près le Tribunal Criminel Extraordinaire, 20 Fructidor An X. ADCS 7.U.1/9.

121 Viale (1855), pp. 106–10; and Saint-Victor (1925) [1887], pp. 357–8, citing a well-known lament.
122 Case v. V. Casile, Assize Court, 1st session 1844. AN BB²⁰125.
123 F. Renucci (1838), pp. 8–14; and Gregorovius (1855), pp. 423–6.
124 Viale (1842); Benson (1825), pp. 129–30, Tommaseo (1841), pp. 138–43; Gregorovius (1855), pp. 417–18; Archer (1924), p. 94; Cavallucci (1930), Ch. III; and Versini (1979), pp. 88–9.
125 Case v. G.-F. Moracchini and L. Antoni, Court of Criminal Justice, 1st session 1830. AN BB²⁰49; and v. A. Casalta, Assize Court, 1st session 1851. AN BB²⁰152. See also, more generally, Report, Prefect to Departmental Council, 1826. AN BB¹⁸1146; and Cesari-Rocca (1908), p. 7.
126 Marcaggi (1932), p. 93; and note 122 above.
127 Coppolani (1949), pp. 77–8; Appolis (1964), pp. 88 and 91–3; Thrasher (1970), pp. 193 and 199; Renucci (1974), p. 60; and Pomponi (1979b), pp. 151–3.
128 Case v. P. Ceccaldi and A.-F. Nesa, Court of Criminal Justice, 1807; and Letter, Procureur-général to Ministry of Justice, 12 June 1807. AN BB¹⁸240.
129 Case v. G. and D. Frimicacci, Assize Court, 1st session 1834. *Gaz. Trib.*, 2 October 1834, No. 2845.
130 Report, Procureur-général, 5 May 1882. Petition for clemency for T. Tomasi(?). AN BB²⁴874; and Lorenzi (1981).
131 See e.g. Lamotte (1956c), p. 57; and Report, Gendarmerie, Ajaccio, 31 July 1842. ADCS 4.M.126 (on threshing-floor shared by people from Pila-Canale, Frasseto, Cognocoli and Ciamannacce).
132 See Stirling (1960), p. 74, for a parallel.

7 *Obligation and organization in the feud*

1 Saint-Germain (1869), p. 182; Reparaz (1961), p. 74; Chiva (1963), pp. 102 and 106; Casanova (1965), II, pp. 3–5; Renucci (1974), p. 178; Pernet and Lenclud (1977), pp. 90–1; Casanova (1978), p. 49; and Lenclud and Pernet (1978), pp. 61–2 and 70–2.
2 Bigot (1890), esp. pp. 442, 460ff and 523; and Lenclud and Pernet (1978), p. 78; see also Casanova (1965), II, pp. 3–7; Pomponi (1974b), pp. 11–12; and Renucci (1974), p. 257.
3 Malaspina (1876), p. 372; Filippi (1906), pp. 14 and 16; and Tommaseo (1841), p. 370; see also Mattei (1867), pp. 49, 52 and 61–2.
4 Maurice (ed.) (1904), p. 120 (26 September 1794); see also Bigot (1890), p. 458; and Busquet (1919), pp. 23–4 and 541–4.
5 Réalier-Dumas (1819), p. 19; and Saint-Germain (1869), p. 252.
6 Bouchez (1843), p. 37 note.
7 Case v. A. Canacci et al., Assize Court, 1st session 1839. *Gaz. Trib.*, 30 March 1839, No. 4229.
8 Marcaggi (1898b), pp. 147–8.
9 Report, Subprefect, Sartène, 21 January 1830. ADCS 4.M.100.
10 Case v. Agostini, Assize Court, 3rd session 1835, *Gaz. Trib.*, 28 October 1835, cit. Sorbier (1863), p. 55.
11 Bouchez (1843), p. 37 note; Barry (1893), p. 141; Blanqui (1841), p. 490; and Vanutberghe (1904), p. 345; see also Bourde (1887), p. 8.
12 Feydel (1799), p. 62; Bourde (1887), p. 9; and Marin-Muracciole (1964), pp. 364–5.
13 E.g. Guitet-Vauquelin (1934), p. 139.
14 Dalmas (1978), p. 42.
15 On memory and oral tradition, see Yates (1966); Vansina (1973); and Finnegan (1977), pp. 135–53.

16 E.g. Case v. M. Vincenti, Assize Court, 2nd session 1845. AN BB^{20}130. Vincenti, a youth of 18 from Pila-Canale, was known in the village as Piazza, his mother's name. His father was dead.

17 Lenclud (1979), p. 42.

18 Cases v. G. Codaccioni, Tribunal correctionnel, Sartène, 24 July 1817. ADCS 3.U.5/167; and v. L. Simoni et al., Extraordinary Criminal Court, Sartène, An X. ADCS 3.U.5/129. On the other hand, some witnesses in trials testified that they were related to parties to the seventh or eighth degree.

19 ADCS 7.U.113.

20 E.g. Anderson (1957); O. Lewis (1964); Kenna (1976), p. 26; and Davis (1977), pp. 223–32.

21 Finelli (n.d.), pp. 48, 114 and 118; and Ceccaldi (1974), p. 282.

22 Viale (1855), p. 113 note.

23 Saint-Germain (1869), p. 296; and Marcaggi (1932), pp. 241–2.

24 Malaspina (1876), p. 374.

25 Letter, V. Roccaserra to Prefect, 4 December 1846. ADCS 2.M.88; see also, more generally, Caisson (1974), pp. 115 and 125; and Pomponi (1978a), p. 23. We will return to this aspect of ritual kinship in Chapter 11.

26 Rossi (1900), pp. 108–9; Bigot (1890), p. 443; Busquet (1919), pp. 124–7; Bourde (1887), pp. 9–12; and Choury (1958), pp. 20–1; see also Pomponi (1978a). On the Genoese *alberghi*, see Heers (1961), pp. 564–76; Hughes (1975); and (1977), esp. pp. 108–11.

27 Lenclud and Ravis-Giordani (1973), pp. 209, 222–4 and 226.

28 E.g. Tommaseo (1841), p. 372.

29 Letter, M.-A. Peretti to Prefect, 26 January 1847. ADCS 2.M.83; see also Comiti (1933), p. 237.

30 E.g. Letter to Prefect, 1860. ADCS 2.M.121 (referring to the Cucchi of Carbini); Barry (1893), p. 141; and Quantin (1914), p. 27.

31 Lenclud (1979); see also Wagner (1968), p. 66.

32 Case v. P. Pianelli, Assize Court, 1st session 1864. AN BB^{20}260. The bond proved to be forged.

33 Lorenzi de Bradi (1928), p. 167.

34 Letter, 9 November 1852. Petition for clemency for F. Bastianesi. AN BB^{24}798.

35 Letters, P. Campi, 8 October 1869; and other documents. ADCS 2.V.19; see also litigation over family chapels. *Gaz. Trib.*, 24 April; and 25–26 May 1829, Nos. 1157 and 1184; Martelli (1960), pp. 264, 266–7 and 274–5; and Finelli (n.d.), p. 12.

36 Burial customs are described and discussed in Chapter 13.

37 AN BB^{18}1586.

38 Filippi (1906), p. 20.

39 Benson (1825), p. 44; see also Lorenzi de Bradi (1928), p. 156; and Deane (1965), p. 65.

40 Abeau (1888), pp. 16–17.

41 Case v. Giovan-Battiste son of the late Anton-Marco, Tribunal correctionnel, Sartène, 31 August 1814. ADCS 3.U.5/166.

42 Privat (1936), p. 16.

43 Saint-Germain (1869), p. 123; Southwell Colucci (1933), p. 202 (citing *vocero*); Martelli (1960), p. 229; Lenclud (1979), p. 23; and author's fieldwork.

44 E.g. in *voceri*; see Tommaseo (1841), p. 206; and Viale (1855), pp. 43–8.

45 Bigot (1890), pp. 460–1; Borel-Léandri (1978), p. 11; Raulin and Ravis-Giordani (1978), esp. pp. 63 and 67; Ravis-Giordani (1978a), pp. 135–6; and Lenclud (1979), p. 21.

46 Such sales did, of course, sometimes occur, but predictably they often led to conflict, e.g. Case v. A.-M. Culioli, Assize Court, 3rd session 1853. AN BB^{20}164.

47 Ardouin-Dumazet (1898), p. 103; Méjean (1932); Arbos (1933); Privat (1936), pp. 15–16; Coppolani (1949), p. 104; Arrighi (1970), pp. 23 and 40–1; Lenclud and Ravis-Giordani (1973), pp. 207–9; Pietri and Nicolas (1977); Borel-Léandri (1978), pp. 18–19 and *passim*; Raulin and Ravis-Giordani (1978); Lenclud (1979), pp. 15–16 and 19; Lenclud (1985), pp. 40–2; and author's fieldwork. On the association of large houses with large family communities elsewhere, see Gaillard-Bans (1976) (Brittany); Collomp (1978) (Haute-Provence); and Gudin de Vallerin (1982) (Burgundy).

48 Lenclud (1979), pp. 20–1 and 31–3; and Lenclud (1985), p. 40.

49 Fontana (1905), p. 75; see also Piobb (n.d.), pp. 47–8; and Borel-Léandri (1978), pp. 138–9.

50 'Matrice cadastrale des Propriétés bâties', Venzolasca 1882. ADHC 3.P.854; and Martelli (1960), p. 229.

51 Vanutberghe (1904), p. 344; Piobb (n.d.), pp. 47–8.

52 See Patin de La Fizelière (1963), p. 77; Robiquet (1835), p. 454; and Blanqui (1841), pp. 497–8.

53 Dupâquier and Jadin (1972). For general and particular criticism, see Berkner (1975); Davis (1977), pp. 169ff; and Lenclud (1979), esp. pp. 7–17. A further possible reason for the inflation of the number of hearths in the statistics is revealed by the arrangements made in 1826 for the partition of common lands, which allotted shares by 'hearths'; see Pomponi (1975), p. 43.

54 Vinciguerra (1962); Lenclud and Ravis-Giordani (1973), pp. 217–18; and Pomponi (1974b), p. 22.

55 Lenclud (1979), p. 17; also Deane (1965), pp. 18–19 and 91–2.

56 Case v. M. Ferrandi, Court of Criminal Justice, Ajaccio, 1812. ADCS 2.U.1/43.

57 Letter, Procureur-général to Minister of Justice, 18 November 1868. AN BB[18]1728.

58 Cases v. G. Orsini, Assize Court, 1st session 1863. AN BB[20]249; v. G. Marcantoni, 1st session 1853. AN BB[20]164; and v. E. Orsini, 4th session 1864. AN BB[20]260.

59 Bigot (1890), p. 460; also Faure (1858), p. 17.

60 Petition for clemency for S.-F. Savelli, 1834. AN BB[24]155–69.

61 Case v. P.-G. Piazzoli and sons, Extraordinary Criminal Court, 17 Messidor An IX. ADCS 7.U.1/16.

62 Case v. P. Giacomoni et al., Assize Court, 2nd session 1848. *Gaz. Trib.*, 12 and 22 July 1848, Nos. 6559 and 6568.

63 Cases v. A. F. Leca, 2nd session 1840. *Gaz. Trib.*, 15 August 1840, No. 4659, cit. Sorbier (1863), pp. 204–5; v. G. Armani, 2nd session 1865. AN BB[20]273; v. C.-A. Peretti, 1st session 1849. AN BB[20]146; v. G.-P. Renucci, 4th session 1865. AN BB[20]273; v. F. Corrazini, 2nd session 1850. AN BB[20]149; and v. M. Corrazini, 1st session 1851. AN BB[20]152. In a modern example, Deane lodged in a village in the Balagna in a house containing her landlord, a shepherd, his wife and daughter, his mother, his wife's two brothers, his sister and her husband and their daughter. All had separate sleeping and living quarters; all but the last three ate together, Deane (1965), pp. 24–6.

64 Lenclud and Ravis-Giordani (1973), p. 217; Marcaggi (1932), p. 150.

65 Reports, Subprefect, Sartène, 24 and 27 February 1829. ADCS 4.M.99; and see, more generally, Dupâquier and Jadin (1972), p. 292; and Lenclud (1985), p. 42.

66 Cases v. V.-D. Marinetti, Assize Court, 2nd session 1859. AN BB[20]213; v. C.-G. Orsini and I. Danesi, 2nd session 1853. AN BB[20]164; v. G.-C. Liccia, 1st session 1857. AN BB[20]194; and v. P. Ordioni, 3rd session 1841. *Gaz. Trib.*, 19 October 1841, No. 4506.

67 Raulin and Ravis-Giordani (1978), p. 67.

68 See pp. 134–5.

69 Cases v. G.-B. Peretti, 1st session 1860. AN BB[20]221; v. A.-P. Ortoli et al., 3rd session 1862. AN BB[20]239; and v. P.-M. Paoli, 4th session 1851. AN BB[20]152.

70 Benson (1825), p. 42; and Cowen (1848), p. 91.
71 Cases v. G. Alessandri, Assize Court, 4th session 1855. AN BB²⁰177; v. F. Luporsi, 2nd session 1853. AN BB²⁰164; v. M.-G. Ferracci, 4th session 1865. AN BB²⁰273; and v. P. Faveletti et al., 3rd session 1841. *Gaz. Trib.*, 4 September 1841, No. 4993.
72 Case v. G.-D. and G. Casanova, 1st session 1865. AN BB²⁰273; see also Lenclud and Ravis-Giordani (1973), p. 207.
73 Cases v. P.-G. Castelli, 2nd session 1848. AN BB²⁰142; v. G.-G. Orsini, 3rd session 1850. AN BB²⁰149; v. L. and A.-G. Cirelli, 2nd session 1893. AN BB²⁰286; v. P.-M. Paoli, 4th session 1843. AN BB²⁰121; v. M. and C.-F. Bonnetti, July 1835. *Gaz. Trib.*, 2 August 1835, No. 3106; and v. B. Marcangeli, 1st session 1862. AN BB²⁰239.
74 Case v. A. Giansilj, Court of Criminal Justice, Ajaccio, 1811. ADCS 2.U.1/42.
75 Case v. Don G. Sampieri, Assize Court, 4th session 1865. AN BB²⁰273.
76 Bigot (1890), p. 449.
77 Cases v. C. Ferrandi, Extraordinary Criminal Court, 25 Floréal An IX. ADCS 7.U.1/14; and v. G. Santucci and A.-F. Stefani, 27 Pluviôse An X. ADCS 7.U.1/19.
78 Indictment of G.-G. Costa et al., 23 November 1815. AN BB¹⁸241.
79 Case v. Degiovanni, Assize Court, 1st session 1833, *Gaz. Trib.*, 5 April 1833, cit. Sorbier (1863), pp. 26–30.
80 On the main hearth, see Saint-Germain (1869), p. 124; Lorenzi de Bradi (1928), p. 153; Arrighi (1970), pp. 41–2; Pietri and Nicolas (1977), p. 22 (Brando); and Raulin and Ravis-Giordani (1978), pp. 54–5.
81 Case v. L. Caizaroni, Assize Court, 3rd session 1853. AN BB²⁰164; see also Privat (1936), pp. 15–16, referring to three hearths in one room of a house at San-Andrea-d'Orcino.
82 E.g. petition for clemency for V. Tomasi, 1844. AN BB²⁴219–50.
83 Case v. B. Comiti, Tribunal correctionnel, Sartène, June 1813. ADCS 3.U.5/139.
84 Arrighi (1970), pp. 40–1; also Lenclud and Ravis-Giordani (1973), pp. 207–9 and 217–18 (Niolo).
85 Case v. F. and N. Cucchi, Assize Court, 4th session 1853. AN BB²⁰164.
86 Banfield (1967), pp. 103 and 110–11; see also Du Boulay (1979), esp. 41 and 47–8. Banfield's influential study is to some extent loaded with specifically North American assumptions, but the concept of 'amoral familism' remains of heuristic value; for a critique, see Silverman (1968).
87 Abeau (1838), p. 17.
88 Ravis-Giordani (1976b), p. 11.
89 Case v. M. Ferrandi, Court of Criminal Justice, Ajaccio, 1812. ADCS 2.U.1/43.
90 Letter, Procureur-général to Minister of Justice, 4 January 1813. AN BB¹⁸241.
91 See Bloch (1965), pp. 123–5.
92 Dalmas (1978), p. 41.
93 Cases v. A.-P. Ortoli et al., Assize Court, 3rd session 1862. AN BB²⁰239; v. P. Toti, 1st session 1858. AN BB²⁰204; v. F. Raffini, 2nd session 1851. AN BB²⁰152; v. P.-L. Pinzuti and G. Manzaggi, 4th session 1852, Extraordinary sitting. AN BB²⁰158; and v. P. Pietri, 4th session 1842. AN BB²⁰116.
94 Chronique départementale, *Gaz. Trib.*, 6 September 1840, No. 4678; and Case v. G.-B. Agostini, Assize Court, 1st session 1841. *Gaz. Trib.*, 10 April 1841, No. 4865.
95 Peters (1967), pp. 263 and 269; and Lewis (1967), pp. 6–7, 170ff and 255; see also Maitland (1911), esp. pp. 213, 219, 221 and 224 (Wales); Philpotts (1913), p. 193, citing Beaumanoir (Beauvaisis); Davies (1969), pp. 345 and 349 (Wales); and Gellner (1969), pp. 126–7 (Atlas region).
96 Wallace-Hadrill (1962), p. 125; Stirling (1965), pp. 247 and 251–2; Turner (1971), p. 365 (medieval Iceland); and Wormald (1980), esp. pp. 70–1.
97 See Westermarck (1934), pp. 365–6 (Moroccan Berbers); Colson (1953), pp. 201–2

(Plateau Tonga); Bloch (1965), pp. 137–42; J. Schneider (1971), pp. 7–11; Roberts (1979), pp. 124, 129 and 133; and Byock (1982), pp. 165 and 169.

98 E.g. Malaspina (1876), pp. 372–3; Vanutberghe (1904), pp. 345–6; and Busquet (1919), pp. 23–4.

99 Tommaseo (1841), p. 23; Gregorovius (1855), p. 138; Bourde (1887), p. 148; Réalier-Dumas (1819), p. 17; Faure (1858), p. 96; and Busquet (1919), pp. 103–6 and 343–4; see also Marin-Muracciole (1964), pp. 10–11; Carrington (1971a), p. 82; and Christophari (1981), p. 173, who writes as if the whole *sterpa* were potentially a vengeance group.

100 Miot (1858), II, pp. 36–7.

101 Case v. G.-B. Scapola, Assize Court, 1st session 1846. *Gaz. Trib.*, 16 April 1846, No. 5860.

102 Marcaggi (1898b), p. 234.

103 Robiquet (1835), p. 394.

104 Case v. P. Giacomoni et al., Extraordinary Criminal Court, 9 Floréal An X. ADCS 3.U.5/129.

105 Cases v. F. Bartoli, Assize Court, 3rd session 1853. AN BB[20]164; and v. P.-P. Giacomi, 1st session 1843. AN BB[20]121.

106 Carrington (1971a), p. 82; also Feydel (1799), pp. 68–9; Malaspina (1876), p. 351; Rossi (1900), p. 115; and Busquet (1919), pp. 341–2.

107 Viale (1855), p. 109; see also Chelhod (1968), for an interesting parallel.

108 See e.g. Filippi (1906), p. 32.

109 Cases v. M. Luciani, Assize Court, 1st session 1851, Extraordinary sitting; v. V. Santoni, 4th session 1851. AN BB[20]152; v. M. Tomasi, 4th session 1852. AN BB[20]158, and v. L. Angeli, 3rd session 1853. AN BB[20]164.

110 Cases v. P. Giacomoni et al., 1848. *Gaz. Trib.*, 12 July 1848, No. 6559; v. F. Pasqualini, 4th session 1852, Extraordinary sitting. AN BB[20]158; v. F. Susini and D.-N. Marcilesi, 3rd session 1854. AN BB[20]170; v. F. di Q. Susini, 2nd session 1860. AN BB[20]221; v. S. Gaffori, 1st session 1849. AN BB[20]146; and v. G.-M. Petrignani, 2nd session 1855. AN BB[20]177.

111 E.g. Reports, Gendarmerie, Vescovato, 31 July; and 1 August; and Bastia, 4 August 1841. ADCS 4.M.125; and Cases v. A. Casalta, Assize Court, 1st session 1851. AN BB[20]152; v. D. Vincenti et al.; and v. M.-A. Peretti, 4th session 1852, Extraordinary sitting. AN BB[20]158.

112 Cases v. G.-F. Lanfranchi, 2nd session 1846. *Gaz. Trib.*, 21 June 1846, No. 5914; v. S. Battini, 2nd session 1851. AN BB[20]152; and v. A. Serra, 2nd session 1850. AN BB[20]149.

113 Ortoli (1887), pp. 272–5.

114 Case v. F. Benedetti, 2nd session 1853, Extraordinary sitting. AN BB[20]164.

115 Faure (1858), pp. 310–11.

116 E.g. Cases v. O.-P. and A.-P. Lorenzi, 3rd and 4th sessions 1844. AN BB[20]125 (Campile); v. G.-F. Giocondi, 2nd session 1851, Extraordinary sitting. AN BB[20]152 (Poggio-Mezzana); and v. G.-A. Nicolai, 1st session 1854. AN BB[20]170 (Fozzano).

117 Case v. P.-P. Paoli, 1st session 1853. AN BB[20]164.

118 Report, Procureur de la République, Calvi, 13 August 1879, Petition for clemency for G.-A. Padovani. AN BB[24]868.

119 Ambrosi (1972), esp. pp. 40–1.

120 Case v. Don Antono Ruffini and F.-A. Grimaldi, Extraordinary Criminal Court, 27 Floréal An XII. ADCS 7.U.1/22.

121 Case v. P.-F. Pasqualini, Assize Court, 4th session 1861. AN BB[20]229.

122 Report, 13 February 1883, Petition for clemency for G.-G. Pietri. AN BB[24]887.

123 Case v. I. Borelli, Assize Court, 3rd session 1849. AN BB[20]146.

124 Cases v. P.-F. Tomasi, 2nd session 1840. *Gaz. Trib.*, 11 June 1840, No. 4604, cit. Sorbier (1863), pp. 177–81; v. G. Muzi, 3rd session 1848. AN BB²⁰142; v. G.-B. Orsini, 3rd session 1850. AN BB²⁰149; and v. G.-A. Franceschi, 3rd session 1848. AN BB²⁰142.

125 E.g. Report, Gendarmerie, Belgodere, 1819. ADCS 4.M.102.

126 Cases v. S. Romanetti, Assize Court, 3rd session 1850. AN BB²⁰149; v. P. Ceccaldi, 2nd session 1851. AN BB²⁰185; and 4th session 1852. AN BB²⁰158.

127 Report, Gendarmerie, Bastia, 5 January 1841. ADCS 4.M.125.

128 Roger (1945), pp. 276–80.

129 E.g. Cases v. A.-M. Pietri Vincenzini, Assize Court, 1st session 1851. AN BB²⁰152 (San Gavino); and v. C.-G. Carlotti, 3rd session 1856. AN BB²⁰185 (Poggio-di-Venaco).

130 Cases v. G. Miliani et al., 2nd session 1847. *Gaz. Trib.*, 18 July 1847, No. 6252; v. P. Chiaroni, 1st session 1851. AN BB²⁰152; v. A.-M. Renucci, 1st session 1843. AN BB²⁰121; v. L. Angeli, 3rd session 1853. AN BB²⁰164; and v. F.-L. Ciamborani, 1st session 1853. AN BB²⁰164.

131 Rossi (1900), p. 115. For examples of vengeance on or by friends, see, e.g., Report, Procureur-général to Minister of Justice, 4 January 1813. AN BB¹⁸241 (Peri); and Case v. F. di Q. Susini, Assize Court, 2nd session 1860. AN BB²⁰221.

132 Black-Michaud (1975), pp. 39–41.

133 Bouchez (1843), p. 8; and Marin-Muracciole (1964), pp. 10–11.

134 Caisson (1974), p. 125 note 4.

135 Réalier-Dumas (1819), p. 19.

136 Ortoli (1887), p. 276 note.

137 Printed Memoir, Captain Frediani, AN BB¹⁸243; and, more generally, Busquet (1919), pp. 351–2.

138 Case v. G. Negroni, Assize Court, 4th session 1838. *Gaz. Trib.*, 5 January 1839, No. 4156; Tommaseo (1841), pp. 32–5 and 98; Gregorovius (1855), p. 145; and Saint-Germain (1869), pp. 228–41.

139 Case v. M. Versini, Assize Court, 1st session 1849. AN BB²⁰146; and Busquet (1919), pp. 345 and 347; also Bourde (1887), p. 148; Mirambel (1943), p. 383; and Carrington (1971a), p. 82.

140 Busquet (1919), pp. 341–4 and 347; and Carrington (1971a), p. 82.

141 Case v. A.-P. Octaviani, Court of Criminal Justice, Ajaccio, 1813. ADCS 2.U.1/43.

142 Report, Procureur-général to Minister of Justice, 12 October 1820, Petitions for clemency for G. Orticoni and M. Graziani. AN BB²⁴8–17.

143 Letter, Miot, to Minister of Justice, 10 Fructidor An IX. AN BB¹⁸236.

144 Réalier-Dumas (1819), p. 18; Faure (1858), p. 20; Busquet (1919), pp. 345–6; and Marin-Muracciole (1964), pp. 10–11; see also Maitland (1911), p. 216, for a parallel.

145 Letter, Mayor to Prefect, 24 July 1860. ADCS 2.M.149.

146 Cases v. A. Serra, Assize Court, 2nd session 1850. AN BB²⁰149; and v. G.-A. Nicolai, 1st session 1854. AN BB²⁰170.

147 Letter, Substitut Poggj to Minister of Justice, 1 Brumaire An VI. AN BB¹⁸237.

148 Interrogation of Anton-Francesco Bozzi, 22 Vendémiaire An X. ADCS 7.U.1/13.

149 Report, Subprefect(?) to Prefect, 18 June 1822. ADCS 1.M.228.

150 Case v. P.-M. Giacomi, Assize Court, 4th session 1842. AN BB²⁰116.

151 E.g. Cases v. A. Lucchini, 2nd session 1839, *Gaz. Trib.*, 20 July 1839, No. 4326 (Ciamannacce – uncle); v. A.-M. Pietri Vincenzini, 1st session 1851. AN BB²⁰152 (San-Gavino – father-in-law); and v. Don G.-T. Peretti, 2nd session 1852. AN BB²⁰158.

152 Malaspina (1876), p. 273; and Filippi (1906), pp. 19, 23 and 27.

153 E.g. Stirling (1960), pp. 63, 68 and 71; and Brögger (1968), p. 133.

154 See Petit-Dutaillis (1908) (medieval Low Countries); Brunner (1943) (medieval S. Germany); Douglas (1948), p. 207 (Capri region); Sonnichsen (1962), pp. 6–7 (Texas); Middleton and Tait (1970) (Africa); Pigliaru (1975) (Sardinia); Sutherland (1975), p. 396 (medieval Lombardy); and F. Du Boulay (1978), pp. 345–6 (medieval Germany).

155 Pompei (1821), p. 209; Bartoli (1898), pp. 233 and 255–6; Surier (1934), pp. 44 and 46–7; Busquet (1919); and Robiquet (1835), p. 394; see also Valéry (1837), p. 204; Saint-Victor (1925) [1887], p. 362; and Marin-Muracciole (1964), p. 9.

156 Faure (1885), I, p. 44; and Saint-Germain (1869), pp. 235–6.

157 Letter, Procureur-général to Minister of Justice, 8 November 1820. AN BB¹⁸1049; Pompei (1821), p. 210; Robiquet (1835), p. 394; and Busquet (1919), pp. 102 and 335–6.

158 'Guardate e moderate i passi!'; 'Guardate, o cantera il prete!'; 'Guardate! se il sol ti vede mio piombo ti tocca!' Cases v. P.-P. Antonmarchi, Assize Court, 3rd session 1837, *Gaz. Trib.*, 20 September 1837, No. 3763; and v. F. Poli, 4th session 1845. AN BB²⁰130; Marin-Muracciole (1964), pp. 9–10; and Montherot (1840), p. 64.

159 Busquet (1919), pp. 102–3 and 347; Police report to Prefect, 22 May 1820. ADCS 4.M.74; and Report, Subprefect, Sartène, 11 December 1821. ADCS 4.M.98; also Bourde (1887), p. 146.

160 Letter, F.-M. Bruni to Miot, An IX. AN BB¹⁸236.

161 Réalier-Dumas (1819), p. 18.

162 Case v. M. Luciani, Assize Court, 1st session 1851, Extraordinary sitting. AN BB²⁰152.

163 Pompei (1821), p. 210; and Busquet (1919), pp. 333–5.

164 Cit. Robiquet (1835), p. 385.

165 Cases v. M. Nicolai, Assize Court, 1st session; and v. Mattei(?), 3rd session 1834. *Gaz. Trib.*, 3 July, and 2 October 1834, Nos. 2769 and 2845; and Chronique départementale, Sartène. *Gaz. Trib.*, 9 June 1842, No. 4233; also Beaumont (1822), p. 28; Mérimée (1840a), pp. 544–5; Régis and Martin (n.d.), pp. 139–43, citing Assize Court cases of 1900; and Carrington (1971a), p. 89.

166 E.g. Marin-Muracciole (1964), pp. 9–10; see also Chelhod (1968), pp. 45–6.

167 Versini (1972), pp. 120–1, citing *Gaz. Trib.*, 31 January 1843; and Montherot (1840), pp. 17–18; see also Réalier-Dumas (1819), p. 17; Mérimée (1840b), p. 731; Bouchez (1843), pp. 53 and 92; Bertrand (1870), p. 124; Malaspina (1876), p. 375; and Busquet (1919), p. 341.

168 Mérimée (1840b), p. 731; also Réalier-Dumas (1819), p. 17; Benson (1825), p. 40; Mérimée (1840a), pp. 492–3; Gregorovius (1855), p. 138; Arrighi (1856b), pp. 13–14; Miot (1858), II, p. 38; Busquet (1919), pp. 101 and 334–5; and Marcaggi (1932), p. 6; for parallels, see Clay (ed.) (1965), p. 121; and Byock (1982), p. 257.

169 Bertrand (1870), p. 19; and Viale (1855), p. 94; see also Mérimée (1840b), pp. 734–7; Viale (1855), pp. 88–9; Ortoli (1887), pp. 314–21; and Natali (1961), pp. 63 and 87.

170 Bourde (1887), pp. 145–6; also Flaubert (1973) [1840], p. 325; and Ortoli (1887), pp. 192–3.

171 Saint-Germain (1869), pp. 299–300.

172 Cases v. G.-B. Peraldi, Assize Court, 2nd session 1843. AN BB²⁰121; v. P. Leonetti, 2nd session, Extraordinary sitting; and v. L. Angeli, 3rd session 1853. AN BB²⁰164.

173 Miot (1858), II, pp. 35–6.

174 Case v. A.-G. Mariotti, 2nd session 1842. AN BB²⁰116.

175 E.g. Cases v. G.-B. Scapola, 1st session 1846. *Gaz. Trib.*, 16 April 1846, No. 5860 (Bastelica); v. S. Bernardi, 1st session 1844. AN BB²⁰125 (Alzi); and v. A. Casalta, 1st session 1851. AN BB²⁰152 (Casalta and Silvareccio).

176 Letter, Conseiller d'Etat to Minister of Justice, 10 Fructidor An IX. AN BB¹⁸236;

Letter, Procureur-général to Minister of Justice, 1818. AN BB[18]243; Dupont de l'Eure, Rapport au roi, 11 November 1830. *Gaz. Trib.*, 14 November 1830, No. 1638; Robiquet (1835), pp. 387 and 393; Miot (1858), I. p. 151; and II, p. 38; Chanal (n.d.), p. 87; Lorenzi de Bradi (1928), p. 236; and Roger (1945), pp. 281–5.

177 Bigot (1890), pp. 449–50; Réalier-Dumas (1819), p. 25.

178 Case v. M.-O. Peraldi, Extraordinary Criminal Court, 23 Vendémiaire An X. ADCS 7.U.1/18.

179 Case v. G.-F. Pasqualini, Assize Court, 4th session 1862. AN BB[20]239.

180 Ortoli (1887), pp. 238–9.

181 E.g. Levi (1948), p. 23; Stirling (1965), p. 253; and Black-Michaud (1975), pp. 17 and 234–7.

182 Cases v. G.-F. Giacomoni et al., Extraordinary Criminal Court, Sartène, 9 Floréal An X. ADCS 3.U.5/129; and v. D. Valentini, 13 Thermidor An IX. ADCS 3.U.5/128.

183 Montherot (1840), pp. 22–3.

184 Letter, General Morand to Minister of Justice, 26 Prairial An XIII. AN BB[18]240; Report, Procureur-général to Minister of Justice, November 1807. AN BB[18]241; Reports, Gendarmerie, Ajaccio, 18 July, and 4 October 1816; 30 April and 12 August 1841; and 26 November 1842. ADCS 4.M.102, 4.M.125 and 4.M.126; *Gaz. Trib.*, 8 October 1834, No. 2846; 25 November 1835, No. 3203; and 16 April 1846, No. 5866; Robiquet (1835), pp. 427, 431 and 438; Petition for clemency for C.-M. Rossy, 1835. AN BB[24]155–69; ADCS 2.M.69; ADCS 2.V.19; Cases v. G.-M. Valle, Assize Court, 2nd session; and v. A. Pantaloni, 3rd session 1845. AN BB[20]130; v. G.-B. Scapola, 1st session 1846. AN BB[20]134; v. N. Ferrolini, 1st session 1849. AN[20]146; v. G.-B. Martinetti and P. Giordani; and v. N. Giordani, 1st session; and v. G. Giordani, 2nd session 1851. AN BB[20]152; v. D. Folacci, 1st session 1852. AN BB[20]158; and v. A. Marietti, 4th session 1859. AN BB[20]213; Faure (1858), pp. 304–13; ADCS 2.M.79; ADCS 2.M.116; Reports, Ministry of Justice and Procureur-général, 1 March, and 12 October 1866. AN BB[18]1726; Fumaroli (1921); Archer (1924), p. 50; and Marcaggi (1932), p. 181.

185 Patorni (1842), pp. 69–70.

186 Case v. A.-M. Lucioni, Assize Court, 1st session 1843. AN BB[20]121.

187 E.g. Durham (1928), p. 168; and Mirambel (1943), p. 382. In Montenegro, the word used to describe the feud also meant 'sacred'.

188 Busquet (1919), p. 31; see also Letter to Minister of Justice, 10 Fructidor An IX. AN BB[18]236; Valéry (1837), p. 204; and Marcaggi (1932), p. 5.

189 Cesari-Rocca (1908), p. 64; Busquet (1919), pp. 108 and 349–50; and Marin-Muracciole (1964), p. 180; also Faure (1858), p. 56; Saint-Germain (1869), p. 235; and Ortoli (1887), pp. 194–7 and 199.

190 Filippi (1906), pp. 30 and 31.

191 Abeau (1888), pp. 38–41.

192 Case v. Agostini, Assize Court, 3rd session 1835. *Gaz. Trib.*, 28 October 1835, cit. Sorbier (1863), pp. 55–60.

193 Case v. G. Codaccioni, Tribunal correctionnel, Sartène, 24 July 1817. ADCS 3.U.5/167.

194 See Rich (1976), pp. 14–15; and Byock (1982), esp. pp. 87ff.

195 Bourde (1887), p. 135.

196 Case v. F. Susini, Tribunal correctionnel, Sartène, 7 June 1830. ADCS 3.U.5/156.

197 Report, Subprefect, Sartène, 15 September 1834. ADCS 4.M.100.

198 Report, Gendarmerie, Vescovato, 2 December 1911. ADCS 1.M.231.

199 See, e.g. Report, Subprefect, Sartène, 20 April 1831. ADCS 2.M.82 (Fozzano); Letter, Municipal councillors to Subprefect, 1845(?). ADCS 2.M.79 (Bisinchi); and Various documents, 1864 etc. ADCS 2.M.138 (Olmeto).

200 Interrogations, Vendémiaire An X. ADCS 7.U.113.
201 Letter to Prefect, n.d. ADCS 2.M.121; see also Dalmas (1978), p. 16.
202 Cases v. Fausti and Ciavaldini, Assize Court, 3rd session 1834; and v. P.-P. Giustiniani et al., 2nd session 1847. *Gaz. Trib.*, 2nd October 1834, No. 2845; and 22 April 1847, No. 6177.
203 E.g. Robiquet (1835), p. 385; and Gregorovius (1855), p. 137.
204 Bartoli (1898), p. 254; also Bourde (1887), p. 135.
205 Report, Subprefect, Sartène, 24 April 1834. ADCS 4.M.100.
206 Marcaggi (1898b), pp. 34–8.
207 Réalier-Dumas (1819), p. 18.
208 Busquet (1919), pp. 108–11, 357–9 and 556–7; also Mérimée (1840a), p. 449; Bouchez (1843), pp. 17 and 52; Gregorovius (1855), p. 138; Ortoli (1887), pp. 196–7; and Rossi (1900), p. 4.
209 See also Case v. G.-B. Martinetti and P. Giordani, Assize Court, 1st session 1851, Extraordinary sitting. AN BB[20]152.
210 Régis and Martin (n.d.), p. 53.
211 Pompei (1821), p. 211; also Barry (1893), pp. 108–9; and, more generally, Dolci (1963), p. 241; and Black-Michaud (1975), pp. 177–81.
212 Report, Subprefect, Sartène, 6 October 1821. ADCS 4.M.98.
213 Report to Ministry of Justice, December 1817. AN BB[18]242; and Case v. P.-F. Angelini, Assize Court, 1st session 1851, Extraordinary sitting. AN BB[20]152; see also e.g. Case v. N. Graziani et al., Court of Criminal Justice, Ajaccio, 1812. ADCS 2.U.1/43 (Pastoreccia); Reports, Procureur-général to Minister of the Interior, 4 January 1813. AN BB[18]241 (Peri); Commissaire spécial, 1 April 1818, cit. Franceschini (1923), p. 76 (Canale); and Procureur-général to Minister of Justice, 4 July 1821. AN BB[18]1049 (Vero); Cases v. G.-B. Martinetti and P. Giordani; and v. N. Giordani, Assize Court, 1st session 1851. AN BB[20]152 (Bastelica); and v. F. Susini and D.-N. Marcilesi, 3rd session 1854. AN BB[20]170 (Figari); and for parallels: Westermarck (1934), p. 365; Gellner (1969), p. 128; and Beames (1978), pp. 83 and 86.
214 Case v. S. Papalini, Assize Court, 1st session 1856. AN BB[20]185.
215 Letter to Prefect, 1816(?). ADCS 1.M.224.
216 Ortoli (1887), pp. 188–9 and 196 note; see also Tommaseo (1841), p. 52, for a contrary view.
217 Cases v. G. Colonna et al., 2nd session 1848. AN BB[20]142; v. V. Luporsi et al., 1st session 1852. AN BB[20]158; v. P. Brignole, 2nd session 1842. AN BB[20]116; v. A.-P. Leca, 2nd session 1837. *Gaz. Trib.*, 12 July 1837, No. 3694; v. L.-A. Leca, 2nd session 1842. AN BB[20]116; and v. G.-G. Renosi, 2nd session 1833. *Gaz. Trib.*, 7 July 1833, cit. Sorbier (1863), pp. 36–8.
218 Mérimée (1840a), p. 468; also Gregorovius (1855), p.142; and Forester (1858), p. 87.
219 Cases v. F. Valerj(?), 4th session 1845. *Gaz. Trib.*, 9 January 1846, No. 5776; v. A. Giacobbi, 1st session 1842. AN BB[20]116; and v. G. Riuscito, 3rd session 1853. AN BB[20]164.
220 Letter, G.-B. Ornano to Prefect, 9 November 1840. ADCS 1.M.229.
221 Case v. G.-A. Nicolai, Assize Court, 1st session 1854. AN BB[20]170.

8 Immunity and disruption

1 Similar immunities existed in other feuding societies; see e.g. Philpotts (1913), p. 194; and Turner (1971), p. 373.
2 According to Cesari-Rocca (1908), p. 64, a man who overtly declined a vendetta was 'inviolable'.

3 We have seen that Antono Bozzi, 'a close friend and relative of the Poli party' at Pila-Canale was apparently given 'a written promise of immunity' by the Bruni around 1798.

4 Malaspina (1876), p. 373.

5 E.g. Durham (1928), p. 169; Mirambel (1943), pp. 383–4; Bieler (1963), pp. 173–5 (mid-seventh-century Irish Canons); Clay (ed.) (1965), pp. 19–21, 28, 38 and 39 (S. Italy); Hocart (1973), pp. 78–86; Black-Michaud (1975), pp. 139–40; and Van Gennep (1977), pp. 26–8. Dennis et al. (1969), pp. 214 and 216, provide the additional explanation that strangers may be categorized as women or children. Edel (1961), p. 128, provides a rare contrary example for non-centralized societies. The Chiga or Kiga of East Africa might kill a stranger 'on the grounds that there may be some forgotten and still unrequited killing on the part of his clan, or on suspicion that he may perhaps himself be about to take revenge for some crime against his clan', but, as this indicates, we are dealing here not with total strangers but with members of rival clans.

6 E.g. Sorbier (1845), p. 45; Gregorovius (1855), pp. 216–19; Saint-Germain (1869), p. vii; Lear (1870), pp. 48 and *passim*; Abeau (1888), pp. 21–6; Spalinowski (1904), pp. 69–71; Lorenzi de Bradi (1928), pp. 170–2; and Caisson (1974).

7 E.g. Réalier-Dumas (1819), pp. 22–3; Benson (1825), pp. 47–50; F. Renucci (1838), pp. 1–5; Malaspina (1876), p. 352; and Vuillier (1896), pp. 191–3 and 217–18.

8 Marcaggi (1898b), pp. 103–6.

9 Chanal (n.d.), pp. 35–53 and 81–92; and Tommaseo (1841), p. 151.

10 Case v. A.-F. Pettinelli and G. Giordani, Assize Court, 2nd session 1853. AN BB²⁰164.

11 See Maitland (1911), pp. 220–1; Durham (1928), p. 165; Westermarck (1934), p. 365; Benedict (1935), p. 170; Colson (1953), pp. 200 and 203; and Mirasyezis (1975), p. 206.

12 E.g. Busquet (1919), p. 349; and Marin-Muracciole (1964), p. 11.

13 Case v. A.-L. Orsini and C.-F. Bernardini, Appeal Court, May–June 1857. ADCS 2.U.1/61.

14 Case v. O.-M. Tristani, Assize Court, 2nd session 1852. AN BB²⁰158; see also Faure (1885), II, pp. 22–49.

15 Marcaggi (1932), pp. 24–6.

16 Case v. G.-M. Guiderdoni, Assize Court, 2nd session 1853, Extraordinary sitting. AN BB²⁰164.

17 Petitions for clemency for G.-D. Santini, 1858–76. AN BB²⁴534–40.

18 Cases v. A. Lucchini, Assize Court, 2nd session 1839. *Gaz. Trib.*, 20 July 1839, No. 4326; and v. D.-A. Mattei, 2nd session 1852. AN BB²⁰158.

19 Petition for clemency for P. Carlotti, 1881. AN BB²⁴876.

20 Letters to Miot, An IX. AN BB¹⁸236; Case v. G. Miliani et al., Assize Court, 2nd session 1847. *Gaz. Trib.*, 18 July 1847, No. 6252; Letter to Prefect, 9 January 1847. ADCS 1.M.224; Report, 4 January 1815. AN BB¹⁸242; and Case v. P. Giacomoni et al., Assize Court, 2nd session 1848, *Gaz. Trib.*, 12 July 1848, No. 6559.

21 Valéry (1837), p. 202; see also Feydel (1799), pp. 74–5; and Surier (1934), pp. 35–6.

22 Busquet (1919), p. 95; and see Hasluck (1954), p. 248, for the parallel situation in Albania.

23 Ortoli (1887), pp. 194–5.

24 Cases v. S. Minichetti, Assize Court, 1st session 1851. AN BB²⁰152; and v. G. Tavera, 2nd session 1853. AN BB²⁰164.

25 Miot (1858), II, pp. 35–6.

26 Cases v. F. di Q. Susini, Assize Court, 2nd session 1860. AN BB²⁰221; and v. P. Toti, 1st session 1858. AN BB²⁰204.

27 Arrighi (1970), p. 127, citing Goury de Champgrand.
28 *Journal du Département de la Corse*, 27 November 1830.
29 Cases v. G. Cotoni, Assize Court, 4th session 1834. *Gaz. Trib.*, 18 January 1835, No. 2936; and v. D. G.-T. Peretti, 2nd session 1852. AN BB²⁰158; also v. G.-A. Anziani, 4th session 1854. Extraordinary sitting. AN BB²⁰ 170; and v. P.-D. Mondolini, 1st session 1855. AN BB²⁰177.
30 Case v. C.-F. Serra, Tribunal correctionnel, Sartène, 9 February 1822. ADCS 3.U.5/171.
31 Cases v. P. Massimi, Assize Court, 1st session 1858. AN BB²⁰204; v. G.-G. Chiari, 4th session 1893. AN BB²⁰286; and v. Ciavaldini and Fausti, 3rd session 1834. *Gaz. Trib.*, 2 October 1834, No. 2845.
32 Busquet (1919), p. 349.
33 Case v. G. Cristini, Assize Court, 4th session 1832. *Gaz. Trib.*, 31 December 1832, cit. Sorbier (1863), pp. 20–1.
34 Marcaggi (1898b), pp. 13–35 and 206.
35 Report, Procureur-général to Minister of Justice, 17 January 1833. Petitions for clemency for S.-P. Agostini, AN BB²⁴116–35; and for G.-G. Pietri, 1883. AN BB²⁴887; Cases v. P.-P. Giustiniani et al., Assize Court, 1st session 1847. *Gaz. Trib.*, 22 April 1847, No. 6177; and v. G.-A. Nicolai, 1st session 1854. AN BB²⁰170; and Bourde (1887), pp. 161–80.
36 See Malaspina (1876), p. 373; and Deane (1965), pp. 17–18 and 23–4.
37 Benson (1825), p. 41; Ballard (1852), p. 16; and Vuillier (1896), p. 218; see also Robiquet (1835), pp. 398–9; Flaubert (1973) [1840], pp. 332–3; Malaspina (1876), p. 371; Lorenzi de Bradi (1928), p. 179; and (1936), Ch. X; Ross (1948), p. 34; Patin de La Fizelière (1963), pp. 65 and 80; Gaste (1965), p. 54; and Ettori (1976).
38 Bigot (1890), p. 448; see also Case v. P. Negroni, Assize Court, 3rd session 1833. *Gaz. Trib.*, 30 October 1833, No. 2562, in which Magdalena Leonetti of Ampriani referred to her dead husband as 'my late master' (*il avio padrone*).
39 Ortoli (1887), pp. 250–1; Martin-Gistucci (1976); and Réalier-Dumas (1819), p. 23; see also Sorbier (1845), p. 40.
40 Robiquet (1835), pp. 451–2; Mattei (1867), pp. 45 and 48; Faure (1885), II, p. 21; Tomasi (n.d.), p. 73; and Rossi (1900), p. 166.
41 See especially Ravis-Giordani (1978b).
42 Saint-Germain (1869), p. 250; and Filippi (1906), p. 20.
43 Malaspina (1876), pp. 371 and 373–4; also Robiquet (1835), pp. 385 and 445; Beaulieu-Delbet (1897), pp. 29–30; Rossi (1900), pp. 142–5; Spinosi (1956), pp. 160–75; and Ravis-Giordani (1978b), p. 200.
44 Deane (1965), pp. 56, 145, 161–2 and 186–7; and Comiti (1933), p. 237; see also Mattei (1867), pp. 29 and 34; Ortoli (1883), pp. 267–73; Patin de La Fizelière (1963), p. 65; and Christophari (1981), p. 32.
45 Juta (1926), p. 157.
46 Morandière (1933), p. 77; and Lenclud (1979), p. 21.
47 Bigot (1890), p. 449; and see Chapter 1, p. 13.
48 See Chapter 5, note 134.
49 E.g. Report, Inspector Carlotti, 1849–50. ADCS 3.X.37c; and see pp. 214–15.
50 Bigot (1890), p. 475; Gregorovius (1855), pp. 107–8; Ross (1948), p. 34; Deane (1965), p. 8; and Christophari (1981), p. 32.
51 See p. 240.
52 Benson (1825), pp. 26–7; Molinari (1886), pp. 254–5; and Saravelli-Retali (1976), p. 103: 'Di e donne e di i boi, casciane quant'e tu poi'; see also Barry (1893), p. 142; Vuillier (1896), p. 219; Baedeker (1902), p. 498; and Ettori (1976), pp. 187–8.
53 Bigot (1890), pp. 448 and 465–7; see also Saint-Germain (1869), pp. 181–2; Deane

(1965), pp. 8, 28–47, 50, 55, 86 and 130 (Balagna); Ravis-Giordani (1976b) and discussion, pp. 9–10, 150–1 and 153; Saravelli-Retali (1976), pp. 103–4; Ravis-Giordani (1978b), p. 192; Finelli (n.d.), pp. 35–6 (Tavera); Ettori (1979), pp. 184–6, citing *vocero* (Zuani); and Christophari (1981), pp. 19, 23 and 32 (Guagno and Balogna). Pig killing was done by men, however.

54 Case v. D.-F. Vargioni, Imperial Court, Ajaccio, 1812. ADCS 2.U.1/42.
55 E.g. Cases v. A.-M. Rughi, Assize Court, 3rd session 1836. *Gaz. Trib.*, 28 September 1836, No. 3443; and v. G.-B. Rustini, 4th session 1864. AN BB^{20}260; Comiti (1933), p. 142; Natali (1934), p. 50; Deane (1965), pp. 86–9 and 158; and Cristofini et al. (1978), p. 105.
56 See Deane (1965), pp. 42, 86 and 112.
57 E.g. Beaumont (1822), p. 182; Ardouin-Dumazet (1898), p. 168; Hauser (1909), p. 545; and Surier (1934), p. 51.
58 Blok (1969), p. 133, writes of southern Italy, for example: 'women are not accustomed to work on the land'. The Corsican pattern of women engaging in heavy agricultural work and porterage is found, however, in the Peloponnese, the Balkans and elsewhere; see Vooys and Piket (1958), pp. 44 and 54; Ferguson (1981), p. 221; and Clay (ed.) (1965), p. 135.
59 Case v. A. Giansilj, Court of Criminal Justice, Ajaccio, 1811. ADCS 2.U.1/42; Report, Gendarmerie, 22 November 1832. ADCS 4.M.100; and Case v. F. Vincileoni and S. Pettinelli, Assize Court, 1st session 1861. AN BB^{20}229.
60 E.g. Viale et al. (1966), pp. 74 and 76.
61 Archer (1924), p. 83.
62 Cases v. P.-O. Orsini, Assize Court, 1st session 1858. AN BB^{20}204; and v. A. Quilichini, Tribunal correctionnel, Sartène, 27 June 1821. ADCS 3.U.5/170; and Saint-Germain (1869), pp. 132–3.
63 E.g. Patin de La Fizelière (1963), p. 63; Case v. E. Nasica, Assize Court, 1st session 1861. AN BB^{20}229; Bazin (1913), p. 203; U. Rutalucciu, 'Images du passé, E spigagliole', *Corse-Matin*, 5 June 1979; Reports, Inspector Carlotti, 1847 and 1849–50. ADCS 3.X.37c; Deane (1965), p. 122; and Renucci (1974), p. 171.
64 E.g. Cases v. A.-G. and C.-D. Santoni, 4th session 1852, Extraordinary sitting. AN BB^{20}158 (Palneca); v. G.-A. Nicolai, 1st session 1854. AN BB^{20}170 (Levie); and v. G.-A. Mercuri, 4th session 1861. AN BB^{20}229 (Asco); Campbell (1868), p. 34; Saint-Germain (1869), p. 332; and Casanova (1978), p. 47.
65 Cases v. P. Giabiconi, 2nd session 1855. AN BB^{20}177; v. M. Giacobetti, 2nd session 1858. AN BB^{20}204; and v. S.-F. Campana, 3rd session 1859. AN BB^{20}213; see also, more generally, Lorenzi de Bradi (1928), p. 174.
66 Carlotti (1936), p. 31.
67 Case v. G. Codaccioni, Tribunal correctionnel, Sartène, 24 July 1817. ADCS 3.U.5/167; and Finelli (n.d.), p. 38.
68 Brady and Pottle (eds.) (1955), p. 163; Montherot (1840), p. 46; Vidalenc (1966), p. 68, citing military report of 1847; Gregorovius (1855), p. 109; Saint-Germain (1869), p. 323; Joanne (1881), p. 479; Black (1892), p. 50; Barry (1893), p. 56; Richardson (1894), pp. 518–19; Beaulieu-Delbet (1897), p. 14; D'Este (1905), pp. 24 and 106 and photos; Lorenzi de Bradi (1928), p. 174; and Ettori (1976), pp. 187–8.
69 Bigot (1890), p. 451.
70 Ravis-Giordani (1976b), p. 9.
71 Reports, Gendarmerie, Ajaccio, 12 August 1841. ADCS 4.M.125; and Vescovato, December 1911. ADCS 1.M.231.
72 See e.g. Fée (1850), p. 47.
73 Case v. A. Francescani, Assize Court, 2nd session 1846. *Gaz. Trib.*, 12 August 1846, No. 5956.

74 See Philpotts (1913), pp. 97–8 and *passim*; Westermarck (1934), pp. 364 and 366; Bateson (1958), p. 138; Davies (1969), p. 346; Gellner (1969), p. 127; Sutherland (1975), pp. 396–8; and Beames (1978), p. 84. In medieval Wales, according to Maitland (1911), pp. 224–5, women of childbearing age paid but did not receive blood money and they paid at half the rate of men. Among the Dakota, women did participate in 'wars' as killers and victims, but 'the conventional female expression of revenge was suicide'. Landes (1959), pp. 46 and 50–2. Among Jordanian Bedouins, a woman's price was generally half that of a man's, but special circumstances could make it more, for example, if she were pregnant, or if she were raped. Chelhod (1968), pp. 58–64.

75 Gray et al. (1909), pp. 721 and 733; Durham (1928), pp. 171–2; Hasluck (1954), pp. 223–4 and 237–8; and Peters (1967), p. 270. In Albania, women occasionally performed vengeance killings (usually where no male relatives were ready or available). However, vengeance against a female killer was taken by the family of her victim not against her but against her male relatives, if she had any. Cozzi (1910), p. 663.

76 Feydel (1799), pp. 75–6; Reports, Police, 22 October and 23 November 1821. ADCS 4.M.74; Mé.imée (1840a), p. 540; Marcaggi (1932), pp. 41–2 and 111; and Busquet (1919), pp. 107 and 349; see also Radclyffe Dugmore (n.d.), p. 36; Marin-Muracciole (1964), p. 11; and Ravis-Giordani (1976b), p. 11.

77 Feydel (1799), pp. 75–6; Cases v. P.-P. Giustiniani et al., Assize Court, 1st session 1847. *Gaz. Trib.*, 1847, No. 6177; and v. G. Agostini and A. Rutilj-Forcioli, 2nd session 1851. AN BB²⁰152; Bertrand (1870), pp. 15–16; Vidalenc (1966), p. 79; and Letter, President of Assize Court, 13 July 1850. AN BB²⁰149.

78 Marcaggi (1932), p. 123.

79 Case v. G.-B. Scapola, Assize Court, 1st session 1846. AN BB²⁰134.

80 P. Casale, Printed memoir, 1817(?). BB¹⁸241; Letter, S. Castelli to Procureur-général, 27 May 1912. ADCS 1.M.231; and Marcaggi (1932), pp. 149–52.

81 Case v. G.-F. Giacomoni et al., Extraordinary Criminal Court, Sartène, 9 Floréal An X. ADCS 3.U.5/129; Letter, Procureur-général to Minister of Justice, 17 February 1819. AN BB¹⁸1049; and Reports, Subprefect, Sartène, 23 May 1823; and 27 May 1826. ADCS 4.M.99.

82 Robiquet (1835), Supplementary Table D and Table LV.

83 Letter, Ex-mayor Pozzi di Borgo to Prefect, 21 September 1850. ADCS 1.M.229; and Marcaggi (1898b), pp. 24–34, 116–19 and 234.

84 Special report, Sartène, 1 May 1839. *Gaz. Trib.*, 9 May 1839, No. 4263.

85 Report, Gendarmerie, Ajaccio, 23 November 1841. ADCS 4.M.125; and Case v. T. Desanti, Assize Court, 1st session 1852. AN BB²⁰158.

86 Cases v. G.-A. Mariani, Assize Court, 2nd session 1865. AN BB²⁰273; v. M. Galloni d'Istria, 2nd session 1851. AN BB²⁰152; and 4th session 1852. AN BB²⁰158.

87 E.g. Cases v. G.-M. Santini, Extraordinary Criminal Court, 8 Thermidor An IX. ADCS 7.U.1/16; and v. P. Quilichini, Assize Court, 2nd session 1842. AN BB²⁰116.

88 Case v. D. Giampierini(?), 4th session 1834. *Gaz. Trib.*, 25 January 1835, No. 2942.

89 Report, Procureur impérial to Ministry of Justice, 21 October 1807. AN BB¹⁸239; Case v. Antonmarchi, Assize Court, 4th session 1831. *Gaz. Trib.*, 1 January 1832; and Chapman (1908), pp. 62–71.

90 Reports, Gendarmerie, Bastia, 22 February; and Corte, 7 March 1842. ADCS 4.M.126.

91 Reports, Gendarmerie; and Subprefect, Bastia, 21 April 1820. ADCS 1.M.228; and Régis and Martin (n.d.), p. 54; see also Christophari (1981), p. 163.

92 E.g. Report, Gendarmerie, Ajaccio, 27 October 1842. ADCS 4.M.126; and Cases v.

G.-A. Roccaserra, Assize Court, 2nd session 1845. AN BB²⁰130; and 3rd session 1846. AN BB²⁰134; and v. B. Zuccarelli, 2nd session 1845. AN BB²⁰130.

93 The female crime rate in Corsica was considerably lower than in France as a whole: 7 per cent as against 19 per cent of crimes were committed by women in the period 1828–31, according to Robiquet (1835), Table XLVI. The proportion for Corsica does not seem to have changed much in subsequent years; see e.g. Bournet (1888), p. 18.

94 Case v. A. Gaffori, Assize Court, 2nd session 1842. AN BB²⁰116.

95 Report, Gendarmerie, Ajaccio, 14 July 1816. ADCS 4.M.102; and Case v. P.-S. Bartoli, Assize Court, 3rd session 1863. AN BB²⁰249.

96 Acte d'accusation against G.-G. Costa et al., 23 November 1815. AN BB¹⁸242.

97 Cases v. S. Gaudeani, Assize Court, 4th session 1844. AN BB²⁰125; and v. F. Mattei, 3rd session 1851. AN BB²⁰152.

98 Report to Ministry of Justice, 4 January 1815. AN BB¹⁸242; and Case v. M.-A. Lucchini, Assize Court, 1st session 1856. AN BB²⁰185.

99 Report, Gendarmerie, Ajaccio, 12 October 1841. ADCS 4.M.125; and Case v. F. Corrazzini, Assize Court, 2nd session 1850. AN BB²⁰149.

100 Case v. S. Panzani et al., Tribunal correctionnel, Sartène, 18 February 1824. ADCS 3.U.5/174; and Christophari (1981), pp. 42–4.

101 E.g. Case v. P.-L. Pinzuti and G. Manzaggi, Assize Court, 2nd session 1852. AN BB²⁰158.

102 Costa (1930), p. 103; and Cases v. M.-I. and L. Fagianelli, Tribunal correctionnel, Sartène, 1812. ADCS 3.U.5/166; and v. M.-V. Battesti, Assize Court, 3rd session 1844. AN BB²⁰125.

103 Robiquet (1835), pp. 398–9; also Saint-Germain (1869), p. 332; and Ortoli (1883), p. 268.

104 A term used by a witness in the case v. F. and P. Susini et al., Tribunal correctionnel, Sartène, 13 August 1822. ADCS 3.U.5/171; see also Marcaggi (1898b), pp. 23–4.

105 Cases v. G.-B. Pianelli, Assize Court, 1st session; and v. P.-P. Peretti, 3rd session 1853. AN BB²⁰164; and Marcaggi (1932), p. 102.

106 See e.g. Davis (1977), pp. 189–90.

107 Marcaggi (1932), pp. 41–2.

108 Report, Gendarmerie to Prefect, 21 April 1820; and other reports. ADCS 1.M.228; and Case v. Suzzarini, Assize Court, 3rd session 1834. *Gaz. Trib.*, 29–30 September 1834, No. 2843.

109 Busquet (1919), p. 349; and Lorenzi de Bradi (1928), pp. 179–80.

110 Mérimée (1840b), pp. 730–3; Viale (1855), pp. 88–9; and Ortoli (1887), pp. 176–9.

111 'Un bandit corse en 1777', *Gaz. Trib.*, 29 October 1841, No. 4540; and Viale (1855), pp. 102–5.

112 Case v. M.-F. Quilichini, Assize Court, 1st session 1846. AN BB²⁰134.

113 E.g. Archer (1924), p. 210 (Marignana).

114 Petition for clemency for M. Sansonetti, widow Murati, 1885. AN BB²⁴877.

115 Ortoli (1887), pp. 314–21; and Vuillier (1896), p. 170; see also Maupassant, 'Une Vendetta' (1883), pp. 117–22, only misleading perhaps in being set in Bonifacio.

116 Valéry (1837), pp. 203–4; Marcaggi (1932), Ch. III, esp. pp. 81–9; Roger (1945), pp. 182–3 and 276–80; and Vrydaghs Fidelis (1962), pp. 213–28.

117 Gregorovius (1855), pp. 399–400; and Cases v. P. Arrighi, Assize Court, 1st session 1851, Extraordinary sitting. AN BB²⁰152; and v. R. Mariani, 2nd session 1853. AN BB²⁰164.

118 E.g. Reports, Gendarmerie, Ajaccio, 29 November 1816. ADCS 4.M.102 (Cozzano); and Subprefect, Sartène, February and March 1829. ADCS 4.M.99 (Olmeto). Poisoning was by no means an exclusively female recourse, however, as some examples have already shown.

119 Case v. R.-M. Nicolai, Assize Court, 2nd session; and Report, Procureur-général, 1865. AN BB²⁰273; see also Saint-Germain (1869), pp. 167 and 259–62; and Malaspina (1876), p. 372.

120 Case v. F. Padovani, 4th session 1845. AN BB²⁰130; Bennet (1876), pp. 37–9; Ortoli (1887), pp. 278–89; and Vuillier (1896), p. 224.

121 Ortoli (1883), pp. 322–8.

122 E.g. Cases v. M.-A. Francescani, Assize Court, 3rd session 1846. AN BB²⁰134; and *Gaz. Trib.*, 12 August 1846, No. 5956; v. A. Giovannoni and G.-B. Pasqualini, 2nd session 1841. *Gaz. Trib.*, 5 June 1841, No. 4913; v. P.-M. Paoli, 4th session 1843. AN BB²⁰121.

123 E.g. Gray et al., (1909), pp. 720 and 733; Durham (1928), p. 164; Westermarck (1934), p. 363; Pareto (1935), IV, pp. 1520–1 (Sardinia); Nash (1967), p. 462 (Maya); Pálsson (1971), pp. 63–4; Black-Michaud (1975), pp. 208–9; and Byock (1982), pp. 95, 256–7 and 267.

124 Bigot (1890), p. 448; Bartoli (1898), pp. 239–40; also Arrighi (1856b), p. 11; Saint-Germain (1869), pp. 299–300; Malaspina (1876), p. 384; Busquet (1919), pp. 111–12; Privat (1936), p. 14; Marin-Muracciole (1964), p. 8; Carrington (1971a), pp. 82 and 92; Ravis-Giordani (1976b), pp. 16–17; and Versini (1979), pp. 151 and 165.

125 Brady and Pottle (eds.) (1955), pp. 182–3.

126 Report, Procureur-général to Minister of Justice, 4 January 1813. AN BB¹⁸241; Marcaggi (1898b), pp. 23–4, 29, 179–80 and 202–9; and Cases v. ... , Assize Court, 2nd session 1890, cit. Régis and Martin (n.d.), p. 54; and v. T. Desanti, 1st session 1852. AN BB²⁰158.

127 Case v. P.-M. Marchi, 2nd session 1895. AN BB²⁰286.

128 Marcaggi (1898b), p. 24; Turner (1971), pp. 367–9; and Deane (1965), p. 39.

129 E.g. Thrasher (1970), p. 76; and Maestrati (1964), p. 48.

130 Case v. Colombani, Assize Court, 4th session 1834. *Gaz. Trib.*, 22 January 1835, No. 2939.

131 Comiti (1933), p. 241; and Durham (1928), pp. 69 and 164. We will discuss the significance of blood and shedding blood in Chapter 13.

132 See Black-Michaud (1975), pp. 208–9.

133 Letter, Deputy Public Prosecutor(?) to Ministry of Justice, 1 Brumaire An VI. AN BB¹⁸237; and Casanova (1931–2), II, esp. p. 148; Thrasher (1970), pp. 14–15, 56–8, 69, 144, 148 and 176; and Casta (1974), pp. 131–3 and 139.

134 Bigot (1890), pp. 443–5 and 448; Filippi (1906), p. 9; and Ortoli (1883), pp. 254–8, 273–7 and 369–73.

135 Griffon (1841), pp. 39–41; and Robiquet (1835), p. 403.

136 See Patin de La Fizelière (1963), p. 66; Susini (1906), pp. 103–4, citing Abbé Gaudin [1787]; Robiquet (1835), pp. 403 and 406; Bessières (1892); Girolami-Cortona (1893), p. 306; Franceschini (1924), pp. 109–10, citing Report, Commissaire spécial, 20 May 1818; Bernardini (1970), II, pp. 21–2; Delarue (1970), pp. 118–20; Casta (1973), esp. p. 189; and Casta (1974), pp. 166, 183–4, 228–9 and 248.

137 Cit. Bernardini (1970), II, p. 22; and Martelli (1960), p. 251; see also Bigot (1890), p. 444.

138 Case re estate of Don G. Renucci, Cour Royale, 1832. *Gaz. Trib.*, 18 January 1833, No. 2472; Robiquet (1835), pp. 392–3; and Case v. G. Poggioli, Assize Court, 2nd session 1851. AN BB²⁰152; also v. A.-P. and F.-A. Ortoli, 3rd session 1862. AN BB²⁰239.

139 Bigot (1890), pp. 444, 446, 448, 454, 469 and 474; Finelli (n.d.), pp. 21–6; Abeau (1888), pp. 20–1; and Ortoli (1887), p. 72 note.

140 Casta (1973), pp. 186–7; also Montherot (1840), p. 64 (Felce); Malaspina (1876), p. 375; and Casta (1974), pp. 168, 172–6, 178, 188–9, 209 and 240.

141 Viale (1855), pp. 51–8; also Tommaseo (1841), pp. 205–20; and Natali (1961), p. 85.
142 Letter, Bishop of Ajaccio to Prefect, 13 February 1851. ADCS 2.V.19; Various documents 'Quêtes à domicile'. ADCS 2.V.25; Chiva (1963), p. 110; Casta (1974), pp. 168 and 228; Finelli (n.d.), p. 35; and Deliberations, Municipal Council, Penta-di-Casinca, 19 December 1856. ADHC E.29/8.
143 Letter, Subprefect, Corte, to Prefect, 28 May 1841; and other documents. ADCS 2.V.25; and Letter, Subprefect to Prefect, 17 February 1849. ADCS 2.V.10.
144 Letter, Juge de paix, San-Martino, to Subprefect, 2 September 1841; and other documents. ADCS 2.V.19; and Cases v. A. and D. Anziani; and v. L. Marcucci, Assize Court, 1st and 3rd sessions 1842. AN BB^{20}116.
145 Letters, Minister of Cults to Prefect, 12 June 1861; and 16 July 1866. ADCS 1.V.44.
146 Case, Appeal Court, 1828. *Gaz. Trib.*, 31 August 1828, No. 956; and Letters, Minister of Cults to Prefect, 10 June 1863; and 29 June 1865. ADCS 1.V.44; and Mayor, San-Andrea-di-Tallano, to Prefect, 27 October 1865. ADCS 2.V.27.
147 See Siegfried (1964), Ch. XVI; and Lewin (1979), p. 143.
148 Réalier-Dumas (1819), p. 57; Ballard (1852), p. 15; Report, Prefect, 23 December 1872. AN F^{7}12849; Bigot (1890), pp. 443–5 and 448; and Pomponi (1978a), p. 18.
149 Casta (1974), p. 165; and Note, Subprefect, 21 May 1887. ADCS 2.V.20 (re Oletta), and see Chapter 11, p. 299.
150 Case v. P. Negroni, Assize Court, 3rd session 1833. *Gaz. Trib.*, 30 October 1833, No. 2562; Reports, Procureur-général to Minister of Justice, 11 November 1847; and 20 January 1848; and other documents. AN BB^{18}1457; and ADCS 2.V.20.
151 Though he subsequently claimed to have been acting under duress. Report, Procureur-général to Minister of Justice, 17 February 1819. AN BB^{18}1049.
152 Letters, Parish priest and others, Avapessa, to Prefect, 25 May 1850. ADCS 2.V.20; Municipal councillors, San-Gavino, to Prefect, 1851; Vicar-general to Prefect, 24 July 1851. ADCS 1.V.44.
153 Case v. A.-P. Octaviani, Court of Criminal Justice, Ajaccio, 1813. ADCS 2.U.1/43; and Versini (1972), p. 218.
154 Report, Procureur-général to Minister of Justice, 2 July 1812. AN BB^{18}241; and Letters, Commissaire de police, Prunelli, 8 January 1855; and Procureur impérial to Subprefect, Corte, 12 January 1856. ADCS 2.V.19.
155 Letters, Conseil de fabrique to Bishop, 15 April; and Bishop, Ajaccio, to Prefect, 20 April 1860. ADCS 2.V.19; and Appolis (1964), pp. 93–100.
156 Various documents. ADCS 2.V.19. Similar conflicts were reported at Levie in 1802, at Aullène in 1848, at Ota in the 1850s, at Sant'Andrea-di-Tallano in 1865, at Ocana in 1868, at Frasseto in 1869–70, at Zoza in 1879, and at Novella in 1890–1. Letter, Administrateur-général, Sartène, to Prefect, 26 Pluviôse An X. ADCS 2.M.54; Case v. Father Lanfranchi et al., Assize Court, 1st session 1848. AN BB^{20}146; Various documents, 1853 and 1855. ADCS 2.M.138; Letter to Prefect, 19 March; and Report, Juge de paix, Bastelica, 29 January 1869. ADCS 2.M.137; Various letters, 1865–70. ADCS 2.V.19; ADCS 2.V.27; ADCS 1.V.44; and Report, Procureur-général to Minister of Justice, 19 June 1891. AN BB^{18}1855.
157 Letter, Subprefect, Sartène, to Prefect, 4 May 1866. ADCS 1.V.44.
158 Letter, Mayor, Piedicroce, to Ministry of Justice, 29 July 1848. AN BB^{18}1466; and Petition for clemency for Santo Biaggini, 1863. AN BB^{24}674–86.
159 De la Rocca (1858a); and 1858(b).
160 Casta (1974), pp. 180, 210–12, 220–1 and 224–6; and Report, Subprefect, Corte, 9 August 1887; and other documents. ADCS 2.V.20; see also Letters relating to Poggio-di-Tallano (1887) and Nonza (1891). ADCS 2.V.20.
161 See, e.g., Burckhardt (1944), pp. 289–90 (fifteenth-century Italy); Huizinga (1955), p. 13 (fifteenth-century Paris); Strubbe (1961) (early medieval France); Barth (1965),

pp. 47, 59, 93, 96–9 and 121–2 (Swat Pathans); Bourdieu (1965), p. 237 (Kabyles); Peters (1967), p. 265 (Bedouin of Cyrenaica); Edwards (ed.) (1969), p. 23 (Serbia); Gellner (1969), esp. pp. 74–80; Cowdrey (1970) (early medieval Europe); Brown (1971), pp. 88–93 (Near East, late Antiquity); Bossy (1973), pp. 138–43 (early modern Europe); Davis (1977), pp. 118–19; Ingram (1977), p. 110 (seventeenth-century England); Ferguson (1981), pp. 217–18.

162 Prefect, Report to Conseil général, 1826. AN BB^{18}1146; Arrighi (1856b), esp. pp. 6–19; Foata (1867), p. 23; and Bartoli (1898), p. 257; see also Bouchez (1843), pp. 14–16 and 53–8; Busquet (1919), Part III, Chapter XIV; and Pomponi (1978a), p. 14.

163 Report, Procureur-général to Minister of Justice, 12 September 1811. AN BB^{18}241; and Cases v. F. Padovani, Assize Court, 4th session 1845. AN BB^{20}130; and v. T. Francisci, 1st session 1854. AN BB^{20}170.

164 Case v. Luporsi(?), Assize Court, 4th session 1834. *Gaz. Trib.*, 25 January 1835, No. 2942; Montherot (1840), p. 65; Case v. C. Tomasini and V. Roccaserra, 4th session 1849. AN BB^{20}146; and v. P. Chiaroni, 1st session 1851, Extraordinary sitting. AN BB^{20}152.

165 There is a parallel here with the situation in the Greek village studied by Du Boulay (1979), p. 180, where the parish priest was *not* expected to conciliate in his own village.

166 Cases v. V. Casile, 1st session 1844. AN BB^{20}125; and v. G.-A. Orabona, 1st session 1845. AN BB^{20}130; Marcaggi (1898b), pp. 289–96; Delarue (1970), pp. 243 and 276; and Casta (1974), pp. 171, 181 and 192–4.

167 Casanova (1931–2), I, Book III, Chapter II; Busquet (1919), pp. 486–513; and Casta (1974), pp. 112 and 125–6 (referring to the missions of St Leonard in the early eighteenth century). Saint-Germain (1869), p. 123, reported that some houses in Bastelica had wooden crosses over the doors still which were 'signs of a reconciliation brought about by the Blessed Leonardo'. See also Cozzi (1910), pp. 678–9, for an Albanian parallel. According to Marin-Muracciole (1964), p. 11, monks had immunity in feuds during the Ancien Régime, but not members of the secular clergy.

168 Report, Subprefect, Ajaccio, 12 September 1827. ADCS 4.M.91; Case v. P. Crudeli, Assize Court, 3rd session 1833, *Gaz. Trib.*, 22 September 1833, cit. Sorbier (1863), pp. 41–5; and Delarue (1970), pp. 175, 185, 191, 198–9, 230 and 238.

169 Moracchini and Carrington (1959), p. 10; and Emmanuelli (1969), pp. 101–2.

170 Reports, Subprefect, Sartène, 27 November 1827; 12 February; and 17 and 20 May 1828. ADCS 4.M.99; Robiquet (1835), p. 404; and Letter, Various inhabitants of Avapessa to Prefect, 25 May 1850. ADCS 2.V.20.

171 Cases v. G.-B. Sanguinetti et al., Assize Court, 1st session 1851. AN BB^{20}152; v. V. Luporsi et al., 1st session; and v. D. Vincenti et al., 4th session 1852. AN BB^{20}158.

172 Arrighi (1976), p. 58, No. 246.

173 Beaulieu-Delbet (1897), p. 42.

174 Report, Gendarmerie, 9 February 1821, cit. E. and J. Franceschini (1919), p. 65; Cases v. G.-B. Orsini, Court of Criminal Justice, 1st session; and v. S. Reginendi, 2nd session 1830. AN BB^{20}49; and Robiquet (1835), pp. 403 and 422–4.

175 Cases v. G.-B. Tomasi, Assize Court, 3rd session 1858. AN BB^{20}204; and v. P.-A. Rossi, 4th session 1861. AN BB^{20}229.

176 Viale (1855), p. 92; Reports, Police to Prefect, 22 May 1820. ADCS 4.M.74; and Gendarmerie, Ajaccio, 23 September 1816. ADCS 4.M.102.

177 Reports, Commissaire du Directoire exécutif près les Tribunaux du Département du Golo, to Ministry of Justice, 20 Messidor An VI. AN BB^{18}237; Gendarmerie, Bastia, 10 July 1816. ADCS 4.M.102; and Cases v. M. Pianelli, Court of Criminal Justice, 2nd session, Cases tried *in absentia*; and v. G.-C. Pietrini, 1st session 1830. AN BB^{20}49;

Reports, Prefect and Procureur-général to Minister of Justice, 27 August and 10 October 1838. AN BB¹⁸1256; Special report, *Gaz. Trib.*, 9 September 1838, No. 4056; Lemps (1844), pp. 153–4; and Cases v. G.-A. Istria, Assize Court, 2nd session 1850. AN BB²⁰149; and v. A. Canacci and O.-F. Lucioni, 1st session 1839. *Gaz. Trib.*, 30 March 1839, No. 4229; Montherot (1840), pp. 76–7; Lorenzi de Bradi (1928), p. 273; and Case v. Don G. Peretti, Assize Court, 2nd session 1852. AN BB²⁰158.

178 Case v. S.-A. Arrii, 2nd session 1849. AN BB²⁰146; Letter, Father Susini to Prefect, 16 May 1850. ADCS 1.M.229; Case v. G. Peres, 2nd session 1854. AN BB²⁰170; and Report, Gendarmerie, Bastia, 5 January 1841. ADCS 4.M.125.

179 For parallels, see Lucarelli (1942), pp. 101–78; and Byock (1982), pp. 110 and 212.

180 Report, Mayor, Santa-Lucia-di-Tallano, 1 November 1820. ADCS 1.V.44; and Saint-Germain (1869), p. 335; also Robiquet (1835), p. 402.

181 AN F⁷3282; and Reports, Subprefect, Ajaccio, 12 April 1825. ADCS 4.M.91; and Sartène, 15 February and 10 April 1824. ADCS 4.M.99.

182 Petition for clemency for B. Peretti, January 1807. AN BB²⁴8–17; Malaspina (1876), p. 352; and Chronique départementale, Corte, 3 June. *Gaz. Trib.*, 10 June 1840, No. 4603.

183 Letter, Mayor, Santa-Lucia-di-Tallano, 1 November 1820. ADCS 1.V.44.

184 Roger (1945), pp. 182–3; and Case v. G. Colonna et al., Assize Court, 2nd session 1848. AN BB²⁰142.

185 Busquet (1919), p. 621; Various documents, 1828 and 1830. ADCS 1.M.224; and Case v. A. Lucchini, Assize Court, 2nd session 1839. *Gaz. Trib.*, 20 July 1839, No. 4326.

186 Letters, Mayor, Santa-Lucia-di-Tallano, to Prefect, 1 November 1820; and 5 March 1821. ADCS 1.V.44; Report, Gendarmerie, Tallano, 3 August 1816. ADCS 4.M.102; Case v. G. Giacomoni, Tribunal correctionnel, Sartène, 13 December 1816. ADCS 3.U.5/167; Cases v. Santa-Lucia, Assize Court, 1st session 1840. *Gaz. Trib.*, 18 April 1840, No. 4559, cit. Sorbier (1863), pp. 166–77; and v. M.-F. Quilichini, 1st session 1846. AN BB²⁰134; and Casta (1974), pp. 193–4.

187 Letter, Bishop of Ajaccio to Prefect, 30 April 1849; and other documents. ADCS 2.V.20; Robiquet (1835), p. 403; and Case v. A.-M. Pietri (?), Assize Court, 1st session 1851. AN BB²⁰152.

188 Evans-Pritchard (1940), p. 156; and Peters (1975), p. xiii (who does concede, however, that feuding might occur between detached parts of a village 'without ... wrecking the basis of ordinary day-to-day economic pursuits'); see also Colson (1953), p. 210; Colson (1962), pp. 119–20; Peters (1967), pp. 265–6, 268 and 270–1; Gellner (1969), p. 127; Middleton and Tait (eds.) (1970), pp. 21–2, 88–9, 163–5, 223 and 228; Koch et al. (1977); and Roberts (1979), pp. 14, 66, 85, 90–1, 99, 110 and 125.

189 Stirling (1960), pp. 68–75; and Stirling (1965), pp. 247–8 and 252–4; see also Byock (1982), pp. 25, 28 and 36, who stresses the 'stabilizing' function of medieval Icelandic feuding, following(?) Gluckman (1956). Ferguson (1981), p. 216, suggests that the famine of 1787 in Montenegro was caused in part by feuding and the consequent disruption of economic life, but feuding there was inter-tribal.

190 Gregorovius (1855), pp. 416–17.

191 Letters, Mayor, Ciamannacce, to Subprefect, 1 October 1828. ADCS 4.M.91; and Poli to Prefect, 1816. ADCS 1.M.224; Delarue (1970), p. 238; Bertrand (1870), pp. 19–20; and Marcaggi (1932), pp. 149–52.

192 Cases v. Agostini, Assize Court, 3rd session 1835. *Gaz. Trib.*, 28 October 1835, cit. Sorbier (1863), pp. 55–60; and v. E. Papalini, 1st session 1856. AN BB²⁰185; also e.g. Bennet (1876), p. 40; and Marin-Muracciole (1964), pp. 9–10.

193 Bertrand (1870), pp. 34–6; Bartoli (1898), p. 254; and Busquet (1919), pp. 340–1.

194 Cit. Vidalenc (1966), p. 79; Report, President, Assize Court, 13 July 1850. AN BB²⁰149; Bertrand (1870), p. 22.

195 Cit. Méjean (1932), p. 660; and Ardouin-Dumazet (1898), p. 103; also Gregorovius (1855), pp. 37–8; and Arrighi (1970), pp. 37–8.
196 See e.g. Forcioli-Conti (1897), p. 44; Vanutberghe (1904), p. 344; Méjean (1932), pp. 661–5 and 671–2; Simi (1966), pp. 128–32; Borel-Léandri (1978); Raulin and Ravis-Giordani (1978); and Lücke (1982), p. 97. Heers (1974), pp. 138–45, sees the high house as a Genoese phenomenon brought to Corsica with colonization, but if this is so it spread well beyond the Genoese coastal towns and served a basic function in Corsican society.
197 Mérimée (1840a), pp. 483–4; and Vrydaghs Fidelis (1962), pp. 57 (photo) and 217 (Fozzano and Arbellara); Gregorovius (1855), pp. 260 and 262 (Santa-Reparata – actually at Palmento – and Monticello); Lear (1870), p. 249 (Santa-Maria-Sicche); Méjean (1932), p. 664; and Raulin and Ravis-Giordani (1978), pp. 41 (esp. photos 31 and 32) and 216–19 (Bonifacio, Stazzona and Santa-Lucia-di-Tallano); also Lücke (1982), pp. 97–8; and author's fieldwork (Olmeta-di-Tuda, Olmeto, Sisco, etc.). For tower houses elsewhere in the Mediterranean region, see Brucker (1969), Ch. I; Weaver (1971); Heers (1974), pp. 190–217; Davis (1977), pp. 254–5; and Waley (1978), pp. 97 and 99–102.
198 Mérimée (1840b), pp. 708–9; Saint-Germain (1869), p. 387; Bertrand (1870), pp. 22–3; Report, President, Assize Court, 13 July 1850. AN BB[20]149; and Case v. P.-P. Giustiniani et al., Assize Court, 1st session 1847, *Gaz. Trib.*, 22 April 1847, No. 6177; see also Miot (1858), I, p. 151 (Cauro and Santa-Maria-Sicche – An V); *Gaz. Trib.*, 2 October 1834, No. 2845 (Gavignano); and Case v. P.-F. Angelini, Assize Court, 1st session 1851, Extraordinary sitting. AN BB[20]152 (Venzolasca).
199 Report, Commissaire du gouvernement près le tribunal criminel du département du Liamone, to Ministry of Justice, 15 Brumaire An IX. AN BB[18]236; Gregorovius (1855), p. 136; Viale (1855), pp. 90–7; Barry (1893), p. 109; Cesari-Rocca (1908), pp. 65–8; and Busquet (1919), pp. 347–8.
200 Report, Procureur-général, 26 May 1832, Petition for clemency for A.-F. Bernardini et al. AN BB[24]116–35; and Valéry (1837), p. 202; see also Mérimée (1840a), esp. pp. 521ff.
201 Letter, Mayor, Arbellara, 22 November 1830. ADCS 4.M.100; Case v. P.-P. Giustiniani et al., Assize Court, 1st session 1847. *Gaz. Trib.*, 22 April 1847, No. 6177; Versini (1972), pp. 96–8; Case v. G.-A. Franceschi, 3rd session 1848. AN BB[20]142; Marcaggi (1898b), pp. 13–17, 22–3, 120–1 and *passim*; Busquet (1919), pp. 632–3; and Report, Procureur-général to Prefect, 11 December 1911. ADCS 1.M.231; also Togab (1905), pp. 289–90.
202 Case v. G.-G. Quilichini, Extraordinary Criminal Court, Sartène, 9 Brumaire An X. ADCS 3.U.5/129.
203 Bourde (1887), p. 149; Cesari-Rocca (1908), pp. 65–8; and Busquet (1919), pp. 347–8.
204 Busquet (1919), pp. 624–5; Bourde (1887), p. 179; and Report, Subprefect to Prefect, 5 February; and 12 April 1831. ADCS 2.M.82.
205 Togab (1905), pp. 165–6; and Report, Gendarmerie, Vescovato, 30 December 1911. ADCS 1.M.231.
206 Report, President, Assize Court, 19 November 1863. AN BB[20]249; and Letter, Mayor, Ciamannacce, and Juge de paix, Tallano, to Subprefect, Ajaccio, 28 February 1828. ADCS 4.M.91; see also Cases v. Giampietri (?), Assize Court, 3rd session 1834. *Gaz. Trib.*, 2 October 1834, No. 2845; and v. P.-P. Giacomi, 4th session 1843. AN BB[20]121 (Gavignano); Report, Gendarmerie, Sartène, 21 October 1841. ADCS 4.M.125 (Pila-Canale); and Busquet (1919), pp. 632–3 (Serra).
207 At Alata, Arbellara Aullène, Bastelica, Canale, Carbini, Frasseto, Levie, Olmiccia, Pila-Canale, Porto-Vecchio, Santa-Lucia-di-Tallano, Santa-Maria-Sicche, Sari-d'Orcino and Ucciani. Letter, Franceschi to Prefect, 9 June 1847. ADCS 1.M.224; also *Gaz.*

Trib., 10 July 1839, No. 4317; Case v. G.-T. Lanfranchi, Assize Court, 1st session 1852. AN BB²⁰158. Notice, October 1824, Cauro. ADCS 1.M.228; Notice, September 1832, Canale, cit. Bertrand (1870), pp. 178–9; Case v. F. Cucchi, Assize Court, 4th session 1853. AN BB²⁰164; Petition for clemency for P.-B. Peretti, 1883. AN BB²⁴876; Cases v. G.-B. Ortoli et al., Extraordinary Criminal Court, Sartène, 4 Nivôse An X. ADCS 3.U./129; Chronique départementale, *Gaz. Trib.*, 12 December 1841, No. 4597; and 18 January 1842, No. 4611; Case v. S. Simoni, Extraordinary Criminal Court, 8 Messidor An IX. ADCS 7.U.1/16; Bourde (1887), p. 179; Letters, Prefect to Procureur-général, 21 March 1842; and G.-B. Ornano to Prefect, 9 November 1840. ADCS 1.M.229; and Petitions for clemency for F. Bastianesi, 1872–4. AN BB²⁴798.

208 Faure (1858), pp. 267–71; Letter, G.-M. Poli, V.-G. Ortoli and F.-M. Quilichini to Prefect, 10 March 1842. ADCS 1.M.229; Marcaggi (1898b), pp. 120–1, 201 and 238; Letter, Pianelli, Military command, Bastia, to Minister of Justice, 18 and 24 March 1809. AN BB¹⁸241; and Case v. S.-F. Ristori, Assize Court, 1st session 1853. AN BB²⁰164; and see Cozzi (1910), p. 680, for a parallel.

209 Busquet (1919), p. 625; and Case v. M. Versini, Assize Court, 1st session 1849. AN BB²⁰146.

210 Robiquet (1835), Table XXX; and Girolami-Cortona (1893), pp. 179–81, 205–8, 237–8, 251–4 and 279–80.

211 Delarue (1970), p. 199.

212 *Journal du Département de la Corse*, 27 November 1830; Report, Gendarmerie, 5 January 1841. ADCS 4.M.125; also Flaubert (1973) [1840], p. 343; and Natali (1961), p. 63.

213 Miot (1858), II, pp. 35–6.

214 Cit. Vidalenc (1966), p. 78; and Malaspina (1876), pp. 351 and 371; see also Hasluck (1954), p. 248, for the parallel situation in Albania.

215 Letter, Commissaire des guerres to Commissaire du gouvernement près le tribunal criminel extraordinaire, 20 Fructidor An X. ADCS 7.U.1/19; and Lenclud and Ravis-Giordani (1973), p. 212; see also, for a parallel, Roberts (1979), p. 111.

216 The French government provided generous aid, for example, when a hurricane damaged trees and crops in the canton of Salice in the late 1860s; see AN BB¹⁸1728.

217 See Vidalenc (1966), p. 71.

218 Maurras (1920), p. 122; Rankin (1930), p. 61; and Hogg (1973), p. 116; see also Vanutberghe (1904), p. 343; Deane (1965), pp. 104–6; Renucci (1974), p. 75; and Chapter 4, p. 99.

219 Scott refers, of course, in *The Heart of Mid-Lothian* to the Scottish gentry of the mid-eighteenth century, 'shut up in their distant and solitary mansion-houses, nursing their revengeful passions just to keep their blood from stagnating'. Scott (n.d.), XI, p. 181.

220 Cit. Vidalenc (1966), p. 70; Rossi (1900), p. 54; and Abeau (1888), p. 37; see also Reparaz (1961), p. 50; Boram (1973), p. 444, on the Kutchin Athabaskan Indians of the Yukon territory; and Roberts (1979), pp. 102–3, more generally. Römer (1977), p. 76, points out that the creation of folk-music and poetry was another, more positive, consequence of the 'leisure' of pastoral life.

221 Robiquet (1835), pp. 392–3; Reports, Gendarmerie, Vescovato, 2 December; and Venzolasca, 29 November 1911. ADCS 1.M.231.

222 E.g. Case v. M. Ferrandi, Court of Criminal Justice, Ajaccio, 1812. ADCS 2.U.1/43; and Report, Subprefect, Sartène, 1 August 1826. ADCS 4.M.99.

223 E.g. Case v. C. M. Balisoni and G.-A. Galloni, Assize Court, 3rd session 1857. AN BB²⁰194.

224 Patin de La Fizelière (1963), p. 59; Albitreccia (1942a), pp. 193 and 235–8; Simi

(1966), pp. 123–8; and Renucci (1974), pp. 16–18 and 177; and, more generally, Agulhon (1966), p. 301; Blok (1969); and Collomp (1978), pp. 301–4.

225 Maurice (ed.) (1904), p. 170; and Vanutberghe (1904), p. 344.

226 Lenclud (1979), p. 18. Some proliferation of hamlets occurred, however, as we shall see.

227 Saint-Germain (1869), pp. 135–6 and 154; also Blanchard (1926), p. 35; Raulin and Ravis-Giordani (1978), p. 64; and Ravis-Giordani (1978a), pp. 138–40.

228 See Méjean (1932), pp. 665 and 669–70; Leca (1978), p. 165; and author's fieldwork.

229 Some students of other feuding and factional societies have suggested that the dispersal of population in time and space reduces tension and conflict, while concentration may exacerbate it. Concomitantly, it has been noted by Wagstaff that a proclivity towards internal conflict inhibits 'the build-up of large population centres'; see Burridge (1957), p. 763; Siegel and Beals (1960b), p. 411; Wagstaff (1965), p. 302; and Boram (1973). Such conclusions, however, have no universal validity and suggest the danger of considering questions of habitat in isolation. Many examples can be found of a high level of conflict in conjunction with both dispersed and agglomerated patterns of settlement; see e.g. Pálsson (1971), pp. 10–11; and Bateson (1958), p. 116.

230 Gregorovius (1855), p. 277; Ardouin-Dumazet (1898), pp. 208–9; Méjean (1932), pp. 661–2 and 668; Morandière (1933), p. 133; Albitreccia (1942a), pp. 189–93; Raulin and Ravis-Giordani (1978), pp. 35, 63–4, 65 and *passim*; and author's fieldwork.

231 Lücke (1982), p. 90; Martelli (1960), p. 289; Saint-Germain (1869), p. 219; Renucci (1974), pp. 129 and 179; Gregorovius (1855), p. 236; Black (1892), p. 27; Forcioli-Conti (1897), p. 39; Archer (1924), p. 50; Hogg (1973), p. 132; Favreau-Cancellieri (1975), pp. 36–7; Finelli (n.d.), pp. 11, 13 and 49; Girolami-Cortona (1893), pp. 288–9; and Defranceschi (1978), pp. 86–7. The unusually dispersed settlement of the Cruzzini was explained in a cosmological legend; see Chanal (n.d.), pp. 83–4.

232 Delarue (1970), p. 232.

233 E.g. Moss and Cappannari (1964); and Tarrow (1967), p. 56 (S. Italy); Nash (1967), pp. 455 and 468; Gellner (1969), pp. 227–8; and Hélias (1978), p. 86 (Brittany).

234 Vassalacci and Santo; Costa and Trucolacci; Dominacci and Stazzona. Saint-Germain (1869), p. 113.

235 Lamotte (1956a), pp. 40–2; Pomponi (1974b), pp. 9–11; and Ravis-Giordani (1978a), pp. 138–141.

236 See Martelli (1960), p. 289 (Ghisoni); Raulin and Ravis-Giordani (1978), pp. 196–7, 233 and 249 (Conca, Pietrosella and Bastelica); and Zuccarelli (n.d.), p. 53.

237 Report, Subprefect, Sartène, 28 November 1829; and other documents. ADCS 2.V.17; Morandière (1933), p. 123; and Ravis-Giordani (1978a), p. 140.

238 ADCS 2.M.65; and Letter, M. Ambrosini et al., to Prefect, 10 April 1860. ADCS 2.M.116.

239 Case v. A. Giansilj, Court of Criminal Justice, Ajaccio, 1811. ADCS 2.U.1/42; and ADCS 2.M.88.

240 See Cases v. A.-D. Mariotti, Assize Court, 2nd session 1854. AN BB^{20}170 (Maja(?)-Campile); and v. G. Mari, 1st session 1859. AN BB^{20}213 (Penta a lu Travu – San-Gavino-d'Ampugnani); and Finelli (n.d.), p. 48 (Tavera).

241 Arrighi (1970), pp. 40–1; Malaspina (1876), p. 374. The identity of large family communities or kindreds with hamlets, villages, compounds or *quartiers* is of course found in other parts of Europe and beyond; see Pocock (1957), p. 298 (Gujerat); Bigay (1964) (Auvergne); Goubert (1973), pp. 92–3 (France); Kent (1977), p. 125 (Renaissance Florence); and Collomp (1978), p. 319 (Haute-Provence).

242 Favreau-Cancellieri (1975), pp. 44–5; Case v. F. Cucchi, Assize Court, 4th session 1853. AN BB^{20}164; also Reparaz (1961), p. 63; Patin de La Fizelière (1963), pp. 60 and 68; Lenclud and Ravis-Giordani (1973), pp. 207–9 and map; Pomponi (1978a),

p. 16; Raulin and Ravis-Giordani (1978), pp. 69–70; Finelli (n.d.), pp. 12 and 56; and Lücke (1982), pp. 97–8.

243 Finelli (n.d.), p. 13; and Cases v. A.-P. Trojani, Assize Court, 2nd session 1850. AN BB²⁰149; and v. A. Padovani, 1st session 1865. AN BB²⁰273; see also Notice, Prefect, 26 August 1825. ADCS 1.M.222.

244 Report, Procureur-général, 9 May 1885; and other documents. Petition for clemency for G.-C. Moracchini. AN BB²⁴887. It is significant in this context that in some villages, herdsmen resided in hamlets and cultivators in the village nucleus; see Comiti (1933), p. 142.

245 Petitions for clemency for G.-A. Piazza, 1885. AN BB²⁴888; and for S. Giannoni, 1886. AN BB²⁴889.

246 Ettori (1979), p. 194; see also Morel (1951), p. 167 (Petreto-Bicchisano).

247 Morel (1951), p. 167; Robiquet (1835), pp. 429–30; and Versini (1972), pp. 49–68.

248 Morandière (1933), pp. 86–8; *Gaz. Trib.*, 23 September 1840, No. 4695; Letter, Juge de paix, San-Martino, 2 September 1841. ADCS 2.V.19; Case, Assize Court, 1st session 1849, Extraordinary sitting. AN BB²⁰146; and Letter, President, Assize Court, 13 July 1850. AN BB²⁰149.

249 Valéry (1837), p. 202; Marcaggi (1932), pp. 45 and 84–5; Case v. O. Giovannoni, Assize Court, 2nd session 1843. AN BB²⁰121; and Marcaggi (1898b), pp. 120–4, 177 and 289–96.

250 Petition for clemency for S.-P. Agostini 1833. AN BB²⁴116–35; and Case v. S. Gaffori, Assize Court, 1st session 1849. AN BB²⁰146.

251 Case v. A. Lucchini, Assize Court, 2nd session 1839. *Gaz. Trib.*, 20 July 1839, No. 4326. Report, Gendarmerie, Tallano, 3 August 1816. ADCS 4.M.102; Cases v. D. Trojani et al., Assize Court, 2nd session 1849. AN BB²⁰146; v. P. Arrighi, 1st session 1851, Extraordinary sitting. AN BB²⁰152; v. N. Tenneroni, 2nd session 1845. AN BB²⁰130; v. G. Filippi et al., 3rd session 1851; and Letter, President, Assize Court, 13 July 1850. AN BB²⁰149; and v. G.-F. Sanguinetti et al., 1st session 1851. AN BB²⁰152; and Deliberations, Municipal Council, Venzolasca, 26 August 1900. ADHC E.18/3.

252 Letter, Subprefect to Prefect, February 1821. ADCS 1.M.224; and Case v. L. Angeli, Assize Court, 3rd session 1853. AN BB²⁰164.

253 Reports, Gendarmerie, 15 August; and 26 November 1842. ADCS 4.M.126; Cases v. G.-A. Nicolai; and A. Peretti, Assize Court, 1st session 1854. AN BB²⁰170; and v. G.-A. Franceschi, 3rd session 1848. AN BB²⁰142; and Letter, Procureur-général to Prefect, 11 December 1911. ADCS 1.M.231.

254 Black-Michaud (1975), p. 178.

9 Conciliation and peacemaking

1 Wallace-Hadrill (1962), pp. 124–5; see also Colson (1962), p. 111; Bourdieu (1965), pp. 236–7; Stirling (1965), p. 248; Peters (1967), p. 266; and Byock (1982), pp. 41–5, 98, 201 and *passim*.

2 E.g. Bigot (1890), p. 451 and Malaspina (1876), p. 351.

3 Saravelli-Retali (1976), p. 103.

4 Deliberations, Municipal Council, Penta-di-Casinca, December 1856. ADHC. E.29/8.

5 Saint-Germain (1869), p. 146; and author's fieldwork.

6 Casta (1974), pp. 75–6; Maestroni (1978), pp. 19 and 70; and Lamotte (1961). A notice on the church door at Pila-Canale in 1981 read: 'Money, politics, pride and jealousy have divided men. Only the true practice of our religion, the love of Christ, reconciles them. Such is the view of the friends of the parish of Pila-Canale.'

7 E.g. the bonfires on the vigils of the feasts of St John the Baptist and Sts Peter and Paul

in medieval London; or the 'pax-cakes' distributed on Palm Sunday in Herefordshire villages; see Stow (1893) [1603], p. 126; and Simpson (1976), p. 142.

8 E.g. Brögger (1968); J. Schneider (1969), p. 116; and J. Schneider (1971), pp. 16–17.

9 Lenclud and Pernet (1978), p. 71; and Barry (1893), pp. 161–2; see also Bialor (1968), pp. 108 and 121–2 (Greece); and Moss (1979), p. 487 (Sardinia).

10 Case v. G.-D. Fumaroli, Assize Court, 1st session 1861. AN BB[20]229; also Case v. G.-L. Angeli, 4th session 1863. AB BB[20]249; and Westermarck (1934), pp. 363 and 369.

11 Case v. S. Stefani, Tribunal correctionnel, Sartène, 1812. ADCS 3.U.5/166.

12 Cases v. P.-E. Carlotti et al., Assize Court, 3rd session 1845. AN BB[20]130; v. P. Giacomoni et al., 2nd session 1848. AN BB[20]142; v. G. Benedetti, 2nd session 1842. AN BB[20]116; and v. F.-A. Desanti, 4th session 1852, Extraordinary sitting. AN BB[20]158.

13 Reports, Procureur-général to Minister of the Interior, 22 December 1864; and 1 February 1865. AN BB[18]1705.

14 Case v. A.-F. Durazzi and P.-G. Paoli, Tribunal correctionnel, Sartène, July 1811. ADCS 3.U.5/165.

15 Case, Fiori v. Pietri, Cour Royale, Bastia, 6 May 1829. *Gaz. Trib.*, 25–26 May 1829, No. 1184.

16 Case v. P. Bartoli, Assize Court, 1st session 1856. AN BB[20]185.

17 Saint-Germain (1869), p. 235; and Case v. G.-C. Santini, Assize Court, 1st session 1862. AN BB[20]239.

18 Robiquet (1835), p. 397; for parallels, see J. Schneider (1969), p. 123 (Sicily); Tait (1970), pp. 190–1 (Konkomba); and Littlewood (1974), pp. 47–9 (S. Italy).

19 Cases v. P. and G.-D. Paolini, Tribunal correctionnel, Sartène, 28 February 1830. ADCS 3.U.5/156; and v. S.-F. Bruselicci, 9 February 1814. ADCS 3.U.5/166.

20 Cases v. Giampierini(?), Assize Court, 4th session 1834. *Gaz. Trib.*, 25 January 1835, No. 2942; and v. F. Padovani, 4th session 1845. AN BB[20]130.

21 Chiva (1963), p. 111; see also Chiva (1958), p. 145; Viale et al. (1966), p. 70; and Pernet and Lenclud (1977), p. 93.

22 Robiquet (1835), p. 385.

23 Cases v. P.-L. Pietri, Extraordinary Criminal Court, 29 Fructidor An IX. ADCS 7.U.1/17; v. A. Guiderdoni, Assize Court, 2nd session 1853. AN BB[20]164; v. A.-L. Orsini and C.-P. Bernardini, Appeal Court, Bastia, 13 May 1857. ADCS 2.U.1/61; and v. G. Poggi, Assize Court, 2nd session 1857. AN BB[20]194; and Bazal (1973), pp. 166–9.

24 Reports, Subprefect, Sartène, 28 July 1821; and 23 February 1823. ADCS 4.M.98–99.

25 Cases v. G.-A. Anziani, Assize Court, 4th session 1854. Extraordinary sitting. AN BB[20]170; and v. A. Fieschi, 2nd session 1850. AN BB[20]149.

26 ADCS 4.U.3.57–60. 'Conciliations An XI – 1880'.

27 Case v. A.-M. Renucci, Assize Court, 1st session 1843. AN BB[20]121; and Report, Police, 27 May 1822. ADCS 4.M.75.

28 E.g. Cases v. N. Paoli, Assize Court, 1st session 1842. AN BB[20]116 (Silvareccio); v. F. Graziani, 1st session 1849, Extraordinary sitting. AN BB[20]146 (Monticello); and v. P. Palmesani et al., 1st session 1865. AN BB[20]273 (Alzi).

29 E.g. Cases v. B. Muraccioli, 2nd session 1844. AN BB[20]125 (Ocana); v. M. Vincenti, 2nd session 1845. AN BB[20]130 (Pila-Canale); v. M. Mattei, 1st session 1849, Extraordinary sitting. AN BB[20]146 (Valpajola); v. D. Folacci, 1st session 1852. AN BB[20]158 (Bastelica); and v. P. Franceschi, 2nd session 1853, Extraordinary sitting. AN BB[20]164 (Piazzole).

30 See also Report, Gendarmerie, Ajaccio, 8 September 1841. ADCS 4.M.125; and Case v. L. Savelli, Assize Court, 3rd session 1861. AN BB[20]229.

31 Cases v. P. Giacomoni, 3rd and 4th sessions 1846. AN BB[20]134; and v. A. Marietti, 4th session 1859. AN BB[20]213; see also Arrighi (1856b), p. 17.

32 Philpotts (1913); Treston (1923), pp. 6–11; Speck (1919); and Quain (1961), p. 271; see also Lane (n.d.), pp. 108–9 (Egypt); Gray et al. (1909), pp. 722–6, 731–2 and 734; Maitland (1911); Westermarck (1934), pp. 362–4 (Berbers); Wallace-Hadrill (1962), pp. 146–7 (Franks); Peters (1967), pp. 263, 265–7 and 276 (Bedouin of Cyrenaica); Chelhod (1968), pp. 42 and 48–51 (Jordanian Bedouin); Gellner (1969), pp. 125–7; Black-Michaud (1975), pp. 9–11 and 109–18; Wormald (1980), pp. 62 and 89; and Byock (1982), pp. 250–2, 261–3 and 268.

33 E.g. Cozzi (1910), pp. 661, 669–70 and 679; Hasluck (1954), pp. 239–41 (Albania); Goldman (1961), p. 198 (Kwakiutl); Lewis (1961), pp. 243–4 (Somali); Winter (1970), p. 147 (Bwamba); and Pálsson (1971), pp. 43–4 (medieval Iceland).

34 Busquet (1919), pp. 91–2; see also Arrighi (1970), p. 217; and Carrington (1971a), p. 80.

35 Cases v. A.-M. Mattei, Court of Criminal Justice, 1st session 1830. AN BB^{20}49; v. F. Santoni et al., Assize Court, 1st session 1849. AN BB^{20}146; v. G.-A. Mariani, 2nd session 1865. AN BB^{20}273; and v. F. Andreani, 1st session 1849, Extraordinary sitting. AN BB^{20}146; and Letter, G.-P. Vincenti to Prefect, 1816. ADCS 1.M.224.

36 Cases v. B. Ottavi, Assize Court, 1st session 1864. AN BB^{20}260; v. G. Filippi et al., 3rd session 1850. AN BB^{20}149; v. Giampietri(?), 3rd session 1834. *Gaz. Trib.*, 2 October 1834, No. 2845; and v. G. Miliani et al., 2nd session 1847. *Gaz. Trib.*, 18 July 1847, No. 6252.

37 E.g. Thrasher (1970), pp. 140 and 146; and Ravis-Giordani (1976a), p. 180.

38 Marcaggi (1898b), pp. 120–30.

39 Busquet (1919), pp. 88 and 364.

40 E.g. Cases v. G. and D. Frimicacci, Assize Court, 1st session; and v. L. Borghetti, 2nd session 1834. *Gaz. Trib.*, 2 October; and 3 July 1834, Nos. 2845 and 2769.

41 Letter, Miot to Minister of Justice, 10 Fructidor An IX. AN BB^{20}236; see also Robiquet (1835), p. 394.

42 Case v. G. Muzi, Assize Court, 3rd session 1848. AN BB^{20}242.

43 E.g. Letter, Poli to Prefect 1816(?). ADCS 1.M.224; Case v. A.-P. Leca, Assize Court, 2nd session 1837. *Gaz. Trib.*, 12 July 1837, No. 3694; and Ambrosi (1972), p. 36; see also Barth (1965) pp. 84–5; and Foster (1961), p. 1185, who suggests that an exact balance – a purely theoretical notion – would lead to stasis, preventing negotiation.

44 Letter, Mayor and Juge de paix, Ciamannacce, to Subprefect, 28 February 1828. ADCS 4.M.91; and Marcaggi (1898b), pp. 120–30 and 239–45.

45 Case v. M. Ferrandi, Imperial Court, Ajaccio, 1812. ADCS 2.U.1/43; and Petitions for clemency for G. Casabianca, 1858 and 1868. AN BB^{24}507–15.

46 Petitions for clemency for G.-D. and S. Santini, 1876. AN BB^{24}534–40; and for F. Bastianesi, 1874 and 1877. AN BB^{24}798.

47 *Gaz. Trib.*, 18 April 1840, No. 4559.

48 Letter, N. Gasparini; and Report, Subprefect, 23 October 1824. ADCS 1.M.228; and Cases v. P. and F. Quastana, Assize Court, 1st session; and v. I. Borelli, 3rd session 1849. AN BB^{20}146.

49 E.g. Maitland (1911), p. 216; Bateson (1958), pp. 80 and 107; Davies (1969), p. 354; Gellner (1969); Hamer (1972) (Ethiopia); and Black-Michaud (1975), pp. 93–9 and 101–3.

50 See Réalier-Dumas (1819), pp. 52–3; Busquet (1919), pp. 254–62; Marin-Muracciole (1964), pp. 13 and 49–50; Viale (1966), p. 70; P. Arrighi (1971), p. 281; and Pomponi (1978a), pp. 10 and 14; also, for parallels, Terrell (1979), pp. 50–1; Wormald (1980), pp. 76–7, 84 and 86–7; and Brown (1983).

51 Miot (1858), II, p. 35; Prefect's Report to Conseil-général, 1827. AN BB^{18}1146; and Report, President Fabrizzi, 29 December 1865. AN BB^{20}273.

52 Letters, Poli to Miot; and Substitut, Commissaire du gouvernement, An IX. AN

BB^{18}236; and Military commander, Bastia, to Minister of Justice, 24 March 1809. AN BB^{18}241; Busquet (1919), p. 621; Letter, Count Willot to Minister of War, 1817(?). AN BB^{18}1014; Printed treaty, Olmeta-di-Tuda, 1818. AN BB^{18}242; Roger (1945), pp. 160–1; and Busquet (1919), pp. 624–35.

53 Reports, Subprefect, Sartène, February 1821. ADCS 1.M.224; and 19 December 1826. ADCS 4.M.99.

54 Letter, Mayor, Ciamannacce to Prefect, 12 July 1830; and other documents. ADCS 1.M.224; Case v. A. Colombani et al., Assize Court, 3rd session 1849. AN BB^{20}146; and Marcaggi (1932), p. 140.

55 Report, Subprefect, 1 May 1835. ADCS 4.M.100; and Busquet (1919), pp. 639–40.

56 See Anderson (1957), p. 50 (S. Italy); and Lienhardt (1970), p. 119 (W. Dinka).

57 Cases v. G. and L. Simoni et al., Extraordinary Criminal Court, Sartène, Thermidor An X. ADCS 3.U.5/129; and Letter, Subprefect, Sartène, to Prefect, 6 Vendémiaire An XI. ADCS 1.M.224; see also, more generally, Facy (1933), p. 68.

58 Busquet (1919), pp. 245–54 and 413–32; Robiquet (1835), pp. 394 and 397 note; and Quantin (1914), p. 280; also Gregorovius (1855), pp. 140 and 423–6; Faure (1858), p. 22; Roger (1945), p. 187; Viale et al. (1966), p. 70; Lenclud and Ravis-Giordani (1973), p. 197; and Desideri (1978), pp. 208–9.

59 E.g. Defacqz (1866), esp. pp. 90–3 (Low Countries); Espinas (1899) (Douai); Maitland (1911), p. 219; Philpotts (1913), pp. 77, 83–7 and *passim* (Germany, N. France and Scandinavia); Brucker (ed.) (1967), pp. 62 and 106; Brucker (1969), p. 205; Brucker (1971), pp. 107 and 110; Becker (1976), pp. 282, 284 and 285; Kent (1977), p. 61 (Florence); and Brown (1983) (Scotland).

60 Letter, Miot to Minister of Justice, 10 Fructidor An IX. AN BB^{18}236; Réalier-Dumas (1819), pp. 19–20; Malaspina (1876), p. 351; Bourde (1887), pp. 150–1; Marin-Muracciole (1964), p. 12; and Letter, Mayor, Ciamannacce, to Prefect, 12 July 1830. ADCS 1.M.224.

61 AN BB^{18}236.

62 Busquet (1919), pp. 624–7; and Roger (1945), pp. 281–5.

63 Letter, Comte Willot, to Minister of War, 1817 (enclosing copies of treaties negotiated under his auspices). AN BB^{18}1014; Case v. M. Versini, Assize Court, 1st session 1849. AN BB^{20}146; and Busquet (1919), pp. 635–9, citing journal of convent of Vico.

64 Busquet (1919), pp. 627–35 and 640–3; Marcaggi (1898b), pp. 120–30 and 289–96; Case v. V. Casile, Assize Court, 1st session 1844. AN BB^{20}125; Bourde (1887), pp. 151–4; and AN BB^{18}1014.

65 E.g. Philpotts (1913), p. 186 (St Omer); and Brown (1983), p. 9.

66 See also AN BB^{18}1014; and Busquet (1919), p. 625.

67 Busquet (1919), pp. 620 and 632; ADCS 1.M.224; Acte de paix, 1 Prairial An IX. AN BB^{18}236; Case v. G.-B. Scapola, Assize Court, 1st session 1846. *Gaz. Trib.*, 16 April 1846, No. 5860; and Letter, Mayor, Sari-d'Orcino, to Prefect, 24 July 1860. ADCS 2.M.149.

68 Busquet (1919), pp. 637–8.

69 Cases v. S. Minichetti, Assize Court, 1st session 1851. AN BB^{20}152; and v. P. Crudeli, 3rd session 1833. *Gaz. Trib.*, 22 September 1833; and Sorbier (1863), pp. 41–5.

70 Letter, Sebastiani Cappellini to Count Berthier, n.d.; and Case v. G.-G. Casalta, Extraordinary Criminal Court, Ajaccio, 16 December 1813. AN BB^{18}242; AN BB^{18}1014; Case v. N. Tenneroni, Assize Court, 2nd session 1845. AN BB^{20}130; and Versini (1972), p. 105.

71 Letter, Substitut, Commissaire du gouvernement, Germinal An IX. AN BB^{18}236; Busquet (1919), pp. 638 and 621; AN BB^{18}1014; and Report, Gendarmerie, Ajaccio, 30 September 1872. AN F^{7}12849.

72 AN BB^{18}242; Letter, Mayor, Frasseto, to Prefect, 20 December 1847. ADCS 1.M.224;

Cases v. G. Muzi, Assize Court, 3rd session 1848. AN BB²⁰142; v. G.-B. Scapola, 1st session 1846. AN BB²⁰134; and v. P. Chiaroni, 1st session 1851, Extraordinary sitting. AN BB²⁰152; and Bazal (1973), pp. 159–60.

73 Banishment was a feature of settlements elsewhere; see Philpotts (1913), pp. 18, 185 and 212; Gellner (1969), pp. 62 and 126; Roberts (1979), pp. 27 and 65–7; and Byock (1982), pp. 112–13, 219–20 and 263–4; and, on pilgrimages of penance, Springer (1950), pp. 96 and 98–9; Sumption (1975), Ch. VII; and Wormald (1980), p. 74. It was also a penalty very generally found in traditional judicial systems, including that of Corsica; see Patin de La Fizelière (1963), p. 73; and Emmanuelli (1969), pp. 90, 92, 94 and 100; also e.g., Jusserand (1891), pp. 152–7 and 159–63 (medieval England); Ganshof (1970), p. 93 (Carolingian France); Foucault (1979), pp. 33 and 313 (eighteenth-century France and Flanders); and Wood (1982) (nineteenth-century Russia). On the expiatory nature of exile, voluntary or not, see Treston (1923), pp. 22–4, 47–52, 62 and 80; Llewellyn and Hoebel (1941), pp. 83–8; and Hasluck (1954), Ch. XXIV.

74 Case v. Luciani, Preliminary proceedings, Vendémiaire An X; and Letter, 1 Brumaire An X. ADCS 7.U.1/4; Case v. M. Ferrandi, Imperial Court, Ajaccio, 1812. ADCS 2.U.1/43; and Letter, Count Willot to Minister of War, 1817. AN BB¹⁸1014; see also Case v. A. Lucchini, Assize Court, 2nd session 1839. *Gaz. Trib.*, 20 July 1839, No. 4326; and Letter, Miot to Minister of Justice, 10 Fructidor An IX. AN BB¹⁸236.

75 Case v. G.-A. Orabona, Assize Court, 1st session 1845. AN BB²⁰130; and Bazal (1973), p. 55.

76 Busquet (1919), pp. 222–32 and 478–9; and Marin-Muracciole (1964), pp. 12–13, 103–4, 112 and 123–4; also Lenclud and Ravis-Giordani (1973), p. 224; Desideri (1978), pp. 209–10 and 212; Pomponi (1978a), p. 23; and Christophari (1981), p. 166.

77 E.g. Barth (1965), p. 96; and Peters (1967), p. 276. For other examples of marriage as an element in feud settlements, see Treston (1923), pp. 89–90; Westermarck (1934), p. 364; Kipling (1964) [1895], p. 192; Stirling (1965), pp. 252 and 254; Chelhod (1968), pp. 51–3; Bossy (1973), p. 132; Wormald (1980), pp. 74–5; and Byock (1982), pp. 53, 106, 180 and 265.

78 Benson (1825), p. 64; Memoir by A. Campocasso. AN BB¹⁸241; Letter, Subprefect, Sartène, to Prefect, 1 February 1821. ADCS 1.M.224; Case v. G. Giacomoni and Don G. Santalucia, Assize Court, 1st session 1840. *Gaz. Trib.*, 18 April 1840, No. 4559; and Sorbier (1863), pp. 166–77; and Marcaggi (1932), p. 53.

79 Middleton and Tait (1970), pp. 216–17; and Black-Michaud (1975), p. 228; see also Benedict (1935), p. 149; and the critical remarks of Pospisil (1968), p. 390.

80 Andrei (1893), pp. 275–7.

81 Byock (1982), p. 104.

82 Robiquet (1835), p. 394; Malaspina (1876), p. 351; Bourde (1887), pp. 153–4; and Emmanuelli (1969), pp. 90 and 102–3.

83 Quantin (1914), p. 280.

84 Letter, Substitut, Commissaire du gouvernement, Germinal An IX. AN BB¹⁸236; and AN BB¹⁸1014.

85 Letters, Fructidor An IX. AN BB¹⁸236; and ADCS 1.M.224; Letters, Substitut, Commissaire du gouvernement, Germinal An IX. AN BB¹⁸236; Military commander, Bastia, to Minister of Justice, 18 and 24 March 1809; and Procureur-général to same, 1809. AN BB¹⁸241; Busquet (1919), pp. 621–2; and Letter, A. Lucchini and S. Gabrielli, 1816. AN BB¹⁸242; and Franceschini (1923), p. 76, citing Report, Commissaire spécial, 1 April 1818.

86 Cases v. S. Poggi, Assize Court, 4th session 1843. AN BB²⁰121; v. A. Moretti and P.-P. Marchetti, 3rd session 1848. AN BB²⁰142.

87 Report, Subprefect, Corte, to Prefect, 12 December 1854. ADCS 2.M.127. According

to Valéry (1837), p. 291, the treaty was concluded under the auspices of General Lallemand in 1834.

10 Feuding and the courts

1 Montherot (1840), pp. 22–3; *Gaz. Trib.*, 18 July 1833, No. 2472; Griffon (1841), p. 35; Patin de La Fizelière (1963), p. 65; and Letter, Mayor Roccaserra to Ministry of Justice, 3 January 1879. AN BB²⁴852; see also Barry (1893), p. 276.
2 Report, Subprefect, Ajaccio, 12 September 1827. ADCS 4.M.91; see also Feydel (1799), p. 82.
3 Cases v. F.-M. Paolini, Assize Court, 3rd session 1856. AN BB²⁰185; and v. M. Nicolai, 1st session 1834. *Gaz. Trib.*, 3 July 1834, No. 2769.
4 Arson as a form of private or 'social vengeance' was also fairly common in continental France in the early nineteenth century; see, for example, cases reported in *Gaz. Trib.*, 26–27 March 1832, No. 2065 (Corrèze and Hautes-Alpes); and 4 May 1834, No. 2719 (Haute-Saône); and Merriman (1976), esp. pp. 454 and 460–4 (Normandy).
5 Cit. Thiers (1977), p. 21; and Case v. F. Stefani, Court of Criminal Justice, 2nd session 1830. AN BB²⁰49; see also Report, Gendarmerie, 8 September 1821, cit. Franceschini (1919), p. 83.
6 Case v. D. Casanova, Court of Criminal Justice, 2nd session 1830. AN BB²⁰49.
7 Cases v. G. Giuliani, Assize Court, 2nd session 1848. AN BB²⁰142; and v. M. and A.-B. Cesari, 1st session 1861. AN BB²⁰229.
8 Case v. Giacomoni, Extraordinary Criminal Court, Sartène, An IX. ADCS 3.U.5/128.
9 Letter, S. Castelli to Procureur-général, 27 May 1912. ADCS I.M.231; see also, more generally, F. Renucci (1838), p. 10; and Busquet (1919), pp. 167–8.
10 Case v. G.-M. Saladini, Extraordinary Criminal Court, 3 Messidor An X. ADCS 7.U.1/22.
11 Case v. S.-A. Arrii, Assize Court, 1st session 1849, Extraordinary sitting. AN BB²⁰146; Petition for clemency for G.-F. Arrii, 1856. AN BB²⁴622–36; and Case v. G.-C. Pietrapiana, 2nd session 1863. AN BB²⁰249; see also Report, Commissaire du gouvernement près le Tribunal Criminel, Liamone, to Minister of Justice, 15 Brumaire An IX. AN BB¹⁸236 (Piana); Report, Subprefect, Ajaccio, 4 August 1827. ADCS 4.M.91 (Tavera); and F. Renucci (1838), pp. 15–19; and Saint-Germain (1869), pp. 300–2 (Monte-d'Olmo). Homicidal arson was of course a feature of Icelandic feuds, viz. *Burnt Njal*; and was found elsewhere; see e.g. Wormald (1980), p. 83.
12 Wagner (1968), pp. 27 and 95–6.
13 Emmanuelli (1969), pp. 90, 93 and 102–3; and Case v. A.-L. Pelliccia, Assize Court, 1st session 1846. AN BB²⁰134.
14 Rovère (1978), pp. 80 and 95–6; Patin de La Fizelière (1963), p. 65; Beaumont (1822), p. 32; Barry (1893), p. 276; and Le Joindre (1904), p. 95; see also Montherot (1840), p. 80; and Griffon (1841), p. 35.
15 Letter, A.-M. Santucci to Minister of Justice, n.d. AN BB¹⁸238; also Report, Procureur-général to Minister of Justice, 29 September 1821. AN BB¹⁸243.
16 Case v. M.-C. Comiti and A.-M. Coscioli, Assize Court, 2nd session 1856. AN BB²⁰185.
17 Petition for clemency for G. Dionisi, 9 November 1879. AN BB²⁴868.
18 E.g. Cases v. M. Moracchini and M.-V. Sebastiani, Assize Court, 4th session 1857. AN BB²⁰194 (San Lorenzo); and v. D.-M. Canioni, 1st session 1860. AN BB²⁰221 (Nessa); see also Cases v. G.-A. Nicolai, 1st session 1854. AN BB²⁰170 (Levie); and v. A.-B. Canacci, 4th session 1862. AN BB²⁰239 (Bisinchi).

19 Letter, S. Castelli to Procureur-général, 27 May 1912. ADCS 1.M.231.
20 Case v. R. Quilichini, Assize Court, 3rd session 1843. AN BB²⁰121.
21 Report, Subprefect, Corte, 4 February 1851. ADCS 2.M.82; and Letters, S. Quilichini to Prefect, 28 September 1843; and Gendarmerie to Prefect, 15 and 19 June 1846. ADCS 2.M.81.
22 Letters, Subprefect to Prefect, 30 April 1843; and F. Susini to Prefect, 2 January 1847. ADCS 2.M.84; Report, Gendarmerie, 10 May 1855. ADCS 2.M.138; Letters, Subprefect to Prefect, 10 September 1861; and 8 March 1864. ADCS 2.M.140; and 2 May; and 14 December 1865. ADCS 2.M.158.
23 Case v. A.-M. Pietri Vincensini, Assize Court, 1st session 1851. Extraordinary sitting. AN BB²⁰152.
24 E.g. *Gaz. Trib.*, 17 April 1841, No. 4871, citing *L'Insulaire Français*; and 1 January 1832.
25 E.g. Montherot (1840), pp. 35–6; and Case v. F.-A. Murati, Assize Court, 3rd session 1848. AN BB²⁰142.
26 E.g. Benedict (1935), pp. 234–5 (on Zuñi mythology).
27 Here the pursuit of vengeance by magical means may be an alternative to direct action (e.g. Villette (1961), pp. 132, 137–8 and 141; Middleton and Tait (1970), pp. 20 and 22; and Favret-Saada (1977), pp. 93–4 and 101–54), or the two modes of vengeance may complement each other (e.g. Evans-Pritchard (1976), pp. xiv, 5–7, 44, 51–3 and *passim*).
28 See e.g. Maitland (1911), pp. 217–18 and 226; Tax Freeman (1968), p. 479; Gellner (1969), p. 123; Middleton (1970), p. 226; Winter (1970), pp. 159–60; Hamer (1972), pp. 241–3; Du Boulay (1979), pp. 171–80; and Roberts (1979), p. 152.
29 E.g. Defacqz (1866), esp. pp. 83–4 and 88–9; Espinas (1899), pp. 3–4, 14–20 and 34–5; Philpotts (1913), pp. 82–5, 144, 162–3 and 178; Davies (1969), esp. pp. 355–9 (all medieval Europe); Dennis (1976); Roberts (1979), pp. 26–7; Wormald (1980), pp. 72–3 and 78–88; Byock (1982), esp. p. 205; and Visser (1984), pp. 194–5 (Ancient Athens).
30 E.g. Gellner (1969), pp. 104–25; Cohen (1972), pp. 9–10; Hanawalt (1977), p. 403; Ingram (1977), pp. 116–22; Roberts (1979), p. 180; Byock (1982), pp. 6, 29, 74ff and 104; and Sharpe (1980), pp. 22–3 (York).
31 On this general aim of 'traditional' judicial systems, see Gluckman (1973); also Chelhod (1968), pp. 43–4 and 62; Du Boulay (1979), pp. 177–80; Becker (1976), pp. 282, 285 and 290–1; and Byock (1982), p. 102.
32 Rémy (1930), p. 93; and, on the autonomy of the traditional system, Lamotte (1964), p. 60; Martini (1964a); and Pernet and Lenclud (1977), p. 93.
33 This line of argument, of course, has much more general currency; see, e.g. Wormald (1980), p. 82; and Pareto (1935), IV, p. 1519: 'whenever judicial process fails, private and group justice replaces it, and vice versa'.
34 Mérimée (1840b), p. 668; and Bartoli (1898), p. 255; see also Letter, Conseiller à la Cour Royal, Ajaccio, 1814 or 1815. AN BB¹⁸242; Réalier-Dumas (1819), p. 21; Blanqui (1841), pp. 530–1; Griffon (1841), pp. 29–32; De la Rocca (1857), p. 77; Malaspina (1876), p. 351; Molinari (1886), p. 259; Bonaparte (1891), p. 93 and Lorenzi de Bradi (1928), p. 236.
35 Busquet (1919), pp. 40–1.
36 Vanutberghe (1904), p. 346.
37 Letters, General Berthier to Minister of Justice, 9 March 1812; and 23 December 1813. AN BB¹⁸241; General Bruslart to same, 9 February 1815. AN BB¹⁸950; and Count Willot to same, 1816. AN BB¹⁸1049.
38 Letters, Substitut du commissaire du gouvernement près le Tribunal Criminel, Liamone, Germinal An IX. AN BB¹⁸236; and C. Mari to Minister of Justice, 1 Nivôse An VI. AN BB¹⁸237; and Petition for clemency for G. Orticoni and M. Graziani, 23

September 1820. AN BB²48–17; see also Réalier-Dumas (1819), p. 20; *Gaz. Trib.*, 23–24 June 1828, No. 989; and Robiquet (1835), pp. 394–5.

39 E.g. Military report, 1846, cit. Vidalenc (1966), p. 79; Ballard (1852), p. 19; Sorbier (1863), p. 210; Bourde (1887), p. 134; Busquet (1919), pp. 119–20; and Quantin (1914), p. 274.

40 E.g. Pitt-Rivers (1965), p. 30; Stirling (1965), pp. 272–3; and Pitt-Rivers (1971), p. 129.

41 Letter, Prefect to Minister of the Interior, 24 March 1823. AN BB¹⁸1095; Barry (1893), p. 275; Filippi (1906), pp. 10–11 and 28; and Saravelli-Retali (1976), pp. 111 and 141. Contrary examples may be cited, however; in a tale collected at Porto-Vecchio in 1881, for example, the courts in Bastia are presented as righters of wrongs, seeing through the ruses of the well-to-do and rendering justice to the poor. Ortoli (1883), pp. 193–204.

42 Robiquet (1835), p. 406; Mancini (1883), p. 73; and Piobb (n.d.), p. 53.

43 E.g. Robiquet (1835), pp. 397 and 407–8; Malaspina (1876), p. 375; Rémy (1930), pp. 23, 29 and *passim*; and Versini (1979), pp. 41–4.

44 Le Joindre (1904), pp. 88–9; and Schnapper (1979), pp. 406–12.

45 Rapport Mottet, 1836, cit. Versini (1979), p. 165; and Ambrosi (1972), p. 35.

46 Saravelli-Retali (1976), p. 118; Valéry (1837), p. 203; and Lorenzi de Bradi (1928), p. 265; see also Letters, Commissaire du Directoire exécutif, Golo, 5 Floréal; and 29 Messidor An VI. AN BB¹⁸237; and Bourde (1887), pp. 124–7 and 135.

47 Letter, Premier président to Minister of Justice, 15 September 1816. AN BB¹⁸242; Rapport Mottet, 1836, cit. Versini (1979), p. 181; Robiquet (1835), pp. 407–8; Bigot (1890), pp. 450 and 459; Report, Procureur-général to Minister of the Interior, 19 June 1871. AN BB³⁰489; and Surier (1934), p. 44; see also Speech, Premier Président Colonna d'Istria, *Journal du Département de la Corse*, 13 November 1828, No. 46; Sorbier (1833); Dufresne (1847), pp. 3–5 and 9; Ballard (1852), pp. 18–19; Metz-Noblat (1885), pp. 33–4; Bournet (1888), pp. 17 and 30–1; Le Joindre (1904), pp. 95–9; and Sacquin-Moulin (1982), p. 654.

48 F. Renucci (1833–4), II, pp. 172ff; Miot (1858), II, pp. 6–7; Rémy (1930), pp. 17–18, 21–2, 44 and 61–3; Cases, Cour de Cassation, 11 May 1827; and 7 February 1828; and Resolution, Conseil-général de la Corse, 6 October 1828. *Gaz. Trib.*, 12 May 1827; 8 February 1828; and 13 March 1829, Nos. 519, 782 and 1121; Réalier-Dumas (1819), pp. 27 and 46–50; and Ballard (1852), p. 19. The main criminal court was called the Cour Extraordinaire Spéciale from 1810 to 1814 and the Cour de Justice Criminelle from 1814 to 1831; it then became a regular Cour d'Assises.

49 Arrighi (1856a), p. 16; *Journal de la Corse*, 21 July 1857; Letters, Premier président; and Procureur-général to Minister of Justice, 26 July; and 11 November 1857. AN BB¹⁸569; and Report, President of Assize Court, 3rd session 1860. AN BB²⁰221.

50 E.g. Rapport Mottet, 1836, cit. Versini (1979), pp. 181–5.

51 Reports, Commissaire spécial, 22 April 1818, cit. Franceschini (1923), pp. 89–91; and Chef du Premier Bureau to Minister of Justice, 29 September 1820; and Letter, Minister of Justice to Procureur-général, 14 February 1821. AN BB¹⁸243; and Versini (1979), p. 95.

52 Report, Commissaire du Directoire exécutif, Golo, to Minister of Justice, 20 Brumaire An VII. AN BB¹⁸237; Letters, General Morand to same, 21 Floréal An XIII; and 3 and 7 August 1807. AN BB¹⁸240; and Report, Procureur-général to same, 4 January 1815. AN BB¹⁸242.

53 Reports, Procureur-général to Minister of Justice, 6 Messidor; and General Morand to same, 9 Messidor An XII. AN BB¹⁸240. In the event an appeal was made against the verdict and Peretti was retried and condemned to death, a sentence commuted to 20 years' hard labour.

54 Dossier, Viale case, 1806; Letter, A.-M. Santucci to Minister of Justice, 1806(?). AN BB¹⁸238; Bernardini (1970), I, pp. 56–7; Versini (1979), pp. 54–6; and Letter, Minister of Justice to President of Assize Court, 9 August 1842. AN BB²⁰116.

55 Cases v. Don G. Peretti, Assize Court, 2nd session; v. D. Mariotti and P.-F. Guerrini, 3rd session 1852. AN BB²⁰158; and v. M.-C. Filippi, 3rd session 1856. AN BB²⁰185.

56 Emmanuelli (1969), p. 102; Letter, Willot to Minister of Justice, 28 May 1816. AN BB¹⁸1049; Rémy (1930), pp. 53 and 61; Robiquet (1835), pp. 438–40; Letters, Procureur-général to Minister of Justice, 11 and 16 November 1820. AN BB¹⁸1049; and Case v. F. Istria, Assize Court, 2nd session 1851, Cases judged *in absentia*. AN BB²⁰152.

57 Rémy (1930), pp. 4, 9, 14ff, 21ff, 65–7 and 77–85.

58 *Ibid.*, pp. 30, 48, 57–9, 68–70, 86–7 and 92; and Sacquin-Moulin (1982).

59 Report, President, Assize Court, 4th session 1843. AN BB²⁰121; see also Rémy (1930), pp. 5–6.

60 Report, Procureur-général to Minister of Justice, 31 October 1825. AN BB¹⁸1132; Bigot (1890), p. 450; and Ceccaldi (1974), p. 253; see also Bournet (1888), pp. 16–17.

61 Cases v. P.-M. Paoli, Assize Court, 4th session 1843. AN BB²⁰121; v. M.-C. Comiti and A.-M. Coscioli, 2nd session 1856. AN BB²⁰185; v. D.-L. Antonmarchi, 4th session 1835. *Gaz. Trib.*, 26 February 1836, cit. Sorbier (1863), pp. 72–6; and v. M.-G. and F. Alcani et al., 4th session 1848. AN BB²⁰142.

62 E.g. Philpotts (1913), p. 129; Croce (1970), p. 37 (Naples); Gluckman (1973), p. 111 (Lozi); Du Boulay (1979), p. 197; and Synge (1979), p. 64 (Aran Islands): 'it is impossible to get reliable evidence in the island – not because the people are dishonest but because they think the claim of kinship more sacred than the claims of abstract truth'.

63 Letter, Substitut du commissaire près le Tribunal Criminel Extraordinaire, 26 Floréal An IX. ADCS 7.U.1/3; Sorbier, Speech at the installation of Mottet as public prosecutor (1833); and Bigot (1890), p. 450; see also Report, President, Assize Court, 3rd session 1844. AN BB²⁰125; Report, Procureur-général, 30 March 1861. AN BB²⁰229; P.-L. Arrighi (1896), p. 23; and *Corse-Matin*, 9 June 1979.

64 Letter, Procureur-général to Minister of Justice, 17 February 1819. AN BB¹⁸1049; Arrighi (1856b), p. 12; and Casta (1974), pp. 194–5.

65 Saravelli-Retali (1976), p. 25; Tommaseo (1841), p. 89; and Ortoli (1887), p. 246, citing *voceri*; Barry (1893), pp. 300–1; and Marcaggi (1898a), p. 308, citing laments by bandits.

66 Petitions for clemency for F. Bastianesi, 1852–77. AN BB²⁴798; and for M. Cristini, 1885. AN BB²⁴887; also for V. Cesari, 1882. AN BB²⁴876; and for C. Terramorsi, 1884. AN BB²⁴885.

67 Report, Procureur-général to Minister of Justice, 6 September 1820. AN BB¹⁸1049; Case, Assize Court, 1st session 1841. *Gaz. Trib.*, 17 April 1841, No. 4871; also Bigot (1890), p. 450; Busquet (1919), pp. 121–4 and 361–4; and Desideri (1978), pp. 205–6.

68 Cases v. F. Venturini et al., Assize Court, 2nd session 1844. AN BB²⁰125; v. F. Antonetti et al., 2nd session; and v. P. Luciani et al., 3rd session 1850. AN BB²⁰149; and v. P.-F. Angelini, 1st session 1851, Extraordinary sitting. AN BB²⁰152.

69 Letter, Greffier, Tribunal correctionnel, Bastia, to Ministry of Justice, 15 Ventôse An VII. AN BB¹⁸236.

70 Cases v. A. Santoni, Assize Court, 3rd session 1850. AN BB²⁰149; v. S. Francisci, 4th session 1853. AN BB²⁰164; v. F. and G.-F. Palmesani, 1st session 1865. AN BB²⁰273.

71 Cases v. L. Colombani, Tribunal correctionnel, Corte, 1st session 1829. AN BB³⁰1211; and v. G.-B. Agostini, Assize Court, 1st session 1841. *Gaz. Trib.*, 10 April 1841. No. 4865.

72 E.g. Cases v. P.-D. Pelliccia, Assize Court, 4th session 1844. AN BB²⁰125; v. G.-B.

Martinetti et al., 1st session 1851. AN BB²⁰152; v. P.-F. Mariani, 3rd session; and v.
P. Ceccaldi, 4th session 1852, Extraordinary sitting. AB BB²⁰158. The defendants
were acquitted in all these cases.

73 Blanqui (1841), pp. 534–5; Letter, Maniez to Minister of Justice, 29 February 1844.
AN BB²⁰121; Petition for clemency for A.-Q. Roccaserra, 1879. AN BB²⁴852; and
Faure (1885), I, p. 44.

74 Case v. P. Negroni, Assize Court, 3rd session 1833. *Gaz. Trib.*, 30 October 1833, No.
2562; and Versini (1972), pp. 69–83.

75 Case v. Follacci, Mariani and Stefani, Cour Royale, Aix-en-Provence, 22 March 1822.
AN BB¹⁸1049; Report, Procureur-général, Liamone, to Minister of Justice, 6 Messi-
dor An XII. AN BB¹⁸240; Cases v. G.-D. Bazziconi, Assize Court, 1st session 1851.
AN BB²⁰152; and v. Don A. Leca, 2nd session 1833. *Gaz. Trib.*, 8 July 1833, cit.
Sorbier (1863), pp. 34–5; and Report, Procureur-général to Minister of Justice, 22
December 1864. AN BB¹⁸1705; see also Sorbier (1833), p. 10; and Bourde (1887),
pp. 137–9.

76 Case v. G.-B. Muselli, Assize Court, 2nd session 1858. AN BB²⁰204; and see Chapter
13, pp. 406–7 and note 209.

77 Robiquet (1835), p. 421; and Cases v. I. Borelli, Assize Court, 3rd session 1849. AN
BB²⁰146; v. M.-F. Quilichini, 1st session 1846. AN BB²⁰134; and Lorenzi de Bradi
(1928), pp. 238–9.

78 Juries were introduced into Corsica in 1792, suspended by the English in 1795, re-
established by the French in 1796, and again suspended in 1800. Report, Procureur-
général to Minister of Justice, 7 Thermidor An XII. AN BB¹⁸240; Benson (1825),
pp. 60–1; Sorbier (1833), pp. 7–9; Costa (1930); Rémy (1930), pp. 10, 12, 15, 17, 21
and 60; and Thrasher (1970), pp. 288, 300 and 317.

79 Réalier-Dumas (1819), pp. 42–4; Pompei (1821), pp. 239ff; Beaumont (1822), p. 75;
Letter, Procureur-général to Minister of Justice, 29 September 1827. AN BB¹⁸1298;
Gaz. Trib., 23–24 June 1828, No. 898; 13 and 14 March 1829, Nos. 1121 and 1122; 29
October 1829, No. 1317; 25 and 29 August 1830, Nos. 1567 and 1571; 5 September
1830, No. 1577; 29 October 1830, No. 1623; 14 November 1830, No. 1638; and 31
March 1831, No. 1757; Patorni (1842); Roger (1945), pp. 62–9; and Sacquin-Moulin
(1982), pp. 652–3.

80 Dufresne (1847), pp. 3–5; Letter, Conseiller, Appeal Court, to Minister of Justice, 3
August 1848. AN BB¹⁸1466; Ballard (1852), pp. 18–22; Arrighi (1856a), p. 22; Rémy
(1930), pp. 63–4; and Luciani (1969), pp. 77–8.

81 Letter, Miot to Minister of Justice, 10 Fructidor An XII. AN BB¹⁸236; Sorbier
(1833), pp. 5–6; Versini (1979), p. 18, citing Rapport Mottet, 1836; Bourde (1887),
p. 137; and Report, Procureur-général to Minister of Justice, 30 December 1896. AN
BB¹⁸1870; see also Letter, Substitut du commissaire du Directoire exécutif près les
Tribunaux Civils et Criminels, Liamone, to Minister of Justice, 25 Vendémiaire An
VI. AN BB¹⁸237; Montherot (1840), pp. 66–7; President Stefanini, Speech to jurors,
Assize Court 4th session 1843. AN BB²⁰121; Reports, Prefect to Minister of Justice,
21 April 1852. AN BB¹⁸1473; and President Montera, Assize Court, 3rd session 1860.
AN BB²⁰221; and P.-L. Arrighi (1896), p. 23.

82 'Rapport au Roi sur l'administration de la justice criminelle pendant l'année 1831',
Gaz. Trib., 24 January 1833, No. 2322; Robiquet (1835), Table XLIV; Patorni
(1842), pp. 68–9 ff; and Barret-Kriegel (1973), p. 290.

83 Cockburn (ed.) (1977), pp. 11–12, 23, 163, 175–7, 179–81 and 183–5; see also Pirastu
(1973), p. 108 (Sardinia).

84 These figures are based mainly on the session reports, but also on Robiquet (1835),
Table XLIV; Ballard (1852), pp. 18–19; and Bernardini (1970), II, p. 20.

85 Cases v. P.-F. Graziani(?) et al., Assize Court, 1st session, Extraordinary sitting; and

v. I. Borelli, 3rd session 1849. AN BB²⁰146; v. F. Agostini, 2nd session 1851, Extraordinary sitting. AN BB²⁰152; and v. G.-A. Bartoli, 4th session 1893. AN BB²⁰286; and Report, Commissaire central, Bastia, to Procureur-général, 25 December 1896, AN BB¹⁸1870.

86 Cases v. C. and P. Maestrati, 4th session 1832. *Gaz. Trib.*, 27 January 1833, No. 2326; and v. G.-D. Bazziconi, 1st session 1851. AN BB²⁰152.

87 Bertrand (1870), pp. 100–1; see also Ballard (1852), p. 19; and Moulin (1973) on 'extenuating circumstances' in French law in the nineteenth century.

88 Report, President, Assize Court, 2nd session 1851. AN BB²⁰152; and Case v. F. Graziani, 1st session 1849. AN BB²⁰146.

89 AN BB²⁰164; and BB²⁰273. Life sentences have been calculated here at 30 years' imprisonment, which is almost certainly an overestimation. Periods of 'surveillance' have been omitted from the calculations.

90 E.g. Petition for clemency for S.-P. Agostini, 1833. AN BB²⁴116–35.

91 Cases v. F.-M. Ortoli et al., Assize Court, 1st session 1851, Extraordinary sitting. AN BB²⁰152; v. G.-D. Fumaroli, 1st session 1861. AN BB²⁰229; and v. L. Ciarini, 2nd session 1857. AN BB²⁰194.

92 See Rémy (1930), p. 61; Franceschini (1919), p. 49; and Bazal (1973), p. 249; see also Barry (1893), pp. 279–80.

93 Cases v. A.-G. Santoni, 4th session 1852. AN BB²⁰158; and v. G.-A. Nicolai, 1st session 1854. AN BB²⁰170.

94 Report, Procureur-général to Minister of Justice, 17 February 1819. AN BB¹⁸1049.

95 See Lawson (1910), p. 443; Fedotov (1966), I, pp. 255–6; and Meligrana (1979), pp. 310–11.

96 *Gaz. Trib.*, 3 July 1834, No. 2769; and Reports, President of Assize Court, 3rd session 1849. AN BB²⁰146; 4th session 1856. AN BB²⁰185; 1st session 1852. AN BB²⁰158; 2nd and 3rd sessions 1857. AN BB²⁰194; and 3rd session 1864. AN BB²⁰260.

97 *Gaz. Trib.*, 18 January 1835, No. 2936; Reports, Procureur-général, 4th session 1865. AN BB²⁰273; and Presidents, Assize Court, 1st session 1845. AN BB²⁰125; 1st session 1856. AN BB²⁰185; 4th session 1857. AN BB²⁰194; and 3rd session 1860. AN BB²⁰221.

98 Reports, Presidents, Assize Court, 1st and 2nd sessions 1844. AN BB²⁰125; 4th session 1846. AN BB²⁰134; 3rd session 1850. AN BB²⁰149; 2nd and 3rd sessions 1852. AN BB²⁰158; 4th session 1857. AN BB²⁰194; and 1st, 2nd and 4th sessions 1864. AN BB²⁰260.

99 Busquet (1919), pp. 121–4 and 361–4.

100 Mattei (1912), p. 1; also *Gaz. Trib.*, 4 March 1827, No. 451; Sorbier (1833), p. 10; Barry (1893), pp. 280–1; Rémy (1930), p. 63; and Guitet-Vauquelin (1934), pp. 143–57.

101 Reports, Commissaire spécial, 17 June 1818, cit. Franceschini (1924), p. 125; and Procureur-général to Minister of Justice, 19 August 1821. AN BB¹⁸243.

102 Cases v. F. Antonetti et al.; and v. C. Ciosi and A. Bottacci, Assize Court, 2nd session; and v. G. Filippi et al., 3rd session 1850. AN BB²⁰149; and v. P.-F. Angelini et al., 1st session 1851, Extraordinary sitting. AN BB²⁰152.

103 Case v. Casanova and Mattei, 2nd session 1833. *Gaz. Trib.*, 4 August 1833, No. 2488.

104 Case v. I. Borelli, Assize Court, 3rd session 1849. AN BB²⁰146.

105 Letter, S. Castelli to Procureur-général, 27 May 1912. ADCS 1.M.231; and Case v. G. M. Borelli, 2nd session 1853, Extraordinary sitting. AN BB²⁰164.

106 Mérimée (1840b), p. 668.

107 Report, Procureur-général to Minister of Justice, 1818; and other documents. AN BB¹⁸243.

108 Cases v. G.-G. Renosi, Assize Court, 2nd session 1833. *Gaz. Trib.*, 7 July 1833, cit. Sorbier (1863), pp. 36–8; v. A.-V. Pacchiarelli and F.-M. Canazzi, 4th session 1865. AN BB^{20}273; and v. O.-M. Chiapperoni, 2nd session 1851, Extraordinary sitting. AN BB^{20}152.

109 Busquet (1919), p. 554; and Petition for clemency for C.-G. Alfonsi et al., 1884. AN BB^{24}882.

110 Cases v. G. Raffaelli, Assize Court, 2nd session 1864. AN BB^{20}260; and v. F. Raffini, 2nd session 1851. AN BB^{20}152; and Patorni (1842), pp. 69–70.

111 Cases v. Don G. Peretti, 4th session 1853, Extraordinary sitting. AN BB^{20}164; and v. P. Arrighi, 1st session 1851, Extraordinary sitting. AN BB^{20}152.

112 Cases v. N. Paoli, 1st session 1842. AN BB^{20}116; v. A.-F. Quilichi, 3rd session 1849. AN BB^{20}146; and v. G.-A. Istria, 2nd session 1850. AN BB^{20}149.

113 Petition for clemency for A.-F. and S. Bernardini and A.-A. Viggioni, 1832. AN BB^{24}116–35; Cases v. Antonmarchi and Morelli, 4th session 1831. *Gaz. Trib.*, 1 January 1832, No. 1991; v. G. Negroni, 4th session 1838. *Gaz. Trib.*, 5th January 1839, No. 4156; and v. M. Luciani, 1st session, Extraordinary sitting. AN BB^{20}152.

114 Case v. G.-F. Giocondi, 1st session 1851, Extraordinary sitting. AN BB^{20}152.

115 Case v. A.-P. Canacci, 1st session 1846. AN BB^{20}134.

116 Marcaggi (1932), p. 46. Régis and Martin (n.d.), pp. 122–3, referring to a case before the Assize Court in December 1900, give a slightly different account.

117 Cases v. N. Giordani, Assize Court, 1st session 1851. Extraordinary sitting. AN BB^{20}152; and v. A.-P. Orsini, 2nd session 1842. AN BB^{20}116.

118 Cases v. F. di Q. Susini, 2nd session 1860. AN BB^{20}221; and v. S. Battini, 2nd session 1851. AN BB^{20}152.

119 Réalier-Dumas (1819), p. 20; and Busquet (1919), p. 621.

120 Letters, Comte Willot to Minister of War, 1817. AN BB^{18}1014; and Procureur-général to Minister of Justice, 14 January 1815. AN BB^{18}242.

121 Cases v. V. Casile, 1st session 1844. AN BB^{20}125; v. N. Tenneroni, 2nd session 1845. AN BB^{20}130; and v. S. Poggi, 3rd session 1842. AN BB^{20}116.

122 Cases v. G.-A. Anziani, 4th session 1854, Extraordinary sitting. AN BB^{20}170; v. A. and D. Anziani, 1st session 1842. AN BB^{20}116; v. C. Balisoni, 2nd session 1853, Extraordinary sitting. AN BB^{20}164; and v. L. Moreschi; and v. M. Versini, 1st session 1849. AN BB^{20}146.

123 Letter re unidentified case, Extraordinary Criminal Court, 26 Floréal An IX. ADCS 7.U.1/3; Letter, Procureur-général to Minister of Justice, 31 October 1825. AN BB^{18}1132; Case v. M. Grimaldi, Assize Court, 3rd session 1865. AN BB^{20}273; and Petition for clemency for G.-A. Santucci, 1882. AN BB^{24}881.

124 Petitions for clemency for S.-P. Agostini, 1833. AN BB^{24}116–35; and for P. Balisoni et al., 1863. AN BB^{24}687–709.

125 Newspapers and presidents for the Assize Court (who reported every session on the state of prisons) agreed generally that they were unhealthy, overcrowded, insecure and promiscuous; see e.g. Chronique départementale, Sartène. *Gaz. Trib.*, 18 January 1842, No. 4611; Reports, Presidents, Assize Court, 2nd session 1852. AN BB^{20}158; and 2nd session 1857. AN BB^{20}194.

126 Bigot (1890), p. 460; Petitions for clemency for F. Serpaggi and B. Pianchi, 1842. AN BB^{24}195–218; and for P. Quastana, 1860. AN BB^{24}605–21.

127 Cases v. G. Chiaroni, Assize Court, 1st session 1843. AN BB^{20}121; v. P. Tafanelli, 2nd session 1853, Extraordinary sitting. AN BB^{20}164; and v. F. di Q. Susini, 2nd session 1860. AN BB^{20}221.

128 Petitions for clemency for G.-D. and S. Santini, 1858–76. AN BB^{24}534–40; and for P.-D. Ficoni, 1878–84. AN BB^{24}875.

11 Patronage and political conflict

1 E.g. Fustel de Coulanges (1916), pp. 128–30, 273–8 and 306–21; Gelzer (1969), pp. 62–110, 136 and 160; Campbell (1964), Ch. IX; Weingrod (1968); Powell (1970); Kaufman (1974); and Mouzelis (1978).

2 See Tarrow (1967), esp. pp. 293, 325ff and 349ff; Weingrod (1968), pp. 381–98; Kaufman (1974), p. 305; and Blok (1975), esp. Ch. V.

3 Gilmore (1977).

4 Littlewood (1974); see also Byock (1982), Ch. V.

5 E.g. Brown (1971), pp. 86–7. This may be more likely where patrons have sacred authority; see also Barth (1965), Ch. 8; and Gellner (1969).

6 Robiquet (1835), p. 396; Galletti (1863), p. 563; and Bourde (1887), pp. 17–19; see also Beaumont (1822), p. 36; Report, President, Assize Court, 2nd session 1850. AN BB²⁰149; Arrighi (1896), p. 18; and Barth (1965), p. 73 (on Swat Pathans): 'Since leaders are permanently in competition, the sources of their authority are most clearly exhibited in situations of conflict.'

7 Report, Commander, Gendarmerie, 8 July 1821, cit. Franceschini (1919), p. 75; and Abeau (1888), p. 18.

8 Versini (1979), pp. 55–6; Bourde (1887), pp. 9–12; Fée (1850), pp. 38–42; Malaspina (1876), pp. 373–4; Lorenzi de Bradi (1928), p. 157; Natali (1934); Roger (1945), pp. 185–6; Gregorovius (1855), p. 139; and Report, Procureur-général to Minister of Justice, 1818. AN BB¹⁸243.

9 Griffon (1841), pp. 24–5; Montherot (1840), pp. 28–9; Mérimée (1840b), p. 668; Abeau (1888), p. 18; see also Bigot (1890), pp. 452 and 459.

10 N. Susini (1871).

11 Rapport Mottet, cit. Versini (1979), p. 181; Bourde (1887), pp. 6–7; also Robiquet (1835), pp. 388–9.

12 Malaspina (1876), p. 374; Abeau (1888), p. 18; also Pomponi (1978a), p. 23.

13 Bigot (1890), pp. 450, 452, 458 and 459.

14 Mérimée (1840a), p. 515; Bourde (1887), pp. 12–14; Bennet (1876), p. 64; Montherot (1840), pp. 12–13; Franceschini (1924), p. 111, citing Report, Commissaire spécial, 27 May 1818; and Petition for clemency for G.-F. Graziani, 1884. AN BB²⁴886.

15 Case v. C.-M. Rossi, Assize Court, 3rd session 1834. *Gaz. Trib.*, 8 October 1834, No. 2850; and Report, Procureur-général, Aix-en-Provence, 28 July 1835, Petition for clemency for C.-M. Rossi. AN BB²⁴155–69. Giulj was acquitted at Aix and Rossi again convicted.

16 Case v. G. Filippi et al., Assize Court, 3rd session 1850. AN BB²⁰149; Versini (1972), pp. 71–9; and Weber (1979), p. 293.

17 E.g. Lists of primary school pupils, 1866–81; and of paupers, 1872. Venzolasca. ADHC E.18/25 and 26; and Report, Prefect, 23 December 1872. AN F⁷12849.

18 Patin de La Fizelière (1963), p. 72; Glatigny (1870), p. 64; Vanutberghe (1904), pp. 338–9; Bourde (1887), pp. 27–8 and 46–7; and Renucci (1974), pp. 84–5, 88–9, 144 and 146; also Bigot (1890), p. 460; Lorenzi de Bradi (1928), p. 140; Southwell Colucci (1933), p. 150; Vidalenc (1966), p. 81; Santoni (1978), p. 226; Versini (1979), pp. 46–9; and Christophari (1981), p. 178.

19 Réalier-Dumas (1819), p. 25; Maurras (1920), p. 147; and Molinari (1886), p. 234; also Robiquet (1835), pp. 406–8; and Ravis-Giordani (1976a), pp. 176–7.

20 ADCS 2.M.86; 2.M.88; 2.M.84; and 2.M.140.

21 Note, Ministry of Justice, 14 January 1893. AN BB¹⁸1927; Casta (1974), p. 189; Note, Subprefect, 21 May; and Letter, Father Maraninchi to Prefect, 11 June 1887. ADCS 2.V.20. Under the concordatory régime in France, ecclesiastical appointments were made by negotiation between the state and church authorities.

22 Casta (1974), p. 176; Delarue (1970), Chs. IX and XIII; 'Faisons une guerre acharnée à la patronage', *Journal de la Corse*, 21 July 1857; and AN BB¹⁸1569.

23 Case v. G. Casalonga et al., Assize Court, 2nd session 1839, *Gaz. Trib.*, 10 July 1839, No.4317; and Sorbier (1863), pp. 150–65; also Lemps (1844), p. 169.

24 Bourde (1887), p. 125; Letters, V. Roccaserra to Prefect, 4 December 1846. ADCS 2.M.88; and Arrighi to Subprefect, 3 December 1850. ADCS 2.V.19.

25 Letter, A.-M. Santuccj to Minister of Justice, An XIII(?). AN BB¹⁸238; Report, Commissaire spécial, 11 March 1817, cit. Franceschini (1922), p. 263; Letters G. Greffini to Commissaire du gouvernement près le Tribunal Criminel Extraordinaire, 23 Vendémiaire An XI. ADCS 7.U.1/9; and Subprefect, Ajaccio, to Prefect, 4 January 1827. ADCS 4.M.91.

26 Bourde (1887), pp. 20–5. In the event, the huge sums proposed led the government to postpone both projects and to introduce a new system of awarding compensation, which attempted to obviate the influence of patronage.

27 Letter, F. Susini to Prefect, 2 January 1847. ADCS 2.M.84.

28 Robiquet (1835), p. 392; also Rapport Mottet, 1836, cit. Versini (1979), pp. 173–4.

29 E.g. Choury (1958), pp. 20–2; Emmanuelli (1971b), p. 409; Cristofini et al. (1978), p. 104; and Versini (1979), pp. 57–9; see also Chapter 7, pp. 179–80.

30 Volney (1825), VII, pp. 316–17; Santoni (1978), pp. 224–6; Pomponi (1978a); and Ravis-Giordani (1976a), pp. 176–86.

31 E.g. Choury (1958), p. 21; and Demailly (1978), pp. 106 and 110; see also Thiers (1977), pp. 21–2; Pomponi (1977), pp. 93–4; and Lenclud and Pernet (1978), pp. 68–9.

32 Casta (1974), pp. 161–2 and 178; Versini (1979), pp. 39–41; and Sacquin-Moulin (1982), p. 651.

33 Balteau et al. (1933), I, Cols. 68–72; and (1956), VII, Cols. 1289–93; Stead (1957), pp. 119–20; Luciani (1969), p. 73; Pomponi (1979b), pp. 366–7; and Versini (1979), p. 74.

34 Saint-Germain (1869), p. 145; and Report, Prefect, 23 December 1872. AN F⁷12849; also Luciani (1969), pp. 70–1.

35 Lorenzi de Bradi (1928), pp. 268–71; Balteau et al. (1939), III, Cols. 474–7; Roger (1945), p. 253; and Christophari (1981), pp. 181–3.

36 Maurras (1920), pp. 146–7; and Christophari (1981), pp. 178–80; also Lorenzi de Bradi (1928), p. 265.

37 Bourde (1887), pp. 9–12; Letters, Mayor, Cozzano, to Prefect, 18 November 1846. ADCS 2.M.81; and Subprefect, Bastia, to Prefect, 2 May 1865. ADCS 2.M.158; Christophari (1981), pp. 182–3; and Lorenzi (1981).

38 Bourde (1887), pp. 46–8 and 50–3; Lorenzi de Bradi (1928), p. 268; Maestrati (1964), esp. pp. 48–9; Renucci (1974), pp. 89–96; and Bigot (1890), p. 158.

39 E.g. *Journal du Département de la Corse*, November-December 1830; Blanqui (1841), p. 531; and Bigot (1890), p. 477.

40 Letter, G.-A. Maestrati to Prefect, 1846. ADCS 2.M.83; and Bourde (1887), pp. 39–41, 44–5 and 53.

41 Lenclud and Pernet (1978), p. 65; also J. Schneider (1971), p. 6.

42 Lorenzi de Bradi (1928), pp. 143–4, 265 and 276; Patin de La Fizelière (1963), p. 65; Metz-Noblat (1885), p. 55; Piobb (n.d.), p. 51; Filippi (1906), p. 28; and Lenclud (1979), p. 13.

43 Bigot (1890), p. 459; Molinari (1886), p. 238; and Petition for clemency for D. Ficoni, 1883. AN BB²⁴875.

44 E.g. Gelzer (1969), pp. 123–36; and Waley (1978), pp. 115–26.

45 E.g. Levi (1948), pp. 20 and 232 (S. Italy); Fenton (1952) (American Indians); Firth et al. (1957) (Indians); Brandon-Albini (1963), p. 65 (S. Italy); Boissevain (1965), esp.

pp. 74–96 (Malta); Morin (1971), pp. 42 and 166 (Brittany); Trueba (1973) (Nahuat); and Zonabend (1980), pp. 25, 45–6, 274–5 and 306 (Burgundy).

46 Gross (1973); Siegel and Beals (1960a); and (1960b); Riegelhaupt (1973), p. 837; and Foster (1961), pp. 1190–1.

47 Maestrati (1964), pp. 48–9; Bourde (1887), pp. 50–3; Lorenzi de Bradi (1928), pp. 268–71; and Choury (1958), pp. 21–2.

48 Letter, Juge de paix Gabrielli, to Prefect, 15 February 1848. ADCS 2.M.88; Case v. A.-F. Quilichi, Assize Court, 3rd session 1849. AN BB^{20}146; and Chiva (1958), p. 146; see also Coppolani (1949), p. 81; Lenclud and Ravis-Giordani (1973), p. 214; Ravis-Giordani (1976a), p. 183; and Pernet and Lenclud (1977), p. 114.

49 Letter, Subprefect, Bastia, 3 April 1866. ADCS 2.M.158; and Report, Procureur-général, 22 August 1879, Petition for clemency for G. Vittori. AN BB^{24}868.

50 Pomponi (1978a), p. 16; also Robiquet (1835), p. 385, citing Cyrnaeus; and Lamotte (1956a), p. 38.

51 Thrasher (1970), Ch. 4 and 17–24; and Pomponi (1979b), Part III.

52 E.g. Lamotte (1956e).

53 Report, Procureur-général, 7 May 1885, Petition for clemency for G.-A. Piazza. AN BB^{24}888; and Letter, Parish priest, Zerubia, to Prefect, 23 November 1846. ADCS 2.M.88.

54 Lenclud and Pernet (1978), p. 62.

55 Letter to Prefect, 24 July 1860. ADCS 2.M.149.

56 Report, Procureur-général, 17 January 1833. AN BB^{24}116–35; Ravis-Giordani (1979a), pp. 67–9; Reports, Prefect, 22 September 1816. AN BB^{18}243; and Subprefect, Sartène, 21 January 1830. ADCS 4.M.100; and, for a parallel, Barth (1965), esp. p. 108.

57 Coppolani (1949), p. 107; Letter, Procureur-général, Golo, to Minister of Justice, 18 Thermidor An XIII. AN BB^{18}238; Surier (1934), p. 226; Ettori (1971), esp. p. 281; Pomponi (1976c), esp. p. 158; and Pomponi (1978a), pp. 13 and 15.

58 E.g. Letters, Subprefects to Prefect, 1836 (Arbellara); and 1840(?) (Bisinchi). ADCS 2.M.79; and Letter, A.-Q. Roccaserra to Minister of Justice, 3 January 1879, Petition for clemency for same. AN BB^{24}852.

59 *Gaz. Trib.*, 9 January 1846, No.5776; and Morandière (1933), pp. 77–8; see also Bourde (1887), p. 12; and Le Joindre (1904), pp. 74–5.

60 Case v. G.-G. Renusi, Assize Court, 4th session 1861. AN BB^{20}229; Printed Judgment, Court of Criminal Justice, Bastia, August 1810. AN BB^{18}239; and Case v. F.-G. Luporsi et al., Assize Court, 3rd session 1849. AN BB^{20}146.

61 Petition for clemency for S.-P. Agostini, 1833. AN BB^{24}116–35; Cases v. A. Canacci and O.-F. Lucioni, Assize Court, 1st session 1839. *Gaz. Trib.*, 30 March 1839, No.4229; v. P.-F. Giannettini, 2nd session 1843. AN BB^{20}121; and v. A.-P. Canacci, 1st session 1846. AN BB^{20}134; Montherot (1840), pp. 76–7; Report, Gendarmerie, Bastia, 5 February 1841. ADCS 4.M.125; and Letter, Municipal councillors, Bisinchi, to Subprefect, 1845(?). ADCS 2.M.79.

62 E.g. Weingrod (1968), pp. 392–3 (Sardinia); and Littlewood (1974), p. 38 (Apulia).

63 Martelli (1960), p. 238.

64 Letters, Mayor, Peri, to Prefect, 16 October 1852. ADCS 2.M.140; Subprefect, Sartène, to Prefect, 20 April 1831. ADCS 2.M.82; and 22 March 1867; and 1869. ADCS 2.M.126; and A.-G. Quilichini to Prefect, 15 November 1846. ADCS 2.M.85.

65 Bourde (1887), pp. 82 and 39–43; also Ravis-Giordani (1976a), pp. 174–5.

66 E.g. Appolis (1964), p. 95, citing the priest of the Greek rite in Cargese in 1830; Rapport Mottet, 1836, cit. Versini (1979), p. 171; Letters, to Prefect, 3 December 1854. ADCS 2.M.126 (Figari); and Subprefect to Prefect, 2 May 1865. ADCS 2.M.158 (Venzolasca); Spalinowski (1909), pp. 86–93; and Deane (1965), pp. 146–50.

67 Case v. P. Franceschi, Assize Court, 2nd session 1853. AN BB[20]164; cit. Pomponi (1976c), p. 158; Report, Commissaire de police, Zicavo, to Prefect, 29 March 1855. ADCS 2.M.124; and Letter to Prefect, 1846. ADCS 2.M.88.

68 ADCS 2.M.83 (Muro); Letter, Curé of Nonza to Prefect, 11 June 1887. ADCS 2.V.20; and Finelli (n.d.), p. 15. It is not implied that these particular mayors were despotic.

69 Report, Subprefect to Prefect, 25 November 1840. ADCS 2.M.87; and Franceschini (1918), p. 56.

70 E.g. Note, Ministry of the Interior to Prefect, 9 September 1809. ADCS 2.M.54 (Tavera); and Letters to Prefect, 1846. ADCS 2.M.84 (Ota); and ADCS 2.M.87 (Santa-Lucia-di-Moriani).

71 Réalier-Dumas (1819), p. 51; Letter to Prefect, 6 November 1850. ADCS 2.V.19; and Letter to Prefect, n.d. ADCS 2.M.83; also Letters, Juge de paix Gabrielli to Prefect, 15 February 1848. ADCS 2.M.88 (Prato); to same, 14 July 1865. ADCS 2.M.144 (Pila-Canale); and Prefect to Subprefect, 23 April 1867; and Arrêté, 9 July 1868. ADCS 2.M.126.

72 ADCS 2.M.65; Letter, Minister of the Interior to Prefect, 31 March 1845. ADCS 2.M.85; and Letters, Procureur-général to Prefect, 17 September; and Prefect to Minister of the Interior, 20 September 1858. ADCS 2.M.140.

73 Letters, Acting Subprefect to Prefect, 24 April 1845. ADCS 2.M.87; Ten municipal councillors, Aullène, to same, 20 September 1846. ADCS 2.M.79; S. Pandolfi to same, 25 October 1846. ADCS 2.M.86; and ADCS 2.M.88.

74 Versini (1979), pp. 60–1 and 171; and Spalinowski (1909), pp. 84–5; also Molinari (1886), pp. 272–3.

75 Letters, Subprefect to Prefect, 20 April 1822. ADCS 2.M.55; and 8 June 1836. ADCS 2.M.83; Ministry of the Interior to Prefect, 23 July 1836. ADCS 2.M.79; and Sergeant Saliceti to General(?), 27 November 1844. ADCS 2.M.82.

76 Letters, Minister of the Interior to Prefect, 31 March; and Prefect to Minister of the Interior, 30 April 1845. ADCS 2.M.85; Letters to Prefect, 1846; and 30 November 1847. ADCS 2.M.88.

77 Cases v. P.-P. Ordioni; and v. G.-A. Mariani, Assize Court, 3rd session 1861. AN BB[20]229.

78 E.g. Bigot (1890), p. 457; and Letters to Prefect, 1 March 1864. ADCS 2.M.116; and Subprefect, Bastia, to Prefect, 28 December 1865. ADCS 2.M.158.

79 Molinari (1886), pp. 272–3; Roger (1945), p. 186; Pomponi (1976c), p. 158; Reports, Procureur-général to Minister of Justice, 12 September 1811. AN BB[18]241 (Lama); and Subprefect to Prefect, 14 December 1865. ADCS 2.M.158 (Venzolasca); and Petition for clemency for A.-A. Moretti. AN BB[24]887 (Pianello).

80 Letters, G. Susini to Prefect, September 1846. ADCS 2.M.81; F.-M. Allegrini et al. to same, 8 July 1847. ADCS 2.M.79; and A.-F. Paolacci to same, 6 November 1850. ADCS 2.V.19; also Pomponi (1976c), p. 156.

81 Appolis (1964), pp. 93 and 95.

82 Letters, Subprefect to Prefect, 8 June 1836. ADCS 2.M.83; and G. Simoni to Subprefect, 25 June 1854. ADCS 2.M.126; also Deliberations, Municipal Council, Penta-di-Casinca, 1840, 1854, 1857 and 1863. ADHC E.29/7–8; and Venzolasca, 1872, 1881 and 1900. ADHC E.18/3 and E.18/26; Bourde (1887), pp. 110–11; Franceschini (1918), p. 44, citing a report by Prefect Arrighi of 15 January 1813 on the low status of field guards; and Pomponi (1976c), p. 160.

83 Letter, A. Lanfranchi to Prefect, 1 February 1847. ADCS 2.M.84.

84 Pomponi (1976c), pp. 161–2; and Ravis-Giordani (1976a), pp. 172–4.

85 E.g. Letters to Prefect, 1846(?). ADCS 2.M.84 (Ota); and 26 January 1847. ADCS 2.M.83 (Levie).

86 Letters, V. Roccaserra to Prefect, 1846. ADCS 2.M.88; and Gendarmerie to same, 30 December 1846. ADCS 2.M.84; and Bourde (1887), pp. 107–8.

87 Letters, P. Santoni, to Prefect, 18 November 1854. ADCS 2.M.127; and Subprefect to same, 26 December 1836. ADCS 2.M.86; Pomponi (1976c), pp. 161–2; and Bourde (1887), pp. 108–9.

88 Report, Procureur-général to Minister of Justice, 12 September 1811; and other documents. AN BB^{18}241. Following a formal complaint, the prefect ordered a new auction, to be held in the subprefect's office in Bastia.

89 Notes, Ministry of the Interior to Prefect, 19 April and 9 May 1865. ADCS 2.M.116; Report, Subprefect to Prefect, 2 May 1865. ADCS 2.M.158; Letters, A. Vincentelli to Prefect, 3 December 1846. ADCS 2.M.87; Limperani et al., to same, 31 August 1867. ADCS 2.M.140; and Bourde (1887), pp. 168–70; also Pomponi (1976c), pp. 161–2.

90 Reports, Subprefect to Prefect, 13 September and 24 November 1853; and Revocation notice, 12 January 1854. ADCS 2.M.126; and Letter, F.-M. Geronimi to Prefect, 28 May 1860. ADCS 2.M.138.

91 Pomponi (1976c), p. 160; Letters, F. Fugianelli to Minister of Justice, 1869. ADCS 2.M.137; L. Luciani et al., to President of the Republic, 31 August 1877; and Acting Subprefect to Mayor, Venzolasca, 18 April 1879. ADHC E.18/26.

92 Letter, Tomasi et al., to Prefect, 14 October 1874. ADCS 2.M.162; and Bourde (1887), pp. 115–18; also Case v. N. Ceccaldi, Assize Court, 4th session 1852, Extraordinary sitting. AN BB^{20}158 (Piana).

93 Case v. D.-L. Antonmarchi, Assize Court, 4th session 1835. *Gaz. Trib.*, 26 February 1836, cit. Sorbier (1863), pp. 72–6; Letter to Prefect, 9 April 1845. ADCS 2.M.85; and Petitions for clemency for F. Bastianesi, 1852–85. AN BB^{24}798.

94 Pomponi (1976c), pp. 162–3; Case v. M. Leoni, Assize Court, 3rd session 1863. AN BB^{20}249; Report, Prefect to Minister of the Interior, 9 September 1862. ADCS 2.M.140; and Revocation notice, 20 January 1862. ADCS 2.M.158.

95 Reports, Commissaire du gouvernement, Liamone, to Minister of Justice, 21 Nivôse An XII. AN BB^{18}236 (Alata); and Minister of the Interior to Prefect, 20 March 1806. ADCS 2.M.54 (Levie); Bourde (1887), pp. 122–3; and Pomponi (1976c), pp. 162–3.

96 Letters, Ministry of the Interior to Prefect, 23 July 1836. ADCS 2.M.79; V. Roccaserra to Prefect, 1846. ADCS 2.M.88; Mayor Castellini to same, 20 January 1853. ADCS 2.M.138; P. Pantalucci to same, 4 July 1843. ADCS 2.M.81; Subprefect to same, 8 June 1836. ADCS 2.M.83; Procureur-général to Minister of Justice, 18 November; and Letter, D. Pietri, 28 September 1868. AN BB^{18}1728; Bourde (1887), pp. 120–2; Spalinowski (1909), pp. 84–5; Letters, F.-M. Allegrini et al. to Prefect, 8 July 1847. ADCS 2.M.79; and Limperani et al. to same, 31 August 1867. ADCS 2.M.140; Deliberations, Municipal Council, Penta-di-Casinca, 20 July 1868; and 9 December 1869. ADHC E.29/8; and Molinari (1886), pp. 272–3.

97 Bourde (1887), pp. 111–14; and Letter, D. Guidicelli et al. to Prefect, 30 November 1847. ADCS 2.M.88.

98 Case v. G. Casalonga, Assize Court, 2nd session 1839, *Gaz. Trib.*, 10 July 1839, No. 4317; and Finelli (n.d.), pp. 25 and 30.

99 Cit. Dalmas (1978), p. 16.

100 Letters, Prefect(?) to Mayor, Balogna, 13 September 1847. ADCS 2.M.79, Subprefect, Bastia, to Prefect, 2 May 1865. ADCS 2.M.158; and S. Quilichini et al. to same, 28 September 1843. ADCS 2.M.81.

101 Case v. G. and D.-F. Casalta, Assize Court, 2nd session 1834, *Gaz. Trib.*, 2 October 1834, No.2845; and Letter, F.-M. Allegrini et al., to Prefect, 8 July 1847. ADCS 2.M.79.

102 Cases v. P. Negroni, Assize Court, 3rd session 1833; and v. P. Giovanelli, 4th session 1832. *Gaz. Trib.*, 30 October and 3 January 1833, Nos. 2562 and 2305.

103 Letters, Procureur-général, Golo, to Minister of Justice, 18 Thermidor An XIII. AN BB¹⁸238; and G. Renucci to Prefect, 2 December 1846. ADCS 2.M.81; also Report, Commissaire spécial, 25 February 1818, cit. Franceschini (1923), p. 45.

104 E.g. Villat (1932), p. 152 (Prunelli-di-Fiumorbo); and see Chapter 12, pp. 368–70.

105 Letter, Mayor, Calenzana, to Minister of Justice, 16 September; and Reports, Prefect, 22 September; and Procureur-général to same, 10 December 1816. AN BB¹⁸243; see also Letter, S. and O.-D. Mondolini to Prefect, 17 July 1847. ADCS 2.M.81 (Cozzano).

106 Report, Prefect to Ministry of the Interior, 11 March 1859. ADCS 2.M.123.

107 Cases v. S.-F. Ristori, Assize Court, 1st session; and v. P. Franceschi, 2nd session 1853. AN BB²⁰164; and Report, Procureur-général to Prefect, 11 April 1864. ADCS 2.M.116.

108 Petition for clemency for O.-T. Campana, 1885. AN BB²⁴888.

109 Case v. ... , Assize Court, 2nd session 1840. *Gaz. Trib.*, 19 July 1840, No. 4637; Letter, Juge de paix Gabrielli to Prefect, 15 February 1848. ADCS 2.M.88; Case v. S. and M.-A. Panzani et al., Tribunal correctionnel, Sartène, 18 February 1824. ADCS 3.U.5/174; Report, Gendarmerie, Ajaccio, 15 January 1841. ADCS 4.M.125; and Letter to Prefect, 24 July 1860. ADCS 2.M.149.

110 See Letters, Mayor(?) to Prefect, 7 February 1847. ADCS 2.M.84 (Petreto-Bicchisano); Juge de paix Gabrielli to same, 15 February 1848. ADCS 2.M.88 (Prato); Finelli (n.d.), pp. 54–5 (Tavera); and Zuccarelli (n.d.), pp. 115–16 (Santa-Lucia-di-Mercurio).

111 *Gaz. Trib.*, 4 August 1833, No.2488; and Report, Procureur-général to Minister of Justice, 2 March 1842. AN BB¹⁸1399.

112 Letter, Procureur-général to Minister of Justice, 22 August 1837. AN BB¹⁸1248; Bourde (1887), p. 94; Letters, Subprefect, Sartène, to Prefect, 23 November 1846; and Mayor, Zerubia to same, 3 February 1848. ADCS 2.M.88; and Report, Subprefect, Corte, to same, 4 February 1851. ADCS 2.M.82; see also Report, Gendarmerie, 10 May 1855. ADCS 2.M.138 (Ota); and Subprefect, Bastia, to Prefect, 4 September 1866. ADCS 2.M.140 (Penta); Letters, Subprefect to Prefect, 9 May 1834; and 30 November 1835. ADCS 2.M.83 (Muro); 26 December 1836. ADCS 2.M.86 (Serra-di-Scopamène); 6 March 1837. ADCS 2.M.79 (Aullène); 30 April and 30 June 1843. ADCS 2.M.84 (Olmeto); Mayor to Prefect, 3 December 1850. ADCS 2.V.19 (Noceta); 1 March 1864. ADCS 2.M.116 (Bastelica); and Prefect to Procureur-général, 20 July 1867. ADCS 2.M.123 (Ciamannacce).

113 E.g. Greffe, Tribunal correctionnel, Ajaccio, 3 July 1815. AN BB¹⁸241 (Ajaccio); Report, Subprefect, Sartène, 17 October 1826. ADCS 4.M.99 (Fozzano); and Case v. P. Giacomoni et al., 2nd session 1848, Assize Court. *Gaz. Trib.*, 22 July 1848, No.6568 (Loreto-di-Tallano).

114 Report, Subprefect, Sartène, 26 March 1826. ADCS 4.M.99; Cases v. N. Ceccaldi, Assize Court, 4th session 1852, Extraordinary sitting. AN BB²⁰158; and v. G. Poggi and P. Antona, 3rd session 1857. AN BB²⁰194.

115 Reports, Gendarmerie, Ajaccio, 4 November 1841. ADCS 4.M.125; Subprefect, 12 November 1827. ADCS 4.M.99; and Case v. A. Costa, Assize Court, 2nd session 1853. AN BB²⁰164.

116 Letter, Procureur-général to Minister of Justice, 4 January 1813. AN BB¹⁸241; Report, Gendarmerie, 4 October 1816. ADCS 4.M.102; Case v. M.-F. Quilichini, Assize Court, 1st session 1846. AN BB²⁰134; Letter to Prefect, 9 September 1846. ADCS 2.M.87; and Case v. R. Mariani, Assize Court, 2nd session 1853. AN BB²⁰164.

117 Cases v. G.-D. Bazziconi, 1st session 1851. AN BB²⁰152; v. C. Susini, 3rd session 1842. AN BB²⁰116; and v. I. Capponi, 3rd session 1848. AN BB²⁰142.

118 Ravis-Giordani (1976a), p. 184. The mayor and *adjoint* of Pietricaggio were suspected

of acting in collusion in 1865 to rig the municipal elections, for instance. Report to Ministry of Justice, 27 January 1866. AN BB[18]1725.

119 Letters, Subprefect to Prefect, 27 August 1834. ADCS 2.M.87; D. Piani et al. to same, 9 April 1858. ADCS 2.M.149; and Mayor, Pila-Canale, to same, 18 March 1866. ADCS 2.M.144.

120 Report, Procureur-général to Minister of Justice, 12 September 1811; and other documents. AN BB[18]241; and Case v. F., G.-F. and L. Palmesani, Assize Court, 1st session 1865. AN BB[20]273.

121 See Chapter 8, pp. 227–9.

122 Letters, Mayor, Bastelica, to Prefect, 15 June 1846. ADCS 2.M.79; and Limperani et al., to same, 31 August 1867. ADCS 2.M.140.

123 Case v. A.-P. Trojani, Assize Court, 2nd session 1850. AN BB[20]149; Letters, S. Mattei et al. to Prefect, 1846(?). ADCS 2.M.84; Parish priest, Zerubia, 23 November 1846; and V. Roccaserra to same, 1846. ADCS 2.M.88; and Municipal councillors, Figari, to same, 3 December 1854. ADCS 2.M.126; and Bourde (1887), p. 62; see also Chapter 8, pp. 243–5.

124 Letters, Castelli to Procureur-général, 27 May 1912. ADCS 1.M.231; and A.-F. Paolacci to Prefect, 6 November 1850. ADCS 2.V.19.

125 Bourde (1887), pp. 58–61 and 115–19; Report, Commissaire spécial, 21 December 1817, cit. Franceschini (1922), p. 339; and Report, Procureur-général to Minister of Justice, 19 June 1871. AN BB[30]489; and Busquet (1919), p. 554.

126 Report, Procureur du Roi, Corte, to Procureur-général, 15 September 1827. AN BB[18]1249; Cases v. D. A. Leca, Assize Court, 2nd session 1833. *Gaz. Trib.*, 8 July 1833, cit. Sorbier (1863), pp. 34–5; and v. 9 persons, Campitello, 1st session 1849, Extraordinary sitting. AN BB[20]146.

127 Circulars, 31 August 1871; and 1 December 1875. AN BB[30]489.

128 E.g. Case v. G.-A. Candeli(?), Assize Court, 1st session 1837. *Gaz. Trib.*, 11 May 1837, No. 3640 (Juge de paix Roccaserra at Porto-Vecchio); Letter, Mayor, Piedicroce, to Minister of Justice, 29 July 1848. AN BB[18]1466 (Juge de paix Battesti); and Case v. G.-G. Renusi, 4th session 1861. AN BB[20]229 (Juge de paix Renucci at Pero-Casevecchie).

129 Reports, Procureur-général to Minister of Justice, 26 April 1876. AN BB[30]489; Ministry of Justice, 14 January 1893; and 27 November 1895. AN BB[18]1927; and Petition for clemency for C. Terramorsi, 1884. AN BB[24]885.

130 Case v. A.-F. Nesa, Assize Court, 1st session 1861. AN BB[20]229; and Réalier-Dumas (1819), p. 50.

131 Patorni (1842), pp. 175–7; Report, Procureur-général, to Minister of Justice, 21 May 1896. AN BB[18]2037; Case v. L. Pianelli, Tribunal correctionnel, Sartène, November 1812. ADCS 3.U.5/166; Petition for clemency for G.-A. Colombani et al., 1880. AN BB[24]868; and Report, Subprefecture, 30 August 1825. ADCS 4.M.99.

132 Cases v. M. Galloni d'Istria, Assize Court, 2nd session 1851. AN BB[20]152; and 4th session, 1852, Extraordinary sitting. AN BB[20]158; Report, Gendarmerie, Piana, 1880. AN F[7]12849; Bourde (1887), pp. 71–4 and 118; and Case v. M. Raffini, Assize Court, 4th session 1860. AN BB[20]221; see also Tommaseo (1841), p. 30.

133 Mérimée (1840b), pp. 734–7; Report, Commissaire spécial, 1 April 1818, cit. Franceschini (1923), p. 76; Benson (1825), pp. 31–2; and Case v. F. Istria, Assize Court, 2nd session 1851. Cases tried *in absentia*. AN BB[20]152.

134 Reports, Procureur-général to Minister of Justice, 1 March 1819. AN BB[18]243; and 29 May 1815. AN BB[18]241.

135 Facy (1933), p. 41; Ravis-Giordani (1976a), p. 181; Bourde (1887), pp. 6 and 9–12; and Barry (1893), pp. 107 and 161–2; also Volney (1825), VII, p. 321; Pomponi (1977), pp. 90–1; and Santoni (1978), p. 232.

136 Griffon (1841), pp. 24–5; Report, Procureur-général, 19 November 1884, Petition for clemency for G.-S. Giacobbi. AN BB²⁴886; Emmanuelli (1971b), p. 409; Renucci (1974), pp. 89–91; and Pomponi (1976c), p. 164.

137 Bourde (1887), pp. 84–5; Rémy (1930), p. 65. Report, Procureur-général, to Minister of Justice, 14 November 1865; and other reports. AN BB¹⁸1724 and 1725.

138 Petition for clemency for V. Cesari, 1884. AN BB²⁴876; see also Report to Ministry of Justice, 12 October 1866. AN BB¹⁸1726; and Petition for clemency for G.-S. Giacobbi, 1884. AN BB²⁴886; for M. Cristini, 1885. AN BB²⁴887; and for M. Agostini, 1885. AN BB²⁴889.

139 Maestrati (1964); Rapport Mottet, 1836, cit. Versini (1979), p. 186; *Gaz. Trib.*, 22 July 1830, No. 1543; Susini della Rocca (1828); and Kent (1937), Ch. IV.

140 Bourde (1887), pp. 61–9; also Lefèbvre (1954), pp. 16–17.

141 'Venzolasca, Correspondance, 1850–89.' ADHC E.18/26; Bourde (1887), pp. 58 and 86; and Ponteil (1966), pp. 364–5.

142 Letters, Electors, Salice, to Minister of Justice, 23 August; and Gendarmerie to Procureur de la République, 14 October 1848. AN BB¹⁸1467A; Petition for clemency for D.-T. Serpentini, 1866. AN BB²⁴718; and Bourde (1887), pp. 86–93.

143 Report, Juge suppléant to Procureur-général, 17 October 1838. AN BB¹⁸1257; and Bourde (1887), pp. 74–81.

144 Letter, Prefect to Minister of the Interior, 14 December 1846. ADCS 2.M.85; Report to Minister of Justice, 16 March 1866. AN BB¹⁸1728; Petitions for clemency for A. Defendini, 1866. AN BB²⁴718; V. Casanova, 1877. AN BB²⁴843; and G.-S. Giacobbi, 1884. AN BB²⁴886.

145 Zuccarelli (n.d.), pp. 64–5; Ravis-Giordani (1976a); Lamotte (1956e), p. 41; and Christophari (1981), pp. 184–5.

146 Reports, Procureur-général, 14 January and 1 March 1884(?). AN BB²⁴876; and Ravis-Giordani (1976a), p. 175.

147 Letter, Mayor, Piedicroce, to Minister of Justice, 29 July 1848. AN BB¹⁸1466; De la Rocca (1858a); and (1858b); Letter, Mayor, Nonza, to Prefect, July 1891. ADCS 2.V.20; Report, Procureur-général to Minister of Justice, 26 April 1876. AN BB³⁰489; and Report, Ministry of Justice, 27 November 1895. AN BB¹⁸1927; also Lorenzi de Bradi (1928), p. 273.

148 Report, Procureur-général, 24 January 1885, Petition for clemency for F.-M. and A.-F. Roccaserra. AN BB²⁴886; and Case v. P.-M. Battesti(?), Assize Court, 2nd session 1893. AN BB²⁰286.

149 Arrêté, 30 March 1872, Venzolasca. ADHC E.18/26; Surier (1934), pp. 227–31; Petition for clemency for A.-A. Moretti, 1885. AN BB²⁴887; and Cases v. Padovani et al., Assize Court, 4th session 1893. AN BB²⁰286.

150 Zeldin (1958), pp. 83–4; Bodley (1899), pp. 338–43; Bourde (1887), p. 103; and Wagner (1968), p. 128, citing Galien.

151 Ravis-Giordani (1976a), pp. 186–8; and Bourde (1887), pp. 98 and 102–4.

152 Reports, Procureur-général to Minister of Justice, 1 March and 12 October 1866. AN BB¹⁸1726; 13 January, 12 April and 12 October 1866. AN BB¹⁸1728; and Petition for clemency for M. Cristini, 1885. AN BB²⁴887.

153 Letters, Procureur-général to Minister of Justice, 11 November 1865; and 10 July 1866; and other documents. AN BB¹⁸1724.

154 Reports, Procureur-général, 25 January 1856, Petition for clemency for L. and D. Saveri. AN BB²⁴484–8; and 12 July 1866. AN BB²⁴717; see also Surier (1934), pp. 227–31; and Ravis-Giordani (1976a), p. 182, on the more recent abuse of postal votes, known as 'the mayor's votes'.

155 Letter, Avocat-général to Minister of Justice, 5 August 1838; and other documents. AB BB¹⁸1255; Report, Ministry of Justice, 27 January 1866. AN BB¹⁸1725; Ravis-

Giordani (1976a), pp. 181–2; and Letters, Procureur-général to Minister of Justice, 28 December 1865; and 12 January 1866. AN BB[18]1726.

156 Bourde (1887), pp. 98–101 and 95–8; Marcaggi (1932), pp. 188–9; Christophari (1981), p. 182; and Surier (1934), pp. 227–9; see also Note 163 below.

157 Bertrand (1870), p. 109; see also Barry (1893), p. 107; Susini (1871); Girolami-Cortona (1893), p. 117; Mattei (1912), p. 53 and Lorenzi de Bradi (1928), p. 275.

158 Bourde (1887), p. 104; Bertrand (1870), pp. 109–10; Rapport Mottet, 1836, cit. Versini (1979), pp. 186–8; and Metz-Noblat (1885), p. 54.

159 Ravis-Giordani (1976a), pp. 181–2; Croze (1911), pp. 77–80; Marcaggi (1926), pp. 62–9; and Southwell Colucci (1933), p. 120.

160 Reports, Procureur-général to Minister of the Interior, 14 April 1896. AN BB[18]2035; Same to Minister of Justice, 27 April, and 10 July 1896. AN BB[18]2036; and Archer (1924), p. 99.

161 Report, Procureur-général, 7 May, Petition for clemency for G.-A. Piazza; and 17 June, Petition for O.-S. Campana; and Letter, E. Arène, 19 December 1885, Petition for G. Antonioli. AN BB[24]888.

162 Cases v. P.-F. Grazioni(?) et al., Assize Court, 1st session 1849, Extraordinary sitting. AN BB[20]146; v. F.-M. Ortoli et al., 1st session, Extraordinary sitting; and v. E. Ortoli et al., 2nd session 1851. AN BB[20]152; Bourde (1887), pp. 102–3; and Petitions for clemency for D. Doria; and P. Matteaccoli, 1879. AN BB[24]868; for G.-G. and E. Moracchini; and A.-A. Moretti, 1885. AN BB[24]887; and for G.-G. Ciccoli, 1885. AN BB[24]888; Reports, Gendarmerie, Soccia, 26 September; and Vico, 2 October 1892. AN F[7]12849; and Cases v. A.-G. Poli et al., Assize Court, 2nd session 1893. AN BB[20]286.

163 Petitions for clemency for G.-F.-E. and D.-A. Graziani, 1884. AN BB[24]886; for O.-M. Bagnoli, 1885. AN BB[24]887; and for L.-N. Graziani, 1885. AN BB[24]889.

164 E.g. Molinari (1886), pp. 272–3; Marcaggi (1932), pp. 17–18; and Pomponi (1976c).

165 Volney (1825), VII, p. 321; Thrasher (1970), pp. 219, 227–8 and 245–7; Miot (1858), II, p. 2; Maestrati (1964); and Versini (1979), pp. 64–73 and 186.

166 Valéry (1837), p. 100; Case v. G.-A. Candeli(?), Assize Court, 1st session 1837, *Gaz. Trib.*, 11 May 1837, No.3640; Report, Ministry of the Interior to Prefect, 24 October 1837. ADCS 2.M.84; Cases v. ... , 4th session 1849. AN BB[20]146; and v. C. Ciosi and A. Bottacci, 2nd session 1850; Report, President, Assize Court, 13 July 1850. AN BB[20]149; and Letter, Mayor, Piedicroce to Minister of Justice, 29 July 1848. AN BB[18]1466.

167 Miot (1858), II, p. 2; Report, President Fabrizzi, 29 December 1865. AN BB[20]273; Marcaggi (1932), pp. 17–18; Facy (1933), p. 41; and Surier (1934), pp. 223–34; see also Ravis-Giordani (1976a), pp. 182–3.

168 Bourde (1887), pp. 151–4; Case v. I. Durazzi and M. Paoli, Assize Court, 4th session 1893. AN BB[20]286; Letters, Avocat-général to Minister of Justice, 9 August and 18 September 1848. AN BB[18]1466; Cases v. C. Cesari et al., 1st session 1849. AN BB[20]146; and v. V. Luporsi et al., 1st session 1852. AN BB[20]158; also v. F. Venturini et al., 2nd session 1844. AN BB[20]125 (Olmeto); and v. F.-M. Ortoli et al., 1st session 1851, Extraordinary sitting. AN BB[20]152 (Olmiccia).

169 Letter, Procureur-général, 20 September 1861. AN BB[18]1638; Zuccarelli (n.d.), p. 65; and Ravis-Giordani (1976a), pp. 180–1.

12 Banditry

1 E.g. Hobsbawm (1972), pp. 18–19 and 37. However, Lewin (1979) has stressed the importance of this factor in late nineteenth- and early twentieth-century Brazil; and

Pereira de Queiroz (1968), esp. p. 194, making the same point in the same context, suggests a parallel between N-E Brazil and Corsica.

2 E.g. Blok (1972); and Lewin (1979). Already a decade before Hobsbawm first tackled the subject, Carleton Beals had noted that 'despite popular sentiment the true nature of the bandit is not that of social reformer. He is essentially selfish and has no fundamental interest in rectifying social evils.' Beals (1949), p. 694. It should be noted that Hobsbawm frequently acknowledges those aspects of banditry highlighted by his critics but gives them little emphasis in his general interpretation.

3 This interpretation of banditry has been favoured by historians of early modern Europe, following Braudel (1947); and (1972), II, pp. 734–56; see also Hobsbawm (1965), pp. 23–4.

4 Report, Prefect, 23 December 1872, 'Banditisme'. AN F⁷12849; Casanova (1931–2), III, pp. 51–5; Villat (1924), I, pp. 157–60 and 264–5; Thrasher (1970), p. 319; and Rovère (1978).

5 Speech, Avocat-général Sorbier. *Gaz. Trib.*, 19 April 1833, No. 2396; *Gaz. Trib.* 23 October 1841, No. 4535; and 14 March 1842, No. 4659; Campbell (1868), p. 160; Malaspina (1876), pp. 351–2; Reports, Prefect, 23 December 1872; and 30 October 1874; Procureur-général, 6 May 1874, and 16 April 1879; and Sûreté Générale, 1887. AN F⁷ 12849; *La Lanterne*, 3 August 1885; Reports, Ministers of War, the Interior and Justice, and Subprefects (1894–6); and Prefect, 1 May 1899; and 1907. AN F⁷ 12850; Mattei (1912) p. 2; Albitreccia (1942a), pp. 211–12; Report, Président du Conseil to Minister of the Interior, 1 December 1917. AN F⁷ 12850; Marcaggi (1932) esp. pp. 18–20, 28 and 33–5; Choury (1958), esp. pp. 32–6, 112–13 and 222–3; and Bazal (1973), Chs. I–IV, and pp. 99, 209 and 214.

6 Figures are taken from: Villat (1924), I, p. 166; List of sentenced fugitives sent to Ministry of Justice, 23 July 1823. AN BB¹⁸1095; Report by Prefect to Conseil-général, 1825, AN BB¹⁸1146; Vidalenc (1966), p. 79; Sacquin-Moulin (1982), p. 654; Faure (1858), pp. 124 and 140; Reports, AN F⁷ 12849–12850; Bennet (1876), p. 41, Maupassant (1928), p. 208; Bourde (1887), p. 183; Barry (1893), p. 283; Facy (1933), pp. 69–70; and Privat (1936), p. 34. It should be noted that these figures were not all arrived at by using the same criteria and that some are 'educated guesses'.

7 Notably in 1852, 1879, 1887, 1896 and 1907. See Ballard (1852); *La Presse*, 26 September 1879; Reports, Commissaire central et spéciale de police, Bastia, to Prefect, 4 December 1896. ADCS 1.M.230; Prefect to Président du Conseil, 10 November 1907, AN F⁷ 12850; and 'Rapport Clemenceau', *Journal Officiel*, 26 September 1908.

8 Report, Prefect to Conseil-général, 1820, cit. Franceschini (1919), p. 51; Le Joindre (1904), p. 104–5; and Report, Prefect to Président du Conseil, 10 November 1907. AN F⁷ 12850.

9 E.g. Report, Sûreté Générale, 1887. AN F⁷ 12849; Mattei (1912); and Report, Commissaire spécial, Bastia, 10 December 1895. AN F⁷ 12850.

10 Marcaggi (1932), pp. 11 and 14; Girolami-Cortona (1893), p. 311; Versini (1979), pp. 174–6, citing Rapport Mottet; Faure (1858), pp. 96–8 and 101–21; Malaspina (1876), pp. 351–2; *La Presse*, 26 September 1879; Report, Prefect, 30 October 1874. AN F⁷ 12849; Faure (1858), pp. 119 and 122ff; and Le Joindre (1904), pp. 104–5.

11 Thrasher (1970), pp. 180–1; and Pomponi (1979b), pp. 285–6 and 318–23.

12 Versini (1979), pp. 177–8; Saint-Germain (1869), p. 187; Marcaggi (1898b), pp. 247ff and 276ff; Reports, Ministry of War to Ministry of the Interior, 22 March 1882; and 11 September 1886; Prefect to Minister of the Interior, 16 December 1882; and Miscellaneous reports 1887–9. AN F⁷ 12849; Note, Ministry of Justice, 29 November 1895. AN BB¹⁸1927; Report, Procureur-général, 11 December 1895; and other reports. AN F⁷ 12850; Report, Gendarmerie; 24 May 1896. ADCS 1.M.

230; Marcaggi (1932), pp. 33–7; and Bazal (1973), pp. 98–9, 115, 135–6, 152 and 200.

13 Especially in the first decades of the century, around 1850, in the 1870s, in the 1890s and again in 1931–2; see ADCS 1.M. 224 (1800–2); Interrogation of hostages, Vendémiaire An X. ADCS 7.U.1/3; Letters, General Morand to Minister of General Police, 30 May and 13 June 1810. AN BB¹⁸ 241; Letter, Commissaire en chef chargé de la haute police to Prefect, 23 August 1812. ADCS 1.M. 228; Report, Prefect to Minister of Justice, 21 April 1852, AN BB¹⁸ 1473; Faure (1858), pp. 35–61 and 139; Malaspina (1876), p. 352; Reports, Procureur-général to Minister of Justice, 1891–3. AN BB¹⁸ 1870; Marcaggi (1932), pp. 33–7; and Bazal (1973), p. 135.

14 Letter, Xavier de Pozzo di Borgo to Prefect(?), 21 September 1850. ADCS 1.M. 229; and Marcaggi (1898b), pp. 287–9. For other examples, see Bennet (1876), p. 43; Reports, Gendarmerie, 24 May 1896; and Subprefect, Sartène, 23 September 1896, ADCS 1.M. 230; and Trésorier-payeur-général, Ajaccio, 30 September 1896. AN F⁷ 12850; and Marcaggi (1932), p. 25.

15 Reports, 15 Germinal and 9 Ventôse An VI, 'Comptabilité de la police départementale, des ports d'armes et des passeports'; and Letter, General Morand to Ministry of Justice, 5 Prairial An IX. AN F⁷ 3247 (mentioning 3000 livres and 45,000 francs respectively).

16 Case v. G. Miliani et al., 2nd session 1847, *Gaz. Trib.*, 18 July 1847, No. 6252; and Marcaggi (1898b), pp. 297–305.

17 Reports, Prefect, 27 March 1873; and Procureur-général, 6 May 1874; Note, Ministry of the Interior, 9 January; and Telegram, Prefect, 1 March 1875; and Report, Procureur-général, 2 August 1876. AN F⁷ 12849; *La Presse*, 26 September 1879; Report, Procureur-général, 16 April 1879; Notes, Ministry of the Interior, 11 February and 20 March 1880; and Prefect, 2 April 1880; Report, Prefect, 7 December 1880; Note, Ministry of the Interior, 16 January 1881; Reports, Ministry of Justice to Ministry of the Interior, 26 April 1882; and Sûreté Générale, 1882. AN F⁷ 12849; Various reports 1895–6; and Report, Minister of War to Minister of the Interior, 1 December 1917. AN F⁷ 12850.

18 Rapport Mottet, cit. Versini (1979), pp. 183–4; and Franceschini (1919), pp. 46–7.

19 Report, Commissaire spécial, Ajaccio. 10 June 1900. AN F⁷ 12850.

20 Thrasher (1970), p. 178; Rovère (1978), pp. 78–9; Dossier, 'Port d'armes', 1806–10. AN F⁷ 3247; Franceschini (1913), p. 81; J. Renucci (1974), p. 51; Report, Commissaire spécial Constant, 10 June 1818, cit. Franceschini (1924), p. 122; Franceschini (1919), pp. 44, 46–7 and 50; Circular, Recteur, Acad. de la Corse, 6 March 1847, cit. Bazal (1973), p. 20; Faure (1858), pp. 132–47; Reports, 1872, ADCS 1.M. 230; Prefect, 23 December 1872; and Sûreté Générale, 1887; Arrêt, Mayor, Ajaccio, 30 December 1875; Report, Prefect, 28 January 1876; Note, Minister of Justice, 25 February 1876; and Letter, Ex-mayor of Ajaccio to Minister of the Interior, 30 April 1882. AN F⁷ 12849; Reports, Gendarmerie, 11 May 1895; and Prefect, 14 February 1896. AN F⁷12850.

21 Report, Prefect, 30 October 1874. AN F⁷ 12849.

22 *La Presse*, 26 September 1879.

23 Braudel (1972), I, p. 102.

24 The term 'bandit' was used to describe peasants in revolt in 1707, the Chouans, and later any violent criminals: e.g. Bercé (1974), pp. 59 and 195; George Sand, *François le Champi* (1848), cit. Gélis et al. (1978), p. 184; and Mirbeau (1977), pp. 122–3 and 241.

25 Moss (1979), pp. 480–2; and Jusserand (1891), p. 253, for medieval England.

26 E.g. Mérimée (1840a), p. 487; Gregorovius (1855), pp. 140–1; Barry (1893), pp. 270–1; Cesari-Rocca (1908), p. 37; and Villat et al. (1951), p. 60.

27 Cit. Vidalenc (1966), p. 79; see also Le Joindre (1904), p. 101; and Radclyffe Dugmore (n.d.), p. 31–2.

28 Tommaseo (1841), p. 7 (my italics); see also Montherot (1840), p. 89; and Bigot (1890), p. 517.

29 Such terms as *macchiaiolu* or *macchiarellu* were used to describe bandits; see Southwell-Colucci (1933), pp. 222–4, citing nineteenth-century laments.

30 See Pitt-Rivers (1971), p. 183.

31 E.g. Hobsbawm (1965), p. 13; and Day (1979), p. 198.

32 See Marcaggi (1932), pp. 59, 186 and *passim*; Bazal (1973), pp. 49–50, 68, 108, 144–5, 152, 156 and 193–4; Reports, Commissaire spécial, Bastia, 10 December 1895; and Subprefect, Corte, 5 February 1896. AN F[7] 12850. This corresponds to some extent to the emic distinction between the 'outlaw' and the 'bandit' referred to by Brögger (1968), p. 234, for southern Italy; see also Hobsbawm (1972), p. 49; and Pitt-Rivers (1971), p. 182, on the 'bandit of honour' in Andalusia.

33 Hobsbawm (1965), pp. 15–16; see also Brögger (1968), pp. 233–4.

34 Montherot (1840), p. 66; Marcaggi (1932), pp. 238–42; Bazal (1973), pp. 101–3; and Tommaseo (1841), p. 36.

35 Robiquet (1835), p. 432; Faure (1858), pp. 214–21; Versini (1979), p. 80; Report, Procureur-général to Minister of Justice, 16 October 1912. ADCS. 1.M. 231; see also Mattei (1912), p. 2; and Southwell Colucci (1933), pp. 220–1, citing lament of c. 1890 celebrating a bandit from the Cinarca, who stayed in the maquis for fourteen years to avoid conscription.

36 Case v. G.-D. Giovanangeli, Assize Court, 3rd session 1862. AN BB[20]239; and Bazal (1973), pp. 50–67. Giovanangeli killed the mayor and wounded his wife.

37 Faure (1858), pp. 213ff; Chiari (1960), p. 141; and Case v. N. Tenneroni, Assize Court, 2nd session 1845. AN BB[20]130.

38 Gregorovius (1855), pp. 131–4; and Case v. F. Raffini, Assize Court, 2nd session 1851. AN BB[20] 152; see also Marcaggi (1932), pp. 133 and 196–8; and Bazal (1973), pp. 130–1, for similar cases.

39 Marcaggi (1932), pp. 127 (Francesco Bocognano), 133–43 (Matteo Poli), 144–55 (Francesco-Maria Castelli), 188 and 200 (Giuseppo Bartoli), and 197 (Francesco Bornea).

40 Barry (1893), pp. 300–1; see also Letter, Mayor of Ucciani and others, 1877, Petition for clemency. AN BB[24] 798; and Bazal (1973), pp. 10, 50, 58 and 122; and Marcaggi (1898a), p. 322, citing the lament of Giovan-Camillo Nicolai of Carbini from the 1890s; 'Disgraced / I go about the forest; / Exposed all winter / To storms, / Always wandering and on the move; / Tell me what kind of a life is this? / A stone for a pillow / At night under my head.'

41 Letter posted on church door at Cauro, 17 October 1824. ADCS 1.M. 288; and Bazal (1973), p. 99; see also *ibid.*, pp. 36, 111–12, 123 and 138; Rossi (1900), p. 4; and, for comparison, Hobsbawm (1972), p. 60; and Day (1979), pp. 186–7. The term *cangaceiro*, used to describe the bandits of NE Brazil, derives from the word *canga* or 'burden', which refers to the arms and equipment carried by them, but which also had a metaphorical sense. Pereira de Queroz (1968), p. 12.

42 Hobsbawm (1965), pp. 17–18; and Hobsbawm (1972), pp. 31–3.

43 This information, taken from a variety of sources, is tabulated below:

Ages of bandits on becoming bandits (B) or when captured or killed (C) (1821–1944)

	15–20	21–25	26–30	31–35	36–40	41–45	46–50	51–55	56–60	61 plus
B	12	5	1	0	0	0	0	0	0	2
C	2	9	8	3	2	2	0	0	2	2
Total	14	14	9	3	2	2	0	0	2	4

44 E.g. Levi (1948), pp. 16–17 and 69–70; and Hobsbawm (1972), p. 136. The 'bandolera' or female bandit was a popular figure in late sixteenth- and early seventeenth-century Spanish plays, but McKendrick (1974), Ch. 4, notes that this was a device for discussing and questioning female roles in society and not a reflection of real life.

45 See Caisson et al. (1978a), p. 190, photograph.

46 Ortoli (1887), pp. 288–90; and Bennet (1876), pp. 38–9: 'Take her to Tallano, / Where are the proud bandits, / Giacomo (sic) and Santa Lucia, / Who have brave and war-like hearts, / And she will keep them company / In going about the forest and the tracks.'

47 Lament collected at Ghisoni *c.* 1930, cit. Southwell Colucci (1933), p. 222, and Bourde (1887), pp. 231–3; see also Pereira de Queiroz (1968), pp. 56–9, 149, 178–88 and photograph, on the Lampião gang, many of whom had wives, though the author emphasizes that this was unusual in Brazil.

48 Faure (1858), pp. 212 and 232; Tommaseo (1841), pp. 341–2; *Gaz. Trib.*, 22 April 1847, No. 6177; Report, Procureur-général to Ministry of Justice, 18 February 1874. AN BB^{24} 798 (Petition for clemency); Marcaggi (1898b), p. 187; and Cases v. G.-T. Lanfranchi, Assize Court, 1st session; and v. C. Pietri, 2nd session 1852. AN BB^{20}158. More generally, see Gregorovius (1855), p. 142; Malaspina (1876), p. 352; Barry (1893), p. 300; and Marcaggi (1932), p. 58. On the status of the medical profession in Corsica and the distinction between doctors and medical officers, see Pomponi (1979a), pp. 251–4.

49 Faure (1858), p. 232.

50 AN F^{7}12849–12850.

51 E.g. Beaulieu-Delbet (1897), pp. 88–103; and Lorenzi de Bradi (1928), pp. 238–9.

52 Marcaggi (1932), pp. 156–7, 188–92 and 238.

53 Tommaseo (1841), p. 34; Faure (1885), II, pp. 11–16ff; Saint-Germain (1869), pp. 235–6; and Versini (1979), p. 85.

54 Faure (1858), p. 264; and Bertrand (1870), p. 178. Their relationship with the wealthy Multedo of Bastia seems to have been distant if it existed at all; see Maestrati (1964), pp. 54 and 58.

55 Letter, Xavier Pozzi di Borgo, former mayor of Marignana, to Prefect, 21 September 1850. ADCS 1.M. 229; and Marcaggi (1898b).

56 Case, Assize Court, 2nd session 1862. AN BB^{20}239.

57 See e.g. Faure (1858), p. 30; Saint-Germain (1869), pp. 165–6; Marcaggi (1932), pp. 188, 221–3 and 268; and Report, Prefect, 23 April 1887. AN F^{7}12849.

58 Letter, Gendarmerie, 17 August 1893. ADCS 1.M. 230; Marcaggi (1932), pp. 193–4; and Bazal (1973), p. 51.

59 One may cite the examples of Carlo Passani and Serafino called the Lucchese, both Italians active in the middle of the century, and of the Spada brothers, whose father was Sardinian, in the inter-war period. Case, v. N. Giordani, Assize Court, 1st session 1851, Extraordinary sitting. AN BB^{20} 152; and Marcaggi (1932), p. 238. Foreigners would be more likely for this reason to be mercenary bandits and/or to serve as agents of élite families, where reliance upon kin was less necessary.

60 Letter, Xavier Pozzo di Borgo to Prefect, 21 September 1850. ADCS 1.M.229.

61 Report, Gendarmerie, Ajaccio, 25 January 1841. ADCS 1.M.125; Cases, Assize Court, November 1831; and April 1834. *Gaz. Trib.*, 1 January 1832; and 3 July 1834. and v. L.-M. Besignani, 1st session 1854. AN BB^{20}134.

62 E.g. in NE Brazil. Pereira de Queiroz (1968), pp. 157ff.

63 Rovère (1978), pp. 88–9; Faure (1858), pp. 276 and 283–7; Case, Assize Court, July 1848. *Gaz. Trib.*, 12 July 1848, No. 6559; Letter, Xavier Castelli to Procureur-général, 27 May 1912. ADCS 1.M.231.

64 On binary or dyadic relationships generally, see Tönnies (1963), pp. 252–3; Bateson

(1958), pp. 238–9 and 243; Foster (1961); Dennis et al. (1969), pp. 45–7; and Blok (1975), pp. 137–8.

65 Report, Gendarmerie, 24 May 1896. ADCS 1.M.230; Marcaggi (1932), pp. 221–3; and Case v. G. Negroni, Assize Court, 4th session 1838. *Gaz Trib.*, 5 January 1839, No. 4156.

66 Letter to Prefect, 18 June 1822. ADCS 1.M.228; and Case, Assize Court, 1st session 1849, Extraordinary sitting. AN BB^{20} 146.

67 Gregorovius (1855), p. 143; Robiquet (1835), pp. 424–5; Tommaseo (1841), pp. 26–7; and Bourde (1887), p. 234.

68 Case v. D. Vignoli, Assize Court, 3rd session 1842. AN BB^{20}116.

69 Faure (1858), pp. 277–82; and Marcaggi (1932), pp. 213–15.

70 Report, Prefect, 30 October 1874. AN F^{7}12849; see also Mérimée (1840a), pp. 487–8; Bourde (1887), pp. 193–4; Barry (1893), pp. 277–9; and Bazal (1973), pp. 36, 67, 144, 154–7 and 215.

71 Cit. Viale (1855), pp. 84ff; and Ortoli (1887), pp. 200–1; see also Southwell Colucci (1933), p. 125; and Note 40.

72 Cit. Versini (1979), pp. 183–4.

73 Marcaggi (1898b), pp. 107 and 263; and Note, Ministry of Justice, 29 November 1895. AN^{18} 1927: see also Bourde (1887), pp. 199–200.

74 Franceschini (1923), p. 6; Malaspina (1876), p. 352; Aurenche (1926), p. 160; Report, Gendarmerie, Ajaccio, 7 May 1842. ADCS 4.M.126; Case v. G.-A. Nicolai, Assize Court, 1st session 1854. AN BB^{20}170; and Morel (1951), p. 179.

75 List of fugitives, Report, Avocat-général to Ministry of Justice, 23 July 1823. AN BB^{18}1095.

76 E.g. Flaubert (1973) [1840], pp. 320–5; and Gregorovius (1855), pp. 143–6.

77 Barry (1893), pp. 278–9; Robiquet (1835), p. 395 note; Report, Gendarmerie, 25 January 1841. ADCS 4.M.125; Marcaggi (1932), Chs. IX–XIII; and Bazal (1973), pp. 86, 115, 144 and 216.

78 Hobsbawm (1965), p. 17; Pitt-Rivers (1971), p. 183; Blok (1972), pp. 497–8; and Rovère (1978), pp. 90–2.

79 Letter, Mayor, Bastelica to Subprefect, 20 August 1824. ADCS 1.M.228; Campbell (1868), p. 72; and Marcaggi (1898b), pp. 269–70.

80 According to Lucarelli (1942) pp. 16–35, Vardarelli led a force of 350 bandits against the French invaders of Naples in 1806–11. Hufton (1974), pp. 266–83 and 304–5, mentions gangs of up to 300 robbers and bandits in eighteenth-century France; and Casey (1979), Ch. 9, gangs of up to 100 in seventeenth-century Valencia. But all these examples seem to be referring to the mobilization of banditry in wider social movements. For early twentieth-century Brazil, police sources referred to gangs of 60–100 men, but such numbers seem only to have been assembled for special operations, and the usual size of a gang was much smaller. A photograph of 1929 shows 29 men in Lampião's gang, but other reports mention 6–12. Pereira de Queiroz (1968), pp. 93–4, 99ff, 122 and photograph. In western Sicily, the Capraro band numbered 15–20 around 1870, but the Grisafi band (1904–17) was much larger. Blok (1975), pp. 109 and 131–6.

81 Rovère (1978), pp. 88–9. Gregorovius (1855), p. 144, usually a reliable informant, denied that they existed at all.

82 Robiquet (1835), p. 422; and Faure (1858), p. 225. Lorenzi de Bradi's figure of 500 (1928) p. 237, is clearly a gross exaggeration.

83 Marcaggi (1898b), pp. 190 and 262–3; Case v. A. Lucchini, Assize Court, 2nd session 1839. *Gaz. Trib.*, 20 July 1839, No. 4326; *Gaz. Trib.*, 23 December 1832, No. 2297; Case, Assize Court, 1st session 1854. AN BB^{20} 170; Letter to Prefect, 1895; and Misc.

reports, 1894 and 1897. AN F⁷12850; Report, Gendarmerie, 16 February 1896.
ADCS 1.M.230; Bourde (1887), pp. 202–3; Mattei (1912), p. 2; and Marcaggi (1932),
pp. 270–1; see also Hobsbawm (1965), pp. 18–19.

84 Case v. A. Fieschi, Assize Court, 2nd session 1850. AN BB²⁰149; Vuillier (1896),
pp. 191–3; Marcaggi (1932), Chs. XII and XIII; and Bazal (1973), pp. 234 and 238.

85 Faure (1858), pp. 225–33; Bazal (1973), p. 216; Marcaggi (1932), pp. 163 and 202; and
Gregorovius (1855), p. 144; and see Brögger (1968), pp. 235–40; and Lewin (1979),
pp. 139–41.

86 Malaspina (1876), p. 352; and Faure (1858), p. 224. Villari (1955) suggests that in
Sicily and southern Italy banditry and mafia were alternatives not found together.

87 Flaubert (1973) [1840], p. 325; see also Bennet (1876), p. 41; and Rossi (1900), p. 191.

88 E.g. Faure (1858), pp. 75 and 304ff; 'Le Banditisme en Corse', *La Presse*, 26
September 1879; and 'Dans le Fiumorbo', *Le Petit Bastiais*, 10 March 1895, which
reassured 'the many people who go to the baths at Pietrapola' that they had nothing
to fear from the bandits active in the region.

89 Ortoli (1887), pp. 236ff; Marcaggi (1898b), pp. 187–9; and Case v. G.-B. Scapola,
Assize Court, 1st session 1846. *Gaz. Trib.*, 16 April 1846, No. 5860.

90 Faure (1858), p. 231; and Marcaggi (1932), pp. 64–5.

91 Vuillier (1896), pp. 216–17; and Bazal (1973), pp. 143 and 236.

92 Hobsbawm (1965), Ch. II; and Hobsbawm (1972), pp. 17–19, 22–4 and 40; see also
Lucarelli (1942), pp. 16–19, 35–7, 50 and *passim*; Levi (1948), pp. 138–9 and 142–3;
Braudel (1947); and (1972), I, p. 102; and II, pp. 738–9.

93 Versini (1979), p. 176; see also Benson (1825), p. 26.

94 Faure (1858), p. 224; and Versini (1979), p. 80.

95 Various reports, 1895–6. AN F⁷12850.

96 Faure (1858), p. 224.

97 Saint-Germain (1869), p. 239; and Cases v. A. Santalucia, Assize Court, 2nd session
1851, Cases judged *in absentia*. AN BB²⁰152; and v. A. Lucchini, 2nd session 1839.
Gaz. Trib., 20 July 1839, No. 4326; and Choury (1958), p. 41.

98 Reports, Commissaire spécial, 6 March 1887. AN F⁷12849; and Police, Bastia, 1 June
1895. AN F⁷12850.

99 Case v. G.-T. Lanfranchi, Assize Court, 1st session 1852. AN BB²⁰158.

100 Malaspina (1876), p. 352; see also Lorenzi de Bradi (1928), p. 237; and Versini (1979),
pp. 83–4. It is doubtful, of course, whether the original Robin Hood legend itself fits
the later stereotype; see Holt (1960).

101 Bazal (1973), p. 214; Archer (1924), pp. 203–4 and 208; Privat (1936), p. 64, and
L'Eveil de la Corse, 14 June 1930, cit. Marcaggi (1932), p. 202.

102 Letter to Prefect, 6 August 1846. ADCS 2.M.79; Report, Prefect, 11 November 1886.
AN F⁷12849; Bourde (1887), pp. 212–14; Letter, Armand Royé to Minister of the
Interior, 1895; Reports, Commissaire spécial, Bastia, 10 December 1895; and Conser-
vateur des forêts, 30 March 1895. AN F⁷12850; see also, more generally, Barry (1893),
p. 300.

103 Letters, Pozzo to President of the Republic, 18 September 1874; and Reports, Prefect, 30 October 1874. AN F⁷12849; and Gendarmerie, 1 and 3 April 1900. ADCS
1.M.230; Marcaggi (1932), pp. 256–7; and Bazal (1973), pp. 96–7.

104 Fontanilles-Laurelli (1963); Franceschi (1923), p. 83 citing Report, 8 April 1818;
Robiquet (1835), pp. 419–22; Valéry (1837), pp. 265–7.

105 Letters, Trésorier-payeur-général, Ajaccio, to Ministry of Finance, 2 April 1895. AN
F⁷12850; and Bazal (1973) p. 147.

106 See Hobsbawm (1972), pp. 31 and 34; Day (1979); Pirastu (1973), p. 173; and Moss
(1979), pp. 483ff.

107 See, for example, Report, Prefect, 30 October 1874. AN F⁷12849; and *Guide Joanne*,

1877, cit. Bazal (1973), p. 195; also Malaspina (1876), p. 353; Marcaggi (1898b), pp. 257–8; and Rovère (1978), p. 84.

108 Case v. G.-F. Sanguinetti and G.-A. Ciosi, Assize Court, 1st session 1851, Extraordinary sitting. AN BB^{20}152; Robiquet (1835), pp. 436–7; Bazal (1973), pp. 96, 105 and 216; see also, generally, Vuillier (1896), p. 184.

109 Marcaggi (1932), pp. 161–2 and 252; and Bazal (1973), pp. 214–17.

110 Case v. G.-D. Bazziconi, Assize Court, 1st session 1851. AN BB^{20}152; Marcaggi (1898b), pp. 280–6; Bourde (1887), pp. 214–16; and Letter, A. Royé, 1895. AN F^{7}12850.

111 Gregorovius (1855), pp. 133 and 146–8; Marcaggi (1898b), pp. 297–305; Reports, Procureur-général, 6 May 1874; and Prefect, 1 December 1893. AN F^{7}12849; and Natali (1934), pp. 77–8. The poet came from Aullène and knew the pastoral milieu extremely well.

112 See Chapter 3, note 85.

113 Hobsbawm (1972), pp. 42 and 44.

114 F. Renucci (1833–4), II, pp. 369–70; Bazal (1973), pp. 48 and 68; and Aurenche (1926), p. 162.

115 Faure (1858), pp. 75, 21–2 and 45; Report, Ministry of Justice to Ministry of the Interior, 30 November 1894. AN F^{7}12850; Privat (1936), pp. 51–2; Bazal (1973), p. 147; and Arrighi (1856b), p. 17.

116 Faure (1858), pp. 76–8; and Case v. L. Ristorucci, Assize Court, 1st session 1841. *Gaz. Trib.*, 7 April 1841, No. 4862.

117 Benson (1825), p. 25; Case v. P.-P. Antonmarchi, 3rd session 1837. *Gaz. Trib.*, 30 September 1837, No. 3763; and Marcaggi (1898b), pp. 242–68. Other examples are cited by Bourde (1887), pp. 211–12; and Chiari (1960), p. 139; see also Hobsbawm (1972), pp. 61–2.

118 Saint-Germain (1869), p. 167.

119 E.g. Marcaggi (1932), pp. 191–2; and Case v. C. and A. Pietri, Assize Court, 2nd session 1852. AN BB^{20}158.

120 Mérimée (1840a), p. 496; Marcaggi (1932), pp. 165 and 252; Darrell (1935), esp. pp. 141ff; and Bazal (1973), pp. 107–15, 212, 214, 216–17 and *passim*; also Case v. G.-T. Lanfranchi, Assize Court, 1st session 1852. AN BB^{20}158; Faure (1858), p. 258; and Hobsbawm (1972), pp. 135–7.

121 Case Assize Court, 1st session 1836. *Gaz. Trib.*, 6 April 1836, cit. Sorbier (1863), pp. 76–80.

122 Marcaggi (1898b), pp. 207–9; see also Quantin (1914), pp. 278–9.

123 Flaubert (1973) [1840], p. 330; Bazal (1973), pp. 218–20; see also Ortoli (1887), pp. 200–1 (lament); Faure (1858), pp. 288–91 and 295–9; Marcaggi (1932), pp. 59 and 152; and Privat (1936), pp. 95–102.

124 E.g. Pereira de Queiroz (1968), pp. 112 and 155.

125 Marcaggi (1932), p. 63; Ortoli (1887), pp. 226–7; see also Faure (1858), pp. 61 and 260–1; a lament cited by Viale (1855), pp. 102–5; and Casanova (1931–2), I, p. xxviii.

126 See Tommaseo (1841), pp. 19–22 and 57–9; Barry (1893), pp. 298–301; and Marcaggi (1898a), pp. 309–10.

127 Faure (1858), p. 61; Saint-Germain (1869), p. 241; Faure (1885), II, pp. 11–16; Marcaggi (1932), pp. 22, 128, 155, 215–16, 247 and 265–6; and Bazal (1973), pp. 107, 79–80, photograph opp. p. 192, and 197–8.

128 Bazal (1973), pp. 86–7. This act of penance, always performed incognito, was a considerable physical ordeal and involved carrying a heavy wooden cross through the streets of the old town; chains were attached to the penitent's bare feet and nails were strewn in his path.

129 Quantin (1914), pp. 278–9; and Vuillier (1896), pp. 231–5 and 211–12.

130 Marcaggi (1932), p. 144; and (1898b), p. 189; see also Mérimée (1840b), p. 715.
131 Mérimée (1840a), pp. 534–5; Bazal (1973), p. 68; Faure (1858), p. 263; and Marcaggi (1898b), pp. 21–22.
132 See Lucarelli (1942), pp. 136–8 (on Don Ciro Annicchiarico 1775–1829); and Hobsbawm (1972), pp. 28–9.
133 See, for example, D'Azeglio (1966), pp. 246–7; Levi (1948), pp. 137–43; Hobsbawm (1965), p. 13; Hobsbawm (1972), pp. 12 and Ch. 9; Blok (1972), pp. 500–1; and Pitt-Rivers (1971), p. 179.
134 Joanne (1881), p. 470; and Le Joindre (1904), p. 102. Le Joindre was director of artillery at Bastia for two years.
135 Bazal (1973), pp. 52, 48 and 193; Vuillier (1896), pp. 191–3; and Marcaggi (1932), p. 60, for example.
136 Gregorovius (1855), p. 144; Bourde (1887), pp. 223 and 231; Rossi (1900), p. 192; Le Joindre (1904), p. 102; Bazin (1913), p. 189; Marcaggi (1932), pp. 121–2; and Bazal (1973), pp. 16, 59–60, 144, 151 and 216.
137 E.g. Tommaseo (1841), pp. 19–22, 24ff and 57–9; Bourde (1887), pp. 234–6; Barry (1893), pp. 298–9; Marcaggi (1898a), pp. 306–22; Southwell Colucci (1933), pp. 124–9; and Dalmas (1978), pp. 47–8.
138 E.g. Lucarelli (1942), pp. 104–5; Brögger (1968), p. 240; Pereira de Queiroz, pp. 60ff, 113ff and 153; and Lewin (1979), pp. 118 and 127.
139 Versini (1979), pp. 81–3; Flaubert (1973) [1840], pp. 321 and 324–5; Gregorovius (1855), pp. 144–5; Faure (1858), pp. 211, 222–3 and 298–9; Saint-Germain (1869), pp. 165–6; and Lorenzi de Bradi (1928), pp. 237–8. According to Faure, Teodoro's legend began in his life-time.
140 Tommaseo (1841), pp. 35–7; Saint-Germain (1869), p. 241; Cesari-Rocca (1908), pp. 111–12; and Versini (1979), pp. 80–4.
141 Ortoli (1887), pp. 278ff; Fée (1850), p. 19; and Metz-Noblat (1885), p. 63.
142 Marcaggi (1898b), pp. 247 and 261; Saint-Germain (1869), pp. 191–2; Chapman (1908), p. 219; and Southwell Colucci (1933), pp. 225–6.
143 Archer (1924), pp. 203–9; Radclyffe Dugmore (n.d.), pp. 32 and 34; Guitet-Vauquelin (1934), pp. 133–4; and Bazal (1973), pp. 131, 211, 216 and 229.
144 Privat (1936), pp. 27–8; and Dalmas (1978), pp. 47–8.
145 Reports, Sub-prefect, Corte, 5 February 1896; and Commissaire spécial, Bastia, 10 December 1895. AN F^{7}12850; Lorenzi de Bradi (1928), p. 239; Albitreccia (1942a), pp. 211–12; and Renucci (1974), p. 73.
146 See Bourde (1887), pp. 207–8; Barry (1893), pp. 279–81; Various reports. AN F^{7}12849; and Bazal (1973), pp. 99, 136, 141 and 152.
147 See Braudel (1947), pp. 129–42; Blok (1972), p. 496; Hobsbawm (1965), p. 13; and Hobsbawm (1972), p. 56.
148 See Montherot (1840), p. 89; Barry (1893), pp. 282–3; and Marcaggi (1932), p. 23 note.
149 Case v. G.-A. Nicolai, Assize Court, 1st session 1854. AN BB^{20}170.
150 Letter to Prefect, 13 February 1823; and Various reports 1822–3. ADCS 1.M.228; and Robiquet (1835), pp. 423–4.
151 See Hobsbawm (1965), pp. 19–20; and Lewin (1979), pp. 136–9, for parallels.
152 See Flaubert (1973) [1840], pp. 324–5; Bourde (1887), p. 250; Reports, Commissaire spécial, Ajaccio, 21 January 1887; and Gendarmerie, Ajaccio, 17 August 1893. AN F^{7}12849; Andrei (1893), p. 157; and Marcaggi (1932), p. 12 note.
153 See Marcaggi (1932), pp. 132, 161, 170, 186, 217 and 232; and Bazal (1973), pp. 68, 214, 230 and 240–1.
154 Rovère (1978), p. 71, referring to the early years of French rule; see also Malaspina (1876), p. 352; Joanne (1881), pp. 470–1; and Emmanuelli (1971a), p. 410.

155 Lament for Teodoro, cit. Tommaseo (1841), pp. 26–7; see also Various reports, 1822–5. ADCS 1.M.228; Robiquet (1835), pp. 423–4; and Cesari-Rocca (1908), p. 49.
156 Letter to Prefect, 9 January 1847. ADCS 1.M.224; and Case, Assize Court, 1st session 1849, Extraordinary sitting. AN BB20146.
157 Bourde (1887), pp. 220–1; Marcaggi (1932), pp. 133–5, 209–12 and 223–32; and Bazal (1973), pp. 232–3 and 238–9.
158 Bourde (1887), pp. 219–21; Report to Prefect, 22 June 1822. ADCS 1.M.228; Letter to Prefect, 2 December 1840. ADCS 2.M.86 (Sari-d'Orcino); and Report, Commissaire spécial, Bastia, 1895 (?). AN F712850.
159 Robiquet (1835), 424–5; Letters, Subprefect to Prefect, 26 July, 1 August and 8 August 1827. ADCS 1.M.228; Report, Gendarmerie, Ajaccio, 23 January 1842. ADCS 4.M.126; Case, Assize Court, 2nd session 1848. AN BB20142; and *Gaz. Trib.*, 12 July 1848, No. 6559; and 15 July 1848, No. 6562; Vuillier (1896), pp. 198–9; and Bourde (1887), p. 250; see also, generally, Gregorovius (1855), p. 143; and Barry (1893), p. 271.
160 Case, Assize Court, 4th session 1835. *Gaz. Trib.*, 25 December 1835, cit. Sorbier (1863), pp. 60–6; Murray (1868), p. 27; and Darrell (1935), pp. 104–7 and 197ff.
161 Reports, Gendarmerie, 13 April; Prefect, 30 October 1874. AN F712849; Gendarmerie, 12 June 1895. ADCS 1.M.230; Commissaire spécial, Bastia, 10 December 1895. AN F712850; and Robiquet (1835), p. 423.
162 Benson (1825), pp. 23–6; Bourde (1887), p. 219; Note, Ministry of Justice, 29 November 1895. AN BB181927; and Letter, Percepteur, Prunelli-di-Fiumorbo to Receveur des finances, 25 September 1896. AN F712850.
163 Gregorovius (1855), p. 143; see also Forester (1858), p. 79.
164 Faure (1858), pp. 232–7; Versini (1979), p. 80; Letter, Trésorier-payeur-général, Ajaccio, 2 April 1895. AN F712850; Bourde (1887), pp. 221 and 250; and Reports, Subprefect, Sartène, 31 July; and Commissaire spécial Bastia, 10 December 1895. AN F712850.
165 Brögger (1968), pp. 236–7; see also Clay (ed.) (1965), pp. 18 and 81.
166 Ortoli (1887), pp. 190–1.
167 Darrell (1935), pp. 99–100; see also Marcaggi (1932), Ch. IX and pp. 198–215 and 252–63; and Bazal (1973), Ch. XIV and pp. 96, 112–14, 131–4 and 228–33.
168 AN BB181095.
169 *Journal du Département de la Corse*, 5 July 1828; *Gaz. Trib.*, 24 April 1839, No. 4250; Case, Assize Court, 3rd session 1846, AN BB20134; *La Lanterne*, 3 August 1885; Bourde (1887), p. 209; and Reports, Directeur-général Postes et Télégraphes, Corse, to Prefect, 26 May 1895; Ministry of Justice to Ministry of the Interior, 20 December 1895; and Commissaire spécial, Ajaccio, 29 April 1899. AN F712850.
170 E.g. Report, Gendarmerie, Sartène, 21 October 1841. ADCS 4.M.125; and Case, Assize Court, 1st session 1849, Extraordinary sitting. AN BB20146.
171 E.g. Report, Procureur-général to Prefect, 11 December 1911. ADCS 1.M.231.
172 Case, Assize Court, 1st session 1862. AN BB20239.
173 *Gaz. Trib.*, 24 April 1829, No. 1157 (Borghello); and 12 July 1848, No. 6559 (Giacomorni and Arrii); Letter to Prefect, 9 January 1847. ADCS 1.M.224 (Antona); Case v. A. Paoletti, Assize Court, 1st session 1862. AN BB20239; and Report, Gendarmerie, 24 May 1896. ADCS 1.M.230 (bandits in Ortolo valley).
174 See Lucarelli (1942), p. 160; Hobsbawm (1972), pp. 58 and 61–5; and Pirastu (1973), p. 126.
175 Bouchez (1843), p. 88; Cases v. G.-D. Bazziconi, 1st session; and v. P.-G. Massoni, 2nd session 1851, Cases judged *in absentia*. AN BB20152; Marcaggi (1898b), pp. 214, 270, 276 and *passim*; and Marcaggi (1932), pp. 149ff.
176 Hobsbawm (1965), pp. 25–6.
177 *Journal du Département de la Corse*, 4 December 1828; Reports, Gendarmerie, Ajaccio,

17 August 1893. AN F⁷12849 and ADCS 1.M.230; Pietrapola, 21 May; and Bastia, 18 June 1895. AN F⁷12850; and Vescovato, 2 and 30 December 1911. ADCS 1.M.231; Letter, X. Castelli to Procureur-général, 27 May 1912. ADCS 1.M.231; and Marcaggi (1932), Ch. VIII.

178 Marcaggi (1932), pp. 142–3; Letters to Prefect, 9 May 1882. AN F⁷12849; and 23 April 1895; and Report, Procureur-général, 11 December 1895. AN F⁷12850; Letters to Procureur-général, 1911; and Procureur de la République to Procureur-général, 17 November 1911. ADCS 1.M.231.

179 Report, Gendarmerie, Vico, 5 November 1816. ADCS 4.M.102; Versini (1979), p. 81; *Journal du Département de la Corse,* 9 April 1829; Tommaseo (1841), p. 37; and *Gaz. Trib.,* 14 March 1842, No. 4659; and 5 January 1845, No. 5522.

180 Rovère (1978), p. 93; Robiquet (1835), p. 396; Report, 1825. ADCS 1.M.228; and Flaubert (1973) [1840], p. 325.

181 Byock (1982), pp. 217–18 and 271–2.

182 Barry (1893), p. 283; Bourde (1887), p. 206; Case v. G. Miliani et al., Assize Court, 5–8 July 1847. *Gaz. Trib.,* 18 July 1847, No. 6252; Marcaggi (1932), pp. 23–4 note, 171–3 and 212–16; and Bazal (1973), pp. 211, 219–20 and 212–16.

183 Bourde (1887), pp. 200–1; Bazal (1973), p. 37; Marcaggi (1898a), pp. 308–20 (lament of Colombani); Southwell Colucci (1933), pp. 127–8 (lament of Leone, collected at Calacuccia in 1925 and at Venzolasca in 1932); Tommaseo (1841), pp. 22–4, 80–4, and 86–91; Viale (1855), pp. 102–5; and Ortoli (1887), pp. 236–46, see also Hobsbawm (1965), p. 14; and (1972), pp. 50–1.

184 Faure (1858), pp. 263 and 287; and Marcaggi (1898b), pp. 210–14.

185 Gregorovius (1855), p. 418; and Bazal (1973), pp. 117 and 146. Some of Ettori's friends apparently accepted small sums for spying on him but then gave false information to the police, which in fact protected him.

186 Faure (1858), pp. 288–9 and 295–9; Versini (1979), p. 86; Reports, Gendarmerie, 17 August 1893; and 29 August 1894; and Letter Prefect to Governor-general, Algeria, 29 November 1893. ADCS 1.M.230.

187 For comparison, see Lucarelli (1942), pp. 112–14 and 136–8; and Pereira de Queiroz (1968), pp. 35ff and 47 (NE Brazil): having acted earlier there as agents in the conflicts of notables, bandits like Antonio Silvino and Lampião became independent powers in the early twentieth century. See also, more generally, Brögger (1968), pp. 239–40.

188 Marcaggi (1898b), pp. 269–70; Report, Prefect, 30 October 1874. AN F⁷12849; Letter, Armand Royé to Minister of the Interior, 1895; Report, Commissaire spécial, Bastia, 10 December 1895; and Various reports and letters 1895–6. AN F⁷12850; *Le Petit Bastiais,* 10 March 1895; *Pascal Paoli,* 3 March 1895; Ardouin-Dumazet (1898), pp. 297–8; Letters, Percepteur, Prunelli-di-Fiumorbo, to Receveur des finances, 20 September 1907; and Président du Conseil to Prefect, 26 October 1907. ADCS 1.M.230.

189 E.g. Lucarelli (1942), pp. 155–6 (early nineteenth-century Naples); Pitt-Rivers (1971), p. 182 (Andalusia); Casey (1979), pp. 207, 212, 214–15 and 217–19 (seventeenth-century Valencia); Day (1979), pp. 195–7 (eighteenth-century Sardinia); and Hughes (1983), p. 14 (Papal States); also Blok (1972), pp. 498–500 and 502; Blok (1975), pp. 99ff; and Lewin (1979), pp. 119, 128ff and 145–6.

190 Faure (1858), pp. 78–80; Report, Prefect, 23 December 1872. AN F⁷12849; Bourde (1887), pp. 196–8; and Robiquet (1835), p. 395 note.

191 See *Gaz. Trib.,* 2 June 1841, No. 4910; Letter to Prefect, 4 July 1843. ADCS 2.M.81; Case v. G. Carlotti, Assize Court, 3rd session 1856. AN BB²⁰185; Faure (1858), pp. 270 and 273; and Bennet (1876), pp. 44–5.

192 Bourde (1887), Ch. XI; Bazal (1973), pp. 199–200; Saint-Germain (1869), p. 220; Report, Prefect, 30 October 1874. AN F⁷12849; Maupassant (1928), pp. 209–16; Vuillier (1896), pp. 197–200; and Marcaggi (1932), pp. 21–2.

193 Marcaggi (1932), pp. 30–2, 165 and 273–9; and Bazal (1973), pp. 216–17 and 83–4.

194 Report, Prefect, 23 December 1872. AN F⁷12849; Bourde (1887), pp. 211 and 214–16; Andrei (1893), p. 93; Submission to Comité des patriotes tendant à la suppression du banditisme en Corse, December 1896; and Letter, Ottomani to Prefect, 25 June 1896; ADCS 1.M.230.

195 Report, President, Assize Court, 13 July 1850. AN BB²⁰149; and Bazal (1973), p. 229.

196 Letter, Mayor Orazj to Subprefect, 20 August 1824. ADCS 1.M.228 (Dossier Gasparini); Marcaggi (1898b), pp. 107 and 248; also Report, Procureur-général, 6 May 1874. AN F⁷12849.

197 Letters to Prefect, 31 March and 9 April 1845. ADCS 2.M.85; Telegram, Subprefect to Prefect, 25 June 1896. ADCS 1.M.230; Various reports, Dossier 'Paoli et Sanguinetti 1910–1912'; and Letter, Xavier Castelli to Procureur-général, 27 May 1912. ADCS 1.M.231; and Reports, Commissaire spécial, Ajaccio, 21 January 1887. AN F⁷12849; and Ministry of Justice to Ministry of the Interior, 8 January 1895. AN F⁷12850.

198 Report, Procureur-général to Minister of Justice, 22 January 1823. AN BB¹⁸1093; Note, Ministry of Justice, 29 November 1895. AN BB¹⁸1927; and see Chapter 7, pp. 204–6.

199 Cases v. P. Arrighi, Assize Court, 1st session 1851, Extraordinary sitting. AN BB²⁰152; and Assize Court, 5–8 July 1847. *Gaz. Trib.*, 18 July 1842, No. 6252.

200 The phenomenon of the 'conservative' political bandit has been identified in a number of societies, for example, eighteenth-century Sardinia [(Day (1979), pp. 195–7)], or western Sicily and Lucania in the 1940s [(Brandon-Albini (1956), pp. 165ff; and Levi (1948), pp. 23–4)]; see also Hobsbawm (1972), p. 89, though in (1965), p. 23, he had asserted that 'the bandit is a pre-political phenomenon', and in both books he stresses the anti-establishment element in banditry, as is well known.

201 Report, Prefect, 23 December 1872. AN F⁷12849; see also Gregorovius (1855), p. 142; and Le Joindre (1904), p. 102.

202 Letters, Gendarmerie to Prefect, 1840. ADCS 1.M.86; and Adjoint and others to Prefect, 9 April 1858. ADCS 2.M.149; Report, Ministry of the Interior, 17 May 1879. AN F⁷12849; Bourde (1887), p. 217; Marcaggi (1932), pp. 156–7, 166 and 189ff; and Privat (1936), pp. 52–3.

203 See 'Le Banditisme en Corse', *La Presse*, 26 September 1879; Marcaggi (1932), pp. 17–18, referring to the 1886 elections; Bourde (1887), pp. 216–17; Report, Commissaire spécial, Bastia, 10 December 1895. AN F⁷12850; Marcaggi (1932), pp. 167–8, 199–200 and 209–10; Privat (1936), pp. 69ff and 154; and Villat (1932), p. 152.

204 Marcaggi (1932), p. 154.

205 For its importance elsewhere, see e.g. Pereira de Queiroz (1968), pp. 60ff and 74ff.

206 Gregorovius (1855), p. 134 and also pp. 141–2; Faure (1858), p. 14; and Marcaggi (1932), pp. 55 and 58; also Malaspina (1876), p. 352; Blanchard (1926), pp. 36–8; Privat (1936), p. 22; Chiari (1960), p. 139; Vidalenc (1966), p. 79; and Bazal (1973), p. 156 (who follows Marcaggi remarkably closely here and elsewhere).

207 See Cases v. A. Valeri, Assize Court, 2nd session 1836. *Gaz. Trib.*, 30 June 1836, cit. Sorbier (1863), pp. 89ff; and v. G. Negroni, 4th session 1839. *Gaz. Trib.*, 5 January 1839, No. 4156; Saint-Germain (1869), pp. 228–41; Faure (1885), II, pp. 11–63; Robiquet (1835), pp. 422 and 431–2; Case, v. S. Romanetti, Assize Court, 3rd session 1850, AN BB²⁰149; and Beaulieu-Delbet (1897), pp. 88–103.

208 Report, Gendarmerie, 21 April 1820. ADCS 1.M.228; Robiquet (1835), p. 438; Case v. G.-B. Scapola, Assize Court, 1st session 1846. AN BB²⁰134; and *Gaz. Trib.*, 16 April 1846, No. 5860; *Journal du Département de la Corse*, 27 November 1830; and *Gaz. Trib.*, 23 December 1832, No. 2297.

209 Letters, 1874–85. AN BB²⁴798, (Petition for clemency for Francesco Bastianesi).

210 Cases v. M. Papini; and v. G.-F. Sanguinetti and v. G.-A. Ciosi, Assize Court, 1st session 1851, Extraordinary sitting. AN BB²⁰152; and Dossier 'Paoli et Sanguinetti 1910–1912'. ADCS 1.M.231; Letter to Procureur-général, 27 May 1912. ADCS 1.M.231; and Marcaggi (1932), Ch. VIII.

211 Cases v. G. Negroni, Assize Court, 4th session 1839. *Gaz. Trib.*, 5 January 1839, No. 4156; v. A. Lucchini, 2nd session 1839. *Gaz. Trib.*, 20 July 1839, No. 4326; and v. F. Poli, 4th session 1845. AN BB²⁰130; Marcaggi (1932), pp. 270–1 note; and Southwell Colucci (1933), p. 222.

212 *Gaz. Trib.*, 20 February 1842, No. 4640; Gregorovius (1855), p. 144; Saint-Germain (1869), p. 187; and Marcaggi (1898b), pp. 271–9 and 286.

213 Letter, 13 May 1822. ADCS 1.M.228; Saint-Germain (1869), p. 241; Faure (1885), II, 53–63; Cases v. G. Mozziconacci et al., Assize Court, 2nd session 1851, Extraordinary sitting. AN BB²⁰152; and v. P.-G. Balisoni, 1st session 1836. *Gaz. Trib.*, 27 May 1836, cit. Sorbier (1863), pp. 85–8.

214 Malaspina (1876), p. 352; Reports, Subprefect, 20 April 1830. ADCS 4.M.99; and Gendarmerie, Ajaccio, 26 November 1842. ADCS 4.M.126; Cases v. A. Fieschi, Assize Court, 2nd session 1850; and v. G.-A. Giansili, 3rd session 1850. AN BB²⁰149; and Note, Ministry of Justice, 29 November 1895. AN BB¹⁸1927.

215 Case, Assize Court, 4th session 1831. *Gaz. Trib.*, 1 January 1832; and Report, Conseil-général, 1826. AN BB¹⁸1146.

216 Faure (1858), pp. 213–15, 263–4, 271 and 300–1 argues that Teodoro's hostility was directed solely against the gendarmerie, but we have seen that this is not strictly true, since Teodoro had been denounced for draft evasion in the first place by enemies in the village and his brother Borghello certainly behaved as if he were engaged in a feud with the latter.

217 Report, Prefect, 7 December 1880. AN F⁷12849.

218 Report, Prefect to Conseil-général, 1826. AN BB¹⁸1146; though, according to these figures, Bastia had a higher percentage of the total than Ajaccio.

219 I.e. those 346 whose domicile is known. Report, Avocat-général to Minister of Justice, 23 July 1832. AN BB¹⁸1095.

220 The other villages, with numbers of fugitives in brackets and feuding villages italicized, were: *Albitreccia*, Barretali, Cambia, Cervione, *Ciammannacce*, *Olmeta-di-Tuda*, Pancheraccia, Scolca and Sorbo-Ocognano (2); Calcatoggio, *Canale*, *Cozzano*, Giuncheto, Monticello, *Oletta*, Piazzole, Poggio-di-Nazza, Rapale, Sollacaro, Speloncato, Taglio and Zigliara (3); Calenzana, Pianello, Vescovato, Ventiseri and Zalana (4); Luri (5); Santa-Maria-Figaniella (6); Zicavo (7); Palneca (9); and Isolaccio (15).

221 E.g. Gregorovius (1855), p. 141; Campbell (1868), p. 72; and Morandière (1933), pp. 89–92.

222 Blanchard (1915), p. 42; and (1926), pp. 35–6.

223 As in Sardinia; see Ferracuti et al. (1970), esp. Maps 3–4 and 7–8; Day (1979); and Moss (1979), pp. 481–2.

224 Reports, Subprefects, Bastia, 31 January 1896; and Calvi, 6 February 1896. AN F⁷12850.

225 Marcaggi (1932), Ch. IX; and Bazal (1973), p. 105.

13 Death and the dead

1 Casta (1979), p. 81.

2 The most important of these are: Galletti (1863), pp. 81ff; Bigot (1890), pp. 445, 446, 449 and 513–15 (Bastelica); Vuillier (1896), pp. 170–4 (Zicavo); Forcioli-Conti (1897), pp. 252–9 and 266–8; Bartoli (1898), pp. 231–40; and Lorenzi de Bradi

(1928), pp. 294–8. See also: Robiquet (1835), p. 453; Mérimée (1840a), pp. 449, 462, 471–2, 501–2 and 504; Mérimée (1840b), p. 723; Tommaseo (1841), pp. 93, 181–5, 187 and 251–3; Bouchez (1843), pp. 5, 13–14, 35, 40 and 83; Lemps (1844), pp. 141–3; Fée (1850); Gregorovius (1855), p. 280; Viale (1855), pp. 19, 21–2, 27, 30–1, 43–8, 48–51, 54, 94 and 106; Faure (1858), pp. 199–202; Miot (1858), II, pp. 36–7; Saint-Germain (1869), pp. 97, 130–1, 195, 296–9 and 334; Malaspina (1876), pp. 373–4; Ortoli (1887), pp. 59, 90–7, 104–6, 133–5, 166–7, 194–5 and 258–71; Saint-Victor (1925) [1887], pp. 349–50 and 362; Barry (1893), pp. 171–5; Beaulieu-Delbet (1897), pp. 42–3 and 71–5; Filippi (1906), p. 12; Chapman (1908), pp. 177–84; Busquet (1919), pp. 97–101 and 337–8; Archer (1924), pp. 126, 141–2 and 220–1; Marcaggi (1926), pp. 26 and 46–7; Casanova (1931), I, pp. xx–xxi; Southwell Colucci (1933), pp. 137ff; Natali (1961), pp. 22, 23, 25–6, 30ff, 70–1 and 80; Carrington (1971a), pp. 90–1; Ettori (1979); Casta (1979); Versini (1979), pp. 140–53; and Christophari (1981), pp. 108–9 and 174.

3 Frediani, *A Messieurs de la Cour Criminelle de la Corse* (Bastia, 1821), p. 8. AN BB^{18}243; and Letter, Mayor of Lopigna to Prefect, 14 May 1849. ADCS 2.V.20.

4 Saint-Germain (1869), p. 334, with special reference to Ghisoni.

5 Vuillier (1896), pp. 170–3.

6 Southwell Colucci (1933), p. 151; see also Case v. A. Giovannoni et al., Assize Court, 1st session 1841. *Gaz. Trib.*, 5 June 1841, No. 4913.

7 Later they simply wore their best clothes.

8 In a *vocero* from Perelli d'Alesani, collected in the 1920s, a mother refers to her dead son as 'mi spegne-fugone' or 'you who put out my fire'. Southwell Colucci (1933), p. 207.

9 In the Niolo, ribbons might be tied to the candles. Southwell Colucci (1933), p. 155.

10 *Tola* is the word for both 'table' and 'bier'. Where an ordinary domestic table was employed, it could not be used for eating for eight days, according to Vuillier.

11 Fée (1850), pp. 132–3 citing a *vocero*.

12 Either 'vitex agnus castus' or a kind of achillea. Bouchez (1843), p. 83; and Tuffelli (1977), p. 27.

13 Southwell Colucci (1933), pp. 188–9.

14 Dalmas (1978), p. 38; and Robiquet (1835), p. 453; and see p. 396.

15 Reports, Gendarmerie, Ajaccio, 21 June 1841; and 18 July 1842. ADCS 4.M.126.

16 E.g. Carrington (1971a), p. 91.

17 Lamotte (1956e).

18 The same assimilation is found in Greece; see Du Boulay (1982), pp. 228–9.

19 Southwell Colucci (1933), pp. 154 and 176.

20 Alexiou (1974), p. 40. In Greece, too, according to Danforth (1982), pp. 72–3, close relatives did not usually lead the laments.

21 The most important are those by Tommaseo (1841) and Viale (1855). Ortoli (1887) and Marcaggi (1898a) add little to these, save translations into French and some background information. Southwell Colucci (1933) is a wholly new collection, which pays far more attention than its predecessors to the provenance of its texts. A team assembled by the late Fernand Ettori is now engaged in making a comprehensive collection of both historical and contemporary *voceri*. Some *voceri* were remembered and repeated after the occasions which gave them birth. Southwell Colucci, for example, collected *voceri* around 1930 that had been composed nearly a century earlier and she found the same *vocero* figuring in the repertoire of a number of women, often from places very far apart. It is these *voceri* in general circulation, as it were, rather than those actually performed at wakes, which were most likely to be collected and written down, that is, shortened and edited versions, divorced from their original context.

22 See e.g. O. Súilleabháin (1967); Ramsay (1872), pp. 54–5; Read (n.d.), p. 1078; De Martino (1975), pp. 179–81; and McNeill and Gamer (1938), pp. 318–19. Parodic *voceri* were sometimes sung, however, on other occasions; see Tommaseo (1841), pp. 244–8; and Marcaggi (1926), pp. 61–2.

23 See e.g. Frediani (1821). AN BB¹⁸243; and Martelli (1960), p. 278. Their use is associated with the spread of burial in the ground or in mortuary chapels as opposed to charnel pits, as we shall see.

24 Versini (1979), pp. 152–3.

25 Lamotte (1957a); see also Ortoli (1883), p. 333; and Borel-Léandri (1978), p. 253. *Bastelli* were 'a special kind of turnover made of bread dough with cooked vegetables inside'.

26 Versini (1979), pp. 152–3; and Bartoli (1898), pp. 231–2.

27 Saint-Germain (1869), pp. 296–9; and Casanova (1931), I, p. xxi.

28 However, the name of the dirge remained the same, *pace* Marcaggi; see Ettori (1978), p. 247.

29 Forcioli-Conti (1897), p. 267.

30 Faure (1858), pp. 199–202.

31 Ortoli (1887), p. 199 note 7.

32 The essential work here is De Martino (1975). See also Lane (n.d.), pp. 441, 517–18, 520–2, 533 and 553 (nineteenth-century Cairo: Muslims and Copts); Cozzi (1910), esp. pp. 680–7 (Albania); Lawson (1910), pp. 345–9 (modern Greece); Brilliant (n.d.), pp. 1166 and 1169 (the Balkans); Durham (1928), pp. 217–28 (Montenegro and Albania); De Martino (1955a) (Lucania); Djilas (1958), pp. 107–8 (Montenegro); Brandon-Albini (1963), pp. 60–2 (S. Italy); Alexiou (1974), pp. 4–10 and 24ff; Du Boulay (1979), p. 44 (Greece); Bonaviri (1980), p. 72 (Sicily); Guiart et al. (n.d.), pp. 13–14 ff; and Beaton (1980), pp. 58–64, 141–5, 148 and 184 (Greece).

33 See, for example: Synge (1912), pp. 56–7, 69, 77 and 79 (modern Ireland); McNeill and Gamer (1938), pp. 318–19 and 333, citing Regino's *Ecclesiastical Discipline* of *c.* 900 and *The Corrector* of Burchard of Worms of *c.* 1000; Wright (1957), p. 101 (the Geats); Leproux (1959), pp. 260ff and 271–2 (Charente – France); Bieler (1963), pp. 162–3, 231 and 273, citing Irish Penitentials and canons of the seventh to ninth centuries; Ó Súilleabháin (1967) (modern Ireland); Ross (1967), p. 135 (twelfth-century Flanders); F. Wilson (1970), pp. 119 and 240, citing eighteenth- and nineteenth-century Russian sources; Brékilien (1966), pp. 170–6; Hélias (1978), pp. 110–13 (nineteenth-century Brittany); Danforth (1982) (modern Greece); and Goldey (1983), pp. 3–4 (nineteenth-century Portugal).

34 See, for example: Benedict (1935), pp. 80 and 173; Mead (1977), pp. 233–4 (Iatmul); and Huntington and Metcalf (1979), p. 30 (Australian Aborigines).

35 See Homer, *The Iliad*, Books XVII, XXII and XXIV (Rieu (1946), pp. 337–8, 345, 408ff and 456–8). It was also present in the Old Testament society of the Hebrew judges and kings.

36 See Busquet (1919), pp. 98–101; Casta (1976), pp. 292–3; and (1979), pp. 83–4, 91 and 95. Similar opposition to wakes and traditional funeral customs was renewed during the Revolutionary period by 'enlightened' opinion; see Lamotte (1964), pp. 63–6.

37 For a vivid description of lamenting and feasting in church in fifteenth-century Portugal, see Letts (1957), pp. 113–14.

38 Case v. Leandri, Extraordinary Criminal Court, 6 Germinal An IX. ADCS 7.U.1/17.

39 The body of Colonel Carlo Frediani was laid out in 1797 in the isolated church of Mezzana (Tavignano), but he was a fugitive who had died of malaria. Frediani (1821). AN BB¹⁸243. When Paolo Santoni was killed in 1821 near Sollacaro, 'the corpse was taken by his father to Sollacaro and placed in the parish church', presumably to await transportation to Palneca from where the Santoni came. Report,

Subprefect, Sartène, 16 December 1821. ADCS 4.M.98. In this, and other cases too, official investigations into deaths by violence or in suspicious circumstances might cause delays and the body would be left in a church; see Southwell Colucci (1933), p. 159, citing a *vocero* for a young girl who was drowned – collected at Olmi-Cappella in 1927. This consideration presumably explains why the Antona bandits were laid out in the church in 1846.

40 E.g. Southwell Colucci (1933), pp. 154, 164, 172–5 and 179; and Fée (1850), p. 219.

41 E.g. Filippi (1906), pp. 13 and 21; Chiari (1960), p. 122; Casta (1978), pp. 176–8 and 183–4; and author's fieldwork.

42 E.g. Sorbier (1863), p. 134 (patronal festival of St Michael at Bisinchi in 1839); Beaulieu-Delbet (1897), pp. 84–8 and 123–6 (festivals of the Virgin at Zilone and of Santa Reparata at Santa-Maria-Sicche); Lorenzi de Bradi (1928), pp. 155–6; and author's fieldwork.

43 Examples of local pilgrimages include those to chapels of the Virgin in the Capo Corso, which occasioned conflict between the villages of Rogliano and Tomino, and Morsiglia respectively. (*Gaz. Trib.* 7 January 1827, No. 396; and 8 October 1828, No. 988); to the chapel of San Petro near Zicavo on 1st August, which dated from 1500. (Saint-Germain (1869), p. 146; and author's fieldwork); and to the top of Monte San Pietro near Piedicroce on 29 June (Archer (1924), p. 250). A few shrines drew pilgrims from all over the island: the fountain of Santa Giulia near Nonza on 22 May (Saint-Germain (1869), p. 433); the chapel of Santa Restitude near Calenzana (author's fieldwork); and the Marian shrine of Lavasina founded in 1677 (Bertoni (1933); and *Corse-Matin*, 7 and 13 September 1977). The pilgrimages of Corbara and of Our Lady of the Snows at the Col de Bavella are of twentieth-century origin and appear to be more 'clerical' in inspiration; see *Corse-Matin*, 5 June 1979: and 1 August 1981.

44 See note 60 below; and Chapter 6, pp. 165–6.

45 Cit. Robiquet (1835), p. 405. A very similar practice is described by Hertz in connection with the cult of St Besse; see Hertz (1983), pp. 60–3.

46 E.g. Fedotov (1966), I, pp. 302 and 304–5, on medieval Russia.

47 Robiquet (1835), p. 403; Ortoli (1887), pp. 314–21; and Bartoli (1898), pp. 240 and 368.

48 Malaspina (1876), p. 374; see also Christophari (1981), p. 92; and Carrington (1971a), pp. 86–7.

49 Viale (1855), p. 110; see also Saint-Victor (1925) [1887], pp. 357–8.

50 Tommaseo (1841), pp. 43–4; and Dalmas (1978), p. 24.

51 As they were more generally in the early medieval period. 'Revenge ... involved both human and divine elements which operated separately and together', Sutherland has written with reference to Liudprand of Cremona in the tenth century. 'It was part of one moral scheme which was supposed to harmonize human and divine vengeance.' Sutherland (1975), esp. p. 400.

52 E.g. *vocero* for Father Larione of the Niolo by his godmother. Viale (1855), pp. 113–15; and Marcaggi (1898a), pp. 186–91.

53 E.g. Viale (1855), pp. 82–3 and 97–9; and Southwell Colucci (1933), pp. 154, 160–1, 184, 193, 195–6 and 218–19.

54 Viale (1855), pp. 111–13; Marcaggi (1898a), pp. 192–7; Ambrosi (1972), pp. 37–8; and Mérimée (1840b), pp. 734–7.

55 Viale (1855), p. 95; and Marcaggi (1898b), p. 29.

56 Versini (1979), p. 152; and Viale (1855), p. 109.

57 In the course of the feud at Orgosolo in 1913, a girl from one family called down divine vengeance on the other: 'God will curse you for the wrong you are doing our family. God will not suffer you to benefit by such a life of infamy.' She then made a gesture of imprecation. Later 'her brother hearkens to her curse and commits murder'. Pareto (1935), IV, p. 1521 note.

58 Malaspina (1876), p. 375.

59 Viale (1855), pp. 35ff; Tommaseo (1841), pp. 85–6, 86–91, 190 and 192; Ortoli (1887), pp. 12–16 and 118–23; and Southwell Colucci (1933), pp. 143, 145, 159, 164, 171, 177 and 187.

60 See Letter, Juge de paix, San-Martino-di-Lota, to Subprefect, 2 September 1841, ADCS 2.V.19; Bouchez (1843), pp. 44–5 note and 92 note; Saint-Germain (1869), p. 292; Malaspina (1876), p. 374; Vuillier (1896), p. 208; Barry (1893), pp. 169–71; Morandière (1933), pp. 84–5; Natali (1961), pp. 26–7; and Renucci (1974), pp. 255–6.

61 E.g. Tommaseo (1841), pp. 192 and 210; Viale (1855), pp. 18 and 34; and Ortoli (1887), pp. 56–7 and 126–9; see also Casta (1979), p. 86; and Carrington and Lamotte (1957), p. 86.

62 Guiart (n.d.), p. 3. In some societies, it appears that commensality could override the demands of vengeance. 'In the olden time in Florence,' according to Longfellow, 'if an assassin could contrive to eat a sop of bread and wine at the grave of the murdered man, within nine days after the murder, he was free from the vengeance of the family; and to prevent this they kept watch at the tomb.' Oelsner et al. (eds.) (1901), p. 428 note.

63 Galletti (1863), p. 84; Ettori (1978), p. 248, citing Cyrnaeus; Viale (1855), pp. 43–8 and 84–8; and Ortoli (1887), pp. 142–53 and 200–16, both citing *voceri* in which enemies address each other; and Ettori (1979).

64 Cases v. A. Marsili, Assize Court, 3rd session 1832. *Gaz. Trib.*, 19 September 1832, cit. Sorbier (1863), p. 19; and v. C. Balisoni, 2nd session 1853. AN BB20164.

65 Boulard (1954), pp. 132–4; Christian (1972), pp. 133ff; and Brandes (1980), Ch. 10. I am grateful for this last reference to Heather Woodward.

66 E.g. Case v. G. Casabianca, Assize Court, 3rd session 1854. AN BB20170; Carrington (1971a), p. 43; and Casta (1976).

67 See Bateson (1958), pp. 152–9, for a similar contrast among the Iatmül of Papua.

68 See Mérimée (1840a), p. 472; and (1840b), p. 723; Ortoli (1887), pp. 158–75 and 186–97; Saint-Victor (1925) [1887], pp. 357; Marcaggi (1898b), pp. 133–46; Southwell Colucci (1933), pp. 207–8 and 216; and Black-Michaud (1975), pp. 78–9.

69 Ettori (1978), p. 250. Men did very occasionally compose *voceri* for women to sing: see Valéry (1837), pp. 396–400 (Bastia region); Tommaseo (1841), pp. 98–101 and 218–19; and Southwell Colucci (1933), pp. 165–6 (Asco); and Saint-Germain (1869), p. 195, refers to the practice at Corscia in the Niolo of 'the man who will carry out the revenge explaining the circumstances of the [original] killing in an improvised *vocero*' – but this is a solitary reference and suggests either participation by the revenger at some stage in the women's singing at the wake or his echoing of their *voceri* on a separate occasion later.

70 Ettori (1978), p. 259 note 18, citing twentieth-century *vocero*; the reference is to the funeral fees and other perquisites which the priest obtained.

71 See Alexiou (1974), pp. 120–2; Eliade (1978), pp. 200 and 304; Breteau and Zagnoli (1979), pp. 296–7ff; and Danforth (1982), pp. 74–95.

72 Ortoli (1887), pp. 26–7 and 34–5; Viale (1855), pp. 35–8; and Southwell Colucci (1933), pp. 214, 144 and 195–6.

73 See Cesari-Rocca (1908), pp. 109–10; and Casta (1965). In an interesting discussion of vampire beliefs in rural Greece, Juliet Du Boulay (1982), pp. 229–36, establishes an analogy between the pattern of marriage exchange – a one-way circle which meant that men always married women of 'strange blood' in the community – and beliefs associated with death. The Corsican material is too fragmentary, at the moment, to explore any such connection there.

74 Southwell Colucci (1933), pp. 137–9; and Ettori (1979), pp. 187–8.

75 See Dalmas (1978), pp. 45–6. For other references, see note 2.

76 See note 33.
77 See also Ettori (1978), pp. 249–50; and Ettori (1979).
78 See Finnegan (1977); and Dégh (1969), pp. 87, 175 and 179.
79 See Mérimée (1840b), pp. 750–3; Tommaseo (1841), pp. 61–2; Bouchez (1843), pp. 6 and 35–7; Viale (1855), pp. 88–9; Ortoli (1887), pp. 176–9; Marcaggi (1898a), pp. 176–9; and Bertrand (1870), pp. 19–20.
80 Fée (1850), pp. 209–10, and Mérimée (1840b), pp. 739–45, give slightly different versions of the well-known 'O caro di la surella'. The opening stanza 'Quandu n'intesi la nova' is attached to two distinct *voceri* from the same region, the Castagniccia; see Mérimée (1840b), pp. 734–7; Tommaseo (1841), pp. 112–13; Fée (1850), Nos. XI and XXII; Viale (1855), pp. 51–4; and Ortoli (1887), pp. 108–15. For other examples, see Ettori (1979), pp. 179–82.
81 The view is based on a reading of some 150 *voceri*.
82 In addition to items in note 2, see Rossi (1900), pp. 178–9; Dalmas (1978), p. 37; and Ettori (1978), pp. 249 and 260.
83 Forcioli-Conti (1897), pp. 251–2 and 270–1; also Girolami-Cortona (1893), p. 118; Rossi (1900), pp. 191–2; Bazin (1913), p. 190; Juta (1926), pp. 147–50; Morandière (1933), pp. 81–3; Natali (1961), p. 73; Carrington (1971a), p. 91; and Ettori (1978), p. 247.
84 See Bouchez (1843), p. 51; Forcioli-Conti (1897), p. 258; Marcaggi (1926), pp. 9–10; Southwell Colucci (1933); and Ettori (1978), pp. 251–3.
85 Patin de La Fizelière (1963), pp. 61 and 67; see also Martelli (1960), p. 278. Burial under the floor of churches was, of course, normal in pre-nineteenth-century Europe as a whole, with some preference in Catholic areas for monastic churches; see Ariès (1977), Ch. 2; and Vovelle (1973), pp. 100–7, 183–202 and 333–9.
86 For example, those of San Francesco near Oletta, of Sant'Antono in the Casinca, and of Venzolasca. Author's fieldwork; and Viale (1855), p. 19 note.
87 Martelli (1960), pp. 278 and 281; and Franceschini (1918), p. 55 (Circular dated 10 July 1818).
88 Martelli (1960), pp. 266–7 and 274–6; Tommaseo (1841), p. 121; Report, 4 October 1828. ADCS 4.M.99; and Marcaggi (1898a), p. 87 note. The municipal council of Penta-di-Casinca, for example, voted 50 francs in November 1861 for the repair of 'the cemetery church'. ADHC E.29/8.
89 Saint-Germain (1869), pp. 113–14, 135–6 and 387; also Martelli (1960), pp. 271 and 274.
90 Southwell Colucci (1933), pp. 197–8 and 200.
91 See, for example, *Gaz. Trib.*, 24 April 1829, No. 1157; and 25–26 May 1829, No. 1184.
92 Report, Prefect to Minister of the Interior, 7 June 1864. ADCS 2.M.116.
93 Hughes (1975), p. 10.
94 Borel-Léandri (1978), p. 253; see also 'Quanda n'intesi la nova', sung for Father Santucci of Alesani. Fée (1850), pp. 188–9. Another *vocero* refers simply to throwing the body 'into a terrible black hole'; see Fée (1850), pp. 130–1; Viale (1855), pp. 21–3; and Ortoli (1887), pp. 98–103.
95 Ravis-Giordani (1978a), p. 138; and Casanova (1931–2), I, p. xxi.
96 Report, Subprefect to Prefect, 10 December 1866. ADCS 1.V.44; Vuillier (1896), pp. 174–5; Martelli (1960), pp. 278 and 281–2; Archer (1924), p. 221; and Casta (1979), p. 87.
97 Bigot (1890), p. 445; Saint-Germain (1869), p. 112; Archer (1924), pp. 220–1; and Casanova (1931–2), I, p. xvi.
98 Archer (1924), pp. 250–1; Carrington, (1971a), p. 302; and Bazal (1973), p. 44.
99 Casanova (1931–2), III, p. 38; and Murray (1868), p. 23. The petition was put forward by representatives at the General Assembly of Estates.

100 Casta (1978), p. 175; (1979), p. 87; and Martelli (1960), pp. 265 and 281.
101 Casanova (1931–2), I, p. xxi.
102 Pina-Cabral and Feijó (1983), p. 20.
103 Franceschini (1918), p. 55.
104 Viale (1855), p. 34; and Ortoli (1887), pp. 22–7 (Pietra-di-Verde and Orezza).
105 Ceccaldi (1974), p. 89; and Casta (1979), p. 87.
106 Case v. M.-C. Filippi, Assize Court, 3rd session 1856. AN BB²⁰185.
107 Martelli (1960), pp. 281–2; Finelli (n.d.), p. 15; Vanutberghe (1904), p. 345; and Casanova (1931–2), I, p. xxi.
108 Lear (1870), pp. 10–11; Beaulieu-Delbet (1897), p. 43; Vuillier (1896), pp. 174–5; and Rankin (1930), p. 11 (with special reference to Bastelica). Similar burial practices occur, of course, in other parts of the world, for example, Rumania (Stahl (1969), Photo 37), Madagascar (Grandidier (n.d.), pp. 898–903), and Mexico (Soustelle (1971), p. 129, citing a Mazahua song), and a comparative study would be of value.
109 Bigot (1890), p. 445; and Murray (1868), p. 23.
110 Archer (1924), p. 142; and Chiari (1960), p. 124.
111 See Leproux (1959), pp. 268 and 280; and Ariès (1977), pp. 515–16.
112 Casta (1979), pp. 87–8; and Martelli (1960), pp. 281–2.
113 Cit. Pomponi (1976c), pp. 166–7.
114 Barry (1893), pp. 185–6. Various observers also commented on the way in which corpses were hurried there and buried without ceremony; see Murray (1868), p. 23; and Archer (1924), pp. 15–16.
115 Spalinowski (1904), p. 65; Renucci (1974), p. 117; and Caisson (1978b), p. 162; see also D'Este (1905), p. 32 and photo; and Radclyffe Dugmore (n.d.), p. 60.
116 Ortoli (1883), p. 330; and Finelli (n.d.), p. 15.
117 Abeau (1888), p. 21; Maurras (1920), p. 123; Bigot (1890), p. 453; and Southwell Colucci (1933), pp. 197–8.
118 Ravis-Giordani (1978a), p. 138; Caisson (1978b), p. 162.
119 Ravis-Giordani relates that in the south ox-yoke mountings might be placed under the pillow of an agitated dying man to calm him, and also notes the sacrilege represented by burning a plough. Ravis-Giordani (1974), p. 46. Also the strips into which the common fields or *presa* were divided were sometimes called *anima* or souls, according to Lamotte (1956a), p. 55.
120 Rocco Filippi of Quenza, killed at Bocognano in 1793 or 1794 was buried, for example, at Afa, many miles away from either place. Case v. G. Rossi, Extraordinary Criminal Court, 4 Messidor An X. ADCS 7.U.1/22.
121 Saint-Germain (1869), pp. 296ff; Letter, Police to Subprefect, 20 December 1821. ADCS 1.M.228; and Benson (1825), p. 69. Benson claims against Saint-Germain that Viterbi himself wished to be buried in Penta.
122 Report, Subprefect, 13 April 1824. ADCS 4.M.91; Southwell Colucci (1933), pp. 149, 165 and 199; Viale (1855), pp. 38–40 and 48–51; Bigot (1890), p. 453; and Renucci (1974), pp. 149 and 152.
123 Bloch (1968).
124 Reports, Gendarmerie, 12 and 21 October 1841. ADCS 4.M.125.
125 Vuillier (1896), p. 207; and Lorenzi de Bradi (1928), p. 298.
126 See Van Gennep (1977), p. 152; Rose (1930), p. 132; and Guiart (n.d.), p. 20.
127 A passage in the thirteenth-century *Dialogue of Miracles* by Caesarius of Heisterbach, describing 'how a feud was contained in the tomb', provides an interesting parallel here. The heads of two peasant families from the Cologne region, that had been feuding for many years, died the same night and were buried in the same grave. 'The corpses were seen to turn on their backs, and dash heads, backs and heels against each

other with great violence. With difficulty one was removed and buried elsewhere.'
See MacCulloch (1932), p. 92.

128 Martelli (1960), pp. 274–5.

129 Caisson (1978b), pp. 162 and 165; see also the parallel situation described by Rose (1930), p. 132.

130 Frazer (1933), pp. 10–11 and *passim*; see also Bendix (1962), p. 131, citing Weber.

131 Carrington (1971a), pp. 38–9, 47, 49, 57, 86 and 303; see also Bartoli (1898), p. 230; and Privat (1936), p. 16.

132 See Ortoli (1883), pp. 316–17 and 337–42; and Martin-Gistucci (1979).

133 Sorbier (1845), p. 58. For parallels see Lombardi-Satriani (1979), p. 332; and Du Boulay (1982), pp. 224–5 and 227ff.

134 Frazer (1933), pp. 33ff; and Van Gennep (1977), p. 164.

135 E.g. Casta (1978), p. 180; and Borel-Léandri (1978), p. 253.

136 Tommaseo (1841), p. 180; Gregorovius (1855), p. 279; Marcaggi (1898a), p. 6; Quantin (1914), p. 205; Chiari (1960), p. 149; and Römer (1977), pp. 82 and 86.

137 Guiart (n.d.), p. 17, referring to Spain.

138 As Carrington (1971a), p. 86, herself emphasizes: 'Each family derived from them its sense of identity and continuation, its pride of being'; see also Lombardi-Satriani (1979), pp. 338–9; and Fribourg (1979), p. 356.

139 E.g. Lombardi-Satriani (1979), p. 332; and Fribourg (1979).

140 See e.g. Breteau and Zagnoli (1979), pp. 300–1; Lombardi-Satriani (1979), p. 356; and Henry (1941), pp. 181–91.

141 Southwell Colucci (1933), pp. 193–4; see also *ibid.*, p. 199 (also from Venzolasca and referring to the deceased's mother, father and sons); Viale (1855), pp. 54–8; and Ortoli (1887), pp. 90–7, where messages are sent to the singer's father and uncle.

142 E.g. Ortoli (1887), pp. 238–9 (great-grandfather).

143 See Ceccaldi (1974), p. 21.

144 Ortoli (1883), pp. 333–7; and Southwell Colucci (1933), p. 142.

145 Tommaseo (1841), p. 101. For parallel situations, see Fox (1963); and Kenna (1976).

146 Lamotte (1956a), pp. 44–6; and (1956e).

147 Giacomo-Marcellesi (1979), pp. 107–9.

148 Rossi (1900), p. 97.

149 For comparison, see Brékilien (1966), p. 230; and Alexiou (1974), p. 55 and *passim*.

150 Mérimée (1840a), pp. 501–2; and see Robiquet (1835) p. 453, Mérimée's probable source here.

151 Fée (1850), pp. 135–6; Viale (1855), pp. 17–20, 51–4 and 77–81; Ortoli (1887), pp. 108–15, 116–17 note, 124–31, 136–9 and 272–6; Southwell Colucci (1933), p. 184; and Mérimée (1840b), pp. 739–45.

152 Dalmas (1978), p. 45; Lamotte (1957a), p. 88; Casta (1979), p. 97; and, for similar customs elsewhere, Durham (1928), pp. 223–5 (Montenegro); Read (n.d.), p. 1081 (Ireland); and Danforth (1982), pp. 43, 46–7, 104–6 and 127–32.

153 Ortoli (1887), p. 59. Another referred to the 500 candles used at the funeral of a priest in the Niolo in 1870. Southwell Colucci (1933), pp. 154 and also 208.

154 Case, Cour Royale, Bastia, 20 December 1844. *Gaz. Trib.*, 5 January 1845. No. 5522; also Letter, Procureur-général to Ministry of Justice, 19 June 1891. AN BB¹⁸1855.

155 See Rossi (1900), p. 182; Privat (1936), p. 16; Borel-Léandri (1978), p. 253; Radclyffe Dugmore (n.d.), p. 60; and Villat et al. (1951), p. 59.

156 Ortoli (1887), pp. 236–46; see also Southwell Colucci (1933), p. 200 (*vocero* referring to visiting the tomb of an uncle near Venzolasca); and Vuillier (1896), p. 216 (relating that the burial place of Massoni in the wild near Calasima was still remembered). In the Greek village studied by Danforth (1982), p. 44, close relatives visited the grave daily for forty days.

157 See, e.g. Southwell Colucci (1933), pp. 164, 193–4 and 195–6; and Natali (1961), pp. 70–1.
158 Archer (1924), pp. 61–2; Martelli (1960), p. 260, for Ghisoni, where the procession was at dusk; Finelli (n.d.), p. 81; Borel-Léandri (1978), p. 253; and Christophari (1981), p. 87. For such practices elsewhere in Europe, see, for example, F. Wilson (1970), p. 240 (Russia); and Guiart (n.d.), pp. 16–19.
159 Cases v. R.-A. Campana, Assize Court, 1st session 1849, Extraordinary session. AN BB²⁰146 (Oletta); and v. G.-A. Giansilj, 3rd session 1850. AN BB²⁰149 (Lozzi) (in each of which attempts were made by the local authorities or others to prevent the 'customary' ringing from taking place); and Saint-Germain (1869), p. 292.
160 Lamotte (1957a), p. 88; and Borel-Léandri (1978), p. 253. This assimilation of the dead with Souls in Purgatory was, of course, very common in Catholic Europe and also found expression in the provision of prayers and masses for the dead; see Casta (1979), pp. 90–1.
161 Finelli (n.d.), pp. 35–6; Lorenzi de Bradi (1928), p. 157; Chiari (1960), p. 122; Rossi (1900), pp. 179–80; Lorenzi de Bradi (1928), p. 157; and Caisson (1978b), p. 164.
162 Arrighi (1856b), p. 3; Carrington and Lamotte (1958), pp. 66–7; Finelli (n.d.), p. 48; Carrington (1971a), p. 303; Ortoli (1883), pp. 237–42; and Martin-Gistucci (1979), p. 215. Sir John Moore noted that children lit bonfires in the streets of Bastia on or before 3 August 1795. This was linked, it appears, by the British authorities with the burning of effigies of Pozzo di Borgo and Colonna in the Casinca and the Castagniccia at the same time by the followers of Paoli, but if this was so, it seems to have been an adaptation of ritual association with the dead that survived intact much later in the south.
163 Tommaseo (1841), pp. 116–17; Rankin (1930), p. 16; Chiari (1960), pp. 112–13. Viale (1855), pp. 77–81; and see Chapter 5, pp. 155–6 and note 137.
164 Cit. Natali (1961), p. 87; Fée (1850), pp. 207–8; and Busquet (1919), pp. 338–9.
165 Bertrand (1870), pp. 18–19; Viale (1855), pp. 82–3; Ortoli (1887), pp. 230–3; and Tommaseo (1841), p. 110. This is similar to the Montenegrin custom by which 'all a man's sisters-in-law cut off their hair and threw it into his grave'. Durham (1928), pp. 217–25.
166 See Mérimée (1840b), p. 731; Tommaseo (1841), p. 23; Fée (1850), pp. 210–11; Viale (1855), pp. 88–9; Bigot (1890), p. 515; Malaspina (1876), p. 375; Lorenzi de Bradi (1928), p. 298; Ortoli (1887), pp. 186–9; and Barry (1893), pp. 298–9, citing a bandit lament; see also, for comparison, Huntington and Metcalf (1979), pp. 45–6.
167 Gregorovius (1855), p. 188; Bartoli (1898), pp. 230–1; Rossi (1900), p. 134; Lorenzi de Bradi (1928), pp. 283–7; and Christophari (1981), pp. 37–8.
168 Southwell Colucci (1933), pp. 193 and 200; and Deane (1965), pp. 6–7.
169 Mérimée (1840a), pp. 491–2; Viale (1855), p. 104; Bigot (1890), pp. 445–6; Saint-Germain (1869), p. 302; Malaspina (1876), p. 375; Ortoli (1887), p. 227 note; Vuillier (1896), p. 151; Lorenzi de Bradi (1928), pp. 100 and 294; Casanova (1931–2), I, p. xxi; Morandière (1933), p. 81; and author's fieldwork.
170 E.g. Cozzi (1910), pp. 664 (Albania); Mirambel (1943), p. 384 (Greece); Hasluck (1954), pp. 230–1 (Albania); Clay (ed.) (1965), p. 96 (S. Italy); Black-Michaud (1975), p. 79 (Balkans and elsewhere); Caisson (1978b), p. 161 (Greece, N. Africa); Hole (1978), pp. 53–4 (Britain); and Goldey (1983), p. 10 (Portugal).
171 *Hrafnkel's Saga*. Pálsson (1971), pp. 26 and 43; and Dante, *Purgatorio*, Canto III, cit. Ariès (1977), p. 50.
172 Viale (1855), p. 104; also Caisson (1978b), p. 161. In Albania and Greece, according to Cozzi, a stone is placed at the site explicitly to record that a death has to be avenged and, when this has been done, the stone is removed.
173 Letter, President, Assize Court, 13 July 1850. AN BB²⁰149; Report, 1858. Petition for

clemency for Gregorio Casabianca. AN BB^{24}507–515; and Letter, Juge de paix, Tallano, and Mayor, Ciamannacce to Subprefect, February 1828. ADCS 4.M.91.

174 Among the Swat Pathans, for example, murdered persons were usually buried where they had been killed, and these spots 'sometimes serve as shrines, and are invariably treated with respect', which implies a continuing presence; see Barth (1965), p. 58. Meligrana relates that it was common in S. Italy to believe more explicitly that the spirit of a person who had been killed remained at the place of the crime until the time when he or she would have died naturally. Meligrana (1979), p. 309.

175 Ortoli (1883), pp. 302–6; and Carrington and Lamotte (1957), p. 84.

176 For comparison, see Mirasyezis (1975), p. 209, on the same belief in Greek popular poetry; and Shakespeare's *Romeo and Juliet*, Act III, Scene 1, where Romeo tells Tybalt who, with his partisans, has just killed Mercutio: 'For Mercutio's soul / Is but a little way above our heads, / Staying for thine to keep him company.'

177 Van Gennep (1977), pp. 150, 156 and 160–1.

178 See Treston (1923), pp. 78, 95–6, and 141–8; and Visser (1984), (Ancient Greece); Benedict (1935), pp. 81–3 (Zuñi); and Llewellyn and Hoebel (1941), pp. 132ff (Cheyenne). Among the Cheyenne, the word meaning 'putrid' was a synonym for 'murder', and a homicide was conceived of as having a bad smell.

179 See Guiart (n.d.), p. 79 on the 'Are 'Are of the Solomon Islands, among whom a sharp distinction is made in funeral ritual, depending on whether the victim was killed by another person, or by the ancestors (i.e. by natural causes). In the latter case, a funeral feast is held, the dead are buried in a cemetery and become ancestors in their turn. In the former, after one victim is killed, a second is killed in revenge. 'Peace money' is then given to the killer of the second victim by the family of the first, and a peace feast takes place. The victims are left without burial; their bodies putrefy and disappear and they never become ancestors. The same annihilation is reserved in rural Greece for those who become vampires. Boiling oil and vinegar were poured into their graves, which destroyed them body and soul. They were then entirely forgotten. Du Boulay (1982), p. 226.

180 In a fourteenth-century deed of reconciliation at Tournai, a man made peace with his brother's killer 'in order to relieve the soul of his brother'. Philpotts (1913), p. 177.

181 Raglan (1940), p. 35; see also Burr (1914), p. 218, citing Cotton Mather; Middleton and Tait (eds.) (1970), pp. 194, 219 and 223 (Konkomba and Lugbara); and Byock (1982), pp. 129–33 and 244 (medieval Iceland).

182 Gough (1958); and Lawson (1910), pp. 434–6, 440 and 441ff; and see Gray et al. (1909), pp. 727–9; and Mirambel (1943), p. 384. In her interesting discussion of vampire beliefs, Du Boulay (1982) specifically leaves aside the category provided by the unavenged dead.

183 See e.g. Gray et al. (1909), pp. 720 and 730ff; Durham (1928), pp. 163ff; Breteau and Zagnoli (1979), pp. 300–1; Meligrana (1979), pp. 309–10; and Nabofa (1985), esp. pp. 392–4 (Africa).

184 Réalier-Dumas (1819), p. 17; Malaspina (1876), p. 374; *Almanacco popolare* (1931), pp. 186–91, citing lament for a young woman of Olmeta-di-Tuda accidentally killed by a salvo of honour fired at a wedding; and Ortoli (1883), pp. 333–7; see also Casanova (1931–2), I, pp. xxii–iv; and Casta (1979), p. 82, on the importance of pre-mortem confession – to a lay person if necessary.

185 Southwell Colucci (1933), pp. 207–8; Case v. P.-A. Rossi, Assize Court, 4th session 1861. AN BB^{20}229; Viale (1855), pp. 106–10; and Ortoli (1887), pp. 258–71.

186 Ortoli (1887), pp. 272–5; and Tommaseo (1841), p. 114. Similar notions were current in the Balkans and the Islamic world; see Durham (1928), pp. 164ff; and Gray et al. (1909), p. 730.

187 Heers (1974), p. 117. Similarly Bloch (1965), p. 126, relates that: 'Among the [early

medieval] Frisians, the very corpse cried out for vengeance; it hung withering in the house till the day when, the vengeance accomplished, the kinsmen had at last the right to bury it'.

188 Ortoli (1887), pp. 250–1; Tommaseo (1841), p. 123; and Southwell Colucci (1933), pp. 225–6; see also a *vocero* from Muro cited by Tommaseo (1841), p. 105; and Fée (1850), pp. 211–12.

189 Report, Commissaire de police, 6 May 1818, cit. Franceschini (1924), p. 101; Case v. I. Borelli, Assize Court, 3rd session 1849. AN BB^{20}146; and Busquet (1919), pp. 95–6; see also Rossi (1900), pp. 115 and 182; Ortoli (1887), p. 215 note 11; Case v. A. Serra, Assize Court, 2nd session 1850. AN BB^{20}149; Marcaggi (1932), p. 149; and Comiti (1933), p. 241.

190 Forcioli-Conti (1897), p. 269; see also Durham (1928), p. 193; and Djilas (1958), p. 106.

191 Ortoli (1887), pp. 250–1; Cases v. A. Marsili, Assize Court, 3rd session 1832. *Gaz. Trib.*, 19 September 1832, cit. Sorbier (1863), p. 19; and v. Balisoni, Assize Court, 2nd session 1853. AN BB^{20}164. Tommaseo (1841), pp. 165–73; Versini (1979), p. 208 note 9; Case v. P. Giovanelli, 4th session 1832. *Gaz. Trib.*, 3 January 1833, No. 2305; and *Gaz. Trib.*, 20 June 1838, No. 3986; see also Bouchez (1843), p. 82; and Ortoli (1883), pp. 322–8.

192 See, e.g., Molinari (1886), p. 261; and Barry (1893), p. 278.

193 See Benson (1825), pp. 165–6; Bouchez (1843), pp. 12–13; Comiti (1933), p. 241; Carrington (1971a), p. 86; and Hogg (1973), p. 27.

194 For parallels, see Breteau and Zagnoli (1979), pp. 300–1; and Lombardi-Satriani (1979), p. 334.

195 Vuillier (1896), p. 170; Bartoli (1898), p. 254; *Almanacco popolare* (1931), pp. 186–91; and Bernardini (1970), II, p. 13.

196 Marcaggi (1898b), pp. 234 and 213. Durilli in fact survived.

197 Cit. Busquet (1919), pp. 95–6; and Carrington (1971a), p. 87.

198 Report, Police to Prefect, 1809. ADCS 4.M.71.

199 Case v. G. Miliani et al., Assize Court, 2nd session 1847. *Gaz. Trib.*, 18 July 1847, No.6252; Versini (1972), pp. 143–5; Letter, Xavier Pozzo di Borgo to Prefect, 21 September 1850. ADCS 1.M.229; and Marcaggi (1932), pp. 120–1 and 124–5.

200 Viale (1855), pp. 90–7; and Ortoli (1887), pp. 158–75; and see also Natali (1961), pp. 56–8; Versini (1979), p. 152; and Christophari (1981), p. 175.

201 Ortoli (1887), pp. 272–5; see also Marcaggi (1898b), p. 29; and Ettori (1978), p. 263 note 77.

202 See e.g. Bassett (1933); and Segal (1971) (Ancient Greece); Soustelle (1962), pp. 96–100; and (1971), p. 82 (Ancient Mexico); Nash (1967), p. 461 (modern Mexico); Landes (1959), p. 50 (the Dakota); Luchaire (1967), pp. 258–60 and 284–5 (medieval France); Foucault (1979), pp. 3ff (early modern France); and Lucarelli (1942), p. 183 (early nineteenth-century Naples).

203 See e.g. Pareto (1935), IV, p. 1520 note; Levi (1948), pp. 70 and 143; and Wormald (1980), p. 74.

204 Ortoli (1887), pp. 190–5.

205 Romeo and Juliet, Act V, Scene 3; see also Hallpike (1973), p. 453.

206 See e.g. Ferguson (1981), p. 213 (Montenegro); and Bercé (1974), p. 157, referring to National Guards cutting off ears of peasant rebels as trophies at the siege of Bressuire in the Vendée in 1792.

207 Lawson (1910), pp. 434–6.

208 Among the Kol of India, for example, it was believed that 'all those who have been mutilated or who have died because of a tiger or an accident remain evil spirits and cannot enter the land of the dead'. Van Gennep (1977), p. 152.

209 Fée (1850), p. 20; Bertrand (1870), pp. 167–8; Maupassant (1962) [1882], p. 56; Faure (1885), II, p. 305; Versini (1972), p. 123; Letters, Franceschi et al. to Prefect, 1847. ADCS 1.M.224; Marcaggi (1932), pp. 270–1; and Marcaggi (1898a), p. 310, citing Colombani's lament; see also Régis and Martin (n.d.), pp. 118–19; and for the general practice, Letter, Minister of War to Minister of Justice, 21 February 1848. AN BB^{18}1460; and Ambrosi (1972), p. 130.

210 Bouchez (1843), p. 88; and Fée (1850), pp. 231–7.

211 Letter, Francesco-Maria Bruni, An IX. AN BB^{18}236; Marcaggi (1898b), pp. 133–46; Caisson (1978b), p. 162; and Ceccaldi (1974), pp. 359–60.

212 Faure (1858), pp. 267–71 and 287; Bertrand (1870), p. 178; Ortoli (1883), pp. 204–19. One of the men is a priest.

213 Captain Frediani, *Mémoire* (1821). AN BB^{18}243; Benson (1825), p. 65; and Case v. A. Paoli et al., Extraordinary Criminal Court, Sartène, 9 Floréal An X. ADCS 3.U. 5/129. In the latter case, the stabbing was done by women.

214 Case v. Vecchioni, Extraordinary Criminal Court, 6 Floréal An X. ADCS 7.U.1/21; Report, Subprefect, 30 September 1824. ADCS 4.M.91.

215 Marcaggi (1898b), p. 24; *Journal du Département de la Corse*, 2 April 1829; Case v. G.-D. Casanova, Assize Court, 1st session 1865. AN BB^{20}273; and Letter, Sebastiano Capellini to Comte Berthier, 1813(?). AN BB^{18}242. In Montenegro, the term 'to drink blood' was a synonym for 'to kill'. Durham (1928), p. 162.

216 Mérimée (1840b), pp. 734–7 and 739–45; Tommaseo (1841), p. 105; Viale (1855), pp. 77–83; Ortoli (1887), pp. 230–3 and 300–11; Ettori (1978), p. 263 note; Flaubert (1973) [1840], p. 325; and Faure (1858), pp. 199–202.

217 For parallels, see Durham (1928), pp. 66ff and 162–72; and Hasluck (1954), pp. 219 and 224–5.

218 Tommaseo (1841), p. 90; and Ceccaldi (1974), p. 346; see also, for comparison, Meligrana (1979), pp. 310–11.

219 Case v. G. Miliani et al., Assize Court, 2nd session 1847. *Gaz. Trib.*, 18 July 1847, No. 6252; and Southwell Colucci (1933), pp. 225–6.

220 Djilas (1958), p. 106.

221 Southwell Colucci (1933), pp. 209–10.

222 The terms 'blood enemy', 'enemies of blood', 'enmities of blood' were all in currency; see, e.g., Case v. G.-S. Casalonga, Assize Court, 3rd session 1848. AN BB^{20}142; and v. S. Costa, 2nd session 1851. AN BB^{20}152; and Petition for clemency for F. Bastianesi. AN BB^{24}798; see also Cozzi (1910), p. 663; Durham (1928), p. 168; Mirambel (1943), pp. 386–91; Chelhod (1968), pp. 45, 55 and 56; and Black-Michaud (1975), pp. 80–5. In Albania the avenger was called the 'father of the blood' and among the Jordanian Bedouin the 'representative of the blood'. In Albania, a state of feud was called 'being in blood', and among the Bedouin the three days after a killing were the time of 'the boiling of the blood'. Also of relevance, among the Bedouin, too, the shedding of the blood of a virgin bride given in marriage to settle a feud was seen as a kind of symbolic vengeance, blood for blood.

223 Filippi (1906), p. 32; Cases v. P.-M. Paoli, Assize Court, 4th session 1843. AN BB^{20}121; and v. … , 1st session 1836. *Gaz. Trib.*, 6 April 1836; and Réalier-Dumas (1819), p. 19.

224 Comiti (1933), p. 241; and see Durham (1928), pp. 69 and 164. In Montenegro, a woman was of a different blood from the men of the tribe into which she married; 'blood', moreover, was only inherited from one's father.

225 See Durham (1928), p. 170.

226 Southwell Colucci (1933), pp. 209–10 and 216; Versini (1972), p. 90; Cesari-Rocca (1908), p. 76, referring to *c.* 1814; Barry (1893), pp. 288–9; and Ambrosi (1972), pp. 37–8, referring to 1920. The term *carne* also had kinship connotations as in *cugine carnale*.

227 Case v. A.-P. Ottaviani, Criminal Court, 1809. ADCS 2.U.1/43; Letters, Francesco-Maria Bruni. AN BB¹⁸236; and Giacomo-Maria Poli et al., to Prefect, 10 March 1842. ADCS 1.M.229; Bertrand (1870), pp. 18–19; Ortoli (1887), pp. 248–55; and Bourde (1887), p. 236. No actual ritual cannibalism, such as is reported in the Balkans, for example, occurred in Corsica, though Tommaseo mentions one case of real cannibalism by bandits unable to get other food; see Durham (1928), pp. 159–62; and Tommaseo (1841), p. 102. All reports of 'real' cannibalism should, of course, be treated with some but not total scepticism; *pace* Arens (1979).

228 Lorenzi de Bradi (1928), p. 168.

229 See e.g. Durham (1928); Lawson (1910), pp. 441ff; Du Boulay (1982); and Gregorovius (1855), p. 149 note, referring to parallel Arab and Hebrew beliefs.

230 E.g. Mérimée (1840b), pp. 734–7, citing *vocero* for Emmanuele de Piazzole, juge de paix of the canton of Orezza, killed in 1813; and Tommaseo (1841), p. 114.

231 Homer, *Odyssey*, Book IX, in Rieu (1946), pp. 175ff; and see comments of Lombardi-Satriani (1979), p. 337.

232 As it might be in certain circumstances, for example among the Berbers of Morocco; see Westermarck (1934), p. 361.

233 Durkheim (1970), p. 356; see also Durham (1928), pp. 162–3.

234 Case v. C.-G. Carlotti, Assize Court, 3rd session 1856. AN BB²⁰185.

235 Carrington and Lamotte (1957), p. 89; and Carrington (1971a), pp. 46–7; see also De Martino (1955a), p. 32 (S. Italy); Evans-Pritchard (1976), pp. xiii and 24ff (Azande); and Guiart (n.d.), p. 6 (Siberia).

236 These are, of course, a nearly universal phenomenon; see, for example, Hole (1978), pp. 7, 40 and *passim*; and Randell (1966), pp. 99–100 (Britain); Brékilien (1966), pp. 236–8 (Brittany); and Guiart (n.d.), pp. 5 and 8.

237 Ortoli (1887), pp. 14–15; Viale (1855), p. 17; and Ortoli (1883), pp. 317–18.

238 Bouchez (1843), pp. 21 and 44–5 note; Gregorovius (1855), p. 188; Galletti (1863), p. 72; Ortoli (1883), pp. 317–18; Andrei (1893), p. 193; Filippi (1897), pp. 460 and 464–7; Bartoli (1898), p. 225 and 243–4; Rossi (1900), p. 172; Lorenzi de Bradi (1928), p. 287; Casanova (1931–2), I, p. xxiii; Southwell Colucci (1933), p. 214; Lorenzi de Bradi (1936), pp. 149–52; Carrington and Lamotte (1957), p. 86; Chiari (1960), p. 133; Carrington (1971a), pp. 49–50; Giacomo-Marcellesi (1979), pp. 113–14; and Ravis-Giordani (1979b), pp. 364–5. The term *squadra d'Arrozza* apparently derives from *squadra* or *squatra*, meaning 'band' or 'team', and *beroda*, *baroca* or *dadora*, relating to the corpse or coffin. According to Ortoli the appearance of the *squadra* was reserved 'for important people'.

239 Case v. Cucchi, Assize Court, 4th session 1853. AN BB²⁰164.

240 The most important account is provided by Carrington and Lamotte (1957); see also Vuillier (1896), pp. 148 and 158–61; Andrei (1893), p. 193; Bartoli (1898), pp. 243–4; Lorenzi de Bradi (1928), p. 290; Casanova (1931–2), I, pp. xxiv–xxv and xxvii; Lorenzi de Bradi (1936), p. 152; Carrington and Lamotte (1958); Chiari (1960), pp. 131–5; Carrington (1971), pp. 51–61; Favreau-Cancellieri (1975), p. 15; Caisson (1978b), p. 160; Casta (1978), p. 182; Ravis-Giordani (1978a), p. 146; and Christophari (1981), pp. 51, 59, 72–3 and 74.

241 Evans-Pritchard (1976), p. 231; Lawrence (1952), pp. 340–2; and Gough (1958), p. 467.

242 Carrington (1971a), pp. 56–7; Ettori (1978), pp. 249 and 260 note 27; Bartoli (1898), p. 230; Ortoli (1883), pp. 317–18; and Ravis-Giordani (1979b), pp. 364–5.

243 Du Boulay (1982), pp. 224, 232 and 237.

244 See, e.g. Southwell Colucci (1933), pp. 146, 151, 155, 197, 199 and *passim*.

245 See e.g. Bateson (1958), Ch. V; Lawrence (1952); and Evans-Pritchard (1976), p. 5 and *passim*.

246 Southwell Colucci (1933), pp. 178 and 162 citing *voceri*.
247 Ginzburg (1983), esp. pp. 2, 16ff, 33ff, 105–6 and 153ff. The *benandanti* ride out at night 'in spirit' and fight with witches or the dead, using sticks of fennel as weapons, in order to ensure the fertility and well-being of their own villages. They act involuntarily and become *benandanti* through having been born with a caul. After their battles, they and the witches visit people's houses and, if there is a clean pail of water there, they drink it and pass on; if not, they enter the houses and spoil the wine in the cellars.
248 Hole (1978), pp. 41–3; Read (n.d.), p. 1076; Briggs (1971), Part B, 2, pp. 505–6, 509–10 and 576; and Brékilien (1966), pp. 214–15.
249 Chiari (1960), p. 122.

14 Conclusion

1 See e.g. Lewis (1961), esp. p. 46; Otterbein (1965), p. 1470; Hallpike (1973), esp. pp. 454–5; Adler (1980), p. 75; Laburthe-Tolra (1980), p. 163; and Boehm (1984), pp. 225 and 241.
2 Boehm (1984), pp. 52–3, 195–6 and 218–19; also Gray et al. (1909), p. 720; and Brögger (1968), p. 231.
3 E.g. Peters (1967), pp. 262 and 268; Peters (1975), p. x; and Black-Michaud (1975), esp. pp. 63–70 and 86. Both writers confusingly use the terms 'vendetta' (finite) and 'feud' (endless) here, inverting or ignoring the assumption in common parlance that vendetta is either a lengthy and serious kind of feud or that the two are synonymous.
4 For examples of the latter, see Boissevain (1965), pp. 137–9 (Malta); Cohen (1972) (central Italy); Pocock (1975), p. 219 (Mundurucu of Brazil); and Bureau (1980) (Gamo of Ethiopia); see also, more generally, Roberts (1979), pp. 15, 33, 47–79 and 154–63.
5 Gregorovius (1855), pp. 134–5; Molinari (1886), pp. 259–60; Le Joindre (1904), p. 93; Rivers (1916); Brögger (1968), pp. 231 and 233; Chelhod (1968), pp. 65–6; Middleton and Tait (eds.) (1970), pp. 20–1; Black-Michaud (1975), pp. 145–9; Pigliaru (1975), esp. pp. 17–18 and 109–27; Du Boulay (1979), pp. 83–4; and Chelhod (1980), p. 128.
6 It is also possible for the system to 'fail', as it were, which it appears to have done among the Kaingáng; see Henry (1941), pp. 49–50.
7 E.g. Gellner (1969), p. 127; and Boehm (1984), p. 203.
8 Bialor (1968), pp. 120–1; and Middleton and Tait (eds.), (1970), pp. 20 and 22.
9 See Maitland (1911), p. 220; Mirambel (1943), pp. 382 and 387–8; Caisson (1974), p. 120; and Verdier (1980), p. 17.
10 E.g. Gellner (1969), p. 123 note.
11 E.g. Cozzi (1910), p. 658; Du Boulay (1979), pp. 177–8; and Otterbein (1965), p. 1470.
12 See e.g. Ganshof (1970), p. 96 (Carolingian Empire); Philpotts (1913), pp. 81, 87 and 109 (medieval and early modern Denmark); and Wormald (1980).
13 See Philpotts (1913), p. 108; Siegel and Beals (1960a), pp. 111–13 and 116; Stirling (1960), p. 74; Stirling (1965), p. 263; Nash (1967), pp. 466 and 468–9; Balikci (1968); Santoni (1978), p. 231; and Du Boulay (1979), pp. 249–50.
14 See Heers (1974), p. 116: 'The vendetta marks the whole of medieval life, especially in the towns.'
15 Vanutberghe (1904), p. 345; Maestrati (1962); Thrasher (1970), pp. 238ff, 326 and 336; and Carrington (1971b).
16 See Levi (1948), pp. 20–1ff; Dolci (1963), p. 59; and, more generally, Verdier (1980), p. 31.
17 See Thurnwald (1949), p. 559; and Barth (1965), p. 85.

18 Montherot (1840), pp. 62–3; Griffon (1841), p. 35; Roger (1945), p. 187; Carrington (1971a), p. 85; and Versini (1979), pp. 63, 90–4 and 213.

19 Tarrow (1967), pp. 40 and 66–7.

20 See Hanawalt (1977); and Beames (1978) for examples of societies with a high rate of 'social homicide'. '

21 Pomponi (1978a), pp. 25–7; and (1976c), pp. 167–8.

22 See Black-Michaud (1975), pp. 24–5 and 158; and Byock (1982), p. 24, citing Heinrich Beck.

23 Malaspina (1876), pp. 372–3; Versini (1979), pp. 76–7; and Black-Michaud (1975), p. 148.

24 See Davis (1977), pp. 89–101.

25 See Gregorovius (1855), pp. 137 and 140; and, for parallels, Scott (n.d.), XII, pp. 261–2; Djilas (1958), p. 107; and Kipling (1964) [1895], p. 197.

26 See, for comparison, Turner (1971), pp. 359 and 363; Garine (1980), p. 92; and Boehm (1984), pp. 88–9 and 187–9.

27 See e.g. Wilson (1983), pp. 29–31 and 401–2, on the former; and Roberts (1979), pp. 91–4; Bureau (1980); and Schott (1980), pp. 192–5, on the latter.

28 See Soustelle (1962).

29 See Bloch (1965), pp. 293–9; Bateson (1958), pp. 6 and 19–20; Hallpike (1977); and Guiart (n.d.), p. 91.

30 See e.g. Henry (1941); Nash (1967); and Hanawalt (1977).

Sources and bibliography

Primary sources

Archives Nationales
BB[18] Ministère de la Justice, Division Criminelle, 1795–1898 (Correspondence and reports, mainly by Procureur-général)
BB[20] Ministère de la Justice, Cours d'assises, 1830–95 (Summaries of trials at the Assize Court in Bastia, made usually by the Président of the session, sometimes by the Procureur-général, and sent to Paris. The full trial papers, kept in Bastia, were destroyed during the Second World War. The official summaries in BB[20] are incomplete and have been complemented by consulting the selected accounts in the *Gazette des Tribunaux*)
BB[24] Ministère de la Justice, Grâces demandées et accordées ou refusées, 1820–85 (Petitions for clemency, with accompanying documents)
BB[30] Ministère de la Justice, Affaires criminelles, etc., 1828–71
F[7] Police générale, 1807–1917 (including reports on banditry)

Archives Départementales de la Corse du Sud
1.M Haute police, 1800–1939 (Prefects' correspondence, banditry, etc.)
2.M Personnel administratif, 1800–76 (Nomination of mayors, etc.)
4.M Police générale, 1800–84 (Reports by subprefects, gendarmerie, etc.)
5.M Santé publique et hygiene, 1803–26 (including cemeteries)
2.U Procédures criminelles, 1800–67
3.U Procédures correctionnelles, etc., 1800–1919
4.U Justices de paix, conciliations, conseils de famille, 1800–1930
7.U Tribunal Criminelle Extraordinaire, etc., 1800–3
1.V Cultes, Plaintes contre ecclésiastiques, 1821–1906
2.V Police du culte, 1801–1909
1 and 3.X Enfants trouvés, etc., 1793–1885

Archives Départementales de la Haute-Corse
E.6 Communes: Tomino, 1779 and 1820–1945
E.18 Communes: Venzolasca, 1866–1912
E.29 Communes: Penta-di-Casinca, 1795–1908
1.J.2/1 Collection Franceschi (Tomino/Rogliano)
3.P.851–4 Cadastre: Venzolasca, 1848–1914

Books, articles, etc. relating to Corsica

Abbatucci, Séverin (1869). *Aux Electeurs de la Corse.* BN Le[77]1781 Broadsheet.
Abeau, M. le Chanoine (1888). *La Corse au double point de vue de l'esprit de famille et de la trempe du caractère*, Conférence donnée au Cercle S. Mitre. Ajaccio. Pamphlet.

Abelleira, Simone (1981). 'Techniques et instruments agricoles à Crosciano', *BSSHNC*, No. 638, pp. 85–117.

Albitreccia, Antoine (1942a). *La Corse, Son évolution au XIXe siècle et au début du XXe siècle.* Paris.

(1942b). *Le Plan terrier de la Corse au XVIIIe siècle.* Paris.

Almanacco popolare di Corsica per l'anno 1931. Oletta.

Ambrosi, Jean (1972). *La Vendetta ne tue pas l'amour.*

Andrei, A. (1893). *A travers la Corse.* Paris.

Anfossi, M.G. (1918). 'Recherches sur la distribution de la population en Corse', *BSSHNC*, Nos. 387–8, pp. 71–135.

Antonetti, Pierre (1979). 'La condition de la femme, du XIIIe au XVIe siècle', I–III, *Corse-Matin*, 2, 5 and 7 June.

Appolis, Emile (1964). 'Les Rapports entre Catholiques de rite grec et de rite latin à Cargèse (Corse)', *ACNSS*, 88, pp. 85–110. Paris.

Arbos, Philippe (1933). 'A propos de la maison corse', *RGA*, XXI, pp. 450–2.

Archer, D. (1924). *Corsica, The Scented Isle.* London.

Ardouin-Dumazet (1898). *Voyage en France, La Corse*, 14th series. Paris and Nancy.

Arrighi, A. (1856a). *Discours prononcé à la rentrée de la Cour Impériale de Bastia.* Bastia. Pamphlet.

Arrighi, A. (1856b). *La Veuve d'Arbellara, Roman historique.* Bastia.

Arrighi, Paul (1970). *La Vie quotidienne en Corse au XVIIIe siècle.* Paris.

(1976). *Le Livre des dictons corses, 500 dictons et surnoms collectifs sur 300 localités de l'Ile.* Toulouse.

(ed.) (1971). *Histoire de la Corse.* Toulouse.

Arrighi, P.-L. (1896). *Discours prononcé à la rentrée de la Cour d'Appel.* Bastia. Pamphlet.

Aurenche, Dr Henri (1926). *Sur les chemins de la Corse.* Paris.

Baedeker, Karl (1895). *South-eastern France from the Loire to the Riviera and the Italian Frontier including Corsica, A Handbook for Travellers.* Leipzig.

(1902). *Southern France including Corsica, Handbook for Travellers.* Leipzig. 4th edn. Also 1914, 6th edn.

Ballard (1852). Lettre du 16 août 1852 rendant compte au ministère d'une mission en Corse. BN Li²⁹12. Ms.

Barry, John Warren (1893). *Studies in Corsica, Sylvan and Social.* London.

Bartoli, Abbé (1898). *Histoire de la Corse*, I. Paris.

Bazal, Jean (1973). *Avec les derniers bandits corses.* Paris.

Bazin, René (1913). *Nord-Sud, Amérique – Angleterre – Corse – Spitzberg.* Paris.

Beaulieu-Delbet, J. (1897). *Souvenirs de Corse.* Tours.

Beaumont, Baron de (1822). *Observations sur la Corse.* Paris.

Bennet, James Henry (1876). *La Corse et la Sardaigne, Etude de voyage et de climatologie.* Paris.

Benson, Robert (1825). *Sketches of Corsica: or A Journal Written during a Visit to that Island in 1823 with an Outline of its History and Specimens of the Language and Poetry of the People.* London.

Bernardini, C. (1970). 'Bastia et sa région sous la Monarchie de Juillet (1830–1848)', *BSSHNC* No. 595, pp. 23–59; and No. 596, pp. 9–49.

Bertarelli, L.V. (1929). *Guida d'Italia del Touring Club Italiano, Sardegna e Córsica.* Milan.

Bertoni, Abbé Modeste (1933). *Le Sanctuaire de N.D. des Grâces de Lavasina, Brando (Corse).* Bastia.

Bertrand, Félix (1852). *Discours prononcé par M. Félix Bertrand, 1er avocat-général, à la rentrée solennelle de la Cour d'Appel de Bastia.* Pamphlet.

(1870). *La Vendetta, le banditisme et leur suppression, Tableau des mœurs corses.* Paris.

Bertrand-Rousseau, Pierrette (1978). *Ile de Corse et magie blanche, Etude des comportements magico-thérapeutiques*, Publications de la Sorbonne, Série 'NS Recherches', 27. Paris.

Bessières, Abbé X. (1892). *Le Recrutement du clergé en Corse à l'heure actuelle.* Bar-le-Duc. Pamphlet.

Bevilacqua, M.V. (1967). 'L'Evolution des structures agraires dans la commune d'Ota', *BSSHNC*, No. 587, pp. 45–63.

Bigot, Maximilien (1890). *Paysans corses en communauté, Porchers-bergers des montagnes de Bastelica, propriétaires ouvriers, dans le système du travail sans engagements d'après les renseignements recueillis sur les lieux en 1869* (contrôleés et confirmés en 1887 par M.F. Escard), *Les Ouvriers des Deux Mondes*, 2nd series, II, No. 64, pp. 433–524.

Bizouard, Patrick (1964). 'Quelques traits relatifs à l'histoire du tabac en Corse', *CH*, IV, Nos. 13–14, pp. 75–80.

Black, C.B. (1892). *Itinerary through Corsica by its Rail, Carriage and Forest Roads.* London and Ajaccio. 3rd edn.

Blanchard, Raoul (1915). 'Les Genres de vie en Corse et leur évolution', *BSSHNC*, Nos. 364–6, pp. 3–63.

(1926). *La Corse.* Grenoble.

Blanqui, J.-A. (1841). 'Rapport sur l'état économique et moral de la Corse en 1838', *Mémoires de l'Académie Royale des Sciences Morales et Politiques de l'Institut de France*, III, pp. 485–568.

Boland, Henri and Leca, Philippe (1929). *La Corse et l'Ile d'Elbe.* Paris.

Bonaparte, Prince Roland (1891). *Une Excursion en Corse.* Paris.

Borel-Léandri, Jean-Marie (1978). *Architecture et vie traditionnelle en Corse.*

Bouchez, E. (1843). *Nouvelles corses tirées de J.V. Grimaldi.* Paris.

Bourde, Paul (1887). *En Corse, L'Esprit de clan – Les moeurs politiques – Les vendettes – Le banditisme.* Paris.

Bournet, A. (1888). *Une Mission en Corse, Notes d'anthropologie criminelle.* Lyon. Pamphlet.

Brady, Frank and Pottle, Frederick A. (eds.) (1955). *Boswell on the Grand Tour: Italy, Corsica and France 1765–1766.* London.

Busquet, J. (1919). *Le Droit de la vendetta et les paci corses.* Paris.

Caisson, Max (1974). 'L'Hospitalité corse comme relation d'ambivalence', *EC*, NS II, pp. 115–27.

Caisson, Max et al. (1978a). *Pieve e Paesi, Communautés rurales corses.* Paris.

Caisson, M. (1978b). 'Les Morts et les limites', in Caisson et al., *Pieve e Paesi*, Ch. VI.

Callon, M. (1931). 'Mouvement de la population de la Corse 1821–1920', *BSSHNC*, Nos. 496–501, pp. 251–97.

Campbell, Thomasina M.A.E. (1868). *Notes on the Island of Corsica in 1868.* London.

Campi, Louis (1901). *Le Plan terrier de l'Ile de Corse, Son histoire et ses vicissitudes.* Ajaccio.

Carlotti, J. (1936). *Sur l'agriculture corse, Etude parue dans 'La Corse Agricole'.* Pamphlet.

Carrington, Dorothy (1971a). *Granite Island, A Portrait of Corsica.* London.

(1971b). 'Les Pozzo di Borgo et les Bonaparte (jusqu'en 1793), d'après les mémoires manuscrits de Charles-André Pozzo di Borgo', *Problèmes d'histoire de la Corse (de l'Ancien Régime à 1815)*, Actes du Colloque d'Ajaccio, 29 October 1969, pp. 101–29. Paris. Société des Etudes Robespierristes.

Carrington, D. and Lamotte, P. (1957). 'Les "Mazzeri"', *EC*, 15–16, pp. 81–91.

(1958). 'A propos des Mazzeri', *EC*, 17, pp. 66–7.

Casabianca, X. de (1853). *Aperçus historiques sur le banditisme, Discours prononcé à la rentrée de la Cour Impériale de Bastia.* Pamphlet.

Casanova, Abbé (1931–2). *Histoire de l'Eglise corse.* Zicavo. 3 vols.

Casanova, Antoine (1965). 'Mariage et Communauté rurale: Exemple corse', *Cahiers du Centre d'Etudes et de Recherches Marxistes*, Nos. 37, pp. 1–29, and 46, pp. 1–30.

(1966). 'Technologie et communautés rurales: Notes sur les pressoirs préindustriels de Corse', *CH*, VI, Nos. 21–2, pp. 37–61.

(1968a). L'Aire de diffusion en Corse au XIXe siècle du type le plus ancien de pressoir (le pressoir à torsion)', *Arts et Traditions Populaires*, pp. 237–57.

(1968b). 'Typologie et diffusion des pressoirs préindustriels dans les communautés rurales de Corse', *CH*, VIII, Nos. 31–2, pp. 39–56.

(1971). 'L'Evolution des techniques rurales en Corse: Le cas du moulin à eau (fin XVIIIe – début XIXe siècle)', in *Problèmes d'histoire de la Corse*, pp. 45–67.

(1973). 'Culture populaire et société rurale traditionnelle: Les problèmes du Carnaval', in *Hommage à Georges Fourrier*, Centre de Recherches d'Histoire et Littérature, Annales Littéraires de l'Université de Besançon, pp. 87–108. Paris.

(1974). 'Technologie et communautés rurales en Corse à la fin du XVIIIe siècle: Aspects de la prédominance des machines élémentaires', *EC*, ns II, No. 3, pp. 83–121.

(1978). 'Techniques et sociétés, Forces productives et rapports de production dans les communautés rurales corses (fin du XVIIIème – début du XIXème), in Caisson, M. et al., *Pieve e Paesi*, Ch. 2.

Casta, Francois-J. (1965). 'La Granitula, Réflexions autour d'une antique tradition corse du Vendredi Saint', *CH*, V, No. 20, pp. 5–10.

(1973). 'L'Histoire religieuse de la Corse, Perspectives et orientations actuelles', *EC*, ns I, pp. 175–91.

(1974). *Le Diocèse d'Ajaccio*. Paris.

(1976). 'L'Eglise corse et la femme', *EC*, ns IV, Nos. 6–7, 'Femmes corses et femmes méditerranéennes', pp. 286–309.

(1978). 'La Religion populaire: A la recherche de ses formes d'expression', in Caisson, M. et al., *Pieve e Paesi*, Ch. 7.

(1979). 'Le Sentiment religieux des Corses face à la mort (Approches d'ethnologie religieuse)', *EC*, ns VII, Nos 12–13, 'La Mort en Corse et dans les Sociétés Mediterranéens', Actes du Colloque, Bonifacio, March 1976, pp. 77–104.

Cavallucci, Giacomo (1930). *Salvator Viale et la littérature corse*. Besançon.

Ceccaldi, Mathieu (1974). *Dictionnaire Corse–Français, Pieve d'Evisa*. Paris. 2nd revised edn.

Cesari-Rocca, Colonna de (1908). *La Vendetta dans l'histoire*. Paris.

(1909). *Vengeances corses, Chroniques et récits*. Paris.

Chanal, Edouard (n.d.). *Voyages en Corse (Descriptions, récits, légendes)*. Paris. c. 1910.

Chapman, John Mitchel (1908). *Corsica, An Island of Rest*. London.

Chiari, Joseph (1960). *Corsica: Columbus's Isle*. London.

Chiva, I. (1958). 'Causes sociologiques du sous-développement régional: L'exemple corse', *Cahiers Internationaux de Sociologie*, 24(1), pp. 141–7.

(1963). 'Social organisation, traditional economy and customary law in Corsica: Outline of a plan of analysis', in Pitt-Rivers, Julian (ed.), *Mediterranean Countrymen, Essays in the Social Anthropology of the Mediterranean*, pp. 97–112. Paris and The Hague.

Choury, Maurice (1958). *Tous bandits d'honneur! Résistance et libération de la Corse (juin 1940 – octobre 1943)*. Paris. 2nd edn.

Christophari, Théophile (1981). *La Corse de mon enfance*. Paris.

Comiti, S. (1933). 'La Corse du Sud: Essai de géographie physique et humaine', *BSSHNC*, Nos. 502–13.

Coppolani, Jean (1949). 'Cargèse, Essai sur la géographie humaine d'un village corse', *RGA*, 37, pp. 71–108.

Costa, A. (1930). 'Le Premier Jury Criminel de la Corse', *BSSHNC*, No. 489, pp. 99–111.

Cowen, William (1848). *Six Weeks in Corsica, Illustrated with Fourteen Highly Finished Etchings*. London.

Cristofini, Bernard, Deffontaines, Jean-Pierre, Raichon, Camille, and Verneuil, Bernard de (1978). 'Pratiques d'élevage en Castagniccia, Explorations d'un milieu naturel et social en Corse', *ER*, 71–2, pp. 89–109.

Croze, Austin de (1911). *La Chanson populaire de l'Ile de Corse*. Paris.

Dalmas, Paul (1978). 'Discours masculin et discours féminin dans les chants de la communauté de San Gavinu di u Castel d'Acqua en Ampugnani', *EC*, ns VI, No. 10, pp. 5–57.

Darrell, Robert (ed.) (1935). *Spada the Bandit, The Autobiography of André Spada – Last of the Corsican Bandits*. London.

Deane, Shirley (1965). *In a Corsican Village*. New York.

Defranceschi, Jean (1974). 'Pasteurs et cultivateurs en Corse au XVIIIe siècle', *Annales Historiques de la Révolution Française*, 46, pp. 542–56.

(1978). 'La communauté rurale corse à la fin de l'Ancien Régime: Recherches sur l'occupation des sols', in Caisson, M. et al., *Pieve e Paesi*, Ch. 3.

De la Rocca, Jean (1857). *La Corse et son avenir*. Paris.

(1858a). *Mission du Prêtre corse*. Paris. Pamphlet.

(1858b). *Mémoire sur la Mission du Prêtre corse*. Pamphlet. (AN BB^{18}1593).

Delarue, Louis (1970). *Prêtre rien que ça, Le Père Charles-Dominique Albini, O.M.I., 1790–1839*. Paris.

Demailly, Serge (1978). 'La Corse en dépendance, Eléments pour une réflexion rétroprospective', *Peuples Méditerranéens*, 3, pp. 89–112.

Desideri, Lucia (1978). 'La Violence humiliée', *TM*, 34, Nos. 385–6, pp. 203–15.

D'Este, Margaret (1905). *Through Corsica with a Camera*. New York.

Dufresne (1847). *Cour Royale de Bastia, Audience solennelle de rentrée du 6 novembre 1847, Discours prononcé par M. Dufresne, Procureur Général du Roi*. Pamphlet.

Dupâquier, Jacques and Jadin, Louis (1972). 'Structure of household and family in Corsica, 1769–71', in Laslett, Peter and Wall, Richard (eds.), *Household and Family in Past Time*, pp. 283–97. Cambridge.

Emmanuelli, René (1969). 'Note sur le Droit pénal corse au XVIIIe siècle', *BSSHNC*, No. 592, pp. 89–106.

(1971a). 'L'Intégration à la France', in Arrighi, P. (ed.), *Histoire de la Corse*, Ch. XI.

(1971b). 'Problèmes d'hier et d'aujourd'hui', in Arrighi, P. (ed.), *Histoire de la Corse*, Ch. XII.

Ettori, Fernand (1971). 'La Paix génoise (1569–1729)', in Arrighi, P. (ed.), *Histoire de la Corse*, Ch. IX.

(1976). 'La Découverte de la femme corse par les français au XVIIIe siècle', *EC*, ns IV, Nos. 6–7, pp. 184–99.

(1979). 'Le Vocero comme catharsis des tensions familiales et sociales', *EC*, ns VII, Nos. 12–13, pp. 177–200.

Facy, Maurice (1933). *Corse du Sud*. Lille and Paris.

Faure, Gracieux (1858). *Le Banditisme et les Bandits célèbres de la Corse*. Paris.

(1885). *Voyage en Corse, Récits dramatiques et pittoresques*. Paris. 2 vols.

Favreau-Cancellieri, M. (1975). 'La Vallée du Cruzzini', *BSSHNC*, No. 614, pp. 9–57.

Fée, A.L.A. (1850). *Voceri, Chants populaires de la Corse, précédés d'une excursion faite dans cette île en 1845*. Paris and Strasburg.

Feydel, Gabriel (1799). *Moeurs et coutumes des Corses*. Paris.

Filippi, J.-M. (1906). *Recueil de sentences et dictons usités en Corse avec traduction et lexique*. Paris.

Filippi, Julie (1897). 'Légendes, croyances et superstitions de la Corse', *Revue des Traditions Populaires*, IX, pp. 457–67.

Finelli, Angèle (n.d.). *Un beau village corse, Tavera et ses légendes*. Ajaccio.

Flaubert, Gustave (1973). 'Voyage aux Pyrénées et en Corse' (1840), *Oeuvres complètes*, 10, pp. 283–349. Paris.

Foata, P.-M. (de la or della) (1856). *Du Parcours et de la vaine pâture*. Bastia. Pamphlet.

(1867). *Litanies du Mois de Marie, Chant du montagnard corse dédiant le mois des fleurs à la Vierge Immaculée*. Bastia. Pamphlet.

(1973). *Poesie giacose in lingua vernacula della Pieve d'Ornano*.

Fontana, Jean (1905). *Essai sur l'histoire du Droit privé en Corse (Etude critique des Statuts Corses du XVIe siècle)*. Paris.

Fontanilles-Laurelli, F. (1963). 'Répartition du Domaine de Migliacciaro entre les communes de Fiumorbo sous le 1er Empire', *BSSHNC*, No. 566, pp. 62–8.

Forcioli-Conti, Comte (1897). *Notre Corse*. Ajaccio.

Forester, Thomas (1858). *Rambles in the Islands of Corsica and Sardinia with Notices of their History, Antiquities and Present Condition*. London.

Franceschini, Emile (1922) (1923) and (1924). 'Notes pour servir a l'histoire de la Corse sous la Restauration, Les Rapports de Constant, Commissaire spécial de police en Corse 1816–1818', *BSSHNC*, Nos. 437–40, pp. 243–346; Nos. 449–52, pp. 3–96; and Nos. 457–68, pp. 99–176 and 273–360.

Franceschini, E. and F. (1913). 'Un préfet de la Corse sous la Restauration, M. de Saint-Genest 1815–1818', *BSSHNC*, Nos. 358–60, pp. 49–101.

Franceschini, Emile and Jules (1916). 'Le Comte de Vignolle, préfet de la Corse (14 mars 1818 – 15 décembre 1819)', *BSSHNC*, Nos. 370–2, pp. 241–56.

  (1918). 'La Corse sous l'administration de M. de Vignolle', *BSSHNC*, Nos. 385–8, pp. 29–86.

  (1919). 'Situation morale et judiciaire de la Corse, 1817–1821', *BSSHNC*, Nos. 397–400, pp. 25–53.

Franzini, Dominique (1975). 'L'Araire de la Castagniccia', *BSSHNC*, No. 617, pp. 35–8.

Fumaroli, D. (1921). 'Esquisse géographique et historique sur le Pieve de Bastelica', *BSSHNC*, Nos. 425–8, pp. 65–92.

Galletti, Abbé Jean-Ange (1863). *Histoire illustrée de la Corse*. Paris.

Gaste, Dr (1965). 'Aspects de la vie à Calvi au début du XIXe siècle d'après une note d'un contemporain, Le docteur Gaste, Médecin adjoint à l'hôpital militaire de cette ville (1822)', *CH*, V, No. 19, pp. 47–56.

Geoffray, B. (1982). 'La Population de Manso et de Galeria (Filosorma)', *BSSHNC*, No. 643, pp. 49–68.

Giacomo-Marcellesi, Mathée (1979). 'Le Vocabulaire de la mort en Corse', *EC*, NS VII, Nos. 12–13, pp. 107–14.

Gil, José (1978). 'Vendetta et pouvoir dans la tradition orale corse', *TM*, 34, Nos. 385–6, pp. 182–202.

Girolami-Cortona, Abbé F. (1893). *Géographie générale de la Corse*. Ajaccio.

Glatigny, Albert (1870). *Le Jour de l'an d'un vagabond*. Paris.

Grandchamps, Conte (1859). *La Corse, Sa colonisation et son rôle dans la Méditerranée*. Paris. 2nd edn.

Gregorovius, Ferdinand (1855). *Corsica in its Picturesque, Social and Historical Aspects: The Record of a Tour in the Summer of 1852*. London.

Griffon, Léon (1841). *Aperçu sur la Corse*. Paris and Bastia.

Guitet-Vauquelin, Pierre (1934). 'Tu ne sera pas bandit', *Les Oeuvres Libres*, 151 (January), pp. 133–58.

Hauser, H. (1909). 'En Corse, Une terre qui meurt', *Revue de Mois*, 10, pp. 539–69.

Hernoux, V. (1852). *Marais de la Corse, Considérations générales et projets de dessèchement des Marais de Calvi, St Florent et du Golo (rive droite), Rapport de l'ingénieur en chef*.

Hogg, Garry (1973). *Corsica, The Fragrant Isle*. London.

Jeoffroy-Faggianelli, P. (1979). *L'Image de la Corse dans la littérature française romantique*. Paris.

Joanne, Adolphe (1881). *Itinéraire général de la France, Provence, Alpes-Maritimes, Corse*. Paris.

Juta, Réné (1926). *Concerning Corsica*. London.

Kofman, Eleonore (1980). 'Differential Modernisation, Social Conflicts and Ethnoregionalism in Corsica'. Unpublished paper.

Kolodny, Yerahmiel (1962). *La Géographie urbaine de la Corse*. Paris.

Laade, Wolfgang (1963). 'The Corsican Tribbiera: A Type of Work Song', *Ethnomusicology*, CI, pp. 181–5.

Lacroix, Jean-Bernard (1981). 'Présentation des collections d'Archives Départementales de la Haute-Corse', *BSSHNC*, Nos. 639–40, pp. 15–37.

Lamotte, Pierre (1956a). 'Deux aspects de la vie communautaire en Corse avant 1768', *EC*, 76, No. 9, pp. 33–46.

(1956b). 'Les Biens communaux', *EC*, 76, No. 9, pp. 47–62.

(1956c). 'Le Système des "prese" et les assolements collectifs', *EC*, 76, No. 10, pp. 54–8.

(1956d). 'A propos de l'Arringo', *EC*, 76, No. 10, p. 59.

(1956e). 'La Structure sociale d'une communauté de La Rocca, Fozzano', *EC*, 76, No. 11, pp. 35–47.

(1956f). 'Le "Caracolu"', *EC*, 76, No. 12, pp. 53–4.

(1956g). 'Note sur la propriété arboraire en Corse', *EC*, 76, No. 12, pp. 60–8.

(1957a). 'Un thème ethnographique et ses différents aspects en Corse, Repas et distributions de vivres en l'honneur des morts', *EC*, 77, No. 13, pp. 84–8.

(1957b). 'Restrictions du droit de propriété et sauvegarde des intérêts de la collectivité dans l'ancienne Corse', *EC*, 77, Nos. 15–16, pp. 68–76.

(1961). 'Confrérie et communauté', *Revue d'Etudes Corses*, I, pp. 44–8.

(1964). 'Aspects inédits de la vie communautaire dans l'ancienne Corse', *CH*, IV, Nos. 13–14, pp. 59–66.

Lear, Edward (1870). *Journal of a Landscape Painter in Corsica*. London.

Leca, Jean Claude (1978). 'Une communauté villageoise au XIXe siècle: Calenzana', in Caisson, M. et al., *Pieve e Paesi*, Ch. IV.

Lefèbvre, Paul (1954). 'Situation démographique du Départment de la Corse', *EC*, 74, No. 2, pp. 11–45.

(1955). 'Population urbaine et population rurale en Corse', *EC*, 75, Nos. 7–8, pp. 86–97.

(1957). 'La Population de la Corse', *RGA*, 45, pp. 557–75.

Léger, Marcel and Arlo, J. (1914). *Le Paludisme en Corse, Deuxième campagne antipaludique (1913)*. Laval.

Le Joindre, R. (1904). *La Corse et les Corses*. Paris and Nancy.

Le Mée, R. (1971). 'Un dénombrement des Corses en 1770', *Problèmes d'histoire de la Corse*, pp. 23–44.

Lemps, Abbé de (1844). *Panorama de la Corse ou histoire abrégée de cette île et description des moeurs et usages de ses habitants*. Paris.

Lenclud, Gérard (1979). 'Des feux introuvables, L'Organisation familiale dans un village de la Corse traditionnelle', *ER*, 76, pp. 7–50.

(1985). 'L'Institution successorale comme organisation et comme représentation, La Transmission du patrimoine foncier dans une communauté traditionnelle de la montagne corse, fin du XIXe siècle, début du XXe', *EF*, 15, pp. 35–44.

Lenclud, G. and Pernet, François (1978). 'Ressources du milieu, gestion du troupeau et évolution sociale: Le cas de la Corse', *ER*, 71–2, pp. 49–87.

Lenclud, G. and Ravis-Giordani, Georges (1973). 'Pour une ethnologie de la Corse, Etat actuel des recherches', *EC*, NS I, pp. 193–232.

Levy, Edouard (1934). 'Prénoms corses', *La Semaine Juridique*, No. 25, 24 June, pp. 601–3.

Lorenzi, Louis (1981). 'La "Catastrophe de Corte"...', *Corse-Matin*, 27 July.

Lorenzi de Bradi (1928). *La Corse inconnue*. Paris.

(1936). *Corse*. Paris.

Luciani, J.-M. (1969). 'La Corse sous Napoléon III', *BSSHNC*, Nos. 591–2, pp. 21–84.

Lücke, Hartmut (1977). 'Interprétation cartographique de l'évolution du sol dans la commune de Vescovato (Corse)', *ER*, 66, pp. 23–36.

(1982). 'Observations concernant la diffusion, l'apparence et les changements de l'habitat traditionnel en Corse', *BSSHNC*, No. 643, pp. 87–118.

McLaren, Moray (1966). *Corsica, Boswell, Paoli, Johnson and Freedom*. London.

Maestrati, Léon (1962). 'Les Origines de la rivalité Bonaparte – Pozzo-di-Borgo', *CH*, III, No. 8, pp. 5–16.

(1964). 'Le Régime censitaire en Corse', *CH*, IV, No. 15, pp. 47–62.

Maestroni, François (1978). *Ajaccio et la Madunnuccia*. Pamphlet.

Malaspina, Toussaint (1876). 'La Corse, Moeurs et coutumes', *Revue Politique et Littéraire, Revue des Cours Littéraires*, 2nd series, 6 (October), pp. 350–3.

Mancini, D.-M. (1883). *Géographie physique, politique, historique et économique de la Corse*. Bastia.

Marcaggi, J.-B. (1898a). *Les Chants de la mort et de la vendetta de la Corse*. Paris.

(1898b). *Fleuve de sang, Histoire d'une vendetta corse*. Paris.

(1908). *L'Ile de Corse, Guide pratique*. Ajaccio.

(1926). *Lamenti, voceri, chansons populaires de la Corse*. Ajaccio.

(1932). *Bandits corses d'hier et d'aujourd'hui*. Reprinted 1978.

Marchetti, Pascale (n.d.). *Le Corse sans peine*. Amsterdam.

Marin-Muracciole, Madeleine-Rose (1960). 'Une étrange coutume corse: l'Attacar', *EC*, 80, Nos. 27–8, pp. 10–20.

(1964). *L'Honneur des femmes en Corse du XIIIe siècle à nos jours*. Paris.

Martelli, Marc-François (1960). *Ghisoni*. Ajaccio.

Martin-Gistucci, Marie-Gracieuse (1976). 'Le Statut de la femme corse à travers les proverbes', *EC*, NS IV, Nos. 6–7, pp. 174–83.

(1979), 'La Mort et les morts dans les contes populaires de l'Ile de Corse', *EC*, NS VII, Nos. 12–13, pp. 201–26.

Martini, Marien (1922). 'Le Cap-Corse (Pieve de Rogliano)', *BSSHNC*, Nos. 437–40, pp. 127–86.

(1964a). 'Aspects de la vie communautaire et des pratiques judiciaires au Cap-Corse (1597–1676)', *CH*, IV, No. 16, pp. 51–63.

(1964b). 'Situation économique et humaine du Cap-Corse en 1770–1775', *CH*, IV, Nos. 13–14, pp. 67–74.

(1965). 'Dénombrement de la population du Cap-Corse en 1770', *BSSHNC*, Nos. 574–5, pp. 10–34.

(1967). Review of Versini, X., *Un siècle de banditisme en Corse*, *BSSHNC*, Nos. 583–4, pp. 115–17.

(1970). 'Les premiers pas de l'administration préfectorale en Corse', *BSSHNC*, No. 597, pp. 7–21.

Mattei, Antoine (1867). *Proverbes, locutions et maximes de la Corse*. Paris.

Mattei, Fernand (1912). *Rapport sur la situation criminelle en Corse et les mesures à prendre pour la répression du banditisme*. Corte. Pamphlet.

Maupassant, Guy de (1928). 'En Corse' (1880); and 'Les Bandits corses' (1880), *Au Soleil, Oeuvres Complètes*, pp. 181–230. Paris.

(1962). 'Histoire corse' (1881); 'Un bandit corse' (1882); and 'Une vendetta' (1883), *Contes et Nouvelles*, I. pp. 43–8, 55–8 and 117–22. Paris.

Maurice, J.F. (ed.) (1904). *The Diary of Sir John Moore*, I. London.

Maurras, Charles (1920). 'Une ville grecque et française'; and 'Figures de Corse' (1898), *Anthinea, D'Athènes à Florence*, Books II and III. Paris.

Méjean, Paul (1932). 'Notes sur la maison corse', *RGA*, XX, pp. 655–76.

Meria, Guy (1970). 'La Castagniccia, Terre d'exode? terre d'avenir?', *BSSHNC*, No. 594, pp. 22–65.

Mérimée, Prosper (1840a). *Colomba, Romans et nouvelles*. Paris. 1957 edn.

(1840b). 'Notes d'un voyage en Corse, 1840', *Notes de voyages*. Paris. 1971 edn.

Metz-Noblat, A. de (1885). 'Dix jours en Corse', *Bulletin de la Société de Géographie de l'Est*, VIII, pp. 47–64, 381–404 and 724–40.

Miot de Melito, Comte (1858). *Mémoires*. Paris. 3 vols.

Molinari, G. de (1886). *Au Canada et aux Montagnes Rocheuses – En Russie – en Corse*. Paris.

Montherot, M. de (1840). *Promenades en Corse, Anecdotes, rencontres, conversations*. Lyon.

Moracchini, Geneviève and Carrington, Dorothy (1959). *Trésors oubliés des églises de Corse*. Paris.

Morandière, Ch. de la (1933). *Au coeur de la Corse, Le Niolo*. Paris.

Morel, Pierre (1951). *La Corse*. Paris and Grenoble.

Murray, John (ed.) (1868). *A Handbook for Travellers in the Islands of Corsica and Sardinia with Maps*. London and Paris.

Natali, Jean (1961). *La Poésie dialectale primitive du peuple corse*. Bastia.

Natali, J.-B. (1934). '*Parmi le Thym et le Rosée', Chez les bergers de Cuscio (en Corse)*. Paris.

Olivesi, Antoine (1969). 'Les Corses dans l'expansion française contemporaine', in *La Méditerranée de 1919 à 1939*, Actes du Colloque de Nice (March 1968), pp. 151–65. Nice.

Orsini, Jean (1981). 'La communauté de Volpajola vers 1800 et une brève analyse de sa population au XIXe siècle', *BSSHNC*, No. 641, pp. 9–44.

Ortoli, J.B. Frédéric (1883). *Les Contes populaires de l'Ile de Corse*. Paris.

(1887). *Les Voceri de l'Ile de Corse*. Paris.

Patin de La Fizelière (1963). 'Mémoire sur la province et juridiction de Sartène ou de La Rocca', ed. Lamotte, *CH*, III, Nos. 9–10, pp. 57–84.

Patorni, F.M. (1842). *La Corse, Documents historiques, législatifs et judiciaires, 1768 à 1842*. Paris.

Pernet, François and Lenclud, Gérard (1977). *Berger corse, Essai sur la question pastorale*. Grenoble.

Perry, P.J. (1967). 'Economy, Landscape and Society in La Castagniccia (Corsica) since the Late Eighteenth Century', *TIBG*, 41, pp. 209–22.

(1969). 'Le Déclin démographique des cantons de La Porta d'Ampugnani et Piedicroce d'Orezza au cours du dix-neuvième siècle', *CH*, IX, No. 33, pp. 37–47.

(1984). 'L'Arbre à pain: le châtaignier en Corse', *Annales du Midi*, 96, pp. 71–84.

Pierangeli, Henri (1907). *Le Paludisme en Corse et l'assainissement de la côte orientale*.

Pietri, Jean, and Nicolas, Marthe (1977). 'Maisons anciennes de Corse, Brando, Sisco, Pietracorbara', *Cahier Corsica*, 64. Bastia.

Piobb, Pierre (Vincenti, Comte Pierre) (n.d.) *La Corse d'aujourd'hui, Ses moeurs – ses ressources – sa détresse*. Paris. *c.* 1909.

Planhol, Xavier de (1968). 'L'Ancien Commerce de la neige en Corse: Neige d'Ajaccio et neige de Bastia', *Méditerranée*, I, pp. 5–22.

Pompei, P.P. (Sebastiani, H.F.B.) (1821). *Etat actuel de la Corse, Caractère et moeurs de ses habitans*. Paris.

Pomponi, Francis (1974a). 'Les Cahiers de doléances des Corses en 1730', *BSSHNC*, No. 610, pp. 7–65.

(1974b). 'Un siècle d'histoire des biens communaux en Corse dans le delà des Monts (1770–1870)', *EC*, NS II, No. 3, pp. 5–41.

(1975). 'Un siècle d'histoire des biens communaux en Corse (1770–1870), Deuxième partie: Evolution et problèmes au XIXe siècle', *EC*, NS III, No. 5, pp. 15–54.

(1976a). 'La Femme corse: Approche monographique et démographique du problème', *EC*, NS IV, Nos 6–7, pp. 323–57.

(1976b). 'Le Problème de la vaine pâture en Corse au XIXe siècle', *BSSHNC*, No. 621, pp. 19–42.

(1976c). 'Pouvoir et abus de pouvoir des maires corses au XIXe siècle', *ER*, 63–4, pp. 153–90.

(1977). 'Crise de structure économique et crise de conscience corse (fin XIXe siècle – début XXe)', in *Typologie des crises dans les pays méditerranéens (XVIe – XXe siècles)*, Actes des journées d'études Bendor, May 1976, pp. 75–114. Nice.

(1978a). 'A la recherche d'un "invariant" historique: La structure clanique dans la société corse', in Caisson, M. et al., *Pieve e Paesi*, Ch. I.

(1978b). 'Introduction, annexes et données cartographiques', in Caisson, M. et al., *Pieve et Paesi*, Pt. II.

(1979a). 'En amont de la mort: Médécine et morbidité en Corse au XIXe siècle', *EC*, ns VII, Nos. 12–13, pp. 251–73.

(1979b). *Histoire de la Corse*. Paris.

Pomponi, Janine (1962). *La Vie rurale de deux communes corses: Serra di Scopamene et Sotta*. Aix-en-Provence.

Privat, Maurice (1936). *Bandits corses*. Neuilly.

Quantin, Albert (1914). *La Corse, La Nature – les hommes – le présent – l'avenir*. Paris.

Radclyffe Dugmore. A. (n.d.). *Corsica the Beautiful, An Impression of the Island as it is Today and of its History*. London. *c.* 1927.

Raichon, C. (1976). 'Activités agricoles et problèmes de développement regional: Un village de Castagniccia', *BSSHNC*, Nos. 619–20, pp. 43–59.

Rankin, Lt.-Colonel Sir Reginald, Bt. (1930). *A Notebook in Corsica, A Night in the Open at 22,000 feet, Pig-sticking at Jodhpur, Canada in '95 and other Essays*. London.

Ratzel, Friedrich (1899). 'La Corse, Etude anthropogéographique', *AG*, VIII, pp. 304–29.

Raulin, H. and Ravis-Giordani, G. (1978). *L'Architecture rurale française, Corpus des genres des types et des variantes, Corse*. Paris.

Ravis-Giordani, G. (1974). 'Typologie et répartition micro-régionale des araires corses', *EC*, ns II, No. 3, pp. 43–82.

(1976a). 'L'*Alta pulitica* et la *bassa pulitica*: valeurs et comportements politiques dans les communautés villageoises corses (XIXe–XXe siècles)', *ER*, 63–4, pp. 171–89.

(1976b). 'La Femme corse dans la société traditionnelle: Statuts et rôles', *EC*, ns IV, Nos. 6–7, pp. 6–19.

(1978a). 'Espaces et groupes sociaux: Organisation objective et apprehension symbolique', in Caisson, M. et al., *Pieve e Paesi*, Ch. V.

(1978b). 'La Femme corse: images et réalités', in Caisson, M. et al., *Pieve e Paesi*, Ch. VIII.

(1978c). Introduction, Raulin, H. and Ravis-Giordani, G., *L'Architecture*.

(1979a). 'Familles et pouvoir en Corse: Endogamie de lignées et préservation d'un patrimoine symbolique, Le pouvoir électif', *Sociologie du Sud-Est*, 21, pp. 63–9.

(1979b). 'Signes, figures et conduites de l'entre-vie-et-mort: Finzione, mazzeri et streie corses', *EC*, ns VII, Nos. 12–13, pp. 361–82.

Réalier-Dumas, M. (1819). *Mémoire sur la Corse*. Paris.

Régis, Max and Martin, J.-C. (n.d.). *La Vendetta, Etude de moeurs corses*. Paris.

Rémy, Emile (1930). 'La Cour d'Appel de la Corse', *BSSHNC*, Nos. 485–9, pp. 1–98.

Renucci, F.O. (1833–4). *Storia di Corsica*. Bastia. 2 vols.

(1838). *Novelle storiche corse.* Bastia. 3rd edn.

Renucci, Janine (1970). *L'Elevage en Corse, Un archaïsme menacé*, *Revue de Géographie de Lyon*, 45, pp. 357–89.

(1974). *Corse traditionnelle et Corse nouvelle, La Géographie d'une île*. Lyon.

Reparaz, G.A. de (1961). 'L'Evolution des structures agraires dans quelques communes typiques de la Corse', *BSSHNC*, No. 559, pp. 31–53; and No. 560, pp. 53–75.

Richardson, Ralph (1894). 'Corsica, Notes on a Recent Visit', *Scottish Geographical Magazine*, X, pp. 505–24.

Robiquet, F. (1835). *Recherches historiques et statistiques sur la Corse*. Paris and Rennes.

Roger, G. (1945). *Prosper Mérimée et la Corse*. Algiers.

(1947). *L'Ame de la Corse à travers la littérature française*. Algiers.

Römer, Markus (1977). 'Quelques aperçus sur la musique corse', *EC*, NS V, No. 9, pp. 73–91.

Ross, Alan (1948). *Time was Away, A Notebook in Corsica*. London.

Rossi, G. (1900). *Les Corses d'après l'histoire, la légende et la poésie*. Poitiers.

Rossi, H. (ed.) (1962). 'L'Arrondissement de Sartène en 1831 (Rapport présenté par Mr Guibega, Sous-Préfet de Sartène au Conseil d'arrondissement – 1831)', *BSSHNC*, No. 564, pp. 47–59.

Rovère, Ange (1978). 'Pacification, résistance et mouvements populaires en Corse: 1770–1774', *EC*, NS VI, No. 10, pp. 69–116.

Sacquin-Moulin, Michèle (1982). 'La Corse au lendemain de la Révolution de 1830: Etienne Cabet, Procureur Général à Bastia, novembre 1830 – mai 1831', *Revue d'Histoire Moderne et Contemporaine*, XXIX, pp. 650–61.

Saint-Germain, Léonard de (1869). *Itinéraire descriptif et historique de la Corse*. Paris.

Saint-Victor, Paul de (1925). 'Les Vocératrices de la Corse' (1887), *Hommes et Dieux, Etudes d'histoire et de littérature*, pp. 349–68. Paris.

Santoni, Charles (1978). 'La Crise de conscience corse', *TM*, 34, Nos. 385–6, pp. 216–39.

Saravelli-Retali, F. (1976). *La Vie en Corse à travers les proverbes et dictons*. 2nd edn.

Simi, Pierre (1966). *L'Adaptation humaine dans la dépression centrale de la Corse*. Etudes et Travaux de 'Méditerranée', III. Gap.

Sorbier, P.-A. (1833). *Procès-verbal de l'installation de M. Mottet en qualité de procureur-général auprès la Cour Royale de Bastia*. Pamphlet.

(1845). *Voyage en Corse de son altesse royale le Duc d'Orléans*. Paris.

(1863). *Dix ans de magistrature en Corse*. Agen.

Southwell Colucci, Edith (1933). *Canti popolari corsi*. Leghorn.

Spalinowski, E. (1904). *Impressions de Corse*. Paris and Lyon.

Spinosi, Caroline (1956). *Le Droit des gens mariés en Corse du XVIe au XVIIIe siècle*. Aix-en-Provence.

Surier, Albert (1934). *Notre Corse, Etudes et souvenirs*. Paris.

Susini, Charles de (1906). *La Corse et les Corses, Opinions et documents*. Paris.

Susini, Napoléon (1871). *Electeurs insulaires, Discours aux Corses*. Ajaccio. Pamphlet.

Susini della Rocca, J.-P. (1828). *Elections de la Corse, Petition aux Chambres*. Pamphlet.

Thiers, Jacques (1977). 'Aspects de la francisation en Corse au cours du XIXe siècle', *EC*, NS V, No. 9, pp. 5–40.

Thompson, Ian (1971). *Corsica*. Newton Abbot.

(1978). 'Settlement and conflict in Corsica', *TIBG*, NS, 3, pp. 259–73.

Thrasher, Peter Adam (1970). *Pasquale Paoli, An Enlightened Hero 1725–1807*. London.

Togab, Arthur (1905). *Souvenirs de Corse*. Brest.

Tomasi, Xavier (n.d.). *Les Chansons de Cyrnos, Anthologie de la chanson populaire de l'Ile de Corse*. Marseille.

Tommaseo, N. (1841). *Canti popolari Toscani, Corsi, Illirici, Greci*, II. Venice.

Tuckett, F.F. (1884). 'Notes on Corsica', *Alpine Journal*, IX, No. 84, pp. 449–59.

Tuffelli, E. (1977). 'Les Noms de plantes en langue corse', *BSSHNC*, No. 622, pp. 21–35.

Valéry, M. (1837). *Voyages en Corse, à l'Ile d'Elbe et en Sardaigne*, I. Paris.

Vanutberghe, H. (1904). 'La Corse, Etude de géographie humaine', *AG*, XIII, pp. 334–47.

Versini, Xavier (1964). *Un Siècle du banditisme en Corse (1814–1914)*. Paris.

(1972). *En Corse, Vieilles affaires et procès oubliés*. Melun.

(1979). *La Vie quotidienne en Corse au temps de Mérimée*. Paris.

Viale, D. and S. et al. (1966). 'L'Homme et le milieu naturel dans la vallée d'Asco', *BSSHNC*, No. 581, pp. 49–97.

Viale, Salvator (1842). *Dionomachia, Poemetto eroi-comico*. Brussels. 3rd revised edn.

(1855). *Canti popolari Corsi con note*. Bastia. 2nd edn.

Vidalenc, Jean (1966). 'La Corse vue par des officiers sous la Monarchie constitutionnelle (1822–1847)', *ACNSS*, 90 (Nice), III, pp. 65–82.

Villat, Louis (1924). *La Corse de 1768 à 1789*. Besançon. 2 vols.

(1932). 'Le Banditisme en Corse', *Larousse Mensuel*, July, No. 305, pp. 151–2.

Villat, L., Ambrosi, C., Arrighi, P. and Guelfi, J.-D. (1951). *Visages de la Corse*. Paris.

Vinciguerra, S.-J. (1962). 'Penta-di-Casinca en 1769', *BSSHNC*, No. 563, pp. 23–7.

(1967). 'Note relative au mariage "alla greca" ou à "mal destino"', *BSSHNC*, No. 582, pp. 27–37.

Volney, C.F. (1825). 'Etat physique de la Corse' and 'Précis de l'état de la Corse', *Oeuvres*, VII, pp. 279–311 and 313–25. Paris.

Vrydaghs Fidelis, R.P. (1962). *Notices historiques sur La Rocca*. Ajaccio.

Vuillier, Gaston (1896). *The Forgotten Isles, Impressions of Travel in the Balearic Isles, Corsica and Sardinia*. London. Original French edn. 1891.

Wagner, Geoffrey (1968). *Elegy for Corsica*. London.

Wilson, Stephen (1981). 'Conflict and its Causes in Southern Corsica, 1800–35', *Social History*, 6, pp. 33–69.

(1988). 'Infanticide, Child-abandonment and Female Honour in Nineteenth-century Corsica', *CSSH*.

Woolsey, Theodore S. (1917). *French Forests and Forestry, Tunisia, Algeria and Corsica*. New York

Yvia-Croce, H. (1966). 'Panorama de la presse corse', *CH*, VI, Nos. 23–4.

Zuccarelli, Dr Charles (n.d.). *En glanant quelques souvenirs*. Toulon.

Other books, articles, etc.

Abbiateci, André, et al. (1971). *Crimes et criminalité en France sous l'Ancien Régime, 17e–18e siècles*, Cahiers des Annales, 33. Paris.

Adler, Alfred (1980). 'La Vengeance chez les Moundang du Tchad', in Verdier, Raymond (ed.), *La Vengeance, Etudes d'ethnologie, d'histoire et de philosophie*, I, *Vengeance et pouvoir dans quelques sociétés extra-occidentales*, pp. 75–89. Paris.

Agulhon, Maurice (1966). 'La Notion de village en Basse-Provence vers la fin de l'Ancien Régime', *ACNSS*, 90, pp. 277–301.

Alexiou, Margaret (1974). *The Ritual Lament in Greek Tradition*. Cambridge.

Anderson, Gallatin (1957). 'Il Comparaggio: The Italian Godparenthood Complex', *SJA*, 13, pp. 32–53.

Annuaire Statistique de la France (1879) (1884) (1889) (1894) and (1899).

Arens, W. (1979). *The Man-Eating Myth, Anthropology and Anthropophagy*. Oxford.

Arensberg, Conrad M. and Kimball, Solon T. (1940). *Family and Community in Ireland*. Cambridge, Mass.

Ariès, Philippe, *L'Homme devant la mort*. Paris.

Balikci, Asen (1968). 'Perspectives on the Atomistic-Type Society, Bad Friends', *Human Organization*, 27, pp. 191–9.

Balteau, J. et al. (1933–). *Dictionnaire de Biographie Française*. Paris.

Banfield, Edward C. (1967). *The Moral Basis of a Backward Society*. New York. Original edn. 1958.

Barley, M.W. (1961). *The English Farmhouse and Cottage*. London.

Barrau, Jacques (1972). 'Culture itinérante, culture sur brûlis, culture nomade, écobuage ou essartage? Un problème de terminologie agraire', *ER*, 45, pp. 99–103.

Barret-Kriegel (1973). 'Régicide-parricide', in Foucault, Michel (ed.), *Moi, Pierre Rivière, ayant égorgé ma mère, ma soeur et mon frère...Un cas de parricide au XIXe siècle*, pp. 285–93. Paris.

Barth, Fredrik (1965). *Political Leadership among Swat Pathans*. London. Revised edn.

Bassett, Samuel Eliot (1933). 'Achilles' Treatment of Hector's Body', *Transactions of the American Philological Association*, 64, pp. 41–65.

Bateson, Gregory (1958). *Naven, A Survey of the Problems suggested by a Composite Picture of the Culture of a New Guinea Tribe from Three Points of View*. Revised edn.

Beals, Carleton (1949). 'Brigandage', *ESS*, II, pp. 693–6.

Beames, M.R. (1978). 'Rural Conflict in Pre-Famine Ireland: Peasant Assassinations in Tipperary 1837–1847', *P and P*, 81, pp. 75–91.

Beaton, Roderick (1980). *Folk Poetry of Modern Greece*. Cambridge.

Becker, Marvin B. (1976). 'Changing Patterns of Violence and Justice in Fourteenth- and Fifteenth-Century Florence', *CSSH*, 18, pp. 281–96.

Bendix, Reinhard (1962). *Max Weber, An Intellectual Portrait*. New York.

Benedict, Ruth (1935). *Patterns of Culture*. London.

Bercé, Y.-M. (1974). *Croquants et Nu-pieds, Les Soulèvements paysans en France du XVIe au XIXe siècle*. Paris.

Berkner, Lutz K. (1975). 'The Use and Misuse of Census Data for the Historical Analysis of Family Structure', *Journal of Interdisciplinary History*, V, pp. 721–38.

Bialor, Perry (1968). 'Tensions leading to Conflict and the Resolution and Avoidance of Conflict in a Greek Farming Community', in Peristiany, J.-G.(ed.), *Contributions to Mediterranean Sociology, Mediterranean Rural Communities and Social Change*, pp. 107–26. Paris and The Hague.

Bieler, Ludwig (ed.) (1963). *The Irish Penitentials*, Scriptores Latini Hiberniae, V. Dublin.

Bigay, Alexandre (1964). 'Les Communautés paysannes de la région de Thiers', *ACNSS*, 88 (Clermont-Ferrand), pp. 843–51.

Billacois, François (1973). 'Bandits', *Ann*, 28, pp. 1160–2.

Birket-Smith, Kaj (1959). *The Eskimos*. London. Original Danish edn. 1927.

Black-Michaud, Jacob (1975). *Cohesive Force, Feud in the Mediterranean and the Middle East*. Oxford.

Bloch, Marc (1965). *Feudal Society*. London. Original French edn. 1939–40.

Bloch, Maurice (1968). 'Tombs and Conservatism among the Merina of Madagascar', *Man*, NS 3, pp. 94–104.

Blok, Anton (1969). 'South Italian Agro-Towns', *CSSH*, 11, pp. 121–35.

(1972). 'The Peasant and the Brigand: Social Banditry Reconsidered', *CSSH*, 14, pp. 494–505.

(1975). *The Mafia of a Sicilian Village, 1860–1960, A Study of Violent Peasant Entrepeneurs*. New York.

Blum, Jerome (1971a). 'The European Village as Community: Origins and Functions', *Agricultural History*, 45, pp. 157–78.

(1971b). 'The Internal Structure and Polity of the European Village Community from the Fifteenth to the Nineteenth Century', *Journal of Modern History*, 43, pp. 541–76.

Bodley, J.E.C. (1899). *France*. London. Revised edn.

Boehm, Christopher (1984). *Blood Revenge, The Anthropology of Feuding in Montenegro and Other Tribal Societies*. Lawrence, Kansas.

Bohannan, Paul (ed.) (1960). *African Homicide and Suicide*. Princeton.

Boissevain, Jeremy (1965). *Saints and Fireworks, Religion and Politics in Rural Malta*. London and New York.

(1974). *Friends of Friends, Networks, Manipulators and Coalitions*. Oxford.

Bonaviri, Giuseppe (1980). *Le Poids du Temps*. Paris. Original Italian edn. 1976.

Boram, Clifford (1973). 'Kutchin Quarrelling', *Ethnology*, 12, pp. 437–48.

Bossy, John (1973). 'Blood and Baptism: Kinship, Community and Christianity in Western Europe from the Fourteenth to the Seventeenth Centuries', in Baker, Derek (ed.), *Sanctity and Secularity: The Church and the World*, Studies in Church History, 10, pp. 129–43. Oxford.

Boulard, Fernand (1954). *Premiers itinéraires en sociologie religieuse*. Paris.

Bourdieu, Pierre (1965). 'The Sentiment of Honour in Kabyle Society', in Peristiany, J. G. (ed.), *Honour and Shame*, pp. 191–241.

Bouvier, J.-C. (1979). 'Noms et usages du glas en Provence et dans les pays méditerranéens', *EC*, NS VII, Nos. 12–13, pp. 115–28.

Brandão, M.F. (1983). 'Death and the Survival of the Rural Household in a Northwestern Municipality', in Feijó, R. et al., *Death in Portugal, Studies in Portuguese Anthropology and Modern History*, Journal of the Anthropological Society of Oxford, Occasional Papers, 2, pp. 75–87.

Brandes, Stanley H. (1973). 'Social Structure and Interpersonal Relations in Navanogal (Spain)', *AA*, 75, pp. 750–65.

(1980). *Metaphors of Masculinity, Sex and Status in Andalusian Folklore*. Philadelphia.

Brandon-Albini, Maria (1956). 'La Véritable Histoire du bandit Giuliano', *TM*, 11, pp. 1656–65.

(1963). *Midi Vivant, Peuple et culture en Italie du Sud*. Paris.

Braudel, Fernand (1947). 'Misère et banditisme', *Ann*, 2, pp. 129–43.

(1972). *The Mediterranean and the Mediterranean World in the Age of Philip II*. London. 2 vols.

Brékilien, Yann (1966). *La Vie quotidienne des paysans en Bretagne au XIXe siècle*. Paris.

Breteau, Claude-H., and Zagnoli, Nello (1979). 'Aspects de la Mort dans deux communautés méditerranéennes: La Calabria et le Nord-Est Constantinois', *EC*, NS VII, Nos. 12–13, pp. 291–308.

Briggs, Katharine M. (1970–1). *A Dictionary of British Folk-Tales in the English Language*. London. 4 vols.

Brilliant, Oscar (n.d.). 'The Balkan Peninsula', in Hutchinson, Walter (ed.), *Customs of the World, A Popular Account of the Manners, Rites and Ceremonies of Men and Women in All Countries*, II, Ch. LV. London, 1912–14.

Brody, Hugh (1973). *Inishkillane, Change and Decline in the West of Ireland*. London.

Brögger, Jan (1968). 'Conflict Resolution and the Role of the Bandit in Peasant Society', *AQ*, 41, pp. 228–40.

(1971). *Montevarese, A Study of Peasant Society and Culture in Southern Italy*. Bergen, Oslo and Tromsö.

Brown, Keith M. (1983). 'Peace and Persuasion: Pacification Procedures in the Early Jacobean Bloodfeud'. Past and Present Society Colloquium, *Police and Policing*, 6 July. Oxford.

Brown, Peter (1971). 'The Rise and Function of the Holy Man in Late Antiquity', *Journal of Roman Studies*, LXI, pp. 80–101.

Brucker, Gene (ed.) (1967). *Two Memoirs of Renaissance Florence, The Diaries of Buonaccorso Pitti and Gregorio Dati*. New York.

(1969). *Renaissance Florence*. New York.

(1971). *The Society of Renaissance Florence, A Documentary Study*. New York.

Brunner, Otto (1943). *Land und Herrschaft, Grundfragen der territorialen Verfassungsgeschichte Südostdeutschlands im Mittelalter*, Veröffentlichungen des Instituts für Geschichtsforschung und Archivwissenschaft in Wien, I, Vienna, Munich and Brünn.

Burckhardt, Jacob (1944). *The Civilization of the Renaissance in Italy*. London. Original edn. 1860.

Bureau, Jacques (1980). 'Une société sans vengeance: Le cas des Gamo d'Ethiopie', in Verdier, R. (ed.), *La Vengeance*, pp. 213–24.

Burr, George Lincoln (1914). *Narratives of the Witchcraft Cases 1648–1706*. New York.

Burridge, Kenelm O.L. (1957). 'Disputing in Tangu', *AA*, 59, pp. 763–80.

Byock, Jesse L. (1982). *Feud in the Icelandic Saga*. Berkeley.

Campbell, J.K. (1964). *Honour, Family and Patronage, A Study of Institutions and Moral Values in a Greek Mountain Community*. Oxford.

Casey, James (1979). *The Kingdom of Valencia in the Seventeenth Century*. Cambridge.

Castan, Nicole (1980). *Justice et répression en Languedoc à l'époque des lumières*. Paris.

Chelhod, Joseph (1968). 'Le Prix du sang dans le droit coutumier jordanien', *Revue de l'Orient Musulman et de la Méditerranée*, 5, pp. 41–67.

(1980). 'Equilibre et parité dans la vengeance du sang chez les Bédouins de Jordanie', in Verdier, R. (ed.), *La Vengeance*, pp. 125–43.

Christian, W.A. (1972). *Person and God in a Spanish Valley*. New York.

Clay, Edith (ed.) (1965). *Ramage in South Italy*. London.

Cockburn, J.S. (1977). 'The Nature and Incidence of Crime in England 1559–1625: A Preliminary Survey', in Cockburn (ed.), *Crime in England 1550–1800*, pp. 49–71. London.

Cohen, Eugene (1972). 'Who Stole the Rabbits? Crime, Dispute and Social Control in an Italian Village', *AQ*, 45, pp. 1–14.

Collomp, Alain (1978). 'Maison, manières d'habiter et famille en Haute Provence aux XVIIe et XVIIIe siècles', *EF*, VIII, pp. 301–19.

Colson, Elizabeth (1953). 'Social Control and Vengeance in Plateau Tonga Society', *Africa*, 23, pp. 199–212.

(1962). *The Plateau Tonga of Northern Rhodesia, Social and Religious Studies*. Manchester.

Cowdrey, H.E.J. (1970). 'The Peace and the Truce of God in the Eleventh Century', *P and P*, 46, pp. 42–67.

Cozzi, D. Ernesto (1910). 'La vendetta del sangue nelle Montagne dell'Alta Albania', *Anthropos*, V, pp. 654–87.

Croce, Benedetto (1970). *History of the Kingdom of Naples*. Chicago. Original edn. 1925.

Cuisenier, Jean (1978). *L'Homme et son corps dans la société traditionnelle*. Paris.

Danforth, Loring M. (1982). *The Death Rituals of Rural Greece*. Princeton.

Davies, R.R. (1969). 'The Survival of the Bloodfeud in Medieval Wales', *History*, 54, pp. 338–57.

Davis, J. (1964). 'Passatella: An Economic Game', *BJS*, 15, pp. 191–206.

(1977). *People of the Mediterranean, An Essay in Comparative Social Anthropology*. London.

Day, John (1979). 'Banditisme social et société pastorale en Sardaigne', in *Les Marginaux et les exclus dans l'histoire*, Cahiers Jussieu, 5, University of Paris 7, pp. 178–214.

D'Azeglio, Massimo (1966). *Things I Remember*. London. Original edn. 1867.

Defacqz (1866). 'De la paix du sang ou paix à partie dans les anciennes coutumes belges', *Bulletin de l'Académie Royale de Belgique*, 2nd series, XXIII, pp. 73–95.

Dégh, Linda (1969). *Folktales and Society, Story-Telling in a Hungarian Peasant Community*. Bloomington.

Delille, Gérard (1982). 'Parenté et alliance en Italie du Sud; analyse de quelques exemples', Paper, Colloquium, *Family and Community in the Mediterranean, 16th–19th Centuries*, University of Essex.

De Martino, Ernesto (1955a). 'Considerazioni storiche sul lamento funebre lucano', *Nuovi Argomenti*, 12, January-February, pp. 1–42.

(1955b), 'La Ritualità del lamento funebre antico come tecnica di reintegrazione', *Studi e Materiali di Storia delle Religioni*, 26, pp. 16–59.

(1975). *Morte e pianto rituale dal lamento funebre antico al pianto di Maria*. Turin. Original edn. 1958.

Dennis, Norman, Henriques, Fernando, and Slaughter, Clifford (1969). *Coal is Our Life, An Analysis of a Yorkshire Mining Community*. London. Original edn. 1956.

Dennis, Philip A. (1976). 'The Uses of Inter-Village Feuding', *AQ*, 49, pp. 174–84.

Depauw, J. (1972). 'Amour illégitime et société à Nantes au XVIIIe siècle', *Ann*, 27, pp. 1155–82; and Eng. trans. in Forster, R. and Ranum, O. (eds.) (1976), *Family and Society, Selections from the Annales*, Ch. 7. Baltimore.

Djilas, Milovan (1958). *Land without Justice*. New York.

Dolci, Danilo (1960). *The Outlaws of Partinico*. London.

(1963). *Waste, An Eye-Witness Report on some Aspects of Waste in Western Sicily*. London.

Douglas, Norman (1948). *Siren Land*. Harmondsworth. Original edn. 1911.

Douxchamps-Lefèvre, Cécile (1975). 'Les Enquêtes judiciaires en Namurois, Source d'histoire rurale', *ER*, 58, pp. 51–61.

Du Boulay, F.R.H. (1978). 'Law Enforcement in Medieval Germany', *History*, 63, pp. 345–55.

Du Boulay, Juliet (1979). *Portrait of a Greek Mountain Village*. Oxford.

(1982). 'The Greek Vampire: A Study of Cyclic Symbolism in Marriage and Death', *Man*, NS 17, pp. 219–38.

Duby, Georges (1985). *The Knight, the Lady and the Priest, The Making of Modern Marriage in Medieval France*. Harmondsworth.

Duby, G. and A. (eds.) (1973). *Les Procès de Jeanne d'Arc*. Paris.

Durham, M.E. (1928). *Some Tribal Origins, Laws and Customs of the Balkans*. London.

Durkheim, Emile (1970). *Suicide, A Study in Sociology*. London. Original edn. 1897.

Dussourd, Henriette (1978). *Les Communautés familiales agricoles du Centre de la France*. Paris.

Edel, May Mandelbaum (1961). 'The Bachiga of East Africa', in Mead, Margaret (ed.), *Cooperation and Competition among Primitive Peoples*, Ch. IV. Boston. Original edn. 1937.

Edwards, Lovett F. (ed.) (1969). *The Memoirs of Prota Matija Nenadović*. Oxford.

Eliade, Mircea (1978). *No Souvenirs, Journal, 1957–1969*. London.

Espinas, G. (1899). *Les Guerres familiales dans la Commune de Douai aux XIIIe et XIVe siècles, Les Trèves et les paix*. Paris.

Evans-Pritchard, E.E. (1940). *The Nuer, A Description of the Modes of Livelihood and Political Institutions of a Nilotic People*. Oxford.

(1949). *The Sanusi of Cyrenaica*. Oxford.

(1976). *Witchcraft, Oracles and Magic among the Azande*. Oxford. Abridged edn.

Falassi, Alessandro (1980). *Folklore by the Fireside, Text and Context of the Tuscan Veglia*. London.

Favret-Saada, Jeanne (1977). *Les Mots, la mort, les sorts, La Sorcellerie dans le Bocage*. Paris.

Fedotov, G.P. (1966). *The Russian Religious Mind*. Cambridge, Mass. 2 vols.

Fenton, William N. (1952). 'Factionalism in American Indian Society', *Actes du IVe Congrès International des Sciences Anthropologiques et Ethnologiques*, II, pp. 330–40. Vienna.

Ferguson, Alan (1981). 'Montenegrin Society 1800–1830', in Clogg, Richard (ed.), *Balkan Society in the Age of Greek Independence*, pp. 205–28. London.

Ferracuti, Franco, Lazzari, Renato, and Wolfgang, Marvin E. (1970). *La Violenza in Sardegna*, Quaderni di Psicologia, 5. Rome.

Finnegan, Ruth (1977). *Oral Poetry, Its Nature, Significance and Social Context*. Cambridge.

Firth, Raymond et al. (1957), 'Factions in Indian and Overseas Indian Societies', *BJS*, 8, pp. 291–342.

Foster, George M. (1961). 'The Dyadic Contract: A Model for the Social Structure of a Mexican Peasant Village', *AA*, 63, pp. 1173–92.

Foucault, Michel (1979). *Discipline and Punish, The Birth of the Prison*. Harmondsworth.

Fox, J.R. (1963). 'Structure of Personal Names on Tory Island', *Man*, No. 192, pp. 153–5.

Frazer, Sir James George (1933). *The Fear of the Dead in Primitive Religion*. London.

Freitas Marcondes, J.V. (1940). 'Mutirao or Mutual Aid', *Rural Sociology*, 13, pp. 374–84.

Fribourg, Jeanine (1979). 'Rapports entre morts et vivants en Espagne (dans des villages du N.-E.: Aragon, Navarre, Catalogne', *EC*, NS VII, Nos. 12–13, pp. 343–59.

Fustel de Coulanges, Numa Denis (1916). *La Cité antique, Etude sur le culte, le droit et les institutions de la Grèce et de Rome*. Paris. Original edn. 1864.

Gaillard-Bans, Patricia (1976). 'Maison longue et famille étendue en Bretagne', *ER*, 62, pp. 73–87.

Ganshof, F.L. (1970). *Frankish Institutions under Charlemagne*. New York.

Garine, Igor de (1980). 'Les étrangers, la vengeance et les parents chez les Massa et les Moussey (Tchad et Cameroun)', in Verdier, R. (ed.), *La Vengeance*, pp. 91–124.

Gélis, J., Laget, M. and Morel, M.-F. (1978). *Entrer dans la vie, Naissances et enfances dans la France traditionnelle*. Paris.

Gellner, Ernest (1969). *Saints of the Atlas*. Chicago and London.

Gelzer, Matthias (1969). *The Roman Nobility*. Oxford. Original German edns. 1912 and 1915.

Gibson, E. and Klein, S. (1961). *Murder, HMSO Studies in the Causes of Delinquency and the Treatment of Offenders*, 4.

Gilmore, David (1977). 'Patronage and Class Conflict in Southern Spain', *Man*, NS 12, pp. 446–58.

Ginzburg, Carlo (1983). *The Night Battles, Witchcraft and Agrarian Cults in the Sixteenth and Seventeenth Centuries*. London. Original Italian edn. 1966.

Girard, René (1977). *Violence and the Sacred*. Baltimore and London.

Given, J.B. (1977). *Society and Homicide in Thirteenth-century England*. Stanford.

Gluckman, Max (1956). *Custom and Conflict in Africa*. Oxford.

(1973). *The Judicial Process among the Barotse of Northern Rhodesia (Zambia)*. Manchester. 3rd revised edn.

Goldey, Patricia (1983). 'The Good Death: Personal Salvation and Community Identity', in Feijó et al. (ed.), *Death in Portugal*, pp. 1–16.

Goldkind, Victor (1966). 'Class Conflict and Cacique in Chan Kom', *SJA*, 22, pp. 325–45.

Goldman, Irving (1961). 'The Kwakiutl Indians of Vancouver Island', in Mead, M. (ed.), *Cooperation and Competition*, Ch. VI.

Goubert, Pierre (1968). *Cent mille provinciaux au XVIIe siècle, Beauvais et le Beauvaisis de 1600 à 1730*. Paris.

(1973). *The Ancien Régime, French Society 1600–1750*. London.

Gough, E. Kathleen (1958). 'Cults of the Dead among the Náyars', *Journal of American Folklore*, 71, pp. 446–78.

Graham, H.D. and Gurr, T.R. (eds.) (1969). *Violence in America: Historical and Comparative Perspectives*, I. Washington, DC.

Grandidier, G. (n.d.). 'Madagascar', in Hutchinson, W. (ed.), *Customs of the World*, Ch. XXXV.

Gray, L.H. et al. (1909). 'Blood-Feud', *Encyclopedia of Religion and Ethics*, 2, pp. 720–35.

Gross, Daniel R. (1973). 'Factionalism and Local Level Politics in Rural Brazil', *JAR*, 29, pp. 123–44.

Gudin de Vallerin Gilles (1982). 'Habitat et communautés de famille en Bourgogne (XVIIe–XIXe siècles)', *ER*, 85, pp. 33–47.

Guiart, Jean, et al. (n.d.). *Rites de la mort*, Exposition du Laboratoire d'Ethnologie du Muséum d'Histoire Naturelle. Paris. *c.* 1980.

Hallowell, A. Irving (1943). 'The Nature and Function of Property as a Social Institution', *Journal of Legal and Political Sociology*, I, pp. 115–38.

Hallpike, C.R. (1973). 'Functionalist Interpretations of Primitive Warfare', *Man*, NS 8, pp. 451–70.

(1977). *Bloodshed and Vengeance in the Papuan Mountains, The Generation of Conflict in Tarade Society*. Oxford.

Hamer, John H. (1972). 'Dispute Settlement and Sanctity: An Ethiopian Example', *AQ*, 45, pp. 232–47.

Hanawalt, Barbara A. (1977). 'Community Conflict and Social Control: Crime and Justice in the Ramsey Abbey Villages', *MS*, 39, pp. 402–23.

Hasluck, Margaret (1954). *The Unwritten Law in Albania*. Cambridge.

Heers, Jacques (1961). *Gênes au XVe siècle, Activité économique et problèmes sociaux*. Paris.

(1974). *Le Clan familial au Moyen Age, Etude sur les structures politiques et sociales des milieux urbains*. Paris.

Hélias, Pierre-Jakez (1978). *The Horse of Pride, Life in a Breton Village*. New Haven.

Henry, Jules (1941). *Jungle People, A Kaingáng Tribe of the Highlands of Brazil*. New York.

Hertz, Robert (1983). 'St Besse: a Study of an Alpine Cult', in Wilson, Stephen (ed.) (1983). Ch. 1. Original French edn. 1913.

Hobsbawm, E.J. (1965). *Primitive Rebels, Studies in Archaic Forms of Social Movement in the 19th and 20th Centuries*. New York. Original edn. 1959.

(1972). *Bandits*. Harmondsworth.

Hocart, A.M. (1973). *The Life-giving Myth and Other Essays*. London.

Hole, Christina (ed.). *Superstitions of Death and the Supernatural* (by Radford, E. and M.) London.

Holt, J.C. (1960). 'The Origins and Audience of the Ballads of Robin Hood', *P and P*, 18, pp. 89–110.

Hufton, Olwen H. (1974). *The Poor of Eighteenth-Century France 1750–1789*. Oxford.

Hughes, Diane Owen (1975). 'Urban Growth and Family Structure in Medieval Genoa', *P and P*, pp. 3–28.

(1977). 'Kinsmen and Neighbors in Medieval Genoa', in Miskimin, Harry A., Herlihy, David, and Udovitch, A.L. (eds.), *The Medieval City*, Ch. 6. New Haven.

Hughes, Steven (1983). 'Fear and Loathing in Bologna and Rome: The Papal Police in Perspective', Past and Present Society Colloquium, *Police and Policing*.

Huizinga, J. (1955). *The Waning of the Middle Ages*. Harmondsworth. Original edn. 1919.

Huntington, Richard and Metcalf, Peter (1979). *Celebrations of Death, The Anthropology of Mortuary Ritual*. Cambridge.

Ingram, M.J. (1977). 'Communities and Courts: Law and Disorder in Early-Seventeenth-Century Wiltshire', in Cockburn, J.S. (ed.), *Crime in England*, pp. 110–34.

Johnston, George, and Foote, Peter (eds.) (1963). *The Saga of Gisli*. London.

Jones, Virgil Carrington (1948). *The Hatfields and the McCoys*. Chapel Hill.

Jusserand, J.J. (1891). *English Wayfaring Life in the Middle Ages (XIVth century)*. London. 8th edn.

Kaufman, Robert R. (1974). 'The Patron-Client Concept and Macro-Politics: Prospects and Problems', *CSSH*, 16, pp. 284–308.

Kenna, Margaret E. (1976). 'Houses, Fields and Graves: Property and Ritual Obligation on a Greek Island', *Ethnology*, 15, pp. 21–34.

Kenny, Michael (1960). 'Patterns of Patronage in Spain', *AQ*, 33, pp. 14–23.

Kent, Francis William (1977). *Household and Lineage in Renaissance Florence, The Family Life of the Capponi, Ginori and Rucellai*. Princeton.

Kent, Sherman (1937). *Electoral Procedure under Louis Philippe*. New Haven.

Kipling, Rudyard (1964). *Soldiers Three, The Story of the Gadsbys, In Black and White*. London. Original edn. 1895.

Koch, Klaus-Friedrich et al. (1977). 'Ritual Reconciliation and the Obviation of Grievances: A Comparative Study in the Ethnography of Law', *Ethnology*, 16, pp. 269–83.

Laburthe-Tolra (1980). 'Notes sur la vengeance chez les Beti', in Verdier, R. (ed.), *La Vengeance*, pp. 157–66.

Landes, Ruth (1959). 'Dakota Warfare', *SJA*, 15, pp. 43–52.

Lane, Edward William (n.d.). *The Manners and Customs of the Modern Egyptians*. Everyman. 5th definitive edn. 1860.

Lawrence, Peter (1952). 'Sorcery among the Garia', *South Pacific*, 6, pp. 340–3.

Lawson, John Cuthbert (1910). *Modern Greek Folklore and Ancient Greek Religion, A Study in Survivals.* Cambridge.

Le Lannou, Maurice (1941). *Pâtres et paysans de la Sardaigne.* Tours.

Leproux, Marc (1959). *Du Berceau à la tombe, Contributions au folklore charentais.* Paris.

Letts, Malcolm (ed.) (1957). *The Travels of Leo of Rozmital through Germany, Flanders, England, France, Spain, Portugal and Italy,* Hakluyt Society, 2nd series, No. CVIII.

Levi, Carlo (1948). *Christ Stopped at Eboli.* London.

Le Vine, Robert A. (1961). 'Anthropology and the Study of Conflict: an Introduction', *JCR*, V, pp. 3–15.

Lewin, Linda (1979). 'The Oligarchical Limitations of Social Banditry in Brazil: The Case of the "Good Thief" Antonio Silvino', *P and P*, 82, pp. 116–46.

Lewis, I.M. (1967). *A Pastoral Democracy, A Study of Pastoralism and Politics among the Northern Somali of the Horn of Africa.* London.

(1971). *Ecstatic Religion, An Anthropological Study of Spirit Possession and Shamanism.* Harmondsworth.

Lewis, Oscar (1964). *The Children of Sánchez.* Harmondsworth.

Lewis, William H. (1961). 'Feuding and Social Change in Morocco', *JCR*, V, pp. 43–54.

Lienhardt, Godfrey (1970). 'The Western Dinka', in Middleton, John and Tait, David (eds.), *Tribes without Rulers,* pp. 97–135.

Lisón-Tolosana, Carmelo (1973). 'Some Aspects of Moral Structure in Galician Hamlets', *AA*, 75, pp. 823–34.

Littlewood, Paul (1974). 'Strings and Kingdoms, The Activities of a Political Mediator in Southern Italy', *Archives Européennes de Sociologie,* XV, pp. 33–51.

Llewellyn, K.N. and Hoebel, E.A. (1941). *The Cheyenne Way, Conflict and Case Law in Primitive Jurisprudence.* Norman, Oklahoma.

Lockwood, William G. (1974). 'Bride Theft and Social Maneuverability in Western Bosnia', *AQ*, 47, pp. 253–67.

Lombardi-Satriani, Luigi M. (1979). 'Il Ritorno dei morti', *EC*, NS VII, Nos. 12–13, pp. 331–41.

Lucarelli, Antonio (1942). *Il Brigantaggio politico del Mezzogiorno d'Italia dopo la seconda restaurazione Borbonica (1815–1818), Gaetano Vardarelli e Ciro Annicchiarico.* Bari.

Luchaire, Achille (1967). *Social France at the Time of Philip Augustus.* New York. Original edn. 1909.

Luomala, Katharine (1960). 'The Native Dog in the Polynesian System of Values', in Diamond, Stanley (ed.), *Culture in History,* pp. 190–240. New York.

MacCulloch, J.A. (1932). *Medieval Faith and Fable.* London.

McKendrick, Melveena (1974). *Woman and Society in the Spanish Drama of the Golden Age, A Study of the Mujer Varonil.* Cambridge.

McNeill, John T. and Gamer, Helena M. (eds.) (1938). *Medieval Handbooks of Penance, A Translation of the Principal Libri Poenitentiales and Selections from Related Documents,* Records of Civilization, Sources and Studies, XXIX. New York.

Mair, Lucy (1971). *Marriage.* Harmondsworth.

Maitland, Frederic William (1911). 'The Laws of Wales. The Kindred and the Blood Feud', in *The Collected Papers,* I, pp. 202–29. Cambridge.

Malcolmson, Robert, W. (1973). *Popular Recreations in English Society 1700–1850.* Cambridge.

Martinez-Alier, Verena (1972). 'Elopement and Seduction in Nineteenth-century Cuba', *P and P*, 55, pp. 91–129.

Mauss, Marcel (with Beuchat, H.) (1979). *Seasonal Variations of the Eskimo, A Study in Social Morphology.* London. Original edn. 1904–5.

Mead, Margaret (1977). *Letters from the Field, 1925–1975.* New York.

Meligrana, Mariano (1979). 'La Vendetta e l'ideologia arcaica della morte nella società meridionale italiana', *EC*, NS VII, Nos. 12–13, pp. 309–29.

Merriman, John M. (1976). 'The Norman Fires of 1830: Incendiaries and Fear in Rural France', *French Historical Studies*, IX, pp. 451–66.

Middleton, John (1970). 'The Political System of the Lugbara of the Nile-Congo Divide', in Middleton, John, and Tait, David (eds.), *Tribes without Rulers*, pp. 203–29.

Middleton, John, and Tait, David (eds.) (1970). *Tribes without Rulers, Studies in African Segmentary Systems*. London. Original edn. 1958.

Mirambel, André (1943). 'Blood Vengeance (*Maina*) in Southern Greece and among the Slavs', *Byzantion*, American Series, 2, pp. 381–92.

Mirasyezis, Maria D. (1975). 'Traits et thèmes communs et particuliers dans la poésie populaire grecque et roumaine', *BS*, 16, pp. 193–216.

Mirbeau, Octave (1977). *L'Abbé Jules*. Paris. Original edn. 1898.

Morel, Alain (1972). 'L'Espace social d'un village picard', *ER*, 45, pp. 62–80.

Morin, Edgar (1971). *Plodémet, Report from a French Village*. Harmondsworth.

Moss, David (1979). 'Bandits and Boundaries in Sardinia', *Man*, NS 14, pp. 477–96.

Moss, Leonard W. and Cappannari, Stephen C. (1964). 'Patterns of Kinship, Comparaggio and Community in a South Italian Village', *AQ*, 33, pp. 24–32.

Moulin, Patricia (1973). 'Les Circonstances atténuantes', in Foucault, Michel (ed.), *Moi Pierre Rivière*, pp. 277–83.

Mouzelis, Nicos (1978). 'Class and Clientelistic Politics: The Case of Greece', *Sociological Review*, 26, pp. 471–97.

Musset, René (1955). 'A propos de la maison normande: Du pays de Caux au Bocage normand, Problèmes et recherches à faire', *Annales de Normandie*, 5, pp. 271–87.

Nabofa, M.Y. (1985). 'Blood Symbolism in African Religion', *Religious Studies*, 21, pp. 389–405.

Nader, Laura and Metzger, Duane (1963). 'Conflict Resolution in Two Mexican Communities', *AA*, 65, pp. 584–92.

Nash, June (1967). 'Death as a Way of Life, The Increasing Resort to Homicide in a Maya Indian Community', *AA*, 69, pp. 455–70.

Oelsner, H. et al. (eds.) (1901). *The Purgatorio of Dante Alighieri*. London.

Ó Súilleabháin, Sean (1967). *Irish Wake Amusements*. Cork.

Otterbein, K.F. and C.S. (1965). 'An Eye for an Eye, a Tooth for a Tooth: A Cross-Cultural Study of Feuding', *AA*, 67, pp. 1470–82.

Pálsson, Hermann (ed.) (1971). *Hrafnkel's Saga and Other Icelandic Stories*. Harmondsworth.

Papanek, Hanna (1973). 'Purdah: Separate Worlds and Symbolic Shelter', *CSSH*, 15, pp. 289–325.

Pareto, Vilfredo (1935). *The Mind and Society*, IV. London.

Pereira de Queiroz, Maria Isaura (1968). *Os Cangaceiros, Les Bandits d'honneur brésiliens*. Paris.

Peristiany, J.G. (ed.) (1965). *Honour and Shame, The Values of Mediterranean Society*. London.

(1976). *Mediterranean Family Structures*. Cambridge.

Peters, E.L. (1967). 'Some Structural Aspects of the Feud among the Camel-herding Bedouin of Cyrenaica', *Africa*, 37, pp. 261–82.

(1975). Foreward to Black-Michaud, Jacob, *Cohesive Force*.

Petit-Dutaillis, C. (1908). *Documents nouveaux sur les moeurs populaires et le droit de vengeance dans les Pays-Bas au XVe siècle, Lettres de rémission de Philippe le Bon*, Bibliothèque du XVe siècle, IX. Paris.

Philpotts, Bertha Surtees (1913). *Kindred and Clan in the Middle Ages and After, A Study in the Sociology of the Teutonic Races*. Cambridge.

Picot, J.B.C. (1864). *Nouveau manuel pratique et complet du Code Napoléon expliqué*. Paris.

Pigliaru, Antonio (1975). *Il Banditismo in Sardegna, La Vendetta barbaricina come ordinamento giuridico*. Milan.

Pina-Cabral, João de and Feijó, Rui (1983). 'Conflicting Attitudes to Death in Modern

Portugal: The Question of Cemeteries', in Feijó, R. et al. (eds.), *Death in Portugal*, pp. 17–43.

Pirastu, Ignazio (1973). *Il Banditismo in Sardegna*. Rome.

Pitt-Rivers, Julian A. (1965). 'Honour and Social Status', in Peristiany, J.G. (ed.), *Honour and Shame*, pp. 19–77.

(1971). *The People of the Sierra*. Chicago. 2nd edn.

Pocock, David (1957). 'The Bases of Faction in Gujerat', *BJS*, 8, pp. 295–306.

(1975). *Understanding Social Anthropology*. London.

Ponteil, F. (1966). *Les Institutions de la France de 1814 à 1870*. Paris.

Porter, Enid (1969). *Cambridgeshire Customs and Folklore*. London.

Pospisil, Leopold (1968). 'Feud', *International Encyclopedia of the Social Sciences*, 5, pp. 388–93.

Powell, John Duncan (1970). 'Peasant Society and Clientelist Politics', *American Political Science Review*, 64, pp. 411–25.

Quain, B.H. (1961). 'The Iroquois', in Mead, M. (ed.), *Cooperation and Competition*, Ch. VIII.

Raglan, Lord (1940). *Jocasta's Crime, An Anthropological Study*. London.

Ramsay, Dean (1872). *Reminiscences of Scottish Life and Character*. 21st edn.

Randell, Arthur (1966). *Sixty Years a Fenman*. London.

Raulin, Henri (1972). 'La Communauté villageoise en Châtillonnais', *ER*, 48, pp. 39–77.

Read, D.H. Moutray (n.d.). 'Great Britain and Ireland', in Hutchinson, W. (ed.), *Customs of the World*, Ch. XLVIII.

Rich, George W. (1976). 'Changing Icelandic Kinship', *Ethnology*, 15, pp. 1–19.

Riegelhaupt, Joyce F. (1973). 'Festas and Padres: The Organisation of Religious Action in a Portuguese Parish', *AA*, 75, pp. 835–52.

Rieu, E.V. (trans.) (1946). Homer, *The Odyssey*. Harmondsworth.

Rivers, W.H.R. (1916). 'Sociology and Psychology', *Sociological Review*, 9, pp. 1–13.

Rivière, P.G. (1967). 'The Honour of Sánchez', *Man*, NS 2, pp. 569–83.

Roberts, Simon (1979). *Order and Dispute, An Introduction to Legal Anthropology*. Harmondsworth.

Robinet, Dr Robert, A. and Le Chaplain, J. (1899). *Dictionnaire historique et biographique de la Révolution et de l'Empire, 1789—1815*. Paris.

Rose, H.J. (1930). 'Ancient Italian Beliefs concerning the Soul', *Classical Quarterly*, XXIV, pp. 129–35.

Ross, James Bruce (ed.) (1967). *The Murder of Charles the Good* (by Galbert of Bruges). New York.

Rossiaud, J. (1976). 'Prostitution, jeunesse et société dans les villes du Sud-Est au XVe siècle', *Ann*, 31, pp. 289–325; and Eng. trans. in Forster, R. and Ranum, O. (eds.) (1978), *Deviants and the Abandoned in French Society, Selections from the Annales*, Ch. 1. Baltimore.

Roubin, Lucienne A. (1970). 'Espace masculin, espace féminin en communauté provençale', *Ann*, 25, pp. 537–60; and Eng. trans. in Forster, R. and Ranum, O. (eds.) (1977), *Rural Society in France*, Ch. 8.

Sabean, David (1976). 'Aspects of Kinship Behaviour and Property in rural Western Europe before 1800', in Goody, Jack et al. (eds.), *Family and Inheritance, Rural Society in Western Europe, 1200–1800*, pp. 96–111. Cambridge.

Salvemini, Gaetano (1955). 'La Piccola borghesia intellettuale nel Mezzogiorno d'Italia', in Caizzi, Bruno (ed.), *Antologia della Questione meridionale*, pp. 382–404. Milan. Original in *La Voce*, 16 May 1911.

Schapera, I. (1955). 'The Sin of Cain', The Frazer Lecture in Social Anthropology, 1954, *JRAI*, 85, pp. 33–43.

Schnapper, Bernard (1979), 'Pour une géographie des mentalités judiciaires: La Litigiosité en France au XIXe siècle', *Ann*, 34, pp. 399–419.

Schneider, Jane (1969). 'Family Patrimonies and Economic Behavior in Western Sicily', *AQ*, 42, pp. 10–29.

(1971). 'Of Vigilance and Virgins: Honor, Shame and Access to Resources in Mediterranean Societies', *Ethnology*, 10, pp. 1–24.

Schneider, Peter (1969). 'Honor and Conflict in a Sicilian Town', *AQ*, 42, pp. 130–54.

Schott, Rüdiger (1980). 'Vengeance and Violence among the Bulsa of Northern Ghana', in Verdier, R. (ed.), *La Vengeance*, pp. 167–99.

Scott, Sir Walter (n.d.), *Waverley Novels*. Edinburgh. 48 vols. Probably 1853–4.

Segal, Charles (1971). *The Theme of the Mutilation of the Corpse in the Iliad*. Leyden.

Sharpe, J.A. (1980). *Defamation and Sexual Slander in Early Modern England: The Church Courts at York*. Borthwick Papers, 58. York.

Siegel, Bernard J. (1961). 'Conflict, Parochialism and Social Differentiation in Portuguese Society', *JCR*, V, pp. 35–42.

Siegel, B.J. and Beals, Alan R. (1960a). 'Conflict and Factionalist Dispute', *JRAI*, 90, pp. 107–17.

(1960b). 'Pervasive Factionalism', *AA*, 62, pp. 394–417.

Siegfried, André (1948). *The Mediterranean*. London.

(1964). *Tableau politique de la France de l'Ouest sous la Troisième République*. Paris.

Silverman, Sydel F. (1968). 'Agricultural Organization, Social Structure and Values in Italy: Amoral Familism Reconsidered', *AA*, 70, pp. 1–20.

Simpson, Jacqueline (1976). *The Folklore of the Welsh Border*. London.

Skinner, Elliott P. (1961). 'Intergenerational Conflict among the Mossi: Father and Son', *JCR*, V, pp. 55–60.

Sonnichsen, C.L. (1957). *Ten Texas Feuds*. Albuquerque.

(1962). *I'll Die Before I'll Run, The Story of the Great Feuds of Texas*. New York. Revised edn.

Soustelle, Jacques (1962). *Daily Life of the Aztecs on the Eve of the Spanish Conquest*. Stanford.

(1971). *The Four Suns, Recollections and Reflections of an Ethnologist in Mexico*. London.

Speck, Frank G. (1919). 'The Functions of Wampum among the Eastern Algonkian', *Memoirs of the American Anthropological Association*, VI, No. 1, pp. 3–71. Lancaster, Pennsylvania.

Springer, Otto (1950). 'Mediaeval Pilgrim Routes from Scandinavia to Rome', *MS*, 12, pp. 92–122.

Stahl, Henri H. (1969). *Les Anciennes Communautés villageoises roumaines – asservissement et pénétration capitaliste*. Bucharest and Paris.

Stead, Philip John (1957). *The Police of Paris*. London.

Steinberg, Jonathan (1982). 'This Modern Mafia', *London Review of Books*, 4, No. 18, 7–20 October, pp. 3–6.

Stirling, Paul (1960). 'A Death and a Youth Club: Feuding in a Turkish Village', *AQ*, 33, pp. 51–75.

(1965). *Turkish Village*. London.

Stow, John (1893). *A Survey of London*. 1603 edn. Morley, Henry (ed.). London.

Strubbe, Egied I. (1961). 'La Paix de Dieu dans le nord de la France', *Recueils de la Société Jean Bodin*, XIV, pp. 485–501.

Sumption, Jonathan (1975). *Pilgrimage, An Image of Mediaeval Religion*. London.

Sutherland, Jon N. (1975). 'The Idea of Revenge in Lombard Society in the Eighth and Tenth Centuries: The Cases of Paul the Deacon and Liudprand of Cremona', *Speculum*, 50, pp. 391–410.

Synge, John M. (1912). *The Tinker's Wedding, Riders to the Sea, and The Shadow of the Glen*. Dublin.

(1979). *The Aran Islands*. Oxford. Original edn. 1907.

Tait, David (1970). 'The Territorial Pattern and Lineage System of the Konkomba', in Middleton, John, and Tait, David (eds.), *Tribes without Rulers*, pp. 167–202.

Tarrow, Sidney G. (1967). *Peasant Communism in Southern Italy*. New Haven.

Tax Freeman, Susan (1968). 'Corporate Village Organisation in the Sierra Ministra: An Iberian Structural Type', *Man*, NS 3, pp. 477–84.

Terrell, Richard (1979). *The Chief Justice, A Portrait from the Raj*. Salisbury.

Thurnwald, R. (1949). 'Blood Vengeance Feud', *ESS*, II, pp. 598–9.

Toch, Hans (1972). *Violent Men, An Inquiry into the Psychology of Violence*. Harmondsworth.

Tönnies, Ferdinand (1963). *Community and Society*. New York. Original edn. 1887.

Treston, Hubert J. (1923). *A Study in Ancient Greek Blood-Vengeance*. London.

Trueba, Henry Torres (1973). 'Nahuat Factionalism', *Ethnology*, 12, pp. 463–74.

Turner, Victor W. (1971). 'An Anthropological Approach to the Icelandic Saga', in Beidelman, T.O. (ed.), *The Translation of Culture, Essays to E.E. Evans-Pritchard*, pp. 349–74. London.

Vailland, Roger (1957). *La Loi*. Paris.

Van Gennep, Arnold (1977). *The Rites of Passage*. London. Original edn. 1909.

Vansina, Jan (1973). *Oral Tradition, A Study in Historical Methodology*. Harmondsworth. Original edn. 1961.

Verdier, R. (1980). 'Le Système vindicatoire, Esquisse théorique', in Verdier (ed.), *La Vengeance*, pp. 11–42.

Villari, Pasquale (1955). 'La Mafia', in Caizzi, Bruno (ed.), *Antologia della Questione meridionale*, pp. 296–313.

Villette, Abbé Pierre (1961). 'La Sorcellerie à Douai', *Mélanges de Sciences Religieuses*, 18, pp. 123–73.

Visser, Margaret (1984). 'Vengeance and Pollution in Classical Athens', *Journal of the History of Ideas*, XLV, pp. 193–206.

Vooys, A.C. de and Piket, J.J.C. (1958). 'A Geographical Analysis of Two Villages in the Peloponnesos', *Tijdschrift van het Koninklijk Nederlandsch Aardrijkundig Genootschap*, 74, pp. 30–55.

Vovelle, Michel (1973). *Piété baroque et déchristianisation en Provence au XVIIIe siècle, Les Attitudes devant la mort d'après les clauses des testaments*. Paris.

Wagstaff, J.M. (1965). 'The Economy of the Máni Peninsula (Greece) in the Eighteenth Century', *BS*, 6, pp. 293–304.

Waley, Daniel (1978). *The Italian City-Republics*. London. 2nd edn.

Wallace-Hadrill, J.M. (1962). *The Long-Haired Kings and Other Studies in Frankish History*. London.

Weaver, Martin E. (1971). 'A Tower House at Yeni Foça Izmir', *BS*, 12, pp. 253–80.

Weber, Eugen (1979). *Peasants into Frenchmen, The Modernization of Rural France 1870–1914*. London.

Weingrod, Alex (1968). 'Patrons, Patronage and Political Parties', *CSSH*, 10, pp. 377–400.

Westermarck, Edward (1922). *The History of Human Marriage*, I. New York.

(1934). 'The Blood-Feud among some Berbers of Morocco', in Evans-Pritchard, E.E. et al. (eds.), *Essays presented to C.G. Seligman*, pp. 361–8. London.

Wilson, Francesca (1970). *Muscovy, Russia through Foreign Eyes 1553–1900*. London.

Wilson, Stephen (ed.) (1983). *Saints and their Cults, Studies in Religious Sociology, Folklore and History*. Cambridge.

Winter, Edward (1970). 'The Aboriginal Political Structure of Bwamba', in Middleton, John and Tait, David (eds.), *Tribes without Rulers*, pp. 136–66.

Wood, Alan (1982). 'General Cuckoo's Army: Siberian Brigands, Bandits and Brodyági'. Unpublished paper.

Wormald, Jenny (1980). 'Bloodfeud, Kindred and Government in Early Modern Scotland', *P and P*, 87, pp. 54–97.

Wright, David (ed.) (1957). *Beowulf*. Harmondsworth.

Yalman, Nur (1963). 'On the Purity of Women in the Castes of Ceylon and Malabar', *JRAI*, 93, pp. 25–58.

Yates, Frances A. (1966). *The Art of Memory*. London.

Zehr, Howard (1976). *Crime and the Development of Modern Society: Patterns of Criminality in Nineteenth-century France and Germany*. London.

Zeldin, Theodore (1958). *The Political System of Napoleon III*. London.

Zonabend, Françoise (1980). *La Mémoire longue, Temps et histoires au village*. Paris.

Index

France 1st republic 1792
1848 - 2nd republic
1870-71 - 3rd republic } July monarchy
4th republic } 1815 - ends
1946 - 5th republic 1830.
1958 -

LaVergne, TN USA
18 August 2010
193679LV00003B/3/A

9 780521 522649